CHAMBERS

POCKET
DICTIONARY
& THESAURUS

CHAMBERS

CHAMBERS
An imprint of Chambers Harrap Publishers Ltd
7 Hopetoun Crescent
Edinburgh, EH7 4AY

First published by Chambers Harrap Publishers Ltd 2003

A CIP catalogue record for this book is available from the British Library.

ISBN 0550 10078 4

Designed and typeset by Chambers Harrap Publishers Ltd, Edinburgh
Printed and bound in Great Britain by Mackays of Chatham Ltd

Contents

Contributors

Project Editor
Mary O'Neill

Editor
Rosalind Fergusson

Editorial Assistance
Amanda Jones

Publishing Manager
Patrick White

Prepress
Marina Karapanovic

Preface

Chambers Pocket Dictionary & Thesaurus provides a concise and up-to-date reference for school, office and home use. It combines a complete yet user-friendly dictionary text with a clear, rapid-access thesaurus, giving coverage of thousands of synonyms and antonyms.

Care has been taken to give users maximum ease of use. Sense numbers and parts of speech in thesaurus sections match those of relevant items in the dictionary section, while irregular and problematic verb, adjective and plural forms are written out in full.

Common errors and easily confused words are given emphasis. Users will find such useful tips as 'Do not confuse with **uninterested**' at the entry for **disinterested**, and 'Do not confuse with **palette** and **palate**' at **pallet**. Particularly interesting word histories are also highlighted, giving an insight into the origins of such words as *bully, scapegoat* and *paraphernalia*.

As well as this information, users of the *Chambers Pocket Dictionary & Thesaurus* will find a fascinating selection of panels giving hundreds of words belonging to selected fields. These include such categories as 'forms of communication' (including *bleeper, e-mail, World Wide Web* and *satellite*) and 'names of collectors and enthusiasts' (including *entomologist* [insects], *campanologist* [bell-ringing] and *arctophile* [teddy-bears]).

Whether for checking meanings or finding alternative words and opposites, *Chambers Pocket Dictionary & Thesaurus* offers a convenient, comprehensive source of reference.

How to use the Dictionary and Thesaurus

Easily confused words are highlighted in a box at the end of relevant entries.

carat *noun* **1** a measure of purity for gold **2** a measure of weight for gem-stones

> **!** Do not confuse with: **carrot**

Phrases that include a headword or related word are grouped together at the end of the main entry.

carbon *noun* an element of which charcoal is one form ◇ **carbonic** *adj* of or made with carbon ◇ **carbon copy 1** a copy of a document made by using carbon paper **2** an exact copy ◇ **carbon paper** paper used in typing to produce exact copies

Alternative spellings and **American spellings** are given after the main entry word.

carburettor or **carburetter** or *US* **carburetor** *noun* the part of a car engine which changes the petrol into vapour

Different meanings are given different sense numbers.

card [1] *noun* [1] cardboard or very thick paper [2] an illustrated, folded piece of card sent in greeting *etc* [3] a rectangular piece of card or plastic used for a special purpose: *playing-card/credit card* **4** (**cards**) any of the many types of games played with a pack of cards

Parts of speech, eg noun, verb, adj, adv, are shown. A change to a new part of speech is signalled by a diamond.

card [2] *noun* a tool for combing wool *etc* ◇ *verb* comb (wool *etc*)

cardboard *noun* stiff material made from paper pulp in sheets

Examples show how the word can be used.

cardiac *adj* of the heart: *cardiac failure*

cardigan *noun* a knitted woollen jacket

Word histories give interesting information about the history of some words.

> Named after the 19th-century Earl of *Cardigan* who advocated the use of buttonable woollen jackets

fungus *noun* (*plural* **fungi** (/'fʌŋgiː/ or /'fʌŋgaɪ/) a soft, spongy plant-like growth, *eg* a mushroom or a disease of animals and plants

> *Types of fungus include*:
> black spot, blight, botritis, brown rot, candida, downy mildew, ergot, grey mould, mushroom, orange-peel fungus, penicillium, potato blight, powdery mildew, rust, scab, smut, sooty mould, toadstool, yeast, brewer's yeast

funky *adj*, *informal* **1** fashionable, trendy **2** odd, eccentric

funnel *noun* **1** a cone ending in a tube, for pouring liquids into bottles **2** a tube or passage for escape of smoke, air *etc* ◇ *verb* (**funnels, funnelling, funnelled**) pass through a funnel; channel

funny *adj* **1** amusing **2** odd ◇ **funnily** *adv* ◇ **funny bone** part of the elbow which gives a prickly feeling when knocked

> ▣ **1** humorous, entertaining, comic, comical, hilarious, witty, droll, absurd, silly **2** strange, peculiar, curious, weird, unusual, puzzling, perplexing, mysterious, dubious
> ▣ **1** serious, solemn, sad **2** normal, ordinary, usual

fur *noun* **1** the short fine hair of certain animals **2** their skins covered with fur **3** a coating on the tongue, on the inside of kettles *etc* ◇ *verb* (**furs, furring, furred**) line or cover with fur ◇ **furrier** *noun* someone who trades in or works with furs ◇ **furry** *adj* covered with fur

Irregular plurals of nouns are shown in full.

Pronunciations are shown for words that could cause difficulty.

'Types of' and other connected words are shown in panels after many entries.

Usage information labels tell you how and where a word is used.

Irregular verb forms are shown in full.

Synonyms or alternative words are listed after the dictionary entry, introduced by the symbol ▣. Sense numbers reflect the senses in the dictionary entry.

Antonyms, words that mean the opposite of the entry word, are introduced by the symbol ▣.

Related words are often included in the entry.

Pronunciation Guide

The following characters are used to represent the sounds underlined in the words.

a	h<u>a</u>t	ɛ̃	*French* v<u>in</u>	ʌ	c<u>u</u>p	aʊ	n<u>ow</u>	ð	<u>th</u>e
ɑː	b<u>aa</u>	ɪ	f<u>i</u>t	ʊ	p<u>u</u>t	oʊ	g<u>o</u>	j	<u>y</u>ou
ɑ̃	*French* gr<u>and</u>	iː	m<u>e</u>	uː	t<u>oo</u>	ɪə	h<u>ere</u>	ŋ	ri<u>ng</u>
ɛ	b<u>e</u>t	ɒ	l<u>o</u>t	aɪ	b<u>y</u>	ɛə	h<u>air</u>	ʃ	<u>sh</u>e
ə	<u>a</u>go	ɔː	r<u>aw</u>	eɪ	b<u>ay</u>	ʊə	p<u>oor</u>	ʒ	vi<u>si</u>on
ɜː	f<u>ur</u>	ɔ̃	*French* b<u>on</u>	ɔɪ	b<u>oy</u>	θ	<u>th</u>in		

Abbreviations used in the Dictionary and Thesaurus

abbrev	abbreviation
adj	adjective
adv	adverb
Brit	British English
comput	computing
conj	conjunction
eg	for example
esp	especially
etc	and so on
exclam	exclamation
hist	history
ie	that is
med	medicine
N	North
orig	originally
prep	preposition
S	South
Scot	Scottish English
sing	singular
US	American English
usu	usually

Aα

a or **an** *adj* **1** one: *a knock at the door* **2** any: *an ant has six legs* **3** in, to or for each: *four times a day*

> The form *a* is used before words beginning with a consonant, *eg* knock; *an* is used before words beginning with a vowel, *eg* ant.

aardvark *noun* a long-nosed S African animal which feeds on termites

aback *adv*: **taken aback** surprised

abacus *noun* (*plural* **abacuses**) a frame with columns of beads for counting and calculating

abandon *verb* (**abandons, abandoning, abandoned**) **1** leave, without intending to return to **2** give up (an idea *etc*) ◇ *noun* lack of inhibition ◇ **abandoned** *adj* **1** deserted **2** uninhibited, unrestrained ◇ **abandonment** *noun*
■ *verb* **1** desert, leave, forsake, jilt, *informal* ditch **2** renounce, relinquish, surrender, yield, drop ◇ **abandonment** desertion, leaving, forsaking, jilting, neglect, scrapping, renunciation, resignation, giving up, discontinuation

abase *verb* humble ◇ **abasement** *noun*

abashed *adj* embarrassed, confused
■ ashamed, mortified, humiliated, bewildered

abate *verb* make or grow less ◇ **abatement** *noun*
■ decrease, reduce, diminish, decline, dwindle, moderate, relieve, alleviate, *informal* let up
⊞ increase, strengthen

abattoir /'abətwɑː(r)/ *noun* a (public) slaughterhouse

abbess *noun* (*plural* **abbesses**) the female head of an abbey or a convent

abbey *noun* (*plural* **abbeys**) **1** a monastery or convent ruled by an abbot or an abbess **2** the church now or formerly attached to it

abbot *noun* the male head of an abbey

abbreviate *verb* shorten (a word, phrase *etc*) ◇ **abbreviation** *noun* a shortened form of a word *etc* used instead of the whole word, *eg maths* for *mathematics*
■ shorten, cut, trim, abridge, summarize, condense, reduce, contract ◇ **abbreviation** shortening, abridgement, reduction, contraction
⊞ extend, lengthen, expand ◇ **abbreviation** extension, expansion, amplification

abdicate *verb* give up (a position, *esp* that of king or queen) ◇ **abdication** *noun*

abdomen *noun* the part of the human body between the chest and the hips ◇ **abdominal** *adj*

abduct *verb* take away by force or fraud ◇ **abduction** *noun*
■ carry off, run away with, *informal* run off with, make off with, seduce, kidnap, snatch, seize

aberration *noun* deviation from what is correct or normal
■ deviation, straying, anomaly, quirk, lapse, defect, divergence, irregularity

abet *verb* (**abets, abetting, abetted**) help or encourage to do wrong

abeyance *noun*: **in abeyance** undecided; not to be dealt with for the time being

abhor *verb* (**abhors, abhorring, abhorred**) regard with horror, hate ◇ **abhorrence** *noun* ◇ **abhorrent** *adj* hateful ◇ **abhorrently** *adv*
■ hate, detest, loathe, shudder at, recoil from, shrink from, despise ◇ **abhorrent** detestable, abominable, offensive, revolting
⊞ love, adore ◇ **abhorrent** delightful, attractive

abide *verb* put up with, tolerate ◇ **abiding** *adj* lasting ◇ **abide by** keep (a law, promise *etc*), act according to
■ bear, stand, endure, tolerate, put up with ◇ **abide by** obey, observe, follow, comply with, adhere to, conform to, submit to, go along with, agree to

ability *noun* (*plural* **abilities**) 1 power or means to do something 2 talent
■ 1 capability, capacity, faculty, facility, power 2 skill, dexterity, deftness, adeptness, competence, proficiency, aptitude, talent, gift, knack, flair, expertise, *informal* know-how, forte, strength

abject *adj* miserable, degraded: *abject poverty*
■ miserable, wretched, forlorn, hopeless, pitiable, pathetic, outcast, degraded

ablaze *adj* 1 burning fiercely 2 gleaming like fire
■ 1 blazing, flaming, burning, on fire, ignited, lighted, alight 2 illuminated, glowing, aglow, radiant, flashing, gleaming

able *adj* 1 having the power or means (to do something) 2 clever ◇ **ably** *adv*

ablutions *noun plural*, *formal* washing of the body

abnormal *adj* not normal (in behaviour *etc*), unusual ◇ **abnormality** *noun* (*plural* **abnormalities**) ◇ **abnormally** *adv*
■ odd, strange, weird, eccentric, singular, peculiar, curious, unusual, uncommon, unnatural, wayward, deviant, irregular, different

aboard *adv* & *prep* on(to) or in(to) (a ship or aeroplane)

abode *noun*, *formal* a dwelling place

abolish *verb* do away with (*eg* a custom) ◇ **abolition** *noun* ◇ **abolitionist** *noun* someone who tries to do away with anything, *esp* slavery
■ do away with, invalidate, revoke, cancel, eradicate, *informal* get rid of, overthrow, overturn
🔁 create, retain, authorize, continue

abominable *adj* hateful; very bad, terrible ◇ **abominably** *adv*
■ detestable, hateful, horrible, abhorrent, repulsive, disgusting, obnoxious, foul, appalling, despicable, wretched
🔁 delightful, pleasant, desirable

abominate *verb* hate very much ◇ **abomination** *noun* 1 great hatred 2 anything hateful

Aboriginal or **Aborigine** a member of the original or native people of Australia ◇ **Aboriginal** *adj*

abort *verb* 1 cause (a plan, mission *etc*) to come to a premature end 2 remove a foetus to terminate a pregnancy ◇ **abortion** *noun* the removal of a foetus to terminate a pregnancy ◇ **abortive** *adj* coming to nothing, useless: *an abortive attempt*
■ 1 stop, arrest, stop, halt, thwart, call off, fail 2 miscarry, terminate, end ◇ **abortive** failed, unsuccessful, fruitless, sterile, useless, ineffective

abound *verb* be very plentiful ◇ **abounding in** full of, having many

about *prep* 1 around: *look about you* 2 here and there in: *scattered about the room* 3 on the subject of: *a book about astrology* ◇ *adv* 1 around: *stood about waiting* 2 in motion or in action: *running about* 3 in the opposite direction: *turned about and walked away* 4 approximately: *about ten miles away* ◇ **about to** on the point of (doing something)
■ *prep* 3 regarding, concerning, connected with, as regards ◇ *adv* 4 roughly, around, close to, nearly

above *prep* 1 over, in a higher position than: *above your head* 2 greater than: *above average* 3 too good for: *above jealousy* ◇ *adv* 1 overhead, on high 2 earlier on (in a letter *etc*) ◇ **above board** *adj* open ◇ *adv* openly
■ *prep* 2 over, higher than, superior to, in excess of, surpassing, beyond ◇ *adv* 1 overhead, aloft
🔁 *prep* 2 below, under ◇ *adv* 1 below, underneath

abrasion *noun* 1 the action of rubbing away 2 a graze on the body

abrasive *adj* 1 able to scrape or wear down 2 having a hurtful manner ◇ *noun* something used for rubbing or polishing ◇ **abrasively** *adv*

◼ *adj* **1** scratching, scraping, grating **2** harsh, annoying, hurtful, nasty, unpleasant

◪ **1** smooth **2** pleasant

abreast *adv* side by side ◇ **abreast of** up to date with: *abreast of current affairs*

abridge *verb* shorten (a book, story *etc*) ◇ **abridgement** or **abridgment** *noun*

◼ shorten, abbreviate, reduce, decrease, condense

◪ expand, amplify, pad out

abroad *adv* **1** in or to another country **2** *formal* outside: *witches go abroad after dark*

◼ overseas, in foreign parts, out of the country

abrupt *adj* **1** sudden, without warning **2** bad-tempered, short, curt ◇ **abruptly** *adv*

◼ **1** unexpected, surprising **2** brusque, curt, terse, gruff, rude, blunt, direct

◪ **1** gradual, slow, leisurely **2** expansive, ceremonious, polite

abscess *noun* (*plural* **abscesses**) a boil or similar collection of pus in the body

abscond *verb* run away secretly: *absconded with the money*

◼ run away, run off, make off, flee, fly, escape, bolt, disappear

absent *adj* away, not present ◇ **absence** *noun* the state of being away ◇ **absentee** *noun* someone who is absent ◇ **absently** *adv* ◇ **absent-minded** *adj* forgetful ◇ **absent yourself** stay away

◼ missing, away, out, unavailable, lacking ◇ **absence** non-attendance, non-appearance, non-existence, lack ◇ **absent-minded** forgetful, scatter-brained, distracted, preoccupied, inattentive

◪ **absent-minded** attentive, practical, matter-of-fact

absolute *adj* complete, not limited by anything: *absolute power* ◇ **absolutely** *adv*

◼ total, complete, entire, full, thorough, sheer, utter ◇ **absolutely** totally, completely, entirely, utterly, fully,

wholly, thoroughly, unconditionally, conclusively, categorically

absolve *verb* pardon: *absolved their sins* ◇ **absolution** *noun* forgiveness, pardon

absorb *verb* **1** soak up (liquid) **2** take up the whole attention of ◇ **absorbed** *adj* ◇ **absorption** *noun*

◼ **1** take in, suck up, soak up **2** engross, involve, fascinate, preoccupy

absorbent *adj* able to soak up liquid

abstain *verb* **1** refuse to cast a vote for or against **2** (with **from**) hold yourself back: *abstain from sex* ◇ **abstainer** *noun* someone who abstains from something, *esp* from alcoholic drink ◇ **abstention** *noun*

◼ **2** refrain, decline, refuse, resist, shun, avoid, keep from, renounce, forgo, go without, deny oneself

abstemious *adj* not greedy, sparing in food, drink *etc* ◇ **abstemiousness** *noun*

abstention *see* abstain

abstinence *noun* abstaining from alcohol *etc* ◇ **abstinent** *adj*

abstract *adj* existing only as an idea, not as a real thing ◇ *noun* a summary ◇ **abstraction** *noun*

◼ *adj* non-concrete, conceptual, intellectual, hypothetical, theoretical, philosophical, academic ◇ *noun* synopsis, outline, summary, résumé

◪ *adj* concrete, real, actual

abstruse *adj* difficult to understand

absurd *adj* clearly wrong; ridiculous ◇ **absurdity** *noun* (*plural* **absurdities**)

◼ ridiculous, ludicrous, preposterous, fantastic, implausible, untenable, nonsensical, foolish, silly, stupid, idiotic, *informal* daft, farcical, laughable

abundant *adj* plentiful ◇ **abundance** *noun* ◇ **abundantly** *adv*

◼ plentiful, full, filled, well-supplied, ample, generous, bountiful, rich, lavish

◪ scarce, sparse

abuse *verb* **1** use wrongly: *abused his power* **2** insult or speak unkindly to **3** treat badly ◇ *noun* **1** wrongful use **2** insulting language or behaviour **3** bad treatment ◇ **abusive** *adj*

■ *verb* **1** misuse, exploit, take advantage of **2** insult, swear at, slander, malign, scold **3** ill-treat, hurt, injure, molest, damage, spoil, harm ◊ *noun* **1** misuse, exploitation **2** insults, swearing, cursing **3** ill-treatment, hurt, injury, molestation, damage, harm, neglect ◊ **abusive** insulting, offensive, rude, hurtful, injurious, cruel

▨ *verb* **2** compliment, praise **3** cherish, care for ◊ *noun* **2** compliment, praise **3** care, attention ◊ **abusive** complimentary, polite

abysmal *adj* **1** *informal* very bad; terrible **2** bottomless ◊ **abysmally** *adv*

abyss *noun* (*plural* **abysses**) a bottomless depth

a/c *abbrev* account

acacia /əˈkeɪʃə/ *noun* a family of thorny shrubs and trees

academic *adj* **1** learned, scholarly **2** not practical: *purely of academic interest* **3** of a university *etc* ◊ *noun* a university or college teacher ◊ **academically** *adv*

▨ *adj* **1** scholarly, well-read, studious, bookish, literary **2** theoretical, hypothetical, speculative, abstract, impractical ◊ *noun* professor, don, master, fellow, lecturer, tutor, scholar, man of letters, woman of letters

academy *noun* (*plural* **academies**) **1** a college for special study or training **2** a society for encouraging science or art **3** in Scotland, a senior school

acanthus *noun* a Mediterranean ornamental shrub

accede *verb*: **accede to** agree to

accelerate *verb* increase in speed ◊ **acceleration** *noun* ◊ **accelerator** *noun* a lever or pedal used to increase the speed of a car *etc*

accent *noun* **1** (a mark indicating) stress on a syllable or word **2** a mark used in some languages, *eg* French, to show how a letter should be pronounced **3** emphasis: *the accent must be on hard work* **4** the way in which words are pronounced in a particular area: *a Scottish accent* ◊ **accentuate** *verb* make more obvious; emphasize

accept *verb* **1** take something offered **2** agree or submit to ◊ **acceptable** *adj* satisfactory; pleasing ◊ **acceptance** *noun*

■ **1** take, receive, obtain **2** allow, approve, agree to, consent to

▨ **1** decline, refuse, turn down **2** reject

> ❗ Do not confuse with: **except**

access *noun* right or means of approach or entry ◊ **accession** *noun* coming to a position, rank *etc*: *accession to the throne*

> ❗ Do not confuse with: **excess**

accessible *adj* easily approached or reached ◊ **accessibility** *noun*

■ reachable, *informal* get-at-able, attainable, achievable, possible, obtainable, available, handy, convenient, nearby

▨ inaccessible, remote

accessory *noun* (*plural* **accessories**) **1** an item chosen to match or complement clothes, *eg* a piece of jewellery, a handbag *etc* **2** a helper, *esp* in crime **3** an additional useful item or part

accident *noun* **1** an unexpected event causing injury or damage **2** something which happens by chance **3** chance ◊ **accidental** *adj* happening by chance ◊ **accidentally** *adv*

■ **1** misfortune, mishap, misadventure, calamity, disaster **2** fluke **3** chance, hazard, fortuity, luck, fortune, fate

acclaim *verb* welcome enthusiastically ◊ *noun* enthusiastic reception: *met with critical acclaim* ◊ **acclamation** *noun*

■ *verb* praise, commend, extol, exalt, honour, hail, welcome, applaud, clap, cheer ◊ *noun* praise, homage, honour, welcome, *formal* approbation, approval, applause, ovation, celebration

acclimatize *verb* accustom to another climate or situation ◊ **acclimatization** *noun*

accommodate *verb* **1** find room for **2** make suitable **3** oblige; fit in with ◊ **accommodating** *adj* obliging ◊ **accommodation** *noun* lodgings

■ **1** lodge, board, put up, house, shelter **2**

adapt, adjust, modify, fit **3** help, assist, aid, serve, provide, supply, comply with ◇ **accommodating** obliging, helpful, kind, considerate, unselfish, friendly, hospitable

accompaniment *noun* **1** something that accompanies **2** the music played while a singer sings *etc*

accompanist *noun* someone who plays an accompaniment

accompany *verb* (**accompanies**, **accompanying**, **accompanied**) **1** go or be with **2** play an instrument (*eg* a piano) while a singer sings *etc*

accomplice *noun* someone who helps another person, *esp* to commit a crime

▣ assistant, helper, abettor, mate, conspirator, collaborator, partner, accessory

accomplish *verb* **1** complete **2** bring about, succeed in doing ◇ **accomplished** *adj* skilled, talented ◇ **accomplishment** *noun* **1** completion **2** a personal talent or skill **3** something done successfully

▣ **2** realize, achieve, effect, produce ◇ **accomplished** gifted, skilful, proficient ◇ **accomplishment 2** aptitude, ability, gift, forte **3** achievement, exploit, feat

accord *verb* **1** agree (with) **2** give, grant ◇ *noun* agreement ◇ **accordance** *noun* ◇ **accordingly** *adv* therefore ◇ **according to 1** as told by **2** in relation to: *paid according to your work* ◇ **of your own accord** of your own free will

▣ *verb* **1** agree, concur, harmonize, match, suit, conform, correspond **2** give, tender, grant, allow, bestow, endow, confer

accordion *noun* a musical instrument with bellows, a keyboard and metal reeds ◇ **accordionist** *noun*

accost *verb* approach and speak to

account *verb* give a reason (for) ◇ *noun* **1** a description of events *etc*; an explanation **2** a record of finances **3** a financial arrangement for banking or credit ◇ **accountable** *adj* answerable, responsible ◇ **on account of** because of

▣ *noun* **1** narrative, story, tale, chronicle, record, statement, report, portrayal, sketch, presentation, explanation

accountant a keeper or inspector of accounts

accoutrements /əˈkuːtrəmənts/ *noun plural* dress and equipment, *esp* military

accredited *adj* having the official power to act

accrue *verb* **1** be given or added to **2** accumulate, collect: *the account accrued no interest* ◇ **accrued** *adj*

accumulate *verb* **1** collect, gather **2** increase ◇ **accumulation** *noun* **1** a collection **2** a mass or pile ◇ **accumulator** *noun* a type of battery used in a car *etc*

accurate *adj* correct, exact ◇ **accuracy** *noun* ◇ **accurately** *adv*

▣ right, unerring, precise, exact, *informal* spot-on, faultless, perfect, true, just, proper, meticulous ◇ **accuracy** correctness, precision, exactness, truth

▣ inaccurate, wrong, imprecise, inexact

accursed *adj*, *formal* **1** under a curse **2** hateful

accuse *verb* bring a (criminal) charge against ◇ **accusation** *noun* ◇ **the accused** the person charged with a crime *etc* ◇ **accuser** *noun*

▣ charge, indict, impugn, denounce, impeach, blame, censure, recriminate, incriminate

accustomed *adj* **1** (with **to**) having much experience or familiarity: *accustomed to travel* **2** usual

▣ **1** used to, in the habit of, given to, confirmed, seasoned, hardened, trained, experienced, adapted, acclimatized, acquainted, familiar **2** habitual, regular, normal, usual, ordinary, everyday, conventional, customary, established, general

AC/DC *abbrev* alternating current/direct current ◇ *adj*, *slang* bisexual

ace *noun* **1** a playing-card with a single spot, usually the highest in a suit **2** an expert: *a computer ace* **3** *tennis* an unreturned first serve

acetylene *noun* a gas used for giving light and heat

ache noun a continuous pain ◊ verb be continuously painful

achieve verb 1 get (something) done, accomplish 2 win ◊ **achievement** noun

acid adj 1 sharp in taste 2 sarcastic ◊ noun a substance containing hydrogen which will dissolve metals (contrasted with: **alkali**) ◊ **acidity** noun the state of being acid ◊ **acid rain** rain containing sulphur and nitrogen compounds and other pollutants

acidify verb (**acidifies, acidifying, acidified**) make or become acid

acknowledge verb 1 admit the truth of 2 (write to) say you have received (something) ◊ **acknowledgement** or **acknowledgment** noun

▣ 1 admit, confess, own up to 2 reply to, confirm, thank for ◊ **acknowledgement 1** admission, confession, declaration, recognition 2 answer, reply, response, reaction, affirmation

acme noun the highest point; perfection

acne noun a common skin disease with pimples

acorn noun the fruit of the oak tree

acoustic /əˈkuːstɪk/ adj of hearing or sound ◊ **acoustics** noun 1 sing the study of sound 2 plural the characteristics of a room etc which affect the hearing of sound in it

acquaint verb make (someone) familiar (with) ◊ **acquaintance** noun 1 knowledge, familiarity 2 someone whom you know slightly

▣ accustom, familiarize, inform, enlighten ◊ **acquaintance 1** awareness, understanding, experience 2 friend, companion, colleague, associate, contact

acquiesce /əkwɪˈɛs/ verb (often with **in**) agree (to) ◊ **acquiescence** noun ◊ **acquiescent** adj

acquire verb obtain, get ◊ **acquired** adj gained; not innate or inherited ◊ **acquisition** noun 1 the act of getting 2 something obtained or bought

▣ buy, purchase, procure, appropriate, obtain, get, collect, gather, net, gain, secure, earn, attain ◊ **acquisition 1** appropriation, securing, procurement, attainment, accession, takeover 2 purchase, informal buy

▣ relinquish, forfeit

acquisitive adj eager to get things ◊ **acquisitiveness** noun

acquit verb (**acquits, acquitting, acquitted**) declare (someone) innocent of a crime ◊ **acquittal** noun a legal judgement of 'not guilty' ◊ **acquit yourself badly** do badly, be unsuccessful ◊ **acquit yourself well** do well, be successful

▣ absolve, clear, reprieve, let off, release

acre noun a land measure containing 4840 square yards or about 4000 square metres ◊ **acreage** noun the number of acres in a piece of land

acrid adj harsh, bitter

acrimonious adj showing bitterness of feeling ◊ **acrimony** noun

▣ bitter, biting, cutting, sharp, virulent, severe, spiteful

▣ peaceable, kindly

acrobat noun someone who performs gymnastic feats, tightrope-walking etc ◊ **acrobatic** adj

acronym noun a word formed from the initial letters of other words, eg radar for radio detecting and ranging

across adv & prep to or at the other side (of): swam across the river/winked at him across the table ◊ **across the board** involving everyone or everything

acrostic noun a poem etc in which the first or last letters of each line, taken in order, spell a word or words

acrylic noun a synthetically produced fibre ◊ adj made with this material

act verb 1 do something 2 behave in a particular way: act foolishly 3 play a dramatic role on stage, film etc ◊ noun 1 something done 2 a government law 3 a section of a play

▣ verb 2 conduct oneself, function, operate ◊ noun 1 deed, action, operation, manoeuvre, move, step, achievement, exploit, feat

action noun 1 a deed, an act 2 a movement 3 a law case 4 dramatic events portrayed in a film, play etc ◇ **actionable** adj likely to cause a law case: an actionable statement

▣ 1 act, move, exploit, feat, performance, effort, process, activity, exercise, operation 2 move, movement, motion 3 litigation, lawsuit, suit, case, prosecution

activate verb start (something) working

▣ start, initiate, trigger, set off, informal kick-start, fire, switch on, mobilize, move, stir, rouse, stimulate

▣ deactivate, stop, arrest

active adj 1 busy; lively 2 able to perform physical tasks 3 grammar describing the form of a verb in which the subject performs the action of the verb, eg 'the dog bit the postman' 4 working, operating: active ingredients

▣ 1 busy, occupied, informal on the go, industrious, diligent, hard-working, enterprising, enthusiastic, devoted, engaged, involved, committed 2 agile, nimble, sprightly, quick, alert, vigorous

activity noun (plural **activities**) 1 action 2 an occupation or pursuit

actor noun someone who acts a part in a play or film

actress noun (plural **actresses**) a female actor

actual adj real, existing in fact ◇ **actuality** noun ◇ **actually** adv really, in fact

actuary noun (plural **actuaries**) someone who works out the price of insurance ◇ **actuarial** adj

actuate verb 1 put into action 2 drive or urge on

acumen noun quickness of understanding

acupressure noun a method of treating illness by applying pressure to certain key points on the body

acupuncture noun a method of treating illness by piercing the skin with needles ◇ **acupuncturist** noun a practitioner of acupuncture

acute adj 1 quick at understanding 2 of a disease: severe, but not lasting very long 3 of an angle: less than a right angle (contrasted with: **obtuse**) ◇ **acuteness** noun ◇ **acute accent** a forward-leaning stroke (´) placed over letters in some languages to show their pronunciation

▣ 1 sharp, keen, incisive, shrewd, discerning, observant, perceptive 2 severe, intense, extreme, violent, dangerous, serious, grave, chronic

▣ 2 mild, slight

AD abbrev in the year of our Lord, eg AD 1900 (from Latin anno Domini)

ad noun, informal an advertisement

adamant adj unwilling to give way to persuasion etc ◇ **adamantly** adv

Adam's apple the natural lump which sticks out from the throat

adapt verb make suitable; alter so as to fit ◇ **adaptable** adj easily altered to suit new conditions ◇ **adaptation** noun

▣ alter, change, qualify, modify, adjust, tweak, customize, tailor, fashion, conform, comply, prepare ◇ **adaptable** changeable, variable, adjustable, flexible, easy-going

▣ **adaptable** inflexible, refractory

add verb 1 make one thing join another to give a total or whole 2 mix in: add water to the dough 3 say further ◇ **addition** noun 1 the act of adding 2 something added ◇ **additional** adj ◇ **additive** noun a chemical etc added to another substance

▣ 1 append, annex, affix, attach, join, combine 2 combine ◇ **addition** 1 extension, enlargement, increasing, increase, gain 2 adjunct, supplement, additive, addendum, appendix, appendage, attachment

▣ 1 take away, remove ◇ **addition** 1 removal

addendum noun (plural **addenda**) something added to a text

adder noun the common name of the viper, a poisonous snake

addict noun someone who is dependent on something, eg a drug or

alcohol, either physically or mentally
◊ **addictive** adj creating dependence,
habit-forming ◊ **addicted to** dependent on

▣ **addicted to** dependent on, hooked on, obsessed with, accustomed to

addition, additional and **additive** see add

address verb **1** speak to **2** write the address on (a letter etc) ◊ noun (plural **addresses**) **1** the name of the house, street, and town where someone lives etc **2** a speech **3** a number identifying where computer data is stored on a system

▣ verb **1** speak to, talk to, greet, approach ◊ noun **2** talk, lecture, sermon, discourse

adenoids noun plural swellings at the back of the nose which hinder breathing

adept adj very skilful

adequate adj satisfactory, esp in quantity ◊ **adequacy** noun ◊ **adequately** adv

▣ enough, sufficient

▣ inadequate, insufficient, unsatisfactory

adhere verb **1** stick (to) **2** give support (to) or be loyal (to) ◊ **adherence** noun ◊ **adherent** adj sticking (to) ◊ noun a follower or supporter of a cause etc

▣ **adherent** noun supporter, upholder, advocate, partisan, follower, disciple, admirer, fan, enthusiast

adhesion noun the act of sticking (to)

adhesive adj sticky, gummed ◊ noun something which makes things stick to each other

▣ adj sticky, tacky, gummy, gluey, gummed, self-adhesive ◊ noun glue, gum, paste, cement

ad hoc adj set up for a particular purpose only

adjacent adj (often with **to**) lying alongside

▣ adjoining, abutting, touching, contiguous, bordering, beside, juxtaposed, neighbouring, closest, nearest, close, near

▣ remote, distant

adjective noun a word which tells

something about a noun, eg 'the black cat,' 'times are hard' ◊ **adjectival** adj

adjoin verb be joined to ◊ **adjoining** adj

adjourn verb **1** stop (a meeting etc) with the intention of continuing it at another time or place **2** (with **to**) go to another place: adjourn to the lounge ◊ **adjournment** noun

▣ **1** interrupt, suspend, discontinue, break off, delay, postpone, put off, recess, retire

▣ **1** assemble, convene

adjudicate verb **1** give a judgement on (a dispute etc) **2** act as a judge at a competition ◊ **adjudication** noun ◊ **adjudicator** noun

adjunct noun something joined or added

adjust verb rearrange or alter to suit the circumstances ◊ **adjustable** adj ◊ **adjustment** noun

▣ modify, change, tweak, adapt, convert, fit, rectify, balance, set, arrange

adjutant noun a military officer who assists a commanding officer

ad-lib verb (**ad-libs, ad-libbing, ad-libbed**) speak without plan or preparation ◊ adj done without preparation

▣ adj impromptu, improvised, extempore, extemporaneous, off-the-cuff, unprepared, unrehearsed, spontaneous

administer verb **1** manage or govern **2** carry out (the law etc) **3** give (help, medicine etc)

▣ **1** rule, lead, head, preside over, officiate, manage, run, organize, direct **3** provide, supply, distribute, dole out, dispense, measure out

administrate verb manage or govern ◊ **administrator** noun someone involved in administration

administration noun **1** management of an organization etc **2** (the body that carries on) the government of a country etc ◊ **administrative** adj

admiral noun the commander of a navy ◊ **admiralty** noun the government office which manages naval affairs

admire verb **1** think very highly of **2** look at with pleasure ◇ **admirable** adj ◇ **admirably** adv ◇ **admiration** noun ◇ **admirer** noun

▣ **1** esteem, respect, revere, venerate, approve, praise, appreciate, value ◇ **admirable** praiseworthy, commendable, worthy, respected, fine, excellent, superior, wonderful, exquisite

▣ **1** despise, censure

admit verb (**admits, admitting, admitted**) **1** let in **2** acknowledge the truth of, confess **3** (with **of**) leave room for, allow: *admits of no other explanation* ◇ **admissible** adj allowable ◇ **admission** noun **1** (the price of) being let in **2** anything acknowledged or confessed ◇ **admittance** noun the right or permission to enter

▣ **1** allow to enter, give access, accept, receive, take in **2** confess, own (up), grant, recognize, allow, concede

▣ **1** shut out, exclude **2** deny

admonish verb **1** warn **2** rebuke, scold ◇ **admonition** noun a warning ◇ **admonitory** adj

ad nauseam adv to a tiresome degree

ado noun trouble, fuss

adobe /əˈdəʊbɪ/ noun clay used for buildings

adolescent noun someone between a child and an adult in age ◇ adj of this age ◇ **adolescence** noun

adopt verb take as your own (*esp* a child of other parents) ◇ **adoption** noun ◇ **adoptive** adj adopting or adopted: *his adoptive parents/her adoptive country*

adore verb **1** love very much **2** worship ◇ **adorable** adj very lovable ◇ **adorably** adv ◇ **adoration** noun

▣ **1** love, cherish, dote on, admire **2** revere, venerate, idolize, glorify ◇ **adorable** lovable, dear, precious, appealing, charming, captivating, winning, delightful, pleasing, attractive

adorn verb decorate (with ornaments *etc*) ◇ **adornment** noun

▣ decorate, bedeck, trim, garnish, enhance, embellish, enrich, grace

adrenaline noun a hormone produced in response to fear, anger *etc*, preparing the body for quick action

adrift adv drifting, floating

adroit adj skilful

ADSL abbrev Automatic Digital Subscriber Line

adulation noun great flattery ◇ **adulatory** adj

adult adj grown up ◇ noun a grown-up person

adulterate verb make impure by adding something else ◇ **adulteration** noun

▣ contaminate, pollute, taint, corrupt, defile, debase

adultery noun unfaithfulness to a husband or wife ◇ **adulterer** or **adulteress** noun

advance verb **1** go forward **2** put forward (a plan *etc*) **3** help the progress of **4** pay before the usual or agreed time ◇ noun **1** movement forward **2** improvement **3** a loan of money ◇ **advanced** adj well forward in progress ◇ **advancement** noun ◇ **in advance** beforehand

▣ verb **1** proceed, move on, progress, flourish, thrive, improve, develop **2** present, submit, suggest, offer, provide **3** further, promote, upgrade, support, assist, benefit, facilitate, increase, grow **4** lend, loan, pay beforehand ◇ noun **1** progress, headway, advancement **2** breakthrough, development **3** credit, loan ◇ **advanced** leading, foremost, cutting-edge, ahead, forward, progressive, forward-looking, sophisticated, complex

▣ verb **1** retreat **3** impede ◇ noun **1** retreat, recession ◇ **advanced** backward, retarded, elementary

advantage noun **1** a better position, superiority **2** gain or benefit ◇ verb help, benefit ◇ **advantageous** adj profitable; helpful ◇ **take advantage of** make use of (a situation, person *etc*) in such a way as to benefit yourself

▣ noun **1** lead, edge, upper hand, superiority, precedence **2** asset, blessing, benefit, good, welfare, interest, service, help, aid, assistance, use, profit ◇ **advantageous** beneficial, favourable, convenient, helpful, useful, worthwhile, valuable, profitable

◪ *noun* **2** disadvantage, drawback, hindrance

advent *noun* **1** coming, arrival: *before the advent of television* **2** (**Advent**) in the Christian church, the four weeks before Christmas

adventure *noun* a bold or exciting undertaking or experience ◇ **adventurer** *noun* ◇ **adventurous** *adj*

▤ exploit, venture, undertaking, enterprise, risk, chance, experience ◇ **adventurous** daring, intrepid, bold, risky, venturesome

◪ **adventurous** cautious, chary, prudent

adverb *noun* a word which gives a more definite meaning to a verb, adjective, or other adverb, *eg* 'eat *slowly*,' '*extremely* hard,' '*very* carefully' ◇ **adverbial** *adj* of or like an adverb

adversary *noun* (*plural* **adversaries**) an enemy; an opponent

adverse *adj* unfavourable: *adverse criticism* ◇ **adversity** *noun* (*plural* **adversities**) misfortune

advert *noun, informal* an advertisement

advertise *verb* **1** make known to the public **2** stress the good points of (a product for sale) ◇ **advertisement** *noun* **1** a photograph, short film *etc* intended to persuade the public to buy a particular product **2** a notice, *eg* in a newspaper, making something known to the public: *job advertisements*

▤ **1** announce, declare, proclaim, broadcast, publish, display, inform, notify **2** publicize, promote, push, *informal* plug, praise, *slang* hype

advice *noun* **1** something said to help someone make a decision *etc* **2** a formal notice

▤ **1** counsel, help, guidance, direction, suggestion, recommendation, opinion, view **2** notification, memorandum, communication

⚠ Do not confuse with: **advise**

advisable *adj* wise, sensible ◇ **advisability** *noun* ◇ **advisably** *adv*

▤ suggested, recommended, sensible, wise, prudent, beneficial, desirable, suitable, appropriate, proper, correct

advise *verb* **1** give advice to **2** recommend (an action *etc*) ◇ **adviser** *noun* ◇ **advisory** *adj* giving advice: *advisory body*

⚠ Do not confuse with: **advice**

advocate *noun* **1** someone who recommends something **2** someone who pleads for another **3** in Scotland, a court lawyer ◇ *verb* **1** plead or argue for **2** recommend

▤ *verb* **1** defend, champion, campaign for, press for, argue for, plead for, urge, encourage **2** recommend, propose, endorse, support, subscribe to, favour

aegis /'iːdʒɪs/ *noun* protection; patronage

aeon or **eon** /'iːɒn/ *noun* a very long period of time, an age

aerate *verb* put air or another gas into (a liquid)

aerial *adj* **1** of, in or from the air: *aerial photography* **2** placed high up or overhead: *aerial railway* ◇ *noun* a wire or rod (or a set of these) by means of which radio or television signals are received or sent

aerobatics *noun plural* stunts performed by an aircraft

aerobics *noun sing* a system of rhythmic physical exercise which aims to strengthen the heart and lungs by increasing the body's oxygen consumption

aerodrome *noun* a landing, take-off and maintenance station for small aircraft

aeronautics *noun sing* the science or art of navigation in the air

aeroplane or *US* **airplane** *noun* an engine-powered flying machine with fixed wings

aerosol *noun* a container of liquid

and gas under pressure, from which the liquid is squirted as a mist

aesthetic or *US* **esthetic** *adj* **1** of beauty or its appreciation **2** artistic, pleasing to the eye ◇ **aesthetically** *adv*

affable *adj* pleasant, easy to speak to ◇ **affability** *noun* ◇ **affably** *adv*

▣ friendly, amiable, approachable, open, kindly, good-humoured, good-natured, amicable, sociable, agreeable

▣ unfriendly, reserved, reticent, cool

affair *noun* **1** events *etc* connected with one person or thing: *the Watergate affair* **2** (**affairs**) personal concerns, transactions *etc*: *his affairs seemed to be in order* **3** business, concern: *that's not your affair* **4** a love affair

affect[1] *verb* **1** act on; have an effect on **2** move the feelings of

▣ **1** act on, change, transform, alter, modify, influence **2** stir, move, touch, influence, sway, upset, disturb, trouble, overcome

❗ Do not confuse with: **effect**

affect[2] *verb* pretend to feel or have: *affecting surprise* ◇ **affectation** *noun* pretence ◇ **affected** *adj* not natural, sham

▣ assume, put on, feign, simulate, imitate, fake, sham, pretend, profess ◇ **affectation** airs, pretentiousness, act, show, appearance, façade, pretence, sham ◇ **affected** assumed, artificial, fake, counterfeit, sham, *informal* phoney, contrived

affection *noun* a strong liking ◇ **affectionate** *adj* loving ◇ **affectionately** *adv*

▣ fondness, attachment, devotion, love, tenderness, care, warmth ◇ **affectionate** fond, loving, tender, caring, warm, kind, friendly, amiable

▣ dislike, antipathy ◇ **affectionate** cold, undemonstrative

affidavit *noun*, *law* a written statement made on oath

affiliated *adj* (with **with** or **to**) connected or attached to a group or organization ◇ **affiliation** *noun*

affinity *noun* (*plural* **affinities**) a close likeness or agreement

affirm *verb* state firmly ◇ **affirmation** *noun* a firm statement ◇ **affirmative** *adj* saying 'yes'

affix *verb* attach

afflict *verb* give continued pain or distress to ◇ **afflicted** *adj* ◇ **affliction** *noun*

▣ strike, burden, oppress, grieve, pain, hurt, wound, harm, torment ◇ **affliction** *noun* distress, grief, sorrow, misery, depression, suffering, pain, torment, disease, illness, sickness, trouble, hardship, misfortune

affluent *adj* wealthy ◇ **affluence** *noun*

▣ wealthy, rich, *slang* loaded, *informal* flush, well-off, prosperous

afford *verb* **1** be able to pay for **2** give, yield

▣ **2** provide, supply, furnish, produce

afforest *verb* cover (land) with forest ◇ **afforestation** *noun*

affray *noun* a fight, a brawl

affront *verb* insult openly ◇ *noun* an insult

▣ *verb* offend, insult, abuse, snub, slight, provoke, displease, irritate, annoy, anger, vex, incense, outrage ◇ *noun* offence, insult, slur, rudeness, discourtesy, indignity, snub, slight, wrong, abuse, vexation, outrage

afloat *adv* & *adj* floating

afoot *adv* happening or about to happen: *I could tell something was afoot*

aforesaid *adj* said, mentioned or named before: *the aforesaid person*

afraid *adj* **1** struck with fear **2** *informal* sorry to have to admit that: *I'm afraid there are no tickets left*

▣ **1** frightened, scared, alarmed, terrified, fearful, timorous, daunted, intimidated, cowardly, reluctant, apprehensive, anxious, nervous, timid

afresh *adv* once again, anew

aft *adv* near or towards the stern of a vessel

after *prep* **1** later in time than: *after dinner* **2** following: *arrived one after* *another; day after day* **3** in memory or honour of: *named after his father* **4** in pursuit of: *run after the bus* **5** about: *asked after her health* **6** despite: *after all my efforts, it still didn't work* **7** in the style of: *after Rubens* ◇ *adv* later in time or place: *we left soon* ◇ *conj* later than the time when: *after she arrived, things improved* ◇ **after-** *prefix* later in time or place: *in after years/aftertaste/afterthought* ◇ **after all** all things considered: *after all, he's still young* **2** despite everything said or done before: *I went after all*

afterbirth *noun* the placenta and membranes expelled from the uterus after giving birth

aftermath *noun* the bad results of something: *the aftermath of the election*

> Originally a second crop coming after the main harvest

afternoon *noun* the time between noon and evening

aftershave *noun* a lotion used on the face after shaving

aftersun *noun* a lotion applied to the skin after sunbathing

afterthought *noun* a later thought

afterwards *adv* later

again *adv* **1** once more: *say that again* **2** in or into the original state, place *etc*: *there and back again* **3** on the other hand: *again, I might be wrong* **4** *informal* at another later time: *see you again*

▣ **1** once more, once again, another time, over again, afresh, anew

against *prep* **1** in opposition to: *against the law/fight against injustice* **2** in the opposite direction to: *against the wind* **3** on a background of: *against the sky* **4** close to, touching: *lean against the wall* **5** as protection from: *guard against infection*

age *noun* **1** a long period of time **2** the time someone or something has lived or existed ◇ *verb* (**ages**, **ageing** or **aging**, **aged**) grow or make visibly older ◇ **aged** *adj* **1** old **2** of the age of: *aged five* ◇ **of age** legally an adult

▣ *noun* **1** era, epoch, generation, period, aeon ◇ *verb* grow old, mature, deteriorate, degenerate

ageism *noun* discrimination on grounds of age ◇ **ageist** *adj*

agency *noun* (*plural* **agencies**) **1** the office or business of an agent **2** action, means by which something is done

agenda *noun* a list of things to be done, *esp* at a meeting

agent *noun* **1** someone who acts for another **2** someone or something that acts **3** a spy

▣ **1** representative, *informal* rep, broker, middleman, go-between, intermediary

agent provocateur someone who deliberately incites others to violence, illegal action *etc*

aggrandize *verb* make greater ◇ **aggrandizement** *noun*

aggravate *verb* **1** make worse **2** *informal* annoy ◇ **aggravating** *adj* ◇ **aggravation** *noun*

▣ **1** exacerbate, worsen, intensify, heighten, magnify, exaggerate **2** annoy, irritate, vex, irk, exasperate, incense, provoke, tease, pester, harass, *informal* bug

aggregate *noun* a total

aggressive *adj* **1** ready to attack **2** quarrelsome ◇ **aggression** *noun* ◇ **aggressively** *adv* ◇ **aggressor** *noun*

▣ **1** hostile, offensive, provocative **2** belligerent, argumentative ◇ **aggression** antagonism, offence, attack, invasion, aggressiveness, belligerence, hostility

▣ **1** peaceable, friendly **2** submissive, timid

aggrieved *adj* hurt, upset

aggro *noun*, *informal* aggression, hostility

aghast *adj* struck with horror

agile *adj* active, nimble ◇ **agility** *noun*

agitate *verb* **1** stir up **2** excite, disturb **3** (often with **for**) campaign, argue ◇ **agitated** *adj* ◇ **agitation** *noun* ◇ **agitator** *noun*

▣ **1** arouse, stimulate, inflame, ferment **2** worry, trouble, upset, alarm, disturb, unsettle, fluster ◇ **agitator** trouble-maker, revolutionary, *slang* stirrer, in-citer, instigator

agnostic *noun* someone who be-lieves it is impossible to know whether God exists or not ◇ **agnosticism** *noun*

ago *adv* in the past: *that happened five years ago*

agog *adj* eager, excited

agony *noun* (*plural* **agonies**) great pain or suffering ◇ **agonizing** *adj* causing great pain ◇ **agony aunt** someone who gives advice in an agony column ◇ **agony column** a regular col-umn in a newspaper or magazine in which readers submit and receive ad-vice about personal problems

▣ anguish, torment, torture, pain, suffer-ing, affliction, distress, misery

agoraphobia *noun* great fear of open spaces and public places ◇ **agor-aphobic** *noun* & *adj*

agrarian *adj* of farmland or farming

agree *verb* **1** be alike in opinions, deci-sions *etc* **2** say that you will do some-thing, consent ◇ **agreeable** *adj* **1** pleasant **2** ready to agree ◇ **agreeably** *adv* ◇ **agree with 1** suit **2** cause no problems in digestion: *the fish didn't agree with me*

▣ **1** concur, see eye to eye, get on, match **2** consent, assent, accede, concede, yield, comply

▤ **1** disagree, differ, conflict **2** refuse

agreement *noun* **1** likeness of opi-nions **2** a written statement of some-thing agreed

agriculture *noun* the cultivation of the land, farming ◇ **agricultural** *adj* ◇ **agriculturalist** *noun*

aground *adj* & *adv* stuck on the bot-tom of the sea or a river: *run aground*

ahead *adv* in front; in advance: *finish-ing ahead of time*

aid *verb* help, assist ◇ *noun* help, assis-tance

▣ *verb* help, assist, rally round, relieve, support, subsidize, sustain ◇ *noun* help, assistance, support, relief, benefit, sub-sidy, grant, funding, sponsorship

▤ *verb* hinder, impede, obstruct ◇ *noun* hindrance, impediment, obstruction

aide-de-camp /eɪddə'kɑ̃/ *noun* (*plural* **aides-de-camp**) an officer who carries messages to and from a general on the field

aide-memoire *noun* (*plural* **aides-memoire**) something to help you re-member; a reminder

AIDS or **Aids** *abbrev* Acquired Immune Deficiency Syndrome

ail *verb* **1** be ill **2** trouble: *what ails you?* ◇ **ailing** *adj*

aileron *noun* a hinged flap on the back edge of an aeroplane's wing, used to control balance

ailment *noun* a minor illness

aim *verb* **1** point (*eg* a weapon or mis-sile) at **2** intend to do **3** direct: *advertis-ing aimed at the young* ◇ *noun* **1** the act of, or skill in, aiming **2** the point aimed at, goal, intention ◇ **aimless** *adj* with-out aim or purpose ◇ **aimlessly** *adv*

▣ *verb* **2** aspire, wish, seek, intend, pro-pose, mean, plan, design, strive, try, at-tempt ◇ *noun* **2** aspiration, ambition, hope, dream, desire, wish, plan, inten-tion, target, goal, objective ◇ **aimless** unmotivated, undirected, random, er-ratic, unpredictable

air *noun* **1** the mixture of gases (mainly oxygen and nitrogen) which we breathe, the atmosphere **2** a light breeze **3** fresh air **4** space overhead **5** a tune **6** the look or manner (of a per-son) ◇ *verb* **1** expose to the air **2** make known (an opinion *etc*) ◇ **airing** *noun* the act of exposing to the air ◇ **airless** *adj* ◇ **on the air** broadcasting

▣ *noun* **6** appearance, look, bearing, character, effect ◇ *verb* **2** voice, give vent to, broadcast ◇ **airless** unventi-lated, stuffy, musty, stifling

airbag *noun* a bag which automati-cally inflates inside a car on impact to protect the driver from injury

airbed *noun* a mattress which can be inflated

airborne *adj* in the air, flying

air-conditioned *adj* equipped with

a system for filtering and controlling the temperature of the air ◇ **air-conditioning** noun

aircraft noun (plural **aircraft**) a flying machine

Types of aircraft include:
aeroplane, plane, jet, jumbo, Concorde, airbus, helicopter, monoplane, two-seater, air-ambulance, freighter, aquaplane, seaplane, glider, hang-glider, microlight, hot-air balloon; fighter, spitfire, bomber, informal kite, jump jet, dive-bomber, slang chopper, spy plane, delta-wing, swing-wing, troop carrier, airship, turbojet, VTOL (vertical take-off and landing), warplane, zeppelin.

air force the branch of the armed forces using aircraft

airgun noun a gun worked by means of compressed air

airlock noun 1 a bubble in a pipe obstructing the flow of a liquid 2 a compartment with two doors for entering and leaving an airtight spaceship etc

air miles credits towards the cost of air tickets

airplane US spelling of **aeroplane**

airport noun a place where aircraft land and take off, with buildings for customs, facilities for passengers etc

air-raid noun an attack by aeroplanes

airship noun a large balloon which can be steered and driven

airstream noun a flow of air

airtight adj made so that air cannot pass in or out

airy adj 1 of or like the air 2 well supplied with fresh air 3 light-hearted ◇ **airily** adv
■ 2 well-ventilated, draughty, breezy, blowy, windy 3 cheerful, happy, light-hearted, high-spirited, lively, nonchalant, offhand

aisle /aɪl/ noun a passage between sections of eg seats in a theatre, church etc

ajar adv partly open: leave the door ajar

aka abbrev also known as: Stevens, aka The Fly

akimbo adv with hand on hip and elbow bent outward

From an Old Norse term meaning 'bowed' or 'curved'

akin adj similar

à la carte adj & adv on or from a menu in which each dish is chosen and priced separately

alacrity noun briskness, cheerful readiness

à la mode adj & adv 1 fashionable 2 US served with ice-cream: apple pie à la mode

alarm noun 1 sudden fear 2 something which rouses to action or gives warning of danger ◇ verb frighten ◇ **alarming** adj ◇ **alarmist** someone who frightens others needlessly
■ noun 1 fright, scare, fear, terror, panic, horror, shock, consternation, dismay, distress 2 danger signal, alert, warning, distress signal, siren, bell, alarm-bell ◇ verb frighten, scare, startle, panic, unnerve, daunt, dismay, distress
■ verb reassure, calm, soothe

alas exclam a cry showing grief

albatross noun (plural **albatrosses**) a type of large sea-bird

albino noun (plural **albinos**) someone or an animal with no natural colour in their skin, hair and eye pupils

album noun 1 a book with blank pages for holding photographs, stamps etc 2 a set of recordings issued on one disc or under one title

albumen noun the white of an egg

alchemy noun an early form of chemistry aimed at changing other metals into gold ◇ **alchemist** noun

alcohol noun 1 the intoxicating substance in drinks such as beer, wine and spirits 2 a drink or drinks containing alcohol ◇ **alcoholic** adj of or containing alcohol ◇ noun someone addicted to alcohol ◇ **alcoholism** noun addiction to alcohol
■ 2 drink, slang booze, liquor, spirits,

intoxicant ◇ **alcholholic** *noun* drunk, drunkard, inebriate, dipsomaniac, *slang* wino, *slang* alkie

alcove *noun* a recess in the wall of a room

alder *noun* a type of tree which grows beside ponds and rivers

ale *noun* a drink made from malt, hops *etc*

alert *noun* a signal to be ready for action ◇ *verb* warn ◇ *adj* **1** watchful **2** quick-thinking ◇ **on the alert** on the watch (for)
■ *verb* warn, notify, inform, signal ◇ *adj* **1** attentive, vigilant, observant, perceptive, *informal* on the ball **2** intelligent, quick-witted, smart, sharp, keen, shrewd, astute, discerning, perceptive, responsive, receptive

alfresco *adj* & *adv* in the open air

algae /'algi:/ or /'aldʒi:/ *noun* a group of simple plants which includes seaweed

algebra *noun* a method of calculating, using letters and signs

algorithm *noun* a series of steps for solving a mathematical problem

alias *adv* also known as: *Mitchell alias Grassic Gibbon* ◇ *noun* (*plural* **aliases**) a false name
■ *noun* pseudonym, false name, assumed name, nom de plume, pen-name, stage name, nickname, sobriquet

alibi *noun* the plea or fact that someone suspected of or charged with a crime was elsewhere when it was committed

alien *adj* **1** foreign **2** extraterrestrial ◇ *noun* **1** a foreigner **2** an extraterrestrial ◇ **alienate** *verb* make unfriendly or unsympathetic ◇ **alien to** not in keeping with: *alien to her nature*
■ *adj* **1** strange ◇ *noun* **1** foreigner, newcomer, stranger, outsider

alight[1] *verb* (**alights**, **alighting**, **alighted**) **1** get off a train, bus *etc* **2** settle, land
■ *verb* **1** descend, get down, dismount, get off, disembark **2** land, touch down, come down, come to rest, settle, perch
▣ **1** board **2** ascend

alight[2] *adj* & *adv* on fire, burning

align *verb* **1** set in line: *align the text with the edge of the picture* **2** take sides in an argument *etc* ◇ **alignment** *noun* arrangement in a line

alike *adj* like one another, similar ◇ *adv* in the same way, similarly
■ *adj* similiar, comparable, akin, analogous, identical, parallel, even, uniform

alimentary *adj* of food ◇ **alimentary canal** the passage through the body which begins at the mouth

alimony *noun* an allowance paid by a husband to his wife, or a wife to her husband, to provide support when they are legally separated

alive *adj* **1** living **2** full of activity ◇ **alive to** aware of
■ **1** living, animate, breathing, existent **2** lively, animated, spirited, alert, energetic, vibrant

alkali *noun* a substance such as soda or potash (*contrasted with*: **acid**) ◇ **alkaline** *adj*

all *adj* & *pronoun* **1** every one (of): *we are all invited/all letters will be answered* **2** the whole (of): *painted all the house* ◇ *adv* wholly, completely: *dressed all in red* ◇ **all in 1** with everything included: *all-in price* **2** *informal* exhausted ◇ **all-in-one** *adj* combining two or more functions ◇ **all over 1** over the whole of **2** everywhere **3** finished, ended ◇ **all right 1** satisfactory **2** well, uninjured ◇ **all-rounder** *noun* someone skilled in many kinds of work, sport *etc*
■ *adj* **1** each, every, each and every, every single, every one of

allay *verb* **1** make less: *tried to allay my fears* **2** calm or relieve
■ **1** reduce, diminish, check, lessen, moderate **2** alleviate, relieve, soothe, ease, calm, tranquillize, quiet, quell, pacify, mollify, soften, blunt

allege *verb* say without proof ◇ **allegation** *noun*
■ assert, claim, maintain, profess ◇ **allegation** accusation, charge, claim

allegiance *noun* loyalty

allegory *noun* (*plural* **allegories**) a

story or fable dealing with a subject in a way which suggests a deeper, more serious meaning ◇ **allegorical** *adj*

allergen *noun* a substance which causes an allergic reaction

allergy *noun* (*plural* **allergies**) abnormal sensitiveness of the body to certain substances ◇ **allergic** *adj*

alleviate *verb* make less severe, distressing, *etc* ◇ **alleviation** *noun*

■ relieve, soothe, ease, palliate, mitigate, soften, cushion, deaden, allay, lessen, reduce, diminish, check, moderate, temper, subdue

🔁 aggravate

alley *noun* (*plural* **alleys**) **1** a narrow passage or lane **2** an enclosure for playing bowls or skittles

alliance *see* ally

alligator *noun* a large reptile which looks like a crocodile

alliteration *noun* the repetition of the same sound at the beginning of two or more words close together, *eg* 'round and round the ragged rocks' ◇ **alliterative** *adj*

allocate *verb* give (*eg* a share of something) to ◇ **allocation** *noun*

■ assign, designate, budget, allow, earmark, set aside, allot, apportion, share out, distribute, dispense, mete out

allot *verb* (**allots**, **allotting**, **allotted**) give (*eg* a share of something) to ◇ **allotment** *noun* **1** the act of distributing **2** a small plot of ground for growing vegetables *etc*

■ divide, ration, apportion, share out, distribute, dispense, dole out, allocate, assign, designate, allow, grant, earmark, set aside

allow *verb* **1** let (someone do something) **2** (with **for**) take into consideration (in calculations, plans *etc*) **3** admit, confess **4** give, *esp* at regular intervals: *she allows him £40 a week* ◇ **allowable** *adj*

■ **1** permit, enable, authorize **2** take into account, make provision for, bear in mind **3** acknowledge, concede **4** allot, allocate, give

🔁 **1** forbid, prevent **3** deny

allowance *noun* a fixed sum or amount given regularly ◇ **make allowances for** treat differently because of special circumstances *etc*

■ payment, pocket money, grant, maintenance

alloy *noun* a mixture of two or more metals

■ blend, compound, composite, amalgam, combination, mixture, fusion, coalescence

allude *verb* (with **to**) refer to indirectly

❗ Do not confuse with: **elude**

allusion *noun* an indirect reference

❗ Do not confuse with: **delusion** and **illusion**

allusive *adj* referring indirectly, hinting ◇ **allusively** *adv*

❗ Do not confuse with: **elusive** and **illusive**

allure *verb* tempt, draw on by promises, attractive appearance *etc* ◇ **allurement** *noun* ◇ **alluring** *adj*

■ lure, entice, seduce, tempt, coax, attract, captivate

alluvium *noun* (*plural* **alluvia**) earth, sand *etc* brought down and left by rivers in flood ◇ **alluvial** *adj*

ally *verb* (**allies**, **allying**, **allied**) join yourself in alliance ◇ *noun* (*plural* **allies**) someone in alliance with another or others; a friend ◇ **alliance** *noun* a joining together of two or more people, nations *etc*, for a common cause ◇ **allied** *adj* **1** joined in alliance **2** similar or related

■ *verb* affiliate, collaborate, join forces, team up, unite ◇ *noun* associate, colleague, helper, accomplice

almanac *noun* a calendar for any year, with information about the phases of the moon *etc*

almighty *adj* having much power ◇ **the Almighty** God

almond *noun* the kernel of the fruit of a small tree

almost *adv* very nearly but not quite:

almost five years old/almost home

alms *noun* gifts to the poor

aloe /'aloʊ/ *noun* a South African plant of the lily family, used in medicine, cosmetics *etc*

aloft *adv* **1** on high **2** upward

alone *adj* not accompanied by others, solitary: *alone in the house* ◇ *adv* **1** only, without anything else: *that alone is bad enough* **2** not with others: *do you live alone?* ◇ **leave alone** let be, leave undisturbed

■ *adj* single, unique, isolated, apart, by oneself, by itself, on one's own

along *prep* over the length of: *walk along the road* ◇ *adv* onward: *come along!* ◇ **alongside** *prep* beside ◇ *adv* near a ship's side ◇ **along with** together with

aloof *adj* distant in manner, showing no interest in others ◇ **aloofness** *noun*

■ distant, remote, standoffish, haughty, cool, chilly, cold, unapproachable, unfriendly

☒ sociable, friendly, concerned

aloud *adv* so as to be heard: *read aloud*

alphabet *noun* the letters of a language given in a fixed order ◇ **alphabetic** or **alphabetical** *adj* in the order of the letters of the alphabet ◇ **alphabetically** *adv*

alpine *adj* of the Alps or other high mountains

already *adv* **1** before this or that time: *I've already done that* **2** now, before the expected time: *you can't have finished already*

Alsatian *noun* a German shepherd dog

also *adv* in addition, besides, too: *I also need to buy milk* ◇ **also-ran** *noun* someone or something that competed (*eg* in a race) but was not among the winners

■ too, as well, and, plus, along with, including, as well as, additionally, in addition, besides, further, furthermore, moreover

altar *noun* **1** a raised place for offerings to a god **2** in Christian churches, the communion table

alter *verb* change ◇ **alteration** *noun*

■ change, vary, modify, adjust, tweak, convert, transform ◇ **alteration** change, variation, adjustment, conversion, transformation

altercation *noun* an argument or quarrel

alternate *verb* of two things: do or happen in turn ◇ *adj* happening *etc* in turns ◇ **alternately** *adv* ◇ **alternation** *noun*

■ *verb* interchange, reciprocate, rotate, take turns, vary, oscillate ◇ *adj* alternating, every other, every second, interchanging, rotating

> ❗ Do not confuse: **alternate** and **alternative**

alternative *adj* offering a second possibility: *an alternative solution* ◇ *noun* a second possibility, a different course of action: *I had no alternative but to agree*

■ *adj* substitute, second, another, other, different ◇ *noun* option, choice, substitute, back-up

although *conj* though, in spite of the fact that

altimeter *noun* an instrument for measuring height above sea level

altitude *noun* height above sea level

alto *noun* (*plural* **altos**) *music* **1** the male voice of the highest pitch **2** the female voice of the lowest pitch

> An alternative term for the female *alto* voice is **contralto**

altogether *adv* **1** considering everything, in all: *there were 20 of us altogether/altogether it was a wonderful holiday* **2** completely: *not altogether satisfied*

■ **1** in all, in total, all in all, on the whole, generally, in general **2** totally, entirely, wholly, fully, utterly, absolutely

altruism *noun* unselfish concern for the good of others ◇ **altruistic** *adj* ◇ **altruistically** *adv*

◼ **altruistic** unselfish, self-sacrificing, disinterested, philanthropic, charitable, humanitarian, benevolent, generous, considerate, humane

aluminium or *US* **aluminum** *noun* a very light metal

alumnus *noun* (*plural* **alumni**) a former student or pupil

always *adv* **1** for ever: *he'll always remember this day* **2** every time: *she always gets it wrong*
◼ **1** eternally, evermore, forever **2** every time, consistently, invariably, without exception, unfailingly, constantly

am [1] or **a.m.** *abbrev* before noon (from Latin *ante meridiem*)

am [2] *see* **be**

amalgam *noun* a mixture (*esp* of metals)

amalgamate *verb* join together, combine; mix ◇ **amalgamation** *noun*
◼ merge, blend, incorporate, integrate, compound, fuse, unite, unify, ally

amass *verb* collect in large quantity

amateur *noun* someone who takes part in an activity for fun, not for money (*contrasted with*: **professional**) ◇ **amateurish** *adj* not done properly; not skilful ◇ **amateurishly** *adv*

amaze *verb* surprise greatly ◇ **amazement** *noun* ◇ **amazing** *adj* ◇ **amazingly** *adv*
◼ surprise, startle, astonish, astound, stun, daze, dumbfound, *informal* flabbergast

Amazon *noun* **1** one of a nation of mythological warrior women **2** a very strong or manlike woman

ambassador *noun* **1** a government minister sent to look after the interests of one country in another country **2** a representative

amber *noun* a hard yellowish fossil resin used in making jewellery ◇ *adj* **1** made of amber **2** of the colour of amber

ambidextrous *adj* able to use both hands with equal skill ◇ **ambidexterity** *noun*

ambience *noun* environment, atmosphere ◇ **ambient** *adj*

ambiguous *adj* having two possible meanings ◇ **ambiguity** *noun* (*plural* **ambiguities**) uncertainty in meaning ◇ **ambiguously** *adv*
◼ equivocal, confusing, obscure, unclear, vague, indefinite, uncertain
◼ clear, definite

❗Do not confuse with: **ambivalent**

ambition *noun* **1** the desire for success, power, fame *etc* **2** a desire to achieve a particular thing: *her ambition is to be a pilot* ◇ **ambitious** *adj* ◇ **ambitiously** *adv*
◼ enterprise, drive, push, commitment, zeal ◇ **ambitious** aspiring, bold, assertive, enterprising, eager

ambivalent *adj* having two contrasting attitudes towards something; undecided ◇ **ambivalence** *noun* ◇ **ambivalently** *adv*
◼ contradictory, conflicting, clashing, opposed, inconsistent, mixed, confused, hesitant, irresolute, undecided, unresolved, uncertain, unsure

❗Do not confuse with: **ambiguous**

amble *verb* walk without hurrying ◇ *noun* an unhurried walk

ambrosia *noun* the mythological food of the gods, which gave eternal youth and beauty

ambulance *noun* a vehicle for carrying the sick or injured

ambush *noun* (*plural* **ambushes**) **1** the act of lying hidden in order to make a surprise attack **2** an attack made in this way **3** the place of hiding for such an attack ◇ *verb* attack suddenly from a position of hiding
◼ *noun* **1** waylaying, surprise **2** trap, snare **3** cover ◇ *verb* lie in wait, waylay, surprise, trap, ensnare

amenable *adj* open to advice or suggestion ◇ **amenably** *adv*
◼ accommodating, flexible, open, agreeable, responsive

amend *verb* **1** correct, improve **2** alter slightly ◇ **amendment** *noun* a change, often in something written ◇ **make**

amends make up for having done wrong
■ **1** revise, improve, correct, rectify, remedy, ameliorate, better **2** alter, adjust, modify, qualify

🛈 Do not confuse with: **emend**

amenity *noun* (*plural* **amenities**) a pleasant or convenient feature of a place *etc*

amethyst *noun* a precious stone of a bluish-violet colour

amiable *adj* likeable; friendly ◇ **amiability** *noun* ◇ **amiably** *adv*
■ affable, friendly, approachable, genial, cheerful, good-natured, kind

amicable *adj* friendly ◇ **amicably** *adv*

amid or **amidst** *prep* in the middle of, among: *staying calm amidst all the confusion*
■ midst, in the midst of, in the thick of, among, amongst, surrounded by, in the middle of

amiss *adv* wrongly; badly

ammonia *noun* a strong-smelling gas made of hydrogen and nitrogen

ammunition *noun* gunpowder, shot, bullets, bombs *etc*

amnesia *noun* loss of memory ◇ **amnesiac** *noun* & *adj* (someone) suffering from amnesia

amnesty *noun* (*plural* **amnesties**) a general pardon of wrongdoers
■ pardon, forgiveness, absolution, mercy, lenience, indulgence, reprieve, remission, dispensation, immunity

amoeba /əˈmiːbə/ *noun* (*plural* **amoebas** or **amoebae**) a very simple form of animal life found in ponds *etc*

amok or **amuck** *adv*: **run amok** go mad and do a lot of damage, run riot

From a Malay word meaning 'fighting frenziedly'

among or **amongst** *prep* **1** in the midst or in the middle of: *among friends* **2** in shares, in parts: *divide it among yourselves* **3** in the group of: *among all her novels, this is the best*

amoral *adj* incapable of distinguishing between right and wrong ◇ **amorality** *noun* ◇ **amorally** *adv*

🛈 Do not confuse with: **immoral**

amorous *adj* loving; ready or inclined to love ◇ **amorously** *adv*

amount *noun* **1** total, sum **2** a quantity ◇ **amount to** add up to
■ **1** number, sum, total **2** quantity, mass, bulk, extent

amp *noun* **1** an ampère **2** *informal* an amplifier

ampère *noun* the standard unit of electric current

ampersand *noun* the character (&) representing *and*

From phrase *and per se and*, 'and by itself and'

amphetamine *noun* a type of drug used as a stimulant

amphibian *noun* **1** a cold-blooded animal that lives on land and in water **2** a vehicle that can operate on land and in water ◇ *adj* living on land and water ◇ **amphibious** *adj*

Amphibians include:
frog, bullfrog, tree frog, toad, horned toad, midwife toad, natterjack, newt, eft, salamander, conger eel, axolotl

amphitheatre *noun* a theatre with seats surrounding a central arena

ample *adj* **1** plenty of **2** large enough
■ **1** abundant, plentiful, plenty of **2** spacious, considerable, substantial
🔁 **1**, **2** insufficient, inadequate, meagre

amplify *verb* (**amplifies**, **amplifying**, **amplified**) **1** make louder or stronger: *the device amplifies the electrical signal* **2** explain more fully ◇ **amplification** *noun* ◇ **amplifier** *noun* an electrical device for increasing loudness
■ **1** boost, intensify, strengthen, heighten

amplitude *noun* **1** largeness **2** size, extent

ampoule or *US* **ampule** *noun* a small glass container of medicine for injection

amputate *verb* cut off (*esp* a human limb) ◊ **amputation** *noun*

amuck *another spelling of* **amok**

amulet *noun* an object worn as a charm against evil

amuse *verb* 1 cause to laugh 2 give pleasure to ◊ **amusement** *noun* ◊ **amusing** *adj* 1 funny 2 giving pleasure
■ 1 make laugh, *informal* tickle 2 entertain, divert, cheer up, gladden, enliven, please, charm, delight, interest, occupy ◊ **amusement** entertainment, fun, enjoyment, pleasure ◊ **amusing** 1 funny, humorous, hilarious, comical 2 enjoyable

an *see* a

anachronism *noun* the mention of something which did not exist at the time spoken about ◊ **anachronistic** *adj*

anaemia or *US* **anemia** *noun* a shortage of red cells in the blood ◊ **anaemic** *adj* 1 suffering from anaemia 2 pale or ill-looking

anaerobic *adj* not requiring oxygen to live

anaesthesia or *US* **anesthesia** *noun* loss of feeling or sensation

anaesthetic or *US* **anesthetic** *noun* a substance which produces lack of feeling for a time in a part of the body, or which makes someone unconscious ◊ **anaesthetist** *noun* a doctor trained to administer anaesthetics

anaesthetize or *US* **anesthetize** *verb* administer an anaesthetic to
■ desensitize, numb, deaden, dull, drug, dope, stupefy

anagram *noun* a word or sentence formed by reordering the letters of another word or sentence, *eg* the word *veil* is an anagram of *evil*

anal *adj* of the anus

analgesic *adj* relieving pain ◊ *noun* a drug that relieves pain

analogy *noun* (*plural* **analogies**) 1 a likeness, resemblance in certain ways 2 a way of explaining one thing by comparing it with another ◊ **analogous** *adj*

similar, alike in some way ◊ **analogously** *adv*
■ 1 resemblance, similarity

analyse or *US* **analyze** *verb* 1 break down, separate into parts 2 examine in detail ◊ **analyst** *noun* 1 someone who analyses 2 a psychiatrist or psychologist
■ 1 break down, separate, divide, take apart, dissect 2 investigate, study, examine, scrutinize, review

analysis *noun* (*plural* **analyses**) 1 a separation into parts 2 a detailed examination (of something)
■ 1 breakdown, separation, dissection 2 investigation, enquiry, examination, review, evaluation

analytic or **analytical** *adj* 1 involving analysis: *an analytic approach* 2 able to make judgements using analysis: *an analytical mind*

analyze *US spelling of* **analyse**

anaphylaxis *noun* a sudden severe reaction to a substance ◊ **anaphylactic** *adj*

anarchy *noun* 1 lack or absence of government 2 disorder or confusion ◊ **anarchic** or **anarchical** *adj* ◊ **anarchist** *noun*
■ **anarchic** lawless, ungoverned, anarchistic, libertarian, rebellious, mutinous, disordered, confused, disorganized

anathema *noun* 1 a hated person or thing: *opera is anathema to him* 2 a curse

anatomy *noun* 1 the study of the parts of the body 2 the body ◊ **anatomist** *noun*

Anatomical terms include:
aural, biceps, bone, cardiac, cartilage, cerebral, cranial, crural, dental, diaphragm, dorsal, duodenal, elbow, epidermis, epiglottis, Fallopian tubes, foreskin, gastric, genitalia, gingival, gristle, groin, gullet, hamstring, helix, hepatic, hock, intercostal, jugular, lachrymal, ligament, lumbar, mammary, membral, muscle, nasal, neural, ocular, oesophagus, optical,

pectoral, pedal, pulmonary, renal, spine, tendon, triceps, umbilicus, uterus, uvula, voice-box, vulva, windpipe, wisdom tooth, womb *see also* **bone**.

ancestor *noun* someone from whom someone is descended by birth ◇ **ancestral** *adj* ◇ **ancestry** *noun* line of ancestors

■ forefather, forebear, progenitor ◇ **ancestry** ancestors, forebears, forefathers, progenitors, parentage, family, lineage, line, descent, blood, race, stock, roots, genealogy, extraction, origin, heredity

anchor *noun* a heavy piece of metal, with hooked ends, for holding a ship fast to the bed of the sea *etc* ◇ *verb* **1** fix by anchor **2** let down the anchor ◇ **anchorman**, **anchorwoman** *noun* the main presenter of a television news programme *etc* ◇ **cast anchor** let down the anchor ◇ **weigh anchor** pull up the anchor

anchorage *noun* a place where a ship can anchor

anchorite *noun* a hermit, a recluse

anchovy *noun* (*plural* **anchovies**) a small fish of the herring family

ancient *adj* **1** very old **2** of times long past

■ **1** old, aged **2** antique, prehistoric, old-fashioned, out-of-date, antiquated, archaic, obsolete

ancillary *adj* serving or supporting something more important

and *conj* **1** joining two statements, pieces of information *etc*: *black and white film/add milk and stir* **2** in addition to: *2 and 2 make 4*

anecdote *noun* a short, interesting or amusing story, usually true ◇ **anecdotal** *adj*

anemone *noun* a type of woodland or garden flower

aneurism *noun* a balloon-like swelling in an artery

angel *noun* **1** a messenger or attendant of God **2** a very good or beautiful person ◇ **angelic** *adj* ◇ **angelically** *adv*

angelic cherubic, seraphic, celestial, heavenly, divine, saintly, virtuous, lovely, beautiful, adorable

angelica *noun* a plant whose candied leaf-stalks are used as cake decoration

anger *noun* a bitter feeling of great displeasure against someone or something ◇ *verb* make angry

■ *noun* annoyance, irritation, displeasure, rage, fury, indignation ◇ *verb* annoy, irritate, *informal* aggravate, antagonize, enrage, infuriate, exasperate

angina *noun* a form of heart disease causing acute chest pains

angle *noun* **1** the V-shape made by two lines meeting at a point **2** a corner **3** a point of view ◇ *verb* present from a particular point of view

■ *noun* **3** standpoint, viewpoint, point of view, slant, perspective

angler *noun* someone who fishes with rod and line ◇ **angling** *noun* the sport of fishing with rod and line

Anglican *adj* of the Church of England ◇ *noun* a member of the Church of England

anglicize *verb* **1** turn into the English language **2** make English in character ◇ **anglicization** *noun*

Anglo-Saxon *adj* & *noun* **1** (of) the people of England before the Norman Conquest **2** (of) their language

angora *noun* wool made from the soft silky hair of a breed of goat or rabbit

angry *adj* feeling or showing anger ◇ **angrily** *adv*

■ annoyed, cross, irritated, displeased, irate, *informal* mad, enraged, incensed, indignant

◨ content, happy, calm

anguish *noun* very great pain or distress

angular *adj* **1** having angles **2** thin, bony ◇ **angularity** *noun*

animal *noun* **1** a living being which can feel and move of its own accord **2** an animal other than a human ◇ *adj* of or like an animal

Animals include:
cat, dog, hamster, gerbil, mouse, rat,

rabbit, hare, fox, badger, beaver, mole, otter, weasel, ferret, ermine, mink, polecat, hedgehog, squirrel, horse, pig, cow, bull, goat, sheep; monkey, lemur, gibbon, ape, chimpanzee, orang-utan, baboon, gorilla; seal, sea lion, dolphin, walrus, whale; lion, tiger, cheetah, puma, panther, cougar, jaguar, ocelot, leopard; aardvark, armadillo, wolf, wolverine, hyena, mongoose, skunk, racoon, wombat, platypus, koala; deer, antelope, gazelle, eland, impala, reindeer, elk, caribou, moose; wallaby, kangaroo, bison, buffalo, gnu, camel, zebra, llama, panda, giant panda, grizzly bear, polar bear, giraffe, hippopotamus, rhinoceros, elephant

animate *verb* **1** give life to **2** make lively ◇ *adj* living ◇ **animated** *adj* **1** lively **2** of a cartoon character: made to move as if alive

▤ **animated 1** lively, spirited, buoyant, vibrant, vivacious, energetic, active

▨ **animated 1** lethargic, sluggish, inert

animation *noun* **1** liveliness **2** a film made from a series of drawings *etc* that give the illusion of movement when shown in sequence ◇ **animator** *noun* an artist who works in animation

animosity *noun* bitter hatred, enmity
▤ ill feeling, acrimony, rancour, hate, hatred, hostility

aniseed *noun* a seed with a flavour like that of liquorice

ankle *noun* the joint connecting the foot and leg

annals *noun plural* yearly historical accounts of events

anneal *verb* toughen glass or metal by heating strongly and cooling slowly

annex *verb* **1** take possession of (*eg* territory) **2** add, attach ◇ *noun* (*also spelled* **annexe**) a building added to another ◇ **annexation** *noun*

▤ *verb* **1** acquire, appropriate, seize, occupy **2** add, append, affix, attach, fasten, connect

annihilate /əˈnaɪəleɪt/ *verb* destroy completely ◇ **annihilation** *noun*
▤ eliminate, eradicate, obliterate, erase, wipe out, *informal* liquidate, murder, assassinate, exterminate, extinguish, raze, destroy, abolish

anniversary *noun* (*plural* **anniversaries**) the day of each year when a particular event is remembered

---

Names of wedding anniversaries include:
1st cotton, 2nd paper, 3rd leather, 4th flowers/fruit, 5th wood, 6th iron/sugar, 7th copper/wool, 8th bronze/pottery, 9th pottery/willow, 10th tin, 11th steel, 12th silk/linen, 13th lace, 14th ivory, 15th crystal, 20th china, 25th silver, 30th pearl, 35th coral, 40th ruby, 45th sapphire, 50th gold, 55th emerald, 60th diamond, 70th platinum

---

annotate *verb* add notes or explanation to (a text) ◇ **annotation** *noun*
▤ **annotation** note, footnote, gloss, comment, commentary, exegesis, explanation

announce *verb* make publicly known ◇ **announcement** *noun* ◇ **announcer** *noun* someone who announces programmes on TV *etc*, or reads the news
▤ declare, proclaim, disclose, divulge, publish, broadcast ◇ **announcement** declaration, proclamation, bulletin, disclosure, broadcast

annoy *verb* make rather angry; irritate ◇ **annoyance** *noun* ◇ **annoyed** *adj* ◇ **annoying** *adj*
▤ rile, displease, anger, irk, exasperate, *informal* wind up

annual *adj* yearly ◇ *noun* **1** a plant that lives only one year **2** a book published yearly ◇ **annualize** *verb* convert to a yearly rate, amount *etc* ◇ **annually** *adv*

annuity *noun* (*plural* **annuities**) a yearly payment made for a certain time or for life

annul *verb* (**annuls, annulling, annulled**) declare no longer valid; put an end to ◇ **annulment** *noun*

◼ nullify, invalidate, void, rescind, abrogate, suspend, cancel, abolish, quash, repeal, revoke, negate, retract, recall, reverse

anode *noun* the conductor through which an electric current enters a battery *etc*

anodyne *adj* soothing, relieving pain ◇ *noun* something that soothes pain

anoint *verb* smear with ointment or oil, *esp* as part of a religious ceremony

anomaly *noun* (*plural* **anomalies**) something unusual or not according to rule ◇ **anomalous** *adj*

◼ abnormality, exception, irregularity, inconsistency, incongruity, aberration, deviation, divergence, peculiarity, oddity

anon. *abbrev* anonymous

anonymous *adj* without the name of the author, giver *etc* being known or given ◇ **anonimity** *noun* ◇ **anonymously** *adv*

anorak *noun* a hooded waterproof jacket

anorexia *noun* **1** (*also called* **anorexia nervosa**) a psychological disorder causing the sufferer to refuse food and become sometimes dangerously thin **2** lack of appetite ◇ **anorexic** *adj & noun*

another *adj* **1** a different (thing or person): *moving to another job* **2** one more of the same kind: *have another biscuit* ◇ *pronoun* an additional thing of the same kind: *do you want another?*

answer *verb* **1** speak, write *etc* in return or reply **2** find the result or solution of (a sum, problem *etc*) **3** (with **for**) be responsible **4** (with **for**) suffer, be punished ◇ *noun* **1** something said, written *etc* in return or reply **2** a solution (*eg* to a problem) ◇ **answerable** *adj* **1** able to be answered **2** responsible: *answerable for her actions*

◼ *verb* **1** reply, acknowledge, respond **2** solve, explain ◇ *noun* **1** reply, acknowledgement, response, reaction **2** solution, explanation

ant *noun* a very small insect which lives in organized colonies ◇ **ant-hill**

noun an earth mound built by ants as a nest ◇ **have ants in your pants** be impatient or restless

antagonist *noun* **1** an enemy **2** an opponent ◇ **antagonism** *noun* hostility, opposition, enmity ◇ **antagonistic** *adj* opposed (to), unfriendly, hostile

◼ **1** enemy, foe, adversary **2** opponent, adversary, rival, competitor, contestant, contender

antagonize *verb* make an enemy of, cause to feel anger or dislike

◼ alienate, estrange, disaffect, repel, embitter, offend, insult, provoke, annoy, irritate, anger, incense

▣ disarm

Antarctic *adj* of the South Pole or regions round it

ante /ˈantɪ/ *noun* a stake in poker *etc*

ante- *prefix* before

anteater *noun* an American animal with a long snout which feeds on ants and termites

antecedent *adj* going before in time ◇ *noun* **1** someone who lived at an earlier time; an ancestor **2** (**antecedents**) previous conduct, history *etc*

antedate *verb* **1** date before the actual date **2** be earlier in date than

antediluvian *adj* very old or old-fashioned

Literally 'before the flood', in allusion to the Biblical story of Noah

antelope *noun* a graceful, swift-running animal like a deer

antenatal *adj* **1** before birth **2** relating to pregnancy: *antenatal clinic*

antenna *noun* (*plural* **antennas** or **antennae**) **1** an insect's feeler **2** an aerial

anteroom *noun* a small room leading into a larger room

anthem *noun* **1** a piece of music for a church choir **2** any song of praise, *eg* a national anthem

anthology *noun* (*plural* **anthologies**) a collection of specially chosen poems, stories *etc*

■ selection, collection, compilation, digest, treasury, miscellany

anthracite *noun* coal that burns with a hot, smokeless flame

anthrax *noun* an infectious disease of cattle, sheep *etc*, sometimes transferred to humans

anthropoid *adj* of apes: resembling humans

anthropology *noun* the study of mankind ◇ **anthropological** *adj* ◇ **anthropologist** *noun*

anti- *prefix* against, opposite: *antiterrorist*

antibiotic *noun* a drug or medicine taken to kill disease-causing bacteria

antibody *noun* (*plural* **antibodies**) a substance produced in the human body to fight bacteria *etc*

anticipate *verb* 1 look forward to, expect 2 see or know in advance 3 act before (someone or something) ◇ **anticipation** *noun* 1 expectation 2 excitement ◇ **anticipatory** *adj*

■ 1 expect, await 2 foresee, predict, forecast 3 pre-empt, intercept

anticlimax *noun* a dull or disappointing ending

anticlockwise *adj & adv* in the opposite direction to the hands of a clock

antics *noun plural* tricks, odd or amusing actions

anticyclone *noun* a circling movement of air round an area of high pressure, causing calm weather

antidote *noun* something given to act against the effect of poison

antifreeze *noun* a chemical with a low freezing-point, added to a car radiator to prevent freezing

antihistamine *noun* a medicine used to treat an allergy

antipathy *noun* extreme dislike

■ aversion, dislike, hate, hatred, loathing, abhorrence, antagonism, animosity, ill-will

antiperspirant *noun* a substance applied to the body to reduce sweating

antipodes *noun plural* places on the earth's surface exactly opposite each other, *esp* Australia and New Zealand in relation to Europe ◇ **antipodean** *adj*

antique *noun* an old, interesting or valuable object from earlier times ◇ *adj* 1 old, from earlier times 2 old-fashioned ◇ **antiquarian** *noun* a dealer in antiques ◇ **antiquated** *adj* grown old or out of fashion

■ antiquity, relic, bygone, period piece, heirloom, curio, museum piece, curiosity, rarity

antiquity *noun* (*plural* **antiquities**) 1 ancient times, *esp* those of the Greeks and Romans 2 great age 3 (**antiquities**) objects from earlier times

antiseptic *adj* germ-destroying ◇ *noun* a chemical *etc* which destroys germs

■ *adj* disinfectant, medicated

antisocial *adj* 1 not fitting in with other people; harmful to other people 2 disliking the company of other people

■ 1 unacceptable, disruptive, disorderly, rebellious 2 hostile, unfriendly, unsociable, uncommunicative, reserved, retiring, withdrawn, alienated, unapproachable

antithesis *noun* (*plural* **antitheses**) the exact opposite: *the antithesis of good taste* ◇ **antithetical** *adj*

antler *noun* the branched horn of a deer

anus /'eɪnəs/ *noun* the lower opening of the bowel through which faeces pass

anvil *noun* a metal block on which blacksmiths hammer metal into shape

anxiety *noun* (*plural* **anxieties**) worry about what may happen, apprehensiveness

■ worry, concern, apprehension, uneasiness, tension, stress

anxious *adj* worried, apprehensive ◇ **anxiously** *adj*

■ worried, concerned, nervous, apprehensive, tense, troubled, tormented

any *adj* 1 some: *is there any milk?* 2 every, no matter which: *any day will suit me* ◇ *pronoun* some: *there aren't any left*

◊ *adv* at all: *I can't work any faster* ◊ **anybody** *pronoun* any person ◊ **anyhow** *adv* **1** in any case: *I think I'll go anyhow* **2** carelessly: *scattered anyhow over the floor* ◊ **anyone** *pronoun* any person ◊ **anything** *pronoun* something of any kind ◊ **anyway** *conj* at any rate ◊ **anywhere** *adv* in any place ◊ **at any rate** in any case, whatever happens

AOB *abbrev* (written on agendas *etc*) any other business

aorta /eɪˈɔːtə/ *noun* the large artery carrying blood from the heart

apart *adv* **1** aside **2** in or into pieces: *came apart in my hands* **3** in opposite directions ◊ **apart from 1** separate, or separately, from **2** except for: *who else knows apart from us?*

apartheid *noun* the political policy of keeping people of different races apart

apartment *noun* **1** a room in a house **2** *US* a flat

apathy *noun* lack of feeling or interest ◊ **apathetic** *adj* ◊ **apathetically** *adv*
▣ indifference, passivity, listlessness, sluggishness ◊ **apathetic** uninvolved, indifferent, unemotional, unmoved, unconcerned, passive, listless

ape *noun* a member of a group of animals related to monkeys but larger, tailless and walking upright ◊ *verb* imitate
▣ *verb* copy, imitate, echo, mirror, parrot, *informal* take off, parody, mock

aperitif *noun* a drink taken before a meal

aperture *noun* an opening, a hole

apex *noun* (*plural* **apexes** or **apices**) the highest point of anything

aphasia *noun* inability to speak or express thoughts verbally

aphid /ˈeɪfɪd/ *noun* a small insect which feeds on plants

aphrodisiac *noun* a drug, food *etc* that increases sexual desire ◊ *adj* causing increased sexual desire

apiary *noun* (*plural* **apiaries**) a place where bees are kept ◊ **apiarist** *noun* someone who keeps bees in an apiary or studies bees

apiece *adv* to or for each one: *three chocolates apiece*

aplomb *noun* calm self-confidence
▣ composure, calmness, equanimity, poise, balance, coolness, confidence, assurance, self-assurance
▣ discomposure

apocalypse *noun* the future destruction of the world ◊ **apocalyptic** *adj*

apocryphal /əˈpɒkrɪfəl/ *adj* unlikely to be true
▣ unauthenticated, unverified, unsubstantiated, unsupported, questionable, spurious, doubtful
▣ authentic, true

apogee /ˈapəʊdʒiː/ *noun* **1** a culmination, a climax **2** the point of an orbit furthest from the earth

apologize *verb* express regret, say you are sorry

apology *noun* (*plural* **apologies**) an expression of regret for having done wrong ◊ **apologetic** *adj*
▣ **apologetic** sorry, repentant, contrite, remorseful, conscience-stricken, regretful, rueful

apoplexy *noun* sudden loss of ability to feel, move *etc*, a stroke ◊ **apoplectic** *adj*

apostle *noun* **1** a religious preacher, *esp* one of the disciples of Christ **2** an advocate for a cause

apostrophe *noun* **1** a mark (') indicating possession: *the minister's cat* **2** a similar mark indicating that a letter *etc* has been missed out, *eg isn't* for *is not*

apothecary *noun* (*plural* **apothecaries**) *old* a chemist or pharmacist

appal *verb* (**appals**, **appalling**, **appalled**) horrify, shock ◊ **appalling** *adj*
▣ horrify, shock, outrage, disgust, dismay ◊ **appalling** horrifying, horrific, harrowing, shocking, outrageous, disgusting, awful, dreadful, terrible, horrible

apparatus *noun* equipment required for a piece of work

apparel *noun* clothing

apparent *adj* easily seen, evident ◊ **apparently** *adv*
▣ seeming, outward, visible, evident,

noticeable, perceptible, plain, clear, manifest, patent

◨ hidden, obscure

apparition *noun* **1** something remarkable which appears suddenly **2** a ghost

appeal *verb* **1** ask earnestly (for help, money *etc*) **2** *law* take a case that has been lost to a higher court **3** be pleasing (to) ◇ *noun* **1** a request for help **2** *law* the taking of a case to a higher court ◇ **appealing** arousing liking or sympathy ◇ **appealingly** *adv*

◨ *verb* **1** plead, beg, beseech, implore, entreat **3** attract, draw, allure, lure, tempt, entice, engage ◇ *noun* **1** request, plea, entreaty

appear *verb* **1** come into view **2** arrive **3** seem ◇ **appearance** *noun* **1** an act of appearing **2** the outward look of someone or something

◨ *verb* **1** materialize, surface **2** enter, turn up, show (up) **3** seem, look

appease *verb* soothe or satisfy, *esp* by giving what was asked for

appendectomy *noun*, *med* surgical removal of the appendix

appendicitis *noun*, *med* inflammation of the appendix

appendix *noun* (*plural* **appendices** or **appendixes**) **1** a part added at the end of a book **2** a small worm-shaped part of the bowels

appertain *verb* (with **to**) **1** belong (to) **2** relate or pertain (to)

appetite *noun* **1** desire for food **2** taste or enthusiasm (for): *no appetite for violence*

◨ **1** hunger **2** relish, zest, taste, propensity, inclination, desire, longing, yearning, craving, eagerness, passion, zeal

appetizer *noun* a snack taken before a main meal

appetizing *adj* tempting to the appetite

◨ mouthwatering, tempting, inviting, appealing, palatable, succulent

applaud *verb* show approval of by clapping the hands ◇ **applause** *noun*

apple *noun* a round firm fruit, usually red or green

appliance *noun* a tool, instrument, machine *etc*

applicable *adj* **1** able to be applied **2** suitable, relevant

◨ **2** relevant, pertinent, apposite, apt, appropriate, fitting, suited, suitable, proper, valid, legitimate

applicant *noun* someone who applies or asks

application *noun* **1** the act of applying **2** something applied, *eg* an ointment **3** a formal request, usually on paper **4** hard work, close attention

appliqué *noun* needlework in which cut pieces of fabric are sewn onto a background to form patterns

apply *verb* (**applies**, **applying**, **applied**) **1** put on (an ointment *etc*) **2** use **3** ask formally (for) **4** (often with **to**) be suitable or relevant, affect: *the rule applies to non-members only* ◇ **apply yourself** work hard

◨ **1** put on, smear, rub **2** exercise, utilize, employ, implement **3** request, ask for, put in for, appeal (for)

appoint *verb* **1** place in a job: *she was appointed manager* **2** fix (a date *etc*) ◇ **appointment** *noun* **1** the act of appointing **2** a job, a post **3** an arrangement to meet someone

◨ **1** employ, take on, commission **2** decide (on), determine, arrange, settle ◇ **appointment 2** job, position, post, office **3** engagement, date, meeting, interview, consultation

◨ **1** reject, dismiss, discharge

apportion *verb* divide in fair shares

apposite *adj* suitable, appropriate

appraise *verb* estimate the value or quality of ◇ **appraisal** *noun*

◨ **appraisal** valuation, rating, survey, inspection, review, examination, evaluation, assessment, estimate, judgement, opinion, appreciation

appreciate *verb* **1** see or understand the good points, beauty *etc* of: *appreciate art* **2** understand: *I appreciate your point* **3** rise in value ◇ **appreciable** *adj* noticeable, considerable ◇ **appreciation** *noun*

■ **1** enjoy, savour, admire, respect, regard **2** comprehend, recognize, acknowledge

apprehend *verb* **1** arrest **2** *formal* understand

apprehension *noun* **1** fear or anxiety about something in the future **2** arrest **3** *formal* understanding

apprehensive *adj* afraid or anxious, feeling apprehension ◇ **apprehensively** *adv*

apprentice *noun* someone who is learning a trade ◇ **apprenticeship** *noun*

approach *verb* **1** come near **2** be nearly equal to **3** speak to in order to ask for something ◇ *noun* (*plural* **approaches**) **1** a coming near: *the approach of winter* **2** a way leading to a place ◇ **approachable** *adj* **1** easy to speak to, friendly **2** able to be reached

■ *verb* **1** move towards, draw near, near, gain on, catch up **2** be like, compare with, approximate, come close **3** apply to, appeal to, sound out

approbation *noun* good opinion, approval

appropriate *adj* suitable, fitting ◇ *verb* **1** take possession of **2** set (money *etc*) aside for a purpose ◇ **appropriately** *adv* ◇ **appropriation** *noun*

■ *adj* applicable, relevant, pertinent, to the point, well-chosen, apt, fitting, suitable, fit, befitting, becoming, proper, correct ◇ *verb* **1** seize, take, expropriate, commandeer, requisition, confiscate, impound

approve *verb* **1** agree to, permit **2** think well (of): *did he approve of the new curtains?* ◇ **approval** *noun* ◇ **on approval** on trial, for return to a shop if not bought

■ **1** consent to, accede to, allow, permit, authorize, ratify, support, accept **2** admire, esteem, like, appreciate

approx. *abbrev* **1** approximate **2** approximately

approximate *adj* more or less accurate ◇ *verb* be or come near (to): *an*

account approximating to the truth ◇ **approximately** *adv* ◇ **approximation** *noun* a rough estimate

■ *adj* estimated, guessed, rough ◇ *verb* approach, border on, verge on ◇ **approximately** roughly, around, about, more or less, close to, nearly

après-ski *adj* taking place after a day's skiing

apricot *noun* an orange-coloured soft fruit like a small peach

April *noun* the fourth month of the year

apron *noun* a garment worn to protect the front of the clothes

apropos *adv*: **apropos of** in connection with, concerning

apse *noun* a rounded domed section, *esp* at the east end of a church

apt *adj* **1** (with **to**) likely: *apt to change his mind* **2** suitable, fitting ◇ **aptness** *noun* suitability

■ **1** liable, prone, disposed, likely **2** relevant, apposite, appropriate, fitting

aptitude *noun* talent, ability

■ ability, capability, capacity, faculty, gift, talent, flair, facility, proficiency

◪ inaptitude

aqualung *noun* a breathing apparatus worn by divers

aquamarine *noun* **1** a type of bluish-green precious stone **2** a bluish-green colour ◇ *adj* bluish-green

aquarium *noun* (*plural* **aquaria**) a tank or tanks for keeping fish or water animals

aquatic *adj* living, growing or taking place in water

aqueduct *noun* a bridge for taking a canal *etc* across a valley

aqueous *adj* of or containing water

aquiline *adj* **1** like an eagle **2** of a nose: curved or hooked

arable *adj* of land: used for growing crops

arachnid /ə'raknɪd/ *noun* a small eight-legged invertebrate creature

arbiter *noun* **1** a judge, an umpire, someone chosen by opposing parties to decide between them **2** someone who sets a standard or has influence: *an arbiter of good taste*

arbitrary *adj* **1** fixed according to opinion rather than objective rules **2** occurring haphazardly ◇ **arbitrarily** *adv* ◇ **arbitrariness** *noun*

⊟ **1** discretionary, subjective, instinctive, unreasoned **2** illogical, irrational, unreasonable

arbitrate *verb* act as a judge between people or their claims *etc* ◇ **arbitration** *noun* the act of judging between claims *etc*, the settlement of a dispute by an arbiter ◇ **arbitrator** *noun* someone who arbitrates

⊟ judge, adjudicate, referee, umpire, mediate, settle, decide, determine ◇ **arbitration** judgement, adjudication, intervention, mediation, negotiation

arboreal *adj* of trees, living in trees

arbour *noun* a seat in a garden shaded by branches *etc*

arc *noun* part of the circumference of a circle, a curve

arcade *noun* a covered walk, *esp* one with shops on both sides

arch¹ *noun* (*plural* **arches**) the curved part at the top of a gateway or supporting a bridge, roof *etc* ◇ *verb* raise or curve in the shape of an arch

arch² *adj* mischievous, roguish

arch- *prefix* chief, main: *arch-enemy*

archaeology *noun* the study of the people of earlier times from the remains of their buildings *etc* ◇ **archaeological** *adj* ◇ **archaeologist** *noun*

archaic *adj* no longer used, old-fashioned ◇ **archaism** *noun* an old-fashioned word *etc*

⊟ antiquated, old-fashioned, outmoded, passé, outdated, out-of-date, obsolete, old, ancient, antique

archangel *noun* a chief angel

archbishop *noun* a chief bishop

archdeacon *noun* a clergyman next in rank below a bishop

archduke *noun*, *hist* the title of the ruling princes of Austria

archer *noun* someone who shoots arrows from a bow ◇ **archery** *noun* the sport of shooting with a bow and arrows

archetype *noun* the original pattern or model from which copies are made ◇ **archetypal** *adj*

⊟ pattern, model, standard, prototype, original, precursor

archipelago *noun* (*plural* **archipelagoes** or **archipelagos**) a group of small islands

From an ancient Greek term for the Aegean Sea, which translates as 'chief sea'

architect *noun* someone who plans and designs buildings

architecture *noun* **1** the study of building **2** the style of a building

archive *noun* **1** historical papers, written records *etc* **2** a building *etc* in which these are kept **3** a place on a computer for keeping data that is rarely used or needed ◇ *verb* store in an archive

archway *noun* a passage or entrance beneath an arch

Arctic *adj* of the regions round the North Pole ◇ **arctic** *adj* very cold

ardent *adj* eager, passionate ◇ **ardently** *adv* ◇ **ardour** *noun*

⊟ fervent, fiery, intense, spirited, enthusiastic, eager, devoted

arduous *adj* difficult ◇ **arduously** *adv* ◇ **arduousness** *noun*

⊟ hard, difficult, tough, rigorous, severe, harsh, strenuous, tiring, exhausting, punishing

are *see* **be**

area *noun* **1** the extent of a surface measured in square metres *etc* **2** a region, a piece of land or ground

⊟ **2** locality, neighbourhood, environment, environs, district, territory, expanse

arena *noun* **1** a place for a public contest, show *etc* **2** *hist* the centre of an amphitheatre *etc* where gladiators fought

argue *verb* (**argues**, **arguing**, **argued**) **1** quarrel in words **2** try to prove by giving reasons **3** suggest or urge ◇ **arguable** adj that can be argued as being true, or as being false ◇ **arguably** adv

▣ **1** squabble, bicker, row, disagree, dispute, debate, discuss **2** reason, assert, demonstrate, indicate, prove

argument noun **1** a heated discussion, a quarrel **2** reasoning (for or against something) ◇ **argumentative** adj fond of arguing

▣ **1** quarrel, squabble, row, controversy, dispute, disagreement, clash, conflict **2** reason, logic, assertion, claim

aria noun a song for a solo voice in an opera

arid adj **1** very dry: arid land **2** uninteresting: arid prose ◇ **aridity** or **aridness** noun

arise verb (**arises, arising, arose, arisen**) **1** rise up **2** come into being

▣ **1** get up, stand up **2** originate, begin, start, commence, emerge, appear, happen, result

aristocracy noun those of the nobility and upper class ◇ **aristocrat** noun ◇ **aristocratic** adj

arithmetic noun a way of counting and calculating by using numbers ◇ **arithmetical** adj

ark noun the covered boat used by Noah in the biblical story of the Flood

arm¹ noun **1** the part of the body between the shoulder and the hand **2** anything jutting out like this

▣ noun **2** bough, branch, projection, extension, offshoot

arm² noun (**arms**) weapons ◇ verb equip with weapons ◇ **armed** adj carrying a weapon, esp a gun

▣ noun weapons, weaponry, firearms, guns, artillery, armaments, ammunition

armada noun a fleet of armed ships

armadillo noun (plural **armadillos**) a small American animal whose body is protected by bony plates

armageddon noun a final battle or devastation, an apocalypse

armaments noun plural equipment for war, esp the guns of a ship, tank etc

armchair noun a chair with arms at each side

armistice noun a halt in fighting during war, a truce

armour noun, hist a protective suit of metal worn by knights ◇ **armoured** adj of a vehicle: protected by metal plates ◇ **armoury** noun (plural **armouries**) an arms store

armpit noun the hollow under the arm at the shoulder

army noun (plural **armies**) **1** a large number of soldiers armed for war **2** a great number of anything

▣ **1** armed force, military, militia, soldiers, troops, legions **2** multitude, throng, host, horde

aroma noun a pleasant smell ◇ **aromatic** adj

▣ smell, odour, scent, perfume, fragrance, bouquet

aromatherapy noun a healing therapy involving massage with plant oils ◇ **aromatherapist** noun

arose past form of **arise**

around prep **1** in a circle about **2** on all sides of, surrounding **3** all over, at several places in: papers scattered around the room **4** somewhere near in time, place or amount: I left him around here/come back around three o'clock ◇ adv all about, in various places: people stood around watching

arouse verb **1** awaken **2** stir, move (a feeling or person) ◇ **arousal** noun

▣ **1** rouse, wake up, waken **2** animate, excite, prompt, provoke, stimulate, agitate, stir up

arpeggio noun, music a chord with the notes played in rapid succession, not at the same time

arraign verb accuse publicly in a lawcourt

arrange verb **1** put in some order **2** make plans, settle a date etc for: arrange a party/arrange to meet ◇ **arrangement** noun

▣ **1** order, tidy, position, set out, lay out, group, class, classify, categorize, sort (out) **2** organize, prepare, devise

array *noun* order, arrangement, display ◇ *verb* put in order

arrears *noun plural*: **in arrears** not up to date; behind with payments

arrest *verb* **1** seize or capture (a suspected criminal) **2** stop (growth, bleeding *etc*) **3** catch (the attention *etc*) ◇ *noun* **1** capture by the police **2** stopping ◇ **arresting** *adj* striking, capturing the attention

■ *verb* **1** capture, catch, seize, *informal* nick, apprehend, detain **2** stop, stem, check, restrain, inhibit, halt, interrupt, stall, delay, slow, retard, block, obstruct, impede, hinder

arrival *noun* **1** the act of arriving **2** someone or something that arrives

arrive *verb* reach a place ◇ **arrive at** reach, come to (a decision *etc*)

■ appear, turn up, *informal* show up, enter

arrogant *adj* proud, haughty, self-important ◇ **arrogance** *noun* ◇ **arrogantly** *adv*

■ haughty, scornful, contemptuous, superior, condescending, patronizing, high and mighty, self-important

☒ humble, unassuming, bashful

arrow *noun* **1** a straight, pointed weapon shot from a bow **2** an arrow-shaped sign showing direction

arrowroot *noun* a starch used in powdered form for thickening liquids

arse *noun, taboo slang* the buttocks

arsenal *noun* a factory or store for weapons, ammunition *etc*

arsenic *noun* an element which, combined with oxygen, makes a strong poison

arson *noun* the crime of setting fire to a house *etc* on purpose ◇ **arsonist** *noun*

art *noun* **1** drawing, painting, sculpture *etc* **2** cleverness, skill **3** cunning **4** (**arts**) non-scientific school or university subjects ◇ **artful** *adj* wily, cunning ◇ **artless** *adj* simple, frank

■ **1** painting, drawing, sculpture, artwork, craft, artistry **2** skill, knack, technique, method, mastery, expertise **3** cunning, craftiness, guile, deceit, trickery

artful cunning, crafty, sly, shrewd

Arts and crafts include:
painting, oil painting, watercolour, fresco, portraiture; architecture, drawing, sketching, caricature, illustration; graphics, film, video, animation, animatronics, digital design; sculpture, modelling, woodcarving, woodcraft, marquetry, metalwork, enamelling, cloisonné, engraving, etching, pottery, ceramics, mosaic, jewellery, stained glass, photography, lithography, calligraphy, collage, origami, spinning, weaving, batik, silk-screen printing, needlework, tapestry, embroidery, patchwork, crochet, knitting

---

artefact or **artifact** *noun* a human-made object

artery *noun* (*plural* **arteries**) a tube which carries blood from the heart through the body ◇ **arterial** *adj* ◇ **arterial road** a main traffic road

artesian well a well in which water rises to the surface by natural pressure

Artex *noun, trademark* a textured plaster coating for walls and ceilings

artichoke *noun* a thistle-like plant with an edible flower-head ◇ **Jerusalem artichoke** a type of sunflower with edible roots

article *noun* **1** a thing, an object **2** a composition in a newspaper, magazine *etc* **3** a section of a document **4** (**articles**) an agreement made up of clauses: *articles of apprenticeship* **5** *grammar* the name of the words *the*, *a*, *an* ◇ *verb* bind (an apprentice *etc*) by articles ◇ **articled** *adj*

■ *noun* **1** item, thing, object **2** feature, report, story, account, piece, review

articulate *adj* expressing thoughts or words clearly ◇ *verb* express clearly ◇ **articulation** *noun* ◇ **articulated lorry** a lorry with a cab which can turn at an angle to the main part of the lorry, making cornering easier

■ *adj* distinct, well-spoken, clear, lucid, intelligible, coherent, fluent, expressive

◇ *verb* utter, pronounce, enunciate, express, state

artifact *another spelling* of **artefact**

artificial *adj* not natural; human-made ◇ **artificiality** *noun* ◇ **artificially** *adv*

▣ false, fake, bogus, counterfeit, *informal* phoney

▣ genuine, true, real, natural

artillery *noun* **1** big guns **2** an army division that uses these

artisan *noun* a skilled worker

artist *noun* **1** someone who paints pictures **2** someone skilled in anything **3** an artiste ◇ **artistry** *noun* skill as an artist

Types of artist include:
architect, graphic designer,
designer, draughtsman,
draughtswoman, graphic artist,
illustrator, cartoonist, animator,
photographer, printer, engraver,
goldsmith, silversmith, blacksmith,
carpenter, potter, weaver, sculptor,
painter; craftsman, craftswoman

artiste /ɑːtiːst/ *noun* a performer in a theatre, circus *etc*

artistic *adj* **1** of artists: *the artistic community* **2** having a talent for art ◇ **artistically** *adv*

as *adv* & *conj* in phrases expressing comparison or similarity: *as good as his brother; the same as this one* ◇ *conj* **1** while, when: *happened as I was walking past* **2** because, since: *we stayed at home as it was raining* **3** in the same way that: *he thinks as I do* ◇ *adv* for instance ◇ **as for** concerning, regarding ◇ **as if** or **as though** as it would be if ◇ **as to** regarding ◇ **as well (as)** too, in addition (to)

asbestos *noun* a thread-like mineral which can be woven and which will not burn ◇ **asbestosis** *noun* a lung disease caused by inhaling asbestos dust

ascend *verb* **1** climb, go up **2** rise or slope upwards ◇ **ascendancy** or **ascendency** *noun* control (over) ◇ **ascendant** or **ascendent** *adj* rising

◇ **ascent** *noun* **1** an upward move or climb **2** a slope upwards; a rise ◇ **ascend the throne** be crowned king or queen

ascertain *verb* **1** find out **2** make certain

▣ **1** find out, learn, discover, determine, fix, establish, settle, locate, detect, identify **2** verify, confirm, make certain

ascetic *noun* someone who avoids all kinds of pleasure

ascribe *verb* think of as belonging to or due to: *the problem is ascribed to poor ventilation*

ash¹ *noun* **1** what is left after anything is burnt **2** (**ashes**) the remains of a body after cremation ◇ **ashen** *adj* very pale

ash² *noun* (*plural* **ashes**) a hardwood tree with silvery bark

ashamed *adj* feeling shame

▣ sorry, apologetic, remorseful, contrite, guilty, conscience-stricken, sheepish, embarrassed, humiliated, abashed, humbled

ashore *adv* on or onto the shore

aside *adv* on or to one side; apart ◇ *noun* words spoken which those nearby are not supposed to hear

asinine *adj* **1** of an ass **2** stupid

ask *verb* **1** put a question to someone, request information: *asked me my name* **2** say that you want (someone to do) something: *asked them to leave/asked for help* **3** invite

▣ **1** inquire, demand, request, seek **2** request, demand, order, bid, require

askance *adv* sideways ◇ **look askance at** look at with suspicion

askew *adv* sideways; awry; to one side

asleep *adj* **1** sleeping **2** of limbs: numbed

asp *noun* a small poisonous snake

asparagus *noun* a plant whose young shoots are eaten as a vegetable

aspect *noun* **1** a part or element of something **2** look, appearance **3** view, point of view **4** a side of a building *etc* or the direction it faces in

■ **1** part, element, facet, feature **2** appearance, look, air, manner, bearing **3** position, standpoint, point of view, view, outlook, angle **4** elevation, side, face, angle, direction

aspen noun a kind of poplar tree

asperity noun **1** harshness, sharpness of temper **2** bitter coldness

aspersion noun: **cast aspersions on** criticize or slander

asphalt noun a tarry mixture used to make pavements, paths etc

asphyxia /as'fɪksɪə/ noun suffocation by choking, drowning, smoke or other fumes etc ◇ **asphyxiate** verb suffocate ◇ **asphyxiation** noun

aspidistra noun a kind of pot plant with large leaves

aspire verb (with **to** or **after**) try to achieve or reach (something difficult, ambitious etc) ◇ **aspiration** noun ◇ **aspiring** adj trying or wishing to be: an aspiring director

■ **aspiration** aim, intent, objective, goal, ambition, hope, dream, desire ◇ **aspiring** ambitious, keen, eager, hopeful

aspirin noun a pain-killing drug

ass noun (plural **asses**) **1** a donkey **2** a stupid person **3** US slang the buttocks

assail verb attack ◇ **assailant** noun an attacker

assassin noun someone who assassinates, a murderer ◇ **assassinate** verb murder (esp a politically important person) ◇ **assassination** noun

■ murderer, killer, slayer, cut-throat, executioner, gunman, slang hitman

Literally 'hashish eater', after an Islamic sect during the Crusades who consumed the drug before assassinating Christians

assault noun an attack, esp a sudden one ◇ verb attack

■ noun attack, offensive, onslaught, raid, invasion ◇ verb invade, strike, hit, informal beat up, slang mug

assemblage noun a collection, a gathering

assemble verb **1** bring (people or things) together **2** put together (a machine etc) **3** meet together

■ **1** gather, collect, muster, round up, mobilize **2** construct, build, manufacture **3** congregate, convene, group

assembly noun (plural **assemblies**) **1** the act of assembling **2** a gathering of people, esp for a special purpose

assent verb agree ◇ noun agreement

assert verb **1** state firmly **2** insist on (a right etc) ◇ **assertion** noun ◇ **assertive** adj not shy, inclined to assert yourself ◇ **assert yourself** make yourself noticed, heard etc

■ **assertive** bold, confident, self-assured, emphatic, strong-willed

◪ **assertive** timid, diffident

assess verb **1** estimate the value, power etc of **2** fix (an amount to be paid in tax etc) ◇ **assessment** noun ◇ **assessor** noun

asset noun **1** an advantage, a helpful feature **2** (**assets**) the property of a person, company etc

assiduous adj persevering; hard-working ◇ **assiduously** adv

assign verb **1** give to someone as a share or task **2** fix (a time or place) ◇ **assignation** /asɪg'neɪʃən/ noun an appointment to meet ◇ **assignment** noun **1** the act of assigning **2** a task given

■ **assignment 2** commission, errand, task, project, job

assimilate verb take in, absorb, integrate ◇ **assimilation** noun

assist verb help ◇ **assistance** noun

■ verb help, aid, abet, rally round, support

assistant noun **1** a helper, eg to a senior worker **2** someone who serves in a shop etc

associate verb **1** keep company (with) **2** join (with) in partnership or friendship **3** connect in thought: I don't associate him with hard work ◇ adj joined or connected: an associate director/an associate member ◇ noun a friend, partner or companion

■ verb **1** socialize, mingle, mix, consort **2** affiliate, join, combine, unite **3** connect, correlate, relate

association noun 1 a club, society, union etc 2 a partnership, friendship 3 a connection made in the mind

■ 1 organization, corporation, company, coalition, confederacy, federation, consortium, cartel, syndicate, union, society, club 2 partnership, companionship, friendship 3 relationship, relation, tie, connection, correlation

assorted adj various, mixed ◇ **assortment** noun a variety, a mixture

assuage verb soothe, ease (pain, hunger etc)

assume verb 1 take as true without further proof, take for granted 2 take on (responsibility, a role etc) 3 put on (a disguise etc) ◇ **assumed** adj false or pretended: an assumed name ◇ **assumption** noun 1 the act of assuming 2 something taken for granted

■ 1 presume, surmise, accept 2 undertake, adopt, take over ◇ **assumed** false, bogus, fake, informal phoney, made-up

assure verb 1 make (someone) sure 2 tell (someone) positively (that) ◇ **assurance** noun 1 a feeling of certainty; confidence 2 a promise 3 insurance ◇ **assured** adj certain; confident

■ 1 hearten, reassure, comfort, ensure, confirm 2 affirm, guarantee, warrant, pledge, swear, tell, promise

asterisk noun a star (*) used in printing for various purposes, esp to point out a footnote or insertion

asthma noun an illness causing difficulty in breathing ◇ **asthmatic** adj suffering from asthma ◇ noun someone with asthma

astonish verb surprise greatly ◇ **astonishing** adj ◇ **astonishment** noun

■ surprise, startle, amaze, astound, stun, stagger, dumbfound, informal flabbergast, shock

astound verb surprise greatly, amaze ◇ **astounding** adj

astral adj of the stars

astray adv out of the right way, straying

astride adv with legs apart ◇ prep with legs on each side of

astringent noun a lotion etc used for closing up the skin's pores ◇ adj 1 used for closing the pores 2 of manner: sharp, sarcastic

astrology noun the study of the stars and their supposed power over the lives of humans ◇ **astrologer** noun

astronaut noun someone who travels in space

astronomy noun the study of the stars, planets and galaxies, and their movements ◇ **astronomer** noun ◇ **astronomical** adj 1 of astronomy 2 of a number: very large

astute adj cunning, clever ◇ **astutely** adv ◇ **astuteness** noun

■ shrewd, wise, canny, knowing, intelligent, sharp, discerning, clever, crafty

asunder adv apart, into pieces

asylum noun 1 a place of refuge or safety 2 old a home for the mentally ill

at prep 1 showing position, time etc: I'll be at home/come at 7 o'clock 2 costing: cakes at 75 pence each ◇ **at all** in any way: not worried at all

ate past form of **eat**

atheism noun belief that there is no God ◇ **atheist** noun someone who does not believe in any god ◇ **atheistic** adj

athlete noun someone good at sport, esp running, gymnastics etc

athletic adj 1 of athletics 2 good at sports; strong, powerful

■ 2 fit, energetic, vigorous, active, sporty, muscular, sinewy, brawny, strapping, robust, sturdy, strong, powerful, wiry

athletics noun sing sports such as running, jumping etc or competitions in these

atlas noun (plural **atlases**) a book of maps

After the mythological Atlas, punished by the Greek gods by having to carry the heavens on his shoulders

ATM abbrev automatic teller machine

atmosphere noun 1 the air round the

earth **2** any surrounding feeling: *a friendly atmosphere* ◇ **atmospheric** *adj* ◇ **atmospheric pressure** the pressure exerted by the atmosphere at the earth's surface, due to the weight of the air

■ **2** ambience, environment, surroundings, aura, mood, character

atoll *noun* a coral island or reef

atom *noun* **1** the smallest part of an element **2** anything very small ◇ **atomic** *adj* ◇ **atom bomb** or **atomic bomb** a bomb in which the explosion is caused by nuclear energy ◇ **atomic energy** nuclear energy

> *subatomic particles include*:
> photon, electron, positron, neutrino, anti-neutrino, muon, pion, kaon, proton, anti-proton, neutron, anti-neutron, lambda particle, sigma particle, omega particle, psi particle

atone *verb* make up for wrongdoing ◇ **atonement** *noun*

atrocious *adj* **1** *informal* very bad **2** cruel or wicked ◇ **atrociously** *adv* ◇ **atrociousness** *noun*

■ **1** shocking, dreadful, terrible, horrible, ghastly **2** heinous, savage, vicious, monstrous, fiendish, ruthless

atrocity *noun* (*plural* **atrocities**) **1** a terrible crime **2** *informal* something very ugly

attach *verb* **1** fasten or join (to) **2** think of (something) as having: *don't attach any importance to it* ◇ **attached** *adj* **1** fastened or joined **2** (*with* **to**) fond (of) ◇ **attachment** *noun* **1** something attached **2** a joining by love or friendship **3** a file sent with an email

■ **1** affix, stick, fasten, secure, tie, bind, unite, connect **2** ascribe, attribute, place, associate

attaché /ə'taʃeɪ/ *noun* a junior member of an embassy staff ◇ **attaché-case** *noun* small case for papers *etc*

attack *verb* **1** cause harm to suddenly or violently **2** speak or write against ◇ *noun* **1** an act of attacking **2** a spell (of an illness *etc*) ◇ **attacker** *noun*

■ *verb* **1** invade, raid, strike, storm, assault,

lay into **2** criticize, blame, denounce, revile ◇ **attacker** assailant, *slang* mugger, aggressor, critic

attain *verb* reach; gain ◇ **attainable** *adj* ◇ **attainment** *noun* **1** the act of attaining **2** something attained, an achievement or accomplishment

■ accomplish, achieve, fulfil, complete, effect, realize, earn, reach, touch, arrive at, get, acquire, obtain, procure, secure, gain, win, net

attempt *verb* try ◇ *noun* **1** a try or effort: *my first attempt* **2** an attack: *an attempt on the president's life*

■ *verb* endeavour, *informal* have a go, aspire, seek, strive, undertake ◇ *noun* **1** try, *informal* shot, *informal* go

attend *verb* **1** be present at or go regularly to **2** pay attention (to) **3** wait on, look after **4** *formal* accompany ◇ **attendance** *noun* **1** the fact of being present: *my attendance was expected* **2** the number of people present: *good attendance at the first night*

attendant *noun* someone employed to look after a public place, shop *etc*: *cloakroom attendant* ◇ *adj* accompanying, related: *stress and its attendant health problems*

■ *noun* helper, assistant, steward, waiter, servant, guide, usher, guard, custodian

attention *noun* **1** careful notice: *pay attention* **2** concentration **3** care and consideration **4** *military* a stiffly straight standing position: *stand to attention*

attentive *adj* **1** giving or showing attention **2** polite and caring ◇ **attentively** *adv* ◇ **attentiveness** *noun*

■ **1** alert, awake, vigilant, watchful, observant **2** considerate, thoughtful, kind, courteous

attic *noun* a room or storage space just under the roof of a house

> From *Attica* in ancient Greece, famous for a type of square architectural column used in upper storeys of classical buildings

attire *verb* dress ◇ *noun* clothing

attitude *noun* **1** a way of thinking or

feeling: *a positive attitude* **2** a position of the body

■ **1** feeling, disposition, mood, point of view, outlook, perspective

attorney *noun* (*plural* **attorneys**) **1** someone with legal power to act for another **2** *US* a lawyer

attract *verb* **1** draw to or towards **2** arouse liking or interest in ◇ **attraction** *noun* **1** the power of attracting **2** something which attracts visitors *etc*: *tourist attractions* ◇ **attractive** *adj* **1** good-looking, likeable **2** pleasing: *attractive price*

■ **1** pull, draw, entice, seduce, tempt **2** engage, fascinate, enchant, charm, captivate ◇ **attractive 1** good-looking, handsome, pretty, sexy **2** pleasing, appealing, inviting

attribute /ə'trɪbjuːt/ *verb* **1** state or consider as the source or cause of: *attribute the accident to human error* **2** state as the author or originator of: *attributed to Rembrandt* ◇ *noun*, /'atrɪbjuːt/ an attendant characteristic: *attributes of power* ◇ **attributable** *adj*

■ *verb* **1** assign, put down, blame, charge, refer **2** ascribe, accredit, credit ◇ *noun* property, quality, idiosyncrasy, peculiarity, quirk, mark, sign, symbol

attributive *adj*, *grammar* of an adjective or noun: placed before the noun it modifies, *eg* the adjective *young* in *young girl*

aubergine /'oʊbəʒiːn/ *noun* an oval dark purple fruit, eaten as a vegetable

auburn *adj* of hair: reddish-brown in colour

auction *noun* a public sale in which articles are sold to the highest bidder ◇ *verb* sell by auction ◇ **auctioneer** *noun* someone who sells by auction

audacious *adj* daring, bold ◇ **audaciously** *adv* ◇ **audacity** *noun*

audible *adj* able to be heard ◇ **audibility** *noun* ◇ **audibly** *adv*

audience *noun* **1** a number of people gathered to watch or hear a performance *etc* **2** a formal interview with someone important: *an audience with the Pope*

■ **1** spectators, onlookers, listeners, viewers, gathering, assembly

audio *noun* the reproduction of recorded or radio sound ◇ *adj* relating to such sound: *an audio tape*

audio-visual *adj* concerned with hearing and seeing at the same time ◇ **audio-visual aids** films, recordings *etc* used in teaching

audit *verb* examine accounts officially ◇ *noun* an official examination of a company's accounts ◇ **auditor** *noun*

audition *noun* a hearing to test an actor, singer *etc*

auditorium *noun* (*plural* **auditoria** or **auditoriums**) the part of a theatre *etc* where the audience sits

auditory *adj* of hearing

au fait /oʊ 'feɪ/ *adj* well-acquainted (with)

augment *verb* increase in size, number or amount ◇ **augmentation** *noun* ◇ **augmentative** *adj*

augur *verb*: **augur ill** be a bad sign for the future ◇ **augur well** be a good sign for the future

August *noun* the eighth month of the year

august *adj* full of dignity, stately

au naturel /oʊ natjʊə'rɛl/ *adv* with no additions; plain, natural

aunt *noun* a father's or a mother's sister, or an uncle's wife

au pair a young, often foreign person who does domestic duties in return for board, lodging and pocket money

aura *noun* (*plural* **auras** or **aurae**) a quality or feeling around a person or in a place

aural *adj* relating to the ear or hearing ◇ **aurally** *adv*

⚠ Do not confuse with: **oral**

auspices *noun plural*: **under the auspices of** under the control or supervision of

■ aegis, authority, patronage, sponsorship, backing, support, supervision, control

auspicious adj favourable; promising luck or success ◊ **auspiciously** adv
▣ favourable, propitious, encouraging, bright, rosy, promising, fortunate, lucky, prosperous

austere adj 1 severe 2 without luxury; simple, sparse ◊ **austerity** noun
▣ 1 stern, strict, cold, formal, rigid, hard, harsh 2 stark, bleak, plain, simple

authentic adj true, real, genuine ◊ **authentically** adv ◊ **authenticity** noun
▣ genuine, true, real, actual, certain, bona fide, legitimate, valid, reliable

authenticate verb show to be true or real ◊ **authentication** noun

author noun the writer of a book, poem, play etc

authoring noun composing, writing, compiling etc using information technology: a course in web authoring

authoritative adj stated by an expert or someone in authority ◊ **authoritatively** adv
▣ authentic, factual, true, accurate, faithful, convincing, sound, reliable, dependable

authority noun (plural **authorities**) 1 power or right 2 someone whose opinion is reliable, an expert 3 someone or a body of people having control (over something) 4 (**authorities**) people in power
▣ 1 authorization, permission, right, prerogative 2 connoisseur, specialist, informal guru

authorize verb 1 give (a person) the power or the right to do something 2 give permission for (something to be done) ◊ **authorization** noun
▣ 1 entitle, license, empower, enable 2 allow, consent to, approve, give the go-ahead

autism noun a disability in children affecting their ability to relate to and communicate with other people ◊ **autistic** adj affected with autism

autobiography noun (plural **autobiographies**) the story of someone's life, written or told by themselves ◊ **autobiographer** noun ◊ **autobiographical** adj

autocrat noun a ruler who has complete power ◊ **autocracy** noun government by such a ruler ◊ **autocratic** adj expecting complete obedience
▣ **autocracy** absolutism, totalitarianism, dictatorship, despotism, tyranny, authoritarianism

autograph noun someone's own signature ◊ verb write your signature on: autograph the book

automate verb make automatic by introducing machines etc ◊ **automation** noun the use of machines for controlling other machines in factories etc

automatic adj 1 of a machine etc: self-working 2 of an action: unconscious, done without thinking ◊ noun 1 something automatic (eg an automatic car or washing-machine) 2 a kind of self-loading gun ◊ **automatically** adv ◊ **automatic pilot** or **autopilot** 1 a device which can be set to control an aircraft on a course 2 the doing of anything unthinkingly or abstractedly
▣ adj 1 automated, self-activating, mechanical, computerized 2 spontaneous, reflex, informal knee-jerk, involuntary, unthinking, instinctive

automaton noun (plural **automatons** or **automata**) 1 a mechanical toy or machine made to look and move like a human 2 someone who acts mindlessly, like a machine

automobile noun, US a motor-car

autonomy noun the power or right of a country to govern itself ◊ **autonomous** adj ◊ **autonomously** adv

autopilot see automatic pilot

autopsy noun (plural **autopsies**) an examination of a body after death

autumn noun the season of the year following summer, when leaves change colour and fruits are ripe ◊ **autumnal** adj 1 relating to autumn 2 like that or those of autumn: autumnal colours

auxiliary adj supplementary, additional ◊ noun (plural **auxiliaries**) a helper, an assistant
▣ adj ancillary, assistant, subsidiary, secondary, supporting, supportive,

helping, assisting, extra, supplementary, spare, reserve, back-up, emergency, substitute

avail verb & noun: **avail yourself of** make use of ◊ **to no avail** without any effect, of no use

available adj able or ready to be made use of ◊ **availability** noun

◼ free, to hand, within reach, at hand, accessible, handy, convenient, on hand, informal off-the-shelf

◼ unavailable

avalanche noun **1** a mass of snow and ice sliding down a mountain **2** a great amount: an avalanche of work

avant-garde adj ahead of fashion, very modern: an avant-garde writer

avarice noun greed, esp for riches ◊ **avaricious** adj greedy

◼ avaricious covetous, grasping, greedy

avenge verb (**avenges**, **avenging**, **avenged**) take revenge for (a wrong) ◊ **avenger** noun

avenue noun **1** a tree-lined street or drive **2** a means, a way: any avenue of escape

aver verb (**avers**, **averring**, **averred**) state firmly

average noun the result obtained by adding a number of amounts and dividing the total by this number, eg the average of 3, 7, 9, 13 is 8 (32÷4) ◊ adj **1** ordinary, usual; of medium size etc **2** obtained by working out an average: the average cost is £10 ◊ verb **1** form an average **2** find the average of ◊ **on average** usually, typically

◼ adj **1** ordinary, everyday, common, standard, typical, unexceptional, run-of-the-mill, informal vanilla

◼ adj **1** extreme, exceptional, remarkable

averse adj not fond of, opposed (to)

aversion noun **1** extreme dislike or distaste: an aversion to sprouts **2** something that is hated

◼ **1** dislike, hate, hatred, loathing, distaste, disgust, revulsion, repulsion

avert verb, formal **1** turn away or aside: avert your eyes **2** prevent from happening: avert the danger

◼ **2** parry, fend off, ward off, stave off, forestall, frustrate, prevent, obviate

aviary noun (plural **aviaries**) a place for keeping birds

aviation noun the practice of flying or piloting aircraft ◊ **aviator** noun, old an aircraft pilot

avid adj eager, greedy: an avid reader ◊ **avidity** noun ◊ **avidly** adv

◼ keen, enthusiastic, fanatical, devoted, fervent, passionate

avocado noun **1** a pear-shaped fruit with a rough peel and rich, creamy flesh **2** a light, yellowish-green colour

avoid verb escape, keep clear of ◊ **avoidable** adj ◊ **avoidance** noun

◼ evade, dodge, shirk, get out of, bypass, refrain from, steer clear of

avoirdupois /avwɑːdjʊˈpwɑː/ or /avədəˈpɔɪz/ noun the system of measuring weights in pounds and ounces (compare with: **metric**)

avow verb, formal declare openly ◊ **avowal** noun ◊ **avowed** adj ◊ **avowedly** adv

avuncular adj **1** of an uncle **2** like an uncle, esp in being kind

await verb wait for

awake verb (**awakes**, **awaking**, **awoke**, **awoken**) **1** rouse from sleep **2** stop sleeping ◊ adj not asleep

◼ verb **1** wake up, rouse, arouse **2** awaken, waken, wake, wake up ◊ adj wide-awake, alert, vigilant, observant, attentive

awaken verb **1** awake **2** arouse (interest etc) ◊ **awakening** noun

award verb **1** give, present, grant (a prize etc) **2** grant legally: award damages to the defendant ◊ noun something that is awarded, a prize etc

◼ verb **1** give, present, bestow, accord, confer **2** grant, allot, apportion, assign, allow ◊ noun prize, trophy, decoration, medal, gift, grant

aware adj **1** having knowledge (of), conscious (of): aware of the dangers **2** alert ◊ **awareness** noun

◼ **1** conscious, alive to, sensitive, appreciative, familiar, conversant, acquainted, informed, *informal* up to speed, enlightened, cognizant **2** heedful, attentive, observant, sharp, alert, *informal* on the ball

away *adv* **1** to a distance: *run away* **2** not here; not at home or work: *she is away all this week* **3** in the opposite direction: *he turned away and left* **4** into nothing: *the sound died away* **5** constantly; diligently: *working away* ◇ **do away with** abolish, get rid of ◇ **get away with** do (something) without being punished ◇ **right away** immediately

awe *noun* wonder or admiration mixed with fear ◇ *verb* affect with awe: *awed by the occasion* ◇ **awestruck** *adj* full of awe

目 *noun* wonder, respect, admiration, amazement, reverence, fear, apprehension

awesome *adj* **1** causing fear **2** *informal* remarkable, admirable

awful *adj* **1** *informal* bad: *an awful headache* **2** *informal* very great: *an awful lot* **3** terrible: *awful crimes* ◇ **awfully** *adv*, *informal* very, extremely: *awfully good of you* ◇ **awfulness** *noun*

目 **1** dreadful, terrible, nasty **3** terrible, dreadful, ghastly, horrible, hideous, horrific, shocking

awkward *adj* **1** clumsy, not graceful **2** difficult to deal with: *an awkward*

customer ◇ **awkwardly** *adv* ◇ **awkwardness** *noun*

目 **1** clumsy, gauche, ham-fisted, unco-ordinated, ungainly, graceless, inelegant, cumbersome, *informal* clunky **2** difficult, delicate, troublesome

F3 **1** graceful, elegant

awl *noun* a pointed tool for boring small holes

awning *noun* a covering of canvas *etc* providing shelter

awry /əˈraɪ/ *adj & adv* **1** not according to plan, wrong **2** crooked

axe *noun* (*plural* **axes**) a tool for chopping ◇ *verb* **1** cancel (a plan *etc*) **2** reduce greatly (costs, services *etc*)

目 *verb* **1** cancel, terminate, discontinue, eliminate, throw out

axiom *noun* a truth, an accepted principle

目 principle, truth, truism, precept, dictum, maxim, adage, aphorism

axis *noun* (*plural* **axes**) **1** the line, real or imaginary, on which a thing turns: *the earth's axis* **2** a fixed line taken as a reference, *eg* in a graph

axle *noun* the rod on which a wheel turns

azalea *noun* a flowering plant related to the rhododendron

azure *adj* sky-coloured, clear blue

Bb

BA *abbrev* **1** British Airways **2** Bachelor of Arts

babble *verb* talk indistinctly or foolishly ◊ *noun* indistinct or foolish talk
📧 *verb* chatter, gabble, jabber, cackle, prate, mutter, mumble, murmur

babe *noun* **1** a baby **2** *informal* a girl or young woman

baboon *noun* a large monkey with a long, dog-like muzzle

baby *noun* (*plural* **babies**) a very young child, an infant ◊ *verb* (**babies, babying, babied**) treat like a baby
📧 babe, infant, suckling, child, tiny, toddler

babyhood *noun* the time when someone is a baby

babysitter *noun* someone who stays in the house with a child while its parents are out ◊ **babysit** *verb* (**babysits, babysitting, babysat**) ◊ **babysitting** *noun*

bachelor *noun* an unmarried man ◊ **Bachelor of Arts, Bachelor of Science** *etc* someone who has gained a degree by passing examinations at a university

bacillus /bə'sɪləs/ *noun* (*plural* **bacilli**) a rod-shaped germ

back *noun* **1** the part of the human body from the neck to the base of the spine **2** the upper part of an animal's body **3** the part of anything situated behind: *sitting at the back of the bus* **4** *football etc* a player positioned behind the forwards ◊ *adj* of or at the back ◊ *adv* **1** to or in the place from which someone or something came: *back at the house/walked back home* **2** to or in a former time or condition: *thinking back to their youth* ◊ *verb* **1** move backwards **2** bet on (a horse *etc*) **3** (often with **up**) help or support ◊ **backer** *noun* a supporter ◊ **back down** change your opinion *etc* ◊ **back out 1** move out backwards **2**

excuse yourself from keeping to an agreement ◊ **put your back into** work hard at ◊ **put someone's back up** irritate someone ◊ **with your back to the wall** in desperate difficulties
📧 *noun* **3** rear, stern, end, tail, tail end, reverse ◊ *adj* rear, hind, end ◊ *verb* **1** reverse, recede, backtrack, retreat, retire, withdraw, back away, recoil **3** support, sustain, assist, side with, encourage, promote, sponsor, finance, subsidize ◊ **back down** concede, yield, give in, surrender, submit, retreat, withdraw
📧 *noun* **3** front

backbone *noun* **1** the spine of the body **2** the main support of something **3** firmness, resolve
📧 **2** mainstay, support, foundation **3** determination, resolve, tenacity, steadfastness, toughness, stamina

backfire *verb* **1** of a vehicle: make an explosive noise in the exhaust pipe **2** of a plan: go wrong

background *noun* **1** the space behind the principal figures of a picture **2** details that explain something **3** someone's family and upbringing
📧 **1** surroundings, environment, setting **2** context, circumstances **3** grounding, preparation, education, upbringing, breeding

backhand *noun* a tennis stroke played with the back of the hand facing the ball ◊ **backhanded compliment** a compliment with a second, unflattering meaning

backing *noun* **1** support **2** material used on the back of a picture *etc* **3** a musical accompaniment on a recording
📧 **1** support, aid, assistance, sponsorship, finance

backlash *noun* a violent reaction against something
📧 reaction, response, repercussion, reprisal, retaliation

backlog *noun* an amount of uncompleted work *etc*

backstroke *noun* a stroke used in swimming on the back

backward *adj* **1** to or towards the back: *a backward glance* **2** slow in learning or development

■ **1** reverse, rearward **2** underdeveloped, retarded

🞸 **2** precocious

backwash *noun* a backward current, such as that caused by an outgoing wave

backwater *noun* **1** a river pool separate from the main stream **2** a place not affected by what is happening in the outside world

backwards *adv* **1** towards the back: *walked backwards out of the room* **2** in a reverse direction; back to front: *written backwards* **3** towards the past

backgammon *noun* a board game for two people played with counters and dice

bacon *noun* pig's flesh salted and dried, used as food

bacteria *noun plural* (*sing* **bacterium**) germs found in air, water, living and dead bodies, and especially decaying matter ◇ **bacterial** *adj*

■ germs, *informal* bugs, viruses, microbes, micro-organisms, bacilli

bad *adj* (**worse**, **worst**) **1** not good; wicked **2** (often with **for**) harmful: *smoking is bad for you* **3** of food: rotten, decaying **4** severe, serious: *bad dose of flu* **5** faulty **6** unwell ◇ **badly** *adv* **1** not well **2** seriously ◇ **badness** *noun* ◇ **bad language** swearing

■ **1** unpleasant, disagreeable, nasty, undesirable, unfortunate, distressing, adverse, evil, wicked, sinful, criminal, corrupt, immoral, vile **2** detrimental, harmful, damaging, injurious **3** rotten, mouldy, decayed, spoilt, putrid, rancid, sour, off, tainted, contaminated **4** serious, grave, severe, harsh **5** inferior, substandard, imperfect, faulty, defective, deficient, unsatisfactory, shoddy, useless ◇ **badly 1** wrongly, incorrectly, improperly, defectively, imperfectly,

inadequately, unsatisfactorily, poorly, incompetently, negligently, carelessly **2** extremely, exceedingly, intensely, deeply, acutely, bitterly, painfully, seriously, desperately, severely, critically, crucially

🞸 **1** good, pleasant, virtuous **3** fresh ◇ **badly 1** well

badge *noun* **1** a brooch-like ornament giving some information about the wearer **2** a mark or sign

■ **1** identification, pin **2** emblem, device, insignia, sign, mark

badger *noun* a burrowing animal of the weasel family which comes out at night ◇ *verb* pester or annoy

badminton *noun* a game resembling tennis, played with shuttlecocks

> Although based on a 16th-century game, this was first played in its modern form in *Badminton* House in Avon

baffle *verb* **1** be too difficult for; puzzle, confound **2** prevent from being carried out; hinder ◇ **baffling** *adj*

■ **1** puzzle, perplex, mystify, bemuse, bewilder, confuse, confound, *informal* bamboozle, *informal* flummox, daze, upset, disconcert, *informal* stump **2** foil, thwart, frustrate, hinder, check, defeat

🞸 **1** enlighten **2** help

BAFTA *abbrev* British Academy of Film and Television Arts

bag *noun* **1** a holder or container, often of a soft material **2** a quantity of fish or game caught ◇ *verb* (**bags**, **bagging**, **bagged**) **1** put in a bag **2** secure possession of, claim: *bag a seat* **3** kill (game) in a hunt

■ *verb* **2** obtain, acquire, get, secure, claim, take, appropriate, commandeer, reserve **3** catch, trap, land, kill, shoot

bagatelle *noun* a board game, in which balls are struck into numbered holes

bagel /'beɪɡəl/ *noun* a ring-shaped bread roll with a dense texture

baggage *noun* luggage

baggy *adj* of clothes: large and loose ◇ **bagginess** *noun*

☐ *adj* loose, roomy, ill-fitting

☒ *adj* tight

bagpipes *noun plural* a wind musical instrument made up of a bag, a pipe with fingerholes on which the tune is played and several other pipes for producing drones

bail[1] *noun* money given to bail out a prisoner ◇ **bail out** *verb* obtain temporary release of (an untried prisoner) by giving money which will be forfeited if they do not return for trial

⚠ Do not confuse with: **bale**

bail[2] *noun* (*usu* **bails**) *cricket* one of the cross-pieces on the top of the wickets

bail[3] *another spelling of* **bale**[2] (sense 2)

bailiff *noun* **1** an officer with the power to seize a debtor's property **2** a landowner's agent

bain-marie /bĕmāri/ *noun* (*plural* **bain-maries**) a double-boiler for cooking

Originally an alchemist's pot, named after the biblical Mary (or Miriam), sister of Moses

bairn *noun, Scot* a child

bait *noun* **1** food put on a hook to make fish bite, or in a trap to attract animals **2** something tempting or alluring ◇ *verb* **1** put bait on a hook *etc* **2** worry, annoy

☐ *noun* **2** lure, incentive, inducement, bribe, temptation, enticement, attraction ◇ *verb* **2** tease, provoke, goad, irritate, annoy, irk, *informal* needle, harass, persecute, torment

☒ *noun* **2** disincentive

baize /beɪz/ *noun* a coarse woollen cloth

bake *verb* **1** cook in an oven **2** dry or harden in the sun or in an oven ◇ **baking powder** a raising agent added to flour in cake-making *etc*

baker *noun* someone who bakes or sells bread *etc* ◇ **bakery** or **bakehouse** *noun* a place where bread, cakes *etc* are baked

baksheesh *noun* a gift of money; a tip

balaclava *noun* a knitted covering for the head and neck

balalaika *noun* a traditional Russian musical instrument like a guitar with a triangular body

balance *noun* **1** steadiness: *lost my balance and fell over* **2** the money needed to make the two sides of an account equal **3** an amount left over **4** a weighing machine ◇ *verb* **1** make or be the same in weight **2** make both sides of an account the same **3** make or keep steady: *balanced it on her head*

☐ *noun* **1** equilibrium, steadiness, stability, poise ◇ *verb* **1** level, square, equalize, equate, match, counterbalance, counteract **3** stabilize

☒ *noun* **1** imbalance, instability

balcony *noun* (*plural* **balconies**) **1** a platform built out from the wall of a building **2** an upper floor or gallery in a theatre *etc*

☐ **2** gallery, upper circle, gods

bald *adj* **1** without hair **2** plain, frank: *a bald statement*

☐ **2** forthright, direct, straight, downright, straightforward

☒ **1** hairy, hirsute

balderdash *noun* nonsense

bale[1] *noun* a large tight bundle of cotton, hay *etc*

bale[2] *verb*: **bale out 1** escape by parachute from an aircraft in an emergency **2** (*also*: **bail out**) scoop water out of a boat

⚠ Do not confuse with: **bail**

baleful *adj* harmful, malevolent: *baleful influence*

balk *verb* **1** hinder, baffle **2** (with **at**) refuse to do something

☐ **1** thwart, frustrate, disconcert, baffle, obstruct, hinder, check, stall, prevent **2** flinch, recoil, shrink, jib, hesitate, refuse, dodge, evade, shirk

ball[1] *noun* **1** a round object used in playing many games **2** anything round: *a ball of wool* ◇ **on the ball** *informal* in touch with the current situation, alert

◇ **play ball** *informal* play along, co-operate

ball [2] *noun* a formal party at which dancing takes place ◇ **have a ball** *informal* have a great time, enjoy yourself

ballad *noun* **1** a narrative poem with a simple rhyme scheme, *usu* in verses of four lines **2** a simple song

ballast *noun* sand, gravel *etc* put into a ship to steady it

ball-bearings *noun plural* small steel balls that sit loosely in grooves and ease the revolving of one part over another in machinery

ballerina *noun* a female ballet dancer

ballet *noun* a form of stylized dancing which tells a story by mime

balloon *noun* a bag filled with gas to make it float in the air, *esp* one made of thin rubber used as a toy *etc* ◇ *verb* puff or swell out

ballot *noun* a way of voting in secret by marking a paper and putting it into a box ◇ *verb* collect votes from by ballot
▪ *noun* poll, vote, referendum

ballpark *noun*, *US* a sports field for ball-games ◇ *adj* approximate, estimated: *a ballpark figure*

ballpoint *noun* a pen with a tiny ball as the writing point

ballroom *noun* a large room used for public dances *etc*

balls *noun plural*, *taboo slang* **1** testicles **2** courage **3** rubbish, nonsense

balls-up *noun*, *taboo slang* a mess; something bungled

balm *noun* **1** something soothing **2** a sweet-smelling healing ointment

balmy *adj* **1** mild, gentle; soothing: *balmy air* **2** sweet-smelling ◇ **balminess** *noun*

balsam *noun* an oily sweet-smelling substance obtained from certain trees

balsawood *noun* a lightweight wood obtained from a tropical American tree

balti *noun* a style of Indian cooking in which food is cooked and served in a wok-like pan

balustrade *noun* a row of pillars on a balcony *etc*, joined by a rail

bamboo *noun* the woody, jointed stem of a very tall Asian grass

bamboozle *verb* trick, puzzle

ban *noun* an order forbidding something ◇ *verb* (**bans**, **banning**, **banned**) forbid officially
▪ *noun* prohibition, embargo, veto, boycott, restriction, suppression, censorship, taboo ◇ *verb* forbid, prohibit, bar, exclude, ostracize, outlaw, banish, suppress, restrict
▫ *noun* permission, dispensation ◇ *verb* allow, permit, authorize

banal *adj* lacking originality or wit, commonplace ◇ **banality** *noun* ◇ **banally** *adv*
▪ trite, commonplace, ordinary, everyday, humdrum, boring, unimaginative, hackneyed, clichéd, stock, stereotyped, *informal* corny, stale, tired
▫ original, fresh, imaginative

banana *noun* the long yellow fruit of a type of tropical tree

band [1] *noun* **1** a strip of some material to put round something **2** a stripe (of colour *etc*) **3** a group of wavelengths for radio broadcasts
▪ **1** strip, belt, tape, binding, tie, strap

band [2] *noun* **1** a group of people **2** a group of musicians playing together ◇ *verb* join together
▪ *noun* **1** troop, gang, crew, group, party, body, club, clique **2** group, orchestra, ensemble ◇ *verb* group, gather, join, unite, ally, collaborate, affiliate
▫ *verb* disband, disperse

bandage *noun* a strip of cloth *etc* or special dressing wrapped around a wound or injury
▪ dressing, plaster, compress

B and B *abbrev* bed and breakfast

bandit *noun* an outlaw or robber, *esp* a member of a gang of robbers
▪ robber, thief, brigand, outlaw, highwayman, gunman, desperado

bandy [1] *adj* of legs: bent outwards at the knee
▪ bow-legged

bandy [2] *verb*: **bandy words** argue

bane *noun* a cause of ruin or trouble: *the bane of my life* ◇ **baneful** *adj* destructive, poisonous

bang *noun* **1** a sudden, loud noise **2** a heavy blow ◇ *verb* **1** close with a bang, slam **2** hit, strike: *banged his head on the door*

■ *noun* **1** explosion, boom, clash, slam, noise, report, shot **2** blow, hit, knock, bump, crash, collision, *informal* whack ◇ *verb* **2** strike, hit, bash, knock, bump, rap, drum, hammer, pound, thump

bangle *noun* a large ring worn on an arm or leg

banish *verb* **1** order to leave a country *etc* **2** drive away (doubts, fear *etc*) ◇ **banishment** *noun*

■ **1** expel, deport, exile, outlaw, ban, bar, debar, exclude, excommunicate, dismiss, oust

◼ **1** recall

banister *noun* the posts and handrail of a staircase

banjo *noun* (*plural* **banjoes** or **banjos**) a stringed musical instrument like a guitar with a long neck and a round body

bank[1] *noun* **1** a mound or ridge of earth *etc* **2** the edge of a river

bank[2] *noun* **1** a place where money is put for safety, lent *etc* **2** a place where blood *etc* is stored till needed **3** a public bin for collecting items for recycling: *a bottle bank* ◇ **banker** *noun* someone who manages a bank ◇ **bank holiday** a day on which all banks and many shops *etc* are closed ◇ **bank on** depend on, count on

bankrupt *noun* someone who has no money to pay their debts ◇ *adj* **1** unable to pay debts **2** utterly lacking in: *bankrupt of ideas* ◇ **bankruptcy** *noun* (*plural* **bankruptcies**)

■ *noun* debtor, pauper ◇ *adj* **1** insolvent, in liquidation, ruined, destitute, *informal* broke **2** exhausted, depleted, lacking

◼ *adj* **1** solvent, wealthy

banknote *noun* a piece of paper money issued by a bank

banner *noun* a flag carried in processions, *etc*

■ flag, standard, colours, ensign, pennant

banns *noun plural* a public announcement of a forthcoming marriage

banquet *noun* a ceremonial dinner ■ feast

bantam *noun* a small kind of chicken

banter *verb* tease in fun ◇ *noun* light teasing

■ *noun* pleasantry, badinage, repartee, word play

baptize *verb* **1** dip in, or sprinkle with, water as a sign of admission into the Christian Church **2** christen, give a name to ◇ **baptism** *noun* ◇ **baptismal** *adj*

■ **baptism** christening, initiation, debut, immersion, sprinkling

bar *noun* **1** a rod of solid material **2** a broad line or band **3** a piece, a cake: *a bar of soap* **4** a hindrance, a block **5** a bank of sand *etc* at the mouth of a river **6** a room, or counter, where drinks are served in a public house, hotel *etc* **7** a public house **8** the rail at which prisoners stand for trial **9** the lawyers who plead in a court **10** a time division in music ◇ *prep* except: *all the runners bar one finished the race* ◇ *verb* (**bars**, **barring**, **barred**) **1** fasten with a bar **2** exclude, shut out: *barred from the competition* ◇ **barring** *prep* except for, but for

■ *noun* **1** rod, stick, shaft, pole, stake, rail, railing **6** saloon, lounge, counter **7** *informal* pub, inn, tavern ◇ *verb* **1** barricade, lock, bolt, fasten, secure **2** exclude, ban, forbid, prohibit, prevent, preclude

barb *noun* the backward-pointing spike on an arrow, fish-hook *etc* ◇ **barbed** *adj* **1** having barbs **2** of a remark: hurtful ◇ **barbed wire** wire with regular clusters of sharp points, used for fencing *etc*

■ **barbed 1** prickly, spiny, thorny, jagged, toothed, pointed

barbarian *noun* an uncivilized person ◇ *adj* uncivilized ◇ **barbaric** *adj* **1** uncivilized **2** extremely cruel ◇ **barbarity** *noun*

■ *noun* savage, brute, ruffian, hooligan,

vandal, lout ◇ **barbaric 1** primitive, wild, savage **2** fierce, cruel, inhuman, brutal, uncivilized

🔄 **barbaric 2** humane, civilized, gracious

barbecue *noun* **1** a frame on which to grill food over an open fire **2** an outdoor party providing food from a barbecue ◇ *verb* cook (food) on a barbecue

> From a Haitian creole term for a wooden grid or frame

barber *noun* a men's hairdresser

barbiturate *noun* a type of sedative drug

bard *noun*, *formal* a poet

bare *adj* **1** uncovered, naked **2** plain, simple **3** empty ◇ *verb* uncover, expose ◇ **barefaced** *adj* impudent, unashamed: *a barefaced lie* ◇ **barely** *adv* hardly, scarcely

🔄 *adj* **1** naked, nude, unclothed, undressed, stripped, denuded, uncovered, exposed **2** plain, simple, unadorned, stark, basic, essential

bargain *noun* **1** an agreement, *esp* about buying or selling **2** something bought cheaply ◇ *verb* argue about a price *etc* ◇ **bargain for** expect: *more than he bargained for* ◇ **into the bargain** in addition, besides

🔄 *noun* **1** deal, transaction, contract, agreement, understanding, arrangement, negotiation **2** discount, reduction, giveaway, special offer ◇ *verb* negotiate, haggle, deal, trade, traffic, barter ◇ **bargain for** expect, anticipate, plan for, reckon on

barge *noun* a flat-bottomed boat used on rivers and canals ◇ *verb* **1** rush clumsily **2** push or bump (into) **3** push your way (into) rudely

🔄 *noun* canal boat, flatboat, narrowboat, houseboat ◇ *verb* **2** bump, hit, collide **3** shove, elbow, push (in), muscle in, butt in, interrupt, gatecrash, intrude, interfere

baritone *noun* **1** a male singing voice between tenor and bass **2** a singer with this voice

bark[1] *noun* the noise made by a dog

etc ◇ *verb* **1** give a bark **2** speak sharply or angrily

🔄 *verb* **1** yap, woof, yelp, snap, snarl, growl, bay, howl

bark[2] *noun* the rough outer covering of a tree's trunk and branches

barley *noun* a grain used for food and for making malt liquors and spirits ◇ **barley sugar** sugar candied by melting and cooling to make a sweet

bar mitzvah a Jewish ceremony to mark a boy's coming of age

barn *noun* a building in which grain, hay *etc* is stored

barnacle *noun* a type of shellfish which sticks to rocks, ships' hulls *etc*

barometer *noun* an instrument which measures the weight or pressure of the air, and shows changes in the weather

baron *noun* **1** a nobleman, the lowest in the British peerage **2** a powerful person, *esp* in a business: *drug baron* ◇ **baronial** *adj*

baroness *noun* (*plural* **baronesses**) a baron's wife or a female baron

baronet *noun* the lowest title that can be passed on to an heir ◇ **baronetcy** *noun*

baroque *adj* extravagantly ornamented

🔄 elaborate, ornate, ornamented, rococo, flamboyant, extravagant

🔄 plain, simple

barracks *noun plural* a place for housing soldiers

🔄 camp, quarters, garrison

barracuda *noun* a voracious West Indian fish

barrage *noun* **1** heavy gunfire against an enemy **2** an overwhelming number: *a barrage of questions* **3** a bar across a river to make the water deeper

🔄 **1** bombardment, shelling, gunfire, volley, salvo, burst, assault, attack, onslaught **2** deluge, torrent, stream, shower, profusion

barrel *noun* **1** a wooden cask with curved sides **2** the metal tube of a gun through which the shot is fired

🔄 **1** cask, keg, butt

barren *adj* not able to produce crops or offspring, infertile ◇ **barrenness** *noun*

■ infertile, sterile, childless, unprolific

■ productive, fruitful, fertile

barricade *noun* a barrier put up to block a street *etc* ◇ *verb* **1** block or strengthen against attack **2** shut behind a barrier

■ *noun* blockade, obstruction, barrier, fence, stockade, bulwark, rampart ◇ *verb* **1** fortify, block, obstruct, bar **2** defend, protect

barrier *noun* **1** a strong fence *etc* used for enclosing or keeping out **2** an obstacle

■ **1** wall, fence, railing, barricade, blockade **2** obstacle, hurdle, stumbling-block, impediment, obstruction, hindrance, handicap

barrister *noun* a lawyer who pleads cases in English or Irish courts

barrow[1] *noun* a small handcart

barrow[2] *noun* a mound built over an ancient grave

Bart or **Bt** *abbrev* baronet

barter *verb* give one thing in exchange for another ◇ *noun* trading by exchanging goods without using money

■ *verb* exchange, swap, trade

basalt *noun* a hard, dark-coloured volcanic rock

base[1] *noun* **1** the part on which a thing stands or rests **2** the lowest part **3** a place from where an expedition, military action *etc* is carried out ◇ *verb* use as a foundation: *based on fact* ◇ **baseless** *adj* without foundation; untrue

■ *noun* **1** pedestal, plinth, stand, rest, support, foundation **2** bottom, foot ◇ *verb* establish, found, ground ◇ **baseless** groundless, unfounded, unsupported, unsubstantiated, unconfirmed, unjustified

base[2] *noun* worthless, cowardly

baseball *noun* a North American ballgame in which players make a circuit of four bases on a field

basement *noun* a storey below ground level in a building

bash *verb* hit hard ◇ *noun* a heavy blow ◇ **have a bash** *informal* make an attempt

bashful *adj* shy ◇ **bashfully** *adv*

■ shy, retiring, reticent, reserved, nervous, timid, coy, self-conscious, embarrassed

■ bold, confident

basic *adj* **1** of or forming a base or basis **2** necessary, fundamental ◇ **basically** *adv* ◇ **basics** *noun plural* fundamental facts or principles

■ **2** fundamental, elementary, primary, root, underlying, key, central, inherent, intrinsic, essential, indispensable, vital, necessary, important ◇ **basics** fundamentals, rudiments, principles, essentials, *informal* brass tacks, grass roots, core, facts

basil *noun* an aromatic herb used in cooking

basilica *noun* a church with a large central hall

basin *noun* **1** a wide, open dish **2** a wash basin **3** a large hollow holding water **4** the land drained by a river and its tributaries

■ **1** bowl, dish **2** sink **3** crater

basis *noun* (*plural* **bases**) **1** something on which a thing is based, a foundation: *the basis of their friendship* **2** the main ingredient

■ **1** base, bottom, footing, support, foundation, ground, groundwork, fundamental, premise **2** principle, essential, heart, core

bask *verb* **1** lie in warmth **2** enjoy, feel great pleasure (in): *basking in glory*

■ **1** sunbathe, lie, lounge, relax, laze, wallow **2** revel, delight in, enjoy, relish, savour, wallow

basket *noun* a container made of strips of wood, rushes *etc* woven together

■ hamper

basketball *noun* a team game in which goals are scored by throwing a ball into a raised net

bas-relief /baːrɪˈliːf/ *noun* sculpture carved to stand slightly out from a background

bass¹ /beɪs/ *noun* (*plural* **basses**) **1** the lowest part in music **2** a deep male singing voice **3** a singer with this voice ◇ *adj* low or deep in tone ◇ **bass clef** *see* **clef**

bass² /bas/ *noun* (*plural* **bass** or **basses**) a kind of fish of the perch family

bassoon *noun* a musical wind instrument with low notes

bastard *noun* **1** a child born to parents who are not married to each other **2** *informal* a general term of abuse

baste¹ *verb* spoon fat over (meat) while roasting

baste² *verb* sew loosely together with big stitches; tack

bastion *noun* **1** a defensive position, a preserve: *the last bastions of male power* **2** a tower on a castle *etc*

bat¹ *noun* a shaped piece of wood *etc* for striking a ball in some games ◇ *verb* (**bats**, **batting**, **batted**) use the bat in cricket *etc* ◇ **batsman**, **batswoman** *noun* someone who bats in cricket *etc*

bat² *noun* a mouse-like flying animal

bat³ *verb* (**bats**, **batting**, **batted**) flutter (eyelids *etc*)

batch *noun* (*plural* **batches**) a quantity of things made *etc* at one time
- lot, consignment, parcel, pack, bunch, set, assortment, collection, amount, quantity

bated *adj*: **with bated breath** anxiously

bath *noun* **1** a vessel which holds water in which you sit to wash your body **2** the water in a bath **3** a washing of the body in a bath **4** (**baths**) a public building with an artificial pool for swimming ◇ *verb* wash (oneself or another) in a bath
- *noun* **1** tub **3** wash, scrub, soak

bathe *verb* **1** swim in water **2** wash gently: *bathe your eyes* **3** take a bath ◇ *noun* a swim ◇ **bathed in** covered with
- *verb* **2** wet, moisten, wash, cleanse ◇ *noun* swim, dip, paddle

bathroom *noun* **1** a room containing a bath, sink, and usually a toilet **2** *US* a room containing a toilet

bathyscaphe or **bathysphere** *noun* a deep-sea observation chamber

batik *noun* a method of dyeing patterns on cloth by waxing certain areas so that they remain uncoloured

batman *noun* an army officer's servant

baton *noun* **1** a small wooden stick **2** a light stick used by a conductor of music

battalion *noun* a part of a regiment of foot soldiers

batten *noun* **1** a long flat piece of wood **2** a strip of wood used to fasten down a ship's hatches during a storm ◇ *verb* (with **down**) fasten down firmly

batter¹ *verb* hit repeatedly ◇ **battered** *adj* **1** beaten, ill-treated **2** worn out by use
- *verb* beat, pound, pummel, buffet, smash, dash, pelt, lash, thrash, *informal* wallop, abuse, maltreat, ill-treat, manhandle, assault, hurt, injure ◇ **battered 1** beaten, abused, ill-treated, injured, bruised **2** weather-beaten, dilapidated, tumbledown, ramshackle, crumbling

batter² *noun* a beaten mixture of flour, milk and eggs, for cooking

battering-ram *noun*, *hist* a weapon comprising a heavy beam for breaking through walls *etc*

battery *noun* (*plural* **batteries**) **1** a device for storing and transmitting electricity **2** a number of large guns **3** a series of cages *etc* in which hens are kept for egg-laying

battle *noun* a fight, *esp* between armies ◇ *verb* fight
- *noun* war, warfare, hostilities, action, conflict, combat, fight, attack, fray, skirmish, clash, struggle ◇ *verb* fight, combat, war, feud, contend, struggle crusade

battleaxe *noun* **1** *hist* a kind of axe used in fighting **2** *informal* a fierce, domineering woman

battlefield *noun* the site of a battle

battlement *noun* a wall on the top of

a building, with openings or notches for firing

battleship *noun* a heavily armed and armoured warship

bauble *noun* **1** a brightly-coloured ornament of little value **2** a round, coloured decoration for a Christmas tree

bawl *verb* shout or cry out loudly ◇ *noun* a loud cry

bay¹ *noun* **1** a wide inlet of the sea in a coastline **2** a space in a room *etc* set back, a recess ◇ **bay window** a window that forms a recess

▤ **1** gulf, bight, inlet, cove **2** recess, alcove, niche, nook

bay² *noun* the laurel tree

bay³ *verb* **1** of dogs: bark **2** of a crowd: shout loudly ◇ **hold at bay** fight off ◇ **stand at bay** stand and face attackers *etc*

▤ **1** howl, bark

bayonet *noun* a steel stabbing blade that can be fixed to the muzzle of a rifle ◇ *verb* stab with this

bazaar *noun* **1** a sale of goods for charity *etc* **2** an Eastern marketplace

▤ **1** sale, fair, fete, bring-and-buy

BB *abbrev* Boys' Brigade

BBQ *abbrev* barbecue

BBC *abbrev* British Broadcasting Corporation

BC *abbrev* before Christ: *55BC*

BCE *abbrev* before Common Era

be *verb* (*present form* **am**, **are**, **is**, *past form* **was**, **were**, *past participle* **been**) **1** live, exist: *there may be some milk left* **2** have a position, quality *etc*: *she wants to be a dentist/if only you could be happy*

▤ **1** exist, breathe, live, inhabit, reside, dwell

> **be** is also used to form tenses of other verbs, *eg* I *was* running for the bus/when *will* you *be* arriving?

beach *noun* (*plural* **beaches**) the shore of the sea *etc*, *esp* when sandy or pebbly ◇ *verb* drive or haul (*eg* a boat) up on the beach

▤ *noun* sand, sands, shore, strand, seashore, seaside, coast

beachcomber *noun* someone who searches beaches for useful or saleable articles

beacon *noun* **1** a flashing light or other warning signal **2** *hist* a fire on a hill used as a signal of danger

▤ **1** signal, light, beam, lighthouse, flare

bead *noun* **1** a small pierced ball of glass, plastic *etc*, used in needlework or jewellery-making **2** a drop of liquid: *beads of sweat*

▤ **2** drop, droplet, drip, globule, blob

beadle *noun* an officer of a church or college

beagle *noun* a small hound used in hunting

beak *noun* **1** the hard, horny part of a bird's mouth with which it gathers food **2** a point, a projection

beaker *noun* a tall cup or glass, usually without a handle

▤ glass, tumbler, jar, cup

beam *noun* **1** a long straight piece of wood or metal **2** a shaft of light **3** a radio signal **4** the greatest breadth of a ship ◇ *verb* **1** shine **2** smile broadly **3** send out by radio

▤ *noun* **1** plank, board, timber, rafter, joist, girder, spar, boom, bar, support **2** ray, shaft, gleam ◇ *verb* **1** radiate, shine, glare **2** smile, grin **3** emit, broadcast, transmit

bean *noun* **1** a pod-bearing plant **2** the seed of this used as food

beanie *noun* a close-fitting woollen hat

bear¹ *verb* (**bears**, **bearing**, **bore**, **borne** or **born**) **1** *formal* carry **2** endure, put up with **3** produce (fruit, children *etc*) ◇ **bearable** *adj* able to be borne or endured ◇ **bearer** *noun* a carrier or messenger ◇ **bear in mind** remember, take into account ◇ **bear out** confirm: *this bears out my suspicions* ◇ **bear with** be patient with

▤ **1** carry, convey, transport, move, take, bring **2** tolerate, stand, put up with, endure, abide, suffer **3** give birth to, breed, propagate, beget, engender, produce, yield ◇ **bearable** tolerable, supportable, sustainable, acceptable, manageable ◇ **bearer** carrier, porter, messenger, runner ◇ **bear out** confirm, endorse, support, prove, demonstrate, corroborate, substantiate, vindicate ◇ **bear with** tolerate, put up with, forbear, be patient with, make allowances for

🔄 **bearable** unbearable, intolerable

> **born** is used for the past participle when referring to the past birth of a child, idea *etc*: *when were you born?*; otherwise the form is **borne**: *I couldn't have borne it any longer*

bear² *noun* a heavy animal with shaggy fur and hooked claws

beard *noun* the hair that grows on a man's chin and cheeks ◇ *verb* face up to, defy

bearing *noun* 1 behaviour 2 direction 3 connection: *it has no bearing on the issue* 4 a part of a machine supporting a moving part

🔄 1 demeanour, manner, mien, behaviour, deportment 2 orientation, position, course, direction 3 relevance, significance, connection

bearskin *noun* the high fur cap worn by the Guards in the British Army

beast *noun* 1 a four-footed animal 2 a brutal person

🔄 1 animal, creature 2 animal, monster, brute

beastly *adj* 1 behaving like an animal 2 horrible 3 *informal* unpleasant ◇ **beastliness** *noun*

beat *verb* (**beats, beating, beat, beaten**) 1 hit repeatedly 2 overcome, defeat 3 of a pulse or the heart: move or throb in the normal way 4 mark (time) in music 5 stir (a mixture *etc*) with quick movements ◇ *noun* 1 a stroke 2 the regular round of a police officer *etc* ◇ **beaten** *adj* 1 of metal: shaped 2 of earth: worn smooth by treading 3 defeated ◇ **beat it** *slang* go away ◇ **beat up** injure by repeated hitting, kicking *etc*

🔄 *verb* 1 whip, flog, lash, cane, thrash, lay into, hit, punch, strike, swipe, knock, bang, bash, pound, hammer, batter,

bruise 2 defeat, trounce, *informal* hammer, *slang* slaughter, conquer, overcome, overwhelm, vanquish, outdo, outstrip, outrun 3 pulsate, pulse, throb, thump, race, palpitate ◇ **beat up** attack, assault, batter, *informal* do over

beatific /biːəˈtɪfɪk/ *adj* of or showing great happiness

beautify *verb* (**beautifies, beautifying, beautified**) make beautiful

beauty *noun* (*plural* **beauties**) 1 very attractive or pleasing appearance, sound *etc* 2 a very attractive person, *esp* a woman ◇ **beautiful** *adj* ◇ **beautifully** *adv*

🔄 **beautiful** attractive, fair, pretty, lovely, good-looking, gorgeous, radiant, ravishing, *informal* stunning, pleasing, appealing, alluring, charming, delightful, fine, exquisite

🔄 **beautiful** ugly, plain, hideous

beaver *noun* 1 a gnawing animal that can dam streams 2 a member of the most junior branch of the Scout Association

becalmed *adj* of a sailing ship: unable to move for lack of wind

because *conj* for the reason that: *we didn't go because it was raining* ◇ **because of** on account of: *because of the holiday, the bank will be shut*

🔄 *conj* as, for, since ◇ **because of** owing to, on account of, thanks to

beck *noun*: **at someone's beck and call** obeying all their orders or requests

beckon *verb* make a sign (with the finger) to summon someone

become *verb* 1 come to be: *she became angry* 2 *formal* suit: *that tie becomes you* ◇ **becoming** *adj* 1 attractive 2 of behaviour: appropriate, suitable

🔄 *verb* 1 turn, grow, get

bed *noun* 1 a place or piece of furniture on which to rest or sleep 2 a plot for flowers *etc* in a garden 3 the bottom of a river *etc* ◇ *verb* (**beds, bedding, bedded**) 1 plant in soil *etc* 2 provide a bed for 3 *informal* have sexual intercourse with

🔄 *noun* 1 divan, couch, bunk, berth, cot, mattress, *slang* sack 2 border, patch

bedclothes *noun plural* sheets, blankets *etc* for a bed

bedding *noun* **1** mattress, bedclothes *etc* **2** straw *etc* for cattle to lie on

bedlam *noun* a place full of uproar and confusion

After St Mary of *Bethlehem* Hospital, a former mental hospital in London

bedraggled *adj* wet and untidy
■ untidy, unkempt, dishevelled, messy, dirty, muddy, muddied, soiled, wet, sodden, drenched
⊟ neat, tidy, clean

bedridden *adj* kept in bed by weakness, illness *etc*

bedrock *noun* the solid rock under the soil

bedroom *noun* a room for sleeping

bedspread *noun* a top cover for a bed

bedstead *noun* a frame supporting a bed

bee *noun* a winged insect that makes honey in wax cells ◇ **make a beeline for** go directly towards

beech *noun* (*plural* **beeches**) a forest tree with grey smooth bark

beef *noun* the flesh of a bull, cow or ox, used as food ◇ **beefy** *adj* stout, muscular

beefeater *noun* **1** a guardian of the Tower of London **2** a member of the Queen's or King's Guard

beehive *noun* a dome or box in which bees are kept

been *see* be

beer *noun* an alcoholic drink flavoured with hops

beet *noun* a plant with a round or carrot-like root, such as sugar beet

beetle *noun* an insect with four wings, the front pair forming hard covers for the back pair

beetroot *noun* a round, dark-red plant root used as a vegetable

befall *verb*, *formal* (**befalls**, **befalling**, **befell**) happen to, strike: *a disaster befell them*

befit *verb* (**befits**, **befitting**, **befitted**) be suitable or right for

before *prep* **1** earlier than: *before three o'clock* **2** in front of: *before the entrance to the tunnel/performing before an audience* **3** rather than, in preference to: *I'd die before telling him* ◇ *adv* **1** earlier **2** in front ◇ *conj* earlier than the time that: *before he was born* ◇ **beforehand** *adv* previously, before the time when something else is done
■ **beforehand** in advance, preliminarily, already, before, previously, earlier, sooner

befriend *verb* act as a friend to, help

beg *verb* (**begs**, **begging**, **begged**) **1** ask for money *etc* from others **2** ask earnestly: *he begged her to stay* ◇ **beggar** someone who begs for money ◇ **beg the question** take as being proved the very point that needs to be proved
■ **2** request, require, desire, beseech, plead, entreat, implore, supplicate

began *past form* of begin

beget *verb*, *formal* (**begets**, **begetting**, **begat**, **begotten**) **1** be the father of **2** cause

begin *verb* (**begins**, **beginning**, **began**, **begun**) **1** make a start on **2** come into existence ◇ **beginner** *noun* ◇ **beginning** *noun*
■ **1** start, commence, set about, embark on, set in motion, *informal* kick-start, activate, originate, initiate, introduce, instigate **2** arise, spring, emerge, appear ◇ **beginner** novice, learner, tenderfoot ◇ **beginning** start, commencement, onset, outset, opening, establishment, birth, dawn, origin, source, emergence, rise
⊟ **1, 2** end, finish, terminate, cease ◇ **beginning** end, finish

begrudge *verb* grudge, envy: *he begrudged me my success*
■ resent, grudge, mind, object to, envy

beguile *verb* **1** amuse, entertain; charm **2** cheat
■ **1** deceive, fool, hoodwink, dupe, trick, cheat, delude, mislead **2** charm, enchant, bewitch, captivate, amuse, entertain, divert, distract

begun past participle of **begin**

behalf noun: **on behalf of 1** as the representative of: on behalf of my client **2** in aid of: collecting on behalf of the homeless

behave verb **1** act (in a certain way): he always behaves badly at parties **2** conduct yourself well: can't you behave for just a minute? ◇ **behaviour** noun ◇ **badly-behaved** adj with bad manners ◇ **well-behaved** adj with good manners

▣ **1** act, react, respond, work, function, run, operate, perform, conduct oneself, formal comport oneself ◇ **behaviour** conduct, formal comportment, manner, manners, demeanour

behead verb cut off the head of

▣ decapitate, execute, guillotine

behind prep **1** at or towards the back of: behind the door **2** after **3** in support of, encouraging: behind him in his struggle ◇ adv **1** at the back **2** not up to date: behind with his work

behold verb (**beholds, beholding, beheld**) formal look (at), see

beholden to adj grateful to because of a good turn

behove verb: **it behoves you to** you ought to

beige noun a light-fawn colour ◇ adj of this colour

▣ adj buff, fawn, mushroom, camel, sandy, khaki, coffee, neutral

being noun **1** existence **2** a living person or thing

▣ **1** existence, actuality, reality, life **2** creature, animal, beast, human being, mortal, person, individual, entity

belabour verb beat, thrash

belated adj arriving late ◇ **belatedly** adv

belch 1 bring up wind from the stomach through the mouth **2** of a fire etc: send up (smoke etc) violently

▣ **1** informal burp **2** emit, discharge, disgorge

beleaguer verb besiege

belfry noun (plural **belfries**) the part of a steeple or tower in which the bells are hung

belie verb, formal (**belies, belying, belied**) prove to be false

belief noun **1** what someone thinks to be true **2** religious faith

▣ **1** conviction, persuasion, confidence, assurance, certainty, sureness, view, opinion, judgement **2** ideology, faith, creed, doctrine, dogma, tenet, principle

▣ **1** disbelief

believe verb **1** think of or accept as true or as existing **2** trust (in) **3** think or suppose ◇ **believable** adj ◇ **make believe** pretend

▣ **2** credit, trust, count on, depend on, rely on **3** think, consider, reckon, suppose, deem, judge

▣ **1** disbelieve, doubt

belittle verb cause to seem small, unimportant or inferior

▣ lessen, diminish, disparage, scorn

▣ exaggerate, praise

bell noun a hollow metal object which gives a ringing sound when struck by the clapper inside

bellicose adj inclined to fight, quarrelsome ◇ **bellicosity** noun

belligerent adj quarrelsome, aggressive ◇ **belligerence** or **belligerency** noun

▣ aggressive, militant, argumentative, quarrelsome, contentious, combative, pugnacious, violent, bullying, antagonistic, warring, warlike, bellicose

▣ peaceable

bellow verb roar like a bull ◇ noun a deep roar

bellows noun plural an instrument for making a blast of air, eg to increase a fire

belly noun (plural **bellies**) **1** the abdomen **2** the underpart of an animal's body ◇ **bellyache** noun a stomach pain ◇ **belly button** informal the navel ◇ **bellyful** noun more than enough (of something) ◇ **belly laugh** a deep laugh

belong verb **1** be someone's property: this book belongs to me **2** be a member (of a club etc) **3** of things or people: have their proper place: those glasses belong in the kitchen ◇ **belongings**

noun plural what someone possesses

■ **belongings** possessions, property, chattels, goods, effects, things, *informal* stuff, *informal* gear

beloved *adj* much loved, very dear ◇ *noun* someone much loved

■ *adj* loved, adored, cherished, dearest

below *prep* lower in position than: *her skirt reached below her knees/a captain ranks below a major* ◇ *adv* in a lower position: *looking down at the street below*

■ *prep* under, beneath, underneath ◇ *adv* beneath, underneath, lower down

▣ above

belt *noun* **1** a strip of leather, cloth *etc* worn round the waist **2** a continuous band on a machine, *eg* for conveying objects in a factory **3** a broad strip, *eg* of land ◇ *verb* **1** put a belt round **2** beat with a belt **3** *informal* beat, hit **4** *informal* move or go very fast

bemoan *verb* weep about, mourn

bench *noun* (*plural* **benches**) **1** a long seat **2** a work-table, *eg* for a carpenter **3** (**the bench**) the judges of a court ◇ **benchmark** *noun* something used as a standard

■ **1** seat, form, settle, pew **2** counter, table **3** court, judiciary

bend *verb* (**bends**, **bending**, **bent**) **1** make or become curved or angled **2** stoop ◇ *noun* **1** a curve or angle **2** a turn in a road

■ *verb* **1** curve, turn, veer, diverge, twist, contort, flex, shape, mould **2** bow, incline, lean, stoop, crouch ◇ *noun* **1** curvature, curve, arc, bow, angle **2** corner, turn

beneath *prep* **1** under, in a lower position than: *sitting beneath the tree reading a book* **2** covered by: *wearing a black dress beneath her coat* **3** considered too low a task *etc* for: *sweeping floors was beneath him* ◇ *adv* below

■ *prep* **1** under, underneath, below **2** under, underneath **3** unworthy of ◇ *adv* below, underneath, lower down

benediction *noun* a blessing

benefactor *noun* someone who does good to others

benefit *noun* **1** something good to

receive or have done to you **2** money received from social security or insurance schemes: *unemployment benefit* ◇ *verb* (**benefits**, **benefiting**, **benefited**) **1** do good to **2** gain advantage: *benefited from the cut in interest rates* ◇ **beneficial** *adj* bringing gain or advantage (to) ◇ **beneficially** *adv*

■ *noun* **1** advantage, good, interest, favour, help, aid, assistance, service, use, gain, profit, asset, blessing **2** welfare, aid, assistance ◇ *verb* help, aid, assist, improve, enhance, better, further, advance, promote ◇ **beneficial** advantageous, favourable, useful, helpful, profitable, rewarding, valuable, improving, edifying, wholesome

▣ *noun* **1** disadvantage, harm, damage ◇ *verb* **1** hinder, harm, undermine ◇ **beneficial** harmful, detrimental, useless

benevolent *adj* tending to do good; kindly ◇ **benevolence** *noun* ◇ **benevolently** *adv*

■ philanthropic, humanitarian, charitable, generous, altruistic, humane, kind, kindly, compassionate, caring, considerate

▣ mean, selfish, malevolent

benign *adj* **1** gentle, kindly **2** of disease: not causing death (*contrasted with*: **malignant**)

bent *noun* a natural liking or aptitude (for something) ◇ *past form* of **bend** ◇ *adj* **1** curved, crooked **2** *informal* dishonest ◇ **be bent on** be determined on

bequeath *verb* leave (money, property *etc*) in a will

bequest *noun* money, property *etc* left in a will

■ gift, donation

berate *verb* scold

bereaved *adj* suffering from the recent death of a relative or friend ◇ **bereavement** *noun*

■ **bereavement** loss

bereft *adj* lacking, deprived (of)

beret /'bereɪ/ *noun* a flat, soft, round hat

bergamot *noun* a citrus fruit whose rind produces an aromatic oil

berry *noun* (*plural* **berries**) a small juicy fruit enclosing seeds

berserk *adv* in a frenzy, mad

■ mad, crazy, demented, insane, deranged, frantic, frenzied, wild, raging, furious, violent, rabid, raving

◼ sane, calm

berth *noun* **1** a room or place for sleeping in a ship *etc* **2** the place where a ship is tied up in a dock ◇ *verb* moor (a ship) ◇ **give a wide berth to** keep well away from

■ *noun* **2** mooring, anchorage ◇ *verb* moor, dock

beryl *noun* a type of precious stone such as an emerald or aquamarine

beseech *verb* (**beseeches**, **beseeching**, **besought** or **beseeched**) ask earnestly

beset *verb* (**besets**, **besetting**, **beset**) attack from all sides; surround

beside *prep* **1** by the side of, near: *the building beside the station* **2** compared with: *beside her sister she seems quite shy* ◇ **be beside yourself** lose self-control ◇ **beside the point** irrelevant

■ **1** next to, adjacent to, next door to, close to, near

besides *prep* **1** in addition to: *he has other friends, besides me* **2** other than, except: *nothing in the fridge besides some cheese* ◇ *adv* **1** also, moreover: *besides, it was your idea* **2** in addition: *plenty more besides*

besiege *verb* (**besieges**, **besieging**, **besieged**) **1** surround (a town *etc*) with an army **2** crowd round; overwhelm: *besieged with letters*

■ **1** lay siege to, surround **2** importune, plague

besmirch *verb* stain, dishonour: *besmirched her good name*

besotted *adj* foolishly fond: *besotted with his cats*

■ infatuated, doting, obsessed, smitten

◼ indifferent

bespoke *adj* of clothes: made to fit a particular person

best *adj* good in the most excellent way ◇ *adv* in the most excellent way

◇ **at best** under the most favourable circumstances ◇ **best man** someone who attends a man who is being married ◇ **best part** the largest or greatest part ◇ **do your best** try as hard as you can ◇ **make the best of** do as well as possible with

■ *adj* optimum, optimal, premium, first, foremost, leading, unequalled, unsurpassed, matchless, incomparable, supreme, greatest

◼ *adj* worst

bestial *adj* like a beast, beastly

bestir *verb* (**bestirs**, **bestirring**, **bestirred**) waken up, make lively

bestow *verb* give

■ award, present, grant, confer, endow, bequeath, impart, donate

◼ withhold, deprive

bestride *verb* stand or sit across, straddle

bestseller *noun* a book *etc* which sells exceedingly well ◇ **bestselling** *adj*

bet *noun* money put down to be lost or kept depending on the outcome of a race *etc* ◇ *verb* (**bets**, **betting**, **bet** or **betted**) place a bet

■ *noun* wager, *informal* flutter, gamble, speculation, risk ◇ *verb* wager, gamble, speculate, risk, hazard, chance, venture, stake, bid

bête noire /bɛt nwɑ:(r)/ a particular dislike

betray *verb* **1** give up (secrets, friends *etc*) to an enemy **2** show signs of: *his face betrayed no emotion* ◇ **betrayal** *noun*

■ **1** inform on, *slang* shop, double-cross, desert, abandon **2** disclose, give away, tell, divulge, expose, reveal, show, manifest ◇ **betrayal** treachery, treason, sell-out, disloyalty, unfaithfulness, duplicity, falseness

◼ **betrayal** loyalty

betroth *verb*, *formal* promise in marriage ◇ **betrothal** *noun* ◇ **betrothed to** engaged to be married to

better *adj* **1** good to a greater degree, of a more excellent kind **2** healthier **3** completely recovered from illness: *don't* *go back to work until you're better* ◇ *adv* in a more excellent way ◇ *verb* **1** improve **2** improve on, surpass ◇ **better off** in a better position, wealthier ◇ **get the better of** defeat, overcome ◇ **had better** ought to, must ◇ **think better of** change your mind about doing

◼ *verb* **1** improve, ameliorate, enhance **2** surpass, beat, outdo

◪ *adj* **1** inferior, worse **2** worse ◇ *verb* **1** worsen, deteriorate

between *prep* **1** in or through the space dividing two people or things: *there was an empty seat between us/between 3 o'clock and 6 o'clock/the road between Edinburgh and Glasgow* **2** in parts, in shares to: *divide the chocolates between you* **3** comparing one to the other: *the only difference between them is the price*

bevel *noun* a slanting edge ◇ *verb* (**bevels**, **bevelling**, **bevelled**) give a slanting edge to ◇ **bevelled** *adj*

beverage *noun* a drink

bevy[1] *noun* (*plural* **bevies**) **1** a group of women or girls **2** a flock of quails

bevy[2] or **bevvy** *noun* (*plural* **bevies** or **bevvies**) *Brit informal* **1** an alcoholic drink **2** a drinking session

bewail *verb* mourn loudly over

beware *verb* watch out for (something dangerous)

◼ watch out, look out, guard against, mind

bewilder *verb* puzzle, confuse ◇ **bewildered** *adj* ◇ **bewildering** *adj* ◇ **bewilderment** *noun*

◼ confuse, muddle, disconcert, confound, *informal* bamboozle, baffle, puzzle, perplex, mystify, daze, stupefy, disorient

◪ **bewildered** unperturbed

bewitch *verb* put under a spell; charm

◼ charm, enchant, allure, beguile, spellbind, captivate, entrance, hypnotize

beyond *prep* **1** on the far side of: *beyond the next set of traffic lights* **2** later than: *beyond January* **3** more than: *beyond the call of duty* **4** too far gone for: *beyond repair* **5** too difficult or confusing for: *it's beyond me!* ◇ *adv* on or to the far side, further away

bi- *prefix* **1** having two: *biped/bipolar* **2** occurring twice in a certain period, or once in every two periods: *bi-monthly*

biannual *adj* happening twice a year

Do not confuse with: **biennial**

bias *noun* **1** the favouring of one person or point of view over any others **2** a tendency to move in a particular direction **3** a weight on or in an object making it move in a particular direction ◇ *verb* (**biases**, **biasing** or **biassing**, **biased** or **biassed**) give a bias to ◇ **biased** *adj* favouring one person or point of view over any others ◇ **on the bias** diagonally across the weave of fabric

◼ **biased** loaded, weighted, influenced, partial, predisposed, prejudiced, one-sided, unfair

◪ impartial, fair

bib *noun* **1** a piece of cloth put under a child's chin to protect their clothes from food stains *etc* **2** a part of an apron, overalls *etc* covering the chest

Bible *noun* the holy book of the Christian Church ◇ **biblical** *adj*

bibliography *noun* (*plural* **bibliographies**) a list of books (about a subject)

bibliophile *noun* a lover of books

bicentenary *noun* (*plural* **bicentenaries**) the two-hundredth year after an event, *eg* someone's birth

biceps *noun sing* the muscle in front of the upper part of the arm

bicker *verb* quarrel over small matters

◼ squabble, quarrel, row

bicycle *noun* a cycle with two wheels, driven by foot-pedals

bid[1] *verb* (**bids**, **bidding**, **bid**) offer a price (for) ◇ *noun* **1** an offer of a price **2** a bold attempt: *a bid for freedom*

◼ *verb* offer, tender, submit, propose ◇ *noun* **1** offer, tender **2** attempt, effort, try, endeavour

bid[2] *verb* (**bids**, **bidding**, **bade** or **bid**, **bidden** or **bid**), *formal* **1** tell, say: *bidding her farewell* **2** command, invite

▧ **2** ask, request, desire, instruct, direct, command

bidet /ˈbiːdeɪ/ *noun* a low washbasin for washing the genital area

biennial *adj* lasting two years; happening once every two years ◇ *noun* a plant that flowers only in its second year ◇ **biennially** *adv*

> ❶ Do not confuse with: **biannual**

bier *noun* a carriage or frame for carrying a dead body

big *adj* (**bigger**, **biggest**) **1** large in size, amount, extent *etc* **2** important **3** boastful or extravagant: *big talk/big ideas*

▧ **1** large, great, sizable, considerable, substantial, huge, enormous, immense, massive, colossal, gigantic, mammoth, burly, bulky, extensive, spacious, vast, voluminous **2** important, significant, momentous, serious, main, principal

▧ **1** small, little **2** insignificant, unknown

bigamy *noun* the crime or fact of having two wives or two husbands at once ◇ **bigamist** *noun* ◇ **bigamous** *adj*

bigot *noun* someone with narrow-minded, prejudiced beliefs ◇ **bigoted** *adj* ◇ **bigotry** *noun*

▧ chauvinist, sectarian, racist, sexist ◇ **bigoted** prejudiced, biased, intolerant, narrow-minded, narrow, blinkered, closed, dogmatic ◇ **bigotry** prejudice, discrimination, bias, intolerance, narrow-mindedness, chauvinism, jingoism, sectarianism, racism, racialism, sexism, dogmatism

▧ liberal ◇ **bigoted** tolerant, liberal, broad-minded ◇ **bigotry** tolerance

bike *noun*, *informal* a bicycle

bikini *noun* (*plural* **bikinis**) a woman's brief two-piece bathing suit

> Named after *Bikini* Atoll atomic test site, because of its supposedly dynamic effect on viewers

bilateral *adj* **1** having two sides **2** affecting two sides, parties *etc*: *bilateral agreement* ◇ **bilaterally** *adv*

bilberry *noun* a type of plant with an edible dark-blue berry

bile *noun* a fluid produced by the liver

bilge *noun* **1** the broadest part of a ship's bottom **2** bilgewater **3** *informal* nonsense ◇ **bilgewater** *noun* water which lies in a ship's bottom

bilingual *adj* using or fluent in two languages

bilious *adj* ill with too much bile; nauseated ◇ **biliousness** *noun*

▧ sick, queasy, *informal* out of sorts

bill[1] *noun* **1** a statement of money owed **2** an early version of a law before it has been passed by parliament **3** a printed sheet of information

▧ **1** invoice, statement, account, charges, reckoning **2** proposal, measure, legislation **3** circular, leaflet, handout, bulletin, handbill, notice, poster

bill[2] *noun* a bird's beak

billet *noun* a lodging, *esp* for soldiers ◇ *verb* lodge (soldiers) in private houses

▧ lodging, accommodation

billiards *noun* a game played with a cue and balls on a table

billion *noun* **1** a thousand millions (1 000 000 000) **2** a million millions (1 000 000 000 000)

billow *noun* a great wave ◇ *verb* rise or swell in billows ◇ **billowy** *adj*

▧ *verb* swell, expand, bulge, puff out, fill out, balloon, rise, heave, surge, roll

billy-goat *noun* a male goat

bimbo *noun* (*plural* **bimbos**) an attractive but not very clever young woman

bin *noun* a container for storing goods or rubbish ◇ *verb* (**bins**, **binning**, **binned**) **1** put in a bin **2** throw away

binary *adj* made up of two ◇ **binary system** a mathematical system in which numbers are expressed by two digits only, 1 and 0

bind *verb* (**binds**, **binding**, **bound**) **1** tie with a band **2** fasten together by wrapping something around **3** place under obligation ◇ **binding** *noun* **1** anything that binds **2** the cover, stitching *etc* which holds a book together **3** a strip sewn to the edge of cloth

■ **2** attach, fasten, secure, tie, lash, strap, bandage, dress **3** oblige, force, compel, constrain ◇ **binding 2** cover, spine **3** edging, trimming, border

bindi or **bhindi** noun a decorative dot worn on the forehead

binge verb eat and drink too much ◇ noun a spell of overeating or drinking too much

bingo noun a popular gambling game using numbers

biochemistry noun the study of the chemistry of cells in living organisms ◇ **biochemist** noun

binoculars noun plural a small double telescope

biodegradable adj able to be broken down into parts by bacteria

biography noun (plural **biographies**) a written account of someone's life ◇ **biographer** noun ◇ **biographical** adj
■ life story, life, curriculum vitae

biology noun the study of living things ◇ **biological** adj ◇ **biologist** noun

biopsy noun (plural **biopsies**) an examination of a small piece of living tissue from the body

biped noun an animal with two feet, eg a bird

birch noun (plural **birches**) a type of hardwood tree

bird noun a feathered, egg-laying creature

Birds include:
sparrow, thrush, starling, blackbird, bluetit, chaffinch, greenfinch, bullfinch, dunnock, robin, wagtail, swallow, tit, wren, martin, swift, crow, magpie, dove, pigeon, skylark, nightingale, linnet, warbler, jay, jackdaw, rook, raven, cuckoo, shrike, woodpecker, yellowhammer; duck, mallard, eider, teal, swan, goose, heron, stork, flamingo, pelican, kingfisher, moorhen, coot, lapwing, peewit, plover, curlew, snipe, avocet, seagull, guillemot, tern, petrel, crane, bittern, petrel, albatross, gannet, cormorant, auk, puffin, dipper; eagle, owl, hawk, sparrowhawk, falcon, kestrel, osprey, buzzard, vulture, condor; emu, ostrich, kiwi, peacock, penguin; chicken, grouse, partridge, pheasant, quail, turkey; canary, budgerigar, informal budgie, cockatiel, cockatoo, lovebird, parakeet, parrot, macaw, toucan, myna bird, mockingbird, kookaburra, bird of paradise

biriyani noun an Indian dish of spiced rice with meat or fish

Biro noun, trademark a type of ballpoint pen

birth noun the very beginning of someone's life; the moment of being born

birthday noun **1** the date on which someone was born **2** an annual celebration on this day

birthmark noun a mark on the body which is present from birth

biscuit noun a small, flat, hard cake of baked dough

bisect verb cut in two equal parts
■ halve, divide, separate, split, intersect

bishop noun a high-ranking member of the clergy (next below an archbishop) in the Roman Catholic Church and the Church of England ◇ **bishopric** noun the district ruled by a bishop

bison noun (plural **bison**) a large wild ox with shaggy hair and a fat hump

bisque noun a rich shellfish soup

bistro noun (plural **bistros**) a small bar or restaurant

bit¹ noun a small piece ◇ **bitty** adj piecemeal, scrappy
■ fragment, part, segment, piece, slice, crumb, morsel, scrap, atom, mite, whit, jot, iota, grain, speck

bit² past form of **bite**

bit³ noun **1** a small tool for boring **2** the part of a bridle which the horse holds in its mouth

bit⁴ noun, comput the smallest unit of information

bitch *noun* (*plural* **bitches**) **1** a female dog, wolf *etc* **2** *slang* an unpleasant woman

bitchy *adj* catty, malicious ◊ **bitchily** *adv* ◊ **bitchiness** *noun*

▣ catty, snide, nasty, mean, spiteful, backbiting

▨ kind

bite *verb* (**bites**, **biting**, **bit**, **bitten**) grip, cut or tear with the teeth ◊ *noun* **1** an act of biting **2** the part bitten off **3** a nibble at a fishing bait **4** a wound caused by an animal's or insect's bite

▣ *verb* chew, gnaw, nibble, champ, crunch, crush, nip

bitten *past participle* of **bite**

bitter *adj* **1** unpleasant to the taste; sour **2** harsh: *bitter cold* **3** resentful, angry through disappointment ◊ **bitterly** *adv* ◊ **bitterness** *noun*

▣ **1** sour, tart, sharp, acid, vinegary, unsweetened **2** intense, severe, harsh, biting, freezing, raw **3** resentful, embittered, cynical, rancorous, acrimonious

▨ **1** sweet **2** mild **3** contented

bittern *noun* a bird resembling a heron

bitty *see* **bit¹**

bivouac *noun* an overnight camp outdoors without a tent

bi-weekly *adj* happening twice a week or once every two weeks

bizarre *adj* odd, strange ◊ **bizarrely** *adv*

▣ strange, odd, queer, curious, weird, peculiar, eccentric, *informal* way-out, *informal* off the wall, outlandish, fantastic, freakish, abnormal, deviant, unusual, left-field, extraordinary

▨ normal, ordinary

blab *verb* (**blabs**, **blabbing**, **blabbed**) **1** talk a lot **2** let out a secret

black *adj* **1** of the dark colour of coal **2** dark-skinned ◊ *noun* black colour ◊ **black belt** an award for skill in judo or karate ◊ **black eye** a bruised area round the eye as result of a blow ◊ **black ice** a thin transparent layer of ice on a road *etc* ◊ **black market** illegal or dishonest buying and selling ◊ **black**

out become unconscious ◊ **black pudding** a dark sausage made with blood and fat ◊ **black sheep** someone who is considered a failure or outsider in a group

black-and-blue *adj* badly bruised

blackberry *noun* (*plural* **blackberries**) a blackish-purple soft fruit growing on a prickly stem

blackbird *noun* a bird with black feathers and a yellow beak

blackboard *noun* a dark-coloured board for writing on in chalk

blacken *verb* **1** make black or dark **2** dishonour, defame: *blackening his name*

blackguard /'blagɑːd/ *noun*, *old* a wicked person

blackleg *noun* someone who works when other workers are on strike

blacklist *noun* a list of people to be refused credit, jobs *etc* ◊ *verb* put on a blacklist

blackmail *noun* the crime of threatening to reveal secrets unless money is paid ◊ *verb* threaten by blackmail

▣ *noun* extortion, protection ◊ *verb* extort, milk, squeeze, hold to ransom, threaten, coerce, demand

blackout *noun* **1** total darkness caused by putting out or covering all lights **2** a temporary loss of consciousness

▣ **2** faint, coma, unconsciousness, oblivion

blacksmith *noun* someone who makes or repairs iron goods, *esp* horseshoes

bladder *noun* **1** the organ in which urine collects in the body **2** a bag with thin, membrane-like walls

blade *noun* **1** the cutting part of a knife, sword *etc* **2** a leaf of grass

▣ **1** edge, knife, dagger, sword, scalpel, razor

blame *verb* find fault with; consider responsible (for) ◊ *noun* responsibility for something bad ◊ **blameless** *adj* ◊ **blameworthy** *adj*

▣ *verb* criticize, find fault with, condemn, accuse, charge ◊ **blameless** innocent, guiltless, clear, irreproachable, unblamable, unimpeachable

◨ *verb* exonerate, vindicate ◇ **blameless** guilty, blameworthy

blanch *verb* **1** become pale **2** prepare (vegetables) by boiling briefly

blancmange /bləˈmɒndʒ/ *noun* a jelly-like pudding made with milk

bland *adj* **1** mild, not strong or irritating: *bland taste* **2** dull

◨ **1** insipid, tasteless, weak, mild, smooth, soft, gentle, non-irritant **2** boring, monotonous, humdrum, tedious, dull, insipid, uninspiring, uninteresting, unexciting, nondescript, characterless, flat

◪ **1** sharp **2** lively, stimulating

blandishments *noun plural* acts or words meant to flatter

blank *adj* **1** clear, unmarked: *a blank sheet of paper* **2** expressionless: *a blank look* ◇ *noun* **1** an empty space **2** a cartridge without a bullet

◨ *adj* **1** empty, unfilled, void, clear, bare, unmarked, plain, clean **2** expressionless, deadpan, poker-faced, impassive, glazed, vacant, uncomprehending ◇ *noun* **1** space, gap, break, void, emptiness, vacuity, nothingness, vacuum

blanket *noun* **1** a bedcover made of wool *etc* **2** a widespread, soft covering: *a blanket of snow*

blare *verb* sound loudly ◇ *noun* a loud sound, *eg* on a trumpet

◨ roar, blast, boom, hoot

blarney *noun* flattery or coaxing talk

blasé /ˈblɑːzeɪ/ *adj* indifferent, unconcerned, *esp* because of being already familiar with something

◨ nonchalant, offhand, unimpressed, unmoved, unexcited, jaded, uninterested, uninspired, indifferent, cool, unconcerned

◪ excited, enthusiastic

blaspheme *verb* **1** speak irreverently of God **2** swear, curse ◇ **blasphemer** *noun* ◇ **blasphemous** *adj* ◇ **blasphemy** *noun* (*plural* **blasphemies**)

◨ **blasphemous** profane, impious, sacrilegious, imprecatory, godless, ungodly, irreligious, irreverent

blast *noun* **1** a blowing or gust of wind **2** a loud note, *eg* on a trumpet **3** an explosion ◇ *verb* **1** break (stones, a bridge *etc*) by explosion **2** produce a loud noise **3** *formal* wither, destroy ◇ *exclam* damn! ◇ **blast-off** *noun* the moment of the launching of a rocket

◨ *noun* **1** draught, gust, gale, squall **2** blow, blare, peal, hoot **3** explosion, detonation, bang, clap, burst, outburst ◇ *verb* **1** explode, blow up, burst, shatter, destroy **2** blare, peal, hoot

blatant *adj* very obvious; shameless: *a blatant lie* ◇ **blatantly** *adv*

◨ flagrant, brazen, barefaced, open, overt, undisguised, glaring, obvious, sheer, outright, unmitigated

blaze *noun* a rush of light or flame ◇ *verb* **1** burn with a strong flame **2** throw out a strong light

◨ *noun* fire, flames, conflagration, bonfire *verb* **1** burn, flare up, flame **2** flare, radiate, glare, flash, gleam, beam, shine

blazer *noun* a light jacket sometimes worn as part of a uniform

blazon *verb* make known publicly; display very obviously

bleach *verb* whiten, remove the colour from ◇ *noun* (*plural* **bleaches**) a substance used for cleaning, whitening clothes *etc*

◨ *verb* whiten, blanch, fade, lighten

bleak *adj* dull and cheerless; cold, unsheltered ◇ **bleakly** *adv* ◇ **bleakness** *noun*

◨ gloomy, sombre, leaden, grim, dreary, dismal, depressing, joyless, cheerless, comfortless, chilly, windy, windswept, exposed, open, barren

◪ bright, cheerful

bleary *adj* of eyes: tired and inflamed ◇ **blearily** *adv*

bleat *verb* **1** cry like a sheep **2** complain in an irritating or whining way ◇ *noun* **1** a sheep's cry **2** an irritating whine

bleed *verb* (**bleeds, bleeding, bled**) **1** lose blood **2** draw blood from ◇ **bleeding** *noun* a flow of blood

◨ **1** haemorrhage, gush, spurt, flow

bleep *noun* a high-pitched intermittent

electronic sound ◊ *verb* give out such a sound

blemish *noun* (*plural* **blemishes**) a stain; a fault or flaw ◊ *verb* stain, spoil

■ *noun* flaw, imperfection, defect, fault, disfigurement, birthmark, spot, mark, speck, smudge, blotch, blot, stain ◊ *verb* flaw, deface, disfigure, spoil, mar, damage, impair, spot, mark, blot, blotch, stain

blend *verb* mix together ◊ *noun* a mixture ◊ **blender** *noun* an electric machine which mixes thoroughly and liquidizes food

■ *verb* merge, amalgamate, coalesce, compound, synthesize, fuse, unite, combine, mix, mingle ◊ *noun* compound, composite, alloy, amalgam, amalgamation, synthesis, fusion, combination, mix, mixture, concoction

☒ *verb* separate

bless *verb* **1** wish happiness to **2** make happy **3** make holy ◊ **blessed** *adj* or (in poetry *etc*) **blest 1** happy; fortunate **2** made holy, consecrated ◊ **blessing** *noun* **1** wish or prayer for happiness **2** a source of happiness or relief: *the extra money was a blessing to them*

■ **blessed 1** happy, lucky, fortunate, favoured **2** holy, sacred, hallowed, sanctified, divine

☒ **blessed 1** cursed

blight *noun* **1** a disease which makes plants wither **2** something that spoils or destroys something ◊ *verb* harm or destroy

■ *noun* **1** disease, canker, fungus, mildew, infestation

blind *adj* unable to see ◊ *noun* **1** a window screen **2** a deception, a trick ◊ *verb* **1** make blind **2** dazzle ◊ **blindness** ◊ **blindfold** *noun* a piece of cloth covering the eyes ◊ *adj* with the eyes covered by a blindfold, so as not to see ◊ *verb* apply a blindfold to

■ *adj* sightless, unseeing, unsighted, partially sighted ◊ *noun* **2** cover, front, smokescreen, *informal* cover-up

☒ *adj* sighted

blink *verb* **1** close the eyes for a moment **2** shine unsteadily ◊ *noun* an act of blinking

blinkers *noun plural* pieces of leather over a horse's eyes which prevent it seeing in any direction except in front

blip *noun* **1** a sudden sharp sound **2** a temporary interruption

bliss *noun* very great happiness ◊ **blissful** *adj* ◊ **blissfully** *adv*

■ blissfulness, ecstasy, euphoria, rapture, joy, happiness, gladness, paradise, heaven

☒ misery, hell, damnation

blister *noun* a thin bubble on the skin full of watery matter ◊ *verb* rise up in a blister

blithe *adj* happy, merry ◊ **blithely** *adv*

blitz *noun* (*plural* **blitzes**) **1** an air attack **2** a sudden violent attack

blizzard *noun* a fierce storm of wind and snow

■ snowstorm, squall, storm

bloated *adj* swollen, puffed out ◊ **bloater** *noun* a type of smoked herring

■ swollen, puffy, blown up, inflated, distended, dilated, expanded, enlarged

blob *noun* **1** a drop of liquid **2** a round spot

■ **1** drop, droplet, globule **2** dab, spot

bloc *noun* an alliance of countries for trade *etc*

block *noun* **1** a lump of wood, stone *etc* **2** a connected group of buildings **3** an obstruction: *road block* **4** an engraved piece of wood or metal for printing ◊ *verb* obstruct, hinder, prevent from progress ◊ **block letters** capital letters

■ *noun* **1** piece, lump, mass, chunk, hunk, square, cube, brick, bar **3** obstacle, barrier, bar, blockage, obstruction, impediment, hindrance ◊ *verb* choke, clog, plug, stop up, dam up, close, bar, obstruct, impede, hinder, stonewall, stop, check, arrest, halt, thwart, scotch, deter

blockage *noun* an obstruction

blockade *verb* surround a fort or country so that food *etc* cannot reach it ◊ *noun* the surrounding of a place in this way

■ *noun* siege

blockhead *noun* a stupid person

blond *adj* **1** of hair: light-coloured **2** fair-haired

blonde *adj* having fair skin and light-coloured hair ◇ *noun* a woman with this colouring

blood *noun* **1** the red liquid which flows in the bodies of human beings and animals **2** someone's descent or parentage: *royal blood* ◇ **blood vessel** a vein or artery in which the blood circulates

bloodshed *noun* violent loss of life, slaughter

bloodshot *adj* of eyes: inflamed with blood

bloodthirsty *adj* murderous, cruel

bloody *adj* **1** covered with blood **2** extremely violent, gory **3** *informal* terrible, awful ◇ **bloodily** *adv*

bloom *verb* **1** of a plant: flower **2** be in good health ◇ *noun* **1** a flower **2** rosy colour **3** freshness, perfection **4** a powder on the skin of fresh fruits

■ *verb* **1** bud, sprout, grow, develop, mature, blossom, flower, open ◇ *noun* **1** blossom, flower, bud

⊞ *verb* **1** fade, wither

bloomers *noun plural* **1** loose underpants with legs gathered above the knee **2** *hist* a woman's outfit of a jacket, skirt and baggy knee-length trousers

After Amelia *Bloomer*, 19th-century US feminist who promoted the use of the outfit for women

blossom *noun* **1** a flower **2** the flowers on a fruit tree ◇ *verb* **1** produce flowers **2** open out, develop, flourish

■ *noun* **1** bloom, flower, bud ◇ *verb* **1** bloom, flower **2** develop, mature, flourish, thrive, prosper

blot *noun* **1** a spot of ink **2** a stain or blemish which spoils something ◇ *verb* (**blots**, **blotting**, **blotted**) spot, stain ◇ **blot out** remove from sight or memory

■ *noun* **2** spot, stain, smudge, blotch, blemish, flaw ◇ *verb* spot, mark, stain, smudge, blur, sully, taint, tarnish, spoil, mar

blotch *noun* (*plural* **blotches**) a spot or patch of colour *etc* ◇ *verb* mark with blotches ◇ **blotched** *adj* ◇ **blotchy** *adj*

■ *noun* splodge, splash, smudge, spot, mark, stain

blotto *adj*, *Brit slang* drunk

blouse *noun* a loose piece of clothing for the upper body

blouson /'bluːzɒn/ *noun* a loose-fitting jacket or blouse gathered at the waist

blow *noun* **1** a hard stroke or knock, *eg* with the fist **2** *informal* a sudden piece of bad luck ◇ *verb* (**blows**, **blowing**, **blew**, **blown**) **1** of wind: move around **2** send air from the mouth: *blow on your soup to cool it* **3** sound (a wind instrument) **4** breathe hard or with difficulty ◇ **blowy** *adj* windy ◇ **blow over** pass and be forgotten ◇ **blow up** destroy by explosion

■ *noun* **1** box, cuff, clip, clout, swipe, bash, slap, smack, *informal* whack, *informal* wallop, *informal* belt, bang, clap, knock, rap, stroke, thump, punch **2** setback, disappointment, upset, jolt, shock, bombshell, *informal* whammy ◇ **blow over** die down, subside, end, finish, cease, pass, fizzle out, peter out

blubber *noun* the fat of whales and other sea animals

bludgeon *noun* a short stick with a heavy end ◇ *verb* hit with (or as with) a bludgeon

blue *noun* the colour of a clear sky ◇ *adj* **1** of this colour **2** *informal* unhappy, depressed **3** containing sexual material: *a blue film* ◇ **the blues** *noun plural* **1** a type of slow, sad jazz music **2** low spirits, depression ◇ **blue blood** royal or aristocratic blood ◇ **out of the blue** unexpectedly

bluebell *noun* **1** a wild plant with blue, bell-shaped flowers **2** in Scotland, the harebell

bluebottle *noun* a large fly with a blue abdomen

blueprint *noun* a plan of work to be done

bluff¹ *verb* try to deceive by pretending

self-confidence ◇ *noun* deception, trickery

◼ *verb* lie, pretend, feign, sham, fake

bluff ² *adj* rough, cheerful and frank ◇ *noun* a steep bank overlooking the sea or a river

blunder *verb* make a bad mistake ◇ *noun* a bad mistake

◼ *verb* stumble, flounder, err, *informal* slip up ◇ *noun* mistake, error, solecism, *informal* howler, *informal* bloomer, *informal* clanger, slip, *informal* boob, indiscretion, gaffe, faux pas, oversight, fault, *slang* cock-up

blunderbuss *noun* (*plural* **blunderbusses**) a short handgun with a wide mouth

blunt *adj* 1 having an edge or point that is not sharp 2 direct and honest in a rough manner ◇ *verb* make less sharp or less painful ◇ **bluntly** *adv* frankly, straightforwardly ◇ **bluntness** *noun*

◼ *adj* 2 direct, forthright, plain-spoken, tactless, insensitive, rude, impolite, uncivil, brusque, curt, abrupt

◳ *adj* 2 subtle, tactful

blur *noun* an indistinct area of something; a smudge, a smear ◇ *verb* (**blurs**, **blurring**, **blurred**) make indistinct, smudge ◇ **blurred** *adj*

◼ *noun* cloudiness, fuzziness, indistinctness, haze ◇ **blurred** out of focus, fuzzy, unclear, indistinct, ill-defined, hazy, foggy, dim, confused

◳ **blurred** clear, distinct

blurt *verb*: **blurt out** say suddenly and without thinking

blush *noun* (*plural* **blushes**) 1 a red glow on the face caused by embarrassment *etc* 2 a reddish glow ◇ *verb* go red in the face

◼ *verb* flush, redden, colour

◳ *verb* pale, blanch

bluster *verb* 1 blow strongly 2 boast loudly ◇ *noun* 1 a blasting wind 2 empty boasting

boa *noun* a long scarf of fur or feathers ◇ **boa constrictor** a large snake which kills its prey by winding itself round it and crushing it

boar *noun* 1 a wild pig 2 a male pig

board *noun* 1 a sheet of wood 2 a group of people who run a business: *board of directors* 3 food: *bed and board* ◇ *verb* 1 cover with boards 2 receive or supply with food and lodging 3 enter (a ship, aeroplane *etc*) ◇ **boarder** *noun* someone who receives food and lodging ◇ **boarding house** a house where paying guests receive meals at a fixed price ◇ **boarding school** a school in which food and lodging is given

◼ *noun* 1 sheet, panel, plank 2 committee, directorate, directors, trustees 3 meals, food, provisions ◇ *verb* 3 get on, embark, enter

boast *verb* brag, speak proudly and exaggeratedly about yourself ◇ *noun* something said in a bragging or boasting manner ◇ **boastful** *adj* ◇ **boastfully** *adv* ◇ **boastfulness** *noun*

◼ *verb* brag, crow, *informal* swank, exaggerate, *informal* talk big, bluster, vaunt, strut, swagger, show off

boat *noun* 1 a vessel for sailing or rowing; a ship 2 a boat-shaped dish: *sauce-boat*

Types of boat or ship include: canoe, dinghy, lifeboat, rowing-boat, kayak, dugout, coracle, skiff, punt, sampan, dhow, gondola, pedalo, catamaran, trimaran, yacht; airboat, cabin-cruiser, motorboat, motor-launch, speedboat, swamp boat, trawler, barge, narrow boat, houseboat, dredger, junk, smack, lugger; hovercraft, hydrofoil; clipper, cutter, ketch, packet, brig, schooner, square-rigger, galleon; ferry, paddle-steamer, tug, freighter, liner, container ship, tanker; warship, battleship, destroyer, submarine, U-boat, frigate, aircraft carrier, cruiser, dreadnought, corvette, minesweeper, man-of-war

---

boater *noun* a straw hat with a brim

boatswain or **bosun** /ˈboʊsən/ *noun* an officer who looks after a ship's boats, rigging *etc*

bob ¹ *verb* (**bobs**, **bobbing**, **bobbed**) move up and down rapidly

bob *noun* a hairstyle cut to neck level

bobbin *noun* a reel or spool on which thread is wound

bobsleigh *noun* a long sledge or two short sledges joined together with one long seat

bode *verb*: **bode well** or **bode ill** be a good or bad sign

bodice *noun* the close-fitting part of a woman's or a child's dress above the waist

bodkin *noun* a large blunt needle

body *noun* (*plural* **bodies**) **1** the whole or main part of a human being or animal **2** a corpse **3** the main part of anything **4** a mass of people **5** *informal* a one-piece woman's undergarment ◇ **bodily** *adj*

☰ **1** figure, trunk, torso **2** corpse, cadaver, carcase, *slang* stiff **4** group, band, crowd, throng, multitude, mob, mass

bodyguard *noun* someone or a group of people whose job is to protect another person from harm or attack

☰ guard, protector, *informal* minder

boffin *noun*, *informal* a research scientist

Said to come from a scientist who gave his colleagues nicknames from Dickens, Mr *Boffin* being a character in *Our Mutual Friend*

bog *noun* **1** a marsh **2** *slang* a toilet ◇ **boggy** *adj* marshy ◇ **bog down** prevent from making progress ◇ **bog-standard** *adj* of the lowest grade

☰ *noun* **1** marsh, swamp, fen, mire, quagmire, marshland, swampland, wetlands ◇ **bog down** encumber, hinder, impede, slow down, delay, stall

bogey *noun* something greatly feared

boggle *verb* be astonished (at)

bogus *adj* false

☰ false, fake, counterfeit, forged, fraudulent, *informal* phoney, sham, pseudo

☲ genuine, true, real, valid

bohemian *noun* someone who lives outside social conventions, *esp* an artist or writer ◇ *adj* of the lifestyle of a bohemian

☰ *adj* unconventional, unorthodox, eccentric, artistic, *informal* arty, offbeat

☲ *adj* bourgeois, conventional

boil *verb* **1** of a liquid: reach the temperature at which it turns to vapour **2** cook in boiling liquid **3** *informal* be hot **4** *informal* be angry

boil *noun* a kind of inflamed swelling

boiler *noun* a container in which water is heated or steam is produced

boisterous *adj* **1** wild, noisy **2** of weather: stormy ◇ **boisterously** *adv* ◇ **boisterousness** *noun*

☰ **1** exuberant, *informal* rumbustious, turbulent, loud, noisy, clamorous, rowdy, rough, riotous, unruly

☲ **1** quiet, calm, restrained

bold *adj* **1** daring, full of courage **2** cheeky **3** striking, well-marked: *bold colours* **4** of printing type: thick and clear ◇ **boldly** *adj* ◇ **boldness** *noun*

☰ **1** fearless, daring, audacious, brave, courageous, plucky, spirited, confident, outgoing **3** eye-catching, striking, conspicuous, prominent, strong, pronounced, bright, vivid, colourful, loud, flashy, showy, flamboyant

bolero *noun* a woman's short open jacket

bollard *noun* **1** a short post on a street used for traffic control **2** a post to which ropes are fastened on a ship or quay

bolshy *adj*, *informal* awkward, uncooperative ◇ **bolshiness** *noun*

bolster *noun* a long cylindrical pillow or cushion ◇ **bolster up** support

bolt *noun* **1** a small metal sliding bar used to fasten a door *etc* **2** a large screw or pin **3** a roll of cloth ◇ *verb* **1** fasten with a bolt **2** swallow (food) hurriedly **3** rush away, escape ◇ **bolt upright** sitting with a very straight back

☰ *verb* **1** fasten, secure, bar, latch, lock **2** gulp, wolf, gobble, gorge, devour, cram, stuff **3** abscond, escape, flee, fly

bomb *noun* a case containing explosive or other harmful material thrown, dropped, timed to go off automatically *etc* ◇ *verb* drop bombs on

☰ *noun* shell, explosive, charge, grenade,

mine, torpedo, rocket, missile ◇ *verb* bombard, shell, torpedo

bombard *verb* **1** attack with artillery **2** overwhelm (with): *bombarded with letters* ◇ **bombardment** *noun*

▪ **1** attack, assault, assail, pelt, pound, strafe, blast, bomb, shell, blitz

bombast *noun* pompous language ◇ **bombastic** *adj*

▪ **bombastic** pompous, high-flown, wordy, verbose

bomber *noun* **1** an aeroplane built for bombing **2** someone who throws or plants bombs

bombshell *noun* **1** a startling piece of news **2** a stunningly attractive woman

bona fide /ˈboʊnə ˈfaɪdɪ/ *adj* real, genuine: *a bona fide excuse*

bond *noun* **1** something which binds, *eg* a rope **2** something which brings people together: *music was a bond between them* **3** a promise to pay or do something ◇ *verb* join together

▪ *noun* **1** fetter, shackle, manacle, chain, cord, band, binding **2** connection, relation, link, tie, attachment, affinity ◇ *verb* connect, fasten, bind, unite, fuse, glue, gum, paste, stick, seal

bondage *noun* slavery

▪ captivity, confinement, slavery, enslavement, servitude

▪▪ freedom, independence

bone *noun* **1** a hard material forming the skeleton of animals **2** one of the connected pieces of a skeleton: *the hip bone* ◇ *verb* take the bones out of (meat *etc*)

> *Human bones include*:
> carpal, clavicle (or collarbone), coccyx, femur (or thigh bone), fibula, hip bone, humerus (or funny bone), ilium, ischium, mandible, maxilla, metacarpal, metatarsal, patella (or kneecap), pelvic girdle, pelvis, phalange, pubis, radius, rib, sacrum, scapula (or shoulder-blade), skull, sternum (or breastbone), tarsal, temporal, tibia, ulna, vertebra

bonfire *noun* a large fire in the open air

bonk *noun* **1** the sound of a blow **2** *slang* an act of sexual intercourse

bon mot /bɔˈmoʊ/ (*plural* **bons mots**) a short, clever saying

bonnet *noun* **1** a decorative woman's or baby's hat, fastened under the chin **2** the covering over a car engine

bonny *adj* good-looking; pretty

bonsai *noun* a miniature or dwarf tree created by special pruning

bonus *noun* (*plural* **bonuses**) **1** an extra payment in addition to wages, interest *etc* **2** something extra

▪ *noun* **1** benefit, extra, *informal* perk, perquisite, commission, dividend, honorarium, tip, gratuity

bony *adj* **1** full of bones **2** not fleshy, thin **3** made of bone or bone-like substance

boo *verb* make a sound of disapproval ◇ *noun* a sound of disapproval

boob *noun* **1** *informal* a mistake **2** *slang* a woman's breast

booby *noun* (*plural* **boobies**) an idiot ◇ **booby prize** a prize for the person who is last in a competition ◇ **booby trap** a hidden device, intended to injure

book *noun* **1** a number of pages bound together **2** a written work which has appeared, or is intended to appear, in the form of a book ◇ *verb* order (places *etc*) beforehand

bookie *noun*, *informal* a bookmaker

book-keeping *noun* the keeping of accounts

booklet *noun* a small book containing instructions, advice *etc*

bookmaker *noun* someone who takes bets and pays winnings

boom *verb* **1** make a hollow sound or roar **2** increase in prosperity, success *etc* ◇ *noun* **1** a loud, hollow sound **2** a rush or increase of trade, prosperity *etc*: *oil boom/property boom* **3** a pole along which a sail is stretched

▪ *verb* **1** bang, crash, roar, thunder, roll, rumble, resound, reverberate, blast, explode **2** flourish, thrive, prosper, succeed, develop, grow, increase, gain, expand ◇ *noun* **1** bang, clap, crash, thunder, rumble, reverberation, blast **2** increase, growth, expansion, gain, upsurge, boost, upturn, improvement, explosion

▣ *verb* **2** fail, collapse, slump ◇ *noun* **2** failure, collapse, slump, recession, depression

boomerang *noun* a curved piece of wood which when thrown returns to the thrower, a traditional hunting weapon of Australian Aboriginals

boon *noun* something to be grateful for, a blessing

▣ blessing, advantage, benefit
▣ disadvantage, blight

boor *noun* a rough or rude person ◇ **boorish** *adj*

▣ **boorish** uncouth, oafish, loutish, ill-mannered, rude, coarse, crude, vulgar, unrefined, uneducated, ignorant
▣ **boorish** polite, refined, cultured

boost *verb* raise, increase: *boost the sales figures* ◇ *noun* an increase, a rise

▣ *verb* raise, elevate, improve, enhance, enlarge, expand, amplify, increase, augment, bolster, supplement ◇ *noun* expansion, increase, rise, jump, increment

booster *noun* **1** a device for increasing the power of a machine, electronic signal *etc* **2** a vaccination given to reinforce an earlier one

boot *noun* **1** a heavy shoe covering the foot and lower part of the leg **2** *Brit* a place for stowing luggage in a car **3** a kick ◇ *verb* kick ◇ **boot up** start (a computer) by running its start-up programs

boot [2] *noun*: **to boot** in addition, as well

bootee *noun* a knitted boot for a baby

booth *noun* **1** a covered stall, *eg* at a market **2** a small compartment for telephoning, voting *etc*

▣ **1** kiosk, stall, stand **2** box, cubicle

bootleg *adj* made illegally ◇ **bootlegger** *noun* a dealer in illegal drink, recordings *etc*

booty *noun* plunder, gains taken in war *etc*

▣ loot, plunder, spoils, *informal* swag, haul, pickings

border *noun* **1** the edge or side of anything **2** the boundary of a country **3** a flowerbed in a garden ◇ *verb* (with **on**) be near to: *bordering on the absurd*

▣ *noun* **1** boundary, bounds, confines, limit, demarcation, margin, fringe, periphery, surround, perimeter, circumference, edge, rim, brim, verge, brink **2** frontier ◇ *verb* approximate, approach, verge (on)

bore [1] *verb* make a hole by piercing ◇ *noun* **1** a pierced hole **2** the diameter of a gun barrel

▣ *verb* drill, mine, pierce, perforate, penetrate, sink, burrow, tunnel

bore [2] *verb* weary, be tiresome to: *this book bores me* ◇ *noun* a tiresome person or thing ◇ **boring** *adj*

▣ *verb* tire, weary, fatigue, jade ◇ **boring** tedious, monotonous, routine, repetitious, uninteresting, unexciting, uneventful, dull, dreary, humdrum, commonplace, trite, unimaginative, uninspired, dry, stale, flat, insipid
▣ **boring** interesting, exciting, stimulating, original

bore [3] *noun* a wave that rushes up a river mouth at high tide

bore [4] *past form* of **bear** [2]

boredom *noun* lack of interest, weariness

▣ tedium, monotony, listlessness, weariness
▣ interest, excitement

born *adj* by birth, natural: *a born actor* ◇ **be born 1** of a baby: come out of the mother's womb **2** come into existence

> ⚠ Do not confuse: **born** and **borne**

borne *past participle* of **bear** [2]

borough *noun* **1** *hist* a town with special privileges granted by royal charter **2** a town that elects Members of Parliament

borrow *verb* get on loan
▣ lend

borzoi *noun* a breed of tall, slender dog with long hair

bosom *noun* **1** the breast **2** midst, centre: *the bosom of her family* ◇ *adj* of a friend: close, intimate

boss *noun* (*plural* **bosses**) a manager, a chief ◇ *verb* (with **around**) order about in a high-handed way

bossy *adj* tending to boss others, domineering ◇ **bossily** *adv* ◇ **bossiness** *noun*
- authoritarian, autocratic, tyrannical, despotic, dictatorial, domineering, overbearing, high-handed, imperious

bosun *see* **boatswain**

botany *noun* the study of plants ◇ **botanic** or **botanical** *adj* ◇ **botanist** *noun*

botch *verb* **1** mend clumsily **2** do badly ◇ *noun* a badly done piece of work

both *adj* & *pronoun* the two, the one and the other: *we're both going to Paris/both the men are dead* ◇ *adv* equally, together: *both willing and able*

bother *verb* **1** be a nuisance to: *stop bothering me!* **2** take time or trouble over something: *don't bother with the dishes* ◇ *noun* trouble, inconvenience
- *verb* **1** disturb, inconvenience, harass, *informal* hassle, pester, plague, nag, annoy, irritate, irk

bottle *noun* a hollow narrow-necked vessel for holding liquids ◇ *verb* put in a bottle ◇ **bottle up** keep in, hold back (feelings)
- *noun* phial, flask, carafe, decanter ◇ **bottle up** keep inside, conceal, hold back, suppress, contain
- **bottle up** unburden

bottleneck *noun* **1** a narrow part of a road likely to become crowded with traffic **2** a stage in a process where progress is held up

bottom *noun* **1** the lowest part or underside of anything **2** the buttocks ◇ **bottomless** *adj* extremely deep
- **1** underside, underneath, base, support, foundation, bed, depths, nadir **2** rump, rear, behind, *informal* posterior, buttocks, seat, *informal* backside, *slang* bum, *US informal* butt, *slang* arse, *US slang* ass

botulism *noun* food poisoning caused by bacteria in infected tinned food *etc*

boudoir /'buːdwɑː(r)/ *noun* a woman's private room

bough *noun* a branch of a tree

bought *past form of* **buy**

boulder *noun* a large stone

bounce *verb* **1** jump up after striking the ground *etc* **2** make (a ball *etc*) do this ◇ *noun* a jumping back up ◇ **bouncing** *adj* full of life, lively ◇ **bounce back** recover after a setback or trouble
- *verb* **1** spring, bob, ricochet, rebound ◇ **bouncing** exuberant, lively, vivacious, energetic, animated

bouncer *noun* someone employed to force troublemakers to leave a club *etc*

bound¹ *past form of* **bind** ◇ **bound to** certain to

bound² *adj*: **bound for** ready to go to, on the way to

bound³ *noun*: **bounds** borders, limits ◇ *verb* enclose, surround ◇ **boundless** *adj* ◇ **out of bounds** beyond the permitted limits

bound⁴ *noun* a leap, a jump ◇ *verb* jump, leap
- *noun* jump, leap, vault, spring, bounce, bob, hop, skip ◇ *verb* jump, leap, vault, spring, bounce, bob, hop, skip

boundary *noun* (*plural* **boundaries**) **1** an edge, a limit **2** a line *etc* marking an edge
- **1** border, frontier, barrier, line, borderline, demarcation, bounds, confines, limits, perimeter

bounteous or **bountiful** *adj* generous; plentiful

bounty *noun* (*plural* **bounties**) **1** a gift; generosity **2** money given as a help

bouquet /bəʊ'keɪ/ *noun* **1** a bunch of flowers **2** a scent, *eg* of wine
- **1** bunch, posy, nosegay, spray

bourgeois /'bɔːʒwɑː/ *adj* of the middle class ◇ **bourgeoisie** *noun*
- middle-class, conservative, traditional, conventional
- bohemian, unconventional

bout *noun* **1** a round in a contest **2** a spell, a fit: *a bout of flu*

boutique *noun* a small shop selling fashionable clothes *etc*

bovine *adj* **1** of or like cattle **2** stupid

bow¹ /baʊ/ *verb* **1** bend **2** nod the head or bend the body in greeting **3** give in: *bow to pressure* **4** weigh down, crush ◇ *noun* a bending of the head or body
∎ *verb* **2** incline, bend, nod, *formal* genuflect, kowtow **3** yield, give in, consent, capitulate, submit, acquiesce, concede, accept, defer

bow² /bəʊ/ *noun* **1** a weapon for shooting arrows **2** a looped knot **3** a wooden rod with horsehair stretched along it, by which the strings of a violin *etc* are played **4** anything in the shape of a curve or arch

bow³ /baʊ/ *noun* the front part of a ship

bowdlerize *verb* expurgate, censor heavily

> After Thomas *Bowdler*, who produced an expurgated edition of Shakespeare in the 19th century

bowels *noun plural* **1** the large and small intestines **2** the innermost or deepest parts of anything: *in the bowels of the earth*
∎ **1** intestines, guts, insides, *informal* innards **2** depths, centre, core, heart

bower *noun* a shady spot in a garden

bowl¹ *noun* **1** a basin for holding liquids **2** a basin-shaped hollow

bowl² *noun* **1** a heavy wooden ball, used in skittles *etc* **2** (**bowls**) a game played on a green with specially weighted bowls ◇ *verb* **1** play at bowls **2** move speedily like a bowl **3** *cricket* throw the ball towards the wicket **4** *cricket* put out by knocking the wicket with the ball ◇ **bowl over 1** knock down **2** surprise greatly
∎ *verb* **3** throw, hurl, fling, pitch, roll ◇ **bowl over 2** surprise, amaze, astound, astonish, stagger, stun, dumbfound, *informal* flabbergast

bowler¹ *noun* someone who bowls *eg* in cricket

bowler² *noun* a hat with a rounded top

box¹ *noun* (*plural* **boxes**) **1** a case for holding anything **2** an enclosure of private seats in a theatre ◇ *verb* **1** put in a box **2** confine in a small space ◇ **box office** an office where theatre tickets *etc* may be bought
∎ *noun* **1** case, crate, carton, packet, chest, coffer, trunk, coffin

box² *verb* **1** engage in the sport of boxing **2** punch, cuff

box³ *noun* **1** an evergreen shrub **2** a hardwood tree

boxer *noun* **1** someone who boxes as a sport **2** a breed of large smooth-haired dog with a head like a bulldog's ◇ **boxer shorts** loose-fitting men's underpants

boxing *noun* the sport of fighting with the fists wearing padded gloves

Boxing Day the first weekday after Christmas Day

boy *noun* **1** a male child **2** a male servant ◇ **boyhood** *noun* the time of being a boy ◇ **boyish** *adj* ◇ **boyishly** *adv*
∎ **1** son, lad, youth

boycott *verb* refuse to do business or trade with ◇ *noun* a refusal to trade or do business
∎ *verb* refuse, reject, embargo, ostracize, cold-shoulder, ignore, spurn
▣ *verb* encourage, support

> After Charles *Boycott*, British estate manager ostracized by the Irish Land League in the 19th century

bra *noun* an article of women's underwear for supporting the breasts

brace *noun* **1** an instrument which holds things firmly together **2** a piece of wire fitted over teeth to straighten them **3** a pair of pheasant, grouse *etc* when shot **4** a carpenter's tool for boring **5** (**braces**) shoulder straps for holding up trousers ◇ *verb* strengthen, give firmness to
∎ *verb* strengthen, reinforce, fortify, bolster, support, steady, tighten, fasten, tie, strap, bind

bracelet noun **1** a circular ornament worn around the wrist **2** slang a handcuff

bracing adj giving strength
■ refreshing, reviving, fortifying, invigorating, brisk
🗷 weakening, debilitating

bracken noun a coarse kind of fern

bracket noun **1** a support for something fastened to a wall **2** each of a pair of written or printed marks, eg ( ), [ ], used to group together several words **3** a grouping, category: in the same age bracket ◊ verb **1** enclose in brackets **2** group together

brackish adj of water: rather salty

brag verb (**brags**, **bragging**, **bragged**) boast ◊ noun a boast

braggart noun someone vain and boastful

braid verb plait (the hair) ◊ noun **1** a plait of hair **2** decorative ribbon used as trimming

braille noun a system of raised marks on paper which blind people can read by feeling

Named after its inventor, French teacher Louis Braille

brain noun the part of the body inside the skull, the centre of feeling and thinking ◊ verb knock out the brains of; hit hard on the head ◊ **brainy** adj, informal clever
■ noun cerebrum, grey matter, head, mind, intellect, informal nous, informal brains, intelligence, reason, sense, common sense ◊ **brainy** intellectual, intelligent, clever, smart, bright, brilliant
🗷 **brainy** dull

brainwash verb force (a person) to change their views ◊ **brainwashing** noun

brainwave noun a good idea

braise verb stew (meat) in a small amount of liquid

brake noun a part of a vehicle used for stopping or slowing down ◊ verb slow down or stop by using the brake(s)
■ verb slow, decelerate, halt, stop, pull up
🗷 verb accelerate

bramble noun **1** the blackberry bush **2** its fruit

bran noun the inner husks of wheat etc, separated from flour after grinding

branch noun (plural **branches**) **1** an arm-like limb of a tree **2** a small shop, bank etc belonging to a bigger one ◊ verb spread out like branches
■ noun **2** department, office, section, division, subdivision ◊ verb diversify, extend, broaden out, multiply, ramify

brand noun **1** a make of goods with a special trademark **2** a burning piece of wood **3** a permanent mark made by a red-hot iron ◊ verb **1** mark with a brand **2** mark permanently; impress deeply **3** mark with disgrace: branded as a thief ◊ **brand-new** adj absolutely new
■ noun **1** make, brand-name, tradename, trademark, logo, label, stamp, hallmark, line, variety ◊ verb **1** mark, stamp, label, burn **3** disgrace, discredit, denounce, censure

brandish verb wave (a weapon etc) about
■ wave, raise, wield, flourish, shake

brandy noun (plural **brandies**) an alcoholic spirit made from wine

brash adj vulgarly self-assured
■ brazen, forward, impertinent, impudent, insolent, rude, cocky, assured, bold, audacious, informal in-your-face

brass noun (plural **brasses**) **1** metal made by mixing copper and zinc **2** music brass wind instruments ◊ adj **1** made of brass **2** playing brass musical instruments: brass band ◊ **brassy** adj **1** like brass **2** of a voice: harsh

brassière noun, formal a bra

brat noun a disapproving name for a child

bravado noun a show of bravery, bold pretence
■ swagger, bragging, talk, showing off, show
🗷 modesty, restraint

brave adj ready to meet danger, pain etc without showing fear; courageous ◊ verb face or meet boldly and without fear ◊ noun a Native American warrior

◇ **bravely** *adv* ◇ **bravery** *noun*

■ *adj* courageous, plucky, unafraid, fearless, undaunted, bold, audacious, daring, intrepid, stout-hearted, valiant ◇ *verb* face, confront, defy, challenge, dare, stand up to, face up to

◘ *adj* cowardly, afraid, timid

bravo *exclam* well done!

bravura *noun* boldness, spirit, dash

brawl *noun* a noisy quarrel; a fight ◇ *verb* quarrel or fight noisily

■ *noun* fight, *informal* punch-up, scrap, scuffle, mêlée, fray, affray, fracas

brawn *noun* muscle power ◇ **brawny** *adj* big and strong

■ **brawny** muscular, sinewy, athletic, well-built, burly, beefy, *informal* hunky, hefty, solid, bulky, hulking, strapping, strong, powerful, sturdy

◘ **brawny** slight, frail

bray *noun* a cry like that of an ass ◇ *verb* cry like an ass

brazen *adj* 1 impudent, shameless: *brazen hussy* 2 of or like brass ◇ **brazenly** *adv*

■ 1 brash, brassy, bold, forward, saucy, pert, barefaced, impudent, insolent, defiant, shameless, unashamed, immodest

◘ 1 shy, shamefaced, modest

brazier *noun* an iron basket for holding burning coals

brazil nut a three-sided nut produced by a tropical tree

breach *noun* (*plural* **breaches**) 1 a break, a gap 2 a breaking of a law, a promise *etc* 3 a quarrel ◇ *verb* make a gap or opening in

■ *noun* 1 break, crack, rift, rupture, fissure, cleft, crevice, opening, aperture, gap, space, hole, chasm 2 violation, contravention, infringement, offence, transgression, lapse

bread *noun* food made of flour or meal and baked

breadth *noun* 1 distance from side to side, width 2 extent: *breadth of knowledge*

■ 1 width, broadness, latitude, thickness, span, spread 2 range, extent, reach, scope, compass

breadwinner *noun* someone who earns a living for a family

break *verb* (**breaks**, **breaking**, **broke**, **broken**) 1 (cause to) fall to pieces or apart 2 act against (a law, promise *etc*) 3 interrupt (a silence) 4 tell (news) 5 check, soften the effect of (a fall) 6 cure (a habit) 7 of a boy's voice: drop to a deep male tone ◇ *noun* 1 an act or instance of breaking 2 an opening 3 a pause 4 *informal* a lucky chance ◇ **breakable** *adj* ◇ **break down 1** divide into parts 2 of an engine, machine *etc*: fail 3 be overcome with weeping or nervous exhaustion ◇ **break in** tame, train (a wild horse *etc*) ◇ **break into** enter by force ◇ **break out 1** appear suddenly 2 escape 3 (with **in**) become covered (with a rash *etc*) ◇ **break up 1** (cause to) fall to pieces or apart 2 separate, leave one another 3 begin school holidays

■ *verb* 1 fracture, crack, snap, split, sever, separate, divide, rend, smash, disintegrate, splinter, shatter, ruin, destroy, demolish 2 violate, contravene, infringe, breach, disobey, flout 4 tell, impart, divulge, disclose, reveal, announce ◇ *noun* 1 fracture, crack, split, rift, rupture, schism, separation, tear, gash 2 crack, fissure, cleft, crevice, opening, gap, hole, breach 3 interruption, pause, halt, lull, *informal* let-up, respite, rest, breather 4 opportunity, chance, advantage, fortune, luck

breakage *noun* 1 the act of breaking 2 something broken

breakdown *noun* 1 a division into parts 2 a collapse from nervous exhaustion *etc* 3 a failure of an engine, *etc*

breaker *noun* a large wave

breakfast *noun* the first meal of the day ◇ *verb* eat this meal

break-in *noun* illegal forced entry of a house *etc* with intent to steal

breakthrough *noun* a sudden success after some effort

breakwater *noun* a barrier to break the force of waves

bream *noun* a small fish

breast *noun* 1 either of the milk-producing glands on a woman's body **2** the front part of a human or animal body between neck and belly **3** a part of a jacket or coat which covers the breast ◊ **breastbone** *noun* the bone running down the middle of the breast; the sternum

breath *noun* **1** the air drawn into and then sent out from the lungs **2** an instance of breathing **3** a very slight breeze

> ⚠ Do not confuse: **breath** and **breathe**

breathalyser *noun* a device into which someone breathes to indicate the amount of alcohol in their blood

breathe *verb* (**breathes**, **breathing**, **breathed**) **1** draw in and send out air from the lungs **2** whisper
≡ **1** respire, inhale, exhale, sigh, gasp, pant, puff **2** murmur, whisper

breather *noun* a rest or pause

breathless *adj* **1** breathing very fast, panting **2** excited ◊ **breathlessly** *adv* ◊ **breathlessness** *noun*
≡ **1** short-winded, out of breath, panting, puffing, puffed (out), winded, gasping, wheezing

bred *past form* of **breed**

breech *noun* the back part, *esp* of a gun

breeches *noun plural* trousers reaching to just below the knee

breed *verb* (**breeds**, **breeding**, **bred**) **1** produce offspring **2** mate and rear (animals) **3** cause: *dirt breeds disease* ◊ *noun* **1** a group of animals *etc* descended from the same ancestor **2** type, sort: *a new breed of salesmen* ◊ **breeding** *noun* **1** the act of producing offspring or mating and rearing animals **2** good manners; education and training
≡ *verb* **1** reproduce, procreate, multiply, propagate, bear, bring forth **3** produce, create, cause, occasion, engender, generate, make, foster, nurture ◊ *noun* **1** species, pedigree, strain, variety, family **2** ilk, sort, kind, type ◊ **breeding 2** manners, politeness, civility, gentility, urbanity, refinement

breeze *noun* a gentle wind
≡ wind, flurry, draught

breezy *adj* **1** windy, gusty **2** bright, lively ◊ **breezily** *adv*
≡ **1** windy, blowy, fresh, airy, gusty, blustery **2** animated, lively, carefree, cheerful, *informal* easy-going, casual, bright

brethren *noun plural, old* brothers

breve /briːv/ *noun* a musical note (◯) equivalent to double a semibreve

brevity *noun* shortness, conciseness

brew *verb* **1** make (beer) **2** make (tea *etc*) **3** be gathering or forming: *there's trouble brewing* **4** plot, plan: *brewing mischief* ◊ **brewer** *noun* someone who brews beer *etc* ◊ **brewery** *noun* (*plural* **breweries**) a place where beer is made ◊ **brewpub** *noun* a pub where beer is made

briar or **brier** *noun* **1** the wild rose **2** a heather plant whose wood is used for making tobacco pipes

bribe *noun* a gift of money *etc* given to persuade someone to do something ◊ *verb* (**bribes**, **bribing**, **bribed**) give a bribe to ◊ **bribery** *noun*
≡ *noun* incentive, inducement, allurement, enticement, *informal* backhander, kickback, payola, *informal* sweetener, *informal* hush money, protection money ◊ *verb* corrupt, buy off, reward

bric-à-brac *noun* small odds and ends

brick *noun* **1** a block of baked clay for building **2** a toy building block of wood *etc*

bride *noun* a woman about to be married, or newly married ◊ **bridal** *adj* of a bride or a wedding
≡ bridal nuptial, matrimonial, marital

bridegroom *noun* a man about to be married, or newly married

bridesmaid *noun* an unmarried woman who attends the bride at a wedding

bridge¹ *noun* **1** a structure built to carry a track or road across a river *etc* **2** the captain's platform on a ship **3** the bony part of the nose **4** a thin piece of wood

holding up the strings of a violin *etc*
◇ *verb* (**bridges, bridging, bridged**) **1**
be a bridge over; span **2** build a bridge
over **3** get over (a difficulty)
▤ *verb* **1** span, cross, link, connect

Types of bridge include:
suspension bridge, arch bridge,
cantilever bridge, flying bridge,
flyover, overpass, footbridge,
railway bridge, viaduct, aqueduct,
humpback bridge, toll bridge,
pontoon bridge, Bailey bridge, rope
bridge, drawbridge, swing bridge

---

bridge² *noun* a card game for two
pairs of players

bridle *noun* the harness on a horse's
head to which the reins are attached
◇ *verb* **1** put a bridle on **2** toss the head
indignantly

Brie /bri:/ *noun* a soft cheese with a yellowish centre and white rind

brief *adj* short; taking a short time
◇ *noun* a set of notes giving information
or instructions, *esp* to a lawyer about a
case ◇ *verb* instruct or inform ◇ **briefly**
adv
▤ *adj* short, terse, succinct, concise, pithy,
crisp, compressed ◇ *noun* orders, instructions, directions, remit, mandate,
directive, briefing, dossier, case, defence ◇ *verb* instruct, direct, explain,
prime, inform, *informal* fill in

briefs *noun plural* close-fitting underpants

brier *another spelling of* **briar**

brigade *noun* a body of soldiers,
usually two battalions

brigadier *noun* a senior army officer

brigand *noun*, *old* a robber, a bandit

bright *adj* **1** shining; full of light **2**
clever **3** cheerful
▤ **1** luminous, illuminated, radiant, shining, gleaming, glittering, sparkling,
twinkling, shimmering, glowing, brilliant, dazzling, glaring, blazing **2** *informal*
brainy, smart, intelligent, quick-witted,
quick, sharp, astute, perceptive **3**
happy, cheerful, upbeat, glad, joyful,
merry, jolly, lively, vivacious

▣ **1** dull **2** stupid **3** sad

brighten *verb* make or grow bright

brilliant *adj* **1** very clever **2** sparkling
or shining brightly **3** *informal* very
good, excellent ◇ **brilliance** *noun*
◇ **brilliantly** *adv*
▤ **1** gifted, talented, accomplished, expert,
skilful, masterly, superb **2** sparkling, glittering,
scintillating, dazzling, glaring, blazing **3**
exceptional, outstanding, superb

brim *noun* **1** the edge of a cup *etc*: *filled
to the brim* **2** the protruding lower edge
of a hat or cap ◇ *verb* (**brims, brim-
ming, brimmed**) be full
▤ *noun* **1** rim, lip

brimstone *noun*, *old* sulphur

brine *noun* salt water ◇ **briny** *adj*

bring *verb* (**brings, bringing,
brought**) **1** fetch, lead or carry (to a
place) **2** cause to happen or come: *the
medicine brings him relief* ◇ **bring about**
cause ◇ **bring up 1** rear, feed and educate: *brought up three children single-
handed* **2** mention: *I'll bring it up at the
meeting* **3** *informal* vomit
▤ **1** carry, bear, convey, transport, fetch,
take, deliver, escort, accompany, usher,
guide, conduct, lead **2** cause, produce,
engender, create, prompt, provoke
◇ **bring up 1** rear, raise, foster, nurture, educate, teach, train, form **2** introduce, broach, mention, submit,
propose **3** vomit, regurgitate, *informal*
throw up

brink *noun* the edge of a cliff *etc* ◇ **on
the brink of** almost at the point of, on
the verge of: *on the brink of tears*

briquette *noun* a small brick of compressed charcoal *etc*

brisk *adj* **1** moving quickly: *a brisk
walk* **2** lively and efficient: *a brisk manner* ◇ **briskly** *adv* ◇ **briskness** *noun*
▤ **1** energetic, vigorous, quick **2** lively,
spirited, active, busy, bustling, alert
▣ **1** sluggish, lazy

bristle *noun* a short, stiff hair on an
animal, a brush, *etc* ◇ *verb* **1** of hair *etc*:
stand on end **2** show anger and indignation: *he bristled at my remark*
◇ **bristly** *adj* having bristles; rough
▤ *noun* hair, whisker

brittle *adj* hard but easily broken
◨ fragile, delicate

broach *verb* **1** begin to talk about: *broached the subject* **2** open, begin using (*eg* a cask of wine)

broad *adj* **1** wide, extensive **2** of an accent *etc*: strong, obvious ◇ **broaden** *verb* make or grow broader ◇ **broadly** *adv*

◨ **1** wide, large, vast, roomy, spacious, capacious, ample, extensive, widespread
◪ **1** narrow

broadcast *verb* transmit (a programme *etc*) on radio or television ◇ *noun* a programme transmitted on radio or television ◇ **broadcaster** *noun* ◇ **broadcasting** *noun*

broadsheet *noun* a large-format quality newspaper

broadside **1** a strong attack in an argument *etc* **2** a shot by all the guns on one side of a ship

brocade *noun* a silk cloth on which fine patterns are sewn

broccoli *noun* a plant with small green or purple flower-heads eaten as a vegetable

brochure /'brəʊʃə/ *noun* a booklet, a pamphlet: *holiday brochures*
◨ leaflet, booklet, pamphlet, prospectus

brogue /brəʊg/ *noun* **1** a strong shoe **2** a broad accent in speaking: *Irish brogue*

broil *verb* **1** make or be very hot **2** *US* grill

broke *past form* of **break** ◇ *adj*, *informal* having no money
◨ *adj* penniless, bankrupt, bust

broken *past participle* of **break**

broker *noun* someone who buys and sells stocks and shares for others ◇ *verb* **1** act as a broker **2** negotiate on behalf of others: *broker a deal*

bromide *noun* **1** a chemical used as a sedative **2** a monochrome photographic print

bronchitis *noun* an illness affecting the windpipe, causing difficulty in breathing ◇ **bronchial** *adj*

bronco *noun* (*plural* **broncos**) *US* a half-tamed horse

brontosaurus *noun* (*plural* **brontosauri**) a large dinosaur

bronze *noun* a golden-brown mixture of copper and tin ◇ *adj* of this colour ◇ **bronzed** *adj* suntanned ◇ **bronze medal** in sports competitions: a medal of bronze awarded for third place

brooch *noun* (*plural* **brooches**) an ornament pinned to the clothing

brood *verb* **1** of a hen *etc*: sit on eggs **2** think anxiously for some time ◇ *noun* **1** a number of young birds hatched at one time **2** young animals or children of the same family
◨ *verb* **2** ponder, ruminate, meditate, muse, mull over, go over, dwell on, mope ◇ *noun* **1** clutch, chicks, hatch **2** litter, young, offspring, issue, progeny, children, family

brook¹ *noun* a small stream
◨ *noun* stream, rivulet, beck, burn

brook² *verb* put up with, endure

broom¹ *noun* a brush for sweeping

broom² *noun* a type of shrub with yellow flowers

broomstick *noun* the handle of a broom

Bros *abbrev* Brothers

broth *noun* soup made with boiled meat or vegetables

brothel *noun* a house where prostitution is practised

Originally *brothel-house*, *brothel* being a general term of abuse that was later applied specifically to prostitutes

brother *noun* **1** a male born of the same parents as yourself **2** a companion, a fellow-worker ◇ **brotherly** *adj* like a brother; affectionate
◨ **2** comrade, friend, mate, partner, colleague, associate, fellow, companion

brotherhood *noun* **1** comradeship between men **2** a men's association
◨ **2** fraternity, society, association

brother-in-law *noun* **1** the brother of your husband or wife **2** the husband of your sister or sister-in-law

brought *past form* of **bring**

brow *noun* **1** a forehead **2** an eyebrow **3** the edge of a hill

browbeat *verb* bully

■ bully, coerce, intimidate, threaten, tyrannize, oppress, hound

brown *noun* the dark colour of wood, soil *etc* ◇ *adj* **1** of this colour **2** *informal* suntanned

■ chocolate, mahogany, coffee, hazel, bay, chestnut, sepia, tan, tawny, russet, rust

brownie *noun* **1** a helpful fairy or goblin **2** a Brownie Guide ◇ **Brownie Guide** a junior Guide

brownfield *noun* an area of land that was previously built on

browse *verb* **1** glance through a range of books, shop merchandise *etc* **2** feed on the shoots or leaves of plants

■ **1** leaf through, flick through, dip into, skim, survey, scan, peruse

bruise *noun* a discoloured area on the skin, the surface of fruit *etc*, where it has been struck ◇ *verb* cause bruises (to)

■ *noun* blemish, mark, discoloration

brunette *noun* a woman with dark brown hair

brunt *noun*: **bear** or **take the brunt** take the most stress or the main force

brush *noun* (*plural* **brushes**) **1** an instrument with tufts of bristles, hair *etc* for smoothing the hair, cleaning, painting *etc* **2** a disagreement, a brief quarrel: *a brush with the law* **3** the tail of a fox **4** undergrowth ◇ *verb* **1** pass a brush over **2** remove by sweeping **3** touch lightly in passing

■ *noun* **1** broom, sweeper, besom **2** confrontation, encounter, clash, conflict, fight, set-to, fracas ◇ *verb* **1** sweep **3** touch, contact, graze, kiss, stroke, rub, scrape

brushwood *noun* **1** broken branches, twigs *etc* **2** undergrowth

brusque *adj* sharp and short in manner, rude ◇ **brusquely** *adv* ◇ **brusqueness** *noun*

■ abrupt, sharp, short, terse, curt, gruff, surly, discourteous, impolite, uncivil

🔁 courteous, polite

Brussels sprouts a type of vegetable like small cabbages, which grow as buds on the stem of a plant

brut /bruːt/ *adj* of champagne: dry

brutal *adj* cruel, extremely harsh ◇ **brutality** *noun* ◇ **brutally** *adv*

■ animal, bestial, beastly, brutish, inhuman, savage, bloodthirsty, vicious, ferocious, cruel, inhumane, remorseless, pitiless, merciless, ruthless, callous, insensitive, unfeeling, heartless, harsh

🔁 kindly, humane, civilized

brute *noun* **1** an animal **2** a cruel person ◇ **brutish** *adj* like a brute, savage, coarse

■ **2** monster, sadist, bully, lout

BSc *abbrev* Bachelor of Science

BSE *abbrev* bovine spongiform encephalopathy, a brain disease of cattle

BST *abbrev* British Summer Time

Bt *abbrev* baronet

BTW *abbrev* by the way

bubble *noun* a thin ball of liquid blown out with air ◇ *verb* rise in bubbles

■ *verb* effervesce, fizz, sparkle, froth

bubbly *adj* **1** full of bubbles **2** lively, vivacious ◇ *noun*, *informal* champagne; sparkling wine

■ *adj* **1** effervescent, fizzy, sparkling, carbonated, frothy, foaming, sudsy **2** lively, bouncy, happy, merry, excited

🔁 *adj* **1** flat, still **2** lethargic

buccaneer *noun*, *old* a pirate

buck[1] *noun* the male of the deer, goat, hare and rabbit ◇ *verb* of a horse *etc*: attempt to throw a rider by rapid jumps into the air

buck[2] *noun*, *US informal* a dollar

bucket *noun* a container for water *etc*

■ pail

buckle *noun* a clip for fastening straps or belts ◇ *verb* **1** fasten with a buckle **2** collapse under weight

■ *noun* clasp, clip, catch, fastener ◇ *verb* **1** fasten, clasp, catch **2** cave in, crumple, collapse

buckshot *noun* large lead shot fired from a shotgun

buckwheat *noun* a plant whose seed

is used to feed animals and ground into flour

bucolic *adj* of the countryside; pastoral, rural

bud *noun* the first shoot of a tree or plant ◇ *verb* (**buds**, **budding**, **budded**) produce buds ◇ **budding** *adj* showing signs of becoming: *budding author*

◼ *noun* shoot, sprout, germ ◇ *verb* shoot, sprout, burgeon, develop, grow ◇ **budding** potential, promising, embryonic, burgeoning, developing

Buddhism *noun* a religion whose followers worship Buddha ◇ **Buddhist** *noun & adj*

budge *verb* (**budges**, **budging**, **budged**) move slightly, stir

◼ move, stir, shift, dislodge, yield, give (way)

budgerigar *noun* a kind of small parrot often kept as a pet

budget *noun* **1** a government plan for the year's spending **2** any plan of future spending ◇ *verb* allow for in a budget: *the project has been budgeted for*

◼ *noun* **2** allotment, allocation, estimate

Originally a small bag; the parliamentary sense of *budget* stems from a political insult directed at Robert Walpole implying that he was a quack or pedlar

---

budgie *noun*, *informal* a budgerigar

buff [1] *noun* a light yellowish-brown colour ◇ *verb* polish

◼ *noun* yellowish-brown, fawn, khaki ◇ *verb* polish, burnish, shine, smooth, rub, brush

buff [2] *noun* an enthusiast, a fan: *film buff*

◼ expert, connoisseur, enthusiast, fan, devotee, addict, fiend, freak

---

The later meaning of 'enthusiast' derives from the *buff*-coloured uniforms once used by volunteer firefighters in New York

---

buffalo *noun* (*plural* **buffaloes**) **1** a large Asian ox, used to draw loads

2 the North American bison

buffer *noun* something which lessens the force of a blow or collision

◼ shock-absorber, bumper, fender

buffet [1] /'bʌfɪt/ *verb* strike, knock about ◇ *noun* a slap or a blow

◼ *verb* batter, hit, strike, knock, bang, bump, push, shove, pound, pummel, beat, thump, box, cuff, clout

buffet [2] /'bʊfeɪ/ *noun* **1** a counter or café serving food and drink **2** a range of dishes set out at a party, *etc* for people to serve themselves

◼ **1** snack-bar, counter, café, cafeteria

buffoon *noun* a clown, fool ◇ **buffoonery** *noun*

bug *noun* **1** a small, *esp* irritating, insect **2** a disease germ: *a tummy bug* **3** a tiny hidden microphone for recording conversations **4** a problem in a computer program causing errors in its execution ◇ *verb* (**bugs**, **bugging**, **bugged**) **1** conceal a microphone in (a room *etc*) **2** record with a hidden microphone **3** *US informal* annoy, harass

◼ *noun* **2** virus, germ **4** fault, gremlin, virus ◇ *verb* **3** annoy, irritate, bother

bugbear *noun* something that frightens or annoys

buggy *noun* (*plural* **buggies**) a child's pushchair

bugle *noun* a small military trumpet ◇ **bugler** *noun*

build *verb* (**builds**, **building**, **built**) put together the parts of anything ◇ *noun* physique, physical character: *a man of heavy build* ◇ **builder** *noun*

◼ *verb* erect, raise, construct, fabricate, make, form, constitute, assemble, knock together ◇ *noun* physique, figure, body, form, shape, size, frame, structure

building *noun* **1** the act or trade of building houses *etc* **2** a house or similar structure ◇ **building society** an institution like a bank which accepts investments and whose main business is to lend people money to buy a house

◼ **1** erection, construction **2** edifice, dwelling, erection, construction, structure

Types of building include:
house, bungalow, cottage, block of flats, cabin, farmhouse, villa, mansion, chateau, castle, palace; church, chapel, cathedral, abbey, monastery, temple, pagoda, mosque, synagogue, gurdwara, mandir; shop, store, garage, factory, warehouse, silo, office block, tower block, skyscraper, high-rise, low-rise, theatre, cinema, multiplex, gymnasium, sports hall, restaurant, café, hotel, *informal* pub, public house, inn, school, college, museum, library, hospital, prison, power station, observatory; barracks, fort, fortress, monument, mausoleum; shed, barn, outhouse, stable, mill, lighthouse, pier, pavilion, boathouse, beach-hut, summerhouse, gazebo, dovecote, windmill

built-up *adj* of an area: containing houses and other buildings

bulb *noun* **1** the rounded part of the stem of an onion, tulip etc, in which they store their food **2** a glass globe surrounding the element of an electric light ◇ **bulbous** *adj* bulb-shaped

bulge *noun* **1** a swelling **2** a noticeable increase ◇ *verb* (**bulges, bulging, bulged**) swell out

◼ *noun* **1** swelling, bump, lump, hump, distension, protuberance, projection **2** rise, increase, surge, upsurge, intensification ◇ *verb* swell, puff out, dilate, expand, enlarge, distend, protrude, project

bulghur or **bulgur** *noun* a kind of cooked, cracked wheat

bulimia *noun* an eating disorder in which bingeing is followed by self-induced vomiting or purging ◇ **bulimic** *adj*

bulk *noun* **1** large size **2** the greater part: *the bulk of the population*

◼ **1** magnitude, volume, mass **2** majority, most

bulkhead *noun* a wall in the inside of a ship

bulky *adj* taking up a lot of room

◼ substantial, big, large, huge, enormous, immense, mammoth, massive, colossal, hulking, hefty, heavy, weighty, unmanageable, unwieldy, awkward, cumbersome

◼ insubstantial, small, handy

bull *noun* the male of cattle, or of the whale, elephant *etc* ◇ **bull bars** a metal grille on the front of a vehicle

bulldog *noun* a breed of strong, fierce-looking dog

bulldozer *noun* a machine for levelling land and clearing away obstacles ◇ **bulldoze** *verb* **1** use a bulldozer on **2** force: *bulldozed his way into the room*

bullet *noun* the piece of metal fired from a gun ◇ **bullet-proof** *adj* not able to be pierced by bullets

◼ shot, pellet, *informal* slug

bulletin *noun* a report of current news, someone's health *etc*

◼ report, newsflash, dispatch, communiqué, statement, announcement, notification, communication, message

bullion *noun* gold or silver in the form of bars *etc*

bullock *noun* a young bull

bullfight *noun* a public entertainment in Spain *etc*, in which a bull is angered and usually killed

bullfrog *noun* a type of large frog

bullring *noun* the arena in which bullfights take place

bull's-eye *noun* the mark in the middle of a target

bully *noun* (*plural* **bullies**) someone who unfairly uses their size, strength or power to hurt or frighten others ◇ *verb* act like a bully

◼ *noun* persecutor, tormentor, browbeater, intimidator, bully-boy, *slang* heavy ◇ *verb* persecute, torment, terrorize, bulldoze, coerce, browbeat, intimidate, tyrannize, push around

Originally a term of affection that developed to mean 'pimp', and so to someone who harasses others

bulrush *noun* (*plural* **bulrushes**) a

large strong reed which grows on wet land or in water

bulwark /'bʊlwək/ *noun* **1** a strong defensive wall **2** a prop, support or defence

bum¹ *noun, Brit slang* the buttocks

bum² *noun, US slang* a tramp ◇ *adj* useless, dud

bumbag *noun, Brit* a carrying pouch strapped round the waist

bumble-bee *noun* a type of large bee

bumf *another spelling of* **bumph**

bump *verb* **1** strike heavily **2** knock by accident ◇ *noun* **1** the sound of a heavy blow **2** an accidental knock **3** a raised lump ◇ **bumpy** *adj*

■ *verb* **1** hit, strike, knock, bang, crash **2** collide (with) ◇ *noun* **1** blow, hit, knock, bang, thump, thud, smash, crash **3** lump, swelling, bulge, hump, protuberance

bumper *noun* a bar round the front and back of a car's body to protect it from damage ◇ *adj* large: *bumper crop*
■ *adj* large, exceptional

bumph or **bumf** *noun, Brit informal* miscellaneous, uninteresting papers, leaflets *etc*

Originally short for 'bum-fodder', *ie* toilet paper

bumpkin *noun* a clumsy, awkward, country person

bumptious *adj* self-important
■ self-important, pompous, conceited, full of oneself, cocky
☲ humble, modest

bun *noun* **1** a sweet roll made from egg dough **2** hair wound into a rounded mass

bunch *noun* (*plural* **bunches**) a number of things tied together or growing together ◇ *verb* crowd together
■ *noun* bundle, sheaf, tuft, clump, cluster, bouquet, posy, spray ◇ *verb* group, bundle, cluster, collect, pack, huddle

bundle *noun* a number of things loosely bound together ◇ *verb* **1** tie in a bundle **2** push roughly: *bundled the children into the car*

■ *noun* bunch, sheaf, roll, bale ◇ *verb* **1** pack, wrap, bale, truss, bind, tie, fasten

bung *noun* the stopper of the hole in a barrel, bottle *etc* ◇ *verb* stop up with a bung

bungalow *noun* a one-storey house

bungle *verb* **1** do badly or clumsily **2** mishandle, mismanage ◇ *noun* a clumsy or mishandled action

■ *verb* **2** mismanage, *slang* cock up, *slang* screw up, *informal* foul up, *informal* mess up, ruin, spoil, mar, botch, fudge

bunion *noun* a lump or swelling on the joint of the big toe

bunk *noun* a narrow bed, *eg* in a ship's cabin

bunkbed *noun* one of a pair of narrow beds one above the other

bunker *noun* **1** a sandpit on a golf course **2** an underground shelter **3** a large box for keeping coal

bunkum *noun* nonsense

From *Buncombe* county in N Carolina, whose representative once gave a rambling speech in Congress

bunny *noun* (*plural* **bunnies**) a child's name for a rabbit

Bunsen burner a gas burner used in laboratories

bunting¹ *noun* **1** small flags on a string **2** a thin cloth used for making flags

bunting² *noun* a bird of the finch family

buoy /bɔɪ/ *noun* **1** a floating mark acting as a guide or warning for ships **2** a float, *eg* a lifebuoy

buoyant *adj* **1** able to float **2** cheerful, bouncy ◇ **buoyancy** *noun* ◇ **buoyantly** *adv*

■ **2** light-hearted, carefree, bright, cheerful, happy, joyful, lively, animated, bouncy
☲ **2** depressed

bur *another spelling of* **burr**

burden *noun* **1** a load **2** something difficult to bear, *eg* poverty or sorrow ◇ *verb* put a burden on ◇ **burdensome** *adj*

◼ *noun* **1** cargo, load, weight, dead-weight **2** encumbrance, millstone, onus, responsibility, obligation, duty, strain, stress, worry, anxiety, care, trouble, trial, affliction, sorrow ◇ *verb* load, weigh down, encumber, tax, strain, overload

burdock *noun* a type of plant with hooked leaves

bureau /'bjʊrəʊ/ *noun* (*plural* **bureaux** or **bureaus**) **1** a writing table **2** an office

◼ **2** agency, service, office

bureaucracy /bjʊ'rɒkrəsɪ/ *noun* **1** government by officials **2** unnecessarily complicated administrative procedures

◼ **1** administration, government, the authorities, the system, officialdom **2** red tape, regulations

bureaucrat *noun* an administrative official ◇ **bureaucratic** *adj* ◇ **bureaucratically** *adv*

burglar *noun* someone who breaks into a house to steal ◇ **burglary** *noun* (*plural* **burglaries**) ◇ **burgle** *verb* commit burglary

◼ housebreaker, robber, thief ◇ **burglary** break-in, robbery, theft

burial *noun* the placing of a body under the ground after death

burlesque *noun* a piece of writing, acting *etc*, making fun of somebody

burly *adj* broad and strong

◼ big, well-built, hulking, hefty, heavy, stocky, sturdy, brawny, beefy, *informal* hunky, muscular, athletic, strapping, strong, powerful

◼ small, puny, thin, slim

burn ¹ *verb* (**burns**, **burning**, **burnt** or **burned**) **1** set fire to **2** be on fire **3** injure by burning or scorching **4** record data onto a compact disk ◇ *noun* an injury or mark caused by fire ◇ **burner** *noun* the part of a lamp or gas-jet from which the flame rises

◼ *verb* **1** ignite, light, kindle, incinerate **2** flame, blaze, flare, glow, flicker **3** scald, scorch, singe, brand

burn ² *noun*, *Scot* a small stream

burnish *verb* & *noun* polish

burnt *past form* of **burn**

burr or **bur** *noun* the prickly seedcase or head of certain plants

burrow *noun* a hole or passage in the ground dug by certain animals for shelter ◇ *verb* make a passage beneath the ground

◼ *noun* warren, hole, earth, set, den, lair, retreat, shelter, tunnel ◇ *verb* tunnel, dig, delve, excavate

burst *verb* **1** break suddenly (after increased pressure) **2** move, speak *etc* suddenly or violently: *burst into the room*

◼ **1** puncture, rupture, tear, split, crack, break, fragment, shatter, explode, blow up

bury *verb* (**buries**, **burying**, **buried**) **1** place (a dead body *etc*) under the ground **2** cover, hide

◼ **1** inter, entomb, lay to rest **2** plant, implant, embed, conceal, hide, cover

bus *noun* (*plural* **buses**) a large road vehicle, often used for public transport ◇ **bus stop** an official stopping place for buses

bush *noun* (*plural* **bushes**) **1** a large plant or small tree **2** wild, unfarmed country in Africa *etc* **bushy** *adj* **1** growing thickly: *bushy hair* **2** full of bushes ◇ **bushily** *adv* ◇ **bushiness** *noun*

◼ **1** shrub, hedge, thicket **2** scrub, brush, scrubland, wilds

business *noun* (*plural* **businesses**) **1** someone's work or job **2** trade, commerce: *business is booming* **3** a matter of personal interest or concern: *none of your business*

◼ **1** job, occupation, work, employment, trade, profession, line, calling, career, vocation, duty, task, responsibility **2** trade, commerce, industry, trading, buying, selling **3** affair, matter, issue, subject, topic, question

businesslike *adj* practical, methodical, alert and prompt

◼ professional, efficient, thorough, organized, methodical, matter-of-fact, formal

businessman, businesswoman

noun someone who works in commerce
▣ trader, tycoon, magnate, executive, entrepreneur

busk *verb* play music or sing in the street for money ◇ **busker** *noun*

bust *noun* 1 a woman's breasts 2 a sculpture of someone's head and shoulders

bustle¹ *verb* busy oneself noisily ◇ *noun* noisy activity, fuss

bustle² *noun hist* a stuffed pad worn under a woman's full skirt

busy *adj* (**busier**, **busiest**) having a lot to do ◇ **busily** *adv* ◇ **busybody** *noun* someone nosey about others ◇ **busy yourself with** occupy yourself with
▣ occupied, engaged, *informal* tied up, working, slaving ◇ **busybody** meddler, *informal* nosey parker, intruder, gossip, eavesdropper, snoop, snooper

but *conj* 1 showing a contrast between two ideas *etc*: *my brother can swim but I can't/that paint isn't black but brown* 2 except that, without that: *it never rains but it pours* ◇ *prep* except, with the exception of: *no one but Tom had any money/take the next road but one* (*ie* the second road) ◇ *adv* only: *we can but hope* ◇ **but for** were it not for: *but for your car, we would have been late*

butane *noun* a gas commonly used for fuel

butch *adj* 1 of a woman: looking or behaving in a masculine way 2 of a man: muscular, tough

butcher *noun* 1 someone who sells meat 2 someone whose work is to kill animals for food and prepare their meat ◇ *verb* 1 kill and carve up (an animal) for food 2 kill cruelly ◇ **butchery** *noun* great or cruel slaughter

butler *noun* the chief manservant in a household

butt¹ *verb* strike with the head ◇ *noun* a push with the head ◇ **butt in** interrupt, interfere ◇ **butt out** *slang* stop interfering
▣ **butt in** interrupt, cut in, interpose, intrude

butt² *noun* 1 the thick heavy end of a

rifle *etc* 2 the end of a finished cigarette or cigar 3 *US slang* the buttocks
▣ 2 stub, end, tip

butt³ *noun* someone of whom others make fun
▣ target, victim, laughing-stock, dupe

butt⁴ *noun* a large cask, a barrel

butter *noun* a fatty food made by churning cream ◇ *verb* spread with butter ◇ **butter up** flatter, soften up

buttercup *noun* a plant with a cup-like yellow flower

butterfly *noun* (*plural* **butterflies**) a kind of insect with large, often patterned wings

---

Types of butterfly include:
red admiral, white admiral, apollo, brown argus, chalkhill blue, common blue, brimstone, meadow brown, Camberwell beauty, Cleopatra, clouded yellow, comma, copper, Duke of Burgundy, fritillary, heath fritillary, marsh fritillary, gatekeeper, grayling, hairstreak, purple hairstreak, white letter hairstreak, heath, map, monarch, orange-tip, painted lady, peacock, purple emperor, ringlet, skipper, chequered skipper, grizzled skipper, swallowtail, tortoiseshell wall, cabbage white

---

buttermilk *noun* the milk that is left after butter has been made

butterscotch *noun* a hard toffee made with butter

buttocks *noun plural* the two fleshy parts of the body on which you sit
▣ rump, hindquarters, rear, *informal* posterior, seat, bottom, behind, *informal* backside, *informal* arse

button *noun* 1 a knob or disc of metal, plastic *etc* used to fasten clothing 2 a knob pressed to work an electrical device ◇ *verb* fasten by means of buttons ◇ **button up** be quiet; shut up

buttonhole *noun* a hole through which a button is passed ◇ *verb* catch the attention of (someone) and force them to listen

∎ *verb* accost, waylay, catch, grab, nab

buttress *noun* (*plural* **buttresses**) a support on the outside of a wall ◇ *verb* support, prop up

∎ *noun* support, prop, shore, stay, brace, pier, strut, mainstay, reinforcement ◇ *verb* support, prop up, shore up, hold up, brace, strengthen, reinforce, bolster up, sustain

buxom *adj* of a woman: plump and pretty

buy *verb* (**buys**, **buying**, **bought**) get in exchange for money ◇ *noun* something bought, a purchase: *a good buy* ◇ **buyer** *noun*

∎ *verb* purchase, invest in, pay for ◇ *noun* purchase, acquisition, bargain, deal

∎ *verb* sell

buzz *verb* **1** make a humming noise like bees **2** *informal* call on the telephone **3** of aircraft: fly close to ◇ *noun* **1** a humming sound **2** *informal* a telephone call

buzzard *noun* a large bird of prey

buzzer *noun* a signalling device which makes a buzzing noise

buzzword *noun* a fashionable word

by *adv* **1** near: *a crowd stood by, watching* **2** past: *people strolled by* **3** aside: *money put by for an emergency* ◇ *prep* **1** next to, near: *standing by the door* **2**

past: *going by the house* **3** indicating the person who does something: *written by Burns* **4** of time: not after: *ready by four o'clock* **5** during: *by night* **6** using as a means: *by train* **7** used to express measurements, compass directions *etc*: *6 metres by 4 metres/north by north-west* **8** in the quantity of: *sold by the pound/paid by the week*

by-election *noun* an election for parliament during a parliamentary session

bygone *adj* past

bygones *noun* old grievances

by-law or **bye-law** *noun* a local law

bypass *noun* a road built round a town *etc*

∎ ring road

by-product *noun* something useful obtained during the manufacture of something else

byroad or **byway** *noun* a side road

bystander *noun* someone who stands watching an event or accident

∎ onlooker, looker-on, watcher, observer, witness, eyewitness, passer-by

byword *noun* someone or something well-known for a particular quality

byte *noun*, *comput* a unit used to measure data or memory

Cc

C *abbrev* degree(s) Celsius or centigrade

c or **ca** *abbrev* about (from Latin *circa*)

cab *noun* **1** a taxi **2** the part of a lorry *etc* where the driver sits

cabaret /ˈkabəreɪ/ *noun* **1** an entertainment consisting of variety acts **2** a restaurant with a cabaret

cabbage *noun* a type of vegetable with edible leaves

cabin *noun* **1** a wooden hut **2** a small room used for living quarters in a ship **3** the part of a commercial aircraft containing passenger seating ◇ **cabin crew** the flight attendants on a commercial airline
■ **1** hut, shack, shed, shelter **2** berth, quarters, compartment, room

cabinet *noun* **1** a cupboard which has shelves and doors **2** a similar container for display, storage *etc* **3** a selected number of government ministers who decide on policy

cable *noun* **1** a strong rope or thick metal line **2** a line of covered electrical or telegraph wires laid under the sea or underground **3** a telegram sent by such a line **4** an insulated electrical wire **5** *informal* cable television ◇ *verb* telegraph by cable ◇ **cable television** a service transmitting television programmes to individual subscribers by underground cable
■ *noun* **1** line, rope, cord, chain **4** wire, flex, lead

cacao *noun* a tree from whose seeds cocoa and chocolate are made

cache /kaʃ/ *noun* **1** a store or hiding place for ammunition, treasure *etc* **2** things hidden **3** a very fast part of a computer's memory

cachet /ˈkaʃeɪ/ *noun* **1** prestige, credit **2** an official stamp or seal

cackle *noun* **1** the sound made by a hen or goose **2** a laugh which sounds like this

cacophony *noun* (*plural* **cacophonies**) an unpleasant noise ◇ **cacophonous** *adj* ◇ **cacophonously** *adv*

cactus *noun* (*plural* **cactuses** or **cacti**) a type of prickly plant

cad *noun, old* a mean, despicable person

cadaver *noun* a human corpse ◇ **cadaverous** *adj* corpse-like, very pale and thin ◇ **cadaverously** *adv* ◇ **cadaverousness** *noun*

caddie or **caddy** *noun* an assistant who carries a golfer's clubs

caddy *noun* (*plural* **caddies**) a box for keeping tea fresh

cadence *noun* **1** a fall of the voice, *eg* at the end of a sentence **2** a group of chords ending a piece of music

cadenza *noun* a musical passage at the end of a movement, concerto *etc*

cadet /kəˈdet/ *noun* **1** an officer trainee in the armed forces or police service **2** a school pupil who takes military training

cadge *verb* (**cadges**, **cadging**, **cadged**) get by asking or begging from others: *cadge a lift* ◇ **cadger** *noun*
■ scrounge, sponge, beg

Caesarean *adj* of a birth: in which the baby is delivered by cutting through the walls of the mother's abdomen ◇ *noun* a Caesarian birth or operation

café *noun* a small restaurant serving coffee, tea, snacks *etc*
■ coffee shop, tea shop, tea room, coffee bar, cafeteria, snackbar, bistro, brasserie

cafeteria *noun* a self-service restaurant

cafetière *noun* a coffee-pot with a plunger mechanism

caffeine *noun* a stimulating drug found in coffee and tea

caftan *noun* a long-sleeved, ankle-length Middle Eastern garment

cage *noun* a barred enclosure for birds or animals ◇ *verb* (**cages**, **caging**, **caged**) keep or confine in a cage

▪ *noun* aviary, coop, hutch, enclosure, pen ◇ *verb* coop up, shut up, confine

cagey or **cagy** *adj* unwilling to speak freely; wary ◇ **caginess** *noun*

cagoule *noun* a lightweight anorak

cahoots *noun plural*: **in cahoots with** in collusion with

cairn *noun* 1 a heap of stones marking a grave, or on top of a mountain 2 a breed of small terrier

cajole *verb* coax by flattery ◇ **cajolery** *noun*

▪ coax, persuade, wheedle, flatter, *informal* sweet-talk, *informal* butter up, tempt, lure, seduce, entice, beguile

cake *noun* 1 a baked lump of dough made from flour, eggs, sugar *etc* 2 something pressed into a lump: *a cake of soap* ◇ *verb* become dry and hard

▪ *noun* 1 gâteau, bun, fancy 2 lump, bar, slab, block ◇ *verb* dry, harden, solidify, consolidate, coagulate, congeal

calamine *noun* a pink powder containing a zinc salt, used to make a skin-soothing lotion

calamity *noun* (*plural* **calamities**) a great disaster, a misfortune ◇ **calamitous** *adj* ◇ **calamitously** *adv*

▪ disaster, catastrophe, mishap, misadventure, mischance, misfortune, adversity, trial, tribulation, tragedy

calcium *noun* a metallic element which forms the chief part of lime

calculable *adj* able to be calculated, counted or measured

calculate *verb* 1 count, work out by mathematics 2 think out in an exact way

▪ 1 compute, work out, count, enumerate, reckon, figure, gauge

calculating *adj* thinking selfishly

▪ crafty, cunning, sly, devious, scheming, designing, contriving

calculation *noun* a mathematical reckoning, a sum

▪ sum, computation, answer, result, reckoning

calculator *noun* a machine which makes mathematical calculations

calculus *noun* a mathematical system of calculation

calendar *noun* a table or list showing the year divided into months, weeks and days

calf[1] *noun* (*plural* **calves**) 1 the young of a cow or ox 2 the young of certain other mammals, *eg* an elephant or whale

calf[2] *noun* (*plural* **calves**) the back of the lower part of the leg

calibrate *verb* 1 mark the scale on (a measuring instrument) 2 check or adjust the scale of (a measuring instrument)

calibre or *US* **caliber** *noun* 1 measurement across the opening of a tube or gun 2 of a person: quality of character, ability

▪ 1 diameter, bore, gauge 2 talent, gifts, strength, worth, merit, quality, character, ability, capacity, stature

calico *noun* a kind of patterned cotton cloth

Originally *Calicut cloth*, after the port in SW India from where it was exported

call *verb* 1 shout, cry 2 name: *what is your cat called?* 3 summon 4 make a short visit 5 telephone ◇ *noun* 1 a loud cry 2 a short visit 3 a telephone conversation ◇ **call centre** an office dealing with telephone queries

▪ *verb* 1 shout, yell, exclaim, cry 2 name, christen, baptize, title, entitle, dub, term, label 3 summon, invite, bid, convene 5 telephone, phone, ring (up), contact ◇ *noun* 1 cry, exclamation, shout, yell, scream

calligraphy *noun* the art of handwriting ◇ **calligrapher** *noun* ◇ **calligraphic** *adj*

calling *noun* a vocation, a job

callipers or **calipers** *noun plural* 1 an instrument like compasses, used to measure thickness **2** a splint to support the leg, made of two metal rods

callous *adj* cruel, hardhearted ◇ **callously** *adv* ◇ **callousness** *noun*

▣ heartless, hard-hearted, cold, indifferent, uncaring, unsympathetic, unfeeling, insensitive

▣ kind, caring, sympathetic, sensitive

> ⚠ Do not confuse with: **callus**

callow *adj* not mature; inexperienced, naive ◇ **callowly** *adv* ◇ **callowness** *noun*

callus *noun* (*plural* **calluses**) an area of thickened or hardened skin

> ⚠ Do not confuse with: **callous**

calm *adj* **1** still or quiet **2** not anxious or flustered ◇ *noun* **1** absence of wind **2** quietness, peacefulness ◇ *verb* make calm ◇ **calmly** *adv* ◇ **calmness** *noun*

▣ *adj* **1** still, mild, tranquil, serene, peaceful, quiet, uneventful, restful **2** composed, self-possessed, collected, cool, placid, sedate, imperturbable, unflappable, *slang* laid back, relaxed, unruffled, unflustered, unperturbed, undisturbed, untroubled ◇ *noun* **2** calmness, stillness, tranquillity, serenity, peacefulness, peace, quiet, hush, repose ◇ *verb* compose, soothe, relax, sedate, tranquillize, quieten, placate, pacify

calorie *noun* **1** a measure of heat **2** a measure of the energy-giving value of food

calumny *noun* (*plural* **calumnies**) a false accusation or lie about a person

calve *verb* give birth to a calf

calypso *noun* (*plural* **calypsos**) a West Indian improvised song

calyx /'keɪlɪks/ *noun* (*plural* **calyces** or **calyxes**) the outer covering or cup of a flower

camaraderie *noun* comradeship, fellowship

camber *noun* a slight curve on a road *etc* making the middle higher than the sides

camcorder *noun* a hand-held device combining a video camera and video recorder

came *past form* of **come**

camel *noun* an animal native to Asia and Africa, with a humped back, used for transport

cameo *noun* (*plural* **cameos**) a gem or stone with a figure carved in relief (*contrasted with*: **intaglio**)

camera¹ *noun* an instrument for taking photographs

camera² *noun*: **in camera** in private

> Literally 'in a room', from the Latin word for 'room' or 'chamber'

camisole *noun* a woman's undervest with thin shoulder straps

camomile *noun* a plant with pale yellow flowers, used as a medicinal herb

camouflage /'kaməflɑːʒ/ *noun* the disguising of appearance by colouring or covering ◇ *verb* disguise by camouflage

▣ *verb* disguise, mask, cloak, veil, screen, cover, conceal, hide, obscure

camp¹ *noun* **1** a group of tents, caravans *etc* forming a temporary settlement **2** fixed military quarters ◇ *verb* **1** pitch tents **2** set up a temporary home ◇ **camp bed** a small portable folding bed

camp² *adj* effeminate ◇ **campness** *noun*

campaign *noun* **1** organized action in support of a cause or movement **2** a planned series of battles or movements during a war ◇ *verb* **1** organize support: *campaigning against the poll tax* **2** serve in a military campaign

▣ *noun* **1** promotion, drive, push, offensive **2** offensive, crusade, movement, attack, battle, expedition, operation ◇ *verb* **1** advocate, fight, battle, crusade, promote, drive, push **2** fight, battle

campanology *noun* bell-ringing ◇ **campanologist** *noun*

camphor *noun* a pungent solid oil obtained from a cinnamon tree, or a synthetic substitute for it, used to repel insects *etc*

campsite *noun* an area set aside for pitching tents

campus *noun* (*plural* **campuses**) the grounds and buildings of a university or college

can¹ *verb* (**can, could**) **1** be able to (do something): *can anybody here play the piano?* **2** have permission to (do something): *asked if I could have the day off* ◇ **can but** can only: *we can but hope*

can² *noun* a sealed metal container for preserving food or liquids, a tin ◇ *verb* (**can, canning, canned**) put into a can to preserve

canal *noun* an artificial waterway for boats

canapé /'kanəpeɪ/ *noun* a small piece of bread *etc* with a topping, served as an appetizer

canary *noun* (*plural* **canaries**) a songbird with yellow plumage, kept as a pet

canasta *noun* a card game similar to rummy

cancan *noun* a high-kicking dance performed by women

cancel *verb* (**cancels, cancelling, cancelled**) **1** put off permanently, call off: *cancel all engagements for the week* **2** mark for deletion by crossing with lines ◇ **cancel out** make ineffective by balancing each other

▪ **1** call off, abort, abandon, drop ◇ **cancel out** neutralize, nullify

cancer *noun* **1** a malignant growth **2** a disease caused by malignant growths ◇ **cancerous** *adj*

▪ **1** tumour, growth, malignancy, carcinoma

candid *adj* giving an honest opinion ◇ **candidly** *adv*

▪ frank, open, truthful, honest, sincere, forthright, straightforward, ingenuous, plain, clear

▪ guarded, evasive, devious

candida *noun* an infection caused by a yeast-like fungus

candidate *noun* someone who enters an examination, or competes for a job, political office *etc* ◇ **candidacy** or **candidature** *noun*

▪ applicant, contender, contestant, competitor, runner, entrant

> From a Latin word meaning 'dressed in white', because of the white togas worn by electoral candidates in ancient Rome

candied *adj* cooked or coated in sugar

candle *noun* a stick of wax containing a wick, used for giving light

candlestick *noun* a holder for a candle

candlewick *noun* a cotton tufted material, used for bedspreads *etc*

candour or *US* **candor** *noun* frankness, honesty

▪ frankness, openness, truthfulness, honesty, sincerity, straightforwardness, directness, ingenuousness, plainness, bluntness, outspokenness

▪ evasiveness, deviousness

candy *noun* **1** sugar crystallized by boiling **2** *US* sweets, chocolate

cane *noun* **1** the woody stem of bamboo, sugar cane *etc* **2** a walking stick ◇ *verb* beat with a cane

canine *adj* of dogs ◇ **canine tooth** a sharp-pointed tooth found on each side of the upper and lower jaw

canister *noun* a tin or other container for tea *etc*

canker *noun* **1** a spreading sore **2** a disease in trees, plants *etc*

cannabis *noun* a narcotic drug obtained from the hemp plant

cannelloni *noun plural* wide hollow tubes of pasta, stuffed with meat, cheese, vegetables *etc*

cannery *noun* (*plural* **canneries**) a factory where food is canned

cannibal *noun* **1** someone who eats human flesh **2** an animal that eats its own kind ◇ **cannibalism** *noun* ◇ **cannibalistic** *adj*

cannon *noun* a large gun mounted on a wheeled carriage

> ⚠ Do not confuse with: **canon**

cannonball *noun* a solid metal ball shot from a cannon

cannot *verb* **1** used with another verb to express inability to do something: *I cannot understand this* **2** used to refuse permission: *you cannot stay here*

canny *adj* wise, shrewd, cautious ◇ **cannily** *adv* ◇ **canniness** *noun*

canoe *noun* a light narrow boat driven by paddles ◇ **canoeing** *noun* ◇ **canoeist** *noun*

canon *noun* **1** a rule used as a standard to judge by **2** a member of the Anglican clergy connected with a cathedral **3** an accepted or established list: *not in the literary canon* **4** a piece of music in which parts follow each other repeating the melody ◇ **canonical** *adj*

⚠ Do not confuse with: **cannon**

canonize *verb* put on the list of saints ◇ **canonization** *noun*

canopy *noun* (*plural* **canopies**) a canvas or cloth covering suspended over a bed *etc*

cant¹ *noun* **1** the slang or vocabulary of a particular group: *thieves' cant* **2** insincere talk

cant² *noun* a slope, an incline ◇ *verb* tilt from a level position

can't *short form* of **cannot**

cantankerous *adj* crotchety, bad-tempered, quarrelsome ◇ **cantankerously** *adv* ◇ **cantankerousness** *noun*
▪ irritable, irascible, grumpy, grouchy, crusty, crotchety, crabbed, crabby, testy, bad-tempered, ill-humoured, cross, peevish, difficult, perverse, contrary, quarrelsome, snappy
▪ good-natured, easy-going

cantata *noun* a short piece of music for a choir

canteen *noun* **1** a place serving food and drink in a workplace *etc* **2** a flask for carrying water **3** a case for storing cutlery

canter *verb* move at an easy gallop ◇ *noun* an easy gallop

Originally *Canterbury gallop*, referring to the pace at which pilgrims rode to the city

cantilever *noun* a large projecting bracket used to support a balcony or staircase ◇ **cantilever bridge** a bridge with two outer spans supporting a central span

canton *noun* a federal state in Switzerland

canvas *noun* (*plural* **canvases**) **1** coarse, strong cloth used for sails, tents *etc* **2** a piece of this stretched and used for painting on

canvass *verb* go round asking for votes, money *etc* ◇ **canvasser** *noun*
▪ electioneer, campaign, solicit, ask for, seek, poll

canyon *noun* a deep, steep-sided river valley
▪ gorge, ravine, gully, valley

cap *noun* **1** a peaked soft hat **2** a lid, a top **3** a contraceptive diaphragm ◇ *verb* (**caps, capping, capped**) **1** put a cap on **2** set a limit to (a budget *etc*) **3** do better than, improve on: *no-one can cap this story* **4** select for a national sports team
▪ *verb* **3** exceed, surpass, transcend, better, beat, outdo, outstrip, crown, top

capable *adj* able to cope without help ◇ **capability** *noun* (*plural* **capabilities**) ◇ **capably** *adv* ◇ **capable of** able or likely to achieve, produce *etc*: *capable of a better performance*
▪ able, competent, efficient, qualified, accomplished, skilful, proficient, disposed ◇ **capability** ability, capacity, potential, means, facility, competence, skill, proficiency, talent
▪ incapable, incompetent, useless ◇ **capability** inability, incompetence

capacious *adj* roomy, wide ◇ **capaciously** *adv* ◇ **capaciousness** *noun*

capacitor *noun* a device for collecting and storing electricity

capacity *noun* (*plural* **capacities**) **1** power of understanding **2** ability to do something: *capacity for growth* **3** the amount that something can hold **4** post, position: *capacity as leader* ◇ **to capacity** to the greatest extent possible: *filled to capacity*

▤ **1** cleverness, intelligence, aptitude, readiness **2** capability, ability, faculty, power, potential, competence, skill, talent, aptitude **3** volume, space, room, size, dimensions, magnitude, extent **4** role, function, position, office, post, job

cape[1] *noun* a thick shawl or covering for the shoulders

▤ cloak, wrap, poncho

cape[2] *noun* a point of land projecting into the sea

▤ headland, head, promontory, point, peninsula

caper[1] *verb* leap, dance about ◇ *noun* **1** a leap **2** *informal* a prank, an adventure

caper[2] *noun* the flower-bud of a shrub, pickled or salted for eating

capillary *noun* (*plural* **capillaries**) **1** a tiny blood vessel **2** a very fine tube

capital *adj* **1** chief, most important **2** punishable by death: *a capital offence* **3** *informal* excellent **4** of a letter: written or printed as at the beginning of a name, *eg* A, B or C ◇ *noun* **1** the chief city of a country: *Paris is the capital of France* **2** a capital letter **3** money for running a business **4** money invested, accumulated wealth ◇ **capital punishment** punishment by death

▤ *noun* **3** funds, finance, money, resources **4** savings, investment(s), wealth, means, resources, assets, property, stock

capitalism *noun* a system in which a country's wealth is owned by individuals, not by the State ◇ **capitalist** ◇ **capitalistic** *adj*

capitalize *verb* **1** write in capital letters **2** (with **on**) turn to your advantage ◇ **capitalization** *noun*

▤ **2** profit from, take advantage of, exploit, cash in on

capitulate *verb* give in to an enemy ◇ **capitulation** *noun*

▤ surrender, throw in the towel, yield, give in, relent, succumb

▣ fight on

capon *noun* a young castrated cock, fattened for eating

cappuccino *noun* white coffee made frothy with pressurized steam

caprice /kə'priːs/ *noun* a sudden, impulsive change of mind or mood

> Originally meaning 'horror', from an Italian word which translates as 'hedgehog head'

capricious *adj* full of caprice; impulsive, fickle ◇ **capriciously** *adv* ◇ **capriciousness** *noun*

▤ unpredictable, changeable, fickle, impulsive, irresolute, vacillating

capsize *verb* upset, overturn

▤ overturn, turn over, turn turtle

capstan *noun* a device used for winding in heavy ropes on a ship or quay

capsule *noun* **1** a small gelatine case containing a dose of medicine *etc* **2** a dry seed-pod on a plant **3** a self-contained, detachable part of a spacecraft

▤ **2** shell, sheath, pod

Capt *abbrev* captain

captain *noun* **1** the commander of a company of soldiers, a ship or an aircraft **2** the leader of a sports team, club *etc* ◇ *verb* lead, be the captain of ◇ **captaincy** *noun* (*plural* **captaincies**)

caption *noun* a heading for a newspaper article, photograph *etc*

captious *adj* quick to find fault; judgemental

captivate *verb* charm, fascinate ◇ **captivating** *adj*

▤ charm, enchant, bewitch, beguile, fascinate, enthral, hypnotize, mesmerize, lure, allure, seduce, win, attract, infatuate, enrapture, dazzle

▣ repel, disgust, appal

captive *noun* a prisoner ◇ *adj* **1** taken or kept prisoner **2** not able to get away: *captive audience*

▤ *noun* prisoner, hostage, detainee, internee, convict ◇ *adj* **1** imprisoned, caged, confined, secure, locked up, ensnared

▣ *adj* **1** free

captivity *noun* **1** the state of being a prisoner **2** the enclosure of an animal

in a zoo *etc*, not in the wild
■ **1** custody, detention, imprisonment, incarceration, internment
■ **1** freedom

captor *noun* someone who takes a prisoner

capture *verb* **1** take by force **2** get hold of; seize: *capture the imagination* ◇ *noun* **1** the act of capturing **2** something captured
■ *verb* **1** catch, trap, snare, take, seize, arrest, apprehend, imprison, secure ◇ *noun* **1** catching, trapping, taking, seizure, arrest, imprisonment

car *noun* **1** a small motor vehicle, usually with four wheels and seats for passengers **2** *US* a train carriage ◇ **car park** a place where cars *etc* may be left for a time

carafe /kəˈraf/ *noun* a bottle for serving wine, water *etc*

caramel *noun* **1** sugar melted and browned **2** a sweet made with sugar and butter

caramelize *verb* cook slowly in butter and sugar

carat *noun* **1** a measure of purity for gold **2** a measure of weight for gemstones

❗ Do not confuse with: **carrot**

caravan *noun* **1** a covered vehicle with living accommodation drawn behind a car **2** a number of travellers *etc* crossing the desert together

caraway *noun* a plant with spicy seeds used in cooking

carbine *noun* a short light musket

carbohydrate *noun* a compound of carbon, hydrogen and oxygen, *eg* sugar or starch

carbon *noun* an element of which charcoal is one form ◇ **carbonic** *adj* of or made with carbon ◇ **carbon copy 1** a copy of a document made by using carbon paper **2** an exact copy ◇ **carbon paper** paper used in typing to produce exact copies

carboniferous *adj* producing or containing coal or carbon

carbuncle *noun* **1** a fiery-red precious stone **2** an inflamed swelling under the skin

carburettor or **carburetter** or *US* **carburetor** *noun* the part of a car engine which changes the petrol into vapour

carcass or **carcase** *noun* the dead body (of an animal)
■ body, corpse, cadaver, remains, relics, skeleton, shell

carcinogen *noun* a substance that encourages the growth of cancer ◇ **carcinogenic** *adj*

carcinoma *noun* (*plural* **carcinomas** or **carcinomata**) a cancerous growth

card[1] *noun* **1** cardboard or very thick paper **2** an illustrated, folded piece of card sent in greeting *etc* **3** a rectangular piece of card or plastic used for a special purpose: *playing-card/credit card* **4** (**cards**) any of the many types of games played with a pack of cards

card[2] *noun* a tool for combing wool *etc* ◇ *verb* comb (wool *etc*)

cardboard *noun* stiff material made from paper pulp in sheets

cardiac *adj* of the heart: *cardiac failure*

cardigan *noun* a knitted woollen jacket

Named after the 19th-century Earl of *Cardigan* who advocated the use of buttonable woollen jackets

cardinal *adj* principal, important ◇ *noun* the highest rank of priest in the Roman Catholic Church ◇ **cardinal number** a number which expresses quantity, *eg* 1,2,3 (*contrasted with*: **ordinal number**)

care *noun* **1** close attention **2** worry, anxiety **3** protection, keeping: *in my care* ◇ *verb* be concerned or worried: *I don't care what happens now* ◇ **carer** *noun* someone who looks after an ill or disabled person at home ◇ **care for 1** look after **2** feel affection or liking for ◇ **care of** at the house of (often written as **c/o**) ◇ **take care** be careful; watch out ◇ **take care of** look after

◼ *noun* **1** carefulness, caution, prudence, vigilance, meticulousness, attention, heed, regard, consideration **2** worry, anxiety, stress, concern, trouble, affliction, tribulation **3** keeping, custody, guardianship, protection, ward, charge, responsibility, control, supervision ◇ **care for 1** look after, nurse, tend, mind, watch over, protect, minister to, attend **2** like, be fond of, love, be keen on, enjoy, delight in

carefree *adj* having no worries
◼ unworried, untroubled, unconcerned, blithe, breezy, happy-go-lucky, light-hearted, cheerful, happy, *informal* easy-going, *informal* laid back
◼ worried, anxious, despondent

careful *adj* attentive, taking care ◇ **carefully** *adv* ◇ **carefulness** *noun*
◼ cautious, prudent, judicious, vigilant, watchful, alert, attentive, mindful, meticulous, painstaking, conscientious, scrupulous, thorough, detailed, punctilious, particular, accurate, precise
◼ careless, reckless

careless *adj* paying little attention; not taking care ◇ **carelessly** *adv* ◇ **carelessness** *noun*
◼ sloppy, neglectful, slipshod, slapdash, hasty, casual

caretaker *noun* someone who looks after a building

career *noun* **1** the work someone does for most of their life; trade, profession **2** course, progress through life **3** headlong rush ◇ *verb* run rapidly and wildly: *careering along the road*
◼ *noun* **1** vocation, calling, life-work, occupation, profession, job, employment, livelihood ◇ *verb* rush, tear, hurtle, race, speed, bolt

caress *verb* touch gently and lovingly ◇ *noun* (*plural* **caresses**) a gentle touch
◼ *verb* stroke, pet, fondle, cuddle, kiss, touch ◇ *noun* stroke, pat, fondle, cuddle, kiss

careworn *adj* worn out by anxiety

carfuffle *noun* commotion, fuss

cargo *noun* (*plural* **cargoes**) a ship's load
◼ freight, shipment, consignment

caribou *noun* (*plural* **caribou** or **caribou**) the North American reindeer

caricature *noun* a picture of someone which exaggerates some of their features ◇ *verb* draw a caricature of ◇ **caricaturist** *noun*
◼ *noun* cartoon, parody, lampoon, burlesque, satire, send-up, take-off, imitation, representation, distortion

caries /ˈkɛəriːz/ *noun* decay, *esp* of the teeth ◇ **carious** *adj*

carillon /kəˈrɪljən/ *noun* **1** a set of bells on which tunes can be played **2** a tune played with bells

carjack *verb* rob or steal a car by attacking the driver ◇ **carjacker** *noun*

carmine *noun* a bright red colour ◇ *adj* of this colour

carnage *noun* slaughter, killing
◼ bloodshed, bloodbath, butchery, slaughter, killing, murder, massacre, holocaust

carnation *noun* a type of garden flower, often pink, red or white

carnival *noun* a celebration with merriment, feasting *etc*

carnivore *noun* a flesh-eating animal ◇ **carnivorous** *adj* eating meat or flesh

carol *noun* a hymn or song sung at Christmas

carouse *verb* take part in a drinking bout ◇ **carousal** *noun*

carousel /karəˈsel/ *noun* **1** *US* a merry-go-round **2** a rotating conveyor belt for luggage at an airport *etc*

carp[1] *noun* (*plural* **carp** or **carps**) a freshwater fish found in ponds

carp[2] *verb* find fault with small errors; complain about nothing

carpenter *noun* a worker in wood, *eg* for building ◇ **carpentry** *noun*

carpet *noun* the tufted woven covering of floors, stairs *etc* ◇ *verb* cover with a carpet

carriage *noun* **1** a vehicle for carrying people: *a railway carriage/a horse-drawn carriage* **2** the act or cost of carrying **3** a way of walking; bearing
◼ **1** coach, wagon, car, vehicle **2** carrying,

conveyance, transport, transportation, delivery **3** deportment, posture, bearing, demeanour

carrier *noun* **1** someone who carries or transports goods **2** a machine or container for carrying **3** someone who passes on a disease

carrion *noun* rotting animal flesh

carrot *noun* a vegetable with an edible orange-coloured root

> ⚠ Do not confuse with: **carat**

carry *verb* (**carries, carrying, carried**) **1** pick up and take to another place **2** contain and take to a destination: *cables carrying electricity* **3** bear, have as a mark: *carry a scar* **4** of a voice: be able to be heard at a distance **5** bear the burden or expense of something **6** keep for sale: *we don't carry cigarettes* ◇ **carried away** overcome by emotion; overexcited ◇ **carry on** continue (doing) ◇ **carry out** accomplish; succeed in doing

■ **1** bring, convey, transport, haul, move, transfer, relay, take, fetch **2** conduct, bring, convey, transport, relay **5** bear, shoulder, support, sustain, suffer, stand ◇ **carry on** continue, proceed, last, endure, maintain, keep on, persist, persevere ◇ **carry out** do, perform, undertake, discharge, conduct, execute, implement, fulfil, accomplish, achieve, realize, bring off

cart *noun* a wheeled vehicle used for carrying loads ◇ *verb* drag, haul: *carted off the stage*

■ *verb* move, haul, *informal* lug, bear, drag, carry

carte blanche freedom of action; a free hand

cartilage *noun* a strong elastic material in the bodies of humans and animals; gristle

cartography *noun* the science of map-making ◇ **cartographer** *noun*

carton *noun* a small container made of cardboard, plastic *etc*

■ box, packet, pack, case, container, package, parcel

cartoon *noun* **1** a comic drawing, or strip of drawings, often with a caption **2** an animated film ◇ **cartoonist** *noun* someone who draws cartoons

cartridge *noun* **1** a case holding the powder and bullet fired by a gun **2** a spool of film or tape enclosed in a case **3** a tube of ink for loading a pen

■ **1** case, shell, round **2** cassette, canister

cartwheel *noun* **1** the wheel of a cart **2** a sideways somersault with arms and legs outstretched

carve *verb* **1** make or shape by cutting **2** cut up (meat) into slices

■ **1** hew, chisel, chip, sculpt, sculpture, shape, form, fashion, mould, etch, engrave, incise, indent **2** cut, slice, hack

cascade *noun* **1** a waterfall **2** an abundant hanging display: *a cascade of curls* ◇ *verb* fall like or in a waterfall

■ *noun* **1** waterfall, falls, torrent, rush, gush

case *noun* **1** a container or outer covering **2** that which happens, an occurrence **3** a statement of facts, an argument **4** state of affairs, what is true: *if that is the case* **5** a trial in a law court: *murder case*

■ **1** container, receptacle, holder, suitcase, trunk, crate, box, carton, chest, cabinet, cartridge, shell, capsule, sheath, cover **5** lawsuit, suit, trial, proceedings, action, process

casement *noun* **1** a window frame **2** a window that swings on hinges

cash *noun* money in the form of coins and notes ◇ *verb* turn into, or change for, money ◇ **cash card** a card issued by a bank *etc* that allows the holder to use a cash dispenser ◇ **cash dispenser** or **cash machine** an electronic panel set in a bank wall which dispenses cash and account information ◇ **cash in on** profit from

■ *noun* money, ready money, bank-notes, notes, coins, change, currency ◇ *verb* encash, exchange, liquidate

cashback *noun* **1** a discount given on payment **2** a service in some supermarkets where customers can withdraw money using a debit card

cashew *noun* a kidney-shaped nut produced by a tropical tree

cashier *noun* someone who looks after the receiving and paying of money

■ clerk, teller, treasurer, bursar, purser, banker

cashmere *noun* fine soft goat's wool

casino *noun* (*plural* **casinos**) a building in which gambling takes place

cask *noun* a barrel containing wine *etc*

casket *noun* 1 a small box for holding jewels *etc* 2 *US* a coffin

cassava *noun* a tropical plant with roots from which tapioca is obtained

casserole *noun* 1 a covered oven-proof dish for cooking and serving food 2 food cooked in a casserole

cassette *noun* 1 a small case for film, recording tape *etc* 2 the tape or film itself

cassock *noun* a long robe worn by priests

cassowary *noun* (*plural* **cassowaries**) a large flightless bird of Australia and New Guinea

cast *verb* (**casts**, **casting**, **cast**) 1 throw, fling 2 throw off; drop, shed 3 shape in a mould 4 choose actors for (a play or film) 5 give a part to (an actor *etc*) ⬦ *noun* 1 something shaped in a mould 2 plaster encasing a broken limb 3 the actors in a play ⬦ **cast iron** unpurified iron melted and moulded into shape ⬦ **cast off** *adj* formerly used by someone else, second-hand

■ *verb* 1 throw, hurl, lob, pitch, fling, toss, sling, launch, impel, drive, direct, project 3 mould, shape, form, model, found ⬦ *noun* 1 casting, mould, shape, form

castanets *noun plural* hollow shells of hard wood, clicked together to accompany a dance

From a Spanish word for 'chestnuts', because of their shape

castaway *noun* a deserted or shipwrecked person

caste *noun* a class or rank of people,

esp in the Indian subcontinent

caster *another spelling of* **castor**

caster sugar very fine granulated sugar

castigate *verb* scold, punish ⬦ **castigation** *noun* ⬦ **castigator** *noun*

castle *noun* a fortified house or fortress

■ stronghold, fortress, citadel, chateau, palace, mansion

Parts of a castle include:
approach, arrow-slit, bailey, barbican, bartizan, bastion, battlements, berm, brattice, buttress, chapel, corbel, courtyard, crenel, crenellation, crosslet, curtain wall, ditch, donjon, drawbridge, dungeon, embrasure, enclosure wall, fosse, gatehouse, inner wall, keep, loophole, merlon, moat, motte, mound, outer bailey, parados, parapet, portcullis, postern, rampart, scarp, stockade, tower, lookout tower, turret, wall walk, ward, watchtower

castor or **caster** *noun* a small wheel, *eg* on the legs of furniture

castor oil a kind of palm oil used medicinally

castrate *verb* remove the testicles of

castrato *noun* (*plural* **castrati**) a male singer who has been castrated to preserve a high voice

casual *adj* 1 happening by chance: *casual encounter* 2 not regular, temporary: *casual labour* 3 informal: *casual clothes* 4 not careful, unconcerned: *casual attitude to work* ⬦ **casually** *adv*

■ 1 chance, fortuitous, accidental, unintentional, unpremeditated, unexpected, unforeseen 3 informal, relaxed, laid back 4 nonchalant, blasé, lackadaisical, negligent, *informal* couldn't-care-less, indifferent, unconcerned

◨ 1 deliberate, planned 3 formal

casualty *noun* (*plural* **casualties**) 1 someone who is killed or wounded 2 a hospital department for treating accidental injuries

◨ **1** victim, sufferer, injured person, wounded

CAT *abbrev* computer-assisted (or -aided) training

cat *noun* **1** a sharp-clawed furry animal kept as a pet **2** an animal of a family which includes lions, tigers *etc*

cataclysm *noun* **1** a violent change; an upheaval **2** a great flood of water

catacombs *noun plural* an underground burial place

catalogue *noun* an ordered list of names, books, objects for sale *etc* ◇ *verb* list in order

◨ *noun* list, inventory, roll, register, schedule, record, table, index, directory, gazetteer, brochure, prospectus ◇ *verb* list, register, record, index, classify, alphabetize, file

catalyst *noun* **1** a substance which helps or prevents a chemical reaction without itself changing **2** something which brings about a change

catamaran *noun* a boat with two parallel hulls

catapult *noun* **1** a small forked stick with a piece of elastic attached, used for firing small stones **2** *hist* a weapon for throwing heavy stones in warfare

cataract *noun* **1** a waterfall **2** a disease of the outer eye

catarrh *noun* inflammation of the lining of the nose and throat causing a discharge

catastrophe /kə'tastrəfɪ/ *noun* a sudden disaster ◇ **catastrophic** *adj* ◇ **catastrophically** *adv*

◨ disaster, calamity, cataclysm, debacle, fiasco, failure, ruin, devastation, tragedy, blow, mischance, misfortune, adversity, affliction, trouble

catch *verb* (**catches**, **catching**, **caught**) **1** take hold of, capture **2** get (a disease): *catch a cold* **3** be in time for: *catch the last train* **4** surprise (in an act): *caught him stealing* ◇ *noun* **1** a haul of fish *etc* **2** something you are lucky to have got or won **3** a hidden flaw or disadvantage: *where's the catch?* **4** a fastening: *window catch* ◇ **catch on** become

popular ◇ **catch-22** *noun* an absurd situation with no way out ◇ **catch up 1** draw level (with), overtake **2** get up-to-date (with work *etc*)

◨ *verb* **1** seize, grab, take, hold, grasp, grip, clutch, capture, trap, entrap, snare, ensnare, hook, net, arrest, apprehend **2** contract, get, develop, go down with **4** surprise, expose, unmask, find (out), discover, detect, discern ◇ *noun* **3** disadvantage, drawback, snag, hitch, obstacle, problem **4** fastener, clip, hook, clasp, hasp, latch, bolt

catching *adj* infectious

catchment area 1 an area from which a river or reservoir draws its water supply **2** an area from which the pupils in a school are drawn

catchphrase or **catchword** *noun* a phrase or word which is popular for a while

catchy *adj* of a tune: easily remembered

catechism /'katəkɪzəm/ *noun* **1** a religious book which teaches by asking questions to which it gives the answers **2** a series of searching questions

categorical *adj* allowing no doubt or argument: *categorical denial* ◇ **categorically** *adv*

◨ absolute, total, utter, unqualified, unreserved, unconditional, positive, definite, unequivocal, clear

◪ tentative, qualified, vague

category *noun* (*plural* **categories**) a class or group of similar people or things ◇ **categorize** *verb* divide into categories

◨ class, classification, group, grouping, sort, type, section, division

cater *verb* **1** provide food **2** supply what is required: *cater for all tastes* ◇ **caterer** *noun* ◇ **catering** *noun*

caterpillar *noun* an insect larva which feeds on plant leaves

> Based on a Latin phrase which translates as 'hairy cat'

caterwaul *verb* howl or yell like a cat

catgut *noun* cord made from sheep's

stomachs, used to make strings for violins, harps *etc*

cathedral *noun* **1** the church of a bishop **2** the chief church in a bishop's district

Catholic *adj* of the Roman Catholic Church

catholic *adj* wide, comprehensive: *a catholic taste in literature*
- broad, wide, wide-ranging, comprehensive, inclusive, broad-minded
- narrow, limited, narrow-minded

catkin *noun* a tuft of small flowers on certain trees, *eg* the willow and hazel

Catseye *noun, trademark* a small mirror fixed in a road surface to reflect light at night

catsup *noun, US* ketchup

cattle *noun plural* animals that eat grass, *eg* oxen, bulls and cows

catty *adj, informal* spiteful

catwalk *noun* a raised platform for models in a fashion show

caucus /ˈkɔːkəs/ *noun, US* a meeting of members of a political party to nominate candidates for election *etc*

caught *past form of* **catch**

cauldron *noun* a large pan

cauliflower *noun* a kind of cabbage with an edible white flower-head

caulk *verb* make (a plank *etc*) watertight by filling in the seams

cause *noun* **1** that which makes something happen **2** a reason for action: *cause for complaint* **3** an aim for which a group or person works: *the cause of peace* ◇ *verb* make happen
- *noun* **1** originator, creator, producer, maker, agent, agency **2** reason, motive, grounds, motivation, stimulus, incentive, inducement, impulse **3** object, purpose, end, ideal, belief, conviction ◇ *verb* give rise to, lead to, result in, occasion, bring about, produce, generate, create, precipitate, motivate, stimulate, provoke, incite, induce

causeway *noun* a raised road over wet ground or shallow water

caustic *adj* **1** burning, corroding **2** bitter, severe: *caustic wit* ◇ **caustically** *adv*
- **1** corrosive, acid, burning, stinging **2** biting, cutting, mordant, trenchant, bitter, acrimonious, sarcastic, scathing, severe

cauterize *verb* burn away flesh with a hot iron *etc* in order to make a wound heal cleanly

caution *noun* **1** carefulness because of potential danger: *approach with caution* **2** a warning ◇ *verb* warn ◇ **cautionary** *adj* giving a warning

cautious *adj* careful, showing caution ◇ **cautiously** *adv*
- careful, prudent, circumspect, judicious, vigilant, watchful, alert, heedful, wary, guarded, unadventurous
- incautious, imprudent, heedless, reckless

cavalcade *noun* a procession on horseback, in cars *etc*
- procession, parade, march-past

cavalier *noun, hist* a supporter of the king in the Civil War of the 17th century ◇ *adj* offhand, careless: *in cavalier fashion*

cavalry *noun* soldiers mounted on horses

cave *noun* a hollow place in the earth or in rock ◇ **caveman, cavewoman** *noun* a prehistoric cave-dweller ◇ **cave in** fall or collapse inwards
- cavern, grotto, pothole ◇ **cave in** collapse, give way, subside

caveat /ˈkavɪət/ *noun* a warning

cavern *noun* a large cave

cavernous *adj* **1** huge and hollow **2** full of caverns ◇ **cavernously** *adv*
- **1** hollow, concave, gaping, yawning, echoing, resonant, deep, sunken

caviare or **caviar** *noun* the pickled eggs of the sturgeon

cavil *verb* (**cavils, cavilling, cavilled**) make objections over small, unimportant details

cavity *noun* (*plural* **cavities**) **1** a hollow place, a hole **2** a decayed hollow in a tooth

cavort *verb* dance or leap around

▄ caper, frolic, skip, dance, romp

caw *verb* call like a crow ◇ *noun* a crow's call

cayenne *noun* a type of very hot red pepper

cayman or **caiman** *noun* (*plural* **caymans** or **caimans**) a South American alligator

CBE *abbrev* Companion of the Order of the British Empire

cc *abbrev* cubic centimetre(s)

CD *abbrev* compact disc

CD-ROM *abbrev* compact disc read-only memory

cease *verb* come or bring to an end ◇ **ceaseless** *adj* ◇ **ceaselessly** *adv*
▄ stop, desist, refrain, *slang* pack in, halt, call a halt, break off, discontinue, finish, end, conclude, terminate, fail, die
▄ begin, start, commence

cedar *noun* a large evergreen tree with a hard sweet-smelling wood

cede *verb* yield, give up
▄ surrender, give up, resign, abdicate, renounce, abandon, yield, relinquish, convey, transfer, hand over

ceilidh /'keɪlɪ/ *noun* an event involving traditional Scottish dancing, sometimes combined with musical performances

ceiling *noun* **1** the inner roof of a room **2** an upper limit

celandine *noun* a small yellow wild flower

celebrate *verb* commemorate an event (*eg* a birthday or marriage) by going out, having a party *etc* ◇ **celebrated** *adj* famous ◇ **celebration** *noun*
▄ commemorate, remember, observe, keep, toast, drink to, honour ◇ **celebrated** famous, well-known, famed, renowned, illustrious, glorious, eminent, distinguished, notable, prominent, outstanding, popular, acclaimed, exalted, revered
▄ **celebrated** unknown, obscure, forgotten

celebrity *noun* (*plural* **celebrities**) **1** a famous person, a star **2** fame

▄ **1** *informal* VIP, personality, name, star, superstar, *informal* celeb
▄ **1** nonentity, nobody

celery *noun* a type of vegetable with edible fibrous stalks

celestial *adj* **1** of the sky: *celestial bodies* **2** heavenly

celibate *adj* abstaining from sexual intercourse ◇ **celibacy** *noun*

cell *noun* **1** a small room in a prison, monastery *etc* **2** the smallest, fundamental part of living things **3** the part of an electric battery containing electrodes

cellar *noun* an underground room used for storing coal, wine *etc*
▄ basement, crypt, vault

cellist /'tʃɛlɪst/ *noun* someone who plays the cello

cello /'tʃɛləʊ/ *noun* (*short for* **violoncello**) a large stringed musical instrument, similar in shape to a violin

cellophane *noun*, *trademark* a thin transparent wrapping material

cellphone *noun* a mobile phone for use in a cellular radio system based on a network of transmitters

cellular *adj* made of or having cells

cellulite *noun* deposits of fat cells under the skin

celluloid *noun* a very hard elastic substance used for making photographic film *etc*

cellulose *noun* a substance found in plants and wood and used to make paper, textiles *etc*

Celsius *adj* **1** of a temperature scale: consisting of a hundred degrees, on which water freezes at 0° and boils at 100° **2** of a degree: measured on this scale: *10° Celsius*

cement *noun* **1** the mixture of clay and lime used *eg* to secure bricks in a wall **2** something used to make two things stick together ◇ *verb* **1** put together with cement **2** join firmly, fix: *cemented their friendship*
▄ *noun* **1** plaster, mortar, concrete ◇ *verb* **2** stick, bond, weld, solder, join, unite, bind, combine

cemetery *noun* (*plural* **cemeteries**) a place where the dead are buried
■ burial-ground, graveyard, churchyard

cenotaph *noun* a monument to someone or a group buried elsewhere

censer *noun* a container for burning incense in a church

> ❗ Do not confuse: **censer**, **censor** and **censure**

censor *noun* someone whose job is to examine books, films *etc* with power to delete any of the contents ◇ *verb* examine (books *etc*) in this way
■ *verb* cut, edit, blue-pencil, expurgate

censorious *adj* fault-finding; judgemental ◇ **censoriously** *adv*
■ condemnatory, disapproving, disparaging, fault-finding, carping, cavilling, critical, hypercritical, severe
🞂 complimentary, approving

censure *noun* blame, expression of disapproval ◇ *verb* blame, criticize
■ *noun* condemnation, blame, disapproval, criticism, admonishment, admonition, reprehension, reproof, reproach, rebuke, reprimand, *informal* telling-off
🞂 *noun* praise, compliments, approval

census *noun* (*plural* **censuses**) a periodical official count of the people who live in a country

> ❗ Do not confuse with: **consensus**

cent *noun* a coin which is the hundredth part of a larger coin, *eg* of a US dollar or a euro

centaur *noun* a mythological monster, half man and half horse

centenarian *noun* someone a hundred or more years old

centenary *noun* (*plural* **centenaries**) a hundredth anniversary; the hundredth year since an event took place

centennial *adj* 1 having lasted a hundred years 2 happening every hundred years ◇ *noun* a centenary

centigrade *adj* 1 of a temperature scale: consisting of a hundred degrees 2 measured on this scale: *5° centigrade* 3 Celsius

centilitre *noun* a hundredth part of a litre

centimetre *noun* a hundredth part of a metre

centipede *noun* a small crawling insect with many legs

central *adj* 1 of or in the centre 2 chief, main: *central point of the argument* ◇ **central heating** heating of a building by water, steam or air from a central point
■ 1 middle, mid, inner, interior, focal 2 main, chief, key, principal, primary, fundamental, vital, essential, important

centralize *verb* 1 group in a single place 2 bring (government authority) under one central control ◇ **centralization** *noun*

centre or *US* **center** *noun* 1 the middle point or part 2 a building used for some special activity: *sports centre/shopping centre* ◇ *verb* (**centres**, **centring**, **centred**) put in the centre
■ *noun* 1 middle, midpoint, bull's-eye, heart, core, nucleus, pivot, hub, focus, crux

centrifugal *adj* moving away from the centre

centripetal *adj* moving towards the centre

centurion *noun*, *hist* a commander of 100 Roman soldiers

century *noun* (*plural* **centuries**) 1 a hundred years 2 *cricket* a hundred runs

ceramic *adj* 1 made of pottery 2 of pottery-making ◇ *noun* 1 something made of pottery 2 (**ceramics**) the art of pottery

cereal *noun* 1 grain used as food 2 a breakfast food prepared from grain

cerebral *adj* of the brain ◇ **cerebrally** *adv* ◇ **cerebral palsy** failure of the brain to develop normally

ceremonial *adj* with or of ceremony ◇ **ceremonially** *adv*
■ formal, official, stately, solemn, ritual, ritualistic
🞂 informal, casual

ceremonious *adj* full of ceremony ◇ **ceremoniously** *adv* ◇ **ceremoniousness**

■ stately, dignified, grand, solemn, ritual, civil, polite, courteous, deferential, courtly, formal, stiff

☲ unceremonious, informal, relaxed

ceremony *noun* (*plural* **ceremonies**) the formal acts that accompany an important event: *marriage ceremony*

cerise /sə'ri:s/ *adj & noun* cherry-red

certain *adj* 1 sure; not to be doubted 2 fixed, settled 3 particular but unnamed: *stopping at certain places/a certain look* ◇ **certainly** *adv* ◇ **certainty** *noun*

■ 1 sure, positive, assured, confident, convinced, undoubted, indubitable, unquestionable, incontrovertible, undeniable, irrefutable, plain, conclusive, absolute, convincing, true 2 established, settled, decided, definite 3 specific, special, particular, individual, precise, express, fixed ◇ **certainty** sureness, positiveness, assurance, confidence, conviction, faith, trust, truth, validity, fact, reality, inevitability

☲ 1 uncertain, unsure, hesitant, doubtful ◇ **certainty** uncertainty, doubt, hesitation

certificate *noun* a written or printed statement giving details of a birth, passed examination *etc*

certify *verb* (**certifies**, **certifying**, **certified**) put down in writing as an official promise or statement *etc*

■ declare, attest, aver, assure, guarantee, endorse, confirm, verify, authenticate, validate, authorize

cervix *noun* the neck of the womb ◇ **cervical** *adj*

cessation *noun* ceasing or stopping; an ending

cesspool *noun* a pool or tank for storing liquid waste or sewage

cf *abbrev* compare (from Latin *confer*)

CFC *abbrev* chlorofluorocarbon

chador /'tʃʌdə(r)/ *noun* a veil worn by Islamic or Hindu women, covering the head and shoulders

chafe *verb* 1 make hot or sore by rubbing 2 wear away by rubbing 3 become annoyed

chaff[1] *noun* 1 husks of corn left after threshing 2 something of little value

chaff[2] *noun* good-natured teasing ◇ *verb* tease jokingly

chaffinch *noun* (*plural* **chaffinches**) a small songbird of the finch family

chagrin /'ʃagrɪn/ *noun* annoyance, irritation ◇ **chagrined** *adj* annoyed

chain *noun* 1 a number of metal links or rings passing through one another 2 (**chains**) these used to tie a prisoner's limbs; fetters 3 a connected series or sequence ◇ *verb* fasten or imprison with a chain ◇ **chain reaction** a chemical process in which each reaction in turn causes a similar reaction ◇ **chain saw** a power-driven saw with teeth on a rotating chain

■ *noun* 2 fetters, manacles, restraints, bonds 3 sequence, succession, progression, string, train, series, set ◇ *verb* tether, fasten, secure, bind, restrain, confine, fetter, shackle, manacle, handcuff

☲ *verb* release, free

chainstore *noun* one of several shops under the same ownership

chair *noun* 1 a seat with a back for one person 2 a university professorship: *the chair of French literature* 3 a chairman or chairwoman ◇ **chairman**, **chairwoman** or **chairperson** *noun* someone who presides at or is in charge of a meeting

chakra *noun* in yoga, a centre of spiritual power in the body

chalet /'ʃaleɪ/ *noun* 1 a small wooden house used by holidaymakers 2 a summer hut used by Swiss herdsmen in the Alps

chalice *noun* a cup for wine, used *eg* in church services

chalk *noun* 1 a type of limestone 2 a compressed stick of coloured powder used for writing or drawing ◇ *verb* mark with chalk ◇ **chalky** *adj* 1 of or like chalk 2 white, pale

challenge *verb* 1 question another's right to do something 2 ask (someone) to take part in a contest, *eg* to settle a quarrel ◇ *noun* **1** a questioning of another's right **2** a call to a contest ◇ **challenger** *noun* ◇ **challenging** *adj* interesting but difficult

■ *verb* **1** dispute, question, query, protest, object to **2** dare, defy, throw down the gauntlet, confront, brave, accost, provoke ◇ *noun* **2** dare, defiance, confrontation, provocation, test

chamber *noun* **1** *old* a room **2** a place where a parliament meets **3** a room where legal cases are heard by a judge **4** an enclosed space or cavity **5** the part of a gun that holds the cartridges ◇ **chamber music** music for a small group of players

chamberlain *noun* an officer appointed by a monarch or a local authority to carry out certain duties

chameleon /kə'mi:lıən/ *noun* a small lizard able to change its colour to match its surroundings

chamois /'ʃamwɑ:/ or /'ʃamı/ *noun* (*plural* **chamois**) **1** a goat-like deer living in mountainous country **2** (*also called* **shammy**) a soft kind of leather made from its skin

champ *verb* chew noisily ◇ **champing at the bit** impatient to act

champagne *noun* a type of white sparkling wine

champion *noun* **1** someone who has beaten all others in a competition **2** a strong supporter of a cause: *champion of free speech* ◇ *verb* support the cause of

■ *noun* **1** winner, victor, conqueror, hero **2** guardian, protector, defender, vindicator, patron, backer, supporter, upholder, advocate ◇ *verb* defend, stand up for, back, support, maintain, uphold, espouse, advocate, promote

championship *noun* **1** a contest to find a champion **2** the title of champion **3** the act of championing

chance *noun* **1** a risk, a possibility **2** something unexpected or unplanned **3** an opportunity ◇ *verb* **1** risk **2** happen by accident ◇ *adj* happening by accident ◇ **chancy** *adj* risky ◇ **by chance** not by arrangement, unexpectedly

◇ **chance upon** meet or find unexpectedly

■ *noun* **1** risk, gamble, speculation, possibility, prospect, probability, likelihood, odds **2** accident, fortuity, coincidence, *informal* fluke, luck, fortune, providence **3** opportunity, opening, occasion ◇ *verb* **1** risk, hazard, gamble, wager, stake, try, venture ◇ *adj* fortuitous, casual, accidental, inadvertent, unintentional, unintended, unforeseen, random, incidental

■ *adj* deliberate, intentional, foreseen, certain

chancel *noun* the part of a church near the altar

chancellor *noun* **1** a high-ranking government minister **2** the head of a university ◇ **Chancellor of the Exchequer** the minister in the British cabinet in charge of government spending

chancery *noun* (in England) the Lord Chancellor's court

chandelier /ʃandə'lıər/ *noun* a fixture hanging from the ceiling with branches for holding lights

change *verb* (**changes**, **changing**, **changed**) **1** make or become different **2** give up or leave (a job, house *etc*) for another **3** put on different clothes **4** give (money of one kind) in exchange for (money of another kind) ◇ *noun* **1** the act of making or becoming different **2** another set of clothing **3** money in the form of coins **4** money returned when a buyer gives more than the price of an article ◇ **changeable** *adj* likely to change; often changing ◇ **changeably** *adv*

■ *verb* **1** alter, modify, convert, reorganize, reform, remodel, restyle, transform, transfigure, metamorphose, mutate, vary, fluctuate **4** exchange, trade ◇ *noun* **1** alteration, modification, conversion, transformation, metamorphosis, mutation, variation ◇ **changeable** variable, mutable, fluid, kaleidoscopic, shifting, mobile, unsettled, uncertain, unpredictable, unreliable, erratic, irregular, inconstant

changeling *noun* in folklore, a child

secretly taken or left in place of another

channel *noun* **1** the bed of a stream **2** a passage for ships **3** a narrow sea **4** a groove; a gutter **5** a band of frequencies for radio or television signals ◇ *verb* (**channels**, **channelling**, **channelled**) direct into a particular course

▪ *noun* **2** canal, watercourse, waterway **3** strait, sound **4** duct, conduit, groove, furrow, trough, gutter ◇ *verb* direct, guide, conduct, convey, send, transmit, force

chant *verb* recite in a singing manner ◇ *noun* a singing recitation

▪ *verb* recite, intone, chorus ◇ *noun* plainsong, psalm, song, chorus, refrain, slogan

chaos /ˈkeɪəs/ *noun* disorder, confusion

chaotic *adj* disordered, confused ◇ **chaotically** *adv*

▪ disordered, confused, disorganized, topsy-turvy, deranged, anarchic, lawless, riotous, tumultuous, unruly, uncontrolled

▪ ordered, organized

chap *noun*, *informal* a man

▪ fellow, *informal* bloke, *informal* guy, man, person, individual, character

chapati *noun* a round of unleavened Indian bread

chapel *noun* **1** a small church **2** a small part of a larger church

chaperone *noun* a woman who accompanies a younger one when she goes out in public ◇ *verb* act as a chaperone to

chaplain *noun* a member of the clergy accompanying an army, navy *etc* ◇ **chaplaincy** *noun*

chapped *adj* of skin: cracked by cold or wet weather

chapter *noun* **1** a division of a book **2** a branch of a society or organization

char¹ *verb* (**chars**, **charring**, **charred**) burn until black

char² *verb* (**chars**, **charring**, **charred**) do odd jobs of housework, cleaning *etc* ◇ *noun*, *informal* a charwoman

charabanc /ˈʃarəbaŋ/ *noun* a long coach with rows of seats

character *noun* **1** the good and bad points which make up a person's nature **2** the nature and qualities of something **3** self-control, firmness, determination *etc* **4** someone noted for eccentric behaviour **5** someone in a play, story or film

▪ **1** personality, nature, disposition, temperament, temper, constitution **2** features, attributes, qualities, nature, type, kind **5** role, part

characteristic *noun* a typical and noticeable feature of someone or something ◇ *adj* typical ◇ **characteristically** *adv*

▪ *noun* peculiarity, idiosyncrasy, mannerism, feature, trait, attribute, property, quality, hallmark, mark ◇ *adj* distinctive, distinguishing, individual, idiosyncratic, peculiar, specific, special, typical, representative

characterize *verb* **1** be typical of **2** describe (as) ◇ **characterization** *noun*

▪ **1** typify, represent **2** portray

charade /ʃəˈrɑːd/ or /ʃəˈreɪd/ *noun* **1** a ridiculous pretence **2** (**charades**) a game in which players have to guess a word from gestures representing its sound or meaning

charcoal *noun* wood burnt black, used for fuel or sketching

charge *verb* (**charges**, **charging**, **charged**) **1** accuse: *charged with murder* **2** ask (a price) **3** ask to do; give responsibility for **4** load (a gun) **5** attack in a rush ◇ *noun* **1** accusation for a crime **2** a price, a fee **3** an attack **4** the gunpowder in a shell or bullet **5** care, responsibility **6** someone looked after by another person ◇ **charger** *noun* a horse used in battle ◇ **in charge** in command or control ◇ **take charge of** take command of

▪ *verb* **1** accuse, indict, impeach, incriminate, blame **2** ask, demand, levy **5** attack, assail, storm, rush ◇ *noun* **1** accusation, indictment, allegation, imputation **2** price, cost, fee, rate, amount **3** attack, assault, onslaught, sortie, rush **5** custody, keeping, care, safe-keeping, guardianship, ward

chariot *noun*, *hist* a two-wheeled carriage used in battle

charisma /kə'rɪzmə/ *noun* a personal quality that impresses others **charismatic** *adj* full of charisma or charm ◇ **charismatically** *adv*

charitable *adj* **1** giving to the poor; generous, kindly **2** of a charity: *charitable status* ◇ **charitably** *adv*

- ▣ **1** philanthropic, humanitarian, benevolent, benign, kind, compassionate, sympathetic, understanding, considerate, generous, magnanimous

charity *noun* (*plural* **charities**) **1** donation of money to the poor *etc* **2** an organization which collects money and gives it to those in need **3** kindness, humanity

- ▣ **1** alms, gift, handout, aid, relief, assistance **3** bountifulness, philanthropy, unselfishness, altruism, benevolence, benignness, kindness, goodness, humanity, compassion
- ▣ **1** selfishness, malice

charlatan /'ʃɑːlətən/ *noun* someone who claims greater powers or abilities than they really have

charm *noun* **1** personal power to attract **2** something thought to have magical powers **3** a magical spell ◇ *verb* **1** please greatly, delight **2** put under a spell ◇ **charming** *adj*

- ▣ *noun* **1** attraction, allure, magnetism, appeal **2** trinket, talisman, amulet, fetish, idol ◇ *verb* **1** please, delight, enrapture, captivate, fascinate, beguile **2** enchant, bewitch, mesmerize ◇ **charming** pleasing, pleasant, attractive, appealing
- ▣ *verb* **1** repel ◇ **charming** ugly, unattractive, repulsive

chart *noun* **1** a table or diagram giving particular information: *temperature chart* **2** a geographical map of the sea ◇ *verb* make into a chart; plot

charter *noun* a written paper showing the official granting of rights, lands *etc* ◇ *verb* hire (a boat, aeroplane *etc*) ◇ *adj* hired for a special purpose: *a charter flight* ◇ **chartered** *adj* **1** qualified under the regulations of a professional body: *chartered surveyor* **2** hired for a special purpose

charwoman *noun* a woman hired to do domestic cleaning *etc*

chary *adj* cautious, careful (of) ◇ **charily** *adv* ◇ **chariness** *noun*

chase *verb* **1** run after, pursue **2** hunt ◇ *noun* a pursuit, a hunt

- ▣ **1** pursue, follow **2** hunt, track

chasm /'kazəm/ *noun* **1** a steep drop between high rocks *etc* **2** a wide difference; a gulf

- ▣ **1** gap, opening, gulf, abyss, void, hollow, cavity, crater, breach, rift, split, cleft, fissure, crevasse, canyon, gorge, ravine **2** gap, gulf, abyss

chassis /'ʃasɪ/ *noun* (*plural* **chassis**) **1** the frame, wheels and machinery of a motor vehicle **2** an aeroplane's landing carriage

chaste *adj* **1** pure, virtuous **2** being a virgin ◇ **chastely** *adv* ◇ **chastity** *noun*

- ▣ **1** pure, undefiled, virtuous, innocent, modest **2** virginal, immaculate

chasten *verb* **1** make humble **2** scold ◇ **chastened** *adj*

chastise *verb* **1** scold **2** punish, *esp* by beating ◇ **chastisement** *noun*

- ▣ **1** reprove, admonish, scold, upbraid, berate, censure **2** punish, discipline, correct, castigate

chat *verb* (**chats**, **chatting**, **chatted**) talk in an easy, friendly way ◇ *noun* a friendly conversation ◇ **chattily** *adv* ◇ **chatty** *adj* willing to talk, talkative

- ▣ *noun* talk, conversation, *informal* natter, schmooze, *informal* chinwag, tête-à-tête, heart-to-heart

chateau /'ʃatəʊ/ *noun* (*plural* **chateaux**) a French castle or country house

chatroom *noun* an area on the Internet where users communicate

chattels *noun plural* movable possessions ◇ **goods and chattels** personal possessions

chatter *verb* **1** talk idly or rapidly; gossip **2** of teeth: rattle together because of cold ◇ **chatterbox** *noun* someone who talks a great deal

◼ **1** prattle, babble, chat, *informal* natter, gossip

chauffeur /ˈʃəʊfə/ or /ʃəʊˈfɜː/ *noun* someone employed to drive another person's car

chauvinism *noun* **1** sexism towards women **2** extreme nationalism or patriotism ◇ **chauvinist** *noun* ◇ **chauvinistic** *adj*

> After Nicholas *Chauvin*, Napoleonic French soldier and keen patriot

cheap *adj* **1** low in price, inexpensive **2** of little value, worthless ◇ **cheapen** *verb* make cheap ◇ **cheaply** *adv*

◼ **1** inexpensive, reasonable, reduced, cut-price, budget, economy, economical **2** tawdry, tatty, *slang* cheapo, *informal* low-rent, shoddy, inferior, secondrate, worthless

cheat *verb* **1** deceive **2** swindle **3** act dishonestly to gain an advantage, *eg* in a game ◇ *noun* **1** someone who cheats **2** a dishonest trick

◼ **1** mislead, deceive, dupe, fool, trick **2** defraud, swindle, diddle, shortchange, *informal* do, *slang* rip off, fleece, *informal* con, double-cross, hoodwink

check *verb* **1** see if (a total *etc*) is correct or accurate **2** see if (a machine *etc*) is in good condition or working properly **3** hold back, restrain **4** bring to a stop ◇ *noun* **1** a test of correctness or accuracy **2** a restraint **3** a sudden stop **4** a pattern of squares **5** *US* a cheque **6** *US* a restaurant bill ◇ **check in** or **check out** record your arrival at or departure from (a hotel *etc*)

◼ *verb* **1** cross-check, confirm, verify **2** examine, inspect, *informal* give the once-over, test, monitor **3** curb, bridle, stop, arrest, halt ◇ *noun* **1** examination, inspection, scrutiny, audit, test **2** curb, restraint, control, limitation, constraint, inhibition

> ⚠ Do not confuse with: **cheque**

checked *adj* patterned with squares

checkered *another spelling of* **chequered**

checkers *another spelling of* **chequers**

checkmate *noun, chess* a position from which the king cannot escape

checkout *noun* a place where payment is made in a supermarket

cheek *noun* **1** the side of the face below the eye **2** a buttock **3** insolence, disrespectful behaviour

cheeky *adj* impudent, insolent ◇ **cheekily** *adv* ◇ **cheekiness** *noun*

◼ impertinent, impudent, insolent, disrespectful, forward, brazen, pert, audacious

cheep *verb* make a faint sound like a small bird ◇ *noun* the sound of a small bird

cheer *noun* a shout of approval or welcome ◇ *verb* **1** shout approval **2** encourage, urge on **3** comfort, gladden ◇ **cheerless** *adj* sad, gloomy ◇ **cheer up** make or become less gloomy

◼ *noun* boo, jeer

cheerful *adj* happy, in good spirits ◇ **cheerfully** *adv* ◇ **cheerfulness** *noun*

◼ happy, glad, contented, joyful, joyous, blithe, carefree, light-hearted, cheery, good-humoured, optimistic, upbeat, enthusiastic, hearty, genial, jovial, jolly, merry, lively, bright, chirpy, breezy

◼ sad, dejected, depressed

cheerio *exclam* goodbye!

cheers *exclam* **1** good health! **2** regards, best wishes

cheery *adj* lively and merry ◇ **cheerily** *adv*

cheese *noun* a solid food made from milk ◇ **cheesy** *adj* **1** tasting of cheese **2** of a smile: broad

> *Varieties of cheese include*:
> Amsterdam, Bel Paese, Bleu d'Auvergne, Blue Cheshire, Blue Vinny, Boursin, Brie, Caboc, Caerphilly, Camembert, Carré, Cheddar, Cheshire, Churnton, cottage cheese, cream cheese, Crowdie, curd cheese, Danish blue,

Derby, Dolcelatte, Dorset Blue, Double Gloucester, Dunlop, Edam, Emmental, Emmentaler, ewe cheese, Feta, fontina, fromage frais, goat cheese, Gloucester, Gorgonzola, Gouda, Gruyère, Huntsman, Jarlsberg®, Killarney, Lancashire, Leicester, Limburg(er), Lymeswold, mascarpone, Monterey Jack, mouse-trap, mozzarella, Neufchâtel, Orkney, Parmesan, pecorino, Petit Suisse, Pont-l'Éveque, Port Salut, processed cheese, provolone, quark, Red Leicester, Red Windsor, ricotta, Roquefort, sage Derby, Saint-Paulin, Stilton, stracchino, vegetarian cheese, Vacherin, Wensleydale

cheesecloth *noun* loosely woven cotton cloth

cheetah *noun* a fast-running animal similar to a leopard

chef *noun* a head cook in a restaurant

chef d'oeuvre a masterpiece

chemical *adj* relating to the reactions between elements *etc* ◇ *noun* a substance formed by or used in a chemical process

The chemical elements (with their symbols) are:
actinium (Ac), aluminium (Al), americium (Am), antimony (Sb), argon (Ar), arsenic (As), astatine (At), barium (Ba), berkelium (Bk), beryllium (Be), bismuth (Bi), boron (B), bromine (Br), cadmium (Cd), caesium (Cs), calcium (Ca), californium (Cf), carbon (C), cerium (Ce), chlorine (Cl), chromium (Cr), cobalt (Co), copper (Cu), curium (Cm), dubnium (Db), dysprosium (Dy), einsteinium (Es), erbium (Er), europium (Eu), fermium (Fm), fluorine (F), francium (Fr), gadolinium (Gd), gallium (Ga), germanium (Ge), gold (Au), hafnium (Hf), hahnium (Ha), helium (He), holmium (Ho), hydrogen (H), indium (In), iodine (I), iridium (Ir), iron (Fe), krypton (Kr), lanthanum (La), lawrencium (Lr), lead (Pb), lithium (Li), lutetium (Lu), magnesium (Mg), manganese (Mn), mendelevium (Md), mercury (Hg), molybdenum (Mo), neodymium (Nd), neon (Ne), neptunium (Np), nickel (Ni), niobium (Nb), nitrogen (N), nobelium (No), osmium (Os), oxygen (O), palladium (Pd), phosphorus (P), platinum (Pt), plutonium (Pu), polonium (Po), potassium (K), praseodymium (Pr), promethium (Pm), protactinium (Pa), radium (Ra), radon (Rn), rhenium (Re), rhodium (Rh), rubidium (Rb), ruthenium (Ru), rutherfordium (Rf), samarium (Sm), scandium (Sc), selenium (Se), silicon (Si), silver (Ag), sodium (Na), strontium (Sr), sulphur (S), tantalum (Ta), technetium (Tc), tellurium (Te), terbium (Tb), thallium (Tl), thorium (Th), thulium (Tm), tin (Sn), titanium (Ti), tungsten (W), uranium (U), vanadium (V), xenon (Xe), ytterbium (Yb), yttrium (Y), zinc (Zn), zirconium (Zr)

chemist *noun* **1** someone who studies chemistry **2** someone who makes up and sells medicines; a pharmacist

chemistry *noun* the study of the elements and the ways they combine or react with each other

chemotherapy *noun* treatment of a disease with strong drugs or other chemicals

chenille /ʃəˈniːl/ *noun* a thick, velvety material or yarn

cheque or *US* **check** *noun* a written order to a banker to pay money from a bank account to another person ◇ **cheque book** a book containing cheques

⚠ Do not confuse with: **check**

chequered or **checkered** *adj* **1** marked with a pattern of squares like a chessboard **2** partly good, partly bad: *a chequered career*

chequers or **checkers** *noun* **1** *plural* a

pattern of squares, *eg* on a chessboard **2** *sing* the game of draughts

cherish *verb* **1** protect and treat with fondness or kindness **2** keep in your mind or heart: *cherish a hope*

■ **1** foster, care for, look after, nurse, nurture, nourish, sustain, support **2** harbour, shelter, entertain, hold dear, value, prize, treasure

cheroot *noun* a small cigar

cherry *noun* (*plural* **cherries**) **1** a small bright-red fruit with a stone **2** the tree that produces this fruit

cherub *noun* (*plural* **cherubs** or **cherubim**) **1** an angel with a plump, childish face and body **2** a beautiful child

chervil *noun* a feathery herb related to the carrot

chess *noun* a game for two players in which pieces are moved in turn on a chequered board ◊ **chessboard** *noun*

chest *noun* **1** a large strong box **2** the part of the body between the neck and the stomach ◊ **chest of drawers** a piece of furniture fitted with a set of drawers

■ **1** trunk, crate, box, case, casket, coffer, strongbox

chesterfield *noun* a kind of sofa

chestnut *noun* **1** a reddish-brown nut **2** the tree that produces this nut, the **horse chestnut** or **sweet chestnut** **3** a reddish-brown horse **4** an old joke

chevron *noun* a V-shape, *eg* on a badge or road-sign

chew *verb* **1** break up (food) with the teeth before swallowing **2** reflect or ponder (on) ◊ **chewy** *adj*

■ **1** masticate, gnaw, munch, champ, crunch, grind

chi *noun* another spelling of **qi**

chic /ʃiːk/ *adj* smart and fashionable ◊ *noun* style, fashionable elegance

chicanery /ʃɪˈkeɪnərɪ/ *noun* dishonest cleverness

chick *noun* **1** the young of birds, *esp* of domestic poultry **2** *slang* a girl, a young woman

chicken *noun* **1** a domestic fowl **2** *in-*

formal a coward ◊ *adj*, *informal* cowardly ◊ **chicken-hearted** *adj* cowardly

chicken-feed *noun* **1** food for poultry **2** something paltry or worthless

chickenpox *noun* an infectious disease which causes red, itchy spots

chickpea *noun* a plant of the pea family with a brown edible seed

chicory *noun* **1** a plant with sharptasting leaves eaten in salads **2** its root, roasted and ground to mix with coffee

chide *verb* scold with words

chief *adj* **1** main, most important **2** largest ◊ *noun* **1** a leader or ruler **2** the head of a department, organization *etc* ◊ **chiefly** *adv* mainly, for the most part

■ *adj* **1** leading, foremost, supreme, grand, arch, premier, principal, main, key, central, prime, prevailing, predominant, pre-eminent, outstanding, vital, essential, primary, major ◊ *noun* **1** ruler, chieftain, lord, master, supremo, head, principal, leader, commander, captain, governor **2** boss, director, manager

☒ *adj* **1** minor, unimportant.

chieftain *noun* the head of a clan or tribe

chiffon *noun* a thin flimsy material made of silk or nylon

chignon /ˈʃiːnjɒn/ *noun* a knot or roll of hair on the back of the head

chihuahua /tʃɪˈwɑːwɑː/ *noun* a breed of very small dog, originally from Mexico

chilblain *noun* a painful swelling on hands and feet, caused by cold weather

child *noun* (*plural* **children**) **1** a young human being **2** a son or daughter: *is that your child?*

■ **1** youngster, *informal* kid, *informal* nipper, *informal* brat, *slang* rugrat, *slang* ankle-biter, baby, infant, toddler, *informal* tot, *slang* sprog, minor, juvenile **2** offspring, issue, progeny, descendant

childhood *noun* the time of being a child

childish *adj* **1** of or like a child **2** silly, immature ◊ **childishly** *adv* ◊ **childishness** *noun*

■ **1** babyish, boyish, girlish **2** infantile,

puerile, juvenile, immature, silly, foolish, frivolous

🔁 **2** mature

childlike *adj* innocent

chill *noun* **1** coldness **2** an illness that causes fever and shivering **3** lack of warmth or enthusiasm ◇ *adj* cold ◇ *verb* **1** make cold **2** refrigerate ◇ **chill out** *slang* relax

📧 *noun* **1** cold, coldness, rawness, bite, nip, crispness **3** coolness, coldness, frigidity

chilli *noun* **1** the hot-tasting pod of a kind of pepper, sometimes dried and powdered for cooking **2** a dish or sauce made with this

chilly *adj* cold: *chilly weather/a chilly reception*

📧 cold, fresh, brisk, crisp, *informal* nippy, wintry, cool, frigid, unsympathetic, unwelcoming, aloof, stony, unfriendly, hostile

🔁 warm, friendly

chime *noun* **1** the sound of bells ringing **2** (**chimes**) a set of bells, *eg* in a clock ◇ *verb* **1** of bells: ring **2** of a clock: strike

chimera /kaɪˈmɪərə/ or /kiˈmɪərə/ *noun* a wild idea or fancy ◇ **chimerical** *adj* wildly fanciful

chimney *noun* (*plural* **chimneys**) a passage allowing smoke or heated air to escape from a fire

chimneypot *noun* a metal or earthenware pipe placed at the top of a chimney

chimpanzee *noun* a type of African ape

chin *noun* the part of the face below the mouth

china *noun* **1** a fine kind of earthenware; porcelain **2** articles made of this

📧 porcelain, ceramic, pottery, earthenware, terracotta

chinchilla *noun* a small S American animal with soft grey fur

chink *noun* **1** a narrow opening **2** the sound of coins *etc* striking together

📧 **1** crack, fissure, crevice, slot, opening, aperture, gap, space

chintz *noun* (*plural* **chintzes**) a cotton cloth with brightly coloured patterning

From a Hindi word for painted or multicoloured cotton

chip *verb* (**chips, chipping, chipped**) **1** break or cut small pieces (from or off) **2** *sport* strike a ball high over a short distance ◇ *noun* **1** a small piece chipped off **2** a part damaged by chipping **3** a long thin piece of fried potato **4** *US* a potato or corn crisp **5** *sport* a short high shot or kick ◇ **chip in** *informal* **1** interrupt **2** contribute (money)

📧 *verb* **1** chisel, whittle, nick, notch ◇ *noun* **1** fragment, wafer, sliver, flake, shaving, paring **2** notch, nick, scratch, dent, flaw

chipmunk *noun* a kind of N American squirrel

chipolata *noun* a type of small sausage

chiropodist *noun* someone who treats minor disorders and diseases of the feet ◇ **chiropody** *noun*

chiropractic *noun* a treatment for muscular pain *etc* involving manipulation of the spinal column ◇ **chiropractor** *noun* a therapist who uses chiropractic

chirp or **chirrup** *verb* of a bird: make a sharp, shrill sound

📧 tweet, cheep, peep, twitter, warble, sing, pipe, whistle

chirpy *adj* merry, cheerful ◇ **chirpily** *adv* ◇ **chirpiness** *noun*

chisel *noun* a metal tool used to cut or hollow out wood, stone *etc* ◇ *verb* (**chisels, chiselling, chiselled**) cut with a chisel

chit [1] *noun* a short note

chit [2] *noun* a child, a young woman: *chit of a girl*

chit-chat *noun* & *verb* gossip, talk

chivalry /ˈʃɪvəlrɪ/ *noun* **1** kindness, *esp* towards women or the weak **2** *hist* the standard of behaviour expected of knights in medieval times ◇ **chivalrous** *adj* ◇ **chivalrously** *adv* ◇ **chivalrousness** *noun*

■ **chivalrous** gentlemanly, polite, courteous, gallant, heroic, valiant, brave, courageous, bold, noble, honourable

🖪 **chivalrous** ungallant, cowardly

chive *noun* an onion-like herb used in cooking

chlorine *noun* a yellowish-green gas with a sharp smell, used as a bleach and disinfectant ◇ **chlorinated** *adj* mixed with chlorine or a substance containing chlorine

chloroform *noun* a liquid whose vapour causes unconsciousness if inhaled

chock-a-block *adj* completely full or congested

chockfull *adj* completely full

chocolate *noun* 1 a sweet made from the seeds of the cacao tree 2 a drink made from cocoa ◇ *adj* dark brown in colour ◇ **chocolatey** *adj* tasting of chocolate

choice *noun* 1 the act or power of choosing 2 something chosen from a selection ◇ *adj* of a high quality: *choice vegetables*

■ *noun* 1 say, choosing, opting, election, discrimination ◇ *adj* best, superior, prime, plum, excellent, fine, exquisite, exclusive, select, special, prize

🖪 *adj* inferior, poor

choir *noun* 1 a group or society of singers 2 a part of a church where a choir sits

🔟 Do not confuse with: **quire**

choke *verb* 1 stop or partly stop the breathing of 2 block or clog (a pipe *etc*) 3 have your breathing stopped or interrupted, *eg* by smoke ◇ *noun* a valve in a petrol engine which controls the inflow of air

■ *verb* 1 throttle, strangle, asphyxiate, suffocate, stifle, smother 2 obstruct, constrict, congest, clog, block, dam, bar, close, stop

cholera /'kɒlərə/ *noun* an infectious intestinal disease, causing severe vomiting and diarrhoea

cholesterol *noun* a substance found

in body cells which carries fats through the bloodstream

chomp *verb*, *informal* munch noisily

choose *verb* (**chooses, choosing, chose, chosen**) 1 select and take from two or several things: *choose whichever book you like* 2 decide, prefer to: *we chose to leave before the film began*

■ 1 pick, select, single out, opt for, plump for, vote for, settle on 2 elect, prefer, wish, desire, see fit

chop *verb* (**chops, chopping, chopped**) 1 cut into small pieces 2 cut with a sudden blow ◇ *noun* 1 a chopping blow 2 a slice of meat containing a bone: *a lamb chop*

■ *verb* 1 cut (up), slice (up), divide, cube, dice, mince 2 cut, hack, hew, lop, sever, truncate, cleave, divide, split, slash

chopper *noun* 1 a knife or axe for chopping 2 *informal* a helicopter

choppy *adj* of the sea: not calm, having small waves

■ rough, turbulent, wavy, uneven

🖪 calm, still

chopsticks *noun plural* a pair of small sticks used for eating Chinese, Japanese *etc* food

Literally 'quick sticks', from Pidgin English *chop* for 'quick'

choral *adj* sung by or written for a choir

chord [1] *noun* a musical sound made by playing several notes together

chord [2] *noun* a straight line joining any two points on a curve

🔟 Do not confuse with: **cord**

chore *noun* 1 a dull, boring job 2 (**chores**) housework

choreography *noun* the arrangement of dancing and dance steps ◇ **choreographer** *noun*

chorister *noun* a member of a choir

chortle *verb* laugh, chuckle

chorus *noun* (*plural* **choruses**) 1 a part of a song repeated after each verse 2 a choir or choral group 3 a band of

singers and dancers in a show **4** something uttered by many people in unison
▪ **1** refrain, response **2** choir, choristers, singers, vocalists, ensemble **4** call, shout

chose *past form* of **choose**

chosen *past participle* of **choose**

chow *noun* a Chinese breed of dog with a bushy coat and a blue-black tongue

chowder *noun* a thick fish soup containing cream

christen *verb* baptize and give a name to ◇ **christening** *noun* the ceremony of baptism

Christian *noun* a believer in Christianity ◇ *adj* of Christianity ◇ **Christian name** a first or personal name

Christianity *noun* the religion which follows the teachings of Christ

Christmas *noun* an annual Christian holiday or festival, in memory of the birth of Christ, held on 25 December ◇ **Christmassy** *adj* suitable for Christmas ◇ **Christmas Eve** 24 December
▪ Xmas, Noel, Yule, Yuletide

chromatic *adj* **1** of colours **2** coloured **3** *music* of or written in a scale in which each note is separated from the next by a semitone

chromium *noun* a metal which does not rust

chromosome *noun* a rod-like part of a body cell that determines the characteristics of an individual

chronic *adj* **1** of a disease: lasting a long time **2** *informal* very bad **3** habitual: *a chronic dieter* ◇ **chronically** *adv*
▪ **1** deep-seated, recurring, incessant, persistent **2** awful, terrible, dreadful, appalling, atrocious **3** inveterate, confirmed, habitual, ingrained, deep-rooted
▪ **1** acute, temporary

chronicle *noun* a record of events in order of time ◇ *verb* write down events in order ◇ **chronicler** *noun*

chronological *adj* arranged in the order of the time of happening ◇ **chronologically** *adv*

▪ historical, consecutive, sequential, progressive, ordered

chronometer *noun* an instrument for measuring time

chrysalis *noun* an insect (*esp* a butterfly or moth) in its early stage of life, with no wings and encased in a soft cocoon

chrysanthemum *noun* a type of garden flower with a large bushy head

chubby *adj* (**chubbier, chubbiest**) attractively plump ◇ **chubbiness** *noun*
▪ plump, podgy, fleshy, flabby, stout, portly, rotund, round, tubby
▪ slim, skinny

chuck *verb* **1** throw, toss **2** pat gently under the chin ◇ **chuck out** *informal* **1** throw away, get rid of **2** expel

chuckle *noun* a quiet laugh ◇ *verb* laugh quietly
▪ *verb* laugh, giggle, titter, snigger, chortle, snort, crow

chuffed *adj*, *informal* very pleased

chum *informal* a close friend ◇ **chummy** *adj* very friendly

chump *noun*: **off your chump** *informal* off your head; mad

chunk *noun* a thick piece ◇ **chunky** *adj* heavy, thick
▪ lump, hunk, mass, *informal* wodge, wedge, block, slab, piece, portion

church *noun* (*plural* **churches**) **1** a building for public, *esp* Christian, worship **2** any group of people who meet together for worship
▪ **1** chapel, house of god, cathedral, abbey, minster, temple

churchyard *noun* a burial ground next to a church

churlish *adj* bad-mannered, rude ◇ **churlishly** *adv* ◇ **churlishness** *noun*

churn *noun* a machine for making butter from milk ◇ *verb* **1** make (butter) in a churn **2** shake or stir about violently

chute /ʃuːt/ *noun* a sloping trough for sending water, parcels *etc* to a lower level

chutney *noun* (*plural* **chutneys**) a sauce made with vegetables or fruits and vinegar

ciabatta /tʃəˈbɑːtə/ *noun* Italian bread made with olive oil

cicada /sɪˈkɑːdə/ *noun* (*plural* **cicadas** or **cicadae** /sɪˈkɑːdiː/) a chirping insect found in warm climates

cicatrice /ˈsɪkətrɪs/ *noun* a scar

cider *noun* an alcoholic drink made from fermented apple juice

cigar *noun* a roll of tobacco leaves for smoking

cigarette *noun* a tube of fine tobacco enclosed in thin paper

cinder *noun* a burnt-out piece of coal

cinema *noun* **1** a place where films are shown **2** films as an art form or industry
◼ **2** films, pictures, *informal* movies

cinnamon *noun* a yellowish-brown spice obtained from tree bark

cipher *noun* **1** a secret writing, a code **2** nought, zero **3** someone of no importance

> Originally meaning 'zero' and later 'number', because of the early use of numbers in encoded documents

circa *prep* about (in dates): *circa 300BC*

circle *noun* **1** a figure formed from an endless curved line **2** something in the form of a circle; a ring **3** a society or group of people **4** a tier of seats in a theatre *etc* ◊ *verb* **1** enclose in a circle **2** move round in a circle
◼ *noun* **3** group, band, company, crowd, set, clique, club, society, fellowship, fraternity ◊ *verb* **1** ring, encircle, surround, gird, encompass, enclose, hem in **2** rotate, revolve, pivot, gyrate, whirl, turn, coil, wind

> *Types of circle include*:
> annulus, ball, band, belt, circuit, circumference, coil, cordon, coronet, crown, curl, cycle, disc, discus, ellipse, girdle, globe, halo, hoop, lap, loop, orb, orbit, oval, perimeter, plate, revolution, ring, rotation, round, saucer, sphere, spiral, turn, tyre, wheel, wreath

circlet *noun* **1** a small circle **2** an ornamental headband

circuit /ˈsɜːkɪt/ *noun* **1** a movement in a circle **2** a connected group of places, events *etc*: *the American tennis circuit* **3** the path of an electric current ◊ **circuitous** *adj* /səˈkjuːɪtəs/ not direct, roundabout: *by a circuitous route* ◊ **circuitously** *adv* ◊ **circuitry** *noun* a system of electrical circuits
◼ **circuitous** roundabout, periphrastic, indirect, oblique, devious, tortuous, winding, meandering, rambling

circular *adj* round, like a circle ◊ *noun* a letter sent to a number of people

circulate *verb* **1** move round **2** send round: *circulate a memo*
◼ **2** spread, diffuse, broadcast, publicize, publish, issue, propagate, pass round, distribute

circulation *noun* **1** the act of circulating **2** the movement of the blood **3** the total sales of a newspaper or magazine

circumcise *verb* cut away the foreskin of (a male) or the clitoris of (a female) ◊ **circumcision** *noun*

circumference *noun* **1** the outside line of a circle **2** the length of this line

circumlocution *noun* a roundabout way of saying something ◊ **circumlocutory** *adj*

circumnavigate *verb* sail round (the world) ◊ **circumnavigation** *noun*

circumscribe *verb* **1** draw a line round **2** put limits on, restrict ◊ **circumscription** *noun*

circumspect *adj* wary, cautious ◊ **circumspection** *noun* caution

circumstance *noun* **1** a condition of time, place *etc* which affects someone, an action or an event **2** (**circumstances**) the state of someone's financial affairs ◊ **circumstantial** *adj* of evidence: pointing to a conclusion without giving absolute proof
◼ **1** detail, particular, fact, item, element, factor, condition, state, state of affairs, situation **2** position, status, lifestyle, means, resources

circumvent *verb* **1** get round (a difficulty) **2** outwit ◊ **circumvention** *noun*

circus noun (plural **circuses**) **1** a travelling company of acrobats, clowns etc **2** a large sports arena

cirrhosis noun a disease of the liver

cirrus noun a fleecy kind of cloud

cissy noun, informal an effeminate person

cistern noun a tank for storing water

citadel noun a fortress within a city
▪ fortress, stronghold, fortification

citation noun **1** something quoted **2** a summons to appear in court **3** official recognition of an achievement or action

cite verb **1** quote as an example or as proof **2** summon to appear in court
▪ **1** quote, adduce, name, specify, enumerate, mention, refer to

⚠ Do not confuse with: **sight** and **site**

citizen noun someone who lives in a city or state ◇ **citizenry** noun plural the inhabitants of a city or state ◇ **citizenship** noun the rights or state of being a citizen
▪ city-dweller, inhabitant, resident, householder, taxpayer

citric acid a sharp-tasting acid found in citrus fruits

citrus fruit one of a group of fruits including the orange, lemon and lime

city noun (plural **cities**) **1** a large town **2** a town with a cathedral ◇ **the City** Brit the part of London regarded as the centre of business
▪ **1** metropolis, town, municipality, conurbation, cosmopolis

civic adj relating to a city or citizens ◇ **civics** noun sing the study of people's duties as citizens

civil adj **1** relating to a community **2** non-military, civilian **3** polite ◇ **civility** noun politeness, good manners ◇ **civil law** law concerned with citizens' rights, not criminal acts ◇ **civil service** the paid administrative officials of the country, excluding the armed forces ◇ **civil war** war between citizens of the same country

▪ **3** polite, courteous, well-mannered, well-bred, refined, civilized, urbane, affable, complaisant, obliging

civilian noun someone who is not in the armed forces ◇ adj non-military

civilization noun **1** making or becoming civilized **2** life under a civilized system **3** a particular culture: a prehistoric civilization
▪ **1** progress, advancement, development, education, enlightenment

civilize verb bring (a people) under a regular system of laws, education etc ◇ **civilized** adj living under such a system; not savage
▪ tame, educate, enlighten, cultivate, refine, sophisticate, improve ◇ **civilized** advanced, developed, educated, enlightened, cultured, refined, sophisticated

clad adj, formal clothed: clad in leather from head to toe

claim verb **1** demand as a right **2** state as a truth; assert (that) ◇ noun an act of claiming or something claimed ◇ **claimant** noun someone who makes a claim
▪ **1** ask for, request, require, need, demand, exact, take, collect **2** allege, profess, state, affirm, assert, maintain, contend, insist

clairvoyant adj able to see into the future, or to contact the spirit world ◇ noun someone with clairvoyant powers ◇ **clairvoyance** noun
▪ noun psychic, fortune-teller, prophet, prophetess, visionary, seer, soothsayer, diviner, telepath

clam noun a large shellfish with two shells hinged together

clamber verb climb awkwardly or with difficulty

clammy adj unpleasantly moist and sticky
▪ damp, moist, sweaty, sticky

clamour noun a loud, continuous noise or outcry ◇ verb **1** cry aloud **2** make a loud demand (for) ◇ **clamorous** adj noisy

clamp noun **1** a piece of metal, wood

etc used to fasten things together **2** a device fitted to a wheel of a illegally parked car to stop it being moved ◇ *verb* **1** bind with a clamp **2** fit a clamp to the wheel of (a parked car) ◇ **clamp down on** suppress firmly

■ **1** vice, grip, brace, bracket

clan *noun* **1** a number of families with the same surname, traditionally under a single chieftain **2** a sect, a clique ◇ **clannish** *adj* loyal to one another, but showing little interest in others ◇ **clansman**, **clanswoman** *noun* a member of a clan

■ **1** tribe, family, house, race **2** brotherhood, fraternity, confraternity, sect, faction, group, band, set, clique, coterie

From Scottish Gaelic *clann* meaning 'children'

clandestine *adj* hidden, secret, underhand ◇ **clandestinely** *adv*

clang *verb* make a loud, deep ringing sound ◇ *noun* a loud, deep ring

clank *noun* a sound like that made by metal hitting metal ◇ *verb* make this sound

clap *noun* **1** the noise made by striking together two things, *esp* the hands **2** a burst of sound, *esp* thunder ◇ *verb* (**claps**, **clapping**, **clapped**) **1** strike noisily together **2** strike the hands together to show approval **3** strike someone gently with the palm as a friendly gesture **4** *informal* put suddenly, throw: *clapped them in jail* ◇ **clapper** *noun* the tongue of a bell

■ *verb* **2** applaud

claptrap *noun* meaningless words, nonsense

claret *noun* **1** a type of red wine **2** the colour of this

clarify *verb* (**clarifies**, **clarifying**, **clarified**) **1** make clear and understandable **2** make (a liquid) clear and pure

■ **1** explain, throw light on, illuminate, elucidate, gloss, define, simplify, resolve, clear up **2** refine, purify, filter, clear

☒ **1** obscure, confuse **2** cloud

clarinet *noun* a musical wind instrument, usually made of wood ◇ **clari-**

nettist *noun* someone who plays the clarinet

clarion *noun, old* **1** a kind of trumpet **2** a shrill, rousing noise ◇ **clarion call** a clear call to action

clarity *noun* clearness

■ clearness, transparency, lucidity, simplicity, intelligibility, comprehensibility, explicitness, unambiguousness, obviousness, definition, precision

☒ obscurity, vagueness, imprecision

clash *noun* (*plural* **clashes**) **1** a loud noise made by striking swords *etc* **2** a disagreement, a conflict, a fight ◇ *verb* **1** bang noisily together **2** disagree **3** of events: take place at the same time **4** of two colours *etc*: not go well together

■ *noun* **1** crash, bang, jangle, clatter **2** confrontation, showdown, conflict, disagreement, fight, brush ◇ *verb* **1** crash, bang, clank, clang, jangle, clatter, rattle **2** disagree, quarrel, wrangle, grapple, fight, feud **3** coincide **4** jar

clasp *noun* **1** a hook or pin for fastening: *hair clasp* **2** a firm grip **3** an embrace ◇ *verb* **1** hold closely; grasp **2** fasten

■ *verb* **1** hold, grip, grasp, clutch, embrace, enfold, hug, squeeze, press

class *noun* (*plural* **classes**) **1** a rank or group of people or things with something in common **2** a group of schoolchildren or students taught together **3** a lesson **4** a grade or type ◇ *verb* **1** place in a class **2** arrange in some order

■ *noun* **1** category, classification, group, set, section, division, department, sphere, grouping, order, league, rank, status, caste, species, genus

classic *noun* **1** a great book or other work of art **2** something typical and influential of its kind **3** (**classics**) the study of ancient Greek and Latin literature ◇ *adj* **1** excellent **2** standard, typical of its kind: *a classic example* **3** simple and elegant in style: *a classic black dress*

classical *adj* **1** of a classic or the classics **2** of music: serious, not light

classify *verb* (**classifies**, **classifying**, **classified**) **1** arrange in classes **2** put into a class or category ◊ **classification** noun

■ **1** sort, grade, rank, arrange, dispose, distribute, systematize, codify, tabulate, file, catalogue **2** categorize, class, group, pigeonhole

classy adj elegant, stylish

clatter noun a noise of plates etc banged together ◊ verb make this noise

clause noun **1** a part of a sentence containing a finite verb **2** a part of a will, act of parliament etc

■ **2** item, part, section, subsection, paragraph, condition, point

claustrophobia noun an abnormal fear of enclosed spaces ◊ **claustrophobic** adj

claw noun **1** an animal's or bird's foot with hooked nails **2** a hooked nail on one of these feet ◊ verb scratch or tear

■ noun **2** talon, nail ◊ verb scratch, scrape, tear, rip, lacerate, maul

clay noun soft, sticky earth, often used to make pottery, bricks etc ◊ **clayey** adj

claymore noun, hist a large sword used by Scottish Highlanders in battle

clean adj **1** free from dirt; pure **2** neat, complete: a clean break ◊ adv completely: got clean away ◊ verb make clean; free from dirt ◊ **cleanliness** noun ◊ **cleanly** adv

■ adj **1** washed, laundered, sterile, antiseptic, hygienic, sanitary, purified, pure, unadulterated, unpolluted, uncontaminated, spotless, unsullied, unblemished ◊ verb wash, launder, rinse, wipe, sponge, scrub, scour, cleanse, purge, purify, decontaminate, disinfect, sanitize, sterilize

✍ adj **1** dirty, polluted

cleaner noun **1** someone employed to clean a building etc **2** a substance which cleans

cleanse /klɛnz/ verb make clean

clear adj **1** transparent **2** free from mist or cloud: clear sky **3** bright, undimmed **4** free from difficulty or obstructions **5** easy to see, hear or understand **6** after deductions and charges have been made: clear profit **7** without a stain or blemish **8** without touching: clear of the rocks ◊ verb **1** make clear **2** empty **3** free from blame **4** leap over without touching **5** of the sky: become clear ◊ **clearance** noun ◊ **clearly** adv ◊ **clearness** noun ◊ **clear out** or **clear off** go away

■ **1** transparent, limpid, crystalline, glassy, see-through, clean, unclouded **3** bright, sunny, light, luminous, undimmed **4** unblocked, open, free, empty, unhindered, unimpeded **5** plain, distinct, comprehensible, intelligible, coherent, lucid, explicit, unambiguous, evident, patent, obvious, manifest, conspicuous, unmistakable, audible

✍ **1** opaque, cloudy **3** dull **4** blocked **5** unclear, vague, ambiguous, confusing, inaudible, indistinct

clear-cut adj distinct, obvious

clearing noun an area of land free of trees

■ space, opening, glade

cleavage noun **1** splitting **2** the way in which two things are split or divided **3** the hollow between a woman's breasts

cleave [1] verb (**cleaves**, **cleaving**, **clove** or **cleft**, **cloven** or **cleft**) **1** divide, split **2** crack

cleave [2] verb stick (to)

cleaver noun a heavy knife for splitting meat carcasses etc

clef noun a musical sign, (𝄞 **treble clef**) or (𝄢 **bass clef**), placed on a stave to fix the pitch of the notes

cleft noun an opening made by splitting; a crack ◊ past form of **cleave**

clematis noun a flowering, climbing shrub

clement adj mild; merciful ◊ **clemency** noun readiness to forgive; mercy

clench verb press firmly together: clenching his teeth

clergy noun plural the ministers of the Christian Church ◊ **clergyman**, **clergywoman** noun a Christian minister

■ **clergyman**, **clergywoman** churchman, churchwoman, cleric, ecclesiastic, minister, priest, reverend, vicar, pastor, parson, rector, canon, dean, deacon, chaplain, curate

cleric *noun* a member of the clergy

clerical *adj* **1** relating to office work **2** of the clergy

■ **1** office, secretarial, white-collar, administrative **2** ecclesiastic(al)

clerk *noun* an office worker who writes letters, keeps accounts *etc* ◇ *verb* act as clerk

clever *adj* **1** quick in learning and understanding **2** intelligent, skilful: *a clever answer* ◇ **cleverly** *adv* ◇ **cleverness** *noun*

■ **1,2** intelligent, *informal* brainy, bright, smart, witty, gifted, expert, knowledgeable, adroit, apt, able, capable, quick, quick-witted, sharp, keen, shrewd, knowing

✦ **1,2** foolish, stupid, senseless, ignorant

cliché /'kliːʃeɪ/ *noun* an idea, phrase *etc* that has been used too much and has little meaning

> From a French word for 'stereotype', in the sense of a fixed printing plate

click *noun* a short sharp sound like a clock's tick ◇ *verb* make this sound

client *noun* **1** a customer **2** someone who goes to a lawyer *etc* for advice

■ **1** customer, patron, regular, shopper, consumer

clientele /kliːɒn'tɛl/ *noun* the customers of a lawyer, shopkeeper *etc*

cliff *noun* a very steep, rocky slope, *esp* by the sea

■ rock-face, escarpment, crag, overhang, precipice

climate *noun* **1** the weather conditions of a particular area **2** general condition or situation: *in the present cultural climate* ◇ **climatic** *adj*

■ **2** environment, ambience, atmosphere, mood, trend

climax *noun* (*plural* **climaxes**) the point of greatest interest, action or importance in a situation

■ culmination, height, high point, highlight, zenith, peak, summit, top, head

✦ nadir

climb *verb* **1** go to towards the top of **2** go up using hands and feet **3** slope upward ◇ *noun* an act of climbing ◇ **climber** *noun* **1** someone who climbs **2** a plant which climbs up walls *etc*

■ **1** ascend **2** scale, shin up, clamber **3** ascend, rise, soar

clinch *verb* **1** grasp tightly **2** settle (an argument, bargain *etc*) ◇ *noun* (*plural* **clinches**) **1** *boxing* a position in which the boxers hold each other with their arms **2** a passionate embrace ◇ **clincher** *noun* something that settles or decides a matter

cling *verb* (**clings, clinging, clung**) stick or hang on (to) ◇ **clingy** *adj*

■ clasp, clutch, grasp, grip, stick, adhere, embrace, hug

clingfilm *noun* thin transparent plastic material used to wrap food

clinic *noun* a place or part of a hospital where a particular kind of treatment is given

clinical *adj* **1** of a clinic **2** based on observation: *clinical medicine* **3** objective, cool and unemotional: *a clinical approach* ◇ **clinically** *adv*

clink *noun* a ringing sound of knocked glasses *etc* ◇ *verb* make such a sound

clinker *noun* waste produced from smelting iron or burning coal

clip¹ *verb* (**clips, clipping, clipped**) **1** cut (off) **2** *informal* hit with a sharp blow ◇ *noun* **1** something clipped off **2** *informal* a smart blow

■ *verb* **1** trim, snip, cut, prune, pare, shear, crop, dock, poll

clip² *noun* a small fastener *eg* for papers or hair ◇ *verb* fasten with a clip

■ *verb* pin, staple, fasten, attach, fix

clipper *noun* **1** a fast-sailing ship **2** (**clippers**) large scissors for clipping

clique /kliːk/ *noun* a small group of friends, colleagues *etc* who keep others at a distance

■ circle, set, coterie, group, bunch, pack, gang, crowd, faction, clan

clitoris *noun* a small sensitive structure at the front of the external female sex organs ◇ **clitoral** *adj*

cloak *noun* **1** a loose outer garment **2** something which hides: *cloak of darkness* ◇ *verb* **1** cover as with a cloak **2** hide

▣ *noun* **1** cape, mantle, wrap **2** cover, shield ◇ *verb* **2** mask, cover, hide, screen, conceal, obscure

cloakroom a place where coats, hats *etc* may be left for a time

clobber *verb, informal* **1** beat, hit very hard **2** defeat completely ◇ *noun, slang* personal belongings

cloche /klɒʃ/ *noun* (*plural* **cloches**) a transparent frame for protecting plants

clock *noun* a machine for measuring time ◇ **clock in** or **clock out** record your time of arrival at, or departure from, work

clockwise *adj* turning or moving in the same direction as the hands of a clock

clockwork *adj* worked by machinery such as that of a clock ◇ **like clockwork** smoothly, without difficulties

clod *noun* **1** a thick lump of earth or turf **2** a stupid person

clog *noun* a shoe with a wooden sole ◇ *verb* (**clogs**, **clogging**, **clogged**) block (pipes *etc*)

▣ *verb* block, choke, stop up, bung up, dam, congest, jam

cloister *noun* **1** a covered-in walk in a monastery or convent **2** a monastery or convent ◇ **cloistered** *adj* **1** shut up in a monastery *etc* **2** sheltered from life

close [1] /kləʊs/ *adj* **1** near in time, place *etc* **2** without fresh air, stuffy **3** narrow, confined **4** mean **5** secretive **6** beloved, very dear: *a close friend* **7** with little difference between competitors: *a close contest* ◇ *noun* **1** a cul-de-sac **2** the gardens, walks *etc* near a cathedral ◇ **closely** *adv* ◇ **closeness** *noun*

▣ *adj* **1** near, nearby, at hand, neighbouring, adjacent, adjoining, impending, imminent **2** oppressive, heavy, airless, suffocating, stuffy, unventilated **6** intimate, dear, familiar, devoted

▣ *adj* **1** far, distant **3** fresh, airy

close [2] /kləʊz/ *verb* **1** shut **2** finish **3** come closer to and fight (with) ◇ *noun* the end of something

▣ *verb* **1** shut, fasten, secure, lock, seal **2** end, finish, complete, conclude, terminate, wind up, stop, cease

▣ *verb* **1** open **2** start

closet *noun, US* a cupboard ◇ *verb* shut in a room for a private conference

close-up *noun* a film or photograph taken very near the subject

closure *noun* the act of closing

clot *noun* **1** a lump that forms in blood, cream *etc* **2** *informal* an idiot ◇ *verb* (**clots**, **clotting**, **clotted**) form into clots

▣ *verb* curdle, coagulate, congeal

cloth *noun* **1** woven material of cotton, wool, silk *etc* **2** a piece of this **3** a tablecloth

▣ **1** fabric, material, stuff, textile **2** rag, flannel, duster, towel

clothe *verb* **1** put clothes on **2** provide with clothes **3** cover

▣ **1** dress, put on, robe, attire, deck, outfit, rig out, vest

▣ **1** undress, strip, disrobe

clothes *noun plural* **1** things worn to cover the body and limbs, *eg* shirt, trousers, skirt **2** sheets and coverings for a bed ◇ **clothing** *noun* clothes

▣ **1** clothing, garments, wear, attire, garb, *informal* gear, *informal* togs, outfit, *informal* get-up, dress, costume

cloud *noun* **1** a mass of tiny drops of water or ice floating in the sky **2** a mass of anything: *a cloud of bees* ◇ *verb* become dim or blurred ◇ **clouded** *adj* ◇ **cloudless** *adj*

cloudy *adj* **1** darkened with clouds **2** not clear or transparent

▣ **1** overcast, dull, nebulous, hazy, misty, foggy **2** blurred, blurry, opaque, muddy, dim, indistinct, obscure

▣ **1** clear, bright, sunny, cloudless

clout *noun, informal* **1** a blow **2** influence, power ◇ *verb* hit

clove [1] *noun* **1** a flower bud used as a spice **2** a small section of a bulb of garlic

clove [2] *past form* of **cleave**

cloven-hoofed *adj* having a divided hoof like an ox, sheep *etc*

clover *noun* a field plant with leaves usually in three parts

clown *noun* **1** a comedian with a painted face and comical clothes in a circus **2** a fool ◇ **clowning** *noun* silly or comical behaviour ◇ **clownish** *adj* like a clown; awkward
■ **2** jester, buffoon, fool

cloy *verb* of something sweet: become unpleasant when too much is taken ◇ **cloying** *adj* ◇ **cloyingly** *adv*

club *noun* **1** a heavy stick **2** a stick used to hit the ball in golf **3** a group of people who meet for social events *etc* **4** the place where these people meet **5** (**clubs**) one of the four suits of playing-cards, with black pips ◇ *verb* (**clubs, clubbing, clubbed**) beat with a club
■ *noun* **1** bat, stick, mace, bludgeon, truncheon, *slang* cosh, cudgel **2** association, society, league, guild, union, group ◇ *verb* hit, strike, beat, bash, clout, *slang* clobber, bludgeon, *slang* cosh

cluck *noun* a sound like that made by a hen ◇ *verb* make this sound

clue *noun* a sign, hint or piece of evidence that helps to solve a mystery *etc*
■ hint, tip, lead, tip-off, pointer, evidence, trace

clump *noun* a cluster of trees or shrubs ◇ *verb* walk heavily
■ *verb* tramp, clomp, stamp, stomp, plod, lumber

clumsy *adj* (**clumsier, clumsiest**) **1** awkward in movement or actions **2** tactless, thoughtless: *a clumsy remark* ◇ **clumsily** *adv* ◇ **clumsiness** *noun*
■ **1** bungling, ham-fisted, inept, bumbling, blundering, lumbering, gauche, ungainly, unco-ordinated, awkward, ungraceful, *informal* clunky
▣ **1** careful, graceful, elegant

clung *past form* of **cling**

cluster *noun* **1** a bunch of fruit *etc* **2** a crowd ◇ *verb* group together in clusters
■ *noun* **2** group, knot, gathering ◇ *verb* bunch, group, gather, collect

clutch *verb* **1** hold firmly **2** seize, grasp ◇ *noun* (*plural* **clutches**) **1** a grasp **2** part of a car engine used for changing gears
■ *verb* **1** hold, clasp, grip, hang on to **2** grasp, seize, snatch, grab, catch

clutter *noun* **1** a muddled or disordered collection of things **2** disorder, confusion, untidiness ◇ *verb* (with **up**) fill or cover in an untidy, disordered way
■ *noun* **2** mess, jumble, untidiness, disorder, disarray, muddle, confusion

cm *abbrev* centimetre

Co *abbrev* **1** Company **2** County

c/o *abbrev* care of

co- *prefix* joint, working with: *co-author/co-driver*

coach *noun* (*plural* **coaches**) **1** a bus for long-distance travel **2** a closed, four-wheeled horse carriage **3** a railway carriage **4** a private trainer for sportspeople ◇ *verb* train or help to prepare for an examination, sports contest *etc*
■ *verb* train, drill, instruct, teach, tutor, prepare

coagulate *verb* thicken; clot
■ clot, curdle, congeal, thicken, solidify, gel

coal *noun* a black substance dug out of the earth and used for burning, making gas *etc*

coalmine *noun* a mine from which coal is dug

coalesce /kəʊəˈlɛs/ *verb* come together and unite

coalition *noun* a joining together of different groups, *esp* in politics
■ merger, amalgamation, combination, integration, fusion, alliance

coarse *adj* **1** not fine in texture; rough, harsh **2** vulgar ◇ **coarsely** *adv* ◇ **coarsen** *verb* make coarse ◇ **coarseness** *noun*
■ **1** rough, unpolished, unfinished, uneven, lumpy, unpurified, unrefined, unprocessed **2** bawdy, ribald, earthy, smutty, vulgar, crude, offensive, foul-mouthed, boorish, loutish, rude, impolite, indelicate, indecent, immodest

coast *noun* the border of land next to

the sea ◇ *verb* move without the use of power on a bike, in a car *etc* ◇ **coastal** *adj* of or on the coast

◼ *noun* coastline, seaboard, shore, beach, seaside ◇ *verb* free-wheel, glide, cruise, drift

coastguard *noun* someone who acts as a guard along the coast to help those in danger in boats *etc*

coat *noun* **1** an outer garment with sleeves **2** an animal's covering of hair or wool **3** a layer of paint ◇ *verb* cover with a coat or layer ◇ **coating** *noun* a covering ◇ **coat of arms** the badge or crest of a family

◼ *noun* **2** fur, hair, fleece, pelt, hide

coax *verb* persuade to do what is wanted without using force

◼ persuade, cajole, wheedle, *informal* sweet-talk, soft-soap

cob *noun* **1** a head of corn, wheat *etc* **2** a male swan

cobalt *noun* **1** a silvery metal **2** a blue colouring obtained from this

cobble *noun* **1** a rounded stone used in paving roads (*also called* **cobble-stone**) ◇ *verb* **1** mend (shoes) **2** repair roughly or hurriedly ◇ **cobbler** *noun* someone who mends shoes

cobra *noun* a poisonous snake found in India and Africa

cobweb *noun* a spider's web

cocaine *noun* a narcotic drug

cochineal *noun* a scarlet dye, used to colour food, made from the dried bodies of certain insects

cock *noun* **1** the male of most kinds of bird, *esp* of the farmyard hen **2** a tap or valve for controlling the flow of liquid **3** a hammer-like part of a gun which fires the shot **4** *slang* the penis ◇ *verb* **1** draw back the cock of (a gun) **2** set (the ears) upright to listen **3** tilt (the head) to one side

cockade *noun* a knot of ribbons worn on a hat

cockatoo *noun* a kind of parrot

cockerel *noun* a young cock

cockle *noun* a type of shellfish

cockney *noun* (*plural* **cockneys**) **1**

someone born in the East End of London **2** the speech characteristic of this area

> Literally 'cock's egg', an old word for a misshapen egg which was later applied to an effeminate person, and so to a soft-living city-dweller

cockpit *noun* **1** the space for the pilot or driver in an aeroplane or small boat **2** a pit where cocks were put to fight

cockroach *noun* (*plural* **cockroaches**) a type of crawling insect

cocktail *noun* a mixed alcoholic drink

cock-up *noun*, *slang* a mess, a mistake

cocky *adj* conceited, self-confident ◇ **cockily** *adv* ◇ **cockiness** *noun*

◼ arrogant, self-important, conceited, vain, swollen-headed, egotistical, swaggering, brash, cocksure, self-assured, self-confident, overconfident

◻ humble, modest, shy

cocoa *noun* the ground seeds of the cacao tree or a drink made from this

coconut *noun* the large, hard-shelled nut of a type of palm tree

> Based on a Portuguese word meaning 'grimace', because of the resemblance of the three holes on the base of the fruit to a human face

cocoon *noun* a protective covering of silk spun by the larva of a butterfly, moth *etc*

cod *noun* a fish much used as food, found in the northern seas

coda *noun* a closing passage in a piece of music, book *etc*

coddle *verb* **1** pamper, overprotect **2** cook (an egg) gently over hot water

code *noun* **1** a way of signalling or sending secret messages, using letters *etc* agreed beforehand **2** a system of laws, rules *etc*

◼ **1** cipher, secret language **2** ethics, rules, regulations, principles, system, custom, convention, etiquette, manners

codger *noun* an old, eccentric man

codicil *noun* a note added to a will or treaty

codify *verb* (**codifies, codifying, codified**) arrange in an orderly way, classify

co-ed *adj, informal* coeducational

coeducation *noun* the education of boys and girls together ◇ **coeducational** *adj*

coerce *verb* make (someone) do something; force, compel ◇ **coercion** *noun* ◇ **coercive** *adj*

◪ force, drive, compel, constrain, pressurize, bully, intimidate, browbeat, bludgeon, bulldoze, dragoon, pressgang

coeval *adj* of the same age or time

coexist *verb* exist at the same time ◇ **coexistence** *noun* ◇ **coexistent** *adj*

C of E *abbrev* Church of England

coffee *noun* 1 a drink made from the roasted, ground beans of an evergreen shrub 2 a pale brown colour

coffer *noun* a chest for holding money, gold *etc*

◪ casket, case, box, chest, trunk, strongbox, treasury, repository

coffin *noun* a box in which a dead body is buried or cremated

cog *noun* a tooth on a wheel

cogent *adj* convincing, believable ◇ **cogency** *noun* ◇ **cogently** *adv*

cogitate *verb* think carefully ◇ **cogitation** *noun*

cognac /ˈkɒnjak/ *noun* a kind of French brandy

cognition *noun* perception, knowledge

◪ perception, awareness, knowledge, discernment, insight, comprehension, understanding, intelligence, reasoning

cognizance *noun* awareness, notice

cogwheel *noun* a toothed wheel

cohere *verb* stick together

coherence *noun* connection between thoughts, ideas *etc*

coherent *adj* 1 clear and logical in thought or speech 2 sticking together ◇ **coherently** *adv*

◪ 1 articulate, intelligible, comprehensible,

meaningful, lucid, consistent, logical, reasoned, rational, sensible, orderly, systematic, organized

◪ 1 incoherent, unintelligible, meaningless

cohesion *noun* the act of sticking together ◇ **cohesive** *adj*

cohort *noun, hist* a tenth part of a Roman legion

coiffure /kwɑːˈfʊə(r)/ *noun* a hairstyle

coil *verb* wind in rings; twist ◇ *noun* 1 a coiled arrangement of hair, rope *etc* 2 a contraceptive device fitted in the uterus

◪ *verb* wind, spiral, curl, loop, twist, twine

coin *noun* a piece of stamped metal used as money ◇ *verb* 1 make metal into money 2 make up (a new word *etc*)

◪ *noun* piece, bit, cash, money, change, small change, loose change, silver, copper ◇ *verb* 1 mint 2 invent, think up, make up

coinage *noun* 1 the system of coins used in a country 2 a newly-made word

coincide *verb* 1 (often with **with**) be the same as: *their interests coincide/his story coincides with mine* 2 (often with **with**) happen at the same time as: *her arrival coincided with his departure*

◪ 1 agree, concur, correspond, square, tally, accord, harmonize, match

coincidence *noun* the occurrence of two related things simultaneously without planning ◇ **coincidental** *adj* ◇ **coincidentally** *adv*

◪ coexistence, conjunction, concurrence, correspondence, correlation

coitus *noun* sexual intercourse

coke *noun* a type of fuel made by heating coal till the gas is driven out

Col *abbrev* Colonel

colander *noun* a bowl with small holes in it for straining vegetables *etc*

cold *adj* 1 low in temperature 2 lower in temperature than is comfortable 3 unfriendly ◇ *noun* 1 the state of being cold 2 an infectious disease causing sneezing, running nose *etc* ◇ **coldly** *adv* ◇ **coldness** *noun* ◇ **get cold feet** decide not to do something because of loss or lack of courage

■ *adj* **1** unheated, cool, chilled **2** chilly, chill, nippy, *informal* parky, raw, biting, bitter, icy, glacial, freezing, arctic, polar **3** unsympathetic, unmoved, unfeeling, stony, unfriendly, distant, aloof, stand-offish, undemonstrative, indifferent, lukewarm

cold-blooded *adj* **1** of animals: having cold blood **2** cruel; lacking in feelings

■ **2** merciless, pitiless, callous, unfeeling, heartless

coleslaw *noun* a salad made from raw cabbage

colic *noun* a severe stomach pain

collaborate *verb* **1** work together (with) **2** work (with an enemy) to betray your country ◇ **collaboration** *noun* ◇ **collaborative** *adj* ◇ **collaborator** *noun*

■ **1** work together, co-operate, join forces, team up, participate **2** conspire, collude ◇ **collaborator** associate, partner, colleague, accomplice, traitor

⚠ Do not confuse with: **corroborate**

collage /kɒˈlɑːʒ/ *noun* a design made of scraps of paper pasted on wood, card *etc*

collagen *noun* a protein found in skin, cartilage *etc*

collapse *verb* **1** fall or break down **2** cave or fall in **3** become unconscious or exhausted ◇ *noun* a falling down or caving in ◇ **collapsible** *adj* of a chair *etc*: able to be folded up

■ *verb* **1** fall, sink, founder, fail, *informal* fold, fall apart, disintegrate **2** crumble, subside, cave in **3** faint, pass out, crumple

collar *noun* **1** a band, strip *etc* worn round the neck **2** part of a garment that fits round the neck ◇ *verb*, *informal* seize

collarbone *noun* either of two bones joining the breastbone and shoulder-blade

collate *verb* **1** examine and compare **2** gather together and arrange in order: *collate the pages for the book*

collateral *noun* an additional security for repayment of a debt

collation *noun* **1** a light, often cold meal **2** the act of collating

colleague *noun* someone who works in the same company *etc* as yourself

■ workmate, co-worker, team-mate, partner, associate, assistant

collect *verb* **1** bring or come together **2** fetch

■ **1** gather, assemble, congregate, convene, muster, rally, converge, cluster, aggregate, accumulate, amass

collected *adj* **1** gathered together **2** calm, composed

■ **2** composed, self-possessed, placid, serene, calm, unruffled, unperturbed, cool

◨ **2** agitated

collection *noun* **1** the act of collecting **2** a number of objects or people gathered together **3** money gathered at a meeting, *eg* a church service

■ **2** assembly, convocation, congregation, crowd, group, cluster, accumulation, conglomeration, mass, heap, pile, hoard, stockpile, store

collective *adj* **1** acting together **2** of several things or people, not of one: *a collective decision* ◇ *noun* a business *etc* owned and managed by the workers

■ *noun* co-operative

Collective nouns (by animal) include: shrewdness of *apes*, cete of *badgers*, sloth of *bears*, swarm of *bees*, obstinacy of *buffaloes*, clowder of *cats*, drove of *cattle*, brood of *chickens*, bask of *crocodiles*, murder of *crows*, herd of *deer*, pack of *dogs*, school of *dolphins*, dole of *doves*, team of *ducks*, parade of *elephants*, busyness of *ferrets*, charm of *finches*, shoal of *fish*, skulk of *foxes*, army of *frogs*, gaggle/skein of *geese*, tribe of *goats*, husk of *hares*, cast of *hawks*, brood of *hens*, bloat of *hippopotamuses*, string of *horses*, pack of *hounds*, troop of *kangaroos*, kindle of *kittens*, exaltation of *larks*, leap of *leopards*, pride of *lions*, swarm of *locusts*, tittering of *magpies*, troop of *monkeys*, watch of *nightingales*, family of *otters*, parliament of *owls*, pandemonium of *parrots*, covey of *partridges*, muster of *peacocks*, rookery of *penguins*, nye of *pheasants*, litter of *pigs*, school of *porpoises*, bury of *rabbits*, colony of *rats*, unkindness of *ravens*, crash of *rhinoceroses*, building of *rooks*, pod of *seals*, flock of *sheep*, murmuration of *starlings*, ambush of *tigers*, rafter of *turkeys*, turn of *turtles*, descent of *woodpeckers*, gam of *whales*, rout of *wolves*, zeal of *zebras*

collector *noun* someone who collects a particular group of things: *stamp collector*

Names of collectors and enthusiasts include:
zoophile (*animals*), antiquary (*antiques*), tegestollogist (*beer mats*), campanologist (*bell-ringing*), ornithologist (*birds*), bibliophile (*books*), audiophile (*broadcast and recorded sound*), lepidopterist (*butterflies*), cartophilist (*cigarette cards*), numismatist (*coins/medals*), gamer (*computer games*), conservationist (*countryside*), cruciverbalist (*crosswords*), environmentalist (*the environment*), xenophile (*foreigners*), gourmet (*good food and drink*), gastronome (*good food and drink*), discophile (*gramophone records*), chirographist (*handwriting*), hippophile (*horses*), entomologist (*insects*), phillumenist (*matches/matchboxes*), monarchist (*the monarchy*), deltiologist (*postcards*), arachnologist (*spiders/ arachnids*), philatelist (*stamps*), arctophile (*teddy bears*), etymologist (*words*)

college *noun* **1** an institute of further or higher education **2** a building housing students, forming part of a university

collegiate *adj* of a university: divided into colleges

collide *verb* come together with great force; clash
⊟ crash, bump, smash, clash

collision *noun* **1** a crash between two moving vehicles *etc* **2** a disagreement, a clash of interests *etc*
⊟ **1** impact, crash, smash, accident, pile-up **2** clash, confrontation, conflict

collie *noun* a breed of long-haired dog with a pointed nose

collier *noun* **1** a coal-miner **2** a ship transporting coal ◇ **colliery** *noun* (*plural* **collieries**) a coalmine

colloquial *adj* used in everyday speech but not in formal writing or speaking ◇ **colloquialism** *noun* a colloquial word or phrase ◇ **colloquially** *adv*
⊟ conversational, informal, familiar, everyday, idiomatic
⊠ formal

collude *verb* conspire ◇ **collusion** *noun* secret or clandestine agreement or co-operation
⊟ conspire, plot, connive, collaborate, scheme, machinate, intrigue

cologne *noun* light perfume made with plant oils and alcohol

colon [1] *noun* a punctuation mark (:) used *eg* to introduce a list of examples

colon [2] *noun* a part of the bowel

colonel /'kɜːnəl/ *noun* a senior army officer fulfilling a staff appointment

colonial *adj* of colonies abroad ◇ **colonialism** *noun* the policy of setting up colonies abroad ◇ **colonialist** *adj*

colonnade *noun* a row of columns or pillars

colony *noun* (*plural* **colonies**) **1** a group of settlers or the settlement they make in another country **2** a group of people, animals *etc* of the same type living together ◇ **colonist** *noun* a settler ◇ **colonize** *verb* set up a colony in
⊟ **1** settlement, outpost, dependency, dominion, territory, province

colossal *adj* of very great size
⊟ huge, enormous, immense, vast, massive, gigantic, *slang* mega, mammoth,

monstrous, monumental

🔁 tiny, minute

colossus *noun* an enormous statue

colour or *US* **color** *noun* **1** a quality that an object shows in the light, *eg* redness, blueness *etc* **2** a shade or tint **3** vividness, brightness **4** (**colours**) a flag or standard ◇ *verb* **1** put colour on **2** blush **3** influence: *coloured my attitude to life* ◇ **coloured** *adj* **1** having colour **2** *offensive* not white-skinned

---

The range of colours includes:
red, crimson, scarlet, vermilion, cherry, cerise, magenta, maroon, burgundy, ruby, orange, tangerine, apricot, coral, salmon, peach, amber, brown, chestnut, mahogany, bronze, auburn, rust, copper, cinnamon, chocolate, tan, sepia, taupe, beige, fawn, yellow, lemon, canary, ochre, saffron, topaz, gold, chartreuse, green, eau de nil, emerald, jade, bottle, avocado, sage, khaki, turquoise, aquamarine, cyan, cobalt, blue, sapphire, gentian, indigo, navy, violet, purple, mauve, plum, lavender, lilac, pink, rose, magnolia, cream, ecru, milky, white, grey, silver, charcoal, ebony, jet, black

---

colour-blind *adj* unable to distinguish certain colours, *eg* red and green

colourful *adj* **1** brightly coloured **2** vivid, interesting ◇ **colourfully** *adv*

🔁 **1** multicoloured, kaleidoscopic, variegated, vivid, bright, brilliant, rich, intense **2** vivid, graphic, picturesque, lively, stimulating, exciting, interesting

colouring *noun* **1** shade or combination of colours **2** complexion

colourless *adj* **1** without colour **2** dull, bland

🔁 **1** transparent, neutral, bleached, washed out, faded, pale, sickly, anaemic **2** insipid, lacklustre, dull, dreary, drab, characterless, uninteresting, tame

🔁 **1** colourful **2** bright, exciting

colt *noun* a young horse

column *noun* **1** an upright stone or wooden pillar **2** something of a long or tall, narrow shape **3** a vertical line of print, figures *etc* on a page **4** a regular feature in a newspaper

🔁 **1** pillar, post, shaft, upright, support, obelisk

columnist *noun* someone who writes a regular newspaper column

coma *noun* unconsciousness lasting a long time

comatose *adj* **1** in or of a coma **2** drowsy, sluggish

comb *noun* **1** a toothed instrument for separating or smoothing hair, wool *etc* **2** the crest of certain birds **3** a collection of cells for honey ◇ *verb* **1** arrange or smooth with a comb **2** search through thoroughly

🔁 *verb* **1** untangle **2** search, scour, screen, hunt

combat *verb* fight or struggle against ◇ *noun* a fight or struggle ◇ **combatant** *noun* someone who is fighting ◇ **combative** *adj* quarrelsome; fighting

🔁 *verb* fight, battle, strive, struggle, contend, contest, oppose, resist, withstand, defy ◇ *noun* war, warfare, hostilities, action, battle, fighting

combination *noun* **1** the act of combining **2** a set of things or people combined; a mixture **3** a series of letters or figures dialled to open a safe

🔁 **1** merger, amalgamation, unification, alliance, coalition, association, federation, confederation, confederacy, consortium, integration, fusion, coalescence **2** blend, mix, mixture, composite, amalgam, synthesis, compound

combine *verb* join together ◇ *noun* a number of traders *etc* who join together ◇ **combine harvester** a large farm machine which cuts and threshes grain

combustible *adj* liable to catch fire and burn ◇ *noun* anything that will catch fire ◇ **combustion** *noun* burning

come *verb* (**comes, coming, came, come**) **1** move towards this place (*opposite* of **go**): *come here!* **2** draw near in time: *Christmas is coming* **3** arrive: *we'll have tea when you come* **4** happen, occur: *the index comes at the end* **5** *slang* achieve a sexual orgasm ◇ **come about** happen ◇ **come across** or **come upon** meet or find accidentally ◇ **come by** obtain ◇ **come over 1** make an impression: *come over well on TV* **2** become: *come over faint* ◇ **come round** or **come to** recover from a faint *etc* ◇ **to come** in the future

▨ **1** advance, move towards, approach, near, draw near **2** approach, near, draw near **3** arrive, enter, appear, materialize ◇ **come about** happen, occur, come to pass, transpire, result, arise ◇ **come across** or **come upon** find, discover, chance upon, happen upon ◇ **come round** or **come to** recover, wake, awake

comedian *noun* a performer who tells jokes, acts in comedy *etc*
▤ comic, humorist, wit

comedy *noun* (*plural* **comedies**) a light-hearted or amusing play (*contrasted with*: **tragedy**)

comely *adj* good-looking, pleasing ◇ **comeliness** *noun*

comet *noun* a kind of star which has a tail of light

comfort *verb* help, soothe (someone in pain or distress) ◇ *noun* **1** ease; quiet enjoyment **2** something that brings ease, happiness or relief

▨ *verb* ease, soothe, relieve, alleviate, assuage, console, reassure ◇ *noun* **1** ease, relaxation, snugness, cosiness, well-being, satisfaction, contentment, enjoyment **2** consolation, compensation, reassurance, alleviation, relief
▨ *noun* **1** discomfort **2** distress

comfortable *adj* **1** at ease; free from trouble, pain *etc* **2** giving comfort ◇ **comfortably** *adv*

comfrey *noun* a plant with hairy leaves, used in herbal medicine

comic *adj* **1** of comedy **2** amusing, funny ◇ *noun* **1** a professional comedian **2** a children's magazine with illustrated stories *etc* ◇ **comical** *adj* funny, amusing ◇ **comically** *adv* ◇ **comic strip** a strip of small pictures telling a story

▨ *adj* **2** funny, hilarious, comical, droll, humorous, witty, amusing, ludicrous
▨ *adj* **1** tragic **2** serious

comma *noun* a punctuation mark (,) indicating a pause in a sentence

command *verb* **1** give an order **2** be in charge of **3** look over or down upon: *commanding a splendid view* ◇ *noun* **1** an order **2** control: *in command of the situation*

▨ *verb* **1** order, bid, charge, enjoin, direct, instruct, demand **2** lead, head, rule, reign, govern, control, dominate, manage, supervise

commandant *noun* an officer in command of a place or of troops

commandeer *verb* seize (something), *esp* for the use of an army

commander *noun* **1** someone who commands **2** a naval officer next in rank below captain

commandment *noun* an order or command

commando *noun* (*plural* **commandoes**) a soldier in an army unit trained for special tasks

commemorate *verb* **1** bring (a person or event) to memory by some solemn act **2** serve as a memorial of ◇ **commemoration** *noun*

▨ **1** celebrate, solemnize, remember, memorialize, mark, honour, salute, immortalize, observe

commence *verb* begin ◇ **commencement** *noun*

▨ begin, start, embark on, originate, initiate, inaugurate, open, launch
▨ finish, end, cease

commend *verb* **1** praise **2** *formal* give into the care of another ◇ **commendable** *adj* praiseworthy ◇ **commendation** *noun* praise ◇ **commendatory** *adj* praising

▨ **1** praise, compliment, acclaim, extol, applaud, approve, recommend **2** commit, entrust, confide, consign, deliver, yield

commensurate *adj*: **commensurate with** proportionate with, appropriate to

comment *noun* **1** a remark **2** a criticism ◇ *verb* remark on; criticize

▣ *noun* **1** statement, remark, observation ◇ *verb* say, mention, interpose, interject, remark, observe, criticize

commentary *noun* (*plural* **commentaries**) **1** a description of an event *etc* by someone who is watching it **2** a set of explanatory notes for a book *etc*

▣ **1** narration, voiceover, description **2** analysis, review, critique, explanation, notes

commentator *noun* someone who gives or writes a commentary

commerce *noun* the buying and selling of goods between people or nations; trade, dealings

commercial *adj* **1** of commerce **2** paid for by advertisements: *commercial radio* ◇ *noun* an advertisement on radio, TV *etc* ◇ **commercially** *adv*

commercialize *verb* **1** involve in the buying and selling of goods **2** exploit for profit

commis /'kɒmɪ/ *noun* an apprentice waiter or chef

commiserate *verb* sympathize (with) ◇ **commiseration** *noun*

commission *noun* **1** the act of committing **2** a document giving authority to an officer in the armed forces **3** an order for a work of art, piece of writing *etc* **4** a fee for doing business on another's behalf **5** a group of people appointed to investigate something ◇ *verb* give a commission or power to ◇ **in** or **out of commission** in or not in use

▣ *noun* **4** percentage, *informal* cut, *informal* rake-off, fee **5** committee, board, delegation ◇ *verb* nominate, select, engage, employ, empower, delegate, order

commissionaire *noun* a uniformed doorkeeper

commissioner *noun* **1** someone with high authority in a district **2** a member of a commission

commit *verb* (**commits, committing, committed**) **1** give or hand over; entrust **2** make a promise to do: *committed to finishing this book* **3** do, bring

about: *commit a crime* ◇ **committal** *noun* the act of committing

▣ **1** entrust, confide, commend, consign, deliver, hand over, give, deposit **2** pledge, promise, swear, undertake **3** do, perform, execute, enact, perpetrate

commitment *noun* **1** a promise **2** a task that must be done

▣ **1** undertaking, guarantee, assurance, promise, obligation **2** duty, responsibility

committed *adj* strong in belief or support: *a committed socialist*

committee *noun* a number of people chosen from a larger body to attend to special business

▣ council, board, panel, commission

commodious *adj* roomy, spacious

commodity *noun* (*plural* **commodities**) **1** an article to be bought or sold **2** (**commodities**) goods, produce

commodore *noun* an officer next above a captain in the navy

common *adj* **1** shared by all or many: *common knowledge* **2** seen or happening often: *a common occurrence* **3** ordinary, normal ◇ *noun* land belonging to the people of a town, parish *etc* ◇ **common law** unwritten law based on custom ◇ **common room** *noun* a sitting-room for the use of a group in a school *etc* ◇ **Commons** or **House of Commons** the lower House of the British Parliament ◇ **common sense** practical good sense

▣ *adj* **1** shared, mutual, joint, collective **2** familiar, customary, habitual, usual, daily, everyday, routine, regular, frequent **3** standard, average, ordinary, plain, simple, undistinguished, unexceptional, conventional

▣ *adj* **2** uncommon, unusual, rare, noteworthy

commoner *noun* someone who is not a noble

commonplace *adj* ordinary

▣ ordinary, everyday, common, humdrum

commonwealth *noun* an association of self-governing states

commotion *noun* a disturbance among a number of people
- agitation, turmoil, tumult, excitement, ferment, fuss, bustle, *informal* to-do, hubbub, rumpus, disorder

communal *adj* common, shared ◇ **communally** *adv*

commune[1] *noun* a group of people living together, sharing work *etc*
- collective, co-operative, kibbutz, community

commune[2] *verb* communicate
- converse, communicate, talk

communicable *adj* able to be passed on to others: *communicable diseases*

communicate *verb* **1** make known, tell; exchange information **2** pass on **3** get in touch (with) **4** have a connecting door ◇ **communication** *noun* **1** a means of conveying or exchanging information **2** a message **3** a way of passing from place to place
- **1** announce, declare, proclaim, report, reveal, disclose, divulge, impart, inform, acquaint, notify, publish **2** disseminate, spread, diffuse, transmit, convey **3** correspond, write, phone, telephone, email, contact

Forms of communication include: broadcasting, radio, wireless, television, TV, cable TV, digital TV, satellite, video, teletext, digicast; newspaper, press, news, newsflash, magazine, journal, advertising, publicity, poster, leaflet, pamphlet, brochure, catalogue; post, dispatch, correspondence, letter, postcard, aerogram, telegram, Telemessage®, cable, *informal* wire, chain letter, junk mail, mailshot; conversation, word, message, dialogue, speech, gossip, *informal* grapevine; notice, bulletin, announcement, communiqué, circular, memo, note, report, statement, press release; telephone, SMS (short message service), text message, intercom, call conferencing, video conferencing, answering machine, voice mail, walkie-talkie, bleeper, pager, tannoy, telex, teleprinter, facsimile, fax, computer, PDA (Personal Digital Assistant), email, Internet, World Wide Web, website, webcast, word processor, typewriter, dictaphone, megaphone, loudhailer; radar, Morse code, semaphore, Braille, sign language

communicative *adj* willing to give information, talkative ◇ **communicatively** *adv*
- talkative, voluble, expansive, informative, chatty, sociable, friendly, outgoing, extrovert, unreserved, free, open, frank, candid

communiqué /kə'mjuːnɪkeɪ/ *noun* an official announcement

communion *noun* **1** the act of sharing thoughts, feelings *etc*; fellowship **2** (**Communion**) in the Christian Church, the celebration of the Lord's Supper with consecrated bread and wine

communism *noun* a form of socialism where industry is controlled by the state ◇ **communist** *adj* of communism ◇ *noun* someone who believes in communism

community *noun* (*plural* **communities**) **1** a group of people living in one place **2** the public in general

commute *verb* **1** travel regularly between two places, *esp* between home and work **2** change (a punishment) for one less severe
- **1** travel, journey **2** reduce, decrease, mitigate, modify, adjust

commuter *noun* someone who travels regularly some distance to work from their home

compact[1] *adj* fitted or packed closely together; small or concise ◇ **compact disc** a small disc on which digitally recorded sound is registered to be read by a laser beam
- small, short, brief, succinct, concise, condensed, compressed, dense

compact[2] *noun* a bargain or agreement

companion noun someone or something that accompanies; a friend ◇ **companionable** adj friendly ◇ **companionship** noun friendship; the act of accompanying

■ fellow, comrade, friend, *informal* buddy, *informal* crony, intimate, confidant(e), ally

company noun (plural **companies**) **1** a gathering of people **2** a business firm **3** a part of a regiment **4** a ship's crew **5** the presence of others; companionship

■ **1** troupe, group, band, ensemble, party, gathering **2** firm, business, concern, corporation, association, partnership **5** guests, companionship, fellowship, support, presence

comparative adj **1** judged by comparing with something else; relative: *comparative improvement* **2** near to being: *a comparative stranger* **3** grammar the degree of an adjective or adverb between positive and superlative, *eg* blacker, better, *more* courageous

compare verb **1** set things together to see how similar or different they are **2** liken ◇ **comparable** adj

■ **1** juxtapose, balance, weigh, correlate **2** liken, equate

comparison noun the act of comparing

■ analogy, parallel, correlation, contrast

compartment noun a separate part or division, *eg* of a railway carriage

■ section, division, subdivision

compass noun (plural **compasses**) **1** an instrument with a magnetized needle for showing direction **2** (**compasses**) an instrument with one fixed and one movable leg for drawing circles

compassion noun pity for another's suffering; mercy ◇ **compassionate** adj pitying, merciful ◇ **compassionately** adv

■ kindness, tenderness, fellow-feeling, humanity, mercy, pity, sympathy, commiseration, condolence, sorrow, concern, care

☒ cruelty, indifference

compatible adj able to live together, work together *etc* ◇ **compatibility**

noun ◇ **compatibly** adv

■ like-minded, well-matched, similar

☒ incompatible

compatriot noun someone from the same country as you

■ fellow-countryman, fellow-countrywoman

compel verb (**compels**, **compelling**, **compelled**) force to do something

■ force, make, constrain, oblige, necessitate, drive, urge, impel, coerce, pressurize

compensate verb make up for wrong or damage done, *esp* by giving money ◇ **compensation** noun something given to make up for wrong or damage

■ repay, refund, reimburse, indemnify, recompense, reward, remunerate, atone, redeem, make good

compère noun someone who introduces acts as part of an entertainment ◇ verb act as compère

compete verb try to beat others in a race *etc*

■ vie, fight, oppose, challenge, rival, emulate, contend, participate

competent adj **1** capable, efficient **2** skilled; properly trained or qualified ◇ **competence** noun ◇ **competently** adv

■ **1** capable, able, adept, efficient **2** trained, qualified, well-qualified, skilled, experienced, proficient, expert

competition noun **1** a contest between rivals **2** rivalry

■ **1** contest, championship, tournament, cup, event, race, match, game **2** rivalry, opposition, challenge, contention, conflict, struggle, competitiveness, combativeness

competitive adj **1** of sport: based on competitions **2** fond of competing with others **3** involving rivalry: *a competitive industry* ◇ **competitively** adv ◇ **competitiveness** noun

■ **2** aggressive, pushy, ambitious, keen **3** cut-throat

competitor noun someone who competes; a rival

■ contestant, contender, candidate, challenger, rival, competition, opposition

compile *verb* make (a book *etc*) from information that has been collected ◇ **compilation** *noun* ◇ **compiler** *noun*
■ compose, put together, collect, gather, assemble, arrange

complacent *adj* self-satisfied ◇ **complacence** or **complacency** *noun* ◇ **complacently** *adv*
■ smug, self-satisfied, self-righteous

complain *verb* 1 express dissatisfaction about something 2 grumble
■ 1 protest, object 2 grumble, grouse, gripe, carp, whinge, *US informal* kvetch, fuss, lament, bemoan, bewail, moan, whine, groan

complainant *noun* 1 someone who complains 2 the plaintiff in a lawsuit

complaint *noun* 1 a statement of dissatisfaction 2 an illness
■ 1 objection, grumble, grouse, beef, grievance, criticism, censure, charge 2 ailment, illness, sickness, disease, disorder

complement *noun* something which completes or fills up ◇ **complementary** *adj* together making up a whole

❗ Do not confuse with: **compliment** and **complimentary**

complete *adj* 1 having nothing missing; whole 2 finished ◇ *verb* 1 finish 2 make whole ◇ **completely** *adv* ◇ **completeness** *noun* ◇ **completion** *noun*
■ *adj* 1 utter, total, whole, perfect, entire, full, intact 2 ended, concluded, over, accomplished, done
◼ *adj* 1 partial, abridged, incomplete 2 unfinished, incomplete

complex *adj* 1 made up of many parts 2 complicated, difficult ◇ *noun* (*plural* **complexes**) 1 a set of repressed emotions and ideas which affect someone's behaviour 2 an exaggerated reaction, an obsession: *has a complex about her height* 3 a group of related buildings: *a sports complex* ◇ **complexity** *noun* (*plural* **complexities**)
■ *adj* 1 multiple, composite, compound, ramified 2 complicated, intricate, elaborate, involved, convoluted ◇ *noun* 2

fixation, obsession, preoccupation, *informal* hang-up, phobia

complexion *noun* 1 the colour or look of the skin of the face 2 appearance

compliant *adj* yielding, giving agreement ◇ **compliance** *noun* ◇ **compliantly** *adv*

complicate *verb* make difficult ◇ **complicated** *adj* difficult to understand; detailed
■ **complicated** complex, intricate, elaborate, involved, convoluted, tortuous, difficult, problematic, puzzling, perplexing

complication *noun* 1 a difficulty 2 a development in an illness which makes things worse

complicity *noun* (*plural* **complicities**) participation with another in a crime or other misdeed

compliment *noun* 1 an expression of praise or flattery 2 (**compliments**) good wishes ◇ *verb* praise, congratulate: *complimented me on my cooking*
■ *noun* 1 flattery, admiration, approval, congratulations, commendation, praise
◼ *noun* 1 insult, criticism

❗ Do not confuse with: **complement**

complimentary *adj* 1 flattering, praising 2 given free: *complimentary ticket*
■ 1 flattering, admiring, favourable, approving, appreciative, congratulatory, commendatory 2 free, gratis, honorary, courtesy

Do not confuse with: **complementary**

comply *verb* (**complies**, **complying**, **complied**) agree to do something that someone else orders or wishes
■ agree, consent, assent, accede, yield, submit, defer, respect, obey

component *adj* forming one of the parts of a whole ◇ *noun* one of several parts, *eg* of a machine
■ *noun* part, ingredient, item, piece, bit, spare part

compose *verb* **1** put together or in order; arrange **2** create (a piece of music, a poem *etc*)

composed *adj* of a person: quiet, calm

▪ calm, tranquil, serene, relaxed, unruffled, level-headed, cool, collected, self-possessed, confident, imperturbable, unflappable

composer *noun* someone who writes music

composite *adj* made up of parts

composition *noun* **1** the act of composing **2** a created piece of writing or music **3** a mixture of things

▪ **1** making, production, creation, design, formulation, compilation, writing **2** work, opus, piece, study, essay **3** combination, mixture, configuration, arrangement

compositor *noun* someone who puts together the type for printing

composure *noun* calmness, self-possession

compos mentis sane, rational

compost *noun* a mixture of natural manures for spreading on soil

compound¹ *adj* **1** made up of a number of different parts **2** not simple ◊ *noun, chemistry* a substance formed from two or more elements

▪ *adj* **1** composite, multiple **2** complex, complicated, intricate

compound² *noun* an enclosure

comprehend *verb* **1** understand **2** include ◊ **comprehensible** *adj* able to be understood ◊ **comprehensibly** *adv* ◊ **comprehension** *noun*

▪ **comprehensible** understandable, intelligible, coherent, explicit, clear, plain, simple, straightforward

comprehensive *adj* taking in or including much or all ◊ **comprehensive school** a state-funded school providing all types of secondary education

▪ thorough, exhaustive, full, complete, broad, wide, extensive, general, inclusive, all-inclusive, all-embracing, across-the-board

compress *verb* **1** press together **2** force into a narrower or smaller space ◊ *noun* a pad used to create pressure on a part of the body or to reduce inflammation ◊ **compression** *noun*

▪ *verb* **1** press, squeeze, crush, squash, flatten **2** compact, concentrate, condense, contract, telescope, shorten, abbreviate, summarize

comprise *verb* **1** include, contain **2** consist of

⚠ Do not confuse with: **consist**

compromise *noun* an agreement reached by both sides giving up something ◊ *verb* **1** make a compromise **2** put in a difficult or embarrassing position

▪ *verb* **1** negotiate, bargain, arbitrate, settle, concede, meet halfway **2** undermine, expose, embarrass

compulsion *noun* a force driving someone to do something

compulsive *adj* unable to stop yourself, obsessional: *compulsive liar* ◊ **compulsively** *adv*

⚠ Do not confuse: **compulsive** and **compulsory**

compulsory *adj* required to be done; forced upon someone ◊ **compulsorily** *adv*

▪ obligatory, mandatory, imperative, forced, required, requisite

▪ voluntary

compunction *noun* regret

compute *verb* count, calculate ◊ **computation** *noun* counting, calculation

computer *noun* an electronic machine that stores, sorts and processes information of various kinds

Types of computer: mainframe, microcomputer, minicomputer, PC (personal computer), Apple Mac®, *informal* Mac, iMac®, desktop, laptop, notebook, palmtop, handheld;
Hardware: chip, silicon chip, circuit board, motherboard, CPU (central processing unit), card, graphics

card, sound card, video card, disk drive, floppy drive, hard drive, joystick, joypad, keyboard, light pen, microprocessor, modem, cable modem, monitor, mouse, pointer, printer, bubblejet printer, dot-matrix printer, inkjet printer, laser printer, screen, scanner, terminal, touchpad, trackball, VDU (visual display unit);

Software: program, application, abandonware, freeware, shareware;

Types of memory: backing storage, external memory, immediate access memory, internal memory, magnetic tape, RAM (Random Access Memory), ROM (Read Only Memory), CD-R (Compact Disc Recordable), CD-ROM (Compact Disc Read Only Memory), DVD-ROM (Digital Versatile Disc Read Only Memory);

Types of disk: Compact Disc (CD), Digital Versatile Disc (DVD), magnetic disk, floppy disk, hard disk, optical disk, zip disk;

Programming languages: BASIC, C, C++, COBOL, Delphi, FORTRAN, Java, Pascal;

Miscellaneous computing terms: access, ASCII, autosave, backup, binary, BIOS (Basic Input/Output System), bitmap, boot, cold boot, reboot, warm boot, buffer, bug, bus, byte, gigabyte, kilobyte, megabyte, terabyte, cache, character, character code, client-server, compression, computer game, computer graphics, computer literate, computer simulation, cracking, cursor, data, databank, database, debugging, default, desktop publishing (DTP), digitizer, directory, DOS (disk operating system), editor, email or e-mail, file, format, FTP (File Transfer Protocol), function, grammar checker, graphics, GUI (graphical user interface), hacking, icon, installation, interface, Internet, Linux, login, log off, log on, Mac OS (Macintosh® operating system),

macro, menu, message box, metafile, MS-DOS (Microsoft® disk operating system), mouse mat, multimedia, network, output, P2P (peer-to-peer), package, password, peripheral, pixel, platform, port, parallel port, serial port, protocol, script, scripting language, scrolling, shell, shellscript, spellchecker, spreadsheet, sprite, subdirectory, template, toggle, toolbar, Unicode, Unix®, upgrade, user-friendly, user interface, utilities, video game, virtual reality (VR), virus, virus checker, window, Windows®, word processing, workstation, World Wide Web (WWW), worm, WYSIWYG (what you see is what you get). *see also* **Internet**

computerize *verb* transfer a system to computer control ◊ **computerization** *noun*

comrade *noun* a companion, a friend

con *verb* (**cons**, **conning**, **conned**) trick, play a confidence trick on ◊ *noun* a confidence trick

▤ trick, hoax, dupe, deceive, mislead, inveigle, hoodwink, *informal* bamboozle, cheat, double-cross, swindle, *slang* sting, defraud, *slang* rip off

concave *adj* hollow or curved inwards (*contrasted with*: **convex**) ◊ **concavity** *noun* (*plural* **concavities**) a hollow

▤ hollow, hollowed, cupped, scooped, sunken, depressed

conceal *verb* hide, keep secret ◊ **concealment** *noun*

▤ hide, disguise, suppress, keep quiet, *informal* hush up

concede *verb* **1** give up, yield **2** admit the truth of something: *I concede that you may be right*

▤ **1** yield, give up, surrender **2** admit, confess, acknowledge, recognize, own, grant, allow, accept

conceit *noun* an excessively high opinion of yourself; vanity ◊ **conceited** *adj* full of conceit; vain ◊ **conceitedness** *noun*

▤ **conceited** vain, boastful, swollen-headed,

informal bigheaded, egotistical, self-important, cocky, self-satisfied, complacent, smug, proud, arrogant, *informal* stuck-up

conceive *verb* 1 form in the mind, imagine 2 become pregnant ◇ **conceivable** *adj* able to be imagined ◇ **conceivably** *adv*

▤ 1 imagine, understand, appreciate, think, grasp, see

concentrate *verb* 1 direct all your attention or effort towards something 2 bring together to one place ◇ **concentrated** *adj* made stronger or less dilute ◇ **concentration** *noun*

▤ **concentrated** condensed, evaporated, reduced, thickened, dense, rich, strong, undiluted

concentric *adj* of circles: placed one inside the other with the same centre point (*contrasted with:* **eccentric**)

concept *noun* a general idea about something ◇ **conception** *noun* 1 the act of conceiving 2 an idea

▤ idea, notion, plan, theory, hyphothesis, thought, abstraction, conception, conceptualization, visualization

concern *verb* 1 have to do with 2 make uneasy 3 interest, affect ◇ *noun* 1 anxiety 2 a cause of anxiety, a worry 3 a business ◇ **concerned** *adj* worried ◇ **concerning** *prep* about: *concerning your application* ◇ **concern yourself with** be worried about

▤ *verb* 1 relate to, refer to, regard 2 upset, distress, trouble, disturb, bother, worry 3 interest, affect, touch, involve, regard ◇ *noun* 1 anxiety, worry, unease, disquiet, care, sorrow, distress 3 company, firm, business, corporation, establishment, enterprise, organization

concert *noun* a musical performance ◇ **in concert** together

⚠ Do not confuse with: **consort**

concerted *adj* planned or performed together

▤ co-ordinated, organized, collaborative, prearranged, planned

▣ unco-ordinated, disorganized

concertina *noun* a type of musical instrument like a small accordion

concerto *noun* (*plural* **concertos**) a long piece of music for a solo instrument with orchestral accompaniment

concession *noun* 1 a granting or allowing of something: *a concession for oil exploration* 2 something granted or allowed 3 a reduction in the price of something for children, the unemployed, senior citizens *etc*

conch *noun* (*plural* **conches**) the shell of a large sea snail

concierge *noun* a warden in a residential building

conciliate *verb* win over (someone previously unfriendly or angry) ◇ **conciliation** *noun* ◇ **conciliatory** *adj*

concise *adj* brief, using few words ◇ **concisely** *adv* ◇ **conciseness** *noun*

▤ short, brief, succinct, pithy, compact, compressed, condensed, abridged

▣ diffuse, wordy

⚠ Do not confuse with: **precise**

conclude *verb* 1 end 2 reach a decision or judgement; settle ◇ **concluding** *adj* last, final

▤ 1 end, close, finish, complete, consummate, cease, terminate, culminate 2 settle, resolve, decide, establish, determine, clinch

conclusion *noun* 1 end 2 a decision, judgement

conclusive *adj* settling, deciding: *conclusive proof* ◇ **conclusively** *adv*

concoct *verb* 1 mix together (a dish or drink) 2 make up, invent: *concoct a story* ◇ **concoction** *noun*

concord *noun* agreement

concourse *noun* 1 a crowd 2 a large open space, *eg* in a railway station

concrete *adj* 1 solid, real 2 made of concrete ◇ *noun* a mixture of gravel, cement *etc* used in building

▤ *adj* 1 real, actual, factual, solid, substantial, tangible, perceptible

▣ *adj* 1 abstract, vague

concur *verb* (**concurs, concurring, concurred**) 1 agree 2 happen together ◇ **concurrence** *noun*

concurrent adj **1** happening together **2** agreeing ◊ **concurrently** adv

■ **1** simultaneous, synchronous, contemporaneous, coinciding, coincident, concomitant, coexisting, coexistent

concussion noun temporary harm done to the brain from a knock on the head

condemn verb **1** blame; express disapproval of **2** sentence (to a certain punishment) **3** declare (a building) unfit for use ◊ **condemnation** noun

■ **1** disapprove, reprehend, reprove, upbraid, reproach, castigate, blame, disparage, revile, denounce, censure, informal slate **2** convict

condensation noun **1** the act of condensing **2** drops of liquid formed from vapour

condense verb **1** make smaller or shorter **2** of steam: turn to liquid

■ **1** contract, compress, compact, summarize, précis, abridge, abbreviate, shorten

condescend verb act towards someone as if you are better than them ◊ **condescending** adj ◊ **condescendingly** adv ◊ **condescension** noun

■ **condescending** patronizing, supercilious, snooty, snobbish, haughty, lofty, superior, imperious

condiment noun a seasoning for food, esp salt or pepper

condition noun **1** the state in which anything is: in poor condition **2** something that must happen before some other thing happens **3** a point in a bargain, treaty etc

conditional adj depending on certain things happening ◊ **conditionally** adv

■ provisional, qualified, limited, restricted, relative, dependent, contingent

condolence noun sharing in another's sorrow; sympathy

condom noun a contraceptive rubber sheath worn by a man

condone verb allow (an offence) to pass unchecked

■ forgive, pardon, excuse, overlook, ignore, disregard, tolerate, brook, allow

Ea condemn, censure

conducive adj helping, favourable (to): conducive to peace

■ leading, tending, contributory, encouraging, favourable

Ea detrimental, adverse, unfavourable

conduct verb /kən'dʌkt/ **1** lead, guide **2** control, be in charge of **3** direct (an orchestra) **4** transmit (electricity etc) **5** behave: conducted himself correctly ◊ noun /'kɒndəkt/ behaviour ◊ **conduction** noun transmission of heat, electricity etc

■ verb **1** accompany, escort, usher, lead, guide, direct, pilot, steer **2** administer, manage, run, organize, orchestrate, chair, control, handle, regulate **4** convey, carry, bear, transmit **5** behave, acquit oneself, act

conductor noun **1** someone who directs an orchestra **2** someone who collects fares on a bus etc **3** something that transmits heat, electricity etc

conduit /'kɒndjʊɪt/ noun a channel or pipe to carry water, electric wires etc

cone noun **1** a shape that is round at the bottom and comes to a point **2** the fruit of a pine or fir tree etc **3** an ice-cream cornet

coney another spelling of **cony**

confection noun a sweet food, eg a cake or sweet ◊ **confectioner** noun someone who makes or sells sweets, cakes etc ◊ **confectionery** noun **1** sweets, cakes etc **2** the shop or business of a confectioner

confederacy noun (plural **confederacies**) a league, an alliance, esp of states

confederate adj joined together by treaty ◊ noun someone acting in an alliance with others

confederation noun a union, a league

confer verb (**confers, conferring, conferred**) **1** talk together **2** give, grant: confer a degree

■ **1** discuss, debate, deliberate, consult,

talk, converse **2** bestow, award, present, give, grant, accord

conference *noun* a meeting for discussion

■ meeting, convention, congress, forum, discussion, debate, consultation

confess *verb* own up, admit to (wrongdoing) ◇ **confessed** *adj* admitted, not secret ◇ **confession** *noun* an admission of wrongdoing

■ admit, confide, own (up), *informal* come clean, grant, concede

confetti *noun plural* small pieces of coloured paper thrown at weddings or other celebrations

confidant *noun* someone trusted with a secret

🚹 Do not confuse with: **confident**

confidante *noun* a female confidant

confide *verb* **1** tell (a secret): *confide your fears* **2** hand over to someone's care ◇ **confiding** *adj* trusting ◇ **confide in** tell secrets to

■ **1** reveal, disclose, tell, impart, unburden

confidence *noun* **1** trust, belief **2** self-assurance, boldness **3** something told privately ◇ **confidence trick** a swindle which involves first winning the trust of the victim

confident *adj* **1** very self-assured **2** certain of an outcome: *confident that they would win* ◇ **confidently** *adv*

■ **1** composed, self-possessed, cool, self-confident, bold, fearless, dauntless, unabashed **2** sure, certain, positive, convinced, assured

🚹 Do not confuse with: **confidant** and **confidante**

confidential *adj* **1** to be kept as a secret: *confidential information* **2** entrusted with secrets ◇ **confidentially** *adv*

■ **1** secret, top secret, classified, *informal* hush-hush, off-the-record, private, personal, privy

confine *verb* **1** shut up, imprison **2** keep within limits ◇ **confinement** *noun* **1** the state of being confined **2**

imprisonment **3** the time of a woman's labour and childbirth ◇ **confines** *noun plural* limits

■ **1** imprison, incarcerate, intern, cage, shut up **2** enclose, circumscribe, bound, limit, restrict, cramp, constrain

confirm *verb* **1** make firm, strengthen **2** make sure **3** show to be true **4** admit into full membership of a church

■ **1** endorse, back, support, reinforce, strengthen, fortify **3** corroborate, substantiate, verify, prove

confirmation *noun* **1** the act of making sure **2** proof **3** the ceremony by which someone is made a full member of a church

confirmed *adj* settled in a habit *etc*: *a confirmed bachelor*

■ inveterate, dyed-in-the-wool, established, long-standing, habitual, seasoned, hardened, incorrigible, incurable

confiscate *verb* take away as a punishment ◇ **confiscation** *noun*

■ seize, appropriate, expropriate, remove, take away, impound, sequester, commandeer

conflagration *noun* a large, widespread fire

conflict *noun* **1** a struggle, a contest **2** a battle **3** disagreement **4** a clash or contradiction ◇ *verb* of statements *etc*: contradict each other ◇ **conflicting** *adj*

■ *verb* differ, disagree, contradict

confluence *noun* a place where rivers join

conform *verb* follow the example of most other people in behaviour, dress *etc* ◇ **conformity** *noun* (*plural* **conformities**) **1** likeness **2** the act of conforming

■ harmonize, match, tally, square, adapt, adjust, comply, follow

conformation *noun* shape, structure or arrangement

confound *verb* puzzle, confuse

■ confuse, bewilder, baffle, perplex, mystify, puzzle

confront *verb* **1** face, meet: *confronted the difficulty* **2** bring face to face

(with): *confronted with the evidence*
◇ **confrontation** *noun*
■ **1** face, meet, encounter, accost, address, oppose, challenge, defy, brave

confuse *verb* **1** mix up, disorder **2** puzzle, bewilder ◇ **confused** *adj* ◇ **confusion** *noun* ◇ **confusing** *adj* puzzling, bewildering ◇ **confusingly** *adv*
■ **confused** puzzled, baffled, perplexed, *informal* flummoxed, nonplussed, bewildered, disorientated

congeal *verb* **1** become solid, *esp* by cooling **2** freeze
■ **1** coagulate, thicken, solidify, set

congenial *adj* agreeable, pleasant
◇ **congenially** *adv*

congenital *adj* of a disease: present in someone from birth

conger *noun* a kind of large sea eel

congested *adj* **1** overcrowded **2** clogged **3** of part of the body: too full of blood, mucus *etc* ◇ **congestion** *noun*
■ **2** clogged, blocked, jammed, packed, stuffed, crammed, full, crowded, overcrowded

conglomeration *noun* a heap or collection
■ mass, accumulation, collection, medley, hotchpotch

congratulate *verb* express joy to (someone) at their success ◇ **congratulations** *noun plural* an expression of joy at someone's success ◇ **congratulatory** *adj*
■ praise, compliment, wish well
◤ commiserate

congregate *verb* come together in a crowd ◇ **congregation** *noun* a gathering, *esp* of people in a church
■ gather, assemble, collect, muster, rally, meet, convene, converge, flock, crowd, throng

congress *noun* (*plural* **congresses**) **1** a large meeting of people from different countries *etc* for discussion **2** (**Congress**) the parliament of the United States, consisting of the Senate and the House of Representatives

congruent *adj* of triangles: exactly matching

congruous *adj* suitable, appropriate
◇ **congruity** *noun* ◇ **congruously** *adv*

conical *adj* cone-shaped

conifer *noun* a cone-bearing tree
◇ **coniferous** *adj*

conjecture *noun* a guess ◇ *verb* guess ◇ **conjectural** *adj*
■ *noun* speculation, guesswork, guess, estimate, supposition, surmise, assumption, presumption, inference, extrapolation, projection

conjoined twins (*also called*: **Siamese twins**) twins joined by their flesh at birth

conjugal *adj* of marriage

conjugate *verb* give the different grammatical parts of (a verb) ◇ **conjugation** *noun*

conjunction *noun* **1** *grammar* a word that joins sentences or phrases, *eg* and, but **2** a union, a combination ◇ **in conjunction with** together with, acting with

conjunctivitis *noun* inflammation of the inside of the eyelid and surface of the eye

conjure *verb* perform tricks that seem magical ◇ **conjuror** or **conjurer** *noun* someone who performs conjuring tricks

conker *noun* **1** the nut of a horse-chestnut tree **2** (**conkers**) a game in which players try to hit and destroy each other's conker, held on the end of a string

conman *noun* someone who regularly cons people, a swindler

connect *verb* join or fasten together
◇ **connected** *adj* related, associated: *inquiries connected with the crime*
■ join, link, unite, couple, combine, fasten, affix, attach

connection *noun* **1** something that connects **2** a state of being connected **3** a train, aeroplane *etc* which takes you to the next part of a journey **4** an acquaintance, a friend ◇ **in connection with** concerning

connive *verb*: **connive at** disregard (a misdeed) ◇ **connivance** *noun*

connoisseur /kɒnɪ'sɜː/ *noun* someone with an expert knowledge of a subject: *wine connoisseur*

▪ authority, specialist, expert, *informal* buff

connotation *noun* 1 a meaning 2 what is suggested by a word in addition to its simple meaning

▪ 2 implication, suggestion, hint, nuance, undertone, overtone, colouring, association

conquer *verb* 1 gain (territory) by force 2 overcome: *conquered his fear of heights* ◇ **conqueror** *noun*

▪ 1 seize, annex, occupy, possess 2 overcome, surmount, overpower, master

conquest *noun* 1 something won by force 2 the act of conquering

conscience *noun* an inner sense of what is right and wrong

conscientious *adj* careful and diligent in work *etc* ◇ **conscientiously** *adv* ◇ **conscientiousness** *noun*

▪ diligent, hard-working, scrupulous, painstaking, thorough

conscious *adj* 1 aware of yourself and your surroundings; awake 2 aware, knowing 3 deliberate, intentional: *a conscious decision* ◇ **consciously** *adv* ◇ **consciousness** *noun*

conscript *noun* someone obliged by law to serve in the armed forces ◇ *verb* compel to serve in the armed forces ◇ **conscription** *noun*

consecrate *verb* set apart for sacred use ◇ **consecrated** *adj* ◇ **consecration** *noun*

consecutive *adj* coming in order, one after the other

consensus *noun* an agreement of opinion

⚠ Do not confuse with: **census**

consent *verb* agree (to) ◇ *noun* 1 agreement 2 permission

▪ *verb* agree, concur, accede, assent, approve, permit, allow, grant, admit, concede, acquiesce, yield

consequence *noun* 1 something that follows as a result 2 importance

▪ 1 result, outcome, upshot, effect, side effect, repercussion 2 importance, significance, concern, value

consequent *adj* following as a result ◇ **consequently** *adv*

▪ resultant, resulting, ensuing, subsequent, following

consequential *adj* 1 following as a result 2 important ◇ **consequentially** *adv*

conservation *noun* the maintaining of old buildings, the countryside *etc* in an undamaged state ◇ **conservationist** *noun* someone who encourages and practises conservation

▪ preservation, protection, ecology, environmentalism

conservative *adj* 1 resistant to change 2 moderate, not extreme: *a conservative estimate* ◇ *noun* 1 someone of conservative views 2 (**Conservative**) a supporter of the Conservative Party ◇ **Conservative Party** a right-wing political party in the UK

▪ *adj* 1 hidebound, reactionary, establishmentarian, unprogressive, conventional, traditional, *informal* button-down 2 moderate, middle-of-the-road, cautious, guarded, sober ◇ *noun* 2 Tory, right-winger

◆ *adj* 1 radical, innovative ◇ *noun* 2 left-winger, liberal

conservatory *noun* (*plural* **conservatories**) a glasshouse attached to a building

conserve *verb* keep from being wasted, damaged or lost; preserve

▪ keep, save, store up, hoard, maintain, preserve, protect, guard, safeguard

◆ use, waste, squander

consider *verb* 1 think about carefully 2 think of as, regard as 3 pay attention to the needs and wishes of (someone) ◇ **considering** *prep* taking into account: *considering your age*

▪ 1 ponder, deliberate, reflect, contemplate, meditate, muse, mull over, chew over, examine, study, weigh, take into account 2 regard, deem, think, believe, judge, count

considerable *adj* large, substantial
◇ **considerably** *adv*

☰ large, sizable, substantial, *informal* tidy, appreciable, significant

🔁 small, slight, insignificant, unremarkable

considerate *adj* taking others' needs and wishes into account; thoughtful

☰ kind, thoughtful, caring, altruistic

🔁 thoughtless, selfish

consideration *noun* **1** serious thought **2** thoughtfulness for others **3** a small payment

☰ **1** thought, deliberation, reflection, meditation, analysis, review

consign *verb* give into the care of another ◇ **consignment** *noun* a load, *eg* of goods

consist *verb*: **consist of** be made up of

☰ comprise, be composed of, contain, include, incorporate, embody, embrace, involve, amount to

❗ Do not confuse with: **comprise**

consistency *noun* (*plural* **consistencies**) **1** thickness, firmness **2** the quality of always being the same

☰ **1** viscosity, thickness, density, firmness **2** evenness, uniformity, sameness, constancy

consistent *adj* **1** not changing, regular **2** of statements *etc*: not contradicting each other ◇ **consistently** *adv*

☰ **1** steady, stable, regular, uniform, unchanging, undeviating, constant, persistent **2** agreeing, accordant, consonant, congruous, compatible

console[1] /'kɒn'soʊl/ *verb* comfort, cheer up ◇ **consolation** *noun* something that makes trouble *etc* more easy to bear

console[2] /'kɒnsoʊl/ *noun* **1** a panel of dials, switches *etc* for operating equipment **2** a cabinet for audio or video equipment

consolidate *verb* **1** make or become strong **2** unite ◇ **consolidation** *noun*

consonant *noun* a letter of the alphabet that is not a vowel, *eg* b, c, d

consort *noun* **1** a husband or wife **2** a companion ◇ *verb* keep company (with)

❗ Do not confuse with: **concert**

conspicuous *adj* clearly seen, noticeable ◇ **conspicuously** *adv* ◇ **conspicuousness** *noun*

☰ apparent, visible, noticeable, marked, clear, obvious, evident, patent, manifest, prominent, striking, blatant, flagrant, glaring, ostentatious

conspiracy *noun* (*plural* **conspiracies**) a plot by a group of people ◇ **conspirator** *noun* someone who takes part in a conspiracy

☰ plot, scheme, intrigue, machination, collusion, league, treason ◇ **conspirator** conspirer, plotter, schemer, intriguer, traitor

conspire *verb* plan or plot together

constable *noun* a police officer of the lowest rank

constant *adj* **1** never stopping **2** never changing **3** faithful ◇ **constancy** *noun* ◇ **constantly** *adv* always

☰ **1** continuous, unbroken, never-ending, non-stop, endless, interminable, ceaseless, incessant **3** loyal, faithful, staunch, steadfast, dependable, trustworthy, true, devoted

🔁 **1** variable, irregular, fitful, occasional **3** disloyal

constellation *noun* a group of stars

consternation *noun* dismay, astonishment

constipation *noun* sluggish working of the bowels ◇ **constipate** *verb* cause constipation in ◇ **constipated** *adj*

constituency *noun* (*plural* **constituencies**) **1** a district which has a member of parliament **2** the voters in such a district

constituent *adj* making or forming a part ◇ *noun* **1** a necessary part **2** a voter in a constituency

☰ *noun* **1** ingredient, element, factor, component, part, bit

constitute *verb* **1** set up, establish **2** form, make up **3** be the equivalent of: *this action constitutes a crime*

☰ **1** form, create, establish, set up, found **2** make up, compose, comprise

constitution *noun* **1** the way in which something is made up **2** the natural condition of a body in terms of health *etc*: *a weak constitution* **3** a set of laws or rules governing a country or organization ◇ **constitutional** *adj* of a constitution ◇ *noun* a short walk for the sake of your health

constrain *verb* force to act in a certain way

☰ force, compel, oblige, necessitate, drive, impel, urge, limit, confine, constrict

constraint *noun* **1** compulsion, force **2** restraint, repression

constrict *verb* **1** press together tightly **2** surround and squeeze

construct *verb* build, make ◇ **construction** *noun* **1** the act of constructing **2** something built **3** the arrangement of words in a sentence **4** meaning

☰ build, erect, raise, elevate, make, manufacture, fabricate, assemble, put together, form, shape, fashion, model, design, engineer, create

constructive *adj* **1** of construction **2** helping to improve: *constructive criticism* ◇ **constructively** *adv*

consul *noun* **1** someone who looks after their country's affairs in a foreign country **2** *hist* a chief ruler in ancient Rome ◇ **consular** *adj*

consulate *noun* **1** the official residence of a consul **2** the duties and authority of a consul

consult *verb* seek advice or information from ◇ **consultation** *noun*

☰ refer to, ask, question, interrogate

consultant *noun* **1** someone who gives professional or expert advice **2** a hospital doctor of the senior grade

consume *verb* **1** eat up **2** use (up) **3** destroy: *consumed by fire* ◇ **consumer** *noun* someone who buys, eats or uses goods

☰ **1** eat, drink, swallow, devour, gobble **2** use, absorb, spend, expend, deplete,

drain, exhaust, use up **3** destroy, demolish, annihilate, devastate, ravage

consummate *verb* /'kɒnsəmeɪt/ **1** complete, perfect **2** make (marriage) legally complete by sexual intercourse ◇ *adj* /kən'sʌmət/ complete, perfect

consumption *noun* **1** the act of consuming **2** an amount consumed **3** *old* tuberculosis

cont. *abbrev* continued

contact *noun* **1** touch **2** meeting, communication **3** an acquaintance; someone who can be of help: *business contacts* ◇ *verb* get into contact with ◇ **contact lens** a plastic lens worn in the eye instead of spectacles

☰ *verb* approach, apply to, reach, get hold of, get in touch with, telephone, phone, ring, call, notify

contagious *adj* of disease: spreading from person to person, *esp* by touch

☰ infectious, catching, communicable, transmissible, spreading

contain *verb* **1** hold or have inside **2** hold back: *couldn't contain her anger*

☰ **1** include, comprise, incorporate, embody, involve, embrace, enclose, hold, accommodate **2** repress, stifle, restrain, control, check, curb, limit

container *noun* a box, tin, jar *etc* for holding anything

contaminate *verb* make impure or dirty ◇ **contamination** *noun*

☰ infect, pollute, taint, soil, adulterate

☲ purify

contd. *abbrev* continued

contemplate *verb* **1** look at or think about attentively **2** intend: *contemplating suicide* ◇ **contemplation** *noun*

☰ **1** meditate, reflect on, ponder, mull over, deliberate, consider, regard, view, survey, observe, study, examine, inspect, scrutinize

contemporary *adj* **1** belonging to the same time **2** modern ◇ *noun* someone of roughly the same age as yourself

contempt *noun* complete lack of respect; scorn

☰ scorn, disdain, disrespect, dishonour, disregard, neglect, dislike

contemptible *adj* deserving scorn, worthless
◼ despicable, detestable, loathsome, worthless

🛇 Do not confuse: **contemptible** and **contemptuous**

contemptuous *adj* scornful
◼ scornful, disdainful, sneering, derisive

contend *verb* **1** struggle against **2** hold firmly to a belief; maintain (that)

content /kɒnˈtɛnt/ *adj* happy, satisfied ◇ *noun* happiness, satisfaction ◇ *verb* make happy, satisfy ◇ **contented** *adj* happy, content ◇ **contentment** *noun* happiness, content
◼ *adj* satisfied, fulfilled, contented, untroubled, pleased, happy

contention *noun* **1** an opinion strongly held **2** a quarrel, a dispute

contentious *adj* quarrelsome ◇ **contentiously** *adv*

contents /ˈkɒntɛnts/ *noun* that which is contained in anything

contest *verb* **1** fight for **2** argue against ◇ *noun* a fight, a competition ◇ **contestant** *noun* a participant in a contest
◼ *noun* competition, game, match, tournament, encounter, fight, battle, set-to, combat, conflict

context *noun* **1** the place in a book *etc* to which a certain word or passage belongs **2** the background of an event, remark *etc*

contiguous *adj* touching, close ◇ **contiguity** *noun* ◇ **contiguously** *adv*

continent *noun* one of the five large divisions of the earth's land surface (Europe, Asia, Africa, Australia, America) ◇ **continental** *adj* **1** of a continent **2** *Brit* of the Continent ◇ **the Continent** *Brit* the mainland of Europe

contingency *noun* (*plural* **contingencies**) a chance happening ◇ **contingency plan** a plan of action in case something does not happen as expected

contingent *adj* depending (on)

◇ *noun* a group, *esp* of soldiers
◼ *noun* body, company, detachment, section, group

continual *adj* going on without stopping or happening repeatedly ◇ **continually** *adv*
◼ constant, perpetual, incessant, interminable, eternal, everlasting, regular, frequent, recurrent, repeated

🛇 Do not confuse with: **continuous**

continuation *noun* **1** the act of continuing **2** a part that continues, an extension

continue *verb* go on (doing something)

continuity *noun* the state of having no gaps or breaks

continuous *adj* coming one after the other without a gap or break ◇ **continuously** *adv*

🛇 Do not confuse with: **continual**

contort *verb* twist or turn violently ◇ **contortion** *noun* a violent twisting ◇ **contortionist** *noun* someone who can twist their body violently out of shape

contour *noun* (often **contours**) outline, shape ◇ **contour line** a line drawn on a map through points at the same height above sea-level

contraband *noun* goods legally forbidden to be brought into a country, smuggled goods

contraception *noun* the prevention of pregnancy

contraceptive *adj* used to prevent the conceiving of children ◇ *noun* a contraceptive device or drug

contract *verb* **1** become or make smaller **2** catch (a disease) **3** promise in writing, make a legal agreement ◇ *noun* a written agreement
◼ *verb* **1** shrink, lessen, diminish, reduce, shorten, curtail, abbreviate

contraction *noun* **1** the act of contracting **2** a shortened form of a word **3** a muscle spasm, *eg* during childbirth

contractor *noun* someone who

promises to do work, or supply goods, at an arranged price

contradict *verb* say the opposite of; deny ◊ **contradiction** *noun* ◊ **contradictory** *adj*

▣ deny, confute, challenge, oppose, dispute, counter, gainsay ◊ **contradictory** contrary, opposite, paradoxical, conflicting, inconsistent, incompatible, irreconcilable

contralto *noun* (*plural* **contraltos**) the lowest singing voice in women

contraption *noun* a machine, a device

contrapuntal *see* **counterpoint**

contrary¹ /'kɒntrərɪ/ *adj* opposite ◊ *noun* the opposite ◊ **on the contrary** in contrast to what has just been said

contrary² /kɒn'trɛərɪ/ *adj* always doing or saying the opposite, perverse ◊ **contrariness** *noun*

▣ perverse, awkward, difficult

contrast *verb* **1** compare so as to show differences **2** show a marked difference from ◊ *noun* a difference between (two) things

▣ *noun* difference, dissimilarity, disparity, divergence, distinction

contravene *verb* break (a law *etc*) ◊ **contravention** *noun*

▣ break, disobey, defy, flout, transgress, infringe

contretemps /'kɒntrətɑ̃/ *noun* **1** a mishap at an awkward moment **2** a slight disagreement

contribute *verb* **1** give (money, help *etc*) along with others **2** supply (articles *etc*) for a publication **3** help to cause: *contributed to a nervous breakdown* ◊ **contribution** *noun* ◊ **contributor** *noun*

▣ **1** donate, subscribe, *informal* chip in, give

contrite *adj* very sorry for having done wrong ◊ **contrition** *noun*

▣ sorry, regretful, remorseful, repentant, penitent, chastened, humble, ashamed

contrive *verb* **1** plan, devise **2** bring about, manage: *contrived to be out of the office* ◊ **contrivance** *noun* **1** an act

of contriving **2** an ingenious device ◊ **contrived** *adj* unnatural

▣ **contrived** unnatural, artificial, false, forced, elaborate

control *noun* **1** authority or ability to rule, manage, restrain *etc* **2** (often **controls**) means by which someone keeps a machine powered or guided ◊ *verb* (**controls**, **controlling**, **controlled**) **1** exercise control over; have power over **2** operate or regulate (a machine, system *etc*) ◊ **controlled** *adj* ◊ **controller** *noun*

▣ *noun* **1** power, charge, authority, mastery, government, rule ◊ *verb* **1** lead, govern, rule, command, direct, manage, oversee, supervise

controversy *noun* (*plural* **controversies**) an argument, a disagreement ◊ **controversial** *adj* likely to cause argument ◊ **controversially** *adv*

▣ **controversial** contentious, polemical, disputed, questionable, debatable, disputable

conundrum *noun* a riddle, a question

conurbation *noun* a group of towns forming a single built-up area

convalesce *verb* recover health gradually after being ill ◊ **convalescence** *noun* ◊ **convalescent** *noun*

convection *noun* the spreading of heat by movement of heated air or water

convector *noun* a heater which works by convection

convene *verb* call or come together for a meeting ◊ **convener** *noun* **1** someone who calls a meeting **2** the chairman or chairwoman of a committee

convenience *noun* **1** suitableness, handiness **2** a means of giving ease or comfort **3** *informal* a public lavatory

convenient *adj* **1** easy to reach or use, handy **2** not causing trouble or difficulty; suitable ◊ **conveniently** *adv*

▣ **1** nearby, at hand, accessible, available, handy, useful, commodious, beneficial, helpful, labour-saving

convent *noun* a building accommodating an order of nuns

convention *noun* **1** a way of behaving that has become usual, a custom **2** a large meeting, an assembly **3** a treaty or agreement ◇ **conventional** *adj* done by habit or custom ◇ **conventionally** *adv*

■ **conventional** traditional, orthodox, formal, correct, proper, accepted, received, expected, ritual, routine, usual, customary, regular

converge *verb* come together, meet at a point ◇ **convergence** *noun* ◇ **convergent** *adj*
🔁 diverge

conversation *noun* talk, exchange of ideas, news *etc* ◇ **conversational** *adj* **1** of conversation **2** talkative

■ talk, chat, gossip, discussion, dialogue, exchange

converse[1] /kən'vɜːs/ *verb* talk ◇ *noun* conversation

converse[2] /'kɒnvɜːs/ *noun* the opposite ◇ *adj* opposite

■ *noun* opposite, reverse, contrary, antithesis

convert *verb* **1** change (from one thing into another) **2** turn from one religion, opinion *etc* to another ◇ *noun* someone who has been converted to another religion *etc* ◇ **conversion** *noun* ◇ **convertible** *adj* able to be changed from one thing to another ◇ *noun* a car with a folding roof

■ *verb* **1** alter, change, turn, transform, adapt, modify, remodel, restyle, revise

convex *adj* curved on the outside (*contrasted with:* **concave**) ◇ **convexity** *noun* (*plural* **convexities**)

■ rounded, bulging, protuberant

convey *verb* **1** carry, transport **2** send **3** *law* hand over: *convey property* ◇ **conveyance** *noun* **1** the act of conveying **2** a vehicle ◇ **conveyor** or **conveyor belt** an endless moving mechanism for conveying articles, *esp* in a factory

■ **1** carry, bear, bring, fetch, move, transport **2** send, forward, deliver, transfer, conduct

convict *verb* declare or prove that someone is guilty ◇ *noun* someone found guilty of a crime and sent to prison ◇ **conviction** *noun* **1** the passing of a guilty sentence on someone in court **2** a strong belief

■ *noun* criminal, felon, culprit, prisoner ◇ **conviction 2** confidence, certainty, persuasion, view, opinion, belief, faith, tenet

convince *verb* make (someone) believe that something is true; persuade (someone)

■ assure, persuade, sway, win over, bring round, reassure

convivial *adj* jolly, festive, sociable ◇ **conviviality** *noun*

convocation *noun* a meeting, *esp* of bishops or heads of a university

convolvulus *noun* a twining plant with trumpet-shaped flowers

convoy *verb* go along with and protect ◇ *noun* a group of lorries, ships *etc* travelling together or protected by an escort

convulse *verb* cause to shake violently: *convulsed with laughter* ◇ **convulsion** *noun* **1** a sudden stiffening or jerking of the muscles **2** a violent disturbance ◇ **convulsive** *adj*

■ **convulsion 1** fit, seizure, paroxysm, spasm, cramp, contraction

cony or **coney** *noun* **1** a rabbit **2** rabbit fur

coo *noun* a sound like that of a dove ◇ *verb* make this sound

cook *verb* **1** prepare (food) by heating **2** *informal* alter (accounts *etc*) dishonestly ◇ *noun* someone who cooks and prepares food

---

Ways of cooking include:
bake, barbecue, boil, braise, broil, casserole, chargrill, coddle, deep-fry, fry, griddle, grill, microwave, poach, pot-roast, roast, sauté, scramble, sear, simmer, spit-roast, steam, stew, stir-fry, toast; prepare, heat

---

cooker *noun* **1** a stove for cooking **2** an apple *etc* used in cooking, not for eating raw

cookery *noun* the art of cooking

cookie *noun*, *US* a biscuit

cool *adj* **1** slightly cold **2** calm, not excited **3** *informal* good, acceptable ◇ *verb* make or grow cool ◇ **coolly** *adj* ◇ **coolness** *noun*
■ *adj* **1** chilly, fresh, breezy, nippy, cold, chilled, iced, refreshing **2** calm, unruffled, unexcited, composed, self-possessed, level-headed, unemotional, quiet, relaxed, *informal* laid-back

coop *noun* a box or cage for hens *etc* ◇ *verb* shut (up) as in a coop

co-operate *verb* work or act together
■ *verb* collaborate, work together, *informal* play ball, combine, unite, conspire

co-operation *noun* **1** working together **2** willingness to help or work together

co-operative *noun* a business or farm *etc* owned by the workers ◇ *adj* co-operating or willing to co-operate ◇ **co-operative society** or **co-op** a trading organization in which the profits are shared among members

co-opt *verb* choose (someone) to join a committee or other body

co-ordinate *verb* make things fit in, match or work smoothly together ◇ **co-ordination** *noun*
■ organize, arrange, systematize, tabulate, integrate, mesh, synchronize, harmonize, match, correlate, regulate

coot *noun* a water-bird with a white spot on the forehead

cop *noun*, *Brit slang* a police officer ◇ *verb* (**cops**, **copping**, **copped**) catch, seize ◇ **cop it** land in trouble ◇ **cop out** avoid responsibility

cope *verb* struggle or deal successfully (with), manage
■ manage, carry on, survive, get by, make do, deal with, contend with, struggle with, grapple with, wrestle with, handle, manage

coping *noun* the top layer of stone in a wall ◇ **coping-stone** *noun* the top stone of a wall

copious *adj* plentiful ◇ **copiously** *adj*
■ abundant, plentiful, inexhaustible, overflowing, profuse, rich, lavish, bountiful, liberal, full, ample, generous, extensive

copper *noun* **1** a hard reddish-brown metal **2** a reddish-brown colour **3** a coin made from copper or similar metal **4** a large metal vessel for boiling water ◇ **copperplate** *noun* a style of very fine and regular handwriting

copse or **coppice** *noun* a wood of low-growing trees

copy *noun* (*plural* **copies**) **1** an imitation **2** a print or reproduction of a picture, document, *etc* **3** an individual example of a certain book *etc* ◇ *verb* (**copies, copying, copied**) **1** make a copy of **2** imitate
■ *noun* **1** counterfeit, forgery, fake, imitation, borrowing, plagiarism, crib **2** duplicate, carbon copy, photocopy, Photostat®, Xerox®, facsimile, reproduction, print, tracing ◇ *verb* **1** duplicate, photocopy, reproduce, print, trace **2** counterfeit, simulate, imitate, impersonate, mimic, ape, parrot, repeat, echo, mirror, follow, emulate

copyright *noun* the right of one person or body to publish a book, perform a play, print music *etc* ◇ *adj* of or protected by the law of copyright

coquette *noun* a flirtatious woman ◇ **coquettish** *adj* flirtatious

coral *noun* a hard substance made from the skeletons of a tiny sea animal ◇ **coral reef** a rock-like mass of coral built up gradually

cord *noun* **1** thin rope or strong string **2** anything resembling this
■ **1** string, twine, rope **2** line, cable, flex, connection, link, bond, tie

> **!** Do not confuse with: **chord**

cordial *adj* cheery, friendly ◇ *noun* a refreshing drink ◇ **cordiality** *noun*

cordon *noun* a line of guards, police *etc* to keep people back

cordon bleu *adj* of a cook or cooking: first-class, excellent

> Literally 'blue ribbon' in French, after the ribbon worn by the Knights of the Holy Ghost

corduroy *noun* a cotton cloth ribbed with velvet-like pile

core *noun* the inner part of anything, *esp* fruit ◇ *verb* take out the core of (fruit)
■ *noun* kernel, nucleus, heart, centre, middle, nub, crux, essence

co-respondent *noun* a man or woman charged with having committed adultery with a wife or husband (the **respondent**)

⚠ Do not confuse with: **correspondent**

corgi *noun* a breed of short-legged dog

coriander *noun* the leaves of the coriander plant, used dried in cooking

cork *noun* 1 the outer bark of a type of oak found in southern Europe *etc* 2 a stopper for a bottle *etc* made of cork ◇ *adj* made of cork ◇ *verb* plug or stop up with a cork

corkscrew *noun* a tool with a screw-like spike for taking out corks ◇ *adj* shaped like a corkscrew

corm *noun* the bulb-like underground stem of certain plants

cormorant *noun* a type of big sea-bird

corn¹ *noun* 1 wheat, oats or a similar crop 2 maize: *corn on the cob* ◇ **corned beef** salted tinned beef

corn² *noun* a small lump of hard skin, *esp* on the foot

cornea *noun* the transparent covering of the eyeball

corner *noun* 1 the point where two walls, roads *etc* meet 2 a small secluded place 3 *informal* a difficult situation ◇ *verb* force into a position from which there is no escape
■ *noun* 1 angle, joint, crook, bend, turning 2 nook, cranny, niche, recess, cavity, hole, hideout, hideaway, retreat

cornerstone *noun* 1 the stone at the corner of a building's foundations 2 something upon which much depends

cornet *noun* 1 a musical instrument like a small trumpet 2 an ice-cream in a cone-shaped wafer

cornflour *noun* finely ground maize flour

cornflower *noun* a type of plant with blue flowers

cornice *noun* an ornamental border round a ceiling

corolla *noun* the petals of a flower

corollary *noun* (*plural* **corollaries**) something which may be taken for granted when something else has been proved; natural result

coronary *noun* (*plural* **coronaries**) (*short for* **coronary thrombosis**) a heart attack caused by blockage of one of the arteries supplying the heart

coronation *noun* the crowning of a king or queen

coroner *noun* a government officer who holds inquiries into the causes of sudden, suspicious or accidental deaths

coronet *noun* 1 a small crown 2 a crown-like piece of jewellery

corporal¹ *noun* the rank next below sergeant in the British army

corporal² *adj* of the body ◇ **corporal punishment** physical punishment by beating

corporate *adj* 1 of or forming a whole, united 2 of a corporation ◇ **corporation** *noun* a body of people acting as one for administrative or business purposes
■ **corporation** council, authorities, association, society, organization, company, firm, conglomerate

corps /kɔː(r)/ *noun* (*plural* **corps**) 1 a division of an army 2 an organized group

⚠ Do not confuse: **corps** and **corpse**

corpse *noun* a dead body
■ body, *slang* stiff, carcass, skeleton, remains

corpulence *noun* obesity, fatness ◇ **corpulent** *adj*

corpus *noun* (*plural* **corpora**) a collection of writing *etc*

corpuscle *noun* a red or white blood cell ◇ **corpuscular** *adj*

corral *noun*, *US* a fenced enclosure for animals ◊ *verb* (**corrals**, **corralling**, **corralled**) enclose, pen

correct *verb* 1 remove errors from 2 set right 3 punish ◊ *adj* 1 having no errors 2 true ◊ **corrective** *adj*

■ *verb* 1 adjust, regulate, improve, amend 2 rectify, put right, right, emend, remedy, cure 3 punish, discipline, reprimand, reprove, reform ◊ *adj* 1 right, accurate, precise, exact, faultless, flawless 2 true, truthful

correction *noun* 1 the putting right of a mistake 2 punishment

correspond *verb* 1 write letters 2 be similar (to), match ◊ **correspondence** *noun* 1 letters 2 likeness, similarity

■ 2 match, fit, answer, conform, tally, square, agree, concur, coincide, correlate, accord, harmonize

correspondent *noun* 1 someone who writes letters 2 someone who contributes reports to a newspaper *etc*

> ⚠ Do not confuse with: **co-respondent**

corridor *noun* a passageway

corrigendum *noun* (*plural* **corrigenda**) a correction to a book *etc*

corroborate *verb* give evidence which confirms or strengthens evidence already given ◊ **corroboration** *noun* ◊ **corroborative** *adj*

■ confirm, prove, bear out, support, endorse, ratify, substantiate, validate

🔁 contradict

> ⚠ Do not confuse with: **collaborate**

corrode *verb* 1 rust 2 eat away at, erode ◊ **corrosion** *noun* ◊ **corrosive** *adj*

corrugated *adj* folded or shaped into ridges: *corrugated iron*

■ ridged, grooved, channelled, crinkled

corrupt *verb* 1 make evil or rotten 2 make dishonest, bribe ◊ *adj* 1 dishonest, taking bribes 2 bad, rotten ◊ **corruptible** *adj* ◊ **corruption** *noun*

■ *verb* 1 contaminate, pollute, adulterate, taint, defile, debase, pervert, deprave, lead astray, lure ◊ *adj* 1 unscrupulous, unprincipled, unethical, immoral, fraudulent, *informal* shady, dishonest, *informal* bent, *informal* crooked

🔁 *adj* 1 ethical, upright, honest, trustworthy

corsair *noun*, old 1 a pirate 2 a pirate ship

corset *noun* a tight-fitting undergarment to support the body

cortège /kɔːˈtɛʒ/ *noun* a funeral procession

corvette *noun* a small swift warship, used against submarines

cosh *noun* (*plural* **coshes**) a short heavy stick ◊ *verb* hit with a cosh

cosmetic *noun* something designed to improve the appearance, *esp* of the face ◊ *adj* 1 applied as a cosmetic 2 superficial, for appearances only

cosmic *adj* 1 of the universe or outer space 2 *informal* excellent

cosmonaut *noun*, *hist* an astronaut of the former USSR

cosmopolitan *adj* 1 including people from many countries 2 familiar with, or comfortable in, many different countries

■ 2 worldly, worldly-wise, well-travelled, sophisticated, urbane, international

cosmos *noun* the universe

cosset *verb* treat with too much kindness, pamper

■ coddle, mollycoddle, baby, pamper, indulge, spoil, cherish

cost *verb* (**costs**, **costing**, **cost**) 1 be priced at 2 cause the loss of: *the war cost many lives* ◊ *noun* 1 the price of something 2 what must be lost or suffered in order to get something ◊ **costly** *adj* high-priced, valuable ◊ **costliness** *noun*

■ *noun* 1 expense, outlay, payment, disbursement, expenditure, charge, price, rate, amount, figure, worth 2 detriment, harm, injury, hurt, loss, deprivation, sacrifice, penalty

costume *noun* 1 a set of clothes 2 clothes to wear in a play 3 fancy dress 4 a swimsuit

cosy adj warm and comfortable ◇ noun (plural **cosies**) a covering to keep a teapot etc warm

■ adj snug, comfortable, informal comfy, warm, sheltered, secure, homely, intimate

🔄 adj uncomfortable, cold

cot noun 1 a small high-sided bed for children 2 US a small collapsible bed; a camp bed ◇ **cot death** the sudden unexplained death in sleep of an apparently healthy baby

coterie /'koʊtərɪ/ noun a number of people interested in the same things who tend to exclude other people

cottage noun a small house, esp in the countryside or a village ◇ **cottager** noun someone who lives in a cottage ◇ **cottage cheese** a soft, white cheese made from skimmed milk

cotton noun 1 a soft fluffy substance obtained from the seeds of a plant 2 thread or cloth made of cotton ◇ adj made of cotton

cotton wool noun cotton in a fluffy state, used for wiping or absorbing

couch noun (plural **couches**) a sofa ◇ verb express verbally: couched in archaic language ◇ **couch potato** someone who spends their free time watching TV etc

■ noun sofa, settee, chesterfield, chaise-longue, ottoman, divan

couchette /'kuː.ʃɛt/ noun a sleeping berth on a train, convertible into an ordinary seat

couch grass a kind of grass, a troublesome weed

cougar noun, US the puma

cough noun a noisy effort of the lungs to throw out air and matter from the throat ◇ verb make this noise or effort

could verb 1 the form of the verb **can** used to express a condition: he could do it if he tried 2 past form of the verb **can**

coulis /'kuːliː/ noun a thin puréed sauce

coulomb noun a unit of electric charge

council noun a group of people elected to discuss or give advice about policy, government etc ◇ **councillor** noun a member of a council

■ committee, panel, board, cabinet, ministry, parliament, congress, assembly

❗ Do not confuse with: **counsel**

counsel noun 1 advice 2 someone who gives legal advice; a lawyer ◇ verb (**counsels, counselling, counselled**) give advice to ◇ **counsellor** noun someone who gives advice

■ noun 1 advice, suggestions, recommendations, guidance, direction 2 lawyer, advocate, solicitor, attorney, barrister ◇ verb advise, warn, caution, suggest, recommend, advocate, guide, direct, instruct

❗ Do not confuse with: **council**

count[1] verb 1 find the total number of, add up 2 say numbers in order (1, 2, 3 etc) 3 think, consider: count yourself lucky! ◇ noun 1 the act of counting 2 the number counted, eg of votes at an election 3 a charge, an accusation 4 a point being considered ◇ **countless** adj too many to be counted, very many ◇ **count on** rely on, depend on

■ verb 1 reckon, calculate, compute, check, add, total, tot up 3 consider, regard, deem, judge, think, reckon ◇ **count on** depend on, rely on, bank on, reckon on, expect, believe, trust

count[2] noun a nobleman in some countries

countenance noun 1 the face 2 the expression on someone's face ◇ verb allow, encourage

counter[1] verb answer or oppose (a move, act, remark etc) by another ◇ adv in the opposite direction ◇ adj opposed; opposite

■ verb parry, answer, respond, retaliate, retort, return

counter[2] noun 1 a token used in counting 2 a small plastic disc used in board games 3 a table across which payments are made in a shop

counter- prefix 1 against, opposing:

counter-argument **2** opposite

counteract *verb* block or defeat (an action, effect *etc*) by doing the opposite
∎ neutralize, counterbalance, offset, oppose, resist, hinder, check, thwart, frustrate, foil, defeat, undo, negate, annul, invalidate
⊞ support, assist

counterattack *noun* an attack made upon an attacker ◊ *verb* launch a counterattack

countercharge *noun* a charge made against an accuser ◊ *verb* make a countercharge against

counterfeit *adj* **1** not genuine, not real **2** made in imitation for criminal purposes: *counterfeit money* ◊ *verb* make a copy of
∎ *adj* **1** fake, false, *informal* phoney, imitation, artificial, simulated **2** fake, false, *informal* phoney, forged, copied, fraudulent, bogus

counterfoil *noun* a part of a cheque, postal order *etc* kept by the payer or sender

countermand *verb* give an order which goes against one already given

counterpane *noun* a top cover for a bed

counterpart *noun* someone or something which is just like or which corresponds to another person or thing
∎ equivalent, opposite number, complement, match, fellow, twin, duplicate, copy

counterpoint *noun* the combining of two or more melodies to make a piece of music ◊ **contrapuntal** *adj* of or in counterpoint

counterpoise *noun* a weight which balances another weight

countersign *verb* sign your name after someone else's signature to show that a document is genuine

counter-tenor *noun* the highest adult male voice

countess *noun* **1** a woman of the same rank as a count or earl **2** the wife or widow of a count or earl

country *noun* (*plural* **countries**) **1** a nation **2** a land under one government **3** the land in which someone lives **4** land which is not in a town or city **5** an area or stretch of land of a particular type ◊ *adj* belonging to the countryside ◊ **country music** a style of music from the USA using banjos, fiddles *etc*
∎ *noun* **1** state, nation, people, kingdom, realm, principality **4** countryside, green belt, farmland, provinces, *informal* sticks, *US informal* boondocks, backwoods, wilds
⊞ *noun* **1** urban

countryside *noun* the parts of a country other than towns and cities

county *noun* (*plural* **counties**) a division of a country
∎ shire, province, region, area, district

coup /kuː/ *noun* **1** a sudden outstandingly successful move or act **2** a coup d'état

coup de grâce /kuː də 'grɑs/ a final blow, a last straw

coup d'état /kuː deɪ'tɑː/ (*plural* **coups d'état**) a sudden and violent change in government

couple *noun* **1** a pair, two of a kind together **2** a husband and wife ◊ *verb* join together
∎ *noun* **1** pair, brace, twosome, duo ◊ *verb* pair, match, marry, wed, unite, join, link, connect, fasten, hitch, clasp, buckle, yoke

couplet *noun* two lines of rhyming verse

coupling *noun* a link for joining railway carriages *etc*

coupon *noun* a piece of paper which may be exchanged for goods or money

courage *noun* bravery, lack of fear ◊ **courageous** *adj* brave, fearless ◊ **courageously** *adv*
∎ **courageous** brave, plucky, fearless, dauntless, indomitable, heroic, gallant, valiant, lion-hearted, hardy, bold, audacious, daring, intrepid, resolute
⊞ **courageous** cowardly, afraid

courgette *noun* a type of small marrow

courier *noun* **1** someone who acts as

guide for tourists **2** a messenger **3** a person or company paid to transport and deliver urgent items

course *noun* **1** a path in which anything moves **2** movement from point to point **3** a track along which athletes *etc* run **4** a direction to be followed: *the ship held its course* **5** line of action: *the best course to follow* **6** a part of a meal **7** a number of things following each other: *a course of twelve lectures* **8** one of the rows of bricks in a wall ◇ *verb* **1** move quickly **2** go coursing ◇ **courser** *noun* ◇ **coursing** *noun* the hunting of hares with greyhounds ◇ **in due course** after a while, in its proper time ◇ **in the course of** during

- *noun* **1** path, road, channel, line, orbit, trajectory, flight path **2** flow, movement, advance, progress, development, sequence, series, succession, progression **4** direction, way, path, track, route, trail, line, circuit

court *noun* **1** an area marked out for playing tennis *etc* **2** a room or building where legal cases are heard or tried **3** an open space surrounded by houses **4** the people who attend a monarch *etc* **5** a royal residence ◇ *verb* **1** woo as a potential lover **2** try to gain: *courting her affections* **3** come near to achieving: *courting disaster* ◇ **courtly** *adj* having fine manners

courtesy *noun* politeness ◇ **courteous** *adj* polite; obliging ◇ **courteously** *adv*

- **courteous** polite, civil, respectful, well-mannered, well-bred, gracious, considerate, attentive, gallant, courtly, urbane, debonair, refined
- discourteous, impolite, rude

courtier *noun* a member of a royal court

- noble, nobleman, lord, lady, page, attendant

court-martial *noun* (*plural* **courts-martial**) an internal court held to try those who break navy or army laws ◇ *verb* (**court-martials**, **court-martialling**, **court-martialled**) try in a court-martial

courtship *noun* the act or time of courting or wooing

courtyard *noun* a court or enclosed space beside a house

couscous /kʊskʊs/ *noun* hard wheat semolina

cousin *noun* the son or daughter of an uncle or aunt

cove *noun* a small inlet on the sea coast; a bay

coven *noun* a gathering of witches

covenant *noun* an important agreement between people to do or not to do something

cover *verb* **1** put or spread something on or over **2** hide **3** stretch over: *the hills were covered with heather/my diary covers three years* **4** include, deal with: *covering the news story* **5** be enough for: *five pounds should cover the cost* **6** travel over: *covering 3 kilometres a day* **7** point a weapon at: *had the gangster covered* ◇ *noun* **1** something that covers, hides or protects **2** protection given by an insurance policy ◇ **cover up 1** cover completely **2** conceal deliberately ◇ **cover-up** *noun* a deliberate concealment, *esp* by people in authority

- *verb* **1** coat, spread, daub, plaster, encase, wrap, envelop, clothe, dress **2** hide, conceal, obscure, shroud, veil, screen, mask, disguise, camouflage **4** deal with, treat, encompass, embrace, incorporate, include, contain, comprise ◇ *noun* **1** coating, covering, top, lid, cup, veil, screen, mask, front, façade, shelter, refuge, protection, shield, guard, defence, concealment, disguise, camouflage ◇ **cover up 1** conceal, hide **2** conceal, hide, whitewash, dissemble, suppress, hush up, keep dark, repress

coverage *noun* **1** an area covered **2** the extent to which a news item is reported

coverlet *noun* a bed cover

covert *adj* secret, not done openly ◇ *noun* a hiding place for animals or birds when hunted ◇ **covertly** *adv*

covet *verb* desire eagerly, *esp* something belonging to another person

◊ **covetous** *adj* ◊ **covetously** *adv*
◊ **covetousness** *noun*

▣ envy, crave, long for, hanker for, want, desire, *informal* fancy, lust after

covey *noun* (*plural* **coveys**) a flock of birds, *esp* partridges

cow[1] *noun* **1** the female of cattle, used for giving milk **2** the female of an elephant, whale *etc*

cow[2] *verb* frighten, subdue ◊ **cowed** *adj* frightened, subdued

coward *noun* someone who has no courage and shows fear easily ◊ **cowardice** *noun* lack of courage ◊ **cowardly** *adj*

▣ craven, faint-heart, *informal* chicken, scaredy-cat, *slang* yellow-belly, *informal* wimp, *slang* wuss, renegade, deserter

cowboy, cowgirl *noun* a man or woman who works with cattle on a ranch

cower *verb* crouch down or shrink back through fear

▣ crouch, grovel, skulk, shrink, flinch, cringe, quail, tremble, shake, shiver

cowl *noun* **1** a hood, *esp* that of a monk **2** a cover for a chimney

cowslip *noun* a yellow wild flower

cox *noun* (*plural* **coxes**) the person who steers a racing boat and directs its crew

coxcomb *noun* **1** *hist* a head-covering notched like a cock's comb, worn by a jester **2** a vain or conceited person

coxswain *noun* **1** someone who steers a boat **2** an officer in charge of a boat and crew

coy *adj* too modest or shy

▣ modest, demure, prudish, diffident, shy, bashful, timid, shrinking, backward, retiring, self-effacing, reserved, evasive

coyote /'kɔɪoʊtiː/ *noun* (*plural* **coyote** or **coyotes**) a type of small North American wolf

coypu *noun* (*plural* **coypus** or **coypu**) a large, beaver-like animal living in rivers and marshes

crab *noun* a sea creature with a shell and five pairs of legs, the first

pair of which have large claws

crab apple a type of small, bitter apple

crabbed /'krabɪd/ *adj* bad-tempered

crack *verb* **1** (cause to) make a sharp, sudden sound **2** break partly without falling to pieces **3** break into (a safe) **4** decipher (a code) **5** break open (a nut) **6** make (a joke) ◊ *noun* **1** a sharp sound **2** a split, a break **3** a narrow opening **4** *informal* a sharp, witty remark **5** *informal* a pure form of cocaine ◊ *adj* excellent: *a crack tennis player* ◊ *adj* **cracked 1** split, damaged **2** mad, crazy ◊ **crack up** have a nervous breakdown, collapse

▣ *verb* **2** split, fracture, break, snap, shatter, splinter, chip **4** decipher, work out, solve ◊ *noun* **1** pop, snap, crash, clap **2** break, fracture, split **3** split, rift, gap, crevice, fissure, chink ◊ **crack up** go mad, go to pieces, break down, collapse

cracker *noun* **1** a hollow paper tube containing a small gift, which breaks with a bang when the ends are pulled **2** a thin, crisp biscuit **3** *informal* something excellent: *a cracker of a story* **4** someone who cracks computer codes to break into systems

crackle *verb* make a continuous cracking noise

crackling *noun* **1** a continuous cracking sound **2** the rind or outer skin of roast pork

cradle *noun* **1** a baby's bed, *esp* one which can be rocked **2** a frame under a ship that is being built or repaired

craft *noun* **1** a trade, a skill **2** a boat, a small ship **3** slyness, cunning ◊ **craftsman**, **craftswoman** or **craftworker** *noun* someone who works at a trade, *esp* making things with their hands

▣ **1** skill, expertise, talent, knack, ability **2** vessel, boat, ship

crafty *adj* cunning, sly ◊ **craftily** *adv* ◊ **craftiness** *noun*

▣ sly, cunning, artful, wily, devious, subtle, scheming, calculating, designing, deceitful, fraudulent

crag *noun* a rough steep rock

craggy *adj* **1** rocky **2** of a face: well-marked, lined

cram *verb* (**crams**, **cramming**, **crammed**) **1** fill full, stuff **2** learn facts for an examination in a short time

■ **1** stuff, jam, ram, force, press, squeeze, crush, compress, pack, crowd, overfill, gorge

cramp *noun* **1** a painful stiffening of the muscles **2** (**cramps**) an acute stomach pain ◇ *verb* **1** confine in too small a space **2** hinder, restrict

■ *verb* **1** confine, shackle, tie, restrict **2** hinder, hamper, impede, restrict, inhibit

cramped *adj* **1** without enough room **2** of handwriting: small and closely-written

crampon *noun* a metal plate with spikes, fixed to boots for climbing on ice or snow

cranberry *noun* (*plural* **cranberries**) a type of red, sour berry

crane *noun* **1** a large wading bird with long legs, neck and bill **2** a machine for lifting heavy weights ◇ *verb* stretch out (the neck) to see round or over something

cranium *noun* (*plural* **crania** or **craniums**) the skull

crank *noun* **1** a handle for turning an axle **2** a lever which converts a horizontal movement into a rotating one **3** an eccentric person ◇ *verb* start (an engine) with a crank

cranky *adj* **1** odd, eccentric **2** cross, irritable

cranny *noun* (*plural* **crannies**) a small opening or crack

crap *noun*, *taboo slang* **1** faeces **2** something worthless, rubbish ◇ *adj* poor, low-quality

craps *noun sing* a gambling game in which a player rolls two dice

crapulent *adj* drinking excessively, intemperate

crash *noun* (*plural* **crashes**) **1** a noise of heavy things breaking or banging together **2** a collision causing damage, *eg* between vehicles **3** the failure of a business ◇ *adj* short but intensive: *a crash course in French* ◇ *verb* **1** be involved in a crash **2** of a business: fail **3** of a computer program: break down, fail **4** *informal* gatecrash ◇ **crash helmet** a protective covering for the head worn by motorcyclists *etc*

■ *noun* **1** bang, clash, clatter, clang, thud, thump, boom, thunder, racket **2** accident, collision, bump, smash, pile-up **3** collapse, failure, ruin, bankruptcy ◇ *verb* **1** collide, hit, knock, bump, bang **2** collapse, fail, fold (up), go under, *informal* go bust

crash-land *verb* land (an aircraft) in an emergency, causing some structural damage ◇ **crash-landing** *noun*

crass *adj* stupid ◇ **crassly** *adv* ◇ **crassness** *noun*

crate *noun* a container for carrying goods, often made of wooden slats

crater *noun* **1** the bowl-shaped mouth of a volcano **2** a hole made by an explosion

cravat *noun* a scarf worn in place of a tie

From a French word for 'Croat', because of the linen neckbands worn by 17th-century Croatian soldiers

crave *verb* **1** long for **2** beg earnestly for

■ **1** hunger for, thirst for, long for, yearn for, pine for, hanker after

craven *adj*, *old* cowardly

crawfish *same as* **crayfish**

crawl *verb* **1** move on hands and knees **2** move slowly **3** be covered (with): *crawling with wasps* **4** be obsequious, fawn ◇ *noun* **1** the act of crawling **2** a swimming stroke of kicking the feet and swinging the arms alternately ◇ **crawler** *noun*, *informal* an obsequious, fawning person

■ *verb* **4** grovel, cringe, toady, fawn, flatter, *slang* suck up

crayfish or **crawfish** *noun* a shellfish similar to a small lobster

crayon *noun* a coloured pencil or stick for drawing or colouring

craze noun a temporary fashion or enthusiasm

▣ fad, novelty, fashion, vogue, mode, trend, obsession, preoccupation, mania, frenzy, passion, infatuation, enthusiasm

crazy adj mad, unreasonable ◇ **crazily** adv ◇ **craziness** noun ◇ **crazy paving** paving with stones of irregular shape

▣ mad, insane, lunatic, unbalanced, deranged, demented, crazed, informal potty, informal barmy, informal daft, silly, foolish, idiotic, senseless, unwise, imprudent, nonsensical, absurd, ludicrous, ridiculous, preposterous, outrageous, irresponsible, wild, berserk

creak verb make a sharp, grating sound like a hinge in need of oiling

cream noun 1 the fatty substance which forms on milk 2 something like this in texture: cleansing cream/shaving cream 3 the best part: the cream of society ◇ verb 1 take the cream from 2 take away (the best part)◇ **creamy** adj full of or like cream

▣ noun 2 emulsion, lotion, ointment, salve 3 best, pick, élite ◇ **creamy** cream-coloured, off-white, milky, buttery, oily, smooth, velvety, rich, thick

crease noun 1 a mark made by folding 2 cricket a line showing the position of a batsman and bowler ◇ verb 1 make creases in 2 become creased

▣ verb 1 fold, pleat, wrinkle, crumple, rumple

create verb 1 bring into being; make 2 informal make a fuss ◇ **creation** noun 1 the act of creating 2 something created ◇ **creator** noun ◇ **the Creator** God

▣ 1 invent, coin, formulate, compose, design, devise, concoct, hatch, originate, initiate, found, establish, set up, institute, cause, occasion, produce, generate, engender, make, form, appoint, install, invest, ordain ◇ **creation 2** invention, brainchild, concept, product, handiwork, chef d'oeuvre, achievement

▣ 1 destroy

creative adj having the ability to create, artistic ◇ **creatively** adv ◇ **creativity** noun

▣ artistic, inventive, original, imaginative, ingenious, resourceful, fertile, productive

▣ unimaginative

creature noun an animal or person

▣ animal, beast, organism, being, mortal, individual

crèche noun a nursery for children

credentials noun plural documents carried as proof of identity, character etc

credible adj able to be believed ◇ **credibility** noun

▣ believable, imaginable, conceivable, thinkable, tenable, plausible, likely, probable, possible, reasonable, reasonable, persuasive, convincing, sincere, honest, trustworthy, reliable, dependable

▣ incredible, unbelievable, implausible, unreliable

⚠ Do not confuse with: **credulous**

credit noun 1 recognition of good qualities, achievements etc: give him credit for some common sense 2 good qualities or honour 3 a source of honour: a credit to the family 4 trustworthiness in ability to pay for goods 5 the sale of goods to be paid for later 6 the side of an account on which payments received are entered 7 a sum of money in a bank account 8 belief, trust 9 (**credits**) the naming of people who have helped in a film etc ◇ verb 1 believe 2 enter on the credit side of an account 3 (with **with**) believe to have: I credited him with more sense ◇ **creditable** adj bringing honour or good reputation to ◇ **creditably** adv ◇ **credit card** a card allowing the holder to pay for purchased articles at a later date

▣ noun 1 acknowledgement, recognition, thanks, approval, commendation, praise, acclaim ◇ **creditable** honourable, reputable, respectable, worthy, deserving

creditor noun someone to whom money is due

credulous adj believing too easily ◇ **credulity** noun ◇ **credulously** adv

▣ naive, gullible, wide-eyed, trusting, unsuspecting, uncritical

▣ sceptical, suspicious

> ❗ Do not confuse with: **credible**

creed *noun* a belief, *esp* a religious one
▣ belief, faith, persuasion, credo, doctrine, principles, tenets

creek *noun* **1** a small inlet or bay on the sea coast **2** a short river

creep *verb* (**creeps, creeping, crept**) **1** move slowly and silently **2** move with the body close to the ground **3** shiver with fear or disgust: *makes your flesh creep* **4** of a plant: grow along the ground or up a wall ◇ *noun* **1** a creeping movement **2** *informal* an unpleasant person ◇ **creep up on** approach silently from behind ◇ **the creeps** *informal* a feeling of disgust or fear
▣ *verb* **1** inch, edge, tiptoe, steal, sneak **2** slink, crawl, slither, worm, wriggle

creeper *noun* a plant growing along the ground or up a wall

creepy *adj* unsettlingly sinister ◇ **creepy-crawly** *noun, informal* a crawling insect
▣ eerie, spooky, sinister, threatening, frightening, scary, terrifying, hair-raising, macabre, gruesome, horrible, unpleasant, disturbing

cremate *verb* burn (a dead body) ◇ **cremation** *noun*

crematorium *noun* a place where dead bodies are burnt

crème fraîche cream thickened with a culture of bacteria

crenellated *adj* of a building: with battlements

Creole *noun* **1** a West Indian of mixed European and black African descent **2** *hist* a French or Spanish settler in Louisiana **3** a hybrid or pidgin language

creosote *noun* an oily liquid made from wood tar, used to keep wood from rotting

crêpe *noun* **1** a type of fine, crinkly material **2** a thin pancake ◇ **crêpe paper** paper with a crinkled appearance

crept *past form* of **creep**

crepuscular *adj* **1** relating to twilight **2** dark, dim

crescendo *noun* **1** a musical passage of increasing loudness **2** a climax

crescent *adj* shaped like the new or old moon; curved ◇ *noun* **1** something with a crescent shape **2** a curved road or street

cress *noun* a plant with small, slightly bitter-tasting leaves, used in salads

crest *noun* **1** a tuft on the head of a cock or other bird **2** the top of a hill, wave *etc* **3** feathers on top of a helmet **4** a badge
▣ **1** tuft, tassel, plume, comb **2** ridge, crown, top, peak, summit, pinnacle, apex, head **4** insignia, device, symbol, emblem, badge

crestfallen *adj* downhearted, discouraged

cretin *noun, informal* an idiot, a fool

crevasse /krə'vas/ *noun* a deep split in snow or ice

> ❗ Do not confuse: **crevasse** and **crevice**

crevice /'krɛvɪs/ *noun* a crack, a narrow opening
▣ crack, fissure, split, rift, cleft, slit, chink, cranny, gap, hole, opening, break

crew[1] *noun* **1** the people who man a ship, aircraft *etc* **2** a gang, a mob ◇ *verb* act as a member of a crew

crew[2] *past form* of **crow**

crewcut *noun* an extremely short hairstyle

crib *noun* **1** a manger **2** *US* a young child's bed **3** a ready-made translation of a school text *etc* ◇ *verb* (**cribs, cribbing, cribbed**) copy someone else's work

cribbage *noun* a type of card game in which the score is kept with a pegged board

crick *noun* a sharp pain, *esp* in the neck ◇ *verb* produce a crick in

cricket[1] *noun* a game played with bats, ball and wickets, between two teams of 11 ◇ **cricketer** noun someone who plays cricket

cricket [2] noun an insect similar to a grasshopper

cried past form of **cry**

crime noun an act or deed which is against the law

■ offence, felony, misdemeanour, misdeed, wrongdoing, misconduct, transgression, violation

---

Crimes include:

theft, robbery, burglary, larceny, pilfering, mugging, carjacking, poaching; assault, rape, grievous bodily harm, informal GBH, battery, manslaughter, homicide, murder, assassination; fraud, bribery, corruption, embezzlement, extortion, blackmail; arson, treason, terrorism, hijack, piracy, kidnapping, sabotage, vandalism, hooliganism, drug smuggling, forgery, counterfeiting, perjury, joyriding, drink-driving, drug-driving, drunk and disorderly

---

criminal adj **1** forbidden by law **2** very wrong ◇ noun someone guilty of a crime

■ noun law-breaker, crook, felon, delinquent, offender, wrongdoer, miscreant

crimson noun a deep red colour ◇ adj of this colour

cringe verb **1** crouch or shrink back in fear **2** behave in too humble a way

■ **1** shrink, recoil, shy, start, flinch, wince, quail, tremble, quiver, cower

crinkle verb **1** wrinkle, crease **2** make a crackling sound ◇ **crinkly** adj wrinkled

crinoline noun a wide petticoat or skirt shaped by concentric hoops

cripple noun a disabled person ◇ verb **1** make lame **2** make less strong, less efficient etc: their policies crippled the economy

■ verb **1** lame, paralyse, disable, handicap, injure, maim, mutilate **2** spoil, destroy, sabotage, incapacitate, weaken, debilitate

crisis noun (plural **crises**) **1** a deciding moment, a turning-point **2** a time of great danger or suspense

■ **1** informal crunch **2** emergency, dilemma, quandary, predicament

crisp adj **1** stiff and dry; brittle **2** cool and fresh: crisp air **3** firm and fresh: crisp lettuce **4** sharp in manner ◇ noun a thin crisp piece of fried potato eaten cold ◇ **crispness** noun ◇ **crispy** adj

■ adj **1** crispy, crunchy, brittle, crumbly, firm, hard **2** bracing, invigorating, refreshing, fresh, brisk

criss-cross adj having a pattern of crossing lines ◇ verb move across and back: roads criss-cross the landscape

---

Based on the phrase Christ's cross

---

criterion noun (plural **criteria**) a means or rule by which something can be judged; a standard

critic noun **1** someone who judges the merits or faults of a book, film etc **2** someone who finds faults in a thing or person

critical adj **1** fault-finding **2** of criticism: critical commentary **3** of or at a crisis **4** very ill **5** serious, very important

■ **1** uncomplimentary, derogatory, disparaging, disapproving, censorious, carping, fault-finding, cavilling, informal nit-picking **2** analytical, diagnostic, penetrating, probing **5** crucial, vital, essential, all-important, momentous, decisive, urgent

criticism noun **1** a judgement or opinion on something or someone esp one showing up faults **2** the act of criticizing

criticize verb **1** find fault with **2** give an opinion or judgement on

■ **1** condemn, informal slate, informal slam, informal knock, disparage, carp, find fault, censure, blame **2** review, assess, evaluate, appraise, judge, analyse

croak verb make a low, hoarse sound ◇ noun a low, hoarse sound ◇ **croakily** adv ◇ **croaky** adj

crochet /'krəʊʃeɪ/ noun a form of knitting done with one hooked needle ◇ verb work in crochet

crock noun 1 an earthenware pot or jar 2 a worthless, old and decrepit person or thing

crockery noun china or earthenware dishes

crocodile noun 1 a large reptile found in rivers in Asia, Africa etc 2 a procession of children walking two by two ◇ **crocodile tears** a false show of grief

crocus noun (plural **crocuses**) a yellow, purple or white flower which grows from a bulb

croft noun a small farm with a cottage, esp in the Scottish Highlands ◇ **crofter** noun someone who farms on a croft ◇ **crofting** noun farming on a croft

croissant noun a curved roll of rich bread dough

crone noun an ugly old woman

crony noun (plural **cronies**) informal a close friend

crook noun 1 a shepherd's or bishop's stick bent at the end 2 a criminal ◇ verb bend or form into a hook

crooked /'krʊkɪd/ adj 1 bent, hooked 2 dishonest, criminal ◇ **crookedly** adv ◇ **crookedness** noun

■ 1 bent, angled, hooked, curved, bowed, warped, distorted, misshapen, deformed, twisted 2 illegal, unlawful, illicit, criminal, nefarious, dishonest, deceitful, informal bent, corrupt, fraudulent, informal shady, shifty, underhand, treacherous, unscrupulous

croon verb sing or hum in a low voice ◇ **crooner** noun ◇ **crooning** noun

crop noun 1 a plant or plants grown for food, esp in fields 2 a part of a bird's stomach 3 a riding whip 4 a short haircut ◇ verb (**crops**, **cropping**, **cropped**) 1 cut short 2 gather a crop (of wheat etc) ◇ **come a cropper** 1 fail badly 2 have a bad fall ◇ **crop up** happen unexpectedly

■ verb 1 cut, snip, clip, shear, trim, pare, lop, shorten, curtail ◇ **crop up** arise

croquet /'krəʊkeɪ/ noun a game in which players use long-handled mallets to drive wooden balls through hoops in the ground

croquette /krəʊ'kɛt/ noun a ball of potato etc coated in breadcrumbs

cross noun 1 a shape (x) or (+) formed of two lines intersecting in the middle 2 the cross-shaped structure on which Christ was crucified, or a representation of this 3 a street monument marking the site of a market etc 4 the result of breeding an animal or plant with one of another kind: a cross between a horse and a donkey 5 a trouble that must be endured ◇ verb 1 mark with a cross 2 go to the other side of (a room, road etc) 3 lie or pass across 4 meet and pass 5 go against the wishes of 6 draw two lines across to validate (a cheque) 7 breed (one kind) with (another) ◇ adj bad-tempered, angry ◇ **crossly** adv ◇ **crossness** noun

▣ noun 4 crossbreed, hybrid, mongrel, blend, mixture, combination 5 burden, load, affliction, misfortune, trouble, worry, trial, tribulation, grief, misery, woe

crossbow noun a bow fixed across a wooden stand with a device for pulling back the bowstring

cross-country adj of a race: across fields etc, not on roads

cross-examine verb question closely in court to test accuracy of a statement etc

cross-eyed adj having the eyes looking in different directions

crossing noun 1 a place where a street, river etc may be crossed 2 a journey over the sea

cross-reference noun a statement in a reference book directing the reader to further information in another section

crossroads noun sing a place where roads cross each other

cross-section noun 1 a surface revealed by cutting across something 2 a sample taken as representative of the whole: a cross-section of voters

crossword noun a puzzle in which letters are written into blank squares to form words

crotch noun the area between the tops of the legs

crotchet noun a musical note (♩) equivalent to a quarter of a semibreve

crotchety adj bad-tempered

crouch verb **1** sit on the heels or stand with the knees well bent **2** of an animal: lie close to the ground

▣ **1** squat, kneel, stoop, bend, bow, hunch, duck

croup[1] /kru:p/ noun a children's disease causing difficulty in breathing and a harsh cough

croup[2] /kru:p/ noun the hindquarters of a horse

croupier noun someone who collects the money and pays the winners at gambling

croûton /'kru:tɒn/ noun a small piece of fried bread, sprinkled on soup etc

crow noun **1** a large bird with shiny black feathers **2** the cry of a cock drymark;verb (**crows**, **crowing**, **crew** or **crowed**) **1** cry like a cock **2** boast **3** of a baby: make happy noises ◇ **crow's feet** fine wrinkles around the eye, produced by ageing ◇ **as the crow flies** in a straight line ◇ **crow's-nest** noun a sheltered and enclosed lookout platform near the masthead of a ship

> **crew** is used as the past form for the first sense only: *the cock crew*; otherwise the form is **crowed**: *crowed about his exam results*

crowbar noun a large iron bar used as a lever

crowd noun a number of people or things together ◇ verb **1** gather into a crowd **2** fill too full **3** keep too close to, impede

▣ noun throng, multitude, host, mob, rabble, horde, swarm, pack, assembly, company, group, bunch

crown noun **1** a jewelled head-dress worn by monarchs on ceremonial occasions **2** the top of the head **3** the highest part of something ◇ verb **1** put a crown on **2** make a monarch **3** informal hit on the head **4** reward, finish

happily: *crowned with success*

▣ noun **1** coronet, diadem, tiara, circlet

crucial adj extremely important, critical: *a crucial question* ◇ **crucially** adv

▣ urgent, pressing, vital, essential, key, pivotal, central, important, momentous, decisive, critical

▣ unimportant, trivial

crucible noun a small container for melting metals etc

crucifix noun (plural **crucifixes**) a figure or picture of Christ crucified ◇ **crucifixion** noun **1** the act of crucifying **2** death on the cross, esp that of Christ

crucify verb (**crucifies**, **crucifying**, **crucified**) put to death by fixing the hands and feet to a cross

cruddy adj, slang dirty or shoddy

crude adj **1** not purified or refined: *crude oil* **2** roughly made or done **3** rude, vulgar ◇ **crudely** adv ◇ **crudity** noun

▣ **1** raw, unprocessed, unrefined, rough, unfinished, unpolished, natural, primitive **3** vulgar, coarse, rude, indecent, obscene, gross, lewd

▣ **1** refined, finished **3** polite, decent

crudités /kru:di'teɪ/ noun plural raw vegetables served as an appetizer

cruel adj **1** causing pain or distress **2** having no pity for others' sufferings ◇ **cruelly** adv ◇ **cruelty** noun (plural **cruelties**)

▣ **1** atrocious, bitter, harsh, severe, cutting, painful, excruciating **2** sadistic, brutal, inhuman, inhumane, unkind, malevolent, spiteful, callous, heartless, unfeeling, merciless, pitiless, flinty, hard-hearted, stony-hearted, implacable, ruthless, remorseless

▣ **2** kind, compassionate, merciful

cruet /'kru:ɪt/ noun **1** a small jar for salt, pepper, mustard etc **2** two or more such jars on a stand

cruise verb travel by car, ship etc at a steady speed ◇ noun a journey by ship made for pleasure ◇ **cruiser** noun a middle-sized warship

crumb noun a small bit of anything, esp bread

crumble *verb* **1** break into crumbs or small pieces **2** fall to pieces; collapse ◊ *noun* a dish of stewed fruit *etc* with a crumbly topping ◊ **crumbly** *adj*

■ **1** crush, pound, grind, powder, pulverize **2** break up, fragment, decompose, disintegrate, decay, degenerate, deteriorate, collapse

crumpet *noun* a soft unsweetened cake, baked on a griddle and eaten with butter

crumple *verb* **1** crush into creases or wrinkles **2** become creased: *her face crumpled* **3** collapse

crunch *verb* **1** chew hard so as to make a noise **2** crush ◊ *noun* **1** a noise of crunching **2** *informal* a testing moment, a turning-point ◊ **crunchy** *adj*

■ *verb* **1** munch, chomp, champ, masticate

crusade *noun* **1** a movement undertaken for some good cause **2** *hist* a Christian expedition to regain the Holy Land from the Turks ◊ **crusader** *noun* someone who goes on a crusade

crush *verb* **1** squeeze violently **2** beat down, overcome **3** crease, crumple ◊ *noun* **1** a violent squeezing **2** a pressing crowd of people **3** a drink made by squeezing fruit ◊ **crushed** *adj* **1** squeezed, squashed **2** completely defeated or miserable

■ **1** squash, compress, squeeze, flatten **2** conquer, vanquish, overpower, overwhelm, overcome, quash, quell, subdue **3** crumple, wrinkle, crease

crust *noun* a hard outside surface, *eg* on bread, a pie, a planet ◊ **crusty** *adj* **1** having a crust **2** cross, irritable

■ exterior, covering, coating, outside, skin, shell, caking

crustacean /krʌ'steɪʃən/ *noun* one of a large group of animals with a hard shell, including crabs, lobsters, shrimps *etc*

crutch *noun* (*plural* **crutches**) **1** a stick held under the armpit or elbow, used for support in walking **2** a support, a prop

crux *noun* (*plural* **cruces** or **cruxes**) the most important or difficult part of a problem

■ nub, heart, core, essence

cry *verb* (**cries**, **crying**, **cried**) **1** weep **2** call loudly ◊ *noun* (*plural* **cries**) a loud call ◊ **cry off** cancel ◊ **cry over spilt milk** be worried about a misfortune that is past

■ *verb* **1** weep, sob, blubber, wail, bawl, whimper, snivel **2** shout, call, exclaim, roar, bellow, yell, scream, shriek, screech ◊ *noun* shout, call, plea, exclamation, roar, bellow, yell, scream, shriek

crying *adj* **1** weeping **2** calling loudly **3** requiring notice or attention: *a crying need*

crypt *noun* an underground cell or chapel, *esp* one used for burial

cryptic *adj* mysterious, difficult to understand: *a cryptic remark* ◊ **cryptically** *adv*

■ enigmatic, ambiguous, equivocal, puzzling, perplexing, mysterious, strange, bizarre, secret, hidden, veiled, obscure

cryptography *noun* the art of coding and reading codes ◊ **cryptographer** *noun*

crystal *noun* **1** very clear glass often used for making bowls, drinking glasses *etc* **2** the regular shape taken by each small part of certain substances, *eg* salt or sugar

crystalline *adj* made up of crystals

crystallize *verb* **1** form into crystals **2** take a form or shape, become clear ◊ **crystallization** *noun*

cub *noun* **1** the young of certain animals, *eg* foxes **2** a Cub Scout ◊ **Cub Scout** a junior Scout

cube *noun* **1** a solid body having six equal square sides **2** the answer to a sum in which a number is multiplied by itself twice: *8 is the cube of 2*

cubic *adj* **1** of cubes **2** in the shape of a cube

cubicle *noun* a small room closed off in some way from a larger one

cubit *noun*, *hist* the distance from the elbow to the tip of the middle finger, used as a measurement

cuckoo *noun* a bird which visits Britain in summer and lays its eggs in the nests of other birds

cucumber *noun* a creeping plant with a long green fruit used in salads

cud *noun* food regurgitated and chewed again by certain animals, *eg* sheep and cows

cuddle *verb* put your arms round, hug ◇ *noun* a hug, an embrace
■ *verb* hug, embrace, clasp, hold, nurse, nestle, snuggle, pet, fondle, caress

cudgel *noun* a heavy stick, a club ◇ *verb* (**cudgels, cudgelling, cudgelled**) beat with a cudgel

cue¹ *noun* a signal to do something
■ signal, sign, nod, hint, suggestion, reminder, prompt

cue² *noun* the stick used to hit a ball in billiards and snooker

cuff *noun* **1** the end of a sleeve near the wrist **2** *US* the turned-back hem of a trouser leg **3** a blow with the open hand ◇ *verb* hit with the hand ◇ **off the cuff** without planning or rehearsal
■ *verb* hit, thump, box, clip, knock, *informal* biff, smack, strike, clout, *slang* clobber, *informal* belt, beat, *informal* whack

cufflinks *noun plural* a pair of ornamental buttons *etc* used to fasten a shirt cuff

cuisine /kwɪ'ziːn/ *noun* **1** the art of cookery **2** a style of cooking: *Mexican cuisine*

cul-de-sac *noun* a street closed at one end

culinary *adj* of or used for cookery

cull *verb* **1** gather **2** choose from a group **3** pick out and kill (seals, deer *etc*) for the good of the herd ◇ *noun* an act of culling

culminate *verb* **1** reach the highest point **2** reach the most important or greatest point, end (in): *culminated in divorce* ◇ **culmination** *noun*
■ **1** climax **2** end (up), terminate, close, conclude, finish, consummate
 2 start, begin

culottes *noun plural* wide-legged shorts or trousers which look like a skirt

culpable *adj* guilty, blameworthy

culprit *noun* someone who is to blame for something
■ guilty party, offender, wrongdoer, miscreant, law-breaker, criminal, felon, delinquent

cult *noun* **1** a religious sect **2** a general strong enthusiasm for something: *the cult of physical fitness*
■ **2** craze, fad, fashion, vogue, trend

cultivate *verb* **1** grow (plants) **2** plough, sow (land) **3** try to develop and improve: *cultivated my friendship* ◇ **cultivated** *adj* **1** farmed, ploughed **2** educated, informed ◇ **cultivation** *noun* ◇ **cultivator** *noun*
■ **1** grow, tend, plant, sow **2** farm, till, work, plough, sow, plant **3** foster, nurture, encourage, promote, further, work on, develop, train, improve, enrich
 3 neglect

cultural *adj* of culture or the arts *etc* ◇ **culturally** *adv*

culture *noun* **1** a type of civilization with its associated customs: *Mediterranean culture* **2** development of the mind by education **3** educated tastes in art, music *etc* **4** cultivation of plants ◇ **cultured** *adj* well-educated in literature, art *etc*
■ **cultured** cultivated, civilized, advanced, enlightened, educated, well-read, well-informed, scholarly, highbrow, well-bred, refined, polished, genteel, urbane
 cultured uncultured, uneducated, ignorant

culvert *noun* an arched drain for carrying water under a road or railway

cum *prep* used for both of two stated purposes: *a newsagent-cum-grocer*

cumbersome *adj* awkward to handle
■ awkward, inconvenient, bulky, unwieldy, *informal* clunky, unmanageable, burdensome, onerous, heavy, weighty
 convenient, manageable

cummerbund *noun* a wide sash worn around the waist

cumulative *adj* increasing with additions: *cumulative effect* ◇ **cumulatively** *adv*

cumulus *noun* (*plural* **cumuli**) a kind of cloud common in summer, made up of rounded heaps

cunning *adj* **1** sly, clever in a deceitful way **2** skilful, clever ◇ *noun* **1** slyness **2** skill, knowledge

■ *adj* **1** crafty, sly, artful, wily, tricky, devious, subtle, deceitful, guileful **2** sharp, shrewd, astute, canny, knowing, deep, imaginative, ingenious, skilful, deft, dexterous ◇ *noun* **1** craftiness, slyness, artfulness, trickery, deviousness, subtlety, deceitfulness, guile **2** sharpness, shrewdness, astuteness, ingenuity, cleverness, adroitness

🇪🇦 *adj* **1** naive, ingenuous, gullible

cup *noun* **1** a hollow container holding liquid for drinking **2** an ornamental vessel given as a prize in sports events ◇ *verb* (**cups**, **cupping**, **cupped**) make (hands *etc*) into the shape of a cup ◇ **cupful** *noun* (*plural* **cupfuls**) as much as fills a cup

cupboard *noun* a shelved recess or box with doors, used for storage

■ cabinet, closet, locker, wardrobe

Cupid *noun* the Roman god of sexual love

cupidity *noun* greed

cupola /'kjuːpələ/ *noun* a curved ceiling or dome on the top of a building

cup-tie *noun* a game in a sports competition for which the prize is a cup

cur *noun* **1** a dog of mixed breed **2** a cowardly person

curable *adj* able to be treated and cured

curate *noun* a Church of England cleric assisting a rector or vicar

curative *adj* likely to cure

curator *noun* someone who has charge of a museum, art gallery *etc*

curb *verb* hold back, restrain ◇ *noun* a restraint

■ *verb* restrain, constrain, restrict, contain, control, check, moderate, suppress, subdue, repress, inhibit, hinder, impede, hamper, retard

❗ Do not confuse with: **kerb**

curd *noun* **1** milk thickened by acid **2** the solid part of curdled milk, as opposed to the **whey**

curdle *verb* cause (*esp* milk) to separate into solid and liquid components ◇ **curdle someone's blood** shock or terrify them

cure *verb* **1** free from disease, heal **2** get rid of (a bad habit *etc*) **3** preserve by drying, salting *etc* ◇ *noun* **1** the act of curing **2** something which cures

■ *verb* **1** heal, remedy, correct, restore, repair, mend **3** preserve, dry, smoke, salt, pickle, kipper ◇ *noun* **2** remedy, antidote, panacea, medicine, specific, corrective, restorative, healing, treatment, therapy

curfew *noun* an order forbidding people to be out of their houses after a certain hour

curio *noun* (*plural* **curios**) an article valued for its oddness or rarity

curiosity *noun* (*plural* **curiosities**) **1** strong desire to find something out **2** something unusual, an oddity

curious *adj* **1** anxious to find out **2** unusual, odd ◇ **curiously** *adv*

■ **1** inquisitive, nosey, prying, meddlesome, questioning, inquiring, interested **2** odd, queer, *informal* funny, strange, peculiar, bizarre, mysterious, puzzling, extraordinary, unusual, rare, unique, novel, exotic, unconventional, unorthodox, quaint

curl *verb* **1** twist (hair) into small coils **2** of hair: grow naturally in small coils **3** of smoke: move in a spiral **4** twist, form a curved shape **5** play at the game of curling ◇ *noun* a small coil or roll, *eg* of hair ◇ **curler** *noun* **1** something used to make curls **2** someone who plays the game of curling ◇ **curliness** *noun* ◇ **curling** *noun* a game played by throwing round, flat stones along a sheet of ice ◇ **curly** *adj* having curls

■ **curly** wavy, kinky, curling, spiralled, corkscrew, curled, crimped, permed, frizzy, fuzzy

🇪🇦 **curly** straight

curlew *noun* a wading bird with a very long slender bill and long legs

curmudgeon *noun* a mean person

currant *noun* **1** a small black dried grape **2** a berry of various kinds of soft fruit: *redcurrant*

!Do not confuse: **currant** and **current**

currency *noun* (*plural* **currencies**) **1** the money used in a particular country **2** the state of being generally known: *the story gained currency*

■ **1** money, legal tender, coinage, coins, notes, bills **2** acceptance, publicity, popularity, vogue, circulation, prevalence, exposure

---

Currencies of the world include: baht (*Thailand*), bolivar (*Venezuela*), cent (*US, Canada, Australia, NZ, S Africa etc*), centavo (*Brazil, Mexico etc*), centime (*Algeria, Andorra etc*), dinar (*Iraq, Jordan etc*), dirham (*Morocco*), dollar (*US, Canada, Australia, NZ etc*), dong (*Vietnam*), euro (*EU*), fils (*Iraq, Jordan etc*), franc (*Switzerland etc*), hryvnia (*Ukraine*), kopeck (*Russia*), koruna (*Czech Republic, Slovakia*), krona (*Sweden*), króna (*Iceland*), krone (*Denmark, Norway*), kyat (*Myanmar*), lek (*Albania*), leu (*Romania*), lev (*Bulgaria*), pence (*UK*), peso (*Mexico, Chile etc*), pfennig (*Germany*), piastre (*Egypt, Syria etc*), pound (*UK, Egypt etc*), rand (*S Africa*), real (*Brazil*), renminbi (*China*), rial (*Iran*), riyal (*Saudi Arabia*), rouble (*Russia*), rupee (*India, Pakistan etc*), shekel (*Israel*), shilling (*Kenya, Uganda etc*), sterling (*UK*), sucre (*Ecuador*), sum (*Uzbekistan*), tolar (*Slovenia*), won (*N Korea, S Korea*), yen (*Japan*), yuan (*China*), zloty (*Poland*)

---

current *adj* **1** belonging to the present time: *the current year* **2** generally known and talked about ◇ *noun* a stream of water, air or electrical power moving in one direction ◇ **current account** a bank account from which money may be withdrawn by cheque

■ *adj* **1** present, ongoing, existing, contemporary, present-day, modern, up-to-date, up-to-the-minute **2** widespread, prevalent, common, general, prevailing, accepted ◇ *noun* draught, stream, jet, flow, drift, tide, course

◼ *adj* **1** obsolete, old-fashioned

curriculum *noun* (*plural* **curricula** or **curriculums**) the course of study at a university, school *etc* ◇ **curriculum vitae** a brief account of a person's education, career *etc*

curry¹ *noun* (*plural* **curries**) a dish containing a mixture of spices with a strong, peppery flavour ◇ *verb* (**curries, currying, curried**) make into a curry by adding spices ◇ **curry powder** a selection of ground spices used in making curry

curry² *verb* rub down (a horse) ◇ **curry favour** try hard to be someone's favourite

curse *verb* **1** use swear words **2** wish evil towards ◇ *noun* **1** a swear word **2** a wish for evil or a magic spell **3** an evil or a great misfortune, or the cause of this ◇ **cursed** *adj* under a curse; hateful

■ *verb* **1** swear, blaspheme **2** damn, condemn, denounce, fulminate ◇ *noun* **3** evil, plague, scourge, affliction, trouble, torment, ordeal, calamity, disaster

◼ *verb* **2** bless

cursor *noun* a flashing device that appears on a VDU screen to show the position for entering data

cursory *adj* hurried ◇ **cursorily** *adv*

curt *adj* impolitely short, abrupt ◇ **curtly** adv ◇ **curtness** *noun*

curtail *verb* make less, reduce ◇ **curtailment** *noun*

■ shorten, truncate, cut, trim, abridge, abbreviate, reduce, restrict

◼ lengthen, extend, prolong

curtain *noun* a piece of material hung to cover a window, stage *etc*

curtsy or **curtsey** *noun* (*plural* **curtsies**) a bow made by bending the knees

curvature *noun* **1** a curving or bending **2** a curved piece **3** an abnormal curving of the spine

curve noun **1** a rounded line, like part of the edge of a circle **2** a bend: *a curve in the road* ◊ verb form a curve

■ noun **1** bend, turn, arc, trajectory, loop, camber, curvature **2** bend, turn ◊ verb bend, arch, arc, bow, hook, crook, turn, wind, twist

cushion noun **1** a casing stuffed with feathers, foam *etc*, for resting on **2** a soft pad ◊ verb reduce the impact of

■ verb soften, deaden, dampen, absorb, muffle, lessen, mitigate, protect

cushy adj, informal easy and comfortable: *a cushy job*

cusp noun **1** a point **2** a division between signs of the zodiac

custard noun a sweet sauce made from eggs, milk and sugar

custody noun **1** care, guardianship **2** imprisonment ◊ **custodian** noun **1** a keeper **2** a caretaker, *eg* of a museum

■ **1** keeping, possession, charge, care, safekeeping, protection, custodianship, guardianship, supervision **2** detention, confinement, imprisonment, incarceration

custom noun **1** something done by habit **2** the regular or frequent doing of something; habit **3** the buying of goods at a shop **4** (**customs**) taxes on goods coming into a country **5** (**customs**) the government department that collects these ◊ **customary** adj usual ◊ **custom-built** adj built to suit a particular purpose

■ **1** practice, convention, formality, observance, ritual, tradition **2** usage, use, habit, routine, procedure, practice, policy, convention, etiquette ◊ **customary** traditional, conventional, accepted, established, habitual, routine, regular, usual, normal, ordinary, everyday, familiar, common, general, popular, fashionable, prevailing

customer noun **1** someone who buys from a shop, pays for a service *etc* **2** informal a person: *an awkward customer*

cut verb (**cuts**, **cutting**, **cut**) **1** make a slit in, or divide, with a blade: *cut a hole/cut a slice of bread* **2** wound **3** trim with a blade *etc*: *cut the grass/my hair needs cutting* **4** reduce in amount **5** shorten (a play, book *etc*) by removing parts **6** refuse to acknowledge (someone you know) **7** divide (a pack of cards) in two **8** stop filming **9** informal play truant from (school) ◊ noun **1** a slit made by cutting **2** a wound made with something sharp **3** a reduction **4** a stroke, a blow **5** the way something is cut **6** the shape and style of clothes **7** a piece of meat ◊ **cut-and-dried** adj decided, settled ◊ **cut down 1** bring down by cutting **2** reduce ◊ **cut down on** reduce the intake of ◊ **cut glass** glass with ornamental patterns cut on the surface ◊ **cut in** interrupt ◊ **cut off 1** separate, isolate: *cut off from the mainland* **2** stop: *cut off supplies* ◊ **cut out 1** shape by cutting **2** informal stop **3** of an engine: fail ◊ **cut-up** adj distressed

■ verb **1** slice, carve, divide, part, split, bisect, dock, lop, sever, prune, excise, incise, penetrate, pierce, nick, gash, slit, slash **2** stab, wound, gash **3** clip, trim, crop, shear, mow, shave, pare **4** reduce, decrease, lower **5** shorten, curtail, abbreviate, abridge, condense, précis, edit **6** ignore, cold-shoulder, spurn, avoid, snub, slight, rebuff ◊ noun **1** incision, slit, slash, rip, laceration **2** wound, gash **3** reduction, decrease, lowering, cutback, saving, economy ◊ **cut down 1** fell, hew, lop, level, raze **2** reduce, decrease, lower, lessen, diminish ◊ **cut in** interrupt, butt in, interject, interpose, intervene

> *Tools for cutting include*:
> axe, billhook, blade, chisel, chopper, clippers, guillotine, hedgetrimmer, knife, flick knife, penknife, pocket knife, Stanley knife®, Swiss army knife, lopper, machete, mower, lawnmower, plane, razor, saw, chainsaw, fretsaw, hacksaw, jigsaw, scalpel, scissors, scythe, secateurs, shears, pinking shears, sickle, Strimmer®, sword

cute adj **1** pretty and pleasing **2** smart, clever

cuticle noun the skin at the bottom

and edges of fingernails and toenails

cutlass *noun* (*plural* **cutlasses**) a short broad sword

cutlery *noun* knives, forks, spoons *etc*

cutlet *noun* a slice of meat with the bone attached

cut-price *adj* sold at a price lower than usual

cut-throat *noun* a ruffian ◇ *adj* fiercely competitive: *cut-throat business*

cutting *noun* **1** a piece cut from a newspaper **2** a trench cut in the earth or rock for a road *etc* **3** a shoot of a tree or plant ◇ *adj* wounding, hurtful: *cutting remarks*
- *noun* **1** clipping, extract, piece ◇ *adj* sharp, keen, pointed, trenchant, incisive, penetrating, piercing, wounding, stinging, caustic, acid, scathing, sarcastic, malicious

cuttlefish *noun* a type of sea creature like a squid

cv *abbrev* curriculum vitae

cwt *abbrev* hundredweight

cyanide *noun* a kind of poison

cyber- *prefix* relating to computers or electronic media: *cyberspace/cyberselling*

cyborg *noun* a robot in human form, an android

cycle *noun* **1** a bicycle **2** a round of events following on from one another repeatedly: *the cycle of the seasons* **3** a series of poems, stories *etc* written about a single person or event ◇ *verb* **1** ride a bicycle **2** move in a cycle; rotate ◇ **cycle lane** a narrow lane reserved for cyclists
- *noun* **2** series, sequence, phase

cyclist *noun* someone who rides a bicycle

cyclone *noun* **1** a whirling windstorm **2** a system of winds blowing in a spiral ◇ **cyclonic** *adj*

cygnet /'sɪgnɪt/ *noun* a young swan

> **!** Do not confuse with: **signet**

cylinder *noun* **1** a solid or hollow tube-shaped object **2** in machines, car engines *etc*, the hollow tube in which a piston works ◇ **cylindrical** *adj* shaped like a cylinder
- **1** column, barrel, drum, reel, bobbin, spool, spindle

cymbals /'sɪmbəlz/ *noun plural* brass, plate-like musical instruments, often beaten together in pairs

cynic /'sɪnɪk/ *noun* someone who believes the worst about people ◇ **cynical** *adj* sneering; believing the worst of people ◇ **cynically** *adv* ◇ **cynicism** *noun*
- sceptic, doubter, pessimist, killjoy, *informal* spoilsport, scoffer ◇ **cynical** sceptical, doubtful, distrustful, pessimistic, negative, scornful, derisive, contemptuous, sneering, scoffing, mocking, sarcastic, sardonic, ironic

cynosure *noun* the centre of attraction or attention

cypress *noun* a type of evergreen tree

cyst /sɪst/ *noun* a liquid-filled blister within the body or just under the skin

cystitis *noun* inflammation of the bladder, often caused by infection

czar *another spelling* of **tsar**

czarina *another spelling* of **tsarina**

Dd

dab verb (**dabs**, **dabbing**, **dabbed**) touch gently with a pad etc to soak up moisture ◇ noun **1** the act of dabbing **2** a small lump of something soft **3** a gentle blow, a pat

  ▣ verb pat, tap, daub, swab, wipe ◇ noun **3** touch, pat, stroke, tap

dabble verb **1** play in water with hands or feet **2** do in a half-serious way or as a hobby: *he dabbles in computers* ◇ **dabbler** noun

  ▣ **2** trifle, tinker, toy, dally, potter

dab hand informal an expert

dace noun (plural **dace**) a type of small river fish

dachshund /'daksənd/ noun a breed of dog with short legs and a long body

dad or **daddy** noun, informal father

dado /'deɪdoʊ/ noun (plural **dadoes**) the lower part of an inside wall, decorated in a different way from the rest

daffodil noun a type of yellow flower which grows from a bulb

daft adj silly ◇ **daftly** adv ◇ **daftness** noun

  ▣ foolish, crazy, stupid, absurd, informal dotty, idiotic, mad

dagger noun a short sword for stabbing

dahlia noun a type of garden plant with large flowers

> Named after Anders *Dahl*, an 18th-century Swiss botanist

daily adj & adv every day ◇ noun (plural **dailies**) **1** a newspaper published every day **2** someone employed to clean a house regularly

dainty adj small and neat ◇ noun (plural **dainties**) a tasty morsel of food ◇ **daintily** adv ◇ **daintiness** noun

  ▣ adj delicate, elegant, exquisite, refined, fine, graceful, neat, charming

dairy noun (plural **dairies**) **1** a building

for storing milk and making butter and cheese **2** a shop which sells milk, butter, cheese etc ◇ **dairy cattle** cows kept for their milk, not their meat ◇ **dairy farm** a farm concerned with the production of milk, butter etc ◇ **dairymaid** or **dairyman** noun a woman or man working in a dairy ◇ **dairy products** food made of milk, butter or cheese

dais noun (plural **daises**) a raised floor at the upper end of a hall

daisy noun (plural **daisies**) a small common flower with white petals ◇ **daisy-chain** noun a string of daisies threaded through each other's stems ◇ **daisy-wheel** noun a flat printing wheel with characters at the end of spokes

> Literally 'day's eye', so called because it opens during the day

dale noun an area of low ground between hills

dally verb (**dallies**, **dallying**, **dallied**) **1** waste time idling or playing **2** play (with) ◇ **dalliance** noun

Dalmatian noun a breed of large spotted dog

dam noun **1** a wall of earth, concrete etc to keep back water **2** water kept in like this ◇ verb (**dams**, **damming**, **dammed**) **1** build a dam across; keep back by a dam **2** hold back, restrain (tears etc)

  ▣ noun **1** barrier, barrage, embankment ◇ verb **1** block, confine, restrict, check, barricade, staunch, stem, obstruct

damage noun **1** harm, injury **2** (**damages**) money paid by one person to another to make up for injury, insults etc ◇ verb spoil, make less effective or unusable

  ▣ noun **1** harm, destruction, devastation, impairment ◇ verb harm, injure, hurt, spoil, ruin, impair, mar, wreck, deface, mutilate, weaken, tamper with, incapacitate

damask *noun* silk, linen or cotton cloth, with figures and designs in the weave

> After *Damascus* in Syria, from where it was exported in the Middle Ages

dame *noun* **1** a comic character in a pantomime, played by a man in drag **2** (**Dame**) the title of a woman of the same rank as a knight

damn *verb* **1** sentence to unending punishment in hell **2** condemn as wrong, bad *etc* ◇ *exclam* an expression of annoyance ◇ **damnable** *adj* **1** deserving to be condemned **2** hateful ◇ **damnably** *adv* ◇ **damnation** *noun* **1** unending punishment in hell **2** condemnation ◇ **damning** *adj* leading to conviction or ruin: *damning evidence*
- *verb* **2** revile, denounce, criticize, censure, *informal* slate, *informal* slam, condemn
- *verb* **1** bless

damp *noun* wetness, moistness ◇ *verb* **1** wet slightly **2** make less fierce or intense ◇ *adj* moist, slightly wet ◇ **dampness** *noun*
- *adj* moist, wet, clammy, dank, humid, dewy, muggy, soggy
- *adj* dry, arid

dampen *verb* **1** make or become damp; moisten **2** lessen (enthusiasm *etc*)
- **2** dash, check, reduce, lessen, moderate

damper *noun* **1** something that lessens enthusiasm *etc* **2** a moveable plate controlling air flow to a fire **3** in a piano *etc*: a pad silencing a note once it is played

damsel *noun*, *old* an unmarried girl

damson *noun* a type of small darkred plum

dance *verb* move in time to music ◇ *noun* **1** a sequence of steps in time to music **2** a social event with dancing ◇ **dancer** *noun* ◇ **dancing** *noun*

> *Dances include*:
> waltz, quickstep, foxtrot, tango,

polka, one-step, military two-step, valeta, Lancers, rumba, samba, mambo, bossanova, beguine, fandango, flamenco, mazurka, bolero, paso doble, salsa, macarena, merengue, can-can; rock 'n' roll, jive, twist, stomp, bop, jitterbug, mashed potato, ceroc; black bottom, Charleston, cha-cha, turkey-trot, kazachoc; Circassian circle, Paul Jones, jig, reel, quadrille, Highland fling, morris-dance, clog dance, hoe-down, hokey-cokey, Lambeth Walk, conga, hora, belly-dance; galliard, gavotte, minuet

> *Types of dancing include*:
> ballet, tap, ballroom, old-time, disco, folk, country, Irish, Highland, set dancing, step dancing, Latin-American, clog-dancing, morris dancing, limbo-dancing, line-dancing, break-dancing, robotics

dandelion *noun* a common plant with a yellow flower

> From the French phrase *dent de lion*, meaning 'lion's tooth'

dandruff *noun* dead skin which collects on the scalp and falls off in flakes

dandy *noun* (*plural* **dandies**) a man who pays great attention to his dress and looks

danger *noun* **1** something potentially harmful: *the canal is a danger to children* **2** potential harm: *unaware of the danger*
- **1**, **2** risk, threat, peril, hazard, menace

dangerous *adj* **1** unsafe, likely to cause harm **2** full of risks ◇ **dangerously** *adv*
- **1**, **2** unsafe, insecure, risky, threatening, hazardous, perilous, precarious, treacherous

dangle *verb* hang loosely

dank *adj* moist, wet ◇ **dankness** *noun*

dapper *adj* small and neat

dappled *adj* marked with spots or splashes of colour
- speckled, mottled, stippled, flecked, variegated

dare *verb* **1** be brave or bold enough (to): *I didn't dare tell him* **2** challenge: *dared him to cross the railway line* **3** lay yourself open to, risk ◇ *noun* a challenge to do something dangerous, or something done for this reason ◇ **daring** *adj* bold, fearless ◇ *noun* boldness ◇ **daringly** *adv* ◇ **dare-devil** *noun* a rash person fond of taking risks ◇ *adj* rash, risky ◇ **I dare say** I suppose: *I dare say you're right*

　▣ *verb* **1** risk, venture, brave, hazard **2** goad, provoke, taunt ◇ **daring** *adj* bold, adventurous, intrepid, fearless, brave, plucky, audacious, dauntless, reckless, rash, impulsive, valiant

　▣ **daring** *adj* cautious, timid, afraid

dark *adj* **1** without light **2** black or near to black **3** gloomy **4** evil: *dark deeds* ◇ *noun* a dark place or time; darkness ◇ **darken** *verb* make or grow dark or darker ◇ **darkness** *noun* ◇ **dark-haired** *adj* having dark-brown or black hair ◇ **dark horse** someone about whom little is known ◇ **in the dark** knowing nothing about something ◇ **keep dark** keep (something) secret

　▣ *adj* **1** unlit, overcast, dim, murky, cloudy, dusky, dingy **3** grim, dismal, bleak **4** forbidding, sombre, sinister

darling *noun* **1** a term of affection **2** someone dearly loved; a favourite

　▣ **1** dear, sweetheart, pet **2** beloved, dearest, favourite, pet

darn *verb* mend (clothes) with interwoven rows of stitches ◇ *noun* a mend done in this way

dart *noun* **1** a pointed missile for throwing or shooting **2** a sewn fold which shapes a garment ◇ *verb* move quickly and suddenly ◇ **darts** *noun sing* a game in which small darts are aimed at a board marked off in circles and numbered sections ◇ **dartboard** *noun* the board used in playing darts

　▣ *verb* dash, sprint, flit, flash, fly, run, tear

dash *verb* **1** rush with speed or violence **2** throw or knock violently, *esp* so as to break **3** ruin (hopes) **4** depress, sadden (spirits) ◇ *noun* (*plural* **dashes**) **1** a rush **2** a short race **3** a small amount, *eg* of a drink **4** liveliness **5** a

short line (–) used to show a break in a sentence *etc* ◇ **dashing** *adj* smart, elegant

　▣ *verb* **1** hurry, race, sprint, run, bolt **2** fling, throw, crash, hurl **3** dampen, confound, blight, ruin, destroy, spoil, frustrate, smash, shatter ◇ *noun* **3** drop, pinch, touch, soupçon, hint, bit

dastardly *adj*, *formal* cowardly

data *noun plural* (*sing* **datum**) **1** available facts from which conclusions may be drawn **2** facts stored in a computer

　▣ **1** information, documents, facts, statistics, figures, details

database *noun*, *comput* a collection of systematically stored files that are often connected with each other

date¹ *noun* **1** a statement of time in terms of the day, month and year, *eg* 23 December 2000 **2** the day or year of an event: *the date of the Battle of Hastings* **3** the period of time to which something belongs **4** a social appointment ◇ *verb* **1** give a date to **2** belong to a certain time: *dates from the 12th century* **3** become old-fashioned: *that dress will date quickly* ◇ **out of date** *adj* **1** old-fashioned **2** no longer valid ◇ **up to date** *adj* **1** in fashion, modern **2** including or aware of the latest information **3** at the appropriate point in a schedule

　▣ *noun* **3** age, era, stage, epoch **4** engagement, assignation, meeting, rendezvous ◇ **out of date 1** old-fashioned, unfashionable, outdated, obsolete, dated, outmoded, antiquated, passé ◇ **up to date 1** fashionable, modern, current, contemporary

　▣ **out of date 1** fashionable, modern ◇ **up to date 1** old-fashioned, dated

date² *noun* **1** a type of palm tree **2** its blackish, shiny fruit with a hard stone

datum *sing* of **data**

daub *verb* **1** smear **2** paint roughly

daughter *noun* a female child ◇ **daughter-in-law** *noun* a son's wife

daunt *verb* **1** frighten **2** discourage ◇ **daunting** *adj* ◇ **dauntless** *adj* unable to be frightened

　▣ **1** intimidate, unnerve, alarm, frighten, scare **2** discourage, dishearten, dispirit, deter ◇ **dauntless** fearless, undaunted, intrepid, valiant, resolute

dawdle *verb* move slowly ◇ **dawdler** *noun*

▣ delay, loiter, lag, hang about, dally, trail, potter, *informal* dilly-dally

dawn *noun* 1 the time of the morning when it begins to get light 2 a beginning: *the dawn of a new era* ◇ *verb* 1 become day 2 begin to appear ◇ **dawning** *noun* dawn ◇ **dawn chorus** the singing of birds at dawn ◇ **dawn on** become suddenly clear to (someone)

▣ *noun* 1 sunrise, daybreak, morning, daylight 2 beginning, start, emergence, onset, origin, birth, advent ◇ *verb* 2 begin, appear, emerge, open, develop, originate, rise

day *noun* 1 the time of light, from sunrise to sunset 2 twenty-four hours, from one midnight to the next 3 the time or hours spent at work 4 (often **days**) a particular time or period: *in the days of steam* ◇ **day in, day out** on and on, continuously ◇ **day-release** *noun* time off from work for training or education ◇ **day trading** buying shares and selling them the same day ◇ **the other day** recently: *saw her just the other day*

daydream *noun* an imagining of pleasant events while awake ◇ *verb* imagine in this way

▣ *noun* fantasy, reverie, musing, imagining

daylight *noun* 1 the light of day, sunlight 2 a clear space

daze *verb* 1 stun with a blow 2 confuse, bewilder ◇ *noun* a confused state of mind

▣ *verb* 1 stun, stupefy 2 bewilder, confuse, baffle, dumbfound, perplex, astonish, *informal* flabbergast, astound, stagger, shock ◇ *noun* bewilderment, confusion, shock

dazzle *verb* 1 shine on so as to prevent from seeing clearly 2 shine brilliantly 3 fascinate, impress deeply ◇ **dazzling** *adj*

▣ 1 daze, blind, confuse, blur 3 fascinate, impress, overwhelm, awe, overawe, bedazzle, bewitch, stupefy

deacon *noun* 1 the lowest rank of clergy in the Church of England 2 a church official in other churches

dead *adj* 1 not living, without life 2 numb 3 not working: *the phones are all dead* 4 no longer in use: *a dead language* 5 complete, utter: *dead silence* 6 exact: *dead centre/a dead shot* ◇ *adv* 1 completely: *dead certain* 2 suddenly and completely: *stop dead* ◇ *noun* 1 those who have died: *speak well of the dead* 2 the time of greatest stillness *etc*: *the dead of night* ◇ **dead-beat** *adj* having no strength left ◇ **dead end** 1 a road *etc* closed at one end 2 a job *etc* not leading to promotion or progress ◇ **dead heat** a race in which two or more runners finish equal ◇ **dead ringer** *informal* someone looking exactly like someone else

▣ *adj* 1 lifeless, deceased, defunct, departed, late, gone 2 unresponsive, dull, indifferent, insensitive, numb, cold, frigid 5 absolute, perfect, utter, outright, total, downright

deaden *verb* lessen (pain *etc*)

▣ blunt, muffle, lessen, numb, alleviate, anaesthetize, desensitize, dampen, paralyse

deadline *noun* a date by which something must be done

Originally a line in a military prison, the penalty for crossing which was death

deadlock *noun* a situation in which complete failure to agree prevents further progress

▣ standstill, stalemate, impasse

deadly *adj* 1 likely to cause death, fatal 2 intense, very great: *deadly hush* ◇ *adv* intensely, extremely ◇ **deadliness** *noun*

▣ *adj* 1 lethal, fatal, dangerous, venomous

deadpan *adj* without expression on the face

deaf *adj* 1 unable to hear 2 refusing to listen: *deaf to our pleas* ◇ **deafness** *noun* ◇ **deaf-mute** *noun* someone who is both deaf and dumb

▣ 1 hard of hearing, stone-deaf 2 indifferent, unmoved, heedless

deafen *verb* **1** make deaf **2** be unpleasantly loud ◇ **deafening** *adj*

■ **deafening** piercing, ear-splitting

deal *noun* **1** an agreement, *esp* in business **2** an amount or quantity: *a good deal of paper* **3** the dividing out of playing-cards in a game ◇ *verb* **1** divide, give out **2** trade (in) **3** do business (with) ◇ **deal with** take action concerning, cope with

■ *noun* **1** contract, understanding, pact, transaction **2** quantity, amount, extent, degree, portion, share ◇ *verb* **1** apportion, distribute, share, dole out, allot **2** trade, traffic

dealer *noun* **1** someone who deals out cards at a game **2** a trader **3** a stockbroker

■ **2** trader, merchant, wholesaler, marketer, merchandiser

dean *noun* **1** the chief religious officer in a cathedral church **2** the head of a faculty in a university

dear *adj* **1** high in price **2** highly valued; much loved ◇ *noun* **1** someone who is loved **2** someone who is lovable or charming ◇ *adv* at a high price ◇ **dearly** *adv* ◇ **dearness** *noun*

■ *adj* **1** expensive, costly, overpriced, *informal* pricey **2** beloved, treasured, valued, cherished, precious

dearth /dɜːθ/ *noun* a scarcity, shortage

death *noun* **1** the end of life, the state of being dead **2** the end of something: *the death of steam railways* ◇ **death-blow** *noun* **1** a blow that causes death **2** an event that causes something to end ◇ **death knell 1** a bell announcing a death **2** something indicating the end of a scheme, hope *etc* ◇ **death mask** a plaster cast taken of a dead person's face ◇ **death rattle** a rattling in the throat sometimes heard before someone dies ◇ **deathwatch beetle** an insect that makes a ticking noise and whose larvae destroy wood ◇ **death wish** a conscious or unconscious desire to die

■ **1** decease, end, demise, passing **2** undoing, downfall, extermination, extinction, obliteration, eradication

deathly *adj* **1** very pale or ill-looking **2** deadly

■ **1** ashen, grim, haggard, pale, pallid, wan

debar *verb* (**debars, debarring, debarred**) prevent (someone) from doing, joining *etc* something: *debarred from the club*

debase *verb* **1** lessen in worth **2** make bad, wicked *etc* ◇ **debased** *adj* ◇ **debasement** *noun*

■ **1** degrade, demean, devalue, dishonour, humiliate **2** contaminate, pollute, corrupt, deprave

debatable *adj* arguable, doubtful: *a debatable point* ◇ **debatably** *adv*

debate *noun* **1** a discussion, *esp* a formal one before an audience **2** an argument ◇ *verb* engage in a debate, discuss

■ *noun* **1** discussion, disputation, deliberation **2** argument, dispute ◇ *verb* dispute, argue, discuss, contend

debauchery *noun* excessive indulgence in drunkenness, lewdness *etc* ◇ **debauched** *adj* inclined to debauchery

■ depravity, intemperance, overindulgence, dissipation, licentiousness, dissoluteness, excess, decadence, wantonness, lewdness, carousal, lust

debilitate *verb* make weak ◇ **debility** *noun* weakness of the body

■ weaken, enervate, undermine, sap, incapacitate, wear out, exhaust, impair

🗗 strengthen, invigorate, energize

debit *noun* **1** a debt **2** an amount taken from an account ◇ *verb* **1** mark down as a debt **2** take from an account ◇ **debit card** a plastic card used to transfer money from a customer's account to a retailer's

debonair *adj* of pleasant and cheerful appearance and behaviour

debouch /dɪ'baʊtʃ/ *verb* come out from a narrow or confined place

debrief *verb* gather information from an astronaut, spy *etc* after a mission ◇ **debriefing** *noun*

debris /'dɛbriː/ *noun* **1** the remains of something broken, destroyed *etc* **2** rubbish

▨ **1** remains, ruins, wreck, wreckage, fragments, rubble **2** rubbish, waste, litter, trash

debt /dɛt/ *noun* what one person owes to another ◇ **debtor** *noun* someone who owes a debt ◇ **in debt** owing money ◇ **in someone's debt** under an obligation to them
▰ creditor

debug *verb* (**debugs**, **debugging**, **debugged**) rewrite sections of a computer program which contain bugs

debut or **début** /'deɪbjuː/ *noun* the first public appearance, *eg* of an actor ◇ *adj* first before the public: *debut concert*

debutante or **débutante** *noun* a young woman making her first appearance in upper-class society

decade *noun* **1** a period of ten years **2** a set or series of ten

decadence *noun* a falling from high to low standards in morals, the arts *etc* ◇ **decadent** *adj*
▨ **decadent** corrupt, debased, debauched, depraved, dissolute, immoral, degenerate, degraded

decaff *adj, informal* decaffeinated ◇ *noun, informal* decaffeinated coffee

decaffeinated *adj* with the caffeine removed

decamp *verb* run away

decant *verb* pour (wine *etc*) from a bottle into a decanter

decanter *noun* an ornamental bottle with a glass stopper for wine, whisky *etc*

decapitate *verb* cut the head from ◇ **decapitation** *noun*

decathlon *noun* an athletics competition combining contests in ten separate disciplines

decay *verb* become bad, worse or rotten ◇ *noun* **1** the process of decaying **2** decayed matter ◇ **decayed** *adj*
▨ *verb* rot, putrefy, decompose, perish, deteriorate, disintegrate, corrode ◇ *noun* **1** decomposition, rotting, decline, deterioration, disintegration **2** rot, mould

decease *noun, formal* death

deceased *adj, formal* dead ◇ *noun* (**the deceased**) a dead person

deceit *noun* the act of deceiving
▨ deception, cheating, duplicity, double-dealing, treachery, hypocrisy
▰ honesty, openness, frankness

deceitful *adj* inclined to deceive; lying ◇ **deceitfully** *adv* ◇ **deceitfulness** *noun*
▨ dishonest, deceptive, deceiving, false, insincere, *informal* two-faced, crafty, hypocritical
▰ genuine, artless, open

deceive *verb* tell lies to so as to mislead ◇ **deceiver** *noun*
▨ mislead, cheat, betray, fool, *informal* take in, double-cross

decelerate *verb* slow down ◇ **deceleration** *noun*

December *noun* the twelfth month of the year

decent *adj* **1** respectable **2** good enough, adequate: *a decent salary* **3** kind: *decent of you to help* ◇ **decency** *noun* ◇ **decently** *adv*
▨ **1** seemly, suitable, presentable, becoming, befitting, nice **2** acceptable, satisfactory, reasonable, proper, fitting, suitable **3** obliging, courteous, helpful

deception *noun* **1** the act of deceiving **2** something that deceives or is intended to deceive

deceptive *adj* misleading: *appearances may be deceptive* ◇ **deceptively** *adv*
▨ illusive, fake, illusory, ambiguous

decibel *noun* a unit of loudness of sound

decide *verb* **1** make up your mind to do something: *I've decided to take your advice* **2** settle (an argument *etc*)
▨ **1** choose, determine, settle, elect, opt **2** resolve, settle, judge, adjudicate

decided *adj* **1** clear: *a decided difference* **2** with your mind made up: *he was decided on the issue* ◇ **decidedly** *adv* definitely
▨ **1** definite, clear-cut, undisputed, unquestionable, distinct **2** certain,

resolute, determined, firm, deliberate

▣ **1** inconclusive **2** irresolute

deciduous *adj* of a tree: having leaves that fall in autumn

decimal *adj* **1** numbered by tens **2** of ten parts or the number 10 ◇ *noun* a decimal fraction *noun* ◇ **decimal currency** a system of money in which each coin or note is either a tenth of another or ten times another in value ◇ **decimal fraction** a fraction expressed in tenths, hundredths, thousandths *etc*, separated by a decimal point ◇ **decimal point** a dot used to separate units from decimal fractions, *eg* $0.1 = \frac{1}{10}$, $2.33 = 2\frac{1}{3}$

decimalize *verb* convert (figures or currency) to decimal form ◇ **decimalization** *noun*

decimate *verb* make much smaller in numbers by destruction

Literally 'reduce by a tenth'

decipher *verb* **1** translate (a code) into ordinary, understandable language **2** make out the meaning of: *can't decipher his handwriting*

decision *noun* **1** the act of deciding **2** clear judgement, firmness: *acting with decision*

▣ **2** decisiveness, firmness, resolve, purpose

decisive *adj* **1** final, putting an end to a contest *etc*: *a decisive defeat* **2** showing decision and firmness: *a decisive manner* ◇ **decisively** *adv*

▣ **1** conclusive, definite, definitive, absolute, final **2** determined, resolute, positive, firm, strong-minded

deck [1] *noun* **1** a platform forming the floor of a ship, bus *etc* **2** a pack of playing-cards **3** the turntable of a record-player ◇ **clear the decks** get rid of old papers, work *etc* before starting something fresh ◇ **deckchair** *noun* a collapsible chair of wood and canvas *etc*

deck [2] *verb* decorate, adorn

declaim *verb* **1** make a speech in impressive, dramatic language **2** speak violently (against) ◇ **declamation** *noun* ◇ **declamatory** *adj*

declare *verb* **1** announce formally or publicly: *declare war* **2** say firmly **3** make known (goods or income on which tax is payable) **4** *cricket* end an innings before ten wickets have fallen ◇ **declaration** *noun*

▣ **1** proclaim, pronounce, decree, broadcast **2** affirm, assert, claim, profess, state, attest

decline *verb* **1** say 'no' to, refuse: *I had to decline his offer* **2** weaken, become worse ◇ *noun* a gradual worsening of health *etc*

▣ *verb* **1** refuse, reject, forgo **2** decay, deteriorate, worsen, degenerate ◇ *noun* deterioration, weakening, worsening, failing, downturn

▣ *verb* **2** improve ◇ *noun* improvement

declivity *noun* (*plural* **declivities**) a downward slope

decode *verb* translate (a coded message) into ordinary, understandable language

▣ decipher, interpret, unscramble, translate, transliterate, uncipher

decompose *verb* **1** rot, decay **2** separate into parts or elements ◇ **decomposition** *noun*

▣ **1** disintegrate, rot, decay, putrefy, break down, crumble, dissolve, fester **2** separate, break down, break up

décor /'deɪkɔːr/ *noun* the decoration of, and arrangement of objects in, a room *etc*

decorate *verb* **1** add ornament to **2** paint or paper the walls of (a room *etc*) **3** pin a badge or medal on (someone) as a mark of honour ◇ **decoration** *noun* ◇ **decorative** *adj* **1** ornamental **2** pretty ◇ **decorator** *noun* someone who decorates houses, rooms *etc*

▣ **1** adorn, beautify, embellish, trim, deck **2** renovate, *informal* do up, paint, paper, refurbish **3** honour, cite, garland, bemedal

decorous *adj* behaving in an acceptable or dignified way

decorum *noun* good behaviour

▣ propriety, seemliness, good manners

decoy *verb* lead into a trap ◇ *noun* something or someone intended to lead another into a trap

◼ *noun* lure, trap, bait

decrease *verb* make or become less ◊ *noun* a lessening

◼ *verb* lessen, lower, diminish, dwindle, decline, fall off, reduce, subside, abate, cut down, contract, drop, ease, shrink, taper, wane, slim, slacken, peter out, curtail ◊ *noun* lessening, reduction, decline, falling-off, dwindling, loss, diminution, abatement, cutback, contraction, downturn, ebb, shrinkage, subsidence, step-down

◼ *verb* increase ◊ *noun* increase

decree *noun* (**decrees, decreeing, decreed**) **1** an order, a law **2** a judge's decision ◊ *verb* give an order

◼ *verb* order, command, rule, lay down, dictate, decide, ordain, prescribe, proclaim, pronounce

decrepit *adj* **1** weak and infirm because of old age **2** in ruins or disrepair ◊ **decrepitude** *noun*

decry *verb* (**decries, decrying, decried**) **1** cause to seem worthless, belittle **2** express disapproval of

dedicate *verb* **1** devote yourself (to): *dedicated to his music* **2** set apart for a sacred purpose **3** inscribe or publish (a book *etc*) in tribute to someone or something: *I dedicate this book to my father* ◊ **dedication** *noun*

◼ **1** commit, assign, pledge **2** consecrate, bless, sanctify, hallow

deduce *verb* think out on the basis of what one knows ◊ **deduction** *noun*

◼ derive, infer, gather, conclude, understand, draw, glean

> ❗ Do not confuse: **deduce** and **deduct**

deduct *verb* subtract, take away (from) ◊ **deduction** *noun*

deed *noun* **1** something done, an act **2** *law* a signed statement or agreement

◼ *noun* **1** action, act, achievement, performance, exploit, feat, fact, truth, reality **2** contract, record, title, transaction

deep *adj* **1** being or going far down **2** hard to understand **3** involved to a great extent: *deep in debt/deep in thought* **4** intense, strong: *a deep red colour/deep affection* **5** low in pitch ◊ **deepen** *verb* ◊ **deep freeze** a low-temperature refrigerator that can freeze and preserve food for a long time ◊ **deep-seated** *adj* firmly fixed, not easily removed ◊ **in deep water** in serious trouble ◊ **the deep** the sea

◼ **1** bottomless, fathomless, yawning **2** obscure, mysterious, abstruse, esoteric **5** low, bass, resonant, booming

deer *noun* (*plural* **deer**) an animal with antlers in the male

deface *verb* spoil the appearance of, disfigure ◊ **defacement** *noun*

◼ damage, spoil, disfigure, blemish, impair, mutilate, mar, sully, tarnish, vandalize, deform

de facto actual, but often not legally recognized

defame *verb* try to harm the reputation of ◊ **defamation** *noun* ◊ **defamatory** *adj*

◼ **defamation** vilification, slander, libel, slur, smear

default *verb* fail to do something you ought to do, *eg* to pay a debt ◊ **defaulter** *noun* ◊ **by default** because of a failure to do something

defeat *verb* beat, win a victory over ◊ *noun* the act of defeating or being defeated

◼ *verb* conquer, beat, subdue, overpower, overthrow, overwhelm, *formal* vanquish ◊ *noun* conquest, beating, *formal* vanquishment

defect *noun*, /ˈdiːfɛkt/ a lack of something needed for completeness or perfection; a flaw ◊ *verb*, /dɪˈfɛkt/ desert a country, political party *etc* to join or go to another ◊ **defection** *noun* **1** failure in duty **2** desertion

◼ *noun* imperfection, fault, flaw, deficiency, failing, mistake, inadequacy, blemish, error, shortcoming, want, weakness

defective *adj* **1** faulty; imperfect **2** not having normal mental or physical ability

■ **1** faulty, imperfect, out of order, flawed, shoddy, broken

> ⚠ Do not confuse with: **deficient**

defence or *US* **defense** *noun* **1** the act of defending against attack **2** a means or method of protection **3** *law* the argument supporting the accused person in a case (*contrasted with*: **prosecution**) **4** *law* the lawyer(s) putting forward this argument ◇ **defenceless** *adj* without defence

■ **defenceless** unprotected, undefended, unarmed, unguarded, vulnerable, helpless, powerless

☲ **defenceless** protected, guarded

defend *verb* **1** guard or protect against attack **2** *law* conduct the defence of ◇ **defender** *noun*

■ **1** protect, guard, safeguard, shield, screen, support, stand up for, stand by

☲ **1** attack **2** accuse

defendant *noun law* the accused person in a case

defensible *adj* able to be defended

defensive *adj* **1** used for defence **2** expecting criticism, ready to justify actions ◇ **on the defensive** prepared to defend yourself against attack or criticism

■ **2** defending, wary, cautious, watchful

defer *verb* (**defers**, **deferring**, **deferred**) **1** put off to another time **2** give way (to): *he deferred to my wishes*

■ **1** delay, postpone, put off, adjourn, hold over, shelve, suspend

deference *noun* **1** willingness to consider or respect the wishes *etc* of others **2** the act of giving way to another ◇ **deferential** *adj* showing deference, respectful

■ **2** submission, submissiveness, acquiescence, obedience, compliance, yielding

defiance *noun* open disobedience or opposition ◇ **defiant** *adj* ◇ **defiantly** *adv*

■ **defiant** resistant, antagonistic, aggressive, rebellious, disobedient, intransigent, bold, insolent

☲ **defiant** compliant, acquiescent, submissive

deficiency *noun* (*plural* **deficiencies**) **1** lack, want **2** an amount lacking

☲ **1**, **2** excess, surfeit

deficient *adj* lacking in what is needed

■ inadequate, insufficient, scarce, wanting

> ⚠ Do not confuse with: **defective**

deficit *noun* an amount by which a sum of money *etc* is too little

■ shortage, shortfall

defile *verb* **1** make dirty, soil **2** corrupt, make bad ◇ **defilement** *noun*

■ **1** pollute, contaminate, soil, stain **2** degrade, dishonour, debase, profane, corrupt, disgrace

define *verb* **1** state the exact meaning of **2** outline or show clearly **3** fix the bounds or limits of

definite *adj* **1** not liable to change, fixed **2** exact **3** certain, sure **4** having clear limits or outlines ◇ **definitely** *adv* ◇ **definiteness** *noun* ◇ **definite article** the grammatical term for the word *the*

■ **1** fixed, firm, decided, determined **2** precise, specific, particular **3** sure, positive **4** clear, clear-cut, explicit, obvious, marked

definition *noun* **1** an explanation of the exact meaning of a word or phrase **2** sharpness or clearness of outline

■ **2** clarity, precision, focus, sharpness

definitive *adj* **1** fixed, final **2** not able to be bettered: *a definitive biography* ◇ **definitively** *adv*

■ **1** decisive, conclusive, final **2** authoritative, standard, correct, ultimate, reliable, exhaustive, perfect, exact, absolute, complete

deflate *verb* **1** let the air out of (a tyre *etc*) **2** reduce in self-importance or self-confidence ◇ **deflation** *noun* **1** the act of deflating **2** a reduction in the amount of available money in a country, lowering economic activity ◇ **deflationary** *adj*

■ **2** debunk, *informal* put down

deflect *verb* turn aside (from a fixed course) ◇ **deflection** *noun*

■ avert, turn (aside)

deform *verb* **1** spoil the shape of; put out of shape **2** make ugly ◇ **deformed** *adj* badly or abnormally formed

▤ **1** distort, contort, disfigure, warp, mar, pervert, ruin, spoil, twist

deformity *noun* (*plural* **deformities**) **1** something abnormal in shape **2** the fact of being deformed

defraud *verb* cheat in order to get something, *esp* money: *they defrauded him of his savings*

▤ cheat, swindle, dupe, *informal* rip off, *informal* do, *informal* con, deceive, embezzle

defray *verb* pay for (expenses)

defrost *verb* remove frost or ice (from); thaw

deft *adj* clever with the hands, handy ◇ **deftly** *adv* ◇ **deftness** *noun*

▤ adept, handy, dexterous, skilful, adroit, nimble, nifty, proficient, neat

▣ clumsy, awkward

defunct *adj* no longer active or in use

▤ obsolete, invalid, inoperative, expired

defy *verb* (**defies, defying, defied**) **1** dare (someone) to do something, challenge **2** resist openly; disobey **3** make impossible: *its beauty defies description*

▤ **1** challenge, dare **2** challenge, confront, resist, brave, face, spurn, beard, flout, disregard, scorn **3** elude, frustrate, baffle, foil

degenerate *adj* having become immoral or very bad ◇ *verb* become bad or worse ◇ **degeneracy** *noun* immorality ◇ **degeneration** *noun* worsening

▤ *adj* dissolute, debauched, depraved, degraded, debased, base, low, decadent, corrupt, fallen, immoral, mean, degenerated, perverted, deteriorated ◇ *verb* decline, deteriorate, sink, decay, rot, slip, worsen, regress

degrade *verb* **1** lower in grade or rank **2** disgrace; humiliate ◇ **degrading** *adj* ◇ **degradation** *noun*

▤ **1** demote, downgrade **2** dishonour, disgrace, debase, shame, humiliate, demean, cheapen

degree **1** a step or stage in a process **2** rank or grade **3** amount, extent: *a degree of certainty* **4** a unit of temperature **5** a unit by which angles are measured, one 360th part of the circumference of a circle **6** a certificate given by a university, gained by examination or given as an honour

dehydrate *verb* **1** remove water from (food *etc*) **2** lose or cause to lose excessive water from the body ◇ **dehydrated** *adj* ◇ **dehydration** *noun*

deify *verb* (**deifies, deifying, deified**) worship as a god

▤ exalt, worship, idolize, idealize, immortalize

deign *verb* act as if doing a favour: *she deigned to answer us*

▤ condescend, stoop, lower oneself, consent, demean oneself

deity *noun* (*plural* **deities**) a god or goddess

déjà vu /deɪʒɑː ˈvuː/ the feeling of having experienced something before

dejected *adj* gloomy, dispirited ◇ **dejection** *noun*

▤ downcast, despondent, depressed, downhearted, disheartened, down, glum, melancholy, dismal, doleful, miserable, cast down, gloomy, glum, crestfallen, doleful, morose

delay *verb* **1** put off, postpone **2** keep back, hinder ◇ *noun* **1** a postponement **2** a situation or period of time in which someone is made to wait

▤ *verb* **1** defer, put off, suspend, shelve **2** obstruct, impede, hold up, hold back, detain ◇ *noun* **1** deferment, suspension **2** hold-up, setback, hindrance, obstruction

delectable *adj* delightful, pleasing ◇ **delectably** *adv*

delectation *noun* delight, enjoyment

delegate *verb* give (a task) to someone else to do ◇ *noun* someone acting on behalf of another; a representative ◇ **delegation** *noun* a group of delegates

▤ *verb* authorize, charge, commission, assign, entrust, devolve, hand over ◇ *noun* representative, agent, deputy, ambassador

delete *verb* erase or strike out (*eg* a piece of writing) ◇ **deletion** *noun*
▣ erase, remove, cross out, rub out, obliterate, edit (out), blot out, efface

deleterious *adj* harmful

deli *noun, informal* a delicatessen

deliberate *verb* think carefully or seriously (about) ◇ *adj* **1** intentional, not accidental **2** not hurried ◇ **deliberately** *adv*
▣ *verb* consider, ponder, reflect, think, cogitate, mull over ◇ *adj* **1** planned, prearranged, premeditated, conscious, intended **2** careful, unhurried, thoughtful, methodical, cautious, circumspect, studied, prudent, slow, ponderous, measured, heedful

deliberation *noun* **1** careful thought **2** calmness, coolness **3** (**deliberations**) formal discussions
▣ **1** consideration, reflection, thought, rumination

delicacy *noun* (*plural* **delicacies**) **1** the state of being delicate **2** something delicious to eat **3** tact
▣ **2** titbit, dainty, sweetmeat **3** sensitivity, subtlety, tact, diplomacy

delicate *adj* **1** not strong, frail; easily damaged **2** fine, dainty: *delicate features* **3** pleasant to taste **4** tactful **5** requiring skill or care: *a delicate operation*
▣ **1** weak, ailing, faint, frail, brittle **2** exquisite, flimsy, elegant, graceful **5** careful, accurate, precise

delicatessen *noun* a shop selling food cooked or prepared for eating, *esp* unusual or imported food

delicious *adj* **1** very pleasant to taste **2** giving pleasure ◇ **deliciously** *adv*
▣ **1** appetizing, palatable, tasty, delectable, *informal* scrumptious, mouthwatering, *informal* yummy **2** enjoyable, pleasant, agreeable, delightful

delight *verb* **1** please greatly **2** take great pleasure (in) ◇ *noun* great pleasure ◇ **delighted** *adj*
▣ *verb* **1** please, charm, gratify, enchant, tickle, thrill, ravish ◇ *noun* bliss, happiness, joy, pleasure, ecstasy, rapture

delightful *adj* very pleasing ◇ **delightfully** *adv*

▣ charming, enchanting, enjoyable, pleasant, pleasurable, attractive, pleasing
▨ nasty, unpleasant

delinquent *adj* **1** guilty of an offence or misdeed **2** not carrying out your duties ◇ *noun* **1** someone guilty of an offence **2** someone who fails in their duty ◇ **delinquency** *noun* **1** wrongdoing, misdeeds **2** failure in duty
▣ *noun* **1** offender, criminal, wrongdoer, law-breaker, hooligan, culprit, *formal* miscreant

delirious *adj* **1** raving, wandering in the mind **2** wildly excited ◇ **deliriously** *adv*
▣ **1** demented, raving, incoherent, deranged, wild, mad, frantic, insane, crazy **2** ecstatic, beside oneself, frenzied, light-headed

delirium *noun* **1** a delirious state, *esp* caused by fever **2** wild excitement ◇ **delirium tremens** a delirious disorder of the brain caused by excessive alcohol

deliver *verb* **1** carry (letters, parcels *etc*) to a person or place **2** hand over **3** give (*eg* a speech, a blow) **4** set free, rescue **5** assist at the birth of (a child) ◇ **deliverance** *noun*
▣ **1** convey, bring, send **2** surrender, relinquish, yield, entrust, commit **4** liberate, release

delivery *noun* (*plural* **deliveries**) **1** a handing over, *eg* of letters **2** the birth of a child **3** a style of speaking
▣ **3** articulation, enunciation, intonation, elocution

delphinium *noun* a branching garden plant with blue flowers

From a Greek word translating as 'little dolphin', because of the shape of the flowerheads

delta *noun* the triangular stretch of land at the mouth of a river

Originally from a Hebrew word meaning 'tent door'

delude *verb* deceive
▣ deceive, mislead, beguile, dupe, take in,

trick, hoodwink, hoax, cheat, misinform

deluge *noun* **1** a great flood of water **2** an overwhelming amount: *deluge of work* ◇ *verb* **1** flood, drench **2** overwhelm

delusion *noun* a false belief, *esp* as a symptom of mental illness ◇ **delusionary** *adj*

▤ hallucination, fancy, misconception, misapprehension, deception, misbelief, fallacy

⚠ Do not confuse with: **allusion** and **illusion**

delve *verb* **1** dig **2** rummage, search through: *delved in her bag for her keys*

demagogue *noun* a leader who appeals to people's emotions and prejudices

demand *verb* **1** require, ask, call for: *demanding attention* **2** insist: *I demand that you listen* ◇ *noun* **1** a forceful request **2** an urgent claim: *many demands on his time* **3** a need for certain goods *etc*: *there's no demand for skiing equipment at this time of year*

▤ *verb* **1** ask, request, call for, require, necessitate **2** insist on, order, need, require ◇ *noun* **1** request, call, order **3** call, need, necessity, order, desire

demanding *adj* difficult; challenging

▤ hard, difficult, taxing, tough, challenging, wearing

demean *verb* lower, degrade

demeanour *noun* behaviour, conduct

demented *adj* mad, insane

▤ mad, insane, lunatic, out of one's mind, crazy, *slang* loony, deranged, unbalanced, frenzied

demise *noun* **1** *formal* death **2** a ceasing to exist: *demise of the shipbuilding industry*

▤ **1** death, decease, passing, departure, expiration **2** end, downfall, fall, collapse, failure, ruin

demob *verb* & *noun*, *informal* **1** demobilize **2** demobilization

demobilize *verb* **1** break up an army after a war is over **2** free (a soldier) from army service ◇ **demobilization** *noun*

democracy *noun* government of the people by the people through their elected representatives

democrat *noun* **1** someone who believes in democracy **2** (**Democrat**) *US* a member of the Democratic Party

democratic *adj* **1** of or governed by democracy **2** (**Democratic**) *US* belonging to one of the two chief political parties in the USA ◇ **democratically** *adv*

▤ **1** self-governing, representative, egalitarian, autonomous, popular, populist

demography *noun* the study of population size and movement ◇ **demographer** *noun* ◇ **demographic** *adj*

demolish *verb* **1** destroy completely **2** pull down (a building *etc*) ◇ **demolition** *noun*

▤ **1** ruin, defeat, destroy, annihilate, wreck, overturn, overthrow **2** dismantle, knock down, pull down, flatten, bulldoze, raze, tear down, level

demon *noun* an evil spirit, a devil ◇ **demonic** *adj*

demonstrable *adj* able to be shown clearly

demonstrate *verb* **1** show clearly; prove **2** show (a machine *etc*) in action **3** express an opinion by marching, showing placards *etc* in public ◇ **demonstrator** *noun*

▤ **1** explain, illustrate, describe, teach **2** show, display, exhibit **3** protest, march, parade, rally, picket, sit in

demonstration *noun* **1** a showing, a display **2** a public expression of opinion by a procession, mass meeting *etc*

demonstrative *adj* **1** pointing out; proving **2** inclined to show feelings openly

▤ **2** affectionate, expressive, expansive, emotional, open, loving

▣ **2** reserved, cold, restrained

demoralize *verb* take away the confidence or enthusiasm of ◇ **demoralization** *noun*

▤ discourage, dishearten, dispirit, depress, deject

▣ encourage

demote verb reduce to a lower rank or grade ◇ **demotion** noun
≡ downgrade, relegate
✷ promote

demur verb (**demurs, demurring, demurred**) object, say 'no'

demure adj shy and modest ◇ **demurely** adv
≡ modest, reserved, reticent, prim, coy, shy, retiring, prissy, prudish, sober, strait-laced, staid

den noun **1** the lair of a wild animal **2** a small private room for working etc

denial noun the act of denying ◇ **in denial** doggedly refusing to accept something
≡ contradiction, negation, dismissal, refusal, rejection

denier /'dɛnɪə(r)/ noun a unit of weight of nylon, silk etc

denigrate verb attack the reputation of, defame
≡ disparage, run down, slander, revile, defame, malign, vilify, decry, besmirch, impugn, belittle, abuse, assail, criticize

denim noun a hard-wearing cotton cloth used for jeans, overalls etc

denizen noun a dweller, an inhabitant

denomination noun **1** name, title **2** a value of a coin, stamp etc **3** a religious sect ◇ **denominational** adj

denominator noun the lower number in a vulgar fraction by which the upper number is divided, eg the 3 in $\frac{2}{3}$

denote verb mean, signify
≡ indicate, stand for, signify, represent, express, designate, typify, mark

dénouement noun the ending of a story where mysteries etc are explained
≡ conclusion, outcome, upshot, resolution

Literally 'untying' or 'unravelling', from French

denounce verb **1** accuse publicly of a crime **2** inform against: denounced him to the enemy **3** condemn strongly ◇ **denunciation** noun

dense adj **1** closely packed together; thick **2** very stupid ◇ **densely** adv

≡ **1** compact, thick, compressed, condensed, close, solid, packed, crowded **2** informal thick, crass, dull, slow, slow-witted

density noun (plural **densities**) **1** the state or degree of being dense: population density **2** weight (of water) in proportion to volume **3** comput the extent to which data can be held on a floppy disk

dent noun a hollow made by a blow or pressure ◇ verb make a dent in
≡ noun hollow, depression, indentation, dimple, pit

dental adj of or for a tooth or teeth

dentist noun a doctor who examines teeth and treats dental problems ◇ **dentistry** noun the work of a dentist

dentures noun plural a set of false teeth

denude verb make bare, strip: denuded of leaves ◇ **denudation** noun

denunciation see denounce

deny verb (**denies, denying, denied**) **1** declare to be untrue: he denied that he had done it **2** refuse, forbid: denied the right to appeal ◇ **deny yourself** do without things you want or need
≡ **1** contradict, oppose, refute, disagree with, disaffirm **2** turn down, forbid, reject, withhold

deodorant noun something that hides unpleasant smells

depart verb **1** go away **2** turn aside (from): departing from the plan ◇ **departed** adj dead ◇ **departure** noun ◇ **a new departure** a new course of action
≡ **1** go, leave, withdraw, exit, make off, set off, disappear **2** deviate, digress, differ, diverge, swerve, veer
✷ **1** arrive, return **2** keep to

department noun a self-contained section within a shop, company, university, government etc

depend verb: **depend on 1** rely on **2** receive necessary financial support from **3** be controlled or decided by: it all depends on the weather ◇ **dependable** adj to be trusted

1 count on, *informal* bank on, lean on **3** hinge on, rest on, be contingent upon, hang on ◇ **dependable** reliable, trustworthy, steady, trusty, responsible, faithful, unfailing

dependant *noun* someone who is kept or financially supported by another

> ⚠ Do not confuse: **dependant** and **dependent**

dependent *adj* relying or depending (on) ◇ **dependence** *noun* the state of being dependent

depict *verb* **1** draw, paint *etc* **2** describe

depilatory *adj* hair-removing: *depilatory cream* ◇ *noun* a hair-removing substance

deplete *verb* make smaller in amount or number ◇ **depletion** *noun*

deplore *verb* disapprove of, regret: *deplored his use of language* ◇ **deplorable** *adj* regrettable; very bad

deplorable grievous, regrettable, unfortunate, distressing, reprehensible, disgraceful, shameful, dishonourable, disreputable

deploy *verb* place in position ready for action

dispose, arrange, position, station, use

depopulate *verb* reduce greatly in population ◇ **depopulated** *adj*

deport *verb* send (someone) out of a country ◇ **deportation** *noun*

banish, exile, transport

deportment *noun* behaviour, bearing

depose *verb* remove from a high position, *esp* a monarch from a throne

unseat, topple, displace, oust

deposit *verb* **1** put or set down **2** put for safekeeping, *eg* money in a bank ◇ *noun* **1** money paid in part payment of something **2** money put in a bank account **3** a solid that has settled at the bottom of a liquid **4** a layer of coal, iron *etc* occurring naturally in rock ◇ **deposit account** a bank account in which money gains interest but cannot be withdrawn by cheque

verb **1** lay, drop, place, put, *informal* dump **2** save, store, hoard, bank, amass, entrust ◇ *noun* **1** security, stake, down payment, retainer, instalment, part payment **3** sediment, dregs, lees, silt

deposition *noun* **1** a written piece of evidence **2** the act of deposing or being deposed

depository (*plural* **depositories**) a place where anything is deposited for safekeeping

depot /'depoʊ/ *noun* **1** a storehouse **2** a building where railway engines, buses *etc* are kept and repaired

deprave *verb* make wicked ◇ **depraved** *adj* wicked ◇ **depravity** *noun*

depraved corrupt, perverted, debauched, immoral, base, shameless, wicked, sinful, vile

moral, upright

deprecate *verb* show disapproval of, condemn ◇ **deprecation** *noun*

deplore, condemn, disapprove of, censure, reject

> ⚠ Do not confuse: **deprecate** and **depreciate**

depreciate *verb* **1** lessen the value of **2** fall in value ◇ **depreciation** *noun*

depredations *noun plural* plundering

depress *verb* **1** make gloomy or unhappy **2** press down **3** lower in value ◇ **depressing** *adj*

1 deject, sadden, dishearten, discourage, upset, daunt, burden ◇ **depressing** gloomy, black, distressing, hopeless

depressed *adj* dispirited, gloomy

low-spirited, melancholy, dispirited, sad, unhappy, low, down, downcast, disheartened, *informal* fed up, miserable, moody, cast down, discouraged, glum, downhearted, distressed, despondent, morose, crestfallen

cheerful

depression *noun* **1** low spirits, gloominess **2** a hollow **3** a low period in a country's economy with unemployment, lack of trade *etc* **4** a region of low atmospheric pressure

■ **1** despair, low spirits, sadness, gloominess, hopelessness **2** indentation, dip, dent, valley, pit

deprive *verb*: **deprive of** take away from ◇ **deprivation** *noun* ◇ **deprived** *adj* suffering from hardship; disadvantaged

■ **deprived** poor, needy, disadvantaged, underprivileged, impoverished, destitute

◨ **deprived** prosperous

depth *noun* **1** deepness **2** a deep place **3** the deepest part: *from the depth of her soul* **4** the middle: *in the depth of winter* **5** intensity, strength: *depth of colour* ◇ **in depth** thoroughly, carefully ◇ **out of your depth** involved in something too difficult to understand or handle

deputation *noun* a group of people chosen and sent as representatives

deputy *noun* (*plural* **deputies**) **1** a delegate, a representative **2** a second-in-command ◇ **deputize** *verb* take another's place, act as substitute

■ **1** representative, agent, delegate, proxy **2** second-in-command, subordinate, assistant

derail *verb* cause to leave the rails ◇ **derailment** *noun*

derange *verb* put out of place, or out of working order; disrupt ◇ **deranged** *adj* mad, insane ◇ **derangement** *noun*

■ **deranged** demented, crazy, mad, insane, disturbed, delirious, berserk

◨ **deranged** sane, calm

derelict *adj* broken-down, ruined, abandoned ◇ **dereliction** *noun* neglect of what should be attended to: *dereliction of duty*

■ neglected, deserted, desolate, discarded, dilapidated, ruined

deride *verb* laugh at, mock ◇ **derision** *noun* ◇ **derisive** *adj*

■ ridicule, mock, scoff, scorn, jeer, *informal* knock, disparage

de rigueur required by custom or fashion

derivative *adj* not original ◇ *noun* **1** a

word formed on the base of another word, *eg fabulous* from *fable* **2** (**derivatives**) stock market trading in futures and options

■ *adj* unoriginal, acquired, copied, borrowed, derived, imitative, second-hand, plagiarized, *informal* cribbed, hackneyed, trite

derive *verb* **1** be descended or formed (from) **2** trace (a word) back to the beginning of its existence **3** receive, obtain: *derive satisfaction* ◇ **derivation** *noun*

■ **1** originate, arise, spring, emanate, descend, stem, issue, develop **3** gain, obtain, get, draw, extract, receive, procure, acquire

dermatitis *noun* inflammation of the skin

dermatology *noun* the study and treatment of skin diseases ◇ **dermatologist** *noun*

derogatory *adj* harmful to reputation, dignity *etc*; scornful

■ defamatory, injurious, insulting, pejorative, offensive, disparaging, depreciative, critical

derrick *noun* **1** a crane for lifting weights **2** a framework over an oil well which holds the drilling machinery

> Named after Derrick, a famous 17th-century hangman in Tyburn, England

dervish *noun* a member of an austere Islamic sect

descant *noun*, *music* a tune played or sung above the main tune

descend *verb* **1** go or climb down **2** slope downwards **3** go from a better to a worse state ◇ **be descended from** have as an ancestor: *claims he's descended from Napoleon*

■ **1** drop, go down, fall, plummet, plunge, tumble **2** dip, slope, subside

descendant *noun* someone descended from another ◇ **descent** *noun* **1** an act of descending **2** a downward slope **3** lineage

describe *verb* **1** give an account of in words **2** draw the outline of, trace

◇ **description** *noun* **1** the act of describing **2** an account in words **3** sort, kind: *people of all descriptions* ◇ **descriptive** *adj*

descry *verb* (**descries**, **descrying**, **descried**) notice, see

desecrate *verb* **1** spoil (something sacred) **2** treat without respect ◇ **desecration** *noun*

⚠ Do not confuse with: **desiccate**

desert[1] *verb* /dɪˈzɜːt/ **1** run away from (the army) **2** leave, abandon: *deserted his wife/his courage deserted him* ◇ **deserter** *noun* ◇ **desertion** *noun*

▣ **1** leave, defect, abscond **2** abandon, forsake, leave, maroon

desert[2] *noun* /ˈdɛzət/ a stretch of barren country with very little water ◇ **desert island** an uninhabited island in a tropical area

⚠ Do not confuse with: **dessert**

deserve *verb* have earned as a right, be worthy of: *you deserve a holiday* ◇ **deservedly** *adv* justly ◇ **deserving** *adj*

▣ earn, be worthy of, merit, be entitled to, warrant, justify

desiccate *verb* **1** dry up **2** preserve by drying: *desiccated coconut*

⚠ Do not confuse with: **desecrate**

design *verb* **1** make a plan of (*eg* a building) before it is made **2** intend ◇ *noun* **1** a plan, a sketch **2** a painted picture, pattern *etc* **3** an intention ◇ **designing** *adj* crafty, cunning ◇ **have designs on** plan to get for yourself

▣ *verb* **1** sketch, draft, outline, draw (up) **2** plan, plot, intend, aim, propose, mean ◇ *noun* **1** blueprint, draft, prototype, sketch, outline, model **3** aim, goal, purpose, object, objective

designate *verb* **1** point out, indicate **2** name **3** appoint, select ◇ *adj* appointed to a post but not yet occupying it: *director designate* ◇ **designation** *noun* a name, a title

desire *verb* wish for greatly ◇ *noun* **1** a

longing **2** a wish ◇ **desirability** *noun* ◇ **desirable** *adj* pleasing; worth having

▣ *verb* want, covet, long for, need, crave, yearn for, *informal* fancy ◇ **desirable** advantageous, worthwhile, beneficial, attractive, seductive

desist *verb*, *formal* stop (doing something)

▣ stop, cease, refrain, discontinue, halt, abstain

desk *noun* a table for writing, reading *etc*

desolate *adj* **1** deeply unhappy **2** empty of people, deserted **3** barren ◇ **desolated** *adj* overcome by grief ◇ **desolation** *noun* **1** deep sorrow **2** barren land **3** ruin

▣ **1** depressed, dejected, despondent, distressed, melancholy, miserable, gloomy, disheartened, dismal, downcast **2** deserted, uninhabited, abandoned, unfrequented

▣ **1** cheerful **2** populous

despair *verb* give up hope ◇ *noun* **1** lack of hope **2** a cause of despair: *she was the despair of her mother* ◇ **despairing** *adj*

▣ *verb* lose heart, lose hope, give up, give in, collapse, surrender ◇ *noun* **1** despondency, gloom, hopelessness, desperation, anguish

despatch *another spelling of* **dispatch**

desperado *noun* (*plural* **desperadoes** or **desperados**) a violent criminal

▣ bandit, brigand, outlaw, cut-throat, thug

desperate *adj* **1** without hope, despairing **2** very bad, awful **3** reckless; violent ◇ **desperately** *adv* ◇ **desperation** *noun*

▣ **1** hopeless, inconsolable, wretched, despondent **2** critical, acute, serious, severe, extreme **3** rash, dangerous, do-or-die, foolhardy, risky, wild, violent, frantic, frenzied

despicable *adj* contemptible, hateful

▣ contemptible, vile, detestable, mean, disgraceful, disreputable, reprobate

▣ admirable, noble

despise *verb* look on with contempt

■ scorn, deride, look down on, condemn, spurn, revile, deplore, dislike, detest, loathe

despite *prep* in spite of: *we had a picnic despite the weather*

■ in spite of, notwithstanding, regardless of, undeterred by

despoil *verb* rob, plunder ◇ **despoliation** *noun*

despondent *adj* downhearted, dejected ◇ **despondency** *noun*

■ depressed, dejected, disheartened, downcast, down, low, gloomy, glum, discouraged, miserable, melancholy, sad, sorrowful, doleful, despairing, heartbroken, inconsolable, mournful, wretched

despot *noun* a ruler with unlimited power, a tyrant ◇ **despotic** *adj* ◇ **despotism** *noun*

■ autocrat, tyrant, dictator, oppressor

dessert *noun* a sweet course served at the end of a meal

⚠ Do not confuse with: **desert**

destination *noun* the place to which someone or something is going

destine *verb* set apart for a certain use ◇ **destined** *adj* 1 bound (for) 2 intended (for) by fate: *destined to succeed*

destiny *noun* (*plural* **destinies**) what is destined to happen; fate

■ fate, fortune, karma, *formal* lot, *formal* portion

destitute *adj* 1 in need of food, shelter *etc* 2 (with **of**) completely lacking in: *destitute of wit* ◇ **destitution** *noun*

■ 1 poor, penniless, poverty-stricken, impoverished, *informal* down and out, bankrupt 2 lacking, wanting, devoid of, bereft, deprived, deficient

destroy *verb* 1 pull down, knock to pieces 2 put an end to: *destroyed his career* 3 kill ◇ **destroyer** *noun* 1 someone who destroys 2 a type of fast warship

■ 1 demolish, wreck, devastate, smash 3 eliminate, extinguish, *formal* slay

destructible *adj* able to be destroyed

destruction *noun* 1 the act of de-

stroying or being destroyed 2 ruin 3 death

destructive *adj* 1 doing great damage 2 of criticism: pointing out faults without suggesting improvements

■ 1 devastating, catastrophic, disastrous 2 hostile, discouraging, disparaging, undermining

desultory *adj* 1 moving from one thing to another without a fixed plan 2 changing from subject to subject, rambling ◇ **desultorily** *adv* ◇ **desultoriness** *noun*

detach *verb* unfasten, remove (from)

■ separate, disconnect, unfasten, disengage, undo, sever, loosen, unhitch

⊞ attach

detachable *adj* able to be taken off: *detachable lining*

detached *adj* 1 standing apart, by itself: *a detached house* 2 not personally involved, showing no emotion

■ 2 aloof, dispassionate, impersonal, disinterested, objective

detachment *noun* 1 the state of being detached 2 a body or group (*eg* of troops on special service)

detail *noun* a small part, fact, item *etc* ◇ *verb* 1 describe fully, give particulars of 2 set to do a special job or task: *detailed to wash the dishes* ◇ **detailed** *adj* with no detail left out ◇ **in detail** giving attention to details, item by item

■ *noun* particular, item, element, feature, point, specific, technicality ◇ **detailed** comprehensive, exhaustive, full, *informal* blow-by-blow, thorough, meticulous

detain *verb* 1 hold back 2 make (someone) late 3 keep under guard

■ 3 confine, arrest, intern, hold, keep

⊞ 3 release

detect *verb* 1 discover 2 notice ◇ **detection** *noun*

■ 1 uncover, catch, discover, disclose, expose, find 2 notice, note, observe, perceive, discern, spot, spy

detective *noun* someone who tries to find criminals or watches suspects

détente /deɪˈtɑːt/ *noun* a lessening of hostility between nations

detention *noun* **1** imprisonment **2** a forced stay after school as punishment
■ **1** detainment, custody, imprisonment, confinement

deter *verb* (**deters, deterring, deterred**) discourage or prevent through fear ◇ **deterrent** *noun* something which deters
■ discourage, put off, inhibit, dissuade, *informal* turn off, restrain, disincline, prevent, prohibit, stop ◇ **deterrent** hindrance, impediment, obstacle, repellent, discouragement, obstruction, restraint

detergent *noun* a soap-like substance used with water for washing clothes, dishes *etc*

deteriorate *verb* grow worse: *her health is deteriorating rapidly* ◇ **deterioration** *noun*
■ worsen, decline, depreciate, fail, decay, disintegrate

determination *noun* **1** the act of determining **2** the fact of being determined; firmness of purpose
■ **2** resoluteness, tenacity, firmness, perseverance, persistence, purpose, *informal* guts, steadfastness, will, conviction, dedication, drive, fortitude

determine *verb* **1** find out **2** fix, settle: *determined his course of action* **3** decide ◇ **determined** *adj* **1** with a firm or strong intention: *determined to succeed* **2** fixed, settled

deterrent *see* **deter**

detest *verb* hate greatly ◇ **detestable** *adj* ◇ **detestation**
■ hate, abhor, loathe, abominate, dislike, deplore, despise
■ adore, love

dethrone *verb* remove from a throne ◇ **dethronement** *noun*

detonate *verb* (cause to) explode ◇ **detonation** *noun* ◇ **detonator** *noun*

detour *noun* a circuitous route
■ deviation, diversion, indirect route, bypass

detox *verb*, *informal* rid the body of toxic substances ◇ *noun* treatment to rid the body of toxic substances

detract *verb* take away (from), lessen ◇ **detraction** *noun*

detriment *noun* harm, damage, disadvantage ◇ **detrimental** *adj* disadvantageous (to), causing harm or damage
■ **detrimental** damaging, harmful, hurtful, adverse, injurious, mischievous, destructive

deuce *noun* **1** a playing-card with two pips **2** *tennis* a score of forty points each

Deutschmark *noun* a former unit of German money

devastate *verb* **1** destroy, ruin **2** overwhelm with grief *etc* ◇ **devastating** *adj* ◇ **devastation** *noun*
■ **1** destroy, lay waste, demolish, spoil, wreck, ruin **2** overwhelm, *informal* shatter

develop *verb* **1** (cause to) grow bigger or become more advanced **2** acquire gradually: *developed a taste for opera* **3** become active or visible **4** unfold gradually: *as the plot develops* **5** use chemicals to make (a photograph) appear ◇ **developer** *noun* **1** a chemical mixture used to make an image appear from a photograph **2** someone who builds on land ◇ **development** *noun*
■ **1** evolve, expand, progress, foster, flourish, mature, prosper, branch out **2** contract, acquire, begin, generate, create

deviate *verb* turn aside, *esp* from a standard course ◇ **deviation** *noun*
■ diverge, veer, digress, stray, wander, err, go astray, *informal* go off the rails

device *noun* **1** a tool, an instrument **2** a plan **3** a design on a coat of arms
■ **1** tool, implement, gadget, *informal* contraption, utensil, instrument, machine **2** scheme, ruse, strategy, plan, plot, manoeuvre, *informal* dodge

⚠ Do not confuse with: **devise**

devil *noun* **1** an evil spirit **2** Satan **3** a wicked person ◇ **devilish** *adj* very wicked ◇ **devilment** or **devilry** *noun* mischief ◇ **devil-may-care** *adj* not caring what happens ◇ **devil's advocate** someone who argues against a proposal simply to encourage discussion

■ **1** demon, fiend, evil spirit, imp **2** Satan, Lucifer, Evil One, Prince of Darkness, Beelzebub, Mephistopheles, *informal* Old Nick, *informal* Old Harry

devious *adj* **1** not direct, roundabout **2** not straightforward or honest ◊ **deviousness** *noun*

■ **1** indirect, circuitous, rambling, roundabout, wandering, winding, tortuous **2** underhand, deceitful, dishonest, scheming, calculating, cunning, wily, sly, *informal* slippery

devise *verb* **1** make up, put together **2** plan, plot

▐ Do not confuse with: **device**

devoid *adj* (with **of**) empty of, free from: *devoid of curiosity*

■ lacking, without, free, deficient, empty, vacant

devolution *noun* the delegation of certain legislative powers to regional or national assemblies ◊ **devolutionist** *noun* a supporter of devolution

devolve *verb* **1** fall as a duty (on) **2** delegate (power) to a regional or national assembly

devote *verb* **1** give up wholly (to) **2** give for a purpose

■ *verb* **1** dedicate, commit, give, sacrifice **2** set apart, set aside, reserve, apply, allocate, allot, sacrifice, assign, appropriate, surrender, pledge

devoted *adj* **1** loving and loyal **2** given up (to): *devoted to her work*

■ **1** attentive, caring, faithful

devotee *noun* a keen follower or supporter

devotion *noun* great love

devour *verb* **1** eat up greedily **2** destroy

■ **1** consume, gorge, gobble, bolt, wolf down, cram, *informal* polish off, *informal* snarf **2** consume, absorb, engulf, ravage

devout *adj* **1** earnest, sincere **2** religious ◊ **devoutly** *adv* ◊ **devoutness** *noun*

■ **1** sincere, earnest, fervent, genuine, ardent, serious, wholehearted, constant, faithful, zealous **2** pious, godly, religious, orthodox

dew *noun* tiny drops of water which form on the ground *etc* as the air cools at night ◊ **dewy** *adj*

dexterity *noun* skill, quickness ◊ **dexterous** or **dextrous** *adj*

diabetes *noun* a disease in which there is too much sugar in the blood ◊ **diabetic** *noun* & *adj* (someone) suffering from diabetes

diabolic or **diabolical** *adj* devilish, very wicked ◊ **diabolically** *adv*

■ fiendish, demonic, hellish, damnable, vile, dreadful, outrageous, shocking, atrocious

diadem *noun* a kind of crown

diagnose *verb* identify (an illness) after making an examination ◊ **diagnosis** *noun* (*plural* **diagnoses**) ◊ **diagnostic** *adj*

diagonal *adj* going from one corner to the opposite corner across the middle ◊ *noun* a diagonal line ◊ **diagonally** *adv*

■ *adj* oblique, slanting, crosswise

diagram *noun* a drawing to explain something ◊ **diagrammatic** or **diagrammatical** *adj* in the form of a diagram

■ plan, sketch, chart, drawing, figure, representation, illustration, outline, graph, picture, layout, table

dial *noun* (**dials**, **dialling**, **dialled**) **1** the face of a clock or watch **2** a rotating disc over the numbers on some telephones ◊ *verb* call (a number) on a telephone using a dial or buttons

dialect *noun* a way of speaking found only in a certain area or among a certain group of people

dialogue *noun* a spoken exchange between two or more people

■ conversation, interchange, discourse, communication, exchange, discussion, debate

diameter *noun* (the length of) a line passing across a circle through its centre

diamond *noun* **1** a very hard precious stone **2** an elongated, four-cornered shape (◇) **3** (**diamonds**) one of the four suits of playing-cards, with red diamond-shaped pips

diaper *noun*, *US* a baby's nappy

Originally a kind of decorated white silk. The current US meaning was used in British English in the 16th century

diaphragm *noun* **1** a layer of muscle separating the lower part of the body from the chest **2** a thin dividing layer **3** a contraceptive device that fits over the cervix

diarrhoea *noun* frequent emptying of the bowels, with too much liquid in the faeces

diary *noun* (*plural* **diaries**) **1** a record of daily happenings **2** a book detailing these

▣ **2** journal, day-book, logbook, chronicle, year-book, appointment book, engagement book

diaspora *noun* a widespread dispersion or migration of people

diatribe *noun* an angry attack in words

dice *noun* (*plural* **dice**) a small cube with numbered sides or faces, used in some games ◇ *verb* cut (food) into small cubes

dictate *verb* **1** speak the text of (a letter *etc*) for someone else to write down **2** give firm commands ◇ *noun* an order, a command ◇ **dictation** *noun*

▣ *verb* **2** command, order, direct, instruct, rule ◇ *noun* decree, principle, rule, direction, order, ruling, statute, ultimatum

dictator *noun* an all-powerful ruler ◇ **dictatorial** *adj* like a dictator; domineering

diction *noun* **1** manner of speaking **2** choice of words

▣ **1** speech, articulation, elocution, enunciation, pronunciation, delivery

dictionary *noun* (*plural* **dictionaries**) **1** a book giving the words of a language in alphabetical order, together with their meanings **2** any alphabetically ordered reference book

did *see* do

die [1] *verb* (**dies**, **dying**, **died**) **1** lose life **2** cease to exist ◇ **be dying for** long for ◇ **diehard** *noun* an obstinate or determined person

▣ **1** decease, perish, pass away, expire, depart, *slang* snuff it, *informal* bite the dust, *slang* kick the bucket, *slang* flatline **2** dwindle, wilt, peter out, decline, decay, lapse, end ◇ **be dying for** pine for, yearn, desire

die [2] *noun* **1** a stamp or punch for making raised designs on money *etc* **2** (*plural* **dice**) a dice

diesel *noun* **1** an internal-combustion engine in which heavy oil is ignited by heat generated by compression **2** fuel for this engine

diet [1] *noun* **1** food **2** a course of recommended foods, *eg* to lose weight ◇ *verb* eat certain kinds of food only, *esp* to lose weight ◇ **dietetic** *adj*

diet [2] *noun* a legislative assembly

differ *verb* (**differs**, **differing**, **differed**) **1** (often with **from**) be unlike **2** disagree

▣ **1** vary, diverge, deviate, contradict, contrast **2** conflict, dispute, quarrel, contend

difference *noun* **1** a point or way in which things or people differ **2** the amount by which one number is greater than another **3** a disagreement

different *adj* not the same or alike

▣ dissimilar, contrasting, divergent, inconsistent, at odds, clashing, opposed

differentiate *verb* make a difference or distinction between

difficult *adj* **1** not easy to do, understand or deal with **2** hard to please

▣ **1** hard, laborious, demanding, tough, complex, complicated, obscure, baffling **2** unmanageable, awkward, troublesome, stubborn, obstinate

difficulty *noun* (*plural* **difficulties**) **1** lack of ease, the quality of being difficult **2** anything difficult **3** anything which makes something difficult; an obstacle, hindrance *etc* **4** (**difficulties**) troubles

diffident *adj* shy, not confident ◇ **diffidence** *noun*

▤ unassertive, modest, shy, timid, bashful, tentative, unsure

diffuse *verb* spread in all directions ◇ *adj* widely spread

▤ *adj* scattered, dispersed, spread out

dig *verb* (**digs, digging, dug**) **1** turn up (earth) with a spade *etc* **2** make (a hole) by this means **3** poke or push (something) into ◇ *noun* **1** a poke, a thrust **2** an archaeological excavation ◇ **digger** *noun* a machine for digging

▤ *verb* **1** scoop, gouge, delve **2** excavate, burrow, mine, tunnel

digest *verb* **1** break down (food) in the stomach into a form that the body can make use of **2** think over ◇ *noun* **1** a summing-up **2** a collection of written material ◇ **digestible** *adj* able to be digested ◇ **digestion** *noun* the act or power of digesting ◇ **digestive** *adj* aiding digestion

digit *noun* **1** a finger or toe **2** any of the numbers 0–9 ◇ **digital** *adj* **1** of a clock *etc*: showing numbers as digits, rather than on a dial or scale **2** using information in the form of binary digits: *digital recording* ◇ **digital television** television signals transmitted in digital form

digitalis *noun* a family of plants, including the foxglove, from which a medicine used to treat heart disease is obtained

dignified *adj* stately, serious

▤ stately, imposing, majestic, noble, formal, distinguished, reserved, honourable
▣ undignified, lowly

dignitary *noun* (*plural* **dignitaries**) someone of high rank or office

dignity *noun* **1** a manner showing a sense of your own worth or the seriousness of the occasion **2** high rank

▤ **1** decorum, self-respect, self-esteem, poise, respectability, pride **2** honour, eminence, importance, nobility, standing, status

digress *verb* wander from the point in

speaking or writing ◇ **digression** *noun*

▤ deviate, go off at a tangent, ramble

dike *another spelling of* **dyke**[1]

dilapidated *adj* falling to pieces, needing repair

▤ ramshackle, shabby, broken-down, neglected, tumbledown, rickety, decrepit, worn-out, ruined, decayed, decaying

dilate *verb* make or grow larger, swell out ◇ **dilatation** *or* **dilation** *noun*

dilatory *adj* slow to act, inclined to delay

dilemma *noun* a situation offering a difficult choice between two options

▤ quandary, conflict, predicament, problem, *informal* catch-22, difficulty, plight

dilettante *noun* someone with a slight but not serious interest in several subjects

diligent *adj* hard-working, industrious ◇ **diligence** *noun* ◇ **diligently** *adv*

▤ hard-working, conscientious, busy, attentive, assiduous, careful, meticulous, persevering, persistent, studious
▣ negligent, lazy

dilly-dally *verb* (**dilly-dallies, dilly-dallying, dilly-dallied**) loiter, waste time

dilute *verb* lessen the strength of a liquid *etc, esp* by adding water ◇ *adj* diluted: *dilute hydrochloric acid* ◇ **dilution** *noun*

▤ *verb* water down, thin (out), weaken

dim *adj* **1** not bright or clear **2** not understanding clearly, stupid ◇ *verb* (**dims, dimming, dimmed**) make or become dim ◇ **dimly** *adv* ◇ **dimness** *noun*

▤ *adj* **1** dark, dull, dusky, cloudy, shadowy, gloomy, sombre, dingy, blurred, hazy, ill-defined **2** stupid, dense, obtuse, *informal* thick ◇ *verb* darken, dull, obscure, cloud, blur, fade, shade
▣ *adj* **1** bright, clear **2** bright, intelligent ◇ *verb* brighten, illuminate

dime *noun* a tenth of a US or Canadian dollar, ten cents

dimension *noun* **1** a measurement of length, width or thickness **2** (**dimensions**) size, measurements

diminish *verb* make or become less

■ decrease, lessen, reduce, lower, contract, decline, dwindle, shrink, recede, taper off, wane, weaken, abate, fade, sink, subside, ebb

diminuendo *noun, music* a fading or falling sound

diminution *noun* a lessening

diminutive *adj* very small

■ undersized, small, tiny, little, miniature, minute, infinitesimal, wee, petite, midget, *informal* teeny-weeny, Lilliputian, *informal* dinky, *informal* pint-size(d)

dimple *noun* a small hollow, *esp* on the cheek or chin

dim sum a Chinese meal made up of many small portions of steamed dumplings *etc*

din *noun* a loud, lasting noise ◇ *verb* (**dins, dinning, dinned**) put (into) someone's mind by constant repetition

■ *noun* noise, row, racket, clamour, pandemonium, uproar, commotion, crash, hubbub

◼ *noun* quiet, calm

dine *verb* eat dinner

dinghy *noun* (*plural* **dinghies**) a small rowing or sailing boat

dingy *adj* dull, faded or dirty-looking ◇ **dinginess** *noun*

■ dark, drab, grimy, faded, dull, dim, shabby, soiled, dreary, gloomy, seedy, run-down

◼ bright, clean

dinner *noun* **1** a main evening meal **2** a midday meal, lunch

dinosaur *noun* any of various types of extinct giant reptile

Coined in the 19th century, from Greek words which translate as 'terrible lizard'

dint *noun* a hollow made by a blow, a dent ◇ **by dint of** by means of

diocese *noun* a bishop's district

dip *verb* (**dips, dipping, dipped**) **1** plunge into a liquid quickly **2** lower (*eg* a flag) and raise again **3** slope down **4** look briefly into (a book *etc*) ◇ *noun* **1** a liquid in which anything is dipped **2** a

creamy sauce into which raw vegetables, biscuits *etc* are dipped **3** a downward slope **4** a hollow **5** a short bathe or swim

■ *verb* **1** immerse, submerge, duck, dunk, douse **3** descend, decline, drop, fall, subside, sink, lower ◇ *noun* **4** basin, hole **5** bathe, immersion, plunge, soaking, swim

diphtheria *noun* an infectious throat disease

diphthong *noun* two vowel sounds pronounced as one syllable, as in *out* or *rain*

diploma *noun* a written statement conferring a qualification, confirming a pass in an examination *etc*

From a Greek word meaning 'a letter folded double'

diplomacy *noun* **1** the business of making agreements, treaties *etc* between countries **2** skill in making people agree, tact

■ **1** statesmanship, politics, negotiation, manoeuvring **2** tact, tactfulness, finesse, delicacy, discretion, savoir-faire, subtlety

diplomat *noun* someone engaged in diplomacy

■ go-between, mediator, negotiator, ambassador, envoy, peacemaker, politician

diplomatic *adj* **1** of diplomacy **2** tactful

dire *adj* **1** dreadful **2** urgent: *in dire need*

■ **1** disastrous, awful, appalling, catastrophic **2** desperate, grave, drastic, crucial, extreme, alarming

direct *adj* **1** straight, not roundabout **2** frank, outspoken ◇ *verb* **1** point or aim **2** show the way **3** order, instruct **4** control, organize **5** put a name and address on (a letter) ◇ **directness** *noun* ◇ **direct speech** speech reported in the speaker's exact words ◇ **direct tax** a tax on income or property

■ *adj* **1** straight, undeviating, uninterrupted **2** straightforward, blunt, unequivocal, candid, explicit ◇ *verb* **1** aim, point, focus **3** instruct, command, order **4** control, manage, run, administer, lead, supervise

direction *noun* **1** the act of directing **2** the place or point to which someone moves, looks *etc* **3** an order **4** guidance **5** (**directions**) instructions on how to get somewhere

directly *adv* **1** in a direct way **2** immediately

■ **2** immediately, instantly, right away, straight away

director *noun* **1** a manager of a business *etc* **2** the person who controls the shooting of a film *etc*

■ **1** manager, controller, executive, administrator

directory *noun* (*plural* **directories**) **1** a book of names and addresses *etc* **2** a named group of files on a computer disk

dirge *noun* a lament; a funeral hymn

dirk *noun* a kind of dagger

dirt *noun* any unclean substance, such as mud, dust, dung *etc* ◇ **dirt track** an earth track for motorcycle racing

dirty *adj* **1** not clean, soiled **2** obscene, lewd ◇ *verb* (**dirties**, **dirtying**, **dirtied**) soil with dirt ◇ **dirtily** *adv* ◇ **dirtiness**

■ *adj* **1** filthy, grimy, grubby, mucky, soiled, unwashed, polluted, squalid, sullied **2** indecent, filthy, smutty, sordid, salacious, vulgar, pornographic

🖬 *adj* **1** clean **2** decent

disability *noun* (*plural* **disabilities**) something which makes someone disabled

disable *verb* take away power or strength from, cripple ◇ **disabled** *adj* restricted in physical or mental ability ◇ **disablement** *noun*

■ cripple, lame, incapacitate, handicap, debilitate, weaken, immobilize

🖬 **disabled** able, able-bodied

disabuse *verb* set right about a wrong belief or opinion: *she soon disabused him of that idea*

disadvantage *noun* an unfavourable

circumstance, a drawback ◇ **disadvantaged** *adj* suffering a disadvantage, *esp* poverty or homelessness ◇ **disadvantageous** *adj* not advantageous

■ snag, hindrance, handicap, impediment, inconvenience, flaw, weakness ◇ **disadvantaged** deprived, underprivileged, poor, handicapped, impoverished

🖬 advantage, benefit

disaffected *adj* discontented, rebellious ◇ **disaffection** *noun*

■ hostile, alienated, antagonistic, rebellious, dissatisfied, discontented

disagree *verb* **1** (often with **with**) be different or opposed; hold different opinions **2** quarrel **3** (with **with**) of food: cause to feel ill ◇ **disagreement** *noun*

■ **1** conflict, clash, contradict, counter, differ **2** quarrel, argue, dispute

disagreeable *adj* unpleasant

■ disgusting, offensive, repulsive, repellent, obnoxious, unsavoury, objectionable, nasty

🖬 agreeable

disallow *verb* not allow or accept

disappear *verb* go out of sight, vanish ◇ **disappearance** *noun*

■ vanish, evaporate, dissolve

disappoint *verb* **1** fail to come up to the hopes or expectations of (someone) **2** fail to fulfil ◇ **disappointed** *adj* ◇ **disappointing** *adj* ◇ **disappointment** *noun*

■ **disappointment** frustration, dissatisfaction, disillusionment, failure, letdown, setback, misfortune

🖬 **disappointment** pleasure, satisfaction, delight, success

disapprove *verb* have an unfavourable opinion (of) ◇ **disapproval** *noun*

disarm *verb* **1** take a weapon away from **2** get rid of war weapons **3** make less angry, charm ◇ **disarmament** *noun* the removal or disabling of war weapons ◇ **disarming** *adj* gaining friendliness, charming: *a disarming smile*

■ **3** appease, mollify, win

disarrange *verb* throw out of order,

make untidy ◇ **disarrangement** noun

disarray noun disorder

■ confusion, disorder, chaos, upset

disaster noun an extremely unfortunate happening, often causing great damage or loss ◇ **disastrous** adj ◇ **disastrously** adv

■ calamity, catastrophe, misfortune, tragedy, accident, mishap, failure, informal flop, fiasco ◇ **disastrous** devastating, dreadful, dire, terrible

disband verb of a group of people: break up, separate ◇ **disbandment** noun

■ assemble, muster

disbelieve verb not believe ◇ **disbelief** noun ◇ **disbeliever** noun

disburse verb pay out ◇ **disbursement** noun

disc noun **1** a flat, round shape **2** a pad of cartilage between vertebrae **3** a gramophone record or compact disc ◇ **disc jockey** someone who introduces and plays recorded music on radio etc

■ **1** circle, plate **3** record, album, LP, CD, MiniDisc

discard verb throw away as useless

■ reject, abandon, dispose of, get rid of, dispense with, cast aside, informal ditch, informal dump, drop, scrap

discern verb see, notice ◇ **discernible** adj noticeable: a discernible difference ◇ **discerning** adj having or showing good judgement: a discerning eye ◇ **discernment** noun

■ **discerning** perceptive, astute, sensitive, shrewd, wise, sharp, acute, discriminating

discharge verb **1** unload **2** set free **3** dismiss, send away **4** fire (a gun) **5** perform (duties) **6** pay (a debt) **7** give off (eg smoke) **8** let out (pus) ◇ noun **1** an act of discharging **2** dismissal **3** pus etc discharged from the body **4** performance (of duties) **5** payment

■ verb **2** liberate, free, release, acquit **4** fire, shoot, let off **5** execute, carry out, perform, fulfil **7** emit

disciple noun **1** someone who believes in another's teaching **2** one of the followers of Christ in the Bible

discipline noun **1** training in an orderly way of life **2** order kept by means of control **3** punishment **4** a subject of study or training ◇ verb **1** bring to order or keep in order **2** punish ◇ **disciplinarian** noun someone who insists on strict discipline ◇ **disciplinary** adj

■ noun **2** restraint, regulation, orderliness, strictness **3** punishment, chastisement, correction ◇ verb **1** control, correct, restrain, govern **2** chastize, chasten, penalize, reprimand, castigate

disclaim verb deny: disclaim responsibility

■ deny, disown, repudiate, renounce

disclaimer noun a denial

disclose verb uncover, reveal, make known ◇ **disclosure** noun **1** the act of disclosing **2** something disclosed

■ divulge, make known, reveal, tell, confess, let slip, relate, publish, informal leak, expose

disco noun (plural **discos**) an event or place where recorded music is played for dancing

discolour or US **discolor** verb spoil the colour of ◇ **discoloration** noun

discombobulate verb, informal confuse greatly

discomfit verb **1** disconcert **2** thwart, defeat ◇ **discomfiture** noun

discomfort noun lack of comfort, uneasiness

■ ache, pain, uneasiness, trouble, distress, disquiet, hardship

discommode verb inconvenience

disconcert verb upset, confuse ◇ **disconcerting** adj

■ **disconcerting** disturbing, confusing, upsetting, unnerving, bewildering, informal off-putting, awkward, baffling, perplexing

disconnect verb separate, break the connection between ◇ **disconnected** adj **1** separated, no longer connected **2** of thoughts etc: not following logically, rambling

disconsolate adj sad, disappointed

■ dejected, dispirited, unhappy, forlorn, heavy-hearted, wretched

discontent *noun* dissatisfaction
◇ **discontented** *adj* dissatisfied, cross
◇ **discontentment** *noun*

▣ **discontented** dissatisfied, *informal* fed up, disgruntled, unhappy, disaffected, miserable, exasperated, complaining

▣ **discontented** contented, satisfied

discontinue *verb* 1 stop 2 cease to produce

discord *noun* 1 disagreement, quarrelling 2 *music* a jarring of notes ◇ **discordant** *adj*

▣ 1 disagreement, conflict, difference, dispute, dissension, contention, friction, division, opposition, strife, split 2 dissonance, disharmony, *formal* cacophony, jangle, jarring

discotheque *noun* a disco

discount *noun* a sum taken off the price of something: *10% discount* ◇ *verb* regard as unlikely or unimportant: *completely discounted my ideas/cannot discount the possibility*

▣ *verb* disregard, ignore, overlook, disbelieve, gloss over

discourage *verb* 1 take away the confidence, hope *etc* of 2 try to prevent by showing dislike or disapproval: *discouraged his advances* ◇ **discouragement** *noun* ◇ **discouraging** *adj* giving little hope or encouragement

▣ 1 dishearten, dampen, dispirit, depress, demoralize, deject, disappoint 2 deter, dissuade, hinder, put off

discourse *noun* 1 a speech, a lecture 2 an essay 3 a conversation ◇ *verb* talk, *esp* at some length

discourteous *adj* not polite, rude ◇ **discourteously** *adv* ◇ **discourtesy** *noun*

▣ rude, bad-mannered, impolite, boorish

discover *verb* 1 find out 2 find by chance, *esp* for the first time ◇ **discoverer** *noun*

▣ 1 ascertain, determine, realize, discern, learn, detect 2 uncover, unearth, dig up, disclose, reveal, locate

discovery *noun* (*plural* **discoveries**) 1 the act of finding or finding out 2 something discovered

discredit *verb* 1 cause to be doubted or disbelieved 2 disgrace ◇ *noun* 1 disgrace 2 disbelief ◇ **discreditable** *adj* disgraceful

▣ *noun* 1 dishonour, shame, reproach, slur, smear, scandal 2 distrust, doubt, mistrust, scepticism, suspicion

discreet *adj* 1 careful to avoid embarrassment; tactful 2 careful to avoid notice ◇ **discreetly** *adv*

▣ 1 tactful, careful, diplomatic 2 cautious, wary, sensible

> ❗ Do not confuse with: **discrete**

discrepancy *noun* (*plural* **discrepancies**) a difference or disagreement between two things: *some discrepancy in the figures*

▣ difference, disparity, variance, inconsistency, disagreement

discrete *adj* separate, distinct

> ❗ Do not confuse with: **discreet**

discretion *noun* 1 discreet behaviour 2 good judgement 3 the freedom to do as you think best

discriminate *verb* 1 make differences (between), distinguish 2 treat people differently because of their gender, race *etc* ◇ **discrimination** *noun* 1 ability to discriminate 2 adverse treatment on grounds of gender, race *etc*

discriminating *adj* having or showing good judgement

▣ discerning, perceptive, sensitive, astute

discus *noun* a heavy disc thrown in an athletic competition

discuss *verb* talk about ◇ **discussion** *noun*

▣ debate, confer, deliberate, converse, consult, examine ◇ **discussion** debate, conference, conversation, dialogue, exchange, discourse, consultation, deliberation, analysis, review, examination

disdain *verb* 1 look down on, scorn 2 be too proud (to do something) ◇ *noun* scorn ◇ **disdainful** *adj*

▣ *noun* scorn, contempt, arrogance, haughtiness, snobbishness

disease *noun* illness ◊ **diseased** *adj*
- sickness, ill-health, infirmity, ailment, malady, condition, affliction, infection, epidemic

disembark *verb* put or go ashore ◊ **disembarkation** *noun*

disembodied *adj* of a soul *etc*: separated from the body

disengage *verb* separate, free ◊ **disengaged** *adj*
- disconnect, detach, loosen, free, extricate, release, separate, disentangle

disentangle *verb* free from entanglement, unravel

disfavour or *US* **disfavor** *noun* dislike, disapproval

disfigure *verb* spoil the beauty or appearance of ◊ **disfigurement** *noun*
- deface, blemish, mutilate, scar, mar, deform, distort, damage, spoil

disgorge *verb* **1** throw or send out (*eg* smoke, passengers) **2** give up (something previously taken) **3** vomit

disgrace *noun* loss of respect or favour; shame ◊ *verb* bring shame on ◊ **in disgrace** out of favour
- *noun* shame, ignominy, disrepute, dishonour, disfavour, humiliation, defamation

disgraceful *adj* shameful; very bad ◊ **disgracefully** *adv*
- shameful, scandalous, shocking, unworthy, dreadful, appalling

disgruntled *adj* sulky, discontented

disguise *verb* **1** change the appearance of, *esp* in order to conceal identity **2** hide (feelings *etc*) ◊ *noun* **1** a disguised state **2** a costume *etc* which disguises

disgust *noun* **1** strong dislike, loathing **2** indignation ◊ *verb* **1** cause loathing in, revolt **2** make indignant ◊ **disgusted** *adj*
- *noun* **1** revulsion, repulsion, distaste, aversion, abhorrence, loathing, detestation ◊ **disgusted** repelled, revolted, offended, appalled, outraged

disgusting *adj* sickening; causing disgust
- repugnant, repellent, revolting, offensive, nauseating, unappetizing, nasty

dish *noun* (*plural* **dishes**) **1** a plate or bowl for food **2** food prepared for eating **3** a saucer-shaped aerial for receiving information from a satellite ◊ *verb* **1** serve (food) **2** deal (out), distribute

dishearten *verb* take away courage or hope from ◊ **disheartened** *adj* ◊ **disheartening** *adj*
- discourage, dispirit, cast down, deject

dishevelled *adj* untidy, with hair *etc* disordered
- tousled, uncombed, untidy, bedraggled, ruffled

dishonest *adj* not honest, deceitful ◊ **dishonesty** *noun*
- untruthful, fraudulent, deceitful, false, lying, deceptive, unprincipled, *informal* shady, corrupt, disreputable
- honest, trustworthy, scrupulous

dishonour *noun* disgrace, shame ◊ *verb* cause shame to ◊ **dishonourable** *adj*
- *noun* disgrace, shame, degradation, discredit, ignominy

disillusion *verb* take away a false but pleasing belief from ◊ **disillusioned** *adj* ◊ **disillusionment** *noun*

disinclined *adj* unwilling
- reluctant, resistant, loath, hesitant

disinfect *verb* destroy germs in

disinfectant *noun* a substance that kills germs

disinherit *verb* take away the rights of an heir ◊ **disinheritance** *noun*

disintegrate *verb* fall to pieces; break up ◊ **disintegration** *noun*
- break up, decompose, fall apart, crumble, rot, separate, splinter

disinterested *adj* unbiased, not influenced by personal feelings
- neutral, unbiased, impartial, unprejudiced, detached, open-minded

> ⚠ Do not confuse with: **uninterested**

disjointed *adj* of speech *etc*: with parts or ideas which are not well connected together
- incoherent, confused, disordered, unconnected, bitty, rambling

disk noun **1** *US spelling* of **disc 2** *comput* a flat round magnetic plate used for storing data ◇ **disk drive** *comput* part of a computer that records data onto and retrieves data from disks

dislike verb not like, disapprove of ◇ *noun* disapproval, hatred
■ *verb* hate, detest, object to, loathe, abhor, disapprove, shun, despise, scorn ◇ *noun* aversion, hatred, hostility, displeasure, disgust, loathing
🔁 *verb* like, favour

dislocate verb **1** put (a bone) out of joint **2** upset, disorder ◇ **dislocation** noun

dislodge verb **1** drive from a place of rest, hiding or defence **2** knock out of place accidentally

disloyal adj not loyal, unfaithful ◇ **disloyalty** noun
■ treacherous, faithless, false, traitorous, *informal* two-faced, unfaithful

dismal adj gloomy; sorrowful, sad

Based on a Latin phrase *dies mali* 'evil days', referring to two days each month which were believed to be unusually unlucky

dismantle verb **1** remove fittings, furniture *etc* from **2** take to pieces
■ **2** demolish, take apart, strip

dismay verb cause to feel alarmed, upset or hopeless ◇ *noun* a feeling of alarm or distress
■ *verb* alarm, frighten, unnerve, unsettle, dispirit, distress, dishearten, discourage, depress, horrify, disappoint ◇ *noun* consternation, alarm, distress, agitation, dread, fright, disappointment

dismember verb **1** tear to pieces **2** cut the limbs from

dismiss verb **1** send away **2** remove (someone) from a job, sack **3** refuse to accept or consider (*eg* an idea) **4** close (a law case) ◇ **dismissal** noun
■ **1** discharge, reject, send away, drop, banish **2** *informal* sack, make redundant, lay off, *informal* fire

dismount verb come down off a horse, bicycle *etc*

disobey verb fail or refuse to do what is commanded ◇ **disobedience** noun ◇ **disobedient** adj refusing or failing to obey

disobliging adj not willing to carry out the wishes of others

disorder noun **1** lack of order, confusion **2** a disease ◇ *verb* throw out of order ◇ **disorderliness** noun ◇ **disorderly** adj **1** out of order **2** behaving in a lawless (noisy) manner
■ *noun* **1** chaos, muddle, disarray, mess, untidiness, *informal* shambles, clutter, disturbance, riot, commotion **2** illness, complaint

disown verb refuse or cease to recognize as your own
■ renounce, disclaim

disparage verb speak of as being of little worth or importance, belittle ◇ **disparagement** noun ◇ **disparaging** adj
■ **disparaging** derisive, derogatory, mocking, scornful, critical, insulting, *informal* snide
🔁 **disparaging** flattering, praising

disparity noun (*plural* **disparities**) great difference, inequality

dispassionate adj **1** favouring no one, unbiased **2** calm, cool ◇ **dispassionately** adv
■ **1** objective, impartial, neutral, disinterested, impersonal, detached

dispatch or **despatch** verb **1** send off (a letter *etc*) **2** kill, finish off **3** do or deal with quickly ◇ *noun* (*plural* **dispatches** or **despatches**) **1** the act of sending off **2** a report to a newspaper **3** speed in doing something **4** killing **5** (**dispatches**) official papers (*esp* military or diplomatic) ◇ **dispatch box 1** a case for official papers **2** the box beside which members of parliament stand to make speeches in the House of Commons ◇ **dispatch rider** a courier who delivers military dispatches by motorcycle

dispel verb (**dispels, dispelling, dispelled**) drive away, make disappear

dispensable adj that can be done without

dispensary noun (plural **dispensaries**) a place where medicines are given out

dispensation noun special permission to break a rule etc

dispense verb **1** give out **2** prepare (medicines) for giving out ◇ **dispenser** noun ◇ **dispense with** do without

◼ **1** distribute, give out, apportion, allot, allocate, assign, share, mete out ◇ **dispense with** dispose of, get rid of, abolish, discard, disregard, forgo

disperse verb **1** scatter, spread **2** (cause to) vanish ◇ **dispersal** or **dispersion** noun

◼ **1** scatter, distribute **2** dissolve, break up, dismiss, dispel, separate

dispirited adj sad, discouraged

displace verb **1** put out of place **2** disorder, disarrange **3** put (someone) out of office ◇ **displacement** noun

display verb set out for show ◇ noun a show, exhibition

◼ verb present, demonstrate, exhibit, show off, parade, flaunt ◇ noun demonstration, presentation, parade, spectacle

displease verb not please; offend, annoy ◇ **displeasure** noun annoyance, disapproval

◼ irritate, anger, upset, informal put out, infuriate, exasperate, incense, slang piss off

disposable adj intended to be thrown away after use

dispose verb **1** arrange, settle **2** get rid (of): they disposed of the body **3** make inclined ◇ **disposal** noun ◇ **at your disposal** available for your use ◇ **disposed** adj inclined, willing

disposition noun **1** temperament, personality **2** arrangement **3** law the handing over of property etc to another

◼ **1** character, nature, temperament, make-up, personality

dispossess verb take something away from (someone), deprive (of)

disproportionate adj too big or too little, not in proportion

◼ unequal, uneven, unreasonable

disprove verb prove to be false

◼ discredit, invalidate, expose

dispute verb argue about ◇ noun an argument, quarrel ◇ **disputable** adj not certain, able to be argued about ◇ **disputation** noun an argument

◼ verb debate, question, contend, challenge, discuss, contest, contradict ◇ noun debate, disagreement, controversy, conflict, contention, quarrel

disqualify verb (**disqualifies**, **disqualifying**, **disqualified**) **1** put out of a competition for breaking rules **2** take away a qualification or right from ◇ **disqualification** noun

disquiet noun uneasiness, anxiety

◼ nervousness, uneasiness, anxiety, worry, concern, restlessness, fear

disregard verb pay no attention to, ignore ◇ noun neglect

◼ verb overlook, discount, neglect, disobey, brush aside ◇ noun neglect, negligence, inattention, oversight, indifference, disrespect, contempt, disdain

disrepair noun bad condition

◼ dilapidation, decay, ruin, shabbiness

disrepute noun bad reputation ◇ **disreputable** adj having a bad reputation, not respectable

◼ **disreputable** unrespectable, shady, dishonourable, discreditable, low

◪ **disreputable** respectable

disrespect noun rudeness, lack of politeness or respect ◇ **disrespectful** adj

◼ **disrespectful** rude, discourteous, impertinent, impolite, impudent, insolent, cheeky, insulting, irreverent

◪ **disrespectful** polite, respectful

disrobe verb, formal undress

disrupt verb disturb the peace, order of progress of (a meeting etc) ◇ **disruption** noun ◇ **disruptive** adj causing disorder

dissatisfy verb (**dissatisfies**, **dissatisfying**, **dissatisfied**) fail to satisfy, displease ◇ **dissatisfaction** noun ◇ **dissatisfied** adj

◼ **dissatisfaction** discontent, displeasure, discomfort, disappointment, frustration, annoyance, irritation, exasperation, regret, resentment

dissect verb 1 cut into parts for examination 2 study and criticize ◇ **dissection** noun

▣ 1 dismember, anatomize 2 analyse, examine

dissemble verb hide, disguise (intentions etc) ◇ **dissembler** noun

disseminate verb scatter, spread ◇ **dissemination** noun

dissension noun disagreement, quarrelling

dissent verb 1 have a different opinion 2 refuse to agree ◇ noun disagreement ◇ **dissenter** noun a member of a church that has broken away from the officially established church

▣ verb 1 disagree, differ 2 protest, object, refuse, quibble ◇ noun disagreement, dissension, resistance, opposition, objection

dissertation noun a long piece of writing or talk on a particular (often academic) subject

disservice noun harm, a bad turn: did him a disservice by telling us

dissident noun someone who disagrees, esp with a political regime

▣ dissenter, nonconformist, rebel, revolutionary

dissimilar adj not the same ◇ **dissimilarity** noun (plural **dissimilarities**)

▣ unlike, different, divergent, disparate, incompatible, mismatched, diverse, various, heterogeneous

▣ similar, alike

dissipate verb 1 (cause to) disappear 2 waste, squander ◇ **dissipated** adj worn out by indulging in pleasures; dissolute ◇ **dissipation** noun

dissociate verb separate ◇ **dissociate yourself from** refuse to be associated with

dissolute adj having loose morals; debauched

▣ dissipated, debauched, degenerate, depraved

dissolve verb 1 (cause to) become part of liquid 2 break up; put an end

to: dissolve a partnership ◇ **dissoluble** adj able to be dissolved ◇ **dissolution** noun

▣ 1 evaporate, disintegrate, liquefy, decompose, disperse 2 end, terminate, separate, sever

dissonance noun 1 discord, esp used deliberately for musical effect 2 disagreement ◇ **dissonant** adj

dissuade verb persuade not to do something ◇ **dissuasion** noun

distaff noun a stick used to hold flax or wool being spun ◇ **the distaff side** the female side or line of descent (contrasted with: **spear side**)

distance noun 1 the space between things 2 a far-off place or point: in the distance 3 coldness of manner

▣ 1 gap, extent, interval, range 3 aloofness, reserve, coolness, coldness, remoteness

distant adj 1 far off or far apart in place or time: distant era/distant land 2 not closely related: distant cousin 3 cold in manner ◇ **distantly** adv

▣ 1 far, faraway, remote 3 aloof, cool, reserved, informal stand-offish, stiff

distaste noun dislike ◇ **distasteful** adj disagreeable, unpleasant

▣ **distasteful** disagreeable, offensive, unpleasant, repulsive, objectionable, obnoxious, repugnant, unsavoury, loathsome, abhorrent

distemper¹ noun a kind of paint used chiefly for walls ◇ verb paint with distemper

distemper² noun a viral disease of dogs, foxes etc

distend verb swell; stretch outwards ◇ **distension** noun

distil verb (**distils, distilling, distilled**) 1 purify (liquid) by heating to a vapour and cooling 2 extract the spirit or essence from ◇ **distillation** noun ◇ **distiller** noun

distillery noun (plural **distilleries**) a place where whisky, brandy etc is made

distinct adj 1 clear; easily seen or noticed: a distinct improvement 2 different: the two languages are quite distinct

■ **1** plain, evident, obvious, apparent, marked, definite, noticeable, recognizable **2** separate, different, detached, individual

> **!** Do not confuse: **distinct** and **distinctive**

distinction *noun* **1** a difference **2** outstanding worth or merit

distinctive *adj* marking as different, special ◊ **distinctively** *adv* ◊ **distinctiveness** *noun*

■ characteristic, distinguishing, individual, unique, singular, original, peculiar, extraordinary

◣ ordinary, common

distinguish *verb* **1** recognize a difference (between) **2** mark as different **3** recognize **4** give distinction to ◊ **distinguished** *adj* **1** outstanding, famous **2** dignified

distort *verb* **1** twist out of shape **2** turn or twist (a statement *etc*) from its true meaning **3** make (a sound) unclear, strange and harsh ◊ **distortion** *noun*

■ **1** deform, contort, bend, misshape, disfigure, twist, warp **2** falsify, misrepresent, pervert, slant, colour **3** garble

distract *verb* **1** divert the attention (of) **2** trouble, confuse **3** make mad ◊ **distracted** *adj* mad with pain, grief *etc*

■ **1** divert, sidetrack, deflect **2** confuse, disconcert, confound

distraction *noun* **1** something which diverts your attention **2** anxiety, confusion **3** amusement, entertainment **4** madness

distraught *adj* extremely agitated or anxious

■ agitated, anxious, overwrought, upset, distressed, distracted, beside oneself, worked up, frantic, hysterical

distress *noun* **1** pain, trouble, sorrow **2** a cause of suffering ◊ *verb* cause pain or sorrow to ◊ **distressed** *adj* ◊ **distressing** *adj*

■ *noun* **1** anguish, grief, misery, heartache, suffering, torment, sadness, worry, anxiety, pain **2** adversity, hardship, poverty, privation, destitution, misfortune, trouble, difficulties, trial ◊ *verb*

upset, afflict, grieve, sadden, worry, torment, trouble

distribute *verb* **1** divide among several **2** spread out widely ◊ **distribution** *noun*

■ **1** dispense, allocate, dole out, dish out, share, deal, divide **2** spread, circulate, diffuse, disperse, scatter

district *noun* a region of a country or town

distrust *noun* lack of trust, suspicion ◊ *verb* have no trust in ◊ **distrustful** *adj*

disturb *verb* **1** confuse, worry, upset **2** interrupt ◊ **disturbance** *noun* ◊ **disturbing** *adj*

■ **1** agitate, unsettle, distress, fluster, annoy, bother **2** disrupt, interrupt, distract ◊ **disturbance** disruption, interruption, intrusion, disorder, commotion

disuse *noun* the state of being no longer used ◊ **disused** *adj* no longer used

ditch *noun* (*plural* **ditches**) a long narrow hollow trench dug in the ground, *esp* for drainage

■ trench, dyke, channel, furrow, drain

dither *verb* **1** hesitate, be undecided **2** act in a nervous, uncertain manner ◊ *noun* a state of indecision

■ *verb* **1** hesitate, *informal* shilly-shally, waver, vacillate

ditto *noun* (often written as **do**) the same as already written or said ◊ **ditto marks** a character (") written below a word in a text, meaning it is to be understood as repeated

ditty *noun* (*plural* **ditties**) a simple, short song

diuretic *adj* increasing the flow of urine ◊ *noun* a medicine with this effect

diva *noun* a leading female opera singer, a prima donna

divan *noun* **1** a long, low couch without a back **2** a bed without a headboard

dive *verb* (**dives**, **diving**, **dived** or *US* **dove**) **1** plunge headfirst into water **2** swoop down through the air **3** go down steeply and quickly ◊ *noun* an act of diving

▣ *verb* **1**, **2**, **3** plunge, plummet, dip, drop, descend

diver *noun* **1** someone who works under water using special breathing equipment **2** a type of diving bird ◊ **dive-bomb** *verb* bomb from an aircraft in a steep downward dive ◊ **dive-bomber** *noun*

diverge *verb* **1** separate and go in different directions **2** differ ◊ **divergence** *noun* ◊ **divergent** *adj*

diverse *adj* different, various

▣ varied, varying, assorted, differing, separate, several, distinct

▣ similar, identical

diversify *verb* (**diversifies, diversifying, diversified**) **1** make or become different or varied **2** engage in different business activities

diversion *noun* **1** deviation **2** an alteration to a traffic route **3** an amusement

▣ **3** amusement, entertainment, distraction, pastime, recreation

diversity *noun* difference; variety

divert *verb* **1** turn aside, change the direction of **2** entertain, amuse ◊ **diverting** *adj* entertaining, amusing

▣ **1** redirect, reroute, sidetrack, avert, distract, switch **2** amuse, entertain, occupy, distract, interest

divest *verb* strip or deprive (of): *divested him of his authority*

divide *verb* **1** separate into parts **2** share (among) **3** (cause to) go into separate groups **4** *maths* find out how many times one number contains another ◊ **dividers** *noun plural* a measuring instrument resembling compasses

▣ **1** split, separate, part, cut, break up, detach **2** distribute, share, allocate, deal out, apportion

dividend *noun* **1** a share of profits from a business **2** an amount to be divided (*compare with*: **divisor**)

divine *adj* **1** of a god; holy **2** *informal* splendid, wonderful ◊ *verb* **1** guess **2** foretell, predict ◊ **divination** *noun* the art of foretelling ◊ **diviner** *noun* someone who claims special powers

in finding hidden water or metals ◊ **divining rod** a forked stick used by diviners to guide them to hidden water *etc*

divinity *noun* (*plural* **divinities**) **1** a god **2** the nature of a god **3** religious studies

division *noun* **1** the act of dividing **2** a barrier, a separator **3** a section, *eg* of an army **4** separation **5** disagreement ◊ **divisibility** *noun* ◊ **divisible** *adj* able to be divided ◊ **divisional** *adj* of a division ◊ **divisor** *noun* the number by which another number (the **dividend**) is divided

▣ **4** separation, parting **5** breach, rupture, split, disunion, disagreement, feud

divorce *noun* **1** the legal ending of a marriage **2** a complete separation ◊ *verb* **1** end a marriage with **2** separate (from) ◊ **divorced** *adj* ◊ **divorcee** *noun* a divorced person

divulge *verb* let out, make known (a secret *etc*)

▣ disclose, reveal, tell, *informal* leak, impart, uncover, let slip, expose

Diwali *noun* the Hindu and Sikh festival of lamps, celebrated in October or November

DIY *abbrev* do-it-yourself

dizzy *adj* **1** giddy, confused **2** causing giddiness: *from a dizzy height* ◊ **dizzily** ◊ **dizziness** *noun*

▣ **1** faint, light-headed, *informal* woozy, shaky, reeling, bewildered, dazed, muddled

DJ *abbrev* disc jockey

DNA *abbrev* deoxyribonucleic acid, a compound carrying genetic instructions for passing on hereditary characteristics

do *verb* (**does, doing, did, done**) **1** carry out, perform (a job *etc*) **2** perform an action on, *eg* clean (dishes), arrange (hair) *etc* **3** *slang* swindle **4** act: *do as you please* **5** get on: *I hear she's doing very well/how are you doing?* **6** be enough: *£10 will do* **7** used to avoid repeating a verb: *I seldom see him now, and when I do, he ignores me* **8** used with a more important verb (1) in questions: *do you see what I mean?*; (2) in sentences with **not**: *I don't know*; or (3) for emphasis: *I do hope she'll be there* ◇ *noun* (*plural* **dos**) *informal* a social event, a party ◇ **doer** *noun* ◇ **doings** *noun plural* actions ◇ **do away with** put an end to, destroy ◇ **do down** *informal* get the better of ◇ **do-gooder** *noun* someone who tries to help others in a self-righteous way ◇ **do in** *informal* **1** exhaust, wear out **2** murder ◇ **done to death** too often repeated ◇ **do or die** a desperate final attempt at something whatever the consequences ◇ **do out of** swindle out of ◇ **do up 1** fasten **2** renovate

■ *verb* **1** perform, execute, implement, undertake, end, finish **2** fix, prepare, arrange, deal with, look after **4** behave, conduct oneself **6** suffice, satisfy, serve

docile *adj* tame, easy to manage ◇ **docilely** *adv* ◇ **docility** *noun*

■ tractable, co-operative, obedient, amenable, obliging

dock¹ *noun* **1** a harbour where ships go for loading, repair *etc* **2** (**docks**) the area around this ◇ *verb* **1** bring into a dock **2** of a spacecraft: join onto another craft in space

dock² *verb* clip or cut short

dock³ *noun* a weed with large leaves

dock⁴ *noun* the box in a law court where the accused person stands

docker *noun* someone who works in the docks

docket *noun* a label listing the contents of something

dockyard *noun* a naval harbour with docks, stores *etc*

doctor *noun* **1** someone trained in and licensed to practise medicine **2** someone with the highest university degree in any subject ◇ *verb* **1** tamper with, alter **2** *informal* castrate or sterilize (an animal)

Types of medical doctor include: general practitioner, GP, family doctor, family practitioner, locum, hospital doctor, houseman, intern, resident, registrar, consultant, medical officer (MO), dentist, veterinary surgeon, *informal* vet

doctrinaire *adj* dogmatic, inflexible or obstinate in beliefs

doctrine *noun* a belief that is taught ◇ **doctrinal** *adj*

■ dogma, creed, belief, tenet, principle, teaching, precept

document *noun* a written statement giving proof, information *etc*

■ paper, certificate, deed, record, report, form

documentary *noun* (*plural* **documentaries**) a film giving information about real people or events ◇ *adj* **1** of or in documents: *documentary evidence* **2** of a documentary

dodder *verb* shake, tremble, *esp* as a result of old age ◇ **doddery** *adj* shaky or slow because of old age

doddle *noun*, *informal* an easy task

dodge *verb* avoid by a sudden or clever movement ◇ *noun* a trick

■ *verb* avoid, elude, evade, swerve, sidestep ◇ *noun* trick, ruse, ploy, scheme

dodo *noun* (*plural* **dodoes** or **dodos**) a type of large extinct bird

doe *noun* (*plural* **does** or **doe**) the female of certain animals, *eg* a deer, rabbit or hare

doer and **does** see **do**

doff *noun* take off (a hat) in greeting

dog *noun* **1** a four-legged animal often kept as a pet **2** one of the dog family which includes wolves, foxes *etc* ◇ *adj* of an animal: male ◇ *verb* (**dogs**, **dogging**, **dogged**) **1** follow and watch constantly **2** hamper, plague: *dogged by ill health* ◇ **dog-collar** *noun* **1** a collar for dogs **2** a clerical collar ◇ **dog-eared** *adj* of a page: turned down at the corner ◇ **dog-eat-dog** *adj* viciously competitive ◇ **dogfight** *noun* a fight between aeroplanes at close quarters ◇ **dogfish** *noun* a kind of small shark ◇ **dog in the manger** someone who stands in the way of a plan or proposal ◇ **dogleg** *noun* a sharp bend ◇ **dogsbody** *noun*, *informal* someone who is given unpleasant or dreary tasks to do ◇ **dog's breakfast** or **dog's dinner** a complete mess ◇ **dog's life** a life of misery ◇ **dog-tag** noun **1** a dog's identity disc **2** an identity disc worn by soldiers etc ◇ **dog-tired** adj completely worn out ◇ **go to the dogs** be ruined

Breeds of dog include:
Afghan hound, alsatian, Australian terrier, basset-hound, beagle, Border collie, borzoi, bull mastiff, bulldog, bull terrier, cairn terrier, chihuahua, chow, cocker spaniel, collie, corgi, dachshund, Dalmatian, Doberman pinscher, foxhound, fox terrier, German Shepherd, golden retriever, Great Dane, greyhound, husky, Irish setter, Irish wolfhound, Jack Russell, King Charles spaniel, komondor, Labrador, lhasa apso, lurcher, Maltese, Old English sheepdog, Pekingese, pit bull terrier, pointer, poodle, pug, Rottweiler, saluki, informal sausage dog, schnauzer, informal Scottie, Scottish terrier, Sealyham, setter, sheltie, shih tzu, springer spaniel, St Bernard, terrier, whippet, Weimaraner, West Highland terrier, informal Westie, wolfhound, Yorkshire terrier

dogged /'dogɪd/ adj determined, stubborn: dogged refusal ◇ **doggedly** adv ◇ **doggedness** noun

▤ resolute, persistent, intent, tenacious, firm, steadfast, staunch, singleminded, steady, obstinate, relentless, unyielding

▤ irresolute, apathetic

doggerel noun badly written poetry

doggy adj, informal of or for dogs ◇ **doggy-bag** noun a bag used to take away left-over food from a restaurant meal ◇ **doggy-paddle** noun a simple style of swimming

dogma noun an opinion, esp religious, accepted or fixed by an authority ◇ **dogmatic** adj **1** of dogma **2** stubbornly stating your opinions or forcing them on others ◇ **dogmatically** adv

▤ **dogmatic 2** opinionated, assertive,

authoritative, dictatorial, categorical, emphatic, overbearing

doily or **doyley** noun (plural **doilies** or **doyleys**) a perforated paper napkin put underneath cakes etc

Originally a light summer fabric, named after Doily's drapery shop in 17th-century London

doldrums noun plural low spirits: in the doldrums

The doldrums take their name from an area of the ocean about the equator famous for calms and variable winds

dole verb deal (out) in small amounts ◇ noun, informal unemployment benefit ◇ **on the dole** informal unemployed

▤ verb distribute, allocate, hand out, dish out, apportion, allot, mete out, share, divide, deal, issue, ration, dispense, administer, assign

doleful adj sad, unhappy ◇ **dolefully** adv ◇ **dolefulness** noun

doll noun a toy in the shape of a small human being

dollar noun the main unit of currency in several countries, eg the USA, Canada, Australia and New Zealand

dolmen noun an ancient tomb in the shape of a stone table

dolphin noun a type of sea mammal like a large fish

dolt noun a stupid person ◇ **doltish** adj

domain noun **1** a kingdom **2** a country estate **3** an area of interest or knowledge ◇ **domain name** the part of a website address identifying the organization, location etc

▤ **1** dominion, realm, territory, empire, province **3** field, speciality, concern, department, sphere, discipline

dome noun **1** the shape of a half sphere or ball **2** the roof of a building etc in this shape ◇ **domed** adj

domestic adj **1** of the home or house **2** of an animal: tame, kept as a pet etc **3** not foreign, of your own country:

domestic products ◇ *noun* a live-in maid, servant *etc* ◇ **domestic help** (someone paid to give) assistance with housework ◇ **domestic science** *old* cookery, needlework *etc*, taught as a subject

■ *adj* **1** family, household, private **3** internal, national, indigenous, native ◇ *noun* servant, maid, char

domesticated *adj* **1** of an animal: tame, used for farming *etc* **2** fond of doing housework, cooking *etc*

domesticity *noun* home life

domicile *noun* the country *etc* in which someone lives permanently

dominant *adj* ruling; most powerful or important ◇ **dominance** *noun*

■ authoritative, controlling, governing, ruling, powerful, assertive, influential, principal, outstanding, chief, prominent, commanding

ℰ submissive, subordinate

dominate *verb* **1** have command or influence over **2** be most strong, or most noticeable: *the taste of garlic dominates* **3** tower above, overlook ◇ **domination** *noun*

■ **1** control, domineer, govern, rule, direct, monopolize, master, lead **3** overshadow, eclipse, dwarf

domineering *adj* overbearing, like a tyrant

■ *informal* bossy, dictatorial, authoritarian, oppressive, arrogant

ℰ meek, servile

dominion *noun* **1** rule, authority **2** an area with one ruler or government

■ **1** power, authority, control, rule, sway, jurisdiction, government, supremacy, sovereignty

domino *noun* (*plural* **dominoes**) **1** a piece used in the game of dominoes **2** *hist* a long silk cloak worn at masked balls ◇ **dominoes** *noun sing* a game played on a table with pieces marked with dots, each side of which must match a piece placed next to it

don[1] *noun* a college or university lecturer

don[2] *verb* (**dons**, **donning**, **donned**) put on (a coat *etc*)

donation *noun* a gift of money or goods ◇ **donate** *verb* present a gift

■ gift, present, offering, contribution, presentation, alms, bequest

done *past participle* of **do**

donkey *noun* (*plural* **donkeys**) (*also called* **ass**) a type of animal with long ears, related to the horse

donor *noun* **1** a giver of a gift **2** someone who gives their blood, body organs, *etc* for medical use

don't *short for* **do not**

doom *noun* **1** judgement; fate **2** ruin ◇ **doomed** *adj* **1** destined, condemned **2** bound to fail or be destroyed

■ **1** fortune, destiny, lot **2** destruction, catastrophe, downfall, ruin, death ◇ **doomed 2** damned, ill-fated, cursed, condemned

door *noun* **1** a hinged barrier which closes the entrance to a room or building **2** the entrance itself ◇ **doorstep** *noun* the step in front of the door of a house ◇ **doorway** *noun* the space filled by a door, an entrance

dope *noun*, *informal* **1** drugs; a drug **2** an idiot ◇ *verb* drug

dormant *adj* sleeping, inactive: *a dormant volcano*

■ inactive, asleep, inert, resting, slumbering

ℰ active, awake

dormer or **dormer window** *noun* a small window jutting out from a sloping roof

dormitory *noun* (*plural* **dormitories**) a room with beds for several people

dormouse *noun* (*plural* **dormice**) a small animal which hibernates

dorsal *adj* of the back: *dorsal fin*

dose *noun* **1** a quantity of medicine to be taken at one time **2** a bout of something unpleasant: *a dose of flu* ◇ *verb* give medicine to

■ *noun* **1** measure, dosage, amount, quantity, prescription, shot ◇ *verb* medicate, administer, prescribe, dispense, treat

doss *verb*, *informal* lie down to sleep

somewhere temporary ◇ **doss-house** *noun, informal* a cheap lodging-house

dossier /'dɒsɪeɪ/ *noun* a set of papers containing information about a person or subject

dot *noun* a small, round mark ◇ *verb* (**dots, dotting, dotted**) **1** mark with a dot **2** scatter ◇ **on the dot** exactly on time

▣ *noun* point, spot, speck, pinpoint, decimal point, full stop, iota, jot

dotage *noun* the foolishness and childishness of old age

dotcom *noun, informal* a company operating mainly on the Internet

dote *verb*: **dote on** be excessively fond of

▣ adore, idolize, treasure, admire, indulge

double *verb* **1** multiply by two **2** make or become twice as big ◇ *noun* **1** twice as much: *he ate double the amount* **2** someone who looks very like another ◇ *adj* **1** containing twice as much: *a double dose* **2** made up of two of the same sort **3** folded over **4** for two people ◇ **doubly** *adv* ◇ **at the double** very quickly ◇ **double agent** a spy paid by each of two rival countries, but loyal to only one of them ◇ **double back** turn sharply and go back the way you have come ◇ **double bass** the largest stringed musical instrument ◇ **double-breasted** *adj* of a coat: with one half of the front overlapping the other ◇ **double-cross** *verb* cheat ◇ **double-dealer** *noun* a deceitful, cheating person ◇ **double-dealing** *noun* ◇ **double-decker** *noun* a bus with two floors ◇ **double-Dutch** *noun* incomprehensible talk, gibberish ◇ **double glazing** two sheets of glass in a window to keep in the heat or keep out noise ◇ **double-take** *noun* a second look at something surprising or confusing ◇ **double-think** *noun* the holding of two contradictory opinions or ideas ◇ **double time** payment for extra work *etc* at twice the usual rate ◇ **double up 1** writhe in pain **2** share accommodation (with)

▣ *noun* **2** twin, copy, clone, replica, dop-

pelgänger, lookalike, *informal* spitting image, *informal* ringer, image

double entendre a word or phrase with two meanings, one of them usually sexual

doublet *noun, hist* a man's close-fitting jacket

doubt *verb* **1** be unsure or undecided about **2** think unlikely: *I doubt that we'll be able to go* ◇ *noun* a lack of certainty, trust or belief ◇ **doubtful** *adj* ◇ **doubtless** *adv* ◇ **no doubt** probably

▣ *verb* **1** be uncertain, be dubious, hesitate, waver ◇ *noun* distrust, scepticism, suspicion, uncertainty, confusion, ambiguity, indecision ◇ **doubtful** uncertain, suspicious, hesitant, tentative, dubious, questionable

douche /duːʃ/ *noun* an instrument which injects water into the body for cleansing

dough *noun* **1** a mass of flour, moistened and kneaded **2** *informal* money

doughnut *noun* a ring-shaped cake fried in fat

doughty /'daʊtɪ/ *adj* strong; brave

dour /dʊə(r)/ *adj* dull, humourless

▣ dismal, grim, morose, unfriendly, dreary, austere, sour, sullen

dove[1] *noun* a pigeon ◇ **dovecote** *noun* a pigeon-house

dove[2] *US past form of* **dive**

dovetail *verb* fit one thing exactly into another

dowdy *adj* not smart, badly dressed

▣ unfashionable, ill-dressed, frumpish, drab, dingy, old-fashioned

down[1] *adv* **1** towards or in a lower position: *fell down/sitting down* **2** to a smaller size: *grind down* **3** to a later generation: *handed down from mother to daughter* **4** on the spot, in cash: *£100 down* ◇ *prep* **1** towards or in the lower part of: *rolled back down the hill* **2** along: *strolling down the road* ◇ *adj* going downwards: *the down escalator* ◇ **go down with** or **be down with** become or be ill with

down[2] *noun* light, soft feathers ◇ **downy** *adj* soft, feathery

down-at-heel *adj* worn down, shabby

downcast *adj* sad
- dejected, depressed, despondent, sad, unhappy, miserable, down, low, disheartened, dispirited, *informal* blue, *informal* fed up
- cheerful, happy, elated

downfall *noun* ruin, defeat
- fall, ruin, disgrace, defeat, undoing

downhearted *adj* discouraged
- depressed, dejected, despondent, sad, downcast, discouraged, disheartened, unhappy, glum

downpour *noun* a heavy fall of rain
- cloudburst, deluge, flood

downs *noun plural* low, grassy hills

downstairs *adj* on a lower floor of a building ◇ *adv* to a lower floor

downstream *adv* further down a river, in the direction of its flow

downtrodden *adj* kept in a lowly, inferior position
- oppressed, exploited, victimized, helpless

downwards *adv* moving or leading down

dowry *noun* (*plural* **dowries**) money and property brought by a woman to her husband on their marriage

doyley *noun another spelling of* **doily**

doze *verb* sleep lightly ◇ *noun* a light, short sleep
- *verb* sleep, nod off, drop off, snooze, *informal* kip, *slang* zizz ◇ *noun* nap, catnap, siesta, *informal* snooze, *informal* forty winks, *informal* kip, *informal* shuteye, *slang* zizz

dozen *adj* twelve

Dr *abbrev* doctor

drab *adj* not brightly coloured, interesting or exciting ◇ **drabness** *noun*
- dull, dingy, dreary, dismal, gloomy, flat, monotonous, grey, lacklustre, cheerless, shabby
- bright, cheerful

draft *noun* **1** a rough written outline or sketch **2** a group of people selected for a special purpose **3** *US* conscription into the army **4** an order for payment of money **5** *US spelling of* **draught** ◇ *verb* **1** make a rough plan of **2** select for a purpose **3** *US* conscript

| ⚠ Do not confuse with: **draught** |

draftsman, draftswoman *US spellings of* **draughtsman, draughtswoman**

drag *verb* **1** pull roughly **2** move slowly and heavily **3** trail along the ground **4** search (a river-bed *etc*) with a net or hook ◇ *noun, informal* **1** a dreary task **2** a tedious person **3** clothes for one sex worn by the other ◇ **drag your feet** or **drag your heels** be slow to do something
- *verb* **1** draw, pull, haul, lug, tug ◇ *noun* **1** *informal* bore, annoyance, nuisance, *informal* pain, bother

dragon *noun* **1** an imaginary, fire-breathing, winged reptile **2** a fierce, intimidating person

dragonfly *noun* a winged insect with a long body and double wings

dragoon *noun* a heavily armed mounted soldier ◇ *verb* force or bully (into)

drain *verb* **1** clear of water, *eg* by trenches or pipes **2** drink the contents of (a glass *etc*) **3** use up completely ◇ *noun* a channel or pipe used to carry off water *etc* ◇ **drained** *adj* **1** emptied of liquid **2** sapped of strength
- *verb* **3** exhaust, consume, sap, use up, deplete ◇ *noun* channel, conduit, culvert, duct, outlet, trench, ditch, pipe

drainage *noun* the removal of water by rivers, pipes *etc*

drake *noun* a male duck

drama *noun* **1** a play for acting in the theatre **2** exciting or tense action

dramatic *adj* **1** relating to plays **2** exciting, thrilling **3** unexpected, sudden ◇ **dramatically** *adv*
- **2** exciting, striking, stirring, thrilling, expressive **3** striking, sudden, significant, impressive

dramatist *noun* a writer of plays

dramatize *verb* **1** turn into a play for

the theatre **2** make vivid or sensational ◇ **dramatization** noun

■ **2** act, play-act, exaggerate, overdo, overstate

drank verb past form of **drink**

drape verb arrange (cloth) to hang gracefully ◇ noun (**drapes**) US curtains ◇ **draper** noun a dealer in cloth ◇ **drapery** noun **1** cloth goods **2** a draper's shop

drastic adj severe, extreme ◇ **drastically** adv

■ extreme, strong, severe, harsh, desperate, dire, radical, forceful

☷ moderate, cautious

draught /drɑːft/ noun **1** a current of air **2** the act of drawing or pulling **3** a drink taken all at once ◇ **draughts** noun sing a game for two, played by moving pieces on a squared board ◇ **draughty** adj full of air currents, chilly

⚠ Do not confuse with: **draft**

draughtsman, draughtswoman noun **1** someone employed to draw plans **2** someone skilled in drawing

draw verb (**draws**, **drawing**, **drew**, **drawn**) **1** make a picture with pencil, crayons etc **2** pull **3** attract: drew a large crowd **4** obtain money from a fund: drawing a pension **5** require (a depth) for floating: this ship draws 20 feet **6** approach, come: night is drawing near **7** score equal points in a game ◇ noun **1** an equal score **2** a lottery **3** an attraction ◇ **draw a blank** get no result ◇ **draw a conclusion** form an opinion from evidence heard ◇ **drawn and quartered** hist cut in pieces after being hanged ◇ **draw on 1** approach **2** use as a resource: drawing on experience ◇ **draw out 1** lengthen **2** persuade (someone) to talk and be at ease ◇ **draw the line at** refuse to allow or accept ◇ **draw up 1** come to a stop **2** move closer **3** plan, write out (a contract etc)

■ verb **1** sketch, portray, trace, pencil, depict, design **2** pull, drag, haul, tow, tug

3 allure, entice, bring in, influence ◇ noun **3** enticement, lure, appeal, interest

drawback noun a disadvantage

■ disadvantage, snag, hitch, impediment, difficulty, informal fly in the ointment, stumbling block, nuisance, trouble

☷ advantage, benefit

drawbridge noun a bridge at the entrance to a castle which can be drawn up or let down

drawer noun **1** a sliding box fitting into a chest, table etc **2** someone who draws

drawing noun a picture made by pencil, crayon etc

drawing-pin noun a pin with a large flat head for fastening paper on a board etc

drawing-room noun a sitting-room

drawl verb speak in a slow, lazy manner ◇ noun a drawling voice

drawn past participle of **draw**

dread noun great fear or apprehension ◇ adj terrifying ◇ verb be greatly afraid of or apprehensive about ◇ **dreaded** adj

■ noun fear, apprehension, trepidation, alarm, horror, terror, fright, disquiet, worry ◇ verb fear, shrink from

☷ noun confidence, security

dreadful adj **1** terrible **2** informal very bad ◇ **dreadfully** adv

■ **1** awful, terrible, frightful, horrible, appalling, dire, shocking, ghastly, horrendous, tragic, grievous, hideous **2** awful, frightful, shocking

☷ **1, 2** wonderful

dreadlock noun a thick, twisted strand of hair

dream noun **1** a series of images and sounds in the mind during sleep **2** something imagined, not real **3** something very beautiful **4** a hope, an ambition: her dream was to go to Mexico ◇ verb (**dreams**, **dreaming**, **dreamt** or **dreamed**) have a dream ◇ **dream up** invent

■ noun **2** illusion, hallucination, delusion, vision, reverie, fantasy **4** aspiration, wish, hope, ambition, desire, goal ◇ *verb* imagine, fantasize, daydream, hallucinate ◇ **dream up** invent, devise, conceive, think up, hatch

dreamy *adj* **1** sleepy, half-awake **2** vague, dim **3** *informal* beautiful ◇ **dreamily** *adv*

dreary *adj* gloomy, cheerless; monotonous ◇ **drearily** *adv* ◇ **dreariness** *noun*

■ depressing, drab, dismal, bleak, boring, tedious, dull

dredge[1] *verb* clear or deepen a river- or sea-bed by bringing up mud *etc* ◇ *noun* an instrument for dredging a river *etc* ◇ **dredger** *noun* a ship which digs or deepens a channel by lifting mud from the bottom

dredge[2] *verb* sprinkle with sugar or flour ◇ **dredger** *noun* a perforated jar for sprinkling sugar or flour

dregs *noun plural* **1** sediment on the bottom of a liquid: *dregs of wine* **2** last remnants **3** a worthless or useless part ■ **1** sediment, deposit, residue

drench *verb* soak

dress *verb* **1** put clothes on **2** prepare (food *etc*) for use **3** arrange (hair) **4** treat and bandage (wounds) ◇ *noun* (*plural* **dresses**) **1** clothes: *in evening dress* **2** a one-piece woman's garment combining skirt and top ◇ *adj* of clothes: for formal use ◇ **dressy** *adj* stylish, smart ◇ **dressing-gown** *noun* a loose, light coat worn indoors over pyjamas *etc* ◇ **dress rehearsal** the final rehearsal of a play, in which the actors wear their costumes

■ *verb* **1** clothe, put on, wear, don **3** arrange, adjust, prepare, groom **4** bandage, tend, treat ◇ *noun* **1** clothing, garment(s), outfit, wear **2** frock, gown, robe

dresser *noun* a kitchen sideboard with shelves above for dishes

dressing *noun* **1** a covering for a wound **2** a seasoned sauce poured over salads *etc*

drew *past form* of **draw**

drey *noun* (*plural* **dreys**) a squirrel's nest

dribble *verb* **1** (cause to) fall in small drops **2** let saliva run down the chin **3** *football* move the ball forward by short kicks

■ **1** trickle, drip, leak, seep, drop, ooze **2** drool, slaver, slobber, drivel

dried *see* **dry**

drift *noun* **1** snow, sand *etc* driven into a pile by the wind **2** the direction in which something is driven **3** the general meaning of someone's words ◇ *verb* **1** go with the tide, current or wind **2** live or wander about aimlessly

■ *noun* **1** accumulation, mound, pile, bank, mass, heap **2** tendency, course, direction, flow **3** meaning, intention, implication, gist ◇ *verb* **1** waft, stray, float **2** wander, meander, roam

drifter *noun* **1** someone who drifts **2** a fishing boat which uses drift-nets

drift-net *noun* a fishing net which stays near the surface of the water

driftwood *noun* wood driven onto the seashore by winds or tides

drill[1] *verb* **1** make a hole in **2** make (a hole) with a drill **3** teach (*eg* soldiers) by repeated exercise ◇ *noun* **1** a tool for making holes in wood *etc* **2** training or military exercise

drill[2] *verb* sow (seeds) in rows ◇ *noun* a row of seeds or plants

drink *verb* (**drinks**, **drinking**, **drank**, **drunk**) **1** swallow (a liquid) **2** take alcoholic drink, *esp* excessively ◇ *noun* **1** liquid to be drunk **2** alcoholic liquids ◇ **drink in** listen to eagerly ◇ **drink to** drink a toast to ◇ **drink up** finish a drink

■ *verb* **1** imbibe, swallow, sip, drain, down, gulp, *informal* swig **2** *informal* booze, *informal* tipple, carouse ◇ *noun* **1** beverage, liquid, refreshment **2** alcohol, *informal* booze, liquor, tipple

drip *verb* (**drips**, **dripping**, **dripped**) **1** fall in drops **2** let (water *etc*) fall in drops ◇ *noun* **1** a drop **2** a continual dropping, *eg* of water **3** a device for adding liquid slowly to a vein *etc* ◇ **dripping** *noun* fat from roasting meat ◇ **drip-dry** *verb* dry (a garment) by hanging it up to dry without wringing or spin-drying it first

drive *verb* (**drives, driving, drove, driven**) **1** control or guide (a car *etc*) **2** go in a vehicle: *driving to work* **3** force or urge along **4** cause to be: *it's driving me mad* **5** hit hard (a ball, nail *etc*) **6** bring about: *drive a bargain* ◇ *noun* **1** a journey in a car **2** a private road or path to a house **3** an avenue or road **4** energy, enthusiasm **5** a campaign: *a drive to save the local school* **6** a games tournament: *a whist drive* **7** a hard stroke with a club or bat ◇ **drive-in** *noun*, *US* a cinema, restaurant *etc* where people stay in their cars ◇ **what are you driving at?** what are you suggesting or implying?

■ *verb* **1** steer, propel **2** motor **3** coerce, press, push, urge ◇ *noun* **1** excursion, outing, ride, spin, trip **4** enterprise, initiative, *informal* get-up-and-go, motivation **5** crusade, appeal, effort, action

drivel *noun*, *informal* nonsense ◇ *verb* (**drivels, drivelling, drivelled**) talk nonsense

driven *past participle* of **drive**

driver *noun* **1** someone who drives a car *etc* **2** a wooden-headed golf club

drizzle *noun* light rain ◇ *verb* rain lightly ◇ **drizzly** *adj*

droll *adj* **1** funny, amusing **2** odd

dromedary *noun* (*plural* **dromedaries**) an Arabian camel with one hump

drone *verb* **1** make a low humming sound **2** speak in a dull boring voice ◇ *noun* **1** a low humming sound **2** a dull boring voice **3** the low-sounding pipe of a bagpipe **4** a male bee **5** a lazy, idle person

drool *verb* produce saliva, dribble

droop *verb* **1** hang down **2** grow weak or discouraged

■ **1** hang (down), dangle, sag **2** flag, falter, slump, lose heart, wilt, wither, drop, faint

drop *noun* **1** a small round or pear-shaped blob of liquid **2** a small quantity: *a drop of whisky* **3** a steep descent **4** a fall from a height **5** a small flavoured sweet: *pear drops* ◇ *verb* (**drops, dropping, dropped**) **1** fall suddenly **2** let fall **3** fall in drops **4** set down from a car *etc*: *drop me at the corner* **5** give up, abandon (a friend, habit *etc*) ◇ **drop off** fall asleep ◇ **drop out** withdraw from a class, society *etc*

■ *noun* **1** droplet, bead, drip **2** dash, spot, sip **3** decline, descent, precipice, slope, plunge ◇ *verb* **1** plunge, plummet, tumble, dive **5** abandon, forsake, desert, give up, reject, jilt, *informal* ditch, leave

droplet *noun* a tiny drop

droppings *noun plural* animal or bird dung

dross *noun* **1** scum produced by melting metal **2** waste material, impurities **3** anything worthless

drought *noun* a period of time when no rain falls

drove *noun* **1** a number of moving cattle or other animals **2** (**droves**) a great number of people ◇ *past form* of **drive** ◇ **drover** *noun* someone who drives cattle

drown *verb* **1** die by suffocating in water **2** kill (someone) in this way **3** flood or soak completely **4** block out (a sound) with a louder one

■ **3** submerge, immerse, inundate, sink, engulf, drench

drowsy *adj* sleepy ◇ **drowsily** *adv* ◇ **drowsiness** *noun*

■ sleepy, tired, lethargic, nodding
▨ alert, awake

drub *verb* (**drubs, drubbing, drubbed**) beat, thrash ◇ **drubbing** *noun* a thrashing

drudge *verb* do very humble or boring work ◇ *noun* someone who does such work ◇ **drudgery** *noun* hard, uninteresting work

■ *verb* plod, toil, work, slave, labour ◇ *noun* menial, *informal* dogsbody, hack, slave

drug *noun* **1** a substance used in medicine to treat illness, kill pain *etc* **2** a stimulant or narcotic substance taken habitually for its effects ◇ *verb* (**drugs, drugging, drugged**) **1** administer drugs to **2** cause to lose consciousness by drugs

▣ *noun* **1** medication, medicine, remedy, potion ◇ *verb* **2** sedate, tranquillize, *informal* dope, anaesthetize, *informal* knock out

druggist *noun* a chemist

drugstore *noun, US* a shop selling newspapers, soft drinks *etc* as well as medicines

drum *noun* **1** a musical instrument of skin *etc* stretched on a round frame and beaten with sticks **2** a cylindrical container: *oil drum/biscuit drum* ◇ *verb* (**drums, drumming, drummed**) **1** beat a drum **2** tap continuously with the fingers ◇ **drummer** *noun*

drumstick *noun* **1** a stick for beating a drum **2** the lower part of the leg of a cooked chicken *etc*

drunk *adj* showing the effects of drinking too much alcohol ◇ *noun* someone who is drunk, or habitually drunk ◇ *past participle* of **drink**

▣ *adj* inebriated, intoxicated, under the influence, drunken, *slang* legless, *informal* paralytic, *informal* sloshed, *informal* merry, *informal* tipsy, *slang* tanked up, *informal* tiddly, *slang* plastered, *informal* sozzled, *informal* well-oiled, *slang* canned

▣ *adj* sober, temperate, abstinent, teetotal

drunkard *noun* a drunk

▣ drunk, inebriate, alcoholic, dipsomaniac, *informal* boozer, *informal* wino, *informal* tippler, *informal* soak, *informal* lush, *informal* sot

drunken *adj* **1** habitually drunk **2** caused by too much alcohol: *drunken stupor* **3** involving much alcohol: *drunken orgy* ◇ **drunkenly** *adv* ◇ **drunkenness** *noun*

dry *adj* **1** not moist or wet **2** thirsty **3** uninteresting: *makes very dry reading* **4** reserved, matter-of-fact **5** of wine: not sweet **6** of humour: ironic ◇ *verb* (**dries, drying, dried**) make or become dry ◇ **dryly** or **drily** *adv* ◇ **dryness** *noun* ◇ **dry-clean** *verb* clean (clothes *etc*) with chemicals, not with water ◇ **dry ice** solid carbon dioxide

◇ **dry rot** a disease causing wood to become dry and crumbly

▣ *adj* **2** parched, dehydrated **3** boring, dull, dreary, tedious **6** cynical, droll, deadpan, sarcastic

dryad *noun* a mythological wood nymph

dual *adj* double; made up of two ◇ **dual carriageway** a wide road on which traffic moving in opposite directions is separated by a central barrier or boundary ◇ **dual-purpose** *adj* able to be used for more than one purpose

▣ double, twofold, duplicate, duplex, paired, twin

> **!** Do not confuse with: **duel**

dub¹ *verb* (**dubs, dubbing, dubbed**) **1** declare (a knight) by touching each shoulder with a sword **2** name or nickname

dub² *verb* (**dubs, dubbing, dubbed**) **1** add sound effects to (a film) **2** give (a film) a new soundtrack in a different language

dubbin or **dubbing** *noun* a grease for softening or waterproofing leather

dubious *adj* **1** doubtful, uncertain **2** probably dishonest: *dubious dealings* ◇ **dubiety** *noun*

▣ **1** doubtful, undecided, unsure, wavering, sceptical, hesitant **2** questionable, unreliable, ambiguous, suspect, *informal* fishy, shady

▣ **1** certain **2** trustworthy

ducal *adj* of a duke

ducat *noun, hist* an old European gold coin

duchess *noun* (*plural* **duchesses**) **1** a woman of the same rank as a duke **2** the wife or widow of a duke

duchy *noun* (*plural* **duchies**) the land owned by a duke or duchess

duck¹ *noun* **1** a web-footed water bird with a broad flat beak **2** *cricket* a score of no runs ◇ **lame duck** an inefficient, useless person or organization

> The meaning in cricket comes from the use of 'duck's egg' to mean a nought on a scoring sheet

duck² *verb* **1** lower the head quickly as if to avoid a blow **2** push (someone's head) under water ◇ **duck out** (**of**) avoid responsibility (for)

■ *verb* **1** stoop, bend, avoid, dodge, evade **2** dip, immerse, plunge, dunk, submerge, douse, wet

duck-billed platypus *see* **platypus**

duckling *noun* a baby duck

duct *noun* a pipe or tube for carrying liquids, electric cables *etc*

ductile *adj* **1** of a metal: that can be drawn out without breaking **2** easily led, yielding

dud *adj, informal* **1** useless, broken **2** counterfeit ◇ *noun, informal* something dud

dudgeon *noun*: **in high dudgeon** very angry, indignant

due *adj* **1** owed, needing to be paid: *the rent is due next week* **2** expected to arrive *etc*: *they're due here at six* **3** proper, appropriate: *due care* ◇ *adv* directly: *due south* ◇ *noun* **1** something you have a right to: *give him his due* **2** (**dues**) the amount of money charged for belonging to a club *etc* ◇ **due to** caused by

■ *adj* **1** owed, owing, payable, unpaid, outstanding **2** expected, scheduled **3** enough, proper, sufficient, ample ◇ *adv* exactly, precisely, *informal* dead

duel *noun, hist* a formalized fight with pistols or swords between two people ◇ *verb* fight in a duel ◇ **duellist** *noun*

⚠ Do not confuse with: **dual**

duet /djʊˈɛt/ *noun* a piece of music for two singers or players

duff *adj, informal* useless, broken

duffel bag a cylindrical canvas bag tied with a drawstring

duffel coat a heavy woollen coat, fastened with toggles

After *Duffel*, a town in Belgium where the fabric was first made

duffer *noun, informal* a stupid or incompetent person

dug *past form* of **dig**

dugout *noun* **1** a boat made by hollowing out the trunk of a tree **2** a rough shelter dug out of a slope or bank or in a trench **3** *football* a bench beside the pitch for team managers, trainers, and extra players

duke *noun* a nobleman next in rank below a prince ◇ **dukedom** *noun* the title, rank or lands of a duke

dulcet *adj, formal* sounding pleasant, melodious

dulcimer *noun* a musical instrument with stretched wires which are struck with small hammers

dull *adj* **1** not bright in colour **2** slow to understand or learn **3** not lively, exciting or interesting **4** of weather: cloudy, not bright or clear **5** of sounds: not clear or ringing **6** of pain, a blade *etc*: not sharp ◇ *verb* make dull ◇ **dullness** *noun* ◇ **dully** *adv*

■ *adj* **2** unintelligent, dense, dim, *informal* dimwitted, *informal* thick, stupid, slow **3** boring, uninteresting, unexciting, flat, dreary, tedious, uneventful **4** dark, gloomy, murky, grey, cloudy, dim, overcast ◇ *verb* deaden, numb, paralyse, dim, obscure, fade

duly *adv* at the expected time or in the proper way: *he duly arrived*

dumb *adj* **1** without the power of speech **2** silent **3** *informal* stupid ◇ **dumbly** *adv* in silence ◇ **dumb down** make less intellectual or challenging ◇ **dumb show** acting without words

dumbfound *verb* astonish

dummy *noun* (*plural* **dummies**) **1** a replica of something used for display **2** a model used for displaying clothes *etc* **3** an artificial teat used to comfort a baby **4** *slang* a stupid person ◇ **dummy run** a try-out, a practice

■ **1** copy, duplicate, substitute, model **2** model, mannequin, figure, form **3** teat, pacifier

dump *verb* **1** drop or throw down heavily **2** unload and leave (rubbish *etc*) **3** sell at a low price ◇ *noun* **1** a place for leaving rubbish **2** an unattractive place ◇ **in the dumps** feeling low or depressed

■ *verb* **1** drop, throw down, let fall **2** get rid of, scrap, throw away, dispose of, ditch, tip ◇ *noun* **1** tip, junk-yard, rubbish-heap, rubbish-tip **2** hovel, slum, shack, *informal* hole

dumpling *noun* a cooked ball of dough

dumpy *adj* short and thick or fat

dun¹ *adj* greyish-brown, mouse-coloured

dun² *verb* (**duns**, **dunning**, **dunned**) demand payment

dunce *noun* a stupid or slow-learning person

Originally a term of abuse applied to followers of the medieval Scottish philosopher, John *Duns Scotus*

dunderhead *noun*, *informal* a stupid person

dune *noun* a low hill of sand

dung *noun* animal faeces, manure ◇ **dunghill** *noun* a heap of dung in a farmyard etc

dungarees *noun plural* trousers made of coarse, hard-wearing material with a bib

dungeon *noun* a dark underground prison

duodenum *noun* the first part of the small intestine

dupe *noun* someone easily cheated ◇ *verb* deceive, trick

■ *noun informal* sucker, fool, *informal* mug, *informal* pushover, *informal* fall guy ◇ *verb* deceive, fool, trick, outwit, *informal* con, cheat, swindle, *informal* rip off

duplicate *adj* exactly the same ◇ *noun* an exact copy ◇ *verb* make a copy or copies of ◇ **duplication** *noun*

■ *adj* identical, matching, twin, matched ◇ *noun* replica, clone, reproduction, photocopy, carbon (copy), facsimile ◇ *verb* copy, reproduce, repeat, photocopy, double

duplicity *noun* deceit, double-dealing ◇ **duplicitous** *adj* ◇ **duplicitously**

adv ◇ **duplicitousness** *noun*

durable *adj* lasting, able to last; wearing well ◇ **durability** *noun*

■ enduring, long-lasting, hard-wearing, strong, sturdy, tough, reliable, dependable, stable, resistant, constant

◼ perishable, weak, fragile

duration *noun* the time a thing lasts ◇ **for the duration** *informal* until something ends; for a long time

duress *noun* illegal force used to make someone do something ◇ **under duress** under the influence of force, threats *etc*

during *prep* **1** throughout all or part of: *we lived here during the war* **2** at a particular point within: *she died during the night*

dusk *noun* twilight, partial dark

■ twilight, sunset, nightfall, evening, sundown, gloaming, shadows

dusky *adj* dark-coloured ◇ **duskiness** *noun*

dust *noun* **1** fine grains or specks of earth, sand *etc* **2** fine powder ◇ *verb* **1** free from dust: *dusted the table* **2** sprinkle lightly with powder ◇ **dusty** *adj* covered with dust ◇ **dust-bowl** *noun* an area with little rain in which the wind raises storms of dust ◇ **dust jacket** a paper cover on a book

dustbin *noun* a container for household rubbish

duster *noun* a cloth for removing dust

dustman *noun* someone employed to collect household rubbish

dutiable *adj* of goods: liable for tax

dutiful *adj* obedient ◇ **dutifully** *adv*

■ obedient, respectful, conscientious, devoted, reverential, submissive

duty *noun* (*plural* **duties**) **1** something a person ought to do **2** an action required to be done, *esp* as part of a job **3** a tax ◇ **duty-free** *adj* not taxed

■ **1** obligation, responsibility **2** task, job, business, function, office, service **3** toll, tariff, levy, customs, excise

duvet /'duːveɪ/ *noun* a quilt stuffed with feathers or synthetic material, used instead of blankets

DV *abbrev* if God is willing (from Latin *deo volente*)

dwarf *noun* (*plural* **dwarfs** or **dwarves**) an undersized person, animal or plant ◊ *verb* cause to appear small by comparison ◊ *adj* not growing to full or usual height: *a dwarf cherry-tree*

dwell *verb* live, inhabit, stay ◊ **dwell on** think habitually about: *dwelling on the past*

dwindle *verb* grow less, fade away
▤ diminish, decrease, decline, lessen, subside, fade, weaken, taper off, tail off, shrink, wane, waste away

dye *verb* (**dyes**, **dyeing**, **dyed**) give a colour to (fabric *etc*) ◊ *noun* a powder or liquid for colouring

dying *present participle* of **die**

dyke¹ or **dike** *noun* **1** a wall or embankment to hold back water **2** a ditch

dyke² *noun, offensive slang* a lesbian

dynamic *adj* forceful, energetic ◊ **dynamically** *adv* ◊ **dynamics** *noun sing* the scientific study of movement and force
▤ forceful, powerful, energetic, vigorous, go-ahead, driving, self-starting, spirited, vital, lively, active
▨ inactive, apathetic

dynamite *noun* a type of powerful explosive

dynamo *noun* (*plural* **dynamos**) a machine for turning the energy produced by movement into electricity

dynasty *noun* (*plural* **dynasties**) a succession of monarchs, leaders *etc* of the same family ◊ **dynastic** *adj*
▤ house, line, succession

dysentery *noun* an infectious disease causing fever, pain and diarrhoea

dyslexia *noun* difficulty in learning to read and in spelling ◊ **dyslexic** *noun* & *adj* (someone) suffering from dyslexia

dyspepsia *noun* indigestion ◊ **dyspeptic** *adj*

Ee

E *abbrev* **1** east; eastern **2** the drug Ecstasy

each *adj* of two or more things: every one taken individually: *there is a post-box on each side of the road/she was late on each occasion* ◇ *pronoun* every one individually: *each of them won a prize* ◇ **each other** used when an action takes place between two (or more than two) people: *we don't see each other very often*

eager *adj* keen, anxious to do or get something ◇ **eagerly** *adv* ◇ **eagerness** *noun*

⬛ keen, enthusiastic, fervent, intent, earnest, zealous

⬛ unenthusiastic, indifferent

eagle *noun* a kind of large bird of prey ◇ **eaglet** *noun* a young eagle

ear¹ *noun* the part of the body through which you hear sounds ◇ **a good ear** the ability to tell one sound from another ◇ **lend an ear** listen

ear² *noun* the part of a cereal plant (*eg* corn) containing seeds

eardrum *noun* the membrane in the middle of the ear

earl *noun* a member of the British aristocracy between a marquis and a viscount ◇ **earldom** *noun* the lands or title of an earl

earlobe *noun* the soft fleshy lower part of the outer ear

early *adj* (**earlier, earliest**) **1** before the usual or expected time **2** at or near the beginning: *in an earlier chapter* **3** sooner than others: *catch the early train* ◇ *adv* at an early time ◇ **earliness** *noun* ◇ **early bird 1** an early riser **2** someone who gains an advantage by acting more quickly than rivals

⬛ *adj* **1** premature, untimely ◇ *adv* ahead of time, in good time, in advance, prematurely

earmark *verb* mark or set aside for a special purpose

earmuffs *noun plural* warm coverings for the ears

earn *verb* **1** receive (money) for work **2** deserve ◇ **earnings** *noun plural* pay for work done

⬛ **1** make, get, *informal* bring in, realize, gross **2** deserve, warrant, merit, win

earnest *adj* serious, serious-minded ◇ *noun* **1** seriousness **2** money *etc* given to make sure that a bargain will be kept ◇ **earnestly** *adv* ◇ **earnestness** *noun* ◇ **in earnest** meaning what you say or do

⬛ *adj* serious, sincere, solemn, resolute, devoted, ardent, keen, fervent, firm, eager, enthusiastic

earphones *noun plural* a pair of tiny speakers fitting in or against the ear for listening to a radio *etc*

ear-piercing *adj* very loud or shrill

earplugs *noun plural* a pair of plugs placed in the ears to block off outside noise

earshot *noun* the distance at which a sound can be heard

earth *noun* **1** the third planet from the sun; our world **2** its surface **3** soil **4** the hole of a fox, badger *etc* **5** an electrical connection with the ground ◇ *verb* connect electrically with the ground ◇ **earthen** *adj* made of earth or clay ◇ **earthly** *adj* of the earth as opposed to heaven

earthenware *noun* pottery, dishes made of clay

earthquake *noun* a shaking of the earth's crust

earthshattering *adj* of great importance

earth tremor a slight earthquake

earthwork *noun* an artificial bank of earth

earthworm *noun* the common worm

earthy *adj* **1** like soil **2** covered in soil **3** coarse, not refined

earwig *noun* a type of insect with pincers at its tail

ease *noun* **1** freedom from difficulty: *finished the race with ease* **2** freedom from pain, worry or embarrassment ◇ *verb* **1** make or become less painful or difficult **2** move carefully and gradually: *ease the stone into position* ◇ **at ease** comfortable, relaxed ◇ **stand at ease** stand with your legs apart and arms behind your back

◼ *noun* **1** effortlessness, facility, skilfulness, deftness **2** comfort, contentment, peace, repose, relaxation, rest, quiet ◇ *verb* **1** alleviate, moderate, lessen, relieve, abate, calm, soothe **2** inch, steer

▨ *verb* **1** aggravate, intensify, worsen

easel *noun* a stand for an artist's canvas while painting *etc*

east *noun* one of the four chief directions, that in which the sun rises ◇ *adj* in or from the east: *an east wind*

Easter *noun* **1** the Christian celebration of Christ's rising from the dead **2** the weekend in spring when this is celebrated each year

easterly *adj* coming from or facing the east

eastern *adj* of the east

eastward or **eastwards** *adj & adv* towards the east

easy *adj* (**easier**, **easiest**) **1** not hard to do **2** free from pain, worry or discomfort ◇ **easily** *adv* ◇ **easiness** *noun*

◼ **1** effortless, simple, uncomplicated, straightforward **2** relaxed, carefree, comfortable, calm, natural ◇ **easily** effortlessly, simply

eat *verb* (**eats**, **eating**, **ate**, **eaten**) **1** chew and swallow (food) **2** destroy gradually ◇ **eatable** *adj* fit to eat, edible

eaves *noun plural* the edge of a roof overhanging the walls

eavesdrop *verb* listen secretly to a private conversation ◇ **eavesdropper** *noun*

◼ listen in, spy, overhear, *informal* tap, *informal* bug, monitor

ebb *noun* **1** the flowing away of the tide after high tide **2** a lessening, a worsening ◇ *verb* **1** flow away **2** grow less or worse

ebony *noun* a type of black, hard wood ◇ *adj* **1** made of ebony **2** black

ebullient *adj* lively and enthusiastic ◇ **ebullience** *noun* ◇ **ebulliently** *adv*

EC *abbrev* European Community

eccentric *adj* **1** odd, acting strangely **2** of circles: not having the same centre (*contrasted with*: **concentric**) ◇ *noun* an eccentric person ◇ **eccentricity** *noun* (*plural* **eccentricities**) oddness of manner or conduct

◼ *adj* **1** odd, peculiar, abnormal, unconventional, strange, quirky, weird, outlandish, bizarre, freakish, dotty

ecclesiastic or **ecclesiastical** *adj* of the church or clergy

echelon /ˈɛʃəlɒn/ *noun* **1** a level, a rank **2** a formation of soldiers, aircraft *etc*

echo *noun* (*plural* **echoes**) **1** the repetition of a sound which echoes **2** an imitation **3** something that evokes a memory: *echoes of the past* ◇ *verb* **1** of sound: strike a surface and be heard again **2** repeat (something said) **3** imitate

◼ *noun* **1** reverberation, reflection

éclair *noun* an oblong sweet pastry filled with cream

eclampsia *noun* a toxic condition that can occur in the final months of pregnancy

eclectic *noun* broadly based, wide-ranging: *eclectic tastes*

eclipse *noun* **1** the covering of the whole or part of the sun or moon, *eg* when the moon comes between the sun and the earth **2** loss of position or prestige ◇ *verb* **1** throw into the shade **2** blot out (someone's achievement) by doing better

◼ *verb* **1** blot out, obscure, cloud, veil, darken, dim **2** outdo, overshadow, outshine, surpass

eco- *prefix* relating to the environment: *eco-friendly/eco-summit*

ecology *noun* **1** the relationship of plants, animals *etc* to their natural surroundings **2** the study of this ◇ **ecological** *adj* ◇ **ecologically** *adv* ◇ **ecologist** *noun*

economic *adj* **1** concerning economy **2** making a profit

economical *adj* **1** thrifty, not wasteful **2** inexpensive
- **1** thrifty, careful, prudent, saving, sparing, frugal **2** cheap, inexpensive, cost-effective, efficient

economics *noun sing* the study of how money is produced and spent

economist *noun* someone who studies or is an expert on economics

economize *verb* be careful in spending or using

economy *noun* (*plural* **economies**) **1** the management of a country's finances **2** the careful use of something, *esp* money

ecstasy *noun* (*plural* **ecstasies**) **1** very great joy or pleasure **2** (**Ecstasy**) a hallucinogenic drug ◇ **ecstatic** *adj* ◇ **ecstatically** *adv*
- **ecstatic** elated, blissful, joyful, rapturous, overjoyed, euphoric

ectoplasm *noun* a substance believed by spiritualists to surround mediums

ecumenical *adj* concerned with the unity of the whole Christian Church

eczema /'ɛksɪmə/ *noun* a skin disease causing red swollen patches on the skin

Edam *noun* a mild Dutch cheese with a red outer skin

eddy *noun* (*plural* **eddies**) a circling current of water or air running against the main stream ◇ *verb* (**eddies**, **eddying**, **eddied**) flow in circles

edelweiss /'eɪdəlvaɪs/ *noun* (*plural* **edelweiss**) an Alpine plant with white flowers

edge *noun* **1** the border of anything, the part farthest from the middle **2** the cutting side of a blade **3** sharpness: *put an edge on my appetite* **4** advantage: *Brazil had the edge at half-time* ◇ *verb* **1** put an edge on **2** move little by little: *edging forward* ◇ **edgeways** *adv* sideways ◇ **edging** *noun* a border, a fringe ◇ **edgy** *adj* unable to relax, irritable ◇ **on edge** nervous, edgy ◇ **set someone's teeth on edge** grate on their nerves, make them wince
- *noun* **1** rim, boundary, limit, fringe, margin, outline, side, verge, line, perimeter, periphery ◇ **edgy** on edge, nervous, tense, anxious, ill at ease, touchy, irritable

edible *adj* fit to be eaten

edict *noun* an order, a command
- command, order, proclamation, decree, pronouncement, ruling

edifice *noun* a large building

edify *verb* (**edifies**, **edifying**, **edified**) improve the mind, enlighten ◇ **edification** *noun* ◇ **edifying** *adj*
- improve, enlighten, educate, inform

edit *verb* prepare (a text, film *etc*) for publication or broadcasting
- correct, revise, rearrange, adapt, check, compile, rephrase, censor

edition *noun* **1** the form in which a book *etc* is published **2** the copies of a book, newspaper *etc* printed at one time **3** a special issue of a newspaper, *eg* for a local area

editor *noun* **1** someone who edits a book, film *etc* **2** the chief journalist of a newspaper or section of a newspaper: *the sports editor*

editorial *adj* of editing ◇ *noun* a newspaper column written by the chief editor

educate *verb* teach (people), *esp* in a school or college ◇ **education** *noun* ◇ **educational** *adj* of or providing education ◇ **educated guess** a guess based on knowledge of the subject involved

> *Educational establishments include*: kindergarten, nursery school, infant school, primary school, middle school, combined school, secondary school, comprehensive

school, secondary modern, upper school, high school, grammar school, community school, foundation school, voluntary school, preparatory school, public school, private school, boarding school, college, sixth-form college, city technical college, CTC, technical college, university, adult-education centre, academy, seminary, finishing school, business school, secretarial college, Sunday school, convent school, summer-school

EEC *abbrev* European Economic Community

EEG *abbrev* electroencephalogram; electroencephalograph

eel *noun* a long, ribbon-shaped fish

eerie *adj* strange and frightening

■ weird, strange, uncanny, *informal* spooky, creepy, frightening, scary, spine-chilling

Originally a Scots word meaning 'afraid' or 'cowardly'

efface *verb* rub out ◇ **efface yourself** try to avoid being noticed

effect *noun* **1** the result of an action **2** strength, power: *the pills had little effect* **3** an impression produced: *the effect of the sunset* **4** general meaning **5** use, operation: *that law is not yet in effect* **6** (**effects**) goods, property ◇ *verb* bring about

■ *noun* **1** outcome, conclusion, consequence, upshot, aftermath **2** force, impact, strength **4** significance, import

🚹 Do not confuse with: **affect**

effective *adj* **1** producing the desired effect **2** actual

effectual *adj* able to do what is required ◇ **effectually** *adv*

effeminate *adj* unmanly, womanish

effervesce *verb* **1** form gas bubbles, froth up **2** be very lively, excited *etc* ◇ **effervescence** *noun* ◇ **effervescent** *adj*

■ **effervescent** bubbly, sparkling, fizzy, frothy, carbonated, foaming, lively, vivacious, animated, exuberant, excited, vital

effete /ɪˈfiːt/ *adj* weak, feeble

efficacious *adj* producing the desired effect, effective ◇ **efficacy** *noun*

efficient *adj* able to do things well; capable ◇ **efficiency** *noun* ◇ **efficiently** *noun*

■ effective, competent, proficient, skilful, capable, able, productive, well-organized

🔁 inefficient, incompetent

effigy /ˈɛfɪdʒɪ/ *noun* (*plural* **effigies**) a likeness of a person carved in stone, wood *etc*

effluent *noun* **1** a stream flowing from another stream or lake **2** liquid industrial waste; sewage

effort *noun* **1** an attempt, *esp* one using a lot of strength or ability **2** hard work ◇ **effortless** *adj*

■ **1** attempt, try, *informal* go, endeavour, shot, stab **2** exertion, strain, application, struggle, trouble, energy ◇ **effortless** easy, simple, undemanding, painless, smooth

effrontery *noun* impudence

effusive *adj* speaking freely, gushing ◇ **effusively** *adv*

■ fulsome, gushing, expansive, profuse, exuberant, talkative

EFL *abbrev* English as a foreign language

eg *abbrev* for example (from Latin *exempli gratia*)

egg *noun* **1** an oval shell containing the embryo of a bird, insect or reptile **2** (*also called* **ovum**) a human reproductive cell **3** a hen's egg used for cooking, eating *etc* ◇ **egg on** urge, encourage

eggplant *noun, US* an aubergine

ego *noun* **1** the conscious self **2** self-conceit, egotism

egoism or **egotism** *noun* the habit of considering only your own interests, selfishness ◇ **egoist** or **egotist** *noun* ◇ **egoistic** or **egotistic** *adj*

■ self-centredness, self-importance,

conceitedness, self-regard, narcissism, self-admiration, vanity, *informal* big-headedness

▣ humility

egregious *adj* outrageous, notoriously bad

egress *noun*, *formal* exit, way out

egret *noun* a type of white heron

eider or **eider-duck** *noun* a northern sea duck ◊ **eiderdown** *noun* **1** soft feathers from the eider **2** a feather quilt

eight *noun* the number 8 ◊ *adj* 8 in number

eighth *adj* the last of a series of eight ◊ *noun* one of eight equal parts

eighteen *noun* the number 18 ◊ *adj* 18 in number

eighteenth *adj* the last of a series of eighteen ◊ *noun* one of eighteen equal parts

eightieth *adj* the last of a series of eighty ◊ *noun* one of eighty equal parts

eighty the number 80 ◊ *adj* 80 in number

either *adj & pronoun* **1** one or other of two: *either bus will go there/either of the dates would suit me* **2** each of two, both: *there is a crossing on either side of the road* ◊ *conj* used with **or** to show alternatives: *either he goes or I do* ◊ *adv* any more than another: *that won't work either*

ejaculate *verb* **1** emit semen **2** shout out, exclaim ◊ **ejaculation** *noun*

▣ **2** call, blurt (out), cry, shout, yell, utter, scream

eject *verb* **1** throw out **2** force to leave a house, job *etc* ◊ **ejection** *noun*

▣ **1** emit, expel, discharge, spout, spew, evacuate, vomit **2** oust, evict, throw out, drive out, turn out, expel

eke *verb*: **eke out** make last longer by adding to: *eked out the stew with more vegetables*

elaborate *verb* **1** work out in detail: *you must elaborate your escape plan* **2** (often with **on**) explain fully ◊ *adj* highly detailed or decorated ◊ **elaboration** *noun*

▣ *verb* **1** develop, devise, polish, refine **2** expand, explain ◊ *adj* intricate, complex, complicated, ornamental, ornate

élan *noun* enthusiasm, dash

eland *noun* a type of African deer

elapse *verb* of time: pass

elastane *noun* a lightweight elastic fabric

elastic *adj* able to stretch and spring back again, springy ◊ *noun* a piece of cotton *etc* interwoven with rubber to make it springy ◊ **elasticity** *noun*

elated *adj* in high spirits, very pleased ◊ **elation** *noun*

▣ exhilarated, excited, euphoric, ecstatic, exultant, jubilant, overjoyed, joyful

▣ despondent, downcast

elbow *noun* the joint where the arm bends ◊ *verb* push with the elbow, jostle ◊ **elbow grease 1** vigorous rubbing **2** hard work, effort ◊ **elbow-room** *noun* plenty of room to move

elder [1] *adj* older ◊ *noun* **1** someone who is older **2** an office-bearer in the Presbyterian church ◊ **elderly** *adj* nearing old age ◊ **eldest** *adj* oldest

elder [2] *noun* a type of tree with purple-black berries ◊ **elderberry** *noun* (*plural* **elderberries**) a berry from the elder tree

elect *verb* **1** choose by voting **2** choose (to) ◊ *adj* **1** chosen **2** chosen for a post but not yet in it: *president elect* ◊ **election** *noun* the choosing by vote of people to sit in parliament *etc* ◊ **electioneer** *verb* campaign for votes in an election ◊ **electorate** *noun* all those who have the right to vote

▣ *verb* **1** choose, pick, opt for, select, vote for, appoint **2** choose, opt for, prefer

electric *adj* **1** (*also* **electrical**) of, produced by or worked by electricity **2** exciting ◊ **electric shock** a convulsion caused by an electric current passing through the body

▣ **2** electrifying, exciting, stimulating, thrilling, charged, dynamic

electrician *noun* someone skilled in working with electricity

electricity *noun* a form of energy used to give light, heat and power

electrify *verb* (**electrifies, electrifying, electrified**) **1** supply with electricity **2** excite greatly
■ **2** thrill, excite, animate, stimulate, amaze, astonish

electrocute *verb* kill by an electric current

electrode *noun* a conductor through which an electric current enters or leaves a battery *etc*

electron *noun* a very light particle within an atom, having the smallest possible charge of electricity

electronic *adj* of or using electrons, small electrical circuits or electronics ◇ **electronics** *noun sing* a branch of physics dealing with electronic circuits and their use in machines *etc*

elegant *adj* **1** graceful, well-dressed, fashionable **2** of clothes *etc*: well-made and tasteful ◇ **elegance** *noun* ◇ **elegantly** *adv*
■ **1, 2** stylish, chic, fashionable, smart, refined, polished, tasteful, exquisite, graceful
⊟ **1, 2** inelegant, unrefined, unfashionable

elegy *noun* (*plural* **elegies**) a poem written on someone's death

element *noun* **1** a part of anything **2** a substance that cannot be split chemically into simpler substances, *eg* oxygen, iron *etc* **3** circumstances which suit someone best: *she is in her element when singing* **4** a heating wire carrying the current in an electrical appliance **5** (**elements**) first steps in learning **6** (**elements**) the powers of nature, the weather ◇ **elemental** *adj* of the elements
■ **1** factor, component, constituent, ingredient, part, piece

elementary *adj* simple; basic
■ basic, fundamental, rudimentary, clear, easy, introductory, straightforward, uncomplicated
⊟ advanced

elephant *noun* a very large animal with a thick skin, a trunk and two ivory tusks ◇ **elephantine** *adj* big and clumsy

elevate *verb* **1** raise to a higher position **2** cheer up **3** improve (the mind) ◇ **elevation** *noun* **1** the act of raising up **2** rising ground **3** height **4** a drawing of a building as seen from the side **5** an angle measuring height: *the sun's elevation* ◇ **elevator** *noun*, *US* a lift in a building
■ **1** lift, raise, hoist, heighten, intensify **2** uplift, rouse, boost, brighten

eleven the number 11 ◇ *adj* 11 in number ◇ *noun* a team of eleven players, *eg* for cricket ◇ **elevenses** *noun plural* coffee, biscuits *etc* taken around eleven o'clock in the morning

eleventh *adj* the last of a series of eleven ◇ *noun* one of eleven equal parts

elf *noun* (*plural* **elves**) a tiny, mischievous supernatural creature ◇ **elfin, elfish** or **elvish** *adj* like an elf

elicit *verb* draw out (information *etc*)
■ draw out, extract, obtain, extort

> 🚫 Do not confuse with: **illicit**

eligible *adj* fit or worthy to be chosen or to do or receive something ◇ **eligibility** *noun*
■ qualified, fit, appropriate, suitable, acceptable, worthy, proper, desirable

eliminate *verb* get rid of or exclude ◇ **elimination** *noun*
■ remove, get rid of, take out, exclude, delete, dispense with, reject, disregard, dispose of, drop, exterminate

elite or **élite** /ɛˈliːt/ or /eˈliːt/ *noun* a part of a group selected as, or believed to be, the best

elixir *noun* a liquid believed to give eternal life, or to be able to turn iron *etc* into gold

elk *noun* a very large deer found in N Europe and Asia, related to the moose

ellipse *noun* an oval shape

ellipsis *noun* (*plural* **ellipses**) **1** the omission of a word or words in a text **2** marks (...) indicating missing words in a text

elliptic or **elliptical** *adj* **1** oval **2** having part of the words or meaning left out

elm *noun* a tree with a rough bark and

leaves with saw-like edges

elocution *noun* 1 the art of what is thought to be correct speech 2 style of speaking

■ 2 delivery, diction, enunciation, pronunciation

elongate *verb* stretch out lengthwise, make longer ◇ **elongation** *noun*

■ lengthen, extend, prolong, protract, stretch

elope *verb* run away from home to get married ◇ **elopement** *noun*

eloquent *adj* 1 good at expressing yourself 2 persuasive ◇ **eloquence** *noun*

■ 1 articulate, fluent, vocal, voluble 2 persuasive, forceful

◨ 1 inarticulate, tongue-tied

else *adv & adj* other than the person or thing mentioned: *someone else has taken her place* ◇ **elsewhere** *adv* in or to another place ◇ **or else** if not; otherwise: *come inside or else you will catch cold*

elucidate *verb* make easy or easier to understand

elude *verb* 1 escape by a trick 2 be too difficult to remember or understand

■ 1 avoid, escape, evade, dodge, shirk, *informal* duck, flee 2 puzzle, frustrate, baffle, confound, stump

⚠ Do not confuse with: **allude**

elusive *adj* 1 hard to catch 2 difficult to understand or remember

■ 1 evasive, shifty, slippery, tricky 2 subtle, puzzling, baffling, transient, transitory

⚠ Do not confuse with: **allusive** and **illusive**

elver *noun* a young eel

elves and **elvish** *see* elf

emaciated *adj* very thin, like a skeleton

■ thin, gaunt, lean, haggard, wasted, scrawny, skeletal, pinched

email or **e-mail** *noun* (short for **electronic mail**) a message or messages sent from one computer to another

emanate *verb* flow, come out from ◇ **emanation** *noun*

emancipate *verb* set free, *eg* from slavery or repressive social conditions ◇ **emancipation** *noun*

■ free, liberate, release, set free, enfranchise, deliver, discharge, loose, unshackle

emasculate 1 castrate 2 deprive of power, weaken

embalm *verb* preserve (a dead body) from decay by treating it with spices or drugs

embankment *noun* a bank of earth or stone to keep back water, or carry a railway over low-lying places

embargo *noun* (*plural* **embargoes**) an official order forbidding something, *esp* trade with another country

■ restriction, ban, prohibition, restraint, bar, barrier, *formal* interdiction

embark *verb* go on board ship ◇ **embarkation** *noun* ◇ **embark on** start (a new career *etc*)

embarrass *verb* cause to feel uncomfortable and self-conscious ◇ **embarrassed** *adj* ◇ **embarrassing** *adj* ◇ **embarrassment** *noun*

■ disconcert, mortify, show up, fluster, humiliate, shame, distress ◇ **embarrassment** self-consciousness, mortification, humiliation, shame, awkwardness, bashfulness

embassy *noun* (*plural* **embassies**) the offices and staff of an ambassador in a foreign country

embellish *verb* 1 decorate 2 add details to (a story *etc*) ◇ **embellishment** *noun*

■ 1 adorn, ornament, decorate, deck, dress up, garnish 2 elaborate, embroider, enrich, exaggerate, enhance

ember *noun* a piece of wood or coal glowing in a fire

embezzle *verb* use for yourself money entrusted to you ◇ **embezzlement** *noun*

emblazon *verb* 1 decorate, adorn 2 show in bright colours or conspicuously

emblem *noun* **1** an image which represents something: *the dove is the emblem of peace* **2** a badge

embody *verb* (**embodies, embodying, embodied**) **1** include **2** express, give form to: *embodying the spirit of the age* ◇ **embodiment** *noun*

■ **1** include, contain, integrate **2** personify, exemplify, represent, symbolize, incorporate, express

embolism *noun* an obstructing clot in a blood vessel

emboss *verb* make a pattern in leather, metal *etc*, which stands out from a flat surface ◇ **embossed** *adj*

embrace *verb* **1** throw your arms round in affection **2** include **3** accept, adopt eagerly ◇ *noun* an affectionate hug

■ *verb* **1** hug, clasp, cuddle, hold, grasp, squeeze **2** encompass, incorporate, contain, comprise, cover, involve **3** accept, take up, welcome

embrocation *noun* an ointment for rubbing on the body, *eg* to relieve stiffness

embroider *verb* **1** decorate with designs in needlework **2** add false details to (a story) ◇ **embroiderer** *noun* ◇ **embroidery** *noun*

embroil *verb* **1** get (someone) into a quarrel, or into a difficult situation **2** throw into confusion

embryo *noun* (*plural* **embryos**) **1** the young of an animal or plant in its earliest stage **2** the beginning of anything ◇ **embryonic** *adj* in an early stage of development

■ **embryonic** undeveloped, rudimentary, immature, early, germinal

emend *verb* remove faults or errors from ◇ **emendation** *noun*

> ❗ Do not confuse with: **amend**

emerald *noun* a bright green precious stone

emerge *verb* **1** come out **2** become known or clear ◇ **emergence** *noun* ◇ **emergent** *adj* **1** arising **2** newly formed or newly independent: *emergent nations*

■ **1** arise, rise, surface, appear, develop, *informal* crop up, turn up, materialize **2** transpire

emergency *noun* (*plural* **emergencies**) an unexpected event requiring very quick action ◇ **emergency exit** a way out of a building for use in an emergency ◇ **emergency services** the police, fire and ambulance services

■ crisis, danger, difficulty, predicament, plight, quandary

emery *noun* a very hard mineral, used for smoothing and polishing

emetic *adj* causing vomiting ◇ *noun* an emetic medicine

emigrate *verb* leave your country to settle in another ◇ **emigrant** *noun* someone who emigrates ◇ **emigration** *noun*

> ❗ Do not confuse with: **immigrate**

émigré *noun* someone who emigrates for political reasons

eminent *adj* famous, notable ◇ **eminence** *noun* **1** distinction, fame **2** a title of honour **3** a hill ◇ **eminently** *adv* very, obviously: *eminently suitable*

■ distinguished, prominent, outstanding, prestigious, celebrated, renowned, esteemed, important, well-known, elevated, respected

🗲 unknown, obscure, unimportant

> ❗ Do not confuse with: **imminent**

emissary *noun* (*plural* **emissaries**) someone sent on private, often secret, business

■ agent, envoy, messenger, courier, representative, ambassador

emit *verb* (**emits, emitting, emitted**) send or give out (light, sound *etc*) ◇ **emission** *noun*

■ discharge, issue, eject, emanate, exude, give out, give off, radiate, release, vent

Emmy *noun* an annual award given by the American Academy of Television Arts and Sciences

emollient *adj* softening and smoothing ◇ *noun* an emollient substance

emolument *noun, formal* wages, salary

emotion *noun* a feeling that disturbs or excites the mind, *eg* fear, love, hatred ◇ **emotional** *adj* **1** moving the feelings **2** of a person: having feelings easily excited **3** of, having or showing emotion: *an emotional response* ◇ **emotionally** *adv* ◇ **emotive** *adj* causing emotion rather than thought

▣ feeling, passion, sentiment, passion, sensation ◇ **emotional 1** moving, poignant, touching, stirring **2** passionate, responsive, sentimental, demonstrative, fervent, hot-blooded

empathy *noun* the ability to share another person's feelings *etc* ◇ **empathize** *verb*

emperor *noun* the ruler of an empire

emphasis *noun* **1** stress placed on a word or words in speaking **2** greater attention or importance: *the emphasis is on playing, not winning* ◇ **emphatic** *adj* spoken strongly: *an emphatic 'no'* ◇ **emphatically** *adv*

▣ **1** stress, weight, accent **2** stress, significance, importance ◇ **emphatic** forceful, positive, definite, insistent, unequivocal, strong, striking

emphasize *verb* put emphasis on; call attention to

emphysema /ɛmfɪ'siːmə/ *noun* a lung disease causing breathing difficulties

empire *noun* **1** a group of nations *etc* under the same ruling power **2** a large business organization including several companies

empirical *adj* based on experiment and experience, not on theory alone ◇ **empirically** *adv* ◇ **empiricism** *noun* ◇ **empiricist** *noun*

employ *verb* **1** give work to **2** use **3** occupy the time of ◇ *noun* employment: *while I was in their employ* ◇ **employee** *noun* someone who works for an employer ◇ **employer** *noun* a person or company employing people

▣ *verb* **1** engage, hire, take on, recruit **2** utilize, make use of

employment *noun* **1** work, occupation **2** the act of employing

▣ job, work, profession, *informal* line, vocation, trade

emporium *noun* (*plural* **emporia** or **emporiums**) a large shop; a market

empower *verb* **1** authorize **2** give self-confidence to

empress *noun* the female ruler of an empire

empty *adj* **1** containing nothing or no one **2** unlikely to result in anything: *empty threats* ◇ *verb* (**empties, emptying, emptied**) make or become empty ◇ *noun* (*plural* **empties**) an empty bottle *etc* ◇ **emptiness** *noun* ◇ **empty-handed** *adj* bringing or gaining nothing ◇ **empty-headed** *adj* flighty, irresponsible

▣ *adj* **1** vacant, void, unoccupied, uninhabited, unfilled, deserted, bare, desolate, blank **2** futile, senseless, useless, ineffective

EMS *abbrev* European Monetary System

EMU *abbrev* European Monetary Union

emu *noun* a type of Australian bird which cannot fly

emulate *verb* try to do as well as, or better than ◇ **emulation** *noun*

▣ match, copy, mimic, follow, imitate, echo, compete with, contend with, rival, vie with

emulsion *noun* a milky liquid, *esp* one made by mixing oil and water

enable *verb* make it possible for, allow: *the money enabled him to retire*

▣ empower, authorize, allow, permit, facilitate, prepare

▣ prevent, inhibit, forbid

enact *verb* **1** act, perform **2** make a law

enamel *noun* **1** a glassy coating fired onto metal **2** a paint with a glossy finish **3** the smooth white coating of the teeth ◇ *verb* (**enamels, enamelling, enamelled**) coat or paint with enamel ◇ **enamelling** *noun*

enamoured *adj*: **enamoured of** fond of

encampment *noun* a military camp

encapsulate *verb* capture the essence

of; describe briefly and accurately

encephalitis *noun* inflammation of the brain

enchant *verb* **1** delight, please greatly **2** put a spell or charm on ◇ **enchanter**, **enchantress** *noun* ◇ **enchantment** *noun*

■ **1** captivate, charm, fascinate, enrapture, attract, allure, appeal, delight, thrill **2** entrance, bewitch, spellbind, hypnotize, mesmerize

enchilada a Mexican tortilla stuffed and cooked in a chilli sauce

enclave *noun* an area enclosed within foreign territory

enclose *verb* **1** put inside an envelope with a letter *etc* **2** put *eg* a wall or fence around ◇ **enclosure** *noun* **1** the act of enclosing **2** something enclosed

■ **2** encircle, encompass, surround, fence, hedge, hem in, envelop, confine, shut in, pen

encompass *verb* **1** surround **2** include

encore /'ɒŋkɔː(r)/ or /ɒŋ'kɔː(r)/ *noun* **1** an extra performance of a song *etc* in reply to audience applause **2** a call for an encore

encounter *verb* **1** meet by chance **2** come up against (a difficulty, enemy *etc*) ◇ *noun* a meeting, a fight

■ *verb* **1** come across, *informal* run into, happen on, chance upon **2** confront, face, experience, fight, clash with, grapple with ◇ *noun* meeting, brush, confrontation, clash, fight, conflict, dispute, run-in

encourage *verb* **1** give hope or confidence to **2** urge (to do) ◇ **encouragement** *noun* ◇ **encouraging** *adj*

■ **1** hearten, reassure, inspire, cheer, support **2** stimulate, spur, urge, *informal* egg on ◇ **encouragement** reassurance, inspiration, stimulation, incentive, support, stimulus ◇ **encouraging** heartening, promising, hopeful, reassuring

🔁 **1** discourage, depress **2** discourage, deter

encroach *verb* intrude or extend gradually (on someone's land *etc*) ◇ **encroachment** *noun*

■ intrude, impinge, trespass, infringe, overstep, *informal* muscle in

encumber *verb* burden, weigh down; hinder, hamper ◇ **encumbrance** *noun* a heavy burden, a hindrance

■ **encumbrance** burden, load, cross, millstone, albatross, difficulty, handicap, impediment, liability

encyclopedia or **encylopaedia** *noun* a reference book containing information on many subjects, or on a particular subject ◇ **encyclopedic** or **encyclopaedic** *adj* giving complete information

end *noun* **1** the last point or part **2** death **3** the farthest point of the length of something: *at the end of the road* **4** a result aimed at **5** a small piece left over ◇ *verb* bring or come to an end ◇ **ending** *noun* the last part ◇ **endless** *adj* ◇ **on end 1** standing on one end **2** in a series, without a stop: *he has been working for days on end*

■ *noun* **1** finish, conclusion, close, completion **2** demise, destruction, extermination, doom **4** outcome, consequence, upshot, objective, goal **5** tip, leftover, remnant, stub, scrap, fragment

🔁 *noun* **1** beginning, start **2** birth

endanger *verb* put in danger or at risk

■ imperil, hazard, jeopardize, risk, expose, threaten, compromise

endear *verb* make dear or liked: *his generosity endeared him to the family* ◇ **endearing** *adj* appealing ◇ **endearment** *noun*

■ **endearing** lovable, charming, appealing, attractive, winsome, delightful, enchanting

endeavour *verb* try hard (to) ◇ *noun* a determined attempt

■ *verb* attempt, try, strive, aim, undertake, venture, aspire, struggle, labour

endemic *adj* of a disease: found regularly in a certain area

endive *noun* a plant with curly leaves eaten as a salad

endocrine *noun* of a gland: secreting hormones *etc* into the blood

endorse verb **1** give your support to something said or written **2** sign the back of a cheque to confirm receiving money for it **3** indicate on a motor licence that the owner has broken a driving law ◇ **endorsement** noun

■ **1** approve, sanction, authorize, support, back, confirm, ratify, advocate, recommend

endow verb **1** give money for the buying and upkeep of: *he endowed a bed in the hospital* **2** give a talent, quality etc to: *nature endowed her with a good brain* ◇ **endowment** noun

■ **1** bestow, bequeath, leave, will, fund, support

endure verb **1** bear patiently, put up with **2** last ◇ **endurable** adj bearable ◇ **endurance** noun the power of enduring

■ **1** bear, stand, put up with, tolerate, weather, brave, cope with, face, go through, suffer, sustain, withstand, survive, stay

enema noun the injection of fluid into the bowels

enemy noun (plural **enemies**) **1** someone hostile to another; a foe **2** someone armed to fight against another **3** someone who is against something: *an enemy of socialism* ◇ **enmity** noun (plural **enmities**)

energy noun (plural **energies**) **1** strength to act, vigour **2** a form of power, eg electricity, heat etc ◇ **energetic** adj active, lively ◇ **energetically** adv

■ **1** vigour, liveliness, animation, drive, dynamism, informal get-up-and-go, life, spirit, vivacity, vitality, zest, zeal ◇ **energetic** lively, vigorous, active, animated, dynamic, spirited, tireless, zestful, forceful

⊟ **energetic** lethargic, sluggish, inactive, idle

enervate verb weaken, enfeeble

enfant terrible /āfǎtɛribl/ (plural **enfants terribles**) someone who behaves outrageously or unconventionally

enfold verb enclose, embrace

enforce verb cause (a law etc) to be carried out

■ impose, administer, implement, apply, execute, insist on, carry out, reinforce

enfranchise 1 set free **2** give the right to vote to

engage verb **1** begin to employ (workers etc) **2** book in advance **3** take or keep hold of (someone's attention etc) **4** be busy with, be occupied (in) **5** of machine parts: fit together **6** begin fighting ◇ **engaging** adj pleasant, charming

■ **1** hire, appoint, take on, commission, recruit **3** occupy, engross, absorb, tie up, grip **6** battle with, attack, take on, encounter, assail, combat

engaged adj **1** bound by a promise of marriage **2** busy with something **3** of a telephone: in use

engagement noun **1** a promise of marriage **2** an appointment, eg to meet someone **3** a fight: *naval engagement*

■ **1** promise, pledge, formal betrothal, commitment **2** meeting, date, arrangement, assignation, fixture

engine noun **1** a machine which converts heat or other energy into motion **2** the part of a train which pulls the coaches

> *Types of engine include*:
> diesel, donkey, fuel-injection, internal-combustion, jet, petrol, steam, turbine, turbojet, turboprop, V-engine

engineer noun **1** someone who works with, or designs, engines or machines **2** someone who designs or makes bridges, roads etc ◇ verb bring about by clever planning ◇ **engineering** noun the science of designing machines, roadmaking etc

engrave verb **1** draw with a special tool on glass, metal etc **2** make a deep impression on: *engraved on his memory* ◇ **engraving** noun a print made from a cut-out drawing in metal or wood

engross verb take up the whole interest or attention of

■ absorb, occupy, engage, grip, preoccupy,

rivet, fascinate, captivate, enthral, involve, intrigue

■ bore

engulf *verb* swallow up wholly

enhance *verb* improve, make greater or better

■ heighten, intensify, increase, improve, lift, boost, strengthen, reinforce, embellish

■ reduce, minimize

enigma *noun* something or someone difficult to understand, a mystery ◇ **enigmatic** *adj*

enjoy *verb* 1 take pleasure in 2 experience, have (something beneficial): *enjoying good health* ◇ **enjoyable** *adj* ◇ **enjoyment** *noun* ◇ **enjoy yourself** have a pleasant time

■ 1 delight in, appreciate, like, relish, revel in ◇ **enjoyable** pleasant, delightful, pleasing, entertaining, amusing, fun

enlarge *verb* 1 make larger 2 (with **on**) say much or more about something ◇ **enlargement** *noun* 1 an increase in size 2 a larger photograph made from a smaller one

enlighten *verb* give more knowledge or information to ◇ **enlightened** *adj* ◇ **enlightenment** *noun*

■ instruct, educate, inform, illuminate, teach, counsel, advise ◇ **enlightened** informed, aware, knowledgeable, educated, refined, wise, open-minded

enlist *verb* 1 join an army *etc* 2 obtain (the support and help of someone)

enliven *verb* make more active or cheerful

en masse /ãmas/ all together, in a body

enmesh *verb* entangle, trap

enmity *see* **enemy**

ennui /ɒˈnwiː/ *noun* boredom

enormity *noun* 1 hugeness 2 extreme badness

■ 2 atrocity, outrage, iniquity, horror, evil, crime, abomination, monstrosity, wickedness, vileness, depravity, atrociousness, viciousness

enormous *adj* very large ◇ **enormously** *adv*

■ huge, immense, vast, gigantic, massive, *slang* mega, colossal, gross, gargantuan, monstrous, mammoth, *informal* jumbo

enough *adj & pronoun* (in) the number or amount wanted or needed: *I have enough coins/have you had enough to eat?* ◇ *adv* as much as is wanted or necessary: *she's been there often enough to know the way*

■ *adj* sufficient, adequate, ample, plenty

enquire, **enquiry** *etc see* **inquire**

enrage *verb* make angry

■ incense, infuriate, anger, madden, provoke, inflame, exasperate, irritate, rile

■ calm, placate

enrich *verb* make rich or richer

■ enhance, improve, refine, adorn, embellish, decorate, grace

enrol or **enroll** *verb* (**enrols**, **enrolling**, **enrolled**) enter the name of (someone) in a register or list of members, or become a member ◇ **enrolment** *noun*

■ register, enlist, sign on, sign up, join up, recruit, record

en route /ɒn ˈruːt/ on the way

ensconce *verb*: **ensconce yourself** settle comfortably

ensemble *noun* 1 the parts of a thing taken together 2 an outfit of clothes 3 a group of musicians

enshrine *verb* treat as sacred, cherish

ensign *noun* 1 the flag of a nation, regiment *etc* 2 *hist* a young officer who carried the flag

enslave *verb* make a slave of

■ subjugate, subject, dominate, bind, enchain, yoke

■ free, emancipate

ensue *verb* 1 follow, come after 2 result (from)

ensure *verb* make sure

■ certify, guarantee, warrant, protect, guard, safeguard, secure

🛈 Do not confuse with: **insure**

entail *verb* 1 bring as a result, involve: *the job entailed extra work* 2 leave land so that the heir cannot sell any part of it

1 involve, require, demand, necessitate, cause, give rise to, lead to, result in

entangle *verb* **1** make tangled or complicated **2** involve (in difficulties)

entente /ä'tät/ *noun* a treaty

enter *verb* **1** go or come in or into **2** put (a name *etc*) on a list **3** take part (in) **4** begin (on)

1 come in, go in, arrive **2** record, log, note, register, take down **4** embark upon

enterprise *noun* **1** an undertaking, *esp* if risky or difficult **2** boldness in trying new things **3** a business concern ◇ **enterprising** *adj*

entertain *verb* **1** amuse **2** receive as a guest **3** give a party **4** consider (*eg* a suggestion) **5** hold in the mind: *entertain a belief* ◇ **entertaining** *adj* amusing ◇ **entertainment** *noun* **1** something that entertains, *eg* a show **2** amusement

1 amuse, divert, please, delight **2** receive, accommodate, put up **4** contemplate, consider, imagine, conceive ◇ **entertainment** amusement, recreation, enjoyment, play, pastime, fun, show, spectacle, performance

entertainer *noun* someone who performs to entertain people

Entertainers include:
acrobat, actor, actress, busker, chat-show host, clown, comedian, comic, conjuror, dancer, disc jockey, *informal* DJ, escapologist, game-show host, hypnotist, ice-skater, impressionist, jester, juggler, magician, mimic, mind-reader, minstrel, musician, presenter, singer, song-and-dance act, stand-up comic, striptease artist, *informal* stripper, trapeze artist, tightrope walker, ventriloquist; performer, artiste

enthral *verb* (**enthrals**, **enthralling**, **enthralled**) give great delight to

enthuse *verb* (cause to) be enthusiastic (about)

enthusiasm *noun* great interest and keenness ◇ **enthusiast** *noun*

passion, keenness, eagerness, vehemence, zeal, excitement, devotion

apathy

enthusiastic *adj* greatly interested, very keen ◇ **enthusiastically** *adv*

keen, ardent, eager, fervent, passionate, excited

unenthusiastic, apathetic

entice *verb* attract with promises, rewards *etc* ◇ **enticement** *noun* a bribe, an attractive promise ◇ **enticing** *adj*

tempt, lure, seduce, attract, lead on, draw, coax, induce

entire *adj* whole, complete ◇ **entirely** *adv* ◇ **entirety** *noun*

complete, whole, total, full, intact, perfect

entitle *verb* **1** give a name to (a book *etc*) **2** give (someone) a right to do something

1 name, call, term, title, label **2** authorize, qualify, enable, allow, permit, license, warrant

entity *noun* (*plural* **entities**) something which physically exists

entomology *noun* the study of insects ◇ **entomologist** *noun*

entourage /'ɒntʊərɑːʒ/ *noun* followers, attendants

entrails *noun plural* the inner parts of an animal's body, the bowels

entrance[1] /'entrəns/ *noun* **1** a place for entering, *eg* a door **2** the act of coming in **3** the right to enter ◇ **entrant** *noun* someone who goes in for a race, competition *etc*

1 opening, way in, door, doorway, gate **3** access, admission, admittance, entry

entrance[2] /ɪn'trɑːns/ *verb* **1** delight, charm **2** bewitch ◇ **entrancing** *adj*

entreat *verb* ask earnestly ◇ **entreaty** *noun* (*plural* **entreaties**)

beg, implore, plead with, beseech, ask, petition, request, appeal to

entrée /'ɒntreɪ/ *noun* **1** *Brit* a dish served between courses **2** *US* a main course

entrenched *adj* **1** firmly established **2** unmoving, inflexible

entrepreneur /ɒntrəprə'nɜː(r)/ *noun*

someone who undertakes an enterprise, often with financial involvement ◇ **entrepreneurial** *adj*

entrust or **intrust** *verb* place in someone else's care

entry (*plural* **entries**) **1** the act of entering **2** a place for entering, a doorway **3** a name or item in a record book
■ **2** opening, entrance, door, doorway, access, threshold, way in, gate **3** record, item, minute, note, statement

E-number *noun* an identification code for food additives, *eg* E102 for tartrazine

enumerate *verb* **1** count **2** mention individually ◇ **enumeration** *noun*

enunciate *verb* **1** pronounce distinctly **2** state formally ◇ **enunciation** *noun*
■ **1** articulate, pronounce **2** state, declare, proclaim, announce

envelop *verb* **1** cover by wrapping **2** surround entirely: *enveloped in mist*
■ **1, 2** wrap, enfold, cover, swathe, enclose, surround, blanket, conceal, obscure, hide, cloak

envelope *noun* a wrapping or cover, *esp* for a letter

environment *noun* surroundings, circumstances in which someone or an animal lives
■ surroundings, conditions, circumstances, atmosphere, habitat, situation, background, ambience, setting, context, territory, domain

environs /ɪnˈvaɪərənz/ *noun plural* surrounding area, neighbourhood

envisage *verb* **1** visualize, picture in the mind **2** consider, contemplate

envoy *noun* a messenger, *esp* one sent to deal with a foreign government

envy *noun* (*plural* **envies**) greedy desire for someone else's property, qualities *etc* ◇ *verb* (**envies**, **envying**, **envied**) feel envy for ◇ **enviable** *adj* worth envying, worth having ◇ **envious** *adj* feeling envy ◇ **enviously** *adv*
■ *noun* jealousy, resentfulness, resentment, grudge, ill-will ◇ **enviable**

desirable, privileged, blessed, fortunate, lucky, excellent

enzyme *noun* a substance produced in a living body which affects the speed of chemical changes

eon *another spelling of* **aeon**

epaulet or **epaulette** *noun* a shoulder ornament on a uniform

ephemeral *adj* very short-lived, fleeting ◇ **ephemerality** *noun*

epic *noun* a long poem, story, film *etc* about heroic deeds ◇ *adj* **1** of an epic; heroic **2** large-scale, impressive

epicentre or *US* **epicenter** *noun* the centre of an earthquake

epicure *noun* a gourmet ◇ **epicurean** *adj*

epidemic *noun* a widespread outbreak of a disease *etc*
■ plague, outbreak, spread, upsurge, wave

epidermis *noun* the top covering of the skin ◇ **epidermal** or **epidermic** *adj*

epidural *noun* (short for **epidural anaesthetic**) the injection of anaesthetic into the spine to ease pain in the lower half of the body

epiglottis *noun* a piece of skin at the back of the tongue which closes the windpipe during swallowing

epigram *noun* a short, witty saying ◇ **epigrammatic** *adj*

epilepsy *noun* an illness causing attacks of unconsciousness and convulsions

epileptic *adj* **1** suffering from epilepsy **2** of epilepsy: *an epileptic fit* ◇ *noun* someone suffering from epilepsy

epilogue or *US* **epilog** *noun* **1** the very end part of a book, programme *etc* **2** a speech at the end of a play

Epiphany *noun* a Christian festival celebrated on 6 January

episcopal *adj* of or ruled by bishops ◇ **episcopalian** *adj* belonging to a church ruled by bishops ◇ **episcopacy** *noun*

episode *noun* **1** one of several parts of

a story *etc* **2** an interesting event ◇ **episodic** *adj* happening at irregular intervals

■ **1** instalment, part, chapter, section, scene **2** incident, event, occurrence, circumstance, experience

epistle *noun* a formal letter, *esp* one from an apostle of Christ in the Bible ◇ **epistolary** *adj* written in the form of letters

epitaph *noun* words on a gravestone about a dead person

epithet *noun* a word used to describe someone; an adjective

epitome /ɪˈpɪtəmɪ/ *noun* **1** a perfect example or representative of something: *the epitome of good taste* **2** a summary of a book *etc*

■ **1** personification, embodiment, representation, archetype, type, essence

epitomize *verb* be the epitome of something

epoch *noun* an extended period of time, often marked by a series of important events ◇ **epochal** *adj* ◇ **epoch-making** *adj* marking an important point in history

Epsom salts a purgative medicine

equable *adj* **1** of calm temper **2** of climate: neither very hot nor very cold ◇ **equably** *adv*

■ **1** even-tempered, placid, calm, serene, unexcitable, tranquil, composed **2** uniform, even, consistent, temperate, unvarying, steady

equal *adj* **1** of the same size, value, quantity *etc* **2** evenly balanced **3** (with **to**) able, fit for: *not equal to the job* ◇ *noun* someone of the same rank, ability *etc* as another ◇ *verb* (**equals**, **equalling**, **equalled**) **1** be or make equal to **2** be the same as ◇ **equality** *noun* ◇ **equally** *adv*

■ *adj* **1** identical, alike, equivalent, corresponding, commensurate, comparable **2** even, uniform, regular, matched **3** competent, able, capable, suitable ◇ *verb* **1** equalize, match, level **2** match, parallel, correspond to ◇ **equality** uniformity, balance, impartiality, fairness

equalize *verb* make equal ◇ **equalizer**

noun a goal *etc* which makes the score equal in a game

equanimity *noun* evenness of temper, calmness

equate *verb* **1** regard or treat as the same **2** state as being equal

equation *noun* a statement, *esp* in mathematics, that two things are equal

equator *noun* an imaginary line around the earth, halfway between the North and South Poles ◇ **equatorial** *adj* on or near the equator

equestrian *adj* **1** of horse-riding **2** on horseback ◇ *noun* a horse-rider

equi- *prefix* equal ◇ **equidistant** *adj* equally distant ◇ **equilateral** *adj* of a triangle: with all sides equal (*compare with*: **isosceles**)

equilibrium *noun* **1** equal balance between weights, forces *etc* **2** a balanced state of mind or feelings

■ **1** balance, poise, symmetry, evenness, stability **2** equanimity, self-possession, composure, calmness, coolness, serenity

equine *adj* of or like a horse

equinox *noun* either of the times (about 21 March and 23 September) when the sun crosses the equator, making night and day equal in length ◇ **equinoctial** *adj*

equip *verb* (**equips**, **equipping**, **equipped**) supply with everything needed for a task

■ provide, fit out, supply, furnish, prepare, arm, kit out, stock, deck out

equipage *noun* attendants, retinue

equipment *noun* a set of tools *etc* needed for a task; an outfit

■ apparatus, gear, supplies, accessories

equipoise *noun* balance

equitable *adj* fair, just ◇ **equitably** *adv*

equity *noun* **1** fairness, just dealing **2** (**Equity**) the trade union for the British acting profession

equivalent *adj* equal in value, power, meaning *etc* ◇ *noun* something that is equivalent to another

■ *adj* equal, same, similar, corresponding, alike, comparable

▪ *adj* unlike, different

equivocal *adj* having more than one meaning; ambiguous, uncertain ◇ **equivocally** *adv*

▪ ambiguous, uncertain, obscure, vague, evasive, misleading, confusing, indefinite

equivocate *verb* use ambiguous words in order to mislead ◇ **equivocation** *noun*

▪ prevaricate, evade, dodge, hedge, mislead

era *noun* a period in history: *the Jacobean era/the era of steam*

▪ age, epoch, period, time

eradicate *verb* get rid of completely ◇ **eradication** *noun*

▪ eliminate, annihilate, get rid of, remove, root out, destroy, exterminate, extinguish, weed out, stamp out, abolish, obliterate

erase *verb* **1** rub out (*eg* pencil marks) **2** delete a recording from a tape **3** remove all trace of ◇ **erasure** *noun*

eraser *noun* something which erases pencil marks *etc*, a rubber

erect *verb* **1** build **2** set upright ◇ *adj* standing straight up ◇ **erection** *noun* **1** the act of erecting **2** something erected **3** an erect penis

▪ *adj* upright, straight, vertical, upstanding, standing, raised, rigid, stiff

ergonomic *adj* of a workplace, machine *etc*: adapted to suit human needs and comfort ◇ **ergonomically** *adv* ◇ **ergonomics** *noun sing* ◇ **ergonomist** *noun*

ermine *noun* **1** a stoat **2** its white fur

erode *verb* wear away, destroy gradually ◇ **erosion** *noun*

▪ eat away, wear down, corrode, consume, grind down ◇ **erosion** wear, corrosion, abrasion, destruction

erotic *adj* of or arousing sexual desire ◇ **erotica** *noun plural* erotic art or literature ◇ **eroticism** *noun* ◇ **eroticize** *verb* make erotic

err *verb* **1** make a mistake **2** sin

▪ 1 be wrong, miscalculate, misjudge **2** do wrong, misbehave, go astray, offend

errand *noun* a short journey to carry a message, buy something *etc*

errant *adj* **1** doing wrong **2** wandering in search of adventure: *knight errant*

erratic *adj* **1** irregular, not following a fixed course or pattern **2** not steady or reliable in behaviour ◇ **erratically** *adv*

▪ 1 variable, inconsistent, irregular, unpredictable **2** changeable, variable, fitful, fluctuating, inconsistent, irregular, unstable, unpredictable

▪ 1,2 steady, consistent, stable

erratum *noun* (*plural* **errata**) an error in a book

erroneous *adj* wrong ◇ **erroneously** *adv*

▪ correct, right

error *noun* **1** a mistake **2** wrongdoing

▪ 1 mistake, inaccuracy, slip, slip-up, gaffe, miscalculation, misprint, oversight, omission, fault

erudite *adj* well-educated or well-read, learned ◇ **erudition** *noun*

erupt *verb* **1** of a volcano: throw out lava *etc* **2** break out: *violence erupted on the streets* ◇ **eruption** *noun* **1** an outburst from a volcano **2** a rash or spot on the skin

▪ *verb* **1** explode, burst, discharge, spout, eject, expel, emit **2** break out, explode, burst, flare up

escalate *verb* increase in amount, intensity *etc* ◇ **escalation** *noun* ◇ **escalator** *noun* a moving stairway

escalope *noun* a slice of meat beaten to make it thinner before cooking

escape *verb* **1** get away safe or free **2** of gas *etc*: leak **3** slip from memory: *his name escapes me* ◇ *noun* the act of escaping

▪ *verb* **1** break free, run away, bolt, abscond, flee, break loose **2** seep, flow, drain, trickle **3** avoid, evade, elude ◇ *noun* getaway, bolt, breakout

escapade *noun* an adventure

escapement *noun* a device which controls the movement of a watch or clock

escapism *noun* the tendency to escape from reality by daydreaming *etc* ◇ **escapist** *noun & adj*

escarpment *noun* a steep side of a hill or rock

eschew *verb*, *formal* shun, avoid

escort *noun* someone who accompanies others for protection, courtesy *etc* ◇ *verb* act as escort to

escutcheon *noun* a shield with a coat of arms

Eskimo *noun* (*plural* **Eskimos**) Inuit

esoteric *adj* understood by a small number of people only
■ recondite, obscure

ESP *abbrev* extrasensory perception

esparto *noun* a strong grass grown in Spain and N Africa, used for making paper and ropes

Esperanto *noun* an international language created in the 19th century

especial *adj* **1** special, extraordinary **2** particular ◇ **especially** *adv*
■ **especially** chiefly, mainly, primarily, above all, particularly, notably, exceptionally, outstandingly, unusually

espionage *noun* spying, *esp* by one country to find out the secrets of another

esplanade *noun* a level roadway, *esp* along a seafront

espouse *verb* adopt, embrace (a cause)

espresso *noun* strong coffee made by forcing boiling water through ground coffee beans

esprit de corps loyalty to, or among, a group

espy /ɪ'spaɪ/ *verb*, *old* catch sight of; watch, observe

Esq *abbrev* or **Esquire** *noun* a courtesy title written after a man's name: *Robert Brown, Esq*

essay *noun* **1** a written composition **2** *formal* an attempt ◇ *verb* try ◇ **essayist** *noun* a writer of essays

essence *noun* **1** the most important part or quality of something **2** a concentrated extract from a plant *etc*: *vanilla essence*
■ **1** nature, quintessence, substance, soul, spirit, core, centre, heart, meaning, significance, crux, character, characteristics, principle

essential *adj* absolutely necessary ◇ *noun* something essential ◇ **essentially** *adv* **1** basically **2** necessarily
■ *adj* crucial, indispensable, vital, needed, important, fundamental, basic ◇ *noun* necessity, prerequisite, must, requirement

establish *verb* **1** settle in position **2** found, set up **3** show to be true, prove (that) ◇ **established** *adj* **1** firmly set up **2** accepted, recognized **3** of a church: officially recognized as national
■ **1** install **2** start, form, create, organize, introduce, instigate **3** prove, demonstrate, verify, certify, confirm

establishment *noun* a place of business, residence *etc* ◇ **the Establishment** the people holding influential positions in a community

estate *noun* **1** a large piece of private land **2** land built on with houses, factories *etc*: *housing estate/industrial estate* **3** someone's total possessions, *esp* at death ◇ **estate agent** someone who sells and leases property for clients ◇ **estate car** a car with an inside luggage compartment and a rear door ◇ **the fourth estate** the press, the media

esteem *verb* think highly of; value ◇ *noun* high value or opinion ◇ **esteemed** *adj*

estimate *verb* judge roughly the size, amount or value of something ◇ *noun* a rough judgement of size *etc* ◇ **estimation** *noun* opinion, judgement
■ *verb* assess, evaluate, calculate, gauge, guess, consider ◇ *noun* valuation, judgement, guess, approximation, assessment, estimation

estranged *adj* no longer friendly; separated
■ separate, alienated, divided, disaffected

estuary *noun* (*plural* **estuaries**) the wide lower part of a river, up which the tide travels

et al *abbrev* and others (from Latin *et alii, aliae* or *alia*)

etc or **&c** *abbrev* and other things of the same sort (from Latin *et cetera*)

etch *verb* draw on metal or glass by eating out the lines with acid ◇ **etching** *noun* a picture printed from an etched metal plate

eternal *adj* **1** lasting for ever **2** unchanging **3** constant ◇ **eternally** *adv* ◇ **eternity** *noun* **1** time without end **2** the time or state after death

■ **1** unending, endless, ceaseless, everlasting, never-ending, infinite, immortal **2** timeless, enduring, lasting, perennial **3** continuous, perpetual, incessant

▣ **1** ephemeral, temporary **2** changeable

ether *noun* a colourless liquid used as an anaesthetic, or to dissolve fats

ethereal *adj* delicate, airy, spirit-like ◇ **ethereally** *adv* ◇ **ethereality** *noun*

ethical *adj* having to do with right behaviour, justice, duty and honour ◇ **ethically** *adv* ◇ **ethics** *noun sing* the study of right and wrong; (belief in) standards leading to ethical behaviour

■ moral, principled, right, proper, virtuous, honest, good, correct, honourable, upright

ethnic *adj* **1** of race or culture **2** of the culture of a particular race or group ◇ **ethnically** *adv* ◇ **ethnicity** *noun* ◇ **ethnic minority** a section of society of a different race from the majority

ethnology *noun* the study of human cultures and civilizations ◇ **ethnological** *adj* ◇ **ethnologist** *noun*

etiolate *verb* **1** of a plant: grow pale through lack of light **2** make feeble ◇ **etiolated** *adj*

etiquette *noun* rules governing correct social behaviour

■ code, standards, correctness, conventions, customs, *formal* protocol, rules, manners, courtesy, decorum

etymology *noun* (*plural* **etymologies**) **1** the study of the history of words **2** the history of a word ◇ **etymological** *adj* ◇ **etymologist** *noun*

EU *abbrev* European Union

eucalyptus *noun* (*plural* **eucalyptuses** or **eucalypti**) a large Australian evergreen tree whose leaves produce a pungent oil

eucharist *noun* **1** the Christian sacrament of the Lord's Supper **2** bread and wine *etc* taken as a sacrament

eugenics *noun sing* the science of trying to improve a race or stock by selective breeding *etc* ◇ **eugenicist** *noun* & *adj*

eulogy *noun* (*plural* **eulogies**) a speech, poem *etc* in praise of someone ◇ **eulogize** *verb* praise greatly

eunuch /ˈjuːnək/ *noun* a castrated man

euphemism *noun* a vague word or phrase used to refer to an unpleasant subject, *eg* 'passed on' for 'died' ◇ **euphemistic** *adj*

euphonious *adj* pleasant in sound, harmonious ◇ **euphony** *noun*

euphonium *noun* a brass musical instrument with a low tone

euphoria *noun* a feeling of great happiness, joy ◇ **euphoric** *adj*

■ elation, ecstasy, bliss, rapture, high spirits, exhilaration, exultation, joy, intoxication, jubilation, transport, exaltation

eurhythmics *noun sing* the art of graceful movement of the body, *esp* to music

euro *noun* the standard unit of money in several European countries, *eg* France, Germany, Spain, Italy and Ireland

Euro- *prefix* of Europe or the European Union: *Euro-budget/Eurocrat* ◇ **Eurosceptic** *noun* & *adj*, *Brit* (someone) opposed to strengthening the powers of the European Union

euthanasia *noun* the killing of someone painlessly, *esp* to end suffering

evacuate *verb* (cause to) leave *esp* because of danger; make empty ◇ **evacuation** *noun*

■ leave, depart, remove, *informal* clear (out), abandon, desert, vacate

evacuee *noun* someone who has been evacuated from a place of danger

evade *verb* avoid or escape *esp* by cleverness or trickery ◇ **evasion** *noun*

◊ **evasive** *adj* with the purpose of evading; not straightforward: *an evasive answer*

▤ elude, dodge, shirk, steer clear of, side-step, prevaricate ◊ **evasive** indirect, *informal* shifty, misleading, deceptive, *informal* cagey

evaluate *verb* find or state the value of

evanescent *adj* passing away quickly

evangelical *adj* 1 spreading Christian teaching 2 strongly advocating some cause ◊ **evangelist** *noun* ◊ **evangelistic** *adj*

evaporate *verb* 1 change into vapour 2 vanish ◊ **evaporation** *noun*

▤ 1 vaporize 2 vanish, disappear, melt (away), dissolve, dissipate, fade

evasion, evasive *see* evade

eve *noun* 1 the evening or day before a festival: *New Year's Eve* 2 the time just before an event: *the eve of the revolution*

even *adj* 1 level, smooth 2 of a number: able to be divided by two without a remainder (*contrasted with:* **odd**) 3 constant, uniform 4 calm: *an even temper* ◊ *adv* used to emphasize another word: *even harder than before/even a child would understand* ◊ *verb* make even or smooth ◊ **evenly** *adv* ◊ **evenness** *noun* ◊ **even-handed** *adv* fair, unbiased ◊ **even out** become equal ◊ **get even with** get revenge on

▤ *adj* 1 flat, horizontal, flush, plane 3 steady, unvarying, regular 4 even-tempered, placid, serene, tranquil, composed, unruffled

evening *noun* the last part of the day and early part of the night

evensong *noun* an evening service in the Anglican Church

event *noun* 1 an important happening 2 an item in a sports programme *etc* ◊ **eventful** *adj* exciting

▤ 1 occurrence, incident, occasion, affair, circumstance, episode, eventuality 2 game, match, competition, contest, tournament ◊ **eventful** busy, exciting, lively, interesting, significant, memorable

eventual *adj* 1 final 2 happening as a result ◊ **eventually** *adv* at last, finally

eventuality *noun* (*plural* **eventualities**) a possible happening

ever *adv* 1 always, for ever 2 at any time, at all: *I won't ever see her again* 3 that has existed, on record: *the best ever*

evergreen *noun* a tree with green leaves all the year round

everlasting *adj* lasting for ever, eternal

▤ eternal, never-ending, endless, immortal, infinite, timeless

▣ temporary, transient

evermore *adv, old* forever

every *adj* each of several things without exception ◊ **everybody** or **everyone** *pronoun* each person without exception ◊ **every other** one out of every two, alternate

everyday *adj* 1 daily 2 common, usual

everything *pronoun* all things

everywhere *adv* in every place

evict *verb* force (someone) out of their house, *esp* by law ◊ **eviction** *noun*

evidence *noun* 1 a clear sign; proof 2 information given in a law case

▤ 1 verification, confirmation, affirmation, grounds, documentation, data 2 testimony, declaration

evident *adj* easily seen or understood ◊ **evidently** *adv*

▤ clear, obvious, apparent, plain, conspicuous, unmistakable, perceptible ◊ **evidently** clearly, plainly, obviously, undoubtedly, doubtless(ly), indisputably

evil *adj* wicked, very bad; malicious ◊ *noun* wickedness ◊ **evilly** *adv*

▤ wrong, sinful, immoral, vicious, malevolent, cruel, heinous

evince *verb, formal* show, display: *they evinced no surprise*

eviscerate *verb, formal* tear out the bowels of; gut

evoke *verb* bring to mind, produce: *evoking memories of their childhood* ◊ **evocative** *adj* evoking memories or atmosphere

evolution *noun* **1** gradual development **2** the belief that the higher forms of life have gradually developed out of the lower forms ◇ **evolutionary** *adj*

evolve *verb* **1** develop gradually **2** work out (a plan *etc*)
◼ **1** develop, grow, increase, mature, progress, expand

ewe *noun* a female sheep

ewer *noun* a large jug with a wide spout

ex *noun*, *informal* a former husband, wife or lover

ex- *prefix* **1** no longer, former: *ex-husband/ex-president* **2** outside, not in: *ex-directory number*

exacerbate *verb* make worse or more severe ◇ **exacerbation** *noun*

> ⚠ Do not confuse with: **exasperate**

exact *adj* **1** accurate, precise **2** punctual **3** careful ◇ *verb* force someone to pay, give *etc*: *exacting revenge* ◇ **exactly** *adv* ◇ **exactness** *noun* accuracy, correctness
◼ *adj* **1** precise, correct, flawless, faultless, specific, strict, unerring **3** scrupulous, particular, methodical, meticulous ◇ *verb* extort, claim, insist on, demand, force, require

exacting *adj* **1** asking too much **2** wearying, tiring

exaggerate *verb* cause to seem larger or greater than reality ◇ **exaggeration** *noun*

exalt *verb* **1** raise in rank **2** praise **3** make joyful ◇ **exaltation** *noun*

exam *noun* an examination

examination *noun* **1** a formal, *esp* written, test of knowledge or skill **2** a close inspection or inquiry **3** formal questioning

examine *verb* **1** look at closely, inquire into **2** look over (someone's body) for signs of illness **3** put questions to (pupils *etc*) to test knowledge **4** question (a witness) ◇ **examiner** *noun*
◼ **1** inspect, investigate, scrutinize, study, analyse, explore, review **4** test, quiz, question, cross-examine, interrogate, *informal* grill

example *noun* **1** something taken as a representative of its kind: *an example of early French glass* **2** behaviour to be copied: *follow her example* ◇ **make an example of** punish as a warning to others
◼ **1** instance, case, case in point, illustration, exemplification, sample, specimen, model, prototype, standard

exasperate *verb* make very angry ◇ **exasperation** *noun*
◼ infuriate, annoy, anger, incense, irritate, madden, provoke, enrage, rankle
◼ appease, pacify

> ⚠ Do not confuse with: **exacerbate**

excavate *verb* **1** dig, scoop out **2** uncover by digging ◇ **excavation** *noun* **1** the act of excavating **2** a hollow made by digging ◇ **excavator** *noun* a machine used for excavating

exceed *verb* go beyond, be greater than
◼ surpass, outdo, outstrip, beat, overtake, outshine, outrun, transcend

exceedingly *adv* very

excel *verb* (**excels**, **excelling**, **excelled**) **1** do very well **2** be better than
◼ **1** succeed, shine, stand out **2** surpass, outdo, beat, outperform, outrank,

excellent *adj* unusually or extremely good ◇ **excellence** *noun* the fact of being excellent, very high quality
◼ superior, first-class, first-rate, outstanding, *informal* blue-chip, remarkable, distinguished, *informal* top drawer, superb, commendable, noteworthy, notable, fine, worthy
◼ inferior, second-rate

except *prep* leaving out, not counting ◇ *conj* with the exception (that) ◇ *verb* leave out, not count ◇ **excepting** *prep* except ◇ **except for** with the exception of

exception *noun* **1** something left out **2** something unlike the rest: *an exception to the rule* ◇ **exceptional** *adj* standing out from the rest ◇ **exceptionally** *adv* very, extremely ◇ **take exception to** object to, be offended by
◼ **exceptional** abnormal, unusual, extraordinary, special, rare, outstanding,

remarkable, phenomenal, superior, marvellous

excerpt /ˈɛksɜːpt/ *noun* a part chosen from a whole work: *an excerpt from a play*

> 🛈 Do not confuse with: **exert**

excess *noun* **1** a going beyond what is usual or proper **2** the amount by which one thing is greater than another or too great **3** (**excesses**) very bad behaviour ◇ *adj* beyond the amount allowed

▤ *adj* extra, surplus, spare, redundant, remaining, residual, left-over, additional, superfluous

> 🛈 Do not confuse with: **access**

excessive *adj* too much, too great *etc* ◇ **excessively** *adv*

▤ extreme, uncalled-for, disproportionate, unnecessary, unneeded, superfluous, exorbitant, extravagant

exchange *verb* give (one thing) and get another in return ◇ *noun* **1** the act of exchanging **2** exchanging money of one country for that of another **3** the difference between the value of money in different places: *rate of exchange* **4** a central office or building: *telephone exchange* **5** a place where business shares are bought and sold

exchequer a government office concerned with a country's finances ◇ **Chancellor of the Exchequer** *see* **chancellor**

> From the chequered cloth used to aid calculation in medieval revenue offices

excise¹ *verb* cut off or out ◇ **excision** *noun*

excise² *noun* tax on goods *etc* made and sold within a country and on certain licences *etc*

excite *verb* **1** rouse the feelings of **2** move to action ◇ **excitable** *adj* easily excited ◇ **excited** *adj* ◇ **excitement** *noun* ◇ **exciting** *adj*

▤ **1** move, agitate, touch, stir up, thrill, elate, impress **2** arouse, rouse, animate,

motivate, stimulate, inspire, induce ◇ **excitement** activity, commotion, fuss, agitation, passion, elation, enthusiasm

exclaim *verb* cry or shout out

exclamation *noun* a sudden shout ◇ **exclamation mark** a punctuation mark (!) used for emphasis, or to indicate surprise *etc*

exclamatory *adj* exclaiming, emphatic

exclude *verb* **1** shut out **2** prevent from sharing **3** leave out of consideration ◇ **exclusion** *noun*

▤ **1** ban, bar, prohibit, disallow, veto, forbid **2** ostracize **3** omit, leave out, reject, ignore, eliminate

exclusive *adj* **1** only open to certain people, select: *an exclusive club* **2** not obtainable elsewhere: *an exclusive offer* ◇ **exclusive of** not including

excommunicate *verb* expel from membership of a church ◇ **excommunication** *noun*

excoriate *verb* **1** strip the skin from **2** criticize strongly

excrement *noun* the waste matter excreted by humans or animals

excrescence *noun* an unwelcome growth, *eg* a wart

excrete *verb* discharge (waste matter) from the body ◇ **excreta** *noun plural* discharged waste products

excruciating *adj* **1** of pain *etc*: very severe **2** painfully bad: *an excruciating performance*

▤ **1** agonizing, painful, severe, tormenting, unbearable, insufferable, acute, intolerable, intense, sharp, piercing, extreme, atrocious, racking

exculpate *verb* absolve from a crime; vindicate ◇ **exculpation** *noun* ◇ **exculpatory** *adj*

excursion *noun* an outing for pleasure, *eg* picnic

excuse *verb* **1** forgive, pardon **2** set free from a duty or task ◇ *noun* an explanation for having done something wrong ◇ **excusable** *adj* pardonable

▤ *verb* **1** overlook, absolve, acquit **2**

release, free, liberate, let off, relieve, spare ◇ *noun* justification, explanation, defence, reason, apology, *informal* cop-out

execrable *adj* very bad

execrate *verb* curse, denounce

execute *verb* 1 carry out: *execute commands* 2 put to death legally ◇ **execution** *noun* 1 the doing or performing of something 2 killing by order of the law ◇ **executioner** *noun* someone with the job of putting condemned prisoners to death

■ 1 perform, do, accomplish, achieve, fulfil, complete, deliver, implement

executive *adj* having power to act or carry out laws ◇ *noun* 1 the part of a government with such power 2 a business manager

■ *adj* administrative, managerial, supervisory, decision-making, organizing, directing, directorial, organizational

executor *noun* someone who sees that the requests stated in a will are carried out

exegesis *noun* a critical discussion of a literary text

exemplary *adj* 1 worth following as an example: *exemplary conduct* 2 acting as a warning: *exemplary punishment*

exemplify *verb* (**exemplifies, exemplifying, exemplified**) 1 be an example of 2 demonstrate by example

■ 1 typify, show, embody, epitomize 2 illustrate, exhibit, depict

exempt *verb* grant freedom from an unwelcome task, payment *etc* ◇ *adj* free (from), not liable for payment *etc* ◇ **exemption** *noun*

exercise *noun* 1 a task for practice 2 a physical routine for training muscles *etc* ◇ *verb* 1 give exercise to 2 use: *exercise great care*

■ *noun* 1 application, practice 2 training, effort, exertion, *informal* work-out ◇ *verb* 1 train, *informal* work out, keep fit 2 use, utilize, apply, practise

❗ Do not confuse with: **exorcize**

exert *verb* bring into action, use: *exerting great influence* ◇ **exertion** *noun* or

exertions *noun plural* effort(s); hard work ◇ **exert yourself** make a great effort

❗ Do not confuse with: **excerpt**

exeunt *verb* leave the stage (a direction printed in a playscript): *exeunt Rosencrantz and Guildenstern*

exfoliant *noun* a substance that removes dead skin layers

exhale *verb* breathe out ◇ **exhalation** *noun*

exhaust *verb* 1 tire out 2 use up completely: *we've exhausted our supplies* 3 say all that can be said about (a subject *etc*) ◇ *noun* a device for expelling waste fumes from fuel engines ◇ **exhaustion** *noun* ◇ **exhaustive** *adj* extremely thorough: *exhaustive research* ◇ **exhaustively** *adv*

exhausted *adj* 1 tired out 2 emptied; used up

■ 1 dead tired, fatigued, weak, washed-out, *informal* whacked, *informal* knackered 2 empty, finished, spent, used up, drained

exhibit *verb* show; put on public display ◇ *noun* 1 something on display in a museum, exhibition *etc* 2 an object produced in court as evidence ◇ **exhibitor** *noun*

exhibition *noun* a public show, an open display

exhibitionism *noun* a tendency to try to draw attention to oneself ◇ **exhibitionist** *noun*

exhilarate *verb* make joyful or lively, refresh ◇ **exhilarating** *adj* ◇ **exhilaration** *noun*

■ thrill, excite, elate, animate, enliven, invigorate, vitalize, stimulate

exhort *verb* urge (to do) ◇ **exhortation** *noun*

exhume *verb* dig up (a buried body) ◇ **exhumation** *noun*

exigency *noun* (*plural* **exigencies**) an urgent need or demand ◇ **exigent** *adj* demanding immediate attention; urgent

exiguous *adj* meagre, scanty

exile *noun* **1** someone who lives outside their own country, by choice or unwillingly **2** a period of living in a foreign country ◇ *verb* drive (someone) away from their own country; banish

exist *verb* **1** be real; live **2** live in poor circumstances ◇ **existence** *noun* ◇ **existent** *adj*
☰ **1** be, live, abide, continue, endure, breathe **2** subsist, survive

exit *noun* **1** a way out **2** the act of going out: *a hasty exit*
☰ **1** door, way out, *formal* egress, doorway, gate **2** departure, going, retreat, withdrawal, farewell

exodus *noun* a departure of many people (*esp* those leaving a place for ever)

exonerate *verb* free from blame ◇ **exoneration** *noun*
☰ absolve, acquit, clear, vindicate, pardon, excuse, spare

exorbitant *adj* going beyond what is usual or reasonable: *exorbitant price* ◇ **exorbitance** *noun*
☰ excessive, unreasonable, inordinate, extravagant, extortionate, enormous, preposterous
☲ reasonable, moderate

exorcize *verb* **1** drive out (an evil spirit) **2** free from possession by an evil spirit ◇ **exorcism** *noun* the act of driving away evil spirits ◇ **exorcist** *noun*

| ❗ Do not confuse with: **exercise** |

exotic *adj* **1** coming from a foreign country **2** unusual, colourful
☰ **1** foreign, alien, imported **2** striking, different, unfamiliar, extraordinary, curious, fascinating

expand *verb* **1** grow wider or bigger **2** open out

expanse *noun* a wide stretch of land *etc*

expansion *noun* a growing, stretching or spreading

expansive *adj* **1** spreading out **2** talkative, telling much ◇ **expansively** *adv*
☰ **1** extensive, broad, comprehensive,

wide-ranging **2** friendly, genial, outgoing, open, affable, sociable, communicative

expat *noun*, *informal* an expatriate

expatiate *verb* talk a great deal (about something)

expatriate *adj* living outside your native country ◇ *noun* someone living abroad

expect *verb* **1** think of as likely to happen or arrive soon: *what did you expect her to say?* **2** think, assume: *I expect he's too busy* ◇ **expectancy** *noun* ◇ **expectant** *adj* **1** hopeful, expecting **2** waiting to become: *an expectant mother* ◇ **expectation** *noun* ◇ **expecting** *adj*, *informal* pregnant
☰ **1** anticipate, await, hope for, look for, bank on, predict, forecast, foresee **2** suppose, surmise, believe, think, imagine

expedient *adj* done for speed or convenience rather than fairness or correctness ◇ *noun* something done to get round a difficulty ◇ **expedience** or **expediency** *noun*

expedite *verb* hasten, hurry on

expedition *noun* **1** a journey with a purpose, often for exploration **2** the people making such a journey ◇ **expeditionary** *adj* of or forming an expedition
☰ **1** journey, excursion, trip, voyage, tour, exploration, trek, safari, quest, pilgrimage, mission, crusade

expeditious *adj* swift, speedy ◇ **expeditiously** *adv*

expel *verb* (**expels, expelling, expelled**) **1** drive or force out **2** send away in disgrace, *eg* from a school ◇ **expulsion** *noun*
☰ **1** drive out, eject, evict **2** banish, throw out, ban, bar, oust, exile

expend *verb* spend, use up

expenditure *noun* an amount spent or used up, *esp* money
☰ spending, expense, outlay, outgoings, payment

expense *noun* **1** cost **2** a cause of spending: *the house was a continual* *expense* **3** (**expenses**) money spent in carrying out a job *etc*

expensive *adj* costing a lot of money ◇ **expensively** *adv*

◧ dear, costly, exorbitant, extortionate, *informal* steep, extravagant, lavish

◩ cheap, inexpensive

experience *noun* **1** an event in which you are involved: *a horrific experience* **2** knowledge gained from events, practice *etc* ◇ *verb* go through, undergo ◇ **experienced** *adj* skilled, knowledgeable

◧ *noun* **1** incident, event, episode, happening, occurrence **2** familiarity, know-how, practice, understanding ◇ *verb* live through, suffer, feel, endure, know ◇ **experienced** practised, capable, competent, expert, skilled

experiment *noun* a trial, a test (of an idea, machine *etc*) ◇ *verb* carry out experiments ◇ **experimental** *adj* ◇ **experimentally** *adv*

◧ **experimental** trial, test, exploratory, speculative, pilot, preliminary

expert *adj* highly skilful or knowledgeable (in a particular subject) ◇ *noun* someone who is highly skilled or knowledgeable (in a subject) ◇ **expertise** /ɛkspɜːˈtiːz/ *noun* skill

◧ *adj* proficient, adept, skilled, skilful, knowledgeable, experienced, professional, qualified ◇ *noun* specialist, authority, professional

expiate *verb* make up for (a crime *etc*) ◇ **expiation** *noun*

expire *verb* **1** die **2** come to an end, become invalid: *your visa has expired* ◇ **expiry** *noun* the act of expiring

explain *verb* **1** make clear or easy to understand **2** give reasons for: *please explain your behaviour*

◧ **1** interpret, clarify, describe, define, simplify, solve **2** justify, excuse, account for

explanation *noun* a statement which makes clear something difficult or puzzling; a reason (*eg* for your behaviour) ◇ **explanatory** *adj* intended to explain

◧ clarification, definition, illustration,

demonstration, account, description

expletive *noun* an exclamation, *esp* a swear word

explicable *adj* able to be explained ◇ **explicably** *adv*

explicit *adj* plainly stated or shown; outspoken, frank ◇ **explicitly** *adv* ◇ **explicitness** *noun*

◧ open, direct, outspoken, straightforward, unreserved, plain, precise, specific, unambiguous

explode *verb* **1** blow up with a loud noise **2** prove to be wrong or unfounded: *that explodes your theory*

◧ **1** blow up, burst, go off, set off, detonate, discharge, erupt **2** discredit, disprove, give the lie to, debunk

exploit *noun* a daring deed; a feat ◇ *verb* **1** make use of selfishly **2** make good use of (resources *etc*) ◇ **exploitation** *noun*

◧ *verb* **1** misuse, abuse, manipulate, take advantage of **2** use, utilize, capitalize on, profit by, turn to account, take advantage of, cash in on, make capital out of

explore *verb* **1** make a journey of discovery **2** inquire into ◇ **exploration** *noun* ◇ **explorer** *noun*

◧ **1** travel, search **2** investigate, examine, research, probe, analyse, search

explosion *noun* a sudden violent burst; an act of exploding

explosive *adj* **1** liable to explode **2** hot-tempered ◇ *noun* something which will explode, *eg* gunpowder ◇ **explosively** *adv*

exponent *noun* someone who shows skill in a particular art or craft: *an exponent of karate*

export *verb* sell goods *etc* in a foreign country ◇ *noun* **1** an act of exporting **2** something exported ◇ **exportation** *noun*

expose *verb* **1** place in full view **2** show up (a hidden crime *etc*) **3** lay open to the sun or wind **4** allow light to reach and act on (a film) ◇ **exposition** *noun* **1** a public display **2** a statement explaining a writer's meaning ◇ **exposure**

noun **1** the act of exposing **2** the amount of film exposed to produce one photograph

▤ **1** reveal, show, exhibit, display, disclose **2** uncover, bring to light, detect, divulge, unmask ◇ **exposure 1** revelation, disclosure, discovery, divulgence

exposé /ɛkˈspoʊzeɪ/ *noun* a report *etc* exposing a scandal or crime

expostulate *verb* protest ◇ **expostulation** *noun*

exposure *see* **expose**

expound *verb* explain fully

express *verb* **1** show by actions or symbols **2** put into words **3** press or squeeze out ◇ *adj* **1** clearly stated: *express instructions* **2** sent in haste: *express messenger* ◇ *noun* a fast train, bus *etc*

▤ *verb* **1** show, manifest, exhibit, indicate, denote, depict **2** articulate, verbalize, voice, state, communicate, pronounce, declare, intimate

expression *noun* **1** the look on someone's face: *an expression of horror* **2** the showing of meaning or emotion through language, art *etc* **3** a show of emotion in an artistic performance *etc* **4** a word or phrase: *an idiomatic expression* **5** pressing or squeezing out

▤ **1** look, air, aspect, countenance, appearance

expressive *adj* expressing meaning or feeling clearly ◇ **expressively** *adv*

▤ meaningful, revealing, informative, moving

expropriate *verb* take (property *etc*) away from its owner

expulsion *see* **expel**

expunge *verb* rub out, remove

expurgate *noun* remove offensive material from (a book *etc*), censor

exquisite *adj* **1** extremely beautiful **2** excellent **3** very great, utter: *exquisite pleasure*

▤ **1** beautiful, attractive, dainty, delicate, charming, elegant, delightful, lovely, pleasing **2** perfect, flawless, precious

extemporize *verb* make up on the spot, improvise

extend *verb* **1** stretch, make longer **2** hold out: *extended a hand* **3** last, carry over: *my holiday extends into next week*

▤ **1** spread, reach, enlarge, increase, lengthen, elongate, draw out, prolong **2** offer, hold out, present

extension *noun* **1** a part added to a building **2** an additional amount of time on a schedule, holiday *etc* **3** a telephone connected with a main one

extensive *adj* wide; covering a large area: *extensive changes* ◇ **extensively** *adv*

▤ large, huge, universal, prevalent, far-reaching, broad, widespread, general, pervasive

extent *noun* **1** the space something covers **2** degree: *to a great extent*

▤ **1** dimension(s), amount, expanse, size, area, spread

extenuate *verb* **1** lessen **2** cause to seem less bad: *extenuating circumstances* ◇ **extenuation** *noun*

exterior *adj* on the outside; outer: *exterior wall* ◇ *noun* the outside of a building *etc*

▤ *noun* outside, surface, covering, coating, face, façade, shell, skin, finish, appearance

▤ *noun* interior

exterminate *verb* kill off completely (a race, a type of animal *etc*), wipe out ◇ **extermination** *noun*

▤ annihilate, eradicate, eliminate, wipe out

external *adj* **1** outside; on the outside **2** not central: *external considerations*

▤ **1** outer, outside, exterior, superficial, outward, outermost, apparent, visible

extinct *adj* **1** no longer active: *extinct volcano* **2** no longer found alive: *the dodo is now extinct* ◇ **extinction** *noun* making or becoming extinct

extinguish *verb* **1** put out (fire *etc*) **2** put an end to ◇ **extinguisher** *noun* a spray containing chemicals for putting out fires

▤ **1** put out, blow out, snuff out, stifle, smother, douse, quench **2** annihilate, erase, remove, end, suppress

extirpate *verb* destroy completely, exterminate

> ⚠ Do not confuse with: **extricate**
> and **extrapolate**

extol _verb_ (**extols, extolling, extolled**) praise greatly

extort _verb_ take by force or threats
◇ **extortion** _noun_
▣ extract, wring, exact, coerce, force, squeeze, _informal_ bleed

extortionate _adj_ of a price: much too high

extra _adj_ more than is usual or necessary; additional ◇ _adv_ unusually; more than is average: _extra large_ ◇ _noun_ **1** something extra **2** someone employed to be one of a crowd in a film
▣ _adj_ added, more, excess, spare, superfluous, surplus, left-over, reserve, redundant ◇ _adv_ especially, exceptionally, particularly, remarkably ◇ _noun_ **1** addition, supplement, extension, attachment

extra- _prefix_ outside, beyond

extract _verb_ **1** draw or pull out, _esp_ by force: _extract a tooth_ **2** remove selected parts of a book _etc_ **3** draw out by pressure or chemical action ◇ _noun_ **1** an excerpt from a book _etc_ **2** a substance obtained by extraction: _vanilla extract_
◇ **extraction** _noun_ **1** the act of extracting **2** someone's descent or lineage: _of Irish extraction_
▣ _verb_ **1** remove, take out, draw out, exact, uproot, withdraw **2** select, cull, abstract, cite, quote **3** derive, draw, distil, obtain

extracurricular _adj_ done outside school or college hours

extradite _verb_ hand over (someone wanted for trial) to the police of another country ◇ **extradition** _noun_

extramarital _adj_ happening outside a marriage: _extramarital affair_

extramural _adj_ of a university department: teaching courses outside the regular degree courses

extraneous _adj_ having nothing to do with the subject: _extraneous information_
◇ **extraneously** _adv_

extraordinary _adj_ **1** not usual, exceptional **2** very surprising **3** specially employed: _ambassador extraordinary_
◇ **extraordinarily** _adv_
▣ **1** unusual, notable, noteworthy, outstanding, unique, special, significant, particular **2** surprising, amazing, wonderful, marvellous, fantastic
▣ **1** commonplace, ordinary

extrapolate _verb_ infer or predict on the basis of known facts

> ⚠ Do not confuse with: **extirpate**
> and **extricate**

extrasensory _adj_ beyond the range of the ordinary senses: _extrasensory perception_

extraterrestrial _adj_ from outside the earth ◇ _noun_ a being from another planet

extravagant _adj_ **1** spending or using too much; wasteful **2** too great, overblown: _extravagant praise_ ◇ **extravagantly** _adv_ ◇ **extravagance** _noun_
▣ **1** spendthrift, thriftless, wasteful, reckless, profligate **2** flamboyant, preposterous, outrageous, ostentatious

extravaganza _noun_ an extravagant creation or production

extravert _another spelling of_ **extrovert**

extreme _adj_ **1** far from the centre **2** far from the ordinary or usual **3** very great: _extreme sadness_ ◇ _noun_ an extreme point ◇ **extremely** _adv_
▣ _adj_ **1** farthest, far-off, faraway, distant **2** extraordinary, exceptional, greatest, highest, unreasonable, inordinate, remarkable **3** intense, utmost, acute, downright, _slang_ full-on ◇ _noun_ limit, maximum, pinnacle, end, climax, edge

extremist _noun_ someone who carries ideas foolishly far ◇ **extremism** _noun_

extremity _noun_ (_plural_ **extremities**) **1** a part or place furthest from the centre **2** great distress or pain **3** (**extremities**) the hands and feet

extricate _verb_ free from (difficulties _etc_)

> ⚠ Do not confuse with: **extirpate**
> and **extrapolate**

extrovert or **extravert** *noun* an outgoing, sociable person

extrude *verb* protrude, stick out

exuberant *adj* in very high spirits ◇ **exuberance** *noun* ◇ **exuberantly** *adv*
■ lively, vivacious, spirited, high-spirited, enthusiastic, effusive, cheerful

exude *verb* give off in large amounts: *exuding sweat/exuded happiness*

exult *verb* be very glad, rejoice greatly: *exulting in their victory* ◇ **exultant** *adj* ◇ **exultation** *noun*
■ rejoice, revel, delight, glory, celebrate, relish, crow, gloat, triumph

eye *noun* 1 the part of the body with which you see 2 the ability to notice: *an eye for detail* 3 sight 4 something the shape of an eye, *eg* the hole in a needle ◇ *verb* (**eyes**, **eyeing**, **eyed**) look at with interest: *eyeing the last slice of cake*

eyeball *noun* the round part of the eye; the eye itself (the part between the eyelids)

eyebrow *noun* the hairy ridge above the eye

eyeglass *noun* a lens to correct faulty eyesight

eyelash *noun* one of the hairs on the edge of the eyelid

eyelet *noun* a small hole for a lace *etc*

eyelid *noun* the skin covering of the eye

eye-opener *noun* that which reveals something unexpected

eyesore *noun* anything that is ugly (*esp* a building)
■ monstrosity, blot on the landscape

eyewash *noun* 1 a liquid for soothing sore eyes 2 *informal* nonsense, insincere talk

eyewitness *noun* someone who sees a thing done (*eg* a crime committed)
■ witness, observer, looker-on, onlooker, bystander, passer-by

eyrie /ˈɪərɪ/ *noun* the nest of an eagle or other bird of prey

Ff

F *abbrev* degree(s) Fahrenheit

FA *abbrev*, *Brit* Football Association

fable *noun* a story about animals *etc*, including a lesson or moral
- allegory, parable, story, tale, myth, legend

fabric *noun* **1** cloth **2** framework; the external parts of a building *etc*
- **1** material, textile, stuff **2** structure, construction, make-up, constitution, organization, foundations

---

Fabrics include:
alpaca, angora, astrakhan, barathea, bouclé, cashmere, chenille, duffel, felt, flannel, fleece, Harris tweed®, mohair, paisley, pashmina, serge, sheepskin, Shetland wool, tweed, vicuña, wool, worsted; buckram, calico, cambric, candlewick, canvas, chambray, cheesecloth, chino, chintz, cord, corduroy, cotton, crepe, denim, drill, jean, flannelette, gaberdine, gingham, jersey, lawn, linen, lisle, madras, moleskin, muslin, needlecord, piqué, poplin, sateen, seersucker, terry towelling, ticking, Viyella®, webbing, winceyette; brocade, grosgrain, damask, lace, Chantilly, Brussels lace, chiffon, georgette, gossamer, voile, organza, organdie, tulle, net, crepe de Chine, silk, taffeta, shantung, satin, velvet, velour; polycotton, polyester, rayon, nylon, Crimplene®, Terylene®, Lurex®, Lycra®, elastane, lamé; hessian, horsehair, chamois, kid, leather, leather-cloth, sharkskin, suede

---

fabricate *verb* make up (lies) ◊ **fabrication** *noun*
- fake, make up, invent, trump up, concoct

fabulous *adj* **1** *informal* very good, excellent **2** imaginary, mythological ◊ **fabulously** *adv* ◊ **fabulousness** *noun*
- **1** wonderful, marvellous, fantastic, superb, breathtaking, spectacular, phenomenal, amazing, astounding **2** mythical, legendary, fantastic, fictitious, invented

façade /fə'sɑːd/ *noun* **1** the front of a building **2** a deceptive appearance or act; a mask

face *noun* **1** the front part of the head **2** the front of anything **3** appearance ◊ *verb* **1** turn or look in the direction of **2** stand opposite to **3** put an additional surface on **4** confront ◊ **face pack** a cosmetic paste applied to the face and left to dry ◊ **face up to** meet or accept boldly: *facing up to responsibilities*
- *noun* **1** features, countenance, visage, physiognomy **2** exterior, outside, surface, cover, front, façade **3** expression, look, appearance, air ◊ *verb* **3** cover, coat, veneer **4** face up to, deal with, cope with, tackle, brave

facet *noun* **1** a side of a many-sided object, *eg* a cut gem **2** an aspect; a characteristic

facetious *adj* not meant seriously; joking ◊ **facetiously** *adv* ◊ **facetiousness** *noun*
- flippant, frivolous, playful, tongue-in-cheek, funny, amusing, humorous, comical, witty
- serious

facial *adj* of the face ◊ **facially** *adv*

facile /'fasaɪl/ *adj* **1** not deep or thorough; superficial, glib **2** fluent ◊ **facilely** *adv*
- **1** complicated, profound

facilitate *verb* make easy

facility *noun* **1** ease **2** skill, ability **3** (**facilities**) buildings, equipment *etc* provided for a purpose: *sports facilities*
- **1** ease, effortlessness **2** proficiency,

talent, gift, knack, ability **3** amenities, services, conveniences, *informal* mod cons

facsimile *noun* an exact copy

fact *noun* **1** something known or held to be true **2** reality ◇ **in fact** actually, really

◼ **2** reality, actuality, truth

◼ **2** fiction

faction *noun* a group which is part of a larger group: *rival factions within the party*

◼ splinter group, minority, division, section, contingent, set

factious *adj* trouble-making, riotous ◇ **factiously** *adv* ◇ **factiousness** *noun*

factitious *adj* produced artificially ◇ **factitiously** *adv* ◇ **factitiousness** *noun*

factor *noun* **1** something affecting the course of events **2** someone who does business for another **3** a number which exactly divides into another (*eg* 3 is a factor of 6)

◼ **1** cause, influence, circumstance, consideration, element, ingredient, component, part, point

factory *noun* (*plural* **factories**) a workshop producing goods in large quantities

◼ works, plant, mill, assembly shop

factotum *noun* someone employed to do all kinds of work

factual *adj* consisting of facts; real, not fictional: *a factual account*

◼ true, actual, real, genuine, authentic, correct, accurate, precise, exact, literal, faithful, close

◼ false, fictitious, imaginary, fictional

faculty *noun* (*plural* **faculties**) **1** a power of the mind, *eg* reason **2** a natural power of the body, *eg* hearing **3** ability, aptitude **4** a department of study in a university: *Faculty of Arts*

fad *noun* **1** a temporary fashion **2** an odd idea, like or dislike ◇ **faddy** *adj* having odd likes or dislikes

◼ **1** craze, *informal* rage, mania, fashion, mode, vogue, trend

fade *verb* **1** (cause to) lose colour or

strength **2** disappear gradually, *eg* from sight or hearing

◼ **1** discolour, bleach, blanch, blench, pale, whiten, dim **2** decline, fall, diminish, dwindle, ebb, wane, disappear, vanish, flag, weaken, droop, wilt, wither, shrivel, perish, die

faeces /'fiːsiːz/ *noun plural* solid excrement

faff *verb*, *informal* dither, fumble: *don't faff about*

fag *noun* **1** *informal* tiring or tedious work **2** *slang* a cigarette **3** *informal* a young schoolboy forced to do jobs for an older one **4** *US slang*, *derogatory* a male homosexual ◇ **fag end** *informal* **1** a cigarette butt **2** the very end, the tail end ◇ **fagged out** *informal* exhausted, tired out

faggot or *US* **fagot** *noun* **1** a bundle of sticks **2** a meatball **3** *US slang*, *derogatory* a male homosexual

Fahrenheit *noun* a temperature scale on which water freezes at 32° and boils at 212° ◇ *adj* measured on this scale: *70° Fahrenheit*

fail *verb* **1** be unsuccessful **2** break down, stop **3** lose strength **4** be lacking or insufficient **5** disappoint ◇ **fail-safe** *adj* made to correct automatically, or be safe, if a fault occurs ◇ **without fail** certainly, for sure

◼ **1** go wrong, fall through, go bankrupt, go bust, go under, founder, sink **2** go wrong, collapse **3** decline, fall, weaken **5** let down, leave, desert, abandon

failing *noun* a fault; a weakness

failure *noun* **1** the act of failing **2** someone or something which fails

faint *adj* **1** lacking in strength, brightness *etc* **2** about to lose consciousness: *feel faint* ◇ *verb* fall down unconscious ◇ *noun* a loss of consciousness ◇ **faintly** *adv* dimly, not clearly ◇ **faintness** *noun*

◼ *adj* **1** slight, weak, feeble, soft, low, muffled, subdued, light, pale, dull, dim, hazy, indistinct, vague **2** dizzy, giddy, *informal* woozy, light-headed, weak, feeble ◇ *verb* black out, pass out, swoon, collapse, *informal* flake out, *informal* keel over, drop

> ⚠ Do not confuse with: **feint**

fair ¹ *adj* **1** of a light colour: *fair hair* **2** of weather: clear and dry **3** unbiased, just: *fair assessment* **4** good enough but not excellent **5** beautiful ◇ **fairly** *adv* ◇ **fairness** *noun* ◇ **fair-haired** *adj* having light-coloured hair; blond ◇ **fair-weather friend** someone who is a friend only when things are going well

▣ **3** just, equitable, impartial, objective, unprejudiced, right, proper, trustworthy, upright **4** average, middling, satisfactory, adequate

fair ² *noun* **1** a large market held at fixed times **2** an exhibition of goods from different producers *etc*: *craft fair* **3** a travelling collection of merry-go-rounds, stalls *etc*

fairway *noun* **1** the mown part on a golf course, between the tee and the green **2** the deep-water part of a river

fairy *noun* (*plural* **fairies**) a small imaginary creature, human in shape, with magical powers ◇ **fairy light** a small coloured light for decorating Christmas trees *etc* ◇ **fairy story** or **fairy tale 1** a traditional story of fairies, giants *etc* **2** *informal* a lie

fait accompli /feɪt əˈkɒmpliː/ (*plural* **faits accomplis**) something already done, an accomplished fact

faith *noun* **1** trust **2** belief in a religion or creed **3** loyalty to a promise: *broke faith with them* ◇ **faithless** *adj*

faithful *adj* **1** loyal; reliable **2** true, accurate: *a faithful account of events* **3** believing in a particular religion or creed **4** keeping your marriage vows ◇ **faithfully** *adv* ◇ **faithfulness** *noun*

▣ **1** devoted, constant, trusty, reliable, dependable, true **2** precise, exact, strict, close, true, truthful

▧ **1** disloyal, treacherous **2** inaccurate, vague

fake *adj* not genuine, forged ◇ *noun* **1** someone who is not what they pretend to be **2** a forgery ◇ *verb* **1** make an imitation or forgery of **2** pretend to feel or have

▣ *adj* forged, counterfeit, false, spurious, bogus, sham, mock, imitation, faux ◇ *noun* **1** fraud, impostor, charlatan **2** forgery, copy, reproduction, imitation ◇ *verb* **1** forge, copy, imitate, simulate **2** simulate, affect, feign

fakir *noun* an Islamic or Hindu holy man

falcon *noun* a kind of bird of prey ◇ **falconer** *noun* someone who trains or uses falcons for hunting ◇ **falconry** *noun* the training or use of falcons for hunting

fall *verb* (**falls, falling, fallen, fell**) **1** go down suddenly, *esp* to the ground **2** become less **3** of a fortress *etc*: be captured **4** die in battle **5** happen, occur: *Christmas falls on a Monday this year* ◇ *noun* **1** an act of falling **2** something that falls: *a fall of snow* **3** lowering in value *etc* **4** *US* autumn **5** an accident involving falling **6** ruin, downfall, surrender **7** (**falls**) a waterfall ◇ **fall guy** a scapegoat ◇ **fall flat** fail to have the intended effect ◇ **fall in love** begin to be in love ◇ **fall out with** quarrel with ◇ **fall through** of a plan: fail, come to nothing

▣ *verb* **1** tumble, stumble, trip, topple, keel over, collapse, slump **2** decrease, lessen, decline, diminish, dwindle, fall off, subside

fallacy *noun* (*plural* **fallacies**) a false belief; something believed to be true but really false ◇ **fallacious** *adj*

▣ misconception, delusion, mistake, error, inconsistency, falsehood

fallible *adj* liable to make a mistake or to be wrong ◇ **fallibility** *noun*

fallopian tubes two tubes along which egg cells pass from a woman's ovaries to her uterus

fallout *noun* radioactive dust resulting from the explosion of an atomic bomb *etc*

fallow *adj* of land: left unsown for a time after being ploughed

▣ uncultivated, unplanted, undeveloped, unused, idle, resting

fallow deer a type of yellowish-brown deer

false *adj* **1** untrue **2** not real, fake **3** not natural: *false teeth* ◇ **falsely** *adv* ◇ **falseness** or **falsity** *noun*

■ **1** wrong, mistaken, inaccurate, misleading **2** fake, forged, sham, bogus **3** artificial, synthetic, imitation, simulated, mock

falsehood *noun* a lie, an untruth

■ fib, story, fabrication, deception

falsetto *noun* a singing voice forced higher than its natural range

falsify *verb* (**falsifies, falsifying, falsified**) make false, alter for a dishonest purpose: *falsified his tax forms*

■ alter, *informal* cook, tamper with, doctor, forge, counterfeit, fake

falter *verb* stumble or hesitate

fame *noun* the quality of being well-known, renown ◇ **famed** *adj* famous

■ renown, celebrity, stardom, prominence, eminence, glory, reputation, name

familiar *adj* **1** well-known **2** seen, known *etc* before **3** well-acquainted (with) **4** friendly, intimate **5** over-friendly, cheeky ◇ **familiarity** *noun*

■ **1** everyday, common, ordinary **3** acquainted, knowledgeable, versed **4** intimate, close, friendly, informal, free-and-easy

familiarize *verb* make accustomed or acquainted (with)

family *noun* (*plural* **families**) **1** a couple and their children **2** the children alone **3** a group of people related to one another **4** a group of animals, languages, *etc* with common characteristics

famine *noun* a great shortage, *esp* of food

■ starvation, hunger, want, scarcity

famished *adj* very hungry

famous *adj* well-known, having fame ◇ **famously** *adv*, *informal* very well: *get along famously*

■ famed, renowned, celebrated, distinguished, legendary, remarkable, notable, prominent

🔁 unheard-of, unknown, obscure

fan [1] *noun* **1** a device or appliance for making a rush of air **2** a small hand-held device for cooling the face ◇ *verb* (**fans, fanning, fanned**) **1** cause a rush of air with a fan **2** increase the strength of: *fanning her anger* ◇ **fan out** spread out in the shape of a fan

fan [2] *noun* an admirer, a devoted follower

fanatic *noun* someone who is over-enthusiastic about something ◇ *adj* fanatical ◇ **fanatical** *adj* wildly or excessively enthusiastic ◇ **fanatically** *adv*

■ **fanatical** overenthusiastic, extreme, passionate, zealous, fervent, obsessive, single-minded

fanciful *adj* **1** inclined to have fancies **2** imaginary, not real ◇ **fancifully** *adv*

fancy *noun* (*plural* **fancies**) **1** a sudden liking or desire: *he had a fancy for ice-cream* **2** imagination **3** something imagined ◇ *adj* not plain, elaborate ◇ *verb* (**fancies, fancying, fancied**) **1** picture, imagine **2** have a sudden wish for **3** *informal* be physically attracted to (someone) **4** think without being sure ◇ **fancier** *noun* someone whose hobby is to keep prize animals, birds *etc* ◇ **fancy dress** an elaborate costume worn *eg* for a party, often representing a famous character

■ *adj* ornate, decorated, elegant, extravagant ◇ *verb* **2** desire, wish for, long for, yearn for **3** like, be attracted to, take a liking to, take to, desire, *slang* have the hots for

fandango *noun* (*plural* **fandangos**) a Spanish dance for two with castanets

fanfare *noun* a loud flourish from a trumpet or bugle

fang *noun* **1** a long tooth of a wild animal **2** the tooth a snake uses to inject poison

fanlight *noun* a window above a door, usually semicircular

fanny *noun*, *taboo slang* **1** *Brit* the vagina **2** *US* the buttocks

fantastic *adj* **1** very unusual, strange or unrealistic **2** *informal* very great **3** *informal* excellent

■ **1** strange, weird, odd, exotic, fanciful, fabulous, imaginative **2** overwhelming, enormous, extreme **3** wonderful, marvellous, sensational, superb, excellent

fantasy *noun* (*plural* **fantasies**) **1** an imaginary scene, story *etc* **2** an idea not based on reality

fanzine *noun, informal* a magazine for a particular group of fans

FAO *abbrev* for the attention of

FAQ *abbrev* frequently asked questions

far (**farther, farthest**) *adv* **1** at or to a long way: *far off* **2** very much: *far better* ◇ *adj* **1** a long way off, distant: *a far country* **2** more distant: *the far side* ◇ **far-fetched** *adj* very unlikely: *a far-fetched story* ◇ **far-flung** *adj* extending over a great distance ◇ **far-sighted** *adj* foreseeing what is likely to happen and preparing for it

◼ *adv* **1** a long way, a good way, *informal* miles **2** much, greatly, considerably, extremely, decidedly ◇ *adj* **1** distant, far-off, far-flung, remote ◇ **far-fetched** implausible, unlikely, incredible, unbelievable, unrealistic

farce *noun* **1** a comedy with farfetched characters and plot **2** a ridiculous situation ◇ **farcical** *adj* absurd, ridiculous

fare *verb* get on (well or badly): *they fared well in the competition* ◇ *noun* **1** the price of a journey **2** a paying passenger in a taxi *etc* **3** food

farewell *exclam & noun* goodbye

farinaceous *adj* floury, mealy

farm *noun* **1** an area of land for growing crops, breeding and feeding animals *etc* **2** a place where certain animals, fish *etc* are reared: *a salmon farm* ◇ *verb* **1** be a farmer **2** cultivate (land) on a farm ◇ **farmer** *noun* the owner or tenant of a farm ◇ **farming** *noun* ◇ **farmhouse** *noun* the house attached to a farm ◇ **farmstead** *noun* a farm and farmhouse ◇ **farmyard** *noun* the yard surrounded by farm buildings ◇ **farm out** give (work) to others to do for payment

farrago *noun* (*plural* **farragoes**) a confused mixture

farrow *noun* a litter of baby pigs ◇ *verb* give birth to a litter of pigs

fart *noun, taboo slang* **1** an outburst of wind from the anus **2** a despised person ◇ *verb* expel wind from the anus

farther and **farthest** *see* far

farthing *noun, hist* an old coin, with the value of one quarter of an old penny

fascia /'feɪʃɪə/ (*plural* **fascias** or **fasciae**) *noun* **1** a signboard above a shop *etc* **2** the dashboard of a car

fascinate *verb* **1** charm, attract irresistibly **2** enthral; interest strongly ◇ **fascinating** *adj* ◇ **fascination** *noun*

◼ **1** delight, charm, captivate **2** engross, intrigue, spellbind, enthral, hypnotize, transfix ◇ **fascination** interest, attraction, lure, pull, charm

◼ **1,2** bore, repel

fascism *noun* a form of authoritarian government characterized by extreme nationalism and suppression of individual freedom ◇ **fascist** *noun* **1** a supporter of fascism **2** a right-wing extremist

From Italian word, *fascio* meaning 'bundle' or 'group'

fashion *noun* **1** the style in which something is made, *esp* clothes **2** a way of behaving or dressing which is popular for a time **3** a manner, a way: *acting in a strange fashion* ◇ *verb* shape, form ◇ **fashionable** *adj* up-to-date, conforming to the latest style ◇ **after a fashion** to some extent, in a way ◇ **in fashion** fashionable

◼ **fashionable** chic, smart, elegant, stylish, à la mode, in vogue, *informal* trendy, in, *informal* all the rage, popular, current, latest, modern, up-to-date

fast¹ *adj* **1** quick-moving **2** of a clock: showing a time in advance of the correct time **3** of dyed colour: fixed, not likely to wash out ◇ *adv* **1** quickly **2** firmly: *stand fast* **3** soundly, completely: *fast asleep* ◇ **fastness** *noun* ◇ **fast-track** *adj* of a career: liable for quick promotion ◇ **in the fast lane** having an exciting but stressful lifestyle

■ *adj* **1** quick, swift, rapid, brisk, accelerated, speedy ◊ *adv* **1** swiftly, rapidly, speedily, like a flash, like a shot, hastily, hurriedly

fast ² *verb* go without food voluntarily, *eg* for religious reasons or as a protest ◊ *noun* abstinence from food

fasten *verb* fix or attach; close or secure by tying, nailing *etc*

■ fix, attach, clamp, grip, nail, seal, close, shut, lock, bolt, secure, tie, bind, chain, link, do up, button, lace, buckle

fastidious *adj* difficult to please ◊ **fastidiously** *adv* ◊ **fastidiousness** *noun*

fat *noun* an oily substance made by the bodies of animals and by plants, used in mammals for insulation and storing energy ◊ *adj* **1** having a lot of fat; plump **2** thick, wide ◊ **fatten** *verb* make or become fat ◊ **fatty** *adj* of meat *etc*: containing a lot of fat

■ *adj* **1** plump, obese, tubby, stout, corpulent, portly, round, pot-bellied, overweight, chubby, podgy, fleshy, flabby

fatal *adj* causing death or disaster ◊ **fatality** *noun* (*plural* **fatalities**) a death, *esp* caused by an accident or disaster

■ deadly, lethal, mortal, incurable, terminal

fate *noun* **1** what the future holds; fortune, luck **2** end, death: *met his fate bravely* ◊ **fated** *adj* doomed ◊ **fateful** *adj* with important consequences; crucial, significant

■ **1** destiny, providence, chance, future, fortune, lot **2** ruin, destruction, death

father *noun* **1** a male parent **2** a priest **3** the creator or inventor of something: *Poe is the father of crime fiction* ◊ *verb* be the father of ◊ **father-in-law** *noun* the father of someone's husband or wife ◊ **fatherland** *noun* someone's native country

fathom *noun* a measure of depth of water (6 feet, 1.83 metres) ◊ *verb* understand, get to the bottom of

fatigue /fə'tiːg/ *noun* **1** great tiredness **2** weakness or strain caused by use: *metal fatigue* ◊ *verb* tire out

■ *noun* **1** tiredness, weariness, exhaustion, lethargy, listlessness, weakness

fatuous *adj* very foolish ◊ **fatuously** *adv* ◊ **fatuousness** *noun*

fatwa *noun* an edict issued by an Islamic authority

faucet *noun*, *US* a tap for water

fault *noun* **1** a mistake **2** a flaw, something bad or wrong, *eg* with a machine **3** responsibility for a wrongdoing ◊ *verb* criticize ◊ **faultless** *adj* perfect ◊ **faultlessly** *adv* ◊ **faulty** *adj* having a fault or faults

■ *noun* **1** error, blunder, *informal* slip-up, slip, offence **2** defect, blemish, imperfection, weakness ◊ *verb* pick holes in, criticize, *informal* knock, find fault with ◊ **faultless** flawless, spotless, immaculate ◊ **faulty** defective, damaged, out of order, broken, wrong

faun *noun* a mythological creature, half human and half animal

fauna *noun* the animals of a district or country as a whole

faux /foʊ/ *adj* imitation: *faux leather*

faux pas /foʊ pɑː/ an embarrassing mistake, a blunder

favour *noun* **1** a kind or helpful action **2** goodwill, approval **3** a gift, a token ◊ *verb* **1** show preference for **2** be an advantage to: *the darkness favoured our escape* ◊ **in favour of 1** in support of **2** for the benefit of

■ *noun* **1** kindness, service, good turn, courtesy **2** support, backing, partiality ◊ *verb* **1** prefer, choose, opt for, like **2** help, assist, benefit

favourable *adj* **1** showing approval **2** advantageous, helpful (to) ◊ **favourably** *adv*

■ **1** agreeable, well-disposed, sympathetic, supportive **2** beneficial, helpful, suitable

favourite *adj* best-liked ◊ *noun* **1** a favourite person or thing **2** a competitor, horse, *etc* expected to win a race ◊ **favouritism** *noun* showing favour towards one person *etc* more than another

■ *adj* preferred, favoured, best-loved, beloved, chosen

fawn[1] *noun* **1** a young deer **2** a light yellowish-brown colour ◇ *adj* of this colour

fawn[2] *verb* (often with **on**) flatter or show affection in a grovelling fashion

fax *noun* **1** a machine which transfers information from a document by a telephone line to a receiving machine which produces a corresponding copy **2** a document sent or received in this way ◇ *verb* **1** send by fax **2** send a fax to

fear *noun* an unpleasant feeling caused by danger, evil *etc* ◇ *verb* feel fear, be afraid of ◇ **fearful** *adj* **1** timid, afraid **2** terrible **3** *informal* very bad: *a fearful headache* ◇ **fearfully** *adv* ◇ **fearless** *adj* brave, daring ◇ **fearlessly** *adv*

■ *noun* alarm, fright, terror, horror, panic, distress, uneasiness, dread ◇ **fearful 1** frightened, scared, nervous, anxious, uneasy **2, 3** dreadful, awful, atrocious, shocking, appalling, horrible

▪ *noun* courage, bravery, confidence

feasible *adj* able to be done, likely ◇ **feasibility** *noun* ◇ **feasibly** *adv*

■ practicable, practical, workable, realizable, reasonable, possible, likely

feast *noun* **1** a rich and plentiful meal **2** a festival day commemorating some event ◇ *verb* eat or hold a feast

feat *noun* a deed requiring some effort

■ exploit, deed, act, accomplishment, achievement, attainment

feather *noun* one of the growths which form the outer covering of a bird ◇ **feathery** *adj* **1** covered in feathers **2** soft **3** light

feature *noun* **1** an identifying mark, a characteristic **2** a special article in a newspaper *etc* **3** the main film in a cinema programme **4** a special attraction **5** (**features**) the various parts of someone's face, eg eyes, nose *etc* ◇ *verb* **1** have as a feature **2** take part (in) **3** be prominent in ◇ **featurette** *noun* a short film relating to a main feature *esp* on a DVD

■ *noun* **1** aspect, attribute, quality, property, trait, characteristic **2** column, article, report, story, piece, item, comment

February *noun* the second month of the year

fecund *adj* fertile ◇ **fecundity** *noun*

fed *past form* of **feed**

federal *adj* of a federation ◇ **federated** *adj* joined by treaty or agreement ◇ **federation** *noun* a group of states *etc* joined together for a common purpose, a league

fee *noun* a price paid for work done, or for a special service

feeble *adj* **1** weak **2** unconvincing: *a feeble excuse* ◇ **feebleness** *noun* ◇ **feebly** *adv*

■ **1** faint, exhausted, frail, delicate, infirm, helpless, inadequate, flimsy, ineffective, incompetent

▪ **1** strong, powerful

feed *verb* (**feeds**, **feeding**, **fed**) **1** give food to **2** eat food **3** supply with necessary materials ◇ *noun* food for animals: *cattle feed* ◇ **fed up** *adj* tired, bored and disgusted

feel *verb* (**feels**, **feeling**, **felt**) **1** explore by touch **2** experience, be aware of: *he felt no pain* **3** believe, consider **4** think (yourself) to be: *I feel ill* ◇ *noun* an act of touching ◇ **feel for** be sorry for: *we felt for her in her grief* ◇ **feel like** want, have an inclination for: *do you feel like going out tonight?*

■ *verb* **1** touch, handle, manipulate, hold, stroke, caress, fondle **2** go through, undergo, suffer, endure, enjoy **3** think, reckon

feeler *noun* one of two thread-like parts on an insect's head for sensing danger *etc*

feelgood *adj* causing a feeling of comfort or security: *a feelgood movie*

feeling *noun* **1** sense of touch **2** emotion: *spoken with great feeling* **3** affection **4** an impression, belief: *I had a feeling I'd met him before* ◇ **feelings** *noun plural* what someone thinks or feels inside: *have mixed feelings/hurt her feelings*

■ **2** passion, intensity, compassion, sympathy, understanding **4** perception, sense, instinct, suspicion, notion

feet *plural* of **foot**

feign /feɪn/ *verb* pretend to feel or have: *feigning illness*

feint *noun* **1** a pretence **2** a move to put an enemy off guard ◇ *verb* make a feint

> ⚠ Do not confuse with: **faint**

feisty *adj, informal* **1** spirited **2** irritable, touchy

felafel *noun* a fried ball of chickpeas and spices

felicity *noun* happiness ◇ **felicitations** *noun plural* good wishes, congratulations ◇ **felicitous** *adj* **1** lucky **2** well-chosen, suiting well

feline *adj* **1** of or relating to cats **2** like a cat

fell[1] *noun* a barren hill

fell[2] *verb* cut down (a tree)

fell[3] *adj, old* cruel, ruthless; destructive

fell[4] *past form* of **fall**

fellow *noun* **1** a companion or equal **2** one of a pair **3** a member of an academic society, college *etc* **4** a man, a boy

> ▤ **1** peer, equal, partner, colleague, companion **2** match, twin, double **4** man, boy, *informal* chap, *informal* bloke, *informal* guy

fellowship *noun* **1** comradeship, friendship **2** an award to a university graduate **3** a society or association

felon *noun* someone who commits a serious crime ◇ **felony** *noun* (*plural* **felonies**) a serious crime

felt[1] *noun* a type of rough cloth made of rolled and pressed wool

felt[2] *past form* of **feel**

female *adj* of the sex which produces offspring ◇ *noun* a human or animal of this sex

feminine *adj* **1** of or relating to the female sex **2** characteristic of women ◇ **femininity** *noun*

feminism *noun* a social and cultural movement aiming to win equal rights for women ◇ **feminist** *noun* a supporter of feminism ◇ *adj* relating to feminism: *feminist literature*

▤ women's movement, women's lib(eration), female emancipation, women's rights

femme fatale /fam fəˈtɑːl/ (*plural* **femmes fatales**) an irresistibly attractive woman who brings disaster on men

femoral *adj* relating to the thigh or thigh bone

femur *noun* the thigh bone

fen *noun* low marshy land, often covered with water

fence *noun* **1** a railing, hedge *etc* for closing in animals or land **2** *slang* a receiver of stolen goods ◇ *verb* **1** close in with a fence **2** fight with swords **3** give evasive answers when questioned

> ▤ *noun* **1** barrier, railing, wall, hedge, guard, defence ◇ *verb* **1** surround, encircle, enclose, pen **3** dodge, evade, hedge

fencing *noun* **1** material for fences **2** the sport of fighting with swords, using blunted weapons

fend *verb*: **fend for yourself** look after and provide for yourself

fender *noun* **1** a low guard round a fireplace to keep in coal *etc* **2** an inflated cylinder, bundle of rope *etc* hung over a ship's side as a buffer against the quay **3** *US* the wing of a car

feng shui /ˈfʌŋ ʃweɪ/ situating buildings, furniture *etc* in a way thought to promote well-being

ferment *verb* **1** change by fermentation **2** stir up (trouble *etc*) ◇ *noun* **1** fermentation **2** excitement

> ▤ *verb* **2** rouse, stir up, work up, agitate, incite

> ⚠ Do not confuse with: **foment**

fermentation *noun* **1** a reaction caused by bringing certain substances together, *eg* in making bread or alcoholic drinks **2** great excitement or agitation

fern *noun* a plant with feather-like leaves and no flowers

ferocious *adj* fierce, savage ◇ **ferociously** *adv* ◇ **ferocity** *noun*

▤ vicious, savage, fierce, wild, barbaric,

brutal, inhuman, cruel, violent, ruthless

ferret *noun* a small weasel-like animal used to chase rabbits out of their warrens ◊ *verb* search busily and persistently

ferrule *noun* a metal tip on a walking stick or umbrella

ferry *verb* (**ferries, ferrying, ferried**) **1** carry over water by boat **2** transport by vehicle or aeroplane ◊ *noun* (*plural* **ferries**) **1** a crossing place for boats **2** a boat which carries passengers and cars *etc* across a channel
■ *verb* **1,2** transport, ship, convey, carry, take, run, move

fertile *adj* **1** able to produce children, young, crops or fruit **2** full of ideas, creative, productive ◊ **fertility** *noun*
■ **1** fruitful, fecund, productive, prolific
◄ **1** infertile, barren, sterile, unproductive

fertilize *verb* **1** of a male cell: to fuse with a female cell **2** of a male animal: to impregnate a female **3** of a flowering plant: to transfer pollen **4** make (soil *etc*) fertile ◊ **fertilization** *noun* ◊ **fertilizer** *noun* manure or chemicals used to make soil more fertile
■ **fertilizer** dressing, compost, manure, dung

fervent *adj* very eager; intense ◊ **fervently** *adv*
■ ardent, earnest, eager, enthusiastic, excited, energetic, vigorous, spirited, intense, passionate, heartfelt
◄ cool, indifferent, apathetic

fervour *noun* ardour, zeal

fester *verb* of a wound: produce pus because of infection
■ ulcerate, suppurate, discharge

festival *noun* **1** a traditional celebration; a feast **2** a season of musical, theatrical or other performances

festive *adj* **1** of a festival or feast **2** in a happy, celebrating mood ◊ **festivity** *noun* (*plural* **festivities**) a celebration, a feast
■ **2** celebratory, happy, joyful, merry, cheery, jolly, jovial ◊ **festivity** jubilation, pleasure, entertainment, amusement, merriment, revelry
◄ **2** gloomy, sombre, sober

festoon *verb* decorate with chains of ribbons, flowers *etc*
■ adorn, deck, bedeck, garland, drape, swathe, decorate, garnish

feta *noun* a crumbly white cheese made from ewes' milk

fetch *verb* **1** go and get **2** bring in (a price): *fetched £100 at auction*
■ **1** get, collect, bring, carry, transport, deliver **2** sell for, go for, yield, make, earn

fetching *adj* attractive, charming
■ pretty, sweet, cute, charming, enchanting, fascinating, captivating

fete or **fête** *noun* a public event with stalls, competitions *etc* to raise money ◊ *verb* entertain lavishly, make much of

fetid *adj* having a rotten smell, stinking

fetish (*plural* **fetishes**) **1** a sacred object believed to carry supernatural power **2** an object of excessive fixation or (*esp* sexual) obsession ◊ **fetishist** *noun* ◊ **fetishistic** *adj*

fetlock *noun* the part of a horse's leg just above the foot

fetters *noun plural, formal* chains for imprisonment

fettle *noun*: **in fine fettle** in good health or condition

fettuccine *noun* pasta shaped in flat, wide strips

feu /fju:/ *noun, Scot* a right to use land, a house *etc* indefinitely in return for an annual payment

feud *noun* a private, drawn-out war between families, clans, *etc*
■ vendetta, quarrel, row, argument, disagreement, dispute, animosity, ill will, bitterness, enmity, hostility, antagonism, rivalry

feudal *adj, hist* of a social system under which tenants were bound to give certain services to the overlord in return for their tenancies ◊ **feudalism** *noun* ◊ **feudalist** *adj*

fever *noun* **1** an above-normal body temperature and quickened pulse **2** a state of excitement ◊ **fevered** *adj* **1** having a fever **2** very excited ◊ **feverish** *adj* **1** having a slight fever **2** excited

3 too eager, frantic: *feverish pace*

■ **2** agitation, turmoil, unrest, restlessness, heat, passion ◊ **feverish 1** delirious, hot, burning, flushed **2** impatient, agitated, restless, nervous **3** frenzied, frantic, hectic, hasty

few *adj* (**fewer**, **fewest**) not many: *only a few tickets left* ◊ **a good few** or **quite a few** several, a considerable number

fey *adj* **1** eccentric, whimsical **2** clairvoyant

fez *noun* (*plural* **fezzes**) a brimless flowerpot-shaped hat, usually with a top tassel

fiancé /fɪˈɑ̃seɪ/ *noun* the man a woman is engaged to marry

fiancée /fɪˈɑ̃seɪ/ *noun* the woman a man is engaged to marry

fiasco *noun* (*plural* **fiascos**) a complete failure

> Based on an Italian phrase *far fiasco* 'make a bottle', meaning forget your lines on stage

fib *verb* (**fibs**, **fibbing**, **fibbed**) lie about something unimportant ◊ *noun* an unimportant lie

fibre *noun* **1** a thread or string **2** the essence or material of something: *the fibre of her being* **3** roughage in foods ◊ **fibrous** *adj* thread-like, stringy

fibreglass *noun* a lightweight material made of very fine threads of glass, used for building boats *etc*

fibre-optic *adj* of a cable: made of glass or plastic filaments which transmit light signals

fibula *noun* (*plural* **fibulae** or **fibulas**) the thinner, outer bone in the lower leg (*compare with*: **tibia**)

fickle *adj* changeable; not stable or loyal

■ inconstant, unreliable, unpredictable, changeable, disloyal, unfaithful

🔄 constant, steady, stable

fiction *noun* **1** stories about imaginary characters and events **2** a lie

■ **1** fantasy, fancy, imagination, invention, fabrication

🔄 **1** non-fiction, fact **2** truth

fictional *adj* imagined, created for a story: *a fictional character*

■ literary, invented, made-up, imaginary, make-believe, legendary, mythical, non-existent, unreal

🔄 factual, real

> ⚠ Do not confuse: **fictional** and **fictitious**

fictitious *adj* **1** not real, imaginary **2** untrue

■ **1** fabricated, imaginary, non-existent, unreal **2** false, untrue, invented, made-up, fabricated

🔄 **2** true, genuine

fiddle *noun*, *informal* **1** a violin **2** a cheat, a swindle **3** a tricky or delicate operation ◊ *verb* **1** play the violin **2** play aimlessly (with) **3** interfere, tamper (with) **4** *informal* falsify (accounts *etc*) with the intention of cheating ◊ **fiddly** *adj* needing delicate or careful handling

fidelity *noun* **1** faithfulness **2** truth, accuracy

■ **1** faithfulness, loyalty, allegiance, constancy **2** accuracy, exactness

fidget *verb* move about restlessly ◊ **fidgety** *adj*

■ squirm, wriggle, shuffle, twitch, jerk, fret, fuss, fiddle ◊ **fidgety** restless, impatient, uneasy, nervous, agitated, jittery, jumpy, twitchy, on edge

field *noun* **1** a piece of enclosed ground for pasture, crops, sports *etc* **2** an area of land containing a natural resource: *goldfield/coalfield* **3** a branch of interest or knowledge **4** those taking part in a race ◊ *verb*, *cricket* catch or retrieve the ball and return it

■ *noun* **3** area, domain, sphere, department, discipline, speciality, line, forte **4** participants, entrants, contestants, competitors, contenders, runners

field-day *noun* a day of unusual activity or success

fieldglasses *noun plural* binoculars

field-marshal *noun* the highest ranking army officer

fiend *noun* **1** an evil spirit **2** a wicked person **3** an extreme enthusiast: *a crossword fiend* ◇ **fiendish** *adj*

▣ **fiendish** devilish, diabolical, infernal, wicked, malevolent, cunning, cruel, inhuman, savage, monstrous

fierce *adj* **1** very angry-looking, hostile, likely to attack **2** intense, strong: *fierce competition* ◇ **fiercely** *adv* ◇ **fierceness** *noun*

▣ **1** ferocious, vicious, savage, cruel, brutal, aggressive, dangerous, murderous, frightening, menacing **2** passionate, intense, strong, powerful

▣ **1** gentle, kind, calm

fiery *adj* **1** like fire **2** quick-tempered, volatile

▣ **1** burning, flaming, aflame, blazing, ablaze, red-hot, glowing, aglow **2** passionate, impatient, excitable, impulsive, hot-headed, fierce, violent, heated

fiesta *noun* a festival, a carnival

FIFA /fiːfə/ *abbrev* (in French) *Fédération Internationale de Football Association*, *ie* the International Football Federation

fife *noun* a small flute

fifteen *noun* the number 15 ◇ *adj* 15 in number

fifteenth *adj* the last of a series of fifteen ◇ *noun* one of fifteen equal parts

fifth *adj* the last of a series of five ◇ *noun* one of five equal parts

fiftieth *adj* the last of a series of fifty ◇ *noun* one of fifty equal parts

fifty *noun* the number 50 ◇ *adj* 50 in number

fig *noun* **1** a soft roundish fruit with thin, dark skin and red pulp containing many seeds **2** the tree which bears it

fight *verb* (**fights**, **fighting**, **fought**) **1** struggle with fists, weapons *etc* **2** quarrel **3** go to war with ◇ *noun* a struggle; a battle ◇ **fighter** *noun* **1** someone who fights **2** a fast military aircraft armed with guns

▣ *verb* **1** wrestle, box, joust, scrap, scuffle, tussle, battle, clash **2** argue, dispute, squabble, bicker

figment *noun* something imagined or invented: *it's just a figment of her imagination*

figurative *adj* of a word: used not in its literal meaning but to show likeness, *eg* 'tiger' for 'ferocious person' ◇ **figuratively** *adv*

▣ metaphorical, symbolic, representative, allegorical, pictorial

figure *noun* **1** outward form or shape **2** a number **3** a geometrical shape **4** an unidentified person: *a shadowy figure approached* **5** a diagram or drawing on a page **6** a set of movements in skating *etc* ◇ *verb* appear, take part: *he figures in the story* ◇ **figured** *adj* marked with a design: *figured silk* ◇ **figurehead** *noun* a leader who has little real power ◇ **figure out** work out, understand

▣ *noun* **1** shape, form, outline, silhouette, body **2** numeral, digit, integer **5** illustration, picture, drawing, sketch, diagram, image, symbol

filament *noun* a slender thread, *eg* of wire in a light bulb

filch *verb*, *informal* steal

file¹ *noun* **1** a folder, loose-leaf book *etc* to hold papers **2** an amount of computer data held under a single name **3** a line of soldiers *etc* walking one behind another ◇ *verb* **1** put (papers *etc*) in a file **2** walk in a file

▣ *noun* **1** folder, dossier, portfolio, binder **3** line, queue, column, row, procession, cortège ◇ *verb* **1** record, register, store, classify, categorize, catalogue

file² *noun* a steel tool with a roughened surface for smoothing wood, metal *etc* ◇ *verb* rub with a file

filial *adj* of or characteristic of a son or daughter

filibeg *noun* a kilt

filibuster *noun* a long speech given in parliament to delay the passing of a law

filigree *noun* very fine gold or silver work in lace or metal

fill *verb* **1** make full: *fill the bucket with water* **2** become full: *her eyes filled with tears* **3** satisfy, fulfil (a requirement *etc*)

4 occupy: *fill a post* **5** appoint someone to (a job *etc*): *have you filled the vacancy?* **6** put something in a hole to stop it up ◇ *noun* as much as is needed to fill: *we ate our fill* ◇ **fill in 1** fill (a hole) **2** complete (a form *etc*) **3** do another person's job while they are absent: *I'm filling in for Anne* ◇ **fill up** fill completely

■ *verb* **1** replenish, stock, supply, pack **6** block, clog, plug, bung, cork, stop, close, seal

filler *noun* **1** a funnel for pouring liquids through **2** a substance added to increase bulk **3** a material used to fill up holes in wood, plaster *etc*

fillet *noun* a piece of meat or fish with bones removed ◇ *verb* (**fillets, filleting, filleted**) remove the bones from

filling *noun* **1** something used to fill a hole or gap, *esp* in a tooth **2** the contents of a pie, sandwich *etc* ◇ *adj* of food: satisfying

filling-station *noun* a garage which sells petrol

filly *noun* (*plural* **fillies**) a young female horse

film *noun* **1** a thin skin or coating **2** a chemically coated strip of celluloid on which photographs are taken **3** a narrative made up of a series of photographed images and shown in a cinema, on television *etc* ◇ *verb* **1** make a film of **2** develop a thin coating: *his eyes filmed over*

■ *noun* **1** covering, dusting, coat, skin, membrane, veil, screen **3** motion picture, picture, *informal* movie, video, feature film

filo /fi:lou/ *noun* Middle Eastern pastry in the form of paper-thin sheets

Filofax *noun*, *trademark* a personal organizer

filter *noun* **1** a device for removing solid material or impurities, *eg* from water or air **2** a green arrow on a traffic light signalling one lane of traffic to move **3** a transparent tinted disc used to change the colour of light ◇ *verb* (**filters, filtering, filtered**) **1** strain through a filter **2** move or arrive gradually: *the news filtered through* **3** of cars

etc: gradually join a stream of traffic

■ *noun* **1** strainer, sieve, sifter, colander, mesh, gauze, membrane ◇ *verb* **1** strain, sieve, sift, screen, purify, clarify, percolate

filth *noun* dirt

■ grime, muck, dung, sewage, refuse, rubbish

🠪 cleanness, cleanliness, purity

filthy *adj* **1** very dirty **2** obscene, lewd ◇ **filthily** *adv* ◇ **filthiness** *noun*

■ **1** soiled, unwashed, grimy, grubby, mucky, muddy **2** pornographic, smutty, suggestive, indecent, coarse

fin *noun* a flexible projecting part of a fish's body used for balance and swimming

final *adj* **1** last **2** allowing no argument: *the judge's decision is final* ◇ *noun* the last contest in a competition: *World Cup final* ◇ **finality** *noun* the quality of being final and decisive ◇ **finally** *adv*

■ **1** latest, closing, concluding, finishing, end, ultimate **2** conclusive, definitive, decisive, definite

finale /fɪ'nɑːlɪ/ *noun* the last part of anything (*eg* a concert)

■ climax, dénouement, culmination, end, conclusion, close

finalize *verb* put (*eg* plans) in a final or finished form

■ conclude, finish, complete, round off, resolve, settle, *informal* wrap up

finance *noun* **1** money affairs **2** the study or management of these **3** (**finances**) the money someone has to spend ◇ *verb* supply with sums of money ◇ **financial** *adj* ◇ **financially** *adv* ◇ **financier** *noun* someone who manages (public) money

■ *noun* **3** income, revenue, resources, assets, capital, wealth, money, cash, funds ◇ *verb* pay for, fund, sponsor, back, support, underwrite, guarantee, subsidize

finch *noun* (*plural* **finches**) a small bird

find *verb* (**finds, finding, found**) **1** come upon accidentally: *I found an earring in the street* **2** discover after searching **3** judge to be: *finds it hard to* *live on her pension* ◇ *noun* something found, *esp* something of interest or value ◇ **find out** discover, detect

■ *verb* **1** come across, chance on, stumble on **2** locate, track down, trace, retrieve, recover, unearth, expose, reveal **3** consider, think, judge

fine¹ *adj* **1** made up of very small pieces, drops *etc* **2** not coarse: *fine linen* **3** thin, delicate **4** slight: *a fine distinction* **5** beautiful, handsome **6** of good quality; pure **7** satisfactory **8** bright, not rainy **9** well, healthy ◇ **fine arts** painting, sculpture, *etc*

■ **3** thin, slender, sheer, flimsy, fragile, delicate, dainty **5** exquisite, splendid, magnificent, attractive, elegant **6** excellent, outstanding, exceptional, superior **7** acceptable, all right, *informal* OK

fine² *noun* money to be paid as a punishment ◇ *verb* compel to pay (money) as punishment

■ *noun* penalty, damages

finery *noun* splendid clothes *etc*

finesse /fɪˈnɛs/ *noun* cleverness and subtlety in handling situations *etc*

finger *noun* one of the five branching parts of the hand ◇ *verb* touch with the fingers

■ *verb* touch, handle, manipulate, feel, stroke, caress, fondle, fiddle with, toy with

fingering *noun* **1** the positioning of the fingers in playing a musical instrument **2** the showing of this by numbers

fingerprint *noun* the mark made by the tip of a finger, used by the police as a means of identification

finish *verb* **1** end **2** complete the making of **3** stop: *when do you finish work today?* ◇ *noun* **1** the end (*eg* of a race) **2** the last coating of paint, polish *etc* ◇ **finished** *adj* **1** ended, complete **2** of a person: ruined, not likely to achieve further success *etc*

■ *verb* **1** conclude, close, wind up, settle, round off, culminate **2** complete, perfect **3** terminate, stop, cease ◇ *noun* **2** surface, appearance, texture, grain, polish, shine, gloss, lustre, smoothness

finite *adj* having an end or limit

fiord or **fjord** *noun* a long narrow inlet between steep hills, *esp* in Norway

fir *noun* a kind of cone-bearing tree ◇ **fir-cone** *noun*

fire *noun* **1** the heat and light given off by something burning **2** a mass of burning material, objects *etc* **3** a heating device: *electric fire* **4** eagerness, keenness ◇ *verb* (**fires**, **firing**, **fired**) **1** set on fire **2** make eager: *fired by his enthusiasm* **3** dismiss (someone) from a job **4** make (a gun) explode, shoot ◇ **fire alarm** a device to sound a bell *etc* as a warning of fire ◇ **fire brigade** a company of firefighters ◇ **fire engine** a vehicle carrying firefighters and their equipment ◇ **fire escape** a means of escape from a building in case of fire

■ *noun* **1** flames **2** blaze, bonfire, conflagration, inferno, burning **4** passion, feeling, excitement, enthusiasm, spirit, intensity, radiance ◇ *verb* **2** excite, enliven, stir, stimulate, inspire **3** dismiss, discharge, *informal* sack

firearm *noun* a gun

firedamp *noun* a dangerous gas found in coal mines

firefighter *noun* a person whose job is to put out fires

firefly *noun* (*plural* **fireflies**) a type of insect which glows in the dark

fireguard *noun* a metal framework placed in front of a fireplace for safety

fireman, firewoman *noun* a firefighter

fireplace *noun* a recess in a room below a chimney for a fire

firewall *noun*, *comput* software that protects a network from unauthorized users

firewood *noun* wood for burning on a fire

fireworks *noun plural* **1** colourful explosive devices set off at night for show **2** *informal* angry behaviour

firkin *noun*, *old* a small barrel

firm *adj* **1** not easily moved or shaken **2** hard or compact **3** with mind made up ◇ *noun* a business company

■ *adj* **1** fixed, embedded, fast, tight, secure, anchored **2** dense, compressed, set, solid **3** adamant, resolute, determined, constant, steadfast, staunch ◇ *noun* corporation, business, enterprise, establishment, partnership

firmament *noun, formal* the heavens, the sky

first *adj & adv* before all others in place, time or rank ◇ **first-aid** *noun* treatment of a wounded or sick person before the doctor's arrival ◇ **first-born** *noun* the eldest child ◇ **first-class** *adj* of the highest standard, best kind *etc* ◇ **first-hand** *adj* direct ◇ **fist minister** the head of government in some countries ◇ **first name** a person's name that is not their surname ◇ **first-rate** *adj* first-class

■ *adj* initial, opening, introductory, basic, original, earliest, earlier, chief, main, key, head, principal ◇ *adv* initially, to begin with, to start with ◇ **first-class** first-rate, A1, second-to-none, top, leading, *informal* top-notch, outstanding ◇ **first name** forename, Christian name, given name

☲ **first-class** inferior

firth *noun* a narrow arm of the sea, *esp* at a river mouth

fiscal *adj* **1** of the public revenue **2** of financial matters

fish *noun* (*plural* **fish** or **fishes**) a kind of animal that lives in water, and breathes through gills ◇ *verb* **1** try to catch fish with rod, nets *etc* **2** search (for): *fishing for a handkerchief in her bag* **3** try to obtain: *fish for compliments*

Types of fish include:
bloater, brisling, cod, coley, Dover sole, flounder, haddock, hake, halibut, herring, hoki, kipper, ling, mackerel, pilchard, plaice, rainbow trout, salmon, sardine, sole, sprat, trout, tuna, turbot, whitebait; bass, Bombay duck, bream, brill, carp, catfish, chub, conger eel, cuttlefish, dab, dace, dogfish, dory, eel, goldfish, guppy, marlin, minnow, monkfish, mullet, octopus, perch, pike, piranha, pollock, ray, roach, roughy, shark, skate, snapper, squid, stickleback, stingray, sturgeon, swordfish, tench, whiting; clam, cockle, crab, crayfish, *US* crawfish, king prawn, lobster, mussel, oyster, prawn, scallop, shrimp, whelk

fisherman *noun* a man who fishes, *esp* for a living

fishmonger *noun* someone who sells fish for food

fishy *adj* **1** like a fish **2** doubtful, arousing suspicion

fission *noun* splitting

fissure *noun* a crack

fist *noun* a tightly shut hand ◇ **fisticuffs** *noun plural, old* a fight with the fists

fit *adj* **1** suited to a purpose; proper **2** in good training or health ◇ *noun* a sudden attack or spasm of laughter, illness *etc* ◇ *verb* (**fits**, **fitting**, **fitted**) **1** be of the right size or shape **2** be suitable ◇ **fitful** *adj* coming or doing something in bursts or spasms ◇ **fitfully** *adv* ◇ **fitness** *noun* ◇ **fitting** *adj* suitable ◇ *noun* something fixed or fitted in a room, house *etc*: *a light fitting* ◇ **fittingly** *adv* ◇ **fittings** *noun plural* fitted furniture or equipment

■ *adj* **1** suitable, appropriate, apt, fitting, right, proper, able, capable, competent, qualified **2** healthy, well, able-bodied, in good shape ◇ **fitting** *adj* apt, appropriate, suitable, deserved

☲ *adj* **1** unsuitable, unworthy **2** unfit

five *noun* the number 5 ◇ *adj* 5 in number

fives *noun sing* a handball game played in a walled court

fix *verb* **1** make firm; fasten **2** mend, repair ◇ *noun* a difficult situation ◇ **fixed** *adj* settled; set in position ◇ **fixedly** *adv* steadily, intently: *staring fixedly*

■ *verb* **1** fasten, secure, tie, bind, attach, stick, glue, cement **2** repair, mend, correct, adjust, restore ◇ *noun* dilemma, quandary, predicament, plight, corner, *informal* spot

fixture *noun* **1** a piece of furniture *etc*

fixed in position **2** an arranged sports match or race

fizz verb make bubbles or a hissing sound ◇ noun **1** a hissing sound **2** bubbles in a drink ◇ **fizzy** adj of a drink: forming bubbles which burst on the surface

■ verb effervesce, sparkle, bubble, froth, fizzle, hiss, sizzle ◇ **fizzy** carbonated, gassy, sparkling, effervescent

fizzle or **fizzle out** verb fail, come to nothing

fjord another spelling of **fiord**

flabbergasted adj informal very surprised

■ amazed, astonished, astounded, staggered, dumbfounded, speechless, stunned, dazed, overwhelmed

flabby adj **1** not firm, soft, limp **2** weak, feeble ◇ **flabbily** adv ◇ **flabbiness** noun

■ **1** fleshy, soft, yielding, flaccid, limp, floppy, drooping, sagging, slack, loose, lax **2** weak, feeble

flaccid /'flasɪd/ adj **1** hanging loosely **2** limp, not firm

flag noun **1** a piece of coloured cloth used to represent a country, in signalling etc **2** a flat paving-stone ◇ verb (**flags**, **flagging**, **flagged**) become tired or weak

■ verb decline, abate, subside, sink, slump, peter out, fade, fail, weaken, slow, falter, tire, weary, wilt, droop, sag

flagellate verb, formal whip, lash ◇ **flagellation** noun whipping

flageolet noun a variety of kidney bean

flagon noun a large container for liquid

flagrant adj **1** conspicuous **2** openly wicked ◇ **flagrancy** noun ◇ **flagrantly** adv

flail verb wave or swing in the air ◇ noun, old a tool for threshing corn

flair noun talent, skill: a flair for languages

■ skill, ability, aptitude, gift, talent, knack, genius, feel, acumen

◼ inability, ineptitude

flak noun **1** anti-aircraft fire **2** strong criticism

flake noun **1** a thin slice or chip of anything **2** a very small piece of snow etc ◇ verb form into flakes ◇ **flaky** adj **1** forming flakes, crumbly: flaky pastry **2** US informal eccentric ◇ **flake off** break off in flakes

flambé /'flɒmbeɪ/ adj, cookery cooked or served in flaming alcohol

flamboyant adj **1** splendidly coloured **2** too showy

■ **1** colourful, brilliant, rich, elaborate **2** ostentatious, gaudy, flashy, dazzling

◼ **2** modest, restrained

flame noun the bright leaping light of a fire ◇ verb **1** burn brightly **2** comput slang send abusive email (to) ◇ **flaming** adj **1** burning **2** red **3** violent: a flaming temper

flamingo noun (plural **flamingoes**) a type of long-legged bird with bright pink plumage

flammable adj easily set on fire

■ inflammable, combustible

◼ non-flammable, incombustible, flameproof, fire-resistant

flan noun a flat, open tart

flange noun a raised edge on the rim of a wheel

flank noun the side of an animal's body, of an army etc ◇ verb go or be at the side of

flannel noun **1** loosely woven woollen fabric **2** a small towel for washing the face

flannelette noun cotton fabric imitating flannel

flannels noun plural trousers made of flannel or similar material

flap noun **1** anything broad, flat and loose-hanging: tent flap **2** the sound of a wing etc moving up and down through air **3** a panic: getting into a flap over nothing ◇ verb (**flaps**, **flapping**, **flapped**) **1** hang down loosely **2** move up and down through air **3** get into a panic

■ noun **3** informal state, fluster, agitation, flutter, dither, informal tizzy

flapjack noun **1** Brit a biscuit made

with rolled oats, butter and sugar **2** US a pancake

flare verb (**flares, flaring, flared**) blaze up ◇ noun a bright light, esp one used at sea as a distress signal ◇ **flare up** erupt

▣ verb flame, burn, blaze, glare, flash, flicker, burst, explode, erupt

flash noun (plural **flashes**) **1** a quick burst of light **2** a moment, an instant **3** a distinctive mark on a uniform etc ◇ verb **1** shine out suddenly **2** pass quickly ◇ **flashy** adj showy, gaudy ◇ **flashlight** noun **1** a burst of light in which a photograph is taken **2** US an electric torch ◇ **in a flash** very quickly or suddenly

▣ noun **1** beam, ray, spark, blaze, flare, sparkle ◇ verb **1** beam, shine, light up, flare, blaze, glare **2** streak, fly, dart, race, dash ◇ **flashy** showy, flamboyant, glamorous, garish, gaudy, jazzy, flash

▣ **flashy** plain, tasteful

flask noun **1** a narrow-necked bottle **2** a small flat bottle **3** an insulated bottle or vacuum flask

flat adj **1** level: a flat surface **2** of a drink: no longer fizzy **3** leaving no doubt, downright: a flat denial **4** below the right musical pitch **5** of a tyre: punctured **6** of a battery: with no electrical charge left **7** dull, uninteresting ◇ adv stretched out: lying flat on her back ◇ noun **1** an apartment on one storey of a building **2** music a sign (♭) which lowers a note by a semitone **3** a punctured tyre ◇ **flatly** adv ◇ **flatness** noun ◇ **flatfish** noun a sea fish with a flat body, eg a sole ◇ **flat race** a race over level ground without hurdles ◇ **flat rate** a rate which is the same in all cases ◇ **flat out** as fast as possible, with as much effort as possible

▣ adj **1** level, plane, even, smooth, horizontal **3** absolute, total, unequivocal, categorical, positive, direct, straight **7** dull, boring, monotonous, tedious, uninteresting, unexciting

flatten verb make or become flat

flatter verb praise insincerely ◇ **flattery** noun

▣ compliment, informal sweet-talk, fawn, informal butter up, play up to, court, curry favour with

flatulence noun wind in the stomach ◇ **flatulent** adj

flaunt verb display in an obvious way: flaunted his wealth

| ⚠ Do not confuse with: **flout** |

flautist or (esp US) **flutist** a flute player

flavour noun **1** taste: lemon flavour **2** quality or atmosphere: an exotic flavour ◇ verb give a taste to ◇ **flavouring** noun an ingredient used to give a particular taste: chocolate flavouring

▣ noun **1** taste, tang, smack, savour **2** quality, property, character, style, aspect, feel, atmosphere

flaw noun a fault, an imperfection ◇ **flawless** adj with no faults or blemishes ◇ **flawlessly** adv

▣ defect, imperfection, fault, blemish, spot, mark, break, fracture, weakness, slip, error, mistake ◇ **flawless** perfect, faultless, unblemished, spotless, immaculate, sound, intact, undamaged

▣ **flawless** flawed, imperfect

flax noun a plant whose fibres are woven into linen cloth ◇ **flaxen** adj **1** made of or looking like flax **2** of hair: fair

flay verb strip the skin off

flea noun a small, wingless, bloodsucking insect with great jumping power

fleck noun a spot, a speck ◇ **flecked** adj marked with spots or patches

fled past form of flee

fledgling noun a young bird with fully-grown feathers

flee verb (**flees, fleeing, fled**) run away from danger etc

▣ run away, bolt, take flight, take off, make off, escape, get away, leave

fleece noun **1** a sheep's coat of wool **2** a warm jacket made of soft fabric ◇ verb **1** clip wool from **2** informal rob by cheating ◇ **fleecy** adj soft and fluffy like wool

fleet *noun* **1** a number of ships **2** a number of cars or taxis ◇ *adj* swift; nimble, quick in movement ◇ **fleeting** *adj* passing quickly: *a fleeting glimpse* ◇ **fleetness** *noun* swiftness

■ **fleeting** short, brief, short-lived, momentary, ephemeral, transient, passing

▣ **fleeting** lasting, permanent

flesh *noun* **1** the soft tissue which covers the bones of humans and animals **2** meat **3** the body **4** the soft eatable part of fruit ◇ **fleshy** *adj* fat, plump ◇ **flesh and blood 1** relations, family **2** human, mortal

flew *past form* of **fly**

flex [1] *verb* bend

flex [2] *noun* a length of covered wire attached to electrical devices

flexible *adj* **1** easily bent **2** willing to adapt to new or different conditions ◇ **flexibility** *noun* ◇ **flexibly** *adv*

■ **1** bendable, *informal* bendy, pliable, malleable, elastic, stretchy, springy, supple, lithe, double-jointed **2** adaptable, adjustable, amenable, accommodating, variable, open

▣ **1** inflexible, rigid

flexitime *noun* a system in which an agreed number of hours' work is done at times chosen by the worker

flick *verb* **1** strike lightly with a quick movement **2** remove (dust *etc*) with a movement of this kind ◇ *noun* a quick, sharp movement: *a flick of the wrist* ◇ **flick-knife** *noun* a knife with a blade which springs out at the press of a button

flicker *verb* **1** flutter **2** burn or shine unsteadily ◇ *noun* **1** a brief or unsteady light **2** a fleeting appearance or occurrence: *a flicker of hope*

■ *verb* **1** flutter, vibrate, quiver, waver **2** blink, wink, twinkle, sparkle, glimmer ◇ *noun* **2** trace, drop, iota, atom, indication

flight *noun* **1** the act of flying **2** a journey by plane **3** the act of fleeing or escaping **4** a flock (of birds) **5** a number (of steps) ◇ **flighty** *adj* changeable, impulsive

■ **3** fleeing, escape, getaway, breakaway, exit, departure, exodus, retreat

flimsy *adj* **1** thin; easily torn or broken *etc* **2** weak: *a flimsy excuse*

■ **1** thin, fine, light, slight, insubstantial, fragile, delicate, shaky, weak **2** feeble, inadequate, shallow, poor, unconvincing, implausible

flinch *verb* move or shrink back in fear, pain *etc*

■ wince, cringe, cower, tremble, shake, quake, shudder, shiver, recoil, draw back, balk, shy away, duck, withdraw, retreat, flee

fling *verb* (**flings**, **flinging**, **flung**) throw ◇ *noun* **1** a throw **2** a period of time devoted to pleasure **3** a brief romantic affair

■ *verb* throw, hurl, pitch, lob, toss, *informal* chuck, cast, sling, launch, send, let fly

flint *noun* a kind of hard stone ◇ *adj* made of flint ◇ **flintlock** *noun* a gun fired by sparks from a flint

flip *verb* (**flips**, **flipping**, **flipped**) toss lightly ◇ *noun* a light toss or stroke ◇ **flip side 1** the reverse side of a record *etc* **2** the converse of anything

flippant *adj* joking, not serious enough ◇ **flippancy** *noun* ◇ **flippantly** *adv*

■ facetious, light-hearted, frivolous, offhand, cheeky *informal* , impudent, impertinent, rude, disrespectful, irreverent

▣ serious, respectful

flipper *noun* **1** a limb of a seal, walrus *etc* **2** a webbed rubber shoe worn by divers

flirt *verb* play at courtship without any serious intentions ◇ *noun* someone who flirts ◇ **flirtation** *noun* ◇ **flirtatious** *adj* fond of flirting

■ chat up, make up to, lead on, philander, dally

flit *verb* (**flits**, **flitting**, **flitted**) move quickly and lightly from place to place

float *verb* **1** (cause to) stay on the surface of a liquid without sinking **2** set going: *float a company* ◇ *noun* **1** a cork *etc* on a fishing line **2** something which keeps a person or thing afloat **3** a van delivering milk *etc* **4** a platform on wheels, used in processions **5** a sum of money set aside for giving change

■ *verb* **1** sail, swim, bob, drift **2** launch, initiate, set up

flock [1] *noun* **1** a group of animals or birds **2** a large number of people **3** the congregation of a church ◇ *verb* (with **together**) gather or move in a crowd

■ *verb* crowd, throng, gather, collect, congregate

flock [2] *noun* **1** particles of wool or other fibre on the surface of wallpaper *etc* **2** wool or cotton waste

floe *noun* a sheet of floating ice

flog *verb* (**flogs, flogging, flogged**) **1** beat, lash **2** *slang* sell ◇ **flogging** *noun*

■ **1** beat, whip, lash, scourge, cane, thrash, *informal* whack, chastise, punish

flood *noun* **1** a great flow, *esp* of water **2** the rise or flow of the tide **3** a great quantity: *a flood of letters* ◇ *verb* **1** (cause to) overflow **2** cover or fill with water

■ *noun* **1** deluge, downpour, torrent, flow, tide, stream, rush **3** excess, rush, spate, abundance, profusion

floodlight *verb* (**floodlights, floodlighting, floodlit**) illuminate with floodlighting ◇ *noun* a light used in floodlighting ◇ **floodlighting** *noun* strong artificial lighting used to illuminate an exterior or stage

floor *noun* **1** the base level of a room on which people walk **2** a storey of a building: *a third-floor flat* ◇ *verb* **1** make a floor **2** *informal* knock flat **3** *informal* puzzle: *floored by the question*

■ *verb* **3** *informal* stump, frustrate, confound, perplex, baffle, puzzle, bewilder, disconcert, throw

flop *verb* (**flops, flopping, flopped**) **1** sway or swing about loosely **2** fall or sit down suddenly and heavily **3** move about clumsily **4** fail badly ◇ *noun* **1** an act of flopping **2** a complete failure ◇ **floppy** *adj* flopping, soft and flexible ◇ **floppy disk** a flexible computer disk, often in a harder case, used to store data

■ *verb* **1** droop, hang, dangle, sag **2** drop, fall, slump, collapse **4** fail, fall flat, founder, fold ◇ *noun* **2** failure, non-starter, fiasco, debacle, *informal* wash-out, disaster ◇ **floppy** droopy, hanging, dangling, sagging, limp, loose, baggy, soft, flabby

flora *noun* the plants of a district or country as a whole

floral *adj* (made) of flowers

florid *adj* **1** with a flushed or ruddy complexion **2** too ornate

■ **2** flowery, ornate, elaborate, fussy, flamboyant, *informal* OTT

florist *noun* a seller or grower of flowers ◇ **floristry** *noun*

floss *noun* **1** fine silk thread **2** thin, often waxed thread for passing between the teeth to clean them ◇ *verb* clean (teeth) with floss

flotilla *noun* a fleet of small ships

flotsam *noun* floating objects washed from a ship or wreck

flounce [1] *verb* walk away suddenly and impatiently, *eg* in anger

flounce [2] *noun* a gathered decorative strip sewn onto the hem of a dress

flounder [1] *verb* **1** struggle to move your legs and arms in water, mud *etc* **2** have difficulty speaking or thinking clearly, or in acting efficiently

■ **1** wallow, struggle **2** struggle, grope, fumble, blunder, stagger, stumble, falter, dither

> **!** Do not confuse with: **founder**

flounder [2] *noun* a small flatfish

flour *noun* **1** finely ground wheat **2** any grain crushed to powder: *rice flour*

flourish *verb* **1** be successful, *esp* financially **2** grow well, thrive **3** be healthy **4** wave or brandish as a show or threat ◇ *noun* (*plural* **flourishes**) **1** a fancy stroke in writing **2** a sweeping movement with the hand, sword *etc* **3** showy splendour **4** an ornamental passage in music

■ *verb* **1** prosper, succeed, get on, do well **2** grow, increase, flower, blossom, bloom, develop, progress, get on, do well **4** shake, swing, display, wield, flaunt, parade

■ *verb* **1** fail **2** decline, languish

floury *adj* **1** covered with flour **2** powdery

> ⚠ Do not confuse with: **flowery**

flout *verb* treat with contempt, defy openly: *flouted the speed limit*

■ defy, disobey, break, disregard, reject

> ⚠ Do not confuse with: **flaunt**

flow *verb* **1** of liquid: run **2** move or come out smoothly or in an unbroken run **3** of the tide: rise ◇ *noun* the action of flowing; a smooth or unbroken run: *flow of ideas*

■ **1** circulate, ooze, trickle, ripple, gush, spill, run, pour, cascade, rush, stream ◇ *noun* course, tide, current, drift, outpouring, stream, cascade, spurt, gush, flood, spate

flower *noun* **1** the showy, colourful part of a plant from which fruit or seeds develop **2** the best of anything ◇ *verb* **1** of plants *etc*: produce a flower **2** be at your best, flourish ◇ **flowering** *noun*

> *Flowers include*:
> African violet, alyssum, anemone, aster, aubrietia, azalea, begonia, bluebell, busy lizzie (impatiens), calendula, candytuft, carnation, chrysanthemum, cornflower, cowslip, crocus, cyclamen, daffodil, dahlia, daisy, delphinium, forget-me-not, foxglove (digitalis), freesia, fuchsia, gardenia, geranium, gladioli, hollyhock, hyacinth, iris (flag), lily, lily-of-the-valley, lobelia, lupin, marigold, narcissus, nasturtium, nemesia, nicotiana, night-scented stock, orchid, pansy, petunia, pink (dianthus), phlox, poinsettia, polyanthus, poppy, primrose, primula, rose, salvia, snapdragon (antirrhinum), snowdrop, stock, sunflower, sweet pea, sweet william, tulip, verbena, viola, violet, wallflower, zinnia
> see also **plant**; **shrub**

flowery *adj* **1** full of or decorated with flowers **2** using fine-sounding, fancy language: *flowery prose style*

■ **2** florid, ornate, elaborate, fancy, baroque, rhetorical

■ **2** plain, simple

> ⚠ Do not confuse with: **floury**

flown *past participle* of **fly**

flu *noun, informal* influenza

fluctuate *verb* be always changing; vary ◇ **fluctuation** *noun*

■ vary, change, alter, shift, rise and fall, seesaw, swing, sway, oscillate, vacillate, waver

flue *noun* a passage for air and smoke in a stove or chimney

fluent *adj* finding words easily in speaking or writing without any awkward pauses ◇ **fluency** *noun* ◇ **fluently** *adv*

■ flowing, smooth, easy, effortless, articulate, eloquent, voluble

■ broken, inarticulate, tongue-tied

fluff *noun* soft, downy material ◇ *verb, slang* bungle ◇ **fluffy** *adj*

fluid *noun* a substance whose particles can move about freely, a liquid or gas ◇ *adj* **1** flowing **2** not settled or fixed: *my plans for the weekend are fluid*

■ *adj* **1** liquid, liquefied, aqueous, watery, running, runny, melted, molten **2** variable, changeable, adaptable, flexible, open

fluke¹ *noun* a small parasitic worm

fluke² *noun* the part of an anchor which holds fast to the bottom

fluke³ *noun* an accidental or unplanned success

flume *noun* a water chute

flummox *verb* bewilder, confuse totally

flung *past form* of **fling**

flunk *verb, slang* fail (an exam *etc*)

fluoride *noun* a chemical added to water or toothpaste to prevent tooth decay ◇ **fluoridize** or **fluoridate** *verb* add fluoride to

flurry *noun* (*plural* **flurries**) a sudden

rush of wind *etc* ◇ *verb* (**flurries, flur-rying, flurried**) excite or agitate

◨ *noun* burst, outbreak, spell, spurt, gust, blast

flush[1] *noun* (*plural* **flushes**) **1** a reddening of the face **2** freshness, glow ◇ *verb* **1** become red in the face **2** clean (*esp* a toilet) by a rush of water

◨ *verb* **1** blush, go red, redden, colour, burn, glow **2** cleanse, wash, rinse, hose, clear, empty

flush[2] *adj* **1** (with **with**) having the surface level with another **2** *informal* well supplied with money

◨ *adj* **1** even, smooth, flat, plane **2** rich, wealthy, prosperous, well-off, well-heeled

fluster *noun* excitement or agitation caused by hurry ◇ *verb* harass, confuse

◨ *verb* bother, upset, embarrass, disturb, perturb, agitate, ruffle, confuse, confound, unnerve, disconcert, *informal* rattle, put off, distract

flute *noun* **1** a high-pitched musical wind instrument **2** a tall narrow wine glass ◇ **fluted** *adj* decorated with grooves

flutter *verb* move (eyelids, wings, *etc*) back and forth quickly ◇ *noun* **1** a quick beating of pulse *etc* **2** nervous excitement: *in a flutter*

◨ *verb* flap, wave, beat, bat, flicker

flux *noun* an ever-changing flow: *in a state of flux*

◨ fluctuation, fluidity, transition

fly[1] *noun* (*plural* **flies**) **1** a small winged insect **2** a fish-hook made to look like a fly to catch fish

fly[2] *noun* (*plural* **flies**) a flap of material with buttons or a zip *esp* at the front of trousers ◇ *verb* (**flies, flying, flew, flown**) **1** move through the air on wings or in an aeroplane **2** move quickly ◇ **flying saucer** a disc-shaped object believed to be an alien spacecraft ◇ **flying squad** a group of police officers organized for fast action or movement

◨ *verb* **1** rise, ascend, mount, soar, glide, float, hover **2** race, sprint, dash, tear, rush, hurry, speed, zoom, shoot, dart, career

flyer *noun* a small poster or advertising sheet

flyover *noun* a road built on pillars to cross over another

flysheet *noun* the outer covering of a tent

flywheel *noun* a heavy wheel which enables a machine to run at a steady speed

foal *noun* a young horse ◇ *verb* give birth to a foal

foam *noun* a mass of small bubbles on liquids ◇ *verb* produce foam ◇ **foam rubber** a sponge-like form of rubber for stuffing chairs, mattresses *etc*

◨ *noun* froth, lather, suds, head, bubbles, effervescence

fob[1] *noun* **1** a decorative attachment to a key ring **2** an ornamental chain attached to a watch

fob[2] *verb* force to accept something worthless: *I won't be fobbed off with a silly excuse*

focaccia /fə'katʃə/ *noun* a flat round of Italian bread topped with olive oil and herbs

focal *adj* central, pivotal: *focal point*

fo'c'sle *another spelling of* **forecastle**

focus *noun* (*plural* **focuses** or **foci**) **1** the meeting point for rays of light **2** the state in which an image is sharp **3** the point to which light, a look, attention, is directed ◇ *verb* (**focuses, focusing, focused**) **1** bring into focus **2** direct (one's attention *etc*) to one point ◇ **focus group** a group set up to review a particular product or service

◨ *verb* **2** concentrate, aim, direct, fix, spotlight, home in, zoom in

fodder *noun* dried food, *eg* hay or oats, for farm animals

foe *noun*, *formal* an enemy

foetus *noun* a young human being or animal in the womb or egg ◇ **foetal** *adj* relating to a foetus

fog *noun* thick mist ◇ *verb* **1** cover in condensation or fog **2** bewilder, confuse ◇ **foggy** *adj* ◇ **foghorn** *noun* a horn used as a warning to or by ships in fog

■ *noun* mist, haze, cloud, gloom, murkiness, smog ◇ *verb* **1** mist, steam up, cloud, dull, dim, darken, obscure **2** confuse, muddle

fogy or **fogey** *noun* someone with old-fashioned views

foie gras /fwɑː grɑː/ fattened goose liver, used for making pâté

foil[1] *verb* defeat, disappoint

■ defeat, outwit, frustrate, thwart, baffle, stop, check, obstruct, block

foil[2] *noun* **1** metal in the form of paper-thin sheets **2** a dull person against whom someone else seems brighter

foil[3] *noun* a blunt sword with a button at the end, used in fencing practice

foist *verb* **1** pass off as genuine **2** palm off (something undesirable) on someone

fold[1] *noun* a part bent and laid on top of another ◇ *verb* **1** bend and lay one part on top of another **2** *informal* fail

■ *noun* bend, turn, layer, overlap, tuck, crease, line, wrinkle ◇ *verb* **1** bend, ply, double, overlap, tuck, crease, crumple **2** go bust, shut down, collapse, crash

fold[2] *noun* an enclosure for sheep *etc*

folder *noun* a cover to hold papers

foliage *noun* leaves

folio *noun* (*plural* **folios**) **1** a leaf (two pages back to back) of a book **2** a page number **3** a sheet of paper folded once

folk *noun* **1** people; a nation, race **2** (**folks**) family or relations ◇ **folk music** traditional music of a particular culture ◇ **folksong** *noun* a traditional song passed on orally

folklore *noun* the study of the customs, beliefs, stories *etc* of a people ◇ **folklorist** *noun* someone who studies or collects folklore

follicle *noun* the pit surrounding a root of hair

follow *verb* **1** go or come after **2** happen as a result **3** act according to: *follow your instincts* **4** understand: *I don't follow you* **5** work at (a trade)

■ *verb* **1** succeed, come next, replace, supersede ◇ obey, comply with, adhere

to, heed, mind, observe, conform to **4** grasp, understand, comprehend, fathom

follower *noun* **1** someone who follows **2** a supporter, disciple: *a follower of Jung*

following *noun* supporters: *the team has a large following* ◇ *adj* next in time: *we left the following day* ◇ *prep* after, as a result of: *following the fire, the house collapsed*

folly *noun* (*plural* **follies**) **1** foolishness **2** a purposeless building

■ **1** stupidity, senselessness, rashness, recklessness, irresponsibility, indiscretion, craziness, madness, lunacy, insanity, absurdity, nonsense

▨ **1** wisdom, prudence, sanity

foment *verb* stir up, encourage growth of (a rebellion *etc*)

⚠ Do not confuse with: **ferment**

fond *adj* loving; tender ◇ **fondly** *adv* ◇ **fondness** *noun* ◇ **fond of** having a liking for

■ affectionate, warm, tender, caring, loving, adoring, devoted, doting

fondle *verb* caress

■ caress, stroke, pat, pet, cuddle

font *noun* **1** a basin holding water for baptism **2** a main source: *a font of knowledge*

food *noun* that which living beings eat ◇ **foodie** *noun*, *informal* someone who takes great interest in food ◇ **food processor** an electrical appliance for chopping, blending *etc* food ◇ **foodstuff** *noun* something used for food

■ provisions, sustenance, nourishment, nutrition, nutriment, subsistence, comestibles, *slang* grub, *slang* nosh

fool[1] *noun* **1** a silly person **2** *hist* a court jester ◇ *verb* deceive ◇ **foolery** *noun* foolish behaviour ◇ **fool about** behave in a playful or silly manner

■ *noun* **1** halfwit, idiot, imbecile, moron, *informal* sucker, *informal* mug, blockhead, dimwit, *informal* nincompoop, *informal* clot, *informal* dope, *slang* wally, *slang* divvy, *informal* twit, *informal* nitwit ◇ *verb* take in, dupe, put one over on, trick, *informal* con, cheat, *informal* have on, tease

fool [2] *noun* a dessert made of fruit, sugar and whipped cream

foolhardy *adj* rash, taking foolish risks

foolish *adj* unwise, ill-considered ◇ **foolishness** *noun* ◇ **foolishly** *adv*
■ stupid, senseless, unwise, crazy, mad, insane, idiotic, simple, unintelligent, ridiculous

foolproof *adj* unable to go wrong

foolscap *noun* paper for writing or printing, 17 x 13 in (43 x 34 cm)

> Referring to the original watermark used on this size of paper, showing a jester's cap and bells

foot *noun* (*plural* **feet**) **1** the part of the leg below the ankle **2** the lower part of anything **3** twelve inches, 30 cm ◇ **foot the bill** pay up ◇ **my foot!** used to express disbelief ◇ **put a foot wrong** make a mistake, act inappropriately

football *noun* **1** a game played by two teams of 11 on a field with a round ball which can be kicked or headed **2** *US* a game played with an oval ball which can be handled or kicked **3** a ball used in the game of football

foothill *noun* a smaller hill at the foot of a mountain

foothold *noun* **1** a place to put the foot in climbing **2** a firm position from which to begin something

footing *noun* **1** balance: *lost my footing* **2** basis, status: *on a friendly footing*

footlight *noun* a light at the front of a stage, which shines on the actors

footloose *adj* unattached, with no responsibilities

footnote *noun* a note at the bottom of a page

footplate *noun* a driver's platform on a railway engine

footprint *noun* a mark of a foot or shoe on the ground

footsore *adj* tired out from too much walking

footstep *noun* the sound of someone's foot touching the ground when walking

footwear *noun* shoes *etc*

footsie *noun*, *informal* the rubbing of a foot against someone's leg *etc* in sexual play

fop *noun* a man who is vain about his dress ◇ **foppish** *adj*

for *prep* **1** sent to or to be given to: *there is letter for you* **2** towards: *headed for home* **3** during (an amount of time): *waited for three hours* **4** on behalf of: *me* **5** because of: *for no good reason* **6** as the price of: *£5 for a ticket* **7** in order to obtain: *only doing it for the money*

forage *noun* food for horses and cattle ◇ *verb* search for food, fuel *etc*
■ *verb* rummage, search, hunt, scavenge

foray *noun* **1** a sudden raid **2** a brief journey

forbade *past form* of **forbid**

forbearance *noun* control of temper ◇ **forbearing** *adj* patient

forbid *verb* (**forbids**, **forbidding**, **forbade**, **forbidden**) order not to do something ◇ **forbidden** *adj* ◇ **forbidding** *adj* rather frightening
■ prohibit, ban, veto, refuse, deny, outlaw, rule out, prevent, block, hinder, inhibit ◇ **forbidding** stern, formidable, awesome, daunting, off-putting, uninviting, menacing, threatening, ominous, sinister, frightening
◪ allow, permit, approve

force *noun* **1** strength, violence **2** the police **3** a group of workers, soldiers *etc* **4** (**forces**) those in the army, navy and air force ◇ *verb* **1** make, compel: *forced him to go* **2** get by violence: *force an entry* **3** break open **4** make vegetables *etc* grow more quickly ◇ **forced** *adj* done unwillingly, with effort: *a forced laugh* ◇ **forceful** *adj* acting with power ◇ **forcefully** *adv* ◇ **forcible** *adj* done by force ◇ **forcibly** *adv*
■ *noun* **1** impulse, influence, aggression, power, might, effort, energy, vigour ◇ *verb* **1** urge, coerce, press, pressurize, oblige, push ◇ **forced** unnatural, stiff, wooden, stilted, strained, false, af-

fected ◇ **forceful** strong, powerful, effective, convincing, persuasive, emphatic

forceps *noun* surgical pincers for holding or lifting

ford *noun* a shallow crossing-place in a river ◇ *verb* cross (water) on foot

fore- *prefix* **1** before **2** beforehand **3** in front

forearm [1] *noun* the part of the arm between elbow and wrist

forearm [2] *verb* prepare beforehand

foreboding *noun* a feeling of coming evil
▪ misgiving, anxiety, worry, apprehension, dread, fear, omen, sign, premonition, warning, prediction, intuition, feeling

forecast *verb* talk about beforehand, predict ◇ *noun* a prediction
▪ *noun* prediction, prophecy, expectation, prognosis, outlook

forecastle or **fo'c'sle** (/ˈfəʊksəl/), *noun* **1** a raised deck at the front of a ship **2** the part of a ship under the deck containing the crew's quarters

foreclose *verb* **1** prevent, preclude **2** bar from redeeming a mortgage

forefather *noun, formal* an ancestor

forefinger *noun* the finger next to the thumb

forefront *noun* the very front
▪ front, front line, firing line, van, vanguard, fore

foregone *adj*: **a foregone conclusion** a result that can be guessed rightly in advance

foreground *noun* the part of a view or picture nearest the person looking at it

forehead *noun* the part of the face above the eyebrows

foreign *adj* **1** belonging to another country **2** not belonging naturally in a place *etc*: *a foreign body in an eye* **3** not familiar ◇ **foreigner** *noun* **1** someone from another country **2** someone unfamiliar
▪ **1** alien, immigrant, imported, international, overseas, exotic, remote **3** unfamiliar, unknown

foreleg *noun* an animal's front leg

forelock *noun* the lock of hair next to the forehead

foreman *noun* (*plural* **foremen**) **1** an overseer of a group of workers **2** the leader of a jury

foremast *noun* a ship's mast nearest the bow

foremost *adj* the most famous or important
▪ first, leading, front, chief, main, principal, primary, central, supreme, prime

forensic *adj* relating to courts of law or criminal investigation: *forensic medicine*

forerunner *noun* an earlier example or sign of what is to follow: *the forerunner of cinema*

foresee *verb* (**foresees, foreseeing, foreseen, foresaw**) see or know beforehand
▪ envisage, anticipate, expect, forecast, predict, foretell

foreshore *noun* the part of the shore between high and low tidemarks

foresight *noun* **1** ability to see what will happen later **2** forethought

forest *noun* a large piece of land covered with trees ◇ **forester** *noun* a worker in a forest ◇ **forestry** *noun* the science of growing trees in forests

forestall *verb* upset someone's plan by acting first or earlier than they expect
▪ pre-empt, anticipate, head off, ward off, frustrate, thwart, prevent, hinder

foretaste *noun* a sample of what is to come
▪ preview, sample, specimen, example, indication, warning

foretell *verb* (**foretells, foretelling, foretold**) tell in advance, prophesy
▪ prophesy, forecast, predict, forewarn

forethought *noun* thought or care for the future
▪ preparation, planning, forward planning, precaution, foresight, prudence, caution
▣ improvidence, carelessness

foretold *past form* of **foretell**

forever *adv* **1** always; eternally **2** continually: *forever whining*
- **1** eternally, always, evermore, for all time, permanently **2** continually, constantly, persistently, incessantly, perpetually, endlessly

forewarn *verb* warn beforehand ◇ **forewarning** *noun*

forewoman *noun* a woman overseer

foreword *noun* a piece of writing at the beginning of a book
- preface, introduction, prologue

⚠ Do not confuse with: **forward**

forfeit *verb* lose (*eg* a right) as a result of doing something: *forfeit the right to appeal* ◇ *noun* something given in compensation or taken as punishment for an action ◇ **forfeiture** *noun* the loss of something as a punishment
- *verb* lose, give up, surrender, relinquish, sacrifice ◇ *noun* loss, surrender, confiscation, penalty, fine, damages

forge *noun* **1** a blacksmith's workshop **2** a furnace in which metal is heated ◇ *verb* (**forges**, **forging**, **forged**) **1** hammer (metal) into shape **2** imitate for criminal purposes **3** move steadily on: *forged ahead with the plan* ◇ **forger** *noun* ◇ **forgery** *noun* (*plural* **forgeries**) **1** something made in imitation for criminal purposes **2** the act of criminal forging
- *verb* **2** fake, counterfeit, falsify, copy, imitate, simulate, feign ◇ **forgery 1** fake, counterfeit, copy, replica, reproduction, imitation, sham, fraud

forget *verb* (**forgets**, **forgetting**, **forgot**, **forgotten**) **1** lose from or put out of the memory **2** leave behind accidentally ◇ **forgetful** *adj* likely to forget ◇ **forgetfully** *adv* ◇ **forgetfulness** *noun*
- **1** overlook, disregard, ignore, lose sight of, think no more of

forgive *verb* (**forgives**, **forgiving**, **forgave**, **forgiven**) **1** be no longer angry with **2** overlook (a fault, debt *etc*) ◇ **forgiveness** *noun* pardon ◇ **forgiving** *adj*
- **1, 2** pardon, absolve, excuse, exonerate,

let off, condone ◇ **forgiving** merciful, lenient, tolerant, kind, humane, compassionate

🔁 **2** punish, censure ◇ **forgiving** merciless, censorious, harsh

forgo *verb* (**forgoes**, **forgoing**, **forwent**, **forgone**) give up, do without
- waive, pass up, do without, abstain from, refrain from

forgot and **forgotten** *see* forget

fork *noun* **1** a pronged tool for piercing and lifting things **2** the point where a road, tree *etc* divides into two branches ◇ *verb* divide into two branches *etc* ◇ **fork-lift truck** a power-driven truck with steel prongs that can lift and carry heavy packages
- *verb* split, divide, part, separate, diverge, branch (off)

forlorn *adj* **1** deserted, forsaken **2** pitiful, unhappy ◇ **forlorn hope** a wish which seems to have no chance of being granted
- **1** deserted, abandoned, forsaken, forgotten, friendless, lonely, lost, destitute **2** desolate, hopeless, unhappy, miserable, wretched, helpless, pathetic

form *noun* **1** shape or appearance **2** kind, type **3** a paper with printed questions and space for answers **4** a long seat **5** a school class **6** the burrow of a hare ◇ *verb* **1** give shape to **2** take shape **3** make
- *noun* **1** mould, cast, outline, figure, build, frame, structure **2** sort, order, species, variety, style, manner, description ◇ *verb* **1** mould, model, fashion, make, create **2** appear, materialize, grow, develop **3** build, construct, assemble, put together

formal *adj* **1** of manner: cold, businesslike, correct **2** done according to custom or convention ◇ **formally** *adv* ◇ **formality** *noun* (*plural* **formalities**) **1** something which must be done but has little meaning: *the nomination was only a formality* **2** cold correctness of manner ◇ **formal dress** clothes required to be worn on formal social occasions, *eg* balls and banquets
- **1** prim, starchy, stiff, strict, rigid, precise,

exact, ceremonious, stilted, reserved **2** official, ceremonial, stately, solemn, conventional, correct, fixed, set

format noun **1** the size, shape etc of a printed book **2** the design or arrangement of an event, eg a television programme **3** comput the description of the way data is arranged on a disk ◇ verb (**formats, formatting, formatted**) **1** arrange into a specific format **2** comput arrange data for use on a disk **3** comput prepare (a disk) for use by dividing it into sectors

formation noun **1** the act of forming **2** arrangement, eg of aeroplanes in flight

former adj **1** of an earlier time **2** of the first-mentioned of two (contrasted with: latter) ◇ adv **formerly** in earlier times; previously
■ **1** past, ex-, one-time, bygone, earlier, previous, preceding

formica noun, trademark a tough, heat-resistant material used for covering work surfaces

formidable adj **1** fearsome, frightening **2** difficult to overcome
■ **1** terrifying, fearful, tremendous, prodigious, impressive, awesome, overwhelming, staggering **2** daunting, challenging, intimidating, threatening

formula noun (plural **formulae** or **formulas**) **1** a set of rules to be followed **2** an arrangement of signs or letters used in chemistry, arithmetic etc to express an idea briefly, eg H_2O = water ◇ **formulate** verb **1** set down clearly: formulate the rules **2** make into a formula

fornicate verb, formal have sexual intercourse outside marriage ◇ **fornication** noun ◇ **fornicator** noun

forsake verb (**forsakes, forsaking, forsook, forsaken**) desert; give up ◇ **forsaken** adj deserted; miserable
■ abandon, jilt, throw over, discard, reject, disown, leave, give up, surrender, relinquish, renounce

fort noun a place of defence against an enemy
■ fortress, castle, citadel, stronghold, garrison, station, camp

forte /'fɔːteɪ/ noun someone's particular talent or specialty

forth adv forward, onward

forthcoming adj **1** happening soon **2** willing to share knowledge; friendly and open

forthright adj outspoken, straightforward
■ direct, straightforward, blunt, frank, candid, plain, open, bold, outspoken
🔁 devious, secretive

forthwith adv immediately

fortieth adj the last of a series of forty ◇ noun one of forty equal parts

fortify verb (**fortifies, fortifying, fortified**) strengthen, esp against attack ◇ **fortifications** noun plural walls etc built to strengthen a position
■ reinforce, brace, shore up, buttress, garrison, defend, protect, secure

fortitude noun courage in meeting danger or bearing pain
■ courage, bravery, valour, grit, pluck, endurance, stoicism

fortnight noun two weeks ◇ **fortnightly** adj & adv once a fortnight

FORTRAN noun a computer language

fortress noun (plural **fortresses**) a fortified place

fortuitous adj happening by chance ◇ **fortuitously** adv ◇ **fortuitousness** noun
■ accidental, chance, random, arbitrary, casual, incidental, unforeseen, lucky, fortunate
🔁 intentional, planned

fortunate adj lucky ◇ **fortunately** adv
■ lucky, happy, successful, well-off, timely, well-timed, convenient, advantageous, favourable

fortune noun **1** (good or bad) luck **2** a large sum of money
■ **1** luck, chance, providence, fate, destiny **2** wealth, riches, informal pile, affluence

forty noun the number 40 ◇ adj 40 in number

forum noun **1** a public place where speeches are made **2** a meeting to talk about a particular subject **3** hist a market-place in ancient Rome

forward *adj* **1** advancing: *a forward movement* **2** near or at the front **3** advanced in development **4** too quick to speak or act ◇ *verb* **1** help towards success: *forwarded his plans* **2** send on (letters) ◇ **forward** or **forwards** *adv* onward, towards the front

▣ *adj* **2** first, leading, onward, progressive **4** confident, assertive, pushy, bold, audacious, brazen, brash, barefaced, *informal* cheeky, impudent, impertinent, pert, *slang* fresh

Do not confuse with: **foreword**

forwent *past form* of **forgo**

fossil *noun* the hardened remains of the shape of a plant or animal found in rock ◇ **fossilize** *verb* change into a fossil

foster *verb* **1** bring up or nurse (a child not your own) **2** help on, encourage ◇ **foster child** a child fostered by a family ◇ **foster parent** someone who fosters a child

▣ **2** support, promote, advance, encourage, cultivate, nurture

fought *past form* of **fight**

foul *adj* **1** very dirty **2** smelling or tasting bad **3** very unpleasant or stormy: *foul weather/in a foul temper* ◇ *verb* **1** become entangled with **2** dirty **3** play unfairly ◇ *noun* a breaking of the rules of a game ◇ **foul play** a criminal act

▣ *adj* **1** filthy, unclean, tainted, polluted, contaminated **2** rank, stinking, smelly, rotten, repulsive, revolting, disgusting, squalid

found[1] *verb* **1** establish, set up (an institution *etc*) **2** shape by pouring melted metal into a mould

▣ **1** start, originate, create, initiate, inaugurate, set up, establish, endow, organize

found[2] *past form* of **find**

foundation *noun* **1** that on which anything rests **2** a sum of money left or set aside for a special purpose **3** an organization *etc* supported in this way

founder[1] *verb* **1** of a ship: sink **2** of a

horse: stumble, go lame **3** of a business: fail

▣ **1** sink, go down, submerge, subside, collapse

❗ Do not confuse with: **flounder**

founder[2] *noun* someone who founds or establishes something

foundling *noun* a child abandoned by its parents

foundry *noun* (*plural* **foundries**) a workshop where metal founding is done

fountain *noun* **1** a rising jet of water **2** the pipe or structure from which it comes **3** the beginning of anything

▣ **1** spray, jet, spout, spring

four the number 4 ◇ *adj* 4 in number

fourteen *noun* the number 14 ◇ *adj* 14 in number

fourteenth *adj* the last of a series of fourteen ◇ *noun* one of fourteen equal parts

fourth *adj* the last of a series of four ◇ *noun* one of four equal parts

fowl *noun* a bird, *esp* a domestic cock or hen

fox *noun* (*plural* **foxes**) a wild animal related to the dog, with reddish-brown fur and a long bushy tail ◇ *verb* **1** trick by cleverness **2** puzzle, baffle ◇ **foxhound** *noun* a breed of dog trained to chase foxes ◇ **fox terrier** a breed of dog trained to drive foxes from their earths

foxglove *noun* a tall wild flower

foxtrot *noun* a ballroom dance involving walking steps and turns

foxy *adj* **1** cunning **2** *US informal* sexually attractive

foyer /'fɔɪeɪ/ or /'fɔɪə(r)/ *noun* an entrance hall to a theatre, hotel *etc*

fracas /'frakɑː/ *noun* **1** uproar **2** a noisy quarrel

fraction *noun* **1** a part, not a whole number, *eg* $\frac{3}{4}$, 0.75 **2** a small part

fractious *adj* cross, quarrelsome

fracture *noun* a break in something hard, *esp* in a bone of the body ◇ *verb* break (something, *esp* a bone)

■ *noun* break, crack, fissure, cleft, rupture, split ◊ *verb* break, crack, rupture, split, splinter, chip

fragile *adj* easily broken ◊ **fragility** *noun*

■ brittle, breakable, frail, delicate, flimsy, dainty, fine, weak, feeble

fragment *noun* a part broken off; something not complete ◊ *verb* break into pieces ◊ **fragmentary** *adj* broken, incomplete ◊ **fragmentation** *noun*

■ *noun* piece, bit, part, portion, fraction, particle, crumb, morsel, scrap, remnant, shred, chip, splinter, sliver, shard ◊ **fragmentary** bitty, piecemeal, broken, separate, scattered, sketchy, partial, incomplete

fragrant *adj* sweet-smelling ◊ **fragrance** *noun* sweet scent ◊ **fragrantly** *adv*

■ perfumed, scented, sweet-smelling, sweet, balmy, aromatic

frail *adj* 1 weak 2 easily tempted to do wrong ◊ **frailty** *noun* (*plural* **frailties**)

■ 1 delicate, fragile, flimsy, insubstantial, weak, feeble

☒ 1 robust, tough, strong

frame *verb* (**frames**, **framing**, **framed**) 1 put a frame round 2 put together, construct 3 *slang* make (someone) appear to be guilty of a crime ◊ *noun* 1 a case or border which supports or surrounds something 2 build of human body ◊ **frame of mind** mood, state of mind ◊ **framework** *noun* the outline or skeleton of something

■ *verb* 2 assemble, build, construct, fabricate, make 3 set up, *slang* fit up, trap ◊ **frame of mind** mood, humour, temper, disposition, spirit, outlook, attitude

franc *noun* 1 a former unit of French of Belgian money 2 the standard unit of Swiss money

franchise *noun* 1 the right to vote in a general election 2 a right to sell the goods of a particular company ◊ *verb* give a business franchise to

Franco- *prefix* of France, French: *Francophile*

franglais *noun* French sprinkled with words borrowed from English

frank *adj* open, speaking your mind ◊ *verb* mark a letter by machine to show that postage has been paid ◊ **frankly** *adv* ◊ **frankness** *noun*

■ *adj* honest, truthful, sincere, candid, blunt, open, free, plain, direct, straightforward, downright, outspoken

☒ *adj* insincere, evasive

frankfurter *noun* a kind of smoked sausage

frankincense *noun* a sweet-smelling resin used as incense

frantic *adj* wildly excited or anxious ◊ **frantically** *adv*

■ agitated, overwrought, fraught, desperate, furious, raging, mad, wild, raving, frenzied, berserk, hectic

☒ calm, composed

fraternal *adj* brotherly; of a brother ◊ **fraternally** *adv*

fraternity (*plural* **fraternities**) 1 a society, a brotherhood 2 a North American male college society (*compare with:* **sorority**)

fraternize *verb* mix or make friends (with)

■ mix, mingle, socialize, associate

fratricide *noun* 1 the murder of a brother 2 someone who murders their brother

fraud *noun* 1 deceit, dishonesty 2 a trick 3 an impostor ◊ **fraudulence** or **fraudulency** *noun* ◊ **fraudulent** *adj* ◊ **fraudulently** *adv*

■ 1 deception, cheating, swindling, double-dealing 2 fake, counterfeit, forgery, hoax, trick 3 *informal* charlatan, *informal* phoney, cheat, swindler, double-dealer, *informal* con man ◊ **fraudulent** dishonest, *informal* crooked, criminal, deceitful, deceptive, double-dealing

fraught *adj* anxious, tense ◊ **fraught with** filled with (danger *etc*)

fray *verb* 1 of cloth, rope *etc*: wear away 2 of tempers, nerves *etc*: become strained ◊ *noun* a fight, a brawl

▣ *noun* brawl, scuffle, *informal* dust-up, clash, conflict, fight, quarrel, row, brawl, riot, rumpus

freak *noun* 1 an unusual event 2 an odd or eccentric person 3 *informal* a keen fan: *film freak*

▣ 3 enthusiast, fanatic, addict, fan, *informal* buff, *informal* fiend, *informal* nut

freckle *noun* a small brown spot on the skin

free *adj* 1 not bound or shut in 2 generous 3 not occupied 4 costing nothing ◊ *verb* 1 make or set free 2 (with **from** or **of**) rid ◊ **free speech** the right to express opinions of any kind

▣ *adj* 1 at liberty, at large, loose, unattached, unrestrained 2 liberal, openhanded, lavish, charitable, hospitable ◊ *verb* 1 release, let go, loose, turn loose, set free, untie, liberate

-free *suffix* not containing or involving: *additive-free/cruelty-free*

freebie *noun*, *informal* a free event, performance *etc*

freedom *noun* liberty

freehand *adj* of drawing: done without the help of rulers, tracing *etc*

freehold *adj* of an estate: belonging to the holder or their heirs for all time

freelance or **freelancer** *noun* someone working independently (such as a writer who is not employed by any one newspaper)

free-range *adj* 1 of poultry: allowed to move about freely and feed out of doors 2 of eggs: laid by poultry of this kind

freestyle *adj* of swimming, skating *etc*: in which any style may be used

freeware *noun* computer software which can legally be copied and distributed, but not resold for profit

freeze *verb* (**freezes**, **freezing**, **froze**, **frozen**) 1 turn into ice 2 make (food) very cold in order to preserve 2 go stiff with cold, fear *etc* 3 fix (prices or wages) at a certain level ◊ **freezing-point** *noun* the point at which liquid becomes solid (of water, 0°C)

freezer *noun* a type of cabinet in which food is frozen or kept frozen

freight *noun* 1 load, cargo 2 a charge for carrying a load ◊ *verb* load with goods ◊ **freighter** *noun* a ship or aircraft that carries cargo ◊ **freight train** a goods train

▣ 1 cargo, load, contents, goods, consignment, shipment 2 transportation, carriage, haulage

French *noun* the official language of France ◊ *adj* of France or French ◊ **French fries** *US* fried potato chips ◊ **French letter** *Brit slang* a condom ◊ **French polish** a kind of varnish for furniture ◊ **French toast** bread dipped in egg and fried ◊ **French window** a long window also used as a door ◊ **take French leave** go or stay away without permission

frenetic *adj* frantic ◊ **frenetically** *adv*

frenzy *noun* 1 a fit of madness 2 wild excitement ◊ **frenzied** *adj* mad ◊ **frenziedly** *adv*

▣ **frenzied** frantic, frenetic, hectic, feverish, desperate, furious, wild, uncontrolled, mad, demented, hysterical

▣ **frenzied** calm, composed

frequent *adj* happening often ◊ *verb* visit often ◊ **frequency** *noun* (*plural* **frequencies**) 1 the rate at which something happens 2 the number per second of vibrations, waves *etc*

▣ *adj* repeated, recurring, regular, common, commonplace, everyday, familiar, usual, customary ◊ *verb* patronize, attend, associate with, *informal* hang about with, *informal* hang out with

fresco *noun* (*plural* **frescoes** or **frescos**) a picture painted on a wall while the plaster is still damp

fresh *adj* 1 new, unused: *a fresh sheet of paper* 2 newly made or picked: *fresh bread/fresh fruit* 3 cool, refreshing: *a fresh breeze* 4 not tired 5 cheeky, impertinent ◊ **freshly** *adv* ◊ **freshness** *noun*

▣ 3 bracing, invigorating, brisk, crisp, keen, cool, bright, clear, pure 4 revived, restored, rested, invigorated, energetic, vigorous, lively, alert 5 disrespectful, impudent, insolent, bold, brazen, pert, *informal* saucy

freshen *verb* make or become fresh

fresher or **freshman** *noun* a first-year university student

freshwater *adj* of inland rivers, lakes *etc*, not of the sea

fret[1] *verb* (**frets, fretting, fretted**) worry or show discontent ◇ **fretful** *adj* ◇ **fretfully** *adv*

■ worry, agonize, brood, pine, vex, irritate, trouble, torment

fret[2] *noun* one of the ridges on the fingerboard of a guitar

fretsaw *noun* a narrow-bladed, fine-toothed saw for fretwork

fretwork *noun* decorated cut-out work in wood

friar *noun* a member of one of the Roman Catholic brotherhoods, *esp* someone who has vowed to live in poverty ◇ **friary** *noun* (*plural* **friaries**) a community of friars or the building where they live

friction *noun* 1 rubbing of two things together 2 the wear caused by rubbing 3 quarrelling, bad feeling

■ 1 chafing, irritation, abrasion, scraping, grating 2 erosion, wearing away, resistance 3 disharmony, conflict, antagonism, hostility, opposition, rivalry, animosity, ill feeling, bad blood, resentment

Friday *noun* the sixth day of the week

fridge *noun, informal* refrigerator

fried *past form of* **fry**

friend *noun* 1 someone who likes another person and knows them well 2 a sympathizer, a helper

■ 1 *informal* mate, *informal* pal, *informal* chum, soul mate, comrade, ally, partner, associate, companion

◪ 1 enemy, opponent

friendly *adj* 1 kind; sociable 2 (**with**) on good terms ◇ *noun* (*plural* **friendlies**) a sports match that is not part of a competition ◇ **friendliness** *noun*

■ 1 amiable, affable, genial, kind, kindly, neighbourly, helpful, sympathetic, sociable,

outgoing, approachable, receptive, amicable 2 intimate, close, *informal* pally, *informal* chummy

◪ 1 hostile, unsociable, cold

-friendly *suffix* 1 not harmful towards: *dolphin-friendly* 2 compatible with or convenient for: *child-friendly*

friendship *noun* the state of being friends; mutual affection

frieze *noun* 1 a part of a wall below the ceiling, often ornamented with designs 2 a picture on a long strip of paper *etc*, often displayed on a wall

frigate *noun* a small warship

fright *noun* sudden fear: *gave me a fright/took fright and ran away*

■ shock, scare, alarm, fear, terror, horror, panic

frighten *verb* make afraid ◇ **frightening** *adj* ◇ **frighteningly** *adv*

■ alarm, daunt, unnerve, intimidate, scare, startle, terrify, petrify, horrify, shock

frightful *adj* 1 causing terror 2 *informal* very bad ◇ **frightfully** *adv*

frigid *adj* 1 frozen, cold 2 cold in manner 3 sexually unresponsive ◇ **frigidity** *noun* ◇ **frigidly** *adv*

■ 1 frozen, icy, frosty, glacial, arctic, cold, chilly, chill, wintry 2 unfeeling, unresponsive, passionless, cool, aloof, passive

frill *noun* 1 an ornamental edging, *esp* on clothing 2 an unnecessary ornament ◇ **frilly** *adj*

■ frilly ruffled, gathered, fancy

fringe *noun* 1 a border of loose threads 2 hair cut to hang over the forehead 3 the outer part or edge of something ◇ *verb* form a fringe round

Frisbee *noun, trademark* a plastic plate-like object skimmed through the air as a game

frisk *verb* 1 skip about playfully 2 *informal* search someone closely for concealed weapons *etc* ◇ **friskily** *adv* ◇ **friskiness** *noun* ◇ **frisky** *adj*

■ 1 jump, leap, skip, hop, bounce, dance, gambol, frolic, romp, play ◇ **frisky** lively, spirited, high-spirited, playful, romping, rollicking, bouncy

frisson /ˈfriːsɒn/ *noun* a shiver, a thrill

fritter *noun* a piece of fried batter containing fruit *etc*

fritter *verb*: **fritter away** waste, squander

frivolous *adj* playful, not serious ◇ **frivolity** *noun* (*plural* **frivolities**) levity, lack of seriousness ◇ **frivolously** *adv*

▣ trifling, trivial, unimportant, shallow, superficial, light, flippant, lighthearted, juvenile, puerile, foolish, silly

▣ serious, sensible

frizzy *adj* of hair: massed in small curls

fro *adv*: **to and fro** forwards and backwards

frock *noun* **1** a woman's or girl's dress **2** a monk's wide-sleeved garment ◇ **frock-coat** *noun* a man's long coat

frog *noun* a small greenish jumping animal living on land and in water

frogmarch *verb* seize (someone) from behind and push them forward while holding their arms tight behind their back

frogman *noun*, *informal* an underwater diver with flippers and breathing apparatus

frolic *noun* a merry, light-hearted playing ◇ *verb* (**frolics**, **frolicking**, **frolicked**) play light-heartedly ◇ **frolicsome** *adj*

▣ *noun* fun, amusement, sport, gaiety, jollity, merriment, revel, romp, prank, lark, caper, antics ◇ *verb* gambol, caper, romp, play, lark around, rollick, prance

from *prep* **1** used before the place, person *etc* that is the starting point of an action *etc*: *sailing from England to France/the office is closed from Friday to Monday* **2** used to show separation: *warn them to keep away from there*

fromage frais /ˈfrɒmɑːʒ ˈfreɪ/ a low-fat cheese with the consistency of whipped cream

frond *noun* a leaf-like growth, *esp* a branch of a fern or palm

front *noun* **1** the part of anything nearest the person who sees it; the most important side **2** the part which faces the direction in which something moves **3** outward appearance **4** the fighting line in a war ◇ *adj* at or in the front ◇ **frontage** *noun* the front part of a building ◇ **frontman** *noun* the main person in a group, TV programme *etc* ◇ **in front of** at the head of, before

▣ *noun* **1** face, aspect, frontage, façade, outside, exterior **3** pretence, show, air, appearance, look, expression, manner, façade, cover, mask, disguise, pretext, cover-up

frontier *noun* a boundary between countries

frontispiece *noun* a picture at the beginning of a book

frost *noun* **1** a layer of ice crystals, *eg* on the ground; frozen dew **2** the coldness of weather needed to form ice ◇ *verb* **1** cover with frost **2** *US* ice (a cake) ◇ **frosted** *adj* ◇ **frosting** *noun*, *US* icing on a cake *etc* ◇ **frosty** *adj* cold, unwelcoming: *gave me a frosty look*

▣ **frosty** icy, unfriendly, unwelcoming, cool, aloof, standoffish, stiff, discouraging

froth *noun* foam on liquids ◇ *verb* throw up foam ◇ **frothy** *adj*

frown *verb* wrinkle the brows in deep thought, disapproval *etc* ◇ *noun* **1** a wrinkling of the brows **2** a disapproving look ◇ **frown on** look upon with disapproval

▣ *verb* scowl, glower, glare, grimace ◇ *noun* **2** scowl, glower, *informal* dirty look, glare, grimace

frowzy *adj* rough and tangled

froze *past form* of **freeze**

frozen *past participle* of **freeze**

frugal *adj* **1** careful in spending, thrifty **2** costing little, small: *a frugal meal* ◇ **frugality** *noun* ◇ **frugally** *adv*

▣ **1** thrifty, penny-wise, parsimonious, careful, provident, saving, economical, sparing

fruit *noun* **1** the part of a plant containing the seed **2** something gained as a result: *all their hard work bore fruit* ◇ **fruiterer** *noun* someone who sells fruit ◇ **fruit machine** a gambling machine into which coins are put

Varieties of fruit include:
apple, crab apple; pear, Asian pear;
orange, mandarin, mineola,
clementine, satsuma, tangerine,
kumquat; apricot, peach, plum,
persimmon, sharon fruit, nectarine,
cherry, sloe, damson, greengage,
grape, gooseberry, *informal*
googegog, physalis, rhubarb,
tomato; banana, pineapple, olive,
lemon, lime, ugli fruit, star fruit,
lychee, date, fig, grapefruit, kiwi
fruit, mango, papaya, pawpaw,
guava, passion fruit, avocado;
melon, honeydew, cantaloupe,
casaba, Galia, watermelon;
strawberry, raspberry, blackberry,
bilberry, loganberry, elderberry,
blueberry, boysenberry, cranberry;
redcurrant, blackcurrant

fruitful *adj* **1** producing plenty of fruit **2** producing good results: *a fruitful meeting*
- **2** rewarding, profitable, advantageous, beneficial, worthwhile, well-spent, useful, successful

fruition *noun* **1** ripeness **2** a good result
- **2** realization, fulfilment, completion, perfection, success

fruitless *adj* useless, done in vain
- unsuccessful, useless, futile, pointless, hopeless
- successful, profitable

frump *noun* a plain, badly or unfashionably dressed woman ◇ **frumpish** *adj*

frustrate *verb* **1** cause to feel powerless **2** bring to nothing: *frustrated his wishes* ◇ **frustration** *noun*
- **1** disappoint, discourage, dishearten, depress **2** thwart, foil, block, defeat, counter, inhibit
- **1** encourage **2** further, promote

fry[1] *verb* (**fries**, **frying**, **fried**) cook in hot fat ◇ *noun* food cooked in hot fat

fry[2] *noun* a young fish ◇ **small fry** unimportant people or things

ft *abbrev* foot, feet

fuchsia /ˈfjuːʃə/ *noun* a plant with long hanging flowers

fuck *verb, taboo slang* have sexual intercourse (with) ◇ *noun, taboo slang* an act of sexual intercourse ◇ **fuck off** go away

fuddle *verb* confuse, muddle

fuddy-duddy *noun* an old fogy, a stick-in-the-mud

fudge[1] *noun* a soft, sugary sweet

fudge[2] *verb* be evasive

fuel *noun* a substance such as coal, gas or petrol, used to keep a fire or engine going ◇ *verb* **1** provide with fuel **2** incite (passion, anger *etc*)
- *verb* **1** feed, nourish, sustain, stoke up **2** incite, fire, encourage, fan, inflame
- *verb* **1** extinguish, damp down, put out **2** discourage

fugitive *adj* running away, on the run ◇ *noun* someone who is running away from the police *etc*

fulcrum *noun* (*plural* **fulcrums** or **fulcra**) the point on which a lever turns, or a balanced object rests

fulfil *verb* (**fulfils**, **fulfilling**, **fulfilled**) carry out (a task, promise *etc*) ◇ **fulfilment** *noun*
- complete, finish, conclude, achieve, accomplish, perform, execute, carry out

full *adj* **1** holding as much as can be held **2** thorough, detailed: *a full report* **3** entire: *the full set* **4** plump: *a full face* ◇ *adv* (used with *adjs*) fully: *full-grown* ◇ **fullness** *noun* ◇ **fully** *adv* ◇ **full moon** the moon when it appears at its largest ◇ **full of** having a great deal or plenty of ◇ **full stop** a punctuation mark (.) placed at the end of a sentence
- *adj* **1** filled, loaded, packed, crowded, crammed, stuffed, jammed **2** comprehensive, exhaustive, all-inclusive, extensive **3** whole, intact, total, complete, unabridged ◇ **fully** completely, totally, entirely, thoroughly, quite

fulminate *verb, formal* **1** speak angrily or passionately against something **2** flash like lightning ◇ **fulmination** *noun*

fulsome *adj, formal* overdone: *fulsome praise*

fumble *verb* **1** use the hands awkwardly **2** drop (a thrown ball *etc*)

■ **1** grope, feel, bungle, botch, mishandle, mismanage

fume *verb* (**fumes**, **fuming**, **fumed**)
1 give off smoke or vapour **2** be in a silent rage ◇ **fumes** *noun plural* smoke, vapour

fumigate *verb* kill germs by means of strong fumes ◇ **fumigation** *noun*

fun *noun* enjoyment, a good time: *are you having fun?* ◇ **make fun of** tease, make others laugh at

■ enjoyment, pleasure, amusement, entertainment, diversion, recreation, play, game, merrymaking, mirth, jollity ◇ **make fun of** rag, jeer at, ridicule, laugh at, mock, taunt, tease, *slang* rib

function *noun* **1** a special job, use or duty of a machine, person, part of the body *etc* **2** an arranged public gathering ◇ *verb* work, operate: *the engine isn't functioning properly*

■ *noun* **1** role, part, office, duty, charge, responsibility, job, task, purpose **2** reception, party, gathering, affair, *informal* do ◇ *verb* work, operate, run, go, serve, perform, behave

functionary *noun* (*plural* **functionaries**) an office holder, an official

fund *noun* **1** a sum of money for a special purpose: *charity fund* **2** a store or supply ◇ *verb* provide money for a particular purpose

■ *noun* **2** pool, treasury, store, reserve, stock, hoard, cache, supply ◇ *verb* finance, capitalize, sponsor, support, promote

fundamental *adj* **1** of great or far-reaching importance; essential **2** basic ◇ *noun* **1** a necessary part **2** (**fundamentals**) the groundwork, the first stages

■ *adj* **1** vital, necessary, essential, crucial, important **2** primary, first, rudimentary, elementary, main, key

funeral *noun* the ceremony of burial or cremation ◇ **funereal** *adj* mournful

funfair *noun* an amusement park

fungus *noun* (*plural* **fungi** (/ˈfʌŋgiː/ or /ˈfʌŋgaɪ/) a soft, spongy plant-like growth, *eg* a mushroom or a disease of animals and plants

---

Types of fungus include:
black spot, blight, botritis, brown rot, candida, downy mildew, ergot, grey mould, mushroom, orange-peel fungus, penicillium, potato blight, powdery mildew, rust, scab, smut, sooty mould, toadstool, yeast, brewer's yeast

funky *adj*, *informal* **1** fashionable, trendy **2** odd, eccentric

funnel *noun* **1** a cone ending in a tube, for pouring liquids into bottles **2** a tube or passage for escape of smoke, air *etc* ◇ *verb* (**funnels**, **funnelling**, **funnelled**) pass through a funnel; channel

funny *adj* **1** amusing **2** odd ◇ **funnily** *adv* ◇ **funny bone** part of the elbow which gives a prickly feeling when knocked

■ **1** humorous, entertaining, comic, comical, hilarious, witty, droll, absurd, silly **2** strange, peculiar, curious, weird, unusual, puzzling, perplexing, mysterious, dubious

■ **1** serious, solemn, sad **2** normal, ordinary, usual

fur *noun* **1** the short fine hair of certain animals **2** their skins covered with fur **3** a coating on the tongue, on the inside of kettles *etc* ◇ *verb* (**furs**, **furring**, **furred**) line or cover with fur ◇ **furrier** *noun* someone who trades in or works with furs ◇ **furry** *adj* covered with fur

furbish *verb* decorate or clean; rub up or burnish

furious *adj* extremely angry ◇ **furiously** *adv*

■ angry, *informal* mad, *informal* up in arms, livid, enraged, infuriated, incensed, raging, fuming

■ calm, pleased

furlong *noun* one-eighth of a mile (220 yards, 201.17 metres)

furnace *noun* a very hot oven for melting iron ore, making steam for heating *etc*

furnish *verb* **1** fit up (a room or house) completely **2** supply: *furnished with enough food for a week* ◇ **furnishings** *noun plural* fittings, furniture

furniture *noun* movable articles in a house, *eg* tables, chairs

furore /fjʊˈrɔːrɪ/ *noun* uproar; excitement

furrow *noun* **1** a groove made by a plough **2** a deep groove **3** a deep wrinkle ◊ *verb* **1** cut furrows in **2** wrinkle: *furrowed brow*

furry *see* **fur**

further *adv* & *adj* to a greater distance or degree; in addition ◊ *verb* help on or forward ◊ **furthest** *adv* to the greatest distance or degree
- *adj* more, additional, supplementary, extra, fresh, new, other ◊ *verb* advance, promote, push, encourage, aid, assist, speed, hasten
- *verb* stop, frustrate

furthermore *adv* in addition to what has been said

furtive *adj* stealthy, sly: *a furtive glance* ◊ **furtively** *adv*
- surreptitious, sly, stealthy, secretive, underhand, hidden, covert, secret

fury *noun* violent anger
- anger, rage, wrath, frenzy, passion, vehemence, madness, ferocity
- calm, peacefulness

furze *another name for* **gorse**

fuse [1] *verb* (**fuses, fusing, fused**) **1** melt **2** join together **3** put a fuse in (a plug *etc*) **4** of a circuit, appliance *etc*: stop working because of the melting of a fuse ◊ *noun* a piece of easily melted wire put in an electric circuit for safety

fuse [2] *noun* any device for causing an explosion to take place automatically

fuselage *noun* the body of an aeroplane

fusion *noun* **1** melting **2** a merging: *a fusion of musical traditions* **3** cookery combining Eastern and Western traditions

fuss *noun* **1** unnecessary activity, excitement or attention, often about something unimportant: *making a fuss about nothing* **2** a strong complaint ◊ *verb* **1** be unnecessarily concerned about details **2** worry too much
- *noun* **1** trouble, *informal* hassle, *informal* hoo-ha, commotion, stir, fluster, confusion, upset, worry, agitation, *informal* flap, excitement

fussy *adj* **1** over-elaborate **2** choosy, finicky ◊ **fussily** *adv* ◊ **fussiness** *noun*
- **2** particular, fastidious, scrupulous, finicky, pernickety, difficult, hard to please, *informal* choosy

fusty *adj* mouldy; stale-smelling

futile *adj* useless; having no effect ◊ **futility** *noun* uselessness
- pointless, useless, worthless, vain, wasted, fruitless, unsuccessful, unprofitable, unproductive
- fruitful, profitable

futon /ˈfuːtɒn/ *noun* a sofa bed with a low frame and detachable mattress

future *adj* happening later in time ◊ *noun* **1** the time to come: *foretell the future* **2** the part of your life still to come: *planning for their future* **3** *grammar* the tense in verbs indicating future actions or events
- *adj* prospective, to be, destined, to come, forthcoming, impending, coming, approaching, expected, planned, later, subsequent, eventual ◊ *noun* **1** hereafter, tomorrow, outlook **2** prospects, expectations

fuzz *noun* **1** fine, light hair or feathers **2** *Brit slang* the police ◊ **fuzzy** *adj* **1** covered with fuzz, fluffy **2** tightly curled: *fuzzy hair*

Gg

g *abbrev* gram

gabble *verb* talk fast, chatter ◇ *noun* fast talk

■ *verb* babble, chatter, jabber, prattle ◇ *noun* babble, chatter, blabber, prattle, twaddle

gaberdine *noun* **1** a heavy fabric **2** a coat made of this

gable *noun* the triangular area of wall at the end of a building with a ridged roof

gadabout *noun* someone who loves going out or travelling

gadget *noun* a small simple machine or tool

■ tool, implement, appliance, device, instrument, apparatus, mechanism

Gaelic *noun* **1** the language of the Scottish Highlands **2** the Irish language; Erse ◇ *adj* written or spoken in Gaelic

gaff¹ *noun* **1** a large hook used for landing fish **2** a spar for raising the top of a sail

gaff² *noun*: **blow the gaff** *informal* let out a secret

gag¹ *verb* (**gags**, **gagging**, **gagged**) silence by stopping the mouth ◇ *noun* a piece of cloth *etc* put in or over someone's mouth to silence them

■ *verb* silence, muffle, muzzle, quiet, stifle, smother, block, plug, throttle, suppress, restrain, curb

gag² *noun*, *informal* a joke

gaggle *noun* a flock of geese

gaiety and **gaily** *see* **gay**

gain *verb* **1** win; earn; obtain **2** reach **3** of a clock: go ahead of correct time **4** have an increase in (*eg* weight, speed) ◇ *noun* **1** something gained **2** profit ◇ **gain on** get closer to, *esp* in a race: *gaining on the leader*

■ *verb* **1** earn, win, make, produce, realize, gross, net, clear, profit, yield, bring in, gather, achieve, obtain, acquire, *formal* procure **2** reach, arrive at, come to, get to, attain, achieve ◇ *noun* **2** profit, earnings, proceeds, income, revenue, winnings, pickings, proceeds, takings, return, reward, yield, *formal* emolument

☒ *verb* **1**, **3**, **4** lose ◇ *noun* **2** loss

gainsay *verb*, *formal* deny

gait *noun* way or manner of walking

⚠ Do not confuse with: **gate**

gaiter *noun* a cloth ankle-covering, fitting over the shoe, sometimes reaching to the knee

gala *noun* **1** a public festival **2** a sports meeting: *swimming gala*

galaxy *noun* (*plural* **galaxies**) **1** a system of stars **2** an impressive gathering ◇ **the Galaxy** the Milky Way

■ **1** stars, star system, solar system, constellation, cluster, nebula **2** array, host, collection, gathering, group, assembly

gale *noun* a strong wind

■ wind, squall, storm, hurricane, tornado, typhoon, cyclone

gall /gɔːl/ *noun* **1** bile, a bitter fluid produced by the liver and stored in the **gallbladder** **2** bitterness of feeling ◇ *verb* annoy ◇ **galling** *adj* annoying, frustrating

gallant *adj* **1** brave; noble **2** polite or attentive towards women ◇ *noun* a gallant man ◇ **gallantry** *noun*

■ *adj* **1** noble, honourable, heroic, valiant, brave, courageous, fearless, dauntless, intrepid, audacious, bold, daring, plucky **2** chivalrous, gentlemanly, courteous, polite, gracious, attentive

☒ *adj* **1** cowardly **2** ungentlemanly

galleon *noun*, *hist* a large Spanish sailing ship

gallery *noun* (*plural* **galleries**) **1** a long passage **2** the top floor of seats in a theatre **3** a room or building for showing artworks

■ **1** arcade, passage, corridor **2** balcony, circle, *informal* gods

galley *noun* (*plural* **galleys**) **1** *hist* a long, low-built ship driven by oars **2** a ship's kitchen

gallivant *verb* travel or go out for pleasure

gallon *noun* a measure for liquids (8 pints, 3.636 litres)

gallop *verb* **1** (cause to) move at a gallop **2** (cause to) move very fast ◇ *noun* a fast pace, *esp* of horses

■ *verb* **2** bolt, run, sprint, race, career, fly, dash, tear, speed, zoom, shoot, dart, rush, hurry

■ *verb* **2** amble

gallows *noun sing* a wooden framework on which criminals were hanged

galore *adv* in plenty: *cards and presents galore*

■ in abundance, lots of, plenty, in numbers, to spare, everywhere; *informal* heaps of, tons of, stacks of, millions of

■ scarce

> Based on an Irish Gaelic phrase *go leor*, meaning 'sufficient'

galosh or **golosh** *noun* (*plural* **galoshes** or **goloshes**) a rubber shoe worn over ordinary shoes in wet weather

galvanic *adj* of electricity produced by the action of acids or other chemicals on metal ◇ **galvanism** *noun*

> Named after the Italian physicist, Luigi *Galvani*

galvanize *verb* **1** stir into activity **2** stimulate by electricity **3** coat (iron *etc*) with zinc

■ **1** jolt, prod, spur, urge, provoke, stimulate, stir, startle, move, rouse, excite

gambit *noun* **1** *chess* a first move involving sacrificing a piece to make the player's position stronger **2** an opening move in a transaction, or an opening remark in a conversation **3** a stratagem

■ **3** device, manoeuvre, move, ploy, tactic(s), ruse, play, stratagem, trick, wile, artifice

gamble *verb* **1** play games for money **2** risk money on the result of a game, race *etc* **3** take a wild chance ◇ *noun* **1** a risk **2** a bet on a result

■ *verb* **1** bet, game, speculate **2** bet, wager, stake, chance, risk, *informal* have a flutter ◇ *noun* **1** chance, risk, lottery, speculation **2** bet, wager, punt, *informal* flutter

gambol *verb* (**gambols**, **gambolling**, **gambolled**) leap playfully

game *noun* **1** a contest played according to rules (**games**) athletic competition **3** wild animals and birds hunted for sport ◇ *adj* **1** plucky **2** of a limb: lame ◇ **gamekeeper** *noun* someone who looks after game birds, animals, fish *etc* ◇ **gamer** *noun* someone who plays computer games ◇ **gaming** *noun* **1** gambling **2** playing computer games

■ *noun* **2** competition, contest, match, round, tournament, event, meeting **3** game birds, animals, wild animals, meat, flesh, wild fowl, prey

> *Indoor games include:*
> board game, backgammon, *US* checkers, chess, Cluedo®, draughts, halma, Jenga®, ludo, mah-jong, Monopoly®, nine men's morris, Pictionary®, Scrabble®, snakes and ladders, Trivial Pursuit®; card game, baccarat, beggar-my-neighbour, bezique, blackjack, brag, bridge, canasta, chemin de fer, *informal* crib, cribbage, faro, gin rummy, rummy, happy families, *informal* nap, napoleon, newmarket, old maid, patience, Pelmanism, picquet, poker, draw poker, stud poker, pontoon, vingt-et-un, snap, solitaire, twenty-one, whist, partner whist, solo whist; bagatelle, pinball, billiards, snooker, pool, bowling, ten-pin bowling, bowls, darts, dice, craps, dominoes, roulette, shove ha'penny, table tennis, ping pong

> *Children's games include:*
> battleships, blind man's buff, charades, Chinese whispers, consequences, fivestones, forfeits,

hangman, hide-and-seek, I-spy, jacks, jackstraws, musical chairs, noughts and crosses, pass the parcel, piggy-in-the-middle, pin the tail on the donkey, postman's knock, sardines, Simon says, spillikins, spin the bottle, tiddlywinks

gammon *noun* meat from the leg of a pig, salted and smoked

gamut *noun* **1** the whole range or extent of anything **2** the range of notes of an individual voice or musical instrument

■ **1** scale, series, range, sweep, scope, compass, spectrum, sequence

From the name of a medieval 6-note musical scale, two notes of which were *gamma* and *ut*

gander *noun* a male goose

gang *noun* **1** a group of people who meet regularly **2** a team of criminals **3** a number of labourers

■ **1** group, crowd, set **2** group, band, ring, mob **3** team, crew, shift

gangrene *noun* the rotting of some part of the body ◊ **gangrenous** *adj*

gangster *noun* a member of a gang of criminals

■ mobster, *US slang* goombah, desperado, hoodlum, tough, thug, *slang* heavy, racketeer, *informal* crook, criminal

gangway *noun* **1** a passage between rows of seats **2** a movable bridge leading from a quay to a ship

gannet *noun* a large white sea bird

gantry *noun* (*plural* **gantries**) a platform or structure for supporting a travelling crane *etc*

gaol *another spelling of* **jail**

gaoler *another spelling of* **jailer**

gap *noun* an opening or space between things ◊ **gappy** *adj* ◊ **gap year** a year between leaving school and starting university or college

■ opening, space, blank, void, hole, cavity, aperture, opening, crack, breach

gape *verb* **1** open the mouth wide (as in surprise) **2** be wide open

■ **1** stare, gaze, wonder, goggle, *informal* gawp, gawk, *US slang* rubberneck **2** open, yawn, crack

garage *noun* **1** a building for storing a car (or cars) **2** a shop which carries out car repairs and sells petrol, oil *etc*

■ **1** lock-up, car port **2** petrol station, service station, *US* gas station

garbage *noun US* rubbish

garble *verb* mix up, muddle: *a garbled account of events*

Originally meaning 'sift', which gradually developed into the sense of confusing by leaving out too much

Garda *noun* **1** the police force of the Republic of Ireland **2** a police officer in the Garda

garden *noun* a piece of ground on which flowers or vegetables are grown ◊ *verb* work in a garden ◊ **gardener** *noun* someone who tends a garden ◊ **gardening** *noun* ◊ **garden party** a large tea party, held out of doors

gardenia *noun* a tropical plant producing large, waxy, white flowers

gargantuan *adj* extremely large, huge

Named after *Gargantua*, a giant with an enormous appetite in a 16th-century French novel by Rabelais

gargle *verb* rinse the throat with a liquid, without swallowing

gargoyle *noun* a grotesque carving of a human or animal head, jutting out from a roof

garish *adj* tastelessly over-bright: *garish book covers* ◊ **garishness** *noun*

■ gaudy, lurid, loud, glaring, flashy, showy, tawdry, vulgar, tasteless, cheap, *informal* glitzy, flash

▨ quiet, tasteful

garland *noun* flowers or leaves tied or woven into a circle

garlic *noun* an onion-like plant with a strong smell and taste, used in cooking

garment *noun* an article of clothing

garner *verb*, *formal* gather; collect and store

garnet *noun* a semi-precious stone, usually red in colour

garnish *verb* decorate (*esp* a dish of food) ◇ *noun* (*plural* **garnishes**) a decoration, *esp* on food ◇ **garnishing** *noun*

◼ *verb* decorate, adorn, ornament, trim, deck (out), festoon, embellish, enhance ◇ *noun* decoration, ornamentation, adornment, trimming, embellishment, enhancement, relish

garret *noun* an attic room

garrison *noun* a body of troops guarding a fortress

garrulous *adj* fond of talking ◇ **garrulousness** or **garrulity** *noun*

garter *noun* a broad elastic band to keep a stocking or sock up

gas *noun* (*plural* **gases** or **gasses**) **1** a substance like air, such as hydrogen, oxygen *etc* **2** a natural or manufactured form of this which will burn and is used as a fuel **3** *US* petrol ◇ *verb* (**gases** or **gasses**, **gassing**, **gassed**) poison with gas ◇ **gaseous** *adj* ◇ **gassy** *adj* ◇ **gas mask** a covering for the face to prevent breathing in poisonous gas

gash *noun* (*plural* **gashes**) a deep, open cut ◇ *verb* cut deeply into

◼ *noun* cut, wound, slash, slit, incision, laceration, tear ◇ *verb* cut, wound, slash, slit, incise, lacerate, tear

gasket *noun* a layer of padding used to make airtight joints

gasoline *noun US* petrol

gasometer *noun* a large tank for storing gas

gasp *noun* the sound made by a sudden intake of breath ◇ *verb* **1** breathe with difficulty **2** say breathlessly **3** *informal* want badly: *gasping for a cup of tea*

◼ *noun* pant, puff, blow, breath, gulp ◇ *verb* **1** pant, puff, blow, breathe, wheeze, heave, choke, gulp

gastric *adj* relating to the stomach: *gastric ulcer*

gasworks *noun sing* a place where gas is made

gate *noun* **1** a door across an opening in a wall, fence *etc* **2** an exit at an airport from which passengers can board or leave a plane **3** the number of people at a football match **4** the total entrance money paid by those at a football match

🛈 Do not confuse with: **gait**

gateau /'gatoʊ/ *noun* (*plural* **gateaus** or **gateaux**) a rich cake, usually layered and filled with cream

gatecrash *verb* go to a party uninvited ◇ **gatecrasher** *noun*

gateway *noun* **1** an opening containing a gate **2** an entrance **3** *comput* a connection between networks

gather *verb* **1** bring together, or meet, in one place **2** pick (flowers *etc*) **3** increase in: *gather speed* **4** learn, come to the conclusion (that): *I gather you don't want to go* ◇ **gathering** *noun* a crowd

◼ **1** congregate, rally, round up, assemble, summon, collect, come/bring together, meet, group, crowd, attract, draw **2** pick, pluck, cull, select, reap, harvest, crop, glean, collect **3** gain, increase, grow, pick up **4** learn, hear, believe, deduce, conclude, assume, understand

🖅 **1** scatter, dissipate

GATT *abbrev* General Agreement on Tariffs and Trade (now **WTO**)

gauche /ɡoʊʃ/ *adj* awkward and clumsy in people's company

Taken from the French word for 'left', because of the supposed awkwardness of using the left hand

gaudy *adj* showy; vulgarly bright in colour ◇ **gaudily** *adv* ◇ **gaudiness** *noun*

◼ showy, kitsch, flaunting, ostentatious, tawdry, vulgar, tasteless, glaring, garish, loud, flashy, *informal* glitzy, flash, snazzy

🖅 drab, plain, simple

gauge *verb* **1** measure **2** estimate or guess ◇ *noun* a measuring device

◼ *verb* **1** count, measure, reckon, figure,

calculate, compute **2** estimate, guess, judge, assess ◇ *noun* measure, meter, test, benchmark, yardstick

gaunt *adj* thin, haggard

◨ haggard, hollow-eyed, angular, bony, thin, lean, lank, skinny, scraggy, scrawny

gauntlet[1] *noun* **1** a long glove (often of leather) with a guard for the wrist used by motorcyclists *etc* **2** *hist* an iron glove worn with armour ◇ **take up the gauntlet** accept a challenge ◇ **throw down the gauntlet** offer a challenge

gauntlet[2] *noun*: **run the gauntlet** expose yourself to criticism, hostility *etc*

> The *gauntlet* was an old military punishment of being made to run past a line of soldiers armed with sticks; the word is of Swedish origin and unrelated to **gauntlet**[1]

gauze *noun* thin cloth that can be seen through

gawky *adj* awkward-looking, and *usu* tall and thin

◨ awkward, ungainly, gangling, graceless

gay *adj* **1** homosexual **2** lively; merry, full of fun **3** brightly coloured ◇ *noun* a homosexual ◇ **gaiety** *noun* ◇ **gaily** *adv*

◨ *adj* **1** homosexual, lesbian, bisexual **2** merry, cheerful, bright, blithe, sunny, carefree, lively, exuberant **3** vivid, bright, brilliant, sparkling, colourful, flamboyant ◇ *noun* homosexual, lesbian

◨ *adj* **1** heterosexual, *informal* straight **2** sad, gloomy ◇ *noun* heterosexual

gaze *verb* look steadily ◇ *noun* a fixed look

◨ *verb* stare, stare fixedly/intently, contemplate, gape, wonder, eye ◇ *noun* stare, look, fixed look, gape

gazelle *noun* a small deer

gazette *noun* a newspaper, *esp* one having lists of government notices

gazetteer *noun* a geographical dictionary

gazump *verb*, *informal* raise the price of property after accepting an offer, but before contracts are signed

GB *abbrev* Great Britain

GBH or **gbh** *abbrev* grievous bodily harm

GC *abbrev* George Cross

GCSE *abbrev* General Certificate of Secondary Education

GDP *abbrev* gross domestic product

gear *noun* **1** clothing and equipment needed for a particular job, sport *etc* **2** a connection by means of a set of toothed wheels between a car engine and the wheels ◇ *verb* (with **to**) adapt to, design for what is needed

◨ *noun* **1** clothes, clothing, equipment, kit, outfit, tackle, apparatus, tools, implements, instruments, appliances, accessories, supplies, belongings, *informal* garb, togs, get-up, stuff, things **2** gearwheel, cogwheel, toothed wheel, ratchet, cog, gearing, mechanism ◇ *verb* adapt, fit, design, devise, prepare

geese *plural* of **goose**

gelatine *noun* a jelly-like substance made from hooves, animal bones *etc*, and used in food

gelatinous *adj* jelly-like

◨ jelly-like, congealed, rubbery, glutinous, gluey, *informal* gooey, sticky, viscous

geld *verb* castrate (an animal)

gelding *noun* a castrated horse

gem *noun* **1** a precious stone, *esp* when cut and polished **2** something greatly valued

◨ **1** gemstone, precious stone, stone, jewel **2** treasure, prize, masterpiece, *informal* pride and joy

> *Gems and gemstones include:*
> diamond, white sapphire, zircon, cubic zirconia, marcasite, pearl, moonstone, onyx, opal, mother-of-pearl, amber, citrine, fire opal, topaz, agate, tiger's eye, jasper, morganite, ruby, garnet, rose quartz, beryl, cornelian, coral, amethyst, sapphire, turquoise, lapis lazuli,

emerald, aquamarine, bloodstone, jade, peridot, tourmaline, jet

gender *noun* **1** the condition of being male or female **2** (in grammar, *esp* in languages other than English) any of three types of noun, masculine, feminine or neuter

gene *noun* the basic unit of heredity responsible for passing on specific characteristics from parents to offspring

genealogy *noun* (*plural* **genealogies**) **1** the study of history of families from generation to generation **2** a personal family history ◇ **genealogical** *adj* ◇ **genealogist** *noun* someone who studies genealogy or makes genealogies

general *adj* **1** not detailed, broad: *a general idea of the person's interests* **2** involving everyone: *a general election* **3** to do with several different things: *general knowledge* **4** of most people: *the general opinion* ◇ *noun* a high-ranking army officer ◇ **generally** *adv* **1** usually, in most cases **2** by most people: *generally known* ◇ **general practitioner** a doctor who treats most ordinary illnesses ◇ **in general** generally

■ *adj* **1** broad, sweeping, blanket, comprehensive, widespread, wide-ranging, vague, ill-defined, indefinite, imprecise **2** universal, global, all-inclusive **3** mixed, varied, assorted, diverse, miscellaneous **4** common, public, usual, regular, normal, typical, ordinary, standard, everyday

◢ *adj* **1** particular, limited, specific, detailed, precise

generalize *verb* make a broad general statement, meant to cover all individual cases ◇ **generalization** *noun* a too general view, statement *etc*

generate *verb* produce, bring into being: *generate electricity/generate goodwill*

■ produce, cause, bring about, bring into being, give rise to, create, originate

◢ prevent

generation *noun* **1** creation, making

2 a step in family descent **3** people born at about the same time: *the younger generation*

■ **1** production, creation, origination, formation, reproduction, propagation, breeding, *formal* genesis, procreation **2**, **3** age group

generator *noun* a machine for making electricity *etc*

generic *adj* general, applicable to any member of a group or class

generous *adj* giving plentifully; kind ◇ **generosity** *noun* ◇ **generously** *adv*

■ kind, big-hearted, benevolent, liberal, free, open-handed, unstinting, unsparing, lavish, magnanimous, charitable, philanthropic, public-spirited, unselfish, selfless

◢ mean, miserly, selfish

genesis *noun* beginning, origin

genetic *adj* **1** relating to genes **2** inherited through genes: *genetic disease* ◇ **genetically** *adv*

genial *adj* good-natured ◇ **geniality** *noun* ◇ **genially** *adv*

■ affable, amiable, friendly, convivial, cordial, jolly, good-natured, agreeable, pleasant

genie *noun* (*plural* **genii**) a spirit with the power to grant wishes

genital *adj* of sexual reproduction ◇ **genitals** *noun plural* the organs of sexual reproduction

genius *noun* (*plural* **geniuses**) **1** unusual cleverness **2** someone who is unusually clever

■ **1** intelligence, brightness, brilliance, cleverness, fine mind, intellect, wisdom, *informal* brains **2** maestro, prodigy, master, expert, intellectual, mastermind, brain, intellect, *informal* egghead, brains, boffin

genocide *noun* the deliberate extermination of a race of people ◇ **genocidal** *adj*

gent *noun*, *informal* a man ◇ **the gents** *informal* a men's public toilet

genteel *adj* good-mannered, *esp* excessively

gentile /ˈdʒɛntaɪl/ *noun* a non-Jew

gentility *noun* **1** aristocracy **2** good manners or refinement, often in excess

gentle *adj* **1** mild-mannered, not brutal **2** light and soft, not extreme: *gentle breeze* ◇ **gently** *adv* ◇ **gentleness** *noun*

▤ **1** kind, kindly, tender, compassionate, sympathetic, humane, merciful **2** mild, light, soft, moderate, calm

▨ **1** unkind, rough, brutal **2** strong, violent, forceful

gentleman *noun* (*plural* **gentlemen**) **1** a man, *esp* one of noble birth **2** a well-mannered man ◇ **gentlemanly** *adj* behaving in a polite manner

gentry *noun* a wealthy, land-owning class of people

genuine *adj* **1** real, not fake: *genuine antiques* **2** honest and straightforward ◇ **genuinely** *adv* ◇ **genuineness** *noun*

▤ **1** real, actual, natural, pure, original, authentic, factual, true, sound, bona fide **2** honest, sincere, frank, candid, earnest, truthful, open, natural

▨ **1** artificial, false, fake, counterfeit **2** insincere, deceitful

genus *noun* (*plural* **genera**) a group of living things made up of a number of species

geography *noun* the study of the surface of the earth and its inhabitants ◇ **geographer** *noun* someone who studies geography ◇ **geographic** or **geographical** *adj*

geology *noun* the study of the earth's history as shown in its rocks and soils ◇ **geological** *adj* ◇ **geologist** *noun* someone who studies geology

geometric or **geometrical** *adj* of a shape or pattern: made up of angles and straight lines

geometry *noun* the branch of mathematics which deals with the study of lines, angles, and figures

Geordie *noun*, *Brit informal* someone who was born or lives in Newcastle

geranium *noun* a plant with thick leaves and bright red or pink flowers

gerbil /ˈdʒɜːbɪl/ *noun* a small, rat-like desert animal, often kept as a pet

germ *noun* **1** a small living organism which can cause disease **2** the earliest or initial form of a plant or animal, *eg* a fertilized egg **3** that from which anything grows: *the germ of an idea* ◇ **germicide** *noun* a germ-killing substance

▤ **1** micro-organism, microbe, bacterium, bacillus, virus, *informal* bug **3** beginning, start, origin, source, fountain, cause

germane *adj* closely related; very relevant ◇ **germanely** *adv*

German shepherd dog (*also called* **Alsatian**) a breed of large wolf-like dog

germinate *verb* begin to grow; sprout ◇ **germination** *noun*

▤ bud, sprout, shoot, develop, originate, grow, swell, spring up, take root

gerrymander *verb* rearrange (voting districts *etc*) to suit a political purpose ◇ **gerrymandering** *noun*

After US governor, Elbridge *Gerry*, who rearranged the map of Massachusetts in 1811 to a shape resembling that of a sala*mander*

gerund *noun* a noun with the ending -*ing*, *eg* watch*ing*, wait*ing*

gesticulate *verb* wave hands and arms about in excitement *etc* ◇ **gesticulation** *noun* ◇ **gesticulatory** *adj*

▤ wave, signal, gesture, motion, indicate, make a sign

gesture *noun* **1** a meaningful action with the hands, head *etc* **2** an action expressing your feelings or intent: *a gesture of goodwill*

▤ **1** movement, motion, indication, sign, signal, wave, gesticulation

get *verb* (**gets**, **getting**, **got**; *US* **gets**, **getting**, **got**, **gotten**) **1** obtain **2** cause to be done: *get your hair cut* **3** receive: *get a letter* **4** cause to be in some condition: *get the car started* **5** go or move; arrive: *what time did you get home?* **6** catch or have (a disease): *I think I've got flu* **7** become: *get rich* ◇ **get at 1** reach **2** hint at: *what are you getting at?* **3** criticize continually: *stop getting at me* ◇ **get away with** escape punishment for

◇ **get on with 1** continue with **2** be on friendly terms with ◇ **get over** recover from ◇ **get to** affect badly, distress: *the pressure is getting to him* ◇ **get up 1** stand up **2** get out of bed

■ **1** obtain, acquire, come by, receive **3** receive, fetch, collect, pick up, bring, take, catch, grab **5** move, go, come, reach, arrive **6** catch, pick up, develop, come down with, become infected with, *formal* contract ◇ **get at 1** reach, attain, find, discover, obtain **2** mean, intend, imply, insinuate, hint, suggest **3** criticize, find fault with, pick on, attack, make fun of, *informal* knock, slate, pick holes in ◇ **get on with 2** get along with, be on friendly terms with, *informal* hit it off with ◇ **get over** recover from, shake off, recuperate from, pull through, get well/better, be restored, survive

■ **1** lose

geyser /ˈgiːzə(r)/ or /ˈgaɪzə(r)/ *noun* **1** a natural hot spring **2** a device which heats domestic water when the tap is turned on

ghastly *adj* **1** very ill: *feeling ghastly* **2** horrible, ugly **3** very pale, death-like **4** very bad ◇ **ghastliness** *noun*

■ **1** ill, sick, unwell, poorly, dreadful, awful, terrible, *informal* lousy, off colour, under the weather **2** gruesome, hideous, horrible, horrid, ugly, nasty, repellent, shocking, appalling **4** awful, terrible, dreadful, frightful, shocking, appalling, unrepeatable

■ **1** well, healthy **2** attractive

gherkin *noun* a small pickled cucumber

ghetto *noun* (*plural* **ghettos**) a poor residential part of a city in which a certain group (*esp* of immigrants) lives

ghost *noun* the spirit of a dead person ◇ **ghostliness** *noun* ◇ **ghostly** *adj* like a ghost

■ spectre, phantom, apparition, visitant, spirit, wraith, *informal* spook

ghoul /guːl/ *noun* **1** someone unnaturally interested in death and disaster **2** an evil spirit which robs graves and eats dead bodies ◇ **ghoulish** *adj*

GHQ *abbrev* general headquarters

giant *noun* **1** an imaginary being, like an enormous human **2** a very tall or large person ◇ *adj* huge

■ *noun* **1** monster, titan, Goliath, Hercules, ogre ◇ *adj* gigantic, colossal, mammoth, huge, enormous, massive, immense, vast, *informal* whopping

gibber *verb* **1** speak nonsense **2** make meaningless noises; babble

gibberish *noun* words without meaning; rubbish

gibbet *noun*, *hist* a gallows where criminals were executed, or hung up after execution

gibbon *noun* a large, tailless ape

gibe *another spelling of* **jibe**

giblets *noun plural* eatable organs from the inside of a chicken *etc*

giddy *adj* **1** unsteady, dizzy **2** causing dizziness: *from a giddy height* ◇ **giddily** *adv* ◇ **giddiness** *noun*

■ **1** dizzy, faint, light-headed, unsteady, reeling, *informal* woozy

gift *noun* **1** something freely given, *eg* a present **2** a natural talent: *a gift for music* **3** *informal* something easily done: *the exam paper was a gift* ◇ **gifted** *adj* having special natural power or ability ◇ **look a gift horse in the mouth** find fault with a gift

■ **1** present, offering, donation, contribution, gratuity, tip, inheritance, legacy, bequest, endowment **2** talent, genius, flair, skill, aptness, bent, power, faculty, ability, capability ◇ **gifted** talented, endowed, adept, skilful, expert, skilled, accomplished, able, capable, proficient

gigantic *adj* huge, of giant size ◇ **gigantically** *adv*

■ huge, enormous, immense, vast, giant, massive, colossal, *slang* mega, mammoth, *informal* jumbo, whopping

■ tiny

giggle *verb* laugh in a nervous or silly manner ◇ *noun* a nervous or silly laugh

■ *verb & noun* titter, snigger, chuckle, chortle, laugh, snicker

gigolo /ˈdʒɪɡələʊ/ *noun* a male lover

kept by a woman at her expense

gild *verb* **1** cover with beaten gold **2** make bright ◇ **gild the lily** try to improve something already beautiful enough

> ⚠ Do not confuse with: **guild**

gill ¹ /dʒɪl/ *noun* a measure ($\frac{1}{4}$ pint, 11.36 centilitres) for liquids

gill ² /gɪl/ *noun* one of the openings on the side of a fish's head through which it breathes

gilt *noun* beaten gold used for gilding ◇ *adj* **1** covered with thin gold **2** gold in colour ◇ **gilt-edged** *adj* not risky, safe to invest in: *gilt-edged stocks*

> ⚠ Do not confuse with: **guilt**

gimlet *noun* a small tool for boring holes by hand

gimmick *noun* something meant to attract attention
 ▤ attraction, publicity, ploy, stratagem, ruse, scheme, trick, stunt

gin ¹ *noun* an alcoholic drink made from grain, flavoured with juniper berries

gin ² *noun* a trap or snare

ginger *noun* a hot-tasting root, used as a seasoning in food ◇ *adj* **1** flavoured with ginger **2** reddish-brown in colour: *ginger hair*

gingerbread *noun* cake flavoured with ginger

gingerly *adv* very carefully and gently: *opened the door gingerly*
 ▤ tentatively, hesitantly, warily, cautiously, carefully, gently, delicately
 ▰ boldly, carelessly

ginseng /ˈdʒɪnsɛŋ/ *noun* a root grown in the Far East believed to have restorative powers

gipsy *another spelling of* **gypsy**

giraffe *noun* an African animal with very long legs and neck

> Called a *camelopard* until the 17th century

gird *verb*, *formal* bind round

girder *noun* a beam of iron, steel or wood used in building

girdle *noun* **1** a belt for the waist **2** a tight-fitting piece of underwear to slim the waist

girl *noun* a female child or young woman ◇ **girlhood** *noun* the state or time of being a girl ◇ **girlie** *adj* **1** girlish **2** pornographic: *girlie magazines* ◇ **girlish** *adj* like a girl
 ▤ lass, young woman, young lady, schoolgirl, girlfriend, daughter, child, teenager, adolescent, au pair

giro /ˈdʒaɪrəʊ/ *noun* (*plural* **giros**) **1** a system by which payment may be made through banks, post offices etc **2** (*also called* **girocheque**) a form like a cheque by which such payment is made **3** *informal* social security paid by girocheque

girth *noun* **1** measurement round the middle **2** a strap tying a saddle on a horse

gismo or **gizmo** *noun* (*plural* **gismos** or **gizmos**) *informal* a gadget, a thingumajig

gist /dʒɪst/ *noun* the main points or ideas of a story, argument *etc*: *the gist of what he said*
 ▤ essence, substance, sense, idea, drift, direction, point, crux, nucleus, nub, core

give *verb* (**gives**, **giving**, **gave**, **given**) **1** hand over freely or in exchange **2** utter (a shout or cry) **3** break, crack: *the bridge gave under the weight of the train* **4** produce: *this lamp gives a good light* ◇ **giver** *noun* ◇ **give away 1** hand over (something) to someone without payment **2** betray (a person or secret) ◇ **give in** yield ◇ **give over** *informal* stop (doing something) ◇ **give rise to** cause ◇ **give up 1** hand over **2** yield **3** stop, abandon (a habit *etc*) ◇ **give way 1** yield **2** collapse **3** let traffic crossing your path go before you
 ▤ **1** present, award, let someone have, slip, offer, donate, contribute, provide, supply, distribute **2** communicate, utter, transmit, convey, tell **3** break (down), collapse, fall apart, sink, yield,

bend, buckle, give way **4** cause, occasion, make, create, produce, do, perform ◇ **give away 2** betray, inform on, expose, uncover, leak, let out, let slip ◇ **give in** yield, give way, surrender, capitulate, submit, admit defeat, give up, *informal* quit, chuck it in, throw in the towel/sponge ◇ **give up 2** surrender, capitulate, give in, admit defeat, *informal* quit, throw in the towel **3** stop, abandon, renounce, *informal* quit, cut out ◇ **give way 1** yield, surrender, submit, capitulate **2** collapse, break, fall in, sink, subside, cave in

glacé *adj* iced or sugared: *glacé cherries*

glacial *adj* **1** of ice or glaciers **2** icy, cold: *glacial expression*

glacier *noun* a slow-moving river of ice in valleys between high mountains

glad *adj* **1** pleased: *I'm glad you were able to come* **2** giving pleasure: *glad tidings* ◇ **gladly** *adv* ◇ **gladness** *noun* ◇ **glad eye** an ogle ◇ **glad rags** best clothes

■ **1** pleased, delighted, contented, satisfied, happy, joyful, thrilled **2** happy, cheerful, welcome

◳ **1** sad, unhappy **2** sad

gladden *verb* make glad

glade *noun* an open space in a wood

gladiator *noun, hist* in ancient Rome, a man trained to fight with other men or with animals for the amusement of spectators ◇ **gladiatorial** *adj*

glamour *noun* fascination, charm, beauty, *esp* false or superficial ◇ **glamorous** *adj* ◇ **glamorously** *adv*

■ **glamorous** smart, elegant, well-dressed, attractive, beautiful, lovely, charming, appealing, fascinating, exciting, thrilling, dazzling, *informal* glitzy, flashy

◳ **glamorous** plain, drab

glance *noun* a quick look ◇ *verb* take a quick look (at) ◇ **glance off** hit and fly off sideways

■ *noun* peep, peek, glimpse, quick/brief look ◇ *verb* peep, peek, glimpse, look quickly/briefly at, scan, skim, leaf, flip, flick, thumb

gland *noun* a part of the body which takes substances from the blood and stores them for later use or elimination by the body ◇ **glandular** *adj*

glare *noun* **1** an unpleasantly bright light **2** an angry or fierce look ◇ *verb* **1** shine with an unpleasantly bright light **2** look angrily

■ *noun***1** brightness, brilliance, glow, flare, dazzle **2** frown, scowl, stare, *informal* dirty look, black look ◇ *verb* **1** dazzle, flare, shine, beam **2** glower, frown, scowl, stare, frown, *informal* look daggers, give someone a dirty look

glaring *adj***1** dazzling **2** very clear, obvious: *glaring mistake* ◇ **glaringly** *adv*

■ **2** blatant, flagrant, open, conspicuous, patent, obvious

◳ **2** hidden, concealed, minor

glasnost *noun* a political policy of openness and forthrightness, originally in the Soviet Union in the 1980s

glass *noun* (*plural* **glasses**) **1** a hard transparent substance used to make windows, bottles *etc* **2** (**glasses**) lenses in a frame worn to improve eyesight **3** a drinking vessel made of glass **4** *old* a mirror ◇ *adj* made of glass ◇ **glass ceiling** a barrier to promotion at work experienced by some women but not officially recognized ◇ **glasshouse** *noun* a greenhouse

glassy *adj* of eyes: without expression ◇ **glassily** *adv*

■ expressionless, blank, empty, vacant, dazed, fixed, glazed, cold, lifeless, dull

glaucoma *noun* an eye disease causing dimness in sight

glaze *verb* **1** cover with a thin coating of glass or other shiny stuff **2** ice (a cake *etc*) **3** put panes of glass in a window **4** of eyes: become glassy ◇ *noun* **1** a shiny surface **2** sugar icing ◇ **glazier** *noun* someone who sets glass in window-frames

■ *verb* **1** coat, cover, enamel, gloss, varnish, lacquer, polish, burnish ◇ *noun* **1** varnish, lacquer, polish, shine, lustre, gloss, enamel

gleam *verb* **1** glow **2** flash ◇ *noun* **1** a beam of light **2** brightness

◼ *verb* **1** glow, glint, glimmer, glitter, shimmer **2** flash, sparkle, glitter, shine ◇ *noun* **1** beam, ray, shaft, glimmer, shimmer **2** brightness, sparkle, glitter, gloss, glow, lustre

glean *verb* **1** collect, gather **2** *old* gather corn in handfuls after the reapers

◼ **1** gather, collect, find out, learn, pick up

glee *noun* **1** joy **2** a song in parts for unaccompanied voices ◇ **gleeful** *adj* merry ◇ **gleefully** *adv*

glen *noun* in Scotland, a long narrow valley

glib *adj* **1** speaking smoothly and fluently (often insincerely and superficially) **2** quick and ready, but showing little thought: *glib reply* ◇ **glibly** *adv* ◇ **glibness** *noun*

◼ **1** fluent, easy, talkative, plausible, insincere, smooth, slick, suave **2** quick, ready, easy, plausible

glide *verb* **1** move smoothly and easily **2** travel by glider ◇ *noun* the act of gliding

◼ *verb* **1** slide, move smoothly/effortlessly, slip, skim, fly, float, drift

glider *noun* an aeroplane without an engine

glimmer *noun* **1** a faint light **2** a faint indication: *a glimmer of hope* ◇ *verb* burn or shine faintly

◼ *noun* **1** glow, shimmer, twinkle, flicker, glint **2** trace, hint, suggestion, flicker, ray ◇ *verb* glow, shimmer, sparkle, twinkle, flicker, gleam, shine

glimpse *noun* a brief view ◇ *verb* get a brief look at

◼ *noun* peep, peek, squint, glance, quick/ brief look, sight, view ◇ *verb* spy, spot, catch sight of, sight, view

glint *verb* sparkle, gleam ◇ *noun* a sparkle, a gleam

◼ *verb* flash, gleam, shine, reflect, glitter, sparkle, glisten, twinkle ◇ *noun* flash, gleam, shine, reflection, glitter, sparkle, glistening

glisten *verb* sparkle: *the wet stones glistened in the moonlight*

◼ shine, gleam, glint, glitter, flash, sparkle, twinkle, flicker, glimmer, shimmer

glitter *verb* sparkle: *glittering diamonds* ◇ *noun* **1** sparkling **2** shiny granules used for decorating paper *etc*

◼ *verb* sparkle, spangle, twinkle, shimmer, glisten, glint, gleam, flash, shine ◇ *noun* **1** sparkling, scintillation, twinkle, shimmer, glimmer, glint, gleam, flash, shine, brightness

glitz *noun* showiness, garishness ◇ **glitzy** *adj*

> Originally a Yiddish word meaning 'glitter'

gloaming *noun* twilight, dusk

gloat *verb* look at or think about with malicious joy: *gloating over their rivals' defeat*

◼ triumph, glory, revel in, delight in, relish, boast

global *adj* **1** of or affecting the whole world: *global warming* **2** applying generally: *a global increase in earnings* ◇ **globalize** *verb* spread across the world ◇ **globalization** *noun*

◼ **1** worldwide, universal, international **2** general, all-encompassing, comprehensive, all-inclusive, wide-ranging

◪ **1** parochial **2** limited

globe *noun* **1** the earth **2** a ball with a map of the world drawn on it **3** a ball, a sphere **4** a glass covering for a lamp

globule *noun* **1** a droplet **2** a small ball-shaped piece

gloom *noun* **1** dullness, darkness **2** sadness ◇ **gloomy** *adj* **1** sad, depressed **2** dimly lit ◇ **gloomily** *adv*

◼ **gloomy 1** depressed, sad, down, low, despondent, dejected, downcast, dispirited, downhearted, miserable, glum, melancholy, in low spirits, *informal* down in the dumps **2** dark, dingy, unlit, shadowy, dim, obscure, overcast

◪ **1** happy, cheerful **2** bright

glorify *verb* (**glorifies, glorifying, glorified**) **1** make glorious **2** praise highly

glorious *adj* **1** splendid **2** deserving great praise **3** delightful ◇ **gloriously** *adv*

◼ **1** marvellous, splendid, beautiful, magnificent, superb, perfect **2** illustrious, eminent, distinguished, famous, renowned, honoured, celebrated **3** delightful, excellent, wonderful

▣ **2** unknown

glory *noun* (*plural* **glories**) **1** fame, honour **2** great show, splendour ◇ *verb* (**glories**, **glorying**, **gloried**) rejoice, take great pleasure (in)

▣ *noun* **1** fame, renown, celebrity, illustriousness, greatness, eminence, distinction, honour, recognition **2** splendour, magnificence, brightness, radiance, brilliance, beauty, grandeur

gloss *noun* brightness on the surface ◇ *verb* make bright or shiny ◇ **glossy** *adj* shiny, highly polished ◇ **gloss over** try to hide (a fault *etc*) by treating it quickly or superficially

▣ *noun* sheen, polish, varnish, lustre, shine, brightness, gleam, shimmer, sparkle, brilliance ◇ **glossy** shiny, sheeny, lustrous, bright, silky, glassy, polished, glazed, gleaming, enamelled

▣ **glossy** matt

glossary *noun* (*plural* **glossaries**) a list of words with their meanings

glove *noun* **1** a covering for the hand with a separate covering for each finger **2** a padded protective covering for a boxer's hand

glow *verb* **1** burn without flame **2** give out a steady light **3** be flushed from heat, cold *etc* **4** be radiant with emotion: *glow with pride* ◇ *noun* **1** a glowing state **2** great heat **3** bright light ◇ **glowing** *adj* **1** giving out a steady light **2** flushed **3** radiant **4** full of praise: *a glowing report* ◇ **glow-worm** *noun* a kind of beetle which glows in the dark

▣ *verb* **1** shine, radiate, gleam, glimmer **3** flush, blush, colour, redden, look pink ◇ *noun* **1** gleam, glimmer, radiance, flush, blush, redness **2** burning **3** light, brightness, brilliance, splendour

glower *verb* stare (at) with a frown ◇ **glowering** *adj* **1** scowling **2** threatening

▣ glare, look daggers, frown, scowl

glucose *noun* a sugar found in fruits *etc*

glue *noun* a substance for sticking

things together ◇ *verb* join with glue ◇ **gluey** *adj* sticky

▣ *noun* adhesive, gum, paste

glum *adj* sad, gloomy ◇ **glumly** *adv* ◇ **glumness** *noun*

glut *verb* (**gluts**, **glutting**, **glutted**) **1** feed greedily till full **2** supply too much to (a market) ◇ *noun* an excessive supply: *a glut of fish on the market*

▣ *noun* surplus, excess, surfeit, saturation, overflow

▣ *noun* scarcity, lack

gluten *noun* a sticky protein found in wheat, oats and other cereals

glutinous *adj* sticky, gluey

glutton *noun* **1** someone who eats too much **2** someone who is eager for something: *a glutton for punishment* ◇ **gluttonous** *adj* **1** fond of overeating **2** eating greedily ◇ **gluttony** *noun* greediness in eating

▣ **1** gourmand, gormandizer, gobbler, *informal* guzzler, *informal* greedy guts, *informal* pig

glycerine *noun* a colourless, sticky, sweet-tasting liquid

GMT *abbrev* Greenwich Mean Time

gnarled *adj* knotty, twisted

gnash *verb* grind (the teeth)

gnat *noun* a small blood-sucking fly, a midge

gnaw *verb* bite at with a scraping action

gnome *noun* a small imaginary human-like creature who lives underground, often guarding treasure

GNP *abbrev* gross national product

gnu /nu:/ *noun* a type of African antelope

GNVQ *abbrev* General National Vocational Qualification

go *verb* (**goes**, **going**, **went**, **gone**) **1** move: *I want to go home/when are you going to Paris?* **2** leave: *time to go* **3** lead: *that road goes north* **4** become: *go mad* **5** work: *the car is going at last* **6** intend (to do): *I'm going to have a bath* **7** be removed or taken: *the best seats have all gone now* **8** be given, awarded *etc*: *the first prize went to Janet* ◇ *noun* **1** the act or process of going **2** energy, spirit **3** *informal* an attempt, a try: *have a go* ◊ **from the word go** from the start ◊ **go about** try, set about ◊ **go ahead** proceed (with), begin ◊ **go-ahead** *adj* eager to succeed ◊ *noun* permission to act ◊ **go along with** agree with ◊ **go back on** fail to keep (a promise *etc*) ◊ **go-between** *noun* someone who helps two people to communicate with each other ◊ **go for 1** aim to get **2** attack ◊ **go-kart** *noun* a small low-powered racing car ◊ **go off 1** explode **2** become rotten **3** come to dislike ◊ **go on 1** continue **2** talk too much ◊ **go out** stop burning or shining ◊ **go out with** have a romantic relationship with ◊ **go round** be enough for everyone: *will the trifle go round?* ◊ **go-slow** *noun* a slowing of speed at work as a form of protest ◊ **go steady with** court, go out with ◊ **go the whole hog** do something thoroughly ◊ **go under** be ruined ◊ **on the go** very active

■ *verb* **1** move, pass, advance, progress, proceed, make for, head, drive, travel, journey, walk **2** depart, leave, take your leave, set off, set out, *informal* make tracks **3** lead, extend, spread, stretch, reach **4** become, turn, get, grow, come to be **5** operate, function, work, run, act, perform, be in working order **8** be given to, be awarded to, be spent on, be allotted to, be assigned to ◊ *noun* **2** energy, vitality, life, spirit, dynamism, vigour, *informal* get-up-and-go, pizzazz **3** attempt, try, endeavour, effort, *informal* shot, *informal* stab ◊ **go ahead** begin, proceed, carry on, continue, advance, make progress ◊ **go-ahead** *adj* enterprising, progressive, ambitious, forward-looking, dynamic, vigorous, energetic, aggressive ◊ *noun* permission, authorization, clearance, approval, *informal* green light, *informal* OK, *informal* thumbs-up ◊ **go along with** accept, agree with, obey, follow, support, abide by ◊ **go back on** renege on, default on, deny, break ◊ **go for 1** aim for, choose, select, prefer, favour, like, enjoy **2** attack, assail, assault, rush at, set about ◊ **go off 1** explode,

blow up, blast, burst, detonate **2** deteriorate, turn, sour, go bad, rot, go stale ◊ **go on 1** continue, carry on, proceed, persist, stay, remain **2** chatter, ramble on, *informal* witter ◊ **go under** close down, collapse, default, fail, go out of business, founder, go down, go bankrupt, *informal* fold, flop

goad *noun* **1** a sharp-pointed stick for driving animals **2** something used to urge action ◊ *verb* urge on by annoying

goal *noun* **1** the upright posts between which the ball is to be driven in football and other games **2** a score in football and other games **3** anything aimed at or wished for: *my goal is to get to the top* ■ **3** target, mark, objective, aim, intention, object, purpose, ambition

goat *noun* an animal of the sheep family with horns and a long-haired coat

gob *noun*, *slang* the mouth ◊ **gob-smacked** *adj*, *slang* shocked, astonished ◊ **gobstopper** *noun* a hard round sweet for sucking

gobble *verb* **1** eat quickly **2** make a noise like a turkey ■ **1** bolt, guzzle, devour, *informal* put away, *informal* scoff, *slang* snarf

goblet *noun*, *hist* **1** a large cup without handles **2** a drinking glass with a stem

goblin *noun* a mischievous, ugly spirit in folklore

god *noun* a supernatural being who is worshipped ◊ **God** *noun* the creator and ruler of the world in the Christian, Jewish *etc* religions ◊ **goddess** *noun* a female god ◊ **godly** *adj* holy, good living ■ **God** Deity, Supreme Being, Divine Being, Godhead, Creator, Maker, Lord

godfather, godmother *noun* someone who agrees to see that a child is brought up according to the beliefs of the Christian Church

godsend *noun* a very welcome piece of unexpected good fortune ■ blessing, boon, stroke of luck, miracle

goggle-eyed *adj* with staring eyes

goggles *noun plural* spectacles for

protecting the eyes from dust, sparks *etc*

goitre *noun* a swelling in the neck

gold *noun* **1** a precious yellow metal **2** riches ◇ *adj* **1** made of gold **2** golden in colour ◇ **gold leaf** gold beaten to a thin sheet ◇ **gold medal** in sports competitions: a medal of gold awarded for first place

golden *adj* **1** of or like gold **2** excellent or prosperous: *a golden opportunity/a golden age* ◇ **golden handshake** money given by a firm to a retiring employee ◇ **golden rule** a guiding principle ◇ **golden wedding** a 50th anniversary of a wedding *etc*

▣ **1** gold, gilded, gilt, gold-coloured, yellow, blond(e), fair, flaxen, shining **2** fine, successful, glorious, excellent

goldfield *noun* a place where gold is found

goldfinch *noun* a small multicoloured bird

goldfish *noun* a golden-yellow Chinese carp, often kept as a pet

goldsmith *noun* a maker of gold articles

golf *noun* a game in which a ball is struck with a club and aimed at a series of holes on a large open course ◇ **golfer** *noun* someone who plays golf ◇ **golf club 1** a club used in golf **2** a society of golf players **3** the place where they meet

golosh *another spelling of* **galosh**

gondola *noun* **1** a canal boat used in Venice **2** a passenger cabin suspended from an airship, cable railway *etc* **3** a shelved display unit in a supermarket ◇ **gondolier** *noun* a boatman who rows a gondola

gone *past participle of* **go**

gong *noun* a round metal plate which makes a booming sound when struck, used to summon people to meals *etc*

good *adj* **1** having desired or positive qualities: *a good butcher will bone it for you* **2** virtuous: *a good person* **3** kind: *she was good to me* **4** pleasant, enjoyable: *a good time* **5** substantial, sufficiently large: *a good income* ◇ **goodly**

adj **1** large **2** ample, plentiful ◇ **goodness** *noun* the quality of being good ◇ **goods** *noun plural* **1** personal belongings **2** things to be bought and sold ◇ **good-for-nothing** *adj* useless, lazy ◇ **good morning, good-day, good afternoon, good evening, good night** or **goodbye** words used when meeting or leaving someone ◇ **good name** good reputation ◇ **good-natured** *adj* kind, cheerful ◇ **good taste** good judgement for what is aesthetically pleasing or socially acceptable ◇ **goodwill** *noun* **1** kind wishes **2** a good reputation in business

▣ **1** competent, proficient, skilled, expert, accomplished, skilful, able, talented, gifted, fit **2** virtuous, moral, upright, honest, trustworthy, worthy, honourable **3** kind, considerate, friendly, sympathetic **4** enjoyable, cheerful, pleasurable, satisfying, fine, wonderful, superb **5** substantial, considerable, sizeable, large ◇ **goods 1** possessions, belongings, things, *informal* gear, stuff **2** merchandise, wares, commodities, products, lines, stock ◇ **goodwill 1** benevolence, kindness, compassion, generosity, favour, friendliness

▣ **1** incompetent **2** wicked, immoral **3** unkind, inconsiderate **4** bad, poor

goose *noun* (*plural* **geese**) a web-footed bird larger than a duck ◇ **goose bumps** or **goose pimples** small bumps on the skin caused by cold or fear ◇ **goosestep** *noun* a military march with straight legs swung high ◇ **goosestepping** *noun*

gooseberry *noun* a sour-tasting, pale green berry

gore [1] *noun* a mass of blood

gore [2] *verb* run through with horns, tusks *etc*

gorge *noun* a narrow valley between hills ◇ *verb* (**gorges, gorging, gorged**) eat greedily till full: *gorging chocolate biscuits*

▣ *noun* **2** canyon, ravine, gully, chasm, pass ◇ *verb* guzzle, gobble, stuff, glut, overeat

gorgeous *adj* **1** beautiful, very attractive **2** showy, splendid **3** *informal* excellent, very enjoyable

■ **1** attractive, beautiful, pretty, glamorous, handsome, good-looking, lovely **2** magnificent, splendid, grand, glorious, superb, fine **3** marvellous, wonderful, delightful

◪ **1, 2** dull, plain

gorgon *noun* **1** a mythological monster whose glance turned people to stone **2** a very stern-looking person

gorgonzola *noun* a strong-flavoured Italian cheese

gorilla *noun* the largest kind of ape

> ⚠ Do not confuse with: **guerrilla**

gormless *adj*, *Brit* stupid, senseless

gorse *noun* a prickly bush with yellow flowers

gory *adj* full of gore; bloody: *a very gory film*

gosling *noun* a young goose

gospel *noun* **1** the teaching of Christ **2** *informal* the absolute truth

gossamer *noun* **1** fine spider-threads floating in the air or lying on bushes **2** a very thin material

gossip *noun* **1** talk, not necessarily true, about other people's personal affairs *etc* **2** someone who listens to and passes on gossip ◇ *verb* (**gossips, gossiping, gossiped**) **1** engage in gossip **2** chatter ◇ **gossiping** *noun* ◇ **gossipy** *adj*

■ *noun* **1** idle talk, prattle, chitchat, tittle-tattle, rumour, hearsay **2** gossipmonger, scandalmonger, busybody, tell-tale ◇ *verb* **1** spread gossip, tell tales, spread/circulate a rumour **2** talk, chat, natter, chatter

> Originally *godsibb*, meaning 'godparent'

got *past form* of **get**

gothic *adj* of an architectural style: with pointed arches

gouge /gaʊdʒ/ *noun* a chisel with a hollow blade for cutting grooves ◇ *verb* (**gouges, gouging, gouged**) scoop (out)

■ *verb* scoop, hollow, extract, chisel, cut, groove, dig

goulash *noun* (*plural* **goulashes**) a stew of meat and vegetables, flavoured with paprika

gourd *noun* **1** a large fleshy fruit **2** the skin of a gourd used to carry water *etc*

gourmand *noun* a glutton

gourmet /ˈɡɔːmeɪ/ *noun* someone with a taste for good wines or food

gout *noun* a painful swelling of the smaller joints, especially of the big toe ◇ **gouty** *adj* suffering from gout

govern *verb* **1** rule, control **2** put into action the laws *etc* of a country

■ **1** rule, dominate, master, control, regulate, curb, check, restrain, subdue **2** reign, be in power, rule, hold office, direct, administer, be responsible for

governess *noun* a woman who teaches young children at their home

government *noun* **1** rule; control **2** those who rule and administer the laws of a country

■ **1** rule, direction, management, command, charge, authority, power, control, regulation, restraint **2** administration, executive, ministry, Establishment, authorities, state, régime, congress, parliament, council, cabinet, leadership

governor *noun* someone who rules a state or country *etc*

■ ruler, commissioner, administrator, executive, director, leader, head, chief, president, viceroy, commander

gown *noun* **1** a woman's formal dress **2** a loose robe worn by members of the clergy, lawyers, teachers *etc*

GP *abbrev* general practitioner

grab *verb* (**grabs, grabbing, grabbed**) **1** seize or grasp suddenly: *grabbed me by the arm* **2** secure possession of quickly: *grab a seat* **3** get in a hurry: *grab a bite to eat* ◇ *noun* a sudden grasp or catch

■ *verb* **1** seize, snatch, take, pluck, snap up, catch hold of, grasp, clutch, grip

grace *noun* **1** beauty of form or movement **2** a short prayer at a meal **3** the

title of a duke or archbishop: *Your Grace*
4 favour, mercy: *by God's grace*
◇ **graceful** *adj* **1** elegant or beautiful in
appearance **2** done in a neat way
◇ **gracefully** *adv* ◇ **grace-note** *noun*
music a short note played before the
main note in a melody ◇ **with good**
(or **bad**) **grace** willingly (or unwillingly)

■ **graceful 1** elegant, beautiful, attractive, appealing, charming, tasteful

⊟ **graceful 1** graceless, awkward,
clumsy, ungainly

gracious *adj* kind, polite ◇ **gra-
ciously** *adv* ◇ **graciousness** *noun*

■ polite, courteous, well-mannered,
refined, considerate, kind, friendly,
pleasant

⊟ ungracious, ill-mannered, inconsiderate

gradation *noun* arrangement in order of rank, difficulty *etc*

grade *noun* a step or placing according to quality or rank; class ◇ *verb* arrange in order, *eg* from easy to difficult
◇ **make the grade** do as well as is necessary

■ *noun* rank, status, standing, place, position, level, stage, degree, step, rating
◇ *verb* sort, arrange, categorize, order,
group, rank

gradient *noun* a slope on a road, railway *etc*

gradual *adj* step by step; going slowly
but steadily ◇ **gradually** *adv*

■ step by step, regular, even, steady, continuous, progressive

⊟ sudden

graduate *verb* **1** divide into regular
spaces **2** pass university examinations
and receive a degree ◇ *noun* someone
who has a university degree ◇ **gradua-
tion** *noun* the act of getting a degree
from a university

■ *verb* **1** calibrate, mark off, measure out,
grade, arrange, order **2** pass, qualify,
complete studies ◇ *noun* qualified person, bachelor, doctor, master, fellow

graffiti *noun plural* words or drawings
scratched or painted on a wall *etc*

graft¹ *verb* **1** fix a shoot or twig of one
plant onto another for growing **2** fix
(skin) from one part of the body onto

another part **3** transfer (a part of the
body) from one person to another
◇ *noun* **1** living tissue (*eg* skin) which is
grafted **2** a shoot grafted

graft² *verb* **1** work hard **2** get illegal
profit ◇ *noun* **1** hard work **2** profit
gained by illegal means

Grail *noun*: **the Holy Grail** the plate or
cup believed to have been used by
Christ at the Last Supper

grain *noun* **1** a seed *eg* of wheat or oats
2 these seeds or crops in general **3** a
very small quantity **4** a very small
measure of weight **5** the run of the lines
of fibre in wood, leather *etc* ◇ **against
the grain** against your natural feelings
or instincts

gram or **gramme** *noun* the basic unit
of weight in the metric system

grammar *noun* **1** the rules applying
to a particular language: *French grammar* **2** the correct use of these rules in
speaking or writing: *his grammar is very
bad* ◇ **grammarian** *noun* an expert on
grammar ◇ **grammar school** a kind of
secondary school

grammatical *adj* correct according
to the rules of grammar ◇ **grammati-
cally** *adv*

gramme *another spelling of* **gram**

gramophone *noun, old* a record-
player

granary *noun* (*plural* **granaries**) a
storehouse for grain

grand *adj* great; noble; fine ◇ **grand-
child** *noun* a son's or daughter's child
◇ **grand-daughter** *noun* a son's or
daughter's daughter ◇ **grand duke** a
duke of specially high rank ◇ **grandfather** *noun* a father's or mother's
father ◇ **grand master** a chess-player
of the greatest ability ◇ **grandmother**
noun a father's or mother's mother
◇ **grand opera** opera without spoken
dialogue ◇ **grandparent** *noun* a
father's or mother's parent ◇ **grand
piano** a piano with a large flat top
◇ **grandson** *noun* a son's or daughter's
son ◇ **grandstand** *noun* rows of raised
seats at a sports ground giving a good
view

▣ splendid, magnificent, glorious, superb, noble, exalting, fine, great, excellent, outstanding

grandee *noun* a man of high rank

grandeur /ˈɡrandʒə(r)/ *noun* greatness

grandiloquent *adj* speaking in a high-sounding language

grandiose *adj* very impressive or imposing

▣ ambitious, extravagant, grand, majestic, stately, magnificent, impressive, imposing

granite *noun* a hard rock of greyish or reddish colour

granny *noun* (*plural* **grannies**) *informal* a grandmother

grant *verb* 1 give, allow (something asked for) 2 admit as true ◇ *noun* money awarded for a special purpose ◇ **granted** or **granting** *conj* (often with **that**) even if, assuming: *granted that you are right* ◇ **take for granted 1** assume that something will happen 2 treat (someone) casually, without respect or consideration

▣ *verb* 1 give, donate, present, award, allot, allocate, provide, supply, allow, permit 2 admit, acknowledge, allow, accept, agree ◇ *noun* allowance, subsidy, award, bursary, scholarship, gift, donation, endowment

▣ *verb* 1 withhold 2 deny

granule *noun* a tiny grain or part ◇ **granular** *adj* made up of grains ◇ **granulated** *adj* broken into grains

grape *noun* the green or black smooth-skinned berry from which wine is made

grapefruit *noun* a sharp-tasting fruit like a large yellow orange

graph *noun* a diagram with a line or lines showing changes in quantity, *eg* in temperature or money spent

graphic *adj* 1 relating to drawing or writing 2 vivid or explicit: *graphic violence* 3 relating to graphs ◇ *noun* a painting, print, illustration or diagram ◇ **graphically** *adv*

▣ 1 visual, pictorial, drawn, illustrative,

representational 2 vivid, descriptive, expressive, striking, telling, lively, realistic, detailed

graphite *noun* a form of carbon used in making pencils

grapple *verb*: **grapple with 1** struggle or fight with 2 try to deal with (a problem *etc*)

▣ 1 struggle with, seize, snatch, grab, grip, lay hold of, wrestle, tussle, battle, fight 2 face, confront, tackle, deal with, cope with, get to grips with

grasp *verb* 1 clasp and grip with the fingers or arms 2 understand ◇ *noun* 1 a grip with the hand or arms 2 someone's power of understanding ◇ **grasping** *adj* greedy, mean

▣ *verb* 1 hold, clasp, clutch, grip, seize, snatch, grab, catch, lay hold of 2 understand, comprehend, follow, see, perceive, master, realize, take in, catch on ◇ *noun* 1 grip, clasp, hold, embrace 2 understanding, comprehension, apprehension, mastery

grass *noun* (*plural* **grasses**) 1 the plant with long narrow leaves which covers lawns and fields 2 a related plant, *eg* wheat, reeds, bamboo 3 *slang* marijuana ◇ **grassy** *adj* covered with grass

grasshopper *noun* a type of jumping insect

grass-snake *noun* a type of green harmless snake

grate¹ *noun* a framework of iron bars for holding a fire ◇ **grating** *noun* a frame of iron bars, *eg* over a window or drain

grate² *verb* 1 rub down into small pieces 2 make a harsh, grinding sound 3 irritate

grateful *adj* 1 feeling thankful 2 showing or giving thanks ◇ **gratefully** *adv*

▣ 1 thankful, appreciative, indebted, obliged, obligated 2 thankful, appreciative

▣ 1, 2 ungrateful

grater *noun* an instrument with a rough surface for rubbing cheese *etc* into small pieces

gratify *verb* (**gratifies, gratifying,**

gratified) please; satisfy ◊ **gratification** *noun* pleasure; satisfaction

gratis *adv* for nothing, without payment

gratitude *noun* thankfulness; desire to repay kindness
■ gratefulness, thankfulness, thanks, appreciation

gratuitous *adj* uncalled-for, done without good reason: *gratuitous violence* ◊ **gratuitously** *adv*

gratuity *noun* (*plural* **gratuities**) a money gift in return for a service; a tip

grave¹ *noun* a pit in which a dead person is buried
■ burial place, tomb, vault, crypt, mausoleum

grave² *adj* 1 serious, important: *grave error* 2 not cheerful, solemn ◊ **gravely** *adv* ◊ **graveness** *noun*
■ *adj* 1 important, significant, serious, critical 2 solemn, dignified, sober, serious, earnest, sombre
⊟ 1 trivial, light 2 cheerful, smiling

gravel *noun* small stones or pebbles

graven *adj*, *old* carved: *graven images*

gravestone *noun* a stone placed to mark a grave

graveyard *noun* a place where the dead are buried, a cemetery

gravitate *verb* move towards as if strongly attracted (to) ◊ **gravitation** *noun*

gravity *noun* 1 seriousness, importance: *the gravity of the situation* 2 lack of levity, solemnity 3 weight 4 the force which attracts things towards earth and causes them to fall to the ground

gravy *noun* (*plural* **gravies**) a sauce made from meat juices, flour *etc* ◊ **gravy train** a situation producing large, easy profits

gray *US spelling of* **grey**

graze¹ *verb* feed on (growing grass) ◊ **grazing** *noun* grassland for animals to graze on
■ grazing crop, feed, fodder

graze² *verb* 1 scrape the skin of 2 touch lightly in passing ◊ *noun* 1 a scraping of the skin 2 a light touch

■ 1 scratch, scrape, bruise, rub, chafe 2 brush, skim, touch, kiss, shave ◊ *noun* 1 scratch, scrape, abrasion

grease *noun* 1 thick animal fat 2 an oily substance ◊ *verb* smear with grease, apply grease to ◊ **greasily** *adv* ◊ **greasiness** *noun* ◊ **greasy** *adj*
■ *noun* 1 fat, lard, dripping 2 oil, lubrication

greasepaint *noun* theatrical make-up

great *adj* 1 very large 2 powerful 3 very important, distinguished 4 very talented: *a great singer* 5 of high rank, noble 6 *informal* excellent, very good ◊ **greatly** *adv* very much ◊ **greatness** *noun* ◊ **great-grandchild** *noun* the son or daughter of a grandson or grand-daughter ◊ **great-grandparent** *noun* the father or mother of a grandfather or grandmother
■ 1 large, big, huge, enormous, massive, colossal, gigantic, immense, vast 3 famous, important, renowned, celebrated, famed, eminent, distinguished, prominent 4 expert, proficient, skilled, skilful, experienced, able, practised, professional 6 excellent, first-rate, superb, wonderful, marvellous, tremendous, fantastic, fabulous, *informal* super, *informal* terrific, *informal* smashing, *slang* cool, *slang* mega, *slang* wicked
⊟ 1 small, limited 3 unknown 4 amateurish

grebe *noun* a freshwater diving bird

greed *noun* great and selfish desire for food, money *etc*

greedy *adj* full of greed ◊ **greedily** *adv* ◊ **greediness** *noun*
■ starving, ravenous, gluttonous, insatiable, covetous, craving, acquisitive

green *adj* 1 of the colour of growing grass *etc* 2 inexperienced, naive 3 concerned with care of the environment ◊ *noun* 1 the colour of growing grass 2 a piece of ground covered with grass 3 a member of the Green Party, an environmentalist 4 (**greens**) green vegetables for food ◊ **green belt** open land surrounding a city ◊ **Green Party** a political party concerned with conserving natural resources and decentralizing political and economic power ◇ **have green fingers** be a skilful gardener ◇ **the green light** permission to go ahead with a plan

greenery *noun* green plants

greenfly *noun* an aphid

greengage *noun* a kind of plum which is green but sweet

greengrocer *noun* someone who sells fresh vegetables and fruit

greenhouse *noun* a building with glass walls and roof in which plants are grown ◇ **greenhouse effect** the warming-up of the earth's surface due to excess carbon dioxide in the atmosphere

greet *verb* **1** meet someone with kind words **2** say hello *etc* to **3** react to, respond to: *greeted the news with relief* **4** become evident to
■ **1, 2** salute, acknowledge, address, say hello to, shake hands with, kiss, wave to, nod to **3** react to, respond to, meet, receive, welcome
Ea **1, 2** ignore

greeting *noun* **1** words of welcome or kindness **2** reaction, response

gregarious *adj* **1** sociable, liking the company of others **2** living in flocks and herds

grenade *noun* a small bomb thrown by hand

From a French word for 'pomegranate', because of its shape

grew *past form* of **grow**

grey or *US* **gray** *adj* **1** of a colour between black and white **2** grey-haired, old ◇ *noun* **1** grey colour **2** a grey horse ◇ **grey matter** *informal* brains

greyhound *noun* a breed of fast-running dog

grid *noun* **1** a grating of bars **2** a network of lines, *eg* for helping to find a place on a map **3** a network of wires carrying electricity over a wide area

grief *noun* deep sorrow, *esp* after bereavement ◇ **come to grief** meet with misfortune

■ sorrow, sadness, unhappiness, desolation, despondency, despair, distress, heartbreak, mourning, bereavement
Ea happiness, delight

grievance *noun* a cause for complaining
■ complaint, *informal* moan, *informal* grumble, charge

grieve *verb* feel grief or sorrow
■ lament, mourn, wail, cry, weep, sob, mope, brood, pine away, ache
Ea rejoice

grievous *adj* **1** painful; serious **2** causing grief

grill *verb* **1** cook directly under heat (provided by an electric or gas cooker) **2** cook on a frame of bars over a fire **3** question closely ◇ *noun* **1** the part of a cooker used for grilling **2** grilled food **3** a frame of bars for grilling food on **4** a restaurant serving grilled food

grille *noun* a metal grating over a door, window *etc*

grim *adj* **1** stern, fierce-looking **2** terrible; very unpleasant: *a grim sight* **3** unyielding, stubborn: *grim determination* ◇ **grimly** *adv* ◇ **grimness** *noun*
■ **1** stern, severe, harsh, dour, forbidding, formidable, fierce **2** unpleasant, horrible, ghastly, gruesome, awful, frightening, terrible, shocking **3** resolute, determined, dogged, persistent, stubborn
Ea **1** attractive **2** pleasant

grimace *noun* a twisting of the face in fun or pain ◇ *verb* twist the face in this way
■ *noun* frown, scowl, pout, smirk, sneer, pull a face

grime *noun* dirt ◇ **grimily** *adv* ◇ **griminess** *noun* ◇ **grimy** *adj*

grin *verb* (**grins, grinning, grinned**) smile broadly ◇ *noun* a broad smile ◇ **grin and bear it** suffer something without complaining

grind *verb* (**grinds, grinding, ground**) **1** crush to powder **2** sharpen by rubbing **3** rub together: *grinding his teeth* ◇ *noun* hard or unpleasant work ◇ **grinder** *noun*
■ *verb* **1** crush, pound, pulverize, crumble,

powder **2** sharpen, whet, smooth, polish, sand, file, rub **3** grate, scrape, rub, rasp, grind

grindstone *noun* a revolving stone for grinding or sharpening tools ◇ **back to the grindstone** back to work ◇ **keep your nose to the grindstone** work hard without stopping

grip *noun* **1** a firm hold, a grasp: *these shoes have a good grip* **2** a way of holding or grasping; control: *a loose grip* **3** a handle or part for holding **4** a travelling bag, a holdall ◇ *verb* (**grips, gripping, gripped**) take a firm hold of ◇ **gripping** *adj* commanding attention, compelling

▪ *noun* **1** hold, grasp, clasp, embrace, clench, hug **4** bag, case, holdall, shoulder-bag, suitcase ◇ *verb* hold, grasp, clasp, get/catch/grab hold of, clutch

gripe *noun* **1** a sharp stomach pain **2** *informal* a complaint ◇ *verb* complain

grisly *adj* frightful, hideous

⚠ Do not confuse with: **grizzly**

grist *noun* corn for grinding ◇ **grist to the mill** something which brings profit or advantage

gristle *noun* a tough elastic substance in meat ◇ **gristly** *adj*

grit *noun* **1** a mixture of rough sand and gravel, spread *eg* on icy surfaces **2** courage ◇ *verb* (**grits, gritting, gritted**) **1** apply grit to (*eg* an icy surface): *has the road been gritted?* **2** clench: *grit your teeth* ◇ **grittily** *adv* ◇ **grittiness** *noun* ◇ **gritty** *adj*

grits *noun plural, US* coarsely ground maize

grizzled *adj* grey; mixed with grey

grizzly *adj* grey in colour ◇ *noun* (*plural* **grizzlies**) *informal* a grizzly bear ◇ **grizzly bear** a type of large bear of North America

⚠ Do not confuse with: **grisly**

groan *verb* **1** moan in pain, disapproval *etc* **2** be full or loaded: *a table groaning with food*

▪ **1** moan, sigh, cry, whine, whimper, complain, grumble

grocer *noun* a dealer in certain kinds of food and household supplies ◇ **groceries** *noun plural* food *etc* sold by grocers

groggy *adj* weak and light-headed after illness or blows

> Originally meaning 'drunk', from *grog*, a mixture of rum and water

groin *noun* the part of the body where the inner thigh joins the torso

groom *noun* **1** a bridegroom **2** someone in charge of horses ◇ *verb* **1** look after (a horse) **2** make smart and tidy

▪ *verb* **2** smarten, neaten, tidy, spruce up, clean

groove *noun* a furrow, a long narrow hollow ◇ *verb* cut a groove (in)

▪ *noun* furrow, hollow, rut, track, slot, channel, canal, gutter, trough, ditch, trench

grope *verb* search (for) by feeling as if blind: *groping for his socks in the dark*

▪ fumble, feel, search, hunt, probe

gross *adj* **1** coarse, vulgar **2** very fat **3** great, obvious: *gross error* **4** of money: total, before any deductions for tax *etc*: *gross profit* **5** *US informal* disgusting, revolting ◇ *noun* **1** the whole taken together **2** twelve dozen ◇ **grossly** *adv* ◇ **grossness** *noun* coarseness

▪ *adj* **1** coarse, obscene, dirty, filthy, indecent, offensive, rude **2** fat, obese, overweight, big, huge **3** serious, blatant, flagrant, glaring

▪▪ **1** decent **2** slight **4** net

grotesque *adj* very odd or unnatural-looking

grotto *noun* (*plural* **grottoes** or **grottos**) a cave

ground[1] *noun* **1** the surface of the earth **2** (*also* **grounds**) a good reason: *ground for complaint* **3** (**grounds**) lands surrounding a large house *etc* **4** (**grounds**) dregs: *coffee grounds* ◇ *verb* **1** of a ship: strike the sea-bed and become stuck **2** prevent (aeroplanes) from flying **3** forbid (a child) from going out, as a punishment ◇ **grounding** *noun* the first steps in learning something ◇ **groundless** *adj* without reason ◇ **ground floor** the storey of a building at street level

■ *noun* **1** earth, land, soil, clay **2** base, foundation, justification, reason, motive, basis **3** estate, property, gardens, park, fields, land **4** dregs, sediment, deposit, residue

ground[2] *past form of* **grind**

groundhog *same as* **marmot**

groundnut *same as* **peanut**

groundswell *noun* **1** broad ocean waves **2** a growing general feeling or opinion

groundwork *noun* the first stages of a task

group *noun* a number of people or things together ◇ *verb* **1** form or gather into a group **2** classify

■ *noun* band, gang, team, unit, club, society, collection, bunch, batch, lot ◇ *verb* **1** gather, collect, mass, cluster **2** classify, categorize, sort, rank, grade

grouse[1] *noun* (*plural* **grouse**) a game bird hunted on moors and hills

grouse[2] *noun* (*plural* **grouses**) a grumble, a complaint ◇ *verb* grumble, complain

grove *noun* a small group of trees

grovel *verb* (**grovels**, **grovelling**, **grovelled**) **1** crawl or lie on the ground **2** be overly humble in order to gain favour

■ **1** crawl, creep, kneel, crouch, stoop, lie low, prostrate yourself **2** ingratiate yourself, crawl, creep, flatter, fawn, cringe, cower, kowtow, *informal* suck up

grow *verb* (**grows**, **growing**, **grew**, **grown**) **1** become bigger or stronger: *the local population is growing* **2** become: *grow old* **3** rear, cause to grow (plants, trees *etc*): *grow from seed*

■ **1** increase, rise, expand, enlarge, spread, extend, stretch, develop **2** become, get, go, turn, change **3** cultivate, farm, produce, propagate, sow, plant, harvest

Fa **1** decrease, shrink

growl *verb* utter a deep sound like a dog ◇ *noun* a dog's deep sound

grown *past participle of* **grow**

growth *noun* **1** growing **2** increase: *growth in market shares* **3** something that grows or has grown **4** something abnormal that grows on the body

■ **2** increase, rise, extension, enlargement, expansion, spread, development **3** germination, shoot, bud, flower **4** tumour, lump, swelling, protuberance, outgrowth

Fa **2** decrease

grub *noun* **1** the form of an insect after being hatched from the egg, *eg* a caterpillar **2** *informal* food ◇ *verb* (**grubs**, **grubbing**, **grubbed**) dig

■ *verb* dig, burrow, delve, rummage

grubby *adj* dirty ◇ **grubbily** *adv* ◇ **grubbiness** *noun*

grudge *verb* **1** be unwilling to grant or allow: *I grudge him his success* **2** give unwillingly or reluctantly ◇ *noun* a feeling of resentment: *she bears a grudge against me*

■ *verb* **1** begrudge, resent, envy, be jealous of ◇ *noun* resentment, bitterness, envy, jealousy, hard feelings

Fa *noun* favour

gruel *noun* a thin mixture of oatmeal boiled in water ◇ **gruelling** *adj* straining, exhausting

gruesome *adj* horrible

Originally a Scots word, from *grue* 'be terrified', popularized by Walter Scott

gruff *adj* **1** rough in manner **2** of a voice: deep and harsh

■ **1** rude, impolite, unfriendly, rough, curt, brusque, abrupt **2** rough, harsh, throaty, husky, hoarse, croaking

Fa **1** friendly, polite

grumble *verb* complain in a bad-tempered, discontented way ◇ *noun* a complaint

■ *verb* complain, moan, object, protest find fault, *informal* gripe, whine, whinge, *US slang* kvetch ◇ *noun* complaint, moan, grievance, objection, protest

grumpy *adj* cross, bad-tempered

◇ **grumpily** *adv* ◇ **grumpiness** *noun*

■ bad-tempered, cross, irritable, surly, sullen, sulky, tetchy, snappy, *informal* ratty, crotchety, grouchy

🇪🇦 contented

grunt *verb* make a sound like that of a pig ◇ *noun* a pig-like snort

guarantee *noun* 1 a promise that something will happen or be done 2 a statement by the maker that something will work well 3 money put down which will be forfeited if a promise is broken ◇ *verb* give a guarantee

■ *noun* 1 assurance, promise, word of honour, pledge 2 warranty, insurance, contract 3 security, collateral, surety ◇ *verb* assure, give an assurance, promise, warrant

guarantor *noun* someone who promises to pay if another person fails to keep an agreement to pay

guard *verb* keep safe from danger or attack ◇ *noun* 1 someone or a group whose duty it is to protect 2 a screen *etc* which protects from danger 3 someone in charge of a railway train 4 *sport* a position of defence ◇ **guarded** *adj* careful, not revealing much: *guarded comments* ◇ **guardedly** *adv*

■ *verb* protect, defend, safeguard, shield, secure, keep watch ◇ *noun* 1 protector, defender, warder, bodyguard, watch, scout, lookout, sentry, patrol 2 screen, shield, defence, wall, barrier, fence

guardian *noun* 1 someone with the legal right to take care of an orphan 2 someone who protects or guards

guava *noun* 1 a yellow pear-shaped fruit 2 the tree that bears this fruit

gubernatorial *adj*, *US* relating to a state governor: *gubernatorial election*

guerrilla *noun* one of a small band which makes sudden attacks on a larger army but does not fight openly ◇ *adj* of fighting: in which many small bands acting independently make sudden raids on an enemy

> ❗ Do not confuse with: **gorilla**

guess *verb* 1 say without sure knowledge: *I can only guess the price* 2 *US*

suppose: *I guess I'll go* ◇ *noun* (*plural* **guesses**) an estimate ◇ **guesswork** *noun* guessing

■ *verb* 1 speculate, make a guess, predict, estimate, judge, reckon 2 suppose, assume, think, believe ◇ *noun* estimate, judgement, reckoning, *informal* guesstimate, ballpark figure

guest *noun* a visitor received and entertained in another's house or in a hotel *etc*

guff *noun*, *informal* rubbish, nonsense

guffaw *verb* laugh loudly ◇ *noun* a loud laugh

GUI *abbrev*, *comput* graphical user interface

guide *verb* 1 show the way to, lead, direct 2 influence ◇ *noun* 1 someone who shows tourists around 2 someone who leads travellers on a route unfamiliar to them 3 a guidebook 4 (**Guide**) a girl belonging to a youth organization ◇ **guided missile** an explosive rocket which after being fired can be guided to its target by radio waves

■ *verb* 1 lead, conduct, direct, usher, escort, show the way 2 influence, educate, teach, advise ◇ *noun* 1 courier, escort, usher 2 leader, navigator, pilot, director, ranger, escort 3 manual, handbook, guidebook

guidance *noun* help or advice towards doing something

guidebook *noun* a book with information for tourists about a place

guild *noun* 1 an association for those working in a particular trade or profession 2 a society, a social club

> ❗ Do not confuse with: **gild**

guile *noun* cunning, deceit

guillemot /ˈɡɪlɪmɒt/ *noun* a diving sea bird

guillotine *noun* 1 *hist* an instrument with a falling blade used for executing by beheading 2 a machine with a blade for cutting paper 3 the limiting of discussion time in parliament by prearranging voting times ◇ *verb* 1 behead with the guillotine 2 cut (paper) with a guillotine **3** use a parliamentary guillotine on

Named after Joseph *Guillotin*, a French doctor who recommended its use during the French Revolution

guilt *noun* **1** a sense of shame or remorse **2** blame for wrongdoing, *eg* breaking the law ◊ **guiltily** *adv* ◊ **guilty** *adj* ◊ **guilt trip** a spell of feeling guilty

▤ **1** conscience, disgrace, dishonour, shame, regret, remorse, contrition **2** responsibility, blame, disgrace, dishonour ◊ **guilty** responsible, to blame, at fault, ashamed, sorry, regretful, conscience-stricken

▣ **1** shamelessness **2** innocence ◊ **guilty** innocent, shameless

🚹 Do not confuse with: **gilt**

guinea *noun* **1** a sum of money equal to £1.05, sometimes used in expressing prices, fees *etc* **2** *hist* a British gold coin worth a guinea

guinea fowl (*plural* **guinea fowl**) a bird resembling a pheasant, with white-spotted feathers

guinea pig 1 a rodent about the size of a rabbit **2** someone used as the subject of an experiment

guise *noun* appearance, dress, *esp* in disguise: *in the guise of a priest*

guiser *noun* a child who dresses up and goes round houses collecting money in return for performing ◊ **guising** *noun*

guitar *noun* a stringed musical instrument with frets which is played by plucking

gulag *noun*, *hist* a labour camp for political prisoners in the former Soviet Union

gulf *noun* a large inlet of the sea

gull *noun* a seagull

gullet *noun* a passage by which food goes down into the stomach

gullible *adj* easily tricked

▤ foolish, naive, green, inexperienced, ingenuous

gully *noun* (*plural* **gullies**) a channel worn by water

gulp *verb* swallow quickly and in large mouthfuls ◊ *noun* a sudden fast swallowing

▤ *verb* swallow, swig, swill, *informal* knock back, guzzle

gum [1] *noun* the firm flesh in which the teeth grow

gum [2] *noun* **1** sticky juice from some trees and plants **2** a flavoured chewy sweet ◊ *verb* (**gums, gumming, gummed**) stick with gum or glue ◊ **gummy** *adj* sticky ◊ **up a gum tree** in a difficult position

gumption *noun* good sense

gun *noun* any weapon firing bullets or shells ◊ **gun dog** a dog trained to fetch birds *etc* after they have been shot ◊ **stick to your guns** keep determinedly to your opinion

gunboat *noun* a small warship with heavy guns

gunfire *noun* the firing of guns

gung-ho *adj* boisterously enthusiastic

Based on a Chinese phrase meaning 'work together'

gunk *noun*, *informal* unpleasantly sticky or dirty material

gunmetal *noun* a mixture of copper and tin

gunpowder *noun* an explosive in powder form

gun-running *noun* bringing guns into a country illegally

gunwale or **gunnel** (both /ˈgʌnəl/) *noun* the upper edge of a boat's side

gurgle *verb* **1** of water: make a bubbling sound **2** of a baby: make such a sound, *eg* in pleasure ◊ *noun* a gurgling sound

▤ *verb* **1** babble, bubble, ripple, lap, splash **2** burble, babble

guru *noun* **1** a Hindu spiritual teacher **2** a revered instructor, a mentor

gush *verb* **1** flow out in a strong stream **2** talk at length with exaggerated emotions: *gushing on about the wedding*

◇ *noun* (*plural* **gushes**) a strong or sudden flow: *gush of tears*

▣ *verb* **1** flow, run, pour, stream, surge, flood, rush, burst **2** enthuse, bubble over, chatter ◇ *noun* flow, stream, torrent, flood, burst, spate

gusset *noun* a piece of material sewn into a seam to strengthen or widen part of a garment

gust *noun* a sudden blast of wind ◇ **gusty** *adj* windy

gusto *noun* enthusiasm

gut *noun* **1** the intestines **2** animal intestines used *eg* as strings for musical instruments **3** (**guts**) spirit, courage ◇ *verb* (**guts**, **gutting**, **gutted**) **1** take out the inner parts of: *gut a fish* **2** destroy completely, *esp* by fire: *gutted the building*

▣ *noun* **1** intestines, bowels, entrails, vital organs, *informal* innards **3** courage, bravery, pluck, boldness ◇ *verb* **1** disembowel, draw, clean (out) **2** destroy, devastate, clear, ravage

gutta-percha *noun* a waterproof material, less elastic than rubber, used *eg* for insulation

gutter *noun* a water channel on a roof, at the edge of a roadside *etc* ◇ **gutter press** newspapers which specialize in sensational journalism ◇ **guttersnipe** *noun, old* a poor child living in the streets

guttural *adj* harsh in sound, as if formed in the throat

guy¹ *noun* **1** *Brit* an effigy of Guy Fawkes, traditionally burned on 5 November **2** *informal* a man

guy² *noun* a steadying rope for a tent *etc*

guzzle *verb* eat or drink greedily

gym *noun, informal* **1** a gymnasium **2** gymnastics

gymkhana *noun* a meeting for competitions, *esp* in horse-riding

gymnasium *noun* (*plural* **gymnasiums** or **gymnasia**) a building or room equipped for physical exercises

gymnast *noun* someone who does gymnastics ◇ **gymnastic** *adj* ◇ **gymnastics** *noun plural* exercises to strengthen the body

gypsum *noun* a softish chalk-like mineral

gypsy or **gipsy** *noun* (*plural* **gypsies** or **gipsies**) a member of a wandering people; a Romany

Based on *Egyptian*, because of the belief that the Romanies came originally from Egypt

gyrate *verb* whirl round ◇ **gyration** *noun* ◇ **gyratory** *adj*

Hh

habeas corpus a request to produce a prisoner in person and give the reasons for their detention

haberdashery *noun* materials for sewing, mending *etc* ◇ **haberdasher** *noun* someone who sells haberdashery

habit *noun* **1** something you are used to doing: *nasty habits* **2** someone's usual behaviour **3** the dress of a monk or nun **4** an addiction ◇ **make a habit of** do regularly or frequently

☐ **1** tendency, mannerism, quirk **2** custom, usage, practice, routine, rule, second nature, way, manner, mode

habitable *adj* fit to live in

habitat *noun* the natural home of an animal or plant

habitation *noun* a dwelling place

habitual *adj* usual, done by habit ◇ **habitually** *adv*

☐ customary, traditional, wonted, routine, ordinary, common, standard, confirmed, inveterate, hardened, addicted, dependent, persistent

☒ occasional, infrequent

habituate *verb* make accustomed

hacienda *noun* a large house on a ranch in Mexico *etc*

hack¹ *verb* **1** cut or chop up roughly **2** (with **into**) use a computer to gain unauthorized access to other systems **3** *slang* bear, tolerate ◇ *noun* a rough cut, a gash

☐ *verb* **1** cut, chop, hew, notch, gash, slash, lacerate, mutilate, mangle

hack² *verb* ride on horseback, *esp* along ordinary roads ◇ *noun* **1** a writer who does hard work for low pay **2** a riding horse kept for hire

hacker *noun* a skilled computer operator, *esp* one who breaks into government or commercial computer systems

hackles *noun, plural* **1** the feathers on the neck of a farmyard cock **2** the hair on a dog's neck ◇ **make someone's hackles rise** make them angry

hackneyed *adj* over-used, not fresh or original: *hackneyed phrases*

☐ stale, overworked, tired, unoriginal, *informal* corny, clichéd, stereotyped, banal, trite, commonplace, common, uninspired

☒ original, new, fresh

hacksaw *noun* a saw for cutting metal

haddock *noun* (*plural* **haddock** or **haddocks**) a small edible N Atlantic fish

haemoglobin or *US* **hemoglobin** /hiːməˈgloʊbɪn/ *noun* the oxygen-carrying substance in red blood cells

haemophilia or *US* **hemophilia** /hiːməˈfɪlɪə/ *noun* a hereditary disease causing uncontrollable bleeding when cut ◇ **haemophiliac** *noun* someone suffering from haemophilia

haemorrhage or *US* **hemorrhage** /ˈhɛmərɪdʒ/ *noun* a large amount of bleeding

haft *noun* a handle of a knife *etc*

hag *noun* **1** an ugly old woman **2** a witch

haggard *adj* gaunt and hollow-eyed from tiredness

☐ drawn, gaunt, thin, wasted, shrunken, pinched, pale, wan, ghastly

> Originally a falconer's term for an untamed hawk

haggis *noun* (*plural* **haggises**) a Scottish dish made from chopped sheep's offal and oatmeal, traditionally cooked in a sheep's stomach

haggle *verb* argue over a price

☐ bargain, negotiate, wrangle, dispute

hagiography *noun* a biography of a saint ◇ **hagiographer** *noun* a saint's biographer ◇ **hagiographic** *adj* **1** of a hagiography **2** highly praising, eulogistic

ha-ha *noun* a sunken fence or wall

haiku *noun* a Japanese form of poem written in three lines of 5, 7 and 5 syllables

hail¹ *verb* **1** greet, welcome **2** call to, attract the attention of ◇ *noun* a call from a distance ◇ **hail-fellow-well-met** *adj* friendly and familiar on first meeting ◇ **hail from** come from, belong to (a place)

∎ *verb* **1** address, acknowledge, salute, wave **2** signal to, flag down, shout, call

hail² *noun* **1** frozen raindrops **2** a falling mass: *a hail of bullets* ◇ *verb* **1** shower with hail **2** descend in a mass ◇ **hailstone** *noun* a piece of hail

hair *noun* **1** a thread-like growth on the skin of an animal **2** the whole mass of these (as on the head) ◇ **hairy** *adj* **1** covered with hair **2** risky, dangerous ◇ **hair-breadth** or **hair's-breadth** *noun* a very small distance ◇ **split hairs** worry about unimportant details; nitpick

hairdresser *noun* someone who cuts, washes and sets hair

hairdryer *noun* an electrical device which blows hot air to dry hair

hair-raising *adj* terrifying

∎ frightening, scary, terrifying, horrifying, shocking, bloodcurdling, spine-chilling, eerie, alarming, startling, thrilling

hairspray *noun* a fine spray to fix a hairstyle

hairspring *noun* a very fine spring in a watch *etc*

hake *noun* an edible sea-fish similar to a cod

halal *noun* meat from animals that have been slaughtered according to Islamic law ◇ *adj* from animals slaughtered in this way

halcyon /'hælsɪən/ *adj*: **halcyon days** a time of peace and happiness

> From the Greek word for 'kingfisher' in the phrase 'kingfisher days', a period of calm weather in mid-winter

hale *adj*: **hale and hearty** healthy

half *noun* (*plural* **halves**) one of two equal parts ◇ *adj* **1** being one of two equal parts: *a half bottle of wine* **2** not full or complete: *a half smile* ◇ *adv* partly, to some extent ◇ **half-baked** *adj* not properly thought out, incomplete ◇ **half-board** *noun* a hotel charge for bed, breakfast and another meal ◇ **half-breed** or **half-caste** *noun*, *derog offensive* someone with a father and mother of different races ◇ **half-brother** or **half-sister** *noun* a brother or sister sharing only one parent ◇ **half-hearted** *adj* not eager ◇ **half-life** *noun* the time in which the radioactivity of a substance falls to half its original value ◇ **half-mast** *adv* of a flag: hoisted half-way up the mast to show that someone important has died ◇ **halfpenny** /'heɪpnɪ/ *noun*, *hist* a coin worth half of a penny ◇ **half-time** *noun* an interval halfway through a sports game ◇ **halfway** *adv* & *adj* at or to a point equally far from the beginning and the end ◇ **half-wit** *noun* an idiot, a fool ◇ **half-witted** *adj* stupid, idiotic

∎ **half-hearted** lukewarm, cool, weak, feeble, passive, apathetic, uninterested, indifferent, neutral

▨ **half-hearted** whole-hearted, enthusiastic

halibut *noun* (*plural* **halibut** or **halibuts**) a large edible flatfish

halitosis *noun* bad breath

hall *noun* **1** a passage at the entrance to a house **2** a large public room **3** a large country house

∎ **1** hallway, corridor, passage, passageway, entrance-hall, foyer, vestibule, lobby

hallmark *noun* **1** a mark put on gold and silver articles to show quality **2** a characteristic sign: *the hallmark of a good editor*

hallo another spelling of **hello**

hallowed *adj*, *old* holy, sacred

Hallowe'en *noun* the evening of 31 October, traditionally a time when spirits are believed to be around

hallucination *noun* the seeing of something that is not really there

◇ **hallucinate** *verb* ◇ **hallucinatory** *adj* causing hallucinations

▣ illusion, mirage, vision, apparition, dream, daydream, fantasy, delusion, *slang* freak-out, *slang* trip

hallucinogen *noun* a substance that causes hallucinations ◇ **hallucinogenic** *adj*

halo *noun* (*plural* **haloes** or **halos**) **1** a circle of light surrounding *eg* the sun or moon **2** a circle of light depicted around the head of a saint *etc* as a sign of holiness

halogen *noun* one of a group of elements that includes chlorine and iodine

halt *verb* come or bring to a stop ◇ *noun* **1** a stop, a standstill: *call a halt* **2** stopping place ◇ **halting** *adj* hesitant, uncertain ◇ **haltingly** *adv*

▣ *verb* stop, draw up, pull up, pause, wait, rest, break off, discontinue, cease, desist, quit, end, terminate, obstruct, impede ◇ **halting** hesitant, stuttering, stammering, faltering, stumbling, broken, imperfect, laboured, awkward

◪ *verb* start, continue

halter *noun* a head-rope for holding and leading a horse ◇ **halterneck** *noun* a woman's sleeveless dress or top with a single strap around the neck

halva *noun* a Middle Eastern sweet made from pounded sesame seeds

halve *verb* divide in two

▣ divide, split, share, cut down, reduce, lessen

halyard *noun* a rope for raising or lowering a sail or flag

ham¹ *noun* **1** meat from a pig's thigh, salted and dried **2** the back of the thigh ◇ **ham-fisted** *adj* clumsy

ham² *noun, informal* **1** an actor who overacts **2** an amateur radio operator

hamburger *noun* a round cake of minced beef, cooked by frying or grilling

hamlet *noun* a small village

hammer *noun* **1** a tool with a heavy metal head for beating metal, driving nails *etc* **2** a striking piece in a clock, piano, pistol *etc* ◇ *verb* **1** drive or shape with a hammer **2** defeat overwhelmingly ◇ **hammer and tongs** determinedly, violently

▣ *verb* **1** hit, strike, beat, drum, bang, bash, pound, batter, knock, drive

hammock *noun* a length of netting, canvas *etc* hung up by the corners, and used as a bed

hamper¹ *verb* hinder, impede

▣ obstruct, slow down, hold up, frustrate, thwart, prevent, restrict, curb, restrain

◪ aid, facilitate

hamper² *noun* a large basket with a lid

hamster *noun* a small rodent with large cheek pouches, often kept as a pet

hamstring *noun* a tendon at the back of the knee ◇ *verb* **1** make lame by cutting the hamstring **2** make ineffective or powerless

hand *noun* **1** the part of the human body at the end of the arm **2** a pointer, *eg* on a clock **3** help, aid: *can you give me a hand?* **4** a measure (four inches, 10.16 centimetres) for the height of horses **5** a worker, a labourer **6** a style of handwriting **7** side, direction: *left-hand side* **8** a group of playing-cards dealt to someone **9** clapping, applause: *a big hand* ◇ *verb* pass (something) with the hand ◇ **at hand** near by ◇ **change hands** pass to another owner ◇ **hand-in-hand** *adj* **1** holding hands **2** in partnership ◇ **hand-me-down** *noun* a second-hand piece of clothing, *esp* one which used to belong to another member of the family ◇ **hand-picked** *adj* chosen carefully ◇ **hands-on** *adj* **1** hand-operated **2** involving practical experience ◇ **hand over** give or transfer possession of ◇ **hand over fist** progressing quickly and steadily ◇ **hand-to-hand** *adj* of fighting: at close quarters ◇ **hand-to-mouth** *adj* with barely enough to live on and nothing to spare ◇ **at hand** near by ◇ **in hand 1** in your possession: *cash in hand* **2** in preparation, under control ◇ **out of hand 1** out of control **2** at once: *dismissed it out* *of hand* ◊ **out of someone's hands** no longer their concern ◊ **take in hand** take charge of ◊ **try your hand at** have a go at, attempt ◊ **wash your hands of** give up all responsibility for

■ *noun* **3** help, aid, assistance, support **5** worker, employee, operative, workman, labourer, farm-hand ◊ *verb* give, pass, offer, submit, present, yield, deliver, transmit, conduct, convey

handbag *noun* a small bag for personal belongings

handbill *noun* a small printed notice

handbook *noun* a small book giving information or instructions

handcuffs *noun plural* steel bands joined by a short chain, put round the wrists of prisoners

handful *noun* (*plural* **handfuls**) **1** as much as can be held in one hand **2** a small amount **3** a child, pet *etc* which is difficult to control

handhold *noun* something which the hand can grip (*eg* in climbing)

handicap *noun* **1** something which makes an action more difficult **2** a disadvantage, such as having to run a greater distance, given to the best competitors in a race **3** a race in which handicaps are given **4** a physical or mental disability ◊ *verb* **1** give a handicap to **2** burden, impede

■ *noun* **1** obstacle, block, barrier, impediment, stumbling-block, hindrance, drawback, disadvantage, restriction, limitation

> Originally a gambling game in which wagers were drawn by *hand* from a *cap*

handicapped *adj* **1** having or given a handicap **2** physically or mentally disabled

handicraft *noun* skilled work done by hand, not machine

handiwork *noun* **1** thing(s) made by hand **2** something done by a particular person *etc*: *the handiwork of a sick mind*

■ **2** doing, responsibility, achievement, product, result, design, invention, creation, production, skill

handkerchief *noun* a small cloth for wiping the nose, eyes *etc*

handle *verb* **1** touch, hold or use with the hand **2** manage, cope with ◊ *noun* **1** the part of anything meant to be held in the hand **2** a way of understanding something

■ *verb* **1** touch, finger, feel, fondle, pick up, hold, grasp **2** tackle, deal with, manage, cope with, control, supervise

handlebars *noun plural* a steering bar at the front of a bicycle with a handle at each end

handler *noun* **1** someone who trains an animal, a sportsman **2** someone who handles something: *a baggage handler*

handout *noun* **1** a sheet or bundle of information given out at a lecture *etc* **2** an amount of money, food *etc* given to someone in need

handsome *adj* **1** good-looking **2** generous: *a handsome gift*

handwriting *noun* writing with pen or pencil

handy *adj* **1** useful or convenient to use **2** easily reached, near **3** clever with the hands ◊ **handily** *adv* ◊ **handiness** *noun* ◊ **handyman** *noun* a man who does odd jobs

■ **1** practical, useful, helpful **2** available, to hand, ready, at hand, near, accessible **3** skilful, proficient, expert, skilled, clever, practical

hang *verb* (**hangs**, **hanging**, **hung** or **hanged**) **1** fix or be fixed to a point off the ground **2** be suspended in the air **3** (with **down**) droop or fall downwards **4** attach (wallpaper) to a wall **5** (*past form* **hanged**) put a prisoner to death by putting a rope round their neck and letting them fall ◊ **get the hang of** understand, learn how to use ◊ **hang about** or **hang around** remain near, loiter ◊ **hang back** hesitate ◊ **hang fire** delay ◊ **hang on 1** depend on **2** wait, linger

■ **1** suspend, dangle, swing, drape, drop **2** float, drift, hover, linger ◊ **hang about** or **hang around** linger, loiter, dawdle ◊ **hang back** hold back, demur, hesitate, shy away, recoil ◇ **hang on 1** hinge on, turn on **2** wait, hold on, remain, hold out

hangar *noun* a shed for aeroplanes

> ⚠ Do not confuse: **hangar** and **hanger**

hangdog *adj* guilty-looking

hanger *noun* a frame on which a garment is hung ◇ **hanger-on** *noun* (*plural* **hangers-on**) someone who stays near another or others in the hope of gaining some advantage

hang-gliding *noun* a form of gliding by hanging in a harness under a large kite

hanging *noun* an execution in which the prisoner is hanged

hangman *noun* an executioner who hangs people

hangnail *noun* a torn shred of skin beside a fingernail

hangover *noun* **1** uncomfortable after-effects of being drunk **2** something remaining: *a hangover from the 60s* ◇ **hungover** *adj* suffering from a hangover

hank *noun* a coil or loop of string, rope, wool *etc*

hanker *verb* long for: *hankering after a chocolate biscuit*

■ crave, hunger for, thirst for, want, wish for, desire, covet, yearn for, long for, pine for, itch for

hankie or **hanky** *noun* (*plural* **hankies**) *informal* a handkerchief

Hanukkah *noun* the Jewish festival of lights held in mid-December

haphazard *adj* depending on chance, without planning or system ◇ **haphazardly** *adv*

■ random, chance, casual, arbitrary, hit-or-miss, disorganized, disorderly, careless, slapdash, slipshod

▣ methodical, orderly

hapless *adj* unlucky

happen *verb* **1** take place **2** chance to do: *did you happen to see the news?* ◇ **happening** *noun* an event

■ **1** occur, arise, crop up, develop, come about, result, ensue, follow, turn out, transpire ◇ **happening** occurrence, phenomenon, event, incident, episode, occasion, adventure, experience, accident, chance, circumstance, case, affair

happy *adj* (**happier**, **happiest**) **1** joyful **2** contented **3** fortunate, lucky: *a happy coincidence* **4** willing: *happy to help* ◇ **happily** *adv* ◇ **happiness** *noun* ◇ **happy-go-lucky** *adj* easy-going, taking things as they come

■ **1** joyful, jolly, merry, cheerful, glad, pleased, delighted, thrilled, elated **2** satisfied, content, contented **3** lucky, felicitous, favourable, appropriate, apt, fitting

▣ **1** unhappy, sad **2** discontented **3** unfortunate, inappropriate

harangue *noun* a loud aggressive speech ◇ *verb* deliver a harangue

harass *verb* annoy persistently, pester ◇ **harassment** *noun*

■ badger, plague, torment, persecute, exasperate, vex, annoy, irritate, bother, disturb, *informal* hassle, trouble, stress, tire, wear out, exhaust, fatigue

harbinger *noun* a sign of something to come: *harbinger of spring*

harbour *noun* **1** a place of shelter for ships **2** a shelter, a place of safety ◇ *verb* **1** give shelter or refuge to **2** store in the mind: *harbouring ill will*

■ *noun* **1** port, dock, quay, wharf, marina, mooring, anchorage **2** haven, shelter, refuge ◇ *verb* **2** hold, retain, entertain, foster, nurse, nurture

hard *adj* **1** solid, firm **2** not easily broken or put out of shape **3** not easy to do, understand *etc* **4** not easy to please: *a hard master* **5** not easy to bear: *hard times* **6** having no kind or gentle feelings **7** of water: containing many minerals and so not forming a good lather **8** of drugs: habit-forming ◇ *adv* strongly, violently ◇ **harden** *verb* make or become hard ◇ **hardness** *noun* the state of being hard ◇ **hard and fast** strict, rigid ◇ **hard disk** *comput* a hard-cased disk able to store large amounts of data, fixed into a base unit ⋄ **hard-headed** adj clever, shrewd ⋄ **hard-hearted** adj having no kind feelings ⋄ **hard hit** badly affected ⋄ **hard lines** or **hard luck** bad luck ⋄ **hard-nosed** adj tough, unsentimental ⋄ **hard of hearing** rather deaf ⋄ **hard shoulder** the surfaced strip on the outer edges of a motorway, used when stopping in an emergency ⋄ **hard up** short of money ⋄ **hardwood** noun the wood of certain trees including oak, ash, elm etc

■ adj **1** tough, strong, dense **2** unyielding, inflexible, stiff, rigid **3** difficult, complex, complicated, baffling, puzzling, perplexing **6** harsh, severe, strict, callous, unfeeling, unsympathetic, cruel, pitiless, merciless, ruthless ⋄ adv strenuously, earnestly, keenly, intently, intensely, energetically, vigorously

🔁 **1** soft **2** yielding **3** easy, simple **6** kind, pleasant

hardback noun a book bound in a rigid cover

hardly adv scarcely; only just; with difficulty

■ barely, scarcely, just, only just, not quite, not at all, by no means

hardship noun something difficult to bear

hardware noun **1** ironmongery **2** the casing, processor, disk drives etc of a computer, not the programs which it runs (contrasted with: **software**)

hardy adj strong, robust, tough ⋄ **hardiness** noun

■ strong, tough, sturdy, robust, vigorous, fit, sound, healthy

🔁 weak, unhealthy

hare noun a fast-running animal which resembles a large rabbit ⋄ **hare-bell** noun a plant with blue, bell-shaped flowers ⋄ **hare-brained** adj mad, foolish ⋄ **harelip** noun a split in the upper lip at birth

harem /ˈhɑːriːm/ or /hɑːˈriːm/ noun **1** the women's rooms in an Islamic house **2** a set of wives and concubines

haricot /ˈharɪkəʊ/ noun a type of bean

hark exclam listen! ⋄ **hark back to** re-call or refer to (a previous time, remark etc)

harlequin noun a comic pantomime character wearing a multicoloured costume

harm noun hurt, damage ⋄ verb **1** hurt, damage **2** do wrong to ⋄ **harmful** adj ⋄ **harmfully** adv ⋄ **harmless** adj ⋄ **harmlessly** adv

■ noun damage, loss, injury, hurt, misfortune, wrong, abuse ⋄ verb **1** impair, blemish, spoil, ruin, hurt, injure **2** ill-treat, maltreat, abuse, misuse ⋄ **harmful** damaging, unhealthy, unwholesome, dangerous, hazardous, poisonous, toxic, destructive

harmonica noun a small wind instrument played by blowing or sucking as you move your mouth along it

harmonious adj **1** pleasant-sounding **2** peaceful, without disagreement ⋄ **harmoniously** adv

■ **1** melodious, tuneful, musical **2** agreeable, cordial, amicable, friendly, sympathetic

harmonium noun a musical wind instrument like a small organ

harmonize verb **1** bring into harmony **2** agree, go well (with) **3** music add the different parts to a melody ⋄ **harmonization** noun

harmony noun (plural **harmonies**) **1** agreement of one part, colour or sound with another **2** agreement between people: living in harmony **3** music a part intended to agree in sound with the melody ⋄ **harmonic** adj relating to harmony ⋄ noun, music a ringing sound produced by lightly touching a string being played

■ **2** accord, compatibility, like-mindedness, peace, goodwill, rapport, sympathy, understanding, friendliness, co-operation

harness noun **1** the leather and other fittings for a workhorse **2** an arrangement of straps etc attaching something to the body: parachute harness ⋄ verb **1** put a harness on a horse **2** use as a resource: harnessing the power of the wind

■ verb **2** control, channel, use, utilize,

exploit, make use of, employ, mobilize, apply

harp *noun* a triangular, stringed musical instrument played upright by plucking with the fingers ◊ *verb* play the harp ◊ **harper** or **harpist** *noun* a harp player ◊ **harp on about** talk too much about

harpoon *noun* a spear tied to rope, used for killing whales ◊ *verb* strike with a harpoon

harpsichord *noun* an early musical instrument with keys, played like a piano

harridan *noun* a bullying or scolding woman

harrier *noun* **1** a bird of prey **2** a cross-country runner **3** a breed of small dog for hunting hares

harrow *noun* a frame with iron spikes for breaking up lumps of earth ◊ *verb* **1** drag a harrow over **2** distress greatly

harrowing *adj* very distressing
■ distressing, upsetting, disturbing, alarming, frightening, terrifying, nerve-racking, traumatic, agonizing, excruciating

harry *verb* (**harries, harrying, harried**) harass, worry
■ badger, pester, nag, harass, annoy, bother, *informal* hassle

harsh *adj* rough, bitter; cruel ◊ **harshly** *adv* ◊ **harshness** *noun*
■ severe, strict, unfeeling, hard, pitiless, austere, bleak, grim, comfortless

hart *noun* the stag or male deer, *esp* from the age of six years

hartebeest or **hartbeest** *noun* a type of S African antelope

harum-scarum *adj* flighty or reckless

harvest *noun* **1** the time of the year when ripened crops are gathered in **2** the crops gathered in at this time ◊ *verb* **1** gather in (a crop) **2** collect internal organs from donors ◊ **harvester** *noun*
■ *noun* **2** crop, yield, return, fruits ◊ *verb* reap, mow, pick, gather, collect

has *see* **have** ◊ **has-been** *noun* someone no longer important or popular

hash *noun* a dish of chopped meat *etc*

◊ **make a hash of** spoil completely

hashish *noun* the strongest form of the drug made from hemp

hasp *noun* a clasp, *eg* on a padlock

hassle *verb* harass or cause problems for ◊ *noun* difficulty, trouble

hassock *noun* a thick cushion used for kneeling on, *esp* in church

haste *noun* speed, hurry ◊ **hasten** *verb* hurry (on) ◊ **hastily** *adv* ◊ **hasty** *adj* hurried; done without thinking ◊ **make haste** hurry
■ *noun* hurry, rush, bustle, speed, rapidity, swiftness, urgency, rashness, recklessness ◊ **hasten** hurry, rush, make haste, run, sprint, dash, tear, race, fly, bolt, accelerate, quicken, urge, press, drive, advance ◊ **hasty** rushed, impatient, headlong, heedless, impetuous, impulsive, fast, brisk
◪ **hasten** dawdle, delay ◊ **hasty** slow, careful, deliberate

hat *noun* a covering for the head ◊ **hatter** *noun* someone who makes or sells hats ◊ **hat trick 1** *football* three goals scored by the same player **2** *cricket* the putting out of three batsmen by three balls in a row **3** any action performed three times in a row ◊ **keep something under your hat** keep it secret

---

Hats include:
trilby, bowler, fedora, top hat, Homburg, *US* derby, pork-pie hat, flat cap, beret, bonnet, Tam o' Shanter, tammy, deerstalker, hunting-cap, stovepipe hat, Stetson®, ten-gallon hat, boater, sunhat, panama, straw hat, picture-hat, pillbox, cloche, beanie, Bronx hat, poke-bonnet, mob cap, turban, fez, sombrero, sou'wester, glengarry, bearskin, busby, peaked cap, sailor hat, baseball cap, jockey cap, balaclava, hood, snood, toque, helmet, mortarboard, skullcap, yarmulka, mitre, biretta

---

hatch[1] *noun* (*plural* **hatches**) a door or covering over an opening in a floor, wall *etc* ◊ **hatchback** *noun* a car with a rear door which opens upwards ◇ **hatchway** noun an opening in a floor or ship's deck

hatch 2 verb **1** produce young from eggs **2** form and set working: *hatch a plan* ◇ **hatchery** noun (*plural* **hatcheries**) a place for hatching eggs (*esp* of fish)

■ verb **2** concoct, formulate, originate, think up, dream up, conceive, devise, contrive, plot, scheme, design, plan, project

hatchet noun a small axe ◇ **hatchet-faced** adj thin-faced, with sharp features ◇ **bury the hatchet** put an end to a quarrel ◇ **hatchet job 1** a severe critical attack on someone or their good reputation **2** a severe reduction

hate verb dislike very much ◇ noun great dislike ◇ **hateful** adj causing hatred ◇ **hatred** noun extreme dislike

■ verb dislike, despise, detest, loathe, abhor, abominate ◇ noun hatred, aversion, dislike, loathing, abhorrence, abomination

haughty adj proud, looking on others with scorn ◇ **haughtily** adv ◇ **haughtiness** noun

■ lofty, imperious, high and mighty, supercilious, *informal* snooty, contemptuous, disdainful, scornful, superior, snobbish, arrogant, proud, *informal* stuck-up, conceited

☒ humble, modest

haul verb drag, pull with force ◇ noun **1** a strong pull **2** *informal* a difficult or tiring journey or job: *a long haul* **3** an amount gathered at one time: *a haul of fish* **4** a rich find, booty ◇ **haulage** noun **1** the carrying of goods **2** money charged for this ◇ **haulier** noun a transporter of goods

■ verb pull, heave, tug, draw, tow, drag, trail, move, transport, convey, carry, cart, lug ◇ noun **4** loot, booty, plunder, *slang* swag, takings, gain, yield, find

haunch noun (*plural* **haunches**) **1** the fleshy part of the hip **2** a leg and loin of meat, *esp* venison

haunt verb **1** visit often **2** of a ghost: inhabit, linger in (a place) **3** torment:

haunted by the memory of the accident ◇ noun a place often visited by someone ◇ **haunted** adj inhabited by ghosts

■ verb **1** frequent, patronize, visit **3** plague, trouble, disturb, prey on, possess ◇ noun resort, *informal* hangout, meeting-place, rendezvous

haute couture high fashion; the fashion industry

haute cuisine cooking of the highest standard

have verb (**has**, **having**, **had**) **1** used with another verb to show that an action is in the past and completed: *we have decided to move house* **2** own, possess: *do you have a cat?* **3** hold, contain: *the hotel has a swimming pool* **4** give birth to: *have a baby* **5** suffer from: *have a cold* **6** cause to be done: *have your hair cut* **7** put up with: *I won't have him being so rude* ◇ **have done with** finish ◇ **have it out** settle by argument ◇ **have on** *informal* trick or tease (someone)

■ **3** include, comprise, incorporate, consist of **5** feel, experience, suffer, undergo, endure, put up with

haven noun a place of safety

■ shelter, refuge, sanctuary, asylum, retreat

haver verb, *Scot* **1** speak nonsense **2** hesitate, be indecisive

haversack noun a bag made of canvas *etc* with shoulder-straps, for carrying on the back

havoc noun great destruction

■ chaos, confusion, disorder, disruption, damage, ruin, wreck, rack and ruin, devastation, waste, desolation

haw noun a berry of the hawthorn tree

hawk 1 noun a bird of prey which resembles a falcon ◇ verb hunt birds with trained hawks

hawk 2 verb carry goods about for sale ◇ **hawker** noun a door-to-door salesman

hawthorn noun a prickly tree with white flowers and small red berries

hay noun cut and dried grass, used as

cattle food ◇ **hay fever** an illness with effects like a bad cold, caused by pollen *etc* ◇ **hayrick** or **haystack** *noun* hay built up into a mound

haywire *adj* in a state of disorder
◼ crazy, mad, wild, chaotic, confused

hazard *noun* **1** chance **2** risk of harm or danger ◇ *verb* **1** risk **2** put forward (a guess) at the risk of being wrong ◇ **hazardous** *adj* dangerous, risky

◼ *noun* **2** risk, danger, peril, jeopardy, threat, death-trap ◇ *verb* **1** risk, endanger, jeopardize, expose **2** chance, gamble, stake, venture, suggest, speculate ◇ **hazardous** risky, dangerous, unsafe, perilous, precarious, insecure, chancy, difficult, tricky

haze *noun* a thin mist ◇ **hazily** *adv* ◇ **haziness** *noun* ◇ **hazy** *adj* **1** misty **2** not clear, vague

◼ **hazy 1** foggy, smoky, clouded, cloudy, fuzzy, blurred, ill-defined **2** obscure, unclear, indistinct, vague, indefinite, uncertain

◪ **hazy 1** clear, bright **2** definite

hazel *noun* a nut-producing tree of the birch family ◇ *adj* greenish brown in colour ◇ **hazelnut** *noun* a nut produced by the hazel tree

H-bomb *noun* a hydrogen bomb

he *pronoun* a male person or animal already spoken about (used only as the subject of a verb): *he ate a banana*

head *noun* **1** the uppermost part of the body, containing the brain, skull *etc* **2** someone's mind: *can't get that tune out of my head* **3** a person in charge, a chief ◇ *verb* **1** lead **2** be at the front of **3** go in the direction of: *heading for home* **4** hit (a ball) with the head **5** (with **off**) turn aside, deflect: *head off an attack* ◇ **heading** *noun* the title of a book or chapter ◇ **heady** *adj* exciting ◇ **head over heels** completely, thoroughly ◇ **off your head** mad, crazy ◇ **per head** per person

◼ *noun* **2** brain, mind, mentality, *informal* brains, intellect, intelligence, understanding, thought **3** leader, chief, captain, boss, director, manager, principal, head teacher, ruler ◇ *verb* **1** rule, govern, command, direct, manage, run, oversee, supervise, control ◇ **heady** intoxicating, strong, stimulating, exhilarating, thrilling, exciting

headache *noun* **1** a pain in the head **2** a worrying problem

headband *noun* a band worn round the head

headboard *noun* a board across the top end of a bed

headdress *noun* a covering for the head, *esp* a decorative ceremonial one

header *noun*, *football* a shot at goal striking the ball with the head

headfirst *adv* **1** with the head first: *fall headfirst down the stairs* **2** rashly, without thinking

headhunt *verb* **1** take the heads of dead enemies as trophies **2** attract (a person) away from their current job ◇ **headhunter** *noun*

headland *noun* a point of land running out into the sea, a cape

headlight *noun* a strong light on the front of a motor vehicle

headline *noun* a line in large letters at the top of a newspaper page

headlong *adv* headfirst ◇ *adj* very fast or reckless: *a headlong rush*

headmaster, headmistress or **headteacher** *noun* the principal teacher of a school

head-on *adj* & *adv* with the head or front first

headphones *noun plural* a listening device that fits over the ears

headquarters *noun sing* & *noun plural* the place from which the operations or activities of an army, business *etc* are controlled

headrest *noun* a support for the head in a vehicle *etc*

headstone *noun* a gravestone

headstrong *adj* determined, stubborn

◼ obstinate, pig-headed, wilful, self-willed

headway *noun* forward movement, progress

headwind *noun* a wind blowing straight in your face

heal *verb* make or become healthy or sound; cure

☰ cure, remedy, mend, restore, treat, soothe, salve

health *noun* **1** someone's physical condition: *improve your health* **2** good or natural physical condition: *restored to health* ◇ **healthy** *adj* **1** in good health or condition **2** encouraging or resulting in good health

☰ **1** tone, state, wellbeing, welfare, constitution, form, shape **2** healthiness, fitness ◇ **healthy 1** well, fit, good, fine, in condition, in good shape, sound, sturdy, robust, strong **2** wholesome, nutritious, nourishing, bracing, invigorating

☰ **2** illness, infirmity

heap *noun* **1** a pile of things thrown one on top of another **2** a great many (of) ◇ *verb* throw in a pile

☰ *verb* pile, stack, mound, amass, accumulate, collect, gather, hoard, stockpile, store, load

hear *verb* (**hears**, **hearing**, **heard**) **1** receive (sounds) by the ear **2** listen to **3** be told, understand: *I hear you want to speak to me* ◇ **hearing** *noun* **1** the act or power of listening **2** a court case ◇ **hear! hear!** a cry to show agreement with a speaker ◇ **will not hear of** will not allow: *he wouldn't hear of her going there alone*

☰ **2** listen, catch, pick up, overhear, eavesdrop, heed, pay attention **3** learn, find out, discover, gather

hearsay *noun* gossip, rumour

hearse *noun* a car for carrying a dead body to a funeral *etc*

heart *noun* **1** the part of the body which acts as a blood pump **2** the inner or chief part of anything: *the heart of the problem* **3** courage: *take heart* **4** will, enthusiasm: *his heart isn't in it* **5** love, affection: *with all my heart* **6** a sign (♡) representing a heart, or often love **7** (**hearts**) one of the four suits of playing-cards, with red heart-shaped pips ◇ **hearten** *verb* cheer, encourage

◇ **heartless** *adj* cruel ◇ **by heart** by or from memory ◇ **take to heart** be deeply affected or upset by

☰ **2** centre, core, nucleus, crux, essence **3** courage, bravery, boldness, spirit **4** resolution, determination **5** emotion, sentiment, love, tenderness, compassion ◇ **heartless** unfeeling, uncaring, cold, hard, hard-hearted, unkind, cruel, inhuman, merciless

heartache *noun* sorrow, grief

heartbroken *adj* very upset, very sad

☰ broken-hearted, miserable, grieved, crushed

heartburn *noun* a burning feeling in the chest after eating, indigestion

heart failure the sudden stopping of the heart's beating

heartfelt *adj* felt deeply, sincere

☰ deep, profound, honest, genuine, earnest, wholehearted, warm

hearth *noun* a fireplace

heart-rending *adj* very moving, very upsetting

heartstrings *noun plural* inmost feelings of love, compassion *etc*

heart-throb *noun* a sexually attractive person, with whom others fall in love

heart-to-heart *noun* a frank, intimate discussion

hearty *adj* **1** strong, healthy **2** of a meal: large, satisfying **3** eager, over-cheerful ◇ **heartily** *adv*

☰ **2** large, substantial, filling, ample, generous **3** enthusiastic, whole-hearted, unreserved, heartfelt, genuine, warm, friendly, cordial, jovial, cheerful, boisterous, energetic, vigorous

heat *noun* **1** high temperature **2** passion, anger **3** a round in a competition, race *etc* ◇ *verb* make or become hot ◇ **heatwave** *noun* a period of hot weather ◇ **in heat** or **on heat** of a female animal: ready for mating in the breeding season

☰ *noun* **1** hotness, warmth, fever **2** ardour, fervour, passion, intensity, fury, excitement, zeal ◇ *verb* warm, boil, toast, cook, bake, roast, reheat, warm up, inflame, excite, animate, rouse, stimulate, flush, glow

heath *noun* **1** barren, open country **2** heather

heathen *noun* someone who does not believe in an established religion, *esp* someone who worships idols ◇ *adj* of heathens, pagan

heather *noun* a plant with small purple or white flowers growing on moorland ◇ *adj* of the colour of purple heather

heave *verb* **1** lift or pull by force **2** throw **3** rise and fall **4** produce, let out (*esp* a sigh)
🔳 **1** hitch, hoist, lever, haul, drag **2** fling, hurl, cast, toss, chuck

heaven *noun* **1** (often **the heavens**) the sky **2** the dwelling place of God; paradise **3** any place of great happiness ◇ **heavenly** *adj* **1** living in heaven **2** *informal* delightful ◇ **heavenly bodies** the sun, moon and stars
🔳 **heavenly 2** blissful, wonderful, glorious, beautiful, lovely, delightful, out of this world

heavy *adj* **1** of great weight **2** great in amount, force *etc*: *heavy rainfall* **3** not easy to bear **4** oppressive ◇ **heavily** *adv* ◇ **heaviness** *noun* ◇ **heavy-handed** *adj* **1** clumsy, awkward **2** overbearing ◇ **heavy metal** a very loud repetitive form of rock music ◇ **heavyweight** *noun* **1** a boxer in the highest weight category **2** someone very important or powerful
🔳 **1** weighty, hefty, ponderous, massive, large, bulky, solid **3** hard, difficult, tough, arduous, laborious, strenuous, demanding, taxing, harsh, severe ◇ **heavy-handed 1** clumsy, awkward, tactless, insensitive, thoughtless **2** oppressive, overbearing, domineering

heckle *verb* ask awkward questions of a public speaker ◇ **heckler** *noun*

hectare *noun* 10 000 square metres

hectic *adj* rushed; feverish
🔳 busy, frantic, frenetic, chaotic, fast, feverish, excited, heated, furious, wild
🔳 leisurely

hector *verb* bully

> After *Hector*, the Trojan hero in the *Iliad*

hedge *noun* a fence of bushes, shrubs *etc* ◇ *verb* **1** make a hedge **2** shut in with a hedge **3** avoid giving a straight answer ◇ **hedgehog** *noun* a small animal with prickly spines on its back ◇ **hedgerow** *noun* a row of bushes forming a hedge ◇ **hedge your bets** keep open two or more possible courses of action

heebie-jeebies *noun plural, slang* feelings of fear, nervousness or anxiety

heed *verb* take notice of (*eg* advice) ◇ *noun* notice, attention: *take heed of their warning/pay heed to what she says* ◇ **heedless** *adj* careless
🔳 *verb* listen, pay attention, mind, note, regard, observe, follow, obey ◇ **heedless** oblivious, unthinking, careless, reckless, inattentive, unobservant, thoughtless, unconcerned
🔳 *verb* ignore, disregard ◇ **heedless** heedful, mindful, attentive

heel *noun* the back part of the foot ◇ *verb* **1** hit (*esp* a ball) with the heel **2** put a heel on (a shoe) ◇ **take to your heels** or **show a clean pair of heels** run away

hefty *adj* powerful, muscular; heavy
🔳 heavy, weighty, big, burly, hulking, beefy, strong, powerful, vigorous, robust, strapping, solid, massive, colossal, bulky
🔳 slight, small

hegemony *noun* complete influence or power over others

Hegira *noun* the Islamic era, dating from AD 622

heifer /'hɛfə(r)/ *noun* a young cow

height *noun* **1** the state of being high **2** distance from bottom to top **3** the highest point **4** (often **heights**) a high place ◇ **heighten** *verb* make higher or more intense
🔳 **2** highness, altitude, elevation **3** top, summit, peak, pinnacle, apex, climax, extremity, maximum, limit, ceiling ◇ **heighten** raise, elevate, increase,

add to, magnify, intensify, strengthen, sharpen, improve, enhance

🔁 **heighten** lower, decrease, diminish

heinous /'heɪnəs/ or sometimes /'hiːnəs/ adj extremely bad, atrocious: heinous crime ◇ **heinously** adv ◇ **heinousness** noun

heir, heiress noun the legal inheritor of a title or property on the death of the owner ◇ **heir apparent** (plural **heirs apparent**) someone expected to receive a title or property when the present holder dies ◇ **heirloom** noun something that has been handed down in a family from generation to generation

heist noun, slang an armed robbery

held past form of **hold**

helicopter noun a flying machine kept in the air by propellers rotating on a vertical axis

> A coinage based on Greek words meaning 'spiral wing'

helium noun a very light gas

helix noun a screw-shaped coil

hell noun 1 a place of punishment of the wicked after death 2 the dwelling place of the Devil 3 any place of great misery or pain ◇ **hellish** adj ◇ **hellishly** adv ◇ **hellbent on** determined to

🔁 **hellish** infernal, devilish, diabolical, fiendish, accursed, damnable, monstrous, abominable, atrocious, dreadful

hello, **hallo** or **hullo** exclam a greeting used between people: I said hello to him/Hello! How are you?

helm noun the wheel or handle by which a ship is steered ◇ **helmsman** noun the person who steers

helmet noun an armoured or protective covering for the head

help verb 1 do something useful for (someone) 2 give (someone) the means for doing something 3 relieve or improve a difficult situation 4 stop yourself from (doing something): I can't help liking him ◇ noun 1 aid, assistance 2 someone who assists ◇ **helpful** adj

useful, able to help ◇ **helpfully** adv ◇ **helping** noun a share, esp of food ◇ **helpless** adj useless; powerless ◇ **helplessly** adv ◇ **helpmate** noun a partner ◇ **help yourself** serve yourself, take what you want

🔲 verb **1, 2** be of use, serve, aid, assist, lend a hand, back, stand by, support **3** relieve, alleviate, ease, facilitate ◇ noun **1** aid, assistance, collaboration, support, advice, guidance ◇ **helpful** practical, constructive, worthwhile, valuable ◇ **helpless** weak, feeble, powerless, dependent, vulnerable, abandoned

🔁 noun **1** hindrance ◇ **helpless** strong, independent, competent

helter-skelter adv in a great hurry, in confusion ◇ noun a spiral slide in a fairground etc

hem noun the border of a garment folded over and stitched ◇ verb (**hems**, **hemming**, **hemmed**) put or form a hem on ◇ **hem in** surround

🔲 **hem in** surround, enclose, box in, confine, restrict

hemisphere noun **1** a half of a sphere or ball-shape **2** a half of the earth: western hemisphere/southern hemisphere ◇ **hemispherical** adj like half a ball in shape

hemlock noun a poisonous plant with spotted leaves

hemoglobin US spelling of **haemoglobin**

hemophilia US spelling of **haemophilia**

hemorrhage US spelling of **haemorrhage**

hemp noun a plant used for making ropes, bags, sails etc and the drug cannabis

hen noun **1** a female bird **2** a female domestic fowl ◇ **henpecked** adj of a husband: dominated by his wife

🔲 **henpecked** dominated, subjugated, browbeaten, bullied, intimidated, meek, timid

🔁 **henpecked** dominant

hence adv **1** from this place or time: ten years hence **2** for this reason: hence,

I am unable to go ◊ **henceforth** or **henceforward** *adv* from now on

henchman *noun* a follower; a servant

henna *noun* a reddish plant dye used for colouring the hair *etc*

hepatitis *noun* inflammation of the liver caused by a virus

heptagon *noun* a seven-sided figure ◊ **heptagonal** *adj*

her *pronoun* a female person or animal already spoken about (used only as the object in a sentence): *have you seen her?* ◊ *adj* belonging to her: *her house* ◊ **hers** *pronoun* something belonging to her: *the idea was hers* ◊ **herself** *pronoun* **1** used reflexively: *she washed herself* **2** used for emphasis: *she herself won't be there but her brother will*

herald *noun* **1** something that is a sign of future things **2** *hist* someone who carries and reads important notices ◊ *verb* **1** announce loudly **2** be a sign of something to come ◊ **heraldic** *adj* of heraldry ◊ **heraldry** *noun* the study of coats of arms, crests *etc*

▣ *noun* **1** omen, token, signal, sign, indication **2** messenger, courier, harbinger ◊ *verb* **1** announce, proclaim, broadcast, advertise, publicize

herb *noun* a plant used in the making of medicines or in cooking ◊ **herbal** *adj* of or using herbs: *herbal remedy* ◊ **herbalism** *noun* the study and use of plants in medicine ◊ **herbalist** *noun*

Herbs and spices include:
angelica, anise, basil, bay, bergamot, borage, camomile, catmint, chervil, chives, cohosh, comfrey, cumin, dill, echinacea, fennel, gaillardia, garlic, hyssop, lavender, lemon balm, lovage, marjoram, mint, oregano, parsley, rosemary, sage, savory, sorrel, St John's wort (or hypericum), tarragon, thyme; allspice, caper, caraway seeds, cardamon, cayenne pepper, chilli, cinnamon, cloves, coriander, curry, ginger, mace, mustard, nutmeg, paprika, pepper, saffron, sesame, turmeric, vanilla

herbaceous *adj* **1** of a plant: with a stem which dies every year **2** filled with such plants: *a herbaceous border*

herbivore *noun* an animal which feeds on grass or other plants *etc* ◊ **herbivorous** *adj*

Herculean *adj* requiring tremendous strength or effort: *a Herculean task*

After the Greek hero, *Hercules*, who was given twelve seemingly impossible tasks to do by the gods

herd *noun* **1** a group of animals of one kind **2** (**the herd**) most people ◊ *verb* group or crowd together like a herd of animals

▣ *noun* **1** drove, flock, swarm, pack **2** mass, horde, throng, multitude, crowd, mob, the masses, rabble ◊ *verb* flock, congregate, gather, collect, assemble, rally

here *adv* at, in or to this place: *he's here already/come here!* ◊ **hereabouts** *adv* approximately in this place ◊ **hereafter** *adv* after this ◊ **the hereafter** life after death ◊ **hereby** *adv* by this means

heredity *noun* the passing on of characteristics from parents to children ◊ **hereditary** *adj* passed on in this way

▣ **hereditary** inherited, handed down, family, ancestral, inborn, inbred, innate, natural, congenital, genetic

heresy /'hɛrəsɪ/ *noun* (*plural* **heresies**) an opinion which goes against the official (*esp* religious) view ◊ **heretic** *noun* someone who holds or teaches such an opinion ◊ **heretical** *adj*

▣ dissidence, blasphemy ◊ **heretic** free-thinker, nonconformist, dissident, dissenter

heritage *noun* **1** something passed on by or inherited from an earlier generation **2** a nation's marks of history, *eg* significant buildings or traditions

▣ **1** inheritance, legacy, bequest, endowment, lot, portion, share, birthright, due **2** history, past, tradition, culture

hermaphrodite *noun* an animal which has the qualities of both male and female sexes

hermetically *adv*: **hermetically sealed** closed completely and airtight

hermit *noun* someone who lives alone, often for religious reasons ◊ **hermitage** *noun* the dwelling of a hermit ◊ **hermit crab** a kind of crab which lives in the abandoned shell of a shellfish

▣ recluse, solitary, monk, ascetic

hernia *noun* the bursting out of part of an internal organ through a weak spot in surrounding body tissue

hero *noun* (*plural* **heroes**), **heroine** *noun* **1** someone much admired for their bravery **2** the chief character in a story, film *etc* ◊ **heroic** *adj* **1** very brave, like a hero **2** of heroes ◊ **heroically** *adv* ◊ **heroism** *noun* bravery

▣ **heroic 1** brave, courageous, fearless, undaunted, valiant, bold, daring, adventurous, gallant, chivalrous, noble, selfless

▣ **heroic 1** cowardly, timid

heroin *noun* a drug derived from morphine

heron *noun* a large water bird, with long legs and neck

herpes *noun* any of various types of skin disease

herring *noun* (*plural* **herring** or **herrings**) an edible sea fish with silvery colouring, which moves in large shoals

hers and **herself** *see* **her**

hertz *noun* a unit of frequency for radio waves *etc*

hesitate *verb* **1** pause because of uncertainty **2** be unwilling (to do something): *I hesitate to ask* ◊ **hesitancy** *noun* ◊ **hesitant** *adj* ◊ **hesitation** *noun*

▣ **1** delay, think twice, hold back, waver, be uncertain, stumble, halt **2** be reluctant, be unwilling, scruple, shrink from ◊ **hesitant** hesitating, reluctant, uncertain, indecisive, wavering, tentative, wary, shy, halting

▣ **hesitant** decisive, resolute, confident, fluent

hessian *noun* a type of coarse cloth

heterodox *noun* heretical, having an opinion other than the accepted one

(*contrasted with*: **orthodox**) ◊ **heterodoxy** *noun*

heterogeneous *adj* composed of many different kinds (*contrasted with*: **homogeneous**)

heterosexual *noun & adj* (someone who is) sexually attracted to the opposite sex ◊ **heterosexuality** *noun*

het up *informal* excited, angry or agitated

heuristic *adj* based on trial and error

hew *verb* (**hews**, **hewing**, **hewed**, **hewn** or **hewed**) cut or shape with an axe *etc*

▣ cut, fell, axe, lop, chop, hack, sever, split, carve, sculpt, sculpture, fashion, model, form, shape, make

hex *noun* a spell to bring bad luck; a curse

hexagon *noun* a six-sided figure ◊ **hexagonal** *adj*

hey *exclam* a call to attract attention: *Hey! You're going the wrong way!*

heyday *noun* the time of greatest strength, the prime

▣ peak, prime, flush, bloom, golden age, boom time

From an old English expression *hey-da*, meaning 'hurrah'. The *-day* ending and current sense developed much later

HGV *abbrev* heavy goods vehicle

hi *exclam*, *informal* **1** hello **2** hey

hiatus /haɪˈeɪtəs/ *noun* a gap, a rift

hibernate *verb* of an animal: pass the winter in a dormant state ◊ **hibernation** *noun* ◊ **hibernator** *noun*

hibiscus *noun* a tropical tree with large colourful flowers

hiccup *noun* **1** an involuntary sharp gasp, caused by laughing, drinking *etc* **2** (**hiccups**) a fit of such gasping **3** a minor setback or difficulty ◊ *verb* make the sound of a hiccup or have hiccups

hickory *noun* (*plural* **hickories**) a N American tree or its wood

hide¹ *verb* (**hides**, **hiding**, **hid**, **hidden**) put or keep out of sight ◊ *noun* a concealed place from which to watch birds *etc* ◇ **hidden** *adj* **1** concealed, out of sight **2** unknown: *hidden meaning*

■ *verb* conceal, cover, shroud, veil, screen, mask, disguise, camouflage, obscure, bury, *informal* stash, withhold, take cover, shelter ◇ **hidden 1** concealed, covered, disguised, camouflaged, unseen **2** secret, covert, cryptic, mysterious

◾ *verb* reveal, show, display

hide[2] *noun* the skin of an animal ◇ **hidebound** *adj* not open to new ideas ◇ **hiding** *noun* a beating

■ skin, pelt, fur, leather ◇ **hiding** flogging, whipping, caning, spanking, thrashing, *informal* walloping

◾ **hidebound** liberal, progressive

hideous *adj* **1** horrible, ghastly **2** very ugly ◇ **hideously** *adv* ◇ **hideousness** *noun*

■ **1**, **2** ugly, repulsive, grotesque, monstrous, horrid, ghastly, awful, dreadful, frightful, terrible, grim, gruesome, macabre, terrifying, shocking, appalling, disgusting, revolting, horrible

◾ **2** beautiful, attractive

hierarchy *noun* a number of people or things arranged in order of rank ◇ **hierarchical** *adj*

■ pecking order, ranking, scale, ladder, echelons, strata

hieroglyphics *noun plural* ancient Egyptian writing, in which pictures are used as letters

hi-fi *adj* short for **high-fidelity** ◇ *noun, informal* a set of high-quality equipment for reproducing recorded sound

higgledy-piggledy *adv* & *adj* in a complete muddle

high *adj* **1** raised far above **2** extending far upwards, tall **3** well up on any scale of measurement, rank *etc* **4** great, large: *high hopes/high prices* **5** of sound: shrill, acute in pitch **6** of meat: beginning to go bad ◇ *adv* **1** far above in the air **2** well up on any scale **3** to a high degree ◇ **Higher** *noun* an examination in Scottish secondary schools, usually taken at the end of the 5th year

◇ **highly** *adv* very: *highly delighted* ◇ **Highness** *noun* a title of a monarch ◇ **for the high jump** expecting trouble or punishment ◇ **High Court** a supreme court ◇ **high-fidelity** *adj* reproducing sound very clearly ◇ **high-five** *noun* a sign of greeting made by slapping together one another's raised palms ◇ **high-flier** *noun* a highly ambitious person ◇ **high-flown** *adj* of language, style: using words that sound too grand or pompous ◇ **high-handed** *adj* thoughtless, overbearing ◇ **high jinks** lively games or play ◇ **highly-strung** *adj* nervous, easily excited ◇ **high road** a main road ◇ **high-spirited** *adj* bold, lively ◇ **high tea** a cooked meal in the late afternoon ◇ **high-tech** *adj* using advanced technology ◇ **high tide** or **high water** the time when the tide is farthest up the shore ◇ **high treason** the crime of acting against the safety of your own country ◇ **the high seas** the open sea ◇ **on your high horse** behaving with exaggerated pride or superiority

■ *adj* **2** tall, elevated, soaring, towering **3** important, influential, powerful, distinguished, chief, senior ◇ **highly** greatly, considerably, extremely, immensely, tremendously, exceptionally

highball *noun, US* an alcoholic drink and mixer (*eg* whisky and soda) with ice in a tall glass

highbrow *adj* intellectual, very literary (*contrasted with*: **lowbrow**)

■ intellectual, sophisticated, cultured, academic

highlight *noun* **1** a bright spot or area in a picture **2** a lighter patch in hair *etc* **3** the most memorable part or experience: *the highlight of the week* ◇ *verb* emphasize, make the focus of attention ◇ **highlighter** *noun* a brightly coloured felt-tip pen used to mark but not obscure lines of text

■ *noun* **3** high point, peak, climax, best

highway *noun* the public road ◇ **highwayman** *noun, hist* a robber who attacked people on the public road ◇ **Highway Code** a set of official rules for road users in Britain

hijack *verb* steal (a car, aeroplane *etc*) while it is moving, forcing the driver or pilot to take a new route ◇ *noun* the action of hijacking a vehicle *etc* ◇ **hijacker** *noun*

hike *verb* travel on foot through countryside ◇ *noun* a long country walk ◇ **hiker** *noun*

hilarious *adj* extremely funny ◇ **hilariously** *adv* ◇ **hilarity** *noun*

▦ amusing, comical, side-splitting, *informal* hysterical, rollicking, merry, jolly, jovial ◇ **hilarity** mirth, laughter, fun, amusement, merriment, high spirits, exhilaration

▨ serious, grave

hill *noun* a mound of high land, less high than a mountain ◇ **hilly** *adj*

hillock *noun* a small hill

hilt *noun* the handle of a sword ◇ **up to the hilt** thoroughly, completely

him *pronoun* a male person or animal already spoken about (used only as the object in a sentence): *I saw him yesterday/what did you say to him?* ◇ **himself** *pronoun* **1** used reflexively: *he cut himself shaving* **2** used for emphasis: *he wrote it himself*

hind[1] *noun* a female deer

hind[2] *adj* placed behind ◇ **hindmost** *adj* farthest behind ◇ **hindsight** *noun* wisdom or knowledge got only after something has happened

▦ back, rear

hinder *verb* keep back, obstruct, prevent ◇ **hindrance** *noun* something that hinders

▦ hamper, obstruct, impede, hold up, delay, slow down, hold back, stop, prevent, frustrate ◇ **hindrance** obstruction, impediment, obstacle, barrier, restriction, drag, disadvantage

▨ help, aid, assist

hinge *noun* a joint on which a door, lid *etc* turns to open or close ◇ *verb* **1** move on a hinge **2** depend (on): *everything hinges on the weather*

▦ *verb* **2** centre, turn, revolve, pivot, hang, depend, rest

hint *noun* **1** a remark which suggests a

meaning without stating it clearly **2** a piece of helpful advice: *I'll give you a hint* **3** a slight impression, a suggestion: *a hint of panic in her voice* ◇ *verb* suggest without stating clearly: *he hinted that he might be there*

▦ *noun* **1** clue, tip-off, reminder, indication, sign, pointer **2** tip, advice, suggestion, help **3** touch, trace, tinge, taste, dash, suggestion ◇ *verb* suggest, prompt, tip off, indicate, imply, insinuate, intimate, allude

hinterland *noun* an area lying inland from the coast

hip[1] *noun* the part of the side of the body just below the waist ◇ **hip flask** a small pocket flask for alcohol

hip[2] *noun* the fruit of the wild rose

hip[3] *adj* very fashionable, trendy

hippie *noun* a member of a youth movement, *esp* of the 1960s, rebelling against conventional society, dress codes *etc*

Hippocratic oath an oath taken by a doctor agreeing to observe a code of medical ethics

hippodrome *noun* **1** an arena for horse-racing **2** a large theatre

hippopotamus *noun* (*plural* **hippopotami** or **hippopotamuses**) a large African animal living in and near rivers

Based on a Greek word which translates as 'river horse'

hire *noun* money paid for work done, or for the use of something belonging to another person ◇ *verb* give or get the use or services of by paying money ◇ **hire-purchase** *noun* a way of buying an article by paying for it in instalments

▦ *verb* rent, let, lease, charter, commission, book, reserve, employ, take on, sign up, engage, appoint, retain

hirsute *adj* hairy, shaggy

his *adj* belonging to him: *his book* ◇ *pronoun* something belonging to him: *that jacket is his*

Hispanic *adj* **1** Spanish **2** Spanish-American

hiss *verb* make a sound like a snake ◊ *noun* (*plural* **hisses**) such a sound, made to show anger or displeasure

histamine *noun* a chemical present in pollen *etc* which can cause an allergic reaction

histology *noun* the study of animal tissue ◊ **histological** *adj* ◊ **histologist** *noun*

history *noun* (*plural* **histories**) **1** the study of the past **2** a description of past events, society *etc* ◊ **historian** *noun* someone who studies or writes history ◊ **historic** *adj* important, likely to be remembered ◊ **historical** *adj* **1** of history **2** true of something in the past

■ **2** record, chronicle, chronology, account, narrative, story, tale, saga, biography, life, autobiography, memoirs ◊ **historic** momentous, important, significant, notable, remarkable, outstanding, extraordinary, celebrated, renowned, famed, famous

✦ **historic** unimportant, insignificant, unknown

histrionic *adj* **1** expressing exaggerated emotion; melodramatic **2** relating to acting or actors ◊ **histrionics** *noun plural* an exaggerated show of strong feeling

hit *verb* **1** strike with a blow, missile *etc* **2** occur suddenly to: *it finally hit me* ◊ *noun* **1** a blow, a stroke **2** a shot which hits a target **3** a success **4** a successful song, recording *etc* **5** *slang* a murder by criminals **6** *slang* a dose of a drug ◊ **hit-and-miss** *adj* haphazard, sometimes working and sometimes not ◊ **hit-and-run** *adj* driving away after causing injury without reporting the accident ◊ **hitman** *noun*, *slang* someone employed to kill or attack others ◊ **hit the ceiling** or **hit the roof** explode with anger ◊ **hit the nail on the head** identify the important point, be exactly right ◊ **hit upon** come upon, discover: *hit upon a solution to the problem*

■ *verb* **1** strike, knock, tap, smack, slap, thrash, *informal* whack, bash, thump, clout, punch, *informal* belt, *informal* wallop, beat, batter ◊ *noun* **1** blow, knock, tap, slap, smack, bash, bump,

collision, impact, crash, smash **3** triumph, *slang* winner

hitch *verb* **1** fasten with a hook *etc* **2** lift with a jerk **3** hitchhike ◊ *noun* (*plural* **hitches**) **1** a jerk **2** an unexpected problem which stops or delays something **3** a type of knot

■ *noun* **2** delay, hold-up, trouble, problem, difficulty, mishap, setback, hiccup, drawback, snag, catch, impediment, hindrance

hitchhike *verb* travel by getting lifts in other people's vehicles ◊ **hitchhiker** *noun*

hither *adv* to this place ◊ **hither and thither** back and forwards ◊ **hitherto** *adv* up till now

HIV *abbrev* human immunodeficiency virus ◊ **HIV-positive** *adj* carrying HIV

hive *noun* **1** place where bees live **2** a busy place: *hive of industry*

hives *noun sing* nettle rash

HM *abbrev* Her or His Majesty

hoard *noun* a hidden store of treasure, food *etc* ◊ *verb* store up secretly

■ *noun* collection, accumulation, mass, heap, pile, supply, reserve, store, cache, *informal* stash ◊ *verb* collect, gather, amass, accumulate, save, put by, store

✦ *verb* use, spend, squander

⚠ Do not confuse with: **horde**

hoarding *noun* **1** a fence of boards **2** a wooden surface for displaying advertisements, posters *etc*

hoarse *adj* having a harsh voice, *eg* from a cold or cough

■ husky, croaky, throaty, gravelly, gruff, rough, harsh, rasping

hoary *adj* **1** white with age **2** very old ◊ **hoar-frost** *noun* white frost

hoax *noun* (*plural* **hoaxes**) a trick played to deceive ◊ *verb* play a hoax on

■ *noun* trick, prank, practical joke, joke, deception, bluff, cheat, swindle, *informal* con ◊ *verb* trick, deceive, take in, fool, dupe, *informal* have on, *informal* pull someone's leg, *informal* con, swindle, *informal* take for a ride, cheat, bluff

hob *noun* the top of a cooker or a flat

surface with rings for heating pans, pots *etc*

hobble *verb* **1** walk with short unsteady steps **2** tie the legs of (a horse *etc*) loosely **3** impede, hamper

▪ **1** limp, stumble, stagger, totter

hobby *noun* (*plural* **hobbies**) a favourite way of passing your spare time

▪ pastime, diversion, recreation, relaxation, pursuit, sideline

> Originally *hobby-horse*, a horse used in morris dances and therefore for amusement or pleasure

hobby-horse *noun* **1** a toy wooden horse **2** a favourite subject of discussion

hobgoblin *noun* a mischievous fairy

hobnail *noun* a large nail used for horseshoes and in the soles of heavy boots

hobnob *verb* (**hobnobs**, **hobnobbing**, **hobnobbed**) be on friendly terms (with); socialize (with)

hobo *noun* (*plural* **hoboes**) a tramp

Hobson's choice the choice of having what is offered, or nothing at all

> Named after *Hobson*, a Cambridge horsekeeper who reputedly gave customers the choice of the horse nearest the door or none at all

hock[1] *noun* a joint on the hind leg of an animal, below the knee

hock[2] *noun* a white German wine

hockey *noun* a ball game played by two teams of 11 players with clubs curved at one end

hocus-pocus *noun* deception, trickery

hod *noun* **1** a wooden trough on a pole, used for carrying bricks and mortar **2** a container for coal

hodge-podge *noun* a hotchpotch

hoe *noun* a tool used for weeding, loosening earth *etc* ◇ *verb* use a hoe

hog *noun* a pig ◇ *verb*, *informal* (**hogs**, **hogging**, **hogged**) take or use selfishly ◇ **hogwash** *noun* nonsense, rubbish

Hogmanay *noun* the name in Scotland for 31 December and the celebrations held that night

> From an old French word *aguillan-neuf*, a gift given at New Year

hoi polloi the masses, the rabble

> Taken from a Greek phrase for 'the people'

hoist *verb* lift, raise ◇ *noun* something which lifts heavy goods

▪ *verb* lift, elevate, raise, erect, heave, rear, uplift

hoity-toity *adj* haughty, superior

hokum *noun*, *US* pretentious rubbish, claptrap

hold *verb* (**holds**, **holding**, **held**) **1** keep in your possession or power; have **2** support or contain **3** occupy (a position *etc*) **4** think, believe **5** put on, organize: *hold a meeting* **6** apply: *that rule doesn't hold any longer* ◇ *noun* **1** grip, grasp **2** influence: *a hold over the others* **3** a large space for carrying a ship's cargo ◇ **holder** *noun* **1** a container **2** someone who holds (a position *etc*) ◇ **holding** *noun* an amount of land, shares *etc* held ◇ **holdall** *noun* a large bag with a zip ◇ **hold forth** speak at length ◇ **hold good** be true ◇ **hold out** refuse to give in ◇ **hold over** keep till later ◇ **hold up 1** support **2** hinder **3** attack and demand money from ◇ **hold-up** *noun* **1** delay **2** an armed attempt at robbery

▪ *verb* **1** have, own, possess, keep, retain **2** bear, support, sustain, carry, accommodate **4** consider, regard, deem, judge, reckon, maintain **5** conduct, call, summon, convene, assemble ◇ *noun* **2** power, sway, dominance, authority, control ◇ **hold-up 1** hitch, setback, snag, difficulty, trouble, obstruction

hole *noun* **1** an opening in something solid **2** a hollow place **3** a miserable or unpleasant place ◇ **in a hole** in a difficult situation

▪ **1** aperture, opening, orifice, puncture, perforation, tear, split, gap, break, crack **2** dimple, depression, hollow, cavity, crater, pit, burrow

holiday *noun* **1** a day when businesses *etc* are closed **2** a period away from work for rest

■ **2** vacation, recess, time off, day off, leave, break, rest

holistic *adj* of medicine: treating the patient as a whole rather than the individual disease or symptoms ◊ **holism** *noun*

hollow *adj* **1** having empty space inside, not solid **2** false, unreal: *hollow victory/hollow smile* ◊ *noun* **1** a sunken place **2** a dip in the land ◊ *verb* scoop (out)

■ *adj* **1** concave, indented, empty, vacant, unfilled **2** artificial, deceptive, insincere, meaningless, empty ◊ *verb* dig, excavate, burrow, tunnel, scoop, gouge, channel

☒ *adj* **1** solid, convex **2** real

holly *noun* (*plural* **hollies**) an evergreen shrub with scarlet berries and prickly leaves

hollyhock *noun* a tall garden plant

Hollywood *noun* the American cinema industry, based in Hollywood, California

holocaust *noun* a great destruction (by fire) ◊ **the Holocaust** the mass killing of Jews by the Nazis in World War II

hologram *noun* a three-dimensional image created by laser beams

holograph *noun* a document written entirely by one person

holster *noun* a case for a pistol

holy *adj* (**holier**, **holiest**) **1** of or like God **2** religious, righteous **3** for religious use; sacred ◊ **holiness** *noun* ◊ **holier than thou** self-righteous ◊ **holy of holies** an inner sanctum ◊ **holy week** the week before Easter

■ **2** pious, devout, godly, God-fearing, saintly, virtuous, good, faithful, pure **3** hallowed, consecrated, sanctified, dedicated, blessed, venerated, revered, spiritual, divine

homage *noun* a show of respect; an acknowledgement of someone's great achievement or superiority: *paying homage to the pioneers of cinema*

■ recognition, acknowledgement, tribute, honour, deference

home *noun* **1** the place where someone lives **2** the house, country *etc* of someone's family **3** a centre or place of origin: *Nashville is the home of country music* **4** a place where children, the elderly *etc* live and are looked after ◊ *adj* **1** of someone's house or family: *home comforts* **2** domestic, not foreign: *home affairs* ◊ *adv* **1** towards home **2** to the full length: *drive the nail home* ◊ **homeless** *noun plural & adj* (people) without a home ◊ **homely** *adj* **1** plain but pleasant **2** *US* not attractive ◊ **homing** *adj* of a pigeon: trained to fly home when released ◊ **bring home to** make (someone) realize ◊ **home economics** the study of how to run a home ◊ **home-made** *adj* made at home ◊ **home rule** government of a country *etc* by its own parliament ◊ **Home Secretary** *Brit* the government minister who deals with domestic issues, *eg* law and order, immigration *etc* ◊ **homesick** *adj* longing for home ◊ **homespun** *adj* plain, unelaborate ◊ **homestead** *noun* a house and surrounding land, *esp* a farmhouse ◊ **home truth** a frank statement of something true but unpleasant ◊ **homewards** *adv* towards home ◊ **homework** *noun* work for school *etc* done at home

■ **1** residence, abode, domicile, house, dwelling-place **2** birthplace, home town, home ground, territory ◊ **homely 1** comfortable, cosy, snug, relaxed, informal, friendly, ordinary, domestic, natural, plain, simple, modest, unassuming, unpretentious, unsophisticated

homeopathy or **homoeopathy** *noun* the treatment of illness by small quantities of substances that produce symptoms similar to those of the illness ◊ **homeopath** *noun* a practitioner of homeopathy ◊ **homeopathic** *adj* of or using homeopathy

homicide *noun* **1** the killing of a human being **2** someone who kills a person ◊ **homicidal** *adj*

◼ **1** murder, manslaughter, assassination, killing

homily *noun* **1** a plain, practical sermon **2** a talk giving advice

homoeopathy *another spelling* of homeopathy

homogeneous *adj* composed of parts of the same kind (*contrasted with*: heterogeneous) ◇ **homogeneity** *noun*

homogenize *verb* treat (milk) so that the cream does not separate and rise to the surface ◇ **homogenization** *noun*

homograph *noun* a word which has the same spelling as, but a different meaning, origin and (sometimes) sound from, another, *eg tear* meaning 'rip' and *tear* meaning 'drop of liquid'

homonym *noun* a word which has the same sound and spelling as, but a different meaning and origin from, another, *eg keen* meaning 'eager' and *keen* meaning 'lament'

homophone *noun* a word which has the same sound as, but a different spelling and meaning from, another, *eg pair* and *pear*

homo sapiens a human being

homosexual *noun & adj* (someone who is) sexually attracted to the same sex ◇ **homosexuality** *noun*

hone *verb* sharpen (a knife *etc*)

honest *adj* truthful; not inclined to steal, cheat *etc* ◇ **honestly** *adv* ◇ **honesty** *noun*

◼ truthful, sincere, frank, candid, blunt, outspoken, direct, straight, forthright, straightforward, plain, simple, open, legitimate, legal, lawful, fair, just, impartial, objective, virtuous, respectable, reliable, trustworthy

◪ dishonest, dishonourable

honey *noun* **1** a sweet, thick fluid made by bees from the nectar of flowers **2** *informal* sweetheart, dear ◇ **honeycomb** *noun* a network of wax cells in which bees store honey ◇ **honeycombed** *adj* patterned with holes like honey cells

honeydew *noun* a sweet-tasting melon with a smooth rind

honeymoon *noun* a holiday spent immediately after marriage ◇ *verb* spend a honeymoon ◇ **honeymooner** *noun*

honeysuckle *noun* a climbing shrub with sweet-smelling flowers

honk *noun* a noise like the cry of the wild goose or the sound of a motor horn ◇ *verb* make this sound

honorary *adj* **1** done to give honour **2** without payment

◼ **2** unpaid, unofficial, nominal, honorific

honour or *US* **honor** *noun* **1** respect for truth, honesty *etc* **2** fame, glory **3** reputation, good name **4** a title of respect, *esp* to a judge: *Your Honour* **5** a privilege **6** (**honours**) recognition given for exceptional achievements ◇ *verb* **1** give respect to **2** give high rank to **3** pay when due: *honour a debt* **4** keep (a promise) ◇ **honourable** *adj* worthy of honour ◇ **honourably** *adv* ◇ **do the honours** perform a (ceremonial) task

◼ *noun* **1** integrity, morality, decency, rectitude **3** reputation, repute, renown, distinction, esteem, regard, respect ◇ *verb* **1** admire, esteem, respect, revere, worship **4** observe, respect, fulfil, carry out ◇ **honourable** great, eminent, distinguished, renowned, respected, worthy, reputable, respectable, virtuous, noble, fair

hood *noun* **1** a covering for the head, often attached to a coat **2** a protective cover for anything **3** *US* the bonnet of a car

hoodwink *verb* deceive

◼ dupe, fool, take in, delude, *informal* have on, mislead, hoax, trick, cheat, *informal* con

hoof *noun* (*plural* **hoofs** or **hooves**) the horny part on the feet of certain animals (*eg* horses)

hook *noun* a bent piece of metal *etc* for hanging, catching or holding things ◇ *verb* hang or catch with a hook ◇ **hooked** *adj* **1** curved, bent **2** *slang* addicted to, fascinated by ◇ **by hook or by crook** by one means or another, whatever the cost

hookah or **hooka** *noun* a tobacco pipe in which the smoke is drawn through water

hooker *noun, slang* a prostitute

hooligan *noun* a wild, unruly person ◊ **hooliganism** *noun* unruly behaviour

▤ ruffian, thug, tough, lout, *slang* yob, vandal, delinquent

hoop *noun* a thin ring of wood or metal

▤ ring, circle, round, loop, band

hooray *another spelling of* **hurrah**

hoot *verb* 1 sound (a siren, car horn *etc*) 2 of an owl: call, cry 3 laugh loudly ◊ *noun* 1 the sound made by a car horn, siren or owl 2 a shout of scorn or disgust 3 *informal* someone or something extremely funny 4 a loud laugh ◊ **hooter** *noun* 1 a siren or horn which makes a hooting sound 2 *slang* a large nose

Hoover *noun, trademark* a vacuum cleaner ◊ **hoover** *verb* vacuum (a floor *etc*)

hop¹ *verb* (**hops**, **hopping**, **hopped**) leap on one leg ◊ *noun* a short jump on one leg ◊ **hopper** *noun* a funnel for shaking down corn to a grinding machine

▤ *verb* jump, leap, spring, bound, vault, skip, dance, prance

hop² *noun* a climbing plant with bitter-tasting fruits which are used in brewing beer

hope *noun* 1 the state of expecting or wishing something good to happen 2 something desired ◊ *verb* expect or wish something good to happen ◊ **hopeful** *adj* ◊ **hopefully** *adv* ◊ **hopeless** *adj* 1 without hope 2 very bad ◊ **hopelessly** *adv*

▤ *noun* 1 hopefulness, optimism, belief, confidence, assurance, conviction, faith 2 wish, desire, longing, dream, expectation ◊ *verb* wish, desire, long, expect, await, look forward, anticipate ◊ **hopeful** optimistic, confident, cheerful, encouraging, promising ◊ **hopeless** pessimistic, despairing, downhearted, dejected, wretched

▨ *noun* 1 pessimism, despair

hopscotch *noun* a hopping game

over lines drawn on the ground

horde *noun* a large crowd or group

▤ band, gang, pack, herd, drove, flock, swarm, crowd, mob, throng, multitude

⚠ Do not confuse with: **hoard**

horizon *noun* 1 the imaginary line where the earth meets the sky 2 the limit of someone's experience or understanding

horizontal *adj* lying level or flat ◊ **horizontally** *adv*

hormone *noun* a substance which is produced by certain glands of the body and acts on a particular organ ◊ **hormonal** *adj*

horn *noun* 1 a hard growth on the heads of certain animals, *eg* deer 2 the bony substance of which this is made 3 something curved or sticking out like an animal's horn 4 a part of a motor vehicle which gives a warning sound 5 a brass wind instrument ◊ **horned** *adj* having horns ◊ **horny** *adj* 1 hard like horn 2 *slang* sexually aroused

hornbill *noun* a bird with a horny growth on its bill

hornet *noun* a kind of large wasp ◊ **stir up a hornet's nest** cause a commotion or violent reaction

hornpipe *noun* a lively sailor's dance

horoscope *noun* a prediction of someone's future based on the position of the stars at their birth

horrendous *adj, informal* awful, terrible ◊ **horrendously** *adv*

horrible *adj* 1 very unpleasant or unkind 2 very bad, awful ◊ **horribly** *adv*

▤ 1 disagreeable, nasty, unkind, horrid 2 revolting, disgusting, offensive, repulsive, hideous, grim, ghastly, awful, dreadful, frightful, fearful, terrible, shocking, appalling, horrific

▨ 1 pleasant, agreeable, lovely, attractive

horrid *adj* hateful; very unpleasant

horrific *adj* 1 terrifying 2 awful, very bad ◊ **horrifically** *adv*

horrify *verb* (**horrifies**, **horrifying**, **horrified**) frighten greatly, shock: *we* *were horrified by his behaviour* ◇ **horrifying** *adj* ◇ **horrifyingly** *adv*

■ outrage, scandalize, appal, disgust, sicken, dismay, alarm, startle, scare, frighten, terrify

🆎 please, delight

horror *noun* **1** great fear, terror **2** something which causes fear **3** an unruly or badly behaved child

■ **1** shock, outrage, disgust, revulsion, abhorrence, loathing, dismay, consternation, alarm, fright, fear, terror, panic, dread **2** ghastliness, awfulness, frightfulness, hideousness

hors d'oeuvre /ɔːˈdɜːvr/ (*plural* **hors d'oeuvre** or **hors d'oeuvres**) an appetizer

horse *noun* **1** a four-footed animal with hooves and a mane **2** a piece of gymnastic equipment for vaulting ◇ **horsy** or **horsey** *adj* **1** fond of horses **2** like a horse ◇ **from the horse's mouth** directly from the source, firsthand ◇ **horse-chestnut** *noun* a tree which produces a shiny, bitter-tasting nut ◇ **horsefly** *noun* a large fly which bites ◇ **horse laugh** a loud, harsh laugh ◇ **horseplay** *noun* rough play, fooling around ◇ **horsepower** *noun* a unit of mechanical power for car engines (*short form* **hp**) ◇ **horseradish** *noun* a plant with a sharp-tasting root which is used in sauces ◇ **horses for courses** people will do best in situations that suit them individually ◇ **horseshoe** *noun* **1** a shoe for horses, made of a curved piece of iron **2** a horseshoe-shaped object

horticulture *noun* the study and art of gardening ◇ **horticultural** *adj* ◇ **horticulturist** *noun*

hosanna *noun* an exclamation of praise to God

hose *noun* **1** (*plural* **hoses**) a rubber tube for carrying water **2** (*plural* **hose**) a covering for the legs and feet, *eg* stockings ◇ **hosiery** *noun* stockings, tights *etc*

hospice *noun* a home providing special nursing care for the terminally ill

hospitable *adj* showing kindness to guests or strangers ◇ **hospitably** *adv*

■ friendly, sociable, welcoming, receptive, cordial, amicable, congenial, convivial, kind, gracious, generous

🆎 inhospitable, unfriendly, hostile

hospital *noun* a building for the treatment of the sick and injured

hospitality *noun* a friendly welcome, food and drink, entertainment *etc* offered to guests or strangers

host¹, hostess *noun* **1** someone who welcomes and entertains guests **2** someone who introduces or talks to participants on a TV or radio show **3** *old* an innkeeper or hotel-keeper

host² *noun* a very large number

hostage *noun* someone held prisoner by an enemy to make sure that an agreement will be kept to

■ prisoner, captive, pawn, surety, security

hostel *noun* a building providing accommodation for students, the homeless *etc*

hostile *adj* **1** of an enemy **2** not friendly; showing dislike or opposition (to) ◇ **hostility** *noun* **1** unfriendliness, dislike **2** (**hostilities**) acts of warfare

■ **1** belligerent, warlike **2** unfriendly, inhospitable, inimical, antagonistic, opposed, adverse, unfavourable, contrary, opposite ◇ **hostility 1** opposition, aggression, animosity, ill-will, hate, hatred, dislike

hot *adj* (**hotter, hottest**) **1** very warm **2** spicy **3** passionate **4** radioactive **5** *slang* stolen **6** *slang* not safe ◇ **hot air** meaningless talk ◇ **hotbed** *noun* a centre or breeding ground for anything: *a hotbed of rebellion* ◇ **hot-blooded** *adj* passionate, easily angered ◇ **hotdog** *noun* a hot sausage in a roll ◇ **hotfoot** *adv* in great haste ◇ **hot-headed** *adj* inclined to act rashly without thinking ◇ **hothouse** *noun* a heated glasshouse for plants ◇ *verb* give (a child) intensive schooling at an early age ◇ **hotline** *noun* a direct telephone line between heads of government ◇ **hot on someone's heels** following them closely ◇ **hot**

potato a touchy subject ◇ **hot seat** a position of responsibility ◇ **hot under the collar** indignant, enraged ◇ **in hot water** in trouble ◇ **sell like hot cakes** sell very quickly

■ **1** warm, heated, fiery, burning, scalding, blistering, scorching, roasting, baking, boiling, sizzling, sweltering **2** spicy, peppery, piquant, sharp, pungent, strong ◇ **hot-headed** headstrong, impetuous, impulsive, hasty, rash, reckless, fiery, volatile, hot-tempered, quick-tempered

hotchpotch *noun* (*plural* **hotchpotches**) a confused mixture

hotel *noun* a building with a number of rooms which people can pay to stay in for one or more nights ◇ **hotelier** *noun* a person who runs a hotel

hound *noun* a dog used in hunting ◇ *verb* hunt, pursue relentlessly

■ *verb* chase, pursue, hunt (down), drive, nag, pester, badger, harry, harass, persecute

hour *noun* **1** sixty minutes, the 24th part of a day **2** a time or occasion: *the hour of reckoning* ◇ **hourly** *adj* happening or done every hour ◇ *adv* every hour ◇ **hourglass** *noun* an instrument which measures the hours by the running of sand from one glass container into another

house *noun* **1** a building in which people live **2** a household **3** a business firm **4** the audience in a theatre ◇ *verb* provide a house for; accommodate ◇ **housing** *noun* **1** accommodation, *eg* houses, flats *etc* **2** a casing for a machine *etc* ◇ **house arrest** confinement under guard in a private house, hospital *etc* ◇ **like a house on fire** very successfully, extremely well ◇ **on the house** free, complimentary

■ *noun* **1** building, dwelling, residence, home **2** family, clan, tribe ◇ *verb* accommodate, put up, take in, shelter, harbour

---

Types of house include:
semi-detached, *informal* semi, detached, terraced, town house, council house, cottage, thatched cottage, *informal* prefab, pied-à-terre, bungalow, chalet bungalow; flat, bedsit, apartment, studio, maisonette, penthouse, granny flat, *US* duplex, *US* condominium; manor, hall, lodge, grange, villa, mansion, rectory, vicarage, parsonage, manse, croft, farmhouse, homestead, ranchhouse, chalet, log cabin, shack, shanty, hut, igloo, hacienda

---

houseboat *noun* a river barge with a cabin for living in

housebreaker *noun* someone who breaks into a house to steal

housecoat *noun* a dressing-gown

household *noun* the people who live together in a house ◇ **householder** *noun* someone who owns or pays the rent of a house ◇ **household name** or **household word** someone or something which everyone is talking about

housekeeper *noun* someone employed to look after the running of a house

house-proud *adj* proud of keeping your house clean and tidy

house-trained *adj* of a pet: trained to urinate and defecate outdoors

housewarming *noun* a party held when someone moves into a new house

housewife *noun* a woman who looks after a house and her family

hovel *noun* a small squalid dwelling

hover *verb* **1** stay in the air in the same spot **2** stay near, linger (about) **3** be undecided or uncertain

■ **1** hang, poise, float, drift, fly **2** pause, linger, hang about, hesitate **3** hesitate, waver, fluctuate

hovercraft *noun* a craft able to travel over land or sea supported on a cushion of air

how *adv* **1** in what manner: *how are they getting there?* **2** to what extent: *how old are you?/how cold is it outside?* **3** to a great extent: *how young he seems/how well you play* **4** by what means: *how* *do you switch this on?* **5** in what condition: *how is she?*

howdah *noun* a seat fixed on an elephant's back

however *adv* **1** no matter how **2** in spite of that

howitzer *noun* a short cannon used to attack a besieged town or trench

howl *verb* **1** make a long, loud sound like that of a dog or wolf **2** yell in pain, anger *etc* **3** laugh loudly ◇ *noun* a howling sound ◇ **howler** *noun, informal* a ridiculous mistake

   ▣ *verb* **1** roar, bellow, bay, yelp **2** wail, cry, shriek, scream, shout, yell, moan, groan

hoyden *noun* a tomboy ◇ **hoydenish** *adj*

HP or **hp** *abbrev* **1** hire-purchase **2** horsepower

HQ *abbrev* headquarters

HRH *abbrev* Her or His Royal Highness

HTML *abbrev, comput* HyperText Mark-up Language

http *abbrev* in web addresses: hypertext transfer protocol

hub *noun* **1** the centre part of a wheel through which the axle passes **2** a thriving centre of anything: *the hub of the entertainment industry*

   ▣ 2 centre, middle, focus, focal point, pivot, linchpin, nerve centre, core, heart

hubbub *noun* a confused sound of many voices

   ▣ noise, racket, din, clamour, commotion, disturbance, riot, uproar, rumpus, confusion, disorder, tumult, chaos

> Originally meaning 'battle' or 'war cry', based on an Irish Gaelic word

hubby *noun, informal* a husband

huddle *verb* crowd together ◇ *noun* a close group

   ▣ *verb* cluster, converge, meet, gather, congregate, crowd, flock, throng, press, cuddle, snuggle, nestle

hue *noun* colour, shade

hue and cry a commotion, a fuss

huff *noun* a fit of bad temper and

sulking ◇ **huffily** *adv* ◇ **huffiness** *noun* ◇ **huffy** *adj* inclined to sulk; peevish

hug *verb* (**hugs**, **hugging**, **hugged**) **1** hold tightly with the arms **2** keep close to: *hugging the kerb* ◇ *noun* a tight embrace

   ▣ *verb* **1** embrace, cuddle, squeeze, enfold, hold, clasp, clutch, grip, cling to ◇ *noun* embrace, cuddle, squeeze, clasp, hold, clinch

huge *adj* extremely big ◇ **hugely** *adv* ◇ **hugeness** *noun*

   ▣ immense, vast, enormous, massive, colossal, giant, gigantic, mammoth, tremendous, great, big, large, bulky

   ▨ tiny, minute

hula-hoop *noun* a light hoop for spinning round the waist

hulk *noun* **1** an old ship unfit for use **2** something big and clumsy ◇ **hulking** *adj* big and clumsy

   ▣ hulking massive, heavy, unwieldy, bulky, awkward, ungainly

hull *noun* the body or framework of a ship

hullabaloo *noun* a noisy disturbance

   ▣ fuss, palaver, outcry, uproar, pandemonium, rumpus, disturbance, commotion, hubbub

   ▨ calm, peace

hullo *another spelling of* **hello**

hum *verb* (**hums**, **humming**, **hummed**) **1** make a buzzing sound like that of bees **2** sing with the lips shut **3** of a place: be noisily busy ◇ *noun* **1** the noise of bees **2** any buzzing, droning sound ◇ **humming-bird** *noun* a small, brightly coloured bird which beats its wings rapidly making a humming noise

   ▣ *verb* **1** buzz, whirr, purr, drone, thrum

human *adj* **1** relating to people as opposed to animals or gods **2** having natural qualities, feelings *etc* ◇ *noun* a man, woman or child ◇ **humanism** *noun* a set of ideas about or interest in ethics and mankind, not including religious belief ◇ **humanist** *noun* ◇ **humanitarian** *adj* kind to fellow human beings ◇ **humanity** *noun* **1** men and women in general **2** kindness, gentleness ◇ **human being** a man, woman or child

humane *adj* kind, showing mercy, gentle ◇ **humanely** *adv*

▪ kind, compassionate, sympathetic, understanding, kind-hearted, good-natured, gentle, tender, loving, mild, merciful, forgiving, kindly

▪ inhumane, cruel

humble *adj* **1** modest, meek **2** not of high rank, unimportant ◇ *verb* cause to feel low and unimportant ◇ **eat humble pie** admit a mistake openly

▪ *adj* **1** meek, submissive, unassertive, polite, respectful, deferential, servile, subservient, sycophantic **2** lowly, insignificant, unimportant, common, commonplace, ordinary, plain, simple, modest

humbug *noun* **1** nonsense, rubbish **2** a kind of hard minty sweet

▪ **1** nonsense, rubbish, *slang* baloney, *informal* bunkum, *informal* claptrap, *informal* eyewash

humdinger *noun, informal* someone or something exceptional

humdrum *adj* dull, not exciting

▪ boring, tedious, monotonous, routine, dull, dreary, uninteresting, uneventful, ordinary, mundane, everyday, commonplace

▪ lively, unusual, exceptional

humerus *noun* the bone of the upper arm

humid *adj* of air *etc*: moist, damp ◇ **humidifier** *noun* a device which controls the amount of humidity in the air ◇ **humidity** *noun*

▪ damp, moist, dank, clammy, sticky, muggy, sultry

humiliate *verb* cause to feel humble, foolish or ashamed, hurt the pride of ◇ **humiliating** *adj* ◇ **humiliation** *noun*

▪ mortify, embarrass, shame, disgrace, confound, crush, break, deflate, demean, humble

▪ dignify, exalt

humility *noun* humble state of mind, meekness

▪ meekness, submissiveness, deference, servility, humbleness, lowliness, modesty

▪ pride, arrogance, assertiveness

hummus *noun* a paste made from ground chickpeas and olive oil

humongous or **humungous** *adj, informal* enormous, huge

humour or *US* **humor** *noun* **1** funniness; the amusing side of anything: *failed to see the humour of the situation* **2** the ability to see things as amusing or ridiculous **3** state of mind; temper, mood ◇ *verb* do as someone else wishes in order to please them ◇ **humorist** *noun* a comedian, a comic writer ◇ **humorous** *adj* funny, amusing ◇ **humorously** *adv*

▪ *noun* **1** wit, jokes, jesting, repartee, comedy, farce, fun, amusement **3** frame of mind, spirits, disposition, temperament ◇ *verb* go along with, gratify, indulge ◇ **humorous** funny, amusing, comic, entertaining, witty, satirical, playful, droll, comical, *informal* zany, absurd, hilarious

hump *noun* **1** a lump, a mound **2** a lump on the back ◇ **humpback** *noun* **1** a back with a hump **2** someone with a hump on their back ◇ **humpbacked** *adj* **1** with a hump on the back **2** of a bridge: rising and falling so as to form a hump shape

humungous *another spelling* of **humongous**

humus /ˈhjuːməs/ *noun* soil made of rotted leaves *etc*

hunch *noun* (*plural* **hunches**) a suspicion that something is untrue, is going to happen *etc* ◇ **hunchback** *noun* a humpback ◇ **hunchbacked** *adj* with a hump on the back

▪ premonition, intuition, suspicion, feeling, impression, idea, guess

hundred the number 100 ◇ *adj* 100 in number ◇ **hundredth** *adj* the last of a series of hundred ◇ *noun* one of a hundred equal parts ◇ **hundredweight** *noun* 112 lb, 50.8 kilograms (often written **cwt**)

hunger *noun* **1** a desire for food **2** a

strong desire for anything ◇ *verb* **1** go without food **2** long (for) ◇ **hungrily** *adv* ◇ **hungry** *adj* wanting or needing food ◇ **hunger strike** a refusal to eat as a protest

▣ *noun* **1** hungriness, emptiness, starvation, malnutrition, famine, appetite **2** desire, craving, longing, yearning, itch, thirst ◇ **hungry** starving, underfed, undernourished, *informal* peckish, empty, hollow, famished, ravenous

hunk *noun* **1** a large lump or piece of something **2** *informal* a muscular, sexually attractive man ◇ **hunky** *adj*

▣ **1** chunk, lump, piece, block, slab, wedge

hunky-dory *adj* in a good situation; well, fine

hunt *verb* **1** chase animals or birds for food or sport **2** search (for) ◇ *noun* **1** the act of chasing wild animals **2** a search ◇ **huntsman**, **huntswoman** *noun* someone who hunts animals

▣ *verb* **1** chase, pursue, hound, dog, stalk, track, trail **2** seek, look for, search, scour, rummage, forage, investigate

hurdle *noun* **1** a light frame to be jumped over in a race **2** a difficulty which must be overcome

▣ **1** jump, fence, wall, hedge, barrier, barricade, obstacle **2** hindrance, impediment, problem, snag, difficulty, complication, stumbling block

hurl *verb* throw with force

▣ throw, toss, fling, sling, catapult, project, propel, fire, launch, send

hurly-burly *noun* a great stir, uproar

hurrah or **hooray** *exclam* a shout of joy, approval *etc*

hurricane *noun* a violent storm of wind blowing at a speed of over 75 miles (120 kilometres) per hour ◇ **hurricane lamp** a lamp designed to keep alight in strong wind

hurry *verb* (**hurries**, **hurrying**, **hurried**) **1** act or move quickly **2** make (someone) act quickly ◇ *noun* haste or speed, or the necessity for this ◇ **hurried** *adj* done in a hurry ◇ **hurriedly** *adv*

▣ *verb* **1** rush, dash, fly, *informal* get a move on, hasten, quicken, speed up **2** speed up, hustle, push ◇ *noun* rush, haste, speed, urgency, hustle, bustle, commotion ◇ **hurried** rushed, hectic, hasty, speedy, swift, rapid, brief, short, careless

hurt *verb* **1** cause pain or distress to **2** injure physically, wound **3** feel pain **4** damage, spoil ◇ *noun* **1** pain, distress **2** damage ◇ **hurtful** *adj* causing pain, distress or damage ◇ **hurtfully** *adv*

▣ *verb* **1** ill-treat, upset, sadden, grieve, distress, afflict, offend, annoy **2** injure, wound, maltreat, ill-treat, bruise, cut, burn, torture **3** ache, throb, sting ◇ **hurtful** upsetting, wounding, vicious, cruel, mean, unkind, nasty, malicious, spiteful, catty, scathing, cutting, harmful, damaging, injurious, destructive

hurtle *verb* rush at great speed

▣ dash, tear, race, fly, shoot, speed, rush, charge

husband *noun* **1** a married man **2** the man to whom a woman is married ◇ *verb* spend or use (*eg* money, strength) carefully ◇ **husbandry** *noun* **1** farming **2** management **3** care with money, thrift

hush *exclam* be quiet! ◇ *noun*, *informal* silence, quiet ◇ *verb* make quiet ◇ **hush-hush** *adj*, *informal* top secret ◇ **hush up** stop (a scandal *etc*) becoming public

▣ *noun* peace, stillness, calm, calmness, tranquillity, serenity ◇ *verb* quieten, silence, still, settle, compose, calm, soothe, subdue

husk *noun* the dry thin covering of certain fruits and seeds

▣ covering, case, shell, pod, hull, bran, chaff

husky[1] *adj* **1** of a voice: deep and rough **2** big and strong ◇ **huskily** *adv* ◇ **huskiness** *noun*

husky[2] *noun* (*plural* **huskies**) a Canadian sledge-dog

hussy *noun* (*plural* **hussies**) a cheeky or immoral girl

hustings *noun plural* political campaigning just before an election

hustle *verb* **1** push rudely **2** hurry
▣ **1** force, push, shove, thrust, elbow, jostle **2** hasten, rush, hurry

hut *noun* a small wooden building
▣ cabin, shack, shed, lean-to, shelter

hutch *noun* (*plural* **hutches**) a box in which pet rabbits are housed

hyacinth *noun* a sweet-smelling flower which grows from a bulb

hyaena *another spelling of* **hyena**

hybrid *noun* **1** an animal or plant bred from two different kinds, *eg* a mule, which is a hybrid of a horse and an ass **2** a word formed of parts from different languages
▣ **1** cross, crossbreed, half-breed, mongrel

hydra *noun* (*plural* **hydras** or **hydrae**) **1** a mythological many-headed snake which grew two heads for each one cut off **2** a sea creature which divide and re-divide itself

hydrant *noun* a connection to which a hose can be attached to draw water from the main water supply

hydraulic *adj* **1** carrying water **2** worked by water or other fluid

hydroelectricity *noun* electricity obtained from water-power ◇ **hydroelectric** *adj*

hydrogen *noun* the lightest gas, which with oxygen makes up water ◇ **hydrogen bomb** an extremely powerful bomb using hydrogen

hydrophobia *noun* **1** a fear of water, a symptom of rabies **2** rabies ◇ **hydrophobic** *adj*

hyena or **hyaena** *noun* a dog-like wild animal with a howl sounding like laughter

hygiene *noun* the maintaining of cleanliness as a means to health ◇ **hygienic** *adj*
▣ **hygienic** sanitary, sterile, germ-free, disinfected, clean, pure
▣ **hygienic** unhygienic, insanitary

hymen *noun* the thin membrane that partially closes the vagina of a virgin

hymn *noun* a religious song of praise ◇ **hymnal** or **hymnary** *noun* (*plural* **hymnaries**) a book of hymns

hype *informal noun* **1** extravagant advertisement or publicity **2** a hypodermic syringe ◇ *verb* **1** promote extravagantly **2** inject yourself with a drug ◇ **hype up** hype

hyper *adj*, *informal* excited

hyper- *prefix* to a greater extent than usual, excessive: *hypersensitive*

hyperbole /haɪˈpɜːbəlɪ/ *noun* exaggeration ◇ **hyperbolical** *adj*

hypermarket *noun* a large self-service store stocking a wide range of goods

hypernym *noun* a general word representing a class containing other members, *eg dance* is a hypernym of *waltz* and *reel* (*contrasted with*: **hyponym**)

hypertension *noun* high blood pressure

hypertext *noun* electronic text containing cross-references which can be accessed by keystrokes *etc*

hyphen *noun* a short stroke (-) used to link or separate parts of a word or phrase: *black-and-white/re-elect*

hypnosis *noun* **1** a sleep-like state in which suggestions are obeyed **2** hypnotism ◇ **hypnotic** *adj* **1** of hypnosis or hypnotism **2** causing a sleep-like state ◇ **hypnotically** *adv* ◇ **hypnotism** *noun* the putting of someone into hypnosis ◇ **hypnotist** *noun* ◇ **hypnotize** *verb* put (someone) into hypnosis
▣ **hypnotic 2** mesmerizing, sleep-inducing, spellbinding, fascinating, compelling, irresistible, magnetic

hypo- *prefix* below, under

hypoallergenic *adj* specially formulated in order to reduce the risk of allergy

hypochondria *noun* over-anxiety about your own health ◇ **hypochondriac** *noun* & *adj*

hypocrite /ˈhɪpəkrɪt/ *noun* someone who pretends to be something they are not, or to believe something they do not ◇ **hypocrisy** *noun* ◇ **hypocritical** *adj*

◼ **hypocritical** insincere, two-faced, self-righteous, false, hollow, deceptive, deceitful

◪ **hypocritical** sincere, genuine

hypodermic *adj* used for injecting drugs just below the skin: *hypodermic syringe/hypodermic needle* ◇ *noun* a hypodermic syringe

hypoglycaemia *noun* an abnormally low amount of sugar in the blood ◇ **hypoglycaemic** *adj*

hyponym *noun* one of a group of words whose meanings are included in a more general term, *eg guitar* and *piano* are hyponyms of *musical instrument* (*contrasted with*: **hypernym**)

hypotenuse *noun* the longest side of a right-angled triangle

hypothermia *noun* an abnormally low body temperature caused by exposure to cold

hypothesis *noun* (*plural* **hypotheses**) something taken as true for the sake of argument ◇ **hypothetical** *adj* supposed ◇ **hypothetically** *adv*

◼ theory, thesis, proposition, supposition, conjecture, speculation ◇ **hypothetical**

theoretical, imaginary, supposed, assumed, proposed, conjectural, speculative

hyssop *noun* an aromatic plant used in perfumes and herbal medicine

hysterectomy *noun* (*plural* **hysterectomies**) surgical removal of the womb

hysteria *noun* **1** a nervous excitement causing uncontrollable laughter, crying *etc* **2** a nervous illness ◇ **hysterical** *adj* **1** affected by hysteria **2** *informal* very funny ◇ **hysterically** *adv* ◇ **hysterics** *noun plural* a fit of hysteria

◼ **hysterical 1** frantic, frenzied, berserk, uncontrollable, mad, raving, crazed, demented, overwrought, neurotic **2** hilarious, uproarious, side-splitting

◪ **hysterical 1** calm, composed, self-possessed

Based on a Greek word for 'womb', because originally thought to be caused by womb disease or abnormalities

Hz *abbrev* hertz

Ii

I *pronoun* the word used by a speaker or writer in mentioning themselves (as the subject of a verb): *I can't find it/I, myself*

ibex *noun* (*plural* **ibexes**) a wild mountain goat

ibid *adv* in the same book, article *etc*

ice *noun* 1 frozen water 2 ice-cream ◇ *verb* 1 cover with icing 2 freeze ◇ **ice age** an age when the earth was mostly covered with ice ◇ **iceberg** *noun* a huge mass of floating ice ◇ **icebox** *noun, US* a refrigerator ◇ **ice-cap** *noun* a permanent covering of ice, as at the north and south poles ◇ **ice-cream** *noun* a sweet creamy mixture, flavoured and frozen ◇ **ice floe** a piece of floating ice ◇ **ice hockey** hockey played with a rubber disc (called a **puck**) on an ice rink ◇ **ice tea** or **iced tea** chilled sweetened tea ◇ **ice-skate** *noun* a skate for moving on ice ◇ **ice-skating** *noun*

■ *noun* 1 frost, rime, icicle, glacier, iciness, frostiness ◇ *verb* 1 frost, glaze 2 freeze, refrigerate, chill, cool

ichthyology *noun* the study of fishes ◇ **ichthyologist** *noun*

icicle *noun* a hanging, pointed piece of ice formed by the freezing of dropping water

icing *noun* a coating for cakes or biscuits made from powdered sugar mixed with water or egg-white ◇ **icing on the cake** something added but not really necessary ◇ **icing sugar** powdered sugar

icky *adj, informal* disgusting, repulsive

icon *noun* 1 a painted or mosaic image of Christ or a saint (*also* **ikon**) 2 a symbol on a computer screen ◇ **iconography** *noun* ◇ **iconographer** *noun*

■ 1 idol, portrait, image, representation, symbol

iconoclasm *noun* 1 the act of breaking

religious images 2 the attacking of long-established beliefs ◇ **iconoclast** *noun* ◇ **iconoclastic** *adj*

icy *adj* 1 covered with ice 2 very cold 3 hostile ◇ **icily** *adv* ◇ **iciness** *noun*

■ 1 frosty, slippery, glassy, frozen 2 ice-cold, arctic, freezing, frozen, bitter, biting, cold, chill, chilly 3 cold, stony, cool, aloof, distant

☲ 1 hot 3 friendly, warm

ID *abbrev* identification ◇ *noun, US* a means of identification, *eg* a driving licence

I'd *short for* **I would**, **I should** or **I had**: *I'd sooner go than stay*

idea *noun* 1 a thought, a notion 2 a plan

■ 1 concept, theory, hypothesis, guess, conjecture, belief, opinion, view, viewpoint, judgement, understanding, inkling, suspicion, clue 2 brainwave, suggestion, proposal, proposition, scheme

ideal *adj* 1 perfect 2 existing in imagination only (*contrasted with*: **real**) ◇ *noun* the highest and best; a standard of perfection ◇ **idealism** *noun* ◇ **idealist** *noun* someone who thinks that perfection can be reached ◇ **idealistic** *adj* ◇ **idealization** *noun* ◇ **idealize** *verb* think of as perfect ◇ **ideally** *adv* in ideal circumstances: *ideally all children should have a place in nursery school*

■ *adj* 1 dream, utopian, best, supreme, highest, model 2 unreal, imaginary, unattainable, impractical, idealistic ◇ **idealize** romanticize, glamorize, glorify, exalt, worship, idolize

identical *adj* the same in all details ◇ **identically** *adv*

■ same, self-same, indistinguishable, interchangeable, twin, duplicate, like, alike, corresponding, matching, equal, equivalent

identify *verb* (**identifies, identifying,**

identified) claim to recognize, prove to be the same: *he identified the man as his attacker* ◇ **identification** *noun* ◇ **identify with 1** feel close to or involved with **2** think of as the same, equate: *identifying money with happiness*

■ recognize, know, pick out, single out, distinguish, perceive, make out, discern, notice, detect, name, label, tag, specify

Identikit *noun*, *trademark* a rough picture of a wanted person which police put together from descriptions

identity *noun* (*plural* **identities**) **1** who or what someone or something is **2** the state of being the same

■ **1** individuality, particularity, singularity, uniqueness, personality, character, existence

ideogram *noun* a written character that represents an idea rather than a sound

ideology *noun* (*plural* **ideologies**) a set of ideas, often political or philosophical ◇ **ideological** *adj* ◇ **ideologically** *adv*

■ philosophy, world-view, ideas, principles, tenets, doctrine(s), convictions, belief(s), faith, creed, dogma

idiocy *see* idiot

idiolect *noun* the language spoken by an individual person, including their vocabulary, pronunciation *etc*

idiom *noun* a common expression whose meaning cannot be guessed from the individual words, eg 'I'm feeling *under the weather*' ◇ **idiomatic** *adj* ◇ **idiomatically** *adv*

idiosyncrasy *noun* (*plural* **idiosyncrasies**) a personal oddness of behaviour ◇ **idiosyncratic** *adj* ◇ **idiosyncratically** *adv*

■ **idiosyncratic** personal, individual, characteristic, distinctive, peculiar, singular, odd, eccentric, quirky

◪ **idiosyncratic** general, common

idiot *noun* a feeble-minded person; a fool ◇ **idiocy** *noun* feeble-mindedness, foolishness ◇ **idiotic** *adj* ◇ **idiotically** *adv*

■ fool, blockhead, dimwit, halfwit, imbecile, moron, cretin, *informal* dork, simpleton, dunce, ignoramus ◇ **idiotic** foolish, stupid, silly, absurd, senseless, *informal* daft, insane, moronic, crazy

idle *adj* **1** not working **2** lazy **3** meaningless: *idle chatter* ◇ *verb* **1** spend time doing nothing **2** of an engine: run without doing any work ◇ **idleness** *noun* ◇ **idler** *noun* ◇ **idly** *adv*

■ *adj* **1** inactive, inoperative, unused, unemployed, jobless, redundant **3** empty, trivial, casual, futile, pointless

idol *noun* **1** an image worshipped as a god **2** someone much loved or honoured ◇ **idolater** *noun* ◇ **idolatrous** *adj* ◇ **idolatry** *noun* **1** the worship of idols **2** excessive admiration or devotion ◇ **idolize** *verb* adore, worship

idyll *noun* **1** a poem on a pastoral theme **2** a time of pleasure and contentment ◇ **idyllic** *adj* very happy or pleasant ◇ **idyllically** *adv*

■ **idyllic** perfect, idealized, heavenly, delightful, charming, picturesque, unspoiled, peaceful, happy, blissful

◪ **idyllic** unpleasant

ie *abbrev* that is, that means (from Latin *id est*)

if *conj* **1** on condition that, supposing that: *if you go, I'll go* **2** whether: *do you know if she'll be there?*

iffy *adj*, *informal* dubious, uncertain

igloo *noun* an Inuit snow hut

igneous *adj* **1** relating to fire **2** of rock: formed by the action of great heat within the earth

ignite *verb* **1** set on fire **2** catch fire

■ **1** set fire to, set alight, burn, fire **2** catch fire, flare up, burn

ignition *noun* **1** the act of setting on fire or catching fire **2** the sparking part of a motor engine

ignoble *adj* dishonourable; of low birth

ignominy *noun* disgrace, dishonour ◇ **ignominious** *adj* ◇ **ignominiously** *adv*

ignoramus *noun* an ignorant person

ignorant *adj* **1** knowing very little **2**

unaware (of) ◊ **ignorance** *noun*

▭ **1** uneducated, illiterate, unread, untaught, untrained, inexperienced, stupid, *informal* clueless, unenlightened, ill-informed **2** unaware, unconscious, oblivious, unenlightened

▣ **1** educated, knowledgeable, clever, wise

ignore *verb* take no notice of

▭ disregard, overlook, pass over, neglect, omit, reject, snub, cold-shoulder, *slang* blank

iguana /ɪˈgwɑːnə/ *noun* (*plural* **iguanas** or **iguana**) a type of tree lizard

ikon *another spelling of* **icon**

I'll *short for* **I shall**, **I will**

ill *adj* **1** unwell, sick **2** evil, bad **3** unlucky ◊ *adv* badly ◊ *noun* **1** evil **2** (**ills**) misfortunes, troubles ◊ **ill-at-ease** *adj* uncomfortable ◊ **ill-feeling** *noun* resentment, animosity ◊ **ill-gotten** *adj* got in a dishonest or unethical way ◊ **ill-humoured** or **ill-natured** *adj* bad-tempered ◊ **ill-starred** *adj* unlucky ◊ **ill-treat** or **ill-use** *verb* treat badly ◊ **ill-will** *noun* dislike, resentment

▭ *adj* **1** poorly, unwell, indisposed, laid up, off-colour, *informal* out of sorts, *informal* under the weather, unhealthy, infirm, frail **2** harmful, injurious, unfavourable, sinister, ominous, threatening **3** unfortunate, difficult, harsh, severe, unkind

illegal *adj* against the law ◊ **illegality** *noun* (*plural* **illegalities**) ◊ **illegally** *adv*

▭ unlawful, illicit, criminal, wrong, forbidden, prohibited, banned, outlawed, unauthorized, black-market

▣ legal, lawful

illegible *adj* impossible to read, indistinct ◊ **illegibility** *noun* ◊ **illegibly** *adv*

▭ unreadable, indecipherable, scrawled, obscure, faint, indistinct

▣ legible

illegitimate *adj* born of parents not married to each other

illicit *adj* unlawful, forbidden ◊ **illicitly** *adv*

▭ illegal, unlawful, criminal, wrong, illegitimate, improper, forbidden, prohibited, unauthorized, unlicensed, blackmarket, contraband, under-the-counter, furtive, clandestine

▣ legal, permissible

❗ Do not confuse with: **elicit**

illiterate *adj* not able to read or write ◊ **illiteracy** *noun*

illness *noun* disease, sickness

illogical *adj* not logical, not showing sound reasoning ◊ **illogicality** *noun* ◊ **illogically** *adv*

▭ irrational, unreasonable, invalid, unsound, faulty, fallacious, inconsistent, senseless, meaningless, absurd

illuminate *verb* **1** light up **2** make more clear ◊ **illuminated** *adj* of a manuscript: decorated with ornamental lettering ◊ **illuminations** *noun plural* a decorative display of lights

▭ **1** light, brighten, decorate **2** enlighten, edify, instruct, elucidate, illustrate, explain, clarify, clear up

illusion *noun* **1** something which deceives the mind or eye **2** a mistaken belief ◊ **illusory** *adj*

❗ Do not confuse with: **allusion** and **delusion**

illusive *adj* misleading, deceptive

❗ Do not confuse with: **allusive** and **elusive**

illustrate *verb* **1** draw pictures for (a book *etc*) **2** explain, show by example ◊ **illustration** *noun* **1** a picture in a book *etc* **2** an example which illustrates ◊ **illustrative** *adj* ◊ **illustrator** *noun* someone who illustrates books *etc*

▭ illustration **2** example, specimen, instance, case, analogy, demonstration, explanation, interpretation

illustrious *adj* famous, distinguished

▭ great, noble, eminent, distinguished, celebrated, famous, famed, renowned, prominent, outstanding, remarkable, notable, brilliant, excellent, splendid, magnificent

▣ ignoble, inglorious

I'm *short for* I am

image *noun* **1** a likeness made of someone or something **2** someone or something strikingly like another: *she is the image of her mother* **3** a picture in the mind **4** public reputation

▣ **1** picture, portrait, icon, effigy, figure, statue, idol, replica **3** idea, notion, concept, impression, perception

imagery *noun* words that suggest images, used to make a piece of writing more vivid

imaginary *adj* existing only in the imagination, not real

▣ imagined, fanciful, visionary, pretend, make-believe, unreal, non-existent, fictional, fabulous, legendary, mythological, made-up, invented, fictitious

⚠ Do not confuse with: **imaginative**

imagination *noun* the power of forming pictures in the mind of things not present or experienced

imaginative *adj* **1** having a lively imagination **2** done with imagination: *an imaginative piece of writing* ◇ **imaginatively** *adv*

▣ **1** resourceful, enterprising, creative, inventive, fanciful **2** creative, inventive, innovative, original, inspired, visionary, ingenious, fantastic, vivid

⚠ Do not confuse with: **imaginary**

imagine *verb* **1** form a picture in the mind, *esp* of something that does not exist **2** think, suppose

▣ **1** visualize, envisage, conceive, fancy, fantasize, pretend, make believe, conjure up, dream up, think up, invent, devise, create **2** think, believe, judge, suppose, guess, assume, gather

imago /ɪˈmeɪgoʊ/ *noun* (*plural* **imagos** or **imagines**) an adult insect that has completed metamorphosis

imam *noun* **1** the priest who leads the prayers in a mosque **2** (**Imam**) an Islamic leader

imbecile *noun* a feeble-minded person; a fool ◇ **imbecility** *noun* feeble-mindedness, stupidity

▣ idiot, halfwit, simpleton, moron, cretin, fool, blockhead

imbibe *verb* drink (in)

imbroglio /ɪmˈbroʊlɪoʊ/ *noun* (*plural* **imbroglios**) a confused situation, a tangle

imbue *verb* fill or affect (with): *imbued her staff with enthusiasm*

imitate *verb* try to be or do the same as, copy ◇ **imitation** *noun* a copy ◇ *adj* made to look like: *imitation leather* ◇ **imitator** *noun*

▣ copy, emulate, follow, mimic, impersonate, caricature, parody, repeat, echo, reproduce, simulate, forge ▪ **imitation** *noun* copy, duplicate, reproduction, replica, simulation, counterfeit, fake

immaculate *adj* spotless; very clean and neat ◇ **immaculately** *adv*

▣ perfect, unblemished, flawless, faultless, impeccable, clean, pure, unsullied, stainless

▣ blemished, stained, contaminated

immaterial *adj* of little importance

immature *adj* not mature ◇ **immaturely** *adv* ◇ **immaturity** *noun*

▣ young, under-age, adolescent, juvenile, childish, puerile, infantile, babyish

immediate *adj* **1** happening straight away: *immediate reaction* **2** close: *immediate family* **3** direct: *my immediate successor* ◇ **immediacy** *noun* ◇ **immediately** *adv* without delay

▣ **1** instant, instantaneous, direct, prompt, swift, current, present, existing, urgent, pressing **2** nearest, adjacent, near, close ◇ **immediately** now, straight away, right away, at once, instantly, directly, without delay, promptly

immemorial *adj* going further back in time than can be remembered ◇ **immemorially** *adv*

immense *adj* very large ◇ **immensely** *adv* ◇ **immensity** *noun*

▣ vast, great, huge, enormous, massive, giant, gigantic, tremendous

▣ tiny, minute

immerse *verb* plunge into liquid

◇ **immersion** *noun* ◇ **immersion heater** an electric water-heater inside a
hot-water tank ◇ **immerse yourself
in** give your whole attention to

▣ plunge, submerge, submerse, sink,
duck, dip, douse, bathe

immigrate *verb* come into a country
and settle there ◇ **immigrant** *noun*
◇ **immigration** *noun*

⚠ Do not confuse with: **emigrate**

imminent *adj* about to happen: *imminent danger* ◇ **imminently** *adv*

▣ impending, forthcoming, approaching,
coming, near, close, looming, threatening, brewing

⚠ Do not confuse with: **eminent**

immobile *adj* **1** not moving **2** not easily moved ◇ **immobility** *noun* ◇ **immobilize** *verb* put out of action

immoderate *adj* going beyond reasonable limits ◇ **immoderately** *adv*

immolate *verb* sacrifice ◇ **immola-
tion** *noun*

immoral *adj* **1** wrong, unscrupulous
2 sexually improper ◇ **immorality**
noun ◇ **immorally** *adv*

▣ **1** unethical, wrong, bad, sinful, evil,
wicked, unscrupulous, unprincipled,
dishonest, corrupt, depraved, degenerate **2** indecent, obscene

▣ **1** moral, right, good

⚠ Do not confuse with: **amoral**

immortal *adj* **1** living for ever **2** famous for ever ◇ **immortality** *noun* unending life or fame ◇ **immortalize** *verb*
make immortal or famous for ever

▣ **1** undying, imperishable, eternal, everlasting, perpetual, endless, ceaseless,
lasting, timeless, ageless

immovable *adj* not able to be moved
or changed ◇ **immovably** *adv*

▣ fixed, rooted, immobile, stuck, fast, secure, stable, constant, firm, set, determined, resolute, adamant, unshakable,
obstinate, unyielding

immune *adj* **1** not likely to catch a
particular disease: *immune to measles* **2**

not able to be affected by something:
she is immune to his charm ◇ **immunity**
noun ◇ **immunize** *verb* make (someone) immune to a disease, *esp* by inoculation ◇ **immune system** the
natural defensive system of an organism which identifies and neutralizes
harmful matter within itself ◇ **immunodeficiency** *noun* weakened ability
to produce antibodies

▣ **1** resistant, protected, safe, exempt,
free, clear **2** invulnerable, unsusceptible

▣ **2** susceptible

immunology *noun* the study of the
human immune system ◇ **immunolo-
gical** *adj* ◇ **immunologist** *noun*

imp *noun* **1** a small malignant spirit **2** a
mischievous child ◇ **impish** *adj*

impact *noun* **1** the blow of one thing
striking another; a collision **2** strong effect: *made an impact on the audience*
◇ *verb* **1** press firmly together **2** have a
strong effect (on)

▣ *noun* **1** collision, crash, smash, bang,
bump, blow, knock, contact, jolt **2** effect, consequences, repercussions, impression, power, influence

impair *verb* damage, weaken ◇ **impairment** *noun*

▣ damage, harm, injure, spoil, undermine,
weaken, reduce, lessen, diminish

▣ improve, enhance

impala *noun* a large African antelope

impale *verb* pierce through with a
spear *etc*

impart *verb* tell (information, news
etc) to others

impartial *adj* not favouring one side
over another; unbiased ◇ **impartiality**
noun ◇ **impartially** *adv*

▣ objective, detached, neutral, unbiased,
unprejudiced, open-minded, fair, just,
equitable

impassable *adj* of a road: not able to
be travelled along

impasse /'ımpas/ or /am'pas/ *noun* a
situation from which there seems to be
no way out

▣ deadlock, stalemate, dead end, cul-de-
sac, blind alley, halt, standstill

impassioned *adj* moved by strong feeling

impassive *adj* not easily moved by strong feeling ◇ **impassively** *adv*

◾ calm, composed, unruffled, unconcerned, cool, unfeeling, unemotional, unmoved, imperturbable, unexcitable, stoical, indifferent

impatient *adj* 1 restlessly eager 2 irritable, short-tempered ◇ **impatience** *noun* ◇ **impatiently** *adv*

◾ 1 eager, keen, restless, fidgety, fretful, edgy 2 irritable, snappy, hot-tempered, quick-tempered, intolerant, brusque, abrupt

impeach *verb* accuse publicly of, or charge with, misconduct ◇ **impeachment** *noun*

impeccable *adj* faultless, perfect ◇ **impeccably** *adv*

◾ perfect, faultless, precise, exact, flawless, unblemished, stainless, immaculate, pure, irreproachable, blameless

◪ faulty, flawed, corrupt

impecunious *adj* having little or no money

impede *verb* hinder, keep back ◇ **impediment** *noun* 1 a hindrance 2 a speech defect, *eg* a stutter or stammer

◾ hamper, obstruct, block, slow, hold up, delay, retard, restrain, disrupt

impel *verb* (**impels**, **impelling**, **impelled**) 1 urge 2 drive on

impending *adj* about to happen: *an impending storm*

◾ imminent, forthcoming, approaching, coming, close, near, looming

impenetrable *adj* 1 not allowing light *etc* through 2 very difficult or impossible to understand

◾ 1 solid, thick, dense 2 unintelligible, baffling, mysterious, cryptic, enigmatic, obscure

impenitent *adj* not sorry for wrongdoing, unrepentant

imperative *adj* 1 necessary, urgent 2 *grammar* expressing command, *eg look!* or *read this* ◇ **imperatively** *adv*

◾ 1 compulsory, obligatory, essential, vital, crucial, pressing, urgent

imperceptible *adj* so small as not to be noticed ◇ **imperceptibly** *adv*

imperfect *adj* having a fault or flaw, not perfect ◇ **imperfection** *noun* a fault or a flaw ◇ **imperfectly** *adv*

◾ faulty, flawed, defective, damaged, broken, chipped, deficient, incomplete

imperial *adj* 1 of an emperor or empire 2 commanding, superior ◇ **imperialism** *noun* the policy of annexing the territory of, and ruling, other nations and people ◇ **imperialist** *adj*

imperil *verb* (**imperils**, **imperilling**, **imperilled**) put in danger

◾ endanger, jeopardize, risk, hazard, expose, compromise, threaten

imperious *adj* having an air of authority, haughty ◇ **imperiously** *adv*

impermanence *noun* lack of permanence, transitoriness ◇ **impermanent** *adj* ◇ **impermanently** *adv*

impermeable *adj* not allowing water *etc* to pass through: *impermeable rock*

impersonal *adj* 1 not influenced by personal feelings 2 not connected with any particular person ◇ **impersonally** *adv*

◾ 1 formal, official, aloof, remote, distant, detached, neutral, objective, cold, frosty, glassy

◪ 1 informal, friendly

impersonate *verb* pretend to be (someone), *esp* to entertain others ◇ **impersonation** *noun* ◇ **impersonator** *noun*

impertinent *adj* 1 cheeky, impudent 2 not pertinent, irrelevant ◇ **impertinence** *noun* ◇ **impertinently** *adv*

◾ 1 rude, impolite, ill-mannered, discourteous, disrespectful, insolent, impudent, *informal* cheeky, bold, brazen, forward, presumptuous

imperturbable *adj* not easily worried, calm ◇ **imperturbably** *adv*

impervious *adj*: **impervious to** not able to be affected by: *impervious to criticism*

◾ immune, invulnerable, untouched, unaffected, unmoved, resistant

impetigo *noun* a kind of skin disease

impetuous *adj* rushing into action, rash ◇ **impetuosity** *noun* ◇ **impetuously** *adv*

▤ impulsive, spontaneous, unplanned, unpremeditated, hasty, reckless, thoughtless

▨ cautious, wary, circumspect

impetus *noun* moving force, motivation

▤ momentum, force, energy, power, drive, boost, push, spur, stimulus, incentive, motivation

impiety *noun* lack of respect for holy things ◇ **impious** *adj* ◇ **impiously** *adv*

impinge *verb*: **impinge on 1** come in contact with **2** trespass on, interfere with

▤ **1** hit, touch (on), affect, influence **2** encroach, infringe, intrude, trespass, invade

impious *see* impiety

implacable *adj* not able to be soothed or calmed ◇ **implacably** *adv*

implant *verb* fix in, plant firmly ◇ *noun* an artificial organ, graft *etc* inserted into the body

implement *noun* a tool ◇ *verb* carry out, fulfil (*eg* a promise) ◇ **implementation** *noun*

▤ *noun* tool, instrument, utensil, gadget, device, apparatus ◇ *verb* enforce, effect, bring about, carry out, execute, perform, do, fulfil, complete, accomplish

implicate *verb* involve: *the statement implicates you in the crime*

implication *noun* **1** something meant though not actually said **2** implicating someone or being implicated

▤ **1** inference, insinuation, suggestion, meaning, significance, ramification, repercussion

implicit *adj* **1** understood, meant though not actually said **2** unquestioning: *implicit obedience* ◇ **implicitly** *adv*

▤ **1** implied, inferred, insinuated, indirect, unsaid, unspoken, tacit, understood **2** unquestioning, utter, total, full, complete, absolute, unqualified, unreserved, wholehearted

implode *verb* collapse inwards suddenly ◇ **implosion** *noun*

implore *verb* beg, entreat

imply *verb* suggest: *her silence implies disapproval*

▤ insinuate, hint, intimate, mean, signify, point to, indicate

⚠ Do not confuse with: **infer**

impolite *adj* not polite, rude ◇ **impolitely** *adv* ◇ **impoliteness** *noun*

▤ rude, discourteous, bad-mannered, ill-mannered, ill-bred, disrespectful, insolent, rough, coarse, vulgar, abrupt

▨ polite, courteous

imponderable *adj* not able to be judged or evaluated

import *verb* bring in (goods) from abroad for sale ◇ *noun* **1** the act of importing **2** goods imported **3** meaning, significance ◇ **importation** *noun* ◇ **importer** *noun*

important *adj* worthy of attention; having great significance or influence ◇ **importance** *noun* ◇ **importantly** *adv*

▤ momentous, noteworthy, significant, meaningful, relevant, urgent, vital, essential, key, primary, substantial, valuable, leading, influential, powerful

importune *verb* keep asking for something ◇ **importunate** *adj* repeatedly asking ◇ **importunity** *noun*

impose *verb* **1** place (a tax *etc*) on something or somebody **2** (with **on**) take advantage of, inconvenience ◇ **imposing** *adj* impressive, commanding attention ◇ **imposition** *noun* a burden, an inconvenience

▤ **1** introduce, institute, enforce, promulgate, exact, levy, set, fix, put, place, lay, inflict, burden, encumber, saddle **2** intrude, butt in, encroach, trespass, obtrude, force oneself on, presume, take liberties

impossible *adj* **1** not able to be done or to happen **2** extremely difficult to deal with, intolerable ◇ **impossibility** *noun* ◇ **impossibly** *adv*

▤ **1** hopeless, impracticable, unworkable, unattainable, unachievable, unobtainable, insoluble, preposterous, absurd, ludicrous, ridiculous

impostor *noun* someone who pretends to be someone else in order to deceive ◇ **imposture** *noun* deceiving in this way

impotent *adj* 1 without power or effectiveness 2 of a male: unable to achieve or maintain an erection ◇ **impotence** *noun* ◇ **impotently** *adv*

🔳 1 powerless, helpless, unable, incapable, ineffective, incompetent, inadequate, weak, feeble, frail, infirm

impound *verb* seize possession of (something) by law

impoverish *verb* 1 make financially poor 2 lessen in quality: *an impoverished culture* ◇ **impoverishment** *noun*

impracticable *adj* not able to be done, used *etc* ◇ **impracticability** *noun*

🔳 unworkable, unfeasible, unattainable, unachievable, impossible, unviable, useless, unserviceable, inoperable

❗ Do not confuse: **impracticable** and **impractical**

impractical *adj* lacking common sense ◇ **impracticality** *noun*

🔳 unrealistic, idealistic, romantic, starry-eyed
🔳 practical, realistic, sensible

imprecation *noun* a curse

imprecise *adj* not precise, vague ◇ **imprecisely** *adv*

🔳 inexact, inaccurate, approximate, estimated, rough, loose, indefinite, hazy, ill-defined, sloppy, ambiguous
🔳 precise, exact

impregnable *adj* too strong to be taken by attack

impregnate *verb* 1 make pregnant 2 saturate: *impregnated with perfume*

impresario *noun* (*plural* **impresarios**) the organizer of an entertainment

impress *verb* 1 arouse the interest or admiration of 2 make a mark on something by pressing 3 fix deeply in the mind: *impressed on them the need for secrecy*

🔳 1 strike, move, touch, affect, influence, stir, inspire, excite

impression *noun* 1 someone's thoughts or feelings about something or someone: *I got the impression she was afraid of him* 2 a deep or strong effect: *the film left a lasting impression on me* 3 a mark made by impressing 4 a quantity of copies of a book printed at one time ◇ **impressionable** *adj* easily influenced or affected ◇ **impressionism** *noun* an artistic or literary style aiming to reproduce personal impressions of things or events ◇ **impressionist** *noun* 1 a follower of impressionism 2 an entertainer who impersonates people ◇ **impressive** *adj* having a strong effect on the mind ◇ **impressively** *adv*

🔳 1 feeling, awareness, sense, idea, notion, opinion, belief, conviction, suspicion, hunch 2 effect, impact, influence ◇ **impressionable** naive, gullible, susceptible, vulnerable, sensitive, responsive, open, receptive ◇ **impressive** striking, imposing, grand, powerful, effective, stirring, exciting, moving, touching

🔳 **impressive** unimpressive, uninspiring

imprint *verb* 1 stamp, press 2 fix in the mind ◇ *noun* 1 a mark made by pressure 2 the printer's or publisher's name *etc* on a book

imprison *verb* shut up as in a prison ◇ **imprisonment** *noun*

🔳 jail, incarcerate, intern, detain, *informal* send down, *informal* put away, lock up, confine

improbable *adj* not likely to happen or to be true ◇ **improbability** *noun*

🔳 uncertain, questionable, doubtful, unlikely, dubious, implausible, unconvincing, far-fetched, preposterous, unbelievable, incredible
🔳 probable, likely, convincing

impromptu *adj* & *adv* without preparation or rehearsal

🔳 *adj* improvised, extempore, ad-lib, off the cuff, unscripted, unrehearsed, unprepared, spontaneous ◇ *adv* extempore, ad lib, off the cuff, off the top of one's head, spontaneously, on the spur of the moment

improper *adj* 1 not suitable; wrong 2

indecent ◇ **improper fraction** a fraction such as $\frac{4}{3}$, with a value greater than 1 ◇ **impropriety** noun (plural **improprieties**) something improper

■ **1** wrong, incorrect, irregular, unsuitable, inappropriate, inopportune, incongruous, out of place **2** indecent, rude, vulgar, unseemly, unbecoming, shocking

improve verb make or become better ◇ **improvement** noun

■ better, ameliorate, enhance, polish, rectify, correct, amend, reform, upgrade, increase, develop, advance, progress, recover, recuperate, turn over a new leaf

🖃 worsen, deteriorate, decline

improvident adj taking no thought for future needs ◇ **improvidence** noun ◇ **improvidently** adv

improvise verb **1** put together from available materials: we improvised a stretcher **2** create (a tune, script etc) spontaneously: the actors had to improvise their lines ◇ **improvisation** noun

imprudent adj unwise

■ ill-advised, foolish, short-sighted, rash, reckless, hasty, irresponsible, careless, heedless, indiscreet

🖃 prudent, wise, cautious

impudent adj cheeky, insolent ◇ **impudence** noun ◇ **impudently** adv

■ impertinent, bold, forward, shameless, cocky, insolent, rude, presumptuous

impugn verb attack in words; criticize

impulse noun **1** a sudden force or push **2** an urge resulting in sudden action ◇ **impulsive** adj acting on impulse, without taking time to consider ◇ **impulsively** adv ◇ **impulsiveness** noun

■ **1** impetus, momentum, force, pressure, drive, thrust, push, stimulus, motive **2** urge, wish, desire, inclination, whim, notion, instinct, feeling, passion ◇ **impulsive** impetuous, rash, reckless, hasty, quick, spontaneous, automatic, instinctive, intuitive

impunity noun freedom from punishment, injury or loss

impure adj mixed with other substances; not clean ◇ **impurity** noun (plural **impurities**)

■ unrefined, contaminated, polluted, tainted, infected, corrupt, debased, unclean, dirty, foul

impute verb think of as being caused, done etc by someone: imputing the mistake to others ◇ **imputation** noun suggestion of fault; blame

in prep **1** showing position in space or time: sitting in the garden/born in the 60s **2** showing state, manner etc: in part/in cold blood ◇ adv **1** towards the inside, not out **2** in power **3** informal in fashion ◇ adj **1** that is in, inside or coming in **2** informal fashionable ◇ **be in for** be about to receive (trouble, punishment) ◇ **go in for** try to win (a competition etc)

in- prefix **1** into, on, towards: inshore **2** not: inaccurate

inability noun (plural **inabilities**) lack of power, means etc (to do something)

■ incapability, incapacity, powerlessness, impotence, inadequacy, weakness, handicap, disability

inaccessible adj difficult or impossible to reach or obtain

inaccurate adj **1** not correct **2** not exact ◇ **inaccuracy** noun (plural **inaccuracies**)

■ **1** incorrect, wrong, erroneous, mistaken, faulty, flawed, defective **2** imprecise, inexact, loose, unreliable, unfaithful, untrue

inactive adj not active ◇ **inaction** noun lack of action ◇ **inactivity** noun idleness; rest

■ immobile, inert, idle, dormant, passive, sedentary, lazy, lethargic, sluggish, sleepy

🖃 active, working, busy

inadequate adj **1** not enough **2** unable to cope with a situation

■ **1** insufficient, short, wanting, deficient, sparse, meagre **2** incompetent, incapable, unequal, unqualified, ineffective, unsatisfactory

inadmissible adj not allowable: inadmissible evidence

inadvertent *adj* unintentional

■ accidental, chance, unintentional, unintended, unplanned, unpremeditated, careless

◨ deliberate, conscious, careful

inadvisable *adj* not advisable, unwise

■ unwise, imprudent, injudicious, foolish, silly, ill-advised, misguided, indiscreet

◨ advisable, wise

inalienable *adj* not able to be removed or transferred: *inalienable rights*

inane *adj* silly, foolish ◇ **inanity** *noun* (*plural* **inanities**) an empty, meaningless remark

■ senseless, stupid, unintelligent, idiotic, frivolous, trifling, puerile, mindless

inanimate *adj* without life

inapplicable *adj* not applicable

inapposite *adj* not suitable, not relevant

inappropriate *adj* not suitable

■ unsuitable, inapt, inapposite, ill-suited, irrelevant, incongruous, out of place, untimely, tactless, improper, unseemly, unbecoming, unfitting

◨ appropriate, suitable

inapt *adj* unsuitable, unfit ◇ **inaptitude** or **inaptness** *noun*

⚠ Do not confuse with: **inept**

inarticulate *adj* 1 unable to express yourself clearly 2 said indistinctly

■ 1 incoherent, speechless 2 unintelligible, incomprehensible, unclear, indistinct, hesitant, faltering

inasmuch as because, since

inattentive *adj* not paying attention ◇ **inattention** *noun*

■ distracted, dreamy, daydreaming, preoccupied, absent-minded, unmindful, heedless, careless, negligent

inaudible *adj* not loud enough to be heard

■ silent, noiseless, imperceptible, faint, indistinct, muffled, muted, low

inaugurate *verb* mark the beginning of (something) or place (someone) in office with a ceremony ◇ **inaugural** *adj* ◇ **inauguration** *noun*

■ launch, introduce, usher in, initiate, induct, ordain, invest, install, commission

inauspicious *adj* unlucky, unlikely to end in success

inborn *adj* existing in someone from birth: *inborn talent*

■ innate, natural, inherent, native, congenital, inbred, hereditary, inherited, ingrained, instinctive, intuitive

inbred *adj* 1 inborn 2 resulting from inbreeding ◇ **inbreeding** *noun* repeated mating within the same family

inc *abbrev* 1 incorporated 2 inclusive 3 including

incalculable *adj* not able to be counted or estimated

■ countless, inestimable, limitless, unlimited, immense, vast

◨ limited, restricted

incandescent *adj* white-hot

incantation *noun* a spell

incapable *adj* 1 unable (to do what is required or expected) 2 helpless (through drink *etc*)

■ 1 unable, powerless, impotent, helpless, weak, feeble, unfit, unsuited, unqualified, incompetent, inept, inadequate, ineffective

◨ 1, 2 capable

incapacitate *verb* 1 take away power, strength or rights from 2 disable ◇ **incapacity** *noun* 1 inability 2 disability

■ 2 disable, cripple, paralyse, immobilize, disqualify, put out of action, lay up, *informal* scupper

incarcerate *verb* imprison ◇ **incarceration** *noun*

incarnate *adj* having human form ◇ **incarnation** *noun* appearance in the form of a human body

incendiary *adj* meant for setting (buildings *etc*) on fire: *an incendiary bomb*

incense [1] /ɪnˈsɛns/ *verb* make angry

■ *verb* anger, enrage, infuriate, madden, exasperate, irritate, rile, provoke, excite

incense [2] /ˈɪnsɛns/ *noun* a mixture of resins, gums, *etc* burned to give off fumes, *esp* in religious ceremonies

incentive *noun* something which encourages someone to do something

■ bait, lure, *informal* carrot, *slang* sweetener, reward, encouragement, motive, impetus, spur, stimulus, motivation

◢ disincentive, discouragement, deterrent

inception *noun* beginning

incessant *adj* going on without pause ◊ **incessantly** *adv*

■ ceaseless, unceasing, endless, continual, persistent, constant, perpetual, eternal, continuous, unbroken, unremitting, non-stop

incest *noun* illegal sexual intercourse between close relatives ◊ **incestuous** *adj* **1** involving incest **2** done within a closely knit group

inch *noun* (*plural* **inches**) one twelfth of a foot (about 2.54 centimetres) ◊ *verb* move very gradually

incidence *noun* the frequency of something occurring

incident *noun* a happening, sometimes causing trouble ◊ **incidental** *adj* **1** happening in connection with something: *an incidental expense* **2** casual ◊ **incidentally** *adv* by the way

■ occurrence, event, episode, adventure, affair, occasion, instance, confrontation, clash, fight

incinerate *verb* burn to ashes ◊ **incineration** *noun* ◊ **incinerator** *noun* an apparatus for burning rubbish *etc*

incipient *adj* beginning to exist: *an incipient dislike*

incise *verb* cut into, engrave ◊ **incision** *noun* **1** a cut, *esp* in surgery **2** cutting into something ◊ **incisive** *adj* sharp, clear, firm ◊ **incisor** *noun* a front tooth

■ incisive cutting, keen, sharp, acute, piercing, penetrating, biting, caustic, acid, astute, perceptive

incite *verb* move to action; urge on ◊ **incitement** *noun*

■ prompt, instigate, rouse, stir up, work up, excite, animate, provoke, stimulate, spur, impel, drive, urge, encourage, *informal* egg on

incivility *noun* (*plural* **incivilities**) impoliteness

inclement *adj* of weather: stormy ◊ **inclemency** *noun*

incline *verb* **1** lean, slope (towards) **2** bend, bow: *inclined his head* ◊ *noun* a slope ◊ **inclination** *noun* **1** liking, tendency **2** a slope, an angle ◊ **inclined** *adj* **1** sloping **2** disposed: *I feel inclined to believe her*

■ **inclination 1** liking, fondness, taste, preference, bias, tendency, trend, disposition, propensity, leaning

include *verb* **1** count in with others **2** contain ◊ **inclusion** *noun* ◊ **inclusive** *adj* including everything mentioned: *from Tuesday to Thursday inclusive is 3 days*

■ **1** add, count, allow for, take into account **2** comprise, incorporate, contain, enclose, embrace, encompass, cover, involve

incognito *adj* & *adv* in disguise, with identity concealed ◊ *noun* (*plural* **incognitos**) a disguise

incoherent *adj* **1** unconnected, rambling **2** speaking or spoken in an unconnected, rambling way ◊ **incoherence** *noun*

■ **1** scrambled, confused, muddled, jumbled, disordered, garbled, broken, unintelligible, incomprehensible **2** inarticulate, rambling, stammering, stuttering

incombustible *adj* not able to be burned by fire

income *noun* **1** personal earnings **2** gain, profit

■ **1** earnings, pay, salary, wages, means **2** revenue, returns, proceeds, gains, profits, interest, takings, receipts

incoming *adj* approaching, next

incommunicado *adj* & *adv* without means of communicating with others

incomparable *adj* without equal

■ matchless, unmatched, unequalled, unparalleled, unrivalled, supreme, superb, brilliant

incompatible *adj* **1** of people: not

suited, bound to disagree **2** of statements: contradicting each other ◇ **incompatibility** *noun*

incompetent *adj* not good enough at doing a job ◇ **incompetence** *noun* ◇ **incompetently** *adv*

☰ incapable, unable, unfit, inefficient, inexpert, unskilful, stupid, useless, ineffective

☲ competent, able

incomplete *adj* not finished

incomprehensible *adj* not able to be understood, puzzling ◇ **incomprehensibly** *adv* ◇ **incomprehension** *noun* lack of understanding

☰ unintelligible, impenetrable, unfathomable, puzzling, perplexing, baffling, mysterious, inscrutable, obscure, opaque

☲ comprehensible, intelligible

inconceivable *adj* not able to be imagined or believed

inconclusive *adj* not leading to a definite decision or conclusion

incongruous *adj* out of place, unsuitable ◇ **incongruity** *noun* (*plural* **incongruities**)

☰ inappropriate, unsuitable, out of place, inconsistent, conflicting, incompatible

inconsequential *adj* unimportant ◇ **inconsequence** *noun* ◇ **inconsequentially** *adv*

inconsiderable *adj* slight, small, unimportant

inconsiderate *adj* not thinking of the needs, feelings *etc* of others

☰ unkind, uncaring, unconcerned, selfish, self-centred, intolerant, insensitive, tactless, rude, thoughtless, unthinking, careless, heedless

inconsistent *adj* not consistent, contradicting

☰ conflicting, incompatible, contradictory, contrary, variable, irregular, unpredictable, varying, unstable, unsteady, inconstant, fickle

inconsolable *adj* not able to be comforted

inconspicuous *adj* not attracting attention

inconstant *adj* often changing ◇ **inconstancy** *noun*

incontinent *adj* unable to control the bladder or bowels ◇ **incontinence** *noun*

incontrovertible *adj* not to be doubted or disrupted

inconvenient *adj* causing awkwardness or difficulty ◇ **inconvenience** *noun* bother or difficulty ◇ *verb* cause trouble or difficulty to

☰ awkward, ill-timed, untimely, inopportune, unsuitable, difficult, embarrassing, annoying, troublesome, unmanageable ◇ **inconvenience** *verb* bother, disturb, disrupt, put out, trouble, upset

incorporate *verb* **1** contain as parts of a whole: *the new building incorporates a theatre, cinema and restaurant* **2** include, take account of: *the new text incorporates the author's changes* ◇ **incorporated** *adj* (short form **inc**) formed into a company or society

incorrect *adj* wrong

☰ wrong, mistaken, erroneous, inaccurate, imprecise, inexact, false, untrue, faulty, inappropriate, unsuitable

incorrigible *adj* unable to be put right or reformed: *incorrigible behaviour*

incorruptible *adj* **1** not able to be bribed **2** not likely to decay

increase *verb* make or become greater or more numerous ◇ *noun* **1** growth **2** the amount added by growth ◇ **increasingly** *adv* more and more

☰ *verb* raise, add to, improve, enhance, advance, step up, intensify, strengthen, heighten, grow, develop, build up, enlarge, extend, prolong, expand, spread, multiply, rise, mount, soar

☲ *verb* decrease, reduce, decline

incredible *adj* impossible to believe ◇ **incredibility** *noun* ◇ **incredibly** *adv*

☰ unbelievable, improbable, implausible, far-fetched, preposterous, absurd, impossible, inconceivable, unthinkable, unimaginable, extraordinary, amazing, astonishing, astounding

☲ credible, believable

⚠ Do not confuse: **incredible** and **incredulous**

incredulous *adj* not believing what is said ◇ **incredulity** *noun* ◇ **incredulously** *adv*

▤ unbelieving, disbelieving, unconvinced, sceptical, doubting, distrustful, suspicious, dubious, doubtful

increment *noun* an annual increase in a salary

incriminate *verb* show that (someone) has taken part in a crime

▤ implicate, involve, accuse, charge, impeach, indict, point the finger at, blame

incubator *noun* **1** a large heated box for hatching eggs **2** a hospital crib for rearing premature babies ◇ **incubate** *verb* brood, hatch ◇ **incubation period** the time that it takes for a disease to develop from infection to the first symptoms

inculcate *verb* impress something on the mind by constant repetition

incumbent *adj* resting (on someone) as a duty: *it is incumbent upon me to warn you* ◇ *noun* someone who holds an official position

incur *verb* (**incurs, incurring, incurred**) bring (blame, debt *etc*) upon yourself

▤ suffer, sustain, arouse, expose oneself to, meet with, run up, gain, earn

incurable *adj* unable to be cured

incursion *noun* an invasion, a raid

indebted *adj* having cause to be grateful: *we are indebted to you for your kindness* ◇ **indebtedness** *noun*

▤ obliged, grateful, thankful

indecent *adj* offending against normal or usual standards of (*esp* sexual) behaviour ◇ **indecency** *noun* ◇ **indecent assault** an assault involving indecency but not rape

▤ improper, immodest, offensive, obscene, pornographic, lewd, vulgar, coarse, crude, dirty, filthy, foul, gross, outrageous, shocking, *informal* X-rated

▣ decent, modest

indecipherable *adj* **1** illegible **2** incomprehensible

indecision *noun* slowness in making up your mind, hesitation ◇ **indecisive** *adj* **1** not producing a definite result **2** unable to make up your mind

▤ indecisiveness, irresolution, vacillation, wavering, hesitation, hesitancy, ambivalence, uncertainty, doubt

indecorous *adj* unseemly, inappropriate ◇ **indecorum** *noun*

indeed *adv* **1** in fact: *she is indeed a splendid cook* **2** (used for emphasis) really: *did he indeed?* ◇ *exclam* expressing surprise

indefatigable *adj* untiring

indefensible *adj* unable to be defended; inexcusable

▤ unjustifiable, unforgivable, unpardonable, insupportable, untenable, wrong, faulty

▣ defensible, excusable

indefinable *adj* not able to be stated or described clearly

indefinite *adj* **1** not fixed, uncertain **2** without definite limits ◇ **indefinitely** *adv* for an indefinite period of time ◇ **indefinite article** the grammatical term for the words *a* and *an*

▤ **1** unknown, unsettled, unresolved, undecided, undetermined, vague, unclear, imprecise, inexact, loose **2** undetermined, undefined, unspecified, unlimited, ill-defined, vague, indistinct ◇ **indefinitely** for ever, eternally, endlessly, continually

▣ **1** definite, clear **2** limited

indelible *adj* unable to be rubbed out or removed

▤ lasting, enduring, permanent, fast, ingrained, indestructible

indelicate *adj* impolite, tactless ◇ **indelicacy** *noun*

indemnify *verb* (**indemnifies, indemnifying, indemnified**) **1** compensate for loss **2** exempt (from)

indemnity *noun* **1** security from damage or loss **2** compensation for loss

indent *verb* **1** begin a new paragraph by going in from the margin **2** (with **for**) apply for (stores, equipment *etc*) ◇ **indentation** *noun* **1** a hollow, a dent **2** an inward curve in an outline, coastline *etc*

indenture *noun* a written agreement ◇ *verb* bind by a written agreement

independent *adj* **1** free to think or act for yourself **2** not relying on someone else for support, guidance *etc* **3** of a country: self-governing ◇ **independence** *noun* ◇ **independently** *adv*

◳ **1** liberated, unconstrained **2** self-sufficient, self-supporting, self-reliant, self-contained, separate **3** autonomous, self-governing, sovereign

indescribable *adj* too extreme, vague *etc* to be described

indestructible *adj* not able to be destroyed

◳ unbreakable, durable, tough, strong, lasting, enduring, abiding, permanent, eternal, everlasting, immortal, imperishable

indetectable *adj* not able to be detected, not noticeable

indeterminate *adj* not fixed, indefinite

◳ unspecified, unstated, undefined, unfixed, imprecise, inexact, indefinite, vague, undecided, undetermined, uncertain

◳▪ known, specified, fixed

index *noun* (*plural* **indexes**) **1** an alphabetical list giving the page number of names, subjects *etc* mentioned in a book **2** an indication **3** (*plural* **indices**) *maths* an upper number which shows how many times a number is multiplied by itself (*eg* 4^3 means 4 x 4 x 4) **4** a numerical scale showing changes in the cost of living, wages *etc*

◳ **1** table, key, list, catalogue, directory, guide **2** indicator, pointer, sign, token, mark, indication, clue

Indian *adj*: **Indian corn** maize ◇ **Indian ink** a very black ink used by artists ◇ **Indian summer** a period of summer warmth in autumn

indiarubber *noun* a rubber eraser

indicate *verb* **1** point out, show **2** be a sign of ◇ **indication** *noun* a sign ◇ **indicative** *adj* indicating: *indicative of his*

attitude ◇ **indicator** *noun* **1** something which indicates; a pointer **2** a flashing light on either side of a vehicle for signalling to other drivers

◳ **1** show, reveal, display, manifest, point to, designate, specify, point out, mark **2** signify, mean, denote, express, suggest, imply ◇ **indication** mark, sign, evidence, symptom, signal, warning, omen, intimation, suggestion, hint, clue, note, explanation

indices *plural of* **index** (sense 3)

indict /ɪn'daɪt/ *verb* accuse formally of a crime ◇ **indictment** *noun*

indie *noun, informal* an independent record, film or television company

indifferent *adj* **1** neither very good nor very bad **2** (with **to**) showing no interest in ◇ **indifference** *noun*

◳ **1** mediocre, average, middling, passable, moderate, fair, ordinary **2** uninterested, unenthusiastic, unexcited, apathetic, unconcerned, unmoved, uncaring, unsympathetic, cold, cool, distant, aloof, detached, neutral, disinterested

◳▪ **1** excellent **2** interested, caring

indigenous *adj* native to a country or area

indigent *adj* poor, impoverished ◇ **indigence** *noun*

indigestion *noun* discomfort or pain caused by difficulty in digesting food ◇ **indigestible** *adj* difficult to digest

indignant *adj* angry, *esp* because of wrong done to yourself or others ◇ **indignation** *noun*

◳ annoyed, angry, irate, heated, fuming, livid, furious, incensed, infuriated, exasperated, outraged

◳▪ pleased, delighted

indignity *noun* (*plural* **indignities**) **1** loss of dignity **2** a cause of shame or humiliation

indigo *noun* a purplish-blue colour ◇ *adj* purplish-blue

indirect *adj* **1** not straight or direct **2** not affecting or affected directly ◇ **indirect speech** speech reported not in the speaker's actual words, *eg* they said *that they'd leave this morning* (contrasted with: **direct speech**) ◊ **indirect tax** a tax on goods, paid by the customer in the form of a higher price

- ▣ **1** roundabout, circuitous, wandering, rambling, winding, meandering, zigzag **2** secondary, incidental, unintended, subsidiary

indiscreet *adj* **1** rash, not cautious **2** giving away too much information ◊ **indiscretion** *noun* a rash or unwise remark or act

- ▣ **1** careless, heedless, imprudent, unwise, foolish, rash, reckless, hasty **2** tactless, undiplomatic ◊ **indiscretion** mistake, error, slip, faux pas, gaffe, tactlessness, rashness

indiscriminate *adj* making no distinction between one person or thing and another: *indiscriminate buying/indiscriminate killing*

- ▣ general, sweeping, random, haphazard, hit-and-miss, aimless, unmethodical, mixed
- ▣ selective, specific, precise

indispensable *adj* not able to be done without, necessary

- ▣ vital, essential, basic, key, crucial, imperative, required, requisite, needed, necessary
- ▣ dispensable, unnecessary

indisposed *adj* unwell ◊ **indisposition** *noun*

indisputable *adj* not able to be denied or doubted

- ▣ incontrovertible, unquestionable, irrefutable, undeniable, absolute, undisputed, definite, positive, certain, sure

indistinct *adj* not clear, *esp* to the eye or ear

- ▣ unclear, ill-defined, blurred, misty, hazy, shadowy, obscure, dim, faint, muffled, confused, unintelligible, vague, woolly, ambiguous, indefinite

indistinguishable *adj* **1** difficult to make out **2** too alike to tell apart

individual *adj* **1** relating to a single person or thing **2** distinctive, unusual ◊ *noun* a single person or thing ◊ **individualist** *noun* someone with an independent or distinctive lifestyle

◊ **individualistic** *adj* ◊ **individuality** *noun* **1** separate existence **2** the quality of standing out from others

- ▣ *adj* **1** peculiar, singular, distinct, specific, single **2** distinctive, characteristic, idiosyncratic, peculiar, unique, special, personal, personalized ◊ *noun* person, being, creature, party, body, soul, character

indivisible *adj* not able to be divided

indoctrinate *verb* fill with a certain teaching or set of ideas

- ▣ brainwash, teach, instruct, school, ground, train

indolent *adj* lazy ◊ **indolence** *noun*

indomitable *adj* unconquerable, unyielding

indoor *adj* done, used *etc* inside a building ◊ **indoors** *adv* in or into a building *etc*

indubitable *adj* not to be doubted

induce *verb* **1** persuade **2** bring on, cause ◊ **inducement** *noun* something which encourages or persuades: *money is an inducement to work*

- ▣ **1** coax, prevail upon, encourage, press, persuade, talk into, move, influence, draw, tempt **2** effect, bring about, occasion, give rise to, lead to, incite, instigate, prompt, provoke, produce ◊ **inducement** lure, bait, attraction, enticement, encouragement, incentive, reward, stimulus, motive
- ▣ **1** discourage, deter

induct *verb* introduce, *eg* into a profession; install

induction *noun* **1** the formal installation of someone in a new post **2** the production of electricity in something by placing it near an electric source **3** the drawing of conclusions from particular cases ◊ **inductive** *adj*

indulge *verb* **1** give in to the wishes of; spoil: *she indulges that child too much* **2** give way to, not restrain: *indulging his sweet tooth* ◊ **indulgence** *noun* **1** the act of indulging **2** a pardon for a sin ◊ **indulgent** *adj* not strict, kind

- ▣ **1** favour, pet, cosset, mollycoddle, pamper, spoil, treat **2** gratify, satisfy, humour, pander to, go along with

◇ **indulgent** tolerant, *informal* easy-going, lenient, generous, liberal, kind, fond, tender, understanding, patient

industrious *adj* working busily or hard

▤ busy, productive, hard-working, diligent, assiduous, conscientious, active, energetic, persistent

▨ lazy, idle

industry *noun* (*plural* **industries**) **1** a branch of trade or manufacture: *the clothing industry* **2** steady attention to work ◇ **industrial** *adj* ◇ **industrialist** *noun* someone involved in organizing an industry

inebriated *adj* drunk

inedible *adj* not eatable

ineffable *adj* not able to be described or expressed in words

ineffective *adj* useless, having no effect

▤ worthless, vain, idle, futile, fruitless, unproductive, unsuccessful, powerless, ineffectual, inadequate, weak, feeble, inept, incompetent

ineffectual *adj* achieving nothing

inefficient *adj* **1** not efficient, not capable **2** wasting time, energy *etc* ◇ **inefficiency** *noun* (*plural* **inefficiencies**)

▤ **1** incompetent, inexpert, slipshod, sloppy, careless, negligent **2** uneconomic, wasteful, money-wasting

inelegant *adj* not graceful ◇ **inelegance** *noun*

▤ graceless, ungraceful, clumsy, *informal* clunky, awkward, ugly, unrefined, crude, rough, unsophisticated

ineligible *adj* not qualified, not suitable to be chosen

ineluctable *adj*, *formal* unavoidable

inept *adj* clumsy, badly done ◇ **ineptitude** *noun*

▤ awkward, clumsy, bungling, incompetent, unskilful, inexpert, foolish, stupid

▨ competent, skilful

> ⚠ Do not confuse with: **inapt**

inequality *noun* (*plural* **inequalities**) **1** lack of equality, unfairness **2** unevenness, *eg* in quantity

▤ **1** disproportion, bias, prejudice **2** unequalness, difference, diversity, dissimilarity, disparity

inert *adj* **1** not moving or able to move **2** disinclined to move or act **3** not lively **4** chemically inactive ◇ **inertia** *noun* ◇ **inertness** *noun*

▤ **1** immobile, motionless, unmoving, still, inactive, inanimate, lifeless, dead, dormant, **2** idle, lazy, lethargic, passive, unresponsive, apathetic **3** sluggish, torpid, sleepy

▨ **3** lively, animated

inescapable *adj* unable to be avoided

inessential *adj* not essential, unnecessary

inestimable *adj* too good or great to be estimated

inevitable *adj* not able to be avoided ◇ **inevitability** *noun* ◇ **inevitably** *adv*

▤ unavoidable, inescapable, definite, certain, sure, decreed, destined, fated, automatic, assured, fixed, irrevocable

▨ avoidable, uncertain, alterable

inexact *adj* not exact, approximate

inexcusable *adj* not to be excused

▤ indefensible, unforgivable, unpardonable, intolerable, unacceptable, outrageous, shameful

inexhaustible *adj* very plentiful; not likely to be used up

▤ unlimited, limitless, boundless, infinite, endless, never-ending, abundant

inexorable *adj* not able to be persuaded; relentless

inexpensive *adj* cheap in price

inexperience *noun* lack of (skilled) knowledge or experience ◇ **inexperienced** *adj*

▤ **inexperienced** inexpert, untrained, unskilled, amateur, apprentice, unfamiliar, unaccustomed, new, fresh, young, immature, naive, unsophisticated, innocent

inexpert *adj* unskilled, amateurish

inexplicable *adj* not able to be explained

▤ unaccountable, strange, mystifying,

puzzling, baffling, mysterious, enigmatic, incomprehensible, incredible, unbelievable, miraculous

inexpressible *adj* not able to be described in words

in extremis in desperate circumstances

inextricable *adj* not able to be disentangled

infallible *adj* **1** never making an error **2** certain to produce the desired result: *an infallible cure* ◇ **infallibility** *noun*

■ **1** accurate, unerring, unfailing, perfect, faultless **2** certain, sure, reliable, dependable, trustworthy, foolproof

infamous *adj* having a very bad reputation; notorious, disgraceful ◇ **infamy** *noun* public disgrace, notoriety

■ notorious, ill-famed, disreputable, disgraceful, shameful, shocking, outrageous, scandalous, wicked
✷ illustrious, glorious

infant *noun* **1** a baby **2** a young schoolchild ◇ **infancy** *noun* **1** early childhood, babyhood **2** the beginning of anything: *when psychiatry was in its infancy* ◇ **infanticide** *noun* **1** the murder of a child **2** a child murderer ◇ **infantile** *adj* **1** of babies **2** childish

■ **1** baby, toddler, *informal* tot, child, *formal* babe, *formal* babe in arms
✷ **1** adult

infantry *noun* soldiers who fight on foot

infatuated *adj* filled with foolish love ◇ **infatuation** *noun*

■ besotted, obsessed, enamoured, *informal* smitten, *informal* crazy, spellbound, mesmerized, captivated, fascinated, enraptured

infect *verb* **1** fill with disease-causing germs **2** pass on disease to **3** pass on or spread *eg* enthusiasm to ◇ **infection** *noun* **1** a disease which can be passed on to others **2** something that spreads widely and affects many people ◇ **infectious** *adj* likely to spread from person to person

■ **infection 1** illness, disease, virus, epidemic, contagion, pestilence, contamination, pollution ◇ **infectious**

contagious, infective, catching, spreading, epidemic, virulent, deadly, contaminating, polluting

infelicitous *adj* unfortunate, inappropriate: *an infelicitous remark*

infer *verb* (**infers, inferring, inferred**) reach a conclusion from facts or reasoning ◇ **inference** *noun*

■ **1** derive, extrapolate, deduce, conclude, assume, presume, surmise, gather, understand

🚹 Do not confuse with: **imply**

inferior *adj* **1** lower in position, status *etc* **2** not of good quality ◇ *noun* someone lower in rank *etc* ◇ **inferiority** *noun* ◇ **inferiority complex** a constant feeling that you are less good in some way than others

■ *adj* **1** lesser, minor, secondary, junior, subordinate, subsidiary, low, humble, menial **2** substandard, second-rate, mediocre, bad, poor, unsatisfactory, slipshod, shoddy

infernal *adj* **1** of hell **2** *informal* annoying, blasted ◇ **inferno** *noun* (*plural* **infernos**) **1** hell **2** a raging fire

infertile *adj* **1** of soil: not supporting the growth of plants **2** not able to bear children or young ◇ **infertility** *noun*

■ **1** barren, sterile, unproductive, unfruitful, arid, parched, dried-up
✷ **1** fertile, fruitful

infest *verb* invade or swarm over: *infested with lice* ◇ **infestation** *noun*

■ swarm, teem, throng, flood, overrun, invade, penetrate, permeate, pervade, ravage

infidel *noun* someone who does not believe in a particular religion (*esp* Christianity)

infidelity *noun* unfaithfulness, disloyalty

■ adultery, unfaithfulness, disloyalty, duplicity, treachery, betrayal, cheating, falseness

infighting *noun* rivalry or quarrelling between members of the same group

infiltrate *verb* enter (an organization

etc) secretly to spy or cause damage ◇ **infiltration** *noun*

■ penetrate, enter, creep into, insinuate, intrude

infinite *adj* without end or limit ◇ **infinity** *noun* space or time without end

■ limitless, unlimited, boundless, endless, never-ending, inexhaustible, innumerable, uncountable, countless, untold, immeasurable, vast, immense, enormous, huge

☒ finite, limited

infinitesimal *adj* very small

infinitive *noun, grammar* the part of a verb which expresses the action but has no subject, *eg* I hate *to lose*

infirm *adj* feeble, weak ◇ **infirmary** *noun* (*plural* **infirmaries**) a hospital ◇ **infirmity** *noun* (*plural* **infirmities**) 1 a physical weakness 2 a character flaw

■ frail, ill, unwell, poorly, sickly, faltering, unsteady, shaky, wobbly

☒ healthy, strong

inflame *verb* 1 make hot or red 2 arouse passion in ◇ **inflamed** *adj*

■ 2 anger, enrage, infuriate, incense, exasperate, madden, provoke, stimulate, excite, rouse, arouse, agitate

inflammable *adj* 1 easily set on fire 2 easily excited ◇ **inflammation** *noun* heat in a part of the body, with pain, redness and swelling ◇ **inflammatory** *adj* arousing passion (*esp* anger)

■ inflammation soreness, painfulness, tenderness, swelling, abscess, infection, redness, heat, rash, irritation

inflate *verb* 1 blow up (a balloon, tyre *etc*) 2 puff up (with pride), exaggerate: *an inflated sense of her own importance* 3 increase to a great extent ◇ **inflation** *noun* 1 the act of inflating 2 an economic situation in which prices and wages keep forcing each other to increase

■ 1 blow up, pump up, blow out, puff out, swell, distend, bloat, expand 2, 3 enlarge, increase, boost, exaggerate, swell

inflect *verb* 1 change the tone of (your voice) 2 vary the endings of (a word) to show tense, number *etc* ◇ **inflection** *noun* ◇ **inflectional** *adj*

inflexible *adj* not yielding, not able to be changed or bent ◇ **inflexibility** *noun*

■ rigid, stiff, hard, solid, set, fixed, firm, immovable, strict, stringent, unyielding, unbending, adamant, resolute, relentless, stubborn, obstinate, intransigent

☒ flexible, yielding, adaptable

inflict *verb* bring down (blows, punishment *etc*) on someone ◇ **infliction** *noun*

■ impose, enforce, wreak, administer, apply, deliver, deal, lay, burden, exact, levy

in-flight *adj* happening or used during a journey in an aeroplane: *in-flight movie*

inflorescence *noun* a blossoming of flowers on a plant

inflow *noun* a flowing in, influx

influence *noun* the power to affect other people or things ◇ *verb* have influence over ◇ **influential** *adj*

■ *noun* power, sway, hold, control, direction, guidance, bias, prejudice, pressure, effect, impact, importance, prestige ◇ *verb* dominate, control, manipulate, direct, guide, change, alter, sway, impress, stir, persuade, prompt, motivate, bias, prejudice

influenza *noun* an infectious illness with fever, headache, muscle pains *etc*

influx *noun* 1 a flowing in 2 the arrival of large numbers of people

info *noun, informal* information

inform *verb* 1 give knowledge to 2 (with **on**) tell on, betray ◇ **informant** *noun* someone who informs ◇ **informative** *adj* giving information ◇ **informer** *noun* someone who gives information to the police or authorities

■ 1 tell, advise, notify, communicate, leak, tip off, acquaint, brief, instruct 2 betray, incriminate, *slang* shop, *informal* tell on, blab, *slang* grass ◇ **informative** educational, instructive, illuminating, revealing, communicative, chatty, newsy, helpful, useful, constructive

informal *adj* not formal; relaxed, friendly ◇ **informality** *noun* ◇ **informally** *adv*

■ casual, relaxed, easy, free, natural, simple,

unpretentious, familiar, colloquial
🔳 formal, solemn

information *noun* knowledge, facts, news

🔳 facts, data, *informal* gen, *informal* SP, intelligence, news, report, notice, instruction, knowledge, evidence

infraction *noun* a breach of a law, rule *etc*

infra-red *adj* of rays of heat: with wavelengths longer than visible light

infrastructure *noun* inner structure, *esp* of a society or organization

infrequent *adj* rare, happening seldom ◊ **infrequently** *adv*

infringe *verb* break (a rule or law) ◊ **infringement** *noun*

🔳 violate, contravene, transgress, overstep, disobey, defy, flout, ignore

infuriate *verb* drive into a rage ◊ **infuriating** *adj*

🔳 anger, vex, enrage, incense, exasperate, madden, provoke, rouse, annoy, irritate, rile, antagonize

🔳 calm, pacify

infuse *verb* **1** pour on or over **2** fill the mind of (with a desire *etc*) ◊ **infusion** *noun* **1** the act of infusing **2** a tea formed by steeping a herb *etc* in water

ingenious *adj* **1** skilful in inventing **2** cleverly thought out ◊ **ingenuity** *noun*

🔳 **1** clever, imaginative, creative, inventive, resourceful, original, innovative **2** clever, shrewd, cunning, crafty, skilful, masterly

> ⚠ Do not confuse: **ingenious** and **ingenuous**

ingenuous *adj* frank; without cunning ◊ **ingenuousness** *noun*

inglorious *adj* shameful, dishonourable

ingot *noun* a block of metal (*esp* gold or silver) cast in a mould

ingrained *adj* deeply fixed: *ingrained laziness*

🔳 fixed, rooted, deep-seated, entrenched, immovable, permanent, inbuilt

ingratiate *verb* work your way into

someone's favour by flattery *etc* ◊ **ingratiating** *adj*

ingratitude *noun* lack of gratitude or thankfulness

ingredient *noun* one of the things of which a mixture is made

🔳 constituent, element, factor, component, part

ingrowing or **ingrown** *adj* of a nail: growing into the flesh

inhabit *verb* live in (a place, building *etc*) ◊ **inhabitant** *noun* someone who lives permanently in a place

🔳 live, dwell, reside, occupy, colonize, settle, populate, stay ◊ **inhabitant** resident, citizen, native, occupier, occupant, tenant, lodger

inhale *verb* breathe in ◊ **inhalant** *noun* a medicine which is inhaled ◊ **inhalation** *noun* **1** the act of inhaling **2** a medicine which is inhaled ◊ **inhaler** *noun* a device for breathing in medicine, steam *etc*

inherent *adj* inborn, belonging naturally

🔳 inbred, innate, inherited, hereditary, native, natural, inbuilt, built-in, intrinsic, ingrained, fundamental, basic

inherit *verb* **1** receive property *etc* as an heir **2** get (a characteristic) from your parents: *she inherits her sense of humour from her father* ◊ **inheritance** *noun* something received by will when a relative dies ◊ **inheritor** *noun* an heir

🔳 **inheritance** legacy, bequest, heritage, birthright

inhibit *verb* hold back, prevent: *inhibit growth* ◊ **inhibited** *adj* unable to act or express yourself without restraint ◊ **inhibition** *noun* a holding back of natural impulses *etc*, restraint

🔳 discourage, repress, hold back, suppress, restrain, hinder, impede, obstruct, interfere with, prevent, stop ◊ **inhibited** repressed, self-conscious, shy, reticent, withdrawn, reserved, guarded, subdued ◊ **inhibition** repression, *slang* hang-up, self-consciousness, shyness, reticence, reserve, restraint, impediment, obstruction

inhospitable *adj* unwelcoming, unfriendly

inhuman *adj* not human; brutal ◇ **inhumanity** *noun*

■ barbaric, barbarous, vicious, savage, sadistic, cold-blooded, brutal, cruel, inhumane

inhumane *adj* cruel

■ unkind, insensitive, callous, unfeeling, heartless, cold-hearted, hard-hearted, pitiless, ruthless, cruel, brutal, inhuman

➤ humane, kind, compassionate

inimical *adj* unfriendly, hostile

inimitable *adj* impossible to imitate

iniquity *noun* (*plural* **iniquities**) wickedness; a sin ◇ **iniquitous** *adj* unjust; wicked

initial *adj* of or at a beginning: *initial difficulties* ◇ *noun* the letter beginning a word, *esp* someone's name ◇ *verb* (**initials**, **initialling**, **initialled**) sign with the initials of your name ◇ **initially** *adv*

■ *adj* first, beginning, opening, introductory, original, primary, early

initiate *verb* **1** begin, start: *initiate the reforms* **2** give introductory lessons to **3** admit formally to a society *etc* ◇ **initiation** *noun*

■ **1** begin, start, commence, originate, set up, introduce, launch, open, activate, trigger, prompt, stimulate, cause

initiative *noun* **1** (the ability to take) the first step **2** readiness to take a lead

■ **2** energy, drive, dynamism, ambition, enterprise, resourcefulness, inventiveness, originality

inject *verb* **1** force (a fluid *etc*) into the veins or muscles of a person or animal with a syringe **2** put (*eg* enthusiasm) into someone or something ◇ **injection** *noun*

■ **1** inoculate, vaccinate, *slang* shoot **2** introduce, insert, add, bring, infuse, instil

in-joke *noun* a joke only understood by a particular group

injudicious *adj* unwise

injunction *noun* an official order or command

injure *verb* harm, damage; cause injury to ◇ **injured** *adj* hurt; offended ◇ **injury** *noun* (*plural* **injuries**) **1** hurt, damage or harm, *esp* to part of the body **2** a wrong

■ hurt, harm, impair, spoil, ruin, wound, cut, break, fracture, ill-treat, maltreat, abuse, offend, wrong, upset ◇ **injury** **1** wound, cut, lesion, fracture, trauma, hurt, mischief, ill, harm, damage, impairment, ruin, disfigurement **2** offence, wrong, injustice

injustice *noun* **1** unfairness **2** a wrong

■ **1** unfairness, inequality, disparity, discrimination, oppression, bias, prejudice

ink *noun* a coloured liquid used in writing, printing *etc* ◇ *verb* mark with ink ◇ **inky** *adj* **1** of or covered in ink **2** very dark ◇ **inkjet printer** a computer printer which forms characters by squirting a fine jet of ink at the paper

inkling *noun* a hint or slight sign

■ suspicion, idea, notion, clue, hint, intimation, suggestion, allusion, indication, sign

inlaid *past form* of **inlay**

inland *adj* **1** not beside the sea **2** happening inside a country ◇ *adv* towards the inner part of a country ◇ **Inland Revenue** the department of the British government which collects taxes

inlay *noun* decoration made by fitting pieces of different shapes and colours into a background ◇ *verb* (**inlays**, **inlaying**, **inlaid**) fit into a background as decoration ◇ **inlaid** *adj*

inlet *noun* a small bay

■ bay, cove, creek, fiord

inmate *noun* a resident, an occupant (*esp* of an institution): *the inmates of the prison*

inmost *adj* the most inward, the farthest in

inn *noun* a small country hotel or pub ◇ **innkeeper** *noun* someone who keeps an inn

innards *noun plural* **1** internal parts **2** entrails

innate *adj* inborn, natural

■ inborn, inbred, inherent, intrinsic, native, natural, instinctive, intuitive

➤ acquired, learnt

inner *adj* **1** farther in **2** of feelings *etc*: hidden ◇ **innermost** *adj* farthest in; most secret

innings *noun sing* **1** a team's turn for batting in cricket **2** a turn, a go at something

innocent *adj* **1** not guilty, blameless **2** harmless **3** naive ◇ **innocence** *noun*

▤ **1** guiltless, blameless, irreproachable, honest, upright, virtuous, righteous, sinless, faultless, incorrupt, inoffensive, harmless, innocuous **3** artless, guileless, inexperienced, fresh, natural, simple, unsophisticated, unworldly, childlike, credulous, gullible, trusting, naive

innocuous *adj* not harmful

▤ harmless, safe, inoffensive, innocent

innovation *noun* a new idea, method *etc* ◇ **innovative** *adj*

▤ **innovative** new, fresh, original, ground-breaking, creative, imaginative, inventive, resourceful, enterprising, bold, daring, adventurous

▣ **innovative** conservative, unimaginative

innuendo *noun* (*plural* **innuendoes**) an indirectly unpleasant or rude remark or allusion

innumerable *adj* too many to be counted

▤ numberless, unnumbered, countless, uncountable, untold, incalculable, infinite, numerous, many

innumerate *adj* not understanding arithmetic or mathematics ◇ **innumeracy** *noun*

inoculate *verb* inject (someone) with a mild form of a disease to prevent them from later catching it ◇ **inoculation** *noun*

inoffensive *adj* harmless, giving no offence

▤ innocuous, innocent, peaceable, mild, unobtrusive, quiet, retiring

▣ offensive, harmful, provocative

inoperative *adj* not active, not working

inopportune *adj* at a bad or inconvenient time

inordinate *adj* going beyond the limit, unreasonably great

▤ excessive, immoderate, unwarranted, undue, unreasonable, disproportionate, great

inorganic *adj* not of animal or vegetable origin

in-patient *noun* a patient who stays in a hospital during their treatment (*contrasted with*: **out-patient**)

input *noun* **1** an amount (of energy, labour *etc*) put into something **2** data fed into a computer (*contrasted with*: **output**) **3** a contribution to a discussion

inquest *noun* a legal inquiry into a case of sudden death

inquire or **enquire** *verb* ask ◇ **inquirer** *noun* ◇ **inquiring** *adj* questioning, curious: *an inquiring mind* ◇ **inquiry** *noun* (*plural* **inquiries**) **1** a question; a search for information **2** an official investigation

▤ question, quiz, query, investigate, look into, probe, examine, inspect, scrutinize, search ◇ **inquiry 1** question, query **2** investigation, inquest, hearing, inquisition, examination, inspection, study, survey, poll

inquisition *noun* a careful questioning or investigation ◇ **inquisitor** *noun* an official investigator

inquisitive *adj* **1** very curious **2** fond of prying, nosey ◇ **inquisitively** *adv* ◇ **inquisitiveness** *noun*

▤ **1** curious, questioning, probing, searching **2** prying, peeping, snooping, nosey, interfering, meddlesome, intrusive

inroad *noun* a raid, an advance ◇ **make inroads into** use up large amounts of: *the holiday made inroads into their savings*

insane *adj* mad, not sane ◇ **insanity** *noun*

▤ crazy, mentally ill, lunatic, *slang* mental, demented, deranged, unhinged, disturbed ◇ **insanity** madness, craziness, lunacy, mental illness, neurosis, psychosis, dementia

insanitary *adj* not sanitary; encouraging the spread of disease

insatiable *adj* not able to be satisfied: *insatiable appetite* ◊ **insatiably** *adv*

inscribe *verb* write or engrave (*eg* a name) on a book, monument *etc* ◊ **inscription** *noun* the words written or engraved on a book, monument *etc*

inscrutable *adj* not able to be understood, mysterious

▣ incomprehensible, impenetrable, deep, inexplicable, unexplainable, baffling, mysterious, enigmatic, cryptic, hidden

insect *noun* a small six-legged creature with wings and a body divided into sections ◊ **insecticide** *noun* powder or liquid for killing insects ◊ **insectivorous** *adj* feeding on insects

---

Insects include:
fly, gnat, midge, mosquito, tsetse fly, locust, dragonfly, cranefly, *informal* daddy longlegs, horsefly, onion fly, mayfly, butterfly, red admiral, cabbage white, moth, tiger moth, bee, bumblebee, wasp, hornet, aphid, blackfly, greenfly, whitefly, froghopper, ladybird, *US* ladybug, water boatman, lacewing; beetle, cockroach, *US* roach, earwig, stick insect, grasshopper, cricket, cicada, flea, louse, nit, leatherjacket, termite, glowworm, woodworm, weevil, woodlouse
Arachnids include:
spider, black widow, tarantula, scorpion, mite, tick

---

insecure *adj* 1 not safe; not firm 2 lacking confidence, not feeling settled ◊ **insecurity** *noun*

▣ 1 dangerous, hazardous, perilous, precarious, unsteady, shaky, loose, unprotected, defenceless, exposed, vulnerable 2 anxious, worried, nervous, uncertain, unsure, afraid

▣▣ 1 secure, safe 2 confident, self-assured

inseminate *verb* 1 put semen into (a female), *esp* artificially 2 plant, introduce (ideas *etc*) ◊ **insemination** *noun*

insensate *adj* without feeling

insensible *adj* 1 unconscious, unaware (of) 2 not having physical feeling

▣ 1 unaware, oblivious, unmindful 2 numb, anaesthetized, dead, cold, insensitive, unresponsive

insensitive *adj* 1 (with **to**) not having physical feeling: *insensitive to cold* 2 showing lack of feeling for others: *an insensitive remark/insensitive to her grief* ◊ **insensitivity** *noun*

▣ 1 hardened, tough, resistant, impenetrable, immune, unsusceptible 2 unfeeling, indifferent, unaffected, unmoved, untouched, uncaring, unconcerned, callous, thoughtless, tactless, crass

inseparable *adj* not able to be separated or kept apart ◊ **inseparably** *adv*

insert *verb* put in something or among other things ◊ *noun* something inserted, *eg* a pullout section in a magazine *etc* ◊ **insertion** *noun*

▣ *verb* put, place, put in, stick in, push in, introduce, implant, embed, set, inset, let in, interleave

in-service *adj* happening as part of someone's work: *in-service training*

inset *noun* something set in or inserted, *eg* a small picture, map *etc* in a corner of a larger one

inshore *adj & adv* towards or near the shore: *inshore waters/fishing inshore*

inside *noun* 1 the side, space or part within 2 indoors ◊ *adj* 1 being on or in the inside 2 indoor 3 coming from or done by someone within an organization: *inside information* ◊ *adv* to, in or on the inside ◊ *prep* to the inside of; within

▣ *noun* 1 interior, content, contents, middle, centre, heart, core ◊ *adv* within, indoors, internally, inwardly, secretly, privately

insidious *adj* 1 likely to trap those who are not careful, treacherous 2 of a disease: coming on gradually and unnoticed

insight *noun* ability to consider a matter and understand it clearly

▣ awareness, knowledge, comprehension, understanding, grasp, perception, intuition, sensitivity, discernment, judgement, acumen, observation, intelligence

insignia *noun plural* signs or badges

showing that someone holds an office, award *etc*

insignificant *adj* of little importance ◇ **insignificance** *noun* ◇ **insignificantly** *adv*

▣ unimportant, irrelevant, meaningless, inconsequential, minor, trivial, trifling, petty, paltry, small, tiny, insubstantial, inconsiderable, negligible

▣ significant, important

insincere *adj* not sincere ◇ **insincerity** *noun*

▣ hypocritical, two-faced, lying, untruthful, dishonest, deceitful, devious, unfaithful, faithless, untrue, false

insinuate *verb* **1** suggest or hint (something unpleasant): *insinuated that I was lying* **2** put in gradually and secretly **3** work yourself into someone's favour *etc* ◇ **insinuation** *noun* a sly hint

insipid *adj* **1** dull, without liveliness or interest **2** tasteless, bland

▣ **1** drab, dull, monotonous, boring, uninteresting, tame, flat, lifeless, characterless **2** flavourless, unsavoury, unappetizing, watery, weak, bland, *informal* wishy-washy

▣ **2** tasty, spicy, piquant, appetizing

insist *verb* **1** urge something strongly: *insist on punctuality* **2** refuse to give way; hold firmly to your intentions **3** go on saying (that): *she insists that she saw a UFO*

▣ **1** demand, require, urge, stress **3** repeat, assert, maintain, claim, vow, swear

insistent *adj* **1** holding fast to what you claim **2** compelling attention ◇ **insistence** *noun* ◇ **insistently** *adv*

▣ **1** emphatic, forceful, pressing, urgent, dogged, tenacious, relentless, unrelenting **2** demanding, importunate, persistent

in situ in position, in place

insolent *adj* showing lack of respect; impolite or insulting ◇ **insolence** *noun*

▣ rude, abusive, disrespectful, *informal* cheeky, impertinent, impudent, bold, arrogant, defiant

▣ polite, respectful

insoluble *adj* **1** not able to be dis-

solved **2** of a problem: not able to be solved

▣ **2** unsolvable, unexplainable, inexplicable, incomprehensible, obscure, mystifying, puzzling, perplexing, baffling

insolvent *adj* not able to pay your debts, impoverished ◇ **insolvency** *noun*

▣ bankrupt, bust, failed, ruined, *informal* broke, penniless, destitute

▣ solvent

insomnia *noun* sleeplessness ◇ **insomniac** *noun* someone who suffers from insomnia

insouciant *adj* indifferent, unconcerned ◇ **insouciance** *noun*

inspect *verb* **1** look carefully at or into, *esp* to find any faults **2** look over (troops *etc*) ceremonially ◇ **inspection** *noun* careful examination ◇ **inspector** *noun* **1** an official who inspects **2** a police officer below a superintendent and above a sergeant in rank

▣ **1** check, vet, look over, investigate, examine, scrutinize, study, scan, survey

inspiration *noun* **1** something which or someone who influences or encourages others **2** a brilliant idea **3** breathing in ◇ **inspirational** *adj* inspiring

▣ **1** influence, encouragement, stimulation, motivation, stimulus **2** brainwave, insight, illumination

inspire *verb* **1** encourage, rouse **2** be the source of creative ideas for someone **3** breathe in ◇ **inspired** *adj* **1** seeming to be aided by higher powers **2** brilliantly good

▣ **1** animate, enliven, kindle, stir, arouse, trigger, motivate, stimulate **2** influence, impress

instability *noun* lack of steadiness or stability (*esp* in the personality)

install or **instal** *verb* (**installs** or **instals**, **installing**, **installed**) **1** place in position, ready for use: *has the cooker been installed?* **2** introduce formally to a new job *etc* ◇ **installation** *noun*

▣ **1** fix, fit, lay, put, place, position, locate, set up **2** settle, inaugurate, ordain

instalment *noun* **1** a part of a sum of

money paid at fixed times until the whole amount is paid **2** one part of a serial story

instance *noun* an example, a particular case ◇ *verb* mention as an example ◇ **at the instance of** at the request of ◇ **for instance** for example

instant *adj* **1** immediate, urgent **2** able to be prepared almost immediately: *instant coffee* ◇ *noun* **1** a very short time, a moment **2** point or moment of time: *I need it this instant* ◇ **instantaneous** *adj* done or happening very quickly ◇ **instantly** *adv* immediately

◼ *adj* **1** instantaneous, immediate, on-the-spot, direct, prompt, urgent, unhesitating, quick, fast, rapid, swift ◇ *noun* **1** flash, trice, moment, *informal* tick, split second **2** second, minute

instead *adv* in place of someone or something: *you can go instead* ◇ **instead of** in place of

instep *noun* the arching, upper part of the foot

instigate *verb* stir up, encourage ◇ **instigation** *noun*

◼ initiate, start, begin, cause, generate, inspire, move, influence, prompt, provoke, stimulate, incite, rouse, excite

instil or **instill** *verb* (**instils** or **instills**, **instilling**, **instilled**) put in little by little (*esp* ideas into the mind)

instinct *noun* a natural feeling or knowledge which someone has without thinking and without being taught ◇ **instinctive** *adj* due to instinct

◼ intuition, sixth sense, *informal* gut reaction, impulse, urge, feeling, hunch, knack, talent, ability, aptitude ◇ **instinctive** natural, native, inborn, innate, inherent, intuitive, impulsive, involuntary, automatic, mechanical, reflex, *informal* knee-jerk, spontaneous, immediate

◪ **instinctive** conscious, voluntary, deliberate

institute *verb* set up, establish, start ◇ *noun* a society, organization *etc* or the building it uses ◇ **institution** *noun* **1** an organization, building *etc* established for a particular purpose (*esp* care

or education) **2** an established custom ◇ **institutional** *adj*

◼ *verb* originate, initiate, introduce, enact, begin, start, commence, create, establish, set up, organize, found, inaugurate, open, launch ◇ *noun* school, college, academy, conservatory, foundation, institution

instruct *verb* **1** teach **2** direct, command ◇ **instruction** *noun* **1** teaching **2** a command **3** (**instructions**) rules or information about how something is to be used ◇ **instructive** *adj* containing or giving information or knowledge ◇ **instructor** *noun* someone who teaches others

◼ **1** educate, tutor, coach, train, drill, ground, school, discipline **2** order, command, inform, notify, advise, counsel, guide ◇ **instructive** informative, educational, edifying, enlightening, illuminating, helpful, useful

instrument *noun* **1** something used for a particular purpose, a tool **2** a device for producing musical sounds, *eg* a piano or a harp ◇ **instrumental** *adj* **1** helpful in bringing something about: *instrumental in their rescue* **2** written for or played by musical instruments, without voice accompaniment ◇ **instrumentalist** *noun* someone who plays a musical instrument

◼ **1** implement, utensil, appliance, gadget, contraption, device, apparatus ◇ **instrumental 1** active, involved, contributory, conducive, influential, useful, helpful

◪ **instrumental 1** obstructive, unhelpful

insubordinate *adj* rebellious, disobedient ◇ **insubordination** *noun*

insufferable *adj* not able to be endured ◇ **insufferably** *adv*

◼ intolerable, unbearable, detestable, loathsome, dreadful, impossible

◪ pleasant, tolerable

insufficient *adj* not enough ◇ **insufficiency** *noun*

◼ inadequate, short, deficient, lacking, sparse, scanty, scarce

insular *adj* **1** of an island or islands **2** narrow-minded, prejudiced ◇ **insularity** *noun*

insulate *verb* **1** cover with a material that electricity, heat, *etc* will not pass through **2** cut off, isolate ◇ **insulation** *noun*

insulin *noun* a substance used in the treatment of diabetes

Based on the Latin word for 'island', because insulin is secreted by cells called the *islets* of Langerhans

insult *verb* treat with scorn or rudeness ◇ *noun* a rude or scornful remark ◇ **insulting** *adj* scornful, rude

■ *verb* abuse, revile, libel, slander, slight, snub, injure, affront, offend, outrage ◇ *noun* abuse, rudeness, insolence, slander, slight, snub, indignity, offence, outrage

insuperable *adj* that cannot be overcome

insure *verb* arrange for payment of a sum of money if (something) is lost, damaged, stolen *etc* ◇ **insurance** *noun*

⚠ Do not confuse with: **ensure**

insurgent *adj* rising up in rebellion ◇ *noun* a rebel ◇ **insurgency** *noun*

insurmountable *adj* not able to be dealt with or overcome

■ insuperable, unconquerable, invincible, overwhelming, hopeless, impossible

insurrection *noun* a rebellion

intact *adj* whole, unbroken

■ unbroken, whole, complete, entire, perfect, sound, undamaged, unhurt, uninjured

🔁 broken, incomplete, damaged

intaglio /ɪnˈtɑːlɪoʊ/ *noun* **1** sculpture carved into a background, not raised from the surface (*contrasted with*: **relief**) **2** a gemstone with a hollowed-out design (*contrasted with*: **cameo**)

intake *noun* an amount of people or things taken in: *this year's intake of students*

intangible *adj* **1** not able to be felt by touch **2** difficult to define or describe, not clear

■ **1** abstract, unreal **2** insubstantial, fleeting, airy, shadowy, vague, indefinite

integer *noun* a whole number, not a fraction

integral *adj* **1** of or essential to a whole: *an integral part of the machine* **2** made up of parts forming a whole

integrate *verb* **1** fit parts together to form a whole **2** enable (racial groups) to mix freely and live on equal terms ◇ **integration** *noun*

■ **1** join, unite, combine, incorporate, fuse, knit, mesh **2** assimilate, merge, mix, blend, harmonize

integrity *noun* **1** honesty **2** wholeness, completeness

■ **1** uprightness, purity, morality, principle, honour, virtue, goodness, righteousness **2** unity, coherence, cohesion

integument *noun* an external layer, a covering

intellect *noun* the thinking power of the mind ◇ **intellectual** *adj* showing or requiring intellect ◇ *noun* someone with academic interests

■ mind, brain(s), brainpower, intelligence, genius, reason, understanding, sense, wisdom, judgement ◇ **intellectual** *adj* academic, scholarly, intelligent, studious, thoughtful, cultural

intelligent *adj* clever, quick at understanding ◇ **intelligence** *noun* **1** mental ability **2** information, news

■ bright, smart, *informal* brainy, quick, alert, quick-witted, sharp, acute, knowing, knowledgeable, well-informed

🔁 unintelligent, stupid, foolish

intelligentsia *noun* the intellectuals within a particular society

intelligible *adj* able to be understood

intemperate *adj* **1** going beyond reasonable limits, uncontrolled **2** tending to drink too much alcohol ◇ **intemperance** *noun*

intend *verb* mean or plan (to do something)

■ aim, propose, plan, project, scheme, plot, design, purpose, resolve, determine

intense *adj* **1** very great **2** tending to

feel strongly, deeply emotional ◇ **intensely** *adv* ◇ **intensity** *noun* (*plural* **intensities**) strength, *eg* of feeling, colour *etc*

intensify *verb* (**intensifies, intensifying, intensified**) increase, make or become more concentrated

■ increase, heighten, aggravate, add to, strengthen, reinforce, sharpen, whet, quicken, deepen, concentrate, emphasize, enhance

🢂 reduce, weaken

intensive *adj* very thorough, concentrated ◇ **intensive care** a unit in a hospital where a patient's condition is carefully monitored

■ concentrated, thorough, exhaustive, comprehensive, detailed, in-depth, intense

intent *noun* purpose ◇ *adj* **1** (often with **on**) with all your concentration, attentive **2** (with **on**) determined ◇ **intention** *noun* **1** what someone means to do, an aim **2** meaning ◇ **intentional** *adj* done on purpose ◇ **intentionally** *adv* ◇ **intently** *adv*

■ *adj* **1** fixed, alert, attentive, concentrating, preoccupied, engrossed, absorbed, occupied **2** resolved, resolute, set, bent, concentrated ◇ **intention 1** aim, purpose, object, end, point, target, goal, objective ◇ **intentional** conscious, planned, deliberate, premeditated, calculated, intended, meant

🢂 *adj* **1** absent-minded, distracted ◇ **intentional** unintentional, accidental

inter- *prefix* between, among, together: *intermingle/interplanetary*

inter /ɪnˈtɜː(r)/ *verb* (**inters, interring, interred**) bury (a dead person *etc*) ◇ **interment** *noun*

interact *verb* act on one another ◇ **interactive** *adj* allowing two-way communication, *eg* between a computer and its user

inter alia among other things

intercede *verb* act as peacemaker between two people, nations *etc* ◇ **intercession** *noun* ◇ **intercessor** *noun*

intercept *verb* stop or seize on the way

■ head off, ambush, interrupt, stop, take, seize, check, delay

interchange *verb* **1** put each in the place of the other **2** alternate ◇ *noun* **1** the act of interchanging **2** a junction of two or more major roads on separate levels ◇ **interchangeable** *adj* able to be used one for the other

■ **interchangeable** reciprocal, equivalent, similar, identical, synonymous, standard

intercom *noun* a telephone system within a building, aeroplane *etc*

intercourse *noun* **1** communication **2** dealings between people *etc* **3** sexual intercourse

interdict *noun* an order forbidding something

interest *noun* **1** special attention, curiosity **2** someone's hobby or field of study **3** advantage, benefit **4** a sum paid for the loan of money ◇ *verb* catch or hold the attention of ◇ **interested** *adj* having or taking an interest ◇ **interesting** *adj* holding the attention

■ *noun* **1** concern, care, attention, notice, involvement, participation **2** activity, pursuit, pastime, hobby, diversion, amusement ◇ *verb* involve, attract, appeal to, divert, amuse, occupy, engage, absorb, engross, fascinate, intrigue ◇ **interesting** attractive, appealing, entertaining, engaging, absorbing, engrossing, fascinating, intriguing, compelling, gripping, stimulating

🢂 **interesting** uninteresting, boring, monotonous, tedious

interface *noun, comput* a connection between two parts of the same system

interfere *verb* **1** (with **in**) take part in what is not your business, meddle **2** (with **with**) get in the way of, hinder: *interfering with her work* ◇ **interference** *noun* **1** the act of interfering **2** the spoiling of radio or television reception by another station or disturbance from traffic *etc*

■ **1** intrude, poke one's nose in, pry, butt in, interrupt, intervene, meddle, tamper **2** hamper, obstruct, block, impede, inhibit, conflict, clash

interim *noun* time between; the meantime ◊ *adj* temporary

interior *adj* **1** inner **2** inside a building **3** inland ◊ *noun* **1** the inside of anything **2** the inland part of a country

interject *verb* **1** make a sudden remark in a conversation **2** exclaim ◊ **interjection** *noun* a word or phrase of exclamation, *eg* Ah! Oh dear!

 ▤ **interjection** exclamation, ejaculation, cry, shout, call, interpolation

interlock *verb* **1** lock or clasp together **2** fit into each other

interlocution *noun* dialogue, conversation ◊ **interlocutor** *noun* someone taking part in a conversation

interloper *noun* someone who enters without permission, an intruder

interlude *noun* **1** an interval **2** a short piece of music played between the parts of a play, film *etc*

intermarry *verb* **1** marry with members of another race *etc* **2** marry with members of the same group *etc*

intermediary *noun* (*plural* **intermediaries**) someone who acts tries to settle a quarrel between two people

intermediate *adj* in the middle; coming between

 ▤ midway, halfway, in-between, middle, mid, median, mean, intermediary, intervening

interment *see* **inter**

 ▯ Do not confuse with: **internment**

intermezzo *noun* (*plural* **intermezzos**) *music* a short movement separating sections of a symphony

interminable *adj* never-ending, boringly long

intermission *noun* an interval, a pause

 ▤ interlude, break, recess, rest, respite, *informal* breather, breathing-space, pause, lull, interruption, halt, stop

intermittent *adj* stopping and then starting again at irregular intervals

 ▤ occasional, periodic, sporadic, fitful, erratic, irregular

 ▣ continuous, constant

intern *verb* keep (someone from an enemy country) prisoner during a war ◊ **internee** *noun* someone who is confined in this way ◊ **internment** *noun*

 ▯ Do not confuse: **internment** and **interment**

internal *adj* **1** of the inner part, *esp* of the body **2** inside, within a country, organization *etc*: *internal affairs*

international *adj* **1** happening between nations **2** concerning more than one nation **3** worldwide ◊ *noun* a sports match between teams of two countries

 ▤ *adj* **1**, **2**, **3** global, worldwide, intercontinental, cosmopolitan, universal, general

internecine *adj* of a conflict: within a group or organization

Internet *noun* an international computer network linking users through telephone lines

interplanetary *adj* between planets

interplay *noun* the action of two or more things on one another

interpose *verb* **1** place or come between others **2** make (a remark *etc*) which interrupts someone

 ▤ **1** insert, introduce, intervene, step in, put in, thrust in **2** interrupt, intrude, interfere, interpolate, interject

interpret *verb* **1** explain the meaning of something **2** translate **3** bring out the meaning of (music, a part in a play *etc*) in performance **4** take the meaning of something to be: *interpreted his silence as disapproval* ◊ **interpretation** *noun* ◊ **interpreter** *noun* someone who translates (on the spot) the words of a speaker into another language

 ▤ **1** explain, expound, elucidate, clarify, define, paraphrase **2** translate, decode, decipher **4** understand, construe, read, take

interregnum *noun* the time between the end of one reign and the beginning of the next

interrogate *verb* question (someone) ◊ **interrogation** *noun* ◊ **interrogative** *noun* a word used in asking a question (*eg* who? where?) ◇ *adj* questioning ◇ **interrogator** *noun*

■ question, quiz, examine, cross-examine, grill, pump, debrief ◇ **interrogation** questioning, examination, cross-examination, grilling, third degree, inquisition, inquiry, inquest

interrupt *verb* 1 stop (someone) while they are saying or doing something 2 stop doing (something) 3 get in the way of, cut off (a view *etc*) ◇ **interruption** *noun*

■ 1 butt in, interject, break in, heckle, disturb, disrupt, intrude, *informal* barge in 2 stop, halt, suspend, discontinue, break off 3 obstruct, check, hinder, break off ◇ **interruption** intrusion, disturbance, disruption, pause, break, suspension

intersect *verb* of lines: meet and cross ◇ **intersection** *noun* 1 the point where two lines cross 2 a crossroads

intersperse *verb* scatter here and there in ◇ **interspersion** *noun*

interstice /ɪnˈtɜːsɪs/ *noun* a small gap between things, a chink

intertwine *verb* twine or twist together

interval *noun* 1 a time or space between two events or things 2 a short pause in a programme *etc*

■ 1 interim, meantime, meanwhile, gap, opening, space 2 interlude, intermission, break, pause, rest

intervene *verb* 1 come or be between or in the way 2 try to stop a fight or quarrel between other people or nations ◇ **intervention** *noun*

■ 1 interfere, interrupt 2 step in, mediate, arbitrate

interview *noun* a formal meeting of one person with another or others to apply for a job, give information to the media *etc* ◇ *verb* 1 ask questions *etc* of in an interview 2 conduct an interview

■ *noun* audience, consultation, talk, dialogue, meeting, conference, press conference, oral examination, viva

intestate *adj* without having made a will: *he died intestate*

intestines *noun plural* the bowels

and passages leading to them ◇ **intestinal** *adj*

intimacy *noun* (*plural* **intimacies**) 1 close friendship 2 familiarity 3 sexual intercourse

intimate *adj* 1 knowing a lot about, familiar (with) 2 of friends: very close 3 private, personal: *intimate details* 4 having a sexual relationship (with) ◇ *noun* a close friend ◇ *verb* 1 hint 2 announce ◇ **intimately** *adv* ◇ **intimation** *noun* 1 a hint 2 announcement

■ *adj* 2 affectionate, dear, close, friendly 3 confidential, secret, private, personal ◇ *noun* friend, bosom friend, confidant(e), associate ◇ *verb* 1 hint, insinuate, imply, suggest, indicate 2 state, declare, announce

🗷 *adj* 2 unfriendly, cold, distant

intimidate *verb* frighten or threaten into submission ◇ **intimidating** *adj* ◇ **intimidation** *noun*

■ daunt, alarm, scare, frighten, terrify, threaten, menace, terrorize, bully, bulldoze, coerce, pressure

into *prep* 1 to the inside: *into the room* 2 towards: *marching into battle* 3 to a different state: *a tadpole changes into a frog* 4 *maths* expressing the idea of division: *2 into 4 goes twice*

intolerable *adj* not able to be endured

■ unbearable, unendurable, insupportable, unacceptable, insufferable, impossible

intolerant *adj* not willing to put up with (people of different ideas, religion *etc*) ◇ **intolerance** *noun*

■ impatient, narrow-minded, small-minded, opinionated, dogmatic

intone *verb* speak in a singing manner, chant ◇ **intonation** *noun* the rise and fall of the voice

intoxicate *verb* 1 make drunk 2 enthuse, excite ◇ **intoxicant** *noun* a strong drink ◇ **intoxicated** *adj* drunk ◇ **intoxication** *noun* drunkenness

intra- *prefix* within

intractable *adj* difficult, stubborn ◇ **intractability** *noun*

intransigent *adj* refusing to change your views or come to an agreement ◊ **intransigence** *noun*

intransitive *adj, grammar* of a verb: not needing an object, *eg* to go, to fall

in-tray *noun* an office tray for letters and work still to be dealt with (*contrasted with*: **out-tray**)

intrepid *adj* without fear, brave ◊ **intrepidity** *noun*
■ bold, daring, brave, courageous, plucky, fearless
◨ cowardly, timid

intricate *adj* complicated, having many details, twists and turns *etc* ◊ **intricacy** *noun* (*plural* **intricacies**)
■ elaborate, fancy, ornate, complicated, complex, sophisticated, involved, convoluted, entangled, knotty, perplexing, difficult
◨ simple, plain, straightforward

intrigue *noun* 1 a secret plot 2 a secret love affair ◊ *verb* 1 plot, scheme 2 rouse the curiosity of, fascinate ◊ **intriguing** *adj*
■ *noun* 1 plot, scheme, conspiracy, trickery, double-dealing 2 romance, liaison, affair, intimacy ◊ *verb* 2 fascinate, rivet, puzzle, tantalize, attract, charm, captivate

intrinsic *adj* belonging to something as part of its nature

introduce *verb* 1 bring in: *introduce a new system* 2 make (someone) known to another person ◊ **introduction** *noun* 1 the introducing of a person or thing 2 an essay at the beginning of a book *etc* briefly explaining its contents ◊ **introductory** *adj* coming at the beginning
■ 1 institute, begin, start, commence, establish, found, inaugurate, launch, open, bring in 2 announce, present, acquaint ◊ **introduction** 1 institution, beginning, start, establishment, inauguration, launch, presentation, debut, initiation 2 foreword, preface, preamble, prologue

introspective *adj* inward-looking, fond of examining your own thoughts and feelings ◊ **introspection** *noun*

intrude *verb* thrust yourself into something or somewhere uninvited ◊ **intruder** *noun* someone who breaks into a place or intrudes ◊ **intrusion** *noun* ◊ **intrusive** *adj*
■ interrupt, butt in, meddle, interfere, violate, infringe, encroach, trespass ◊ **intruder** trespasser, burglar, prowler, raider, invader ◊ **intrusion** interruption, interference, violation, infringement, encroachment, trespass, invasion
◨ withdraw, stand back

intuition *noun* 1 ability to understand something without thinking it out 2 an instinctive feeling or belief ◊ **intuitive** *adj*
■ 1 insight, instinct, sixth sense, perception 2 hunch, feeling, *informal* gut feeling ◊ **intuitive** instinctive, spontaneous, involuntary, innate, untaught

Inuit *noun* 1 the Eskimo people, *esp* those in Greenland, Canada and N Alaska 2 their language

inundate *verb* 1 flood 2 overwhelm: *inundated with work* ◊ **inundation** *noun*

inure *verb* make accustomed (to): *inured to pain*

invade *verb* 1 enter (a country *etc*) as an enemy to take possession 2 interfere with (someone's rights, privacy *etc*) ◊ **invader** *noun* ◊ **invasion** *noun*
■ 1 attack, raid, seize, occupy, overrun 2 encroach, infringe, violate ◊ **invasion** attack, offensive, onslaught, raid, intrusion, encroachment, infringement, violation

invalid¹ /ɪn'valɪd/ *adj* not valid, not legally effective ◊ **invalidate** *verb* make invalid ◊ **invalidity** *noun*
■ false, fallacious, unfounded, illegal, null, void, worthless

invalid² /'ɪnvəlɪd/ *noun* someone who is ill or disabled ◊ *adj* for or being an invalid ◊ *verb* 1 make an invalid of 2 (with **out**) discharge from the army as an invalid

invaluable *adj* extremely useful, important *etc*
■ priceless, inestimable, incalculable, precious, valuable, useful
◨ worthless, cheap

invariable adj unchanging ◇ **invariably** adv always

■ **invariably** always, without exception, without fail, unfailingly, consistently, regularly, habitually

invasion see **invade**

invective noun abusive words; scorn

inveigle verb coax, entice ◇ **inveiglement** noun

invent verb 1 make or think up for the first time 2 make up (a story, an excuse) ◇ **invention** noun something invented ◇ **inventive** adj good at inventing, resourceful ◇ **inventor** noun

■ 1 conceive, think up, design, discover, create, originate, formulate, devise 2 make up, concoct, cook up, dream up, contrive, fabricate ◇ **inventive** imaginative, creative, innovative, original, ingenious, resourceful, inspired, gifted, clever

inventory noun (plural **inventories**) a detailed list of contents

inverse adj opposite, reverse ◇ noun the opposite ◇ **inversely** adv

invert verb 1 turn upside down 2 reverse the order of ◇ **inversion** noun 1 a turning upside-down 2 a reversal ◇ **inverted commas** noun plural quotation marks

■ 1 upturn, turn upside down, overturn, capsize, upset 2 transpose, reverse

◼ 1 right

invertebrate adj of an animal: not having a backbone ◇ noun an animal with no backbone, eg a worm or insect

Invertebrates include:
sponges: calcareous, glass, horny; jellyfish, corals and sea anemones: Portuguese man-of-war, box jellyfish, sea wasp, dead-men's fingers, sea pansy, sea gooseberry, Venus's girdle; echinoderms: sea lily, feather star, starfish, crown-of-thorns, brittle star, sea urchin, sand dollar, sea cucumber; worms: annelid worm, arrow worm, blood fluke, bristle worm, earthworm, fluke, hookworm, leech, liver fluke, lugworm, peanut worm, pinworm, ragworm, ribbonworm, roundworm, sea mouse, tapeworm, threadworm; crustaceans: acorn barnacle, barnacle, brine shrimp, crayfish, daphnia, fairy shrimp, fiddler crab, fish louse, goose barnacle, hermit crab, krill, lobster, mantis shrimp, mussel shrimp, pill bug, prawn, sand hopper, seed shrimp, spider crab, spiny lobster, tadpole shrimp, water flea, whale louse, woodlouse; centipede, millipede, velvet worm

invest verb 1 put money in a company, property etc to make a profit 2 give a particular quality to ◇ **investiture** noun a ceremony before taking on an important office ◇ **investment** noun 1 money invested 2 something in which money is invested ◇ **investor** noun someone who invests money

■ 1 spend, lay out, put in, sink

investigate verb try to find out about by detailed examination, searching etc ◇ **investigation** noun ◇ **investigator** noun

■ inquire into, look into, consider, examine, study, inspect, scrutinize, analyse, go into, probe, explore, search ◇ **investigation** inquiry, inquest, hearing, examination, study, research, survey, review, inspection, analysis

inveterate adj 1 firmly fixed in a habit: an inveterate gambler 2 deep-rooted ◇ **inveteracy** noun

invidious adj likely to cause ill-will or envy

invigilate verb supervise (an examination etc) ◇ **invigilator** noun

invigorate verb strengthen, refresh ◇ **invigorating** adj

■ vitalize, energize, animate, enliven, liven up, quicken, strengthen, fortify, stimulate, perk up, refresh, freshen, revitalize, rejuvenate

◼ tire, weary, dishearten

invincible adj not able to be defeated or overcome ◇ **invincibility** noun

■ unbeatable, unconquerable, insuperable, unsurmountable, impenetrable, invulnerable, indestructible

inviolable *adj* sacred, not to be disregarded or harmed ◇ **inviolability** *noun* ◇ **inviolate** *adj* not violated, free from harm *etc*

invisible *adj* not able to be seen ◇ **invisibility** *noun*

■ unseen, out of sight, hidden, concealed, disguised, inconspicuous, indiscernible, microscopic, imaginary, nonexistent

invite *verb* **1** ask (someone) to come for a meal, to a party *etc* **2** seem to ask for: *inviting punishment* ◇ **invitation** *noun* a written or spoken message inviting someone to come ◇ **inviting** *adj* tempting, attractive

■ **1** ask, call, summon, welcome, encourage **2** bring on, provoke, ask for ◇ **inviting** welcoming, appealing, attractive, tempting, seductive, enticing, alluring, pleasing, delightful, captivating, fascinating

Eɜ inviting uninviting, unappealing

in vitro of fertilization: carried out in a test tube, in a laboratory

invocation *see* invoke

invoice *noun* a letter sent with goods with details of price and quantity ◇ *verb* request payment from or for by means of an invoice

invoke *verb* **1** call upon in prayer **2** ask for (*eg* help) ◇ **invocation** *noun*

■ **1** call upon, conjure, appeal to, petition, solicit, implore, entreat, beg, beseech, supplicate, pray

involuntary *adj* not done willingly or intentionally ◇ **involuntarily** *adv*

■ spontaneous, unconscious, automatic, mechanical, reflex, *informal* knee-jerk, instinctive, conditioned, impulsive, uncontrolled, unintentional, accidental

Eɜ deliberate, intentional

involve *verb* **1** have as a consequence, require **2** cause to take part or be concerned **3** implicate (in): *involved in the scandal* **4** engage: *involved in organizing a conference* ◇ **involved** *adj* complicated ◇ **involvement** *noun*

■ **1** require, necessitate, mean, imply, entail, include **3** implicate, incriminate, in-

culpate, draw in, mix up, embroil, associate ◇ **involved** complex, intricate, elaborate, tangled, knotty, tortuous, confusing ◇ **involvement** concern, interest, responsibility, association, connection, participation

invulnerable *adj* not vulnerable, not able to be hurt ◇ **invulnerability** *noun*

■ safe, secure, unassailable, impenetrable, invincible, indestructible

inward *adj* **1** placed or directed within **2** situated in the mind or soul ◇ *adv* (also **inwards**) towards the inside ◇ **inwardly** *adv* **1** within **2** in your heart, privately

in-your-face *adj, slang* aggressive, demanding attention

iodine *noun* a liquid chemical used to kill germs

ion *noun* an electrically charged atom or group of atoms ◇ **ionizer** *noun* a device which sends out negative ions to improve the quality of the air

iota *noun* a little bit, a jot

■ scrap, bit, mite, jot, speck, trace, hint, grain, particle, atom

IOU *short for* **I owe you**, a note given as a receipt for money borrowed

ipso facto by that fact, thereby

IQ *abbrev* intelligence quotient

IRA *abbrev* Irish Republican Army

irascible *adj* easily made angry ◇ **irascibility** *noun* ◇ **irascibly** *adj*

irate *adj* angry

■ annoyed, irritated, indignant, enraged, *informal* mad, furious, incensed, worked up, fuming, livid, exasperated

Eɜ calm, composed

IRC *abbrev* Internet Relay Chat

ire *noun, formal* anger

iridescent *adj* **1** coloured like a rainbow **2** shimmering with changing colours ◇ **iridescence** *noun*

iris *noun* (*plural* **irises**) **1** the coloured part of the eye around the pupil **2** a lily-like flower which grows from a bulb

irk *verb* annoy ◇ **irksome** *adj* tiresome, annoying

iron *noun* **1** a common metal, widely

used to make tools *etc* **2** an iron instrument: *a branding iron* **3** an appliance for pressing clothes **4** a golf club (originally with an iron head) **5** (**irons**) a prisoner's chains ◇ *adj* **1** made of iron **2** stern, resolute: *iron will* **3** of a rule: not to be broken ◇ *verb* **1** press (clothes) with an iron **2** (with **out**) smooth out (difficulties) ◇ **Iron Age** human culture at the stage of using iron for tools *etc*

■ *adj* **2** adamant, determined, hard, steely, tough, strong **3** rigid, inflexible ◇ *verb* **2** resolve, settle, sort out, straighten out, clear up, put right, reconcile, deal with, get rid of, eradicate, eliminate

ironmonger *noun* a shopkeeper selling household tools, gardening equipment *etc* ◇ **ironmongery** *noun* goods sold by an ironmonger

irony *noun* (*plural* **ironies**) **1** a form of humour in which someone says the opposite of what is obviously true **2** an absurd contradiction or paradox: *the irony of it was that she was planning to give him the money which he stole* ◇ **ironic** or **ironical** *adj* ◇ **ironically** *adv*

■ **ironic** sarcastic, sardonic, scornful, contemptuous, derisive, sneering, scoffing, mocking, satirical, wry, paradoxical

irrational *adj* against logic or common sense ◇ **irrationality** *noun*

■ unreasonable, unsound, illogical, absurd, crazy, wild, foolish, silly, senseless, unwise

irregular *adj* **1** uneven, variable **2** against the rules ◇ **irregularity** *noun* (*plural* **irregularities**)

■ **1** rough, bumpy, uneven, crooked, fluctuating, wavering, erratic, fitful, random, haphazard **2** abnormal, unconventional, improper, unusual, exceptional

irrelevant *adj* not having anything to do with the matter or subject ◇ **irrelevancy** *noun* (*plural* **irrelevancies**)

■ immaterial, beside the point, inapplicable, inappropriate, unrelated, unconnected

irreparable *adj* not able to be repaired

irreplaceable *adj* too good or rare to be replaced

irrepressible *adj* not restrainable or controllable

■ ebullient, bubbly, uninhibited, buoyant, resilient, boisterous, uncontrollable, unstoppable

irreproachable *adj* not able to be criticized or blamed

irresistible *adj* too strong or too charming to be resisted

■ overwhelming, overpowering, unavoidable, inevitable, uncontrollable, compelling, tempting, seductive, enchanting, charming, fascinating

☒ resistible, avoidable

irresolute *adj* not able to make up your mind or keep to a decision

irrespective *adj* taking no account (of): *irrespective of the weather*

irresponsible *adj* having no sense of responsibility, thoughtless

■ unreliable, untrustworthy, careless, negligent, thoughtless, heedless, rash, reckless, wild, carefree, light-hearted, immature

☒ responsible, cautious

irreverent *adj* having no respect, *eg* for holy things ◇ **irreverence** *noun*

irrevocable *adj* not to be changed

■ unalterable, unchangeable, invariable, final, fixed, settled, irreversible, irretrievable

☒ alterable, flexible, reversible

irrigate *verb* supply (land) with water by canals *etc* ◇ **irrigation** *noun*

irritate *verb* **1** annoy **2** cause discomfort to (the skin, eyes *etc*) ◇ **irritable** *adj* cross, easily annoyed ◇ **irritation** *noun*

■ **1** get on one's nerves, *informal* aggravate, provoke, anger, enrage, infuriate, exasperate, peeve ◇ **irritable** cross, bad-tempered, crotchety, short-tempered, short, impatient, touchy, edgy, prickly, peevish, fretful

☒ **irritable** good-tempered, cheerful

ISA *abbrev* Individual Savings Account

ISBN *abbrev* International Standard Book Number, an identification number given to a published book

ISDN *abbrev* Integrated Services Digital Network

Islam *noun* **1** the Muslim religion, founded by the prophet Mohammed **2** the Muslim world ◇ **Islamic** *adj*

island *noun* **1** an area of land surrounded by water **2** an isolated place, a haven ◇ **islander** *noun* an inhabitant of an island

isle *noun*, *formal* an island

-ism *suffix* **1** indicating a system, set of beliefs *etc*: *socialism/Catholicism* **2** indicating prejudice against a particular group: *racism/sexism*

isobar *noun* a line on a map connecting places where atmospheric pressure is the same

isolate *verb* **1** place or keep separate from other people or things **2** consider (something) by itself: *isolate the problem* ◇ **isolation** *noun*

▣ **1** keep apart, segregate, quarantine, insulate, cut off, detach, remove, disconnect, separate ◇ **isolation** quarantine, solitude, loneliness, seclusion, retirement, withdrawal, exile, segregation, insulation, separation, detachment

isosceles *adj* of a triangle: having two sides equal (*compare with*: **equilateral**)

isotherm *noun* a line on a map connecting places which have the same temperature

isotonic *adj* of muscles: having the same tension

isotope *noun* an atom with the same atomic number as, but different mass number from, another

issue *verb* **1** go or come out **2** give out (orders *etc*) **3** publish or make available ◇ *noun* **1** a flowing out **2** *formal* children: *he died without issue* **3** the copies of a book *etc* published or made available at one time **4** one in a series of magazines *etc*: *an article in last week's issue* **5** result, consequence **6** the matter which is being discussed ◇ **take issue with** disagree with

▣ *verb* **1** originate, stem, spring, rise, emerge, burst forth, gush, flow, proceed, emanate **3** release, distribute, supply, deliver, circulate, broadcast, announce ◇ *noun* **3** publication, release, distribution, supply, delivery, circulation **6** matter, affair, concern, problem, point, subject, topic, question, debate, argument, dispute

isthmus *noun* (*plural* **isthmuses**) a narrow neck of land connecting two larger portions

it *pronoun* **1** the thing spoken of: *I meant to bring the book, but I left it at home* **2** used in sentences with no definite subject: *it snowed today/it is too late now* **3** used in phrases as a kind of object: *go it alone/brave it out*

italics *noun plural* a kind of type which slopes to the right ◇ **italic** *adj* ◇ **italicize** *verb* print in italics

itch *noun* **1** an irritating feeling in the skin, made better by scratching **2** a strong desire ◇ *verb* **1** have an itch **2** be impatient (to), long (to): *itching to open his presents* ◇ **itchy** *adj*

▣ *noun* **1** itchiness, tickle, irritation, prickling **2** eagerness, keenness, desire, longing, yearning, craving

item *noun* a separate article or detail in a list ◇ **itemize** *verb* list item by item, detail

▣ object, article, thing, piece, component, ingredient, element, factor, point, detail, aspect, feature, consideration, matter

itinerant *adj* travelling from place to place, *esp* on business ◇ *noun* someone who travels around, *esp* a tramp, pedlar *etc*

▣ *adj* travelling, roving, roaming, wandering, rambling, nomadic, migratory, rootless, unsettled

▣ *adj* stationary, settled

itinerary *noun* (*plural* **itineraries**) a route or plan of a journey

its *adj* belonging to it: *keep the hat in its box*

⚠ Do not confuse: **its** and **it's**

it's *short for* it is

itself *pronoun* **1** used reflexively: *the cat licked itself* **2** used for emphasis or contrast: *after I've read the introduction, I'll begin the book itself*

IU or **IUD** *abbrev* intra-uterine (contraceptive) device

IV *abbrev* intravenous (drip)

ivory *noun* (*plural* **ivories**) the hard white substance which forms the tusks of the elephant, walrus *etc*

ivy *noun* (*plural* **ivies**) a creeping evergreen plant

Jj

jab *verb* (**jabs**, **jabbing**, **jabbed**) poke, stab ◇ *noun* **1** a poke, a stab **2** *informal* an injection

■ *verb* poke, prod, dig, nudge, stab, push, elbow, tap, thrust

jabber *verb* talk rapidly and indistinctly

jack *noun* **1** a device with a lever for raising heavy weights **2** (*also called* **knave**) the playing-card between ten and queen ◇ **jack-in-the-box** *noun* a doll fixed to a spring inside a box which leaps out when the lid is opened ◇ **jackknife** *noun* **1** a large folding knife **2** a dive forming a sharp angle and then straightening ◇ *verb* of a vehicle and its trailer: swing together to form a sharp angle ◇ **jack up 1** raise with a jack **2** raise (prices *etc*) steeply

jackal *noun* a dog-like wild animal

jackass *noun* **1** a male ass **2** *informal* an idiot ◇ **laughing jackass** the kookaburra

jackboots *noun plural* large boots reaching above the knee

jackdaw *noun* a type of small crow

jacket *noun* **1** a short coat **2** a loose paper cover for a book ◇ **jacket potato** a baked potato

jackpot *noun* a fund of prize money which increases until someone wins it

■ prize, winnings, kitty, pool, pot, reward, award

Jacobean *noun, hist* relating to the period of James, I of England (1603–1625), VI of Scotland

jacuzzi *noun, trademark* a bath fitted with a device that agitates the water

jade *noun* a hard green mineral substance used for ornaments

jaded *adj* tired

■ fatigued, exhausted, dulled, played-out, tired, tired out, weary, spent, bored, *informal* fagged

jagged *adj* having a rough, uneven edge

■ uneven, irregular, notched, indented, rough, serrated, toothed, ragged, pointed, barbed

■ even, smooth

jaguar *noun* a S American animal like a leopard

jail *noun* a prison ◇ **jailer** *noun* someone in charge of a jail or prisoners

■ prison, jailhouse, custody, lock-up, penitentiary, *US slang* pen, *informal* inside, *slang* nick, *slang* clink

jailbird *noun* a convict or ex-convict

jalapeño /haːləˈpeɪnjoʊ/ or **jalapeño pepper** *noun* a hot Mexican chilli pepper

jalopy *noun* (*plural* **jalopies**) an old motor car or aeroplane

jam¹ *noun* fruit boiled with sugar till it is set

jam² *noun* **1** a crush or blockage caused by crowding **2** *informal* a difficult situation ◇ *verb* (**jams**, **jamming**, **jammed**) **1** press or squeeze tight **2** crowd full **3** stick and so be unable to move: *the back wheel has jammed* **4** cause interference with another radio station's broadcast **5** *music* play with other musicians in an improvised style ◇ **jam-packed** *adj* packed tightly, congested ◇ **jam session** an informal gathering to play improvised music

■ *noun* **1** crush, crowd, press, congestion, pack, mob, throng, bottleneck, traffic jam, gridlock **2** predicament, trouble, quandary, plight, *informal* fix ◇ *verb* **1** cram, pack, wedge, squash, squeeze, press, crush **2** crowd, congest, stuff

jamb *noun* the side post of a door

jamboree *noun* **1** a large, lively gathering **2** a rally of Scouts

jangle *verb* **1** make a harsh ringing noise **2** irritate: *jangling my nerves*

▣ **1** clank, clash, clatter, jingle, chime, rattle, vibrate

janitor *noun* **1** a caretaker **2** a doorkeeper

January *noun* the first month of the year

jape *noun, informal* a trick, a practical joke

japonica *noun* a Japanese flowering plant

jar *noun* a glass or earthenware container with a wide mouth ◇ *verb* (**jars, jarring, jarred**) **1** jolt or vibrate **2** have a harsh, startling effect **3** be discordant, not agree ◇ **jarring** *adj* harsh, startling

▣ *noun* pot, crock, pitcher, urn, flagon ◇ *verb* **1** jolt, agitate, rattle, shake, vibrate, rock **2** jangle, disturb, discompose ◇ **jarring** discordant, jangling, harsh, grating, irritating, cacophonous, rasping, disturbing, jolting

jargon *noun* special words used within a particular trade, profession *etc*

▣ parlance, cant, argot, vernacular, idiom

jasmine *noun* a shrub with white or yellow sweet-smelling flowers

jaundice *noun* a disease which causes the skin and eyes to turn yellow ◇ **jaundiced** *adj* **1** having jaundice **2** discontented, bitter

▣ **jaundiced 2** bitter, cynical, pessimistic, sceptical, distrustful, disbelieving, envious, jealous, hostile, jaded, suspicious, resentful

jaunt *noun* a short journey for pleasure

jaunty *adj* **1** cheerful, lively **2** stylish ◇ **jauntily** *adv*

▣ **1** sprightly, lively, perky, breezy, buoyant, high-spirited, self-confident, carefree, airy, cheeky **2** debonair, dapper, smart, showy, spruce

▣▣ **1** depressed **2** dowdy

Java *noun, comput* a programming language

javelin *noun* a long spear for throwing

jaw *noun* **1** the lower part of the face, including the mouth and chin **2** (**jaws**) an animal's mouth

jay *noun* a brightly coloured bird like a crow

jaywalker *noun* someone who walks carelessly among traffic

jazz *noun* a style of music with a strong rhythm, syncopation, improvisation *etc* ◇ **jazzy** *adv* colourful, flamboyant ◇ **jazz something up** make it more lively or colourful

jealous *adj* **1** wanting to have what someone else has; envious **2** guarding closely (possessions *etc*) ◇ **jealousy** *noun*

▣ **1** envious, covetous, grudging, resentful, *informal* green, *informal* green-eyed **2** suspicious, distrustful, possessive, protective

jeans *noun plural* denim trousers

jeep *noun* a small army motor vehicle

jeer *verb* make fun of, scoff ◇ *noun* a scoff

▣ *verb* mock, scoff, taunt, jibe, ridicule, sneer, deride, make fun of, heckle

Jehovah *noun* the Hebrew God of the Old Testament

jejune /dʒɪ'dʒuːn/ *adj* naive, inexperienced

From a Latin word meaning 'hungry' or 'fasting'

jelly *noun* (*plural* **jellies**) **1** a transparent wobbly food, often fruit-flavoured **2** fruit juice boiled with sugar till it becomes firm **3** any jelly-like substance

jellyfish *noun* (*plural* **jellyfish** or **jellyfishes**) a sea animal with a jelly-like body

jemmy *noun* (*plural* **jemmies**) a burglar's iron tool for forcing open doors, windows *etc*

jeopardy *noun* danger ◇ **jeopardize** *verb* put in danger or at risk

▣ danger, peril, risk, hazard, endangerment, vulnerability, precariousness, insecurity, exposure, liability ◇ **jeopardize** endanger, imperil, risk, hazard, venture, gamble, chance, threaten, menace, expose

▣▣ safety, security ◇ **jeopardize** protect, safeguard

Originally a gambling term, based on

French *jeu parti* meaning 'even chance'

jerk *verb* give a sudden sharp movement ◇ *noun* a sudden sharp movement ◇ **jerkily** *adv* ◇ **jerky** *adj* moving or coming in jerks

■ *verb* jolt, tug, twitch, jog, yank, wrench, pull ◇ *noun* jolt, tug, twitch, jar, jog, yank, wrench, pull ◇ **jerky** fitful, spasmodic, jumpy, jolting, convulsive, disconnected, bumpy, shaky, rough, unco-ordinated, uncontrolled

☲ **jerky** smooth

jerkin *noun* a type of short coat

jerry-built *adj* hastily and badly built

jersey *noun* (*plural* **jerseys**) 1 a sweater, pullover 2 a machine-knitted stretchy fabric

jest *noun* a joke ◇ *verb* joke ◇ **in jest** as a joke, not seriously

■ *noun* joke, quip, *informal* wisecrack, witticism, *informal* gag, prank, *informal* leg-pull, trick ◇ *verb* joke, quip, fool, *informal* tease, mock, jeer

jester *noun*, *hist* a fool employed to amuse a royal court *etc*

jet¹ *noun* 1 a spout of flame, air or liquid 2 a jet plane ◇ **jet-engine** an engine using jet propulsion ◇ **jet lag** tiredness caused by the body's inability to cope with being in a new time zone ◇ **jet plane** an aeroplane driven by jet propulsion ◇ **jet propulsion** high speed forward motion produced by sucking in air or liquid and forcing it out from behind ◇ **jet set** rich people who enjoy frequent expensive holidays ◇ **jet stream 1** a band of high-speed winds far above the earth 2 the exhaust of a jet engine

■ **2** gush, spurt, spout, spray, spring, fountain, flow, stream, squirt

jet² *noun* a hard black mineral, used for ornaments and jewellery ◇ **jet-black** *adj* very black

jetsam *noun* goods thrown overboard and washed ashore

jettison *verb* 1 throw overboard 2 abandon

jetty *noun* (*plural* **jetties**) a small pier

■ breakwater, pier, dock, groyne, quay, wharf

Jew *noun* someone who is of the Hebrew race or religion ◇ **Jewish** *adj* of the Jews ◇ **Jew's harp** a small harp-shaped musical instrument played between the teeth

jewel *noun* 1 a precious stone 2 someone or something highly valued ◇ **jewelled** or *US* **jeweled** *adj* set with jewels ◇ **jeweller** or *US* **jeweler** *noun* someone who makes or sells articles made of precious jewels and metals ◇ **jewellery** or *US* **jewelry** *noun* articles made of precious jewels or metals and worn for personal adornment

■ **1** gem, precious stone, gemstone, ornament, *slang* rock **2** treasure, find, prize, rarity, paragon, pearl

Types of jewellery include:
bangle, bracelet, charm bracelet, anklet, cufflink, tiepin, hatpin, lapel pin, brooch, cameo, earring, nose-ring, ring, signet-ring, solitaire ring, toe ring, necklace, necklet, choker, pendant, locket, chain, beads, amulet, torque, tiara, coronet, diadem, body jewel, nail jewel, tooth jewel, bindi

Jezebel *noun* a wicked, scheming woman

jib¹ *noun* a three-cornered sail in front of a ship's foremast ◇ *verb* (**jibs, jibbing, jibbed**) **jib at** refuse or object to (doing something)

jib² *noun* the jutting-out arm of a crane

jibe or **gibe** *verb* jeer, scoff ◇ *noun* a jeer

Jiffy bag *trademark* a padded envelope for posting

jig *noun* a lively dance or tune ◇ *verb* (**jigs, jigging, jigged**) jump about

■ *verb* jerk, prance, caper, hop, jump, twitch, skip, bounce, bob, wiggle

jiggery-pokery *noun*, *informal* trickery, deceit

jigsaw or **jigsaw puzzle** *noun* a puzzle consisting of many different shaped pieces that fit together to form a picture

jihad /dʒɪ'hɑːd/ *noun* an Islamic holy war

jilt *verb* cast aside (a lover)

■ *verb* abandon, reject, desert, discard, brush off, *informal* ditch, drop, spurn, betray

jingle *noun* 1 a clinking sound like that of coins 2 a simple rhyme or tune ◇ *verb* make a clinking sound

■ *noun* 1 clink, tinkle, ringing, clang, rattle 2 rhyme, verse, song, tune, ditty, melody, poem, chant, chorus ◇ *verb* clink, tinkle, ring, chime, chink, jangle, clatter

jingoism *noun* chauvinism, narrow-minded nationalism ◇ **jingoistic** *adj*

■ chauvinism, flag-waving, patriotism, nationalism, imperialism, warmongering, insularity

jinx *noun* someone or something thought to bring bad luck

> Probably from the *Jynx* bird which was once invoked in spells and charms

jitterbug *noun* a dance like the jive

jitters *noun plural*: **have the jitters** be very nervous ◇ **jittery** *adj* very nervous, shaking with nerves

jive *noun* a style of fast dancing to jazz music

job *noun* 1 someone's daily paid work 2 any piece of work ◇ **job centre** a government office providing information about available jobs ◇ **job-lot** *noun* a collection of odds and ends ◇ **job-share** *noun* the division of one job between two people, each working part-time

■ 1 work, employment, occupation, position, post, situation, profession, career, calling, vocation, trade, métier, capacity, business, livelihood 2 task, chore, duty, responsibility, charge, commission, mission, activity

jock *noun*, *slang* 1 *derog* a Scotsman or Scotswoman 2 *US* an athletic college student

jockey *noun* (*plural* **jockeys**) someone who rides a horse in a race ◇ *verb* push your way into a good position

jockstrap *noun* a genital support for men while playing sports

jocose *adj formal* humorous, merry ◇ **jocosity** *noun*

jocular *adj* joking, merry ◇ **jocularity** *noun* ◇ **jocularly** *adv*

■ joking, jesting, funny, *formal* jocose, humorous, jovial, amusing, comical, entertaining, facetious, droll, whimsical, teasing, witty

🔁 serious

jodhpurs *noun plural* riding breeches, fitting tightly from knee to ankle

joey *noun* (*plural* **joeys**), *Austral informal* a young kangaroo

jog *verb* (**jogs**, **jogging**, **jogged**) 1 nudge, push slightly 2 run at a gentle pace ◇ *noun* ◇ **jogger** *noun* someone who runs gently to keep fit ◇ **jogging** *noun*

■ *verb* 1 jolt, jar, bump, jostle, jerk, nudge, poke, prod, push 2 run, trot

joggle *verb* shake slightly

joie de vivre /ʒwɑː də 'viːvrə/ enthusiasm for life; sparkle, spirit

join *verb* 1 put or come together 2 connect, fasten 3 become a member of ◇ *noun* the place where two or more things join ◇ **joiner** *noun* someone who makes wooden fittings, furniture *etc* ◇ **joint** *noun* 1 the place where two or more things join 2 the place where two bones are joined, *eg* an elbow or knee 3 meat containing a bone ◇ *adj* 1 united 2 shared ◇ **jointly** *adv* together ◇ **join battle** begin fighting in battle

■ *verb* 1, 2 unite, connect, combine, conjoin, attach, link, amalgamate, fasten, meet, merge, marry, couple, yoke, tie, splice, knit, cement, adhere, annex 3 associate, affiliate, accompany, ally, enlist, enrol, enter, sign up, opt in ◇ **joint** *noun* 1 junction, connection, union, juncture, intersection, hinge, knot, articulation, seam ◇ *adj* 1 combined, joined, united, collective, amalgamated, mutual, co-operative, co-ordinated, consolidated, concerted 2 common, communal, shared

🔁 *verb* 1, 2 divide, separate 3 leave

joist *noun* the beam to which the boards of a floor or the laths of a ceiling are nailed

jojoba /hoʊˈhoʊbə/ *noun* a desert shrub with edible seeds whose oil is used in cosmetics

joke *noun* something said or done to cause laughter ◊ *verb* make a joke, say something in jest ◊ **joker** *noun* **1** someone who jokes **2** an extra playing-card in a pack

▤ *noun* quip, *informal* crack, *informal* gag, witticism, *informal* wisecrack, *informal* one-liner, pun, yarn, trick, jape, lark, prank, spoof

jolly *adj* merry ◊ **jollification** *noun* noisy festivity or celebration ◊ **jolliness** or **jollity** *noun* merriment

▤ jovial, merry, cheerful, playful, hearty, happy, exuberant

▣ sad

jolt *verb* **1** shake suddenly **2** go forward with sudden jerks ◊ *noun* a sudden jerk

▤ *verb* **1** jerk, jog, bump, jostle, knock, bounce, shake, push

joss-stick *noun* a stick of gum which gives off a sweet smell when burned

jostle *verb* push or knock against

▤ push, shove, jog, bump, elbow, hustle, jolt, crowd, shoulder, joggle, shake, squeeze, throng

jot *noun* a very small part ◊ *verb* (**jots**, **jotting**, **jotted**) write down hurriedly or briefly ◊ **jotter** *noun* a book for taking notes

▤ *verb* write down, take down, note, list, scribble down

joule *noun* a unit of energy

journal *noun* **1** a personal account of each day's events; a diary **2** a newspaper, a magazine

▤ **1** chronicle, diary, daybook, log, record **2** newspaper, periodical, magazine, paper, publication, review, weekly, monthly, gazette, fanzine

journalist *noun* a person whose job is to write for a newspaper or magazine ◊ **journalism** *noun* ◊ **journalistic** *adj*

▤ reporter, news-writer, hack, correspondent, editor, columnist, feature-writer, commentator, broadcaster, contributor

journey *noun* (*plural* **journeys**) a distance travelled ◊ *verb* travel ◊ **journeyman** *noun* someone whose apprenticeship is finished

▤ *noun* voyage, trip, travel, expedition, passage, trek, tour, ramble, outing, wanderings, safari, progress ◊ *verb* travel, voyage, go, trek, tour, roam, rove, proceed, wander, tramp, ramble, range

journo *noun* (*plural* **journos**) *informal* a journalist

joust *noun*, *hist* the armed contest between two knights on horseback at a tournament ◊ *verb* fight on horseback at a tournament

jovial *adj* cheerful, good-humoured ◊ **joviality** *noun*

▤ jolly, cheery, merry, affable, cordial, genial

▣ gloomy

jowl *noun* the lower part of the jaw or cheek

joy *noun* gladness ◊ **joyless** *adj* dismal

▤ happiness, gladness, delight, pleasure, bliss, ecstasy, elation, joyfulness, exultation, gratification, rapture

▣ despair, grief

joyful or **joyous** *adj* full of joy

▤ happy, pleased, delighted, glad, elated, ecstatic, triumphant

▣ sorrowful

joy-ride *noun* a reckless trip for amusement in a stolen car

JP *abbrev* Justice of the Peace

Jr *abbrev* Junior: *John Brown Jr*

jubilant *adj* full of rejoicing, triumphant ◊ **jubilation** *noun*

▤ joyful, rejoicing, overjoyed, delighted, elated, triumphant, exuberant, excited, euphoric, thrilled

jubilee *noun* celebrations arranged for the anniversary of a wedding, coronation *etc*

> From a Hebrew word for 'ram's horn', which was blown to announce the start of a celebratory Jewish year

Judaism *noun* the Jewish religion or way of life ◊ **Judaic** *adj*

Judas *noun* a traitor

judder *noun* a strong vibration or jerky movement

judge *verb* **1** make a decision on (a law case) after hearing all the evidence **2** form an opinion **3** decide the winners in a competition *etc* ◇ *noun* **1** an official who judges law cases in a court **2** someone who judges a competition **3** someone skilled in evaluating anything: *a good judge of character*

■ *verb* **1** try, sentence, rule, find **2** decide, assess, appraise, evaluate, value, discern, reckon, believe, think, consider, conclude, rate **3** adjudicate, arbitrate, referee, umpire, decree, mediate, examine ◇ *noun* **1** magistrate, arbiter, justice **3** connoisseur, authority, expert, evaluator, assessor, critic

judgement or **judgment** *noun* **1** a decision in a law case **2** an opinion **3** good sense in forming opinions

■ **1** verdict, sentence, ruling, decree **2** assessment, evaluation, appraisal, estimate, opinion, view, belief, diagnosis **3** discernment, discrimination, understanding, wisdom, prudence, common sense, sense, intelligence, taste, shrewdness, penetration

judicial *adj* of a judge or court of justice ◇ **judicially** *adv*

judiciary *noun* the judges of a country or state

judicious *adj* wise ◇ **judiciously** *adv*

■ wise, prudent, careful, cautious, astute, discerning, informed, shrewd, thoughtful, reasonable, sensible, sound, well-judged, well-advised, considered

☒ injudicious

judo *noun* a Japanese form of wrestling for self-defence

jug *noun* a container for liquids with a handle and a shaped lip for pouring

juggernaut *noun* a large articulated lorry

From a Hindi word for a large wagon used to carry the image of the god Krishna in religious processions

juggle *verb* **1** toss a number of things (*eg* balls, clubs *etc*) into the air and catch them in order **2** handle or present in a deceitful way: *juggle the facts* ◇ **juggler** *noun*

■ **2** alter, change, manipulate, falsify, rearrange, rig, *informal* doctor, *informal* cook, disguise

jugular vein the large vein at the side of the neck

juice *noun* the liquid in vegetables, fruits *etc* ◇ **juicy** *adj* **1** full of juice **2** sensational, scandalous

■ liquid, fluid, extract, essence, sap, secretion, nectar ◇ **juicy 1** succulent, moist, lush, watery **2** interesting, colourful, sensational, racy, risqué, suggestive, lurid

jujitsu *noun* a Japanese martial art similar to judo

jujube /dʒuːdʒuːb/ *noun* a soft, jelly-like, fruit-flavoured sweet

jukebox *noun* a coin-operated machine which plays selected records automatically

julep *noun*, *US* a sweet cocktail made with alcohol, sugar and mint

julienne *adj* of vegetables *etc*: cut into thin strips for cooking

July *noun* the seventh month of the year

Juma *noun* the Islamic Sabbath, held on Friday

jumble *verb* throw together without order, muddle ◇ *noun* a confused mixture ◇ **jumble sale** a sale of odds and ends, cast-off clothing *etc*

■ *verb* disarrange, confuse, disorganize, mix (up), muddle, shuffle, tangle ◇ *noun* disorder, disarray, confusion, mess, chaos, mix-up, muddle, clutter, mixture, hotch-potch, *informal* mish-mash, medley

☒ *verb & noun* order

jumbo *noun* (*plural* **jumbos**) a child's name for an elephant ◇ *adj* very large ◇ **jumbo jet** a large jet aircraft

jump *verb* **1** spring off the ground or over an obstacle **2** make a sudden startled movement ◇ *noun* **1** an act of jumping **2** a sudden increase ◇ **jump-suit** *noun* a one-piece garment combining trousers and top

■ *verb* **1** leap, spring, bound, vault, clear, bounce, skip, hop, prance, frolic, gambol **2** start, flinch, jerk, recoil, *informal* jump out of one's skin, wince ◇ *noun* **1** leap, spring, bound, vault, hop, skip, bounce, prance, frisk, frolic, pounce, start, jerk, jolt, jar, shock

jumpy *adj* easily startled ◇ **jumpily** *adv*

■ nervous, anxious, agitated, apprehensive, jittery, tense, edgy, fidgety, shaky
❐ calm, composed

jumper *noun* a knitted garment for the top half of the body

junction *noun* a place or point of joining, *esp* of roads or railway lines

■ joint, join, joining, connection, juncture, union, intersection, linking, coupling, meeting-point, confluence

juncture *noun* a point in time: *it's too early to decide at this juncture*

June *noun* the sixth month of the year

jungle *noun* a dense growth of trees and plants in tropical areas

junior *adj* **1** younger **2** in a lower class or rank ◇ *noun* **1** someone younger: *he is my junior* **2** someone in a lower class or rank

■ *adj* **1** younger **2** minor, lesser, lower, subordinate, secondary, subsidiary, inferior
❐ *adj* **1**, **2** senior

juniper *noun* an evergreen shrub with edible berries and prickly leaves

junk¹ *noun* worthless articles, rubbish ◇ **junkie** or **junky** *noun* (*plural* **junkies**), *slang* a drug addict ◇ **junk food** convenience food with little nutritional value ◇ **junk mail** unsolicited mail, *esp* advertising material

■ rubbish, refuse, trash, debris, garbage, waste, scrap, litter, clutter, oddments, rummage

junk² *noun* a Chinese flat-bottomed sailing ship, high in the bow and stern

junket *noun* a dish made of curdled milk sweetened and flavoured ◇ **junketing** *noun* feasting, merriment

junta /'dʒʌntə/ or /'hʊntə/ *noun* a government formed following a successful coup d'état

jurisdiction *noun* **1** a legal authority or power **2** the district over which a judge, court *etc* has power

jurisprudence *noun* the study or knowledge of law

jury *noun* (*plural* **juries**) **1** a group of men or women selected to reach a decision on whether an accused prisoner is guilty or not **2** a group of judges for a competition *etc* ◇ **juror**, **juryman** or **jurywoman** *noun* someone who serves on a jury

just *adj* **1** fair in judgement **2** rightly deserved **3** correct ◇ *adv* **1** exactly: *just right* **2** not long since: *only just arrived* **3** merely, only **4** really: *just beautiful* ◇ **justly** *adv*

■ *adj* **1** fair, equitable, impartial, unbiased, unprejudiced, fair-minded, even-handed, objective, righteous, upright, virtuous, honourable, good, honest, irreproachable

justice *noun* **1** fairness in making judgements **2** what is right or rightly deserved **3** a judge ◇ **Justice of the Peace** (*short form* **JP**) a citizen who acts as a judge for certain matters

■ **1** fairness, equity, impartiality, objectivity, equitableness, justness, reasonableness **2** rectitude **3** judge, Justice of the Peace, JP, magistrate

justifiable *adj* able to be justified or defended ◇ **justifiably** *adv*

■ defensible, excusable, warranted, reasonable, justified, lawful, legitimate, acceptable, explainable, forgivable, pardonable, understandable, valid, well-founded, right, proper, explicable, tenable
❐ unjustifiable

justification *noun* good reason

■ defence, plea, mitigation, explanation, excuse, vindication, warrant, rationalization, reason, grounds

justify *verb* (**justifies**, **justifying**, **justified**) **1** prove or show to be right or desirable **2** *printing* make (text) form an even margin down the page

jut *verb* (**juts**, **jutting**, **jutted**) stand or stick out

■ project, protrude, stick out, overhang, extend

jute *noun* fibre from certain plants for making sacking, canvas *etc*

juvenile *adj* **1** young; of or for young people **2** childish ◇ *noun* a young person

▤ *adj* **1** young, youthful **2** immature, childish, puerile, infantile, adolescent, babyish, unsophisticated ◇ *noun* child, youth, minor, young person, youngster, adolescent, teenager, boy, girl, *informal* kid, infant

▣ *adj* **2** mature

juxtapose *verb* place side by side ◇ **juxtaposition** *noun*

Kk

k or **K** *abbrev* kilo-; one thousand

kabuki *noun* a stylized form of Japanese theatre

kaftan *another spelling of* **caftan**

kaiser /'kaɪzə(r)/ *noun, hist* a German emperor

kalanchoe *noun* a plant with flower clusters on long stems

kale *noun* a cabbage with open curled leaves

kaleidoscope *noun* a tube held to the eye and turned, so that loose, coloured shapes reflected in two mirrors change patterns ◇ **kaleidoscopic** *adj* **1** with changing colours **2** changing quickly ◇ **kaleidoscopically** *adv*

kamikaze *noun, hist* a Japanese pilot trained to make a suicidal attack ◇ *adj* suicidal, self-destructive

kangaroo *noun* a large Australian animal with long hindlegs and great jumping power, the female carrying its young in a pouch on the front of her body

kaolin *noun* a soft white clay used for making porcelain (*also called*: **China clay**)

kapok /'keɪpɒk/ *noun* light waterproof fibre fluff from the seeds of a tropical tree, used for padding

kaput /kə'pʊt/ *adj, slang* broken, not working

karaoke /karɪ'oʊkɪ/ *noun* a form of entertainment which involves singing well-known songs to pre-recorded backing music

karate /kə'rɑːtɪ/ *noun* a Japanese form of unarmed fighting using blows and kicks

karma *noun* in Buddhist belief, someone's destiny as determined by their actions in a previous life

kayak *noun* **1** an Inuit sealskin canoe **2** a lightweight canoe for one person, manoeuvred with a single paddle

KB *abbrev, comput* kilobyte

KBE *abbrev* Knight Commander of the British Empire

kcal *abbrev* kilocalorie

kebab *noun* small pieces of meat or vegetables cooked on a skewer

kedgeree *noun* a dish made with rice, fish and hard-boiled eggs

keel *noun* the piece of a ship's frame that lies lengthways along the bottom ◇ **keel over** overturn, fall over, collapse

■ **keel over** overturn, capsize, founder, collapse, upset, faint, pass out, swoon, fall, drop, stagger, topple over

keelhaul *verb, hist* punish by hauling under the keel of a ship with ropes

keen[1] *adj* **1** eager, enthusiastic **2** very sharp; bitingly cold ◇ **keenly** *adv* ◇ **keenness** *noun*

■ **1** eager, avid, fervent, enthusiastic, earnest, devoted, diligent, industrious **2** sharp, piercing, penetrating, incisive, acute, pointed, intense, pungent, trenchant

◪ **1** apathetic **2** dull

keen[2] *verb* wail in grief; lament ◇ **keening** *noun*

keep *verb* (**keeps, keeping, kept**) **1** hold on to, not give or throw away **2** look after; feed and clothe **3** have or use **4** fulfil (a promise) **5** remain in a position or state **6** (also with **on**) continue (doing something): *keep taking the tablets* **7** of food: stay in good condition **8** celebrate: *keep Christmas* ◇ *noun* **1** food, board: *earn your keep* **2** a castle stronghold ◇ **keeper** *noun* someone who looks after something, *eg* animals at a zoo ◇ **keeping** *noun* care, charge ◇ **in keeping with** suited to ◇ **keep out 1** exclude **2** stay outside ◇ **keep up** go on with, continue ◇ **keep up with** go as fast *etc* as

■ *verb* **1** retain, hold, preserve, hold on to, hang on to, store, stock, amass, accumulate, collect, stack, conserve **2** tend, care for, have charge of, have custody of, maintain, provide for, subsidize, support, sustain, be responsible for, foster, mind, protect, feed **6** carry on, keep on, continue, persist ◇ *noun* **1** living, maintenance, support, upkeep, means, food, nourishment **2** fort, fortress, tower, castle, citadel, stronghold, dungeon

keepsake *noun* a gift in memory of an occasion *etc*

■ memento, souvenir, reminder, token

keg *noun* a small cask or barrel

kelp *noun* a type of large brown seaweed

kelpie *noun* a Celtic water-sprite in the shape of a horse

kelvin *noun* a measure of temperature

ken *noun* the extent of someone's knowledge or understanding: *beyond the ken of the average person* ◇ *verb* (**kens, kenning, kent** or **kenned**), *Scot* know

kendo *noun* a Japanese martial art using bamboo staves

kennel *noun* **1** a hut for a dog **2** (**kennels**) a place where dogs can be looked after

kept *past form of* **keep**

keratin *noun* the substance from which horns and nails are made

kerb *noun* the edge of a pavement ◇ **kerb-crawling** *noun* driving a car slowly in order to pick up prostitutes

! Do not confuse with: **curb**

kerchief *noun* a square of cloth used as a headscarf

kernel *noun* **1** a soft substance in the shell of a nut, or inside the stone of a fruit **2** the important part of anything

■ **1** core, grain, seed **2** nucleus, heart, nub, essence, germ, marrow, substance, *informal* nitty-gritty, gist

kerosine *noun* paraffin oil

kestrel *noun* a type of small falcon which hovers

ketch *noun* (*plural* **ketches**) a two-masted sailing ship

ketchup *noun* a sauce made from tomatoes *etc*

Originally spelt *catsup*, as it still is in US English; based on a Chinese word for 'fish brine'

kettle *noun* a pot with a spout for heating liquids

kettledrum *noun* a drum made of a metal bowl covered with stretched skin *etc*

key *noun* **1** a device which is turned in a corresponding hole to lock or unlock, tighten, tune *etc* **2** a lever pressed on a piano *etc* to produce a note **3** a button on a typewriter or computer keyboard which is pressed to type letters **4** the chief note of a piece of music **5** something which explains a mystery or deciphers a code **6** a table explaining the symbols used on a map *etc* **7** a book containing answers to exercises ◇ *verb* type on a typewriter or computer ◇ *adj* important, essential ◇ **keyed-up** *adj* excited

■ *noun* **5** clue, cue, indicator, pointer, explanation, sign, answer, solution, interpretation, means, secret **6** legend, code, table **7** guide, glossary, translation, index ◇ *adj* important, essential, vital, crucial, necessary, principal, decisive, central, chief, main, major, basic, fundamental

keyboard *noun* **1** the keys in a piano or organ arranged along a flat board **2** the keys of a typewriter or computer **3** an electronic musical instrument with keys arranged as on a piano *etc*

keyhole *noun* the hole in which a key of a door is placed ◇ **keyhole surgery** surgery peformed through very small openings in body tissue

keynote *noun* **1** the chief note of a piece of music **2** the chief point about anything

keypad *noun* a device with buttons that can be pushed to operate a television, telephone *etc*

keystone *noun* the stone at the highest

point of an arch holding the rest in position

kg *abbrev* kilogram(s)

KGB *abbrev, hist* Committee of State Security (in Russian, *Komitet Gosudarstvennoi Bezopasnosti*)

khaki *adj* greenish-brown in colour ◇ *noun* **1** a greenish-brown colour **2** cloth of this colour used for military uniforms

From an Urdu word meaning 'dusty'

kibbutz *noun* (*plural* **kibbutzim**) a farming settlement in Israel in which all share the work

kibosh *noun, informal*: **put the kibosh on** ruin, destroy, get rid of

kick *verb* **1** hit or strike out with the foot **2** of a gun: spring back violently when fired ◇ *noun* **1** a blow with the foot **2** the springing back of a gun when fired **3** *informal* stimulation: *get a kick out of gambling* ◇ **for kicks** *informal* for fun ◇ **kick-off** *noun* the start (of a football game)

■ *verb* **1** boot, hit, strike **2** recoil ◇ *noun* **1** blow, striking **2** recoil **3** thrill, excitement

kid¹ *noun* **1** *informal* a child **2** a young goat **3** the skin of a young goat ◇ *adj* made of kid leather ◇ **kids' stuff** *informal* something very easy or tame ◇ **with kid gloves** very carefully or tactfully

■ *noun* **1** child, youngster, youth, juvenile, infant, girl, boy, teenager, lad, *informal* nipper, *informal* tot

kid² *verb* (**kids, kidding, kidded**), *informal* tease, deceive playfully

■ tease, joke, *informal* have on, hoax, fool, *informal* pull someone's leg, pretend, trick, delude, dupe, *informal* con, hoodwink

kidnap *verb* (**kidnaps, kidnapping, kidnapped**) carry off (someone) by force, often demanding money in exchange ◇ **kidnapper** *noun* ◇ **kidnapping** *noun*

■ abduct, capture, seize, hold to ransom, snatch, hijack, steal

kidney *noun* (*plural* **kidneys**) either of a pair of organs in the lower back which filter waste from the blood and produce urine ◇ **kidney bean** a bean with a curved shape like a kidney

kilim *noun* a Middle-Eastern woven rug

kill *verb* **1** put to death **2** put an end to **3** *informal* cause severe pain to: *my feet are killing me* ◇ *noun* **1** the act of killing **2** the animals killed by a hunter ◇ **killer** *noun* a murderer ◇ **be in at the kill** be there at the most exciting moment

■ *verb* **1** slaughter, murder, slay, put to death, exterminate, assassinate, *informal* do in, *informal* bump off , finish off, massacre, *formal* smite, execute, eliminate, destroy **2** stifle, quash, quell, suppress, do away with ◇ **killer** murderer, assassin, executioner, destroyer, slaughterer, exterminator, gunman, *slang* hit-man

kiln *noun* a large oven or furnace for baking pottery, bricks *etc* or for drying grain, hops *etc*

kilo- *prefix* **1** 1000 **2** *comput* 1024

kilobyte *noun, comput* a measure of capacity equal to 1024 bytes

kilocalorie *noun* a measure of energy equal to 1000 calories

kilogram *noun* a measure of weight equal to 1000 grams (about 2 lb)

kilometre *noun* a measure of length equal to 1000 metres (about $\frac{5}{8}$ of a mile)

kilowatt *noun* a measure of electrical power equal to 1000 watts

kilt *noun* a pleated tartan skirt reaching to the knee, worn by men as part of traditional Scottish dress

kilter *noun*: **out of kilter** out of sequence, off balance

kimono *noun* (*plural* **kimonos**) a loose Japanese robe, fastened with a sash

kin *noun* members of the same family, relations ◇ **kith and kin** *see* **kith** ◇ **next of kin** your nearest relative

kind *noun* **1** a sort, type **2** nature, character: *differ in kind* **3** goods, not money: *paid in kind* ◇ *adj* having good feelings towards others; generous, gentle ◇ **kind-hearted** *adj* kind ◇ **kindness** *noun*

◼ *noun* **1** sort, type, class, category, set, variety, genus, genre, style, brand, family, breed, race, nature, species ◇ *adj* benevolent, kind-hearted, kindly, good-hearted, good-natured, helpful, obliging, generous, compassionate, charitable, thoughtful, warm, warm-hearted, considerate, sympathetic, gentle, giving, good

◼ *adj* cruel, inconsiderate

kindly *adv* in a kind way ◇ *adj* kind, warm-hearted ◇ **kindliness** *noun*

kindergarten *noun* a nursery school

kindle *verb* **1** light a fire **2** catch fire **3** stir up (feelings)

◼ **1** ignite, light, set alight, set on fire **3** fire, stir, thrill, stimulate, rouse, arouse, awaken, excite, fan, incite, inspire, induce, provoke

kindling *noun* material for starting a fire

kindred *noun* relatives, relations ◇ *adj* of the same sort; related: *a kindred spirit*

kinesiology *noun* the study of human movement and posture

kinesis *noun* movement, change in position

kinetic *adj* of or expressing motion: *kinetic sculpture*

king *noun* **1** the hereditary male ruler of a nation **2** a playing-card with a picture of a king **3** the most important chess piece, which must be protected from checkmate ◇ **kingly** *adj* like a king; royal

◼ **1** monarch, ruler, sovereign, majesty, emperor, chief, chieftain, supremo

kingcup *noun* marsh marigold

kingdom *noun* **1** the area ruled by a king **2** any of the three major divisions of natural objects, *ie* animal, vegetable or mineral

◼ **1** monarchy, sovereignty, reign, realm, empire, dominion, commonwealth, nation, principality, state, country, domain, dynasty, province, sphere, territory, land, division

kingfisher *noun* a type of fish-eating bird with brightly coloured feathers

kingpin *noun* the most important person in an organization

kink *noun* **1** a bend or curl in a rope, hair *etc* **2** a peculiarity of the mind

◼ **1** curl, twist, bend, dent, indentation, knot, loop, crimp, coil, tangle, wrinkle **2** quirk, eccentricity, idiosyncrasy, foible, perversion

kinky *adj* **1** twisted, bent, curled **2** *informal* sexually unusual or perverted

kinsfolk *noun plural* relations, relatives

kinsman, kinswoman *noun* a close relation

kiosk *noun* **1** a small stall for the sale of newspapers, sweets *etc* **2** a telephone box

◼ **1** stall, stand, news-stand, bookstall, counter **2** booth, box, cabin

kip *slang*, *noun* a bed ◇ *verb* (**kips**, **kipping**, **kipped**) go to bed, sleep

kipper *noun* a smoked and dried herring

kir /kɪə(r)/ *noun* a drink of white wine mixed with blackcurrant syrup or liqueur

kirk *noun*, *Scot* a church

kirsch /kɪəʃ/ *noun* a liqueur made from cherries

kismet *noun* destiny, fate

kiss *verb* **1** touch lovingly with the lips **2** touch gently ◇ *noun* (*plural* **kisses**) an affectionate touch with the lips ◇ **kiss of life** a mouth-to-mouth method of restoring breathing

◼ *verb* **1** caress, *informal* peck, *informal* smooch, *informal* neck, *slang* snog **2** touch, graze, glance, brush, lick, scrape, fan ◇ *noun informal* peck, *informal* smack, *slang* smacker

kit *noun* an outfit of clothes, tools *etc* necessary for a particular job ◇ **kit out** provide with the necessary equipment, clothes, *etc*

◼ equipment, gear, apparatus, supplies, tackle, provisions, outfit, implements, set, tools, rig, instruments, paraphernalia ◇ **kit out** equip, fit out, outfit, supply, fix up, furnish, prepare, arm, deck out, dress

kitchen *noun* a room where food is cooked ◇ **kitchenette** *noun* a small kitchen ◇ **kitchen garden** a vegetable garden

kite *noun* **1** a light frame, covered with paper or other material, for flying in the air **2** a kind of hawk

kith *noun*: **kith and kin** friends and relatives

kitsch *noun* vulgarly tasteless art *etc*

kitten *noun* a young cat ◇ **kittenish** *adj* behaving like a kitten, playful ◇ **have kittens** *informal* make a great fuss

kittiwake *noun* a type of gull

kitty¹ *noun* (*plural* **kitties**) a sum of money set aside for a purpose

kitty² *noun* (*plural* **kitties**) *informal* a kitten

kiwi *noun* **1** a fast-running almost wingless bird of New Zealand **2** a kiwi fruit ◇ **kiwi fruit** an edible fruit with a thin hairy skin and bright green flesh

kleptomania *noun* an uncontrollable desire to steal ◇ **kleptomaniac** *noun & adj*

km *abbrev* kilometre(s)

knack *noun* a special clever ability

■ flair, faculty, facility, bent, skill, talent, genius, gift, trick, ability, expertise, skilfulness, handiness, dexterity, quickness

knacker *noun* a buyer of old horses for slaughter ◇ *verb, informal* exhaust, tire out ◇ **knackered** *adj, informal*

knapsack *noun* a bag for food, clothes *etc* carried on the back

■ bag, pack, haversack, rucksack, backpack

knave *noun* **1** a cheating rogue **2** in playing-cards, the jack ◇ **knavery** *noun* dishonesty ◇ **knavish** *adj* cheating, wicked

knead *verb* **1** work (dough *etc*) by pressing with the fingers **2** massage

■ **1** manipulate, press, massage, work, ply, squeeze, shape, rub, form, mould **2** manipulate, massage, rub

knee *noun* the joint at the bend of the leg

kneecap *noun* the flat round bone on the front of the knee joint ◇ **kneecapping** *noun* a form of torture or punishment in which the victim is shot or otherwise injured in the kneecap

kneel *verb* (**kneels, kneeling, knelt**) go down on one or both knees

knell *noun* **1** the tolling of a bell for a death or funeral **2** a warning of a sad end or failure

knew *past form* of **know**

knickerbockers *noun plural* loose breeches tucked in at the knee

Named after Diedrich *Knickerbocker*, a fictional Dutchman invented by US author Washington Irving in the 19th century

knickers *noun plural* women's or girls' underpants

knick-knack *noun* a small, ornamental article

■ trinket, trifle, bauble, gewgaw, gimcrack, bric-à-brac

knife *noun* (*plural* **knives**) a tool for cutting ◇ *verb* stab ◇ **at knifepoint** under threat of injury from a knife

■ *noun* blade, cutter, carver, dagger, penknife, pocket-knife, switchblade, jackknife, flick-knife, machete ◇ *verb* cut, rip, slash, stab, pierce, wound

knight *noun* **1** *hist* an aristocrat trained to use arms **2** a man awarded the title *Sir* **3** a piece used in chess ◇ *verb* raise to the rank of knight ◇ **knighthood** *noun* the rank of a knight ◇ **knightly** *adj* **1** of knights **2** gallant, courageous ◇ **knight-errant** *hist* a knight who travelled in search of adventures

knit *verb* (**knits, knitting, knitted**) **1** form a garment from yarn by interlocking loops **2** join closely ◇ **knitting** *noun* work done by knitting ◇ **knitting needles** *noun plural* a pair of thin pointed rods used in knitting

■ **2** join, unite, secure, connect, tie, fasten, link, mend, interlace, intertwine

knob noun **1** a small rounded projection **2** a round door-handle

knock verb **1** strike, hit **2** drive or be driven against **3** make a noise by striking something **4** tap on a door to have it opened ◇ noun **1** a sudden stroke **2** a tap (on a door) ◇ **knocker** noun a hinged weight on a door for knocking with ◇ **knock back** informal eat or drink greedily ◇ **knock down 1** demolish **2** informal reduce in price ◇ **knock-kneed** adj having knees that touch in walking ◇ **knock off** informal **1** stop work for the day **2** plagiarize, copy illegally ◇ **knock out** hit (someone) hard enough to make them unconscious ◇ **knock up 1** put together hastily **2** slang make pregnant

☰ verb **1** hit, strike, rap, thump, pound, slap, smack ◇ noun **1** blow, box, rap, thump, cuff, clip, pounding, hammering, slap, smack ◇ **knock down 1** demolish, destroy, fell, floor, level, wreck, raze

knoll noun a small rounded hill

knot noun **1** a join or fastening made by tying string etc **2** a tangle **3** a small gathering, a cluster of people **4** a hard lump, eg in wood **5** a measure of speed for ships (about 1.85 kilometre per hour) ◇ verb (**knots, knotting, knotted**) tie in a knot ◇ **knotted** adj full of knots ◇ **get knotted!** exclam, informal expressing anger or defiance towards someone ◇ **knotty** adj **1** having knots **2** difficult, complicated: knotty problem

☰ noun **1** tie, bond, joint, fastening, loop, splice, hitch **3** bunch, cluster, clump, group

Types of knot include:
bend, Blackwall hitch, blood knot, bow, bowline, running bowline, carrick bend, clove hitch, common whipping, double-overhang, Englishman's tie (or knot), figure of eight, fisherman's bend, fisherman's knot, flat knot, granny knot, half hitch, highwayman's hitch, hitch, Hunter's bend, loop knot, overhand knot or thumb knot, reef knot or square knot, rolling hitch, round

turn and two half hitches, seizing, sheepshank, sheet bend or common bend or swab hitch, slipknot, spade-end knot, surgeon's knot, tie, timber hitch, Turk's head, turle knot, wall knot, weaver's knot, Windsor knot

know /noʊ/ verb (**knows, knowing, known, knew**) **1** be aware or sure of **2** recognize ◇ **knowing** adj clever; cunning ◇ **knowingly** adv intentionally

☰ **1** understand, comprehend, apprehend, perceive, be aware of, fathom, experience, realize, see **2** be acquainted with, be familiar with, recognize, identify

knowledge noun **1** that which is known **2** information **3** ability, skill

knowledgeable adj showing or having knowledge ◇ **knowledgeably** adv

☰ educated, scholarly, learned, well-informed, lettered, aware, acquainted, conscious, familiar, au fait, informal in the know, conversant, experienced

knuckle noun a joint of the fingers ◇ **knuckle under** give in, yield

knuckleduster noun a metal covering worn on the knuckles as a weapon

koala bear an Australian tree-climbing animal resembling a small bear

kohl noun a black powder used as an eyeliner

kohlrabi noun a type of cabbage with a turnip-shaped stem

kookaburra noun the Australian giant kingfisher (also called: **laughing jackass**)

kooky adj, informal eccentric

kopeck noun a Russian coin, equal to a hundredth of a rouble

Koran noun the sacred book of Islam

kosher adj **1** pure and clean according to Jewish law **2** informal acceptable, all right

kowtow verb (often with **to**) treat someone with too much respect

☰ defer, cringe, fawn, grovel, pander, informal suck up, informal toady, flatter, kneel

Based on a Chinese phrase meaning to prostrate yourself before the emperor

kraal *noun* a South African village

krill *noun* a small shrimplike creature eaten by whales *etc*

Krugerrand *noun* a South African coin used only for investment

krypton *noun* an inert gas present in the air, used in fluorescent lighting

Kt *abbrev* Knight

kudos /'kjuːdɒs/ *noun* fame, glory

kulfi *noun* Indian ice-cream made with boiled, reduced milk

kumquat *noun* a small Chinese orange with a sweet rind

kung-fu *noun* a Chinese form of self-defence

kw *abbrev* kilowatt(s)

kyrie /'kɪərɪ/ *noun* **1** a prayer in the Roman Catholic mass following the opening anthem **2** a musical setting for this

Ll

l *abbrev* litre(s)

lab *noun*, *informal* a laboratory

label *noun* a small written note fixed onto something listing its contents, price *etc* ◇ *verb* (**labels**, **labelling**, **labelled**) **1** fix a label to **2** call something by a certain name

■ *noun* tag, ticket, mark, marker, sticker, badge ◇ *verb* **2** define, describe, classify, categorize, characterize, identify, class, designate, brand, call, name

labial *adj* of the lips

laboratory *noun* (*plural* **laboratories**) a scientist's workroom

laborious *adj* requiring hard work; wearisome

■ hard, arduous, difficult, strenuous, tough, backbreaking, wearisome, tiresome, heavy

🔁 easy, effortless

labour or *US* **labor** *noun* **1** hard work **2** workers on a job **3** the process of childbirth ◇ *verb* **1** work hard **2** move slowly or with difficulty **3** emphasize (a point) too greatly ◇ **laboured** *adj* showing signs of effort ◇ **labourer** *noun* someone who does heavy unskilled work ◇ **Labour Party** one of the chief political parties of Great Britain

■ *noun* **1** work, task, job, chore, toil, effort, exertion **2** workers, employees, workforce, labourers ◇ *verb* **3** overdo, overemphasize, dwell on, elaborate, overstress

labrador *noun* a large black or fawn-coloured dog, often used for retrieving game

laburnum *noun* a tree with large clusters of yellow flowers and poisonous seeds

labyrinth *noun* a maze

lace *noun* **1** a cord for fastening shoes *etc* **2** decorative openwork fabric made with fine thread ◇ *verb* **1** fasten with a

lace **2** add alcohol to (a drink)

■ *noun* **1** string, cord, tie, shoelace, bootlace **2** netting, meshwork, openwork ◇ *verb* **1** tie, do up, fasten, thread, bind, attach, string **2** add to, mix in, *informal* spike

lacerate *verb* **1** tear, cut roughly **2** wound ◇ **laceration** *noun*

■ **1** tear, rip, rend, cut, gash, slash **2** wound, mangle, maim, torture

lachrymal *adj* of tears

lack *verb* be without or have too little of ◇ *noun* want, need

■ *noun* need, want, scarcity, shortage, insufficiency, deficiency, absence

🔁 *noun* abundance, profusion

lackadaisical *adj* bored, half-hearted ◇ **lackadaisically** *adv*

lackey *noun* (*plural* **lackeys**) **1** a manservant **2** someone who acts like a slave

lacklustre or *US* **lackluster** *adj* dull, insipid

■ drab, dull, flat, boring, leaden, lifeless, unimaginative, dim

🔁 brilliant, inspired

laconic *adj* using few words to express meaning ◇ **laconically** *adv*

■ terse, succinct, pithy, concise, crisp, taciturn, short, curt, brief

lacquer *noun* a varnish ◇ *verb* varnish

lacrosse *noun* a twelve-a-side ball game played with sticks having a shallow net at the end

lactate *verb* produce or secrete milk

lactic *adj* of milk

lactose *noun* (*also called* **milk sugar**) a sugar obtained by evaporating whey

lacuna *noun* (*plural* **lacunae**) a gap, a space

lad *noun* a boy, a young man

■ boy, youth, youngster, *informal* kid, schoolboy, chap, *informal* guy, fellow

ladder *noun* **1** a set of rungs or steps

between two supports, for climbing up or down **2** a run from a broken stitch in a stocking *etc*

laden *adj* loaded, burdened

lading *noun* a load; cargo

ladle *noun* a large spoon for lifting out liquid ◇ *verb* lift or serve with a ladle

lady *noun* (*plural* **ladies**) **1** a woman of good manners **2** (**Lady**) a title for the wife of a knight, lord or baronet, or a daughter of a member of the aristocracy **3** (**ladies**) a public lavatory for women ◇ **Her Ladyship** the title used in addressing a titled Lady

ladybird *noun* a small beetle, usually red with black spots

lag¹ *verb* (**lags, lagging, lagged**) move slowly and fall behind ◇ *noun* a delay

   ▣ *verb* dawdle, loiter, hang back, linger, straggle, trail, delay, shuffle, idle
   ▣ *verb* hurry, lead

lag² *verb* (**lags, lagging, lagged**) cover (a boiler or pipes) with insulation ◇ **lagging** *noun* insulating material for covering pipes *etc*

lager *noun* a light beer ◇ **lager lout** a drunken pugnacious youth

laggard *noun* someone who lags behind

lagoon *noun* a shallow stretch of water separated from the sea by low sandbanks, rocks *etc*

laid *past form of* **lay**¹ ◇ **get laid** *slang* have sexual intercourse

laid-back *adj, informal* relaxed, easygoing

laid-up *adj* ill in bed

lain *past participle of* **lie**²

lair *noun* the den of a wild beast
   ▣ den, burrow, hole, nest, hideout

   ⚠ Do not confuse with: **layer**

laird *noun* in Scotland, a landowner

laissez-faire /lɛseɪˈfɛə(r)/ *noun* a general principle of not interfering

laity *see* **lay**²

lake *noun* a large stretch of water surrounded by land

lama *noun* a Buddhist priest of Tibet

lamb *noun* **1** a young sheep **2** the meat of this animal **3** a gentle person

lambast *verb* beat or reprimand severely

lame *adj* **1** unable to walk, crippled **2** not good enough: *a lame excuse* ◇ *verb* make lame ◇ **lamely** *adv* ◇ **lameness** *noun* ◇ **lame duck** an inefficient or weak person or organization

   ▣ *adj* **1** disabled, handicapped, crippled, limping, hobbling **2** weak, feeble, flimsy, inadequate, unsatisfactory, poor
   ▣ **1** able-bodied **2** convincing

lamé /ˈlɑːmeɪ/ *noun* a fabric interwoven with metallic thread

lament *verb* **1** mourn, feel or express grief for **2** regret ◇ *noun* **1** a show of grief **2** a mournful poem or piece of music ◇ **lamentation** *noun*

   ▣ *verb* **1** grieve, sorrow, weep, wail **2** deplore, regret
   ▣ **1** rejoice, celebrate

lamentable *adj* **1** pitiful **2** very bad or inadequate ◇ **lamentably** *adv*

   ▣ **1** deplorable, regrettable, mournful, distressing, tragic, unfortunate, sorrowful **2** meagre, low, inadequate, insufficient, mean, unsatisfactory, poor, disappointing, *informal* pathetic

laminated *adj* made by putting layers together: *laminated glass*

Lammas *noun* 1 August, an old feast day celebrating the beginning of the harvest

lamp *noun* a device that gives out light, containing an electric bulb, candle *etc* ◇ **lamp-post** *noun* a pillar supporting a street lamp

lampoon *noun* a piece of ridicule or satire directed at someone ◇ *verb* ridicule, satirize

   ▣ *noun* satire, caricature, parody, *informal* send-up, spoof, *informal* take-off, burlesque ◇ *verb* satirize, caricature, parody, send up, *informal* take off, ridicule, mock

lamprey *noun* (*plural* **lampreys**) a type of fish like an eel

lance *noun* a long shaft of wood with a

spearhead ◇ *verb* cut open (a boil *etc*) with a knife ◇ **lance-corporal** *noun* a soldier of the rank below a corporal

lancet *noun* a sharp surgical instrument

land *noun* 1 the solid portion of the earth's surface; ground or soil 2 a country: *from foreign lands* 3 a part of a country; an area of ground ◇ *verb* 1 arrive on land or on shore 2 set (an aircraft, ship *etc*) on land or on shore ◇ **landed** *adj* owning much land: *landed gentry*
■ *noun* 1 earth, ground, soil, terra firma 3 region, territory, province, estate ◇ *verb* 1 alight, disembark, wind up, end up, drop, settle 2 dock, berth, touch down, deposit, drop

landau *noun, hist* a horse-drawn carriage with a removable top

landfall *noun* 1 an approach to land after a voyage 2 the land approached

landing *noun* 1 a coming ashore or to ground 2 a place for getting on shore 3 the level part of a staircase between the flights of steps or at the top

landlocked *adj* shut in by land

landlord, landlady *noun* 1 the owner of land or accommodation for rent 2 the owner or manager of a pub *etc*
■ 1 owner, proprietor 2 proprietor, host, publican, innkeeper, hotel-keeper

landlubber *noun* someone who works on land and knows little about the sea

landmark *noun* 1 an object on land that serves as a guide 2 an important event
■ 1 feature, monument, signpost, milestone, beacon 2 turning-point, milestone

land mine a bomb laid on or near the surface of the ground which explodes when someone passes over it

landscape *noun* a painting, photograph *etc* of inland scenery ◇ **landscape gardening** gardening for picturesque effect
■ scene, scenery, view, panorama, vista, prospect, countryside, aspect

landslide *noun* 1 a mass of land that slips down a hill 2 an election in which a great mass of votes goes to one side

lane *noun* 1 a narrow street or passage 2 a part of the road, sea or air to which cars, ships, aircraft *etc* must keep

language *noun* 1 words used for communication 2 the words used by a particular people or nation
■ 1 speech, talk, discourse, expression, utterance, diction 2 speech, vocabulary, terminology, tongue

---

Language terms include:
brogue, dialect, idiolect, idiom, patois, tongue, pidgin, creole, lingua franca, vernacular, argot, cant, jargon, doublespeak, gobbledygook, buzzword, journalese, *informal* lingo, patter, slang, cockney rhyming slang; etymology, lexicography, linguistics, phonetics, semantics, syntax, usage, grammar, orthography, sociolinguistics; language engineering, natural language processing, machine translation, speech recognition

---

languid *adj* lacking liveliness and spirit

languish *verb* 1 grow weak, droop 2 long (for) ◇ **languishing** *adj*
■ 1 wilt, droop, fade, fail, flag, wither, waste away, weaken, sink, faint, decline, mope, grieve, sorrow, sigh, sicken 2 pine, yearn, want, long, desire, hanker, hunger

languor *noun* a languid state, listlessness

laniard *another spelling of* **lanyard**

lank *adj* 1 tall and thin 2 of hair: straight and limp

lanky *adj* tall and thin
■ gaunt, gangling, scrawny, tall, thin, scraggy, weedy
◪ short, squat

lanolin *noun* a fat extracted from sheep's wool

lantern *noun* a case for holding or carrying a light ◇ **lantern-jawed** *adj* having hollow cheeks and long jaws

lanyard or **laniard** noun **1** a short rope used for fastening on a ship **2** a cord for hanging a whistle etc round the neck

lap¹ verb (**laps**, **lapping**, **lapped**) **1** lick up with the tongue **2** wash or flow against (a shore etc) **3** (with **up**) accept (praise etc) greedily
■ verb **1** drink, sip, sup, lick

lap² noun the front part, from waist to knees, of someone seated

lap³ noun **1** one round of a racetrack or competition course **2** a fold ◊ verb **1** wrap round, surround **2** get a lap ahead of in a race
■ noun **1** circuit, round, orbit, tour, loop, course, circle ◊ verb **1** wrap, fold, envelop, enfold, swathe, surround, cover, swaddle, overlap

laparoscope noun a long optical tube used for examining internal organs without cutting ◊ **laparoscopy** noun surgical examination with a laparoscope

lapdog noun a small pet dog

lapel noun the part of a coat joined to the collar and folded back on the chest

lapidary noun (plural **lapidaries**) someone who cuts, polishes and shapes gems and stones ◊ adj engraved on stone

lapis lazuli a deep-blue stone containing several minerals

lapsang souchong a Chinese tea with a smoky flavour

lapse verb **1** fall into bad habits **2** cease, be no longer valid ◊ noun **1** a mistake, a failure **2** a period of time passing
■ verb **1** decline, fall, sink, drop, deteriorate, slide, slip, fail, worsen, degenerate, backslide **2** expire, run out, end, stop, terminate ◊ noun **1** error, slip, mistake, negligence, omission, oversight, fault, failing, indiscretion, aberration, relapse

laptop noun a compact portable computer combining screen, keyboard and processor in one unit

lapwing noun (also called **peewit**) a type of bird of the plover family

larceny noun stealing, theft

larch noun (plural **larches**) a cone-bearing deciduous tree

lard noun the melted fat of a pig ◊ verb **1** put strips of bacon in meat before cooking **2** smear, lay on thickly

larder noun **1** a room or place where food is kept **2** a stock of food

large adj great in size, amount etc ◊ **largely** adv mainly, to a great extent ◊ **largeness** noun ◊ **at large 1** at liberty, free **2** in general: the public at large
■ big, huge, immense, massive, vast, sizable, great, giant, gigantic, bulky, enormous, informal mega, broad, considerable, monumental, substantial, full, extensive, generous, roomy, plentiful, spacious, grand, sweeping ◊ **largely** mainly, principally, chiefly, generally, primarily, predominantly, mostly, considerably, widely, extensively
🗲 small, tiny

largesse noun a generous giving away of money etc

largo adj & adv, music (to be played) in a broad and slow manner

lariat noun **1** a rope for fastening horses while they are grazing **2** a lasso

lark¹ noun a general name for several kinds of singing bird

lark² noun a piece of fun or mischief ◊ verb fool about, behave mischievously
■ noun escapade, antic, fling, prank, romp, revel, mischief, frolic, caper, game

larkspur noun a tall plant with blue, white or pink spurred flowers, a kind of delphinium

larva noun (plural **larvae**) an insect in its first stage after coming out of the egg, a grub

laryngitis noun inflammation of the larynx

larynx noun (plural **larynxes** or **larynges**) the upper part of the windpipe containing the vocal cords

lasagne noun **1** flat sheets of pasta **2** a baked dish made with this

lascivious *adj* lustful; indecent, lewd
◇ **lasciviously** *adv* ◇ **lasciviousness** *noun*

laser *noun* **1** a very narrow powerful beam of light **2** an instrument that concentrates light into such a beam

An acronym of 'light amplification by stimulated emission of radiation'

lash *noun* (*plural* **lashes**) **1** a thong or cord of a whip **2** a stroke with a whip **3** an eyelash ◇ *verb* **1** strike with a whip **2** fasten tightly with a rope *etc* **3** attack with bitter words ◇ **lash out 1** kick or hit out suddenly **2** speak angrily **3** spend extravagantly

◼ *noun* **2** blow, whip, stroke, swipe, hit ◇ *verb* **1** whip, flog, beat, hit, thrash, strike, scourge **2** tie, bind, fasten, secure, join, affix, rope, tether, strap **3** attack, criticize, lay into, scold

lass *noun* (*plural* **lasses**) a girl

lassitude *noun* lack of energy, weariness

lasso *noun* (*plural* **lassoes** or **lassos**) a long rope with a loop that tightens when the rope is pulled, used for catching wild horses *etc* ◇ *verb* (**lassoes**, **lassoing**, **lassoed**) catch with a lasso

last¹ *adj* **1** coming after all the others: *the last person to arrive* **2** the final one remaining: *the last ticket* **3** most recent: *my last employer* ◇ *adv* **1** at the end **2** most recently ◇ *noun* a foot-shaped tool on which shoes are made or repaired ◇ **lastly** *adv* finally ◇ **at last** in the end ◇ **last rites** religious ceremonies performed for the dying ◇ **last straw** the last in a series of unpleasant events, which makes a situation unbearable ◇ **last word** the final comment or decision about something ◇ **on your last legs** completely worn out, about to collapse ◇ **to the last** to the end

◼ *adj* **1** final, latest, rearmost, terminal, furthest, concluding, remotest ◇ *adv* **1** finally, ultimately, behind, after ◇ **at last** eventually, finally, in the end, in due course, at length

◪ *adj* **1** first, initial ◇ *verb* **1** cease, stop, fade

last² *verb* **1** continue, go on **2** remain in good condition

◼ **1** continue, endure, remain, persist, keep (on) **2** survive, hold out, wear

latch *noun* (*plural* **latches**) **1** a wooden or metal catch used to fasten a door **2** a type of door lock ◇ *verb* fasten with a latch ◇ **latchkey** *noun* a key used to raise the latch of a door ◇ **latchkey child** a child who regularly returns home to an empty house

late *adj* **1** coming after the expected time: *his train was late* **2** far on in time: *it's getting late* **3** recent: *our late disagreement* **4** recently dead: *the late author* **5** recently, but no longer, holding an office or position: *the late chairman* ◇ *adv* **1** after the expected time **2** far on in time: *He arrived late on Thursday* **3** recently: *sent as late as this morning* ◇ **lately** *adv* recently ◇ **lateness** *noun* ◇ **of late** recently

◼ *adj* **1** overdue, behind, slow, unpunctual, delayed, last-minute **3** recent, up-to-date, current, fresh, new ◇ **lately** recently, of late, latterly

◪ *adj* **1** early, punctual

latent *adj* hidden, undeveloped as yet: *latent ability/latent hostility*

◼ potential, dormant, undeveloped, unrealized, lurking, unexpressed, unseen, secret, concealed, hidden, invisible, underlying, veiled

◪ active, conspicuous

lateral *adj* of, at, to or from the side ◇ **lateral thinking** looking at a problem in new ways rather than proceeding in logical stages

latex *noun* the milky juice of plants, *esp* of the rubber tree

lath /lɑːθ/ *noun* a thin narrow strip of wood

❗ Do not confuse: **lath** and **lathe**

lathe /leɪð/ *noun* a machine for turning and shaping articles of wood, metal *etc*

lather *noun* **1** foam or froth, *eg* from soap and water **2** *informal* a state of agitation ◇ *verb* cover with lather

◼ *noun* **1** foam, suds, soap-suds, froth,

bubbles, soap, shampoo **2** agitation, fluster, fuss, *informal* state, flutter, *informal* flap, fever

Latin *noun* the language of ancient Rome

latitude *noun* **1** the distance, measured in degrees, of a place north or south of the equator (*compare with:* **longitude**) **2** freedom of action or choice: *the new job allows him far more latitude than his previous one*

■ **2** freedom, liberty, licence, leeway, indulgence

latrine *noun* a toilet in a camp, barracks *etc*

latter *adj* **1** the last of two things mentioned (*contrasted with:* **former**): *between working and sleeping, I prefer the latter* **2** recent ◇ **latterly** *adv* recently ◇ **latter-day** *adj* of recent times

■ **1** last-mentioned, last, later, closing, concluding, ensuing, succeeding, successive, second

lattice *noun* **1** a network of crossed wooden *etc* strips **2** a window constructed this way

laud *verb, formal* praise ◇ **laudatory** *adj* expressing praise

laudable *adj* worthy of being praised ◇ **laudably** *adv*

laudanum /lɔːdənəm/ *noun* a solution prepared from opium

laugh *verb* make sounds with the voice in showing amusement, scorn *etc* ◇ *noun* a sound of laughing ◇ **laughable** *adj* ridiculous ◇ **laughably** *adv* ◇ **laughing stock** an object of scornful laughter

■ *verb* chuckle, giggle, guffaw, snigger, titter, chortle, *informal* fall about, *informal* crease up ◇ *noun* giggle, chuckle, snigger, titter, guffaw, chortle, *informal* scream ◇ **laughable** farcical, ridiculous, absurd, ludicrous, preposterous, nonsensical

laughter *noun* the act or noise of laughing

■ laughing, giggling, chuckling, chortling, guffawing, tittering, hilarity, amusement, merriment, mirth, glee, convulsions

launch *verb* **1** slide (a boat or ship) into water, *esp* on its first voyage **2** fire off (a rocket *etc*) **3** start (something or someone) off on a course **4** put (a product) on the market with publicity **5** throw, hurl ◇ *noun* (*plural* **launches**) **1** the act of launching **2** a large motor boat

■ *verb* **1** float, set in motion **2** send off, project, fire **3** begin, commence, start, embark on, establish, found, open, initiate, inaugurate, introduce, instigate

launder *verb* wash and iron clothes *etc*

launderette *noun* a shop where customers may wash clothes *etc* in washing machines

laundry *noun* (*plural* **laundries**) **1** a place where clothes *etc* are washed **2** clothes *etc* to be washed

laurel *noun* **1** the bay tree, from which ceremonial wreaths were made **2** (**laurels**) honours or victories gained ◇ **rest on your laurels** be content with past successes and not try for any more

lava *noun* molten rock *etc* thrown out by a volcano, becoming solid as it cools

lavatory *noun* (*plural* **lavatories**) a toilet

lavender *noun* **1** a sweet-smelling plant with small pale purple flowers **2** a pale purple colour

lavish *verb* spend or give very freely ◇ *adj* **1** very generous **2** abundant

■ *adj* **1** generous, liberal, open-handed, extravagant, fulsome, thriftless, prodigal **2** abundant, lush, luxuriant, plentiful, profuse, unlimited, prolific

law *noun* **1** the official rules which apply in a country or state **2** one such rule **3** a scientific rule stating the conditions under which certain things always happen ◇ **lawful** *adj* allowed by law ◇ **lawfully** *adv* ◇ **lawless** *adj* **1** ignoring or breaking the law **2** having no laws ◇ **law court** a place where people accused of crimes are tried

■ **2** rule, act, decree, edict, order, statute, regulation, command **3** principle, axiom, criterion, standard, precept, formula, code, canon ◇ **lawful** legal, legitimate, permissible, legalized, authorized, allowable, warranted, valid, proper, rightful

▣ **lawful** illegal, unlawful, illicit

law-abiding *adj* obeying the law

▤ obedient, upright, orderly, lawful, honest, honourable, decent, good

lawn[1] *noun* an area of smooth grass *eg* as part of a garden ◊ **lawn tennis** tennis played on a hard or grass court

lawn[2] *noun* a kind of fine linen

lawnmower *noun* a machine for cutting grass

lawsuit *noun* a quarrel or dispute to be settled by a court of law

lawyer *noun* someone whose work it is to give advice in matters of law

lax *adj* **1** not strict **2** careless, negligent ◊ **laxity** or **laxness** *noun*

▤ **1** casual, easy-going, slack, lenient **2** negligent, remiss

laxative *noun* a medicine which loosens the bowels

lay[1] *verb* (**lays, laying, laid**) **1** place or set down **2** put (*eg* a burden, duty) on someone **3** cause to lie **4** cause to leave or subside: *lay a ghost* **5** set in order, arrange **6** of a hen: produce (eggs) **7** bet, wager ◊ **lay about someone** beat them all over ◊ **lay down 1** assert: *laying down the law* **2** store (*eg* wine) ◊ **lay off 1** dismiss (workers) temporarily **2** *informal* stop: *lay off arguing* ◊ **lay up** store for future use ◊ **lay waste** ruin, destroy

▤ **1** put, place, deposit, set down, settle, lodge, plant, set, establish, leave **5** arrange, position, set out, locate, work out, devise, prepare ◊ **lay off 1** dismiss, discharge, make redundant, *informal* sack, pay off, let go **2** give up, drop, stop, quit, cease, let up

❗ Do not confuse with: **lie**

lay[2] *adj* **1** not of the clergy **2** without special training in a particular subject ◊ **laity** *noun* ordinary people, not clergymen ◊ **layman, laywoman** *noun* someone without special training in a subject

lay[3] *noun, old* a short poem or song

layabout *noun* a lazy idle person

layby *noun* a parking area at the side of a road

layer *noun* a thickness forming a covering or level ◊ **layered** *adj* having a number of distinct layers: *layered cake*

▤ cover, coating, coat, covering, film, blanket, mantle, sheet, stratum, seam, thickness, bed, plate, row

❗ Do not confuse with: **lair**

layette *noun* a complete outfit for a baby

laze *verb* be lazy; idle

▤ idle, *informal* loaf, lounge, sit around, lie around, loll

lazy *adj* (**lazier, laziest**) not inclined to work; idle ◊ **lazily** *adv* ◊ **laziness** *noun* ◊ **lazybones** *noun sing, informal* an idler

▤ idle, slothful, slack, inactive, lethargic

▣ industrious

lb *abbrev* pound(s) (in weight)

lbw *abbrev, cricket* leg before wicket

lea *noun, old* a meadow

leach *verb* seep slowly through or out of something

❗ Do not confuse with: **leech**

lead[1] /liːd/ *verb* (**leads, leading, led**) **1** show the way by going first **2** direct, guide **3** persuade **4** live (a busy, quiet *etc* life) **5** of a road: go (to) ◊ *noun* **1** the first or front place **2** guidance, direction **3** a leash for a dog *etc* ◊ **leading question** one asked in such a way as to suggest the desired answer

▤ *verb* **2** guide, conduct, escort, steer, pilot, usher **3** influence, persuade, incline

lead[2] /lɛd/ *noun* **1** a soft bluish-grey metal **2** the part of a pencil that writes, actually made of graphite **3** a weight used for sounding depths at sea *etc* ◊ **lead-free** *adj* of petrol: unleaded

leaden *adj* **1** made of lead **2** lead-coloured **3** dull, heavy

leader *noun* **1** someone who leads or goes first; a chief **2** a column in a newspaper expressing the editor's opinions

◇ **leadership** *noun* **1** the state of being a leader **2** the ability to lead

■ **1** head, chief, director, ruler, principal, commander, *informal* boss, superior, ringleader, guide, conductor

leaf *noun* (*plural* **leaves**) **1** a flat green part of a plant growing from the side of a stem **2** a page of a book **3** a hinged flap on a table *etc* ◇ **leafy** *adj* ◇ **turn over a new leaf** begin again and do better

leaflet *noun* a small printed sheet

league ¹ *noun* **1** a union of people, nations *etc* for the benefit of each other **2** an association of clubs for games ◇ **in league with** allied with

■ **1** association, confederation, alliance, union, federation, confederacy, coalition

league ² *noun*, *old* a measure of distance, approximately 3 miles (about 4.8 kilometres)

leak *noun* **1** an unwanted hole through which liquid or gas passes **2** an escape of liquid, gas *etc* **3** a release of secret information ◇ *verb* **1** escape, pass out **2** give (secret information) to the media *etc* ◇ **leakage** *noun* the act or result of leaking

■ *noun* **1** crack, hole, opening, puncture, crevice, chink **2** leakage, seepage, drip ◇ *verb* **1** seep, drip, ooze, escape, spill, trickle, exude, discharge **2** divulge, disclose, reveal, let slip, make known, make public, tell, give away, pass on

lean ¹ *verb* (**leans**, **leaning**, **leant**) **1** slope over to one side **2** rest (against) **3** rely (on) ◇ **lean-to** *noun* a shed *etc* built against another building or wall

■ *verb* **1** slant, slope, bend, tilt, list, tend, incline **2** recline, prop, rest

lean ² *adj* **1** thin **2** poor, scanty **3** of meat: with little fat

■ **1** thin, skinny, bony, gaunt, lank, angular, slim, scrawny, emaciated **2** scanty, inadequate, bare, barren

leaning *noun* a liking for, or interest in, something

■ tendency, inclination, propensity, partiality, liking, bias, disposition

leap *verb* (**leaps**, **leaping**, **leapt**) **1** move with jumps **2** jump (over) ◇ *noun* a jump ◇ **leap year** a year which has 366 days (February having 29), occurring every fourth year

■ *verb* **1** skip, hop, bounce, prance, caper, gambol **2** jump (over), bound, spring, vault, clear

leapfrog *noun* a game in which one player leaps over another's bent back

learn *verb* (**learns**, **learning**, **learnt** or **learned**) **1** get to know (something) **2** gain skill **3** discover ◇ **learned** *adj* having or showing great knowledge ◇ **learner** *noun* ◇ **learning** *noun* knowledge

■ **1** grasp, comprehend, understand, gather, assimilate, discern **2** master, acquire, pick up **3** find out, ascertain, hear, detect, determine ◇ **learned** scholarly, well-informed, well-read, cultured, academic, lettered, literate, intellectual, versed ◇ **learner** novice, beginner, student, trainee, pupil, scholar, apprentice

🖪 **learned** uneducated, illiterate

lease *noun* **1** an agreement giving the use of a house *etc* on payment of rent **2** the period of this agreement ◇ *verb* let or rent

leaseback *noun* an arrangement in which the buyer of a property leases it back to the seller

leasehold *noun* property or land held by lease

leash *noun* (*plural* **leashes**) a strip of leather, cord or chain by which a dog *etc* is held *eg* when walking ◇ *verb* put (a dog *etc*) on a leash

least *adj & noun* the smallest amount of anything: *he had the least money* ◇ *adv* (often with **the**) the smallest or lowest degree: *I like her least* ◇ **at least** at any rate, anyway ◇ **not in the least** not at all

■ *adj* smallest, lowest, minimum, fewest, slightest, poorest

leather *noun* the skin of an animal, prepared by tanning for use ◇ *verb* beat ◇ **leathering** *noun* a thrashing ◇ **leathery** *adj* like leather; tough

leave ¹ *verb* (**leaves**, **leaving**, **left**) **1**

depart (from) **2** allow to remain **3** abandon, forsake **4** hand down to someone in a will **5** give over to someone's responsibility, care *etc*: *leave the choice to her* ◇ **leavings** *noun plural* things left over and unwanted

■ **1** depart, go, go away, set out, take off, exit, move, quit, retire, withdraw, pull out, disappear **3** abandon, desert, forsake, give up, drop, relinquish, renounce, surrender **4** bequeath, will, hand down, leave behind **5** commit, entrust, consign

leave **2** *noun* **1** permission to do something (*eg* be absent) **2** a holiday, *esp* from work ◇ **take your leave of 1** part from **2** say goodbye to

■ **1** permission, authorization, consent, allowance, sanction, concession, indulgence, liberty, freedom **2** holiday, time off, vacation, sabbatical

◨ **1** refusal, rejection

leaven *noun* yeast ◇ **leavened** *adj* raised with yeast

lecher *noun* a lustful man ◇ **lecherous** *adj* lustful in a sexual way ◇ **lechery** *noun*

lectern *noun* a stand for a book to be read from

lecture *noun* **1** a talk about a certain subject given to an audience **2** a scolding ◇ *verb* **1** deliver a lecture **2** scold ◇ **lecturer** *noun* someone who lectures, *esp* to students

■ *noun* **1** discourse, address, lesson, speech, talk, instruction **2** reprimand, rebuke, reproof, scolding, chiding, *informal* telling-off, *informal* talking-to, *informal* dressing-down

LED *abbrev* light-emitting diode

led *past form of* **lead¹**

ledge *noun* **1** a shelf or projecting rim: *window ledge* **2** an underwater ridge

■ **1** shelf, sill, mantle, ridge, projection, step

ledger *noun* the accounts book of an office or shop

lee *noun* the side away from the wind, the sheltered side

leech *noun* (*plural* **leeches**) a kind of blood-sucking worm

⚠ Do not confuse with: **leach**

leek *noun* a long green and white vegetable of the onion family

leer *noun* a sly, sidelong or lustful look ◇ *verb* look sideways or lustfully (at) ◇

lees *noun plural* dregs that settle at the bottom of liquid, *esp* wine

leeward *adj & adv* in the direction towards which the wind blows

leeway *noun* **1** a ship's drift off course **2** lost time, ground *etc*: *a lot of leeway to make up* **3** room to manoeuvre, latitude

■ **3** space, room, latitude, elbow-room, play, scope

left¹ *adj* on or of the side of the body that in most people has the less skilful hand (*contrasted with*: **right**) ◇ *adv* on or towards the left side ◇ *noun* **1** the left side **2** a political grouping with left-wing ideas *etc*

left² *past form of* **leave**

left-field *adj*, *informal* odd, eccentric

left-handed *adj* **1** using the left hand rather than the right **2** awkward

left-wing *adj* of or holding socialist or radical political views, ideas *etc*

leg *noun* **1** one of the limbs by which humans and animals walk **2** a long slender support for a table *etc* **3** one stage in a journey, contest *etc*

legacy *noun* (*plural* **legacies**) **1** something which is left by will **2** something left behind by the previous occupant of a house, job *etc*

■ **1** bequest, endowment, gift, heritage, heritance, inheritance, birthright, estate, heirloom

legal *adj* **1** allowed by law, lawful **2** of law ◇ **legalize** *verb* make lawful

■ **1** lawful, legitimate, permissible, allowed, authorized, allowable, legalized, constitutional, valid, warranted, aboveboard, proper, rightful

Legal terms include:
courts: county court, courthouse, courtroom, Court of Appeal, Court of Protection, Court of Session, Crown Court, European Court of

Human Rights, European Court of Justice, High Court of Justice, House of Lords, International Court of Justice, juvenile court, magistrates' court, Old Bailey, sheriff court, small claims court, *US* Supreme Court; *criminal law*: acquittal, age of consent, alibi, arrest, bail, caution, charge, confession, contempt of court, dock, fine, guilty, indictment, innocent, malice aforethought, pardon, parole, plead guilty, plead not guilty, prisoner, probation, remand, reprieve, sentence; *marriage and divorce*: adultery, alimony, annulment, bigamy, decree absolute, decree nisi, divorce, maintenance, settlement; *people*: accessory, accomplice, accused, advocate, Attorney General, barrister, *informal* brief, clerk of the court, client, commissioner for oaths, convict, coroner, criminal, defendant, Director of Public Prosecutions, DPP, executor, felon, judge, jury, justice of the peace, JP, juvenile, Law Lord, lawyer, Lord Advocate, Lord Chancellor, Lord Chief Justice, liquidator, magistrate, notary public, offender, plaintiff, procurator fiscal, receiver, Queen's Counsel, QC, sheriff, solicitor, witness, young offender; *property or ownership*: asset, conveyance, copyright, deed, easement, endowment, estate, exchange of contracts, fee simple, foreclosure, freehold, inheritance, intestacy, lease, leasehold, legacy, local search, mortgage, patent, tenancy, title, trademark, will; *miscellaneous*: act of God, Act of Parliament, adjournment, affidavit, agreement, allegation, amnesty, appeal, arbitration, bar, Bill of Rights, bench, brief, by-law, charter, civil law, claim, codicil, common law, constitution, contract, covenant, cross-examine, courtcase, court martial, custody, damages, defence, demand, equity, eviction, evidence, extradition, grant, hearing, hung jury, indemnity,

injunction, inquest, inquiry, judgement, judiciary, lawsuit, legal aid, liability, mandate, misadventure, miscarriage of justice, oath, party, penalty, power of attorney, precedent, probate, proceedings, proof, proxy, public inquiry, repeal, sanction, settlement, statute, subpoena, sue, summons, testimony, trial, tribunal, verdict, waiver, ward of court, warrant, will, writ

legalism *noun* rigid adherence to the law or rules ◇ **legalist** *noun* ◇ **legalistic** *adj* sticking rigidly to the law or rules

legality *noun* (*plural* **legalities**) the state of being legal

legate *noun* an ambassador, *esp* from the Pope

legatee *noun* someone to whom a legacy is left

legation *noun* an official body of people acting on behalf of their government abroad

legato *adj & adv, music* (to be played) smoothly

legend *noun* **1** a traditional story handed down, a myth **2** a caption ◇ **legendary** *adj* **1** of legend **2** famous **3** not to be believed

▤ **1** myth, story, tale, folk-tale, fable, fiction, narrative **2** inscription, caption, key, motto ◇ **legendary 1** mythical, fabulous **2** famous, celebrated, renowned, well-known

legerdemain /lɛdʒədə'meɪn/ *noun* conjuring by quickness of the hand

leggings *noun plural* close-fitting coverings for the legs

leggy *adj* having long legs

legible *adj* able to be read easily ◇ **legibility** *noun* ◇ **legibly** *adv*

▤ readable, intelligible, decipherable, clear, distinct, neat

legion *noun, hist* **1** a body of from 3000 to 6000 Roman soldiers **2** a great many ◇ **legionary** *noun* (*plural* **legionaries**) a soldier of a legion

legionnaire's disease a serious

disease similar to pneumonia caused by a bacterium

> So called after an outbreak of the disease at an American *Legion* convention in 1976

legislate *verb* make laws ◇ **legislation** *noun* **1** the making of laws **2** a law or laws ◇ **legislator** *noun* someone who makes laws

legislative *adj* law-making

legislature *noun* the part of the government which has the powers of making laws

legitimate *adj* **1** lawful **2** of a child: born of parents married to each other **3** correct, reasonable ◇ **legitimacy** *noun*
≡ **1** legal, lawful, authorized, statutory, rightful, proper, correct, real **3** reasonable, sensible, admissible, acceptable, justifiable, warranted, well-founded, valid, true

legless *adj, informal* drunk

legroom *noun* room for the legs, *eg* between rows of seats

legume *noun* a plant of the pea or bean family

leisure *noun* time free from work, spare time ◇ **leisured** *adj* not occupied with business ◇ **leisurely** *adj* unhurried: *leisurely pace*
≡ relaxation, rest, spare time, time off, ease, freedom, liberty, recreation, retirement, holiday, vacation ◇ **leisurely** unhurried, slow, relaxed, comfortable, easy, tranquil, restful, gentle, carefree, *informal* laid-back, lazy
✂ **leisurely** rushed, hectic

leitmotif or **leitmotiv** /ˈlaɪtmoʊtiːf/ *noun* **1** a musical theme in an opera associated with a particular character *etc* **2** a recurring theme

lemming *noun* **1** a small rat-like animal of the arctic regions, reputed to follow others of its kind over cliffs *etc* when migrating **2** someone who follows others unquestioningly

lemon *noun* **1** an oval fruit with pale yellow rind and sour juice **2** the tree which bears this fruit

lemonade *noun* a soft drink flavoured with lemons

lemur *noun* an animal related to the monkey with a pointed nose, large eyes and a long bushy tail

lend *verb* (**lends, lending, lent**) **1** give use of (something) for a time **2** give or add (a quality) to someone or something: *his presence lent an air of respectability to the occasion* ◇ **lend itself to** be suitable for, adapt easily to
≡ **1** loan, advance **2** give, grant, bestow, provide, furnish, confer, supply, impart, contribute

length *noun* **1** extent from end to end in space or time **2** the quality of being long **3** a great extent **4** a piece of cloth *etc* ◇ **lengthen** *verb* make or grow longer ◇ **at length 1** in detail **2** at last
≡ **1** extent, distance, measure, reach, duration, period, term, stretch, span ◇ **lengthen** stretch, extend, elongate, draw out, prolong, spin out, increase, expand, continue
✂ **lengthen** reduce, shorten

lengthways or **lengthwise** *adv* in the direction of the length

lengthy *adj* **1** long **2** tiresomely long
≡ **1** long, prolonged, extended, lengthened **2** long-winded, rambling, diffuse, verbose, drawn-out, interminable
✂ **2** brief, concise

lenient *adj* merciful, punishing only lightly ◇ **lenience** or **leniency** *noun*
≡ tolerant, forbearing, sparing, indulgent, merciful, forgiving, soft-hearted, kind, mild, gentle, compassionate
✂ strict, severe

lens *noun* (*plural* **lenses**) **1** a piece of glass curved on one or both sides, used in spectacles, cameras *etc* **2** a part of the eye

Lent *noun* in the Christian church, a period of fasting before Easter, lasting forty days

lent *past form* of **lend**

lentil *noun* the seed of a pod-bearing plant, used in soups *etc*

leonine *adj* like a lion

leopard *noun* a large wild animal of

the cat family with a spotted skin ◇ **leopardess** *noun* a female leopard

leotard *noun* a tight-fitting garment worn for dancing, gymnastics *etc*

leper *noun* **1** someone with leprosy **2** an outcast ◇ **leprosy** *noun* a contagious skin disease causing thickening or numbness in the skin

lepidopterist *noun* someone who studies butterflies and moths

leprechaun *noun* a mischievous elf in Irish folklore

lesbian *noun* a female homosexual ◇ *adj* of a woman: homosexual

lesion *noun* a wound

less *adj* **1** not as much: *take less time* **2** smaller: *think of a number less than 40* ◇ *adv* not as much, to a smaller extent: *he goes less often than he should* ◇ *noun* a smaller amount: *he has less than I have* ◇ *prep* minus: *5 less 2 equals 3* ◇ **lessen** *verb* make or become less ◇ **lesser** *adj* smaller

■ **lessen** decrease, reduce, diminish, lower, ease, abate, contract, die down, dwindle, lighten, slow down, weaken, shrink, minimize, narrow, moderate, slack, flag, fail, deaden, impair ◇ **lesser** lower, secondary, inferior, smaller, subordinate, slighter, minor

■ **lessen** grow, increase

lessee *noun* someone with a lease for a property, business *etc*

lesson *noun* **1** something which is learned or taught **2** a period of teaching **3** a part of the Bible read in church

■ **2** class, period, instruction, lecture, tutorial, teaching, coaching

lest *conj* for fear that, in case

let *verb* (**lets**, **letting**, **let**) **1** allow **2** grant use of (*eg* a house, shop) in return for payment ◇ **let down** fail to act as expected by, disappoint ◇ **let off** excuse, not punish ◇ **let up** become less

■ **1** permit, allow, give leave, give permission, authorize, consent to, agree to, sanction, grant, enable, tolerate **2** lease, hire, rent ◇ **let off** excuse, absolve, pardon, forgive, acquit, spare, ignore, liberate, release ◇ **let up** abate,

subside, ease (up), slacken, diminish, decrease

■ **1** prohibit, forbid

lethal *adj* causing death

■ fatal, deadly, deathly, mortal, dangerous, poisonous, noxious, destructive, devastating

■ harmless, safe

lethargy *noun* a lack of energy or interest; sleepiness ◇ **lethargic** *adj*

■ listlessness, sluggishness, dullness, inertia, slowness, apathy, inaction, indifference, sleepiness, drowsiness, stupor

■ liveliness

letter *noun* **1** a mark representing a sound **2** a written message **3** (**letters**) learning: *a woman of letters* ◇ **to the letter** according to the exact meaning of the words: *following instructions to the letter*

■ **2** note, message, line, missive, communication, chit, acknowledgement

lettering *noun* the way in which letters are formed

lettuce *noun* a kind of green plant whose leaves are used in a salad

leucocyte *noun* a white blood corpuscle

leukaemia *noun* a cancerous disease of the white blood cells in the body

levee *noun*, *US* a river embankment

level *noun* **1** a flat, smooth, horizontal surface **2** a height, position *etc* in comparison with some standard: *water level* **3** an instrument for showing whether a surface is level: *spirit level* **4** personal rank or degree of understanding: *a bit above my level* ◇ *adj* **1** flat, smooth **2** horizontal **3** equal ◇ *verb* (**levels**, **levelling**, **levelled**) **1** make flat, smooth or horizontal **2** make equal **3** aim (a gun *etc*) **4** pull down (a building *etc*) ◇ **level crossing** a place where a road crosses a railway track ◇ **level playing-field** a position of equality from which to compete fairly

■ *noun* **2** height, elevation, altitude **4** position, rank, status, class, degree, grade, standard, standing ◇ *adj* **1** flat, smooth, even, plane ◇ *verb* **4** demolish, destroy, devastate, flatten, knock down, pull down, bulldoze, tear down

level-headed *adj* having good sense

■ calm, balanced, even-tempered, sensible, steady, reasonable, composed, cool, unflappable, sane, dependable

lever *noun* **1** a bar of metal, wood *etc* used to raise or shift something heavy **2** a handle for operating a machine **3** a method of gaining advantage

leverage *noun* **1** the use of a lever **2** power, influence

leveret *noun* a young hare

leviathan *noun* **1** a huge mythological sea monster **2** anything huge or powerful

levitation *noun* the illusion of raising a heavy body in the air without support ◇ **levitate** *verb* (cause to) float in the air

levity *noun* lack of seriousness, frivolity

■ light-heartedness, frivolity, facetiousness, flippancy, irreverence, triviality, silliness

◼ seriousness

levy *verb* (**levies, levying, levied**) collect by order (*eg* a tax, army conscripts) ◇ *noun* (*plural* **levies**) money, troops *etc* collected by order

■ *verb* tax, impose, exact, demand, charge ◇ *noun* tax, toll, subscription, contribution, duty, fee, tariff, collection

lewd *adj* taking delight in indecent thoughts or acts ◇ **lewdness** *noun*

■ obscene, smutty, indecent, pornographic, salacious, licentious, lascivious, impure, vulgar, unchaste, lustful

◼ decent, chaste

lexical *adj* of words

lexicographer *noun* someone who compiles or edits a dictionary ◇ **lexicography** *noun*

lexicon *noun* **1** a dictionary **2** a glossary of terms

liability *noun* (*plural* **liabilities**) **1** legal responsibility **2** a debt **3** someone or something which is a problem

■ **1** accountability, duty, obligation, responsibility, onus **2** debt, arrears **3**

drawback, disadvantage, hindrance, impediment, *informal* drag

liable *adj* **1** legally responsible (for) **2** inclined or apt (to do something or happen) **3** (with **to**) likely to have or suffer from: *liable to colds*

■ **1** responsible, answerable, accountable **2** inclined, likely, apt, disposed **3** prone, tending, susceptible

liaise /lɪˈeɪz/ *verb* communicate (with), be in contact (with)

liaison /lɪˈeɪzən/ *noun* **1** contact, communication **2** a sexual affair

■ **1** contact, connection, link **2** love affair, affair, romance, *informal* fling, intrigue, amour, entanglement

liar *see* **lie¹**

lib *noun, informal* liberation: *women's lib*

libation *noun* wine poured to honour a god

Lib Dem *short for* Liberal Democrat

libel *noun* something written to hurt another's reputation ◇ *verb* (**libels, libelling, libelled**) write something libellous about ◇ **libellous** *adj*

■ *noun* defamation, slur, smear, slander, vilification, aspersion ◇ *verb* defame, slur, smear, slander, vilify, malign ◇ **libellous** defamatory, vilifying, slanderous, derogatory, maligning, injurious, scurrilous, untrue

liberal *adj* **1** generous **2** broadminded, tolerant ◇ **Liberal** *noun* a member of the former Liberal Party ◇ **liberality** *noun* ◇ **Liberal Democrats** one of the chief political parties of Great Britain

■ **1** generous, ample, bountiful, lavish, plentiful **2** broad-minded, openminded, tolerant, lenient

◼ **1** mean, miserly **2** narrow-minded

liberate *verb* set free ◇ **liberation** *noun*

■ free, emancipate, release, let go, let out, set free, deliver, unchain, discharge, rescue

◼ imprison, enslave

libertine *noun* someone who lives a wicked, immoral life

liberty noun (plural **liberties**) 1 freedom, esp of speech or action 2 (**liberties**) rights, privileges ◇ **take liberties** behave rudely or impertinently

☰ 1 freedom, emancipation, release, independence, licence, permission, sanction, right, authorization

libido noun sexual drive or urge ◇ **libidinous** adj

library noun (plural **libraries**) 1 a collection of books, records etc 2 a building or room housing these ◇ **librarian** noun the keeper of a library

libretto noun (plural **libretti** or **librettos**) the words of an opera, musical show etc

lice plural of **louse**

licence noun 1 a form giving permission to do something, eg to keep a television set, drive a car etc 2 too great freedom of action

☰ 1 permission, permit, leave, warrant, authorization, authority, certificate, charter, right, privilege, dispensation 2 abandon, dissipation, indulgence, unruliness, anarchy, disorder

🗲 1 prohibition, restriction 2 decorum, moderation

⚠ Do not confuse: **licence** and **license**

license verb permit, give a licence to or for ◇ **licensee** noun someone to whom a licence is given

licentious adj given to behaving immorally or improperly ◇ **licentiousness** noun

☰ debauched, lascivious, immoral, abandoned, lewd, promiscuous, impure, lax, lustful, disorderly, wanton, unchaste

🗲 modest, chaste

lichen /ˈlaɪkən/ noun a moss-like plant that grows on rocks etc

licit adj legal, allowable

lick verb 1 pass the tongue over 2 of flames: reach up, touch ◇ noun 1 the act of licking 2 a tiny amount ◇ **lick into shape** make vigorous improvements to

☰ verb 1 tongue, lap, taste 2 touch, flick, flicker, play over

licorice another spelling of **liquorice**

lid noun 1 a cover for a box, pot etc 2 an eyelid

lido /ˈliːdoʊ/ noun 1 a bathing beach 2 an open-air swimming pool

lie[1] noun a false statement meant to deceive ◇ verb (**lies**, **lying**, **lied**) tell a lie ◇ **liar** noun someone who tells lies

☰ noun falsehood, untruth, fabrication, invention, fiction, deceit, informal fib, falsity, falsification, white lie, informal whopper ◇ verb perjure, misrepresent, fabricate, falsify, informal fib, invent

lie[2] verb (**lies**, **lying**, **lay**, **lain**) 1 rest in a flat position 2 be or remain in particular a state or position ◇ noun the position or situation in which something lies ◇ **lie in wait** keep hidden in order to surprise someone ◇ **lie low** keep quiet or hidden ◇ **the lie of the land** the present state of affairs

⚠ Do not confuse with: **lay**

liege /liːdʒ/ noun 1 a loyal subject 2 a lord or superior

lieu /ljuː/ or /luː/ noun: **in lieu of** instead of

Lieut abbrev Lieutenant

lieutenant /lɛfˈtɛnənt/ or US /luːˈtɛnənt/ noun 1 an army officer next below captain 2 in the navy, an officer below a lieutenant-commander 3 a rank below a higher officer: lieutenant-colonel

life noun (plural **lives**) 1 the period between birth and death 2 the state of being alive 3 liveliness 4 manner of living 5 the story of someone's life 6 living things: animal life ◇ **lifeless** adj 1 dead 2 not lively, spiritless ◇ **life-support machine** a device for keeping a human being alive during severe illness, space travel etc

☰ 2 being, existence, animation, breath, entity, soul 3 liveliness, vigour, vitality, vivacity, verve, zest, energy, spirit, sparkle, activity ◇ **lifeless** 1 dead, deceased, defunct, cold, unconscious, inanimate **2** lethargic, listless, sluggish, dull, apathetic, passive, insipid, colourless, slow

lifebelt *noun* a ring of cork or filled with air for keeping someone afloat

lifeboat *noun* a boat for rescuing people in difficulties at sea

lifeblood *noun* a source of necessary strength or life

lifebuoy *noun* a float to support someone awaiting rescue at sea

life-cycle *noun* the various stages through which a living thing passes

life-jacket *noun* a buoyant jacket for keeping someone afloat in water

lifelike *adj* like a living person or thing; realistic

■ realistic, true-to-life, real, true, vivid, natural, authentic, faithful, exact, graphic

◼ unrealistic, unnatural

lifeline *noun* a vital means of communication

lifelong *adj* lasting the length of a life

■ lifetime, long-lasting, long-standing, persistent, lasting, enduring, abiding, permanent, constant

◼ impermanent, temporary

life-size *adj* full size, as in life

lifespan *noun* the length of somone's life

lifestyle *noun* the way in which someone lives

lifetime *noun* the period during which someone is alive

lift *verb* **1** raise, take up **2** *informal* steal **3** of fog: disappear, disperse ◇ *noun* **1** a moving platform or compartment carrying goods or people between floors in a large building **2** a ride in someone's car *etc* **3** a boost

■ *verb* **1** raise, elevate, hoist

lift-off *noun* the take-off of a rocket, spacecraft *etc*

ligament *noun* a tough substance which connects the bones of the body

ligature *noun* **1** something which binds **2** a printed character formed of two or more letters, *eg* æ

light¹ *noun* **1** the brightness given by the sun, moon, lamps *etc* which makes things visible **2** a source of light, *eg* a lamp **3** a flame on a cigarette lighter **4** a way of thinking about something or someone ◇ *adj* **1** having light, not dark **2** of a colour: pale ◇ *verb* (**lights**, **lighting**, **lit** or **lighted**) **1** give light to **2** set fire to ◇ **lighten** *verb* **1** make or become lighter **2** of lightning: to flash ◇ **lightening** *noun* a making or becoming lighter ◇ **bring to light** reveal, cause to be noticed ◇ **come to light** be revealed or discovered ◇ **in the light of** taking into consideration (information *etc*)

■ *noun* **1** illumination, brightness, brilliance, luminescence, radiance, glow, ray, shine, glare, gleam, glint, lustre, flash, blaze **2** lamp, lantern, lighter, match, torch, candle, bulb, beacon ◇ *adj* **1** illuminated, bright, brilliant, luminous, glowing, shining **2** pale, pastel, fair, blond, blonde, bleached, faded, faint ◇ **lighten 1** illuminate, illumine, brighten, light up, pale, fade, bleach

light² *adj* **1** not heavy **2** easy to bear or do **3** easy to digest **4** nimble **5** lively **6** cheerful **7** not serious: *light music* **8** of rain *etc*: little in quantity ◇ **lighten** *verb* make less heavy ◇ **lightly** *adv*

■ *adj* **1** weightless, insubstantial, delicate, buoyant, flimsy, feathery, slight **5** lively, blithe **6** cheerful, cheery, carefree, merry **7** entertaining, amusing, funny, humorous, frivolous, witty, pleasing ◇ **lighten** ease, lessen, unload, lift, relieve, reduce, mitigate, alleviate

light³ *verb* (**lights**, **lighting**, **lit** or **lighted**) *old* (with **on**) **1** land, settle on **2** come upon by chance

lighter¹ *noun* a device with a flame *etc* for lighting

lighter² *noun* a large open boat used in unloading and loading ships

light-fingered *adj* apt to steal

light-headed *adj* dizzy

light-hearted *adj* cheerful

■ cheerful, joyful, jolly, bright, carefree, untroubled, merry, happy-go-lucky, elated, jovial, playful

◼ sad, unhappy, serious

lighthouse *noun* a tower-like building with a flashing light to warn or guide ships

lighting *noun* a means of providing light

lightning *noun* an electric flash in the clouds ◇ **lightning conductor** a metal rod on a building *etc* which conducts electricity down to earth

> ⚠ Do not confuse with: **lightening**

lightship *noun* a ship anchored in a fixed position to serve as a lighthouse

lightweight *noun* a weight category in boxing

light-year *noun* the distance light travels in a year (6 million million miles)

ligneous *adj* woody; wooden

lignite *noun* brown, woody coal

like¹ *adj* the same as or similar to ◇ *adv* in the same way as: *he sings like an angel* ◇ *noun* something or someone that is the equal of another: *you won't see her like again* ◇ **likelihood** *noun* probability ◇ **likely** *adj* **1** probable **2** liable (to do something) ◇ *adv* probably ◇ **liken** *verb* think of as similar, compare ◇ **likeness** *noun* **1** similarity, resemblance **2** a portrait, photograph *etc* of someone ◇ **likewise** *adv* **1** in the same way **2** also

▪ *adj* similar, resembling, alike, same, identical, equivalent, corresponding, related, relating, parallel ◇ **likelihood** likeliness, probability, possibility, chance, prospect, liability ◇ **likely** *adj* **1** probable, possible, anticipated, expected **2** liable, prone, tending, predictable, inclined ◇ *adv* probably, presumably, in all probability, no doubt, doubtlessly ◇ **likeness 1** similarity, resemblance, affinity **2** representation, image, copy, reproduction, replica, facsimile, effigy, picture, portrait, photograph

▪ *adj* unlike, dissimilar ◇ **likelihood** improbability, unlikeliness

like² *verb* **1** be pleased with **2** be fond of ◇ **liking** *noun* **1** fondness **2** preference: *to my liking*

▪ **liking 1** fondness, love, affection, appreciation, desire **2** preference, partiality, penchant, taste

▪ **liking 1** dislike, aversion, hatred

likeable or **likable** *adj* attractive, lovable

▪ lovable, pleasing, appealing, agreeable, charming, engaging, pleasant, amiable, congenial, attractive, sympathetic

▪ unpleasant, disagreeable

lilac *noun* a small tree with hanging clusters of pale purple or white flowers ◇ *adj* of pale purple colour

lilliputian *adj* tiny, minuscule

> After *Lilliput*, a country on a tiny scale in Jonathan Swift's 18th-century satirical novel, *Gulliver's Travels*

lilt *noun* a striking rhythm or swing ◇ *verb* have this rhythm

lily *noun* (*plural* **lilies**) a tall plant grown from a bulb with large white or coloured flowers ◇ **lily-of-the-valley** *noun* a plant with small white bell-shaped flowers

limb *noun* **1** a leg or arm **2** a branch

▪ **1** arm, leg, member, appendage **2** branch, projection, offshoot, extension, part, extremity, bough

limber *adj* easily bent, supple ◇ **limber up** exercise so as to become supple

▪ **limber up** loosen up, warm up, work out, exercise, prepare

limbo¹ *noun* the borderland of hell, reserved for those unbaptized before death ◇ **in limbo** forgotten, neglected

limbo² *noun* a West Indian dance in which the dancer passes under a low bar

lime¹ *noun* **1** (*also called* **quicklime**) a white substance left after heating limestone, used in making cement

lime² *noun* **1** a tree related to the lemon **2** its greenish-yellow fruit

lime³ *noun another name* for **linden**

limelight *noun*: ◇ **in the limelight** attracting publicity or attention

limerick *noun* a type of humorous rhymed poetry in five-line verses

After *Limerick* in Ireland, the name of which was repeated in nonsense songs in an old Victorian parlour game

limestone *noun* a rock composed mainly of calcium carbonate

limit *noun* **1** the farthest point or place **2** a boundary **3** largest (or smallest) extent, degree *etc* **4** restriction ◇ *verb* set or keep to a limit ◇ **limitation** *noun* **1** something which limits **2** a weak point, a flaw

◼ *noun* **2** boundary, bound, border, frontier, confines, edge, verge, brim, end, perimeter, rim **4** check, curb, restraint, restriction, limitation, ceiling, maximum, cut-off point, saturation point ◇ *verb* check, curb, restrict, restrain, constrain, confine, delimit, bound, hem in, ration, specify, hinder ◇ **limitation** **2** inadequacy, shortcoming, disadvantage, drawback, condition, reservation

limo *noun, informal* a limousine

limousine *noun* a kind of large motor car, *esp* one with a separate compartment for the driver

Named after a type of cloak worn in *Limousin* in France, because the car's roof was supposedly similar in shape

limp [1] *verb* **1** walk lamely **2** move with difficulty ◇ *noun* **1** the act of limping **2** a limping walk

◼ *verb* **1** hobble, falter, stumble, hop, shuffle

limp [2] *adj* **1** not stiff, floppy **2** weak

◼ **1** drooping, flaccid, floppy, loose, slack, relaxed, lax, soft, flexible, pliable **2** tired, weary, exhausted, spent, weak, worn out, lethargic

limpet *noun* **1** a small cone-shaped shellfish which clings to rocks **2** someone who is difficult to get rid of

limpid *adj* clear, transparent

linchpin *noun* a pin-shaped rod used to keep a wheel on an axle

linctus *noun* a syrupy medicine for sore throats *etc*

linden *noun* (*also called* **lime**) a tree

with small flowers and heart-shaped leaves

line [1] *noun* **1** a cord, rope *etc* **2** a long thin stroke or mark **3** a wrinkle **4** a row of people, printed words *etc* **5** a company running a service of ships or aircraft **6** a railway **7** a telephone connection **8** a short letter **9** a family from generation to generation **10** course, direction **11** a subject of interest, activity *etc* **12** (**lines**) a series of military defences **13** (**lines**) a written school punishment exercise ◇ *verb* **1** mark out with lines **2** (often with **up**) place in a row **3** form lines along (a street) ◇ **line dancing** dancing without partners and in rows, to country music ◇ **out of line 1** not aligned **2** *informal* behaving unacceptably

◼ *noun* **1** string, rope, cord, cable, thread, filament, wire **2** stroke, band, bar, stripe, mark, strip, rule, strand, streak, underline, score, scratch **3** crease, wrinkle, furrow **4** row, rank, queue, file, column, sequence, series, procession, chain, trail **9** ancestry, family, descent, extraction, lineage, race, breed **10** course, path, direction, track, route, axis

line [2] *verb* cover on the inside

lineage *noun* descent traced back to your ancestors

◼ ancestry, descent, extraction, family, line, pedigree, race, stock, birth, breed, genealogy

lineal *adj* directly descended through the father, grandfather *etc*

lineament *noun* a feature, *esp* of the face

linear *adj* **1** made of lines **2** in one dimension (length, breadth or height) only

linen *noun* **1** cloth made of flax **2** articles made of linen: *table linen/bed linen*

liner *noun* a ship or aeroplane working on a regular service

linesman, lineswoman *noun* an umpire at a boundary line

ling [1] *noun* a long slender fish like the cod

ling[2] *noun* heather

linger *verb* **1** stay for a long time or for longer than expected **2** loiter, delay
■ **1** wait, remain, stay, hang on **2** loiter, delay, dally, idle, dawdle

lingerie /'lɛ̃ʒərɪ/ *noun plural* women's underwear

lingo *noun* (*plural* **lingoes**) a language, a dialect

lingua franca a language used amongst people from different nations *etc* so that they can communicate

linguini *noun plural* pasta in long thin flat strands

linguist *noun* **1** someone skilled in languages **2** someone who studies language ◇ **linguistic** *adj* ◇ **linguistics** *noun sing* the scientific study of languages and of language in general

liniment *noun* an oil or ointment rubbed into the skin to cure stiffness in the muscles, joints *etc*

lining *noun* a covering on the inside

link *noun* **1** a ring of a chain **2** a single part of a series **3** anything connecting two things ◇ *verb* **1** connect with a link **2** join closely **3** be connected ◇ **linkage** *noun*
■ *noun* **2** part, piece, element, member, constituent, component, division **3** connection, bond, tie, association, joint, relationship, union, knot, attachment, communication
◙ *verb* **1, 2** separate, unfasten

links *noun plural* **1** a stretch of flat or slightly hilly ground near the seashore **2** a golf course

linnet *noun* a small songbird of the finch family

lino *noun, informal* linoleum ◇ **linocut** *noun* a design for printing cut into a block of linoleum

linoleum *noun* a type of smooth, hard-wearing covering for floors

linseed *noun* flax seed ◇ **linseed oil** oil from flax seed

lint *noun* **1** a soft woolly material for putting over wounds **2** fine pieces of fluff

lintel *noun* a timber or stone over a doorway or window

lion *noun* a powerful animal of the cat family, the male of which has a shaggy mane ◇ **lioness** *noun* a female lion ◇ **the lion's share** the largest share

lionize *verb* treat as a celebrity

lip *noun* **1** either of the two fleshy flaps in front of the teeth forming the rim of the mouth **2** the edge of a container *etc*
■ **2** edge, brim, border, brink, rim, margin, verge

liposuction *noun* a surgical operation to remove unwanted body fat

lip-reading *noun* reading what someone says from the movement of their lips

lip-service *noun* saying one thing but believing another: *paying lip-service to the rules*

lipstick *noun* a stick of red, pink *etc* colouring for the lips

liquefy *verb* (**liquefies, liquefying, liquefied**) make or become liquid ◇ **liquefaction** *noun*

liqueur *noun* a strong alcoholic drink, strongly flavoured and sweet

> 🛈 Do not confuse with: **liquor**

liquid *noun* a flowing, water-like substance ◇ *adj* **1** flowing **2** looking like water
■ *noun* liquor, fluid, juice, drink, sap, solution, lotion ◇ *adj* **1** fluid, flowing, liquefied, watery, wet, runny, smooth

liquidate *verb* **1** close down, wind up the affairs of (a bankrupt business company) **2** *slang* kill, murder ◇ **liquidation** *noun* ◇ **liquidator** *noun*
■ **1** pay (off), close down, clear, discharge, wind up, sell **2** annihilate, terminate, do away with, kill, murder, massacre, assassinate, destroy, dispatch, abolish, eliminate, exterminate, remove, finish off

liquidize *verb* **1** make liquid **2** make into a purée ◇ **liquidizer** *noun* a machine for liquidizing

liquor *noun* an alcoholic drink, *esp* a spirit (*eg* whisky)

> 🛈 Do not confuse with: **liqueur**

liquorice or **licorice** *noun* **1** a plant with a sweet-tasting root **2** a black, sticky sweet flavoured with this root

lira /'lɪərə/ *noun* a former unit of Italian money

lisp *verb* **1** say *th* for *s* or *z* because of being unable to pronounce these letters correctly **2** speak imperfectly, like a child ◇ *noun* a speech disorder of this kind

lissome *adj* nimble, bending easily

list¹ *noun* a series of names, numbers, prices *etc* written down one after the other ◇ *verb* write (something) down in this way ◇ **listed building** one protected from being knocked down because it is of architectural or historical interest

■ *noun* catalogue, roll, inventory, register, schedule, index, listing, record, file, directory, table, tabulation, tally, series ◇ *verb* register, itemize, catalogue, index, tabulate, record, file, enrol, enter, note, bill, book

list² *verb* of a ship: lean over to one side ◇ *noun* a slope to one side

■ *verb* lean, incline, tilt, slope, heel (over), tip

listen *verb* hear and pay attention to ◇ **listener** *noun*

■ hark, attend, pay attention, hear, heed, prick up one's ears, take notice, lend an ear, eavesdrop, overhear

listeria *noun* a bacterium found in certain foods which can damage the nervous system if not killed during cooking ◇ **listeriosis** *noun* a brain disease caused by eating food contaminated with listeria bacteria

listless *adj* weary, without energy or interest ■ **listlessness** *noun*

■ sluggish, lethargic, languid, spiritless, limp, lifeless, inert, inactive, impassive, indifferent, apathetic, indolent, depressed, bored, heavy

🞎 energetic, enthusiastic

lists *noun plural, hist* the ground enclosed for a battle between knights on horseback

lit *past form* of **light**¹ and **light**³

litany *noun* (*plural* **litanies**) **1** a set form of prayer **2** a long list or catalogue

liter *US spelling* of **litre**

literal *adj* following the exact or most obvious meaning ◇ **literally** *adv* exactly as stated: *he was literally blinded by the flash*

■ verbatim, word-for-word, strict, close, actual, precise, faithful, exact, accurate, factual, true, genuine, unexaggerated

🞎 imprecise, loose

literary *adj* **1** relating to books, authors *etc* **2** knowledgeable about books ◇ **literacy** *noun* ability to read and write ◇ **literate** *adj* able to read and write

■ **2** educated, well-read, bookish, learned, scholarly, literate, cultured, cultivated, refined

🞎 **2** ignorant, illiterate

literature *noun* **1** the books *etc* that are written in any language, *esp* those regarded as being well-written **2** anything in written form on a subject

■ **2** information, leaflet(s), pamphlet(s), circular(s), brochure(s), hand-out(s), *informal* bumf

lithe *adj* bending easily, supple, flexible

lithium *noun* a metallic element whose salts are used in treating some mental illnesses

lithograph *noun* a picture made from a drawing done on stone or metal ◇ **lithographer** *noun* ◇ **lithography** *noun* printing done by this method

litigation *noun* a law case

litigious *adj* fond of taking your grievances to court

litmus paper treated paper which changes colour when dipped in an acid or alkaline solution ◇ **litmus test** something which indicates underlying attitudes *etc*

litre *noun* a metric measure of liquids (1.76 pint)

litter *noun* **1** discarded paper, rubbish *etc* in a public place **2** a heap of straw as bedding for animals **3** a number of animals born at one birth **4** *hist* a bed for carrying the sick and injured ◇ *verb* **1** scatter rubbish carelessly about **2** produce a litter of young

■ *noun* **1** rubbish, debris, refuse, waste, mess, disorder, clutter, untidiness, *informal* junk **3** offspring, young, *formal* progeny, brood, family ◇ *verb* **1** strew, scatter, mess up, disorder, clutter

little *adj* small in quantity or size ◇ *adv* **1** in a small quantity or degree **2** not much **3** not at all: *little does she know* ◇ *pronoun* a small amount, distance *etc*: *have a little more/move a little to the right*

■ *adj* small, short, tiny, minute, slender, insufficient, sparse, scant, meagre, paltry, skimpy ◇ *adv* **2** barely, hardly, scarcely, rarely, seldom, infrequently

liturgy *noun* (*plural* **liturgies**) the form of service of a church ◇ **liturgical** *adj*

live¹ /lɪv/ *verb* **1** have life **2** dwell **3** pass your life **4** continue to be alive **5** survive **6** be lifelike or vivid ◇ **live and let live** allow others to live as they please ◇ **live down** live until (an embarrassment *etc*) is forgotten by others ◇ **live on 1** keep yourself alive **2** be supported by ◇ **live up to** be as good as expected

■ **1** be, exist, breathe, draw breath **2** inhabit, reside, lodge **5** last, endure, continue, remain, persist

live² /laɪv/ *adj* **1** having life, not dead **2** full of energy **3** of a television broadcast *etc*: seen as the event takes place, not recorded **4** charged with electricity and apt to give an electric shock ◇ **liven** *verb* make lively

■ **1** alive, living, existent **2** lively, vital, active, energetic, dynamic, alert

livelihood *noun* someone's means of living or earning money (*eg* their daily work)

livelong *adj*, *old* whole: *the livelong day*

lively *adj* full of life or high spirits ◇ **liveliness** *noun*

■ animated, alert, active, energetic, spirited, feisty, vivacious, vigorous, sprightly, cheerful, blithe, merry, breezy, *informal* chirpy

liver *noun* a large gland in the body that carries out several important functions including purifying the blood

livery *noun* (*plural* **liveries**) the uniform of a servant, employee *etc* ◇ **livery stable** a stable where horses are kept for hire

livestock *noun* farm animals

liveware *noun*, *comput*, *informal* the people operating a system, as opposed to the hardware and software

livewire *noun* a very lively, energetic person

livid *adj* **1** very angry **2** of a bluish lead-like colour

■ **1** angry, furious, infuriated, irate, outraged, enraged, raging, fuming, indignant, incensed, exasperated, *informal* mad **2** leaden, black-and-blue, bruised, discoloured, greyish, purple

living *adj* **1** having life **2** active, lively **3** of a likeness: exact ◇ *noun* livelihood ◇ **living wage** a wage on which it is possible to live comfortably

■ *adj* **1** alive, breathing, existing **2** active, lively, vital, animated ◇ *noun* livelihood, support, income, sustenance, work, job, occupation, profession, way of life

▣ *adj* **1** dead **2** sluggish

living-room *noun* an informal sitting-room

lizard *noun* a four-footed reptile with a long body and tail

llama *noun* a S American animal of the camel family without a hump

lo *exclam*, *old* look

loach *noun* (*plural* **loaches**) a type of small river fish

load *verb* **1** put on what is to be carried **2** put the ammunition in (a gun) **3** put a film in (a camera) **4** weight for some purpose: *loaded dice* ◇ *noun* **1** something carried, or as much as can be carried at once **2** cargo **3** a heavy weight or task **4** the power carried by an electric circuit ◇ **loaded question** one meant to trap someone into making a damaging admission

■ *verb* **1** burden, weigh down, overburden, pack, pile, heap ◇ *noun* **3** burden, onus

loadline *noun* a line along a ship's side to mark the waterline when fully loaded

loaf[1] *noun* (*plural* **loaves**) a shaped mass of bread

loaf[2] *verb* pass time idly or lazily ◇ **loafer** *noun* **1** an idler **2** (**loafers**) casual shoes

■ **loafer 1** *informal* idler, *informal* layabout, shirker, *informal* skiver, wastrel, lounger, *informal* lazybones

loam *noun* a rich soil ◇ **loamy** *adj*

loan *noun* something lent, *esp* a sum of money ◇ *verb* lend

■ *noun* advance, credit, mortgage, allowance ◇ *verb* lend, advance, credit, allow

loath or **loth** /loʊθ/ *adj* unwilling (to)

⚠ Do not confuse: **loath** and **loathe**

loathe /loʊð/ *verb* dislike greatly ◇ **loathing** *noun* great hate or disgust ◇ **loathsome** *adj* causing loathing or disgust, horrible

■ hate, detest, abominate, abhor, despise, dislike ◇ **loathing** hatred, detestation, abhorrence, abomination, repugnance, revulsion, repulsion, dislike, disgust ◇ **loathsome** detestable, odious, repulsive, hateful, repugnant, repellent, offensive, horrible, disgusting, vile, revolting, nasty

🄵 adore, love ◇ **loathing** affection, love

loaves *plural* of **loaf**[1]

lob *noun* **1** *cricket* a slow, high ball bowled underhand **2** *tennis* a ball high overhead dropping near the back of the court ◇ *verb* (**lobs**, **lobbing**, **lobbed**) **1** send such a ball **2** *informal* throw

lobby *noun* (*plural* **lobbies**) **1** a small entrance hall **2** a passage off which rooms open **3** a group of people who try to influence the government or other authority ◇ *verb* (**lobbies, lobbying, lobbied**) **1** try to influence (public officials) **2** conduct a campaign to influence public officials

■ *verb* **1** influence, solicit, pressure **2** campaign for, press for, demand, persuade, call for, urge, push for, promote

lobe *noun* **1** the hanging-down part of

an ear **2** a division of the brain, lungs *etc*

lobelia *noun* a garden plant with flowers twisted upside-down

lobotomy *noun* surgical incision into a lobe, *esp* of the brain ◇ **lobotomize** *verb* **1** perform a lobotomy on **2** make bland or spiritless

lobster *noun* a kind of shellfish with large claws, used for food ◇ **lobster pot** a basket in which lobsters are caught

local *adj* of or confined to a certain place ◇ *noun*, *informal* **1** the public house nearest someone's home **2** (**locals**) the people living in a particular place or area ◇ **local colour** details in a story which make it more interesting and realistic ◇ **local government** administration of the local affairs of a district *etc* by elected inhabitants

■ *adj* regional, provincial, parochial, small-town, limited, narrow, restricted

locale /loʊˈkɑːl/ *noun* scene, location

locality *noun* a particular place and the area round about

■ neighbourhood, vicinity, district, area, locale, region, position, place, site, spot, scene, setting

localize *verb* confine to one area, keep from spreading

locate *verb* **1** find **2** set in a particular place: *a house located in the Highlands*

■ **1** find, discover, unearth, track down, detect, pinpoint, identify **2** situate, settle, fix, establish, place, put, set, seat

location *noun* **1** the act of locating **2** position or situation ◇ **on location** of filming *etc*: in natural surroundings, not in a studio

■ **2** position, situation, place, locus, whereabouts, venue, site, locale, bearings, spot, point

loch *noun* in Scotland, a lake or a long narrow sea inlet

lock[1] *noun* **1** a fastening for doors *etc* needing a key to open it **2** a part of a canal for raising or lowering boats **3** the part of a gun by which it is fired **4** a tight hold ◇ *verb* **1** fasten or become fastened with a lock **2** make or become unable to move or be moved **3** (with **up**) shut in with a lock ◇ **lock, stock and barrel** completely

■ *noun* **1** fastening, bolt, clasp, padlock ◇ *verb* **1** fasten, secure, bolt, latch, seal, shut

lock² *noun* **1** a section of hair **2** (**locks**) hair

locker *noun* a small cupboard

locker-room *noun* a room for changing clothes and storing personal belongings

locket *noun* a little ornamental case hung round the neck

lock-in *noun* a period of drinking in a pub after it has closed

lockjaw *noun* a form of tetanus which stiffens the jaw muscles

lockout *noun* the locking out of workers by their employer during industrial disputes

locksmith *noun* a person who makes locks

lock-up *noun* a lockable garage or small shop

locomotion *noun* movement from place to place ◇ **locomotive** *noun* a railway engine ◇ *adj* of or capable of locomotion

locum *noun* (*plural* **locums**) a doctor, dentist *etc* taking another's place for a time

locus *noun* (*plural* **loci**) a place, a locality

locust *noun* a large insect of the grasshopper family which destroys growing plants

lode *noun* a vein containing metallic ore

lodestar *noun* the Pole star

lodestone *noun* **1** a form of the mineral magnetite with magnetic properties **2** a magnet

lodge *noun* **1** a small house, often at the entrance to the grounds of a larger building **2** a beaver's dwelling **3** a house occupied during the shooting or hunting season **4** a branch of a society such as the Freemasons ◇ *verb* **1** live in

rented rooms **2** (cause to) become fixed (in) **3** put in a safe place **4** make (a complaint, appeal, *etc*) officially

■ *noun* **3** hut, cabin, cottage, chalet, shelter, retreat, den, hunting-lodge, meeting-place, club ◇ *verb* **2** fix, imbed, implant, get stuck **3** deposit, place, put **4** submit, register

lodger *noun* someone who lives in rented rooms

■ boarder, paying guest, resident, tenant, guest

lodging *noun* **1** a place to stay, sleep *etc* **2** (**lodgings**) a room or rooms rented in someone else's house

■ **1** dwelling, abode, residence **2** accommodation, *informal* digs, quarters, boarding-house, rooms, *informal* pad

loess /'loʊɪs/ *noun* a loamy deposit found in river valleys

loft *noun* **1** a room or storage space just under a roof **2** a gallery in a hall, church *etc*

lofty *adj* **1** high up **2** noble, proud ◇ **loftily** *adv* ◇ **loftiness** *noun*

log *noun* **1** a thick, rough piece of wood, part of a felled tree **2** a device for measuring a ship's speed **3** a logbook ◇ *verb* (**logs, logging, logged**) write down (events) in a logbook ◇ **log in** or **log on** start a session on a computer system ◇ **log out** or **log off** end a session on a computer system

■ *noun* **1** timber, trunk, block, chunk **3** record, diary, journal, logbook, daybook, account, tally ◇ *verb* record, register, write up, note, book, chart, tally

loganberry *noun* a kind of fruit like a large raspberry

logbook *noun* **1** an official record of a ship's or aeroplane's progress **2** a record of progress, attendance *etc* **3** the registration documents of a motor vehicle

loggerhead *noun*: **at loggerheads** quarrelling

loggia /'lɒdʒɪə/ *noun* (*plural* **loggie** or **loggias**) a covered arcade

logic *noun* **1** the study of reasoning correctly **2** correctness of reasoning ◇ **logical** *adj* according to the rules of logic or sound reasoning ◇ **logically** *adv*

◧ **logical** reasonable, rational, reasoned, coherent, consistent, valid, sound, well-founded, clear, sensible, methodical, well-organized

◨ **logical** illogical, irrational

log-jam *noun* **1** a piling up of floating logs **2** congestion which brings traffic *etc* to a standstill

logo *noun* (*plural* **logos**) a symbol of a company, organization *etc* consisting of a simple picture or lettering

loin *noun* **1** the back of an animal cut for food **2** (**loins**) the lower part of the back

loincloth *noun* a piece of cloth worn round the hips, *esp* in India and south-east Asia

loiter *verb* **1** linger **2** stand around **3** proceed slowly

◧ **1** hang about, idle, linger, dally **3** mooch, lag, saunter, dawdle

loll *verb* **1** lie lazily about **2** of the tongue: hang down or out

lollipop *noun* a large boiled sweet on a stick ◇ **lollipop man**, **lollipop woman** *Brit* someone employed to stop cars to allow schoolchildren to cross the street, who carries a pole with a disc at the top

lollop *verb* **1** bound clumsily **2** lounge, idle

lolly *noun* (*plural* **lollies**), *informal* **1** a lollipop **2** money

lone *adj* alone; standing by itself

◧ single, sole, one, only, isolated, solitary, separate, separated

lonely *adj* **1** lacking or needing companionship **2** of a place: having few people **3** lone ◇ **loneliness** *noun*

◧ **1** alone, friendless, lonesome, solitary, abandoned, forsaken, companionless, unaccompanied, destitute **2** isolated, uninhabited, remote, out-of-the-way, secluded, abandoned, deserted, forsaken, desolate

◨ **1** popular **2** crowded, populous

lonesome *adj* **1** lone **2** feeling lonely

long *adj* **1** not short, measuring a lot

from end to end **2** measuring a certain amount: *cut a strip 2 cm long/the film is 3 hours long* **3** far-reaching **4** slow ◇ *adv* **1** for a great time **2** through the whole time: *all day long* ◇ *verb* wish very much (for): *longing to see him again* ◇ **before long** soon ◇ **in the long run** in the end ◇ **long johns** underwear resembling close-fitting trousers ◇ **so long** *informal* goodbye

◧ *adj* **1** lengthy, extensive, extended, expanded, prolonged, protracted, stretched, spread out **3** expansive, far-reaching **4** long-drawn-out, interminable, slow

◨ *adj* **1**, **4** brief, short, fleeting, abbreviated

longbow *noun* a large bow bent by the hand in shooting

longevity *noun* great length of life

longhand *noun* writing in full (*contrasted with*: **shorthand**)

longing *noun* a strong desire

◧ craving, desire, yearning, hankering, thirst, wish, urge, coveting, aspiration, ambition

longitude *noun* the distance, measured in degrees, of a place east or west of the Greenwich meridian (*compare with*: **latitude**)

long-range *adj* **1** able to reach a great distance **2** looking a long way into the future

longship *noun*, *hist* a Viking sailing ship

long-sighted *adj* able to see things at a distance but not those close at hand

long-standing *adj* begun a long time ago, having lasted a long time

◧ established, long-lived, long-lasting, enduring, abiding, traditional

long-suffering *adj* putting up with troubles without complaining

◧ uncomplaining, forbearing, forgiving, tolerant, easy-going, patient, stoical

long-term *adj* **1** extending over a long time **2** taking the future, not just the present, into account

long-wave _adj_ of radio: using wave-lengths over 1000 metres (_compare with_: **short wave**)

long-winded _adj_ using too many words

▣ lengthy, overlong, prolonged, wordy, long-drawn-out, repetitious, rambling, tedious

◫ brief, terse

loo _noun_, _informal_ a toilet

loofah _noun_ the fibrous fruit of a tropical plant, used as a rough sponge

look _verb_ **1** turn the eyes towards so as to see **2** appear, seem: _you look tired/it looks as if I can go after all_ **3** face: _his room looks south_ ◊ _noun_ **1** the act of looking **2** the expression on someone's face **3** appearance **4** (**looks**) personal appearance ◊ **look alive** _informal_ rouse yourself, get ready for action ◊ **look down on** think of as being inferior ◊ **look for** search for ◊ **look forward to** anticipate with pleasure ◊ **look into** investigate ◊ **look on 1** stand by and watch **2** think of (as): _he looks on her as his mother_ ◊ **look out!** be careful! ◊ **look over** examine briefly ◊ **look sharp** _informal_ be quick, hurry up

▣ _verb_ **1** watch, see, observe, view, survey, regard, gaze, study, stare, examine, inspect, scrutinize, glance, contemplate, scan ◊ _noun_ **2** expression, bearing, face **3** appearance, aspect, manner ◊ **look forward to** anticipate, await, expect, hope for, long for, count on, wait for ◊ **look into** investigate, probe, research, study, examine, inquire about, explore, check out, inspect

lookalike _noun_ someone who looks very much like another

looker _noun_, _informal_ someone attractive or good-looking

look-in _noun_ a chance of doing something

looking-glass _noun_ a mirror

lookout _noun_ **1** (someone who keeps) a careful watch **2** a high place for watching from **3** concern, responsibility: _that's your lookout_

▣ **1** guard, sentry, watch, watchman, sentinel **2** tower, post **3** concern, responsibility, worry, affair, business, problem

loom[1] _noun_ a machine for weaving cloth

loom[2] _verb_ appear indistinctly, often threatening

▣ appear, emerge, take shape, menace, threaten, hang over, dominate, tower, overhang, rise, soar, overshadow

loony _noun_ (_plural_ **loonies**), _informal_ a lunatic, an insane person ◊ _adj_ mad, insane

loop _noun_ **1** a rounded doubled-over part in a piece of string _etc_ **2** a U-shaped bend ◊ **loop the loop** fly (an aircraft) upwards, back and down as if going round a circle

loophole _noun_ a way of avoiding a difficulty without breaking a law

loose _adj_ **1** not tight, slack **2** not fastened or firmly fixed **3** not closely packed **4** vague, not exact **5** careless ◊ _verb_ **1** make loose, slacken **2** untie ◊ **loosely** _adv_ ◊ **break loose** escape ◊ **on the loose** free

▣ _adj_ **1** slack, lax, baggy, hanging **2** free, unfastened, untied, movable, unattached, insecure, wobbly **4** imprecise, vague, inexact, ill-defined, indefinite, inaccurate, indistinct

❗ Do not confuse with: **lose**

loose-leaf _adj_ having a cover that allows pages to be inserted or removed

loosen _verb_ make loose or looser

▣ free, set free, release, let go, let out, ease, relax, loose, slacken, undo, unbind, untie, unfasten

loot _noun_ goods stolen or plundered ◊ _verb_ plunder, ransack

lop _verb_ (**lops**, **lopping**, **lopped**) cut off the top or ends of

lope _verb_ run with a long stride

lop-eared _adj_ of an animal: having ears hanging down

lopsided _adj_ leaning to one side, not symmetrical

▣ asymmetrical, unbalanced, off balance, uneven

■ balanced, symmetrical

loquacious *adj* talkative ◇ **loquaciousness** or **loquacity** *noun*

lord *noun* 1 the owner of an estate 2 a title for a male member of the aristocracy, bishop, judge *etc* 3 *old* a master, a ruler ◇ **lordly** *adj* 1 relating to a lord 2 noble, proud ◇ **lordship** *noun* 1 power, rule 2 used in addressing a lord: *His Lordship* ◇ **drunk as a lord** extremely drunk ◇ **House of Lords** the upper house of the British parliament ◇ **lord it over someone** act in a domineering manner towards them ◇ **the Lord** God or Christ ◇ **Lord's day** Sunday

■ **lordly** 2 noble, dignified, aristocratic, proud, arrogant, disdainful, haughty, imperious, condescending, domineering, overbearing

lore *noun* knowledge, beliefs *etc* handed down

■ knowledge, wisdom, learning, erudition, scholarship, traditions, teaching, beliefs, sayings

lorgnette *noun* eyeglasses with a handle

lorry *noun* (*plural* **lorries**) a large motor vehicle for carrying heavy loads

lose *verb* (**loses**, **losing**, **lost**) 1 cease to have (something) 2 have (something) taken away 3 put (something) where it cannot be found 4 waste (time) 5 miss (a train, a chance *etc*) 6 not win (a game) ◇ **loser** *noun* someone unlikely to succeed at anything

■ 1, 2 forfeit 3 mislay, misplace, forget 4 waste, squander, use up, exhaust, expend, drain

⚠ Do not confuse with: **loose**

loss *noun* (*plural* **losses**) 1 the act of losing or being lost 2 something which is lost ◇ **at a loss** uncertain what to do or say

■ 1 privation, mislaying, defeat, failure, losing, disappearance, destruction 2 waste, deficiency, deficit

lost *adj* 1 not able to be found 2 no longer possessed; thrown away 3 not won 4 ruined ◇ *past form of* **lose** ◇ **lost in** completely taken up by, engrossed in: *lost in thought*

■ 1 mislaid, missing, vanished, disappeared, misplaced, astray 2 wasted, squandered 4 ruined, destroyed

lot *noun* 1 a large number or quantity 2 someone's fortune or fate 3 a separate portion ◇ **draw lots** decide who is to do something by drawing names out of a hat *etc*

loth *another spelling* of **loath**

lotion *noun* a liquid for treating or cleaning the skin or hair

lottery *noun* (*plural* **lotteries**) an event in which money or prizes are awarded through drawing numbers at random

■ draw, raffle, sweepstake

lotus *noun* (*plural* **lotuses**) 1 a kind of water-lily 2 a mythical tree whose fruit caused forgetfulness

loud *adj* 1 making a great sound; noisy 2 showy, over-bright ◇ **loud** or **loudly** *adv* ◇ **loudness** *noun*

■ 1 noisy, deafening, booming, resounding, ear-piercing, ear-splitting, piercing, thundering, blaring, clamorous 2 garish, gaudy, glaring, flashy, showy, ostentatious, tasteless

🔲 1 quiet 2 subdued

loudhailer *noun* a megaphone

loudmouth *noun, informal* someone who talks offensively and too much

loudspeaker *noun* a device for converting electrical signals into sound

lounge *verb* 1 lie back in a relaxed way 2 move about lazily ◇ *noun* a sitting-room ◇ **lounger** *noun* 1 a reclining chair for relaxing on outdoors 2 a lazy person ◇ **lounge suit** a man's suit for everyday (but not casual) wear

■ *verb* 1 relax, loll, sprawl, recline, lie back, slump 2 idle, laze, waste time, kill time, lie about, take it easy

lour *see* **lower²**

louse *noun* (*plural* **lice**) a small bloodsucking insect sometimes found on the bodies of animals and people

lousy *adj* 1 swarming with lice 2 *informal* inferior, of poor quality

lout *noun* a clumsy or boorish man

louvre or *US* **louver** *noun* a slat set at an angle ◊ **louvre door** a slatted door allowing air and light to pass through ◊ **louvre window 1** a window covered with sloping slats **2** a window with narrow panes that can be set open at an angle

love *noun* **1** a great liking or affection **2** a loved person **3** *tennis* no score, zero ◊ *verb* be very fond of; like very much ◊ **lovable** *adj* worthy of love ◊ **in love** (**with**) feeling love and desire (for) ◊ **love affair** a relationship between people in love but not married ◊ **make love to 1** have sexual intercourse with **2** make sexual advances to, court

▣ *noun* **1** adoration, affection, fondness, attachment, regard, liking, devotion, passion, tenderness, warmth, infatuation ◊ *verb* adore, cherish, dote on, treasure, idolize, worship, like, take pleasure in, enjoy, delight in, appreciate, desire ◊ **lovable** adorable, endearing, captivating, charming, engaging, attractive, fetching, sweet, lovely, pleasing, delightful

▣ *verb* detest, hate ◊ **lovable** detestable, hateful

lovebite *noun* a mark on the skin caused by sucking or biting during lovemaking

love-child *noun* an illegitimate child

lovely *adj* beautiful; delightful ◊ **loveliness** *noun*

▣ beautiful, charming, delightful, attractive, enchanting, pleasing, pleasant, pretty, adorable, agreeable, enjoyable, sweet, winning, exquisite

▣ ugly, hideous

lovemaking *noun* **1** courtship **2** sexual play and intercourse

lover *noun* **1** someone who loves another, *esp* in a relationship outside marriage **2** an admirer, an enthusiast: *an art lover*

▣ **1** beloved, admirer, boyfriend, girlfriend, sweetheart, suitor, mistress, fiancé(e), *informal* flame

lovesick *adj* languishing with love

loving *adj* full of love ◊ **lovingly** *adv*

▣ amorous, affectionate, devoted, doting, fond, ardent, passionate, warm, warm-hearted, tender

low¹ *adj* **1** not high in position or size; not lying or reaching far up **2** of a voice or sound: not loud or high in pitch **3** cheap: *low air-fare* **4** feeling sad, depressed **5** humble **6** mean, unworthy ◊ *adv* **1** in or to a low position **2** not loudly **3** cheaply ◊ **lowness** *noun* ◊ **keep a low profile** not make your feelings or presence known

▣ *adj* **1** short, small, squat, stunted, little, shallow, deep, depressed, sunken **4** unhappy, depressed, downcast, gloomy

low² *verb* make the noise of cattle; bellow; moo

lowbrow *adj* populist, not intellectual (*contrasted with*: **highbrow**)

lowdown *noun*, *informal* the relevant information about something

lower¹ /lɔʊə(r)/ *adj* **1** less high **2** inferior ◊ *verb* **1** make less high: *lower the price* **2** let or come down: *lower the blinds* ◊ **lower-case** *adj* of a letter: not a capital, *eg a* not *A* (*contrasted with*: **upper-case**)

▣ *adj* **2** inferior, lesser, subordinate, secondary, minor, second-class, low-level, lowly, junior ◊ *verb* **1** reduce, decrease, cut, lessen, diminish **2** drop, depress, sink, descend, let down

lower² or **lour** /laʊə(r)/ *verb* **1** of the sky: become dark and cloudy **2** frown ◊ **lowering** *adj*

low-key *adj* not elaborate, unpretentious

lowland *noun* flattish country, without high hills

lowly *adj* low in rank, humble ◊ **lowliness** *noun*

▣ humble, low-born, obscure, poor, plebeian, plain, simple, modest, ordinary, inferior, meek, mild, mean, submissive, subordinate

▣ lofty, noble

loyal *adj* faithful, true ◊ **loyalist** *noun* someone loyal to their sovereign or country ◊ **loyally** *adv* ◊ **loyalty** *noun* (*plural* **loyalties**)

■ true, faithful, steadfast, staunch, devoted, trustworthy, sincere, patriotic
✷ disloyal, treacherous

lozenge *noun* **1** a diamond-shaped figure **2** a small sweet for sucking

LP *noun* a long-playing record

Lt *abbrev* Lieutenant

Ltd *abbrev* limited liability

lubricate *verb* apply oil *etc* to (something) to overcome friction and make movement easier ◇ **lubricant** *noun* something which lubricates; an oil ◇ **lubrication** *noun*

lucerne *noun* a type of plant used for feeding cattle; alfalfa

lucid *adj* **1** easily understood **2** clear in mind; not confused ◇ **lucidity** *noun* ◇ **lucidly** *adv*

Lucifer *noun* Satan, the Devil

luck *noun* **1** fortune, either good or bad **2** chance: *as luck would have it* **3** good fortune: *did you have any luck?* ◇ **luckless** *adj* unfortunate, unhappy
■ **2** chance, fortune, accident, fate, *informal* fluke, destiny **3** good fortune, success, *informal* break, godsend

lucky *adj* (**luckier, luckiest**) **1** fortunate, having good luck **2** bringing good luck: *lucky charm* ◇ **luckily** *adv*
■ **1** fortunate, favoured, successful, timely ◇ **luckily** fortunately, happily

lucrative *adj* profitable
■ profitable, well-paid, remunerative, advantageous
✷ unprofitable

lucre /'luːkə(r)/ *noun* gain; money

Luddite *noun* an opponent of technological innovation

Originally a group of protesters against the Industrial Revolution in the early 19th century, who based their name on Ned *Ludd*, an earlier opponent of machines for weaving stockings

ludicrous *adj* ridiculous ◇ **ludicrously** *adv*
■ absurd, ridiculous, preposterous, nonsensical, laughable, farcical, silly, comical, funny
✷ serious

ludo *noun* a game played with counters on a board

lug **1** *verb* (**lugs, lugging, lugged**) pull or drag with effort ◇ **lugger** *noun* a small sailing vessel

lug **2** *noun*, *informal* the ear ◇ **lughole** *noun*, *informal* the earhole

luggage *noun* suitcases and other travelling baggage

lugubrious *adj* mournful, dismal ◇ **lugubriously** *adv* ◇ **lugubriousness** *noun*

lugworm *noun* a large worm found on the seashore, used for fishing bait

lukewarm *adj* **1** neither hot nor cold **2** not very keen, unenthusiastic
■ **2** cool, half-hearted, apathetic, tepid, indifferent, unenthusiastic, uninterested, unresponsive, unconcerned

lull *verb* soothe or calm ◇ *noun* a period of calm
■ *verb* soothe, subdue, calm, hush, pacify, quieten down, quiet, quell ◇ *noun* calm, peace, quiet, tranquillity, stillness, pause, hush, silence

lullaby *noun* (*plural* **lullabies**) a song to lull children to sleep

lumbago *noun* a pain in the lower part of the back

lumbar *adj* of or in the lower part of the back

lumber **1** *noun* **1** sawn-up timber **2** discarded old furniture *etc*
■ **2** clutter, jumble, rubbish, bits and pieces, odds and ends, junk

lumber **2** *verb* move about clumsily
■ clump, shamble, plod, shuffle, stump, trundle

lumberjack *noun* someone who fells, saws and shifts trees

luminary *noun* (*plural* **luminaries**) an exemplary teacher or leader; an expert or authority

luminescent *adj* giving out light ◇ **luminescence** *noun*

luminous *adj* **1** giving light **2** shining; bright ◇ **luminosity** *noun* ◇ **luminously** *adv*
■ **1, 2** glowing, illuminated, lit, lighted, radiant, shining, fluorescent, brilliant, lustrous, bright

lump noun **1** a small, solid mass of indefinite shape **2** a swelling **3** the whole taken together: *considered in a lump* **4** a heavy, dull person ◇ *verb* **1** form into lumps **2** treat as being alike: *lumped all of us together* ◇ **lumpy** *adj* full of lumps ◇ **lump sum** an amount of money given all at once

◼ *noun* **1** mass, cluster, clump, clod, ball, bunch, piece, chunk, hunk, nugget, wedge **2** swelling, growth, bulge, bump, protuberance, protrusion, tumour

lumpectomy noun (*plural* **lumpectomies**) surgery to remove a lump in the breast

lumpish *adj* heavy, dull or awkward

lunacy *noun* madness, insanity

◼ madness, insanity, aberration, derangement, mania, *informal* craziness, idiocy, folly, absurdity, stupidity

lunar *adj* of the moon: *lunar eclipse*

lunatic *noun* someone who is insane or crazy ◇ *adj* insane, mad

◼ *noun* psychotic, psychopath, madman, maniac, *informal* loony, *informal* nutcase, *informal* nutter, *informal* fruitcake ◇ *adj* mad, insane, deranged, psychotic, irrational, *informal* crazy, *informal* bonkers

lunch *noun* (*plural* **lunches**) a midday meal ◇ *verb* eat lunch

luncheon *noun* lunch

lung *noun* either of the two bag-like organs which fill with and expel air in the course of breathing

lunge *noun* a sudden thrust or push ◇ *verb* thrust or plunge forward suddenly

◼ *noun* thrust, stab, pounce, charge, jab, pass, cut, spring ◇ *verb* thrust, jab, stab, pounce, plunge, charge, dart, dash, dive, poke, fall upon, grab (at), hit (at), leap

lupin *noun* a type of plant with flowers on long spikes

lurch *verb* roll or pitch suddenly to one side; stagger ◇ *noun* a pitch to one side ◇ **leave in the lurch** leave in a difficult position without help

◼ *verb* roll, rock, pitch, sway, stagger, reel, list

lure *noun* something which entices; a bait ◇ *verb* attract, entice away

◼ *noun* temptation, enticement, attraction, bait, inducement ◇ *verb* tempt, entice, draw, attract, allure, seduce

lurex *noun*, *trademark* a plastic-coated aluminium thread woven into fabric

lurid *adj* **1** glaring, garish: *lurid book covers* **2** horrifying, sensational: *a lurid story* **3** pale, ghostly

◼ **1** brightly coloured, garish, glaring, loud, vivid **2** macabre, gruesome, gory, ghastly, grisly, sensational, shocking, startling, graphic, exaggerated

lurk *verb* **1** keep out of sight; be hidden **2** move or act secretly and slyly ◇ **lurker** *noun* ◇ **lurking** *adj* vague, hidden

◼ *verb* **1** hide, lie low, crouch, lie in wait **2** skulk, prowl, snoop

luscious *adj* sweet, delicious, juicy

◼ delicious, juicy, succulent, appetizing, mouth-watering, sweet, tasty, savoury, desirable

lush *adj* of grass *etc*: thick and plentiful

◼ flourishing, luxuriant, abundant, prolific, overgrown, green, verdant

lust *noun* **1** a greedy desire (for power, riches *etc*) **2** a strong sexual desire ◇ *verb* have a strong desire (for) ◇ **lustful** *adj* ◇ **lustfully** *adv*

◼ *noun* **1** craving, desire, appetite, longing, passion, greed, covetousness **2** sensuality, libido, lechery, licentiousness

lustre or *US* **luster** *noun* brightness, shine, gloss ◇ **lustrous** *adj* bright, shining, glossy

◼ *noun* shine, gloss, sheen, gleam, glow, brilliance, brightness, radiance, sparkle

lusty *adj* hearty, strong ◇ **lustily** *adv* ◇ **lustiness** *noun*

◼ robust, strong, sturdy, vigorous, hearty, healthy, *informal* gutsy, energetic, lively, strapping, powerful

lute *noun* a stringed musical instrument with a pear-shaped, round-backed body and fretted fingerboard ◇ **lutenist** *noun* a lute player

luxuriant *adj* **1** thick with leaves, flowers *etc* **2** richly ornamented

> ❗ Do not confuse with: **luxurious**

luxuriate *verb* **1** be luxuriant **2** enjoy; take delight (in)

luxurious *adj* full of luxuries; very comfortable ◇ **luxuriously** *adv* ◇ **luxuriousness** *noun*

- sumptuous, opulent, lavish, de luxe, plush, magnificent, splendid, expensive, costly, self-indulgent, pampered
- austere, spartan

> ❗ Do not confuse with: **luxuriant**

luxury *noun* (*plural* **luxuries**) **1** something very pleasant or expensive but not necessary: *having a car is a luxury* **2** the use or enjoyment of such things

- **2** sumptuousness, opulence, hedonism, splendour, affluence, richness, magnificence, pleasure, indulgence, gratification, comfort, extravagance, satisfaction
- **2** austerity

lychee /laɪˈtʃiː/ *noun* a small Chinese fruit with rough skin and translucent flesh

lychgate *noun* a churchyard gate with a porch

lycra *noun*, *trademark* a lightweight synthetic elastic fabric

lying *see* **lie**

lymph *noun* a colourless fluid in the body ◇ **lymph gland** one of the glands carrying lymph

lynch *verb* condemn and put to death without legal trial ◇ **lynch mob** a group of people intent on lynching someone

> Named after William *Lynch*, 19th-century Virginian planter who organized unofficial trials of suspected criminals

lynx *noun* (*plural* **lynxes**) a wild animal of the cat family, noted for its keen sight

lyre *noun* an ancient stringed musical instrument like a small, U-shaped harp

lyrebird *noun* an Australian bird with a lyre-shaped tail

lyric *noun* **1** a short poem, often expressing the poet's feelings **2** (**lyrics**) the words of a song ◇ *adj* **1** of a lyric **2** full of joy

lyrical *adj* **1** lyric **2** song-like **3** full of enthusiastic praise ◇ **lyrically** *adv*

Mm

M *abbrev* a thousand (from Latin *mille*)

m *abbrev* **1** metre(s) **2** mile(s) **3** married **4** male **5** masculine

MA *abbrev* Master of Arts

mac *short for* mackintosh

macabre *adj* gruesome, horrible

▤ gruesome, grisly, grim, horrible, frightful, dreadful, ghostly, eerie

macadamia *noun* an edible nut from an Australian evergreen tree

macadamize *verb* surface (a road) with small broken stones bound with tar

> Named after the 19th-century Scottish engineer John *McAdam* who invented the process

macaroni *noun* pasta shaped into short hollow tubes

macaroon *noun* a sweet cake or biscuit made with ground almonds and sugar

macassar *noun* oil obtained from ylang-ylang flowers, once popular as a hair oil

macaw *noun* a long-tailed, brightly coloured parrot

mace¹ *noun* a heavy staff with an ornamental head, carried as a sign of office

mace² *noun* a spice made from the covering of a nutmeg

macerate *verb* **1** make into pulp by steeping **2** *old* emaciate

machete /ma'ʃɛtɪ/ *noun* a heavy knife used to cut through foliage *etc*

machinations *noun plural* a crafty scheme, a plot

machine *noun* **1** a device with moving parts used to perform a task **2** a political party organization **3** *informal* a car, motorcycle *etc* ◇ *verb* sew *etc* with a machine ◇ **machinist** *noun* a machine

maker or operator ◇ **machine code** a system of symbols which can be understood by a computer

▤ **1** instrument, device, contrivance, tool, mechanism, engine, apparatus, appliance

machinery *noun* **1** machines in general **2** the working parts of a machine **3** organization: *machinery of local government*

▤ **1** instruments, tools, apparatus, equipment, tackle, gear **2** mechanism, works **3** organization, channels, structure, system, procedure

machine-gun *noun* an automatic rapid-firing gun

machismo /ma'kɪzmoʊ/ *noun* overt or aggressive masculinity

Mach number the ratio of the speed of an aircraft to the speed of sound (*eg* Mach 5 = 5 times the speed of sound)

macho /'matʃoʊ/ *adj* overtly or aggressively masculine

mackerel *noun* an edible sea-fish with wavy markings

mackintosh *noun* (*plural* **mackintoshes**) a waterproof overcoat

macramé *noun* ornamental knotted threadwork

macro *noun*, *comput* a single instruction that prompts a computer to carry out a series of short instructions

macrobiotic *adj* of diet: consisting of organic unprocessed food, especially vegetables

macula *noun* a spot or mark, *eg* on the skin

mad *adj* **1** out of your mind, insane **2** wildly foolish **3** furious with anger ◇ **madhouse** *noun* **1** a place of confusion and noise **2** *hist* an asylum for the insane ◇ **madman, madwoman** *noun* someone who is insane ◇ **madness**

noun ◇**like mad** very quickly or energetically

■ **1** insane, lunatic, unbalanced, psychotic, deranged, demented, out of one's mind, *informal* crazy, *informal* nuts, *informal* barmy, *informal* bonkers **3** angry, furious, enraged, infuriated, incensed

ᴇᴀ **1** sane **3** calm

madam *noun* a polite form of address to a woman

madcap *noun* a rash, hot-headed person ◇*adj* foolishly rash: *a madcap scheme*

madden *verb* make angry or mad ◇**maddening** *adj* extremely annoying

■ anger, enrage, infuriate, incense, exasperate, provoke, annoy, irritate

ᴇᴀ calm, pacify

made *past form* of **make**

madeira *noun* **1** a kind of fortified white wine **2** a plain rich sponge cake

madly *adv* **1** insanely **2** extremely: *madly in love*

■ **1** insanely, dementedly, hysterically, wildly **2** intensely, extremely, exceedingly, fervently, devotedly

Madonna *noun* the Virgin Mary as depicted in art

madrigal *noun* a part-song for several voices

maelstrom /ˈmeɪlstroʊm/ *noun* **1** a whirlpool **2** any place of great confusion

maestro /ˈmaɪstroʊ/ *noun* (*plural* **maestros**) someone highly skilled in an art, especially music

MAFF *abbrev* Ministry of Agriculture, Fisheries and Food

magazine *noun* **1** a periodical paper containing articles, stories and pictures **2** a storage place for military equipment **3** a place for extra cartridges in a rifle

■ **1** journal, periodical, paper, weekly, monthly, quarterly **2** arsenal, storehouse, ammunition dump, depot, ordnance

The sense of *magazine* as a periodical developed from the military use, being intended as a storehouse or treasury of information

magenta *noun* a reddish-purple colour ◇*adj* of this colour

maggot *noun* a small worm-like creature, the grub of a bluebottle *etc* ◇**maggoty** *adj* full of maggots

Magi *see* **magus**

magic *noun* **1** a supernatural process producing results which cannot be explained or which are remarkable **2** conjuring tricks ◇*adj* **1** using magic **2** used in magic **3** magical ◇**black magic** magic performed for an evil purpose; witchcraft

■ *noun* **1** sorcery, enchantment, occultism, black art, witchcraft, spell **2** conjuring, illusion, sleight of hand, trickery

magical *adj* **1** of or produced by magic **2** very wonderful or mysterious ◇**magically** *adv*

■ **2** charming, enchanting, bewitching, fascinating, spellbinding

magician *noun* someone skilled in magic

■ sorcerer, miracle-worker, conjuror, illusionist, enchanter, wizard, witch, warlock, spellbinder

magisterial *adj* **1** of magistrates **2** having an air of authority ◇**magisterially** *adv*

magistrate *noun* someone with the power to enforce the law, *eg* a justice of the peace or a provost

magma *noun* molten rock

magnanimous *adj* very generous ◇**magnanimously** *adv* ◇**magnanimity** *noun* generosity

■ generous, liberal, open-handed, benevolent, selfless, charitable, big-hearted, kind, noble, unselfish, ungrudging

magnate *noun* someone with great power or wealth

■ tycoon, captain of industry, industrialist, mogul, entrepreneur, plutocrat, baron, personage, notable

magnesia *noun* a white powder formed from magnesium

magnesium *noun* a white metal which burns with an intense white light

magnet *noun* **1** a piece of iron, steel

etc which has the power to attract other pieces of metal **2** someone or something which attracts strongly

magnetic *adj* **1** having the powers of a magnet **2** strongly attractive: *magnetic personality* ◇ **magnetic north** the direction in which the magnetized needle of a compass points ◇ **magnetic tape** tape on which sound, pictures, computer data *etc* can be recorded

■ **2** attractive, alluring, fascinating, charming, mesmerizing, seductive, irresistible, entrancing, captivating, gripping, absorbing, charismatic

magnetism *noun* **1** the attractive power of a magnet **2** attraction, great charm

■ **2** attraction, allure, fascination, charm, lure, appeal, drawing power, draw, pull, hypnotism, mesmerism, charisma, grip, magic, power, spell

magnetize *verb* **1** make magnetic **2** attract, influence

magneto *noun* (*plural* **magnetos**) a device producing electric sparks, *eg* for lighting the fuel in a car engine

magnificent *adj* **1** splendid in appearance or action **2** excellent, very good ◇ **magnificence** *noun* ◇ **magnificently** *adv*

■ **1** splendid, grand, imposing, impressive, glorious, gorgeous, brilliant, excellent, majestic, superb, sumptuous, noble, elegant, fine, rich

🖪 **1** modest, humble, poor

magnify *verb* (**magnifies, magnifying, magnified**) **1** cause to appear larger *eg* by using special lenses **2** exaggerate ◇ **magnification** *noun*

■ **1** enlarge, amplify, increase, expand, *informal* blow up, intensify, boost, enhance, greaten, heighten **2** build up, exaggerate, dramatize, overemphasize, overplay, overstate, overdo, *informal* blow up

magniloquent *adj* of speech: overly grand; pompous ◇ **magniloquence** *noun*

magnitude *noun* size, importance

■ size, extent, measure, amount, expanse, dimensions, mass, proportions, quantity, volume, bulk, largeness, space, strength, amplitude, importance, significance, consequence, moment

magnolia *noun* a tree which produces large white or purplish sweet-scented flowers

magnum *noun* a bottle of wine or champagne equal to two ordinary bottles

magnum opus a great work, a masterpiece

magpie *noun* a black-and-white bird of the crow family, known for its habit of collecting objects

Originally *maggot pie*, meaning 'pied Margaret'

magus *noun* (*plural* **magi**) an ancient Persian priest or astrologer ◇ **the Magi** the three wise men who brought gifts to the infant Christ

Magyar *noun* the Hungarian language

maharajah *noun* an important Indian prince, especially the ruler of a state

maharani *noun* a maharajah's wife

maharishi *noun* a Hindu sage or religious leader

Mahdi *noun* the Islamic messiah

mah-jong *noun* a Chinese table game played with small painted bricks

mahogany *noun* **1** a tropical American hardwood tree **2** its hard reddish-brown wood, often used for furniture

maid *noun* **1** a female servant **2** *old* an unmarried woman; a young girl

maiden *noun*, *old* an unmarried girl; a virgin ◇ *adj* **1** of a maiden **2** unmarried: *maiden aunt* **3** first, initial: *maiden speech/maiden voyage* ◇ **maiden name** the surname of a married woman before her marriage ◇ **maiden over** *cricket* an over in which no runs are made

■ girl, virgin, lass, lassie, *formal* damsel, miss

mail[1] *noun* letters, parcels *etc* carried

by post ◇ *verb* post ◇ **mail order** an order for goods to be sent by post ◇ **mail shot** unsolicited advertising material sent by post

■ *noun* post, letters, correspondence, packages, parcels, delivery ◇ *verb* post, send, dispatch, forward

mail[2] *noun* body armour of steel rings or plates

maim *verb* cripple, disable

■ mutilate, wound, incapacitate, injure, disable, hurt, impair, cripple, lame

main *adj* chief, most important ◇ *noun, old* 1 the ocean 2 (**the mains**) a chief pipe, wire *etc* supplying gas, water or electricity ◇ **mainly** *adv* chiefly, mostly ◇ **in the main** for the most part

■ *adj* principal, chief, leading, first, foremost, predominant, pre-eminent, primary, prime, supreme, paramount, central, cardinal, outstanding, essential, critical, crucial, necessary, vital ◇ **mainly** primarily, principally, chiefly, in the main, mostly, on the whole, for the most part, generally, in general, especially, as a rule, above all, largely, overall

▣ *adj* minor, unimportant, insignificant

mainframe *noun* the central processing unit and storage unit of a computer ◇ *adj* of a computer: of the large, powerful type rather than the small-scale kind

mainland *noun* a large piece of land off whose coast smaller islands lie

mainline *verb, slang* inject drugs intravenously

mainsail *noun* the principal sail of a ship or boat

mainspring *noun* 1 the chief spring causing the wheels to move in a watch or clock 2 the chief cause of any action: *mainspring of the revolution*

mainstay *noun* the chief support

■ support, buttress, bulwark, linchpin, prop, pillar, backbone, foundation

maintain *verb* 1 keep (something) as it is 2 continue to keep in good working order 3 support (a family *etc*) 4 state (an opinion) firmly

■ 1 carry on, continue, keep (up), sustain, retain, preserve 2 conserve, look after, take care of, service 4 assert, affirm, claim, contend, declare, hold, state, insist, believe, fight for

▣ 2 neglect

maintenance *noun* 1 the act of maintaining; upkeep, repair 2 means of support, *esp* money for food, clothing *etc*

■ 1 conservation, repairs, upkeep, running 2 subsistence, living, livelihood, allowance, alimony, keep

maize *noun* a cereal crop producing corncobs

Maj *abbrev* Major

majesty *noun* (*plural* **majesties**) 1 a title used in addressing a king or queen: *Your Majesty* 2 greatness of rank or manner ◇ **majestic** *adj* stately, regal

■ **majestic** magnificent, grand, dignified, noble, royal, stately, splendid, imperial, impressive, exalted, imposing, regal, superb, lofty, monumental, pompous

▣ **majestic** lowly, unimpressive, unimposing

majolica *noun* tin-glazed decorative earthenware

major *adj* great in size, importance *etc* (*contrasted with*: **minor**) ◇ *noun* a senior army officer

■ *adj* greater, chief, main, larger, bigger, higher, leading, outstanding, notable, supreme, uppermost, significant, crucial, important, key, keynote, great, senior, older, superior, pre-eminent, vital, weighty

▣ *adj* minor, unimportant, trivial

majority *noun* (*plural* **majorities**) 1 the greater number or quantity 2 the difference in amount between the greater and the lesser number: *won by a majority of 46 votes* 3 the age when someone becomes legally an adult (18 in the UK)

■ 1 bulk, mass, preponderance, most, greater part

make *verb* (**makes, making, made**) 1 form, construct 2 cause to be: *he makes me mad at times* 3 bring about: *make trouble* 4 amount to: *2 and 2 make 4* 5 earn: *she made £800 last week* **6** force: *I made him do it* **7** undergo (a journey *etc*) **8** prepare (a meal *etc*): *I'll make some tea* ◇ *noun* a brand of commercial product ◇ **maker** *noun* ◇ **make believe** pretend ◇ **make good 1** do well **2** carry out (a promise) **3** make up for (a loss) ◇ **make light of** treat as unimportant ◇ **make much of** fuss over, treat as important ◇ **make nothing of 1** be unable to understand, do *etc* **2** make light of ◇ **make off** run away ◇ **make out 1** see in the distance or indistinctly; understand with difficulty **2** declare, prove **3** write out (a bill *etc*) formally ◇ **make-up** *noun* cosmetics ◇ **make up 1** form a whole: *eleven players make up the side* **2** put together, invent (a false story) **3** put make-up on the face **4** be friendly again after a quarrel ◇ **make up for** give or do something in return for damage done ◇ **on the make** *informal* **1** looking for personal gain **2** looking for a sexual partner

◼ *verb* **1** create, manufacture, fabricate, construct, build, produce, put together, originate, compose, form, shape **3** cause, bring about, effect, accomplish, occasion, give rise to, generate **5** earn, gain, net, obtain, acquire **6** coerce, force, oblige, constrain, compel, prevail upon, pressurize, press, require ◇ *noun* brand, sort, type, style, variety, manufacture, model, mark, kind, form, structure ◇ **make off** run off, run away, depart, bolt, leave, fly, *informal* cut and run, *informal* beat a hasty retreat, *informal* clear off ◇ **make out 1** discern, perceive, decipher, distinguish, recognize, see, detect, discover, understand, work out, grasp, follow, fathom **2** claim, assert, describe, demonstrate, prove **3** draw up, complete, fill in, write out ◇ **make up 1** complete, fill, supply, meet, supplement **2** create, invent, devise, fabricate, construct, originate, formulate, dream up, compose **4** be reconciled, make peace, settle differences, forgive and forget, bury the hatchet ◇ **make up for** compensate for, make good, make amends for, redress, recompense, redeem, atone for

makeover *noun* a series of improvements to the appearance of someone or something

makeshift *adj* used for a time for want of something better

◼ temporary, improvised, rough and ready, provisional, substitute, stopgap

◪ permanent

malachite *noun* a green mineral, basic copper carbonate

maladjusted *adj* unable to fit in happily in your environment, society *etc*

◼ disturbed, unstable, confused, alienated, neurotic, estranged

◪ well-adjusted

maladministration *noun* bad management, especially of public affairs

maladroit *adj* **1** clumsy, awkward **2** tactless

malady *noun* (*plural* **maladies**) illness, disease

malaise *noun* a feeling or general air of depression or despondency

malapropism *noun* the use of a wrong word which sounds similar to the one intended, *eg contemptuous* for *contemporary*

After Mrs *Malaprop* in Sheridan's play, *The Rivals* (1775), who habitually used the wrong word

malaria *noun* a fever caused by the bite of a mosquito ◇ **malarial** *adj*

From an Italian phrase meaning 'bad air', malarial fever being originally thought to be caused by poisonous marsh gases

male *adj* of the sex that is able to father children or young, masculine ◇ *noun* a member of this sex

malediction *noun* a curse; cursing ◇ **maledictory** *adj*

malefactor *noun* an evildoer

malevolent *adj* wishing ill to others; spiteful ◇ **malevolence** *noun* ◇ **malevolently** *adv*

◼ malicious, malign, spiteful, vindictive, ill-natured, hostile, vicious, venomous, evil-minded

▪ benevolent, kind

malformation noun faulty or wrong shape

▪ irregularity, deformity, distortion, warp

malfunction verb fail to work or operate properly ◇ noun failure to operate

▪ verb break down, go wrong, fail ◇ noun fault, defect, failure, breakdown

malice noun ill will; spite

▪ malevolence, enmity, animosity, ill-will, hatred, hate, spite, vindictiveness, bitterness

▪ love

malicious adj intending harm; spiteful ◇**maliciously** adv ◇**maliciousness** noun

▪ malevolent, ill-natured, malign, spiteful, venomous, vicious, vengeful, evil-minded, bitter, resentful

▪ kind, friendly

malign /mə'laɪn/ verb speak ill of

▪ defame, slander, libel, disparage, abuse, informal run down, harm, injure

▪ praise

malignant adj 1 wishing harm, spiteful 2 of a disease or tumour: likely to cause death (contrasted with: **benign**) ◇**malignantly** adv

▪ 1 malevolent, malicious, spiteful, evil, hostile, vicious, venomous, destructive, harmful, hurtful, pernicious 2 fatal, deadly, incurable, terminal, dangerous, cancerous, uncontrollable, virulent

▪ 1 kind 2 benign

malinger verb pretend to be ill to avoid work etc ◇**malingerer** noun

mall /mɔːl/ or /mæl/ noun a shopping centre

mallard noun common wild duck, the male of which has a green head

malleable adj 1 of metal: able to be beaten out by hammering 2 of people: easy to influence ◇**malleability** noun

mallet noun a heavy wooden hammer

malnutrition noun lack of sufficient or proper food; undernourishment

malodorous adj having a bad smell

malpractice noun 1 wrongdoing 2

professional misconduct

▪ 2 misconduct, mismanagement, negligence, impropriety, formal dereliction of duty, abuse, misdeed

malt noun 1 barley or other grain prepared for making beer or whisky 2 a malt whisky

maltreat verb treat roughly or unkindly ◇**maltreatment** noun

▪ ill-treat, mistreat, misuse, abuse, injure, harm, damage, hurt

▪ care for

mama or **mamma** noun, informal mother

mamba noun a large deadly African snake, black or green in colour

mammal noun a member of the class of animals in which the female parent feeds the young with her own milk ◇**mammalian** adj

---

Mammals include:
aardvark, anteater, antelope, armadillo, baboon, badger, bat, bear, beaver, bushbaby, camel, cat, chimpanzee, chipmunk, cow, deer, dog, dolphin, duck-billed platypus, dugong, echidna, elephant, flying lemur, fox, gerbil, gibbon, giraffe, goat, gorilla, guinea pig, hamster, hare, hedgehog, hippopotamus, horse, human being, hyena, kangaroo, koala, lemming, leopard, lion, manatee, marmoset, marmot, marsupial mouse, mole, mouse, opossum, orang utan, otter, pig, porcupine, porpoise, rabbit, raccoon, rat, rhinoceros, sea cow, seal, sea lion, sheep, shrew, sloth, squirrel, tamarin, tapir, tiger, vole, wallaby, walrus, weasel, whale, wolf, zebra
see also **dog**; **rodent**

---

mammary adj of a female breast or breasts: mammary gland

mammogram noun an X-ray taken of a woman's breast to detect early signs of cancer

mammon noun money considered as the root of evil

mammoth noun a very large elephant, now extinct ◇*adj* enormous, huge: *mammoth savings*

▣ *adj* enormous, huge, vast, colossal, gigantic, giant, massive, immense, monumental, mighty

▣ *adj* tiny, minute

man *noun* (*plural* **men**) **1** a grown-up human male **2** a human being **3** the human race **4** *informal* a husband **5** a piece in chess or draughts ◇*verb* (**mans**, **manning**, **manned**) supply with workers, crew *etc*: *man the boats* ◇**mannish** *adj* of a woman: behaving or looking like a man ◇**man-of-war** *noun* a warship ◇**the man in the street** the ordinary person

▣ *noun* **1** male, gentleman, fellow, *informal* bloke, *informal* chap, *informal* guy **2** person, individual, adult, human **3** humanity, humankind, mankind, human race, people, Homo sapiens, mortals ◇ *verb* staff, crew, take charge of, operate, occupy

manacle *noun*, *formal* a handcuff ◇*verb* handcuff

manage *verb* **1** have control or charge of; deal with **2** cope: *can't manage on his own* **3** succeed: *managed to finish on time*

▣ **1** control, influence, deal with, handle, operate, manipulate, guide **2** cope, fare, survive, get by, get along, get on, make do

manageable *adj* easily managed or controlled ◇**manageably** *adv*

management *noun* **1** those in charge of a business *etc* **2** the art of managing a business *etc*

▣ **1** managers, directors, directorate, executive, executives, governors, board, *informal* bosses, supervisors

manager *noun* someone in charge of a business *etc*

▣ director, executive, administrator, controller, superintendent, supervisor, overseer, governor, organizer, head, *informal* boss

manageress *noun*, *noun* a woman manager

mañana /man'jɑ:nə/ *noun* tomorrow; sometime in the future

Mancunian *noun* someone born or living in Manchester

mandarin *noun* **1** a small orange-like citrus fruit **2** *hist* a senior Chinese official

mandate *noun* **1** power to act on someone else's behalf **2** a command

▣ **1** warrant, authorization, authority, instruction, commission **2** injunction, charge, directive, order, command, decree, edict

mandatory *adj* compulsory ◇**mandatorily** *adv*

▣ obligatory, compulsory, binding, required, necessary, requisite, essential

▣ optional

mandible *noun* the jaw or lower jawbone

mandolin or **mandoline** *noun* a round-backed stringed instrument similar to a lute

mandrake *noun* a poisonous plant of the potato family with a forked root

mandrill *noun* a large baboon from W Africa with a red and blue muzzle

mane *noun* **1** long hair on the head and neck of a horse or male lion **2** a long or thick head of hair

maneuver *US spelling* of **manoeuvre**

manful *adj* courageous ◇**manfully** *adv*

manganese *noun* a hard, easily broken metal of a greyish-white colour

mange /meɪndʒ/ *noun* a skin disease of dogs, cats *etc* ◇**mangy** *adj*

mangel-wurzel *noun* a kind of beetroot used as cattle food

manger *noun* a box or trough holding dry food for horses and cattle

mangetout /mɒndʒ'tu:/ *noun* a thin pea with an edible pod

mangle[1] *noun* a machine for squeezing water out of clothes or for smoothing them ◇*verb* squeeze (clothes) through a mangle

mangle[2] *verb* crush, tear, damage badly

▣ mutilate, disfigure, mar, maim, spoil,

butcher, destroy, deform, wreck, twist, maul, distort

mango noun (plural **mangoes**) **1** the fruit of a tropical Indian tree, with juicy orange flesh **2** the tree which produces mangoes

mangrove noun a type of tree which grows in swamps in hot countries and has roots above the ground

manhandle verb handle roughly

▤ haul, heave, hump, pull, push, shove, tug, maul, mistreat, maltreat, misuse, abuse, informal knock about

manhole noun a hole (into a drain, sewer etc) large enough to let a person through

manhood noun the state of being a man

mania noun **1** a form of mental illness in which the sufferer is over-active, over-excited and unreasonably happy **2** extreme fondness or enthusiasm: a mania for stamp-collecting

▤ **1** madness, insanity, lunacy, psychosis, derangement, disorder, aberration, informal craziness, frenzy **2** passion, craze, rage, obsession, compulsion, enthusiasm, informal fad, infatuation, fixation, craving

---

Manias (by name of disorder) include: dipsomania (alcohol), bibliomania (books), ailuromania (cats), demomania (crowds), necromania (dead bodies), thanatomania (death), cynomania (dogs), narcomania (drugs), pyromania (fire-raising), anthomania (flowers), hippomania (horses), mythomania (lying and exaggerating), egomania (oneself), ablutomania (personal cleanliness), hedonomania (pleasure), megalomania (power), theomania (religion), nymphomania (sex), monomania (single idea or thing), kleptomania (stealing), tomomania (surgery), logomania (talking), ergomania (work)
see also **phobia**

---

maniac noun **1** a mad person **2** a very rash or over-enthusiastic person

▤ **1** lunatic, madman, madwoman, psychotic, psychopath, informal loony, slang nutter **2** enthusiast, informal fan, fanatic, informal fiend, informal freak

manic adj **1** suffering from mania **2** very energetic or excited ◇**manically** adv

manicure noun **1** the care of hands and nails **2** professional treatment for the hands and nails ◇verb perform a manicure on ◇**manicurist** noun someone who performs manicures

manifest adj easily seen or understood ◇verb show plainly ◇**manifestation** noun ◇**manifestly** adv obviously, clearly

▤ adj obvious, evident, clear, apparent, plain, open, patent, noticeable, conspicuous, unmistakable, visible, unconcealed ◇ verb show, exhibit, display, demonstrate, reveal, expose, prove, illustrate

manifesto noun (plural **manifestoes** or **manifestos**) a public announcement of intentions, eg by a political party

manifold adj many and various

▤ many, numerous, varied, various, diverse, multiple, abundant, copious

manila noun strong brown paper used for envelopes etc

manipulate verb **1** handle so as to turn to your own advantage **2** move or work (something) with the hands ◇**manipulation** noun ◇**manipulative** adj

▤ **1** influence, engineer, guide, direct, steer, negotiate, work, falsify, rig, juggle with, informal doctor, informal cook, informal fiddle

mankind noun the human race

manky adj, slang dirty, grubby ◇**mankiness** noun

manly adj brave, strong ◇**manliness** noun

manna noun an unexpected or delicious treat

The name given in the Bible to the food miraculously provided for the Israelites in the wilderness

mannequin *noun* **1** someone who models clothes for prospective buyers **2** a display dummy

manner *noun* **1** the way in which something is done **2** the way in which someone behaves **3** (**manners**) polite behaviour towards others ◇ **mannerly** *adj* polite ◇ **all manner of** all kinds of
◼ **1** way, method, means, fashion, style, procedure, process **2** behaviour, conduct, bearing, demeanour, air, character **3** etiquette, politeness, courtesy, formalities, social graces, p's and q's

mannerism *noun* an odd and obvious habit or characteristic
◼ idiosyncrasy, peculiarity, characteristic, quirk, trait, feature, foible, habit

manoeuvre or *US* **maneuver** *noun* **1** a planned movement, *eg* of troops, ships or aircraft **2** a trick, a cunning plan ◇ *verb* **1** perform a manoeuvre **2** manipulate to gain an advantage
◼ *verb* **1** move, manipulate, handle, guide, pilot, steer, navigate, direct, drive, exercise **2** contrive, engineer, plot, scheme, *informal* wangle, *informal* pull strings, manipulate, manage, plan, devise, negotiate

manor *noun* **1** a large house, usually attached to a country estate **2** *hist* the land belonging to a lord or squire ◇ **manorial** *adj*

manpower *noun* the number of people available for work

manqué /'mɒŋkeɪ/ *adj* unfulfilled in a particular ambition: *a poet manqué*

mansard roof a roof with a divided slope which is steeper in the lower part

manse *noun* the house of a minister in certain Christian churches

mansion *noun* a large house

manslaughter *noun* killing someone without deliberate intent

mantelpiece *noun* a shelf over a fireplace

mantis *noun* an insect of the cockroach family, with large spiny forelegs (*also called*: **praying mantis**)

mantle *noun* **1** a cloak or loose outer garment **2** a covering: *a mantle of snow* **3** a thin, transparent shade around the flame of a gas or paraffin lamp
◼ **1** cloak, cape, hood, shawl, veil, wrap **2** shroud, screen, cover, covering, blanket

mantra *noun* a word or phrase chanted or repeated inwardly in meditation

manual *adj* **1** of the hand or hands **2** worked by hand **3** working with the hands: *manual worker* ◇ *noun* a handbook giving instructions on how to use something: *a car manual* ◇ **manually** *adv*
◼ *adj* **2** hand-operated, by hand, physical, human ◇ *noun* handbook, guide, guidebook, instructions, Bible, vade mecum, directions
◪ *adj* **2** automatic

manufacture *verb* make (articles or materials) in large quantities, *usu* by machine ◇ *noun* **1** the process of manufacturing **2** a manufactured article ◇ **manufacturer** *noun*
◼ *verb* make, produce, construct, build, fabricate, create, assemble, mass-produce, turn out, process, forge, form ◇ *noun* **1** production, construction, fabrication, mass-production, assembly, formation

manure *noun* a substance, especially animal dung, spread on soil to make it more fertile ◇ *verb* treat with manure

manuscript *noun* **1** the prepared material for a book *etc* before it is printed **2** a book or paper written by hand

Manx cat a tailless breed of cat

many *adj* a large number of: *many people were present* ◇ *pronoun* a large number: *many survived* ◇ **many a** a large number of: *many a voice was raised*
◼ *adj* numerous, countless, *informal* lots of, *formal* manifold, various, varied, sundry, diverse, *informal* umpteen
◪ *adj & pronoun* few

map *noun* a flat drawing of all or part of the earth's surface, showing geographical features ◇ *verb* (**maps, mapping, mapped**) make a map of ◇ **map out** plan

maple *noun* **1** a tree related to the

sycamore, one variety of which produces sugar **2** its hard light-coloured wood used for furniture *etc*

mar *verb* (**mars**, **marring**, **marred**) spoil, deface

▱ spoil, impair, harm, hurt, damage, deface, disfigure, mutilate, injure, maim, scar, detract from, mangle, ruin, wreck, tarnish

▱ enhance

maracas *noun plural* a pair of filled gourds shaken as a percussion instrument

maraschino /marə'ʃiːnoʊ/ *noun* a liqueur distilled from cherries

marathon *noun* a long-distance race on foot, usually covering 26 miles 385 yards

After the distance run by a Greek soldier from *Marathon* to Athens with news of the victory over the Persians

maraud *verb* plunder, raid ◇ **marauder** *noun* a plundering robber ◇ **marauding** *adj*

▱ **marauder** bandit, brigand, robber, raider, plunderer, pillager, pirate, buccaneer, outlaw, ravager, predator

marble *noun* **1** limestone that takes a high polish, used for sculpture, decorating buildings *etc* **2** a small glass ball used in a children's game

marcasite *noun* crystals formed from iron and used in jewellery

March *noun* the third month of the year

march¹ *verb* **1** (cause to) walk in time with regular steps **2** go on steadily: *time marches on* ◇ *noun* (*plural* **marches**) **1** a marching movement **2** a procession **3** a piece of music for marching to **4** the distance covered by marching **5** a steady progression of events: *the march of time*

▱ *verb* **1** walk, stride, parade, pace, file ◇ *noun* **2** parade, demonstration, *informal* demo **5** development, progress, evolution, passage

march² *noun* a boundary or border ◇ **riding the marches** the traditional

ceremony of riding around the boundaries of a town *etc*

marchioness *noun* (*plural* **marchionesses**) a woman marquess

Mardi Gras a carnival held on Shrove Tuesday in certain countries

mare *noun* a female horse

margarine *noun* an edible spread similar to butter, made mainly of vegetable fats

margarita *noun* a cocktail made with tequila and lime juice *etc*

margin *noun* **1** an edge, a border **2** the blank edge on the page of a book **3** additional space or room; allowance: *margin for error*

▱ **1** border, edge, boundary, bound, periphery, perimeter, rim, brink, limit, confine, verge, side, skirt **3** allowance, play, leeway, latitude, scope, room, space, surplus, extra

marginal *adj* **1** of or in a margin **2** borderline, close to a limit **3** of a political constituency: without a clear majority for any one candidate or party **4** of little effect or importance: *marginal improvement* ◇ *noun* a marginal political constituency ◇ **marginalize** *verb* make less important or central ◇ **marginally** *adv*

▱ *adj* **2** borderline, peripheral **4** negligible, minimal, insignificant, minor, slight, doubtful, low, small

▱ *adj* **2** central, core

marguerite *noun* a kind of large daisy

marigold *noun* a kind of plant with a yellow flower

marijuana *noun* a drug made from the plant hemp

marimba *noun* an African instrument like a xylophone, often used in jazz music

marina *noun* a place with moorings for yachts, dinghies *etc*

marinade *noun* a mixture of oil, wine, herbs, spices *etc* in which food is steeped for flavour ◇ **marinade** or **marinate** *verb* steep in a marinade

marine *adj* of the sea ◇ *noun* a soldier

serving on board a ship

■ *adj* sea, maritime, naval, nautical, seafaring, sea-going, ocean-going, saltwater

mariner /'marɪnə(r)/ *noun*, *old* a sailor

■ sailor, seaman, seafarer, deckhand, navigator, *informal* tar, *informal* sea-dog, *informal* salt

marionette *noun* a puppet moved by strings

marital *adj* of marriage ◊ **maritally** *adv*

■ conjugal, matrimonial, married, wedded, *formal* nuptial, *formal* connubial

maritime *adj* 1 of the sea or ships 2 lying near the sea

marjoram *noun* a sweet-smelling herb used in cooking

Mark *noun* a Deutschmark, a former unit of German money

mark *noun* 1 a sign that can be seen 2 a stain, spot *etc* 3 a target aimed at 4 a trace left behind 5 a point used to assess the merit of a piece of schoolwork *etc* 6 the starting-line in a race: *on your marks!* ◊ *verb* 1 make a mark on; stain 2 observe, pay heed to 3 stay close to (an opponent in football *etc*) 4 award marks to (a piece of schoolwork *etc*) ◊ **marked** *adj* easily noticed: *marked improvement* ◊ **markedly** *adv* noticeably ◊ **marker** *noun* 1 something used to mark a position 2 someone who marks exam papers *etc* ◊ **mark off** separate, distinguish ◊ **marksman, markswoman** *noun* someone who shoots well ◊ **mark time** 1 move the feet up and down, as if marching, but without going forward 2 keep things going without progressing ◊ **up to the mark** coming up to the required standard

■ *noun* 1 symbol, sign, indication, emblem, brand, stamp, token, characteristic, feature, proof, evidence, badge 2 spot, stain, blemish, blot, blotch, smudge, scar, scratch, bruise, line 3 goal, aim, objective, purpose 4 dent, impression, print, scratch, scar ◊ *verb* 1 stain, blemish, blot, smudge, dent,

scar, scratch, bruise 2 heed, mind, note, observe, regard, notice 4 evaluate, assess, correct, grade ◊ **marked** noticeable, obvious, conspicuous, evident, pronounced, distinct, decided, emphatic, considerable, remarkable, apparent, glaring

■ **marked** imperceptible, slight

market *noun* 1 a public place for buying and selling 2 (a country, place *etc* where there is) a need or demand (for certain types of goods) ◊ *verb* put on sale ◊ **marketing** *noun* the act or practice of advertising and selling ◊ **market forces** commerce not restricted by government intervention ◊ **market garden** a garden in which fruit and vegetables are grown to be sold ◊ **market leader** a company, or brand of goods, that outsells its competitors ◊ **on the market** for sale

■ *noun* 1 mart, marketplace, bazaar, fair, exchange, outlet

marlin *noun* a large ocean fish related to the swordfish

marlinspike *noun* a spike for separating the strands of a rope *etc*

marmalade *noun* a jam made from citrus fruit, *esp* oranges

marmite *noun*, *trademark* a savoury spread made from yeast and vegetable extracts

marmoset *noun* a type of small monkey found in America

marmot *noun* a burrowing animal of the squirrel family (*also called*: **woodchuck** or **groundhog**)

maroon¹ *noun* 1 a brownish-red colour 2 a firework used as a distress signal ◊ *adj* brownish-red

maroon² *verb* 1 abandon on an island *etc* without means of escape 2 leave in a helpless or uncomfortable position

■ 1 cast away, desert, put ashore, strand, isolate 2 desert, strand, leave, isolate

marquee /maː'kiː/ *noun* a large tent used for large gatherings, *eg* a wedding reception or circus

marquetry *noun* the inlaying of

wood with small pieces of different coloured wood, ivory etc

marquis or **marquess** /'ma:kwɪs/ noun (plural **marquises** or **marquesses**) a nobleman below a duke in rank

marriage noun 1 the ceremony by which two people become husband and wife 2 a joining together: marriage of minds ◊**marriageable** adj suitable or old enough for marriage
▪ 2 union, alliance, merger, coupling, amalgamation, link, association, confederation

marrow noun 1 the soft substance in the hollow part of bones 2 a long thick-skinned vegetable

marry verb (**marries, marrying, married**) join, or be joined, together in marriage
▪ wed, join in matrimony, informal tie the knot, informal get hitched, informal get spliced

marsh noun (plural **marshes**) a piece of low-lying wet ground ◊**marsh gas** methane ◊**marsh marigold** a marsh plant with yellow flowers (also called: **kingcup**)

marshal noun 1 a high-ranking officer in the army or air force 2 someone who directs processions, controls crowds at public events etc 3 US a law-court official 4 US the head of a police force ◊verb (**marshals, marshalling, marshalled**) 1 arrange (troops, facts, arguments etc) in order 2 show the way, conduct, lead
▪ verb 1 arrange, dispose, order, line up, align, array, rank, organize, assemble, gather, muster, group, collect, draw up, deploy 2 guide, lead, escort, conduct, usher

marshmallow noun 1 a spongy jelly-like sweet made from sugar and egg-whites etc 2 a marsh plant with pink flowers, similar to the hollyhock

marshy adj wet underfoot; boggy

marsupial noun an animal which carries its young in a pouch, eg the kangaroo

martello tower a round coastal fort

marten noun an animal related to the weasel

martial adj 1 of war or battle 2 warlike ◊**martial art** a combative sport or method of self-defence ◊**martial law** the government of a country by its army

Martian noun a potential or imaginary being from the planet Mars

martin noun a bird of the swallow family

martinet noun someone who keeps strict order; a disciplinarian

> Named after Jean Martinet, a 17th-century French officer who invented a type of military drill

martini noun (plural **martinis**) a cocktail made with gin and vermouth

Martinmas noun 11 November, the feast of St Martin

martyr noun someone who suffers death or hardship for their beliefs ◊verb execute or make suffer for beliefs ◊**martyrdom** noun the death or suffering of a martyr

marvel noun something astonishing or wonderful ◊verb (**marvels, marvelling, marvelled**) feel amazement (at)
▪ noun wonder, miracle, phenomenon, prodigy, spectacle, sensation, genius ◊ verb wonder, gape, gaze, be amazed at

marvellous adj 1 astonishing, extraordinary 2 informal excellent, very good ◊**marvellously** adv
▪ 1 extraordinary, amazing, astonishing, astounding, miraculous, remarkable, surprising, unbelievable, incredible 2 wonderful, excellent, splendid, superb, magnificent, glorious, informal terrific, super, informal fantastic

Marxist noun a follower of the theories of Karl Marx; a communist ◊**Marxism** noun

marzipan noun a mixture of ground almonds, sugar etc, used in cake-making and confectionery

mascara noun a cosmetic used to colour the eyelashes

mascot *noun* a person, animal or thing believed to bring good luck

masculine *adj* **1** of the male sex **2** manly ◇ **masculinity** *noun*

mash *verb* beat or crush into a pulp ◇ *noun* **1** mashed potato **2** a mixture of bran, meal *etc*, used as animal food

◨ *verb* crush, pulp, beat, pound, pulverize, pummel, grind, smash

mask *noun* **1** a cover for the face for disguise or protection **2** a pretence, a disguise ◇ *verb* **1** hide, disguise **2** cover for protection ◇ **masked** *adj* wearing a mask

◨ *noun* **1** disguise, camouflage, veil, visor **2** front, façade, concealment, cover-up, cover, guise, pretence, semblance, cloak, show, veneer

masochism *noun* an unnatural pleasure in being dominated or treated cruelly ◇ **masochist** *noun* someone who takes such pleasure ◇ **masochistic** *adj*

> After Leopold von Sacher-*Masoch*, 19th-century Austrian novelist

mason *noun* **1** someone who carves stone **2** a Freemason ◇ **masonic** *adj*

masonry *noun* stonework

masque *noun* an old type of theatre performance with actors wearing masks

masquerade *noun* **1** a pretence **2** a dance at which masks are worn ◇ *verb* pretend to be someone else: *masquerading as a journalist*

◨ *noun* **1** cover-up, cover, deception, front, pose, pretence, guise ◇ *verb* disguise, impersonate, pose, pass oneself off, mask, play, pretend, profess

Mass or **mass** *noun* **1** (in some Christian churches) the celebration of Christ's last supper with his disciples **2** part of the text of a Mass set to music and sung

mass *noun* (*plural* **masses**) **1** a lump or quantity gathered together **2** a large quantity **3** the main part or body **4** a measure of quantity of matter in an object ◇ *adj* **1** of a mass **2** of or consisting of large numbers or quantities ◇ *verb* form into a mass or crowd ◇ **mass media** means of communicating information to a large number of people, *eg* television ◇ **mass production** production in large quantities of articles all exactly the same ◇ **the masses** ordinary people

◨ *noun* **1** heap, pile, load, accumulation, collection, conglomeration, combination, entirety, whole, totality, sum, lot, group, batch, bunch **3** majority, body, bulk ◇ *adj* **2** widespread, large-scale, extensive, comprehensive, general, indiscriminate, popular, across-the-board, sweeping, wholesale, blanket ◇ *verb* collect, gather, assemble, congregate, crowd, rally, cluster, muster, swarm, throng

◨ *adj* **2** limited, small-scale ◇ *verb* separate

massacre *noun* the merciless killing of a large number of people ◇ *verb* kill (a large number) in a cruel way

◨ *noun* slaughter, murder, extermination, carnage, butchery, holocaust, blood bath, annihilation, killing ◇ *verb* slaughter, butcher, murder, mow down, wipe out, exterminate, annihilate, kill, decimate

massage *noun* the rubbing of parts of the body to remove pain or tension ◇ *verb* perform massage on

masseur *noun* someone who performs massage

masseuse *noun* a female masseur

massive *adj* bulky, heavy, huge ◇ **massively** *adv*

◨ huge, immense, enormous, vast, colossal, *informal* mega, gigantic, big, bulky, monumental, solid, substantial, heavy, large-scale, extensive

◨ tiny, small

mast *noun* a long upright pole holding up the sails *etc* in a ship, or holding an aerial, flag *etc*

mastectomy *noun* the surgical removal of a woman's breast or breasts

master *noun* **1** someone who controls or commands **2** an owner of a dog *etc* **3** an employer **4** a male teacher **5** the commander of a merchant ship **6** someone who is very skilled in something, an expert **7** (**Master**) (someone with) a higher degree awarded by universities: *Master of Arts* ◇ *adj* chief, controlling: *master switch* ◇ *verb* **1** overcome, defeat **2** become able to do or use properly: *I've finally mastered this computer program* ◇ **master of ceremonies** someone who directs the form and order of events at a public occasion; a compère

■ *noun* **1** ruler, chief, governor, head, lord, captain, *informal* boss, commander, controller, director, manager, superintendent, overseer, principal, overlord, owner **3** *informal* boss, employer, director, manager ◇ *verb* **1** conquer, defeat, subdue, subjugate, vanquish, triumph over, overcome, quell, rule, control **2** learn, grasp, acquire, *informal* get the hang of, manage

masterful *adj* strong-willed

■ authoritative, domineering, overbearing, high-handed, despotic, dictatorial, autocratic, *informal* bossy, tyrannical, powerful

🖝 humble

master key a key which opens a number of different locks

masterly *adj* showing the skill of an expert or master

■ expert, skilled, skilful, dexterous, adept, adroit, first-rate, *informal* ace, excellent, superb, superior, supreme

mastermind *verb* plan, work out the details of (a scheme *etc*)

masterpiece *noun* the best example of someone's work, *esp* a very fine picture, book, piece of music *etc*

■ master-work, magnum opus, pièce de résistance, chef d'oeuvre

mastery *noun* **1** victory (over) **2** control (of) **3** great skill (in)

■ **3** proficiency, skill, ability, command, expertise, virtuosity, knowledge, know-how, dexterity, familiarity, grasp

🖝 **3** incompetence

mastic *noun* a gum resin from Mediterranean trees, used as a varnish or glue

masticate *verb*, *formal* chew ◇ **mastication** *noun*

mastiff *noun* a breed of large, powerful dog

mastodon *noun* an extinct animal similar to an elephant

masturbate *verb* stimulate the sexual organs to a state of orgasm ◇ **masturbation** *noun*

mat *noun* **1** a piece of material (coarse plaited plant fibre, carpet *etc*) for wiping shoes on, covering the floor *etc* **2** a piece of material, cork *etc* put below dishes at table ◇ *adj*, another spelling of **matt** ◇ **matted** *adj* thickly tangled ◇ **matting** *noun* material from which mats are made

matador *noun* the person who kills the bull in bullfights

match¹ *noun* (*plural* **matches**) a small stick of wood *etc* tipped with a substance which catches fire when rubbed against an abrasive surface

match² *noun* (*plural* **matches**) **1** a contest or game **2** a person or thing similar to, or the same as, another **3** a person or thing that goes well with another **4** an equal: *she's met her match* **5** someone suitable for marriage ◇ *verb* **1** be of the same make, size, colour *etc* **2** set (two things, teams *etc*) against each other **3** hold your own with, be equal to ◇ **matchless** *adj* having no equal

■ *noun* **1** contest, competition, bout, game, test, trial **2** equivalent, rival, copy, double, replica, duplicate **4** equal, peer, counterpart, fellow, mate ◇ *verb* **1** co-ordinate, blend, adapt, go together, relate, tone with **3** equal, compare, measure up to, rival, compete, vie

matchbox *noun* a box for holding matches

matchmaker *noun* someone who tries to arrange marriages or partnerships

matchstick *noun* the wooden stem of a match

matchwood *noun* wood broken into small pieces

mate noun **1** a friend, a companion **2** an assistant worker: *plumber's mate* **3** a husband or wife **4** the sexual partner of an animal, bird *etc* **5** a merchant ship's officer, next in rank to the captain ◇ *verb* **1** bring or come together to breed **2** marry

▣ *noun* **1** friend, companion, comrade, *informal* pal **2** assistant, helper, subordinate ◇ *verb* **1** couple, pair, breed, copulate **2** join, match, marry, wed

material *adj* **1** made of matter, able to be seen and felt **2** not spiritual, concerned with physical comfort, money *etc*: *a material outlook on life* **3** important, essential: *material difference* ◇ *noun* **1** something out of which anything is, or may be, made **2** cloth, fabric ◇ **materially** *adv* to a large extent, greatly

▣ *adj* **1** physical, concrete, tangible, substantial **3** relevant, significant, important, meaningful, pertinent, essential, vital, indispensable, serious ◇ *noun* **1** stuff, substance, body, matter **2** fabric, textile, cloth

◪ *adj* **1** abstract **3** irrelevant

materialism *noun* **1** a tendency to attach too much importance to material things (*eg* physical comfort, money) **2** the belief that only things we can see or feel really exist or are important ◇ **materialist** *noun* ◇ **materialistic** *adj*

materialize *verb* **1** appear in bodily form **2** happen, come about

▣ **1** appear, arise, take shape, turn up **2** happen, occur

◪ **1** disappear

maternal *adj* **1** of a mother **2** like a mother, motherly **3** related through your mother: *maternal grandmother* ◇ **maternally** *adv*

maternity *noun* the state of being a mother, motherhood ◇ *adj* of or for a woman having or about to have a baby: *maternity clothes*

math *noun*, *US informal* mathematics

mathematics *noun sing* the study of measurements, numbers and quantities ◇ **mathematical** *adj* **1** of or done by mathematics **2** very exact ◇ **mathe-**

matician *noun* an expert in mathematics

maths *noun*, *informal* mathematics

matinée *noun* an afternoon performance in a theatre or cinema ◇ **matinée coat** a baby's short jacket

matins *noun plural* the morning service in certain churches

matriarch *noun* a woman who controls a family or community ◇ **matriarchal** *adj*

matrices *plural* of **matrix**

matricide *noun* **1** the killing of your own mother **2** someone who kills their own mother

matriculate *verb* admit, or be admitted, to a university ◇ **matriculation** *noun*

matrimony *noun*, *formal* marriage ◇ **matrimonial** *adj* relating to marriage ◇ **matrimonially** *adv*

matrix *noun* (*plural* **matrices**) **1** a mould in which metals *etc* are shaped **2** a mass of rock in which gems *etc* are found **3** a rectangular table of data

matron *noun* **1** a married woman **2** formerly, a senior nurse in charge of a hospital **3** *old* a woman in charge of housekeeping or nursing in a school, care home *etc* ◇ **matronly** *adj* **1** of a woman: dignified, staid **2** rather plump

matt or **mat** *adj* having a dull surface; not shiny or glossy

matter *noun* **1** anything that takes up space, can be seen, felt *etc*; material, substance **2** a subject written or spoken about **3** (**matters**) affairs, business **4** trouble, difficulty: *what is the matter?* **5** importance: *of no great matter* **6** pus ◇ *verb* be of importance: *it doesn't matter* ◇ **a matter of course** something that is to be expected ◇ **a matter of opinion** a subject on which different opinions are held ◇ **as a matter of fact** in fact ◇ **matter-of-fact** *adj* keeping to the actual facts; unimaginative, uninteresting

▣ *noun* **1** substance, stuff, material, body, content **2** subject, issue, topic, question, affair, business, concern, event, episode, incident **4** trouble, problem, difficulty, worry **5** importance, significance, consequence, note ◇ *verb* count, be important, make a difference, mean something

mattock *noun* a tool like a pickaxe

mattress *noun* (*plural* **mattresses**) a thick layer of padding covered in cloth, usually as part of a bed

mature *adj* **1** fully grown or developed **2** ripe, ready for use ◇ *verb* **1** (cause to) become mature **2** of an insurance policy *etc*: be due to be paid out ◇ **maturely** *adv*
■ *adj* **1** adult, grown-up, grown, full-grown, fully fledged, complete **2** ripe, ripened, seasoned, mellow, ready ◇ *verb* **1** grow up, come of age, develop, mellow, ripen, age, bloom

maturity *noun* **1** adulthood **2** ripeness
■ **1** adulthood, majority, womanhood, manhood, wisdom, experience **2** ripeness, readiness, mellowness, perfection
◪ **1** childishness

matzo *noun* (*plural* **matzos** or **matzoth**) a wafer or cracker eaten during Passover

maudlin *adj* foolishly sad or sentimental

From Mary *Magdalene*, who was frequently depicted crying in paintings

maul *verb* hurt badly by rough or savage treatment
■ abuse, ill-treat, manhandle, maltreat, molest, paw, beat (up), knock about, rough up, claw, batter

Maundy Thursday the day before Good Friday in the Christian calendar

mausoleum *noun* a large or elaborate tomb

mauve *adj* of a purple colour

maverick *noun* someone who refuses to conform; a determined individualist

After Samuel *Maverick*, Texas rancher who never branded his cattle

maw *noun* **1** an animal's jaws or gullet

2 a wide or gaping cavity

mawkish *adj* weak and sentimental ◇ **mawkishly** *adv*

maxi- *prefix* very large or long: *maxiskirt*

maxim *noun* a general truth or rule about behaviour *etc*
■ saying, proverb, adage, axiom, aphorism, epigram, motto, byword, precept, rule

maximum *adj* greatest, most ◇ *noun* (*plural* **maxima**) **1** the greatest number or quantity **2** the highest point or degree
■ *adj* greatest, highest, largest, biggest, most, utmost, supreme ◇ *noun* **1** most, top (point), utmost, upper limit **2** peak, pinnacle, summit, height, ceiling, extremity, *formal* zenith
◪ *adj & noun* minimum

May *noun* the fifth month of the year

may *verb* (**may**, **might**) **1** used with another verb to express permission or possibility: *you may watch the film/I thought I might find him there* **2** used to express a wish: *may your wishes come true*

maybe *adv* perhaps
■ perhaps, possibly, *formal* perchance

Mayday *noun* the first day of May

mayday *noun* an international distress signal

mayfly *noun* a short-lived insect which appears in May

mayhem *noun* widespread chaos or confusion

mayo *noun*, *informal* mayonnaise

mayonnaise *noun* a cold sauce made of eggs, oil and vinegar or lemon juice

mayor *noun* the chief elected public official of a city or town ◇ **mayoress** *noun* a mayor's wife

maypole *noun* a decorated pole traditionally danced around on Mayday

maze *noun* **1** a network of winding paths, planned to make exit difficult **2** something complicated and confusing: *maze of regulations*
■ **1** labyrinth, network **2** tangle, web,

complex, confusion, puzzle, intricacy

mazurka *noun* a lively Polish dance or dance music

Mb *abbrev* megabyte(s)

MBE *abbrev* Member of the Order of the British Empire

mbyte *abbrev* megabyte

MD *abbrev* **1** Doctor of Medicine (from Latin *Medicinae Doctor*) **2** Managing Director

MDMA *abbrev* methylene-dioxymethamphetamine, the drug Ecstasy

ME *abbrev* myalgic encephalomyelitis, a condition of chronic fatigue and muscle pain following a viral infection

me *pronoun* the word used by a speaker or writer in mentioning themselves: *she kissed me/give it to me*

mea culpa my fault

mead *noun* an alcoholic drink made with honey

meadow *noun* a field of grass
▣ field, grassland, pasture, lea

meadowsweet *noun* a wild flower with sweet-smelling cream-coloured flowers

meagre or *US* **meager** *adj* **1** thin **2** poor in quality **3** scanty, not enough ◇ **meagreness** *noun*
▣ **1** thin, puny, insubstantial, bony, emaciated, scrawny, slight **3** scanty, sparse, inadequate, deficient, skimpy, paltry, negligible

meal[1] *noun* the food taken at one time, *eg* breakfast or dinner

meal[2] *noun* grain ground to a coarse powder

mealy-mouthed *adj* not frank and straightforward in speech

mean[1] *adj* **1** not generous with money *etc* **2** unkind, selfish **3** lowly, humble ◇ **meanly** *adv* ◇ **meanness** *noun*
▣ **1** miserly, niggardly, parsimonious, *informal* tight, tight-fisted, *informal* stingy, *informal* penny-pinching **2** unkind, unpleasant, nasty, bad-tempered, cruel, spiteful **3** lowly, base, poor, humble, wretched
▣ **1** generous **2** kind **3** splendid

mean[2] *adj* **1** midway between two other points, quantities *etc*; middle **2** average ◇ *noun* a mean point or amount; a middle course ◇ **in the meantime** meanwhile ◇ **meanwhile** *adv* in the time between two happenings
▣ *adj* **1** intermediate, middle, halfway **2** average, normal ◇ *noun* average, middle, midpoint, norm, median, compromise, middle course, middle way, happy medium

mean[3] *verb* (**means, meaning, meant**) **1** intend to express; indicate: *what do you mean?/when I say no, I mean no* **2** intend: *how do you mean to do that?* ◇ **mean well** have good intentions
▣ **1** signify, represent, denote, stand for, symbolize, suggest, indicate, imply **2** intend, aim, propose, design

meander /mɪˈandə(r)/ *verb* **1** of a river: flow in a winding course **2** wander about slowly and aimlessly
▣ **1** wind, zigzag, turn, twist, snake, curve **2** wander, stray, amble, ramble, stroll

> After the winding *Maeander* river in Turkey

meaning *noun* **1** what is intended to be expressed or conveyed **2** purpose, intention

meaningful *adj* full of significance; expressive ◇ **meaningfully** *adv*

meaningless *adj* lacking significance

means *noun plural* **1** an action or instrument by which something is done **2** money, property *etc*: *a woman of means* ◇ **by all means 1** certainly, of course **2** in every way possible ◇ **by no means** certainly not; not at all
▣ **1** method, mode, way, medium, course, agency, process, instrument, channel, vehicle **2** resources, funds, money, income, wealth, riches, substance, wherewithal, fortune, affluence

measles *noun* an infectious disease causing red spots

measly *adj*, *informal* mean, stingy: *gave me a measly five pounds*

measure *noun* **1** size or amount

(found by measuring) **2** an instrument or container for measuring **3** musical time **4** (**measures**) a plan of action: *measures to prevent crime* **5** a law brought before parliament to be considered ◇ *verb* **1** find out the size, quantity *etc* by using an instrument or container marked with units **2** be of a certain length, amount *etc* **3** indicate the measurement of **4** mark (off) or weigh (out) in portions ◇ **for good measure** as a bonus

■ *noun* **1** size, quantity, magnitude, amount, degree, extent, range, scope, proportion **2** rule, gauge, scale, yardstick, meter **4** step, course, action, deed, procedure **5** act, bill, statute ◇ *verb* **1** quantify, evaluate, assess, weigh, value, gauge, determine, calculate, estimate, plumb, survey, compute, measure out

measured *adj* steady, unhurried

measurement *noun* **1** the act of measuring **2** the size, amount *etc* found by measuring

meat *noun* animal flesh used as food

meaty *adj* **1** full of meat; tasting of meat **2** of a book *etc*: full of information

Mecca *noun* **1** the birthplace of Mohammed **2** a place of pilgrimage

mechanic *noun* a skilled worker with tools or machines

mechanical *adj* **1** of machinery: *mechanical engineering* **2** worked by machinery **3** done without thinking ◇ **mechanically** *adv*

■ **3** automatic, involuntary, instinctive, routine, habitual, impersonal, emotionless, cold, matter-of-fact, unfeeling, lifeless, dead, dull

☒ **3** conscious

mechanics *noun* **1** *sing* the study and art of constructing machinery **2** *plural* the actual details of how something works: *the mechanics of the plan are beyond me*

mechanism *noun* **1** a piece of machinery **2** the way a piece of machinery works **3** an action by which a result is produced

■ **1** machine, machinery, engine, appli-

ance, instrument, tool, motor, works, workings, gadget, device, apparatus, contrivance, gears, components **3** means, method, agency, process, procedure, system, technique, operation

mechanize *verb* **1** equip (a factory *etc*) with machinery **2** supply (troops) with armoured vehicles ◇ **mechanization** *noun*

Med *noun, informal* the Mediterranean

medal *noun* a metal disc stamped with a design, inscription *etc*, made to commemorate an event or given as a prize ◇ **medallist** *noun* someone who has gained a medal

medallion *noun* a large medal or a piece of jewellery like one

meddle *verb* **1** concern yourself with things that are not your business **2** interfere or tamper (with) ◇ **meddler** *noun* ◇ **meddlesome** *adj* fond of meddling

■ **1** intervene, pry, *informal* snoop, intrude, butt in, interfere

media *noun*: **the media** television, newspapers *etc* as a form of communication

mediaeval *another spelling of* **medieval**

median *noun* **1** a straight line from an angle of a triangle to the centre of the opposite side **2** the middle value or point of a series ◇ *adj* mid, middle

mediate *verb* act as a peacemaker (between) ◇ **mediation** *noun* ◇ **mediator** *noun* someone who tries to make peace between people who are quarrelling

■ arbitrate, conciliate, intervene, referee, umpire, intercede, moderate, reconcile, negotiate, settle, step in

medic *noun, informal* a medical student or doctor

medical *adj* of doctors or their work ◇ *noun* a health check, a physical examination

Medical terms include:
abortion, allergy, amniocentesis, amputation, analgesic, antibiotics,

antiseptic, assisted conception, bandage, barium meal, biopsy, blood bank, blood count, blood donor, blood group, blood pressure, blood test, caesarean, cardiopulmonary resuscitation (CPR), case history, casualty, cauterization, cervical smear, check-up, childbirth, circulation, circumcision, clinic, complication, compress, consultant, consultation, contraception, convulsion, cure, diagnosis, dialysis, dislocate, dissection, doctor, donor, dressings, enema, examination, gene, genetic counselling, health screening, home visit, hormone replacement therapy (HRT), hospice, hospital, immunization, implantation, incubation, infection, inflammation, injection, injury, inoculation, intensive care, in-vitro fertilization (IVF), keyhole surgery, labour, laser treatment, microsurgery, miscarriage, mouth-to-mouth, nurse, ointment, operation, paraplegia, post-mortem, pregnancy, prescription, prognosis, prosthesis, psychosomatic, quarantine, radiotherapy, recovery, rehabilitation, relapse, remission, respiration, resuscitation, scan, side effect, sling, smear test, specimen, splint, sterilization, steroid, surgery, suture, symptom, syndrome, therapy, tourniquet, tranquillizer, transfusion, transplant, trauma, treatment, tumour, ultrasound scanning, vaccination, vaccine, virus, X-ray

medicate *verb* give medicine to ◇ **medicated** *adj* including medicine or disinfectant

medication *noun* **1** medical treatment **2** a medicine

medicinal *adj* **1** used in medicine **2** used as a medicine ◇ **medicinally** *adv*
■ **2** therapeutic, healing, remedial, curative, restorative

medicine *noun* **1** something given to a sick person to make them better **2** the science of the treatment of illness ◇ **medicine man** a tribal healer
■ **1** medication, drug, cure, remedy, medicament, prescription, panacea

medieval *adj* of or in the Middle Ages

mediocre *adj* not very good, ordinary ◇ **mediocrity** *noun*
■ ordinary, average, middling, medium, indifferent, unexceptional, undistinguished, *informal* so-so, run-of-the-mill, commonplace, insignificant, second-rate, inferior, uninspired
☒ exceptional, extraordinary, distinctive

meditate *verb* **1** think deeply and in quietness **2** contemplate religious or spiritual matters **3** consider, think about ◇ **meditative** *adj* thoughtful ◇ **meditatively** *adv*
■ **1** reflect, ponder, ruminate, contemplate, muse, brood, think **3** think over, consider, deliberate, mull over, study, speculate

meditation *noun* **1** deep, quiet thought **2** contemplation on a religious or spiritual theme

medium *noun* **1** (*plural* **media**) a means or substance through which an effect is produced **2** (*plural* **mediums**) someone through whom spirits (of dead people) are said to speak ◇ *adj* middle or average in size, quality *etc* ◇ **the media** *see* **media**
■ *noun* **1** means, agency, channel, vehicle, instrument, way, mode, form, avenue, organ **2** psychic, spiritualist, spiritist, clairvoyant ◇ *adj* average, middle, median, mean, medial, intermediate, middling, midway, standard, fair

medley *noun* (*plural* **medleys**) **1** a mixture **2** a piece of music put together from a number of other pieces

meek *adj* gentle, uncomplaining ◇ **meekly** *adv* ◇ **meekness** *noun*
■ modest, long-suffering, forbearing, humble, docile, patient, unassuming, unpretentious, resigned, gentle, peaceful, tame, timid, submissive, spiritless
☒ arrogant, assertive, rebellious

meerkat *noun* a South African animal related to the mongoose

meerschaum *noun* **1** a fine white clay used to make tobacco pipes **2** a pipe made of this

meet¹ *verb* (**meets, meeting, met**) **1** come face to face (with) **2** come together, join **3** make the acquaintance of **4** pay (bills *etc*) fully **5** be suitable for, satisfy: *able to meet the demand* ◇ *noun* a gathering for a sports event

▣ *verb* **1** encounter, come across, run across, run into, chance on, *informal* bump into, experience, encounter, face, go through, undergo, endure **2** gather, collect, assemble, congregate, convene, join, converge, come together, connect, cross, intersect, touch, abut, unite **5** fulfil, satisfy, match, answer, measure up to, equal, discharge, perform

meet² *adj, old* proper, suitable

meeting *noun* a gathering of people for a particular purpose

▣ assembly, gathering, congregation, conference, convention, rally, get-together, forum, conclave, session

mega *adj, slang* **1** huge **2** excellent, very good

mega- *prefix* **1** great, huge **2** one million

megabyte *noun, comput* approximately one million bytes

megalith *noun* a huge stone erected in prehistoric times

megalomania *noun* an exaggerated idea of your own importance or abilities ◇ **megalomaniac** *noun* someone suffering from megalomania

megaphone *noun* a portable cone-shaped device with microphone and amplifier to increase the sound of the voice

megaton *adj* of a bomb: having an explosive force equal to a million tons of TNT

melancholy *noun* lowness of spirits, sadness ◇ *adj* sad, depressed ◇ **melancholic** *adj*

▣ *noun* depression, dejection, gloom, despondency, low spirits, *informal* blues, sadness, unhappiness, sorrow ◇ *adj* depressed, dejected, downcast, down, down-hearted, gloomy, low, low-spirited, heavy-hearted, sad, unhappy, despondent, dispirited, miserable, mournful, dismal, sorrowful, moody

▣ *noun* elation, joy ◇ *adj* cheerful, elated, joyful

mélange *noun* a mixture, a medley

melanin *noun* the dark pigment in human skin or hair

melanoma *noun* a skin tumour which usually develops from a mole

melba toast thin curled slices of toasted bread

meld *verb* merge, blend

mêlée /'mɛleɪ/ *noun* a confused fight between two groups of people

mellifluous *adj* sweet-sounding ◇ **mellifluously** *adv* ◇ **mellifluousness** *noun*

mellow *adj* **1** of fruit: ripe, juicy, sweet **2** pleasant or agreeable **3** of light, sound, colour *etc*: soft, not harsh ◇ *verb* make or become mellow ◇ **mellowness** *noun*

▣ *adj* **1** mature, ripe, juicy, full-flavoured, sweet, tender **2** genial, cordial, affable, pleasant, relaxed, placid, serene, tranquil, cheerful, happy, jolly **3** smooth, melodious, rich, rounded, soft, warm ◇ *verb* mature, ripen, improve, sweeten, soften, temper, season, perfect

▣ *adj* **1** unripe **2** cold **3** harsh

melodeon *noun* a type of accordion

melodious *adj* pleasant-sounding; tuneful ◇ **melodiously** *adv* ◇ **melodiousness** *noun*

▣ tuneful, musical, melodic, harmonious, dulcet, sweet-sounding, *formal* euphonious, silvery

▣ discordant, grating, harsh

melodrama *noun* a type of play with a sensational or exaggerated plot

melodramatic *adj* exaggerated, sensational, overdramatic ◇ **melodramatically** *adv*

▣ histrionic, theatrical, overdramatic, exaggerated, over the top, *informal* OTT, overemotional, sensational, *informal* hammy

melody *noun* (*plural* **melodies**) **1** a tune **2** pleasant music ◇**melodic** *adj* of melody ◇**melodically** *adv*
▤ **1** tune, music, song, refrain, harmony, theme, air, strain

melon *noun* a large round fruit with soft juicy flesh

melt *verb* **1** make or become liquid, *eg* by heating **2** disappear gradually: *the crowd melted away* **3** soften in feeling: *his heart melted at the sight*
▤ **1** liquefy, dissolve, thaw, *formal* deliquesce
▧ **1** freeze, solidify

meltdown *noun* **1** the process in which the radioactive fuel in a nuclear reactor overheats and melts through the insulation into the environment **2** *informal* total breakdown

member *noun* **1** someone who belongs to a group or society **2** a limb or organ of the body ◇**Member of Parliament** (*shortened to:* **MP**) someone elected to the House of Commons
▤ **1** adherent, associate, subscriber, representative, comrade, fellow

membership *noun* **1** the members of a club *etc* **2** the state of being a member

membrane *noun* a thin skin or covering, especially as part of a human or animal body, plant *etc*

memento *noun* (*plural* **mementos**) something by which an event is remembered ◇**memento mori** an object used as a reminder of human mortality
▤ souvenir, keepsake, remembrance, reminder, token, memorial, record, relic

memo *noun* (*plural* **memos**) *short for* **memorandum**

memoirs *noun plural* a personal account of someone's life; an autobiography

memorable *adj* worthy of being remembered; famous ◇**memorably** *adv*
▤ unforgettable, remarkable, significant, impressive, notable, noteworthy, extraordinary, important, outstanding, momentous

▧ forgettable, trivial, unimportant

memorandum *noun* (*plural* **memoranda**) **1** a brief note sent to colleagues in an office *etc* **2** a note which acts as a reminder **3** a written statement of something under discussion

memorial *noun* a monument commemorating a historical event or person ◇*adj* commemorating an event or person
▤ *noun* remembrance, monument, souvenir, memento, record, stone, plaque, mausoleum ◇ *adj* commemorative, celebratory

memorize *verb* learn by heart

memory *noun* (*plural* **memories**) **1** the power to remember **2** the mind's store of remembered things **3** something remembered **4** *comput* a store of information ◇**in memory of** in remembrance of, as a memorial of
▤ **1** recall, retention **3** recollection, remembrance, reminiscence, commemoration

menace *noun* **1** potential harm or danger **2** someone persistently threatening or annoying ◇*verb* be a danger to; threaten
▤ *noun* **1** danger, peril, hazard, jeopardy, risk **2** nuisance, annoyance, pest ◇ *verb* threaten, frighten, alarm, intimidate, terrorize, loom

menacing *adj* looking evil or threatening

ménage *noun* a household

menagerie /məˈnadʒərɪ/ *noun* **1** a collection of wild animals **2** a place where these are kept

mend *verb* repair; make or grow better ◇*noun* a repaired part ◇**on the mend** getting better, recovering
▤ *verb* repair, renovate, restore, refit, fix, patch, cobble, darn, heal, recover, get better, improve

mendacious *adj* not true; lying ◇**mendaciously** *adv* ◇**mendacity** *noun*

mendicant *noun* **1** a beggar **2** a monk who is dependent on charity ◇*adj* begging; dependent on charity

menhir /ˈmɛnhɪə(r)/ *noun* a prehistoric standing stone

menial *adj* of work: unskilled, unchallenging

▣ low, lowly, humble, base, dull, humdrum, routine, degrading, demeaning, ignominious, unskilled

meningitis *noun* an illness caused by inflammation of the covering of the brain

menopause *noun* the ending of menstruation in middle age

menorah *noun* a candelabrum used in Jewish ceremonies

menses *noun plural* the discharge of blood *etc* during menstruation

menstruation *noun* the monthly discharge of blood from a woman's womb ◇ **menstrual** *adj* of menstruation ◇ **menstruate** *verb* undergo menstruation

mensurable *adj* measurable

mensuration *noun* measurement of length, height *etc*

mental *adj* 1 of the mind 2 done, made, happening *etc* in the mind: *mental arithmetic* 3 of illness: affecting the mind ◇ **mentally** *adv* ◇ **mental hospital** a hospital for people suffering from mental illness

▣ 1 cognitive, cerebral 2 intellectual, abstract, conceptual, theoretical, rational

mentality *noun* (*plural* **mentalities**) 1 mental power 2 type of mind; way of thinking

▣ 1 intellect, brains, understanding, faculty, rationality 2 character, disposition, personality, psychology, outlook

menthol *noun* a sharp-smelling substance obtained from peppermint oil

mention *verb* 1 speak of briefly 2 remark (that) ◇ *noun* a mentioning, a remark

▣ *verb* 1 refer to, speak of, allude to, touch on, name, cite, acknowledge, bring up 2 report, make known, impart, declare, communicate, broach, divulge, disclose, intimate, point out, reveal, state

mentor *noun* someone who gives advice as a tutor or supervisor

After *Mentor*, a friend of Odysseus, who guides Telemachus in his search for his father

menu *noun* (*plural* **menus**) 1 (a card with) a list of dishes to be served at a meal 2 *comput* a list of options

MEP *abbrev* Member of the European Parliament

mercantile *adj* of buying and selling; trading

Mercator's projection a map of the globe in the form of a rectangle evenly marked with lines of latitude and longitude

mercenary *adj* 1 working for money 2 influenced by the desire for money ◇ *noun* (*plural* **mercenaries**) a soldier paid by a foreign country to fight in its army

▣ *adj* 2 greedy, avaricious, covetous, grasping, acquisitive, materialistic

mercerized *adj* of thread *etc*: treated with caustic soda to increase its strength and absorbency

merchandise *noun* goods to be bought and sold

▣ goods, commodities, stock, produce, products, wares, cargo, freight

merchant *noun* someone who carries on a business in the buying and selling of goods, a trader ◇ *adj* of trade ◇ **merchant bank** a bank providing *esp* commercial banking services; **merchantman** *noun* a merchant ship ◇ **merchant navy** ships and crews employed in trading ◇ **merchant ship** a trading ship

merciful *adj* willing to forgive or be lenient ◇ **mercifully** *adv* 1 luckily; thankfully 2 in a merciful way

▣ compassionate, forgiving, forbearing, humane, lenient, sparing, tenderhearted, pitying, gracious, humanitarian, kind, liberal, sympathetic, generous, mild

▨ hard-hearted, merciless

merciless *adj* showing no mercy; cruel ◇ **mercilessly** *adv*

▣ pitiless, relentless, unmerciful, ruthless,

hard-hearted, hard, heartless, implacable, inhumane, unforgiving, remorseless, unpitying, unsparing, severe, cruel, callous, inhuman

☒ compassionate, merciful

mercury *noun* an element, a heavy, silvery, liquid metal (*also called*: **quicksilver**) ◇**mercurial** *adj* changeable, volatile

mercy *noun* (*plural* **mercies**) lenience or forgiveness towards an enemy, wrongdoer *etc*; pity ◇**at someone's mercy** in their power

☰ compassion, clemency, forgiveness, forbearance, leniency, pity, humanitarianism, kindness, grace

mere *adj* nothing more than: *mere nonsense* ◇**merely** *adv* only, simply

☰ sheer, plain, simple, bare, utter, pure, absolute, complete, stark, unadulterated

meretricious *adj, formal* superficially attractive, flashy

❗ Do not confuse with: **meritorious**

merge *verb* **1** combine or join together **2** blend, come together gradually

☰ **1** join, unite, combine, converge, amalgamate, blend, coalesce, mix, intermix **2** mingle, melt into, fuse, meet, meld, incorporate, consolidate

merger *noun* a joining together, *eg* of business companies

☰ amalgamation, union, fusion, combination, coalition, consolidation, confederation, incorporation

meridian *noun* **1** an imaginary line around the globe passing through the north and south poles **2** the highest point of the sun's path **3** *Chinese med* a main energy channel in the body

meringue /məˈraŋ/ *noun* a baked cake or shell made of sugar and egg-white

merino *noun* (*plural* **merinos**) **1** a sheep with very fine soft wool **2** its wool, or a soft fabric made from it

merit *noun* **1** positive worth or value **2** a commendable quality ◇*verb* deserve

☰ *noun* **1** worth, excellence, value, quality,

good, goodness, virtue **2** virtue, asset, credit, advantage, strong point, talent ◇ *verb* deserve, be worthy of, earn, justify, warrant

meritorious *adj, formal* deserving honour or reward

❗ Do not confuse with: **meretricious**

mermaid *noun* an imaginary sea creature with a woman's upper body and a fish's tail

merry *adj* **1** full of fun; cheerful and lively **2** slightly drunk ◇**merrily** *adv*

☰ **1** jolly, light-hearted, mirthful, joyful, happy, convivial, festive, cheerful, glad

☒ **1** gloomy, melancholy **2** sober

merry-go-round *noun, Brit* a fairground roundabout with wooden horses *etc* for riding on

mesh *noun* (*plural* **meshes**) **1** network, netting **2** the opening between the threads of a net ◇*verb* of gears *etc*: interconnect, engage

☰ *noun* **1** net, network, netting, lattice, web ◇ *verb* engage, interlock, dovetail, fit, connect, co-ordinate

mesmeric *adj* **1** hypnotic **2** commanding complete attention, fascinating ◇**mesmerically** *adv*

mesmerize *verb* **1** hypnotize **2** hold the attention of completely; fascinate

An earlier term than *hypnotize*, the word comes from the name of the 18th-century Austrian doctor, Franz Anton Mesmer, who claimed to be able to cure disease through the influence of his will on patients

mesolithic *adj* referring to the period of the Stone Age between palaeolithic and neolithic

meson *noun* a particle with a mass between that of a proton and an electron

mess (*plural* **messes**) **1** an untidy or disgusting sight **2** disorder, confusion **3** a place where a group of soldiers *etc* take their meals together ◇**mess up** make untidy, dirty or muddled ◇**mess**

with *US informal* interfere with, fool with

□ *noun* **2** untidiness, disorder, disarray, confusion, muddle, jumble, clutter, disorganization, mix-up, *informal* shambles ◇ **mess up** disarrange, jumble, muddle, tangle, dishevel, disrupt

message *noun* **1** a piece of news or information sent from one person to another **2** a lesson, a moral ◇ **get the message** *informal* understand, get the point

□ **1** communication, bulletin, dispatch, communiqué, report, *formal* missive, errand, letter, memorandum, note, notice **2** meaning, idea, point, theme, moral

messenger *noun* someone who carries a message

□ courier, *formal* emissary, envoy, go-between, herald, runner, carrier, bearer, harbinger, agent, ambassador

messiah *noun* a saviour, a deliverer

Messrs *plural* of Mr

messy *adj* **1** dirty **2** untidy, disordered ◇ **messily** *adv* ◇ **messiness** *noun*

□ **1** dirty, grubby **2** untidy, unkempt, dishevelled, disorganized, chaotic, sloppy, slovenly, confused, muddled, cluttered

metabolic *adj* of metabolism ◇ **metabolically** *adv*

metabolism *noun* **1** the combined chemical changes in the cells of a living organism which provide energy for living processes and activity **2** the conversion of nourishment into energy

metal *noun* any of a group of substances (*eg* gold, silver, iron *etc*) able to conduct heat and electricity

⚠ Do not confuse with: **mettle**

metallic *adj* **1** made of metal **2** shining like metal: *metallic thread*

metallurgy *noun* the study of metals ◇ **metallurgic** or **metallurgical** *adj* ◇ **metallurgist** *noun*

metamorphose *verb* change completely in appearance, form or character

metamorphosis *noun* (*plural* **metamorphoses**) **1** a complete change in appearance, form or character; a transformation **2** a physical change that occurs during the growth of some creatures, *eg* from a tadpole into a frog

□ **1** change, alteration, transformation, rebirth, regeneration, transfiguration, conversion, modification

metaphor *noun* a way of describing something by suggesting that it is, or has the qualities of, something else, *eg the camel is the ship of the desert*

□ figure of speech, allegory, analogy, symbol, picture, image

metaphorical *adj* using a metaphor or metaphors ◇ **metaphorically** *adv*

□ figurative, allegorical, symbolic

metaphysics *noun* **1** the study of being and knowledge **2** any abstruse or abstract philosophy ◇ **metaphysical** *adj* ◇ **metaphysician** *noun*

mete *verb*: **mete out** *formal* deal out (punishment *etc*)

□ allot, apportion, deal out, dole out, hand out, measure out, share out, ration out, portion, distribute, dispense, divide out, assign, administer

meteor *noun* a small piece of matter moving rapidly through space, becoming bright as it enters the earth's atmosphere

meteoric *adj* **1** of a meteor **2** extremely rapid: *meteoric rise to fame*

□ **2** rapid, speedy, swift, sudden, overnight, instantaneous

meteorite *noun* a meteor which falls to the earth as a piece of rock

meteorologist *noun* someone who studies or forecasts the weather

meteorology *noun* the study of weather and climate ◇ **meteorological** *adj*

meter[1] *noun* an instrument for measuring the amount of gas, electricity, *etc* used ◇ *verb* measure with a meter

⚠ Do not confuse with: **metre**

meter[2] *US spelling* of **metre**

methadone *noun* a synthetic drug

similar to morphine, used to treat addiction

methane *noun* a colourless gas produced by rotting vegetable matter (*also called*: **marsh-gas**)

methanol *noun* methyl alcohol (*also called*: **wood spirit**)

method *noun* **1** a planned or regular way of doing something **2** orderly arrangement

■ **1** way, approach, means, course, manner, mode, fashion, process, procedure, route, technique, style, plan, scheme, programme **2** organization, order, structure, system, pattern, form, planning, regularity, routine

methodical *adj* orderly, done or acting according to some plan ◇ **methodically** *adv*

■ systematic, structured, organized, ordered, orderly, tidy, regular, planned, efficient, disciplined, businesslike, deliberate, neat, scrupulous, precise, meticulous, painstaking

◪ chaotic, irregular, confused

meths *noun, informal* methylated spirits

methyl alcohol a poisonous alcohol found in nature

methylated spirits an alcohol with added violet dye, used as a solvent or fuel

meticulous *adj* careful and accurate about small details ◇ **meticulously** *adv* ◇ **meticulousness** *noun*

■ precise, scrupulous, exact, punctilious, fussy, detailed, accurate, thorough, fastidious, painstaking, strict

◪ careless, slapdash

métier /'mɛtɪeɪ/ *noun, formal* occupation, profession

metonym *noun* the use of the name of part of a thing to stand for the whole, *eg the ring* for *boxing* ◇ **metonymy** *noun*

metre or *US* **meter** *noun* **1** the chief unit of length in the metric system (about 1.1 yards) **2** the arrangement of syllables in poetry, or of musical notes, in a regular rhythm

⚠ Do not confuse with: **meter**

metric *adj* **1** of the metric system **2** metrical ◇ **metric system** the system of weights and measures based on tens (1 metre = 10 decimetres = 100 centimetres *etc*)

metrical *adj* **1** of or in metre or verse **2** relating to measurement

metrication *noun* the change-over of a country's units of measurements to the metric system

metronome *noun* an instrument that keeps a regular beat, used for music practice

metropolis *noun* (*plural* **metropolises**) a large city, usually the capital city of a country ◇ **metropolitan** *adj*

■ capital, city, municipality, megalopolis

mettle *noun, formal* courage, pluck ◇ **on your mettle** out to do your best

■ spirit, courage, vigour, nerve, boldness, daring, indomitability, pluck, resolve, valour, bravery, fortitude

⚠ Do not confuse with: **metal**

mew *noun* a whining cry made by a cat *etc* ◇ *verb* cry in this way

mews *noun* buildings (originally stables) built around a yard or in a lane

Originally a cage for hawks, *mews* took on its present meaning after royal stables were built in the 17th century on a site formerly used to house the King's hawks

mezzanine *noun* **1** a low storey between two main storeys **2** *US* a balcony in a theatre

mezzo-soprano *noun* (*plural* **mezzo-sopranos**) **1** a singer whose voice is between alto and soprano **2** a singing voice between alto and soprano

mg *abbrev* milligram(s)

MHz *abbrev* megahertz

MI5 *noun, informal* a British government counter-espionage agency

MI6 *noun, informal* a British espionage and intelligence agency

miaow *noun* the sound made by a cat ◇ *verb* make the sound of a cat

miasma /mɪ'azmə/ *noun* an unhealthy or depressing atmosphere

mica *noun* a mineral which glitters and divides easily into thin transparent layers

mice *plural* of **mouse**

Michaelmas *noun* the festival of St Michael, 29 September

mickey *noun*: **take the mickey** *informal* tease, make fun of someone

micro *noun, informal* (*plural* **micros**) **1** a microwave oven **2** a microcomputer

micro- *prefix* very small

microbe *noun* a minute living organism

▣ micro-organism, bacterium, bacillus, germ, virus, pathogen, *informal* bug

microchip *noun* a tiny piece of silicon designed to act as a complex electronic circuit

microcomputer *noun* a small desktop computer containing a microprocessor

microcosm *noun* a version on a small scale: *a microcosm of society*

microfiche /'maɪkrəfiːʃ/ *noun* a sheet of microfilm with text on it

microfilm *noun* narrow photographic film on which books, newspapers, *etc* are recorded in miniaturized form ◇ *verb* record on microfilm

microphone *noun* an instrument which picks up sound waves for broadcasting, recording or amplifying

microprocessor *noun* a computer processor consisting of one or more microchips

microscope *noun* a scientific instrument which magnifies very small objects placed under its lens

microscopic *adj* tiny, minuscule ◇ **microscopically** *adv*

▣ minute, tiny, minuscule, infinitesimal, indiscernible, imperceptible, negligible

▣ huge, enormous

microsecond *noun* a millionth of a second

microsurgery *noun* delicate surgery carried out under a microscope ◇ **microsurgeon** *noun* a surgeon who performs microsurgery

microwave *noun* **1** a microwave oven **2** a very short radio wave ◇ **microwave oven** an oven which cooks food by passing microwaves through it

mid- *prefix* placed or occurring in the middle: *mid-morning*

midday *noun* noon

midden *noun* a rubbish or dung heap

middle *noun* the point or part of anything equally distant from its ends or edges; the centre ◇ *adj* **1** occurring in the middle or centre **2** coming between extreme positions *etc*: *trying to find a middle way* ◇ **in the middle of** in the process of doing, busy doing ◇ **middle-aged** *adj* between youth and old age ◇ **Middle Ages** the time roughly between AD500 and AD1500 ◇ **middle class** the class of people between the working and upper classes ◇ **middle-of-the-road** *adj* bland, unadventurous; with widespread appeal

▣ *noun* centre, halfway point, midpoint, mean, heart, core, midst, inside, bull's eye ◇ *adj* **1** central, halfway, mean, median, intermediate, inner, inside, intervening

middling *adj* **1** of middle size or quality **2** neither good nor bad; mediocre

▣ **1** medium, ordinary, moderate, average **2** mediocre, unremarkable, unexceptional, run-of-the-mill, indifferent, modest, passable, tolerable, *informal* so-so, *informal* OK

midge *noun* a small biting insect

midget *noun* an abnormally small person or thing ◇ *adj* very small

midnight *noun* twelve o'clock at night ◇ *adj* occurring at midnight

midriff *noun* the middle of the body, just below the ribs

midst *noun* the middle ◇ **in our midst** among us

▣ middle, centre, midpoint, heart, hub, interior

midsummer *noun* the time around

21 June, the summer solstice and the longest day in the year

midway *adv* halfway

midwife *noun* (*plural* **midwives**) a nurse trained to assist women during childbirth ◇ **midwifery** *noun* the practice or occupation of being a midwife

Meaning literally 'with woman'

midwinter *noun* the time around 21 December, the winter solstice and shortest day in the year

mien /miːn/ *noun, formal* look, appearance, aspect

might[1] *noun* power, strength

might[2] *past tense* of **may**

mighty *adj* (**mightier**, **mightiest**) very great or powerful ◇ *adv, US informal* very ◇ **mightily** *adv* ◇ **mightiness** *noun*

migraine *noun* a severe form of headache

migrant *noun* 1 someone migrating, or who has recently migrated, from another country 2 a bird which migrates annually

migrate *verb* 1 change your home to another area or country 2 of birds: fly to a warmer region for the winter ◇ **migration** *noun* ◇ **migratory** *adj* 1 migrating 2 wandering

■ 1 move, resettle, relocate, wander, roam, rove, journey, emigrate

mike *noun, informal* a microphone

milch cow 1 a cow kept for milk production 2 a ready source of money

mild *adj* 1 not harsh or severe; gentle 2 of taste: not sharp or bitter 3 of weather: not cold ◇ **mildly** *adv* ◇ **mildness** *noun*

■ 1 gentle, calm, peaceable, placid, tender, soft, good-natured, kind, amiable, lenient, compassionate 2 bland, mellow, smooth, subtle, soothing 3 calm, temperate, warm, balmy, clement, fair, pleasant

mildew *noun* a whitish mark on plants, fabric *etc* caused by fungus ◇ **mildewed** *adj*

mile *noun* a measure of length (1.61 kilometre or 1760 yards)

mileage *noun* distance in miles

milestone *noun* 1 a stone beside the road showing the number of miles to a certain place 2 something which marks an important event

milieu /ˈmiːljɜː/ *noun* surroundings

militant *adj* 1 fighting, warlike 2 aggressive, favouring or taking part in forceful action ◇ *noun* someone who is militant

■ *adj* 1 fighting, warring, belligerent 2 aggressive, vigorous

military *adj* of soldiers or warfare ◇ *noun* (**the military**) the army

■ *adj* martial, armed, soldierly, warlike, service ◇ *noun* army, armed forces, soldiers, forces, services

militate *verb*: militate against fight or work against; act to the disadvantage of

■ oppose, counter, counteract, contend, resist, count against, tell against, weigh against

⚠ Do not confuse with: **mitigate**

militia *noun* a group of fighters, not regular soldiers, trained for emergencies

milk *noun* 1 a white liquid produced by female animals as food for their young 2 this liquid, *esp* from cows, used as a drink ◇ *verb* 1 draw milk from 2 take (money *etc*) from ◇ **milky** *adj* 1 like milk, creamy 2 white ◇ **milk tooth** any of the first set of teeth in children and young mammals ◇ **Milky Way** a bright band of stars seen in the night sky

■ *verb* 2 drain, bleed, tap, extract, draw off, exploit, use, press, pump, squeeze

milkman *noun* a man who sells or delivers milk

mill *noun* 1 a machine for grinding or crushing grain, coffee *etc* 2 a building where grain is ground 3 a factory ◇ *verb* 1 grind 2 cut grooves round the edge of (a coin) 3 move round and round in a crowd ◇ **miller** *noun* someone who grinds grain

■ *noun* **1** grinder, crusher, quern, roller **3** factory, plant, works, workshop, foundry ◇ *verb* **1** grind, pulverize, powder, pound, crush, roll, press

millennium *noun* (*plural* **millennia**) a period of a thousand years

millet *noun* a type of grain used for food

milli- *prefix* thousand; a thousandth part of

milligram *noun* a thousandth of a gram

millilitre *noun* a thousandth of a litre

millimetre *noun* a thousandth of a metre

milliner *noun* someone who makes and sells women's hats ◇ **millinery** *noun* the goods sold by a milliner

million *noun* a thousand thousands (1 000 000)

millionaire *noun* someone who has a million pounds (or dollars) or more

millionth *adj* the last of a series of a million ◇ *noun* one of a million equal parts

millipede *noun* a small crawling insect with a long body and many pairs of legs

millisecond *noun* a thousandth of a second

millstone *noun* **1** one of two heavy stones used to grind grain **2** something felt as a burden or hindrance

millwheel *noun* a waterwheel which drives the machinery of a mill

mime *noun* **1** a theatrical art using body movements and facial expressions in place of speech **2** a play performed through mime ◇ *verb* **1** perform a mime **2** express through gestures *etc* rather than speech

■ *noun* **1** pantomime, gesture, mimicry **2** dumb show, pantomime, charade ◇ *verb* **2** gesture, signal, act out, represent

mimic *verb* (**mimics**, **mimicking**, **mimicked**) imitate, *esp* in a mocking way ◇ *noun* someone who mimics ◇ **mimicry** *noun*

■ *verb* imitate, parody, caricature, *informal* take off, ape, parrot, impersonate,

informal send up, echo, mirror, simulate ◇ *noun* imitator, impersonator, impressionist, caricaturist, *informal* copy-cat

mimosa *noun* a tree producing bunches of yellow, scented flowers

min *abbrev* **1** minimum **2** minute (of time)

minaret *noun* a slender tower on an Islamic mosque

mince *verb* **1** cut or chop into small pieces **2** walk primly with short steps ◇ *noun* meat chopped finely ◇ **mincer** *noun* a machine for mincing food ◇ **not mince matters** not try to soften an unpleasant fact or statement

■ *verb* **1** chop, cut, hash, dice, grind, crumble

mincemeat *noun* a chopped-up mixture of dried fruit, suet *etc* ◇ **make mincemeat of** pulverize, destroy

mince pie a pie filled with mincemeat

mind *noun* **1** consciousness, intelligence, understanding **2** intention: *I've a good mind to tell him so* ◇ *verb* **1** see to, look after: *will you mind the children for me?* **2** watch out for, be careful of: *mind the step* **3** object to: *do you mind if I open the window?* ◇ **change your mind** change your opinion or intention ◇ **in two minds** undecided ◇ **make up your mind** decide ◇ **mindful of** paying attention to ◇ **out of your mind** mad, crazy ◇ **presence of mind** ability to act calmly and sensibly ◇ **speak your mind** speak frankly

■ *noun* **1** intelligence, intellect, brains, reason, sense, understanding, wits, mentality, thinking, thoughts, *informal* grey matter, head, genius, concentration, attention, spirit, psyche **2** inclination, disposition, tendency, will, wish, intention, desire ◇ *verb* **1** look after, take care of, watch over, guard, have charge of, *informal* keep an eye on **3** care, object, take offence, resent, disapprove, dislike

minder *noun* **1** someone who looks after a child *etc* **2** an aide or adviser to a public figure

mindless *adj* **1** foolish, unthinking; pointless **2** involving no mental effort

◇ **mindlessly** *adv*

■ **1** thoughtless, senseless, illogical, irrational, stupid, foolish, gratuitous, negligent

🇪🇦 **2** thoughtful, intelligent

mine[1] *noun* **1** an underground pit or system of tunnels from which metals, coal *etc* are dug **2** an explosive device placed in the ground or in water ◇ *verb* **1** dig or work a mine **2** obtain (metal, coal) from a mine **3** lay explosive mines in ◇ **miner** *noun* someone who works in a mine

■ *noun* **1** pit, colliery, coalfield, excavation, vein, seam, shaft, deposit ◇ *verb* **1** excavate, delve, tunnel **2** dig for, dig up, quarry, extract, unearth

mine[2] *pronoun* something belonging to me: *that drink is mine*

minefield *noun* an area covered with explosive mines

mineral *noun* a natural substance mined from the earth, *eg* coal, metals, gems *etc* ◇ *adj* of or containing minerals ◇ **mineral water** water containing small amounts of minerals

mineralogy *noun* the study of minerals ◇ **mineralogist** *noun*

minestrone /mɪnə'strəʊnɪ/ *noun* a thick Italian vegetable soup containing rice or pasta

minesweeper *noun* a ship which removes explosive mines

mingle *verb* mix

■ mix, intermingle, intermix, combine, blend, merge, unite, alloy, coalesce, join, compound

mingy /'mɪndʒɪ/ *adj, informal* stingy, mean

Mini *noun, trademark* a small, two-doored British car

mini- *prefix* smaller than average; compact: *minibus/minicab*

miniature *noun* **1** a small-scale painting **2** a small bottle of spirits ◇ *adj* on a small scale

■ *adj* tiny, small, scaled-down, minute, diminutive, baby, pocket-size(d), *informal* pint-size(d), little, *informal* mini

🇪🇦 *adj* giant

minibus *noun* (*plural* **minibuses**) a type of small bus

minim *noun, music* a note (♩) equal to two crotchets, or half a semibreve, in length

minimal *adj* very small; of the least amount ◇ **minimally** *adv*

■ least, smallest, minimum, slightest, littlest, negligible, minute, token

minimize *verb* **1** cause to seem small or unimportant **2** make as small as possible

■ **1** belittle, make light of, make little of, disparage, deprecate, discount, play down, underestimate, underrate **2** reduce, decrease, diminish

minimum *noun* (*plural* **minima**) the smallest possible quantity ◇ *adj* the least possible

■ *noun* least, lowest point, slightest, bottom ◇ *adj* minimal, least, lowest, slightest, smallest, littlest, tiniest

🇪🇦 *noun & adj* maximum

minion *noun* a slave-like follower

minister *noun* **1** the head a government department: *minister of trade* **2** a member of the clergy **3** an agent, a representative ◇ *verb* (with **to**) help, supply the needs of ◇ **ministerial** *adj* of a minister

■ *noun* **1** official, office-holder, politician, cabinet minister, agent, aide, administrator, executive **2** clergyman, clergywoman, churchman, churchwoman, cleric, parson, priest, pastor, vicar, preacher, *formal* ecclesiastic, divine

ministry *noun* (*plural* **ministries**) **1** a government department or its headquarters **2** the work of a member of the clergy

mink *noun* a small weasel-like animal or its fur

minneola *noun* a hybrid fruit grown from a tangerine and a grapefruit

minnow *noun* a type of very small river or pond fish

minor *adj* of less importance, size *etc*; relatively small or unimportant (*contrasted with*: **major**) ◇ *noun* someone not yet legally of age (*ie* in the UK, under 18)

■ *adj* lesser, secondary, smaller, inferior, subordinate, subsidiary, junior, younger, insignificant, inconsiderable, negligible, petty, trivial, trifling, second-class, unclassified, slight

☒ *adj* major, significant, important

minority *noun* (*plural* **minorities**) 1 the smaller number or part 2 the state of being a minor

Minotaur *noun* a mythological creature with a bull's head, living in the Cretan labyrinth

minster *noun* a large church or cathedral

minstrel *noun* 1 *hist* a medieval travelling musician 2 a singer, an entertainer

mint¹ *noun* a plant with strong-smelling leaves, used as flavouring

mint² *noun* 1 a place where coins are made 2 *informal* a large sum of money: *cost a mint* ◇ *verb* make coins ◇ **in mint condition** in perfect condition

■ **in mint condition** perfect, brand-new, fresh, immaculate, unblemished, excellent, first-class

minuet *noun* 1 a kind of slow, graceful dance 2 the music for this

minus *prep* 1 used to show subtraction, represented by the sign (−): *five minus two equals three* 2 *informal* without: *I'm minus my car today* ◇ *adj* of a quantity less than zero

minuscule *adj* tiny, minute

minute¹ /ˈmɪnɪt/ *noun* 1 a sixtieth part of an hour 2 in measuring an angle, the sixtieth part of a degree 3 a very short time 4 (**minutes**) notes taken of what is said at a meeting

minute² /maɪˈnjuːt/ *adj* 1 very small 2 very exact

■ 1 tiny, infinitesimal, minuscule, microscopic, miniature, inconsiderable, negligible, small 2 detailed, precise, meticulous, painstaking, close, critical, exhaustive

minutiae *noun plural* minute or exact details

minx *noun* (*plural* **minxes**) a cheeky young girl

miracle *noun* 1 a wonderful act beyond normal human powers 2 a fortunate happening with no natural cause or explanation ◇ **miraculous** *adj* ◇ **miraculously** *adv*

■ **miraculous** wonderful, marvellous, phenomenal, extraordinary, amazing, astounding, astonishing, unbelievable, supernatural, incredible, inexplicable, unaccountable, superhuman

mirage *noun* something imagined but not really there, *eg* an oasis seen by travellers in the desert

mire *noun* deep mud ◇ **miry** *adj*

mirror *noun* a backed piece of glass which shows the image of someone looking into it ◇ *verb* 1 reflect like a mirror 2 copy exactly

■ *verb* 1 reflect 2 echo, imitate, copy, mimic

mirth *noun* merriment, laughter ◇ **mirthful** *adj* ◇ **mirthless** *adj*

■ merriment, hilarity, gaiety, fun, laughter, jollity, jocularity, amusement, revelry, glee, cheerfulness

☒ gloom, melancholy

mis- *prefix* wrong(ly), bad(ly): *mispronounce/misapply*

misadventure *noun* an unlucky happening

misanthropist *noun* someone who hates humanity ◇ **misanthropic** *adj* ◇ **misanthropy** *noun*

misappropriate *verb* put to a wrong use; use (someone else's money) for yourself

■ steal, embezzle, peculate, pocket, *informal* swindle, misspend, misuse, misapply, abuse, pervert

misbehave *verb* behave badly ◇ **misbehaviour** *noun*

■ offend, transgress, get up to mischief, mess about, *informal* muck about, play up, *informal* act up

misc *abbrev* miscellaneous

miscarriage *noun* 1 the accidental loss of a foetus during pregnancy 2 a going wrong, failure: *miscarriage of justice*

■ **2** failure, breakdown, mishap, mismanagement, error, disappointment

☒ **2** success

miscarry *verb* (**miscarries, miscarrying, miscarried**) **1** have a miscarriage in pregnancy **2** go wrong or astray; be unsuccessful

■ **2** fail, abort, come to nothing, fall through, misfire, founder, come to grief

☒ **2** succeed

miscellaneous *adj* assorted, made up of several kinds ◇ **miscellaneously** *adv*

■ mixed, varied, various, assorted, diverse, diversified, sundry, motley, jumbled, indiscriminate

miscellany *noun* (*plural* **miscellanies**) a mixture or collection of things, *eg* pieces of writing

mischance *noun* an unlucky accident

mischief *noun* **1** naughtiness **2** *old* harm, damage

mischievous *adj* naughty, teasing; causing trouble ◇ **mischievously** *adv*

■ naughty, impish, rascally, roguish, playful, ludic, teasing

misconceive *verb* **1** misunderstand **2** plan badly ◇ **misconception** *noun* a wrong idea, a misunderstanding

■ **misconception** misapprehension, misunderstanding, misreading, mistake, error, fallacy, delusion, *informal* the wrong end of the stick

misconduct *noun* bad or immoral behaviour

■ misbehaviour, impropriety, misdemeanour, malpractice, mismanagement, wrongdoing

misconstrue *verb* misunderstand ◇ **misconstruction** *noun*

miscreant *noun* a wicked person

misdeed *noun* a bad deed; a crime

misdemeanour *noun* a minor offence

miser *noun* someone who hoards money and spends very little ◇ **miserly** *adj* stingy, mean

■ niggard, skinflint, *informal* penny-pincher, Scrooge

☒ spendthrift

miserable *adj* very unhappy; wretched

■ unhappy, sad, dejected, despondent, downcast, heartbroken, wretched, distressed, crushed

☒ cheerful, happy

misery *noun* (*plural* **miseries**) great unhappiness, pain, poverty *etc*

■ unhappiness, sadness, suffering, distress, depression, despair, gloom, grief, wretchedness, affliction, privation, hardship, deprivation, poverty, want, oppression, destitution

misfire *verb* **1** of a plan: go wrong **2** of a gun: fail to go off

■ **1** miscarry, go wrong, abort, fail, fall through, *informal* flop, founder, fizzle out, come to grief

misfit *noun* **1** someone who cannot fit in happily in society *etc* **2** something that fits badly

misfortune *noun* **1** bad luck **2** an unlucky accident

■ **1** bad luck, mischance, ill-luck, trouble, hardship **2** mishap, setback, calamity, catastrophe, disaster, blow, accident, tragedy

misgiving *noun* fear or doubt, *eg* about the result of an action

■ doubt, uncertainty, hesitation, qualm, reservation, apprehension, scruple, suspicion, second thoughts, niggle, anxiety, worry, fear

misguided *adj* led astray, mistaken, showing bad judgement ◇ **misguidedly** *adv*

■ ill-considered, ill-advised, ill-judged, imprudent, rash, misplaced, deluded, foolish, erroneous, mistaken

mishandle *verb* treat badly or roughly

mishap *noun* an unlucky accident

■ misfortune, ill-fortune, misadventure, accident, setback, calamity, disaster, adversity

mishmash *noun* a hotchpotch, a medley

misinform *verb* inform wrongly

misinterpret *verb* interpret wrongly

misjudge *verb* judge unfairly or wrongly

■ miscalculate, mistake, misinterpret, misconstrue, misunderstand, overestimate, underestimate

mislay *verb* (**mislays**, **mislaying**, **mislaid**) forget where (something) is; lose

■ lose, misplace, miss, lose sight of

mislead *verb* (**misleads**, **misleading**, **misled**) give a false idea (to); deceive ◇ **misleading** *adj*

■ misinform, misdirect, deceive, delude, lead astray, fool, trick

mismatch *noun* an unsuitable match

misnomer *noun* a wrong or unsuitable name

misogynist /mɪˈsɒdʒɪnɪst/ *noun* a man who hates women ◇ **misogyny** *noun*

misplace *verb* put in the wrong place; mislay

misprint *noun* a mistake in printing

■ mistake, error, erratum, literal, *informal* typo

misquote *verb* make a mistake in repeating something written or said

misrepresent *verb* give a wrong idea of (someone's words, actions *etc*)

■ distort, falsify, slant, pervert, twist, garble, misquote, exaggerate, minimize, misconstrue, misinterpret

Miss *noun* (*plural* **Misses**) **1** a form of address used before the surname of an unmarried woman **2** (**miss**) a young woman or girl

miss *verb* **1** fail to hit, catch, see, hear, understand *etc* **2** discover the loss or absence of **3** feel the lack of: *missing old friends* ◇ *noun* (*plural* **misses**) an act of missing; a failure to hit a target, catch a ball *etc* ◇ **missing** *adj* lost ◇ **miss out 1** leave out **2** fail to benefit from something worthwhile or advantageous

■ *verb* **3** pine for, long for, yearn for, regret, grieve for, mourn, sorrow for, want, wish, need, lament

missal *noun* the Mass book of the Roman Catholic Church

misshapen *adj* badly or abnormally shaped

■ deformed, distorted, twisted, malformed, warped, contorted, crooked, crippled, grotesque, ugly, monstrous

missile *noun* a weapon or other object that is thrown or fired

■ projectile, shot, guided missile, arrow, shaft, dart, rocket, bomb, shell, flying bomb, grenade, torpedo, weapon

mission *noun* **1** a task that someone is sent to do **2** a group of representatives sent to another country **3** a group sent to spread a religion **4** the headquarters of such groups **5** someone's chosen task or purpose: *his only mission is to make money*

■ **1** task, undertaking, assignment, operation, campaign, crusade, business, errand **2** commission, ministry, delegation, deputation, legation **5** calling, duty, purpose, vocation, raison d'être, aim, charge, office, job, work

missionary *noun* (*plural* **missionaries**) someone sent abroad *etc* to spread a religion

missive *noun* something sent, *eg* a letter

misspell *verb* (**misspells**, **misspelling**, **misspelled** or **misspelt**) spell wrongly ◇ **misspelling** *noun*

misspent *adj* spent unwisely, wasted: *misspent youth*

mist *noun* a cloud of moisture in the air; thin fog or drizzle ◇ **misty** *adj* ◇ **mist up** or **mist over** cover or become covered with condensation

■ haze, fog, vapour, smog, cloud, condensation, film, spray, drizzle, dew, steam, veil, dimness ◇ **misty** hazy, foggy, cloudy, blurred, fuzzy, murky, unclear, dim, indistinct, obscure, opaque, vague, veiled

mistake *verb* (**mistakes**, **mistaking**, **mistaken**, **mistook**) **1** be wrong or make an error about **2** take (one thing or person) for another ◇ *noun* a wrong action or statement; an error ◇ **mistaken** *adj* making an error, wrong: *mista-*

ken belief ◇ **mistakenly** *adv*

■ *verb* **1** misunderstand, misapprehend, misconstrue, misjudge, misread, miscalculate, confound, confuse, slip up, blunder, err ◇ *noun* error, inaccuracy, slip, slip-up, oversight, lapse, blunder, *informal* boob, gaffe, fault, faux pas, *formal* solecism, indiscretion, misjudgement, miscalculation, misunderstanding, misprint, misspelling, misreading, mispronunciation, *informal* howler

mister *full form* of Mr

mistletoe *noun* a plant with white berries, used as a Christmas decoration

mistreat *verb* treat badly; abuse

mistress *noun* (*plural* **mistresses**) **1** a female teacher **2** a female owner of a dog *etc* **3** a woman skilled in an art **4** a woman who is the lover though not the legal wife of a man

mistrust *noun* a lack of trust or confidence in someone or something ◇ *verb* have no trust or confidence in

■ *noun* distrust, doubt, suspicion, wariness, misgiving, reservations, qualm, hesitancy, chariness, caution, uncertainty, scepticism, apprehension ◇ *verb* distrust, doubt, suspect, be wary of, beware, have reservations, fear

■ *noun & verb* trust

misunderstand *verb* (**misunderstands**, **misunderstanding**, **misunderstood**) take a wrong meaning from what is said or done ◇ **misunderstanding** *noun* **1** a mistake about a meaning **2** a slight disagreement

■ misapprehend, misconstrue, misinterpret, misjudge, mistake, get wrong, miss the point, mishear, *informal* get hold of the wrong end of the stick

misuse *noun* **1** wrong use **2** bad treatment ◇ *verb* **1** use wrongly **2** treat badly

■ *noun* **1** abuse, harm, misapplication, misappropriation, waste **2** mistreatment, ill-treatment, maltreatment, abuse, corruption, exploitation ◇ *verb* **1** abuse, misapply, misemploy, misappropriate **2** ill-treat, harm, mistreat, wrong, distort, injure, corrupt

mite *noun* **1** something very small, *eg* a tiny child **2** a very small spider

3 *hist* a very small coin

mitigate *verb* make (punishment, anger *etc*) less great or severe ◇ **mitigation** *noun*

■ extenuate, justify, vindicate, modify, qualify

⚠ Do not confuse with: **militate**

mitre *noun* **1** the pointed head-dress worn by archbishops and bishops **2** a slanting joint between two pieces of wood

mitt or **mitten** *noun* a glove without separate divisions for the four fingers

mix *verb* **1** unite or blend two or more things together **2** associate with other people ◇ *noun* a mixture, a blending ◇ **mix up** confuse, muddle

■ *verb* **1** combine, blend, mingle, intermingle, intermix, amalgamate, compound, homogenize, synthesize, merge, join, unite, coalesce, fuse, incorporate, fold in **2** associate, consort, fraternize, socialize, mingle, join, *informal* hobnob ◇ **mix up** confuse, bewilder, muddle, perplex, puzzle, confound, mix, jumble, complicate, garble

mixed *adj* **1** jumbled together **2** confused, muddled **3** consisting of different kinds **4** for both sexes: *mixed doubles* ◇ **mixed-up** *adj* confused, bewildered ◇ **mixed up in** involved in (*esp* something illegal)

mixer *noun* **1** a machine that mixes food **2** someone who mixes socially **3** a soft drink added to alcohol

mixture *noun* a number of things mixed together

■ mix, blend, combination, amalgamation, amalgam, compound, conglomeration, composite, coalescence, alloy, brew, synthesis, union, fusion, concoction, assortment, variety, miscellany, medley, mélange, mixed bag, potpourri, jumble, hotchpotch

mizzen-mast *noun* the mast nearest the stern of a ship

ml *abbrev* millilitre(s)

MLitt *abbrev* Master of Letters or Literature (from Latin *Magister Litterarum*)

Mlle *abbrev* mademoiselle

mm *abbrev* millimetre(s)

Mme *abbrev* madame

mnemonic /nɪˈmɒnɪk/ *noun* a rhyme *etc* which helps you to remember something

MO *abbrev* medical officer

moan *noun* a low sound of grief or pain ◇ *verb* **1** make this sound **2** complain
   ■ *verb* **1** lament, wail, sob, weep, howl, groan, whimper, mourn, grieve **2** complain, grumble, *informal* whine, *informal* whinge, gripe, carp, *US slang* kvetch
   ☒ *verb* **1**, **2** rejoice

moat *noun* a deep trench round a castle *etc*, often filled with water

mob *noun* a noisy crowd ◇ *verb* (**mobs**, **mobbing**, **mobbed**) crowd round, or attack, in disorder
   ■ *noun* crowd, mass, throng, multitude, horde, host, swarm, gathering, group, collection, herd, pack, set, crew, gang ◇ *verb* crowd round, crowd round, surround, swarm round, jostle, overrun, set upon, besiege, descend on, throng, pack, pester, charge

mobile *adj* **1** able to move or be moved easily **2** not fixed, changing quickly **3** portable, not relying on fixed cables *etc*: *mobile phone* ◇ *noun* **1** a decoration or toy hung so that it moves slightly in the air **2** *informal* a mobile phone ◇ **mobility** *noun*
   ■ *adj* **1** moving, movable, peripatetic, travelling, roaming, roving, itinerant, wandering, migrant **2** flexible, agile, active, energetic, nimble, changing, changeable, mutable, ever-changing, mutable, expressive, lively
   ☒ *adj* **1** immobile

mobilize *verb* gather (troops *etc*) together ready for active service ◇ **mobilization** *noun*

Möbius strip *maths* a one-sided surface made by twisting and joining together the ends of a rectangular strip

moccasin *noun* a soft leather shoe of the type originally worn by Native Americans

mocha /ˈmɒkə/ *noun* **1** a fine coffee **2** coffee and chocolate mixed together **3** a deep brown colour

mock *verb* laugh at, make fun of ◇ *adj* false, pretended, imitation: *mock battle* ◇ **mockery** *noun* (*plural* **mockeries**) **1** the act of mocking **2** a ridiculous imitation
   ■ *verb* ridicule, jeer, make fun of, laugh at, disparage, deride, scoff, sneer, taunt, scorn, tease ◇ *adj* imitation, faux, counterfeit, artificial, sham, simulated, *informal* phoney, pseudo, feigned, faked, pretended, dummy

MOD *abbrev* Ministry of Defence

modal verb *grammar* a verb which modifies the sense of a main verb, *eg* can, may, must *etc*

mode *noun* **1** a manner of doing or acting **2** kind, sort; fashion

model *noun* **1** a design or pattern to be copied **2** a small-scale copy of something: *model railway* **3** a person who poses for an artist **4** someone employed to wear and display new clothes ◇ *adj* **1** being or acting as a model **2** fit to be copied, perfect: *model behaviour* ◇ *verb* (**models**, **modelling**, **modelled**) **1** make a model of **2** shape according to a particular pattern **3** wear and display (clothes)
   ■ *noun* **2** replica, representation, facsimile, imitation, mock-up, copy **3** sitter, subject, poser ◇ *adj* **2** exemplary, perfect, typical, ideal ◇ *verb* **2** make, form, fashion, mould, sculpt, carve, cast, shape, work, create, design, plan **3** display, wear, show off

modem *noun* a device which transmits information from a computer along telephone cables

moderate *verb* make or become less great or severe ◇ *adj* **1** keeping within reason, not going to extremes **2** of medium or average quality, ability *etc* ◇ **moderately** *adv* ◇ **moderation** *noun* **1** a lessening or calming down **2** the practice of not going to extremes
   ■ *verb* control, regulate, decrease, lessen, soften, restrain, tone down, play down, diminish, ease, curb, calm, check, mod-

ulate, repress, subdue, tame, subside, pacify, mitigate, allay, alleviate, abate, dwindle ◊ *adj* **1** reasonable, restrained, sensible, calm, controlled, cool, mild, well-regulated **2** mediocre, medium, ordinary, fair, indifferent, average, middle-of-the-road

modern *adj* belonging to the present or to recent times; not old ◊ **modernity** *noun* ◊ **modernize** *verb* bring up to date

▤ current, contemporary, up-to-date, new, fresh, latest, late, novel, present, present-day, recent, up-to-the-minute, *informal* newfangled, advanced, avant-garde, progressive, modernistic, innovative, state-of-the-art, fashionable, stylish, in vogue, in style, *informal* trendy

modest *adj* **1** not exaggerating achievements; not boastful **2** not very large: *modest salary* **3** behaving decently; not shocking ◊ **modestly** *adv* ◊ **modesty** *noun*

▤ **1** unassuming, humble, self-effacing, self-deprecating, quiet, reserved, retiring, unpretentious, discreet, bashful, shy **2** moderate, ordinary, unexceptional, fair, reasonable, limited, small

modicum *noun* a small quantity or amount: *a modicum of kindness*

modify *verb* (**modifies, modifying, modified**) **1** make a change in: *modified my design* **2** make less extreme: *modified his demands* ◊ **modification** *noun*

▤ **1** change, alter, redesign, revise, vary, adapt, adjust, *informal* tweak, transform, reform, convert, improve, reorganize **2** moderate, reduce, temper, tone down, limit, soften, qualify

modish *adj* fashionable, smart ◊ **modishly** *adv* ◊ **modishness** *noun*

modular *adj* of or composed of modules

modulate *verb* **1** vary or soften in tone or pitch **2** *music* change key ◊ **modulation** *noun*

▤ **1** modify, adjust, balance, alter, soften, lower, regulate, vary, harmonize, inflect, tune

module *noun* **1** a set course forming a unit in an educational scheme **2** a separate, self-contained section of a spacecraft **3** a self-contained unit which combines with others to form a structure

modus operandi a method of working

modus vivendi a way of life or living

mogul *noun* **1** an influential person; a magnate

mohair *noun* **1** the long silky hair of an Angora goat **2** fabric made from this

Mohammed *noun* a prophet, the founder of Islam

moiety *noun* a half share or division

moist *adj* damp, slightly wet

▤ damp, clammy, humid, wet, dewy, rainy, muggy, marshy, drizzly, watery, soggy

▣ dry, arid

moisten *verb* make slightly wet or damp

moisture *noun* slight wetness; water or other liquid in tiny drops in the atmosphere or on a surface

▤ water, liquid, wetness, wateriness, damp, dampness, dankness, humidity, vapour, dew, mugginess, condensation, steam, spray

▣ dryness

moisturize *verb* add moisture to ◊ **moisturizer** *noun* a cosmetic cream which restores moisture to the skin

molar *noun* a back tooth used for grinding food

molasses *noun sing* a thick dark syrup left when sugar is refined

mole¹ *noun* **1** a small burrowing animal, with tiny eyes and soft fur **2** a spy who infiltrates a rival organization

mole² *noun* a small dark spot on the skin, often raised

molecule *noun* the smallest part of a substance which has the same qualities as the substance itself

molehill *noun* a small heap of earth created by a burrowing mole

molest *verb* **1** annoy or torment **2** injure or abuse, *esp* sexually ◇ **molestation** *noun* ◇ **molester** *noun*

◼ **1** annoy, disturb, bother, harass, irritate, persecute, pester, plague, tease, torment, hound, upset, worry, trouble, badger **2** attack, accost, assail, hurt, ill-treat, maltreat, mistreat, abuse, harm, injure

moll *noun* a gangster's girlfriend

mollify *verb* (**mollifies**, **mollifying**, **mollified**) calm down; lessen the anger of

mollusc *noun* any of a group of boneless animals, usually with hard shells, *eg* shellfish and snails

mollycoddle *verb* pamper, overprotect

molten *adj* of metal *etc*: melted

moment *noun* **1** a very short space of time; an instant **2** importance, consequence

◼ **1** second, instant, minute, split second, trice, *informal* jiffy, *informal* tick

momentary *adj* lasting for a moment ◇ **momentarily** *adv*

◼ brief, short, short-lived, temporary, transient, transitory, fleeting, ephemeral, hasty, quick, passing

◼◼ lasting, permanent

momentous *adj* of great importance

◼ significant, important, critical, crucial, decisive, weighty, grave, serious, vital, fateful, historic, earth-shaking, epoch-making, eventful, major, *informal* seismic

◼◼ insignificant, unimportant, trivial

momentum *noun* (*plural* **momenta**) **1** the force of a moving body **2** speed of progress: *the campaign gained momentum*

monarch *noun* a king, queen, emperor or empress ◇ **monarchist** *noun* someone who believes in government by a monarch

monarchy *noun* (*plural* **monarchies**) **1** government by a monarch **2** an area governed by a monarch

◼ **1** royalism, sovereignty, autocracy, monocracy, absolutism, despotism, tyranny **2** kingdom, empire, principality, realm, domain, dominion

monastery *noun* (*plural* **monasteries**) a building housing a group of monks ◇ **monastic** *adj* of or like monasteries or monks: *monastic life* ◇ **monasticism** *noun* the way of life in a monastery

◼ **monastic** reclusive, withdrawn, secluded, cloistered, austere, ascetic, celibate, contemplative

Monday *noun* the second day of the week

monetarism *noun* an economic policy based on control of a country's money supply ◇ **monetarist** *noun* & *adj*

monetary *adj* of money or coinage

money *noun* **1** coins and banknotes used for payment **2** wealth ◇ **moneyed** or **monied** *adj* wealthy

◼ **1** currency, cash, legal tender, banknotes, coin, funds, capital, *informal* dough, *informal* dosh

mongoose *noun* (*plural* **mongooses**) a small weasel-like animal which kills snakes

mongrel *noun* an animal of mixed breed, *esp* a dog

monicker *noun*, *slang* a nickname, an alias

monitor *noun* **1** an instrument used to check the operation of a system or apparatus **2** a screen in a television studio showing the picture being transmitted **3** a computer screen **4** a school pupil given certain responsibilities ◇ *verb* **1** keep a check on **2** listen to and report on (foreign broadcasts *etc*)

◼ *verb* **1** check, watch, keep track of, keep under surveillance, keep an eye on, follow, track, supervise, observe, note, survey, trace, scan, record, plot, detect

monk *noun* a member of a male religious group living in a monastery

monkey *noun* (*plural* **monkeys**) **1** a long-tailed mammal which walks on four legs and is related to the apes **2** a mischievous child ◇ **monkey about** fool about ◇ **monkey nut** *noun* a peanut ◇ **monkey puzzle** a pine tree with

prickly spines along its branches
◇**monkey wrench** an adjustable
spanner

▣ **1** primate, simian, ape **2** scamp, imp,
urchin, brat, rogue, *informal* scallywag,
rascal

monkfish *noun* a type of sea-fish,
used as food

mono- *prefix* one, single

monochrome *adj* **1** in (shades of)
one colour **2** black and white: *monochrome photography*

monocle *noun* a single eyeglass

monogamy *noun* marriage to one
spouse at a time ◇**monogamous** *adj*

monogram *noun* two or more letters,
usually initials, made into a single design

monolith *noun* **1** an upright block of
stone **2** something unmovable or intractable ◇**monolithic** *adj*

monologue *noun* a long speech by
one person

monoplane *noun* an aeroplane with
a single pair of wings

monopolize *verb* **1** have exclusive
rights to or control of **2** take up the
whole of: *monopolizing the conversation*

▣ **1** corner, control **2** dominate, take over,
appropriate, *informal* hog, occupy, take
up

monopoly *noun* (*plural* **monopo-
lies**) **1** an exclusive right to make or sell
something **2** complete unshared possession, control *etc*

monorail *noun* a railway on which
the trains run along a single rail

monosyllable *noun* a word of one
syllable ◇**monosyllabic** *adj*

monotone *noun* a single, unchanging tone

monotonous **1** unchanging, dull **2**
in a single tone ◇**monotonously** *adv*
◇**monotony** *noun* lack of variety

▣ **1** boring, dull, tedious, uninteresting,
tiresome, wearisome, unchanging, uneventful, unvaried, uniform, toneless,
flat, colourless, repetitive, routine,
plodding, humdrum, soul-destroying

▣ **1** lively, varied, colourful

monsoon *noun* **1** a wind that blows in
the Indian Ocean **2** the rainy season
caused by the southwest monsoon in
summer

monster *noun* **1** a huge terrifying
creature **2** something of unusual size
or appearance **3** an evil person ◇*adj*
huge

▣ *noun* **1** giant, ogre, troll, dragon **3**
beast, fiend, brute, barbarian, savage,
villain

monstrosity *noun* (*plural* **mon-
strosities**) **1** something unnatural **2**
something very ugly

monstrous *adj* huge, horrible

▣ huge, enormous, colossal, gigantic,
gargantuan, vast, immense, massive,
mammoth, grotesque, hideous, deformed, malformed, misshapen

montage /mɒnˈtɑːʒ/ *noun* **1** a composite picture **2** a film made up of parts of
other films

month *noun* a twelfth part of a year,
approximately four weeks

monthly *adj & adv* happening once a
month ◇*noun* (*plural* **monthlies**) a magazine *etc* published once a month

monument *noun* **1** a building, pillar,
tomb *etc* built in memory of someone or
an event **2** a building, grave *etc* remaining from ancient times

▣ **1**, **2** memorial, cenotaph, headstone,
gravestone, tombstone, shrine, mausoleum, cairn, cross, obelisk, pillar, statue

monumental *adj* **1** of a monument **2**
huge, enormous ◇**monumentally** *adv*

▣ **2** huge, immense, enormous, colossal,
vast, tremendous, massive, great

moo *noun* the sound made by a cow

mooch *verb* slouch, skulk

mood *noun* the state of a person's feelings or temper

▣ disposition, frame of mind, state of
mind, temper, humour, spirit, tenor,
whim

moody *adj* **1** often changing in mood
2 ill-tempered, cross ◇**moodily** *adj*
◇**moodiness** *noun*

▣ **1** changeable, temperamental, unpredictable, capricious **2** irritable, short-

tempered, *informal* crabby, crotchety, testy, touchy, morose, angry, broody, mopy, sulky, sullen

moon[1] *noun* the heavenly body which travels round the earth once each month and reflects light from the sun

moon[2] *verb* 1 wander (about) 2 gaze dreamily (at)

moonbeam *noun* a beam of light from the moon

moonlight *noun* the light of the moon

moonshine *noun* 1 the shining of the moon 2 rubbish, foolish ideas or talk

moonstone *noun* a precious stone with a pearly shine

moor[1] *noun* a large stretch of open ground, often covered with heather

moor[2] *verb* tie up or anchor (a ship *etc*)

■ fasten, secure, tie up, drop anchor, anchor, berth, dock, make fast, fix, hitch, bind

moorhen *noun* a kind of water bird with black plumage and a red beak

moorings *noun plural* 1 the place where a ship is moored 2 the anchor, rope *etc* holding it

moorland *noun* a stretch of moor
■ moor, heath, fell, upland

moose *noun* (*plural* **moose**) a large deer-like animal, found in N America

moot point a debatable point; a question with no obvious solution

mop *noun* 1 a pad of sponge or a bunch of short pieces of coarse yarn *etc* on a handle for washing or cleaning 2 a thick head of hair ◇ *verb* (**mops, mopping, mopped**) 1 clean with a mop 2 clean or wipe: *mopped his brow* ◇ **mop up** clean up

mope *verb* be unhappy and gloomy
■ brood, fret, sulk, pine, languish, droop, despair, grieve

moped /'moʊpɛd/ *noun* a pedal bicycle with a motor

moquette *noun* fabric with a velvety pile and canvas backing, used for upholstery

moraine *noun* a line of rocks and gravel left by a glacier

moral *adj* 1 relating to standards of behaviour and character 2 of correct or acceptable behaviour or character ◇ *noun* 1 the lesson of a story 2 (**morals**) principles and standards of (*esp* sexual) behaviour ◇ **morality** *noun* moral standards ◇ **moralize** *verb* draw a lesson from a story or event ◇ **moral support** encouragement without active help ◇ **moral victory** a failure that can really be seen as a success

■ *adj* 1 ethical, principled 2 honourable, decent, upright, upstanding, virtuous, good, right, righteous, high-minded, honest, incorruptible, proper, blameless, chaste, clean-living, pure, just, noble

morale /məˈrɑːl/ *noun* spirit and confidence

morass *noun* (*plural* **morasses**) 1 a marsh or bog 2 a bewildering mass of something: *a morass of regulations*

moratorium *noun* (*plural* **moratoria**) an official suspension or temporary ban

morbid *adj* 1 too concerned with gloomy, unpleasant things 2 diseased, unhealthy ◇ **morbidity** *noun* ◇ **morbidly** *adv*

■ 1 gloomy, pessimistic, melancholy, sombre, dark 2 sick, unhealthy, unwholesome, insalubrious

mordant *noun* a substance used to fix dye or make paint stick to a surface

more *adj* a greater or additional number or amount of: *more money* ◇ *adv* to a greater extent: *more beautiful/more than I can say* ◇ *noun* 1 a greater proportion or amount 2 a further or additional number: *more where this came from*

■ *adj* further, extra, additional, added, new, fresh, increased, other, supplementary, repeated, alternative, spare ◇ *adv* further, longer, again, besides, moreover, better

🔁 *adj* less, fewer ◇ *adv* less

moreish *adj* of food *etc*: enjoyable, making you want more

morel /məˈrɛl/ *noun* a mushroom with

a honeycombed cap

morello *noun* a sour-tasting cherry

moreover *adv* besides

■ furthermore, further, besides, in addition, as well, also, additionally, what is more

morganatic *adj* of a marriage: in which the woman has no claim to the title or property of her husband

From early German *morgengabe* 'morning gift', a present given to a spouse on the morning after the wedding

morgue *noun* a place where dead bodies are laid, awaiting identification *etc*

MORI *abbrev* Market & Opinion Research International

moribund *adj* 1 dying 2 lacking activity or vitality

morn *noun*, *formal* morning

morning *noun* the part of the day before noon ◇*adj* of or in the morning ◇**morning star** Venus when it rises before the sun

■ *noun* daybreak, daylight, dawn, sunrise, break of day

morocco *noun* a fine goatskin leather first brought from Morocco

moron *noun*, *informal* a very stupid person ◇**moronic** *adj*

morose *adj* bad-tempered, gloomy ◇**morosely** *adv*

■ ill-tempered, bad-tempered, moody, sullen, sulky, surly, gloomy, grim, gruff, sour, taciturn, glum, *informal* grouchy, *informal* crabby, saturnine

■ cheerful, communicative

morphine *noun* a drug which causes sleep or deadens pain

morphology *noun* the study of the forms of words ◇**morphological** *adj* ◇**morphologist** *noun*

morris dance a traditional English country dance in which male dancers carry sticks and wear bells

Originally a *Moorish* dance brought from Spain

morrow *noun*, *old*: **the morrow** tomorrow, the day after

Morse *noun* a code of signals made up of dots and dashes

morsel *noun* a small piece, *eg* of food

■ bit, scrap, piece, fragment, crumb, bite, mouthful, nibble, taste, soupçon, titbit, slice, fraction, modicum, grain, atom, part

mortal *adj* 1 liable to die 2 causing death; deadly: *mortal injury* ◇*noun* a human being ◇**mortally** *adv* fatally: *mortally wounded*

■ *adj* 1 earthly, bodily, human, perishable, temporal 2 fatal, lethal, deadly ◇ *noun* human being, human, individual, person, being, body, creature

■ *adj* 1 immortal ◇ *noun* immortal, god

mortality *noun* (*plural* **mortalities**) 1 the state of being mortal 2 death 3 frequency of death; death-rate: *infant mortality*

mortar *noun* 1 a heavy bowl for crushing and grinding substances with a pestle 2 a short gun for throwing shells 3 a mixture of lime, sand and water, used for fixing stones *etc*

mortarboard *noun* a university or college cap with a square flat top

mortgage *noun* a sum of money lent through a legal agreement for buying buildings, land *etc* ◇*verb* offer (buildings *etc*) as security for money borrowed

mortice *another spelling of* **mortise**

mortician *noun*, *US* an undertaker

mortify *verb* (**mortifies**, **mortifying**, **mortified**) cause to feel ashamed or humble ◇**mortification** *noun*

■ humiliate, shame, humble, embarrass, crush

mortise or **mortice** *noun* a hole in a piece of wood to receive the shaped end (**tenon**) of another piece ◇**mortise lock** or **mortice lock** a lock whose mechanism is sunk into the edge of a door

mortuary *noun* (*plural* **mortuaries**) a place where dead bodies are kept before burial or cremation

mosaic noun a picture or design made up of many small pieces of coloured glass, stone etc

Moses basket a portable cot for babies

Moslem another spelling of **Muslim**

mosque noun an Islamic place of worship

mosquito noun (plural **mosquitoes** or **mosquitos**) a biting or blood-sucking insect, often carrying disease

moss noun (plural **mosses**) a very small flowerless plant, found in moist places ◇ **mossy** adj covered with moss

most adj the greatest number or amount of: most children attend school regularly ◇ adv **1** very, extremely: most grateful **2** to the greatest extent: the most expensive car in the showroom ◇ noun the greatest number or amount: he got most ◇ **at most** not more than ◇ **for the most part** mostly

mostly adv mainly, chiefly
▣ mainly, on the whole, principally, chiefly, generally, usually, largely, for the most part, as a rule

MOT noun a compulsory annual check, originally on behalf of the Ministry of Transport, on vehicles over a certain age

mote noun a particle of dust; a speck

motel noun a hotel built to accommodate motorists and their vehicles

moth noun **1** a flying insect, seen mostly at night **2** the cloth-eating grub of the clothes moth ◇ **moth-eaten** adj **1** full of holes made by moths **2** tatty, shabby

mothball noun a small ball of chemical used to protect clothes from moths ◇ verb (also **put in mothballs**) put aside for later use etc

mother noun **1** a female parent **2** the female head of a convent ◇ verb **1** be the mother of **2** care for like a mother ◇ **motherly** adj of or like a mother ◇ **mother-in-law** noun the mother of your husband or wife ◇ **mother-of-pearl** noun a hard shiny substance which forms inside certain shells

◇ **mother tongue** a native language
▣ noun **1** parent, birth mother, formal procreator, formal progenitress, dam, informal mamar, informal mamma, informal mum, informal mummy, matriarch ◇ verb **1** bear, produce, nurture, raise, rear, nurse **2** care for, cherish, pamper, spoil, baby, indulge, overprotect, fuss over ◇ **motherly** maternal, caring, comforting, affectionate, kind, loving, protective, warm, tender, gentle, fond
▣ **motherly** neglectful, uncaring

motherboard noun, comput a printed circuit board into which other boards can be slotted

motherhood noun the state of being a mother

motherland noun the country of your birth

motif noun (plural **motifs**) **1** a design or part of a pattern **2** a distinctive feature or idea in a piece of music, a play etc
▣ **2** theme, idea, topic, concept

❗ Do not confuse with: **motive**

motion noun **1** the act or state of moving **2** a single movement **3** a suggestion put before a meeting for discussion ◇ verb **1** make a signal by a movement or gesture **2** direct (someone) in this way: the policeman motioned us forward
▣ noun **1** movement, action, mobility, moving, activity, locomotion **2** gesture, gesticulation, action, movement, signal, sign, wave, nod ◇ verb **1** signal, gesture, gesticulate, sign, wave, nod **2** beckon, direct, usher

motionless adj not moving
▣ unmoving, still, stationary, static, immobile, at a standstill, fixed, halted, at rest, resting, standing, paralysed, inanimate, lifeless, frozen, rigid, stagnant
▣ active, moving

motivate verb cause (someone) to act in a certain way ◇ **motivation** noun
▣ prompt, incite, impel, spur, provoke, stimulate, drive, lead, stir, urge, push, propel, persuade, move, inspire, encourage, cause, trigger, induce, kindle, draw, arouse, bring

motive *noun* the cause of someone's actions; a reason

■ ground(s), cause, reason, purpose, motivation, object, intention, influence, rationale, incentive, impulse, stimulus, inspiration, incitement

| **!** Do not confuse with: **motif** |

motley *adj* made up of different colours or kinds

motocross *noun* the sport of motorcycle racing across rough terrain

motor *noun* 1 an engine which causes motion 2 a car ◇ *verb* travel by car ◇ **motorize** *verb* supply with an engine

motorbike *noun*, *informal* a motorcycle

motorcade *noun* a procession of cars carrying a head of state *etc*

motorcycle *noun* a bicycle with a petrol-driven engine ◇ **motorcyclist** *noun*

motorist *noun* someone who drives a car

motorway *noun* a dual carriageway for fast-moving traffic

mottled *adj* marked with spots or blotches

■ speckled, dappled, blotchy, flecked, piebald, stippled, streaked, tabby, spotted, freckled, variegated

motto *noun* (*plural* **mottoes**) a phrase which acts as a guiding principle or rule

■ saying, slogan, maxim, watchword, catchword, byword, precept, proverb, adage, formula, rule, golden rule, dictum

mould[1] *noun* a shape into which a liquid is poured to take on that shape when it cools or sets: *jelly mould* ◇ *verb* 1 form in a mould 2 shape

■ *verb* 1 cast 2 forge, shape, stamp, make, form, create, design, construct, sculpt, model, work

mould[2] *noun* 1 a fluffy growth on stale food *etc* 2 soil containing rotted leaves *etc* ◇ **mouldy** *adj* affected by mould; stale

■ **mouldy** mildewed, blighted, musty, decaying, corrupt, rotten, fusty, putrid, bad, spoiled, stale

F3 mouldy fresh, wholesome

moulder *verb* decay or crumble away

moulding *noun* a decorated border of moulded plaster round a ceiling *etc*

moult *verb* of a bird: shed its feathers

mound *noun* 1 a bank of earth or stones; a hill 2 a heap

■ 1 hill, hill, hillock, hummock, rise, knoll, bank, dune, elevation, ridge, embankment, earthwork 2 heap, pile, stack

mount *verb* 1 go up, ascend 2 climb on to (a horse, bicycle *etc*) 3 fix (a picture *etc*) on to a backing or support 4 fix (a gemstone) in a casing 5 organize (an exhibition) ◇ *noun* 1 a support or backing for display 2 a horse, bicycle *etc* to ride on 3 *old* a mountain ◇ **the Mounties** *informal* the Canadian mounted police

■ *verb* 1 climb, ascend, go up, scale 2 get on, clamber up, get astride 5 put on, set up, prepare, stage, exhibit, display, launch

F3 *verb* 1 descend 2 dismount, get down

mountain *noun* 1 a large hill 2 a large quantity ◇ **mountaineer** *noun* a mountain climber ◇ **mountain ash** the rowan tree

■ 1 mount, peak, alp, tor, massif 2 heap, pile, stack, mound, mass, abundance, backlog

mountainous *adj* 1 having many mountains 2 huge

■ 1 craggy, rocky, hilly, high, highland, upland, alpine 2 huge, towering, enormous, immense

mountebank *noun* a charlatan, a quack

Originally a street pedlar who climbed on a mound or bench to sell his goods

mourn *verb* 1 grieve for 2 be sorrowful ◇ **mourner** *noun* ◇ **mournful** *adj* sad

■ 1 grieve, lament, bemoan, miss, regret, deplore 2 sorrow, grieve, weep, wail

mourning *noun* 1 the showing of grief 2 the period during which someone grieves after a person's death **3** dark-coloured clothes traditionally worn by mourners

■ **1** grief, grieving, lamentation, sadness, sorrow, desolation, weeping **2** bereavement

mouse noun (plural **mice**) **1** a small gnawing animal, found in houses and fields **2** a shy, timid, uninteresting person **3** comput a device moved by hand which causes corresponding cursor movements on a screen

moussaka noun a Greek dish of minced lamb topped with a cheese sauce

mousse /muːs/ noun a frothy set dish including eggs, cream etc, either sweet or savoury

moustache noun unshaved hair above a man's upper lip

mousy adj **1** of a light-brown colour **2** shy, timid, uninteresting

mouth noun **1** the opening in the head through which an animal or person eats and makes sounds **2** the part of a river where it flows into the sea **3** an opening, an entrance ◇ verb **1** speak **2** shape (words) in an exaggerated way without speaking ◇ **mouthful** noun (plural **mouthfuls**) as much as fills the mouth ◇ **mouth organ** a harmonica

■ noun **1** lips, jaws, informal trap, slang gob **2** inlet, estuary **3** opening, aperture, orifice, cavity, entrance, gateway ◇ verb **1** enunciate, articulate, utter, pronounce, whisper

mouthpiece noun **1** the part of a musical instrument, tobacco-pipe etc held in the mouth **2** someone who speaks for others

move verb **1** (cause to) change place or position **2** change your house **3** rouse or affect the feelings of **4** rouse into action **5** propose, suggest formally: I move that the concert be postponed ◇ noun **1** an act of moving **2** a step, an action **3** a shifting of pieces in a game of chess etc ◇ **movable** adj able to be moved, changed etc

■ verb **1** stir, go, advance, budge, change, proceed, progress, make strides, trans-

port, carry, transfer **3** affect, touch, agitate, stir, impress, excite **4** prompt, stimulate, urge, impel, drive, propel, motivate, incite, provoke, persuade, induce, inspire

movement noun **1** the act or manner of moving **2** an action or change of position **3** a division of a piece of music **4** a group of people united in a common aim: the peace movement **5** an organized attempt to achieve an aim: the movement to reform the divorce laws

■ **1** activity, action, agitation, stirring, moving, transfer, passage **2** move, action, gesture, repositioning, relocation **4** group, organization, party, faction **5** campaign, crusade, drive

movie noun a cinema film ◇ **the movies** the cinema

moving adj **1** in motion **2** causing emotion ◇ **movingly** adv

■ **1** mobile, active, in motion **2** touching, affecting, poignant, impressive, emotive, arousing, stirring, inspiring, inspirational, exciting, thrilling, persuasive, stimulating

mow verb cut (grass, hay etc) with a scythe or machine ◇ **mower** noun a machine for mowing ◇ **mow down** destroy in great numbers

mozzarella noun a mild-tasting spongy Italian cheese

MP abbrev **1** Member of Parliament **2** Military Police

mpg abbrev miles per gallon

mph abbrev miles per hour

MPhil abbrev Master of Philosophy

Mr noun the form of address used before a man's surname

Mrs noun the form of address used before a married woman's surname

MS abbrev **1** multiple sclerosis **2** manuscript

Ms noun a form of address used before the surname of a married or unmarried woman

MSc abbrev Master of Science

MSG abbrev monosodium glutamate

much adj a great amount of ◇ adv to or by a great extent: much loved/much *faster* ◊*pronoun* **1** a great amount **2** something important: *made much of it* ◊ **much the same** nearly the same

▤ *adj* copious, plentiful, ample, considerable, a lot, abundant, great, substantial ◊ *adv* greatly, considerably, a lot, frequently, often

mucilage *noun* a sticky or gluey substance

muck *noun* dung, dirt, filth ◊ **muckraking** *noun* looking for scandals to expose

▤ dirt, dung, manure, mire, filth, mud, sewage, slime, *informal* gunge, ordure, scum, sludge

mucous *adj* like or covered by mucus

⚠ Do not confuse: **mucous** and **mucus**

mucus *noun* slimy fluid secreted from the nose *etc*

mud *noun* wet, soft earth

▤ clay, mire, ooze, dirt, sludge, silt

muddle *verb* **1** confuse, bewilder **2** mix up **3** make a mess of ◊ *noun* **1** a mess **2** a state of confusion

▤ *verb* **1** confuse, bewilder, bemuse, perplex **3** disorganize, disorder, mess up, jumble, scramble, tangle ◊ *noun* **1** mess, jumble, clutter, tangle **2** chaos, confusion, disorder, mix-up

muddy *adj* **1** covered with mud **2** unclear, confused

▤ **1** dirty, foul, miry, mucky, marshy, boggy, swampy, quaggy, grimy **2** cloudy, indistinct, obscure, opaque, murky, hazy, blurred, fuzzy, dull

▣ **1** clean **2** clear

mudguard *noun* a shield or guard over wheels to catch mud splashes

muesli *noun* a mixture of grains, nuts and fruit eaten with milk

muezzin *noun* an Islamic priest who calls out the hour of prayer from a mosque

muff[1] *noun* a tube of warm fabric to cover and keep the hands warm

muff[2] *verb, informal* fail in an opportunity, *eg* to catch a ball

muffin *noun* **1** a round, flat spongy cake, toasted and eaten hot with butter **2** a small sweet cup-shaped cake: *blueberry muffins*

muffle *verb* **1** wrap up for warmth *etc* **2** deaden (a sound)

▤ **1** wrap, envelop, cloak, swathe, cover **2** deaden, dull, quieten, silence, stifle, dampen, muzzle, suppress

muffler *noun* **1** a scarf **2** *US* a silencer for a car

mufti *noun* clothes worn by soldiers *etc* when off duty

mug[1] *noun* **1** a straight-sided cup **2** *informal* a stupid or gullible person **3** *informal* the face

mug[2] *verb* (**mugs**, **mugging**, **mugged**) attack and rob (someone) in the street ◊ **mugger** *noun*

▤ set upon, attack, assault, waylay, steal from, rob, beat up, jump (on)

mug[3] *verb* (**mugs**, **mugging**, **mugged**): **mug up** *informal* study hard; swot up

muggy *adj* of weather: close and damp ◊ **mugginess** *noun*

▤ humid, sticky, stuffy, sultry, close, clammy, oppressive, sweltering, moist, damp

mulatto *noun* (*plural* **mulattoes**) *old* someone with one black and one white parent

mulberry *noun* (*plural* **mulberries**) **1** a tree on whose leaves silkworms are fed **2** its purple berry

mulch *noun* loose straw *etc* laid down to protect plant roots ◊ *verb* cover with mulch

mule[1] *noun* an animal bred from a horse and an ass

mule[2] *noun* a backless slipper

mulish *adj* stubborn

mull *verb*: **mull over** think over, ponder

▤ reflect on, ponder, contemplate, think over, think about, ruminate, consider, weigh up, chew over, meditate, study, examine, deliberate

mullah *noun* an Islamic teacher

mulled *adj* of wine, *etc*: mixed with spices and served warm

mullet *noun* **1** an edible small sea-fish **2** a man's hairstyle that is short at the top but long at the back

mulligatawny *noun* an East Indian curried soup

mullion *noun* an upright division in a window

multi- *prefix* many

multicoloured *adj* many-coloured

multifarious *adj* of many kinds

multimedia *adj* of a computer: able to run various sound and visual applications

multimillionaire *noun* someone who has property worth several million pounds (or dollars)

multinational *adj* of a company: having branches in several different countries

multiple *adj* **1** affecting many parts: *multiple injuries* **2** involving many things of the same sort: *a multiple crash* ◇ *noun* a number or quantity which contains another an exact number of times ◇ **multiple sclerosis** a progressive nerve disease resulting in paralysis (shortened to **MS**)

▣ *adj* **1** many, numerous, manifold, various, several, sundry, collective

multiplex *adj* of a cinema: including several screens and theatres in one building

multiply *verb* (**multiplies, multiplying, multiplied**) **1** increase **2** increase a number by adding it to itself a certain number of times: *2 multiplied by 3 is 6* ◇ **multiplication** *noun* the act of multiplying ◇ **multiplier** *noun* the number by which another is to be multiplied ◇ **a multiplicity of** a great number of

▣ **1** increase, proliferate, expand, spread, reproduce, propagate, breed, accumulate, intensify, extend, build up, augment, boost

multitasking *noun*, *comput* the action of running several processes simultaneously

multitude *noun* a great number; a crowd ◇ **multitudinous** *adj* very many

▣ crowd, throng, horde, swarm, mob,

mass, herd, congregation, host, lot, lots, legion, public, people, populace

▣ few, scattering

mum[1] *noun*, *informal* mother

mum[2] *adj* silent

mumble *verb* speak indistinctly

mummy[1] *noun* (*plural* **mummies**) *informal* mother

mummy[2] *noun* (*plural* **mummies**) a dead body preserved by wrapping in bandages and treating with wax, spices *etc* ◇ **mummify** *verb* (**mummifies, mummifying, mummified**) make into a mummy

mumps *noun sing* an infectious disease affecting glands at the side of the neck, causing swelling

munch *verb* chew noisily ◇ **the munchies** hunger pangs

▣ eat, chew, crunch, *formal* masticate

mundane *adj* dull, ordinary

▣ banal, ordinary, everyday, commonplace, prosaic, humdrum, workaday, routine

municipal *adj* of or owned by a city or town

▣ civic, city, town, urban, borough, community, public

municipality *noun* a city or town; an area covered by local government

munificent *adj* very generous ◇ **munificence** *noun*

munitions *noun plural* weapons and ammunition used in war

Munro *noun* (*plural* **Munros**) a British or Irish mountain above 3000 feet

Originally applied only to mountains in Scotland, from a list prepared by the Scottish mountaineer, Hugh *Munro*

mural *adj* of or on a wall ◇ *noun* a painting or design on a wall

murder *verb* kill someone unlawfully and deliberately ◇ *noun* the act of murdering ◇ **murderer** *noun* someone who commits murder ◇ **murderess** *noun*, *old* a woman who commits murder ◇ **murderous** *adj* capable or guilty of murder; wicked

■ *verb* kill, slaughter, slay, assassinate, butcher, massacre ◇ *noun* homicide, killing, manslaughter, slaying, assassination, massacre

murky *adj* dark, gloomy ◇ **murkiness** *noun*

■ dark, dismal, gloomy, dull, overcast, misty, foggy, dim, cloudy, obscure, shadowy, veiled, grey

✎ bright, clear

murmur *noun* **1** a low indistinct continuous sound **2** something said in a hushed tone ◇ *verb* **1** make a murmur **2** complain, grumble

■ *noun* **1** undertone, humming, rumble, drone **2** mumble, muttering, whisper ◇ *verb* **1** mutter, mumble, buzz, hum

Murphy's Law the law that if something can go wrong, it will

muscat *noun* a musky variety of grape, used to make wine

muscle *noun* **1** fleshy tissue which contracts and stretches to cause body movements **2** a structure composed of this in the body **3** physical strength or power

muscular *adj* **1** of muscles **2** strong ◇ **muscular dystrophy** a hereditary disease in which the muscles gradually deteriorate

■ **2** brawny, *informal* beefy, sinewy, athletic, powerfully built, strapping, hefty, powerful, husky, robust, stalwart, vigorous, strong

✎ **2** puny, flabby, weak

Muse *noun* one of the nine goddesses of poetry, music, dancing *etc* in classical mythology

muse *verb* think (over) in a quiet, leisurely way

museum *noun* (*plural* **museums**) a building for housing and displaying objects of artistic, scientific or historic interest

mush *noun* **1** something soft and pulpy **2** an overly sentimental film, song *etc*

mushroom *noun* an edible fungus, usually umbrella-shaped ◇ *verb* grow

very quickly: *buildings mushroomed all over town*

mushy *adj* **1** soft and pulpy **2** overly sentimental ◇ **mushiness** *noun*

music *noun* **1** the art of arranging, combining *etc* certain sounds produced by the voice or by instruments **2** an arrangement of such sounds or its written form **3** a sweet or pleasant sound

musical *adj* **1** of music **2** sounding sweet or pleasant **3** having a talent for music ◇ **musically** *adv*

■ **2** tuneful, melodious, melodic, harmonious, dulcet, sweet-sounding, lyrical

✎ **2** discordant, unmusical

Musical instruments include:
balalaika, banjo, cello, double-bass, guitar, harp, hurdy-gurdy, lute, lyre, mandolin, sitar, spinet, ukulele, viola, violin, *informal* fiddle, zither; accordion, concertina, *informal* squeeze-box, clavichord, harmonium, harpsichord, keyboard, melodeon, organ, Wurlitzer®, piano, grand piano, Pianola®, player-piano, synthesizer, uillean pipes, virginals; bagpipes, bassoon, bugle, clarinet, cor anglais, cornet, didgeridoo, euphonium, fife, flugelhorn, flute, French horn, harmonica, horn, kazoo, mouth organ, oboe, Pan-pipes, piccolo, recorder, saxophone, sousaphone, trombone, trumpet, tuba; castanets, cymbal, glockenspiel, maracas, marimba, tambourine, triangle, tubular bells, xylophone; bass-drum, bodhran, bongo, kettle-drum, snare-drum, steel pan, tenor-drum, timpani, tom-tom

---

Musical terms include:
accelerando, acciaccatura, accidental, accompaniment, acoustic, adagio, ad lib, a due, affettuoso, agitato, al fine, al segno, alla breve, alla cappella, allargando, allegretto, allegro, al segno, alto,

amoroso, andante, animato, appoggiatura, arco, arpeggio, arrangement, a tempo, attacca, bar, bar line, double bar line, baritone, bass, beat, bis, breve, buffo, cadence, cantabile, cantilena, chord, chromatic, clef, alto clef, bass clef, tenor clef, treble clef, coda, col canto, con brio, concert, con fuoco, con moto, consonance, contralto, counterpoint, crescendo, crotchet, cross-fingering, cue, da capo, decrescendo, demisemiquaver, descant, diatonic, diminuendo, dissonance, dolce, doloroso, dominant, dotted note, dotted rest, downbeat, drone, duplet, triplet, quadruplet, quintuplet, sextuplet, encore, ensemble, expression, finale, fine, fingerboard, flat, double flat, forte, fortissimo, fret, glissando, grave, harmonics, harmony, hemidemisemiquaver, hold, imitation, improvisation, interval, augmented interval, diminished interval, second interval, third interval, fourth interval, fifth interval, sixth interval, seventh interval, major interval, minor interval, perfect interval, intonation, key, key signature, langsam, larghetto, largo, leading note, ledger line, legato, lento, lyric, maestoso, major, manual, marcato, mediant, medley, melody, metre, mezza voce, mezzo forte, microtone, middle C, minim, minor, moderato, mode, modulation, molto, mordent, movement, mute, natural, non troppo, note, obbligato, octave, orchestra, ostinato, part, pause, pedal point, pentatonic, perdendo, phrase, pianissimo, piano, piece, pitch, pizzicato, presto, quarter tone, quaver, rallentando, recital, refrain, resolution, rest, rhythm, ritenuto, root, scale, score, semibreve, semiquaver, semitone, semplice, sempre, senza, sequence, sforzando, shake, sharp, double sharp, slur, smorzando, solo, soprano, sostenuto, sotto voce,

spiritoso, staccato, staff, stave, subdominant, subito, submediant, sul ponticello, supertonic, swell, syncopation, tablature, tacet, tanto, tempo, tenor, tenuto, theme, tie, timbre, time signature, compound time, simple time, two-two time, three-four time, four-four time, six-eight time, tone, tonic sol-fa, transposition, treble, tremolo, triad, trill, double trill, tune, tuning, turn, tutti, upbeat, unison, vibrato, vigoroso, virtuoso, vivace

musician *noun* **1** a specialist in music **2** someone who plays a musical instrument

musicology *noun* the study of music ◇**musicologist** *noun*

musk *noun* a strong perfume, obtained from the male musk deer or artificially ◇**musky** *adj* ◇**musk deer** a small hornless deer found in Central Asia ◇**muskrat** *noun* a musquash

musket *noun* a kind of gun formerly used by soldiers ◇**musketeer** *noun* a soldier armed with a musket

Muslim *noun* a follower of the Islamic religion ◇*adj* Islamic

muslin *noun* a fine, soft cotton cloth

musquash *noun* (*plural* **musquashes**) a large North American water-rat

mussel *noun* an edible shellfish with two separate halves to its shell

must *verb* **1** used with another verb to express necessity: *I must finish this today* **2** expressing compulsion: *you must do as you're told* **3** expressing certainty or probability: *that must be the right answer* ◇*noun* something that must be done; a necessity

mustache *US spelling* of **moustache**

mustang *noun* a North American wild horse

mustard *noun* **1** a plant with sharp-tasting seeds **2** a hot yellow paste made from its seeds

muster *verb* gather up or together (*eg* troops, courage) ◇**pass muster** be accepted as satisfactory

■ assemble, convene, gather, call together, mobilize, round up, marshal, come together, congregate, collect, group, meet, rally, mass, throng, call up, summon

musty *adj* smelling old and stale ◇ **mustiness** *noun*

■ mouldy, mildewy, stale, stuffy, fusty, dank, airless, decayed, smelly

mutable *adj* changeable

mutation *noun* **1** change, alteration **2** something that has changed in form

mute *adj* **1** not able to speak; dumb **2** silent **3** of a letter in a word: not pronounced ◇ *noun* **1** a mute person **2** a device which softens the sound of a musical instrument ◇ **muted** *adj* **1** of a sound: made quieter, hushed **2** of a colour: not bright

■ *adj* **1** silent, dumb, voiceless, wordless, speechless **2** noiseless, silent **3** silent, unpronounced

◨ *adj* **1** vocal, talkative

mutilate *verb* **1** inflict great physical injury on; maim **2** damage greatly: *mutilate a text* ◇ **mutilation** *noun*

■ **1** maim, injure, wound, dismember, disable, disfigure, lame, mangle, cut to pieces, cut up, butcher **2** spoil, mar, damage, cut, censor

mutiny *verb* (**mutinies, mutinying, mutinied**) **1** rise against those in power **2** refuse to obey the commands of military officers ◇ *noun* (*plural* **mutinies**) refusal to obey commands; rebellion ◇ **mutineer** *noun* someone who takes part in a mutiny ◇ **mutinous** *adj* rebellious; refusing to obey orders

■ *verb* **1** rebel, revolt, rise up, protest, disobey, strike ◇ *noun* rebellion, insurrection, revolt, revolution, rising, uprising, insubordination, disobedience, defiance, resistance, riot, strike

mutt *noun*, *informal* **1** a dog **2** an idiot

mutter *verb* speak in a low voice; mumble

mutton *noun* meat from a sheep, used as food

mutual *adj* **1** given by each to the other(s): *mutual help* **2** shared by two or more: *a mutual friend* ◇ **mutually** *adv*

■ **1** reciprocal, interchangeable, interchanged, exchanged, complementary **2** shared, common, joint

Muzak *noun*, *trademark* recorded music played in shops *etc*

muzzle *noun* **1** an animal's nose and mouth **2** a fastening placed over an animal's mouth to prevent it biting **3** the open end of a gun ◇ *verb* **1** put a muzzle on (a dog *etc*) **2** prevent from speaking freely

■ *verb* **2** restrain, stifle, suppress, gag, mute, silence, censor, choke

muzzy *adj* cloudy, confused ◇ **muzziness** *noun*

my *adj* belonging to me: *this is my book*

mycology *noun* the study of fungi ◇ **mycologist** *noun*

myna or **mynah** *noun* a black Asiatic bird which can be trained to imitate human speech

myopia *noun* short-sightedness ◇ **myopic** *adj* short-sighted

myriad *noun* a very great number ◇ *adj* very many, countless

myrrh *noun* a bitter-tasting resin used in medicines, perfumes *etc*

myrtle *noun* a type of evergreen shrub with aromatic berries

myself *pronoun* **1** used reflexively: *I can see myself in the mirror* **2** used for emphasis: *I wrote this myself*

mysterious *adj* **1** puzzling, difficult to understand **2** secret, hidden ◇ **mysteriously** *adv* ◇ **mysteriousness** *noun*

■ **1** enigmatic, cryptic, mystifying, inexplicable, incomprehensible, puzzling, perplexing, obscure, strange, unfathomable, unsearchable, mystical, baffling, curious **2** hidden, secret, weird, secretive, veiled, dark, furtive

◨ **1** straightforward, comprehensible

mystery *noun* (*plural* **mysteries**) **1** something that cannot be or has not been explained; something puzzling **2** a deep secret

mystic *noun* someone who seeks knowledge of sacred or mystical things by going into a state of spiritual ecstasy

mystical *adj* having a secret or sacred meaning beyond ordinary human understanding

▭ occult, arcane, mystic, esoteric, supernatural, paranormal, transcendental, metaphysical, hidden, mysterious

mystify *verb* (**mystifies, mystifying, mystified**) puzzle greatly; confuse, bewilder

▭ puzzle, bewilder, baffle, perplex, confound, confuse, nonplus

mystique /mɪˈstiːk/ *noun* an atmosphere of mystery about someone or something

myth *noun* **1** a story about gods, heroes *etc* of ancient times **2** something imagined or untrue ◇ **mythical** *adj* **1** of a myth **2** invented, imagined

▭ **1** legend, fable, fairy tale, allegory, parable, saga, story **2** fiction, tradition, fancy, fantasy, superstition

mythology *noun* **1** the study of myths **2** a collection of myths ◇ **mythological** *adj* of myth or mythology; mythical ◇ **mythologist** *noun*

Mythological creatures and spirits include:

abominable snowman (or yeti), afrit, basilisk, Bigfoot, brownie, bunyip, centaur, Cerberus, Chimera, cockatrice, Cyclops, dragon, dryad, dwarf, Echidna, elf, Erinyes (or Furies), Fafnir, fairy, faun, Frankenstein's monster, genie, Geryon, giant, gnome, goblin, golem, Gorgon, griffin, hamadryad, Harpies, hippocampus, hippogriff, hobgoblin, imp, kelpie, kraken, lamia, leprechaun, Lilith, Loch Ness monster, mermaid, merman, Minotaur, naiad, nereid, nymph, ogre, ogress, orc, oread, Pegasus, phoenix, pixie, roc, salamander, sasquatch, satyr, selkie, sea serpent, Siren, Sphinx, sylph, troll, Typhoeus, unicorn, vampire, werewolf, wivern, yaksha

myxomatosis *noun* a contagious disease of rabbits

Nn

N *abbrev* **1** north **2** northern

nab *verb* (**nabs, nabbing, nabbed**) *informal* **1** snatch, seize **2** arrest

nacre *noun* mother-of-pearl

nadir *noun* **1** the point of the heavens opposite the zenith **2** the lowest point of anything

naevus or *US* **nevus** /'niːvəs/ *noun* a birthmark

naff *adj, slang* inferior, crass, tasteless

nag[1] *verb* (**nags, nagging, nagged**) find fault with constantly
▪ scold, berate, irritate, annoy, pester, badger, plague, torment, harass

nag[2] *noun* a horse

naiad *noun* a mythological river nymph

nail *noun* **1** a horny covering protecting the tips of the fingers and toes **2** a thin pointed piece of metal for fastening wood *etc* ◇ *verb* **1** fasten with nails **2** *informal* catch, trap
▪ *noun* **2** fastener, pin, tack, spike, skewer ◇ *verb* **1** fasten, attach, secure, pin, tack, fix, join

naive or **naïve** /naɪˈiːv/ *adj* **1** simple in thought, manner or speech **2** inexperienced and lacking knowledge of the world ◇ **naivety** *noun*
▪ **1** unsophisticated, ingenuous, innocent, *informal* green, unaffected, artless, guileless, simple **2** natural, childlike, open, trusting, unsuspecting, gullible, wide-eyed
▪ **1** sophisticated **2** experienced

naked *adj* **1** without clothes **2** having no covering: *a naked flame* **3** bald, blatant: *a naked lie* ◇ **nakedly** *adv* ◇ **nakedness** *noun*
▪ **1** nude, bare, undressed, unclothed, uncovered, stripped, stark-naked, disrobed, denuded **3** open, unadorned, undisguised, unqualified, plain, stark, overt, blatant, barefaced, exposed

namby-pamby *adj* childish, feeble

Originally a nickname of the 18th-century sentimental English poet, *Ambrose* Philips

name *noun* **1** a word by which a person, place or thing is known **2** fame, reputation: *making a name for himself* **3** an offensive description: *don't call people names* **4** authority: *I arrest you in the name of the king* ◇ *verb* **1** give a name to **2** speak of by name, mention **3** appoint ◇ **nameless** *adj* without a name, not named ◇ **namely** *adv* that is to say
▪ *noun* **1** title, *formal* appellation, designation, label, term **2** reputation, character, repute, renown, esteem, eminence, fame, honour, distinction, note ◇ *verb* **1** call, christen, baptize, term, title, entitle, label **3** designate, nominate, cite, choose, select, specify, commission, appoint ◇ **nameless** unnamed, anonymous, unidentified, unknown, obscure ◇ **namely** that is, ie, specifically, that is to say

nameplate *noun* a small panel having on it the name of a person, house *etc*

namesake *noun* someone with the same name as another

nan or **naan** *noun* a flat round Indian bread

nanny *noun* (*plural* **nannies**) a children's nurse

nanny-goat *noun* a female goat

nap[1] *noun* a short sleep ◇ *verb* (**naps, napping, napped**) take a short sleep ◇ **caught napping** taken unawares
▪ *noun* **1** rest, sleep, siesta, catnap, *informal* forty winks, *informal* kip ◇ *verb* doze, sleep, *informal* snooze, nod (off), drop off, rest, *informal* kip

nap[2] *noun* a woolly or fluffy surface on cloth

nap[3] *noun* **1** a kind of card game **2** a

horse-racing tip claimed to be a certainty

napalm *noun* a type of flammable jelly used to make bombs

nape *noun* the back of the neck

naphtha *noun* a highly flammable, clear liquid, obtained from coal and other substances

napkin *noun* a small piece of cloth or paper for wiping the lips or protecting the clothes at meals

nappy *noun* (*plural* **nappies**) a piece of cloth, or a thick pad, put between a baby's legs to absorb urine and faeces

narcissus *noun* (*plural* **narcissi** or **narcissuses**) a plant like a daffodil with a white, star-shaped flower

narcotic *noun* a type of drug that brings on sleep or stops pain
■ drug, opiate, sedative, tranquillizer, painkiller

nark *noun* 1 a persistent complainer 2 *slang* a police informer ◇ **narky** *adj* irritable, complaining

narrate *verb* tell a story ◇ **narration** *noun* ◇ **narrator** *noun*
■ tell, relate, report, recount, describe, recite

narrative *noun* a story ◇ *adj* telling a story
■ *noun* story, tale, chronicle, account, history, report, detail, statement

narrow *adj* 1 of small extent from side to side, not wide: *a narrow road* 2 with little to spare: *win by a narrow margin* 3 lacking wide interests or experience: *narrow views* 4 only just achieved: *a narrow escape* ◇ *verb* make or become narrow ◇ **narrowly** *adv* closely; barely ◇ **narrows** *noun plural* a narrow sea passage, a strait
■ *adj* 1 slim, slender, thin, fine, tapering, close 2 tight, confined, constricted, cramped, limited, restricted 3 narrow-minded, biased, bigoted, exclusive, dogmatic ◇ *verb* constrict, limit, tighten, reduce, diminish, simplify
■ *adj* 1 wide, broad 3 broad-minded, tolerant ◇ *verb* broaden, widen, increase

narrow-minded *adj* unwilling to accept or tolerate new ideas
■ biased, bigoted, prejudiced, reactionary, small-minded, conservative, intolerant, insular, petty
■ broad-minded

narwal or **narwhal** *noun* a kind of whale with a large tusk

NASA *abbrev, US* National Aeronautics and Space Administration

nasal *adj* 1 of the nose 2 sounded through the nose

nascent *adj* beginning to develop, in an early stage ◇ **nascency** *noun*

nasturtium *noun* a climbing plant with brightly coloured flowers

nasty *adj* 1 very disagreeable or unpleasant 2 of a problem *etc*: difficult to deal with ◇ **nastily** *adv* ◇ **nastiness** *noun*
■ 1 malicious, mean, spiteful, wicked, vicious, malevolent, unpleasant, repellent, repugnant, repulsive, offensive, disgusting, sickening, horrible, filthy, foul, polluted, obscene
■ 1 agreeable, pleasant, decent

natal *adj* of birth

nation *noun* 1 the people living in the same country, or under the same government 2 a race of people: *the Jewish nation*

national *adj* of or belonging to a nation or race ◇ *noun* someone belonging to a nation: *a British national* ◇ **nationally** *adv* ◇ **national anthem** a nation's official song or hymn
■ *adj* countrywide, civil, domestic, nationwide, state, internal, general, governmental, public, widespread, social

nationalism *noun* the desire to bring the people of a nation together under their own government ◇ **nationalist** *noun* & *adj* ◇ **nationalistic** *adj*

nationality *noun* (*plural* **nationalities**) membership of a particular nation
■ race, nation, ethnic group, birth, tribe, clan

nationalize *verb* place (industries *etc*) under the control of the government ◇ **nationalization** *noun*

native *adj* **1** in a person from birth: *native intelligence* **2** of someone's birth: *my native land* **3** originating in a certain place ◇ *noun* **1** someone born in a certain place: *a native of Scotland* **2** an inhabitant of a country from earliest times ◇ **the Nativity** the birth of Christ

▣ *adj* **1** inborn, inherent, innate, inbred, hereditary, inherited, congenital, instinctive, natural, intrinsic, natal **2** home **3** local, indigenous, domestic, natural

▣ *noun* **1** foreigner, outsider, stranger

natty *adj* trim, tidy, smart ◇ **nattily** *adv*

natural *adj* **1** of nature **2** produced by nature, not artificial **3** of a quality *etc*: present at birth, not learned afterwards **4** unpretentious, simple **5** of a result, reaction *etc*: expected, normal: *it's natural to be afraid of the unknown* ◇ *noun* **1** an idiot **2** someone with a natural ability **3** *music* a note which is neither a sharp nor a flat, shown by the sign (♮) ◇ **naturally** *adv* **1** by nature **2** simply **3** of course ◇ **natural gas** gas suitable for burning found in the earth or under the sea ◇ **natural history** the study of animals and plants ◇ **natural selection** evolution by survival of the fittest, who pass their characteristics onto the next generation ◇ **natural resources** the natural wealth of a country in its forests, minerals, water *etc*

▣ *adj* **2** genuine, pure, authentic, unrefined, unprocessed, real **3** innate, inborn, instinctive, intuitive, inherent, congenital, native **4** sincere, unaffected, genuine, artless, ingenuous, guileless, simple, unsophisticated, open, candid, spontaneous ◇ **naturally 3** of course, obviously, logically, typically, certainly, absolutely

naturalist *noun* someone who studies animal and plant life

naturalize *verb* give the rights of a citizen to (someone born in another country)

nature *noun* **1** the things which make up the physical world, *eg* animals, plants, rivers, mountains *etc* **2** the qualities which characterize someone or something: *a kindly nature*

▣ **2** essence, quality, character, disposition, personality, make-up, constitution, temperament, mood, outlook, temper

naturism *noun* (the belief in) nudity practised openly ◇ **naturist** *noun*

naturopathy *noun* treatment of disease through a combination of herbs, diet, exercise *etc* ◇ **naturopath** *noun* a practitioner of naturopathy

naught *noun* nothing: *our plans came to naught*

⚠ Do not confuse with: **nought**

naughty *adj* bad, misbehaving ◇ **naughtily** *adv* ◇ **naughtiness** *noun*

▣ bad, badly behaved, mischievous, disobedient, exasperating, playful, roguish

▣ good, well-behaved

nausea *noun* a feeling of sickness ◇ **nauseate** *verb* cause to feel sick, fill with disgust ◇ **nauseous** *adj* sickening; disgusting

▣ vomiting, sickness, retching, queasiness ◇ **nauseate** sicken, disgust, revolt, repel, offend, *informal* turn one's stomach

nautical *adj* of ships or sailors ◇ **nautical mile** 1.85 kilometre (6080 ft)

nautilus *noun* (*plural* **nautiluses** or **nautili**) a small sea creature related to the octopus

naval *see* **navy**

nave *noun* the middle or main part of a church

navel *noun* the small hollow in the centre of the front of the belly

navigate *verb* **1** steer or pilot a ship, aircraft *etc* on its course **2** sail on, over or through **3** give directions to a driver ◇ **navigable** *adj* able to be used by ships ◇ **navigation** *noun* the art of navigating ◇ **navigator** *noun* someone who navigates

▣ **1** steer, drive, direct, pilot, guide, handle, manoeuvre **2** cruise, sail **3** direct, guide

navvy *noun* (*plural* **navvies**) a labourer working on roads *etc*

navy noun (plural **navies**) **1** a nation's fighting ships **2** the men and women serving on these ◇**naval** adj of the navy ◇**navy blue** dark blue

nay exclam, old no

Nazi /'nɑːtsɪ/ noun, hist a member of the German National Socialist Party, a fascist party ruling Germany in 1933–45 ◇**Nazism** noun

NB or **nb** abbrev note well (from Latin nota bene)

NE abbrev north-east; north-eastern

neap adj of the tide: at its smallest extent between low and high level

near adj **1** not far away in place or time **2** close in relationship, friendship etc **3** barely avoiding or almost reaching (something): a near disaster ◇adv to or at a short distance; nearby ◇prep close to ◇verb approach ◇**nearness** noun
◼ adj**1** nearby, close, bordering, adjacent, adjoining, alongside, neighbouring **2** dear, familiar, close, related, intimate

nearby adj & adv to or at a short distance: do you live nearby?/a nearby housing estate
◼ adv near, within reach, at close quarters, close at hand, not far away

nearly adv almost: nearly four o'clock
◼ almost, practically, virtually, approximately, more or less, as good as, just about

nearside adj of the side of a vehicle: furthest from the centre of the road (contrasted with: **offside**)

near-sighted adj short-sighted

neat adj **1** trim, tidy **2** skilfully done **3** of an alcoholic drink: not diluted with water etc
◼ **1** tidy, orderly, smart, trim, clean, informal spick-and-span **2** deft, clever, adroit, skilful, expert **3** undiluted, unmixed, straight, pure

nebula noun (plural **nebulae**) a shining cloud-like appearance in the night sky, produced by very distant stars or by a mass of gas and dust

nebulous adj hazy, vague
◼ imprecise, indefinite, indistinct, cloudy, misty, obscure, uncertain, unclear, dim, ambiguous, confused, fuzzy, shapeless
◪ clear

necessary adj not able to be done without ◇noun (plural **necessaries**) something that cannot be done without, such as food, clothing etc ◇**necessarily** adv
◼ adjneeded, required, essential, compulsory, indispensable, vital, imperative, obligatory, unavoidable, inevitable
◪ adj unnecessary, inessential, unimportant

necessitate verb make necessary; force
◼ require, involve, entail, call for, demand, oblige, force, constrain, compel

necessity noun (plural **necessities**) **1** something necessary **2** great need; want, poverty
◼ **1** requirement, obligation, prerequisite, essential, fundamental, indispensability **2** need, want, demand, poverty, destitution, hardship

neck noun **1** the part between the head and body **2** a narrow passage or area: neck of a bottle/neck of land ◇**necktie** noun, US a man's tie ◇**neck and neck** running side by side, staying exactly equal

necklace noun a string of beads or precious stones etc worn round the neck

necromancer noun someone who works with black magic ◇**necromancy** noun

necropolis noun (plural **necropolises**) a cemetery

nectar noun **1** the sweet liquid collected from flowers by bees to make honey **2** the drink of the ancient Greek gods **3** a delicious drink

nectarine noun a kind of peach with a smooth skin

née adj born (in stating a woman's surname before her marriage): Mrs Janet Brown, née Phillips

need verb **1** be without **2** require ◇noun **1** necessity, needfulness; something needed **2** difficulty, want, poverty ◇**needful** adj necessary ◇**needless**

adj unnecessary ◇ **needlessly** *adv*

▣ *verb* **1** miss, lack **2** want, require, demand, call for, necessitate, crave ◇ *noun* **1** necessity, demand, obligation, requirement **2** want, lack, insufficiency, inadequacy, neediness, shortage ◇ **needless** unnecessary, gratuitous, uncalled-for, unwanted, redundant, superfluous, useless, pointless

▣ **needless** necessary, essential

needle *noun* **1** a small, sharp piece of steel used in sewing, with a small hole at the top for thread **2** a long thin piece of metal, wood *etc* used *eg* in knitting **3** a thin hollowed-out piece of steel attached to a hypodermic syringe *etc* **4** the moving pointer in a compass **5** the long, sharp-pointed leaf of a pine, fir *etc* **6** a stylus on a record-player ◇ **needlework** *noun* sewing

needy *adj* poor

▣ poor, destitute, impoverished, penniless, disadvantaged, deprived, poverty-stricken, underprivileged

▣ affluent, wealthy, well-off

neep *noun*, *Scot* a turnip

ne'er *adj*, *poetic* never ◇ **ne'er-do-well** *noun* a lazy, worthless person who makes no effort

nefarious *adj* very wicked; villainous, shady

negate *verb* **1** prove the opposite of; cancel the effect of **2** refuse to accept, reject (a proposal *etc*)

▣ **1** nullify, annul, cancel, invalidate, undo, countermand, neutralize, quash, reverse, revoke, wipe out, void **2** deny, contradict, oppose, disprove, refute, repudiate

▣ **1, 2** affirm

negative *adj* **1** meaning or saying 'no' (*contrasted with*: **positive**) **2** of a person, attitude *etc*: timid, lacking spirit or ideas **3** less than zero ◇ *noun* **1** a word or statement by which something is denied **2** the photographic film, from which prints are made, in which light objects appear dark and dark objects appear light ◇ **negative equity** the situation where the selling value of a property is less than the mortgage on it

▣ *adj* **1** contradictory, contrary, denying, opposing, invalidating, neutralizing, nullifying, annulling **2** unco-operative, cynical, pessimistic, unenthusiastic, uninterested, unwilling ◇ *noun* **1** contradiction, denial, opposite, refusal

▣ *adj* **1** affirmative, positive **2** constructive, positive

neglect *verb* **1** treat carelessly **2** fail to give proper attention to **3** fail (to do something): *she neglected to inform us that the trip had been cancelled* ◇ *noun* lack of care and attention ◇ **neglectful** *adj*

▣ *verb* **2** disregard, ignore, abandon, rebuff, scorn, disdain, slight, spurn **3** forget, omit, overlook, let slide, shirk, skimp ◇ *noun* negligence, disregard, carelessness, failure, inattention, indifference, forgetfulness, heedlessness, oversight, slight, disrespect

▣ *verb* **1** cherish, appreciate **2** attend to **3** remember ◇ *noun* care, attention, concern

négligée *noun* a women's loose dressing-gown made of thin material

negligent *adj* careless ◇ **negligence** *noun* ◇ **negligently** *adv*

▣ **negligence** inattentiveness, carelessness, neglect, thoughtlessness, forgetfulness, indifference, omission, oversight, disregard, failure

▣ **negligence** attentiveness, care, regard

▣ Do not confuse: **negligent** and **negligible**

negligible *adj* not worth thinking about, very small: *a negligible amount*

▣ unimportant, insignificant, small, imperceptible, trifling, trivial, minor, minute

▣ significant

negotiate *verb* **1** discuss a subject (with someone) in order to reach agreement **2** arrange (a treaty, payment *etc*) **3** get past (an obstacle or difficulty) ◇ **negotiable** *adj* able to be negotiated ◇ **negotiation** *noun* ◇ **negotiator** *noun*

▣ **1** confer, deal, mediate, arbitrate, bargain, arrange, settle, consult, contract **2** arrange, settle **3** get round, cross, surmount, traverse, pass

Negro *noun* (*plural* **Negroes**), *now offensive* a black African, or black person of African descent ◇**Negress** *noun* a black woman ◇**negroid** *adj* black, dark-skinned

neigh *verb* cry like a horse ◇*noun* a horse's cry

neighbour or *US* **neighbor** *noun* someone who lives near another

neighbourhood *noun* surrounding district or area: *in the neighbourhood of Paris/a poor neighbourhood* ◇**in the neighbourhood of** approximately, nearly

▣ district, locality, vicinity, community, environs, confines, surroundings, region, proximity

neighbouring *adj* near or next in position

▣ adjacent, bordering, near, nearby, adjoining, connecting, surrounding

▣ distant, remote

neighbourly *adj* friendly

▣ sociable, friendly, amiable, kind, helpful, genial, hospitable, obliging, considerate, companionable

neither *adj* & *pronoun* not either: *neither bus goes that way/neither of us can afford it* ◇*conj* (sometimes with **nor**) used to show alternatives in the negative: *neither Bill nor David knew the answer/she is neither eating nor sleeping*

nematode *noun* (*also called* **threadworm**) a parasitic worm with a cylindrical body

nemesis *noun* fate, punishment that is bound to follow wrongdoing

neo- *prefix* new

neolithic *adj* relating to the later Stone Age

neologism *noun* a new word or expression ◇**neologistic** *adj*

neonatal *adj* of newborn babies

neon lighting a form of lighting in which an electric current is passed through a small quantity of gas

neophyte *noun* **1** a new convert **2** a novice, a beginner

nephew *noun* the son of a brother or sister, or of a brother-in-law or sister-in-law

nerd *noun* a socially inept, irritating person ◇**nerdish** *adj*

nerve *noun* **1** one of the fibres which carry feeling from all parts of the body to the brain **2** courage, coolness **3** *informal* impudence, cheek ◇*verb* strengthen the nerve or will of ◇**nervy** *adj* excitable, jumpy

▣ *noun* **2** courage, bravery, mettle, *informal* guts, spirit, vigour, daring, fearlessness, firmness, resolution, fortitude, steadfastness, will, determination, endurance, force **3** audacity, impudence, *informal* cheek, boldness, impertinence, insolence

nervous *adj* **1** of the nerves **2** easily excited or frightened; timid or anxious ◇**nervously** *adv* ◇**nervousness** *noun* ◇**nervous system** the brain, spinal cord and nerves

▣ **2** highly-strung, excitable, *informal* hyper, anxious, agitated, *informal* nervy, on edge, edgy, *informal* jumpy, tense, fidgety, apprehensive, neurotic, shaky, uneasy, worried, flustered, fearful

▣ **2** calm, relaxed

nest *noun* **1** a structure in which birds (and some animals and insects) live and rear their young **2** a shelter, a den ◇*verb* build a nest and live in it ◇**nestling** *noun* a young, newly hatched bird

nestle /ˈnesəl/ *verb* **1** lie close together as in a nest **2** settle comfortably

Net *noun*: **the Net** *informal* the Internet

net[1] *noun* **1** a loose arrangement of crossed and knotted cord, string or thread, used for catching fish, wearing over the hair *etc* **2** fine meshed material, used to make curtains *etc* ◇*verb* (**nets**, **netting**, **netted**) **1** catch or cover with a net **2** put (a ball) into a net

▣ *verb* **1** catch, trap, capture, bag, ensnare, entangle, *informal* nab

net[2] *adj* (*also* **nett**) **1** of profit *etc*: remaining after expenses and taxes have been paid **2** of weight: not including packaging ◊ *verb* make by way of profit

■ *verb* bring in, clear, earn, make, realize, receive, gain, obtain, accumulate

netball *noun* a team game in which a ball is thrown into a high net

nether *adj* lower ◊ **nethermost** *adj* lowest

nett *see* net

netting *noun* fabric of string, wire *etc* knotted or twisted to form an open mesh

nettle *noun* a plant covered with hairs which sting sharply ◊ *verb* make angry, provoke ◊ **nettle rash** a skin rash, like that caused by a sting from a nettle

network *noun* **1** an arrangement of lines crossing one another **2** a widespread organization **2** a system of linked computers, radio stations *etc*

neur- or **neuro-** *prefix* of the nerves

neuralgia *noun* pain in the nerves, *esp* in those of the head and face

neurosis *noun* a type of mental illness in which the patient suffers from extreme anxiety

■ disorder, affliction, abnormality, disturbance, derangement, deviation, obsession, phobia, mania

neurotic *adj* **1** suffering from neurosis **2** showing excessive anxiety or obsession ◊ *noun* someone suffering from neurosis ◊ **neurotically** *adv*

■ *adj* **1** disturbed, maladjusted, anxious, nervous, overwrought, unstable **2** overanxious, unhealthy, abnormal, compulsive, obsessive, manic, phobic

neuter *adj* **1** *grammar* neither masculine nor feminine **2** of an animal: neither male nor female **3** of an animal: infertile, sterile ◊ *verb* sterilize (an animal)

neutral *adj* **1** taking no side in a quarrel or war **2** of a colour: not strong or definite ◊ *noun* **1** someone or a nation which takes no side in a war *etc* **2** the gear position used when a vehicle is remaining still ◊ **neutrality** *noun*

■ *adj* **1** impartial, unbiased, disinterested, unprejudiced, undecided, non-commit-

tal, objective, indifferent **2** dull, non-descript, colourless, drab, indistinct

◨ *adj* **1** biased, partisan **2** colourful

neutralize *verb* **1** cancel out the effect of **2** make useless or harmless

neutron *noun* one of the uncharged particles which, together with protons, make up the nucleus of an atom ◊ **neutron bomb** a nuclear bomb that kills people by intense radiation but leaves buildings intact

never *adv* **1** not ever; at no time **2** under no circumstances

nevertheless *adv* in spite of that: *I hate opera, but I shall come with you nevertheless*

■ nonetheless, still, anyway, even so, yet, however, anyhow, but, regardless

nevus *US spelling of* **naevus**

new *adj* **1** recent; not seen or known before **2** not used or worn; fresh ◊ **newly** *adv* ◊ **newness** *noun*

■ **1** novel, original, fresh, different, unfamiliar, unknown, unusual **2** brand-new, mint, unused, virgin

newcomer *noun* someone lately arrived

■ immigrant, alien, foreigner, settler, arrival, outsider, stranger, novice, beginner

newfangled *adj* new and disliked or despised

news *noun sing* **1** information about a recent event **2** new and interesting information

■ **1** report, account, story, information, intelligence, dispatch, bulletin, statement **2** gossip, hearsay, rumour, word, latest, scandal, revelation, disclosure, *informal* lowdown

newsagent *noun* a shopkeeper who sells newspapers

newsgroup *noun*, *comput* a special-interest group of Internet users

newspaper *noun* a paper printed daily or weekly containing news

newt *noun* a small lizard-like animal, living on land and in water

next *adj* nearest; closest in place, time *etc* after: *the next page* ◊ *adv* in the nearest place or at the nearest time after: *she won and I came next/what shall we do next?*

■ *adj* adjacent, adjoining, neighbouring, nearest, closest, following, subsequent, succeeding, ensuing, later ◇ *adv* afterwards, subsequently, later, then

◨ *adj* previous, preceding

nexus *noun* a bond, a connection

NHS *abbrev* National Health Service

nib *noun* a pen point

nibble *verb* take little bites (of) ◇ *noun* a little bite

■ *verb* bite, eat, peck, pick at ◇ *noun* bite, morsel, taste, titbit, bit, crumb, snack, piece

NICAM or **Nicam** *noun* near-instantaneous companded audio multiplexing, a system for transmitting digital sound with standard TV signals

nice *adj* 1 agreeable, pleasant 2 careful, precise, exact: *a nice distinction* ◇ **nicely** *adv* pleasantly; very well

■ **1** pleasant, agreeable, delightful, charming, likable, attractive, good, kind, friendly, well-mannered, polite, respectable **2** scrupulous, precise, exact, accurate, careful, strict

◨ **1** nasty, disagreeable, unpleasant **2** careless

nicety *noun* (*plural* **niceties**) a small fine detail ◇ **to a nicety** with great exactness

■ delicacy, refinement, subtlety, distinction, nuance

niche /niːʃ/ *noun* 1 a hollow in a wall for a statue, vase *etc* 2 a suitable place in life: *she hasn't yet found her niche* 3 a gap in a market for a type of product

■ **1** recess, alcove, hollow, nook, cubbyhole, corner, opening **2** position, place, vocation, calling

nick *noun* 1 a little cut, a notch 2 *slang* prison, jail ◇ *verb* 1 cut notches in 2 *slang* steal

■ *noun* **1** notch, indentation, chip, cut, groove, dent, scar, scratch, mark **2** *slang* prison, jail, police station ◇ *verb* **2** steal, pilfer, *informal* knock off, *informal* pinch

nickel *noun* 1 a greyish-white metal

used for mixing with other metals and for plating 2 *US* a 5-cent coin

nickname *noun* an informal name used instead of someone's real name

■ pet name, sobriquet, epithet, diminutive

nicotine *noun* a poisonous substance contained in tobacco

> Named after Jean *Nicot*, 16th-century French ambassador who sent tobacco samples back from Portugal

niece *noun* the daughter of a brother or sister, or of a brother-in-law or sister-in-law

niff *noun, slang* a bad smell

nifty *adj, slang* 1 fine, smart, neat 2 speedy, agile

niggardly *adj* mean, stingy

niggle *verb* irritate, rankle ◇ *noun* 1 an irritation 2 a minor criticism ◇ **niggling** *adj* 1 unimportant, trivial, fussy 2 of a worry or fear: small but always present

nigh *adj, old* near

night *noun* 1 the period between sunset and sunrise, or between going to bed and getting up 2 darkness ◇ *adj* 1 of or for night 2 happening, active *etc* at night ◇ **nightly** *adj & adv* 1 by night 2 every night

■ *noun* **1** night-time, darkness, dark, dead of night **2** darkness, dark

nightdress or **nightgown** *noun* a garment worn in bed

nightfall *noun* the beginning of night

■ sunset, dusk, twilight, evening, gloaming

◨ dawn, sunrise

nightingale *noun* a small bird, the male of which sings beautifully by night and day

nightjar *noun* a kind of bird like a swallow which is active at night

nightmare *noun* a frightening dream

■ bad dream, hallucination

> The *-mare* ending comes from an old English word meaning 'incubus', nightmares being thought to be

caused by an evil spirit pressing on the body

nightshade *noun* a family of plants some of which have poisonous berries, *eg* deadly nightshade

night-watchman *noun* someone who looks after a building during the night

nihilism *noun* belief in nothing, extreme scepticism ◇ **nihilist** *noun* ◇ **nihilistic** *adj*

nil *noun* nothing

▤ nothing, zero, none, nought, naught, cipher, love, duck, *slang* zilch

nimble *adj* quick and neat, agile ◇ **nimbleness** *noun* ◇ **nimbly** *adv*

▤ agile, active, lively, sprightly, spry, smart, quick, brisk, deft, alert, light-footed, prompt, ready, swift, quick-witted

▣ clumsy, slow

nimbus *noun* a rain cloud

NIMBY *abbrev* not in my back yard, *ie* not wanting something to take place in your neighbourhood

nincompoop *noun* a weak, foolish person

nine *noun* the number 9 ◇ *adj* 9 in number ◇ **ninth** *adj* the last of a series of nine ◇ *noun* one of nine equal parts

ninepins *noun sing* a game in which nine bottle-shaped objects are set up and knocked down by a ball

nineteen *noun* the number 19 ◇ *adj* 19 in number ◇ **nineteenth** *adj* the last of a series of nineteen ◇ *noun* one of nineteen equal parts

ninety *noun* the number 90 ◇ *adj* 90 in number ◇ **ninetieth** *adj* the last of a series of ninety ◇ *noun* one of ninety equal parts

ninny *noun* (*plural* **ninnies**) a fool

nip *verb* (**nips, nipping, nipped**) 1 pinch, squeeze tightly 2 be stingingly painful 3 bite, cut (off) 4 *informal* go nimbly or quickly ◇ *noun* 1 a pinch 2 a sharp coldness in the weather: *a nip in the air* 3 a small amount: *a nip of whisky* ▤ *verb* 1 pinch, squeeze, tweak, catch,

grip ◇ *noun* 3 dram, draught, shot, swallow, mouthful, drop, sip, taste, portion

nipper *adj, informal* 1 a child, a youngster 2 (**nippers**) pincers, pliers

nipple *noun* the pointed part of the breast from which a baby sucks milk

nippy *adj, informal* 1 speedy, nimble 2 frosty, very cold

Nirvana *noun* 1 the state to which a Buddhist or Hindu aspires as the best attainable 2 (**nirvana**) a blissful state

nit *noun* 1 the egg of a louse or other small insect 2 *informal* an idiot, a nitwit

nitrate *noun* a substance formed from nitric acid, often used as a soil fertilizer

nitric acid a strong acid containing nitrogen

nitrogen *noun* a gas forming nearly four-fifths of ordinary air

nitroglycerine *noun* a powerful kind of explosive

nitwit *noun* a very stupid person

No or **no** *abbrev* number

no *adj* 1 not any: *they have no money* 2 not a: *she is no beauty* ◇ *adv* not at all: *the patient is no better* ◇ *exclam* expressing a negative: *are you coming? No* ◇ *noun* (*plural* **noes**) 1 a refusal 2 a vote against ◇ **no dice** no answer, no success ◇ **no doubt** surely ◇ **no go** *informal* not possible, futile ◇ **no joke** not something to laugh about or dismiss ◇ **no one** or **no-one** *pronoun* not any person, nobody ◇ **no way** *informal* under no circumstances

no-ball *noun, cricket* a bowled ball disallowed by the rules

nobble *verb, slang* 1 interfere with (*eg* a racehorse) to stop it winning 2 persuade, coerce 3 seize, arrest

Nobel prize an annual international prize awarded for achievements in arts, science, politics *etc*

nobility *noun* 1 the aristocracy 2 goodness, greatness of mind or character

▤ 1 aristocracy, peerage, nobles, gentry, élite, lords, high society 2 nobleness, dignity, grandeur, majesty, magnificence, eminence, excellence, superiority, honour, virtue, worthiness

■ **1** proletariat **2** baseness

Titles of the nobility include:
aristocrat, baron, baroness,
baronet, count, countess, dame,
dowager, duchess, duke, earl, grand
duchess, grand duke, governor,
knight, lady, laird, liege, liege lord,
life peer, lord, marchioness,
marquess, marquis, noble,
nobleman, noblewoman, peer,
peeress, ruler, seigneur, squire,
thane, viscount, viscountess

---

noble *adj* **1** great and good, fine **2** of aristocratic birth ◇*noun* an aristocrat ◇**nobly** *adv* ◇**nobleman, noblewoman** *noun*

■ *adj***1** magnificent, magnanimous, splendid, stately, generous, dignified, distinguished, eminent, grand, great, honoured, honourable, impressive, majestic, virtuous, worthy, excellent, elevated, fine **2** aristocratic, high-born, titled, high-ranking, patrician, *informal* blue-blooded

■ **1** ignoble, base, contemptible **2** lowborn

noblesse oblige /nou'blɛs ou'bli:ʒ/ the duty of the privileged to help the less fortunate

nobody *pronoun* not any person ◇*noun* (*plural* **nobodies**) someone of no importance: *just a nobody*

nocturnal *adj* happening or active at night ◇**nocturnally** *adv*

nocturne *noun* a piece of music intended to have an atmosphere of night-time

nod *verb* (**nods, nodding, nodded**) **1** bend the head forward quickly, often as a sign of agreement **2** let the head drop in weariness ◇*noun* an action of nodding ◇**nodding acquaintance with** a slight knowledge of ◇**nod off** fall asleep

■ *verb***1** gesture, indicate, sign, signal, salute, acknowledge, agree **2** sleep, doze, drowse, nap ◇*noun* gesture, indication, sign, signal, salute, greeting, acknowledgement

noddle *noun*, *slang* head; intelligence

node *noun* **1** the swollen part of a branch or twig where leaf-stalks join it **2** a swelling

nodule *noun* a small rounded lump

Noël *noun* Christmas

noise *noun* a sound, often one which is loud or harsh ◇*verb*, *old* spread (a rumour *etc*) ◇**noiseless** *adj*

■ *noun* sound, din, racket, row, clamour, clash, clatter, commotion, outcry, hubbub, uproar, cry, talk, pandemonium, tumult, babble ◇*verb* report, rumour, publicize, announce, circulate ◇**noiseless** silent, inaudible, soundless, quiet, mute, still, hushed

■ *noun* quiet, silence

noisy *adj* (**noisier, noisiest**) making a loud sound

■ loud, deafening, ear-splitting, clamorous, piercing, vocal, vociferous, tumultuous, boisterous

■ quiet, silent, peaceful

nomad *noun* **1** one of a group of people without a fixed home who wander with their animals in search of pasture **2** someone who wanders from place to place ◇**nomadic** *adj*

no-man's-land *noun* land owned by no one, *esp* that lying between two opposing armies

nom de plume (*plural* **noms de plume**) a pen-name

nomenclature *noun* **1** a system of naming **2** names

nominal *adj* **1** in name only **2** very small: *a nominal fee*

■ **2** token, minimal, trifling, trivial, insignificant, small

nominate *verb* propose (someone) for a post or for election; appoint ◇**nomination** *noun* ◇**nominee** *noun* someone whose name is put forward for a post

■ *verb* propose, choose, select, name, designate, submit, suggest, recommend, put up, present, elect, appoint, assign, commission, elevate ◇**nomi-**

nation proposal, choice, selection, submission, suggestion, recommendation, designation, election, appointment ◊ **nominee** candidate, entrant, contestant, appointee, runner

non- *prefix* not: *non-aggression/non-event/non-smoking*

nonagenarian *noun* someone from ninety to ninety-nine years old

nonce *noun*: **for the nonce** for the moment, in the meantime

nonchalant *adj* not easily roused or upset, cool ◊ **nonchalance** *noun* ◊ **nonchalantly** *adv*
■ unconcerned, detached, dispassionate, offhand, blasé, indifferent, casual, cool, collected, apathetic, careless, insouciant
◼ concerned, careful

non-commissioned *adj* belonging to the lower ranks of officers in the armed forces

non-committal *adj* unwilling to express, or not expressing, an opinion
■ guarded, unrevealing, cautious, wary, reserved, ambiguous, discreet, equivocal, evasive, circumspect, careful, neutral, indefinite, politic, tactful, tentative, vague

nonconformist *noun* someone who does not agree with those in authority, *esp* in church matters ◊ *adj* not agreeing with authority
■ *noun* dissenter, rebel, individualist, dissident, radical, protester, heretic, iconoclast, eccentric, maverick

nondescript *adj* not easily described, lacking anything noticeable or interesting
■ featureless, indeterminate, undistinctive, undistinguished, unexceptional, ordinary, commonplace, plain, dull, uninspiring, uninteresting, unclassified
◼ distinctive, remarkable

none *adv* not at all: *none the worse* ◊ *pronoun* not one, not any

nonentity *noun* (*plural* **nonentities**) someone of no importance

non-existent *adj* not existing, not real

nonplussed *adj* taken aback, confused

■ disconcerted, confounded, taken aback, stunned, bewildered, astonished, astounded, dumbfounded, perplexed, stumped, flabbergasted, flummoxed, puzzled, baffled, dismayed, embarrassed

nonsense *noun* **1** words that have no sense or meaning **2** foolishness ◊ **nonsensical** *adj* ◊ **nonsensically** *adv*
■ **1** rubbish, trash, drivel, balderdash, gibberish, gobbledygook, *informal* rot, twaddle, *informal* claptrap **2** stupidity, silliness, foolishness, folly, ridiculousness ◊ **nonsensical** ridiculous, meaningless, senseless, foolish, inane, irrational, silly, incomprehensible, ludicrous, absurd, fatuous, *informal* crazy
◼ **1** sense **2** wisdom ◊ **nonsensical** reasonable, sensible, logical

non sequitur a remark unconnected with what has gone before

non-stop *adj* going on without a stop
■ never-ending, uninterrupted, continuous, incessant, constant, endless, interminable, unending, unbroken, ongoing
◼ intermittent, occasional

noodle *noun* a long thin strip of pasta, eaten in soup or served with a sauce

nook *noun* **1** a corner **2** a small recess ◊ **every nook and cranny** *informal* everywhere
■ **2** recess, alcove, cranny, niche, cubbyhole, hide-out, retreat, shelter, cavity

noon *noun* twelve o'clock midday

no one *see* no

noose *noun* a loop in a rope *etc* which tightens when pulled

nor *conj* used (often with **neither**) to show alternatives in the negative: *neither James nor I can speak Japanese*

Nordic *adj* **1** relating to Finland or Scandinavia **2** of skiing: involving cross-country and jumping events

norm *noun* a pattern or standard to judge other things from
■ average, mean, standard, rule, pattern, criterion, model, yardstick, benchmark, measure, reference

normal *adj* ordinary, usual according

to a standard ◇ **normality** *noun* ◇ **normally** *adv*

■ usual, standard, general, common, ordinary, conventional, average, regular, routine, typical, mainstream, natural, accustomed, well-adjusted, straight, rational, reasonable ◇ **normality** ordinariness, regularity, routine, conventionality, balance, adjustment, reason, rationality ◇ **normally** ordinarily, usually, as a rule, typically, commonly, characteristically

☒ abnormal, irregular, peculiar ◇ **normality** abnormality, irregularity, peculiarity ◇ **normally** abnormally, exceptionally

north *noun* **1** one of the four chief directions, that to the left of someone facing the rising sun ◇ *adj & adv* in or to the north ◇ **north pole** the northern end of the imaginary axis on which the earth turns

north-east *noun* the point of the compass midway between north and east

northerly *adj* of, from or towards the north

northern *adj* of the north ◇ **northerner** *noun* someone from a northern region or country

northward or **northwards** *adj & adv* towards the north

north-west *noun* the point of the compass midway between north and west

nose *noun* **1** the part of the face by which people and animals smell and breathe **2** a jutting-out part, *eg* the front of an aeroplane ◇ *verb* **1** track by smelling **2** *informal* interfere in other people's affairs, pry (into) **3** push a way through: *the ship nosed through the ice* **4** move forward cautiously

nosedive *noun* a headfirst dive by an aeroplane ◇ *verb* dive headfirst

nosegay *noun*, *old* a bunch of flowers

nosey or **nosy** *adj* inquisitive, fond of prying

■ inquisitive, meddlesome, prying, interfering, snooping, curious, eavesdropping

no-show *noun* someone expected who does not arrive

nostalgia *noun* **1** a longing for past times **2** a longing for home ◇ **nostalgic** *adj* ◇ **nostalgically** *adv*

■ **nostalgic** yearning, longing, wistful, emotional, regretful, sentimental, homesick

nostril *noun* either of the two openings of the nose

not *adv* expressing a negative, refusal or denial: *I am not going/give it to me, not to him/I did not break the window*

notable *adj* worth taking notice of; important, remarkable ◇ *noun* an important person ◇ **notability** *noun* (*plural* **notabilities**) a well-known person ◇ **notably** *adv* **1** in a notable or noticeable way **2** particularly

■ *adj* noteworthy, remarkable, noticeable, striking, extraordinary, impressive, outstanding, unusual, distinguished, famous, eminent, well-known, notorious, renowned, rare ◇ **notably 1** markedly, noticeably, remarkably, strikingly, conspicuously, distinctly, especially, impressively, outstandingly

☒ *adj* ordinary, commonplace, usual

notary *noun* (*plural* **notaries**) an official who sees that written documents are drawn up in a way required by law

notation *noun* **1** the showing of numbers, musical sounds *etc* by signs: *sol-fa notation* **2** a set of such signs

notch *noun* (*plural* **notches**) a small V-shaped cut ◇ *verb* make a notch ◇ **notched** *adj*

■ *noun* cut, nick, indentation, incision, score, groove, mark ◇ *verb* cut, nick, score, scratch, indent, mark

note *noun* **1** a piece of writing used as a record, reminder *etc*: *keep a note of what you spend* **2** (**notes**) details for a speech, from a talk *etc* set down in a short form **3** a short explanation **4** a short letter **5** a piece of paper used as money: *£5 note* **6** attention **7** a single sound or the sign standing for it in music **8** a key on the piano *etc* ◇ *verb* **1** make a note of **2** notice ◇ **noted** *adj* well-known ◊ **of note** well-known, distinguished ◊ **take note of** notice particularly

■ *noun* **3** annotation, comment, gloss, remark **4** communication, letter, message **6** heed, attention, regard, notice, observation ◊ *verb* **1** record, register, write down, enter **2** notice, observe, perceive, heed, detect, mark, remark, mention, see, witness ◊ **noted** famous, well-known, renowned, notable, eminent, prominent, great, distinguished, respected, recognized

◨ **noted** obscure, unknown

notebook *noun* **1** a small book for taking notes **2** a small laptop computer

notepaper *noun* paper for writing letters

noteworthy *adj* notable, remarkable

■ remarkable, significant, important, notable, memorable, exceptional, extraordinary, unusual, outstanding

◨ commonplace, unexceptional, ordinary

nothing *noun* **1** no thing, not anything **2** nought, zero **3** something of no importance ◊ *adv* not at all: *he's nothing like his father* ◊ **nothingness** *noun* **1** non-existence **2** space, emptiness

■ **1** non-existence, emptiness, nothingness, void **2** nought, cipher, zero, *slang* zilch

notice *noun* **1** a public announcement; a sign giving information **2** attention: *the colour attracted my notice* **3** a warning given *eg* before leaving or dismissing someone from a job ◊ *verb* see, observe, take note of ◊ **noticeable** *adj* easily noticed, standing out ◊ **take notice** pay attention; see or hear and obey: *I told her to stop but she took no notice*

■ *noun* **1** announcement, information, declaration, communication, intelligence, news **2** attention, observation, awareness, note, regard, consideration **3** notification, warning, instruction ◊ *verb* note, remark, perceive, observe, mind, see, discern, distinguish, mark, detect, heed, spot ◊ **noticeable** perceptible, observable, unmistakable,

conspicuous, evident, clear, distinct, significant, striking, obvious

◨ *verb* ignore, overlook ◊ **noticeable** inconspicuous, unnoticeable

notify *verb* (**notifies, notifying, notified**) **1** inform **2** give notice of ◊ **notifiable** *adj* that must be reported: *a notifiable disease* ◊ **notification** *noun*

■ **1** inform, tell, advise, acquaint **2** warn, alert, publish, disclose, announce ◊ **notification** announcement, information, notice, declaration, advice, warning, message, publication, statement, communication

notion *noun* **1** an idea **2** a vague belief or opinion

■ **1** idea, thought, concept **2** belief, impression, view, opinion, understanding

notorious *adj* well known because of badness: *a notorious criminal* ◊ **notoriety** *noun*

■ infamous, disreputable, scandalous, dishonourable, disgraceful ◊ **notoriety** infamy, disrepute, dishonour, disgrace, scandal

notwithstanding *prep* in spite of: *notwithstanding his poverty, he refused all help*

nougat /ˈnuːɡɑː/ or /ˈnʌɡət/ *noun* a sticky kind of sweet containing nuts *etc*

nought *noun* the figure 0, zero

❗ Do not confuse with: **naught**

noun *noun*, *grammar* the word used as the name of someone or something, *eg John* and *tickets* in the sentence *John bought the tickets*

nourish *verb* **1** feed **2** encourage the growth of ◊ **nourishing** *adj* giving the body what is necessary for health and growth ◊ **nourishment** *noun* **1** food **2** the act of nourishing

■ *verb* **1** nurture, feed, foster, care for, provide for, sustain, support, tend **2** strengthen, encourage, promote, cultivate, stimulate ◊ **nourishment 1** nutrition, food, sustenance, diet

nous /naʊs/ *noun* common sense

nouveau riche /ˈnuːvoʊ riːʃ/ (*plural* **nouveaux riches**) someone who has recently acquired wealth but not good taste

nouvelle cuisine a style of cooking using light sauces and fresh ingredients

nova *noun* (*plural* **novae** or **novas**) a star that suddenly increases in brightness for a period

novel /ˈnɒvəl/ *adj* new and strange ◇ *noun* a book telling a long story ◇ **novelist** *noun* a writer of novels

■ *adj* new, original, fresh, innovative, unfamiliar, unusual, uncommon, different, imaginative, unconventional, strange ◇ *noun* fiction, story, tale, narrative, romance

✗ *adj* hackneyed, familiar, ordinary

novelty *noun* (*plural* **novelties**) **1** something new and strange **2** newness **3** a small, cheap souvenir or toy

■ **2** newness, originality, freshness, innovation, unfamiliarity, uniqueness, difference, strangeness **3** gimmick, gadget, trifle, memento, curiosity, souvenir, trinket

November *noun* the eleventh month of the year

novice *noun* a beginner

■ beginner, learner, pupil, trainee, apprentice, amateur, newcomer

✗ expert

now *adv* **1** at the present time: *I can see him now* **2** in the present circumstances: *I can't go now because my mother is ill* ◇ *conj* (often with **that**) because, since: *you can't go out now that it's raining* ◇ **just now 1** a moment ago **2** at this moment ◇ **now and then** or **now and again** sometimes, from time to time

■ *adv* **1** at present, nowadays, these days

nowadays *adv* in present times, these days

nowhere *adv* not in, or to, any place

no-win *adj* of a situation: in which you are bound to lose or fail

noxious *adj* harmful: *noxious fumes*

■ harmful, poisonous, pernicious, toxic, injurious, unhealthy, deadly, destructive

✗ innocuous, wholesome

> **!** Do not confuse with: **obnoxious**

nozzle *noun* a spout fitted to the end of a pipe, tube *etc*

NSPCC *abbrev* National Society for the Prevention of Cruelty to Children

nuance *noun* a slight difference in meaning or colour *etc*

■ subtlety, suggestion, shade, hint, suspicion, distinction, overtone, refinement, touch, trace, tinge, degree

nub *noun* a small lump, a knob

nubile *adj* of a woman: sexually attractive ◇ **nubility** *noun*

nuclear *adj* **1** of a nucleus, *esp* that of an atom **2** produced by the splitting of the nuclei of atoms ◇ **nuclear energy** energy released or absorbed during reactions taking place in atomic nuclei ◇ **nuclear family** the family unit made up of the mother and father with their children ◇ **nuclear fission** the splitting of atomic nuclei ◇ **nuclear fusion** the creation of a new nucleus by merging two lighter ones, with release of energy ◇ **nuclear missile** a missile whose warhead is an atomic bomb ◇ **nuclear reactor** an apparatus for producing nuclear energy

nucleus *noun* (*plural* **nuclei**) **1** the central part of an atom **2** the central part round which something collects or from which it grows: *the nucleus of my book collection* **3** the part of a plant or animal cell which controls its development

■ **2** centre, heart, nub, core, focus, kernel, pivot, basis, crux

nude *adj* without clothes, naked ◇ *noun* **1** an unclothed human figure **2** a painting or statue of such a figure ◇ **in the nude** naked

■ *adj* naked, bare, undressed, unclothed, stripped, stark-naked, uncovered, *informal* starkers, *informal* in one's birthday suit

✗ *adj* clothed, dressed

nudge *noun* a gentle push, *eg* with the elbow or shoulder ◇ *verb* push gently

■ *verb & noun* poke, prod, shove, dig, jog,

prompt, push, elbow, bump

nudist *noun* someone who advocates going without clothes in public ◇**nudism** *noun*

nudity *noun* the state of being nude

nugget *noun* a lump, *esp* of gold

nuisance *noun* someone or something annoying or troublesome

▪ annoyance, inconvenience, bother, irritation, pest, *informal* pain, *informal* drag, bore, problem, trial, trouble, drawback

NUJ *abbrev* National Union of Journalists

nuke *noun*, *slang* a nuclear weapon ◇*verb*, *slang* **1** attack with a nuclear weapon **2** cook in a microwave

null *adj*: **null and void** having no legal force

nullify *verb* (**nullifies, nullifying, nullified**) **1** make useless or of no effect **2** declare to be null and void

▪ **1** negate, counteract **2** annul, revoke, cancel, invalidate, abrogate, abolish, rescind, quash, repeal

▪▪ **2** validate

NUM *abbrev* National Union of Mineworkers

numb *adj* having lost the power to feel or move ◇*verb* make numb

▪ *adj* insensible, unfeeling, deadened, insensitive, frozen, benumbed, immobilized ◇ *verb* deaden, anaesthetize, freeze, immobilize, paralyse, dull, stun

▪▪ *adj* sensitive

number *noun* **1** a word or figure showing how many, or showing a position in a series **2** a collection of people or things **3** a single issue of a newspaper or magazine **4** a popular song or piece of music ◇*verb* **1** count **2** give numbers to **3** amount to in number ◇**numberless** *adj* more than can be counted

▪ *noun* **1** figure, numeral, digit, integer, unit **2** total, sum, collection, amount, quantity, company, crowd, multitude, throng, horde **3** copy, issue, edition, impression, volume, printing ◇ *verb* **1** count, calculate, enumerate, reckon,

total, add, compute, include

numeral *noun* a figure (*eg* 1, 2 *etc*) used to express a number

numerate *adj* having some understanding of mathematics and science

numerator *noun* the number above the line in vulgar fractions, *eg* 2 in $\frac{2}{3}$

numerical *adj* of, in, using or consisting of numbers

numerology *noun* prediction of future events by studying numbers ◇**numerologist** *noun*

numerous *adj* many

▪ many, abundant, several, plentiful, copious, profuse

numismatics *noun sing* the study of coins ◇**numismatist** *noun* someone who collects and studies coins

numskull *noun* a stupid person

nun *noun* a member of a female religious group living in a convent

nunnery *noun* (*plural* **nunneries**) a house where a group of nuns live

nuptial *adj* of marriage ◇**nuptials** *noun plural* a wedding ceremony

nurse *noun* someone who looks after sick or injured people, or small children ◇ *verb* **1** look after sick people *etc* **2** give (a baby) milk from the breast **3** hold or look after with care: *he nurses his tomato plants* **4** encourage (feelings) in yourself: *nursing her wrath*

▪ *noun* sister, matron, nursemaid, nanny ◇ *verb* **1** tend, care for, look after, treat **2** breast-feed, feed, suckle, nurture, nourish **3** preserve, sustain, support, cherish, encourage, keep

nursery *noun* (*plural* **nurseries**) **1** a place where young children are looked after during the day **2** a room for young children in a house **3** a place where young plants are reared ◇**nursery school** a school for very young children

▪ **1** crèche, playgroup ◇**nursery school** kindergarten, playschool

nursing home a small private hospital

nurture *verb* bring up, rear; nourish: *nurture tenderness* ◇ *noun* care, upbringing; food, nourishment

■ *verb* bring up, rear, cultivate, develop, educate, instruct, train, school, discipline, feed, nourish, tend, care for, support, sustain ◇ *noun* rearing, upbringing, training, care, cultivation, development, education, discipline, food, nourishment

NUS *abbrev* National Union of Students

NUT *abbrev* National Union of Teachers

nut *noun* **1** a fruit with a hard shell which contains a kernel **2** a small metal block with a hole in it for screwing on the end of a bolt ◇ **nutty** *adj* **1** containing or having the flavour of nuts **2** *informal* mad, insane ◇ **in a nutshell** expressed very briefly

---

Varieties of nut include:
almond, beech nut, brazil nut, cashew, chestnut, cobnut, coconut, filbert, hazelnut, macadamia, monkey nut, peanut, pecan, pine nut, pistachio, walnut

---

nutcrackers *noun plural* an instrument for cracking nuts open

nuthatch *noun* (*plural* **nuthatches**) a small bird living on nuts and insects

nutmeg *noun* a hard aromatic seed used as a spice in cooking

nutrient *noun* a substance which provides nourishment

nutriment *noun* nourishment; food

nutrition *noun* nourishment; food

nutritious or **nutritive** *adj* valuable as food, nourishing

■ nourishing, nutritive, wholesome, healthful, health-giving, good, beneficial, strengthening, substantial, invigorating

◨ bad, unwholesome

nuzzle *verb* **1** press, rub or caress with the nose **2** lie close to, snuggle, nestle

NVQ *abbrev, Brit* National Vocational Qualification

NW *abbrev* north-west; north-western

NY *abbrev* New York (city or state)

nylon *noun* **1** a synthetic material made from chemicals **2** (**nylons**) stockings made of nylon

nymph *noun* **1** a mythological female river or tree spirit **2** a beautiful girl **3** an insect not yet fully developed

nymphomania *noun* excessively strong sexual desire in women ◇ **nymphomaniac** *noun* someone suffering from nymphomania

NZ *abbrev* New Zealand

Oo

O or **Oh** *exclam* expressing surprise, admiration, pain *etc*

oaf *noun* (*plural* **oafs**) a stupid or clumsy person

oak *noun* **1** a tree which produces acorns as fruit **2** its hard wood ◇ **oak** or **oaken** *adj* made of oak ◇ **oak apple** a growth on the leaves and twigs of oaks, caused by insects

OAP *abbrev* **1** old age pensioner **2** old age pension

oar *noun* a pole for rowing, with a flat blade on the end ◇ **oarsman, oarswoman** *noun* someone who rows ◇ **put your oar in** interfere

oasis *noun* (*plural* **oases**) a place in a desert where water is found and trees *etc* grow

oatcake *noun* a thin flat cake made of oatmeal

oath *noun* (*plural* **oaths**) **1** a solemn promise to speak the truth, keep your word, be loyal *etc* **2** a swear-word
- **1** vow, pledge, promise, word, affirmation, assurance, word of honour **2** curse, imprecation, swear-word, profanity, expletive, blasphemy

oatmeal *noun* meal made by grinding oats

oats *noun plural* a type of grassy plant or its grain, used as food

obbligato *noun* (*plural* **obbligatos**), *music* an instrumental accompaniment

obdurate *adj* stubborn, firm, unyielding

OBE *abbrev* Officer of the Order of the British Empire

obedience *noun* **1** the act of obeying **2** willingness to obey ◇ **obedient** *adj* ◇ **obediently** *adv*
- **obedient** compliant, docile, yielding, dutiful, law-abiding, deferential, respectful, subservient, observant, submissive
- **obedient** disobedient, rebellious, wilful

obeisance *noun* a bow or curtsy showing respect

obelisk *noun* a tall four-sided pillar with a pointed top

obese *adj* very fat ◇ **obesity** *noun*

obey *verb* do what you are told to do (by someone): *obey the instructions/ obey your commanding officer*
- comply, surrender, yield, take orders from, follow, observe, abide by, adhere to, conform, heed, carry out, execute, act upon

obfuscate *verb* make unclear; obscure, confuse

obituary *noun* (*plural* **obituaries**) a notice in a newspaper *etc* of someone's death, sometimes with a brief biography

object /ˈɒbdʒɪkt/ *noun* **1** something that can be seen or touched **2** an aim, a purpose: *the object is to score as many points as possible* **3** *grammar* the word in a sentence which stands for the person or thing on which the action of the verb is done, *eg* me in the sentence *he gave me some good advice* ◇ *verb* /əbˈdʒɛkt/ (often with **to**) feel or show disapproval of
- *noun* **1** thing, entity, article, body **2** aim, objective, purpose, goal, target, intention, motive, end, reason, point, design ◇ *verb* protest, oppose, take exception, disapprove, refuse, complain, rebut, repudiate
- *verb* agree, acquiesce

objection *noun* **1** the act of objecting **2** a reason for objecting
- **1** protest, dissent, disapproval, opposition, demur, complaint, challenge

objectionable *adj* nasty, disagreeable
- unacceptable, unpleasant, offensive, obnoxious, disgusting, repugnant, dis-

objective *adj* not influenced by personal interests, fair ◇*noun* aim, purpose, goal

■ *adj* impartial, unbiased, detached, unprejudiced, open-minded, dispassionate, neutral, non-partisan, disinterested, just, fair ◇ *noun* object, aim, goal, end, purpose, ambition, mark, target, intention, design

■ *adj* subjective

objet d'art /ˈɒbʒeɪ dɑː(r)/ (*plural* **objets d'art**) an article with artistic value

obligation *noun* 1 a promise or duty by which someone is bound: *under an obligation to help* 2 a debt of gratitude for a favour received

■ 1 duty, responsibility, onus, charge, commitment 2 debt, burden

obligatory *adj* compulsory; required as a duty

■ compulsory, mandatory, statutory, required, binding, essential, necessary, enforced

oblige *verb* 1 force, compel: *we were obliged to go home* 2 do a favour or service to: *oblige me by shutting the door*

■ 1 compel, constrain, coerce, require, make, necessitate, force, bind 2 help, assist, accommodate, do a favour, serve, gratify, please

obliged *adj* owing or feeling gratitude

obliging *adj* ready to help others

■ accommodating, co-operative, helpful, considerate, agreeable, friendly, kind, civil

■ unhelpful

oblique *adj* 1 slanting 2 indirect, not straight or straightforward: *an oblique reference* ◇**obliquely** *adv* ◇**obliqueness** *noun*

obliterate *verb* 1 blot out (writing *etc*), efface 2 destroy completely ◇**obliteration** *noun*

■ 1 delete, blot out, wipe out, erase 2 eradicate, destroy, annihilate, wipe out

oblivion *noun* 1 forgetfulness 2 the state of being forgotten ◇**oblivious**

adj 1 unaware (of), not paying attention (to) 2 forgetful

■ **oblivious** 1 unaware, unconscious, unmindful, inattentive, blind, insensible 2 careless, heedless, negligent

oblong *noun* a rectangle with touching sides unequal in length ◇*adj* of the shape of an oblong

obloquy *noun* strong criticism, censure

obnoxious *adj* offensive, causing great dislike ◇**obnoxiously** *adv*

■ unpleasant, disagreeable, disgusting, loathsome, nasty, horrid, odious, repulsive, revolting, repugnant

■ pleasant

⚠ Do not confuse with: **noxious**

oboe *noun* (*plural* **oboes**) a high-pitched woodwind instrument ◇**oboist** *noun* someone who plays the oboe

obscene *adj* 1 sexually indecent, lewd 2 disgusting, repellent ◇**obscenity** *noun* (*plural* **obscenities**)

■ 1 indecent, improper, immoral, impure, filthy, dirty, bawdy, lewd, licentious, pornographic, X-rated 2 disgusting, foul, shocking, shameless, offensive

■ 1 decent, wholesome

obscure *adj* 1 dark 2 not clear or easily understood 3 unknown, not famous: *an obscure poet* ◇*verb* 1 darken 2 make less clear ◇**obscurity** *noun*

■ *adj* 1 indistinct, shadowy, cloudy, shady, murky, gloomy, dusky 2 incomprehensible, enigmatic, cryptic, mysterious, deep, abstruse, confusing, esoteric 3 unknown, unimportant, little-known, unheard-of, humble, minor ◇ *verb* 1 shroud, darken, dim, eclipse, screen, block out 2 cloud, blur, disguise, mask, overshadow, shadow, shade

■ *adj* 2 intelligible, straightforward 3 famous, renowned

obsequies *noun plural* funeral rites

obsequious *adj* trying to win favour by flattery, willingness to agree *etc* ◇**obsequiousness** *noun*

■ servile, ingratiating, grovelling, fawning, sycophantic, flattering, *informal* smarmy, submissive, subservient

observance *noun* the act of keeping (a law, tradition *etc*)

observant *adj* good at noticing
- attentive, alert, vigilant, watchful, perceptive, eagle-eyed, wide-awake, heedful
- unobservant

observation *noun* **1** the act of seeing and noting; attention **2** a remark
- **1** attention, notice, examination, inspection, scrutiny, monitoring, study, watching, consideration, discernment **2** remark, comment, utterance, thought, statement, reflection, opinion

observatory *noun* (*plural* **observatories**) a place for making observations of the stars, weather *etc*

observe *verb* **1** notice **2** watch with attention **3** remark (that) **4** obey (a law *etc*) **5** keep, preserve: *observe a tradition* ◇ **observer** *noun* someone who observes; someone sent to listen to, but not take part in, a discussion *etc*
- **1** notice, see, perceive **2** watch, study, keep an eye on **3** remark, comment, say, mention ◇ **observer** watcher, spectator, viewer, witness, looker-on, onlooker, eyewitness, commentator, bystander, beholder

obsess *verb* fill the mind completely ◇ **obsessed** *adj* having an obsession

obsession *noun* **1** a feeling or idea which someone cannot stop thinking about **2** the state of being obsessed
- **1** preoccupation, fixation, ruling passion, compulsion, fetish, infatuation, mania

obsessive *adj* **1** forming an obsession **2** having or likely to have an obsession
- **1** consuming, compulsive, gripping, fixed, haunting, tormenting, maddening

obsidian *noun* a glassy black volcanic rock

obsolescent *adj* going out of date ◇ **obsolescence** *noun*

❗ Do not confuse: **obsolete** and **obsolescent**

obsolete *adj* no longer in use

- outmoded, disused, out of date, old-fashioned, passé, dated, old, antiquated, antique, dead, extinct
- modern, current, up-to-date

obstacle *noun* something which stands in the way and hinders ◇ **obstacle race** a race in which obstacles have to be passed, climbed *etc*
- barrier, bar, obstruction, impediment, hurdle, hindrance, check, snag, stumbling-block, drawback, difficulty, hitch, catch, stop, interference, interruption
- advantage, help

obstetrics *noun sing* the study of helping women before, during and after childbirth ◇ **obstetric** or **obstetrical** *adj* of obstetrics ◇ **obstetrician** *noun* a doctor trained in obstetrics

obstinate *adj* stubborn; not yielding ◇ **obstinacy** *noun* stubbornness
- inflexible, immovable, *informal* pig-headed, unyielding, intransigent, persistent, headstrong, strong-minded, self-willed, steadfast, firm, determined, wilful

obstreperous *adj* noisy, unruly

obstruct *verb* **1** block, keep from passing **2** hold back ◇ **obstruction** *noun* **1** a hindrance or blockage **2** the act of obstructing
- **1** block, clog, choke **2** impede, hinder, hamper, stall, inhibit, hold up
- **2** assist, further

obtain *verb* **1** get, gain **2** be in use, be valid: *that rule still obtains* ◇ **obtainable** *adj* able to be got
- **1** acquire, get, gain, come by, attain, procure, secure, earn, achieve **2** prevail, exist, hold, be in force, stand

obtrude *verb* **1** be or become undesirably noticeable **2** thrust (yourself or your opinions) forward when not wanted ◇ **obtrusion** *noun*

obtrusive *adj* **1** too noticeable **2** pushy, impudent ◇ **obtrusiveness** *noun*
- **1** prominent, protruding, noticeable, obvious, blatant **2** forward, intrusive, interfering, prying, meddling, *informal* nosey, *informal* pushy

obtuse *adj* **1** of an angle: greater than

a right angle (*contrasted with*: **acute**) **2** blunt, not pointed **3** stupid, not quick to understand ◇ **obtuseness** *noun*

■ **3** slow, stupid, *informal* thick, dull, dense, dull-witted, *informal* dumb

◪ **3** bright, sharp

obverse *noun* the side of a coin showing the head or main design

obviate *verb* remove, prevent or get round (a difficulty *etc*)

obvious *adj* easily seen or understood; plain, evident ◇ **obviously** *adv*

■ evident, self-evident, patent, clear, plain, distinct, transparent, undeniable, unmistakable, glaring, apparent, open, visible, noticeable, perceptible, pronounced, recognizable, self-explanatory, straightforward, prominent

◪ unclear, indistinct, obscure

ocarina *noun* a musical toy with holes, played like a flute

occasion *noun* **1** a particular time: *on that occasion* **2** a special event: *a great occasion* **3** a cause, a reason: *have no occasion to be angry* **4** opportunity ◇ *verb* cause

■ **1** event, occurrence, time, instance **2** celebration, function, affair, party **3** reason, cause, excuse, justification, ground(s) **4** chance, case, opportunity

occasional *adj* happening or used now and then ◇ **occasionally** *adv*

■ periodic, intermittent, irregular, sporadic, infrequent, uncommon, incidental, odd, rare, casual ◇ **occasionally** sometimes, on occasion, from time to time, at times, now and then, now and again, irregularly, periodically, infrequently

◪ frequent, regular, constant ◇ **occasionally** frequently, often, always

Occident *noun* the countries of the West ◇ **occidental** *adj*

occlude *verb* **1** shut out, exclude **2** of the teeth: bite or come together ◇ **occlusion** *noun*

occult *adj* **1** secret, mysterious **2** supernatural

occupation *noun* **1** the state of being occupied **2** an activity which occupies someone **3** someone's trade or job **4**

possession of a house *etc*

■ **3** job, profession, work, vocation, employment, trade, post, calling, business, line, pursuit, craft, walk of life, activity **4** occupancy, possession, holding, tenancy, tenure, residence, habitation, use

occupy *verb* (**occupies**, **occupying**, **occupied**) **1** dwell in **2** keep busy **3** take up, fill (space, time *etc*) **4** seize, capture (a town, fort *etc*) ◇ **occupancy** *noun* (*plural* **occupancies**) the act, fact or period of occupying ◇ **occupant** *noun* someone who occupies a house, position, seat *etc* ◇ **occupier** *noun* someone who occupies a house *etc*

■ **1** inhabit, live in, possess, reside in **2** absorb, take up, engross, engage, hold, involve, preoccupy, amuse, busy, interest **4** invade, seize, capture, overrun, take over

occur *verb* (**occurs**, **occurring**, **occurred**) **1** happen **2** appear, be found **3** (with **to**) come into the mind of: *that never occurred to me*

■ **1** happen, come about, take place, transpire **2** crop up, appear, turn up, result, exist, be present, be found

occurrence *noun* **1** a happening, an event **2** the act or fact of occurring

■ **1** incident, event, happening, affair, circumstance, episode, instance, case, development, action **2** incidence, existence, appearance, manifestation

ocean *noun* **1** the stretch of salt water surrounding the land of the earth **2** one of five main divisions of this, *ie* the Atlantic, Pacific, Indian, Arctic or Antarctic

ocelot *noun* a wild American cat like a small leopard

ochre *noun* a fine pale-yellow or red clay, used for colouring

octa- or **octo-** or **oct-** *prefix* eight

octagon *noun* an eight-sided figure ◇ **octagonal** *adj* having eight sides

octane *noun* a colourless liquid found in petroleum and used in petrol

octave *noun*, *music* a range of eight notes, *eg* from one C to the C next above or below it

octet *noun* a group of eight lines of poetry, singers *etc*

October *noun* the tenth month of the year

octogenarian *noun* someone from eighty to eighty-nine years old

octopus *noun* (*plural* **octopuses**) a deep-sea creature with eight arms

ocular *adj* of the eye

oculist *noun* someone who specializes in diseases and defects of the eye

OD /oʊˈdiː/ *noun, slang* an overdose of drugs ◇*verb, slang* (**OD's**, **OD'ing**, **OD'd**) take an overdose

odd *adj* **1** of a number: leaving a remainder of one when divided by two, *eg* the numbers 3, 17, 31 (*contrasted with:* **even**) **2** unusual, strange **3** not one of a matching pair or group, left over: *an odd glove/an odd screw* ◇**oddly** *adv* ◇**oddments** *noun plural* scraps ◇**odds** *noun plural* chances or probability: *the odds are that they will win* ◇**at odds** quarrelling ◇**it makes no odds** it makes no difference ◇**odd jobs** jobs of different kinds, not part of regular employment ◇**odds and ends** objects, scraps *etc* of different kinds

▣ *adj* **2** unusual, strange, uncommon, peculiar, abnormal, exceptional, curious, different, queer, bizarre, left-field, eccentric, remarkable, unconventional, weird, irregular, extraordinary, rare **3** unmatched, unpaired, single, spare, surplus, left-over, remaining

oddity *noun* (*plural* **oddities**) **1** queerness, strangeness **2** a strange person or thing

▣ **1** abnormality, peculiarity, rarity, eccentricity, idiosyncrasy **2** curiosity, character, freak, misfit, phenomenon, quirk

ode *noun* a type of poem, often written to someone or something: *ode to autumn*

odious *adj* hateful ◇**odiously** *adv*

▣ offensive, loathsome, unpleasant, obnoxious, disgusting, hateful, repulsive, revolting, repugnant, foul, detestable, abhorrent, horrible, horrid, abominable

▣ pleasant

odium *noun* dislike, hatred

odour *noun* smell, either pleasant or unpleasant ◇**odourless** *adj* without smell

▣ smell, scent, fragrance, aroma, perfume, stench, *informal* stink

oedema *or US* **edema** /ɪˈdiːmə/ *noun* (*plural* **oedemata** *or* **oedemas**) an accumulation of fluid in body tissue, causing swelling

oenology /iːˈnɒlədʒɪ/ *noun* the study of wines ◇**oenological** *adj* ◇**oenologist** *noun*

oesophagus *or US* **esophagus** /ɪˈsɒfəgəs/ *noun* (*plural* **oesophagi**) the gullet

oestrogen *or US* **estrogen** /ˈiːstrədʒən/ *noun* a female sex hormone which regulates the menstrual cycle, prepares the body for pregnancy *etc* ◇**oestrogenic** *adj*

oestrus *or US* **estrus** /ˈiːstrəs/ *noun* the period during which a female mammal is ready for conceiving; heat

of *prep* **1** belonging to: *the house of my parents* **2** from (a place, person *etc*): *within two miles of his home* **3** from among: *one of my pupils* **4** made from: *a house of bricks* **5** indicating an amount, measurement *etc*: *a spoonful of sugar* **6** about, concerning: *talk of old friends* **7** with, containing: *a class of twenty children/a cup of coffee* **8** indicating a cause: *die of hunger* **9** indicating removal or taking away: *robbed her of her jewels* **10** indicating a connection between an action and its object: *the joining of the pieces* **11** indicating character, qualities *etc*: *a man of good taste/it was good of you to come* **12** *US* (in telling the time) before, to: *ten of eight*

off *adv* **1** away from a place, or from a particular state, position *etc*: *he walked off rudely/switch the light off* **2** entirely, completely: *finish off your work* ◇*adj* **1** cancelled: *the holiday is off* **2** rotten, bad: *the meat is off* **3** not working, not on: *the control is in the off position* **4** not quite pure in colour: *off-white* ◇*prep* **1** not on, away from: *fell off the table* **2** taken away: *10% off the usual price* **3** below the normal standard: *off his game* ◇ **badly off** poor ◇ **be off** go away, leave quickly ◇ **off and on** occasionally ◇ **well off** rich

■ *adv* **1** away, elsewhere, out, at a distance, apart, aside ◇ *adj* **1** cancelled, postponed **2** rotten, bad, sour, turned, rancid, mouldy, decomposed

offal *noun* the internal organs of an animal (heart, liver *etc*) which are eaten

off-beat *adj* not standard, eccentric

off-chance *noun* a slight chance ◇ **on the off-chance** just in case

off-colour *adj* not feeling well

■ indisposed, under the weather, unwell, sick, out of sorts, ill, poorly

offcut *noun* a piece of wood, fabric *etc* remaining from a larger piece

offence or *US* **offense** *noun* **1** displeasure, hurt feelings **2** a crime, a sin ◇ **take offence** be angry or feel hurt (at)

■ **1** resentment, indignation, pique, outrage, hurt, hard feelings **2** misdemeanour, transgression, violation, wrong, wrongdoing, infringement, crime, misdeed, sin, trespass

offend *verb* **1** hurt the feelings of; insult, displease **2** do wrong, commit a crime or sin ◇ **offender** *noun*

■ **1** hurt, insult, injure, affront, wrong, wound, displease, snub, upset, annoy, outrage

offensive *noun* **1** the position of someone who attacks: *on the offensive* **2** an attack ◇ *adj* **1** insulting, disgusting **2** used for attack or assault: *an offensive weapon*

■ *noun* **2** attack, assault, onslaught, invasion, raid ◇ *adj* **1** insolent, abusive, rude, disrespectful, insulting, impertinent, disagreeable, unpleasant, disgusting, odious, repellent, repugnant, revolting, loathsome, vile, nauseating, nasty

offer *verb* **1** put forward (a gift, payment *etc*) for acceptance or refusal **2** lay (a choice, chance *etc*) before someone **3** say that you are willing to do something ◇ *noun* **1** an act of offering **2** a bid of money **3** something proposed

■ *verb* **1** present, make available, advance,

extend, put forward, submit, suggest, hold out, sell **2** give, present, provide **3** volunteer, come forward, *informal* show willing ◇ *noun* **3** proposal, bid, submission, tender, suggestion, proposition

offering *noun* **1** a gift **2** a collection of money in church

offhand *adj* **1** said or done without thinking or preparation **2** rude, curt ◇ *adv* without preparation; impromptu

■ *adj* **1** casual, unconcerned, uninterested, careless **2** brusque, abrupt ◇ *adv* impromptu, off the cuff, off the top of one's head, immediately

■ *adj* **1** calculated, planned

office *noun* **1** a place where administrative or clerical work is done **2** the people working in such a place **3** a duty, a job **4** a position of authority, *esp* in the government **5** (**offices**) services, helpful acts ◇ **officer** *noun* **1** someone who carries out a public duty **2** someone holding a commission or a position of authority in the armed forces

■ **3** occupation, situation, post, employment, function, appointment, responsibility, duty, obligation, charge

official *adj* **1** done or given out by those in power: *official announcement/ official action* **2** forming part of the tasks of a job or office: *official duties* **3** having full and proper authority ◇ *noun* someone who holds an office in the service of the government *etc* ◇ **officially** *adv* **1** formally **2** as announced or said in public (though not necessarily truthfully): *officially, he resigned for family reasons*

■ *adj* **3** authorized, authoritative, legitimate, formal, licensed, certified, approved, authenticated, authentic, proper

🛈 Do not confuse with: **officious**

Officials include:
agent, ambassador, bailiff, bureaucrat, captain, chairman, chairwoman, chairperson, chancellor, chief, clerk, commander, commissar,

commissioner, congressman, congresswoman, consul, coroner, councillor, delegate, diplomat, director, elder, envoy, equerry, Eurocrat, executive, Euro-MP, gauleiter, governor, hakim, inspector, justice of the peace (JP), magistrate, manager, mandarin, marshal, mayor, mayoress, member of parliament, minister, monitor, notary, ombudsman, overseer, prefect, president, principal, proctor, proprietor, public prosecutor, registrar, *US* senator, sheriff, steward, superintendent, supervisor, usher

officiate *verb* perform a duty or service, *esp* as a clergyman at a wedding *etc*

officious *adj* fond of interfering, *esp* in a pompous way ◊ **officiously** *adv* ◊ **officiousness** *noun*

■ obtrusive, dictatorial, intrusive, *informal* bossy, interfering, meddlesome, self-important, *informal* pushy, forward

🛈 Do not confuse with: **official**

offing *noun*: **in the offing** expected to happen soon, forthcoming

off-licence *noun* a shop selling alcohol which must not be drunk on the premises

offline *adj*, *comput* not connected

offload *verb* **1** unload **2** get rid of (something) by passing onto someone else

■ **1** unburden, unload, jettison, dump, drop, deposit, get rid of, discharge

off-peak *adj* not at the time of highest use or demand

off-putting *adj* causing aversion

■ intimidating, daunting, disconcerting, discouraging, disheartening, unnerving, unsettling, demoralizing, disturbing

offset *verb* counterbalance, make up for: *the cost of the project was partly offset by a government grant*

offshoot *noun* **1** a shoot growing out of the main stem **2** a small business,

project *etc* created out of a larger one: *an offshoot of an international firm*

■ **1** branch, outgrowth **2** branch, arm, development, spin-off, by-product

offshore *adj & adv* **1** in or on the sea close to the coast **2** at a distance from the shore **3** from the shore: *offshore winds*

offside *adj & adv, sport* **1** illegally ahead of the ball, *eg* in football, in a position between the ball and the opponent's goal **2** of the side of a vehicle: nearest to the centre of the road (*contrasted with*: **nearside**)

offspring *noun* **1** someone's child or children **2** the young of animals *etc*

■ **1** child, children, young, heirs, successors, descendants **2** young, issue, *formal* progeny, brood

often *adv* many times

■ frequently, repeatedly, regularly, generally, again and again, time after time

🔁 rarely, seldom, never

ogle *verb* eye (someone) impudently in an amorous or lecherous way

ogre *noun* **1** a mythological man-eating giant **2** someone extremely frightening or threatening

ohm *noun* a unit of electrical resistance

oil *noun* **1** a greasy liquid obtained from plants (*eg* olive oil), from animals (*eg* whale oil), and from minerals (*eg* petroleum) **2** (**oils**) oil colours for painting ◊ *verb* smear with oil, put oil on or in ◊ **oily** *adj* **1** of or like oil **2** obsequious, too friendly or flattering ◊ **oil colour** paint made by mixing a colouring substance with oil ◊ **oil painting** a picture painted in oil colours

■ **oily 1** greasy, fatty **2** unctuous, smooth, ingratiating, *informal* smarmy, glib, flattering

oilfield *noun* an area where mineral oil is found

oilrig *noun* a structure set up for drilling an oil-well

oilskin *noun* **1** cloth made waterproof with oil **2** a heavy coat made of this

oil-well *noun* a hole drilled into the

earth's surface or into the sea bed to extract petroleum

oink *noun* the noise of a pig ◇ *verb* make this noise

ointment *noun* a greasy substance rubbed on the skin to soothe, heal *etc*

OK or **okay** *exclam, adj & adv* all right ◇ *verb* (**OK's**, **OK'ing**, **OK'd** or **okays**, **okaying**, **okayed**) mark or pass as being all right

▣ *adj* acceptable, all right, fine, permitted, fair, satisfactory, reasonable, tolerable, passable, not bad, good, adequate, convenient, correct, accurate ◇ *verb* approve, authorize, pass, *informal* give the green light to, rubber-stamp, agree to

okapi *noun* a Central African animal related to the giraffe

okra *noun* a tropical plant with edible pods

old *adj* 1 advanced in age, aged 2 having a certain age: *ten years old* 3 not new, having existed a long time: *an old joke* 4 belonging to far-off times 5 worn, worn-out 6 out-of-date, old-fashioned ◇ **of old** long ago ◇ **old age** the later part of life ◇ **old guard** the conservative element in an organization *etc* ◇ **old hand** someone with long experience in a job *etc* ◇ **old maid** 1 a spinster 2 a game played by passing and matching playing cards ◇ **old timer** 1 an old person 2 a veteran, someone with experience

▣ *adj* 1 aged, elderly, advanced in years, grey 4 ancient, original, primitive, antiquated 5 worn-out, decayed, decrepit 6 obsolete, old-fashioned, out-of-date

old-fashioned *adj* in a style common in the past, out-of-date

▣ outmoded, out-of-date, outdated, dated, unfashionable, obsolete, antiquated, archaic, passé, obsolescent

▣ modern, up-to-date

oleander *noun* an evergreen shrub with spiky leaves and red or white flowers

olfactory *adj* of or used for smelling: *olfactory glands*

oligarchy *noun* government by a small exclusive group ◇ **oligarch** *noun*

a member of an oligarchy ◇ **oligarchic** or **oligarchical** *adj*

olive *noun* 1 a small oval fruit with a hard stone, which is pressed to produce a cooking oil 2 the Mediterranean tree that bears this fruit ◇ *adj* of a yellowish-green colour ◇ **olive branch** a sign of a wish for peace

ombudsman *noun* an official appointed to look into complaints against the government

From a Swedish word meaning 'administration man', introduced into English in the 1960s

omega *noun* the last letter of the Greek alphabet

omelette or **omelet** *noun* beaten eggs fried in a single layer in a pan

omen *noun* a sign of future events

▣ portent, sign, warning, premonition, foreboding, indication

ominous *adj* suggesting future trouble

▣ portentous, inauspicious, foreboding, menacing, sinister, fateful, unpromising, threatening

▣ auspicious, favourable

omission *noun* 1 something omitted 2 the act of omitting

omit *verb* (**omits**, **omitting**, **omitted**) 1 leave out 2 fail (to do something): *she omitted to mention that she couldn't drive*

▣ 1 leave out, exclude, miss out, pass over, overlook, disregard, drop, skip, eliminate 2 forget, neglect, leave undone, fail

omnibus *noun* (*plural* **omnibuses**) 1 *old* a bus 2 a book *etc* made up of miscellaneous contents 3 a radio or TV programme made up of material from preceding editions or previous episodes

omnipotent *adj* having absolute, unlimited power: *an omnipotent ruler* ◇ **omnipotence** *noun*

omnipresent *adj* being present everywhere at the same time ◇ **omnipresence** *noun*

omniscient *adj* knowing everything ◊ **omniscience** *noun*

omnivorous *adj* feeding on all kinds of food ◊ **omnivorousness** *noun*

on *prep* **1** touching or fixed to the outer or upper side: *on the table* **2** supported by: *standing on one foot* **3** receiving, taking *etc*: *suspended on half-pay/on antibiotics* **4** occurring in the course of a specified time: *on the following day* **5** about: *a book on Scottish history* **6** with: *do you have your cheque book on you?* **7** next to, near: *a city on the Rhine* **8** indicating membership of: *on the committee* **9** in the process or state of: *on sale/on show* **10** by means of: *can you play that on the piano* **11** followed by: *disaster on disaster* ◊ *adv* **1** so as to be touching or fixed to the outer or upper side: *put your coat on* **2** onwards, further in space or time: *they carried on towards home/later on* ◊ *adj* **1** working, performing: *the television is on* **2** arranged, planned: *do you have anything on this afternoon?* ◊ **from now on** after this time, henceforth ◊ **on and off** occasionally, intermittently ◊ **you're on!** I agree, accept the challenge *etc*

once *adv* **1** at an earlier time in the past: *people once lived in caves* **2** for one time only: *I've been to Paris once before* ◊ *noun* one time only: *do it just this once* ◊ *conj* when: *once you've finished, you can go* ◊ **all at once** suddenly ◊ **at once 1** immediately: *come here at once!* **2** (sometimes with **all**) at the same time, together: *trying to do several things all at once* ◊ **once and for all** for the last time ◊ **once upon a time** at some time in the past

■ *adv* **1** formerly, previously, in the past, at one time, long ago, once upon a time

oncology *noun* the study of tumours ◊ **oncological** *adj* ◊ **oncologist** *noun*

oncoming *adj* approaching from the front: *oncoming traffic*

■ approaching, advancing, upcoming, looming, onrushing, gathering

one *noun* **1** the number 1 **2** a particular member of a group: *she's the one I want to meet* ◊ *pronoun* **1** a single person or thing: *one of my cats* **2** in formal or pompous English used instead of **you,** meaning anyone: *one must do what one can* ◊ *adj* **1** 1 in number, a single: *we received only one reply* **2** identical, the same: *we are all of one mind* **3** some, an unnamed (time *etc*): *one day soon* ◊ **one another** used when an action takes place between two or more people: *they looked at one another*

■ *adj* **1** single, solitary, lone, individual, only **2** equal, identical, alike

onerous *adj* heavy, hard to bear or do: *an onerous task*

■ oppressive, demanding, laborious, hard, taxing, difficult, troublesome, exacting, exhausting, heavy, weighty

🔁 easy, light

oneself *pronoun* **1** used reflexively: *wash oneself* **2** used for emphasis: *one usually has to finish the job oneself*

one-sided *adj* with one person, side *etc* having a great advantage over the other

■ unbalanced, unequal, unfair, unjust, prejudiced, biased

one-way *adj* meant for traffic moving in one direction only

ongoing *adj* continuing: *ongoing talks*

onion *noun* a bulb vegetable with a strong taste and smell ◊ **oniony** *adj* tasting of onions ◊ **know your onions** *informal* know your subject or job well

online *adj, comput* connected to or using a computer

onlooker *noun* someone who watches an event, but does not take part in it

■ bystander, observer, spectator, eye-witness, witness, watcher, viewer

only *adv* **1** not more than: *only two weeks left* **2** alone, solely: *only you are invited* **3** not longer ago than: *I saw her only yesterday* **4** indicating an unavoidable result: *he'll only be offended if you ask* ◊ *adj* single, solitary: *an only child* ◊ *conj, informal* but, except that: *I'd like to go, only I have to work* ◊ **only too** extremely: *only too pleased to help*

■ *adv* **2** exclusively, solely ◊ *adj* sole,

single, solitary, lone, unique, exclusive, individual

ono *abbrev* or nearest offer

onomatopoeia *noun* the forming of a word which sounds like the thing it refers to, *eg* moo, swish ◇ **onomatopoeic** *adj*

onrush *noun* a rush forward

onset *noun* 1 beginning 2 a fierce attack

▣ 1 beginning, start, commencement, outset, outbreak 2 assault, attack, onslaught, onrush

onslaught *noun* a fierce attack

▣ attack, assault, offensive, charge, bombardment, blitz

ontology *noun* the study of pure being or essence ◇ **ontologic** or **ontological** *adj* ◇ **ontologist** *noun*

onus *noun* burden; responsibility

▣ burden, responsibility, load, obligation, duty, liability, task

onward *adj* going forward in place or time ◇ **onward** or **onwards** *adv*

onyx *noun* a precious stone with layers of different colours

oodles *noun plural, informal* lots (of), many

ooze *verb* flow gently or slowly ◇ *noun* 1 soft mud 2 a gentle flow

▣ *verb* seep, exude, leak, percolate, escape, dribble, drip, drop, discharge, secrete, emit, overflow with, filter, drain

op *abbrev* 1 opus 2 optical: *op art*

opacity *see* opaque

opal *noun* a bluish-white precious stone, with flecks of various colours

opalescent *adj* milky and iridescent ◇ **opalescence** *noun*

opaque *adj* not able to be seen through ◇ **opacity** *noun*

▣ cloudy, clouded, murky, dull, dim, hazy, muddy

▣ transparent

open *adj* 1 not shut, allowing entry or exit 2 not enclosed or fenced 3 showing the inside or inner part; uncovered 4 not blocked 5 free for all to enter: *an open competition* 6 honest, frank 7 of land: without many trees ◇ *verb* 1 make

open; unlock or uncover 2 begin ◇ **openly** *adv* without trying to hide or conceal anything ◇ **in the open** 1 out-of-doors, in the open air 2 widely known, not secret ◇ **open air** any place not indoors or underground ◇ **open book** something that can be easily seen or understood ◇ **open to** likely or willing to receive: *open to attack/open to suggestions* ◇ **open verdict** a verdict of death, with no cause stated, given by a coroner's jury ◇ **with open arms** warmly, enthusiastically

▣ *adj* 1 unclosed, ajar, unlocked 2 unrestricted, accessible 3 uncovered, gaping, exposed 4 free, unobstructed, clear, accessible 6 frank, candid, honest, guileless, natural, ingenuous, unreserved ◇ *verb* 1 unfasten, undo, unlock, unseal 2 begin, start, commence, initiate, launch ◇ **openly** overtly, frankly, candidly, blatantly, plainly, unashamedly, unreservedly, in full view, shamelessly

▣ *adj* 1 shut 2 enclosed 6 reserved ◇ *verb* 1 close, shut 2 end, finish

open-air *adj* happening outside

▣ outdoor, alfresco

▣ indoor

open-cast *adj* of a mine: excavated in the open, above ground

open-ended *adj* without definite limits

opener *noun* something which opens: *tin-opener*

open-heart *adj* of surgery: performed on a heart which has been temporarily stopped, with blood being circulated by a heart-lung machine

opening *noun* 1 a hole, a gap 2 an opportunity 3 a vacant job 4 a beginning

▣ 1 aperture, breach, gap, orifice, break, crack, hole, split, vent 2 opportunity, chance, occasion, *informal* break 3 place, vacancy 4 start, onset, beginning, inauguration, launch

open-minded *adj* ready to take up new ideas

open-plan *adj* of an office: with desks *etc* in the same room, not divided by walls

opera[1] *noun* a play in which the characters sing accompanied by an orchestra ◇ **operatic** *adj*

opera[2] *plural* of **opus**

operate *verb* **1** act, work **2** control (a machine) **3** bring about an effect **3** perform a surgical operation ◇ **operating** *adj* of or for an operation on someone's body: *operating theatre*
  🔲 **1** function, act, perform, run, work, go **2** control, handle, manage, use, utilize, manoeuvre

operation *noun* **1** action **2** method or way of working **3** the cutting of a part of the human body to examine or treat disease **4** (**operations**) movements of armies, troops

operative *adj* **1** working, in action **2** of a rule *etc*: in force, having effect ◇ *noun* a worker in a factory *etc*
  🔲 *adj* **1** operational, in operation, functioning, active, functional **2** in force, active, effective, efficient
  ⛝ *adj* **1** inoperative, out of service

operator *noun* **1** someone who works a machine **2** someone who connects telephone calls

operetta *noun* a play with music and singing

ophthalmic *adj* relating to the eye: *an ophthalmic surgeon* ◇ **ophthalmologist** *noun* a doctor who specializes in eye diseases and injuries

opiate *noun* **1** a drug containing opium used to make someone sleep **2** anything that calms or dulls the mind or feelings

opine *verb*, *formal* give as an opinion

opinion *noun* **1** what someone thinks or believes **2** professional judgement or point of view: *he wanted another opinion on his son's case* **3** judgement of the value of someone or something: *I have a low opinion of her* ◇ **opinionated** *adj* having and expressing strong opinions
  🔲 **1** belief, view, point of view, feeling, sentiment **2** judgement, estimation, assessment **3** impression, perception ◇ **opinionated** dogmatic, dictatorial, arrogant, inflexible, obstinate, stubborn, uncompromising, single-minded,

prejudiced, biased, bigoted
  ⛝ **opinionated** open-minded

opium *noun* a drug made from the dried juice of a type of poppy

opossum *noun* a small American animal which carries its young in a pouch

opponent *noun* someone who opposes; an enemy, a rival
  🔲 adversary, enemy, antagonist, foe, competitor, contestant, challenger, opposer, opposition, rival
  ⛝ ally

opportune *adj* coming at the right or convenient time

opportunist *noun* someone who takes advantage of a situation ◇ **opportunism** *noun* ◇ **opportunistic** *adj*

opportunity *noun* (*plural* **opportunities**) a chance (to do something)
  🔲 chance, opening, *informal* break, occasion, possibility, hour, moment

oppose *verb* **1** struggle against, resist **2** stand against, compete against
  🔲 **1** resist, withstand **2** attack, combat, contest, stand up to, confront, defy, fight
  ⛝ **1** defend, support

opposite *adj* **1** facing, across from **2** lying on the other side (of) **3** as different as possible ◇ *prep* **1** facing, across from: *he lives opposite the post office* **2** acting a role in a play *etc* in relation to another: *she played Ophelia opposite his Hamlet* ◇ *noun* something as different as possible (from something else): *black is the opposite of white*
  🔲 *adj* **1** facing, fronting, corresponding **3** unlike, reverse, different, contrasted, differing ◇ *noun* reverse, converse, contrary, antithesis, contradiction, inverse, antonym

opposition *noun* **1** resistance **2** those who resist **3** the political party which is against the governing party
  🔲 **1** antagonism, hostility, resistance, obstructiveness, unfriendliness, disapproval **2** opponents, antagonists, rivals, foes
  ⛝ **1** co-operation, support **2** allies, supporters

oppress *verb* **1** govern harshly like a tyrant **2** treat cruelly **3** distress, worry greatly ◇ **oppression** *noun*

■ **1** subjugate, suppress, subdue, overpower **2** crush, trample, tyrannize, persecute, maltreat, abuse **3** burden, afflict, depress, sadden, torment, vex

oppressive *adj* **1** oppressing **2** cruel, harsh **3** of weather: close, tiring ◇ **oppressively** *adv*

■ **1** tyrannical, despotic, overbearing, overwhelming, repressive **2** harsh, unjust, inhuman, cruel, brutal **3** airless, stuffy, close, stifling, suffocating, sultry, muggy, heavy

ऒ **2** just, gentle **3** airy

opprobrium *noun* **1** great or public disgrace **2** something that brings great disgrace ◇ **opprobrious** *adj* disgraceful; scornful

opt *verb* **1** (with **for**) choose **2** decide (to do) ◇ **opt out** decide not to do something

optic or **optical** *adj* relating to the eyes or sight ◇ **optical illusion** an impression that something seen is different from what it is ◇ **optics** *noun sing* the science of light

optician *noun* someone who makes and sells spectacles

optimal *adj* very best, optimum

optimism *noun* the habit of taking a bright, hopeful, positive view of things (*contrasted with*: **pessimism**) ◇ **optimist** *noun* ◇ **optimistic** *adj*

■ **optimistic** confident, assured, sanguine, hopeful, positive, cheerful, buoyant, bright, idealistic, expectant

ऒ **optimistic** pessimistic

optimum *adj* best, most favourable: *optimum conditions*

■ best, ideal, perfect, optimal, superlative, top, choice

ऒ worst

option *noun* **1** choice; the right or power to choose **2** something which is or may be chosen ◇ **optional** *adj* left to choice, not compulsory

■ **optional** voluntary, discretionary, elective, free, unforced

ऒ **optional** compulsory

opulent *adj* wealthy; luxurious ◇ **opulence** *noun* riches

opus *noun* (*plural* **opuses** or **opera**) an artistic work, *esp* a musical composition

or *conj* **1** used (often with **either**) to show alternatives: *would you prefer tea or coffee?* **2** because if not: *you'd better go or you'll miss your bus*

oracle *noun* **1** someone thought to be very wise or knowledgeable **2** *hist* a sacred place where a god answered questions **3** someone through whom such answers were made known ◇ **oracular** *adj*

oral *adj* **1** spoken, not written: *oral literature/an oral examination* **2** relating to the mouth: *oral hygiene* ◇ **oral** *noun* an oral examination or test ◇ **orally** *adv* by mouth: *the drug is administered orally*

■ *adj* **1** verbal, spoken, unwritten, vocal

❗ Do not confuse with: **aural**

orange *noun* a juicy citrus fruit, with a thick reddish-yellow skin

orang-utan *noun* a large man-like ape

Based on a Malay phrase which translates as 'wild man'

oration *noun* a public speech, *esp* one in fine, formal language ◇ **orator** *noun* a public speaker ◇ **oratory** *noun* the art of speaking well in public

oratorio *noun* (*plural* **oratorios**) a sacred story set to music, performed by soloists, choir and often orchestra

orb *noun* anything in the shape of a ball, a sphere

orbit *noun* **1** the path of a planet or moon round a sun, or of a spacecraft, satellite *etc* round the earth **2** range or area of influence: *within his orbit* ◇ *verb* go round (the earth *etc*) in space

■ *noun* **1** circuit, cycle, circle, course, path, trajectory, track, revolution, rotation **2** range, scope, domain, influence, sphere of influence, compass

orchard *noun* a large garden of fruit trees

orchestra *noun* a group of musicians playing together under a conductor ◇ **orchestrate** *verb* **1** arrange (a piece of music) for an orchestra **2** organize so as to produce the best effect

orchid *noun* a plant with unusually shaped, often brightly coloured, flowers

ordain *verb* **1** declare something to be law **2** receive (a member of the clergy) into the Church ◇ **ordinance** *noun* a command; a law ◇ **ordination** *noun* ordaining or being ordained into the Church

ordeal *noun* **1** a hard trial or test **2** suffering, painful experience

■ **2** affliction, trouble(s), suffering, anguish, agony, pain, persecution, torture, nightmare

order *noun* **1** an instruction to act made by someone in authority **2** a request or list of requests: *an order for ten boxes of paper* **3** arrangement according to a system: *in alphabetical order* **4** an accepted way of doing things **5** a tidy or efficient state **6** peaceful conditions: *law and order* **7** rank, position, class **8** a society or brotherhood, *eg* of monks ◇ *verb* **1** give an order to, tell to do something **2** put in an order for: *I've ordered another copy of the book* **3** arrange ◇ **in order 1** correct according to what is regularly done **2** in a tidy or systematic arrangement ◇ **in order to** for the purpose of: *in order to live you must eat* ◇ **out of order 1** not working **2** not the correct way of doing things **3** not in a tidy or systematic arrangement

■ *noun* **1** command, directive, decree, instruction, direction **2** requisition, request, booking, commission, reservation **3** arrangement, organization, grouping, disposition, sequence, categorization, classification, method, pattern, plan, system, layout, structure **6** peace, quiet, calm, tranquillity, harmony, discipline **7** class, kind, sort, type, rank, hierarchy **8** association, society, community, fraternity, brotherhood, sisterhood, lodge, guild, company, organization, denomination, sect, union ◇ *verb* **1** command, instruct, direct, require, authorize **2** request, re-

serve, apply for, requisition **3** arrange, organize, classify, group, sort out, lay out, manage, control, catalogue

orderly *adj* **1** in proper order **2** well-behaved, quiet ◇ *noun* (*plural* **order-lies**) **1** a soldier who carries the orders and messages of an officer **2** a hospital attendant who does routine jobs

■ *adj* **1** ordered, systematic, neat, tidy, regular, methodical, in order, well-organized, well-regulated **2** well-behaved, controlled, disciplined, law-abiding

🖪 *adj* **1** chaotic **2** disorderly

ordinal *adj* of or in an order ◇ **ordinal number** a number which shows order in a series, *eg* 1st, 2nd, 3rd (*contrasted with*: **cardinal number**)

ordinance *see* ordain

ordinary *adj* common, usual; not exceptional ◇ **ordinarily** *adv* ◇ **ordinariness** *noun* ◇ **out of the ordinary** unusual

■ common, commonplace, regular, routine, standard, average, everyday, run-of-the-mill, usual, unremarkable, typical, normal, customary, plain, *informal* vanilla, familiar, habitual, simple, conventional, mediocre

🖪 extraordinary, unusual

ordination *see* ordain

Ordnance Survey a government office which produces official detailed maps

ordure *noun* excrement, dung

ore *noun* a mineral from which a metal is obtained: *iron ore*

oregano /ɒrɪˈgɑːnoʊ/ or *US* /əˈrɛɡənoʊ/ *noun* a Mediterranean herb used in cooking

organ *noun* **1** an internal part of the body, *eg* the liver **2** a large musical wind instrument with a keyboard **3** a means of spreading information or propaganda, *eg* a newspaper: *an organ of conservatism* ◇ **organist** *noun* someone who plays the organ

■ **3** medium, agency, forum, vehicle, voice, publication, newspaper, periodical, journal

organic *adj* **1** of or produced by the

bodily organs **2** of living things **3** made up of parts each with its separate function **4** of food: grown without the use of artificial fertilizers *etc* ◇ **organically** *adv*

organism *noun* any living thing

organization *noun* **1** the act of organizing **2** a group of people working together for a purpose

■ **1** arrangement, system, classification, methodology, order, formation **2** association, institution, society, company, firm, corporation, federation, group, league, club, confederation, consortium

organize *verb* **1** arrange, set up (an event *etc*) **2** form into an ordered or unified whole

■ **1** establish, found, set up, develop, form, frame, construct, shape, run

orgasm *noun* the climax of sexual excitement ◇ **orgasmic** *adj*

orgy *noun* (*plural* **orgies**) a drunken or other unrestrained celebration ◇ **orgiastic** *adj*

oriel *noun* a small room with a bay window built out from a wall

Orient *noun*, *old* the countries of the East ◇ **oriental** *adj* eastern; from the East

orientate *verb* **1** find your position and sense of direction **2** set or put facing a particular direction ◇ **orientation** *noun*

■ **orientation** situation, bearings, location, direction, position, alignment, attitude

orienteering *noun* the sport of finding your way across country with the help of map and compass

orifice *noun*, *formal* an opening

origami *noun* the Japanese art of folding paper into decorative shapes

origin *noun* **1** the starting point **2** that from which someone or something comes into being **3** the cause of something

■ **1** beginning, commencement, start, inauguration, launch **2** ancestry, descent, extraction, heritage, family, lineage,

parentage, source, spring, fount, foundation, base

original *adj* **1** first in time **2** not copied **3** able to think of or do something new ◇ *noun* **1** the earliest version **2** a model from which other things are made ◇ **originally** *adv* ◇ **original sin** the supposed sinful nature of all human beings since Adam disobeyed God

■ *adj* **1** first, early, earliest, initial, primary, commencing, first-hand **2** novel, new, fresh, unusual, unique **3** innovative, creative, imaginative, inventive, unconventional, ground-breaking ◇ *noun* **2** prototype, model, pattern

☒ *adj* **1** latest **2** hackneyed, unoriginal

originate *verb* **1** bring or come into being **2** produce

■ **1** create, invent, inaugurate, introduce, develop, discover, establish, begin, commence, start, set up, launch, pioneer **2** conceive, form, produce, generate

Orion *noun* a constellation containing seven bright stars, forming the shape of a hunter

ormolu *noun* gilded bronze or other metal, used for ornamentation

ornament *noun* something added to give or enhance beauty ◇ *verb* adorn, decorate ◇ **ornamentation** *noun*

■ *noun* decoration, adornment, embellishment, garnish, trimming, accessory, frill, jewel ◇ *verb* decorate, adorn, embellish, garnish, trim, beautify, brighten, dress up, deck, gild

ornamental *adj* used for ornament; decorative

■ decorative, embellishing, adorning, attractive, showy

ornate *adj* richly decorated ◇ **ornately** *adv*

■ elaborate, ornamented, fancy, decorated, florid, flowery, fussy, busy, sumptuous

☒ plain

ornithologist *noun* someone who studies or is an expert on birds ◇ **ornithological** *adj* ◇ **ornithology** *noun*

orotund *adj* of a voice: full, round

orphan *noun* a child whose parents

are dead ◇**orphanage** *noun* a home for orphans

orthodox *adj* agreeing with the prevailing or established religious, political *etc* views (*contrasted with*: **heterodox**) ◇**orthodoxy** *noun*

☰ conformist, conventional, accepted, official, traditional, usual, established, received, customary, recognized

🖝 nonconformist, unorthodox

orthography *noun* an established system of spelling ◇**orthographic** or **orthographical** *adj*

orthopaedics or *US* **orthopedics** *noun sing* the branch of medicine which deals with bone diseases and injuries ◇**orthopaedic** *adj*

Oscar *noun* an annual award given by the American Academy of Motion Picture Arts and Sciences

oscillate *verb* **1** swing to and fro like the pendulum of a clock **2** keep changing your mind ◇**oscillation** *noun*

From Latin *oscillum*, literally 'small face', a mask of the god Bacchus which hung in Roman vineyards and swayed in the wind

osier *noun* **1** a type of willow tree whose twigs are used for weaving baskets *etc* **2** a twig from this tree

osmosis *noun* **1** diffusion of liquids through a membrane **2** gradual absorption or assimilation

osprey *noun* (*plural* **ospreys**) a type of eagle which eats fish

ostensible *adj* of a reason *etc*: apparent, but not always real or true

☰ alleged, apparent, presumed, seeming, supposed, so-called, professed, outward, pretended, superficial

🖝 real

ostentatious *adj* showy, meant to catch the eye ◇**ostentation** *noun*

☰ showy, flashy, pretentious, vulgar, loud, garish, gaudy, flamboyant, flash, conspicuous, extravagant

🖝 restrained

osteopath *noun* someone who treats injuries to bones, muscles *etc* by ma-

nipulating the patient's body, not by drugs or surgery ◇**osteopathy** *noun*

osteoporosis *noun* a disease which makes bones porous and brittle, caused by lack of calcium

ostler *noun*, *hist* someone who attends to horses at an inn

ostracize *verb* banish (someone) from the company of a group of people ◇**ostracism** *noun*

☰ exclude, banish, exile, expel, excommunicate, blacklist, blackball, reject, shun, snub, avoid, *informal* cold-shoulder

🖝 accept, welcome

Based on *ostrakon*, a piece of pottery used in ancient Greece to cast votes to decide if someone was to be exiled

ostrich *noun* (*plural* **ostriches**) a large African bird with showy plumage, which cannot fly but runs very fast ◇**ostrich-like** *adj* avoiding facing up to difficulties (after the ostrich's supposed habit of burying its head in the sand when chased)

other *adj* **1** the second of two: *where is the other sock?* **2** remaining, not previously mentioned: *these are for the other children* **3** different, additional: *there must be some other reason* **4** recently past: *the other day* ◇*pronoun* **1** the second of two **2** (**others**) those remaining, those not previously mentioned: *the others arrived the next day* **3** the previous one: *one after the other* ◇**every other** alternate, second: *see him every other day* ◇**other than** except: *no hope other than to retreat* ◇**someone or other** or **something or other** someone or something not named or specified: *there's always someone or other here*

otiose *adj*, *formal* superfluous, redundant

OTT *abbrev* over-the-top, extravagant

otter *noun* a type of river animal which eats fish

ottoman *noun* a low, cushioned seat without a back

ought *verb* **1** used with other verbs to

indicate duty or need: *we ought to set an example/I ought to practise more* **2** used to indicate what can be reasonably expected: *the weather ought to be fine*

ounce *noun* a unit of weight, one-sixteenth of a pound, 2.35 grams

our *adj* belonging to us: *our house*
◇ **ours** *pronoun* something belonging to us: *the green car is ours*

ourselves *pronoun* **1** used reflexively: *we exhausted ourselves swimming* **2** used for emphasis: *we ourselves don't like it, but other people may*

oust *verb* **1** drive out (from) **2** take the place of: *she ousted him as leader of the party*
■ **1** expel, eject, depose, displace, turn out, throw out, overthrow, evict, drive out, unseat, topple
▣ **1** install, settle

out *adv* **1** into or towards the open air: *go out for a walk* **2** from within: *take out a handkerchief* **3** not inside: *out of prison* **4** far from here: *out in the Far East* **5** not at home, not in the office *etc*: *she's out at the moment* **6** aloud: *shouted out* **7** to or at an end: *hear me out* **8** inaccurate: *the total was five pounds out* **9** *informal* on strike **10** published: *is the book out yet?* **11** no longer hidden: *the secret is out* **12** openly admitting to being homosexual **13** dismissed from a game of cricket, baseball *etc* **14** finished, having won at cards *etc* **15** no longer in power or office **16** determined: *out to win*
■ **5** away, absent, elsewhere, not at home, gone, outside **11** revealed, exposed, disclosed, public, evident, manifest

out-and-out *adj* complete, total, thorough

outback *noun* the wild interior parts of Australia

outbid *verb* (**outbids**, **outbidding**, **outbid**) offer a higher price than (someone else)

outboard *adj* on the outside of a ship or boat: *an outboard motor*

outbreak *noun* a beginning, a breaking out, *eg* of war or disease
■ eruption, outburst, explosion, flare-up,

rash, burst, epidemic

outbuilding *noun* a building that is separate from the main buildings

outburst *noun* a bursting out, *esp* of angry feelings
■ outbreak, eruption, explosion, flare-up, outpouring, burst, fit, gush, surge, storm, spasm, seizure

outcast *noun* someone driven away from friends and home

outcome *noun* result
■ result, consequence, upshot, conclusion, effect, end result

outcrop *noun* the part of a rock formation that can be seen at the surface of the ground

outcry *noun* (*plural* **outcries**) a widespread show of anger, disapproval *etc*
■ protest, complaint, protestation, objection, indignation, uproar, cry, exclamation, row, commotion, noise, outburst

outdo *verb* (**outdoes**, **outdoing**, **outdid**, **outdone**) do better than
■ surpass, exceed, beat, excel, outshine, overcome, outclass, outdistance

outdoor *adj* of or in the open air
◇ **outdoors** *adv* **1** outside the house **2** in or into the open air

outer *adj* nearer, at or on the edge, surface *etc*; further away

outermost *adj* nearest the edge; furthest away

outfit *noun* a set of clothes worn together, often for a special occasion *etc*
◇ **outfitter** *noun* a seller of outfits, *esp* men's clothes
■ clothes, costume, ensemble, *informal* get-up, *informal* togs, *formal* apparel

outgoings *noun plural* money spent or being spent

outgrow *verb* (**outgrows**, **outgrowing**, **outgrew**, **outgrown**) get too big or old for (clothes, toys *etc*)

outhouse *noun* a shed

outing *noun* a trip, excursion
■ excursion, expedition, jaunt, pleasure trip, trip, spin, picnic

outlandish *adj* looking or sounding very strange

▤ unconventional, unfamiliar, bizarre, strange, odd, weird, eccentric, alien, exotic, foreign, extraordinary

▧ familiar, ordinary

outlaw noun **1** someone put outside the protection of the law **2** a criminal, a robber or bandit ◇ verb **1** place beyond the protection of the law **2** ban, forbid

▤ noun **2** bandit, brigand, robber, desperado, highwayman, criminal, fugitive ◇ verb **2** ban, disallow, forbid, prohibit, exclude, bar, banish, condemn

outlay noun money paid out

outlet noun **1** a passage to the outside, eg for a water-pipe **2** a means of expressing or getting rid of (a feeling, energy etc) **3** a market for goods; a shop

▤ **1** exit, way out, vent, escape, opening, safety valve, channel **2** vent, escape, release **3** retailer, shop, store, market

▧ **1** entry, inlet

outline noun **1** the outer line of a figure in a drawing etc **2** a sketch showing only the main lines **3** a rough sketch **4** a brief description ◇ verb **1** draw an outline of **2** describe briefly

outlive verb live longer than

outlook noun **1** a view from a window etc **2** attitude **3** what is thought likely to happen: the weather outlook

▤ **2** view, viewpoint, point of view, attitude, perspective, frame of mind, mindset, opinion **3** expectations, future, forecast, prospect, prognosis

outlying adj far from the centre, distant

outnumber verb be greater in number than: their team outnumbered ours

out-of-date or **out of date** adj obsolete, no longer valid or fashionable: this voucher is out of date/an out-of-date ticket

out-patient noun a patient who does not stay in a hospital while receiving treatment (contrasted with: **in-patient**)

outpost noun **1** a military station in front of or far from the main army **2** an outlying settlement

output noun **1** the goods produced by a machine, factory etc; the amount of work done by a person **2** data produced by a computer program (contrasted with: **input**)

▤ **1** production, productivity, product, yield, manufacture

outrage noun **1** an act of great violence **2** an act which shocks or causes offence ◇ verb **1** insult, shock **2** injure, hurt by violence

▤ noun **2** atrocity, offence, injury, enormity, crime, violation, evil, scandal ◇ verb **1** affront, incense, enrage, madden, disgust, injure, offend, shock, scandalize

outrageous adj **1** highly offensive **2** not moderate, extravagant

▤ **1** atrocious, shocking, scandalous, offensive, disgraceful, monstrous, unspeakable, horrible **2** excessive, exorbitant, immoderate, unreasonable, extortionate, inordinate, preposterous

▧ **2** acceptable, reasonable

outré /'u:treɪ/ adj beyond what is normal, extravagant

outright adv completely; openly ◇ adj **1** complete, thorough: an outright lie **2** clear: the outright winner

▤ adv totally, absolutely, completely, utterly, thoroughly, openly, without restraint, straightforwardly, positively, directly, explicitly ◇ adj **1** total, utter, absolute, complete, downright, pure, thorough, direct, straightforward **2** definite, categorical

▧ adj **2** ambiguous, indefinite

outset noun start, beginning

outshine verb (**outshines, outshining, outshone**) **1** shine more brightly than **2** do better than

outside noun the outer surface or place: the outside of the box ◇ adj **1** in, on or of the outer surface or place: the outside seat **2** relating to leisure rather than your full-time job: outside interests **3** slight: an outside chance of winning ◇ adv **1** beyond the limits of: go outside **2** out-of-doors; in or into the open air: let's eat outside ◇ prep beyond the range of, not within ◇ **outsider** noun **1** someone not included in a particular social group **2** a runner *etc* whom no one expects to win ◇ **at the outside** at the most: *ten miles at the outside*

■ *noun* exterior, façade, front, surface, face, appearance, cover ◇ *adj* **1** exterior, outer, outdoor **3** remote, marginal, distant, faint, slight, slim, negligible ◇ **outsider** stranger, intruder, alien, foreigner, newcomer, visitor, intruder, misfit, odd man out

outsize *adj* of a very large size

outskirts *noun plural* the outer parts or borders of a city *etc*

outspoken *adj* bold and frank in speech

■ candid, frank, forthright, blunt, unreserved, plain-spoken, direct, explicit

☒ diplomatic, reserved

outstanding *adj* **1** excellent **2** of a debt: unpaid

■ **1** excellent, distinguished, exceptional, remarkable, superb, impressive, special, extraordinary, notable, noteworthy **2** owing, unpaid, due, unsettled, unresolved, uncollected, payable, remaining

☒ **1** ordinary, unexceptional **2** paid, settled

outstretched *adj* reaching out

out-tray *noun* an office tray for letters and work already dealt with (*contrasted with*: **in-tray**)

outvote *verb* defeat by a greater number of votes

outward *adj* **1** towards or on the outside **2** of a journey: away from home, not towards it ◇ **outwardly** or **outwards** *adv* on the outside, externally

■ **1** external, exterior, outer, outside, surface, superficial, visible, apparent

☒ **1** inner, private

outweigh *verb* be more important than: *the advantages outweigh the disadvantages*

outwit *verb* (**outwits**, **outwitting**, **outwitted**) defeat by cunning

■ outsmart, get the better of, trick, better, beat, dupe, cheat, deceive, defraud, swindle

outwith *prep*, *Scot* outside

ouzo /ˈuːzoʊ/ *noun* a Greek aniseed-flavoured liqueur

ova *plural* of **ovum**

oval *adj* having a flattened round shape like an egg ◇ *noun* an oval shape

ovary *noun* (*plural* **ovaries**) one of two organs in the female body in which eggs are formed

ovation *noun* an outburst of cheering, hand-clapping *etc*

oven *noun* an enclosed place for baking; a small furnace

over *prep* **1** higher than, above: *the number is over the door/we've lived here for over thirty years* **2** across: *going over the bridge* **3** on the other side of: *the house over the road* **4** on top of: *threw his coat over the body* **5** here and there on: *paper scattered over the carpet* **6** about: *they quarrelled over their money* **7** by means of: *over the telephone* **8** during, throughout: *over the years* **9** while doing, having *etc*: *fell asleep over his dinner* ◇ *adv* **1** above, higher up: *two birds flew over* **2** across a distance: *he walked over and spoke to her* **3** downwards: *did you fall over?* **4** above in number *etc*: *aged four and over* **5** as a remainder: *three left over* **6** through: *read the passage over* ◇ *adj* finished: *the sale is over* ◇ *noun*, *cricket* a fixed number of balls bowled from one end of the wicket ◇ **overly** *adv* too, excessively ◇ **over again** once more

■ *adv* **1** above, beyond, overhead, on high **5** extra, remaining, surplus, superfluous, left, unused, unwanted, in excess, in addition

over- *prefix* too much, to too great an extent: *overcook/over-excited*

overall *noun* **1** a garment worn over ordinary clothes to protect them against dirt **2** (**overalls**) hard-wearing trousers with a bib worn as work clothes ◇ *adj* **1** from one end to the other: *overall length* **2** including everything: *overall cost* ◇ *adv* altogether; as a whole

■ *adj* **1** total, general, complete **2** total, all-inclusive, comprehensive, inclusive, general, universal, global, broad, blanket, complete, all-over

■ *adj* 2 narrow, specific

overawe *verb* frighten or astonish into silence

overbalance *verb* lose your balance and fall

overbearing *adj* over-confident, domineering

■ imperious, domineering, arrogant, dictatorial, tyrannical, high-handed, haughty, *informal* bossy, oppressive

■ meek, unassertive

overboard *adv* out of a ship into the water: *man overboard*

overcast *adj* of the sky: cloudy

overcharge *verb* 1 charge too great a price 2 fill or load too heavily

overcoat *noun* an outdoor coat worn over all other clothes

overcome *verb* (**overcomes, overcoming, overcame, overcome**) get the better of, defeat ◇ *adj* helpless from exhaustion, emotion *etc*

■ *verb* conquer, defeat, beat, triumph over, vanquish, rise above, master, overpower, overwhelm, overthrow, subdue

overdo *verb* (**overdoes, overdoing, overdid, overdone**) 1 do too much 2 exaggerate: *they rather overdid the sympathy* 3 cook (food) too long

■ 1 carry to excess, *informal* go overboard, overwork 2 exaggerate, go too far, overstate

overdose *noun* too great an amount (of medicine, a drug *etc*) ◇ *verb* give or take too much medicine *etc*

overdraw *verb* (**overdraws, overdrawing, overdrew, overdrawn**) draw more money from the bank than you have in your account ◇ **overdraft** *noun* the amount of money overdrawn from a bank

overdue *adj* 1 later than the stated time: *the train is overdue* 2 of a bill *etc*: still unpaid although the time for payment has passed

■ 1 late, behind schedule, delayed, unpunctual, slow 2 late, owing

overflow *verb* 1 flow or spill over: *the river overflowed its banks/the crowd overflowed into the next room* 2 be so full as to flow over: *an overflowing bucket* ◇ *noun* 1 a running-over of liquid 2 a pipe or channel for getting rid of excess water *etc*

overgrown *adj* 1 covered with wild plant growth 2 grown too large

overhang *verb* jut out over

overhaul *verb* examine carefully and carry out repairs ◇ *noun* a thorough examination and repair

■ *verb* renovate, repair, service, recondition, mend, examine, inspect, check, survey, fix ◇ *noun* reconditioning, repair, renovation, check, service, examination, inspection, *informal* going-over

overhead *adv* directly above: *the aeroplane flew overhead* ◇ *adj* placed high above the ground: *overhead cables* ◇ **overheads** *noun plural* the general expenses of a business *etc*

overhear *verb* (**overhears, overhearing, overheard**) hear what you were not meant to hear

overjoyed *adj* filled with great joy

■ delighted, elated, euphoric, ecstatic, enraptured, thrilled, jubilant, *informal* over the moon

■ sad, disappointed

overland *adv* & *adj* on or by land, not sea

overlap *verb* (**overlaps, overlapping, overlapped**) 1 extend over and partly cover: *the two pieces of cloth overlapped* 2 cover a part of the same area or subject as another; partly coincide ◇ *noun* the amount by which something overlaps

overleaf *adj* on the other side of a leaf of a book

overload *verb* load or fill too much

overlook *verb* 1 look down on from a higher point; have or give a view of: *the house overlooked the village* 2 fail to see, miss 3 pardon, not punish: *minor offences will be overlooked*

■ 1 front on to, face, look on to, look over, command a view of 2 miss, disregard,

ignore, neglect, pass over **3** excuse, forgive, pardon, condone, turn a blind eye to, ignore, let pass, let ride
⊠ 2 notice **3** penalize

overlord *noun*, *hist* a lord with power over other lords

overmuch *adv* too much

overnight *adv* **1** during the night: *staying overnight with a friend* **2** in a very short time: *he changed completely overnight* ◇ *adj* **1** for the night: *an overnight bag* **2** got or made in a very short time: *an overnight success*

overpass *noun* a road going over above another road, a railway, canal *etc*

overpower *verb* defeat through greater strength; overwhelm
▤ overcome, conquer, overwhelm, vanquish, defeat, beat, subdue, overthrow, crush, immobilize, floor

overpowering *adj* **1** unable to be resisted **2** overwhelming, very strong: *overpowering smell*
▤ 2 overwhelming, powerful, strong, forceful, compelling, extreme, oppressive

overrate *verb* value more highly than is deserved: *his new film is overrated*
▤ overestimate, overvalue, overpraise, magnify, blow up, make too much of
⊠ underrate

overreach *verb*: **overreach yourself** try to do or get more than you can and so fail

override *verb* (**overrides**, **overriding**, **overrode**, **overridden**) ignore, set aside: *overriding the teacher's authority*

overrule *verb* go against or cancel an earlier judgement or request

overrun *verb* (**overruns**, **overrunning**, **overran**, **overrun**) **1** grow or spread over: *overrun with weeds* **2** take possession of (a country)
▤ 1 infest, overwhelm, inundate, swarm over, surge over, ravage, overgrow **2** invade, occupy, overwhelm

overseas *adj* & *adv* abroad; beyond the sea

oversee *verb* (**oversees**, **oversee-** **ing**, **oversaw**, **overseen**) watch over, supervise ◇ **overseer** *noun*

overshadow *verb* lessen the importance of by doing better than
▤ outshine, eclipse, excel, surpass, dominate, rise above, tower above

oversight *noun* something left out or forgotten by mistake or through failure to notice it
▤ omission, fault, error, slip-up, mistake, blunder, lapse, carelessness, neglect

overstep *verb* (**oversteps**, **overstepping**, **overstepped**) go further than (a set limit, rules *etc*)

overt *adj* not hidden or secret; openly done
▤ open, manifest, plain, evident, observable, obvious, apparent, public, professed, unconcealed
⊠ covert, secret

overtake *verb* (**overtakes**, **overtaking**, **overtook**, **overtaken**) catch up with and pass
▤ pass, catch up with, outdistance, outstrip, draw level with, pull ahead of

overthrow *verb* (**overthrows**, **overthrowing**, **overthrew**, **overthrown**) defeat or overturn (a government *etc*)
▤ depose, oust, bring down, topple, conquer, vanquish, beat, defeat, crush, overcome, overpower, overturn, overwhelm, subdue, master, abolish
⊠ install, protect, reinstate, restore

overtime *noun* **1** time spent working beyond the agreed normal hours **2** payment for this, usually at a higher rate

overtone *noun* an additional meaning or association, not directly stated
▤ suggestion, intimation, nuance, hint, undercurrent, insinuation, association, feeling, implication, sense

overture *noun* **1** a proposal intended to open discussions: *overtures of peace* **2** a piece of music played as an introduction to an opera

overturn *verb* **1** turn upside down **2** bring down or destroy (*eg* a government)

overweening *adj* **1** arrogant, extremely conceited **2** of pride: excessive

overwhelm verb **1** defeat completely **2** load with too great an amount: overwhelmed with work **3** overcome, make helpless: overwhelmed with grief ◇ **overwhelming** adj

■ **1** overpower, destroy, defeat, crush, rout, devastate **2** overrun, inundate, snow under, submerge, swamp, engulf **3** bowl over, stagger, floor

overwork verb work more than is good for you ◇ **overworked** adj

overwrought adj excessively nervous or excited, agitated

■ tense, agitated, keyed up, on edge, worked up, wound up, frantic, overcharged, overexcited, excited, informal hyper, beside oneself, informal uptight

◨ calm

ovum noun (plural **ova**) the egg from which a baby or young animal develops

owe verb **1** be in debt to: I owe Peter three pounds **2** have someone or something to thank for: he owes his success to his family ◇ **owing to** because of

owl noun a bird of prey which comes out at night ◇ **owlet** noun a young owl

own verb **1** have as a possession **2** (often with **up**) admit, confess to be true ◇ adj belonging to the person mentioned: is this all your own work? ◇ **hold your own** keep your place or position, not weaken ◇ **on your own 1** by your own efforts **2** alone: walking home on her own ◇ **own goal** a goal scored by mistake against your own side

■ verb **1** possess, have, hold, retain, keep **2** admit, confess ◇ adj personal, individual, private, particular, idiosyncratic

owner noun someone who possesses something ◇ **ownership** noun possession

ox noun (plural **oxen**) a male cow, usually castrated, used for drawing loads etc

Oxbridge noun Oxford and Cambridge Universities ◇ adj of or typical of Oxbridge

oxide noun a compound of oxygen and another element

oxidize verb **1** combine with oxygen **2** become rusty

oxygen noun a gas with no taste, colour or smell, forming part of the air and of water ◇ **oxygenate** verb

oyster noun a type of edible shellfish ◇ **oystercatcher** noun a black and white wading bird which eats limpets and mussels ◇ **oyster mushroom** an edible mushroom often found on dead wood

oz abbrev ounce(s)

ozone noun a form of oxygen ◇ **ozone layer** a layer of the upper atmosphere which protects the earth from the sun's ultraviolet rays

Pp

p *abbrev* **1** page **2** pence

PA *abbrev* **1** public address (system) **2** personal assistant

pa *abbrev* per annum

pace *noun* **1** a step **2** rate of walking, running *etc* ◇ *verb* **1** measure by steps **2** walk backwards and forwards

■ *noun* **1** motion, progress, rate, speed, velocity, celerity, quickness, rapidity, measure ◇ *verb* **1** mark out, measure **2** step, stride, walk, march, tramp, pound

pacemaker *noun* **1** someone who sets the pace in a race **2** a device used to correct weak or irregular heart rhythms

pachyderm *noun* a thick-skinned animal such as an elephant

pacify *verb* (**pacifies, pacifying, pacified**) **1** calm, soothe **2** make peaceful ◇ **pacifist** *noun* someone who is against war and works for peace

■ *verb* **1** appease, conciliate, placate, calm, compose, soothe, assuage, soften, tame, subdue

◳ *verb* **1** anger

pack *noun* **1** a bundle, *esp* one carried on the back **2** a set of playing-cards **3** a group of animals, *esp* dogs or wolves ◇ *verb* **1** place (clothes *etc*) in a case or trunk for a journey **2** press or crowd together closely ◇ **pack animal** an animal which carries loads on its back ◇ **pack in** cram in tightly

■ *noun* **1** bundle, burden, load, backpack, rucksack, haversack, knapsack **3** group, company, troop, herd, flock ◇ *verb* **2** charge, cram, stuff, crowd, throng, press

package *noun* a bundle, a parcel ◇ *verb* **1** put into a container **2** wrap ◇ **package holiday** or **package tour** a holiday or tour arranged by an organizer with all travel and accommodation included in the price

packet *noun* **1** a small parcel **2** a container made of paper, cardboard *etc* and its contents: *a packet of biscuits*

pack ice a mass of large pieces of floating ice driven together by wind, currents *etc*

packing *noun* **1** the act of putting things in cases, boxes *etc* **2** material for wrapping goods **3** something used to fill an empty space ◇ **packing case** a wooden box for transporting goods ◇ **send packing** send (someone) away forcefully

pact *noun* an agreement; a treaty, a contract

■ treaty, convention, covenant, bond, alliance, contract, deal, bargain, compact, agreement, arrangement, understanding

◳ disagreement, quarrel

pad *noun* **1** a soft cushion-like object to prevent jarring or rubbing *etc* **2** a bundle of sheets of blank paper fixed together **3** the paw of certain animals **4** a rocket-launching platform ◇ *verb* (**pads, padding, padded**) **1** stuff or protect with a soft material **2** (often with **out**) fill up with unnecessary material: *padded out her essay with lengthy quotations* **3** walk making a dull, soft, noise

■ *noun* **1** cushion, pillow, wad, buffer, padding, protection **2** writing-pad, note-pad, jotter, block ◇ *verb* **1** fill, stuff, wad, pack, wrap, line, cushion, protect **2** expand, inflate, fill out, flesh out

padding *noun* **1** stuffing material **2** words included in a speech, book *etc* just to fill space or time

■ **1** filling, stuffing, wadding, packing, protection **2** verbiage, verbosity, wordiness, *informal* waffle, hot air

paddle¹ *verb* wade in shallow water

paddle² *noun* a short, broad, spoon-shaped oar ◇ *verb* row with a paddle or paddles ◊ **paddle-steamer** noun a steamer driven by two large wheels made up of paddles

paddock noun a small closed-in field used for pasture

paddy field a muddy field in which rice is grown

padlock noun a removable lock with a hinged hook

paean /piən/ noun a song of praise or thanksgiving

paediatrics or US **pediatrics** noun sing the treatment of children's diseases ◊ **paediatrician** noun

paedophile or US **pedophile** noun someone who has sexual desire for children

pagan noun someone who does not believe in any religion; a heathen ◊ adj heathen ◊ **paganism** noun

page noun 1 a blank, written or printed sheet of paper 2 a section of information from a website or teletext service 3 a boy servant or messenger 4 a boy who attends the bride in a marriage service
■ noun 1 leaf, sheet, folio, side

pageant noun 1 a show or procession made up of scenes from history 2 an elaborate parade or display ◊ **pageantry** noun elaborate show or display
■ noun 1 play, scene, tableau 2 procession, parade, show, display, spectacle, extravaganza ◊ **pageantry** pomp, ceremony, grandeur, magnificence, splendour, glamour, glitter, spectacle, parade, display, show, extravagance, theatricality, drama, melodrama

pagoda noun an Eastern temple, esp in China or India

paid past form of **pay**

pail noun an open vessel of metal, plastic etc for carrying liquids; a bucket

pain noun 1 feeling caused by hurt to body or mind 2 threat of punishment: under pain of death 3 (pains) care: takes great pains with his work 4 informal a nuisance ◊ verb cause suffering to, distress ◊ **pained** adj showing pain or distress ◊ **painful** adj ◊ **painfully** adv

◊ **painless** adj ◊ **painlessly** adv
■ noun 1 hurt, ache, throb, cramp, spasm, twinge, pang, stab, sting, smart, soreness, tenderness, discomfort, distress, suffering, affliction, trouble, anguish, agony, torment, torture 4 nuisance, bother, informal bore, annoyance, burden ◊ verb hurt, afflict, torment, torture, agonize, distress, upset, sadden, grieve ◊ **pained** hurt, injured, wounded, stung, offended, aggrieved, distressed, upset
Fa verb please, delight, gratify

painkiller noun a drug or medicine taken to lessen pain

painstaking adj very careful ◊ **painstakingly** adv
■ careful, meticulous, scrupulous, thorough, conscientious, diligent, assiduous, industrious, hardworking, dedicated, devoted, persevering
Fa careless, negligent

paint noun a liquid substance used for colouring and applied with a brush, a spray etc ◊ verb 1 apply paint to 2 create a picture (of) with paint ◊ **painter** noun 1 someone whose trade is painting 2 an artist who works in paint 3 a rope used to fasten a boat ◊ **painting** noun 1 the act or art of creating pictures with paint 2 a painted picture

pair noun 1 two of the same kind 2 a set of two ◊ verb 1 join to form a pair 2 go in twos 3 mate
■ noun 1 twins, two of a kind 2 couple, twosome, partnership ◊ verb 1 match (up), twin, team, partner

pajamas another spelling of **pyjamas**

pakora noun an Indian dish of balls of chopped vegetables coated in batter and fried

pal noun, informal a friend

palace noun the house of a king, queen, archbishop or aristocrat

palaeography noun the study of historical styles of handwriting ◊ **palaeographer** noun ◊ **palaeographic** or **palaeographical** adj

palaeolithic or **paleolithic** adj relating to the early Stone Age when people used stone tools

palaeontology *noun* the study of fossils ◇ **palaeontological** *adj* ◇ **palaeontologist** *noun*

palatable *adj* **1** pleasant to the taste **2** acceptable, pleasing: *the truth is not always palatable*
■ **1** tasty, appetizing, eatable, edible **2** acceptable, satisfactory, pleasant, agreeable, enjoyable, attractive
☲ **1** unpalatable **2** unacceptable, unpleasant, disagreeable

palate *noun* **1** the roof of the mouth **2** taste

⚠ Do not confuse with: **palette** and **pallet**

palatial *adj* like a palace, magnificent

palaver *noun* an unnecessary fuss

pale¹ *noun* a wooden stake used in making a fence to enclose ground ◇ **paling** *noun* a row of wooden stakes forming a fence

pale² *adj* **1** light or whitish in complexion **2** not bright in colour ◇ *verb* make or turn pale
■ *adj* **1** pallid, livid, ashen, ashy, white, chalky, pasty, pasty-faced, waxen, waxy, wan, sallow, anaemic **2** light, pastel, faded, washed-out, bleached, colourless, insipid ◇ *verb* whiten, blanch, bleach, fade
☲ *adj* **1** ruddy **2** dark ◇ *verb* colour, blush

palette *noun* a board or plate on which an artist mixes paints

⚠ Do not confuse with: **pallet** and **palate**

palindrome *noun* a word or phrase that reads the same backwards as forwards, *eg* level

From Greek *palindromos*, meaning 'running back'

paling *see* **pale**

palisade *noun* a fence of pointed wooden stakes

pall /pɔːl/ *noun* **1** the cloth over a coffin at a funeral **2** a dark covering or cloud: *a pall of smoke* ◇ *verb* become dull or uninteresting ◇ **pallbearer** *noun* one of those carrying or walking beside the coffin at a funeral

pallet *noun* **1** a straw bed or mattress **2** a platform that can be lifted by a fork-lift truck for stacking goods

⚠ Do not confuse with: **palette** and **palate**

palliative *adj* making less severe or harsh ◇ *noun* something which lessens pain, *eg* a drug

pallid *adj* pale in the face

pallor *noun* unhealthy paleness of complexion

palm¹ *noun* a tall tree with broad fan-shaped leaves, which grows in hot countries

palm² *noun* the inner surface of the hand between the wrist and the base of the fingers ◇ **palm off** give with the intention of cheating: *that shopkeeper palmed off a foreign coin on me*
■ **palm off** foist, impose, fob off, off-load, unload, pass off

palmist *noun* someone who claims to tell fortunes by the lines and markings of the hand ◇ **palmistry** *noun* the telling of fortunes in this way

palpable *adj* **1** able to be touched or felt **2** easily noticed, obvious
■ **1** solid, substantial, material, touchable, tangible **2** apparent, clear, plain, obvious, evident, manifest, conspicuous, blatant, unmistakable

palpate *verb* examine by touch ◇ **palpation** *noun*

palpitate *verb* of the heart: beat rapidly, throb ◇ **palpitations** *noun plural* uncomfortable rapid beating of the heart
■ flutter, quiver, tremble, shiver, vibrate, beat, pulsate, pound, thump, throb

palsy *noun* a loss of power and feeling in the muscles ◇ **palsied** *adj*

paltry *adj* of little value: *a paltry sum*
■ meagre, mean, low, miserable, wretched, poor, sorry, small, slight, trifling, inconsiderable, negligible, trivial, minor, petty, unimportant, insignificant, worthless

☛ substantial, significant, valuable

pampas *noun plural* the vast treeless plains of South America

pamper *verb* spoil (a child *etc*) by giving too much attention *etc*

☐ cosset, coddle, mollycoddle, gratify, indulge, overindulge, spoil, pet, fondle

☒ neglect, ill-treat

pamphlet *noun* a small book or leaflet giving information, opinions *etc*: *a pamphlet about social security benefits* ◇ **pamphleteer** *noun* a writer of political pamphlets

☐ leaflet, brochure, booklet, folder, circular, handout, notice

pan¹ *noun* **1** a broad shallow pot used in cooking, a saucepan **2** a shallow dent in the ground: *a salt pan* **3** the bowl of a toilet ◇ **pan out 1** turn out (well or badly) **2** come to an end

pan² *verb* (**pans, panning, panned**) move a television or film camera so as to follow an object or give a wide view

panacea /panəˈsɪə/ *noun* a cure for all things

panache *noun* a sense of style, swagger

☐ flourish, flamboyance, style, flair, dash, spirit, enthusiasm, zest, energy, vigour, verve

pancake *noun* a thin cake of flour, eggs and milk, fried in a pan

panda *noun* **1** a large black-and-white bear-like animal found in Tibet *etc* **2** a raccoon-like animal found in the Himalayas ◇ **panda car** *Brit informal* a police patrol car

pandemic *adj* of a disease *etc*: occurring over a wide area and affecting a large number of people

pandemonium *noun* a state of confusion and uproar

☐ chaos, disorder, confusion, commotion, rumpus, turmoil, tumult, uproar, din, bedlam

☒ order, calm, peace

> The name of the capital of Hell in Milton's *Paradise Lost* (1667)

pander *noun* a pimp ◇ **pander to** indulge, easily comply with

☐ **pander to** humour, indulge, pamper, please, gratify, satisfy, fulfil, provide, cater to

> After *Pandarus*, who acts as a go-between in the story of Troilus and Cressida

Pandora's box something which causes unexpected havoc

> After the story of *Pandora*, who disobeyed the Greek gods and opened a box containing all the troubles of the world

p and p or **p & p** *abbrev* postage and packing

pane *noun* a sheet of glass

panegyric /panəˈdʒɪrɪk/ *noun* a speech highly praising someone, an achievement *etc*

panel *noun* **1** a flat rectangular piece of wood such as is set into a door or wall **2** a group of people chosen to judge a contest, take part in a television quiz *etc* ◇ **panelled** *adj*

pang *noun* a sudden sharp pain; a twinge

☐ pain, ache, twinge, stab, sting, prick, jab, stitch, gripe, spasm, agony, anguish, discomfort, distress

panic *noun* **1** a sudden and great fright or loss of nerve **2** fear that spreads from person to person ◇ *verb* (**panics, panicking, panicked**) **1** throw into panic **2** act wildly through fear

☐ *noun* **1** alarm, dismay, consternation, fear, horror, terror, *informal* flap **2** frenzy, hysteria ◇ *verb* **2** lose one's nerve, lose one's head, lose the place, go to pieces, *informal* flap, overreact

☒ *noun* **1** calmness, confidence

pannier *verb* **1** a basket slung on a horse's back **2** a light container attached to a bicycle *etc*

panoply *noun* (*plural* **panoplies**) **1** the ceremonial dress, equipment *etc* associated with a particular event: *the panoply of a military funeral* **2** *hist* a full suit of armour

panorama *noun* a wide view of a landscape, scene *etc*
◙ view, vista, prospect, scenery, landscape, scene, spectacle, perspective, overview, survey

pansy *noun* (*plural* **pansies**) a plant with flat, five-petalled flowers

pant *verb* **1** gasp for breath **2** say breathlessly **3** wish eagerly (for)

pantechnicon *noun* a large van for transporting furniture

pantheism *noun* **1** the belief that all things in the physical universe are part of God **2** belief in many gods ◊ **pantheist** *noun* a believer in pantheism ◊ **pantheistic** or **pantheistical** *adj*

panther *noun* **1** a large leopard **2** *US* a puma

panties *noun plural* women's or children's underpants

pantihose *noun plural*, *US* tights

pantomime *noun* a Christmas play, with songs, jokes *etc*, based on a popular fairy tale

pantry *noun* (*plural* **pantries**) a room for storing food

pants *noun plural* **1** underpants or knickers **2** *US* trousers

papa *noun*, *informal* father

papacy *noun* the position or power of the Pope ◊ **papal** *adj* of the Pope

paparazzo *noun* (*plural* **paparazzi**) a press photographer who hounds celebrities *etc*

papaya *noun* a green-skinned edible fruit from S America (*also called*: **pawpaw**)

paper *noun* **1** a material made from rags, wood *etc* used for writing or wrapping **2** a single sheet of this **3** a newspaper **4** an essay on a learned subject **5** a set of examination questions **6** (**papers**) documents proving someone's identity, nationality *etc* ◊ *verb* cover (*esp* walls) with paper
◙ *noun* **3** newspaper, daily, broadsheet, tabloid, *slang* rag, journal, organ, *slang* blatt **4** essay, composition, dissertation, thesis, article, report **6** docu-

ments, credentials, authorization, identification, certificate, deeds

paperback *noun* a book bound in a flexible paper cover

paperweight *noun* a heavy glass, metal *etc* object used to keep a pile of papers in place

papier-mâché /papɪeɪ ˈmaʃeɪ/ *noun* a substance consisting of paper pulp and glue, shaped into models, bowls *etc*

papoose *noun*, *old* a Native American baby

paprika *noun* a type of ground red pepper

papyrus *noun* (*plural* **papyri** or **papyruses**) **1** a reed used by the ancient Egyptians *etc* to make paper **2** paper made from these reeds

par *noun* **1** an accepted standard, value *etc* **2** *golf* the number of strokes a good golfer would take for a hole or course ◊ **below par 1** not up to standard **2** not feeling very well ◊ **on a par with** equal to or comparable with

parable *noun* a story (*eg* in the Bible) which teaches a moral lesson
◙ fable, allegory, lesson, moral tale, story

parabola *noun* **1** a curve **2** the intersection of a cone with a plane parallel to its side

paracetamol *noun* a pain-relieving drug

parachute *noun* an umbrella-shaped device made of light material and rope which supports someone or something dropping slowly to the ground from an aeroplane ◊ *verb* drop by parachute ◊ **parachutist** *noun* someone dropped by parachute from an aeroplane

parade *noun* **1** an orderly arrangement of troops for inspection or exercise **2** a procession of people, vehicles *etc* in celebration of some event ◊ *verb* **1** arrange (troops) in order **2** march in a procession **3** display in an obvious way
◙ *noun* **2** procession, cavalcade, motorcade, ceremony, spectacle, pageant, show, display, exhibition ◊ *verb* **3** show, display, exhibit, show off, vaunt, flaunt

paradigm *noun* an example showing a certain pattern

paradise *noun* **1** heaven **2** a place or state of great happiness

paradox *noun* (*plural* **paradoxes**) a saying which seems to contradict itself but which may be true ◇ **paradoxical** *adj* ◇ **paradoxically** *adv*

🔲 contradiction, inconsistency, incongruity, absurdity, oddity, anomaly, mystery, enigma, riddle, puzzle ◇ **paradoxical** self-contradictory, contradictory, conflicting, inconsistent, incongruous, absurd, illogical, improbable, impossible, mysterious, enigmatic, puzzling, baffling

paraffin *noun* an oil which burns and is used as a fuel (for heaters, lamps *etc*)

paragliding *noun* the sport of gliding, supported by a modified type of parachute

paragon *noun* a model of perfection or excellence: *a paragon of good manners*

🔲 ideal, exemplar, epitome, quintessence, model, pattern, archetype, prototype, standard, criterion

paragraph *noun* **1** a division of a piece of writing shown by beginning the first sentence on a new line **2** a short item in a newspaper

parakeet *noun* a type of small parrot

parallel *adj* **1** of lines: going in the same direction and never meeting, always remaining the same distance apart **2** similar or alike in some way: *parallel cases* ◇ *noun* **1** a parallel line **2** something comparable in some way with something else **3** a line to mark latitude, drawn across a map or round a globe at a set distance from the equator ◇ **parallel processing** *comput* the use of two or more processors at the same time to carry out a single task

🔲 *adj* **2** analogous, equivalent, corresponding, matching, like, similar, resembling ◇ *noun* **2** similarity, resemblance, likeness, correspondence, correlation, equivalence, analogy, comparison

🔁 *adj* **2** divergent, different

parallelogram *noun* a four-sided figure, the opposite sides of which are parallel and equal in length

paralyse or *US* **paralyze** *verb* **1** affect with paralysis **2** make helpless or ineffective **3** bring to a halt: *the strike paralysed the industry*

🔲 **1** cripple, lame, disable, incapacitate, immobilize, anaesthetize, numb **3** freeze, transfix, halt, stop

paralysis *noun* loss of the power to move and feel in part of the body

paralytic *adj* **1** suffering from paralysis **2** *informal* helplessly drunk ◇ *noun* a paralysed person

paramedic *noun* someone helping doctors and nurses, *eg* a member of an ambulance crew ◇ **paramedical** *adj*

parameter *noun* a boundary, a limiting factor

🔲 guideline, indication, criterion, specification, limitation, restriction, limit, boundary

❗ Do not confuse with: **perimeter**

paramilitary *adj* **1** on military lines and intended to supplement the military **2** organized illegally as a military force ◇ *noun* a member of a paramilitary force

paramount *adj* **1** above all others in rank or power **2** very greatest: *of paramount importance*

🔲 **1** supreme, principal, chief, primary, premier **2** supreme, highest, utmost, prime, primary

paramour *noun, old* a lover

paranoia *noun* **1** a form of mental disorder characterized by delusions of grandeur, persecution *etc* **2** intense, irrational fear or suspicion

paranormal *adj* beyond what is normal in nature; supernatural, occult

parapet *noun* a low wall on a bridge or balcony to prevent people falling over the side

paraphernalia *noun plural, used as singular* belongings; gear, equipment

🔲 equipment, gear, tackle, apparatus, accessories, trappings, bits and pieces, odds and ends, belongings, effects, stuff, things, baggage

> Originally a woman's property apart from her dowry, which remained her own after marriage

paraphrase *verb* express (a piece of writing) in other words ◊ *noun* an expression in different words

■ *verb* reword, rephrase, restate, interpret, render, translate ◊ *noun* rewording, rephrasing, version, interpretation, rendering, translation

paraplegia *noun* paralysis of the lower part of the body and legs ◊ **paraplegic** *adj* of paraplegia ◊ *noun* someone who suffers from paraplegia

parasite *noun* an animal, plant or person living on another without being any use in return ◊ **parasitic** *adj*

parasol *noun* a light umbrella used as a sunshade

paratroops *noun plural* soldiers carried by air to be dropped by parachute into enemy country ◊ **paratrooper** *noun*

parboil *verb* boil (food) slightly

parcel *noun* a wrapped and tied package ◊ *verb* (**parcels**, **parcelling**, **parcelled**) 1 (with **out**) divide into portions 2 (with **up**) wrap up as a package ◊ **part and parcel** an absolutely necessary part

■ *noun* package, packet, pack, box, carton ◊ *verb* divide, carve up, apportion, allocate, allot, share

parch *verb* 1 make hot and very dry 2 make thirsty ◊ **parched** *adj*

■ **parched** arid, waterless, dry, dried up, dehydrated, scorched, withered, shrivelled, *informal* thirsty, *informal* gasping

parchment *noun* 1 the dried skin of a goat or sheep used for writing on 2 paper resembling this

pardon *verb* 1 forgive 2 allow to go unpunished ◊ *noun* 1 forgiveness 2 the act of pardoning ◊ **pardonable** *adj* able to be forgiven

■ *verb* 1 forgive, condone, excuse 2 acquit, absolve, remit, let off, reprieve,

free, liberate, release ◊ *noun* 1 forgiveness, mercy, clemency 2 amnesty, acquittal, absolution ◊ **pardonable** forgivable, excusable, justifiable, warrantable, understandable, allowable, permissible

◪ *verb* 2 punish, discipline ◊ *noun* 1, 2 punishment, condemnation

pare *verb* 1 peel or cut off the edge or outer surface of 2 make smaller gradually ◊ **parings** *noun plural* small pieces cut away or peeled off

parent *noun* a father or mother ◊ **parentage** *noun* descent from parents or ancestors ◊ **parental** *adj* 1 of parents 2 with the manner or attitude of a parent

■ father, mother, progenitor, procreator, guardian

parenthesis *noun* (*plural* **parentheses**) 1 a word or group of words in a sentence forming an explanation or comment, often separated by brackets or dashes, *eg* he and his wife (*so he said*) were separated 2 (**parentheses**) brackets ◊ **parenthetical** *adj*

par excellence superior to all others of the kind

pariah *noun* someone driven out from a community or group; an outcast

> Originally a member of a low caste in southern India

parish *noun* (*plural* **parishes**) 1 a district with its own church and minister or priest 2 members of such a community ◊ **parishioner** *noun* a member of a parish

■ 1 district, church 2 parishioners, community, churchgoers, congregation, flock, fold

parity *noun* equality

park *noun* 1 a public place for walking, with grass and trees 2 an enclosed piece of land surrounding a country house ◊ *verb* stop and leave (a car *etc*) in a place for a time

■ *noun* 1 woodland, reserve, pleasure-ground 2 grounds, estate, parkland, gardens

parka *noun* a type of thick jacket with a hood

Parkinson's disease a disease causing trembling in the hands *etc* and rigid muscles

parley *verb* (**parleys, parleying, parleyed**) hold a conference, *esp* with an enemy ◇ *noun* (*plural* **parleys**) a meeting between enemies to settle terms of peace *etc*

parliament *noun* **1** the chief lawmaking council of a nation **2** *Brit* the House of Commons and the House of Lords ◇ **parliamentary** *adj*
∎ **parliamentary** governmental, senatorial, congressional, legislative, lawmaking

parlour *noun* **1** *old* a sitting-room in a house **2** a commercial premises used for a particular purpose: *a funeral parlour*

Parma ham an Italian smoked ham

Parmesan *noun* a hard Italian cheese, often grated over dishes

parochial *adj* **1** relating to a parish **2** interested only in local affairs; narrow-minded ◇ **parochially** *adv*
∎ **2** petty, small-minded, narrow-minded, inward-looking, blinkered, limited, restricted, confined
∎∎ **2** national, international

parody *noun* (*plural* **parodies**) an amusing imitation of someone's writing style, subject matter *etc* ◇ *verb* (**parodies, parodying, parodied**) make a parody of
∎ *noun* caricature, lampoon, satire, send-up, spoof, skit, mimicry, imitation, take-off, travesty, distortion, burlesque

parole *noun* the release of a prisoner before the end of a sentence on condition that they will have to return if they break the law ◇ *verb* release on parole

From French *parole* meaning 'word' because prisoners are released on their word of honour

paroxysm *noun* a fit of pain, rage, laughter *etc* ◇ **paroxysmal** *adj*
∎ fit, seizure, spasm, convulsion, attack, outbreak, outburst, explosion

parquet *noun* a floor covering of wooden blocks arranged in a pattern

parr *noun* a young salmon before it leaves a river for the sea

parricide *noun* **1** the murder of a parent or close relative **2** someone who commits such a crime

parrot *noun* a bird found in warm countries with a hooked bill and often brightly coloured feathers

parry *verb* (**parries, parrying, parried**) deflect, turn aside (a blow, question *etc*)
∎ ward off, fend off, repel, repulse, field, deflect, block, avert, avoid, evade, duck, dodge, sidestep, shun

parse *verb* name the parts of speech of (words in a sentence) and say how the words are connected with each other

parsimony *noun* great care in spending money, meanness ◇ **parsimonious** *adj*

parsley *noun* a bright green leafy herb, used in cookery

parsnip *noun* a plant with an edible yellowish root shaped like a carrot

parson *noun* a member of the clergy, *esp* one in charge of a parish ◇ **parsonage** *noun* a parson's house ◇ **parson's nose** the piece of flesh at the tail-end of a cooked chicken or other bird

part *noun* **1** a portion, a share **2** a piece forming part of a whole: *the various parts of a car engine* **3** a character taken by an actor in a play **4** a role in an action or event: *played a vital part in the campaign* **5** *music* the notes to be played or sung by a particular instrument or voice **6** (**parts**) talents: *a man of many parts* ◇ *verb* **1** divide **2** separate, send or go in different ways **3** put or keep apart ◇ **in good part** without being hurt or taking offence ◇ **part of speech** one of the grammatical groups into which words are divided, *eg* noun, verb, adjective, preposition ◇ **part-song** *noun* a song in which singers sing different parts in harmony ◇ **part with** let go, be separated from: *I didn't want to part with my old car* ◇ **take someone's part** support them in an argument *etc*

- ▣ *noun* **1** portion, share, helping, slice **2** component, constituent, element, factor, piece, bit, particle, fragment, scrap **3** role, character ◇ *verb* **1** split, divide, tear, break, dismantle, take apart **2** separate, break up, disunite, part company, disband, disperse, scatter, leave, depart, withdraw, go away
- ▣ *noun* **2** whole, totality

partake *verb* (**partakes**, **partaking**, **partook**, **partaken**): **partake of 1** eat or drink some of something **2** take a part in

parthenogenesis *noun* reproduction from an unfertilized egg

partial *adj* **1** in part only, not total or complete: *partial payment* **2** having a liking for (someone or something): *partial to cheese* ◇ **partially** *adv*
- ▣ **1** incomplete, limited, restricted, imperfect, fragmentary, unfinished

partiality *noun* **1** the favouring of one thing more than another, bias **2** a particular liking (for something)
- ▣ **1** inclination, preference, predisposition **2** liking, fondness, *formal* predilection

participant or **participator** *noun* someone who takes part in something
- ▣ entrant, contributor, member, party, co-operator, helper, worker

participate *verb* **1** take part (in) **2** have a share in ◇ **participation** *noun* ◇ **participatory** *adj*
- ▣ **1** take part, join in, contribute, engage, be involved, enter **2** share, partake

participle *noun* a form of a verb which can be used with other verbs to form tenses, *eg* 'he was *eating*' or 'she has *arrived*', as an adjective, *eg* '*stolen* jewels', or as a noun, *eg* '*running* makes me tired'

particle *noun* a very small piece: *a particle of sand*
- ▣ bit, piece, fragment, scrap, shred, sliver, speck, morsel, crumb, iota, atom, grain, drop

particoloured *adj* variegated

particular *adj* **1** relating to a single definite person, thing *etc* considered separately from others: *I want this particular colour* **2** special: *take particular care of the china* **3** fussy, difficult to please: *particular about her food* ◇ **particularly** *adv* especially ◇ **particulars** *noun plural* the facts or details about someone or something
- ▣ *adj* **1** specific, precise, exact, distinct **2** exceptional, thorough **3** fussy, discriminating, *informal* choosy, finicky, fastidious ◇ **particularly** especially, exceptionally, remarkably, notably, extraordinarily, unusually, uncommonly, surprisingly, specifically, explicitly, distinctly ◇ **particulars** details, specifics, points, features, items, facts, circumstances

parting *noun* **1** the act of separating or dividing **2** a place of separation **3** a going away (from each other), a leave-taking **4** a line dividing hair on the head brushed in opposite directions
- ▣ *noun* **1** divergence, separation, division, partition, rift, split, rupture, breaking **3** departure, going, leave-taking, farewell, goodbye, adieu

partisan *adj* giving strong support or loyalty to a particular cause, theory *etc*, often without considering other points of view ◇ *noun* someone with partisan views
- ▣ *adj* biased, prejudiced, partial, predisposed, discriminatory, one-sided, sectarian ◇ *noun* devotee, adherent, follower, backer, supporter
- ▣ *adj* impartial

partition *noun* **1** a division **2** something which divides, *eg* a wall between rooms ◇ *verb* **1** divide into parts **2** divide by making a wall *etc*
- ▣ *noun* **1** division, break-up, splitting, separation, parting, severance **2** divider, barrier, wall, panel, screen ◇ *verb* **1** share, divide, split up **2** separate, divide, subdivide, wall off, fence off, screen

partly *adv* not wholly or completely
- ▣ somewhat, to some extent, slightly, fractionally, moderately, relatively, in part, partially, incompletely
- ▣ completely, totally

partner *noun* **1** someone who shares the ownership of a business *etc* with another or others **2** one of a pair in games, dancing *etc* **3** a husband, wife or lover ◇ *verb* act as someone's partner ◇ **partnership** *noun*

▣ **1** associate, ally, confederate, colleague **3** companion, spouse, husband, wife

partridge *noun* a type of bird which is shot as game

parturient *adj* **1** relating to childbirth **2** giving or about to give birth

party *noun* (*plural* **parties**) **1** a gathering of guests: *birthday party/dinner party* **2** a group of people travelling together: *a party of tourists* **3** a number of people with the same plans or ideas: *a political party* **4** someone taking part in, or approving, an action: *one of the parties to the agreement* ◇ **party line 1** a shared telephone line **2** policy laid down by the leaders of a political party

▣ **1** celebration, festivity, social, *informal* do, *slang* knees-up, *slang* rave-up, get-together, gathering, reunion, function, reception **2** team, squad, crew, gang, band, group, company, detachment

parvenu *noun* (*plural* **parvenus**) an upstart, someone with newly acquired wealth or power

PASCAL *noun* a high-level computer programming language

pashmina *noun* a shawl made from the fleece of the **pashm**, an Indian goat

pass *verb* (**passes**, **passing**, **passed**) **1** go, move, travel *etc*: *he passed out of sight over the hill* **2** give, hand on: *pass the salt/stories passed from generation to generation* **3** go by: *I saw the bus pass our house* **4** overtake **5** put (a law) into force **6** be successful in an examination **7** be declared satisfactory, healthy or in good condition after an inspection **8** come to an end: *the feeling of dizziness soon passed* **9** spend (time): *passing a pleasant hour by the river* **10** make, utter (*eg* a remark) ◇ *noun* **1** a narrow passage over or through a range of mountains **2** a ticket or card allowing someone to go somewhere **3** success in an examination **4** a sexual

advance: *he made a pass at her sister* ◇ **pass off** present (a forgery *etc*) as genuine ◇ **pass on 1** go forward, proceed **2** hand on **3** die ◇ **pass out** faint ◇ **pass up** fail to take up (an opportunity)

▣ *verb* **2** give, hand, transfer, transmit **3** go past, go by **4** exceed, go beyond, outdo, outstrip, overtake, leave behind **5** enact, ratify, validate, adopt, authorize, sanction, approve **6** succeed, get through, qualify, graduate **8** go, disappear, vanish **9** spend, while away, fill, occupy ◇ *noun* **1** gorge, ravine, canyon, gap, passage **2** permit, passport, identification, ticket, licence, authorization, warrant, permission

passable *adj* **1** fairly good **2** of a river *etc*: able to be crossed ◇ **passably** *adv*

▣ **1** satisfactory, acceptable, allowable, tolerable, average, ordinary, unexceptional, moderate, fair, adequate, all right, *informal* OK, mediocre **2** clear, open, navigable

▣ **1** unacceptable **2** blocked, impassable

passage *noun* **1** the act of passing: *passage of time* **2** a journey in a ship **3** a corridor **4** a way through **5** a part of the text of a book ◇ **passageway** *noun* a passage, a way through

▣ **2** journey, voyage, trip, crossing **3** passageway, aisle, corridor, hall, hallway **4** thoroughfare, way, route, road, avenue, path, lane, alley **5** extract, excerpt, quotation, text, paragraph, section, piece, clause, verse

passé /ˈpæseɪ/ *adj* no longer used or done, out of date

passenger *noun* a traveller, not a driver or member of the crew, in a bus, train, ship, aeroplane *etc*

▣ traveller, voyager, commuter, rider, fare

passer-by *noun* (*plural* **passers-by**) someone who happens to pass by when something happens

passing *adj* **1** going by: *a passing car* **2** not lasting long: *passing interest* **3** casual: *passing remark* ◇ *noun* **1** the act of someone or something which passes **2** a going away, a coming to an end **3** death

■ *adj* **2** ephemeral, transient, short-lived, temporary, momentary, fleeting, brief, short, cursory

⊞ *adj* **2** lasting, permanent

passion *noun* strong feeling, *esp* anger or love ◊ **the Passion** the sufferings and death of Christ

■ feeling, emotion, love, adoration, infatuation, fondness, affection, lust, desire, craving, mania, obsession, craze, eagerness, keenness, avidity, zest, enthusiasm, ardour, fervour, warmth, heat, fire, spirit, intensity, anger, indignation, fury, rage, outburst

⊞ coolness, indifference, self-possession

passionate *adj* **1** easily moved to passion **2** full of passion ◊ **passionately** *adv*

■ **1** emotional, excitable, hot-headed, impetuous, impulsive, quick-tempered, irritable **2** ardent, fervent, eager, keen, avid, enthusiastic, fanatical, warm, hot, fiery, aroused, excited, impassioned, intense, strong, fierce, violent, stormy, tempestuous, wild, frenzied, affectionate, lustful, erotic, sexy, sensual, sultry

⊞ **1** phlegmatic, *informal* laid back

passionflower *noun* a tropical climbing plant with flowers thought to resemble a crown of thorns

passionfruit *noun* the edible, oblong fruit of the passionflower

passive *adj* **1** not active; making no resistance **2** acted upon, not acting ◊ **passively** *adv* ◊ **passiveness** or **passivity** *noun* ◊ **passive smoking** the involuntary inhaling of smoke from tobacco smoked by others

■ **1** indifferent, apathetic, lifeless, inert, inactive, non-participating **2** receptive, unassertive, submissive

⊞ **1** active, lively, responsive, involved

pass key a key which can open several locks

Passover *noun* a Jewish festival celebrating the exodus of the Israelites from Egypt

passport *noun* a card or booklet which gives someone's name and personal details, and which is needed to enter another country

password *noun* **1** a secret word which allows those who know it to pass **2** a word typed into a computer to allow access to restricted data

past *noun* **1** time gone by: *methods used in the past* **2** someone's previous life or career **3** *grammar* the tense used for time gone by, *eg* I *bought* a ticket ◊ *adj* **1** of an earlier time: *past kindnesses* **2** just over, recently ended: *the past year* **3** gone, finished: *the time for argument is past* ◊ *prep* **1** after: *it's past midday* **2** up to and beyond, further than: *go past the traffic lights* ◊ *adv* by: *she walked past*

■ *noun* **1** history, former times, olden days, antiquity **2** life, background, experience, track record ◊ *adj* **1** former, previous, preceding, late, recent **2, 3** over, ended, finished, completed, done

pasta *noun* **1** a dough used in making spaghetti, macaroni *etc* **2** the prepared shapes of this, *eg* spaghetti, lasagne

paste *noun* **1** a gluey liquid for sticking paper *etc* together **2** any soft, kneadable or spreadable mixture: *almond paste/salmon paste* **3** fine glass used to make imitation gems

■ *noun* **1** adhesive, glue, gum, mastic, putty, cement

pasteboard *noun* cardboard

pastel *adj* of a colour: soft, pale ◊ *noun* **1** a chalk-like crayon used for drawing **2** a drawing made with this

pasteurize *verb* heat food (*esp* milk) in order to kill harmful germs in it

Named after Louis *Pasteur*, the 19th-century French chemist who invented the process

pastiche /paˈstiːʃ/ *noun* a humorous imitation, a parody

pastille *noun* a small sweet, sometimes sucked as a medicine

pastime *noun* a hobby, a spare-time interest

■ hobby, activity, game, sport, recreation, play, fun, amusement, entertainment, diversion, distraction, relaxation

⊞ work, employment

pastor *noun* a member of the clergy

pastoral *adj* **1** relating to country life **2** of a pastor or clerical work
▪ **1** rural, country, rustic, bucolic, agricultural, agrarian **2** ecclesiastical, clerical, priestly, ministerial

pastrami *noun* a smoked, seasoned cut of beef

pastry *noun* (*plural* **pastries**) **1** a flour paste used to make the bases and crusts of pies, tarts *etc* **2** a small cake

pasture *noun* ground covered with grass on which cattle graze ◇ **pasturage** *noun* grazing land

pasty¹ /'peɪstɪ/ *adj* **1** like paste **2** pale
▪ **2** pale, pallid, wan, anaemic, pasty-faced, sickly, unhealthy
▪ **2** ruddy, healthy

pasty² /'pastɪ/ *noun* a pie containing meat and vegetables in a covering of pastry

pat *noun* **1** a light, quick blow or tap with the hand **2** a small lump of butter *etc* **3** a cake of animal dung ◇ *verb* (**pats, patting, patted**) strike gently, tap ◇ **off pat** memorized thoroughly, ready to be said when necessary
▪ *noun* **1** tap, dab, slap, touch, stroke, caress ◇ *verb* tap, dab, slap, touch, stroke, caress, fondle, pet

patch *verb* **1** mend (clothes) by putting a new piece of material over a hole **2** (with **up**) mend, *esp* hastily or clumsily **3** (with **up**) settle (a quarrel) ◇ *noun* (*plural* **patches**) **1** a piece of material sewn over a hole **2** a small piece of ground
▪ *verb* **1** mend, repair, fix, cover, reinforce ◇ *noun* **1** piece, bit, scrap **2** plot, lot

patchouli *noun* a perfume oil obtained from the dried branches of an Asian tree

patchwork *noun* fabric formed of small patches or pieces of material sewn together

patchy *adj* uneven, mixed in quality ◇ **patchily** *adv* ◇ **patchiness** *noun*
▪ uneven, irregular, inconsistent, variable, random, fitful, erratic, sketchy, spotty, blotchy
▪ even, uniform, regular, consistent

pate *noun*, *formal* the head: *a bald pate*

pâté /'pateɪ/ *noun* a paste made of finely minced meat, fish or vegetable, flavoured with herbs, spices *etc*

patella *noun* the knee-cap

patent *noun* an official written statement granting someone the sole right to make or sell something which they have invented ◇ *adj* **1** protected from copying by a patent **2** open, easily seen ◇ *verb* obtain a patent for ◇ **patently** *adv* openly, clearly: *patently obvious* ◇ **patent leather** leather with a very glossy surface
▪ *adj* **2** obvious, evident, conspicuous, manifest, clear, transparent, apparent, visible, open, overt, blatant, glaring
▪ *adj* **2** hidden, opaque

paterfamilias *noun* the male head of a family or household

paternal *adj* **1** of a father **2** like a father, fatherly **3** on the father's side of the family: *my paternal grandfather* ◇ **paternalism** *noun* excessive benevolence; overprotectiveness ◇ **paternalistic** *adj*

paternity *noun* the state or fact of being a father ◇ **paternity leave** leave of absence from work for a father after the birth of a child

path *noun* **1** a way made by people or animals walking on it, a track **2** the route to be taken by someone or a vehicle: *in the lorry's path* **3** a course of action, a way of life
▪ *noun* **1** footpath, trail, track, walk **2** route, course, direction, way, road, avenue

pathetic *adj* **1** causing pity **2** *informal* causing contempt; feeble, inadequate: *a pathetic attempt* ◇ **pathetically** *adv*
▪ **1** pitiable, poor, sorry, lamentable, miserable, sad, distressing, moving, touching, poignant, plaintive, heartbreaking **2** contemptible, derisory, deplorable, useless, worthless, inadequate, meagre, feeble, *informal* sad
▪ **1** cheerful **2** admirable, excellent, valuable

pathology *noun* the study of diseases ◇ **pathological** *adj* **1** relating to disease **2** *informal* compulsive, obsessive: *pathological liar* ◇ **pathologist** *noun* **1** a doctor who studies the causes and effects of disease **2** a doctor who makes post-mortem examinations

pathos /'peɪθɒs/ *noun* a quality that arouses pity: *the pathos of the situation made me weep*

pathway *noun* a path

patience *noun* **1** the ability or willingness to be patient **2** (*also called:* **solitaire**) a card game played by one person

patient *adj* suffering delay, discomfort *etc* without complaint or anger ◇ *noun* someone under the care of a doctor *etc* ◇ **patiently** *adv*

■ *adj* calm, composed, self-possessed, self-controlled, restrained, even-tempered, mild, lenient, understanding, forgiving, tolerant, accommodating, uncomplaining, submissive, resigned, philosophical, stoical, persistent, persevering

◪ *adj* impatient, restless, intolerant, exasperated

patina *noun* a film that forms on the surface of exposed metals *etc*

patio *noun* (*plural* **patios**) a paved open area attached to a house

patisserie *noun* a shop selling French pastries and cakes

patois /ˈpatwɑː/ *noun* (*plural* **patois**) a dialect of language spoken by the ordinary people of a certain area

patriarch *noun* **1** the male head of a family or tribe **2** the head of the Greek Orthodox Church ◇ **patriarchal** *adj* ◇ **patriarchy** *noun*

patrician *adj* aristocratic ◇ *noun* an aristocrat, *esp* in ancient Rome

patricide *noun* **1** the murder of your own father **2** someone who murders their own father ◇ **patricidal** *adj*

patrimony *noun* property handed down from a father or ancestors

patriot *noun* someone who loves and is loyal to their country ◇ **patriotic** *adj* ◇ **patriotically** *adv* ◇ **patriotism** *noun* love of and loyalty to your country

■ **patriotic** nationalistic, chauvinistic, jingoistic, loyal

patrol *verb* (**patrols**, **patrolling**, **patrolled**) keep guard or watch by moving regularly around an area *etc* ◇ *noun* **1** the act of keeping guard in this way **2** a person or people keeping watch **3** a small group of Scouts or Guides ◇ **patrol car** a police car used to patrol an area

■ *verb* police, guard, protect, defend, tour, inspect ◇ *noun* **1** watch, surveillance, policing, protection, defence **2** guard, sentry, sentinel, watchman

patron *noun* **1** someone who protects or supports (an artist, a form of art *etc*) **2** a customer of a shop *etc* ◇ **patron saint** a saint chosen as the protector of a country *etc*

■ **1** benefactor, philanthropist, sponsor, supporter, sympathizer, advocate, defender, protector, guardian, helper **2** customer, client, frequenter, regular, shopper, buyer, purchaser, subscriber

patronage *noun* the support given by a patron

■ custom, business, trade, sponsorship, backing, support

patronize *verb* **1** be a patron of: *patronize your local shops* **2** treat (someone) as an inferior, look down on: *don't patronize me* ◇ **patronizing** *adj*

■ **patronizing** condescending, stooping, overbearing, haughty, high-handed, superior, snobbish, supercilious, disdainful

◪ **patronizing** humble, lowly

patronymic *noun* a name derived from a father or male ancestor

patter[1] *verb* of rain, footsteps *etc*: make a quick tapping sound ◇ *noun* the sound of falling rain, of footsteps *etc*

■ *verb* tap, pat, pitter-patter, beat, pelt, scuttle, scurry ◇ *noun* pattering, tapping, pitter-patter, beating

patter[2] *noun* **1** chatter, rapid talk, *esp* that used by salesmen to encourage people to buy their goods **2** the jargon of a particular group

■ **1** chatter, gabble, jabber, line, pitch, *slang* spiel

pattern noun **1** an example suitable to be copied **2** a model or guide for making something **3** a decorative design **4** a sample, eg of fabric ◇ **patterned** adj having a decorative design

▣ **1** original, prototype, standard **2** template, stencil, guide **3** decoration, ornamentation, ornament, figure, motif, design, style ◇ **patterned** decorated, ornamented, figured, printed

▣ **patterned** plain

patty noun (plural **patties**) a small flat cake of chopped meat etc

paucity noun smallness of number or quantity

paunch noun (plural **paunches**) a fat stomach

pauper noun a very poor person

pause noun **1** a short stop, an interval **2** a break or hesitation in speaking or writing **3** music a symbol (⌒) showing the holding of a note or rest ◇ verb stop for a short time

▣ **1** interval, interlude, intermission, halt, stoppage, interruption, break, rest, informal breather, respite **2** delay, hesitation, break, interruption

pave verb lay (a street etc) with stone or concrete to form a level surface for walking on ◇ **pave the way for** prepare or make the way easy for

pavement noun a paved footway at the side of a road for pedestrians

pavilion noun **1** a building in a sports ground with facilities for changing clothes **2** a large ornamental building **3** a large tent

paw noun the foot of an animal ◇ verb **1** of an animal: scrape with the front feet **2** handle or touch roughly or rudely **3** strike out wildly with the hand: paw the air

▣ verb **2** maul, manhandle, mishandle, molest

pawn verb put (an article of some value) in someone's keeping in exchange for a sum of money which, when repaid, buys back the article ◇ noun **1** chess a small piece of the lowest rank **2** someone who lets themselves be used by another for some purpose

◇ **in pawn** having been pawned

▣ verb deposit, pledge, stake, mortgage ◇ noun **2** dupe, puppet, tool, instrument, toy, plaything

pawnbroker noun someone who lends money in exchange for pawned articles

pawnshop noun a pawnbroker's place of business

pawpaw another word for **papaya**

pay verb (**pays, paying, paid**) **1** give (money) in exchange for goods, services etc: I paid £30 for it **2** suffer the punishment (for) **3** be advantageous or profitable: it pays to be prepared **4** give (eg attention) ◇ noun money given or received for work; wages ◇ **pay off 1** pay in full and discharge (workers) owing to lack of work **2** have good results: his hard work paid off ◇ **pay out 1** spend **2** give out (a length of rope etc)

▣ verb **1** remit, settle, discharge, reward, remunerate, pay out **3** pay off, bring in, yield, return ◇ noun wages, salary, earnings, income, fee, payment, reward, compensation, reimbursement ◇ **pay off 1** discharge, settle, square, clear **2** succeed, work

payable adj requiring to be paid

▣ owed, owing, unpaid, outstanding, in arrears, due

pay-as-you-earn adj of income tax: deducted from a salary before it is given to the worker

PAYE abbrev pay as you earn

payee noun someone to whom money is paid

payment noun **1** the act of paying **2** money paid for goods etc

▣ **1** settlement, discharge **2** premium, outlay, advance, deposit, instalment, contribution, allowance, reward, remuneration, pay, fee, fare

payphone noun a coin- or card-operated public telephone

payroll noun a list of workers entitled to receive pay

PC abbrev **1** police constable **2** privy councillor **3** political correctness **4** personal computer

pc *abbrev* **1** postcard **2** per cent

PE *abbrev* physical education

pea *noun* **1** a climbing plant which produces round green seeds in pods **2** the seed itself, eaten as a vegetable ◇ **peashooter** *noun* a small toy weapon consisting of a tube for blowing peas through

peace *noun* **1** quietness, calm **2** freedom from war or disturbance **3** a treaty bringing this about

▤ **1** silence, quiet, hush, stillness, rest, relaxation, tranquillity, calm, calmness, composure, contentment

▥ **1** noise, disturbance

peaceable *adj* of a quiet nature, fond of peace

peaceful *adj* **1** quiet; calm **2** free from war or aggression ◇ **peacefully** *adv*

▤ **1** quiet, still, restful, relaxing, tranquil, serene, calm, placid, unruffled, undisturbed **2** friendly, amicable, peaceable, pacific, non-violent

▥ **1** noisy, disturbed, troubled **2** violent

peace offering something offered to bring about peace

peach *noun* (*plural* **peaches**) **1** a juicy, velvet-skinned fruit **2** the tree that bears it **3** an orange-pink colour

peacock *noun* a large bird, the male of which has brightly coloured, patterned tail feathers

peahen *noun* a female peacock

peak *noun* **1** the pointed top of a mountain or hill **2** the highest point **3** the jutting-out part of the brim of a cap ◇ *verb* **1** rise to a peak **2** reach the highest point: *prices peaked in July and then fell steadily* ◇ **peaked** *adj* **1** pointed **2** of a cap: having a peak

▤ *noun* **1** top, summit, pinnacle, crest, crown **2** height, maximum, climax, culmination, apex, tip, point ◇ *verb* **2** climax, culminate, come to a head

▥ *noun* **2** nadir, trough

peaky *adj* looking pale and unhealthy

peal *noun* **1** a set of bells tuned to each other **2** the changes rung on such bells **3** a succession of loud sounds: *peals of laughter* ◇ *verb* sound loudly

▤ *noun* **2** chime, carillon, toll, knell, ring, clang, ringing

! Do not confuse with: **peel**

peanut *noun* **1** a type of nut similar to a pea in shape (*also called* **groundnut**, **monkey nut**) ◇ **peanut butter** a paste of ground roasted peanuts, spread on bread *etc*

pear *noun* **1** a fruit which narrows towards the stem and bulges at the end **2** the tree that bears it ◇ **pear-shaped** *adj* ◇ **go pear-shaped** go wrong

pearl *noun* **1** a gem formed in the shell of the oyster and several other shellfish **2** a valuable remark *etc*: *pearls of wisdom* ◇ **pearly gates** the entrance to heaven

peasant *noun* someone who works and lives on the land, *esp* in an underdeveloped area

pease pudding a dish of boiled, mashed peas

peat *noun* turf cut out of boggy places, dried and used as fuel

pebble *noun* a small, roundish stone ◇ **pebbly** *adj* **1** full of pebbles **2** rough, knobbly ◇ **pebbledash** *noun* a coating for outside walls with small stones set into the mortar

pecan *noun* **1** an oblong, thin-shelled nut common in N America **2** the tree bearing this nut

peccadillo *noun* (*plural* **peccadilloes** or **peccadillos**) a slight misdemeanour or wrong

peck *verb* **1** strike with the beak **2** pick up with the beak **3** eat little, nibble (at) **4** kiss quickly and briefly ◇ *noun* **1** a sharp blow with the beak **2** a brief kiss ◇ **peckish** *adj* slightly hungry

pectoral *adj* of the breast or chest: *pectoral muscles*

peculiar *adj* **1** belonging to one person, place or thing only: *a custom peculiar to England* **2** strange, odd: *he is a very peculiar person* ◇ **peculiarly** *adv*

▤ **1** characteristic, distinctive, specific, particular, special, individual, unique, singular **2** strange, odd, curious, funny, weird, bizarre, extraordinary, unusual, abnormal, exceptional, unconventional, eccentric, *slang* way-out, left-field

☒ **1** general **2** ordinary, normal

peculiarity *noun* (*plural* **peculiarities**) that which marks someone or something off from others in some way; something odd

▭ oddity, abnormality, exception, eccentricity, quirk, mannerism, feature, trait, mark, quality, attribute, characteristic, distinctiveness, particularity

pecuniary *adj* of money

pedagogue *noun* a teacher ◇ **pedagogic** or **pedagogical** *adj* of a teacher or of education

pedal *noun* a lever worked by the foot on a bicycle, piano, harp *etc* ◇ *verb* (**pedals**, **pedalling**, **pedalled**) **1** work the pedals of **2** ride on a bicycle

pedant *noun* **1** someone who makes a great show of their knowledge **2** someone overly fussy about minor details ◇ **pedantic** *adj* ◇ **pedantry** *noun* **1** fussiness about unimportant details **2** a display of knowledge

▭ **pedantic** stilted, fussy, particular, precise, exact, hair-splitting, nit-picking

☒ **pedantic** imprecise, informal, casual

peddle *verb* travel from door to door selling goods

pedestal *noun* the foot or support of a pillar, statue *etc*

▭ plinth, stand, support, mounting, foot, base, foundation, platform, podium

pedestrian *adj* **1** going on foot **2** for those on foot **3** unexciting, dull: *a pedestrian account* ◇ *noun* someone who goes on foot ◇ **pedestrian crossing** a place where pedestrians may cross the road when the traffic stops ◇ **pedestrian precinct** a shopping street from which traffic is excluded

pediatrics, pediatrician *US spelling* of **paediatrics, paediatrician**

pedicure *noun* a treatment for the feet including treating corns, cutting nails *etc* ◇ **pedicurist** *noun* someone who gives a pedicure

pedigree *noun* **1** a list of someone's

ancestors **2** the ancestry of a pure-bred animal **3** a distinguished descent or ancestry ◇ *adj* of an animal: pure-bred, from a long line of ancestors of the same breed

▭ **1** genealogy, family tree, lineage, ancestry, descent, line, family, parentage

> Literally 'crane's foot', because the forked feet of the bird were thought to resemble the lines of a family tree

pediment *noun* a triangular structure over the front of an ancient Greek building

pedlar *noun* someone who peddles, a hawker

pedometer *noun* an instrument for measuring the distance covered by a walker

pee *verb* (**pees**, **peeing**, **peed**) *informal* urinate ◇ *noun* **1** the act of urinating **2** urine

peek *verb* peep, glance *esp* secretively ◇ *noun* a secret look

peel *verb* **1** strip off the outer covering or skin of: *peel an apple* **2** of skin, paint *etc*: come off in small pieces **3** lose skin in small flakes, *eg* as a result of sunburn ◇ *noun* the skin or rind of vegetables or fruit

▭ *verb* **1** pare, skin, strip **2** scale, flake (off) ◇ *noun* skin, rind, zest, peeling

> ⚠ Do not confuse with: **peal**

peep *verb* **1** look through a narrow opening, round a corner *etc* **2** look slyly or quickly (at) **3** begin to appear: *the sun peeped out* **4** make a high, small sound ◇ *noun* **1** a quick look, a glimpse, often from hiding **2** a high, small sound ◇ **peeping Tom** someone who spies secretly on others, a voyeur

▭ *verb* **1**, **2** look, peek, glimpse, spy, squint, peer ◇ *noun* **1** look, peek, glimpse, glance, squint

peer ¹ *verb* look at with half-closed eyes, as if with difficulty

▭ look, gaze, scan, examine, inspect, peep, squint

peer ² *noun* **1** someone's equal in rank,

merit or age **2** a nobleman of the rank of baron upwards **3** a member of the House of Lords ◊ **peerage** *noun* **1** a peer's title **2** the peers as a group

◼ *noun* **1** equal, counterpart, equivalent, match, fellow **2** aristocrat, noble, nobleman, lord, duke, marquess, marquis, earl, count, viscount, baron

peerless *adj* without any equal, better than all others

peeve *verb, informal* irritate ◊ **peeved** *adj* annoyed

peevish *adj* cross, bad-tempered, irritable

◼ petulant, touchy, irritable, cross, grumpy, *informal* ratty, ill-tempered, crabbed, cantankerous, crusty, snappy, short-tempered, surly, sullen, sulky

◪ good-tempered

peewit *noun* the lapwing

peg *noun* **1** a pin or stake of wood, metal *etc* used for fastening, marking *etc* **2** a hook fixed to a wall for hanging clothes *etc* ◊ *verb* (**pegs**, **pegging**, **pegged**) **1** fasten with a peg **2** fix (prices *etc*) at a certain level

◼ *verb* **1** fasten, secure, fix, attach, join **2** control, stabilize, limit, freeze, fix, set

peignoir /'peɪnwɑ:(r)/ *noun* a woman's light dressing-gown

pejorative *adj* showing disapproval, scorn *etc*: *a pejorative remark* ◊ **pejoratively** *adv*

◼ derogatory, disparaging, belittling, slighting, unflattering, uncomplimentary, unpleasant, bad, negative

◪ complimentary

Pekinese or **Pekingese** *noun* a breed of small dog with a long coat and flat face

pelican *noun* a large waterbird with a pouched bill for storing fish

pelican crossing a street-crossing with traffic lights operated by pedestrians

Taken from the phrase '*pe*destrian *li*ght *con*trolled crossing'

pellagra *noun* a disease marked by shrivelled skin and paralysis caused by the lack of certain vitamins

pellet *noun* **1** a small ball of shot *etc* **2** a small pill

pell-mell *adv* in great confusion; headlong

pellucid *adj* clear, transparent

pelmet *noun* a strip or band hiding a curtain rail

pelota *noun* a Basque ball game played against a marked wall with a basket-like racket strapped to the players' wrists

peloton *noun* the leading group of cyclists in a race

pelt¹ *noun* the untreated skin of an animal

pelt² *verb* **1** throw things at: *they pelted us with stones* **2** run fast **3** of rain: fall heavily ◊ **at full pelt** at top speed

◼ *verb* **1** throw, hurl, bombard, shower, assail, batter, beat, hit, strike **2** rush, hurry, charge, *informal* belt, tear, dash, speed, career **3** pour, teem, *informal* rain cats and dogs

pelvis *noun* the frame of bone which circles the body below the waist

pen¹ *noun* an instrument for writing in ink ◊ *verb* (**pens**, **penning**, **penned**) write (*eg* a letter)

◼ *verb* write, compose, draft, scribble, jot down

pen² *noun* a small enclosure for sheep, cattle *etc* ◊ *verb* (**pens**, **penning**, **penned**) enclose in a pen

◼ *noun* enclosure, fold, stall, sty, coop, cage, hutch ◊ *verb* enclose, fence, hedge, hem in, confine, cage, coop, shut up

pen³ *noun* a female swan

penal *adj* of or as punishment ◊ **penal servitude** imprisonment with hard labour as an added punishment

penalize *verb* **1** punish **2** put under a disadvantage

◼ **1** punish, discipline, correct, fine **2** handicap

◪ **1** reward

penalty *noun* (*plural* **penalties**) **1** punishment **2** a disadvantage put on a player or team which breaks a rule of a game

🔲 **1** punishment, retribution, fine **2** forfeit, handicap, disadvantage

penance *noun* punishment willingly suffered by someone to make up for a wrong

pence *plural* of **penny**

penchant /'pãʃã/ *noun* an inclination (for), a liking or tendency

pencil *noun* an instrument containing a length of graphite or other substance for writing, drawing *etc* ◇ *verb* (**pencils**, **pencilling**, **pencilled**) draw, mark *etc* with a pencil

pendant *noun* **1** an ornament hung from a necklace *etc* **2** a necklace with such an ornament

pendent *adj* hanging

pending *adj* awaiting a decision or attention: *this matter is pending* ◇ *prep* awaiting, until the coming of: *pending confirmation*

🔲 *adj* impending, in the offing, forthcoming, imminent, undecided, in the balance

🔲 *adj* finished, settled

pendulous *adj* hanging down, drooping ◇ **pendulosity** *noun*

pendulum *noun* a swinging weight which drives the mechanism of a clock

penetrate *verb* **1** pierce or pass into or through **2** enter, *esp* with difficulty or by force ◇ **penetrating** *adj* **1** of a sound: piercing **2** keen, probing: *penetrating questions* ◇ **penetration** *noun*

🔲 **1** pierce, stab, prick, jab, puncture, probe, sink, bore, enter ◇ **penetrating 1** piercing, shrill **2** sharp, keen, acute, shrewd, discerning, perceptive, observant, profound, deep, searching, probing

pen-friend *noun* someone you have never seen (*usu* living abroad) with whom you exchange letters

penguin *noun* a large sea bird of Antarctic regions, which cannot fly

penicillin *noun* a medicine obtained from mould, which kills many bacteria

penile *adj* of or for the penis

peninsula *noun* a piece of land almost surrounded by water ◇ **peninsular** *adj*

penis *noun* the part of the body of a male human or animal used in sexual intercourse and for urinating

penitent *adj* sorry for your sins ◇ *noun* a penitent person ◇ **penitential** *adj* ◇ **penitentiary** *noun*, *US* a prison

🔲 *adj* repentant, contrite, sorry, apologetic, remorseful, regretful, conscience-stricken, shamefaced, humble

🔲 *adj* unrepentant, hard-hearted, callous

penknife *noun* a pocket knife with folding blades

pen-name *noun* a name adopted by a writer instead of their own name

pennant *noun* a long flag coming to a point at the end

pennate *adj* wing-shaped

penniless *adj* having no money

🔲 poor, poverty-stricken, impoverished, destitute, bankrupt, ruined, bust, *informal* broke, *slang* stony-broke, *slang* skint

🔲 rich, wealthy, affluent

penny *noun* **1** a coin worth $\frac{1}{100}$ of £1 **2** (*plural* **pence**) used to show an amount in pennies: *the newspaper costs forty-two pence* **3** (*plural* **pennies**) used for a number of coins: *the coffee machine doesn't take pennies*

penny-farthing *noun* a old type of bicycle with a large front wheel and small rear wheel

penny-pinching *adj* mean, stingy

pension *noun* a sum of money paid regularly to a retired person, a widow, someone wounded in war *etc* ◇ **pensionable** *adj* having or giving the right to a pension: *of pensionable age* ◇ **pensioner** *noun* someone who receives a pension, *esp* an old age pension ◇ **pension off** dismiss or allow to retire with a pension

pensive *adj* thoughtful ◇ **pensively** *adv* ◇ **pensiveness** *noun*

🔲 thoughtful, reflective, contemplative, meditative, absorbed, preoccupied, absent-minded, wistful, solemn, serious, sober

🔲 carefree

pent or **pent-up** adj **1** of emotions: not freely expressed **2** shut up, not allowed to go free

◻ **1** repressed, inhibited, restrained, bottled-up, suppressed, stifled

pentagon noun a five-sided figure ◇**pentagonal** adj ◇**the Pentagon** the headquarters of the US armed forces in Washington, DC

pentathlon noun a five-event contest in the Olympic Games etc ◇**pentathlete** noun an athlete who takes part in this event

pentatonic adj, music of a scale: consisting of five notes, ie a major scale omitting the fourth and seventh

Pentecost noun **1** a Jewish festival held fifty days after Passover **2** a Christian festival held seven weeks after Easter

penthouse noun a luxurious flat at the top of a building

penultimate adj last but one

penumbra noun a light shadow surrounding the main shadow of an eclipse

penury noun poverty, want ◇**penurious** adj impoverished, penniless

peony noun (plural **peonies**) a type of garden plant with large red, white or pink flowers

people noun plural **1** the men, women and children of a country or nation **2** persons generally ◇verb **1** fill with people **2** inhabit, make up the population of

◻ noun **1** population, inhabitants, citizens, community, society, race, nation **2** persons, individuals, humans, human beings, mankind, humanity, folk, public, general public, populace, rank and file ◇verb **2** populate, inhabit, occupy, settle, colonize

PEP abbrev personal equity plan

pep noun, informal spirit, verve ◇**pep pill** a pill containing a stimulating drug ◇**pep talk** a talk meant to encourage or arouse enthusiasm ◇**pep up** invigorate, enliven

◻ energy, vigour, verve, spirit, vitality, liveliness, informal get-up-and-go, exuberance, high spirits ◇**pep up** invigorate, vitalize, liven up, quicken, stimulate, excite, exhilarate, inspire

◻ **pep up** tone down

pepper noun **1** a plant whose berries are dried, powdered and used as seasoning **2** the spicy powder so produced **3** a hot-tasting hollow fruit containing many seeds, eaten raw or cooked ◇verb **1** sprinkle with pepper **2** (with **with**) throw at or hit: peppered with bullets ◇**pepper mill** a small device for grinding peppercorns over food

pepper-and-salt adj mixed black and white: pepper-and-salt hair

peppercorn noun the dried berry of the pepper plant

peppermint noun **1** a type of plant with a powerful taste and smell **2** a flavouring taken from this and used in sweets etc

pepperoni noun a spicy beef and pork sausage

peppery adj **1** containing much pepper **2** inclined to be hot-tempered

peptic adj of the digestive system: peptic ulcer

per prep **1** in, out of: five parts per thousand **2** for each: £2 per dozen **3** in each: six times per week ◇**per annum** in each year ◇**per capita** or **per head** for each person ◇**per cent** in or for every hundred: two-fifths of the population, or forty per cent

peradventure adv, old by chance

perambulator noun, formal a pram

perceive verb **1** become aware of through the senses **2** see **3** understand

◻ **1** sense, feel, be aware of **2** see, discern, make out, detect, spot, catch sight of, notice, observe, view, distinguish, recognize **3** know, grasp, understand, gather, deduce, appreciate, conclude

percentage noun the rate per hundred

perceptible adj able to be seen or understood

◻ perceivable, discernible, detectable, appreciable, distinguishable, observable, noticeable, obvious, evident, conspicuous, clear, plain, apparent, visible

▣ imperceptible, inconspicuous

perception *noun* the ability to perceive; understanding

▤ sense, feeling, impression, idea, conception, apprehension, awareness, consciousness, observation, recognition, grasp, understanding, insight, discernment

perceptive *adj* able or quick to perceive or understand ◊ **perceptively** *adv*

▤ discerning, observant, sensitive, responsive, aware, alert, quick, sharp, astute, shrewd

▣ unobservant

perch[1] *noun* (*plural* **perches**) **1** a rod on which birds sit or roost **2** a high seat or position ◊ *verb* sit, roost

▤ *verb* land, alight, settle, sit, roost, balance, rest

perch[2] *noun* (*plural* **perches**) a type of freshwater fish

perchance *adv, old* by chance; perhaps

percolate *verb* **1** of a liquid: drip or drain through small holes **2** cause (a liquid) to do this **3** of news *etc*: pass slowly down or through ◊ **percolator** *noun* a device for percolating: *a coffee percolator*

percussion *noun* **1** a striking of one object against another **2** musical instruments played by striking, *eg* drums, cymbals *etc* ◊ **percussionist** *noun* a musician who plays percussion ◊ **percussive** *adj* making the noise of percussion; loud, striking

perdition *noun* **1** utter loss or ruin **2** everlasting punishment

peregrinations *noun plural* wanderings

peregrine *noun* a type of falcon used in hawking

peremptory *adj* **1** urgent **2** of a command: to be obeyed at once **3** domineering, dictatorial

▤ **3** imperious, commanding, dictatorial, authoritative, assertive, high-handed,

overbearing, domineering, *informal* bossy, abrupt

perennial *adj* **1** of a plant: growing from year to year without replanting **2** everlasting, perpetual **3** lasting through the year ◊ *noun* a perennial plant

▤ *adj* **2** lasting, enduring, everlasting, eternal, immortal, undying, imperishable, unceasing, incessant, never-ending, constant, continual, perpetual, persistent

perestroika *noun* reconstruction, restructuring of the state (originally in the former Soviet Union)

perfect *adj* **1** complete, finished **2** faultless **3** exact ◊ *verb* **1** make perfect **2** finish

▤ *adj* **2** faultless, impeccable, flawless, immaculate, spotless, blameless, pure, superb, excellent, matchless, incomparable **3** exact, precise, accurate, right, correct, true ◊ *verb* **1** polish, refine **2** complete, finish

▣ *adj* **2** imperfect, flawed, blemished **3** inaccurate, wrong ◊ *verb* **1** spoil, mar

perfection *noun* **1** the state of being perfect **2** the highest state of excellence ◊ **perfectionist** *noun* someone who is satisfied only by perfection

▤ **1** faultlessness, flawlessness, excellence, superiority, ideal **2** paragon, crown, pinnacle, model ◊ **perfectionist** idealist, purist, pedant, stickler

perfidious *adj* treacherous, unfaithful ◊ **perfidiousness** *noun* ◊ **perfidy** *noun*

perforate *verb* make a hole or holes through ◊ **perforated** *adj* pierced with holes ◊ **perforation** *noun* a small hole

▤ hole, punch, drill, bore, pierce, prick, stab, puncture, penetrate

perforce *adv, old* of necessity, unavoidably

perform *verb* **1** do, act **2** act (a part) or present (a play) on the stage **3** provide entertainment for an audience **4** play (a piece of music) ◊ **performer** *noun* someone who acts or performs

▤ **1** do, carry out, execute, discharge, fulfil, complete, achieve, accomplish, bring off, pull off, effect, act, behave **2** stage, put on, present, enact, represent, act, play

performance *noun* **1** an entertainment in a theatre *etc*: *tickets for the evening performance* **2** the act of doing something **3** the level of success of a machine, car *etc*

perfume *noun* **1** smell, fragrance **2** a fragrant liquid put on the skin, scent ◇ *verb* **1** put scent on or in **2** give a sweet smell to ◇ **perfumery** *noun* a shop or factory where perfume is sold or made

■ **1** scent, fragrance, smell, odour, aroma, bouquet, sweetness **2** scent, essence, cologne, toilet water, incense

perfunctory *adj* done carelessly or half-heartedly: *perfunctory inspection* ◇ **perfunctorily** *adv*

perhaps *adv* it may be (that), possibly: *perhaps she'll resign*

peri- *prefix* around

peril *noun* great danger ◇ **at your peril** at your own risk

■ danger, hazard, risk, jeopardy, uncertainty, insecurity, threat, menace

▣ safety, security

perilous *adj* very dangerous ◇ **perilously** *adv*

■ dangerous, unsafe, hazardous, risky, precarious, insecure, unsure, vulnerable, exposed, menacing, threatening

▣ safe, secure

perimeter *noun* **1** the outside line enclosing a figure or shape **2** the outer edge of any area

⚠ Do not confuse with: **parameter**

perinatal *adj* relating to the period between the seventh month of pregnancy and the first week of the baby's life

perineum *noun* the part of the body between the genitals and the anus ◇ **perineal** *adj*

period *noun* **1** a stretch of time **2** a stage in the earth's development or in history **3** *US* a full stop after a sentence **4** a time of menstruation

■ **1** generation, years, time, term, season,

stage, phase, stretch, turn, session, interval, spell, cycle **2** era, epoch, age

periodic *adj* **1** of a period **2** happening at regular intervals, *eg* every month or year **3** happening every now and then: *a periodic clearing out of rubbish*

■ **2** recurrent, repeated, regular **3** occasional, infrequent, sporadic, intermittent, periodical, seasonal

periodical *adj* issued or done at regular or irregular intervals; periodic ◇ *noun* a magazine which appears at regular intervals

peripatetic *adj* moving from place to place; travelling: *a peripatetic teacher*

peripheral *adj* **1** of or on a periphery; away from the centre **2** not essential, of little importance **3** *comput* supplementary, separate from the main unit

■ **2** minor, secondary, incidental, unimportant, irrelevant, unnecessary, marginal, borderline, surface, superficial

periphery *noun* (*plural* **peripheries**) **1** the line or region surrounding something **2** an outer boundary or edge

periphrastic *adj* roundabout, using more words than necessary

periscope *noun* a tube with mirrors by which a viewer in a submarine *etc* is able to see objects on the surface

perish *verb* **1** be destroyed, pass away completely; die **2** decay, rot ◇ **perishable** *adj* liable to go bad quickly

■ **1** crumble, collapse, fall, die, expire, pass away **2** rot, decay, decompose, disintegrate ◇ **perishable** destructible, biodegradable, decomposable, short-lived

▣ **perishable** imperishable, durable

peristyle *noun* a group of columns surrounding a building

peritoneum *noun* a membrane in the stomach and pelvis ◇ **peritonitis** *noun* inflammation of the peritoneum

periwig *noun*, *hist* a wig

periwinkle *noun* **1** a small shellfish, shaped like a small snail, eaten as food when boiled **2** a creeping evergreen plant with a small blue flower

perjure *verb*: **perjure yourself** tell a lie when you have sworn to tell the truth, *esp* in a court of law ◇ **perjurer** *noun* ◇ **perjury** *noun*

perk[1] *noun* something of value allowed in addition to payment for work; a side benefit: *cheap rail travel is one of the perks of the job*

■ fringe benefit, benefit, bonus, dividend, gratuity, tip, extra, *informal* plus, perquisite

perk[2] *verb*: **perk up** recover energy or spirits

■ brighten, cheer up, *informal* buck up, revive, liven up

perky *adj* jaunty, in good spirits ◇ **perkily** *adv* ◇ **perkiness** *noun*

perm *noun* short for **permanent wave** ◇ *verb* give a permanent wave to (hair)

permaculture *noun* farming without using artificial fertilizers and with minimal weeding

permafrost *noun* permanently frozen subsoil

permanent *adj* lasting, not temporary ◇ **permanence** *noun* ◇ **permanently** *adv* ◇ **permanent wave** a wave or curl put into the hair by a special process and *usu* lasting for some months

■ fixed, stable, unchanging, imperishable, indestructible, unfading, eternal, everlasting, lifelong, perpetual, constant, steadfast, perennial, long-lasting, lasting, enduring, durable

☒ temporary, ephemeral, fleeting

permeate *verb* **1** pass into through small holes, soak into **2** fill every part of ◇ **permeable** *adj*

■ **1** soak through, filter through, seep through, penetrate **2** infiltrate, pervade, imbue, saturate, impregnate, fill

permissible *adj* allowable

■ permitted, allowable, allowed, admissible, acceptable, proper, authorized, sanctioned, lawful, legal, legitimate

☒ prohibited, banned, forbidden

permission *noun* freedom or authorization given to do something

■ consent, assent, agreement, approval, authorization, sanction, leave, warrant,

permit, licence, dispensation, freedom

☒ prohibition

permissive *adj* **1** allowing something to be done **2** too tolerant ◇ **permissiveness** *noun*

permit *verb* **1** say that someone may do something **2** make possible ◇ *noun* a written order, allowing someone to do something: *a fishing permit*

■ *verb* **1** allow, let, consent, agree, admit, grant, authorize, sanction, warrant, license, *informal* green-light ◇ *noun* pass, passport, visa, licence, warrant, authorization, sanction, permission

☒ *verb* **1** prohibit, forbid

permutation *noun* **1** the arrangement of numbers, letters *etc* in a certain order **2** the act of changing the order of things

pernicious *adj* destructive ◇ **perniciousness** *noun*

pernickety *adj* fussy about small details

peroration *noun* **1** the closing part of a speech **2** a speech

peroxide *noun* a chemical (hydrogen peroxide) used for bleaching hair *etc* ◇ **peroxide blonde** *informal* a woman whose hair has been bleached

perpendicular *adj* **1** standing upright, vertical **2** at right angles (to) ◇ *noun* a line at right angles to another

perpetrate *verb* commit (a sin, error *etc*) ◇ **perpetration** *noun* ◇ **perpetrator** *noun*

■ commit, carry out, execute, enact, do, perform, inflict, wreak

⚠ Do not confuse with: **perpetuate**

perpetual *adj* everlasting; continually recurring ◇ **perpetually** *adv*

■ eternal, everlasting, infinite, endless, unending, never-ending, interminable, ceaseless, incessant, continuous, uninterrupted, constant, persistent, continual, repeated, recurrent, lasting, enduring, abiding

☒ intermittent, temporary, ephemeral, transient

perpetuate *verb* cause to last for

ever or for a long time ◇ **perpetuity** *noun* ◇ **in perpetuity 1** for ever **2** for the length of someone's life

■ continue, keep up, maintain, preserve, keep alive, immortalize, commemorate

> **!** Do not confuse with: **perpetrate**

perplex *verb* **1** puzzle, bewilder **2** make more complicated

■ **1** puzzle, baffle, mystify, stump, confuse, muddle, confound, bewilder, dumbfound

perplexity *noun* **1** a puzzled state of mind **2** something which puzzles

perquisite *noun*, *formal* a perk

per se in itself, essentially

persecute *verb* **1** harass over a period of time **2** cause to suffer, *esp* because of religious beliefs ◇ **persecution** *noun* ◇ **persecutor** *noun*

■ **1** hound, pursue, hunt, bother, annoy, pester, harass **2** oppress, tyrannize, victimize, martyr, torment, torture, molest, abuse, ill-treat

■ **1** pamper, spoil

> **!** Do not confuse with: **prosecute**

persevere *verb* keep trying to do a thing (in spite of difficulties) ◇ **perseverance** *noun*

■ continue, carry on, *informal* stick at it, keep going, soldier on, persist

■ give up, quit, stop, discontinue

persimmon *noun* a plum-like fruit from an African or American tree

persist *verb* **1** continue to do something in spite of difficulties, discouragement *etc* **2** survive, last

■ **1** continue, carry on, keep at it, persevere **2** remain, linger, last, endure

persistent *adj* **1** obstinate, refusing to be discouraged **2** lasting, not dying out ◇ **persistence** *noun* ◇ **persistently** *adv*

■ **1** persevering, determined, resolute, stubborn, obstinate, steadfast, tireless **2** incessant, endless, never-ending, continuous, relentless, constant, steady, continual, repeated, perpetual, lasting, enduring

person *noun* **1** a human being **2** someone's body: *jewels hidden on his person* **3** *grammar* a class of pronouns or verbs: *third person singular* ◇ **in person** personally, not represented by someone else

persona *noun* the outward part of the personality presented to others; social image

personable *adj* good-looking

personage *noun* a well-known person

personal *adj* **1** of a particular person; your own; private: *personal belongings/ her personal life* **2** of a remark: insulting, offensive to the person it is aimed at ◇ **personal column** a newspaper column containing personal messages, advertisements *etc* ◇ **personal organizer** a small loose-leaf filing system containing a diary and an address book, maps, indexes *etc* ◇ **personal stereo** a small portable cassette player with earphones

■ **1** own, private, confidential, intimate, special, particular, individual, exclusive, idiosyncratic, distinctive

■ **1** public, general, universal

> **!** Do not confuse with: **personnel**

personality *noun* (*plural* **personalities**) **1** all of a person's characteristics as seen by others **2** a well-known person

■ **1** character, nature, disposition, temperament, individuality **2** celebrity, personage, public figure, *informal* VIP, star

personally *adv* **1** speaking from your own point of view **2** by your own action, not using an agent or representative: *he thanked me personally*

persona non grata someone disliked or out of favour

personify *verb* (**personifies**, **personifying**, **personified**) **1** talk about things, ideas *etc* as if they were living persons (*eg* 'Time marches on') **2** typify, be a perfect example of ◇ **personification** *noun*

■ **2** embody, epitomize, typify, exemplify, symbolize, represent

personnel *noun* the people employed in a company *etc*

> ⚠ Do not confuse with: **personal**

perspective *noun* **1** a point of view **2** the giving of a sense of depth, distance *etc* in a painting like that in real life ◇ **in perspective 1** of an object in a painting *etc*: of a size in relation to other things that it would have in real life **2** of an event: in its true degree of importance when considered in relation to other events: *keep things in perspective*
- **1** aspect, angle, slant, attitude, standpoint, viewpoint, point of view, mindset, prospect, outlook

Perspex *noun, trademark* a transparent plastic which looks like glass

perspicacious *adj* of clear or sharp understanding ◇ **perspicacity** *noun* keenness of understanding

perspicuity *noun* clearness in expressing thoughts ◇ **perspicuous** *adj*

perspire *verb* sweat ◇ **perspiration** *noun* sweat

persuade *verb* cause someone to do or think something, by arguing with them or advising them
- coax, cajole, wheedle, talk into, induce, bring round, win over, convince, sway, influence, incite, prompt, urge
- dissuade, deter, discourage

persuasion *noun* **1** the act of persuading **2** a firm belief, *esp* a religious belief

persuasive *adj* having the power to persuade or convince ◇ **persuasiveness** *noun*
- convincing, plausible, sound, valid, influential, forceful, weighty, effective, compelling, moving, touching
- unconvincing

pert *adj* saucy, cheeky

pertain *verb* (with **to**) belong, have to do with: *duties pertaining to the job*

pertinacious *adj* holding strongly to an idea, obstinate ◇ **pertinacity** *noun*

pertinent *adj* connected with the subject spoken about, to the point
- appropriate, suitable, fitting, apt, relevant, to the point, material, applicable

perturb *verb* disturb greatly; make anxious or uneasy ◇ **perturbation** *noun* great worry, anxiety
- disturb, bother, trouble, upset, worry, alarm, disconcert, unsettle, discompose, ruffle, fluster, agitate, vex
- reassure, compose

peruse *verb* read (with care) ◇ **perusal** *noun*
- study, pore over, read, browse, look through, scan, scrutinize, examine, inspect, check

pervade *verb* spread through: *silence pervaded the room*

perverse *adj* obstinate in holding to an opposite point of view; unreasonable ◇ **perverseness** or **perversity** *noun* stubbornness
- contrary, wayward, wilful, headstrong, stubborn, obstinate, intransigent, disobedient, rebellious, troublesome, unmanageable, ill-tempered, unreasonable, incorrect, improper
- obliging, co-operative, reasonable

perversion *noun* **1** the act of perverting **2** an unnatural or perverted act

pervert *verb* **1** turn away from what is normal or right: *pervert the course of justice* **2** turn (someone) to crime or evil; corrupt ◇ *noun* someone who commits unnatural or perverted acts
- *verb* **1** twist, warp, distort, misrepresent, falsify **2** corrupt, lead astray, deprave, debauch, debase, degrade, abuse ◇ *noun* deviant, degenerate, *informal* weirdo, *slang* perv

peseta *noun* a former unit of Spanish money

pessary *noun* a cotton plug containing medicine *etc* inserted into the vagina

pessimism *noun* the habit of thinking that things will always turn out badly (*contrasted with:* **optimism**) ◇ **pessimist** *noun* ◇ **pessimistic** *adj* ◇ **pessimistically** *adv*
- **pessimistic** negative, cynical, fatalistic, defeatist, resigned, hopeless, despairing, despondent, dejected, downhearted, glum, morose, melan-

choly, depressed, dismal, gloomy, bleak
Ea pessimistic optimistic

pest noun 1 a troublesome person or thing 2 a creature that is harmful or destructive, eg a mosquito

■ 1 nuisance, bother, annoyance, irritation, vexation, trial, curse, scourge, bane

pester verb annoy continually

■ nag, badger, hound, informal hassle, harass, plague, torment, provoke, worry, bother, disturb, annoy, irritate

pesticide noun any substance which kills animal pests

pestilence noun a deadly, spreading disease ◇**pestilent** or **pestilential** adj 1 very unhealthy 2 troublesome

pestle noun a tool for pounding things to powder

pesto noun a sauce made with ground pine nuts, basil, olive oil and parmesan cheese

pet¹ noun 1 a tame animal kept in the home, such as a cat 2 a favourite ◇adj 1 kept as a pet 2 favourite 3 chief: my pet hate ◇verb (**pets, petting, petted**) fondle ◇**pet name** one used to express affection or love

■ adj 2 favourite, favoured, preferred, dearest, cherished, special ◇verb stroke, caress, fondle, cuddle, kiss, slang neck, slang snog

pet² noun a fit of sulks

petal noun one of the coloured, leaf-like parts of a flower

petard noun: **hoist with your own petard** caught in a trap of your own making

peter verb: **peter out** fade or dwindle away to nothing

■ dwindle, taper off, fade, wane, ebb, fail, cease, stop

petite adj small and neat in appearance

petit fours small fancy cakes or biscuits

petition noun a request or note of protest signed by many people and sent to a government or authority ◇verb send a petition to ◇**petitioner** noun

■ noun appeal, application, request, plea, entreaty

petrel noun a small, long-winged seabird

petrify verb (**petrifies, petrifying, petrified**) 1 turn into stone 2 turn (someone) stiff with fear ◇**petrifaction** noun ◇**petrified** adj

■ 2 terrify, horrify, appal, paralyse, numb, stun, dumbfound

petrol noun petroleum when refined as fuel for use in cars etc

petroleum noun oil in its raw, unrefined form, extracted from natural wells below the earth's surface

petticoat noun an underskirt worn by women

pettifogger noun someone who argues over trivial details

pettish adj sulky

petty adj 1 of little importance, trivial 2 childishly spiteful ◇**pettiness** noun ◇**petty cash** money used for small expenses, eg in an office ◇**petty officer** a non-commissioned officer in the navy

■ 1 minor, unimportant, insignificant, trivial, secondary, lesser, small, little, slight, trifling, paltry, inconsiderable, negligible

Ea important, significant

petulant adj 1 cross, irritable 2 unreasonably impatient ◇**petulance** noun ◇**petulantly** adv

■ 1 fretful, peevish, cross, irritable, snappish, bad-tempered, ill-humoured, moody, sullen, sulky, sour, ungracious

petunia noun a S American flowering plant related to tobacco

pew noun a seat or bench in a church

pewter noun a mixture of tin and lead

phalanx noun (plural **phalanxes**) 1 a company of foot soldiers in an oblong-shaped formation 2 a group of supporters

phallus noun (plural **phalluses** or **phalli**) a representation of a penis ◇**phallic** adj

phantasm noun a vision, an illusion

phantasmagoria noun a dreamlike

series of visions or hallucinations

phantom *noun* a ghost

Pharaoh *noun, hist* a ruler of ancient Egypt

pharmaceutical *adj* relating to the making up of medicines and drugs

pharmacist *noun* someone who prepares and sells medicines

pharmacology *noun* the scientific study of drugs and their effects ◇ **pharmacological** *adj* ◇ **pharmacologist** *noun*

pharmacopoeia *noun* a list of drugs with directions for their preparation

pharmacy *noun* (*plural* **pharmacies**) **1** the art of preparing medicines **2** a chemist's shop

pharynx *noun* the back part of the throat behind the tonsils ◇ **pharyngitis** *noun* inflammation of the pharynx

phase *noun* a stage in the change or development of something ◇ **phase in** introduce in steps or stages ◇ **phase out** get rid of or abolish gradually
▣ stage, step, time, position, point, aspect, state, condition

PhD *abbrev* Doctor of Philosophy

pheasant *noun* a bird with brightly coloured feathers which is shot as game

phenobarbitone *noun* a sedative and hypnotic drug

phenol *noun* an acid used as a powerful disinfectant

phenomenal *adj* very unusual, remarkable ◇ **phenomenally** *adv* extremely: *phenomenally successful*
▣ marvellous, sensational, stupendous, amazing, remarkable, extraordinary, exceptional, unusual, unbelievable, incredible

phenomenon *noun* (*plural* **phenomena**) **1** an event (*esp* in nature) which is observed by the senses: *the phenomenon of lightning* **2** something remarkable or very unusual, a wonder
▣ **2** wonder, marvel, miracle, prodigy, rarity, curiosity, spectacle, sensation

pheronome *noun* a chemical secreted by the body which attracts or in-

fluences other people or animals

phew *exclam* used to express relief

phial *noun* a small glass bottle

philander *verb* of a man: have casual love affairs, flirt ◇ **philanderer** *noun*

philanthropy *noun* love of mankind, often shown by giving money for the benefit of others ◇ **philanthropic** *adj* ◇ **philanthropist** *noun*
▣ **philanthropic** humanitarian, public-spirited, altruistic, unselfish, benevolent, kind, charitable, generous, liberal, open-handed
▣ **philanthropic** misanthropic

philately *noun* the study and collecting of postage stamps ◇ **philatelist** *noun*

philharmonic *adj* (in names of orchestras *etc*) music-loving

philistine *noun* someone ignorant of, or hostile to, culture and the arts

> After a people of ancient Palestine, enemies of the Israelites

philology *noun* the study of words and their history ◇ **philologist** *noun*

philosopher *noun* someone who studies philosophy

philosophical *adj* **1** of philosophy **2** calm, not easily upset
▣ **2** resigned, patient, stoical, unruffled, calm, composed

philosophy *noun* (*plural* **philosophies**) **1** the study of the nature of the universe, or of human behaviour **2** someone's personal view of life

philtre *noun* a love potion

phlegm /flɛm/ *noun* **1** thick slimy matter brought up from the throat by coughing **2** coolness of temper, calmness

phlegmatic *adj* not easily aroused
▣ placid, stolid, impassive, unemotional, unconcerned, indifferent, matter-of-fact, stoical, philosophical
▣ emotional, passionate

phlox *noun* a garden plant with flat white or purplish flowers

phobia *noun* an intense, often irrational, fear or dislike

■ fear, terror, dread, anxiety, neurosis, obsession, mania, *informal* hang-up, *informal* thing, aversion, dislike, hatred, horror, loathing, revulsion, repulsion

弓 love, liking

Phobias (by object of fear) include: zoophobia (*animals*), apiphobia (*bees*), ailurophobia (*cats*), necrophobia (*corpses*), scotophobia (*darkness*), cynophobia (*dogs*), claustrophobia (*enclosed places*), panphobia (*everything*), pyrophobia (*fire*), xenophobia (*foreigners*), phasmophobia (*ghosts*), acrophobia (*high places*), hippophobia (*horses*), entomophobia (*insects*), astraphobia (*lightning*), autophobia (*loneliness*), agoraphobia (*open spaces*), toxiphobia (*poison*), herpetophobia (*reptiles*), ophiophobia (*snakes*), tachophobia (*speed*), arachnophobia (*spiders*), triskaidekaphobia (*thirteen*), brontophobia (*thunder*), hydrophobia (*water*)

---

phoenix /fiːnɪks/ *noun* a mythological bird believed to burn itself and to rise again from its ashes

phone *noun, short for* **telephone** ◇ **phonecard** *noun* a card that can be used instead of cash to operate certain public telephones

phoneme *noun* the smallest meaningful unit of sound in any language

phonetic *adj* 1 relating to the sounds of language 2 of a spelling: representing the sound of a word, *eg* flem for 'phlegm' ◇ **phonetics** *noun sing* 1 the study of the sounds of language 2 a system of writing according to sound

phoney or **phony** *adj, informal* fake, not genuine

■ fake, counterfeit, forged, bogus, trick, false, assumed, affected, put-on, sham, pseudo, imitation, faux

phosphate *noun* a soil fertilizer containing phosphorus

phosphorescence *noun* faint glow

of light in the dark ◇ **phosphorescent** *adj*

phosphorus *noun* a wax-like, poisonous substance that gives out light in the dark

photo *noun* (*plural* **photos**) *informal* a photograph

photocopy *noun* (*plural* **photocopies**) a copy of a document made by a device which photographs and develops images of the document ◇ *verb* (**photocopies**, **photocopying**, **photocopied**) make a photocopy of

photofit *noun, trademark* a method of making identification pictures by combining photographs of individual features

photogenic *adj* being a good subject for a photograph; photographing well

photograph *noun* a picture taken with a camera ◇ *verb* take a picture with a camera ◇ **photographer** *noun*

■ *noun* photo, snap, snapshot, print, shot, slide, transparency, picture, image, likeness

photography *noun* the art of taking pictures with a camera

photosensitive *adj* affected by light

photostat *noun, trademark* 1 a special camera for making photographic copies of documents, pages of books *etc* 2 a photographic copy so made

photosynthesis *noun* the conversion of light into complex compounds by plants

phrase *noun* 1 a small group of words expressing a single idea, *eg* 'after dinner', 'on the water' 2 a short saying or expression 3 *music* a short group of bars forming a distinct unit ◇ *verb* express in words: *he could have phrased it more tactfully*

■ *noun* 1 construction, utterance, remark 2 idiom, expression, saying ◇ *verb* word, formulate, present, put, express, say, utter, pronounce

phraseology *noun* someone's personal choice of words and phrases

phrenology *noun* the study of the surface of the skull as a sign of personality *etc* ◇ **phrenologist** *noun*

phut *adj*: **go phut** break down

phylactery *noun* a small box containing a piece of Scripture worn on the wrist or forehead by Orthodox Jews

phylum *noun* a main division of the animal or vegetable kingdoms

physical *adj* **1** relating to the body: *physical strength/physical exercises* **2** relating to things that can be seen or felt ◇ **physically** *adv*
▤ **1** bodily, corporeal, fleshy, incarnate, mortal **2** material, concrete, solid, substantial, tangible, visible, real, actual
▨ **1** mental, spiritual

physician *noun* a doctor specializing in medical rather than surgical treatment

physics *noun sing* the science which includes the study of heat, light, sound, electricity, magnetism *etc* ◇ **physicist** *noun* someone who specializes in physics

physiognomy *noun* the features or expression of the face

physiology *noun* the study of the way in which living bodies work, including blood circulation, food digestion *etc* ◇ **physiological** *adj* ◇ **physiologist** *noun*

physiotherapy *noun* the treatment of injury or disease by bodily exercise, massage *etc* ◇ **physiotherapist** *noun*

physique *noun* **1** the build of someone's body **2** bodily strength
▤ **1** body, figure, shape, form, build, frame, structure

pianist *noun* someone who plays the piano

piano *noun* (*plural* **pianos**) a large musical instrument played by striking keys

piazza *noun* a market-place or town square surrounded by buildings

picador *noun* a bullfighter armed with a lance and mounted on a horse

piccalilli *noun* a vegetable pickle

piccolo *noun* (*plural* **piccolos**) a small, high-pitched flute

pick *verb* **1** choose **2** pluck, gather (flowers, fruit *etc*) **3** peck, bite, nibble (at) **4** poke, probe (teeth *etc*) **5** open (a lock) with a tool other than a key ◇ *noun* **1** choice: *take your pick* **2** the best or best part: *the pick of the crop* **3** a pickaxe **4** an instrument for picking, *eg* a toothpick ◇ **pick a quarrel** start a quarrel deliberately ◇ **pick on 1** single out unfairly for criticism *etc* **2** nag at ◇ **pick up 1** lift up **2** learn (a language, habit *etc*) **3** give (someone) a lift in a car **4** find or get by chance **5** improve, gain strength
▤ *verb* **1** select, choose, opt for, decide on, settle on, single out **2** gather, collect, pluck, harvest, cull ◇ *noun* **1** choice, selection, option, decision, preference **2** best, cream, élite, elect ◇ **pick up 1** lift, raise, hoist **2** learn, master, grasp **3** call for, fetch, collect **5** improve, recover, *informal* perk up, strengthen

pickaxe *noun* a heavy tool for breaking ground, pointed at one or both ends

picket *noun* **1** a pointed stake **2** a small sentry-post or its guard **3** a number of workers on strike who prevent others from going into work ◇ *verb* place a guard or a group of strikers at (a place)

pickle *noun* **1** vegetables preserved in vinegar **2** a liquid in which food is preserved **3** *informal* an awkward, unpleasant situation ◇ *verb* preserve with salt, vinegar *etc*

pickpocket *noun* someone who robs people's pockets or handbags

picky *adj* choosy, fussy ◇ **pickiness** *noun*

picnic *noun* a meal eaten out-of-doors, often during an outing *etc* ◇ *verb* (**picnics**, **picnicking**, **picnicked**) have a picnic

picot /ˈpiːkoʊ/ *noun* an ornamental loop in a lace edging

pictorial *adj* **1** having pictures **2** consisting of pictures **3** calling up pictures in the mind

picture *noun* **1** a painting or drawing **2** a portrait **3** a photograph **4** a film **5**

(**pictures**) the cinema **6** a vivid description ◊ *verb* **1** make a picture of **2** see in the mind, imagine

◼ *noun* **1** painting, landscape, drawing, sketch, illustration, engraving, print, representation **2** portrait, likeness, image, effigy **6** depiction, portrayal, description, account, report, impression ◊ *verb* **1** depict, describe, represent, show, portray, draw, sketch, paint, photograph, illustrate **2** imagine, envisage, envision, conceive, visualize, see

picturesque *adj* charming to look at; pretty, quaint

piddling *adj* trifling, minor

pidgin *noun* a language made up of two others in a distorted form

| ⚠ Do not confuse with: **pigeon** |

pie *noun* meat, fruit or other food baked in a casing or covering of pastry ◊ **pie-eyed** *adj, informal* drunk

piebald *adj* white and black in patches: *a piebald horse*

piece *noun* **1** a part or portion of anything **2** a single article or example: *a piece of paper* **3** an artistic work: *a piece of popular music* **4** a coin **5** any of the shapes or discs moved across the board in chess, draughts *etc* ◊ *verb* put (together)

◼ *noun* **1** fragment, bit, scrap, morsel, bite, lump, chunk, slice, sliver, snippet, shred, offcut, sample, component, constituent, element, part, segment, section, division, fraction, share, portion **2** article, item, specimen, example

pièce de résistance /pɪˈɛs də reɪˈzɪstãs/ the best item or work

piecemeal *adv* by pieces, little by little

piecework *noun* work paid according to how much is done, not to the time spent on it

pied *adj* with two or more colours in patches

pier *noun* **1** a platform stretching from the shore into the sea as a landing

place or promenade **2** a pillar supporting an arch, bridge *etc*

pierce *verb* make a hole through; force a way into

◼ penetrate, enter, stick into, puncture, drill, bore, perforate, punch, prick, jab, stab, lance, spear, skewer, spike, impale

piercing *adj* shrill, loud; sharp

◼ shrill, high-pitched, loud, ear-splitting, sharp

piety *see* **pious**

piffle *noun* nonsense

pig *noun* **1** a farm animal, from whose flesh ham and bacon are made **2** an oblong moulded piece of metal (*eg* iron)

pigeon *noun* a bird of the dove family

pigeonhole *noun* a small division in a case or desk for papers *etc* ◊ *verb* **1** lay aside **2** classify, put into a category

◼ *noun* compartment, niche, slot, cubbyhole, cubicle, locker, box, place, section ◊ *verb* **1** shelve **2** compartmentalize, label, classify, sort, file, catalogue, alphabetize

piggyback *noun* a ride on someone's back with your arms round their neck

piggy bank a china pig with a slit along its back to insert coins for saving

pig-headed *adj* stubborn

pigment *noun* **1** paint or other substance used for colouring **2** a substance in animals and plants that gives colour to the skin *etc* ◊ **pigmentation** *noun* colouring of skin *etc*

pigmy *another spelling of* **pygmy**

pigskin *noun* leather made from a pig's skin

pigsty *noun* (*plural* **pigsties**) or **piggery** *noun* (*plural* **piggeries**) a place where pigs are kept

pigtail *noun* hair formed into a plait

pike¹ *noun* a freshwater fish

pike² *noun* a weapon like a spear, with a long shaft and a sharp head

Pilates /pɪˈlɑːtəz/ *noun* a system of exercises to tone the muscles

pilau or **pilaff** *noun* an Indian dish of spiced rice, containing or served with meat *etc*

pilchard *noun* a small sea-fish like a herring, often tinned

pile¹ *noun* **1** a number of things lying one on top of another, a heap **2** a great quantity **3** a large building ◇ *verb* (often with **up**) make or form a pile or heap

■ *noun* **1** stack, heap, mound, mountain **2** mass, accumulation, collection, assortment, hoard, stockpile ◇ *verb* stack, heap, mass, amass, accumulate, build up, gather, assemble, collect, hoard, stockpile, store, load, pack

pile² *noun* a large stake or pillar driven into the earth as a foundation for a building, bridge *etc*

■ post, column, upright, support, bar, beam, foundation

pile³ *noun* the thick, soft surface on carpets and on cloth such as velvet

pilfer *verb* steal small things ◇ **pilfering** *noun*

■ steal, *informal* pinch, *informal* nick, *slang* knock off, filch, lift, shoplift, rob, thieve

pilgrim *noun* a traveller to a holy place ◇ **pilgrimage** *noun* a journey to a holy place

pill *noun* **1** a tablet of medicine **2** (often with **the**) a contraceptive in the form of a small tablet taken by mouth

pillage *verb* seize goods and money, *esp* as loot in war ◇ *noun* the act of plundering in this way

pillar *noun* **1** an upright support for roofs, arches *etc* **2** an upright post or column as a monument **3** someone or something that gives support: *a pillar of the community*

pillarbox *noun* a tall cylindrical box with a slot through which letters *etc* are posted

pillion *noun* **1** a seat for a passenger on a motorcycle **2** *old* a light saddle for a passenger on horseback, behind the main saddle

pillory *noun* (*plural* **pillories**) *hist* a wooden frame fitted over the head and hands of wrongdoers as a punishment ◇ *verb* (**pillories**, **pillorying**, **pilloried**) mock in public

pillow *noun* a soft cushion for the head ◇ *verb* rest or support on a pillow ◇ **pillowcase** or **pillowslip** *noun* a cover for a pillow

pilot *noun* **1** someone who flies an aeroplane **2** someone who steers a ship in or out of a harbour **3** a guide, a leader ◇ *verb* steer, guide ◇ **pilot light 1** a small gas flame from which larger jets are lit **2** an electric light showing that a current is switched on ◇ **pilot scheme** a scheme introduced on a small scale as an experiment or as preparation for a full-scale one

■ *noun* **1** flyer, aviator, airman **2** navigator, steersman, helmsman, coxswain, captain ◇ *verb* fly, drive, steer, direct, control, handle, manage, operate, run, conduct, lead, guide, navigate

pimento *noun* (*plural* **pimentos**) a mild type of red pepper

pimp *noun* a man who finds clients for prostitutes and takes money from them

pimpernel *noun* a plant of the primrose family, with small pink or scarlet flowers

pimple *noun* a small round infected swelling on the skin ◇ **pimpled** or **pimply** *adj* having pimples

PIN /pɪn/ *abbrev* personal identification number (for automatic teller machines *etc*)

pin *noun* **1** a short pointed piece of metal with a small round head, used for fastening fabric **2** a wooden or metal peg **3** a skittle ◇ *verb* (**pins**, **pinning**, **pinned**) **1** fasten with a pin **2** hold fast, pressed against something: *the bloodhound pinned him to the ground*

■ *verb* **1** tack, nail, fix, affix, attach, join, staple, clip, fasten, secure **2** hold down, restrain, immobilize

pinafore *noun* **1** an apron to protect the front of a dress **2** a sleeveless dress worn over a jersey, blouse *etc*

pinball *noun* a game played on a slot-machine in which a ball runs down a sloping board between obstacles

pince-nez /ˈpansneɪ/ *noun* a pair of eyeglasses with a spring for gripping the nose

pincers *noun plural* **1** a tool like pliers, but with sharp points for gripping, pulling out nails *etc* **2** the claws of a crab or lobster

pinch *verb* **1** squeeze (*esp* flesh) between the thumb and forefinger, nip **2** grip tightly, hurt by tightness **3** *informal* steal ◊ *noun* (*plural* **pinches**) **1** a squeeze, a nip **2** a small amount (*eg* of salt) ◊ **pinched** *adj* of a face: looking cold, pale or thin ◊ **at a pinch** if really necessary or urgent ◊ **feel the pinch** suffer from lack of money

■ *verb* **1** squeeze, compress, tweak, nip **2** crush, press, hurt, grip, grasp **3** steal, *slang* nick, pilfer, filch, snatch

pinchbeck *adj* sham, in poor imitation

From Christopher *Pinchbeck*, a 17th-century watchmaker who invented a copper alloy to imitate gold

pine¹ *noun* **1** an evergreen tree with needle-like leaves which produces cones **2** the soft wood of such a tree used for furniture *etc*

pine² *verb* **1** waste away, lose strength **2** long (for something)

■ **2** long, yearn, ache, sigh, grieve, mourn, wish, desire, crave, hanker, hunger, thirst

pineapple *noun* a large tropical fruit shaped like a pine cone

ping *noun* a short, light, ringing sound ◊ *verb* make such a sound

ping-pong *noun, trademark* table-tennis

pinion¹ *noun* a bird's wing ◊ *verb* **1** hold (someone) fast by binding or holding their arms **2** cut or fasten the wings of (a bird)

pinion² *noun* a small toothed wheel

pink¹ *noun* **1** a pale red colour **2** a sweet-scented garden flower like a carnation ◊ **in the pink** in a healthy or good state

pink² *verb* of an engine: make a faint clinking noise

pink³ *verb* cut (cloth *etc*) with pinking scissors ◊ **pinking scissors** or **pinking**

shears scissors with blades which give cloth a zig-zag edge

pinkie *noun, informal* the little finger

pinnacle *noun* **1** a slender spire or turret **2** a high pointed rock or mountain **3** the highest point: *the pinnacle of his career*

■ **1** spire, steeple, turret, pyramid, cone, obelisk, needle **2** peak, summit, top, cap, crown, crest, apex **3** height, eminence

pinnie *noun, informal* an apron or overall

pint *noun* a liquid measure equal to 0.568 litre

pioneer *noun* **1** an explorer **2** an inventor, or an early exponent of something: *pioneers of the cinema* ◊ *verb* act as a pioneer of

■ *noun* **2** developer, innovator, inventor, discoverer, founder ◊ *verb* invent, discover, originate, create, initiate, instigate, begin, start, launch, institute, found, establish, set up, develop, open up

pious *adj* respectful in religious matters ◊ **piety** *noun*

■ devout, godly, saintly, holy, spiritual, religious, reverent, good, virtuous, righteous, moral

☒ impious, irreligious, irreverent

pip¹ *noun* **1** a seed of a fruit **2** a spot or symbol on dice or cards **3** a star on an army officer's tunic **4** a short bleep as part of a time signal *etc* on the radio or telephone

pip² *verb* (**pips, pipping, pipped**) defeat (someone) narrowly

pipe *noun* **1** a tube for carrying water, gas *etc* **2** a tube with a bowl at the end, for smoking tobacco **3** a metal or wooden tube which is part of a musical instrument **4** (**pipes**) bagpipes ◊ *verb* **1** play (notes, a tune) on a pipe or pipes **2** whistle, chirp **3** speak in a shrill high voice **4** convey (*eg* water) by pipe ◊ **pipeclay** *noun* a fine white clay used to whiten leather and in making clay pipes ◊ **piped music** continuous background music played throughout a building ◊ **pipe down** become silent, stop talking ◊**pipe up** speak up, express an opinion

◼ *noun* **1** tube, hose, piping, tubing, pipeline, line, main, channel, passage, conveyor ◊ *verb* **4** channel, funnel, siphon, carry, convey, conduct, transmit, supply, deliver

pipeline *noun* a long line of pipes, *eg* to carry oil from an oilfield ◊**in the pipeline** in preparation, soon to become available

piper *noun* someone who plays a pipe or the bagpipes

pipette *noun* a small glass tube used in laboratories

piping *adj* high-pitched, shrill ◊**piping hot** very hot ◊ *noun* **1** a length of tubing **2** a system of pipes **3** a narrow ornamental cord for trimming clothes **4** a strip of decorative icing round a cake

pippin *noun* a kind of apple

pipsqueak *noun, informal* an insignificant, or very small, person

piquant /'pi:kənt/ *adj* **1** sharp-tasting, spicy **2** arousing interest

◼ **1** spicy, tangy, savoury, salty, peppery, pungent, sharp, biting, stinging, *informal* nippy **2** spirited, stimulating, provocative, interesting, sparkling

pique /'pi:k/ *noun* anger caused by wounded pride, spite, resentment ◊ *verb* **1** wound the pride of **2** arouse (curiosity)

◼ *noun* annoyance, irritation, vexation, displeasure, offence, *informal* huff, resentment, grudge

piranha *noun* a S American river-fish which eats flesh

pirate *noun* **1** someone who robs ships at sea **2** someone who steals or plagiarizes another's work ◊**piracy** *noun* ◊**piratical** *adj*

pirouette *noun* a rapid whirling on the toes in dancing ◊ *verb* twirl in a pirouette

piss *verb, slang* urinate ◊ *noun, slang* **1** urine **2** an act of urinating ◊**piss about** or **piss around** *slang* behave foolishly, waste time ◊**pissed** *adj, slang* extremely drunk ◊**pissed off** *slang* annoyed, fed up ◊**piss off** *exclam, slang* go away

pistachio *noun* (*plural* **pistachios**) a greenish nut, often used as a flavouring

piste /pi:st/ *noun* a ski track

pistil *noun* the seed-bearing part of a flower

pistol *noun* a small gun held in the hand

piston *noun* a round piece of metal that moves up and down inside a cylinder, *eg* in an engine

pit *noun* **1** a hole in the ground **2** a place from which coal and other minerals are dug **3** the ground floor of a theatre behind the stalls **4** (often **pits**) a place beside the racetrack for repairing and refuelling racing cars *etc* ◊ *verb* (**pits**, **pitting**, **pitted**) set one thing or person against another: *pitting my wits against his*

◼ *noun* **1** dent, hole, cavity, crater, pothole, gulf, chasm, abyss **2** mine, coalmine, excavation

pitch *verb* **1** fix (a tent *etc*) in the ground **2** throw **3** fall heavily; lurch: *pitch forward* **4** set the level or key of a tune ◊ *noun* (*plural* **pitches**) **1** a throw **2** an attempt at selling or persuading: *sales pitch* **3** the height or depth of a note **4** a peak, an extreme point: *reach fever pitch* **5** the field for certain sports **6** *cricket* the ground between wickets **7** the slope of a roof *etc* **8** the spot reserved for a street seller or street entertainer ◊**pitched battle** a battle on chosen ground between sides arranged in position beforehand

◼ *verb* **1** erect, put up, set up, place, station, settle, plant, fix **2** throw, fling, toss, *informal* chuck, lob, hurl, heave, sling, fire, launch, aim, direct **3** plunge, dive, plummet, drop, fall headlong, tumble, lurch ◊ *noun* **7** gradient, incline, slope, tilt, angle, degree, steepness

pitch² *noun* a thick dark substance obtained by boiling down tar

pitchblende *noun* a black mineral made up of uranium oxides

pitch-dark *adj* very dark

pitcher *noun* a kind of large jug

pitchfork *noun* a fork for lifting and throwing hay ◇*verb* throw suddenly and violently

piteous *see* **pity**

pitfall *noun* a trap, a possible danger

■ danger, peril, hazard, trap, snare, stumbling-block, catch, snag, drawback, difficulty

pith *noun* **1** the soft substance in the centre of plant stems **2** the white substance under the rind of an orange, lemon *etc* **3** the important part of anything

■ **3** importance, significance, moment, weight, value, consequence, substance, matter, gist, essence, crux

pithy *adj* **1** full of pith **2** full of meaning, to the point: *a pithy saying*

■ **2** succinct, concise, compact, terse, short, brief, pointed

◨ **2** wordy, verbose

pitiable *see* **pity**

piton *noun* an iron peg for attaching a rope to in mountaineering

pitta *noun* a flat oval Mediterranean bread

pittance *noun* a very small wage or allowance

■ modicum, crumb, *informal* chickenfeed, *slang* peanuts, *slang* buttons, trifle

pitted *adj* marked with small holes

■ dented, holey, potholed, pockmarked, blemished, scarred, marked, notched, indented, rough

pituitary gland a gland in the brain affecting growth

pity *noun* **1** feeling for the sufferings of others, sympathy **2** a cause of grief **3** a regrettable fact: *it's a pity you can't go* ◇*verb* (**pities**, **pitying**, **pitied**) feel sorry for ◇**piteous** *or* **pitiable** *adj* deserving pity; wretched ◇**pitiful** *adj* poor, wretched ◇**take pity on** show pity for

■ *noun* **1** sympathy, commiseration, regret, understanding, empathy, compassion, kindness, tenderness, mercy **3** shame, misfortune, bad luck ◇ *verb* feel for, sympathize with, commiserate with, grieve for, weep for ◇ **pitiful** pit-

eous, doleful, mournful, distressing, heart-rending, pathetic, pitiable, sad, miserable, wretched, poor, sorry

◨ *noun* **1** cruelty, anger, scorn

pivot *noun* **1** the pin or centre on which anything turns **2** something or someone greatly depended on ◇*verb* **1** turn on a pivot **2** depend (on) ◇**pivotal** *adj*

■ *noun* **1** axis, hinge, axle, spindle, linchpin, swivel, centre, heart ◇ *verb* **1** swing, turn, spin, revolve, rotate, swing **2** depend, rely, hinge, hang, lie

pixel *noun*, *comput* the smallest element in a screen display

pixie *or* **pixy** *noun* (*plural* **pixies**) a kind of fairy

pizza *noun* a flat piece of dough spread with tomato, cheese *etc* and baked

pizzazz *noun* flamboyant style, panache

pizzicato /pɪtsɪˈkɑːtoʊ/ *adv*, *music* played by plucking the strings rather than bowing

placard *noun* a printed notice (*eg* an advertisement) placed on a wall *etc*

placate *verb* calm, soothe, make less angry *etc*

■ appease, pacify, conciliate, mollify, calm, assuage, soothe, lull, quiet

◨ anger, enrage, incense, infuriate

place *noun* **1** a physical location; any area or building **2** a particular spot **3** an open space in a town: *market place* **4** a seat in a theatre, at a table *etc* **5** a position on a course, in a job *etc* **6** a position in order: *in third place* **7** rank ◇*verb* (**places**, **placing**, **placed**) **1** put in a particular place **2** find a place for **3** give (an order for goods *etc*) **4** remember who someone is: *I can't place him at all* ◇**placed** *adj* **1** having a place **2** among the first three in a competition ◇**in place** in the proper position ◇**in place of** instead of ◇**out of place 1** not in the proper position **2** unsuitable

■ *noun* **1** site, locale, venue, location, situation **2** spot, point **4** position, seat, space, room ◇ *verb* **1** put, set, plant, fix, position **2** locate, situate, rest, settle, lay, stand, deposit, leave ◇ **out of place 2** inappropriate, unsuitable, unfitting, unbecoming, unseemly

placebo *noun* (*plural* **placebos**) an inactive medicine given to humour a patient, or used in drug trials

placenta *noun* a part of the womb that connects an unborn mammal to its mother, shed at birth

placid *adj* calm, not easily disturbed ◇ **placidity** *noun*

☰ calm, composed, unruffled, untroubled, cool, self-possessed, level-headed, mild, gentle, equable, even-tempered, serene, tranquil, still, quiet, peaceful, restful

☲ excitable, agitated, disturbed

plagiarize *verb* steal or borrow from the writings or ideas of someone else without permission ◇ **plagiarism** *noun* ◇ **plagiarist** *noun*

☰ crib, copy, reproduce, imitate, counterfeit, pirate, infringe copyright, poach, steal, lift, appropriate, borrow

plague *noun* **1** a fatal infectious disease carried by rat fleas **2** a great and troublesome quantity: *a plague of flies* ◇ *verb* pester or annoy continually

☰ *noun* **1** pestilence, epidemic, disease, infection, contagion, infestation **2** nuisance, annoyance, curse, scourge, trial, affliction, torment, calamity ◇ *verb* annoy, vex, bother, disturb, trouble, distress, upset, pester, harass, hound, haunt, afflict, torment, torture, persecute

plaice *noun* a type of edible flatfish

plaid *noun* a long piece of cloth (*esp* tartan) worn over the shoulder

plain *adj* **1** simple, ordinary **2** without ornament or decoration **3** clear, easy to see or understand **4** not good-looking, not attractive ◇ *noun* a large, flat stretch of land

☰ *adj* **1** ordinary, basic, simple, unpretentious, modest **2** unadorned, unelaborate, restrained, unpatterned **3** obvious, evident, patent, clear, understandable, apparent, visible, manifest, unmistakable **4** unattractive, ugly, unprepossessing, unlovely

☲ **1** fancy, elaborate **3** unclear, obscure **4** attractive, good-looking

plain-clothes *adj* of a police officer: wearing ordinary clothes, not in uniform

plain-spoken *adj* speaking your thoughts frankly

plaintiff *noun* someone who takes action against another in the law courts

plaintive *adj* sad, sorrowful

☰ doleful, mournful, melancholy, wistful, sad, sorrowful, grief-stricken, piteous, heart-rending, high-pitched

plait *noun* **1** a length of hair arranged by intertwining three or more separate pieces **2** threads *etc* intertwined in this way ◇ *verb* form into a plait

plan *noun* **1** a diagram of a building, town *etc* as if seen from above **2** a scheme or arrangement to do something ◇ *verb* (**plans**, **planning**, **planned**) **1** make a sketch or plan of **2** decide or arrange to do (something)

☰ *noun* **1** layout, diagram, chart, map, drawing, sketch, representation **2** idea, suggestion, proposal, proposition, project, scheme, plot, system, method, procedure, strategy, programme, schedule ◇ *verb* **1** plot, scheme, design, invent, devise, contrive, formulate, frame, draft, outline, prepare, organize, arrange **2** aim, intend, propose, contemplate, envisage

plane¹ *short for* **aeroplane**

plane² *noun* **1** a level surface **2** a carpentry tool for smoothing wood **3** a standard (of achievement *etc*): *on a higher intellectual plane* ◇ *adj* flat, level ◇ *verb* **1** smooth with a plane **2** glide over water *etc*

plane³ *noun* a type of tree with broad leaves

planet *noun* any of the bodies (*eg* the earth, Venus) which move round the sun or round another fixed star ◇ **planetary** *adj*

Planets within the Earth's solar system (nearest the sun shown first) are:
Mercury, Venus, Earth, Mars, Jupiter, Saturn, Uranus, Neptune, Pluto

plangent *adj* resonant, resounding

plank *noun* a long, flat piece of timber

plankton *noun* tiny living creatures floating in seas, lakes *etc*

plant *noun* 1 a living growth from the ground, with a stem, root and leaves 2 a factory or machinery ◇ *verb* 1 put (something) into the ground so that it will grow 2 put (an idea) into the mind 3 put in position: *plant a bomb* 4 set down firmly: *plant your feet on the floor* 5 *informal* place (something) as false evidence

---

Plants include:
annual, biennial, perennial, herbaceous plant, evergreen, succulent, cultivar, hybrid, house plant, pot plant; flower, herb, shrub, bush, tree, vegetable, grass, vine, weed, cereal, wild flower, air plant, water plant, cactus, fern, moss, algae, lichen, fungus; bulb, corm, seedling, sapling, bush, climber *see also* **flower**; **shrub**

---

plantain *noun* a coarse green-skinned tropical fruit like a banana

plantation *noun* 1 an area planted with trees 2 an estate for growing cotton, sugar, rubber, tobacco *etc*

planter *noun* the owner of a plantation

plaque *noun* 1 a decorative plate of metal, china *etc* for fixing to a wall 2 a film of saliva and bacteria which forms on the teeth

plasma *noun* the liquid part of blood and certain other fluids

plaster *noun* 1 a mixture of lime, water and sand which sets hard, for covering walls *etc* 2 (*also called* **plaster of Paris**) a fine mixture containing gypsum used for moulding, making casts for broken limbs *etc* 3 a small dressing which can be stuck over a wound ◇ *adj* made of plaster ◇ *verb* 1 apply plaster to 2 cover thickly (with) ◇ **plastered** *adj, slang* drunk ◇ **plasterer** *noun* someone who plasters walls

▣ *verb* 2 daub, smear, coat, cover, spread

plastic *adj* 1 easily moulded or shaped 2 made of plastic ◇ *noun* a chemically manufactured substance that can be moulded when soft, formed into fibres *etc* ◇ **plastic bullet** a cylinder of PVC fired from a gun ◇ **plastic explosive** mouldable explosive material ◇ **plastic surgery** an operation to repair or replace damaged areas of skin, to improve the appearance of facial features *etc*

▣ *adj* 1 soft, pliable, flexible, supple, malleable, mouldable, ductile

▣ *adj* 1 rigid, inflexible

Plasticine *noun, trademark* a soft clay-like substance used for modelling

plasticity *noun* the quality of being easily moulded

plate *noun* 1 a shallow dish for holding food 2 a flat piece of metal, glass, china *etc* 3 gold and silver articles 4 a sheet of metal used in printing 5 a book illustration 6 the part of false teeth that fits to the mouth ◇ *verb* cover with a coating of metal

plateau *noun* (*plural* **plateaus** or **plateaux**) 1 a broad level stretch of high land 2 a steady, unchanging state: *prices have now reached a plateau*

plate glass glass in thick sheets, used for shop windows, mirrors *etc*

platelet *noun* a tiny blood particle which plays a part in clotting

platform *noun* 1 a raised level surface for passengers at a railway station 2 a raised floor for speakers, entertainers *etc* 3 a computer system's hardware and operating system

▣ 2 stage, podium, dais, rostrum, stand

plating *noun* a thin covering of metal

platinum *noun* a heavy and very valuable steel-grey metal

platitude *noun* a dull, ordinary remark made as if it were important

▣ banality, commonplace, truism, cliché

platonic *adj* of a relationship: not sexual

platoon *noun* a section of a company of soldiers

platter *noun* a large, flat plate

platypus *noun* (*plural* **platypuses**) a small water animal of Australia that has webbed feet and lays eggs (*also called*: **duck-billed platypus**)

plaudits *noun plural* applause, praise

plausible *adj* **1** seeming to be truthful or honest **2** seeming probable or reasonable ◇**plausibility** *noun*

▣ **1** credible, believable **2** reasonable, logical, likely, possible, probable, convincing, persuasive

play *verb* **1** amuse yourself **2** take part in a game **3** gamble **4** act (a role) **5** perform on (a musical instrument) **6** carry out (a trick) **7** trifle or fiddle (with): *don't play with your food* **8** move over lightly: *the firelight played on his face* ◇*noun* **1** amusement, recreation **2** gambling **3** a story for acting, a drama **4** a way of behaving: *foul play* **5** freedom of movement ◇**play along** co-operate ◇**play off** set off (one person) against another to gain some advantage for yourself ◇**play on** make use of (someone's feelings) to your own advantage ◇**play on words** make a pun ◇**play the game** act fairly and honestly

▣ *verb* **1** have fun, enjoy oneself, revel, sport, romp, frolic, caper **2** participate, take part, join in, compete ◇ *noun* **1** fun, amusement, entertainment, diversion, recreation, sport **3** drama, tragedy, comedy, farce, show, performance **5** movement, action, flexibility, give, leeway, margin, scope, range, room, space ◇ **play on** exploit, take advantage of, profit by, trade on, capitalize on

playboy *noun* an irresponsible rich man only interested in pleasure

player *noun* **1** an actor **2** someone who plays a game, musical instrument *etc*: *a lute player*

playful *adj* **1** wanting to play: *a playful kitten* **2** fond of joking, not serious ◇**playfully** *adv* ◇**playfulness** *noun*

▣ **1** lively, spirited, frolicsome, ludic **2** mischievous, roguish, impish, good-natured, jesting, teasing, humorous, tongue-in-cheek

▣ **2** serious

playground *noun* an open area for playing at school, in a park *etc*

playgroup *noun* a group of young children who play together supervised by adults

playing-card *noun* one of a pack of cards used to play card games

playmate *noun* a friend with whom you play

play-off *noun* **1** a game to decide a tie **2** a game between the winners of other competitions

playschool *noun* a nursery school or playgroup

plaything *noun* a toy

playwright *noun* a writer of plays

PLC or **plc** *abbrev* public limited company

plea *noun* **1** an excuse **2** an accused person's answer to a charge in a lawcourt **3** an urgent request ◇**plea bargaining** the arranging of lenient terms for an accused person willing to plead guilty before their trial begins

▣ **1** defence, justification, excuse, explanation, claim **3** appeal, petition, request, entreaty, supplication, prayer, invocation

plead *verb* **1** state your case in a lawcourt **2** (*with* **with**) beg earnestly **3** give as an excuse: *plead ignorance* ◇**plead guilty** or **not guilty** admit or deny guilt in a law court

▣ **2** beg, implore, beseech, entreat, appeal, petition

pleasant *adj* giving pleasure; agreeable ◇**pleasantly** *adv* ◇**pleasantness** *noun*

▣ agreeable, nice, fine, lovely, delightful, charming, likable, amiable, friendly, affable, good-humoured, cheerful, congenial, enjoyable, amusing, pleasing, gratifying, satisfying, acceptable, welcome, refreshing

▣ unpleasant, nasty, unfriendly

pleasantry *noun* (*plural* **pleasantries**) a good-humoured joke

please *verb* **1** give pleasure or delight to **2** satisfy **3** choose, like (to do): *do as you please* ◇*exclam* added for politeness to a command or request: *please* *keep off the grass* ◇ **if you please** please

■ **1** delight, charm, captivate, entertain, amuse, cheer, gladden **2** indulge, humour, gratify, satisfy, content, suit **3** want, will, wish, desire, like, prefer, choose, think fit

☎ **1** displease, annoy, anger, sadden

pleasurable *adj* delightful, pleasant

pleasure *noun* **1** enjoyment, joy, delight **2** what you wish: *what is your pleasure?* ◇ **at your pleasure** when or if you please

■ **1** amusement, entertainment, recreation, fun, enjoyment, gratification, satisfaction, contentment, happiness, joy, delight, comfort, solace

☎ **1** sorrow, pain, trouble, displeasure

pleat *noun* a fold in cloth, which has been pressed or stitched down ◇ *verb* put pleats in ◇ **pleated** *adj*

pleb *noun*, *informal* someone of no taste or culture, a boor; a plebeian

plebeian *adj* **1** of the ordinary or common people **2** vulgar, lacking culture or taste ◇ *noun* a member of the common people

plebiscite *noun* a vote by everyone in an area on a special issue, for or against

plectrum *noun* a small piece of horn, metal *etc* used for plucking the strings of a guitar

pledge *noun* **1** something handed over as security for a loan **2** a solemn promise ◇ *verb* **1** give as security, pawn **2** promise solemnly

■ *noun* **1** deposit, security, surety, bail **2** promise, vow, word of honour, oath, bond, covenant, guarantee, warrant, assurance, undertaking ◇ *verb* **2** promise, vow, swear, contract, engage, undertake, vouch, guarantee

plenary *adj* **1** full, complete **2** of a meeting *etc*: attended by all members or delegates

plentiful or **plenteous** *adj* not scarce, abundant

■ ample, abundant, profuse, copious, overflowing, lavish, generous, liberal, bountiful, fruitful, productive

☎ scarce, scanty, rare

plenty *noun* **1** a full supply, as much as is needed **2** a large number or quantity (of)

■ **1** enough, sufficiency **2** quantity, mass, volume, fund, mine, abundance, profusion, plethora, *informal* lots, *informal* loads, *informal* masses, *informal* heaps, *informal* piles, *informal* stacks

plethora *noun* too large a quantity of anything: *a plethora of politicians*

pleurisy *noun* an illness in which the covering of the lungs becomes inflamed

pliable *adj* **1** easily bent or folded **2** easily persuaded ◇ **pliant** *adj* pliable

■ **1** pliant, flexible, bendable, *informal* bendy, supple, lithe, malleable, plastic, yielding **2** persuadable, responsive, receptive, impressionable, susceptible

☎ **2** rigid, inflexible, headstrong

pliers *noun plural* a tool used for gripping, bending and cutting wire *etc*

plight¹ *noun* a bad state or situation

■ predicament, quandary, dilemma, trouble, difficulty, straits, state, condition, situation, circumstances, case

plight² *verb*, *old* promise solemnly, pledge

plimsoll *noun* a light rubber-soled canvas shoe for sports ◇ **Plimsoll line** a ship's loadline

plinth *noun* **1** the square slab at the foot of a column **2** the base or pedestal of a statue, vase *etc*

PLO *abbrev* Palestine Liberation Organization

plod *verb* (**plods**, **plodding**, **plodded**) **1** travel slowly and steadily **2** work on steadily ◇ **plodder** *noun* a dull but hard-working person

■ **1** trudge, tramp, stump, lumber, clump **2** drudge, labour, toil, grind, slog, persevere, soldier on

plonk *noun*, *informal* cheap wine

plop *noun* the sound made by a small object falling into water ◇ *verb* (**plops**, **plopping**, **plopped**) make this sound

plot *noun* **1** a small piece of ground **2** a plan for an illegal or malicious action **3** the story of a play, novel *etc* ◇ *verb* (**plots**, **plotting**, **plotted**) **1** plan secretly **2** make a chart, graph *etc* of **3** mark points on a map, chart *etc* ◇ **plotter** *noun*

■ *noun* **1** patch, tract, area, allotment, lot **2** conspiracy, intrigue, scheme, plan, stratagem, machination **3** story, narrative, subject, theme, storyline, thread, outline, scenario ◇ *verb* **1** conspire, intrigue, scheme, hatch, lay, cook up, devise, contrive, plan, project, design, draft

plough *noun* a farm tool for turning up the soil ◇ *verb* **1** turn up the ground in furrows **2** work through slowly: *ploughing through the ironing* ◇ **the Plough** a group of seven stars forming a shape like an old plough

ploughman's lunch a cold dish of bread, cheese and pickle *etc*

ploughshare *noun* the blade of a plough

plover *noun* any of several kinds of bird that nest on the ground in open country

ploy *noun* a stratagem or manoeuvre

■ manoeuvre, stratagem, tactic, contrivance, scheme, game, trick, dodge, wile, ruse, subterfuge

pluck *verb* **1** pull out or off **2** pick (flowers, fruit *etc*) **3** strip off the feathers of (a bird) before cooking ◇ *noun* courage, spirit ◇ **pluck up courage** prepare yourself to face a danger or difficulty

■ *verb* **1** pull, draw, tug, snatch, pull off, remove **2** pick, collect, gather, harvest ◇ *noun* courage, bravery, spirit, mettle, *informal* nerve, *informal* guts, backbone, fortitude, resolution, determination

◤ *noun* cowardice

plucky *adj* brave, determined

■ brave, courageous, bold, daring, intrepid, heroic, valiant, spirited, feisty

◤ cowardly, weak, feeble

plug *noun* **1** an object fitted into a hole to stop it up **2** a fitting on an appliance put into a socket to connect with an electric current **3** *informal* a brief advertisement ◇ *verb* (**plugs**, **plugging**, **plugged**) **1** stop up with a plug **2** *informal* advertise, publicize

■ *noun* **1** stopper, bung, cork **3** *informal* advertisement, publicity, mention ◇ *verb* **1** stop (up), bung, cork, block, choke, close, seal, fill, pack, stuff **2** *informal* advertise, publicize, promote, push, *informal* hype, mention

plum *noun* **1** a soft fruit, often dark red or purple, with a stone in the centre **2** the tree that produces this fruit ◇ *adj* very good, very profitable *etc*: *a plum job* ◇ **plum pudding** a rich pudding containing dried fruit

plumage *noun* the feathers of a bird

plumb *noun* a lead weight hung on a string (**plumbline**), used *eg* to test if a wall is vertical ◇ *adj* & *adv* standing straight up or falling straight down, vertical ◇ *verb* test the depth of (the sea *etc*)

plumber *noun* someone who fits and mends water, gas and sewage pipes

plumbing *noun* **1** the work of a plumber **2** the drainage and water systems of a building *etc*

plume *noun* **1** a feather, *esp* an ornamental one **2** something looking like a feather: *a plume of smoke*

plummet *verb* plunge ◇ *noun* a weight of lead hung on a line, for taking depths at sea

■ *verb* plunge, dive, nose-dive, descend, drop, fall, tumble

◤ *verb* soar

plump *adj* fat, rounded, well filled out ◇ *verb* **1** grow fat, swell **2** beat or shake (cushions *etc*) back into shape **3** sit or sink down heavily ◇ **plump for** choose, vote for

■ *adj* fat, obese, dumpy, tubby, stout, round, rotund, portly, chubby, podgy, fleshy, full, ample, buxom ◇ **plump for** opt for, choose, select, favour, back, support

◤ *adj* thin, skinny

plunder *verb* carry off goods by force, loot, rob ◇ *noun* goods seized by force

■ *verb* loot, pillage, ravage, devastate, sack, raid, ransack, rifle, steal, rob, strip

plunge *verb* **1** dive (into water, through air *etc*) **2** thrust suddenly (into): *he plunged the knife into the ani-*

mal's neck ◇ *noun* a thrust; a dive

■ *verb* **1** dive, jump, nose-dive, swoop, dive-bomb, plummet, descend, go down, sink, drop, fall, pitch, tumble, hurtle, career, charge, dash, rush, tear ◇ *noun* dive, jump, swoop, descent, drop, fall, tumble, immersion, submersion

pluperfect *noun, grammar* showing an action which took place before the main past actions being described, *eg* he *had already left*, when you phoned

plural *adj* more than one ◇ *noun, grammar* the form which shows more than one, *eg* mice is the plural of *mouse* ◇ **plurality** *noun*

plus *prep* used to show addition, represented by the sign (+): *five plus two equals seven* ◇ *adj* of a quantity more than zero ◇ *adv, informal* and a bit extra: *she earns £20 000 plus*

plus fours baggy trousers reaching to just below the knees

> So called from the four additional inches of cloth needed for their length

plush *noun* cloth with a soft velvety surface on one side ◇ *adj* luxurious

plutocrat *noun* someone who is powerful because of their wealth ◇ **plutocratic** *adj*

ply¹ *verb* (**plies, plying, plied**) **1** work at steadily **2** make regular journeys: *the ferry plies between Oban and Mull* **3** use (a tool) energetically **4** keep supplying with (food, questions to answer *etc*)

ply² *noun* (*plural* **plies**) a thickness, layer or strand: *two-ply wool*

plywood *noun* a board made up of thin sheets of wood glued together

PM *abbrev* prime minister

pm *abbrev* after noon (from Latin *post meridiem*)

PMS *abbrev* premenstrual syndrome

PMT *abbrev* premenstrual tension

pneumatic /njʊˈmatɪk/ *adj* **1** filled with air **2** worked by air: *pneumatic drill*

pneumonia /njʊˈmoʊnɪə/ *noun* a disease in which the lungs become inflamed

PO *abbrev* **1** post office **2** postal order

poach *verb* **1** cook gently in boiling water or stock **2** catch fish or hunt game illegally ◇ **poacher** *noun* someone who hunts or fishes illegally

pocket *noun* **1** a small pouch or bag, *esp* as part of a garment **2** a personal supply of money: *well beyond my pocket* **3** a small isolated area: *a pocket of unemployment* ◇ *verb* **1** put in a pocket **2** steal ◇ **in** or **out of pocket** having gained or lost money on a deal *etc* ◇ **pocket-book** *noun* **1** a wallet **2** *US* a handbag ◇ **pocket money** an allowance of money for personal spending

■ *noun* **1** pouch, bag, envelope, receptacle, compartment, hollow, cavity ◇ *verb* **2** take, appropriate, help oneself to, lift, pilfer, filch, steal, *informal* nick, *informal* pinch

pockmark *noun* a scar or small hole in the skin left by disease

pod *noun* a long seed-case of the pea, bean *etc* ◇ *verb* (**pods, podding, podded**) **1** remove from a pod **2** form pods

podgy *adj* short and fat

podium *noun* a low pedestal, a platform

poem *noun* a piece of imaginative writing set out in lines which often have a regular rhythm or rhyme

poesy *noun, old* poetry

poet *noun* someone who writes poetry

poetaster *noun* a writer of bad poetry

poetic *adj* of or like poetry ◇ **poetically** *adv* ◇ **poetic justice** a fitting reward or punishment ◇ **poetic licence** a departure from truth, logic *etc* for the sake of effect

■ poetical, lyrical, moving, artistic, graceful, flowing, metrical, rhythmical, rhyming

▰ prosaic

poetry *noun* **1** the art of writing poems **2** poems

po-faced *adj* stupidly solemn, humourless

pogo stick a child's stick with a spring in it for jumping up and down

pogrom *noun* an organized killing or massacre of a group of people

poignant *adj* **1** sharp, keen **2** very painful or moving; pathetic ◇**poignancy** *noun*
- **2** moving, touching, affecting, tender, distressing, upsetting, heartbreaking, pathetic, sad, painful, agonizing

poinsettia *noun* a plant, originally from Mexico, with large scarlet or white petal-like leaves

point *noun* **1** a sharp end of anything **2** a headland **3** a dot: *points of light* **4** a full stop in punctuation, *esp* one used in a decimal fraction **5** an exact place or spot **6** an exact moment of time **7** the chief matter of an argument **8** the meaning of a joke *etc* **9** a mark in a competition **10** a purpose, an advantage: *there is no point in going* **11** a movable rail to direct a railway engine from one line to another **12** an electrical wall socket **13** a mark of character: *he has many good points* ◇*verb* **1** make pointed: *point your toes* **2** direct, aim **3** indicate with a gesture: *pointing to the building* **4** fill (wall joints) with mortar
- *noun* **3** dot, spot, mark, speck **5** place, position, situation, location, site, spot **6** moment, instant, juncture, stage, time, period **7** essence, crux, core, gist, thrust, meaning, drift **10** use, purpose, motive, reason, object, intention, aim, end, goal, objective **13** feature, attribute, aspect ◇*verb* **2** aim, direct, train, level **3** indicate, signal, show

point-blank *adj* **1** of a shot: fired from very close range **2** of a question: direct
- **2** direct, forthright, straightforward, plain, explicit, open, unreserved, blunt, frank, candid

pointed *adj* **1** having a point, sharp **2** of a remark: obviously aimed at someone
- **2** sharp, keen, edged, barbed, cutting, incisive, biting, penetrating, telling

pointer *noun* **1** a rod for pointing **2** a type of dog used to show where game has fallen

pointless *adj* having no meaning or purpose
- useless, futile, vain, fruitless, unproductive, unprofitable, worthless, senseless, absurd, meaningless, aimless
- useful, profitable, meaningful

poise *verb* **1** balance, keep steady **2** hover in the air ◇*noun* **1** a state of balance **2** dignity, self-confidence
- *noun* **2** composure, coolness, equanimity, aplomb, assurance, dignity, elegance, grace

poised *adj* **1** balanced, having poise **2** prepared, ready: *poised for action*
- **1** dignified, graceful, calm, composed, unruffled, collected, self-possessed, cool, self-confident, assured **2** prepared, ready, set, waiting, expectant

poison *noun* **1** a substance which, when taken into the body, kills or harms **2** anything harmful ◇*verb* **1** kill or harm with poison **2** add poison to **3** make bitter or bad: *poisoned her mind* ◇**poison ivy** a N American plant whose juice causes a skin rash ◇**poison-pen letter** a malicious anonymous letter ◇**poison pill** *informal* an action taken to prevent a threatened takeover bid by making a company seem undesirable
- *verb* **1** infect, contaminate, pollute **3** adulterate, corrupt, deprave, pervert, warp

poisonous *adj* **1** containing poison **2** causing evil
- **1** toxic, venomous, lethal, deadly, fatal, mortal, noxious **2** pernicious, malicious

poke *verb* **1** push (*eg* a finger or stick) into something **2** prod, thrust at **3** search about inquisitively ◇*noun* **1** a nudge, a prod **2** a prying search
- *verb* **1** prod, stab, jab, stick **2** thrust, push, shove, nudge, elbow, dig, butt

poker *noun* **1** a rod for stirring up a fire **2** a card game in which players bet on their chance of winning

poky *adj* cramped and shabby

polar *adj* of the regions round the north or south poles

polarity *noun* the state of having two opposite poles

polarize *verb* **1** give polarity to **2** split into opposing sides

polaroid *noun*, *trademark* **1** a plastic through which light is seen less brightly **2** a camera which develops individual pictures in a few seconds

pole *noun* **1** a long rounded rod or post **2** either end of the earth's axis **3** either of the opposing points of a magnet or electric battery ◇**pole star** the star most directly above the north pole ◇**pole vault** a sport in which an athlete jumps over a bar with the aid of a flexible pole

≡ **1** bar, rod, stick, shaft, spar, upright, post, stake, mast, staff

polecat *noun* **1** a large kind of weasel **2** *US* a skunk

polemic or **polemical** *adj* expressing strong, often controversial views ◇**polemicist** *noun* someone who writes polemic material

police *noun* the body of men and women whose work it is to see that laws are obeyed *etc* ◇*verb* keep law and order in (a place) by use of police ◇**policeman, policewoman** *noun* ◇**police station** the headquarters of the police in a district

≡ *verb* check, control, regulate, monitor, watch, observe, supervise, oversee, patrol, guard, protect, defend, keep the peace

policy *noun* (*plural* **policies**) **1** an agreed course of action **2** a written agreement with an insurance company

≡ **1** course of action, line, course, plan, programme, scheme, stance, position

polio *short for* **poliomyelitis**

poliomyelitis *noun* a disease of the spinal cord, causing weakness or paralysis of the muscles

polish *verb* **1** make smooth and shiny by rubbing **2** improve ◇*noun* **1** a gloss on a surface **2** a substance used for polishing **3** fine manners, style *etc*

≡ *verb* **1** shine, brighten, smooth, rub, buff, burnish, clean, wax **2** improve, enhance, brush up, touch up, finish, perfect, refine, cultivate ◇*noun* **3** refinement, cultivation, class, breeding, sophistication, finesse, style, elegance, grace, poise

◫ *verb* **1** tarnish, dull

polite *adj* having good manners, courteous ◇**politely** *adv* ◇**politeness** *noun*

≡ courteous, well-mannered, respectful, civil, well-bred, refined, cultured, gracious, obliging, thoughtful, considerate, tactful, diplomatic

◫ impolite, discourteous, rude

politic *adj* wise, cautious

political *adj* of government, politicians or politics

Political ideologies include:
absolutism, anarchism,
authoritarianism, Bolshevism,
Christian democracy, collectivism,
communism, conservatism,
democracy, egalitarianism, fascism,
federalism, holism, imperialism,
individualism, liberalism, Maoism,
Marxism, nationalism, Nazism,
neocolonialism, neo-fascism, neo-
nazism, pluralism, republicanism,
social democracy, socialism,
syndicalism, Thatcherism,
theocracy, totalitarianism,
unilateralism, Trotskyism, Whiggism

---

politician *noun* someone involved in politics, *esp* a member of parliament

politicize *verb* make aware of political issues

politicking *noun* working in politics, vote-seeking

politico *noun* (*plural* **politicos** or **politicoes**) *informal* a politician

politics *noun sing* the art or study of government

≡ public affairs, civics, affairs of state, statecraft, government, diplomacy, statesmanship, political science

polka *noun* a lively dance or the music for it

poll *noun* **1** an election **2** total number of votes **3** (*also called* **opinion poll**) a test of public opinion by questioning

◇ *verb* **1** receive (votes): *they polled 5000 votes* **2** cut or clip off (hair, branches *etc*) ◇ **polling station** a place where voting is done ◇ **poll tax** *Brit hist* the community charge

pollard *noun* a tree with its top cut off to allow new growth ◇ *verb* cut the top off (a tree)

pollen *noun* the fertilizing powder of flowers

pollinate *verb* fertilize with pollen ◇ **pollination** *noun*

pollutant *noun* something that pollutes

pollute *verb* **1** make dirty or impure **2** make (the environment) harmful to life
■ **1** contaminate, infect, poison, taint, adulterate, dirty, foul, soil, sully, stain, mar, spoil

pollution *noun* **1** the act of polluting **2** something which pollutes
■ **1** contamination, adulteration, corruption **2** impurity, infection, taint, corruption, dirtiness, foulness
Ⓔ **1** purification **2** purity, cleanness

polo *noun* a game like hockey played on horseback ◇ **polo neck 1** a close-fitting neck with a part turned over at the top **2** a jumper with a neck like this

polonaise *noun* a slow Polish dance

poltergeist *noun* a kind of ghost believed to move furniture and throw objects around a room

poly- *prefix* many, much

polyanthus *noun* a hybrid plant which produces many flowers

polyester *noun* a synthetic material often used in clothing

polygamy *noun* the fact of having more than one wife or husband at the same time ◇ **polygamist** *noun* ◇ **polygamous** *adj*

polyglot *adj* speaking, or written in, many languages ◇ *noun* someone fluent in many languages

polygon *noun* a figure with many angles and sides ◇ **polygonal** *adj*

polygraph *noun* an instrument which measures pulse rate *etc*, used as a lie-detector

polymath *noun* someone with knowledge of a wide range of subjects

polymer *noun* a chemical compound with large molecules

polyp *noun* **1** a small sea-animal with arms or tentacles **2** a kind of tumour

polyphony *noun* musical composition in parts, each with a separate melody ◇ **polyphonic** *adj*

polystyrene *noun* a synthetic material which resists moisture, used for packing, disposable cups *etc*

polysyllable *noun* a word of two or more syllables ◇ **polysyllabic** *adj*

polytechnic *noun* formerly, a college which taught technical and vocational subjects

polythene *noun* a type of plastic that can be moulded when hot

polyunsaturated *adj* of oil: containing no cholesterol

polyurethane *noun* a resin used to produce foam materials

pomegranate *noun* a fruit with a thick skin, many seeds and pulpy edible flesh

pommel *noun* **1** the knob on the hilt of a sword **2** the high part of a saddle

pomp *noun* solemn and splendid ceremony, magnificence
■ ceremony, ritual, solemnity, formality, state, grandeur, splendour, magnificence, pageantry, show, display, parade, ostentation, flourish
Ⓔ austerity, simplicity

pompous *adj* self-important, excessively dignified ◇ **pomposity** *noun*
■ self-important, arrogant, grandiose, supercilious, overbearing, imperious, magisterial, bombastic, overblown, affected, pretentious, ostentatious
Ⓔ unassuming, modest, simple, unaffected

poncho *noun* (*plural* **ponchos**) a S American cloak made of a blanket with a hole for the head

pond *noun* a small lake or pool

ponder *verb* think over, consider ◇ **ponderous** *adj* **1** weighty **2** clumsy **3** sounding very important

pontiff *noun* **1** a Roman Catholic bishop **2** the Pope

pontifical *adj* **1** of a pontiff **2** pompous in speech

pontificate *verb* speak in a pompous manner

pontoon¹ *noun* a flat-bottomed boat used to support a temporary bridge

pontoon² *noun* a card game in which players try to collect 21 points

pony *noun* (*plural* **ponies**) a small horse ◇ **pony-trekking** *noun* riding cross-country in small parties

poodle *noun* a breed of dog, with curly hair often clipped in a fancy way

pool *noun* **1** a small area of still water **2** a deep part of a river **3** a joint fund or stock (of money, typists *etc*) **4** the money played for in a gambling game ◇ *verb* put (money *etc*) into a joint fund ◇ **football pools** organized betting on football match results

■ *noun* **1** puddle, pond, lake, watering-hole, paddling-pool, swimming-pool **3** fund, reserve, accumulation, bank, kitty, purse, pot, jackpot ◇ *verb* contribute, *informal* chip in, combine, amalgamate, merge, share

poop *noun* **1** a ship's stern, or back part **2** a high deck in the stern

poor *adj* **1** having little money or property **2** not good: *this work is poor* **3** lacking (in): *poor in sports facilities* **4** deserving pity: *poor Tom has broken his leg* ◇ **the poor** those with little money

■ **1** impoverished, poverty-stricken, badly off, hard-up, *informal* broke, *slang* stony-broke, *slang* skint, bankrupt, penniless, destitute **2** bad, substandard, unsatisfactory, inferior, mediocre, second-rate, third-rate, shoddy, imperfect, faulty, weak, feeble **3** lacking, deficient, insufficient, meagre, sparse **4** unfortunate, unlucky, luckless, ill-fated, unhappy, miserable, pathetic, pitiable, pitiful

■ **1** rich, wealthy, affluent **2** superior, impressive **4** fortunate, lucky

poorly *adj* in bad health, ill

■ ill, sick, unwell, indisposed, ailing, sickly, off colour, *informal* out of sorts, *informal* under the weather, seedy, groggy, *informal* rotten

■ well, healthy

pop *noun* **1** a sharp quick noise, *eg* that made by a cork coming out of a bottle **2** a fizzy soft drink **3** popular music ◇ *verb* (**pops**, **popping**, **popped**) **1** (cause to) make a short, quick noise, *eg* by bursting **2** move quickly, dash: *pop in/pop along the road* ◇ *adj* of music: popular

■ *noun* **1** bang, crack, snap, burst, explosion

popadom or **popadum** *noun* a thin circle of dough fried in oil until crisp

popcorn *noun* a kind of maize that bursts open when heated

Pope or **pope** *noun* the bishop of Rome, head of the Roman Catholic Church

poplar *noun* a tall, narrow quick-growing tree

poplin *noun* strong cotton cloth

poppy *noun* (*plural* **poppies**) a plant growing wild in fields *etc* with large scarlet flowers

populace *noun* the people of a country or area

popular *adj* **1** of the people: *popular vote* **2** liked by most people **3** widely held or believed: *popular belief* ◇ **popularity** *noun* the state of being generally liked ◇ **popularize** *verb* make popular or widely known ◇ **popularly** *adv*

■ **2** well-liked, favourite, liked, favoured, approved, in demand, sought-after, fashionable, modish, *informal* trendy, *informal* in **3** conventional, standard, stock, common, prevalent, widespread, universal, general, household, famous, well-known ◇ **popularly** commonly, widely, universally, generally, usually, customarily, conventionally, traditionally

populate *verb* fill (an area) with people

■ people, occupy, settle, colonize, inhabit, live in, overrun

population *noun* the number of people living in a place

◨ inhabitants, natives, residents, citizens, occupants, community, society, people

populist *adj* appealing to the mass of people ◇**populism** *noun*

populous *adj* full of people ◇**populousness** *noun*

◨ crowded, packed, swarming, teeming, crawling, overpopulated

◧ deserted

porcelain *noun* a kind of fine china

porch *noun* (*plural* **porches**) a covered entrance to a building

porcupine *noun* a large gnawing animal, covered with sharp quills

pore *noun* **1** a tiny hole **2** the hole of a sweat gland in the skin

> ⚠ Do not confuse with: **pour**

pore over study closely or eagerly

pork *noun* the flesh of the pig, prepared for eating

porn *noun*, *informal* pornography

pornography *noun* literature or art that is sexually explicit and often offensive ◇**pornographic** *adj*

porous *adj* **1** having pores **2** allowing fluid to pass through ◇**porosity** *noun*

◨ **1** honeycombed, pitted **2** permeable, pervious, penetrable, absorbent, spongy

◧ **2** impermeable, impervious

porpoise *noun* a blunt-nosed sea animal of the dolphin family

porridge *noun* a food made from oatmeal boiled in water or milk

porringer *noun* a small bowl for soup, porridge *etc*

port¹ *noun* **1** a harbour **2** a town with a harbour

port² *noun* the left side of a ship as you face the front

port³ *noun* a strong, dark red sweet wine

port⁴ *noun* **1** an opening in a ship's side for loading *etc* **2** *comput* a socket connecting the main processor to a peripheral device

portable *adj* able to be lifted and carried ◇*noun* a computer, telephone *etc*

that can be carried around ◇**portability** *noun*

◨ *adj* movable, transportable, compact, lightweight, manageable, handy, convenient

◧ *adj* fixed, immovable

portal *noun* a grand entrance or doorway

portcullis *noun* (*plural* **portcullises**) a grating which is let down quickly to close a gateway

portend *verb* give warning of, foretell

portent *noun* a warning sign

portentous *adj* **1** strange, wonderful **2** important, weighty ◇**portentousness** *noun*

porter *noun* **1** someone employed to carry luggage, push hospital trolleys *etc* **2** a doorkeeper **3** a kind of dark brown beer

portfolio *noun* (*plural* **portfolios**) **1** a case for carrying papers, drawings *etc* **2** the job of a government minister

porthole *noun* a small round window in a ship's side

portico *noun* (*plural* **porticoes** or **porticos**) a row of columns in front of a building forming a porch or covered walk

portion *noun* **1** a part **2** a share, a helping ◇*verb* divide into parts

◨ *noun* **1** part, section, division, fraction, percentage, piece, segment, slice **2** allocation, allotment, share, allowance, ration, quota, measure, serving, helping

portly *adj* stout and dignified

◨ stout, corpulent, rotund, round, fat, plump, obese, overweight, heavy, large

◧ slim, thin, slight

portmanteau *noun* a large leather travelling bag

portrait *noun* **1** a drawing, painting, or photograph of a person **2** a description of a person, place *etc*

◨ **1** picture, painting, drawing, sketch, caricature, miniature, icon, photograph, likeness, image, representation **2** profile, characterization, description, depiction, portrayal

portray verb (**portrays**, **portraying**, **portrayed**) **1** make a painting or drawing of **2** describe in words **3** act the part of ◇ **portrayal** noun

■ **1** draw, sketch, paint **2** depict, describe **3** impersonate, characterize, personify

Portuguese man-of-war a stinging jellyfish

pose noun **1** a position of the body: *a relaxed pose* **2** behaviour put on to impress others, a pretence ◇ verb **1** position yourself for a photograph *etc* **2** (with **as**) pretend or claim to be what you are not: *posing as an expert* **3** put forward (a problem, question *etc*)

■ noun **1** position, stance, air, bearing, posture, attitude **2** pretence, sham, affectation, façade, front, masquerade, role, act, charade ◇ verb **1** model, sit, position **2** pretend, feign, affect, put on an act, masquerade, pass oneself off, impersonate **3** set, put forward, submit, present

poser noun **1** a poseur **2** a difficult question

poseur noun someone who behaves in an affected way to impress others

posh adj, informal high-class; smart

■ smart, stylish, fashionable, high-class, upper-class, grand, luxurious, lavish, informal swanky, luxury, deluxe, up-market, exclusive, select, informal classy

✤ inferior, cheap

posit verb postulate, assume as true for the sake of argument

position noun **1** place, situation **2** manner of standing, sitting *etc*: *in a crouching position* **3** a rank or job: *a high position in a bank* ◇ verb place

■ noun **1** place, situation, location, site, spot, point **2** posture, stance, pose, arrangement, disposition **3** rank, grade, level, status, standing, job, post, occupation, employment, office, duty, function, role ◇ verb put, place, set, fix, stand, arrange, dispose, lay out, deploy, station, locate, situate, site

positive adj **1** meaning or saying 'yes': *a positive answer* (contrasted with: **negative**) **2** not able to be doubted: *positive proof* **3** certain, convinced: *I am positive*

that she did it **4** definite: *a positive improvement* **5** greater than zero **6** grammar of an adjective or adverb: of the first degree of comparison, *eg big*, not *bigger* or *biggest*

■ **2** definite, decisive, conclusive, clear, unmistakable, explicit, unequivocal, express, firm, undeniable, irrefutable, indisputable **3** sure, certain, convinced, confident, assured

✤ **2** indefinite, vague **3** uncertain

positron noun a particle with a positive electrical charge

posse /'pɒsɪ/ noun a body of police *etc*

possess verb **1** own, have **2** take hold of your mind: *anger possessed her*

■ **1** own, have, hold, obtain, acquire **2** seize, take, take over, occupy, control, dominate, bewitch, haunt

possessed adj **1** in the power of an evil spirit **2** obsessed **3** self-possessed, calm

possession noun **1** the state of possessing **2** the state of being possessed **3** something owned

possessive adj **1** grammar showing possession, *eg* the adjectives *my, your, their etc* **2** over-protective and jealous in attitude

■ **2** selfish, clinging, overprotective, domineering, dominating, jealous, covetous, acquisitive, grasping

✤ **2** unselfish, sharing

possessor noun an owner

possibility noun (plural **possibilities**) something that may happen or that may be done

possible adj **1** able to happen or to be done **2** not unlikely

■ **1** workable, achievable, attainable, accomplishable, realizable, practicable, feasible, viable **2** potential, promising, likely, probable, imaginable, conceivable

✤ **1** impracticable, unattainable **2** impossible, unthinkable

possibly adv perhaps

■ perhaps, maybe

possum noun a tree-dwelling animal which carries its young in a pouch **play**

possum pretend to be asleep or dead

post[1] *noun* an upright pole or stake ◊ *verb* put up, stick up (a notice *etc*)

■ *noun* pole, stake, picket, pale, pillar, column, shaft, support, upright, stanchion, strut ◊ *verb* display, stick up, pin up

post[2] *noun* **1** a job: *teaching post* **2** a place of duty: *the soldier remained at his post* **3** a settlement, a camp: *military post/trading post* ◊ *verb* send or station somewhere: *posted abroad*

■ *noun* **1** office, job, employment, position, situation, place, vacancy, appointment **2** assignment, station, beat ◊ *verb* station, locate, situate, position, place, put, appoint, assign, second, transfer, move, send

post[3] *noun* (the service which delivers) letters and other mail ◊ *verb* put (a letter) in a postbox for collection ◊ **post office** an office for sending mail, buying stamps *etc*

■ *verb* mail, send, dispatch, transmit

post- *prefix* after

postage *noun* money paid for sending a letter *etc* by post ◊ **postage stamp** a small printed label to show that postage has been paid

postal *adj* of or by post ◊ **postal order** a document bought at a post office which can be exchanged for a stated amount of money

postbox *noun* a box with an opening in which to post letters *etc*

postcard *noun* a card for sending a message by post

postcode *noun* a short series of letters and numbers, used for sorting mail by machine

post-date *verb* mark (a cheque) with a date in the future, so that it cannot be cashed immediately

poster *noun* **1** a large notice or placard **2** a large printed picture

■ **1** notice, bill, sign, placard, sticker, advertisement, announcement

posterior *adj* situated behind, coming after ◊ *noun* the buttocks

posterity *noun* **1** all future genera-

tions **2** someone's descendants

postern *noun* a back door or gate to a castle *etc*

post-free *adv* without charge for postage

postgraduate *adj* of study *etc*: following on from a first university degree ◊ *noun* someone continuing to study after a first degree

post-haste *adv* with great speed

posthumous *adj* **1** of a work: published after the author's or composer's death **2** of a child: born after the father's death

postilion or **postillion** *noun*, *old* a carriage driver who rides on one of the horses

postman, postwoman *noun* someone who delivers letters

postmark *noun* a date stamp put on a letter at a post office

postmaster, postmistress *noun* an official in charge of a post office

postmortem *noun* an examination of a dead body to find out the cause of death

postpone *verb* put off to a future time, delay ◊ **postponement** *noun*

■ put off, defer, put back, hold over, delay, adjourn, suspend, shelve, pigeonhole, freeze, put on ice

🔁 advance, forward

postscript *noun* an added remark at the end of a letter, after the sender's name

postulant *noun* someone applying to enter a religious order

postulate *verb* assume or take for granted (that)

■ theorize, hypothesize, suppose, assume, propose, advance, lay down, stipulate

posture *noun* **1** the manner in which someone holds themselves in standing or walking **2** a pose adopted for effect

■ **1** disposition, bearing, carriage, deportment, position, stance, pose, attitude

postwar *adj* relating to the time after a war

posy *noun* (*plural* **posies**) a small bunch of flowers

pot¹ *noun* **1** a deep vessel used in cooking, as a container, or for growing plants **2** (**pots**) *informal* a great deal: *pots of money* ◇ *verb* (**pots**, **potting**, **potted**) **1** plant in a pot **2** make articles of baked clay ◇ **pot belly** a protruding stomach ◇ **pot plant** a household plant kept in a pot ◇ **pot shot** a casual or random shot ◇ **take pot luck** take whatever is available or offered

■ *noun* **1** receptacle, vessel, teapot, coffee pot, urn, jar, vase, bowl, basin, pan, cauldron, crucible

pot² *noun, slang* marijuana

potash *noun* potassium carbonate, obtained from the ashes of wood

potassium *noun* a type of silvery-white metal

potato *noun* (*plural* **potatoes**) **1** a plant with round starchy roots which are eaten as a vegetable **2** the vegetable itself ◇ **couch potato** *see* couch

potboiler *noun* a book with a sensational plot, written simply to make money

poteen *noun* illicit Irish whiskey

potent *adj* powerful, strong ◇ **potency** *noun*

■ powerful, mighty, strong, intoxicating, pungent, effective, impressive, convincing, persuasive, compelling, forceful, dynamic, vigorous, authoritative, commanding, dominant, influential, overpowering

🖃 impotent, weak

potentate *noun* a powerful ruler

potential *adj* that may develop, possible ◇ *noun* the possibility of further development ◇ **potentiality** *noun* (*plural* **potentialities**) a possibility ◇ **potentially** *adv*

■ *adj* possible, likely, probable, prospective, future, aspiring, promising, budding, undeveloped, dormant, latent, hidden, concealed, unrealized ◇ *noun* possibility, ability, capability, capacity, aptitude, talent, powers, resources

pothole *noun* **1** a deep cave **2** a hole

worn in a road surface ◇ **potholer** *noun* someone who explores caves

potion *noun* a drink, often containing medicine or poison

■ mixture, concoction, brew, beverage, drink, draught, dose, medicine, tonic, elixir

potpourri /poʊˈpʊəri/ *noun* **1** a scented mixture of dried petals *etc* **2** a mixture or medley

■ **2** medley, mixture, jumble, hotchpotch, mix, miscellany, collection

potted *adj* **1** of meat: pressed down and preserved in a jar **2** condensed and simplified: *potted history*

potter¹ *noun* someone who makes articles of baked clay

potter² *verb* **1** do small odd jobs **2** dawdle

■ *verb* **1** tinker, fiddle, *informal* mess about, dabble

pottery *noun* (*plural* **potteries**) **1** articles made of baked clay **2** a place where such things are made **3** the art of making them

potty¹ *adj, informal* mad, eccentric

potty² *noun, informal* a child's receptacle for urine and faeces

pouch *noun* (*plural* **pouches**) **1** a pocket or small bag **2** a bag-like fold on the front of a kangaroo *etc*, for carrying its young

pouffe *noun* a low, stuffed seat without back or arms

poulterer *noun* someone who sells poultry and game

poultice *noun* a semi-liquid mixture spread on a bandage and put on inflamed skin ◇ *verb* put a poultice on

poultry *noun* farmyard fowls, *eg* hens, ducks, geese, turkeys

pounce *verb* (often with **on**) seize, attack ◇ *noun* **1** a sudden attack **2** a bird's claw

■ *verb* fall on, dive on, swoop, drop, attack, strike, ambush, spring, jump, leap, snatch, grab

pound¹ *noun* **1** the standard unit of money in Britain, shown by the sign (£), equal to 100 pence **2** a measure of weight, written lb, equal to 16 ounces (about 0.45 kilogram)

pound² 1 an enclosure for animals 2 a place where illegally parked cars are kept after being taken into police charge

pound³ *verb* 1 beat into powder 2 beat heavily 3 walk or run with heavy steps

▪ *verb* 1 pulverize, powder, grind, mash, crush 2 strike, thump, beat, drum, pelt, pummel, hammer, batter, bang, throb, pulsate, palpitate, thud

pour *verb* 1 flow in a stream: *the blood poured from the wound/the crowd poured into the square* 2 cause to flow (out): *pour the tea* 3 rain heavily

▪ 1 spill, issue, discharge, flow, stream, run, rush, spout, spew, gush, cascade, crowd, throng, swarm 2 serve, decant, tip

⚠ Do not confuse with: **pore**

pout *verb* push out the lips sulkily to show displeasure ◇ *noun* a sulky look

▪ *verb* scowl, glower, grimace, pull a face, sulk, mope ◇ *noun* scowl, glower, grimace, moue, long face

poverty *noun* 1 the state of being poor 2 lack, want: *poverty of ideas*

▪ 1 poorness, impoverishment, insolvency, bankruptcy, pennilessness, penury, destitution, distress, hardship, privation 2 need, necessity, want, lack, deficiency, shortage, inadequacy, insufficiency, depletion, scarcity

▪ 1 wealth, richness 2 affluence, plenty

POW *abbrev* prisoner of war

powder *noun* 1 a substance made up of very fine particles 2 gunpowder 3 cosmetic powder for the face ◇ *verb* 1 sprinkle or dab with powder 2 grind down to powder ◇ **powdered** *adj* 1 in fine particles 2 covered with powder ◇ **powdery** *adj* 1 covered with powder 2 like powder: *powdery snow*

▪ **powdery** 1 dusty, sandy 2 grainy, granular, powdered, pulverized, ground, fine, loose, dry, crumbly, chalky

power *noun* 1 strength, force 2 ability to do things 3 authority or legal right 4 a strong nation 5 someone in authority 6 the force used for driving machines: *electric power/steam power* 7 *maths* the product obtained by multiplying a number by itself a given number of times (*eg* $2 \times 2 \times 2$ or 2^3 is the third power of 2) ◇ **powerful** *adj* ◇ **power station** a building where electricity is produced

▪ 1 potency, strength, intensity, force, vigour, energy 2 ability, capability, capacity, potential, faculty, competence 3 right, privilege, prerogative, authorization, warrant ◇ **powerful** dominant, prevailing, leading, influential, high-powered, authoritative, commanding, potent, effective, strong, mighty, robust, muscular, energetic, forceful, impressive, convincing, persuasive, compelling, overwhelming

▪ **powerful** impotent, ineffective, weak

power-driven or **powered** *adj* worked by electricity, not by hand

powerless *adj* without power or ability: *we were powerless to help*

▪ impotent, incapable, ineffective, weak, feeble, frail, infirm, incapacitated, disabled, paralysed, helpless, vulnerable, defenceless, unarmed

▪ powerful, potent, able

pow-wow *noun* 1 *hist* a Native American gathering for debate 2 *informal* a conference, a debate

pp *abbrev* pages

PR *abbrev* 1 proportional representation 2 public relations

practicable *adj* able to be used or done

▪ possible, feasible, performable, achievable, attainable, viable, workable, practical, realistic

▪ impracticable

practical *adj* 1 preferring action to thought 2 efficient 3 involving or learned by actually doing something: *practical knowledge* ◇ **practical joke** a joke consisting of action, not words

▪ 2 experienced, trained, qualified, skilled, accomplished, proficient

▪ 1 impractical 2 unskilled 3 theoretical

practically *adv* 1 in a practical way 2

in effect, in reality **3** almost: *practically empty*

■ **1** sensibly, reasonably, rationally, pragmatically **2** realistically, in principle, in effect, essentially, fundamentally **3** almost, nearly, virtually, pretty well, all but, just about

practice *noun* **1** habit: *it is my practice to get up early* **2** the actual doing of something: *putting their ideas into practice* **3** repeated performance to improve skill: *piano practice/in practice for the race* **4** the business of a doctor, lawyer *etc*

■ *noun* **1** custom, tradition, convention, usage, habit, routine, way, method, system, procedure, policy **2** effect, reality, actuality, action, operation, performance, use, application **3** rehearsal, run-through, try-out, training, drill, exercise, work-out, study, experience

ᴇᴈ **2** theory, principle

🛈 Do not confuse: **practice** and **practise**

practise or *US* **practice** *verb* **1** perform or exercise repeatedly to improve a skill: *he practises judo nightly* **2** make a habit of: *practise self-control* **3** follow (a profession): *practise dentistry*

■ **1** rehearse, run through, repeat, drill, exercise, train, study, perfect **2** do, perform, execute, implement, carry out, apply **3** follow, pursue, engage in, undertake

practitioner *noun* someone engaged in a profession: *a medical practitioner*

pragmatic or **pragmatical** *adj* relating to fact, rather than ideas or theories, practical ◇ **pragmatism** *noun* ◇ **pragmatist** *noun*

■ practical, realistic, sensible, matter-of-fact, businesslike, efficient, hard-headed, *informal* hard-nosed, unsentimental

ᴇᴈ unrealistic, idealistic, romantic

prairie *noun* a stretch of level grassland in N America

praise *verb* **1** speak highly of **2** glorify (God) by singing hymns *etc* ◇ *noun* an expression of approval

■ *verb* **1** commend, congratulate, admire, compliment, flatter, applaud, cheer **2** acclaim, hail, recognize, honour, laud, glorify, magnify, exalt, worship, adore, bless ◇ *noun* approval, admiration, commendation, congratulation, compliment, flattery, adulation, applause, ovation, cheering, acclaim, recognition, tribute, accolade, homage, honour, glory, worship, adoration, devotion

ᴇᴈ *verb* **1** criticize, revile

praiseworthy *adj* deserving to be praised

■ commendable, fine, excellent, admirable, worthy, deserving, honourable, reputable, estimable, sterling

ᴇᴈ blameworthy, dishonourable, ignoble

pram *noun* a small wheeled carriage for a baby, pushed by hand

prance *verb* **1** strut or swagger about **2** dance about **3** of a horse: spring from the hind legs

prank *noun* a trick played for mischief

■ trick, practical joke, joke, jape, stunt, caper, frolic, lark, antic, escapade

prat *noun*, *slang* an idiot

prate *verb* talk foolishly

prattle *verb* talk or chatter meaninglessly ◇ *noun* meaningless talk

prawn *noun* a type of shellfish like the shrimp

pray *verb* **1** ask earnestly, beg **2** speak to God in prayer ◇ **praying mantis** *see* mantis

■ **1** entreat, implore, plead, beg, beseech, petition, ask, request, crave, solicit

🛈 Do not confuse with: **prey**

prayer *noun* **1** an earnest request for something **2** a request, or thanks, given to God

pre- *prefix* before

preach *verb* **1** give a sermon **2** teach, speak in favour of: *preach caution* ◇ **preacher** *noun* someone who gives religious sermons

preamble *noun* something said as an introduction

prearrange *verb* arrange beforehand

precarious *adj* uncertain, risky, dangerous ◇**precariously** *adv*

■ unsafe, dangerous, treacherous, risky, hazardous, chancy, uncertain, unsure, dubious, doubtful, unpredictable, unreliable, unsteady, unstable, shaky, wobbly, insecure, vulnerable

◪ safe, certain, stable, secure

precaution *noun* care taken beforehand to avoid an accident *etc* ◇**precautionary** *adj*

■ safeguard, security, protection, insurance, providence, caution, prudence, foresight, anticipation, preparation ◇**precautionary** safety, protective, preventive, cautious, prudent, preparatory

precede *verb* go before in time, order, rank or importance

■ come before, lead, come first, go before, take precedence, introduce, herald, usher in

◪ follow, succeed

⚠ Do not confuse with: **proceed**

precedence *noun* the right to go before; priority

■ priority, preference, pride of place, superiority, supremacy, lead, first place, seniority, rank

precedent *noun* a past action which serves as an example or rule for the future

■ example, instance, pattern, model, standard, criterion

preceding *adj* going before; previous

precentor *noun* someone who leads the singing in a church

precept *noun* a guiding rule, a commandment

precinct *noun* **1** an area enclosed by the boundary walls of a building **2** (**precincts**) the area closely surrounding any place **3** *US* an administrative district ◇**shopping precinct** a shopping centre, often closed to traffic

precious *adj* **1** highly valued or valuable **2** over-fussy or precise

■ **1** valued, treasured, prized, cherished, beloved, favourite, loved, adored, idolized, valuable, expensive, costly, dear, priceless, rare, choice, fine

precipice *noun* a steep cliff

precipitate *verb* **1** throw head foremost **2** force into hasty action *etc* **3** hasten (death, illness *etc*) ◇*adj* headlong; hasty, rash ◇*noun* sediment at the bottom of a liquid

■ *verb* **3** hasten, hurry, speed, accelerate, quicken, expedite, advance, further, bring on, induce, trigger, cause, occasion ◇*adj* headlong, breakneck, frantic, violent, impatient, hot-headed, impetuous, impulsive, rash, reckless, heedless, indiscreet, sudden, unexpected, abrupt, quick, swift, rapid, brief, hasty, hurried

precipitation *noun* **1** great hurry **2** rainfall

precipitous *adj* very steep ◇**precipitousness** *noun*

■ steep, sheer, perpendicular, vertical, high

◪ gradual

précis /'preɪsiː/ *noun* (*plural* **précis**) a summary of a piece of writing

precise *adj* **1** definite **2** exact, accurate ◇**precisely** *adv*

■ **1** definite, explicit, unequivocal, unambiguous, clear-cut, distinct, detailed, specific, fixed, rigid, strict, careful, meticulous, scrupulous **2** exact, accurate, right, punctilious, correct, factual, faithful, authentic, literal, word-for-word ◇**precisely** exactly, absolutely, just so, accurately, correctly, literally, verbatim, word for word, strictly, minutely, clearly, distinctly

◪ **1**, **2** imprecise, inexact, ambiguous, careless

⚠ Do not confuse with: **concise**

precision *noun* **1** certainty, definiteness **2** exactness, accuracy

■ **1** certainty, definiteness, explicitness, distinctness **2** exactness, accuracy, correctness, faithfulness

◪ **2** imprecision, inaccuracy

preclude *verb* prevent, make impossible ◇**preclusion** *noun* ◇**preclusive** *adj*

precocious *adj* of a child: unusually

advanced in mental development, behaviour *etc* ◇ **precocity** *noun*

◾ forward, ahead, advanced, early, premature, mature, developed, gifted, clever, bright, smart, quick, fast

◪ backward

precognitive *adj* knowing beforehand, foretelling ◇ **precognition** *noun*

preconceive *verb* form (ideas *etc*) before having actual knowledge or experience

preconception *noun* an idea formed without actual knowledge

◾ presupposition, presumption, assumption, conjecture, anticipation, expectation, prejudgement, bias, prejudice

precondition *noun* a condition which must be met before something can happen

◾ condition, stipulation, requirement, prerequisite, essential, necessity, must

precursor *noun* someone or something which goes before, an early form of something: *the precursor of jazz*

◾ antecedent, forerunner, sign, indication, herald, harbinger, messenger, usher, pioneer

◪ follower, successor

predate *verb* happen before in time

predator *noun* a bird or animal that kills others for food ◇ **predatory** *adj* **1** of a predator **2** using other people for your own advantage

predecease *verb* die before (someone)

predecessor *noun* the previous holder of a job or office

◾ ancestor, antecedent, forerunner, precursor

◪ successor, descendant

predestine *verb* destine beforehand, preordain

predetermine *verb* settle or decide beforehand

predicament *noun* an unfortunate or difficult situation

◾ situation, plight, trouble, mess, fix, *informal* spot, quandary, dilemma, impasse, crisis, emergency

predicate *noun*, *grammar* something

said about the subject of a sentence, *eg has green eyes* in the sentence *Anne has green eyes*

predict *verb* foretell, forecast

◾ foretell, prophesy, foresee, forecast, prognosticate, project

predictable *adj* able to be foretold, expected: *a predictable response*

◾ foreseeable, expected, anticipated, likely, probable, imaginable, foreseen, certain, sure, reliable, dependable

◪ unpredictable, uncertain

prediction *noun* the act of predicting; something predicted

◾ prophecy, forecast, augury, divination, fortune-telling, soothsaying

predilection *noun* a preference, a liking for something

predispose *verb* **1** make (someone) in favour of something beforehand: *we were predisposed to believe her* **2** make liable (to): *predisposed to colds* ◇ **predisposition** *noun*

◾ **1** dispose, incline, prompt, induce, make, sway, influence, affect, bias, prejudice

predominant *adj* **1** ruling **2** most noticeable or outstanding ◇ **predominance** *noun* ◇ **predominantly** *adv*

◾ **1** dominant, prevailing, preponderant, chief, main, principal, primary, capital, paramount, supreme, sovereign, ruling, controlling, leading, powerful, potent, prime, important, influential, forceful, strong

◪ **1** minor, lesser, weak

predominate *verb* **1** be the strongest or most numerous **2** have control (over)

pre-eminent *adj* outstanding, surpassing all others ◇ **pre-eminence** *noun* ◇ **pre-eminently** *adv*

◾ supreme, unsurpassed, unrivalled, unequalled, unmatched, matchless, incomparable, inimitable, chief, foremost, leading, eminent, distinguished, renowned, famous, prominent, outstanding, exceptional, excellent

◪ inferior, unknown

pre-empt *verb* block or stop by making a first move ◇ **pre-emptive** *adj*

preen *verb* **1** of a bird: arrange its feathers **2** smarten your appearance in a conceited way ◇ **preen yourself** show obvious pride in your achievements

prefabricated *adj* made of parts made beforehand, ready to be fitted together

preface *noun* an introduction to a book *etc* ◇ *verb* precede or introduce (with)

- ▣ *noun* foreword, introduction, preamble, prologue, prelude, preliminaries ◇ *verb* precede, prefix, lead up to, introduce, launch, open, begin, start
- ▨ *noun* epilogue, postscript ◇ *verb* end, finish, complete

prefect *noun* **1** a senior pupil in some schools with certain powers **2** the head of an administrative district in France *etc*

prefecture *noun* an administrative district controlled by a prefect

prefer *verb* (**prefers**, **preferring**, **preferred**) **1** like better: *I prefer tea to coffee* **2** put forward (a claim or request): *do you wish to prefer charges?*

- ▣ **1** favour, like better, want, wish, desire, choose, select, pick, opt for, go for, plump for, single out, advocate, recommend, back, support, fancy, elect, adopt

preferable *adj* more desirable

- ▣ better, superior, nicer, preferred, favoured, chosen, desirable, advantageous, advisable, recommended
- ▨ inferior, undesirable

preference *noun* **1** greater liking **2** something preferred: *what is your preference?*

- ▣ **1** liking, fancy, inclination, predilection, partiality, favouritism, preferential treatment **2** favourite, first choice, choice, pick, selection, option, wish, desire

preferential *adj* giving special favours or advantages

- ▣ better, superior, favoured, privileged, special, favourable, advantageous
- ▨ equal

preferment *noun* promotion

prefix *noun* (*plural* **prefixes**) an element at the beginning of a word which adds to or changes its meaning, *eg dis-*, *un-*, *re-*, in *dis*like, *un*happy, *re*gain

pregnant *adj* **1** carrying a foetus in the womb **2** full of meaning: *pregnant pause* ◇ **pregnancy** *noun* (*plural* **pregnancies**) the state of being pregnant

- ▣ **2** meaningful, significant, eloquent, expressive, suggestive, charged, loaded, full

prehensile *adj* able to grasp or hold: *prehensile tail*

prehistoric *adj* relating to the time before history was written down ◇ **prehistory** *noun*

prejudge *verb* decide (something) before hearing the facts of a case

prejudice *noun* **1** an unfair feeling for or against something or someone **2** an opinion formed without careful thought **3** harm, injury ◇ *verb* **1** fill with prejudice **2** do harm to, damage: *his late arrival prejudiced his chances of success*

- ▣ *noun* **1** bias, partiality, unfairness, injustice, intolerance, narrow-mindedness, discrimination **3** harm, damage, impairment, hurt, injury, detriment, disadvantage, loss, ruin ◇ *verb* **1** bias, predispose, incline, sway, influence, condition, colour, slant, distort, load, weight **2** harm, damage, impair, hinder, undermine, hurt, injure, mar, spoil, ruin, wreck
- ▨ *noun* **1** fairness, impartiality, tolerance **3** benefit, advantage ◇ *verb* **2** benefit, help, advance

prejudiced *adj* showing prejudice

- ▣ biased, partial, predisposed, subjective, partisan, one-sided, discriminatory, unfair, unjust, intolerant, narrow-minded, bigoted, chauvinist, racist, sexist, distorted, warped, influenced, conditioned, blinkered
- ▨ impartial, fair, tolerant

prejudicial *adj* damaging, harmful

- ▣ harmful, damaging, hurtful, injurious, detrimental, disadvantageous, unfavourable, inimical
- ▨ beneficial, advantageous

prelate *noun* a bishop or archbishop

◇**prelacy** (*plural* **prelacies**) the office of a prelate

preliminary *adj* going before, preparatory: *preliminary investigation* ◇*noun* (*plural* **preliminaries**) something that goes before

▪ *adj* preparatory, prior, advance, exploratory, experimental, trial, test, pilot, early, earliest, first, initial, primary, qualifying, introductory, opening ◇ *noun* preparation, groundwork, foundation, basics, rudiments, formality, introduction, preface, prelude, opening, beginning, start

▣ *adj* final, closing

prelude *noun* **1** a piece of music played as an introduction to the main piece **2** a preceding event: *a prelude to a brilliant career*

▪ **2** introduction, preface, opening, opener, preliminary, preparation, beginning, start, commencement, precursor

▣ **1** finale **2** epilogue

premarital *adj* before marriage

premature *adj* coming, born *etc* before the right, proper or expected time

▪ early, immature, green, unripe, embryonic, half-formed, incomplete, undeveloped, hasty, ill-considered, rash, untimely, inopportune, ill-timed

▣ late, tardy

premeditate *verb* think out beforehand, plan: *premeditated murder* ◇**premeditation** *noun*

premenstrual *adj* in or of the days immediately before menstruation: *premenstrual tension*

premier *adj* first, leading, foremost ◇*noun* a prime minister

❗Do not confuse: **premier** and **première**

première *noun* a first performance of a play, film *etc*

premise or **premiss** *noun* (*plural* **premises** or **premisses**) something assumed from which a conclusion is drawn

▪ proposition, statement, assertion, argument, basis, supposition, hypothe-

sis, presupposition, assumption

premises *noun plural* a building and its grounds

premium *noun* (*plural* **premiums**) **1** a reward **2** a payment on an insurance policy ◇**at a premium** very desirable and therefore difficult to obtain

premonition *noun* a feeling that something is going to happen; a forewarning

▪ presentiment, feeling, intuition, hunch, idea, suspicion, foreboding, misgiving, fear, apprehension, anxiety, worry, warning, omen, sign

prenatal *adj* before birth, or before giving birth

prenuptial *adj* before marriage ◇**prenuptial agreement** an agreement made by two people before marriage about how to share their money *etc* if they separate

preoccupied *adj* deep in thought or engrossed in other activity

▪ intent, immersed, engrossed, engaged, taken up, wrapped up, involved, distracted, abstracted, absent-minded, daydreaming, absorbed

preoccupy *verb* completely engross the attention of (someone) ◇**preoccupation** *noun*

preordain *verb* determine beforehand

prep *noun*, *informal* preparation ◇**prep school** a preparatory school

prepaid *past form* of **prepay**

preparation *noun* **1** the act of preparing **2** study for a lesson **3** something prepared for use, *eg* a medicine

▪ **1** provision, foundation, groundwork, spadework, basics, rudiments, preliminaries, plans, arrangements **3** mixture, compound, concoction, potion, medicine, lotion, application

preparatory *adj* **1** acting as an introduction or first step **2** (with **to**) before, in preparation for ◇**preparatory school** a private school educating children of primary-school age

prepare *verb* **1** make or get ready **2** train, equip

▣ **1** make, produce, construct, assemble, concoct, contrive, devise, draft, draw up, organize, arrange **2** warm up, train, coach, study, equip, fit out, rig out

prepared *adj* **1** ready **2** willing
▣ **1** ready, waiting, set, fit

prepay *verb* (**prepays, prepaying, prepaid**) pay beforehand ◇ **prepayment** *noun*

preponderance *noun* greater amount or number: *a preponderance of young people in the audience* ◇ **preponderant** *adj*

preposition *noun*, *grammar* a word placed before a noun or pronoun to show its relation to another word, *eg* '*through* the door', '*in* the town', 'written *by* me'

⚠ Do not confuse with: **proposition**

prepossessing *adj* pleasant, making a good impression

preposterous *adj* very foolish, absurd
▣ incredible, unbelievable, absurd, ridiculous, ludicrous, foolish, crazy, nonsensical, unreasonable, monstrous, shocking, outrageous, intolerable, unthinkable, impossible
▣ sensible, reasonable, acceptable

prequel *noun* a book, film *etc* which deals with events happening before an existing one

pre-Raphaelite *noun* one of a group of 19th-century British artists who painted in a naturalistic style

prerequisite *noun* something necessary before another thing can happen
▣ precondition, condition, proviso, qualification, requisite, requirement, imperative, necessity, essential, must

prerogative *noun* a right enjoyed by someone because of rank or position

presage *verb* foretell, warn of

presbyter *noun* a minister or elder in a Presbyterian church

Presbyterian *adj* **1** of a church: managed by ministers and elders **2** belonging to such a church ◇ *noun* a member of a Presbyterian church

presbytery *noun* (*plural* **presbyteries**) **1** a body of presbyters **2** the house of a Roman Catholic priest

prescient *adj* having foresight ◇ **prescience** *noun*

prescribe *verb* **1** lay down as a rule **2** order the use of (a medicine)
▣ **1** ordain, decree, dictate, rule, command, order, require, direct, assign, specify, stipulate, lay down, set, appoint, impose, fix, define, limit

⚠ Do not confuse with: **proscribe**

prescription *noun* **1** a doctor's written instructions for preparing or supplying a medicine **2** something prescribed
▣ **1** instruction, direction, formula **2** medicine, drug, preparation, mixture, remedy, treatment

⚠ Do not confuse with: **proscription**

prescriptive *adj* laying down rules

presence *noun* **1** the state of being present (*contrasted with*: **absence**) **2** someone's personal appearance, manner *etc* ◇ **in your presence** while you are present ◇ **presence of mind** calmness, ability to act sensibly in an emergency, difficulty *etc*
▣ **1** attendance, occupancy, residence, existence **2** aura, air, demeanour, bearing, carriage, appearance, poise, self-assurance, personality, charisma

present[1] /ˈprɛzənt/ *adj* **1** here, in this place **2** happening or existing now: *present rates of pay/the present situation* ◇ *noun* **1** the time now **2** *grammar* the tense used for events happening now, *eg* 'we *are* on holiday'
▣ *adj* **1** attending, here, there, near, at hand, to hand, available, ready **2** current, contemporary, present-day, immediate, instant, existent, existing
▣ **1** absent **2** past, out-of-date

present[2] /prɪˈzɛnt/ *noun* a gift ◇ *verb* **1** hand over (a gift, prize *etc*) formally **2** offer, put forward **3** introduce (someone) to another ◇ **present yourself** **1**

introduce yourself **2** arrive

■ *verb* **1** award, confer, bestow, grant, give, donate, hand over **2** entrust, extend, hold out, offer, tender, submit **3** introduce, announce

presentable *adj* fit to be seen or to appear in company

presentation *noun* **1** the giving of a present, award *etc* **2** something presented **3** a formal talk or demonstration **4** a showing of a play *etc*

■ **3** demonstration, talk, delivery **4** show, performance, production, staging, representation, portrayal, display

presentiment *noun* a feeling that something bad is about to happen, a foreboding

presently *adv* soon

■ soon, shortly, in a minute, before long, by and by

preservative *noun* a substance added to food to prevent it from going bad

preserve *verb* **1** keep safe from harm **2** keep in existence, maintain **3** treat (food) so that it will not go bad ◇ *noun* **1** a place where game animals, birds *etc* are protected **2** jam, pickle *etc*: *jars of home-made preserves* ◇ **preservation** *noun*

■ *verb* **1** protect, safeguard, guard, defend, shield, shelter **2** care for, maintain, uphold, sustain, continue, keep, retain, conserve, save, store **3** bottle, tin, can, pickle, salt, cure, dry

☒ *verb* **1** destroy, ruin

preside *verb* be in charge at a meeting *etc*

■ chair, officiate, conduct, direct, manage, administer, control, run, head, lead, govern, rule

president *noun* **1** the leading member of a society, club *etc* **2** the head of a republic ◇ **presidency** *noun* (*plural* **presidencies**) the (term of) office of a president

press *verb* **1** push on, against or down **2** urge, force **3** iron (clothes *etc*) ◇ *noun* **1** a crowd **2** a printing machine **3** the news media, journalists

■ *verb* **1** crush, squash, squeeze, com-

press, stuff, cram, crowd, push, depress **2** urge, plead, petition, campaign, demand, insist on, compel, constrain, force, pressure, pressurize, harass **3** iron, smooth, flatten ◇ *noun* **1** crowd, throng, multitude, mob, horde, swarm, pack, crush, push **3** journalists, reporters, correspondents, the media, newspapers, papers, Fleet Street, fourth estate

pressgang *noun*, *hist* a group of men employed to carry off people by force into the army or navy ◇ *verb* **1** *hist* carry off in a pressgang **2** force (someone) to do something: *pressganged into joining the committee*

pressing *adj* requiring immediate action

■ urgent, high-priority, burning, crucial, vital, essential, imperative, serious, important

☒ unimportant, trivial

pressure *noun* **1** force on or against a surface **2** strong persuasion, compulsion **3** stress, strain **4** urgency ◇ **pressure cooker** a pan in which food is cooked quickly by steam under pressure ◇ **pressure group** a group of people who try to influence the authorities on a particular issue

■ *noun* **1** force, power, load, burden, weight, heaviness, compression **3** stress, strain, difficulty **4** constraint, obligation, urgency

pressurize *verb* **1** fit (an aeroplane *etc*) with a device that maintains normal air pressure **2** force (someone) to do something

■ **2** force, compel, constrain, oblige, drive, bulldoze, coerce, press, pressure, *informal* lean on, browbeat, bully

prestige *noun* reputation, influence due to rank, success *etc*

■ status, reputation, standing, stature, eminence, distinction, esteem, regard, importance, authority, influence, fame, renown, kudos, credit, honour

☒ humbleness, unimportance

prestigious *adj* having or giving prestige

■ esteemed, respected, reputable, important, influential, great, eminent, prominent, illustrious, renowned, celebrated, exalted, imposing, impressive, up-market

🖪 humble, modest

presumably *adv* as is assumed, probably: *presumably you know the way back*

presume *verb* **1** take for granted, assume (that) **2** (with **on**) take advantage of (someone's kindness *etc*)

🖻 **1** assume, take it, think, believe, suppose, surmise, infer, presuppose, take for granted, count on, rely on, depend on, bank on, trust

presumption *noun* **1** a strong likelihood **2** impertinent behaviour

presumptuous *adj* unsuitably bold ◇ **presumptuousness** *noun*

🖻 bold, audacious, impertinent, impudent, insolent, over-familiar, forward, pushy, arrogant, over-confident, conceited

🖪 humble, modest

presuppose *verb* take for granted

pretence *noun* **1** the act of pretending **2** a false claim

🖻 **1** show, display, appearance, cover, front, façade, veneer, cloak, mask, guise, sham, feigning, faking, simulation, deception, trickery, ruse, excuse, pretext, bluff, falsehood, deceit, fabrication, invention, make-believe, charade, acting, play-acting, posturing, posing, affectation, pretension

🖪 **1** honesty, openness

pretend *verb* **1** make believe, fantasize: *let's pretend we're stranded on a desert island* **2** give a false impression; make a false claim: *pretending to be ill*

🖻 **1** simulate, act, play-act, mime **2** fake, feign, affect, simulate, bluff, impersonate, claim, allege, profess, purport

pretender *noun* someone who lays claim to something (*esp* to the crown)

pretension *noun* **1** a claim (whether true or not) **2** self-importance

🖻 **1** claim, profession, demand, aspiration, ambition **2** pretentiousness, pomposity, self-importance, airs, conceit, vanity, snobbishness, affectation, pretence,

show, showiness, ostentation

🖪 **2** modesty, humility, simplicity

pretentious *adj* self-important; showy, ostentatious ◇ **pretentiousness** *noun*

🖻 pompous, self-important, conceited, immodest, snobbish, affected, mannered, showy, ostentatious, extravagant, over-the-top, *informal* OTT, exaggerated, inflated, grandiose, ambitious, overambitious

🖪 **2** modest, humble, simple, straightforward

preterite *noun*, *grammar* the past tense in verbs

preternatural *adj* beyond what is natural, abnormal

pretext *noun* a false reason given for doing something

🖻 excuse, ploy, ruse, cover, cloak, mask, guise, semblance, appearance, pretence, show

pretty *adj* pleasing or attractive to see, listen to *etc* ◇ *adv* fairly, quite: *pretty good* ◇ **prettiness** *noun*

🖻 *adj* attractive, good-looking, beautiful, fair, lovely, cute, winsome, appealing, charming, dainty, graceful, elegant, fine, delicate, nice ◇ *adv* fairly, somewhat, rather, quite, reasonably, moderately, tolerably

🖪 *adj* plain, unattractive, ugly

pretzel *noun* a crisp salted biscuit, twisted in shape

prevail *verb* **1** (with **against** or **over**) gain control over **2** win, succeed **3** (with **on**) persuade: *she prevailed on me to stay* **4** be most usual or common

🖻 **1** overcome, overrule, reign, rule **2** win, triumph, succeed **3** persuade, talk into, prompt, induce, sway, influence, convince, win over

prevailing *adj* **1** controlling **2** most common: *the prevailing mood*

🖻 **1** predominant, main, principal, dominant, controlling, powerful, compelling, influential, reigning, ruling **2** current, fashionable, popular, mainstream, accepted, established, set, usual, customary, common, prevalent, widespread

🖪 **1** minor, subordinate

prevalent adj common, widespread ◇ **prevalence** noun

■ widespread, extensive, rampant, rife, frequent, general, customary, usual, universal, ubiquitous, common, everyday, popular, current, prevailing

✎ uncommon, rare

prevaricate verb avoid telling the truth ◇ **prevarication** noun ◇ **prevaricator** noun

■ hedge, equivocate, quibble, dodge, evade, shift, shuffle, lie, deceive

prevent verb hinder, cause not to happen ◇ **prevention** noun ◇ **preventive** adj

■ stop, avert, avoid, head off, ward off, stave off, intercept, forestall, anticipate, frustrate, thwart, check, restrain, inhibit, hinder, hamper, impede, obstruct, block, bar ◇ **preventive** preventative, anticipatory, inhibitory, obstructive, precautionary, protective, counteractive, deterrent

✎ cause, help, foster, encourage, allow ◇ **preventive** causative

preview noun a view of a performance, exhibition etc before its official opening

previous adj going before in time; former ◇ **previously** adv

■ preceding, foregoing, earlier, prior, past, former, one-time, sometime, erstwhile ◇ **previously** formerly, once, earlier, before, beforehand

✎ following, subsequent, later

prey noun 1 an animal killed by others for food 2 a victim ◇ verb (with **on**) 1 seize and eat: preying on smaller birds 2 stalk and harass

| ⚠ Do not confuse with: **pray** |

price noun 1 the money for which something is bought or sold 2 something that must be given up in order to gain something: the price of fame

■ 1 value, worth, cost, expense, outlay, expenditure, fee, charge, toll, rate, bill, valuation, estimate, quotation, figure, amount, sum, payment 2 penalty, forfeit, sacrifice, consequences

priceless adj 1 very valuable 2 informal very funny

■ 1 invaluable, inestimable, incalculable, expensive, costly, dear, precious, valuable, prized, treasured, irreplaceable 2 funny, amusing, comic, hilarious, side-splitting

✎ 1 cheap, run-of-the-mill

prick verb 1 pierce slightly 2 give a sharp pain to 3 (often with **up**) stick up (the ears) ◇ noun 1 a pricking feeling on the skin 2 slang an idiot

■ verb 1 pierce, puncture, perforate 2 punch, jab, stab, sting, bite, prickle, itch, tingle

prickle noun a sharp point on a plant or animal ◇ verb 1 be prickly 2 feel prickly

■ noun thorn, spine, barb, spur, point, spike, needle ◇ verb 2 tingle, itch, smart, sting, prick

prickly adj 1 full of prickles 2 stinging, scratching, pricking 3 irritable

■ 1 thorny, brambly, spiny, barbed, spiky 2 bristly, rough, scratchy 3 irritable, edgy, touchy, grumpy, short-tempered

✎ 2 smooth 3 relaxed, informal easy-going

pride noun 1 too great an opinion of yourself 2 pleasure in having done something well 3 dignity 4 a group of lions ◇ **pride yourself on** feel or show pride in

■ 1 conceit, vanity, egotism, bigheadedness, boastfulness, smugness, arrogance, self-importance, haughtiness, snobbery, pretentiousness 2 satisfaction, gratification, pleasure, delight 3 dignity, self-respect, self-esteem, honour

✎ 1 humility, modesty 3 shame

priest noun 1 a member of the clergy in the Roman Catholic and Anglican churches 2 an official in a non-Christian religion ◇ **priestess** noun a female, non-Christian priest ◇ **priesthood** noun those who are priests

prig noun a smug, self-righteous person ◇ **priggish** adj ◇ **priggishly** adv

■ **priggish** smug, self-righteous, informal goody-goody, sanctimonious,

holier-than-thou, puritanical, prim, prudish, narrow-minded
◨ priggish broad-minded

prim *adj* unnecessarily formal and correct
◫ prudish, strait-laced, formal, demure, proper, priggish, prissy, fussy, particular, precise, fastidious
◨ informal, relaxed, *informal* easy-going

prima ballerina the leading female dancer of a ballet company

prima donna 1 a leading female opera singer **2** a woman who is over-sensitive and temperamental

primaeval *another spelling* of **primeval**

prima facie /ˈpraɪmə ˈfeɪʃɪ/ of evidence: apparent at first sight

primary *adj* **1** first **2** most important, chief ◇**primary colours** those from which all others can be made, *ie* red, blue and yellow ◇**primary school** a school for the early stages of education
◫ **1** first, earliest, original, initial, introductory, beginning, basic, fundamental, essential **2** chief, principal, main, dominant, leading, foremost, supreme, cardinal, capital, paramount, greatest, highest, ultimate, premier
◨ **2** secondary, subsidiary, minor

primate *noun* **1** a member of the highest order of mammals including humans, monkeys and apes **2** an archbishop

prime *adj* **1** first in time or importance **2** of best quality, excellent ◇*noun* the time of greatest health and strength: *the prime of life* ◇*verb* **1** prepare the surface of for painting: *prime a canvas* **2** supply with detailed information: *she was well primed before the meeting* ◇**prime minister** the head of a government
◫ *adj* **1** pre-eminent, superior, senior, leading, ruling, chief, principal, main, predominant, primary, supreme **2** best, choice, select, quality, first-class, first-rate, excellent, top, premium ◇ *noun* height, peak, zenith, heyday, flower, bloom, maturity, perfection
◨ *adj* **1** secondary **2** second-rate

primer *noun* **1** a simple introductory book on a subject **2** a substance for preparing a surface for painting

primeval or **primaeval** *adj* **1** relating to the beginning of the world **2** primitive **3** instinctive

primitive *adj* **1** belonging to very early times **2** old-fashioned **3** not skilfully made, rough
◫ **1** early, elementary, rudimentary, primary, first, original, earliest **3** crude, rough, unsophisticated

primogeniture *noun* **1** the fact of being born first **2** the rights of a first-born child

primrose *noun* a pale-yellow spring flower common in woods and hedges

prince *noun* **1** the son of a king or queen **2** a ruler of certain states

princely *adj* splendid, impressive: *a princely reward*
◫ generous, liberal, lavish, sumptuous, magnificent, handsome

princess *noun* (*plural* **princesses**) the daughter of a king or queen

principal *adj* most important, chief ◇*noun* **1** the head of a school or university **2** a leading part in a play *etc* **3** money in a bank on which interest is paid
◫ *adj* main, chief, key, essential, primary, first, foremost, leading, dominant, prime, paramount, pre-eminent, supreme, highest
◨ *adj* minor, subsidiary, lesser, least

❗Do not confuse: **principal** and **principle**

principality (*plural* **principalities**) a state ruled by a prince

principally *adv* chiefly, mostly
◫ mainly, mostly, chiefly, primarily, predominantly, above all, particularly, especially

principle *noun* **1** a general truth or law **2** the theory on which the working of a machine is based **3** (**principles**) someone's personal rules of behaviour, sense of right and wrong *etc*

▤ **1** rule, formula, law, canon, axiom, precept, maxim, truth, tenet, doctrine, creed, standard, criterion, proposition, fundamental, essential **3** morality, morals, ethics, standards, scruples, conscience

print *verb* **1** mark letters on paper with type **2** write in separate or capital letters **3** publish in printed form **4** stamp patterns on (cloth *etc*) **5** make a finished photograph ◇*noun* **1** a mark made by pressure: *footprint* **2** printed lettering **3** a photograph made from a negative **4** a printed reproduction of a painting *etc* **5** cloth printed with a design ◇**in print** of a book: published and available to buy

▤ *verb* **3** run off, publish, issue **4** mark, stamp, imprint, impress, engrave ◇ *noun* **1** mark, impression, fingerprint, footprint **2** letters, characters, lettering, type, typescript, typeface, font **4** copy, reproduction, picture, engraving, lithograph

printer *noun* **1** someone who prints books, newspapers *etc* **2** a machine that prints, attached to a computer system

printout *noun* the printed information produced by a computer

prior[1] *adj* **1** earlier **2** previous (to)

prior[2] *noun* the head of a priory ◇**prioress** *noun* the female head of a priory ◇**priory** *noun* (*plural* **priories**) a building where a community of monks or nuns live

priority *noun* (*plural* **priorities**) **1** the right to be first: *ambulances must have priority in traffic* **2** something that must be done first: *our priority is to get him into hospital* **3** first position

▤ **1** right of way, precedence, seniority, rank, superiority, pre-eminence, supremacy

prise *verb* force open or off with a lever: *prised off the lid*

prism *noun* a glass tube with triangular ends which breaks light into different colours

prison *noun* **1** a building for holding criminals **2** a place where someone is

confined against their will

▤ **1** jail, *slang* nick, *slang* clink, *slang* cooler, *informal* slammer, penitentiary, cell, lock-up, cage, dungeon, imprisonment, confinement, detention, custody

prisoner *noun* someone held under arrest or locked up ◇**prisoner of war** someone captured by the enemy forces during war

pristine *adj* in the original or unspoilt state

privacy *noun* freedom from observation; secrecy

▤ secrecy, confidentiality, solitude, isolation, seclusion, concealment, retirement, retreat

private *adj* **1** relating to an individual, not to the general public; personal **2** not open to the public **3** secret, not generally known ◇*noun* the lowest rank of ordinary soldier (not an officer) ◇**privately** *adv* ◇**private eye** *informal* a detective ◇**private parts** the external sexual organs

▤ *adj* **1** intimate, personal, individual, own, exclusive, particular, special, independent **2** isolated, secluded, hidden, concealed, reserved **3** secret, classified, *informal* hush-hush, off the record, unofficial, confidential

privation *noun* **1** want, poverty, hardship **2** taking away, loss

privatize *verb* transfer from state to private ownership, denationalize

privet *noun* a type of shrub used for hedges

privilege *noun* a right available to one person or a few people only ◇**privileged** *adj* having privileges

▤ advantage, benefit, concession, birthright, title, due, right, prerogative, entitlement, freedom, liberty, franchise, licence, sanction, authority, immunity, exemption ◇ **privileged** advantaged, favoured, special, authorized, immune, exempt, élite, honoured, ruling, powerful

▣ disadvantage ◇ **privileged** disadvantaged, under-privileged

privy *adj*: **privy council** an appointed

group of advisers to a king or queen ◇**privy to** knowing about (something secret)

prize noun **1** something won in a competition **2** something given for great achievement **3** something captured **4** something highly valued ◇adj very fine, worthy of a prize ◇verb value highly ◇**prize fight** a boxing match fought for money

▣ noun **1** trophy, medal, award, winnings, jackpot, premium, stake(s) **2** reward, award, honour, accolade ◇ adj best, top, first-rate, excellent, outstanding, champion, winning, prize-winning, award-winning ◇ verb treasure, value, appreciate, esteem, revere, cherish

▣ adj second-rate

pro short for **professional**

pro- prefix **1** before, forward, front **2** in favour of: pro-devolution ◇**pros and cons** the arguments for and against anything

probability noun (plural **probabilities**) **1** likelihood **2** something likely to happen

probable adj **1** likely to happen **2** likely to be true

▣ **1** likely, odds-on, expected, anticipated **2** credible, believable, plausible, feasible, possible, apparent, seeming

▣ **1, 2** improbable, unlikely

probably adv very likely

probation noun **1** a trial period in a new job etc **2** a system of releasing prisoners on condition that they commit no more offences and report regularly to the authorities ◇**probationer** noun someone who is training to be a member of a profession

probe noun **1** a long, thin instrument used to examine a wound etc **2** a thorough investigation **3** a spacecraft for exploring space ◇verb **1** examine very carefully **2** investigate thoroughly to find out information

▣ noun **2** inquiry, inquest, investigation, exploration, examination, test, scrutiny, study, research ◇ verb **1** sound, plumb, explore, examine, scrutinize **2** investigate, go into, look into, search

probity noun honesty, goodness of character

problem noun **1** a question to be solved **2** a matter which is difficult to deal with

▣ **1** question, poser, puzzle, brain-teaser, conundrum, riddle, enigma **2** trouble, worry, predicament, quandary, dilemma, difficulty, complication, snag

problematic or **problematical** adj **1** causing problems **2** doubtful, uncertain

proboscis noun (plural **proboscises**) **1** an animal's nose, esp an elephant trunk **2** an insect's mouth

procedure noun **1** the established method of doing something **2** a course of action

▣ **1** routine, process, method, system, technique **2** course, scheme, strategy, plan of action, operation

proceed verb **1** go on with, continue **2** begin (to do something) **3** take legal action (against) ◇**proceeds** noun plural profit made from a sale etc

▣ **1** advance, go ahead, move on, progress, continue, carry on, press on ◇ **proceeds** revenue, income, returns, receipts, takings, earnings, gain, profit, yield, produce

▣ **1** stop, retreat ◇ **proceeds** expenditure, outlay

⚠ Do not confuse with: **precede**

proceeding noun **1** a step forward **2** (**proceedings**) a record of the meetings of a society etc **3** a law action

process noun (plural **processes**) **1** a series of operations, eg in manufacturing goods **2** a series of events producing change or development **3** a law case ◇**in the process of** in the course of

▣ **1** procedure, operation, practice, method, system, technique, means **2** course, progression, advance, progress, development, evolution, formation, growth, movement **3** action, proceeding

procession noun a line of people or vehicles moving forward in order

▣ march, parade, cavalcade, motorcade, cortège, file

proclaim *verb* announce publicly, declare openly ◇ **proclamation** *noun* an official announcement made to the public

▤ announce, declare, pronounce, affirm, give out, publish, advertise, make known, profess, testify, show, indicate ◇ **proclamation** announcement, declaration, pronouncement, affirmation, publication, promulgation, notice, notification, manifesto, decree, edict

procrastinate *verb* put things off, delay doing something till a later time ◇ **procrastination** *noun*

▤ defer, put off, postpone, delay, retard, stall, temporize, play for time, dally, drag one's feet, prolong, protract

▰ advance, proceed

procurator fiscal the law officer of a district in Scotland

procure *verb* obtain

▤ acquire, buy, purchase, get, obtain, find, come by, pick up, lay hands on, earn, gain, win, secure, appropriate, requisition

▰ lose

prod *verb* (**prods, prodding, prodded**) 1 poke 2 urge on 3 remind ◇ *noun* 1 a poke 2 a stimulus 3 a reminder

▤ *verb* 1 poke, jab, dig, stab, elbow, nudge, push, shove 2 urge, *informal* egg on, prompt, stimulate, motivate ◇ *noun* 1 poke, jab, dig, stab, elbow, nudge, push, shove 2 stimulus, motivation 3 prompt, reminder

prodigal *adj* spending money recklessly, wasteful ◇ **prodigality** *noun*

prodigious *adj* 1 strange, astonishing 2 enormous

prodigy (*plural* **prodigies**) 1 a wonder 2 someone astonishingly clever: *child prodigy*

produce *verb* 1 bring out: *he produced a knife from his pocket* 2 bring about, cause 3 prepare (a play *etc*) for the stage 4 make, manufacture; bring into being ◇ *noun* food grown or produced on a farm or in a garden ◇ **producer** *noun* someone who produces a play, film *etc*

▤ *verb* 2 cause, occasion, give rise to, provoke, bring about, result in, effect 4 invent, make, manufacture, fabricate, construct, compose, generate, yield, bear, deliver

product *noun* 1 something produced 2 a result 3 *maths* the number that results from the multiplication of two or more numbers ◇ **production** *noun*

▤ 1 commodity, merchandise, goods, end-product, artefact, work, creation, invention, offshoot, spin-off, by-product 2 result, consequence, outcome, issue, upshot

productive *adj* fruitful, producing results ◇ **productivity** *noun* the rate of work done

▤ fruitful, profitable, rewarding, valuable, worthwhile, useful, constructive, creative, inventive, fertile, rich, busy, energetic, vigorous, efficient, effective ◇ **productivity** productiveness, yield, output, work rate, efficiency

▰ unproductive, fruitless, useless

profane *adj* 1 not sacred 2 treating holy things without respect

▤ 1 secular, temporal, lay, unconsecrated, unhallowed, unsanctified, unholy, irreligious, sacrilegious, blasphemous, ungodly 2 disrespectful, abusive, crude, coarse, foul, filthy, unclean

▰ 1 sacred, religious 2 respectful

profanity *noun* (*plural* **profanities**) 1 swearing 2 lack of respect for sacred things

profess *verb* 1 declare (a belief *etc*) openly 2 pretend, claim: *he professes to be an expert on Scott* ◇ **professed** *adj* 1 declared 2 pretended

▤ 1 confirm, certify, declare, announce, proclaim, state, assert, affirm 2 maintain, claim, allege, make out, pretend

profession *noun* 1 an occupation requiring special training, *eg* that of a doctor, lawyer, teacher *etc* 2 an open declaration

▤ 1 career, business, vocation, calling, office 2 admission, confession, acknowledgement, declaration, announcement, statement, testimony, assertion, affirmation, claim

professional *adj* **1** of a profession **2** earning a living from a game or an art (*contrasted with*: **amateur**) **3** skilful, competent ◇ *noun* **1** someone who works in a profession **2** someone who earns money from a game or art ◇ **professionalism** *noun* ◇ **professionally** *adv*

▪ *adj* **3** qualified, licensed, trained, experienced, practised, skilled, expert, masterly, proficient, competent, businesslike, efficient ◇ *noun* **1** expert, authority, specialist

▪ *adj* **2** amateur **3** amateurish, unprofessional

professor *noun* **1** a teacher of the highest rank in a university **2** *US* a university teacher

proffer *verb* offer

proficiency *noun* skill ◇ **proficient** *adj* skilled, expert

▪ skill, skilfulness, expertise, mastery, talent, knack, aptitude, ability, competence ◇ **proficient** able, capable, skilled, qualified, trained, experienced, accomplished, expert, masterly, gifted, talented, clever, skilful, competent, efficient

▪ incompetence ◇ **proficient** unskilled, incompetent

profile *noun* **1** an outline **2** a side view of a face, head *etc* **3** a short description of someone's life, achievements *etc*

▪ **1** outline, contour, silhouette, shape, form, figure, sketch, drawing **3** biography, portrait, study, analysis, examination, survey, review

profit *noun* **1** gain, benefit **2** money got by selling something for more than it cost: excess of income over expenditure ◇ *verb* gain (from), benefit

▪ *noun* **1** gain, advantage, benefit, use **2** surplus, excess, return, yield, proceeds, receipts, takings, earnings

profitable *adj* bringing profit or gain

▪ cost-effective, economic, commercial, money-making, lucrative, paying, rewarding, successful, fruitful, productive, advantageous, beneficial, useful, valuable, worthwhile

▪ unprofitable, loss-making, non-profit-making

profiteer *noun* someone who makes large profits unfairly ◇ *verb* make large profits

profligate *adj* **1** living an immoral life **2** very extravagant ◇ *noun* a profligate person ◇ **profligacy** *noun*

pro forma or **pro-forma** *adj* of an invoice: showing the market price of specified goods, with goods being paid for before dispatch

profound *adj* **1** very deep or great **2** deeply felt **3** showing great knowledge or understanding: *a profound comment* ◇ **profoundly** *adv* ◇ **profundity** *noun*

▪ **1** deep, great, intense, extreme, marked, far-reaching, extensive **2** heartfelt **3** serious, weighty, penetrating, thoughtful, philosophical, wise, learned, erudite, abstruse

▪ **1** shallow, slight, mild

profuse *adj* abundant, lavish, extravagant ◇ **profusion** *noun*

▪ ample, abundant, plentiful, copious, generous, liberal, lavish, rich, luxuriant, excessive, extravagant, overabundant, overflowing

▪ inadequate, sparse

progenitor *noun* an ancestor ◇ **progeny** *noun* children

progesterone *noun* a female sex hormone which maintains pregnancy

prognosis *noun* a prediction of the course of a disease

prognosticate *verb* foretell ◇ **prognostication** *noun*

program *noun* a set of instructions telling a computer to carry out certain actions ◇ *verb* (**programs**, **programming**, **programmed**) **1** give instructions to (a computer *etc*) **2** prepare instructions to be carried out by a computer ◇ **programmer** *noun* ◇ **programming** *noun*

programme or *US* **program** *noun* **1** a TV or radio broadcast **2** a booklet with details of an entertainment, ceremony *etc* **3** a scheme, a plan

▪ **1** broadcast, transmission, show, performance, production, presentation **2** schedule, timetable, agenda, order of events, listing, line-up **3** plan, scheme, project

progress noun **1** advance, forward movement **2** development, improvement ◇ verb **1** go forward **2** develop, improve ◇ **progression** noun

■ noun **1** movement, progression, passage, journey, way, advance, headway **2** breakthrough, development, evolution, growth, increase, improvement, promotion ◇ verb **1** proceed, advance, go forward, forge ahead, make progress, make headway **2** develop, grow, mature, blossom, improve, better, prosper, increase ◇ **progression** cycle, chain, string, succession, series, sequence, order, course, advance, headway, progress, development

✷ noun **1** recession **2** deterioration, decline

progressive adj **1** going forward, progressing **2** favouring reforms

■ **1** advancing, continuing, developing, growing, increasing, intensifying **2** modern, avant-garde, advanced, forward-looking, enlightened, liberal, radical, revolutionary, reformist, dynamic, enterprising

✷ **1**, **2** regressive

prohibit verb **1** forbid **2** prevent

■ **1** forbid, ban, bar, veto, proscribe, outlaw, rule out, preclude **2** prevent, stop, hinder, hamper, impede, obstruct, restrict

✷ **1** permit, allow, authorize

prohibition noun **1** the act of forbidding **2** the forbidding by law of making and selling alcoholic drinks

prohibitive adj **1** prohibiting **2** of price: too expensive, discouraging

project noun **1** a plan, a scheme **2** a task **3** a piece of study or research ◇ verb **1** throw out or up **2** jut out **3** cast (an image, a light etc) onto a surface **4** plan, propose

■ noun **1** venture, plan, scheme, programme, design, proposal, idea **2** assignment, contract, task, job, work, activity ◇ verb **1** throw, fling, hurl,

launch, propel **2** protrude, stick out, bulge, jut out, overhang

projectile noun a missile

projection noun **1** an act of projecting **2** a forecast based on known data **3** something which juts out

■ **2** estimate, reckoning, calculation **3** protuberance, overhang, ledge, sill, shelf, ridge

projectionist noun someone who operates a film projector

projector noun a machine for projecting photographs or films on a screen

prolapse verb of a body organ: fall out of place

prole noun, informal a proletarian

proletariat noun the ordinary working people ◇ **proletarian** noun a member of the proletariat

proliferate verb grow or increase rapidly ◇ **proliferation** noun

■ multiply, reproduce, breed, increase, build up, intensify, escalate, mushroom, snowball, spread, expand, flourish, thrive

✷ dwindle

prolific adj producing a lot, fruitful

■ productive, fruitful, fertile, profuse, copious, abundant

✷ unproductive

prolix adj using too many words, tiresomely long ◇ **prolixity** noun

prologue noun a preface or introduction to a play etc

prolong verb make longer

■ lengthen, extend, stretch, protract, draw out, spin out, drag out, delay, continue, perpetuate

✷ shorten

prom informal, short for **1** promenade **2** promenade concert

promenade noun **1** a level roadway or walk, esp by the seaside **2** a walk, a stroll ◇ verb walk for pleasure ◇ **promenade concert** a concert at which a large part of the audience stands instead of being seated

prominent adj **1** standing out, easily seen **2** projecting, bulging **3** famous, distinguished ◇ **prominence** *noun*

■ **1** noticeable, conspicuous, obvious, unmistakable, striking, eye-catching **2** protuberant, projecting, jutting, protruding, obtrusive **3** famous, well-known, celebrated, renowned, noted, eminent, distinguished, respected, leading, foremost, chief, main, important, popular, outstanding

☶ **1** inconspicuous **3** unknown, unimportant, insignificant

promiscuous *adj* **1** having many sexual relationships **2** mixed in kind **3** not making distinctions between people or things ◇ **promiscuity** *noun*

■ **1** licentious **3** indiscriminate

☶ **1** chaste

promise *verb* **1** give your word (to do or not do something) **2** show signs for the future: *the weather promises to improve* ◇ *noun* **1** a statement of something promised **2** a sign of something to come **3** a sign of future success: *his painting shows great promise*

■ *verb* **1** vow, pledge, swear, take an oath, contract, undertake, give one's word **2** augur, presage, indicate, suggest, hint at ◇ *noun* **1** vow, pledge, oath, word of honour, bond, compact, covenant **3** potential, ability, capability, aptitude, talent

promising *adj* showing signs of being successful

■ favourable, rosy, bright, encouraging, hopeful, talented, gifted, budding, up-and-coming, auspicious

☶ unpromising, inauspicious, discouraging

promontory *noun* (*plural* **promontories**) a headland jutting out into the sea

promote *verb* **1** raise to a higher rank **2** help onwards, encourage **3** advertise, encourage the sales of ◇ **promotion** *noun* ◇ **promotional** *adj* used in advertising

■ **1** upgrade, advance, move up, raise, elevate, exalt, honour **2** help, aid, assist, foster, nurture, further, forward, encourage, boost, stimulate, urge **3** advertise, *informal* plug, publicize, *slang* hype, popularize, market, sell, push, recommend, sponsor ◇ **promotion** advancement, upgrading, rise, advertising, plugging, publicity, *slang* hype, campaign, propaganda, marketing, development, encouragement

☶ **1** demote **2** hinder **3** disparage

prompt *adj* **1** quick, immediate **2** punctual ◇ *verb* **1** move to action: *what prompted her to leave so suddenly?* **2** supply words to an actor who has forgotten their lines ◇ **prompter** *noun* someone who prompts actors ◇ **promptly** *adv* ◇ **promptness** *noun*

■ *adj* **1** quick, swift, rapid, speedy, unhesitating, willing, responsive, timely, early, immediate, instantaneous, instant **2** punctual, on time ◇ *verb* **1** cause, give rise to, result in, instigate, elicit, provoke, incite, urge, encourage, inspire, move, stimulate, motivate

☶ *adj* **1** slow, hesitant **2** late

promulgate *verb* make widely known ◇ **promulgation** *noun*

prone *adj* **1** inclined (to): *prone to laziness* **2** lying face downwards

■ **1** given, inclined, disposed, predisposed, bent, apt, liable, subject, susceptible, vulnerable **2** face down, prostrate, flat, horizontal, full-length, stretched, recumbent

☶ **1** unlikely, immune **2** upright, supine

prong *noun* the spike of a fork ◇ **pronged** *adj* having prongs

pronoun *noun* a word used instead of a noun, *eg* I, you, who

pronounce *verb* **1** speak (words, sounds) **2** announce (an opinion), declare

■ **1** say, utter, speak, express, voice, vocalize, sound, articulate, enunciate, stress **2** declare, announce, proclaim, decree, judge, affirm, assert, state

pronounced *adj* noticeable, marked

■ clear, distinct, definite, positive, decided, marked, noticeable, conspicuous, evident, obvious, striking, unmistakable, strong, broad

☶ faint, vague

pronouncement *noun* a statement, an announcement

pronto *adv*, *informal* quickly

pronunciation *noun* the way a word is said

■ diction, elocution, enunciation, articulation, delivery, accent, stress, inflection, intonation, modulation

proof *noun* 1 evidence that something is true 2 the standard strength of whisky *etc* 3 a copy of a printed sheet for correction before publication ◇ *adj* able to keep out or withstand: *waterproof*

■ *noun* 1 evidence, documentation, demonstration, verification, confirmation, corroboration, substantiation

proofread *verb* read printed page proofs of a text ◇ **proofreader** *noun*

prop *noun* 1 a support 2 *short for* **propeller** 3 an item of furniture *etc* used on stage ◇ *verb* (**props**, **propping**, **propped**) hold up, support

■ *noun* 1 support, sustain, stay, strut, buttress, brace, truss

propaganda *noun* 1 the spreading of ideas to influence public opinion 2 material used for this, *eg* posters, leaflets ◇ **propagandist** *noun* someone who spreads propaganda

propagate *verb* 1 spread 2 produce seedlings or young ◇ **propagation** *noun* ◇ **propagator** *noun*

■ 1 spread, transmit, broadcast, diffuse, disseminate, circulate, publish, promulgate, publicize, promote 2 multiply, proliferate, generate, produce, breed, spawn, procreate, reproduce

propane *noun* a gas used as fuel

propel *verb* (**propels**, **propelling**, **propelled**) drive forward

■ move, drive, impel, force, thrust, push, shove, launch, shoot, send

propellant *noun* 1 an explosive for firing a rocket 2 the gas in an aerosol spray

propeller *noun* a shaft with revolving blades which drives forward a ship, aircraft *etc*

propensity *noun* (*plural* **propensities**) a natural inclination: *a propensity for bumping into things*

proper *adj* 1 right, correct: *the proper way to do it* 2 full, thorough: *a proper search* 3 prim, well-behaved ◇ **properly** *adv* 1 in the right way 2 thoroughly ◇ **proper noun** or **proper name** *grammar* a name for a particular person, place or thing, *eg Shakespeare, the Parthenon*

■ 1 right, correct, accurate, exact, precise, true, genuine, real, actual 3 decent, respectable, polite, formal

■ 1 wrong 3 improper, indecent

property *noun* (*plural* **properties**) 1 land or buildings owned 2 belongings 3 a quality 4 (**properties**) the furniture *etc* required by actors in a play

■ 1 estate, land, real estate, acres, premises, buildings, house(s), wealth, riches, resources, means, capital, assets 2 belongings, possessions, effects, goods, chattels 3 feature, trait, quality, attribute, characteristic, peculiarity, mark

prophecy *noun* (*plural* **prophecies**) 1 foretelling the future 2 something prophesied

❗ Do not confuse: **prophecy** and **prophesy**

prophesy *verb* (**prophesies**, **prophesying**, **prophesied**) foretell the future, predict

■ predict, foresee, augur, foretell, forewarn, forecast

prophet *noun* 1 someone who claims to foretell events 2 someone who tells what they believe to be the will of God

prophylactic *noun* 1 something which helps to prevent disease 2 a condom

propinquity *noun* nearness

propitiate *verb* calm the anger of ◇ **propitious** *adj* favourable: *propitious circumstances*

proponent *noun* someone in favour of a thing, an advocate

proportion *noun* 1 a part of a total amount: *a large proportion of income is taxed* 2 relation in size, number *etc* compared with something else: *the proportion of girls to boys is small* ◇ **in** or **out of proportion** appropriate or inappropriate in size or degree when compared with other things

- **1** percentage, fraction, part, division, share, quota, amount **2** ratio, relationship, correspondence, symmetry, balance, distribution

proportional or **proportionate** *adj* in proportion ◇ **proportional representation** a voting system in which parties are represented in proportion to their voting strength

- relative, consistent, corresponding, analogous, comparable, equitable, even
- disproportionate

proposal *noun* **1** an act of proposing **2** anything proposed **3** an offer of marriage

- **2** proposition, suggestion, recommendation, motion, plan, scheme, project, design

propose *verb* **1** put forward for consideration, suggest **2** intend: *what do you propose to do about it?* **3** make an offer of marriage (to)

- **1** suggest, recommend, move, advance, put forward, introduce, bring up, submit, present, offer, tender **2** intend, mean, aim, purpose, plan, design
- **1** withdraw

proposition *noun* **1** a proposal, a suggestion **2** a statement **3** a situation that must be dealt with: *a tough proposition*

! Do not confuse with: **preposition**

propound *verb* state, put forward for consideration

proprietor, proprietress *noun* an owner, *esp* of a hotel

- landlord, landlady, title-holder, freeholder, leaseholder, landowner, owner, possessor

propriety *noun* (*plural* **proprieties**) **1** fitness, suitability **2** correct behaviour, decency

propulsion *noun* the act of driving forward

pro rata in proportion

prorogue *verb* discontinue meetings

of (parliament *etc*) for a period ◇ **prorogation** *noun*

prosaic *adj* dull, not interesting ◇ **prosaically** *adv*

proscenium /prou'si:nɪəm/ *noun* the front part of a stage

prosciutto /prou'ʃuːtou/ *noun* cured, uncooked Italian ham

proscribe *verb* ban, prohibit ◇ **proscription** *noun* ◇ **proscriptive** *adj*

! Do not confuse with: **prescribe**

prose *noun* **1** writing which is not in verse **2** ordinary written or spoken language

prosecute *verb* **1** bring a law-court action against **2** *formal* carry on (studies, an investigation *etc*)

- **1** accuse, indict, sue, charge, prefer charges, take to court, litigate, summon, put on trial, try

! Do not confuse with: **persecute**

prosecution *noun* **1** an act of prosecuting **2** *law* those bringing the case in a trial (*contrasted with*: **defence**)

proselyte *noun* a convert ◇ **proselytize** *verb* make converts

prosody *noun* study of the rhythms and construction of poetry

prospect *noun* **1** a view, a scene **2** a future outlook or expectation: *the prospect of a free weekend/a job with good prospects* ◇ *verb* search for gold or other minerals

- *noun* **2** chance, odds, probability, likelihood, possibility, hope, expectation, anticipation, outlook, future
- *noun* **2** unlikelihood

prospective *adj* soon to be, likely to be: *the prospective election*

- future, intended, designate, destined, forthcoming, approaching, coming, imminent, awaited, expected, anticipated, likely, possible, probable, potential, aspiring, would-be
- current

prospector *noun* someone who prospects for minerals

prospectus *noun* (*plural* **prospec-**

tuses) a booklet giving information about a school, organization *etc*
■ programme, syllabus, manifesto, outline, synopsis, pamphlet, leaflet, brochure, catalogue, list

prosper *verb* get on well, succeed
■ boom, thrive, flourish, flower, bloom, succeed, get on, advance, progress, grow rich
◼ fail

prosperity *noun* success, good fortune, financial well-being
■ boom, plenty, affluence, wealth, riches, fortune, well-being, luxury, the good life, success, good fortune
◼ adversity, poverty

prosperous *adj* successful, wealthy
■ booming, thriving, flourishing, blooming, successful, fortunate, lucky, rich, wealthy, affluent, well-off, well-to-do
◼ unfortunate, poor

prostate *noun* a gland in a man's bladder which releases a fluid used in semen

prosthesis *noun* (*plural* **prostheses**) an artificial replacement part for the body ◇ **prosthetics** *noun sing* the study and use of artificial body parts

prostitute *noun* someone who offers sexual intercourse for payment

prostrate *adj* 1 lying flat face downwards 2 worn out by grief, tiredness *etc* ◇ *verb* exhaust, tire out completely ◇ **prostration** *noun* ◇ **prostrate yourself** lie on the ground as a sign of respect: *prostrated themselves before the emperor*
■ *adj* 1 flat, horizontal, prone, fallen 2 exhausted, drained, crushed, paralysed, powerless, helpless ◇ *verb* overwhelm, crush, overthrow, tire, wear out, fatigue, exhaust, drain ◇ **prostrate yourself** bow down, kneel, kowtow, submit, grovel
◼ *verb* strengthen

protagonist *noun* a chief character in a play *etc*
■ hero, heroine, lead, principal, leader, champion

protean *adj* changing shape often and easily

protect *verb* shield from danger, keep safe
■ safeguard, defend, guard, escort, cover, screen, shield, secure, watch over, look after, care for, support, shelter, harbour, keep
◼ attack, neglect

protection *noun* 1 the act of protecting 2 safety, shelter ◇ **protectionism** *noun* the system of protecting home industries against foreign competition by taxing imports ◇ **protectionist** *noun*
■ 1 care, custody, charge, guardianship, safekeeping, conservation, preservation, safeguard 2 safety, barrier, buffer, defence, guard, shield, armour, screen, cover, shelter, refuge

protective *adj* giving protection; intended to protect
■ defensive, motherly, maternal, fatherly, paternal, possessive, watchful, vigilant, careful, waterproof, fireproof, windproof, insulating
◼ aggressive, threatening

protector *noun* a guardian, a defender

protectorate *noun* a country which is partly governed and defended by another country

protégé, protégée *noun* a pupil or employee who is taught or helped in their career by someone important or powerful

protein *noun* a substance present in milk, eggs, meat *etc* which is a necessary part of a human or animal diet

protest *verb* 1 object strongly 2 declare solemnly: *protesting his innocence* ◇ *noun* a strong objection ◇ **protestation** *noun* 1 a solemn declaration 2 a protest
■ *verb* 1 object, take exception, complain, appeal, demonstrate, oppose, disapprove, disagree, argue 2 assert, maintain, contend, insist, profess ◇ *noun* objection, disapproval, opposition, dissent, complaint, protestation, outcry, appeal, demonstration, *informal* demo
◼ *verb* 1 accept ◇ *noun* acceptance

Protestant *noun* a member of one of the Christian churches which broke away from the Roman Catholic Church at the time of the Reformation

protocol *noun* 1 correct procedure 2 a set of rules for transmitting electronic data

▣ 1 procedure, formalities, convention, custom, etiquette, manners, good form, propriety

proton *noun* a particle with a positive electrical charge, forming part of the nucleus of an atom (*compare with*: **electron**)

protoplasm *noun* a semi-liquid substance which is the chief material of all living cells

prototype *noun* the original model from which something is copied

protozoan *noun* a tiny creature made up of a single cell

protract *verb* lengthen in time

protractor *noun* an instrument for drawing and measuring angles on paper

protrude *verb* stick out, thrust forward ◇ **protrusion** *noun*

▣ stick out, poke out, come through, bulge, jut out, project, extend, stand out, obtrude

protuberance *noun* a swelling, a bulge ◇ **protuberant** *adj*

proud *adj* 1 thinking too highly of yourself, conceited 2 feeling pleased at an achievement *etc* 3 dignified, self-respecting: *too proud to accept the money*

▣ 1 conceited, vain, egotistical, big-headed, boastful, smug, complacent, arrogant, self-important, cocky, presumptuous, haughty, high and mighty, overbearing, supercilious, *informal* snooty, snobbish, *informal* stuck-up 2 satisfied, contented, gratified, pleased, delighted, honoured 3 dignified, noble, honourable, worthy, self-respecting

▣ 1 humble, modest, unassuming 2 ashamed 3 ignoble

prove *verb* 1 show to be true or correct 2 try out, test 3 turn out (to be): *his prediction proved correct*

▣ 1 show, demonstrate, attest, verify,

confirm 2 try, test, check, examine, analyse

▣ 1 disprove, discredit, falsify

provenance *noun* source, origin

provender *noun* food, *esp* for horses and cattle

proverb *noun* a well-known wise saying, *eg* 'nothing ventured, nothing gained'

proverbial *adj* well-known, widely spoken of

▣ accepted, conventional, traditional, customary, time-honoured, famous, well-known, legendary, notorious, typical, archetypal

provide *verb* give or make available (what is needed) ◇ **providing that** on condition that

▣ supply, furnish, stock, equip, outfit, prepare for, cater, serve, present, give, contribute, yield, lend, add, bring

▣ take, remove

providence *noun* 1 foresight; thrift 2 (**Providence**) God seen as a protector

▣ 1 prudence, far-sightedness, foresight, caution, care, thrift 2 fate, destiny, divine intervention, God's will, fortune, luck, karma, kismet

provident *adj* thinking of the future; thrifty ◇ **providential** *adj* fortunate, coming as if by divine help

▣ prudent, far-sighted, judicious, cautious, careful, thrifty, economical, frugal ◇ **providential** timely, opportune, convenient, fortunate, lucky, happy, welcome, heaven-sent

▣ **providential** untimely

province *noun* 1 a division of a country 2 the extent of someone's duties or knowledge 3 (**provinces**) all parts of a country outside the capital

▣ 1 region, area, district, zone, county, shire, department, territory, colony, dependency 2 responsibility, concern, duty, office, role, function, field, sphere, domain, department, line

provincial *adj* 1 of a province or provinces 2 narrow-minded, parochial

▣ 1 regional, local, rural, rustic 2 parochial, insular, inward-looking, limited, narrow, narrow-minded, small-minded

1 cosmopolitan, urban, sophisticated

provision *noun* **1** the act of providing or preparing: *make provision for the future* **2** a rule or condition **3** (**provisions**) a supply of food

provisional *adj* used for the time being; temporary

☐ temporary, interim, transitional, stopgap, makeshift, conditional, tentative

☒ permanent, fixed, definite

proviso *noun* (*plural* **provisos**) a condition laid down beforehand

☐ condition, term, requirement, stipulation, qualification, reservation, restriction, limitation, provision

provocative *adj* **1** tending to rouse anger **2** likely to arouse sexual interest

☐ **1** annoying, *informal* aggravating, galling, outrageous, offensive, insulting, abusive **2** erotic, titillating, arousing, sexy, seductive, alluring, tempting, inviting, tantalizing, teasing, suggestive

provoke *verb* **1** cause, result in **2** rouse to anger or action: *don't let him provoke you* ◇ **provocation** *noun*

☐ **1** cause, occasion, give rise to, produce, generate, induce, elicit, evoke, excite, inspire, move, stir, prompt, stimulate, motivate, incite, instigate **2** annoy, irritate, rile, *informal* aggravate, offend, insult, anger, enrage, infuriate, incense, madden, exasperate, tease, taunt

☒ **2** please, pacify

provost *noun* the chief magistrate of a burgh in Scotland

prow *noun* the front part of a ship

prowess *noun* skill, ability

☐ accomplishment, attainment, ability, aptitude, skill, expertise, mastery, command, talent, genius

prowl *verb* go about stealthily

proximity *noun* nearness

☐ closeness, nearness, vicinity, neighbourhood, adjacency, juxtaposition

☒ remoteness

proxy *noun* (*plural* **proxies**) someone who acts or votes on behalf of another

☐ agent, factor, deputy, stand-in, substitute, representative, delegate

prude *noun* an over-modest, priggish

person ◇ **prudery** *noun* ◇ **prudish** *adj*

prudent *adj* wise and cautious ◇ **prudence** *noun* ◇ **prudently** *adv*

☐ wise, sensible, politic, judicious, shrewd, discerning, careful, cautious, wary, vigilant, circumspect, discreet, provident, far-sighted, thrifty

☒ imprudent, unwise, careless, rash

prune¹ *verb* **1** trim (a tree) by cutting off unneeded twigs **2** shorten, reduce

prune² *noun* a dried plum

prurient *adj* excessively concerned with sexual matters ◇ **prurience** *noun*

pry *verb* (**pries**, **prying**, **pried**) look closely into things which are not your business ◇ **prying** *adj*

☐ meddle, interfere, poke one's nose in, intrude, peep, peer, snoop, nose, ferret, dig, delve

☒ mind one's own business

psalm *noun* a sacred song ◇ **psalmist** *noun* a writer of psalms

psalter *noun* a book of psalms

psaltery *noun* a medieval stringed instrument played by plucking

p's and q's correct social manners

psephologist *noun* someone who studies elections and voting trends

Coined in the 1950s, based on Greek *psephos*, a pebble used in the ancient Greek system of casting votes

pseudo /ˈsjuːdoʊ/ or (*US*) /ˈsuːdoʊ/ *adj*, *informal* false, fake, pretended: *his Spanish accent is pseudo* ◇ **pseud** *noun*, *informal* a pretentious person; a fraud

pseudo- /ˈsjuːdoʊ/ or (*US*) /ˈsuːdoʊ/ *prefix* false

pseudonym *noun* a false name used by an author

☐ false name, assumed name, alias, incognito, pen name, nom de plume, stage name

psoriasis /səˈraɪəsɪs/ *noun* a skin disease causing red scaly patches

psychedelic *adj* bright and multicoloured

psychiatrist *noun* someone who treats mental illness

psychiatry *noun* the treatment of mental illness ◇**psychiatric** *adj*

psychic /'saɪkɪk/ or **psychical** *adj* **1** relating to the mind **2** able to read other people's minds, or tell the future

▣ **1** mental, psychological, intellectual, cognitive **2** spiritual, supernatural, occult, mystic(al), clairvoyant, extrasensory, telepathic

psycho- /'saɪkoʊ/ or **psych-** /saɪk/ *prefix* relating to the mind

psychoanalysis *noun* a method of treating mental illness by discussing with the patient its possible causes in their past ◇**psychoanalyse** *verb* treat by psychoanalysis ◇**psychoanalyst** *noun*

psychology *noun* the science which studies the human mind ◇**psychological** *adj* of psychology or the mind ◇**psychologist** *noun*

▣ **psychological** mental, cerebral, intellectual, cognitive, emotional, subjective, subconscious, unconscious, psychosomatic, irrational, unreal

▣ **psychological** physical, real

psychosis *noun* a mental illness ◇**psychotic** *adj*

psychosomatic *adj* of an illness: having a psychological cause

psychotherapy *noun* treatment of mental illness by psychoanalysis *etc* ◇**psychotherapist** *noun*

PT *abbrev* physical training

pt *abbrev* **1** part **2** pint

PTA *abbrev* parent teacher association

ptarmigan /'tɑːmɪgən/ *noun* a mountain-dwelling bird of the grouse family, which turns white in winter

pterodactyl /tɛrə'daktɪl/ *noun* an extinct flying reptile

PTO *abbrev* please turn over

pub *noun, informal* a public house

puberty *noun* the time during youth when the body becomes sexually mature

pubic *adj* of the lowest part of the abdomen: *pubic hair*

public *adj* **1** relating to or shared by the people of a community or nation in general: *public opinion/public library* **2** generally or widely known: *a public figure* ◇*noun* people in general ◇**in public** in front of or among other people ◇**public address system** a system of microphones, amplifiers and loudspeakers used to enable an audience to hear voices, music *etc* ◇**public house** a building where alcoholic drinks are sold and consumed ◇**public relations 1** the relations between a business *etc* and the public **2** a department of a business *etc* dealing with this

▣ *adj* **1** state, national, civil, community, social, collective, communal, common, general, universal, open, unrestricted **2** known, well-known, recognized, acknowledged, overt, open, exposed, published ◇*noun* people, nation, country, population, populace, masses, citizens, society, community, voters, electorate

▣ *adj* **1** private, personal **2** secret

publican *noun* the keeper of an inn or public house

publication *noun* **1** the act of making news *etc* public **2** the act of publishing a book, newspaper *etc* **3** a published book, magazine *etc*

▣ **1** announcement, declaration, notification, disclosure **2** release, issue, printing, publishing **3** book, newspaper, magazine, periodical, booklet, leaflet, pamphlet

publicist *noun* an advertising agent

publicity *noun* advertising; bringing to public notice or attention

▣ advertising, *informal* plug, *slang* hype, promotion, build-up, boost, attention, limelight, splash

publicize *verb* make public, advertise

▣ advertise, *informal* plug, *slang* hype, promote, push, spotlight, broadcast, make known, blaze

publish *verb* **1** make generally known **2** prepare and put out (a book *etc*) for sale ◇**publisher** *noun* someone who publishes books

▣ **1** announce, declare, communicate, make known, divulge, disclose, reveal, release, publicize, advertise **2** produce, print, issue, bring out, distribute, circulate, spread, diffuse

puce *adj* of a brownish-purple or purplish-pink colour

pucker *verb* wrinkle ◇ *noun* a wrinkle, a fold

▪ *verb* gather, ruffle, wrinkle, shrivel, crinkle, crumple, crease, furrow, purse, screw up, contract

pudding *noun* **1** the sweet course of a meal **2** a dish made with eggs, flour, milk *etc* **3** a type of sausage: *black pudding*

puddle *noun* a small pool, *esp* of rainwater

pudendum *noun* (*plural* **pudenda**) the female external sex organs

puerile *adj* childish, silly ◇ **puerility** *noun*

▪ childish, babyish, infantile, juvenile, immature, irresponsible, silly, foolish, inane, trivial

▪ mature

puerperal *adj, formal* relating to childbirth

puff *verb* **1** blow out in small gusts **2** breathe heavily, *eg* after running **3** blow up, inflate; swell (up or out) ◇ *noun* **1** a short, sudden gust of wind, breath *etc* **2** an act of inhaling and exhaling smoke from a cigarette *etc* **3** a piece of advertising ◇ **puff pastry** a light, flaky kind of pastry

▪ *verb* **2** pant, gasp, gulp, blow, wheeze **3** inflate, expand, swell, balloon, bloat

puffball *noun* a ball-shaped mushroom containing a powdery mass of spores

puffin *noun* a type of sea bird, with a short, thick beak

puffy *adj* swollen, flabby

▪ puffed up, inflated, swollen, bloated, distended, enlarged

pug *noun* a breed of small dog with a snub nose

pugilist *noun, old* a boxer ◇ **pugilism** *noun, old* boxing

pugnacious *adj* quarrelsome, fond of fighting ◇ **pugnacity** *noun*

puke *noun & verb, slang* vomit

pull *verb* **1** move or try to move (something) towards yourself by force **2** drag, tug **3** stretch, strain: *pull a muscle* **4** remove or destroy by pulling: *pull to pieces* ◇ *noun* **1** the act of pulling **2** a pulling force, *eg* of a magnet **3** a handle for pulling **4** *informal* advantage, influence ◇ **pull through** get safely to the end of a difficult or dangerous experience ◇ **pull up** stop, halt ◇ **pull yourself together** regain self-control or self-possession

▪ *verb* **2** tow, drag, haul, draw, tug, jerk, *informal* yank **3** dislocate, sprain, wrench, strain **4** remove, take out, extract, pull out, pluck, uproot, pull up, rip, tear ◇ *noun* **1** tow, drag, tug, jerk, *informal* yank ◇ **pull up** stop, halt, park, draw up, pull in, pull over, brake

▪ *verb* **1, 2** push, press

pullet *noun* a young hen

pulley *noun* (*plural* **pulleys**) a grooved wheel fitted with a cord and set in a block, used for lifting weights *etc*

Pullman *noun* luxurious or superior seating on a train, in a cinema *etc*

Named after George M *Pullman*, an American who made the first luxury sleeping car for railways in the 19th century

pullover *noun* a knitted garment for the top half of the body, a jersey

pulmonary *adj* relating to the lungs

pulp *noun* **1** the soft fleshy part of a fruit **2** a soft mass of wood *etc* which is made into paper **3** any soft mass ◇ *verb* reduce to pulp

▪ *verb* crush, squash, pulverize, mash, purée, liquidize

pulpit *noun* an enclosed platform in a church for the minister or priest

pulsar *noun* a distant source of regular radio signals in space, possibly a star

pulsate *verb* beat, throb

▪ pulse, beat, throb, pound, hammer, drum, thud, thump, vibrate, oscillate, quiver

pulse *noun* the beating or throbbing of the heart and blood vessels as blood flows through them ◊ *verb* throb, pulsate

■ *noun* beat, stroke, rhythm, throb, pulsation, beating, pounding, drumming, vibration

pulses *noun plural* beans, peas, lentils and other edible seeds

pulverize *verb* 1 crush into powder 2 defeat

■ 1 crush, pound, grind, mill, powder 2 defeat, destroy, demolish, annihilate

puma *noun* an American wild animal like a large cat

pumice or **pumice stone** *noun* a piece of light solidified lava used for smoothing skin and for rubbing away stains

pummel *verb* (**pummels, pummelling, pummelled**) beat with the fists

pump[1] *noun* 1 a machine used for making water rise to the surface 2 a device for drawing out or forcing in air, gas, liquid *etc*: *bicycle pump* ◊ *verb* 1 raise or move with a pump 2 *informal* draw out information from by clever questioning

pump[2] *noun* a kind of thin- or soft-soled shoe used for dancing, gymnastics *etc*

pumpernickel *noun* a coarse dark rye-bread

pumpkin *noun* a large, roundish, thick-skinned, yellow fruit, with stringy edible flesh

pun *noun* a play on words which sound similar but have different meanings, *eg* 'two *pears* make a *pair*' ◊ *verb* (**puns, punning, punned**) make a pun

■ *noun* play on words, double entendre, witticism, quip

punch[1] *verb* hit with the fist ◊ *noun* (*plural* **punches**) a blow with the fist

■ *verb* hit, strike, pummel, jab, bash, clout, cuff, box, thump, *slang* sock, *informal* wallop ◊ *noun* blow, jab, bash, clout, thump, *informal* wallop

punch[2] *verb* make a hole in with a tool: *punch a ticket* ◊ *noun* a tool for punching holes

■ *verb* perforate, pierce, puncture, prick, bore, drill, stamp, cut

punch[3] *noun* a drink made of spirits or wine, water, sugar *etc*

punch-bowl *noun* a bowl for mixing punch

punch-drunk *adj* dizzy from being hit

punchline *noun* the words that give the main point to a joke

punchy *adj* having a powerful effect, striking

punctilious *adj* paying attention to details, *esp* in behaviour; fastidious

■ scrupulous, conscientious, meticulous, careful, exact, precise, strict, formal, proper, particular, finicky, fussy

🖙 lax, informal

punctual *adj* 1 on time, not late 2 habitually arriving on time ◊ **punctuality** *noun* ◊ **punctually** *adv*

■ 1 prompt, on time, on the dot, exact, precise, early, in good time

🖙 1 unpunctual, late

punctuate *verb* 1 divide up sentences by commas, full stops *etc* 2 interrupt at intervals: *the silence was punctuated by occasional coughing* ◊ **punctuation** *noun* ◊ **punctuation marks** the symbols used in punctuating sentences, *eg* full stop, comma, colon, question mark *etc*

puncture *noun* 1 an act of pricking or piercing 2 a small hole made with a sharp point 3 a hole in a tyre

■ 2 leak, hole, perforation, cut, nick

pundit *noun* an expert

pungent *adj* 1 sharp-tasting or sharp-smelling 2 of a remark: strongly sarcastic

■ 1 strong, hot, peppery, spicy, aromatic, tangy, piquant 2 stinging, biting, cutting, incisive, pointed, piercing, penetrating, sarcastic, scathing

🖙 1 mild, bland, tasteless

punish *verb* 1 make (someone) suffer for a fault or crime 2 impose a penalty for (an offence) **3** treat roughly or harshly

■ **1** penalize, discipline, correct, chastise, castigate **3** beat, flog, lash, cane

punishable *adj* likely to bring punishment

punishment *noun* suffering or constraints inflicted for a fault or crime

■ discipline, correction, chastisement, beating, flogging, penalty, fine, imprisonment, sentence, revenge

☶ reward

punitive *adj* inflicting punishment or suffering

■ penal, disciplinary, retributive, retaliatory, vindictive, punishing

punnet *noun* a small basket for holding fruit

punt *noun* a flat-bottomed boat with square ends which is propelled by pushing a pole against the bottom of a river ◇*verb* move (a punt) in this way

punter *noun, informal* **1** a professional gambler **2** a customer, a client **3** an ordinary person

puny *adj* little and weak ◇**puniness** *noun*

■ weak, feeble, frail, sickly, undeveloped, underdeveloped, stunted, undersized, diminutive, little, tiny, insignificant

☶ strong, sturdy, large, important

pup *noun* **1** a young dog **2** the young of certain animals, *eg* a seal

pupa *noun* (*plural* **pupae**) the stage in the growth of an insect in which it changes from a larva to its mature form, *eg* from a caterpillar into a butterfly ◇**pupate** *verb* become a pupa

pupil[1] *noun* someone who is being taught by a teacher

■ student, scholar, schoolboy, schoolgirl, learner, apprentice, beginner, novice, disciple, protégé(e)

pupil[2] *noun* the round opening in the middle of the eye through which light passes

puppet *noun* **1** a doll which is moved by strings or wires **2** a doll that fits over the hand and is moved by the fingers **3**

someone who acts exactly as they are told to

puppy *noun* a young dog ◇**puppy fat** temporary fat in childhood or adolescence ◇**puppy love** immature love when very young

purblind *adj, old* nearly blind, dim-sighted

purchase *verb* buy ◇*noun* **1** the act of buying **2** something which is bought **3** firm grip or hold **4** the power to lift by using a lever *etc* ◇**purchaser** *noun* someone who buys

■ *verb* buy, pay for, *informal* invest in, procure, acquire, obtain, get, secure, gain, earn ◇ *noun* **1** buying, acquisition **2** acquisition, *informal* buy, investment, asset, possession, property

☶ *verb* sell ◇ *noun* **1**, **2** sale

purdah *noun, hist* the seclusion of Hindu or Islamic women from strangers, behind a screen or under a veil

pure *adj* **1** clean, spotless **2** not contaminated or polluted **3** not mixed with other substances **4** free from faults or sin, innocent **5** utter, absolute, nothing but: *pure nonsense*

■ **1** clean, immaculate, spotless, clear **2** sterile, uncontaminated, unpolluted, germ-free, aseptic, antiseptic, disinfected, sterilized, hygienic, sanitary **3** unadulterated, unalloyed, unmixed, undiluted, neat, solid, simple, natural, real, authentic, genuine, true **4** chaste, virginal, undefiled, unsullied, moral, upright, virtuous, blameless, innocent, *informal* squeaky-clean **5** sheer, utter, complete, total, thorough, absolute, perfect

☶ **2** contaminated, polluted **3** impure, adulterated **4** immoral

purée *noun* food made into a pulp by being put through a sieve or liquidizing machine ◇*verb* make into a purée, pulp

purely *adv* **1** in a pure way **2** wholly, entirely: *purely on merit* **3** merely, only: *purely for the sake of appearance*

■ **2** utterly, completely, totally, entirely, wholly, thoroughly, absolutely **3** only, simply, merely, just, solely, exclusively

purgative *noun* a medicine which clears waste matter out of the body ◇*adj* of a medicine: having this effect

purgatory *noun* **1** in the Roman Catholic Church, a place where souls are made pure before entering heaven **2** a state of suffering for a time

purge *verb* **1** make clean, purify **2** clear (something) of anything unwanted: *purged the party of those who disagreed with her*

▣ **1** purify, cleanse, clean out, scour, clear, absolve

purify *verb* (**purifies, purifying, purified**) make pure ◇**purification** *noun*

▣ refine, filter, clarify, clean, cleanse, decontaminate, sanitize, disinfect, sterilize, fumigate, deodorize

▣ contaminate, pollute, defile

purist *noun* someone who insists on correctness

puritan *noun* **1** someone of strict, often narrow-minded, morals **2** (**Puritan**) *hist* one of a group believing in strict simplicity in worship and daily life ◇**puritanical** *adj* ◇**puritanism** *noun*

▣ **puritanical** puritan, moralistic, disciplinarian, abstemious, austere, severe, stern, strict, strait-laced, prim, proper, prudish, disapproving, stuffy, stiff, rigid, narrow-minded, bigoted, fanatical

▣ **puritanical** hedonistic, liberal, indulgent, broad-minded

purity *noun* the state of being pure

▣ clearness, clarity, cleanliness, simplicity, authenticity, genuineness, truth, chastity, decency, morality, integrity, virtue, innocence

purl *verb* knit in stitches made with the wool in front of the work

purloin *verb* steal

purple *noun* a dark colour formed by the mixture of blue and red

purport *noun* meaning ◇*verb* **1** mean **2** seem, pretend: *he purports to be a film expert*

purpose *noun* **1** aim, intention **2** use, function (of a tool *etc*) ◇*verb* intend ◇**purposely** *adv* intentionally ◇**on purpose** intentionally ◇**to the purpose** to the point

▣ *noun* **1** intention, aim, objective, end, goal, target, plan, design, idea, point, object, reason, motive **2** use, function, application, good, advantage, benefit, value ◇**on purpose** purposely, deliberately, intentionally, consciously, knowingly, wittingly, wilfully

▣ **on purpose** accidentally, impulsively, spontaneously

purposeful *adj* determined ◇**purposefully** *adv*

purr *noun* the low, murmuring sound made by a cat when pleased ◇*verb* of a cat: make this sound

purse *noun* **1** a small bag for carrying money **2** *US* a handbag ◇*verb* close (the lips) tightly ◇**purse strings** the control of a source of money: *I can see who holds the purse strings in this family!*

purser *noun* the officer who looks after a ship's money

pursue *verb* **1** follow after (in order to overtake or capture), chase **2** be engaged in, carry on (studies, an enquiry *etc*) **3** follow (a route, path *etc*) ◇**pursuer** *noun* someone who pursues

▣ **1** chase, go after, follow, track, trail **2** perform, engage in, practise, conduct, carry on, continue, keep on, keep up, maintain, persevere in, persist in

pursuit *noun* **1** the act of pursuing **2** an occupation or hobby

▣ **1** chase, tracking, stalking, trail, hunt, quest, search **2** activity, interest, hobby, pastime, occupation, trade, craft, line

purulent *adj* full of, or like, pus

purvey *verb* supply (food *etc*) as a business ◇**purveyor** *noun*

pus *noun* a thick yellowish liquid produced from infected wounds

push *verb* **1** press hard against **2** thrust (something) away with force, shove **3** urge on **4** make a big effort ◇*noun* **1** a thrust **2** effort **3** *informal* energy and determination

▣ *verb* **1** press, depress, squeeze, squash **2** propel, thrust, ram, shove, jostle, elbow, drive, force **3** encourage, urge, *in-*

formal egg on, incite, spur, influence, persuade, pressurize ◇ *noun* **1** knock, shove, nudge, jolt, prod, poke, thrust **2** drive, effort **3** energy, vigour, vitality, *informal* go, ambition, determination

☒ *verb* **1, 2** pull **3** discourage, dissuade

pushchair *noun* a folding chair on wheels for a young child

pushy *adj* aggressively assertive

☰ assertive, self-assertive, ambitious, forceful, aggressive, over-confident, forward, bold, brash, *slang* in-your-face, arrogant, presumptuous, assuming, *informal* bossy

☒ unassertive, unassuming

pusillanimous *adj* cowardly ◇ **pusillanimity** *noun*

pussy *noun, informal* a cat, a kitten

pussyfoot *verb* act timidly or non-committally

pussy-willow *noun* an American willow tree with silky catkins

pustule *noun* a small pimple containing pus

put *verb* (**puts, putting, put**) **1** place, lay, set: *put the book on the table* **2** bring to a certain position or state: *put the light on/put it out of your mind* **3** express: *put the question more clearly* ◇ **put about** spread (news) ◇ **put by** set aside, save up ◇ **put down** defeat ◇ **put in for** make a claim for, apply for ◇ **put off 1** delay **2** turn (someone) away from their plan or intention ◇ **put out 1** extinguish (a fire, light *etc*) **2** annoy, embarrass, inconvenience: *I hope I'm not putting you out by staying an extra night/she seemed put out by the news* ◇ **put up 1** build **2** propose, suggest (a plan, candidate *etc*) **3** let (someone) stay in your house *etc* **4** stay as a guest ◇ **put-up job** *informal* a dishonest scheme ◇ **put up with** bear patiently, tolerate

☰ **1** place, lay, deposit, *informal* plonk, set, stand, position, dispose, situate, station, post **3** word, phrase, formulate, frame, couch, express, voice, utter, state ◇ **put down** crush, quash, suppress, defeat, quell, silence ◇ **put off**

1 delay, defer, postpone, reschedule **2** deter, dissuade, discourage, dishearten, demoralize ◇ **put out 1** extinguish, quench, douse, smother, switch off, turn off **2** inconvenience, impose on, bother, disturb, trouble, upset, hurt, offend, annoy, irritate, irk, anger, exasperate ◇ **put up with** stand, bear, abide, endure, suffer, tolerate, allow, accept, stand for, take

putative *adj* supposed, commonly accepted ◇ **putatively** *adv*

putrefy *verb* (**putrefies, putrefying, putrefied**) go bad, rot ◇ **putrefaction** *noun*

putrescent *adj* going bad, rotting ◇ **putrescence** *noun*

putrid *adj* rotten; stinking

☰ rotten, decayed, decomposed, mouldy, off, bad, rancid, addled, corrupt, contaminated, tainted, polluted, foul, rank, fetid, stinking

☒ fresh, wholesome

putt *verb, golf* send a ball gently forward ◇ **putter** *noun* a golf club used for this

putty *noun* a cement made from ground chalk, used in putting glass in windows *etc*

puzzle *verb* **1** present with a difficult problem or situation *etc* **2** be difficult for (someone) to understand: *her moods puzzled him* **3** (with **out**) consider long and carefully in order to solve (a problem) ◇ *noun* **1** a problem or situation which is difficult to understand or solve **2** a toy, game or question which needs a lot of thought, tests knowledge or skill *etc*: *crossword puzzle/jigsaw puzzle*

☰ *verb* **1, 2** baffle, mystify, perplex, confound, *informal* stump, confuse, bewilder, *informal* flummox **3** solve, work out, figure out, decipher, decode, crack, unravel, untangle, sort out, resolve, clear up ◇ *noun* **1** mystery, enigma, paradox **2** question, poser, brainteaser, mind-bender, crossword, rebus, anagram, riddle, conundrum

PVC *abbrev* polyvinyl chloride, a tough type of plastic

pygmy or **pigmy** (*plural* **pygmies** or **pigmies**) *noun* one of a race of very small human beings

pyjamas or **pajamas** *noun plural* a sleeping suit consisting of trousers and a jacket

pylon *noun* a high, steel tower supporting electric power cables

pyramid *noun* **1** a solid shape with flat triangular sides which come to a point at the top **2** a building of this shape used as a tomb in ancient Egypt

pyre *noun* a pile of wood on which a dead body is burned

Pyrex *noun, trademark* a type of glassware for cooking which will withstand heat

pyromaniac *noun* someone who gets pleasure from starting fires ◊ **pyromania** *noun*

pyrotechnics *noun plural* a display of fireworks

Pyrrhic victory a victory gained at so great a cost that it is equal to a defeat

After the costly defeat of the Romans by *Pyrrhus*, king of Epirus, in 280 BC

python *noun* a large, non-poisonous snake which crushes its victims

Qq

QC *abbrev* Queen's Counsel

qed *abbrev quod erat demonstrandum*, which was to be demonstrated (from Latin)

qt *abbrev* quart

qua *adv* in the capacity of, thought of as

quack¹ *noun* the cry of a duck ◇ *verb* make the noise of a duck

quack² *noun* someone who falsely claims to have medical knowledge or training

quad *short for* **1** quadruplet **2** quadrangle

quadrangle *noun* **1** *maths* a figure with four equal sides and angles **2** a four-sided courtyard surrounded by buildings in a school, college *etc* ◇ **quadrangular** *adj*

quadrant *noun* **1** one quarter of the circumference or area of a circle **2** an instrument used in astronomy, navigation *etc* for measuring heights

quadraphonic *adj* of recorded sound: relayed through four speakers

quadrennial *adj* happening every four years

quadri- *prefix* four

quadrilateral *noun* a four-sided figure or area ◇ *adj* four-sided

quadrille *noun* a dance for four couples arranged to form a square

quadriplegia *noun* paralysis of both arms and both legs ◇ **quadriplegic** *noun* someone suffering from quadriplegia

quadruped *noun* a four-footed animal

quadruple *adj* **1** four times as much or many **2** made up of four parts ◇ *verb* make or become four times greater: *quadrupled the price* ◇ **quadruplet** *noun* one of four children born to the

same mother at one birth

quaff *verb* drink up eagerly

quagmire *noun* wet, boggy ground
▤ bog, marsh, quag, fen, swamp, morass, mire

quail¹ *verb* shrink back in fear
▤ recoil, back away, shy away, shrink, flinch, cringe, cower, tremble, quake

quail² *noun* a type of small bird like a partridge

quaint *adj* pleasantly odd, *esp* because of being old-fashioned
▤ picturesque, charming, *informal* twee, old-fashioned, antiquated, old-world, *informal* olde-worlde, unusual, strange, odd, curious, bizarre, fanciful

quake *verb* (**quakes**, **quaking**, **quaked**) shake, tremble with fear ◇ *noun*, *informal* an earthquake
▤ *verb* shake, tremble, shudder, quiver, shiver, quail

Quaker *noun* a member of a religious group opposed to violence and war, founded in the 17th century

> Originally a nickname given to the group because their founder, George Fox, told them to *quake* at the word of God

qualification *noun* **1** a qualifying statement **2** a skill, or the fact of having passed an examination or undergone training, which makes someone suitable for a job
▤ **1** caveat, provision, proviso, stipulation, modification **2** skill, competence, ability, capability, capacity, aptitude

qualify *verb* **1** be suitable for a job or position **2** pass a test **3** lessen the force of (a statement) by adding or changing words ◇ **qualified** *adj* having the necessary qualifications for a job
▤ **3** moderate, reduce, lessen, diminish, temper, soften, weaken, mitigate,

ease, adjust, modify ◊ **qualified** certified, chartered, licensed, professional, trained, experienced, practised, skilled, accomplished, expert, knowledgeable, skilful, talented, proficient, competent, efficient, able, capable, fit, eligible

qualitative *adj* relating to quality rather than quantity

quality *noun* (*plural* **qualities**) **1** an outstanding feature of someone or something: *kindness is a quality admired by all* **2** degree of worth: *cloth of poor quality*

▣ **1** property, characteristic, peculiarity, attribute, aspect, feature, trait, mark **2** standard, grade, class, kind, sort, nature, character, calibre, status, rank, condition

qualm *noun* doubt about whether something is right

▣ misgiving, apprehension, fear, anxiety, worry, disquiet, uneasiness, scruple, hesitation, reluctance, uncertainty, doubt

quandary *noun* (*plural* **quandaries**) **1** a state of uncertainty **2** a situation in which it is difficult to decide what to do

▣ **1** perplexity, bewilderment, confusion, mess **2** dilemma, predicament, impasse, fix, *informal* hole, problem, difficulty, *informal* spot

quango *noun* (*plural* **quangos**) an official body, funded and appointed by government, which supervises some national activity *etc*

quantify *verb* (**quantifies, quantifying, quantified**) state or determine the quantity of ◊ **quantifiable** *adj* ◊ **quantification** *noun*

quantitative *adj* relating to quantity, not quality

quantity *noun* (*plural* **quantities**) **1** amount: *a large quantity of paper* **2** a symbol which represents an amount: *x is the unknown quantity*

▣ **1** amount, number, sum, total, aggregate, mass, lot, share, portion, quota, allotment, measure, dose, proportion, capacity, volume, weight, bulk, size, magnitude, expanse, extent, length, breadth

quantum leap a huge, dramatic transition or advance

quarantine *noun* the isolation of people or animals who might be carrying an infectious disease ◊ *verb* put in quarantine

quark[1] /kwɔːk/ or /kwɑːk/ *noun, physics* a subatomic particle

> A word invented by James Joyce in *Finnegans Wake* (1939)

quark[2] /kwɑːk/ *noun* a type of soft cheese

quarrel *noun* an angry disagreement or argument ◊ *verb* (**quarrels, quarrelling, quarrelled**) **1** disagree violently or argue angrily (with) **2** find fault (with) ◊ **quarrelsome** *adj* fond of quarrelling, inclined to quarrel

▣ *noun* row, argument, *informal* slanging match, wrangle, squabble, tiff, misunderstanding, disagreement, dispute, dissension, controversy, difference, conflict, clash, contention, strife, fight, scrap, brawl, feud, vendetta, schism ◊ *verb* **1** row, argue, bicker, squabble, wrangle, be at loggerheads, fall out, disagree, differ, be at variance, clash, contend, fight, scrap, feud

quarry[1] *noun* (*plural* **quarries**) a pit from which stone is taken for building ◊ *verb* (**quarries, quarrying, quarried**) dig (stone *etc*) from a quarry

quarry[2] *noun* **1** a hunted animal **2** someone or something eagerly looked for

▣ prey, victim, target, game, kill, prize

quart *noun* a measure of liquids, 1.136 litre (2 pints)

quarter *noun* **1** one of four equal parts of something **2** a fourth part of a year, three months **3** direction: *no help came from any quarter* **4** a district **5** mercy shown to an enemy: *no quarter was given by either side* **6** (**quarters**) lodgings, accommodation ◊ *verb* **1** divide into four equal parts **2** accommodate

▣ *noun* **6** accommodation, lodgings, billet, *informal* digs, residence, dwelling, habitation, domicile, rooms, barracks, station, post ◇ *verb* **2** station, post, billet, accommodate, put up, lodge, board, house, shelter

quarterdeck *noun* the upper deck of a ship between the stern and the mast nearest it

quarter-final *noun* a match in a competition immediately before a semi-final

quarterly *adj* happening every three months ◇*adv* every three months ◇*noun* (*plural* **quarterlies**) a magazine *etc* published every three months

quartermaster *noun* an officer who looks after soldiers' accommodation and supplies

quartet *noun* **1** *esp* in classical music, a group of four players or singers **2** a piece of music written for such a group

quarto *noun* (*plural* **quartos**) a paper size produced by folding each sheet into four leaves

quartz *noun* a hard substance often in crystal form, found in rocks

quasar *noun* a star-like object which gives out light and radar waves

quash *verb* **1** crush, put down (*eg* a rebellion) **2** wipe out, annul (*eg* a judge's decision)
 ▤ **1** squash, crush, quell, suppress, subdue, defeat, overthrow **2** annul, revoke, rescind, overrule, cancel, nullify, void, invalidate, reverse

quasi- *prefix* to some extent, but not completely: *quasi-historical*

quatrain *noun* a poetic stanza of four lines

quaver *verb* **1** shake, tremble **2** speak in a shaking voice ◇*noun* **1** a trembling of the voice **2** *music* a note (♪) equal to half a crotchet in length
 ▤ *verb* **1** shake, tremble, quake, shudder, quiver

quay /kiː/ *noun* a solid landing place for loading and unloading boats
 ▤ wharf, pier, jetty, dock, harbour

queasy *adj* **1** feeling nauseous **2** easily shocked or disgusted ◇**queasiness** *noun*
 ▤ **1** sick, ill, unwell, queer, groggy, green, nauseated, sickened, bilious, squeamish

queen *noun* **1** the hereditary female ruler of a nation **2** the wife of a king **3** the most powerful chesspiece, which can move in any direction **4** a playing-card with a picture of a queen **5** an egg-laying female bee, ant or wasp
 ◇**queenly** *adj* of or like a queen
 ◇**queen bee 1** an egg-laying female bee **2** a woman who is the centre of attention ◇**queen mother** the mother of the reigning king or queen who was once herself queen
 ▤ **1** monarch, sovereign, ruler, majesty, empress

queer *adj* **1** odd, strange **2** *informal* (*sometimes derogatory*) homosexual ◇*noun, informal* (*sometimes derogatory*) a homosexual
 ▤ *adj* **1** odd, mysterious, strange, unusual, uncommon, weird, unnatural, bizarre, eccentric, peculiar, funny, puzzling, curious
 ▨ *adj* **1** ordinary, usual, common

quell *verb* **1** crush (a rebellion *etc*) **2** remove (fears, suspicions *etc*)
 ▤ **1** subdue, quash, crush, squash, suppress, put down, overcome, conquer, defeat, overpower **2** allay, alleviate, quiet, silence, stifle, extinguish

quench *verb* **1** drink and so satisfy (thirst) **2** put out (*eg* a fire)
 ▤ **1** slake, satisfy, sate, cool **2** extinguish, douse, put out, snuff out

quenelle *noun* a poached dumpling of chicken, fish *etc*

querulous *adj* complaining
 ▤ peevish, fretful, fractious, cantankerous, cross, irritable, complaining, grumbling, discontented, dissatisfied, critical, carping, captious, fault-finding
 ▨ placid, uncomplaining, contented

query *noun* (*plural* **queries**) **1** a question **2** a question mark (?) ◇*verb* (**queries**, **querying**, **queried**) question (*eg* a statement)
 ▤ *noun* **1** question, inquiry, problem ◇ *verb* ask, inquire, question, challenge, dispute, quarrel with, doubt

quest *noun* a search

search, hunt, pursuit, investigation, inquiry, mission, crusade, enterprise, undertaking, venture, journey, voyage, expedition, exploration, adventure

question *noun* **1** something requiring an answer, *eg* 'where do you live?' **2** a subject, matter *etc: the energy question/ a question of ability* **3** a matter for dispute or doubt: *there's no question of her leaving* ◇ *verb* **1** ask questions of (someone) **2** express doubt about ◇ **out of the question** not even to be considered, unthinkable ◇ **question mark** a symbol (?) put after a question in writing

noun **1** query, inquiry, poser, problem, difficulty **2** issue, matter, subject, topic, point, proposal, proposition, motion, debate, dispute, controversy ◇ *verb* **1** interrogate, quiz, grill, pump, interview, examine, cross-examine, debrief, ask, inquire **2** query, challenge, dispute, doubt, disbelieve

questionable *adj* doubtful

debatable, disputable, unsettled, undetermined, unproven, uncertain, arguable, controversial, vexed, doubtful, dubious

unquestionable, indisputable, certain

questionnaire *noun* a written list of questions to be answered, *eg* to provide information for a survey

queue *noun* a line of people waiting, *eg* for a bus ◇ *verb* stand in, or form, a queue

quibble *verb* argue over trivial details ◇ *noun* a petty argument or complaint

verb carp, cavil, split hairs, nit-pick, equivocate, prevaricate ◇ *noun* complaint, objection, criticism, query

quiche /kiːʃ/ *noun* an open pastry case filled with beaten eggs, cheese *etc* and baked

quick *adj* **1** done or happening in a short time **2** acting without delay, fast-moving: *a quick brain* ◇ *noun* a tender area of skin under the nails ◇ *adv, informal* quickly ◇ **quicken** *verb* speed up, become or make faster ◇ **quickly** *adv* without delay, rapidly ◇ **quick-**

tempered *adj* easily made angry ◇ **the quick** *old* the living: *the quick and the dead*

adj **1** fast, swift, rapid, speedy, express, hurried, hasty, cursory, fleeting, brief, prompt, ready, immediate, instant, instantaneous, sudden **2** brisk, nimble, sprightly, agile, intelligent, quick-witted, smart, sharp, keen, shrewd, astute, discerning, perceptive, responsive, receptive

adj **1** slow **2** dull, sluggish, lethargic

quicklime *noun* lime which has not been mixed with water

quicksand *noun* sand which sucks in anyone who stands on it

quicksilver *noun* mercury

quickstep *noun* a ballroom dance like a fast foxtrot

quid *noun, slang* a pound (£1)

quiddity *noun* (*plural* **quiddities**) **1** the essence or nature of something **2** a quibble

quid pro quo **1** a returned favour **2** a retaliation

quiescent *adj* not active ◇ **quiescence** *noun*

quiet *adj* **1** making little or no noise **2** calm: *a quiet life* ◇ *noun* **1** the state of being quiet **2** lack of noise, peace ◇ *verb* make or become quiet ◇ **quieten** *verb* make or become quiet ◇ **quietly** *adv* ◇ **quietness** *noun*

adj **1** silent, noiseless, inaudible, hushed, soft, low, muted **2** peaceful, still, tranquil, serene, calm, composed, undisturbed, untroubled, placid ◇ **quieten** silence, hush, mute, soften, lower, diminish, reduce, stifle, muffle, deaden, dull

adj **1** noisy, loud **2** excitable

🚫 Do not confuse with: **quite**

quiff *noun* a tuft of hair brushed up and back from the forehead

quill *noun* **1** a large feather of a goose or other bird made into a pen **2** one of the sharp spines of a porcupine

quilt *noun* a bedcover filled with down, feathers *etc* ◇ **quilted** *adj* made of two layers of material with padding between them

■ bedcover, coverlet, bedspread, counterpane, eiderdown, duvet

quin *short for* **quintuplet**

quince *noun* a pear-like fruit with a sharp taste, used to make jams *etc*

quincunx *noun* an arrangement of five things, one at each corner and one in the centre of a square

quinine *noun* a bitter drug taken from the bark of a S American tree, used to treat malaria

quinquennial *adj* 1 happening once every five years 2 lasting five years

quinsy *noun* acute inflammation of the tonsils with pus forming round them

quintessence *noun* 1 the most important part of anything 2 the purest part or form of something ◇ **quintessential** *adj* ◇ **quintessentially** *adv*

Literally 'fifth essence', sought after by medieval alchemists as the highest essence or ether

quintet *noun* 1 *esp* in classical music, a group of five players or singers 2 a piece of music written for such a group

quintuplet *noun* one of five children born to a mother at the same time

quip *noun* a witty remark or reply ◇ *verb* (**quips**, **quipping**, **quipped**) make a witty remark

■ *noun* joke, jest, crack, *informal* gag, witticism, riposte, retort, gibe

quire *noun* a set of 24 sheets of paper

⚠ Do not confuse with: **choir**

quirk *noun* 1 an odd feature of someone's behaviour 2 a trick, a sudden turn: *quirk of fate*

■ 1 eccentricity, curiosity, oddity, peculiarity, idiosyncrasy, mannerism, habit, trait, foible 2 turn, twist

quirky *adj* full of sudden twists or changes; unpredictable, inconsistent ◇ **quirkily** *adv* ◇ **quirkiness** *noun*

quisling *noun* someone who collaborates with an enemy, *esp* a puppet ruler

After Vidkun *Quisling*, head of the Norwegian fascist party during the German occupation

quit *verb* (**quits**, **quitting**, **quit** or **quitted**) 1 give up, stop: *I'm going to quit smoking* 2 *informal* leave, resign from (a job) ◇ **be quits** be even with each other, *eg* in a dispute

■ 1 stop, cease, end, discontinue, desist, drop, give up, *slang* pack in 2 leave, depart, go, exit, desert, forsake, abandon, renounce, relinquish, surrender, give up, resign, retire

quite *adv* 1 completely, entirely: *quite empty* 2 fairly, moderately: *quite good*

⚠ Do not confuse with: **quiet**

quiver[1] *noun* a tremble, a shake ◇ *verb* tremble, shake

■ *verb* shake, tremble, shudder, shiver, quake, quaver, vibrate, palpitate, flutter, flicker, oscillate, wobble

quiver[2] *noun* a carrying case for arrows

qui vive: on the qui vive on the alert, ready for action

quixotic *adj* having noble but foolish and unrealistic aims ◇ **quixotically** *adv*

After Don *Quixote*, the knight in Cervantes's 16th-century Spanish romance

quiz *verb* (**quizzes**, **quizzing**, **quizzed**) question ◇ *noun* (*plural* **quizzes**) a competition to test knowledge ◇ **quizzical** *adj* of a look: as if asking a question, *esp* mockingly

■ *verb* question, interrogate, grill, pump, examine, cross-examine ◇ *noun* questionnaire, test, examination, competition ◇ **quizzical** questioning, inquiring, curious, amused, humorous, teasing, mocking, satirical, sardonic, sceptical

quoits *noun sing* a game in which heavy flat rings (**quoits**) are thrown onto small rods

quorum *noun* the least number of people who must be present at a meeting before any business can be done

> From Latin phrase *quorum vos .. esse volumus* 'of whom we wish that you be (one, two etc)', used in legal commissions

quota *noun* a part or share to be given or received by each member of a group
- ration, allowance, allocation, assignment, share, portion, part, slice, *informal* cut, percentage, proportion

quotation *noun* **1** the act of repeating something said or written **2** the words repeated **3** a price stated for a job to be done ◇ **quotation marks** marks used in writing to show that someone's words are being repeated exactly, *eg* 'he said "I'm going out"'
- **2** citation, *informal* quote, extract, excerpt, passage, piece, cutting, reference **3** estimate, *informal* quote, tender, figure, price, cost, charge, rate

quote *verb* **1** repeat the words of (someone) exactly as said or written **2** state (a price for something)
- **1** cite, refer to, mention, name, reproduce, echo, repeat, recite, recall, recollect

quoth *verb*, *old* said

quotidian *adj*, *formal* daily

quotient *noun*, *maths* the result obtained by dividing one number by another, *eg* 4 is the quotient when 12 is divided by 3

qv *abbrev* which see (from Latin *quod vide*)

qwerty *noun* (*plural* **qwertys**) a standard arrangement of keys on a typewriter or computer keyboard, with the top line of letters beginning Q,W,E,R,T,Y

Rr

R *abbrev* King or Queen (from Latin *rex* or *regina*)

RA *abbrev* Royal Academy

rabbi *noun* (*plural* **rabbis**) a Jewish priest or teacher of the law ◇ **rabbinical** *adj*

rabbit *noun* a small, burrowing, long-eared animal

rabble *noun* a disorderly, noisy crowd
▣ crowd, throng, horde, herd, mob, populace, riff-raff

rabid *adj* **1** of a dog: suffering from rabies **2** violently enthusiastic or extreme: *a rabid nationalist*

rabies *noun* (*also called* **hydrophobia**) a disease transmitted by the bite of an infected animal, causing fear of water and madness

raccoon or **racoon** *noun* a small furry animal of N America with black eye patches

race¹ *noun* **1** a group of people with the same ancestors and physical characteristics **2** descent: *of noble race*
▣ **1** nation, people, tribe, clan, house, dynasty, family, kindred **2** ancestry, line, blood, stock, genus, species, breed

race² *noun* a competition to find the fastest person, animal, vehicle *etc* ◇ *verb* **1** run fast **2** take part in a race
▣ *noun* sprint, steeplechase, marathon, scramble, regatta, competition, contest ◇ *verb* **1** run, sprint, dash, tear, fly, gallop, speed, career, dart, zoom, rush, hurry, hasten

racecourse or **racetrack** *noun* a course over which races are run

racehorse *noun* a horse bred and used for racing

raceme *noun* a plant stalk with flowers growing along it

racial *adj* of or according to race
▣ national, tribal, ethnic, folk, genealogical, ancestral, inherited, genetic

racism or **racialism** *noun* **1** the belief that some races of people are superior to others **2** prejudice on the grounds of race ◇ **racist** or **racialist** *noun* someone who believes in, or practises, racism ◇ *adj* involving racism
▣ **2** xenophobia, chauvinism, jingoism, discrimination, prejudice, bias

rack *noun* **1** a framework for holding letters, plates, coats *etc* **2** *hist* an instrument for torturing victims by stretching their joints **3** a bar with teeth which fits into and moves a toothed wheel: *rack and pinion* ◇ **rack and ruin** a state of neglect and decay ◇ **rack your brains** think hard about something

racket¹ or **racquet** *noun* **1** a bat made up of a strong frame strung with gut or nylon for playing tennis, badminton *etc* **2** (**rackets**) a form of tennis played against a wall

racket² *noun* **1** a great noise, a din **2** *informal* a dishonest way of making a profit ◇ **racketeer** *noun* someone who makes money dishonestly
▣ **1** noise, din, uproar, row, fuss, clamour, commotion, disturbance, pandemonium, hurly-burly, hubbub **2** swindle, *informal* con, fraud, fiddle, deception, trick, dodge, scheme, business, game

raconteur *noun* someone who tells stories, *esp* in an entertaining way

racoon *another spelling of* **raccoon**

racquet *another spelling of* **racket**

racy *adj* of a story: full of action, and often involving sexual exploits
▣ ribald, risqué, naughty, indecent, indelicate, suggestive, *informal* saucy

RADA *abbrev* Royal Academy of Dramatic Art

radar *noun* a method of detecting solid objects using radio waves which bounce back off the object and form a picture of it on a screen

radiant *adj* **1** sending out rays of light, heat *etc* **2** showing joy and happiness: *a radiant smile* ◇**radiance** *noun* brightness, splendour

■ **1** bright, luminous, shining, gleaming, glowing, beaming, glittering, sparkling, brilliant **2** resplendent, splendid, glorious, happy, joyful, delighted, ecstatic

◨ **1** dull **2** miserable

radiate *verb* **1** send out rays of light, heat *etc* **2** spread or send out from a centre

■ **1** shine, gleam, glow, beam, shed, pour, give off, emit, emanate, diffuse **2** issue, disseminate, scatter, spread (out), diverge, branch

radiation *noun* **1** the giving off of rays of light, heat *etc* or of those from radioactive substances **2** radioactivity

radiator *noun* **1** a device (*esp* a series of connected hot-water pipes) which sends out heat **2** the part of a car which cools the engine

radical *adj* **1** thorough: *a radical change* **2** basic, deep-seated: *radical differences* **3** advocating dramatic changes in the method of government ◇*noun* someone who has radical political views

■ *adj***1** drastic, comprehensive, thorough, sweeping, far-reaching, thorough-going, complete, total, entire **2** basic, fundamental, primary, essential, natural, native, innate, intrinsic, deep-seated, profound **3** militant, extreme, extremist

radicchio *noun* a purple-leaved variety of chicory

radio *noun* (*plural* **radios**) a device for sending and receiving sound signals by means of electromagnetic waves ◇*verb* (**radios**, **radioing**, **radioed**) send a message to (someone) in this way

radioactive *adj* giving off rays which are often dangerous but which can be used in medicine ◇**radioactivity** *noun*

radiography *noun* photography of the interior of the body by X-rays ◇**radiographer** *noun*

radiology *noun* **1** the study of radioactive substances and radiation **2** the branch of medicine involving the use of X-rays and radium ◇**radiologist** *noun*

radiotherapy *noun* the treatment of certain diseases by X-rays or radioactive substances ◇**radiotherapist** *noun*

radish *noun* (*plural* **radishes**) a plant with a sharp-tasting root, eaten raw in salads

radium *noun* a radioactive metal used in radiotherapy

radius *noun* (*plural* **radii**) **1** a straight line from the centre to the circumference of a circle **2** an area within a certain distance from a central point

RAF *abbrev* Royal Air Force

raffia *noun* strips of fibre from the leaves of a palm tree, used in weaving mats *etc*

raffish *adj* flashy, dashing

raffle *noun* a way of raising money by selling numbered tickets, one or more of which wins a prize ◇*verb* give as a prize in a raffle

■ *noun*draw, lottery, sweepstake, sweep, tombola

raft *noun* a number of logs *etc* fastened together and used as a boat

rafter *noun* one of the sloping beams supporting a roof

rag[1] *noun* **1** a torn or worn piece of cloth **2** (**rags**) worn-out, shabby clothes ◇*adj* made of rags: *a rag doll*

rag[2] *verb* (**rags**, **ragging**, **ragged**) tease, play tricks on

ragamuffin *noun* a ragged, dirty child

rag-bag *noun* a random or confused collection

rag doll a floppy doll made of scrap material

rage *noun* great anger, fury ◇*verb* **1** be violently angry **2** of a storm, battle *etc*: be violent ◇**all the rage** very fashionable or popular

■ *noun* anger, wrath, fury, frenzy, tantrum, temper ◇ *verb* **1** fume, seethe, rant, rave **2** storm, thunder, explode, rampage

ragga *noun* a style of rap music

ragged *adj* **1** in torn, shabby clothes **2** torn and tattered
▣ **1** shabby, scruffy, unkempt, down-at-heel **2** frayed, torn, ripped, tattered, worn-out, threadbare, tatty, shabby, scruffy

raglan *noun* a cardigan or coat with the sleeves in one piece with the shoulders

Named after Lord *Raglan*, British commander in the Crimean war

ragout /ra'gu:/ *noun* a highly seasoned meat-and-vegetable stew

ragtime *noun* a style of jazz music with a highly syncopated melody

rag trade the fashion or clothes industry

ragwort *noun* a large coarse weed with a yellow flower

raid *noun* **1** a short, sudden attack **2** an unexpected visit by the police to catch a criminal, recover stolen goods *etc* ◇ *verb* make a raid on ◇ **raider** *noun*
▣ *noun* **1** attack, onset, onslaught, invasion, incursion, foray, sortie, strike, blitz, swoop, robbery, break-in, hold-up ◇ *verb* loot, pillage, plunder, ransack, rifle, maraud, attack, descend on, invade, storm

rail[1] *noun* **1** a bar of metal used in fences **2** (**rails**) strips of steel which form the track on which trains run **3** the railway: *I came here by rail*

rail[2] *verb* (with **against** or **at**) speak angrily or bitterly

railing *noun* a fence or barrier of rails
▣ fence, paling, barrier, parapet, rail, balustrade

railway or *US* **railroad** *noun* a track laid with steel rails on which trains run

raiment *noun, old* clothing

rain *noun* **1** water falling from the clouds in drops **2** a great number of things falling ◇ *verb* pour or fall in drops: *It's raining today* ◇ **rainy** *adj* **1** full of rain: *rainy skies* **2** showery, wet: *a rainy day*

▣ *verb* spit, drizzle, shower, pour, teem, pelt, *informal* bucket, deluge ◇ **rainy 2** wet, damp, showery, drizzly
▨ **rainy 2** dry

rainbow *noun* **1** the brilliant coloured bow or arch sometimes to be seen in the sky opposite the sun when rain is falling **2** a member of the most junior branch of the Guides

raincheck *noun, US* an arrangement to keep an appointment *etc* at a later, postponed date

raincoat *noun* a waterproof coat to keep out the rain

rainfall *noun* the amount of rain that falls in a certain time

rainforest *noun* a tropical forest with very heavy rainfall

raise *verb* **1** lift up: *raise the flag* **2** make higher: *raise the price* **3** bring up (a subject) for consideration **4** bring up (a child, family *etc*) **5** breed or grow (*eg* pigs, crops) **6** collect, get together (*eg* a sum of money)
▣ **1** lift, elevate, hoist, jack up, erect **2** increase, augment, escalate, magnify, heighten, strengthen, intensify, amplify, boost, enhance **3** bring up, broach, introduce, present, put forward, suggest **5** rear, breed, propagate, grow, cultivate, develop **6** get, obtain, collect, gather, assemble, rally, muster, recruit
▨ **1** lower **2** decrease, reduce

❗ Do not confuse with: **raze**

raisin *noun* a dried grape

raison d'être reason for existing

Raj *noun, hist* the time of British rule in India, 1858–1947

rajah *noun, hist* an Indian prince

rake[1] *noun* a tool, like a large comb with a long handle, for smoothing earth, gathering hay *etc* ◇ *verb* **1** draw a rake over **2** scrape (together) **3** aim gunfire at (*eg* a ship) from one end to the other

rake[2] *noun, old* someone who lives an immoral life ◇ **rakish** *adj* at a slanting, jaunty angle

rally *verb* (**rallies**, **rallying**, **rallied**) **1**

gather again: *rally troops* **2** come together for a joint action or effort: *the club's supporters rallied to save it* **3** recover from an illness ◇ *noun (plural rallies)* **1** a gathering **2** a political mass meeting **3** an improvement in health after an illness **4** *tennis* a long series of shots before a point is won or lost **5** a competition to test driving skills over an unknown route ◇ **rallying** *noun* long-distance motor-racing over public roads

☰ *verb* **1** gather, collect, assemble, congregate, convene, muster, summon, round up, unite, marshal, organize, mobilize, reassemble, regroup, reorganize **3** recover, recuperate, revive, improve, pick up ◇ *noun* **1** gathering, assembly, convention, convocation, conference, meeting, jamboree, reunion **2** march, demonstration **3** recovery, recuperation, revival, comeback, improvement, resurgence, renewal

RAM *abbrev, comput* random access memory

ram *noun* **1** a male sheep **2** something heavy, *esp* as part of a machine, for ramming ◇ *verb* (**rams, ramming, rammed**) **1** press or push down hard **2** of a ship, car *etc*: run into and cause damage to

☰ *verb* **1** force, drive, thrust, cram, stuff, jam, wedge **2** hit, strike, butt, hammer, pound, drum, crash, smash, slam

Ramadan *noun* **1** the ninth month of the Islamic calendar, a period of fasting by day **2** the fast itself

ramble *verb* **1** walk about for pleasure, *esp* in the countryside **2** speak in an aimless or confused way ◇ *noun* a country walk for pleasure ◇ **rambler** *noun* **1** someone who rambles **2** a climbing rose or other plant

☰ *verb* **1** walk, hike, trek, tramp, traipse, stroll, amble, saunter, straggle, wander, roam, rove, meander, wind, zigzag **2** chatter, babble, *informal* rabbit (on), *informal* witter (on), expatiate, digress, drift ◇ *noun* walk, hike, trek, tramp, stroll, saunter, tour, trip, excursion ◇ **rambler** hiker, walker, stroller, rover, roamer, wanderer, wayfarer

rambunctious *adj* boisterous, exuberant

ramekin *noun* **1** a baking dish for a single portion **2** something served in this

ramification *noun* **1** a branch or part of a subject, plot *etc* **2** a consequence, usually indirect and one of several

☰ **1** branch, offshoot, development, complication **2** result, consequence, upshot, implication

ramp *noun* a sloping surface (*eg* of a road)

rampage *verb* rush about angrily or violently ◇ **on the rampage** rampaging

☰ run wild, run amok, run riot, rush, tear, storm, rage, rant, rave ◇ **on the rampage** wild, amok, berserk, violent, out of control

rampant *adj* **1** widespread and uncontrolled **2** *heraldry* standing on the left hind leg: *lion rampant*

☰ **1** unrestrained, uncontrolled, unbridled, unchecked, wanton, excessive, fierce, violent, raging, wild, riotous, rank, profuse, rife, widespread, prevalent

rampart *noun* a mound or wall built as a defence

ram-raid *noun* a raid by smashing into a shop window with a stolen car

ramrod *noun* **1** a rod for pushing the charge down a gun barrel **2** someone strict or inflexible in their views

ramshackle *adj* badly made, falling to pieces

☰ dilapidated, tumbledown, broken-down, crumbling, ruined, derelict, jerry-built, unsafe, rickety, shaky, unsteady, tottering, decrepit

☲ solid, stable

ran *past form* of **run**

ranch *noun* (*plural* **ranches**) a large farm in North America for rearing cattle or horses

rancid *adj* of butter: smelling or tasting stale

☰ sour, off, bad, musty, stale, rank, foul, fetid, putrid, rotten

☲ fresh

rancour *noun* ill-will, hatred ◇ **rancorous** *adj*

rand *noun* the standard unit of South African money

R and B *abbrev* rhythm and blues

R and D *abbrev* research and development

random *adj* done without any aim or plan; chance: *a random sample* ◇ **at random** without any plan or purpose ◇ **random access memory** a computer memory in which data can be directly located

■ arbitrary, chance, fortuitous, casual, incidental, haphazard, irregular, unsystematic, unplanned, accidental, aimless, purposeless, indiscriminate, stray

⏛ systematic, deliberate

randy *adj* lustful

range *noun* 1 a line or row: *a range of mountains* 2 a number of different things, often of the same kind: *the shop sells a wide range of footwear* 3 a piece of ground with targets for shooting or archery practice 4 the distance which an object can be thrown, or across which a sound can be heard 5 the distance between two limits, *eg* the top and bottom notes of a singing voice 6 a large kitchen stove with a flat top ◇ *verb* 1 set in a row or in order 2 wander (over) 3 stretch, extend; vary: *prices ranging from £5 to £500* ◇ **ranger** *noun* a keeper who looks after a forest or park ◇ **Ranger Guide** an older member of the Guide movement

■ *noun* 2 variety, diversity, assortment, selection 4 scope, compass, scale, spectrum, sweep, spread, extent, distance, reach, span, limits, bounds, parameters, area, field, domain, province, sphere, orbit

rank¹ *noun* 1 a row or line (*eg* of soldiers) 2 class, order: *the upper ranks of society/the rank of captain* 3 (**ranks**) private soldiers, not officers ◇ *verb* 1 place in order of importance, merit *etc* 2 have a place in an order: *apes rank above dogs in intelligence* ◇ **rank and file** 1 soldiers of the rank of private 2 ordinary people, the majority

■ *noun* 1 row, line, range, column, file, series, order, formation 2 grade, degree, class, caste, status, standing, position, station, condition, estate, echelon, level, stratum, tier, classification ◇ *verb* 1 grade, class, rate, place, position, range, sort, classify, categorize, order, arrange, organize, marshal

---

Ranks in the armed services include:
air force: aircraftsman, aircraftswoman, corporal, sergeant, warrant officer, pilot officer, flying officer, flight lieutenant, squadron-leader, wing commander, group-captain, air-commodore, air-vice-marshal, air-marshal, air-chief-marshal, marshal of the Royal Air Force; *army:* private, lance-corporal, corporal, sergeant, warrant officer, lieutenant, captain, major, lieutenant-colonel, colonel, brigadier, major general, lieutenant-general, general, field marshal; *navy:* able seaman, rating, petty officer, chief petty officer, sublieutenant, lieutenant, lieutenant-commander, commander, captain, commodore, rear admiral, vice-admiral, admiral, admiral of the fleet
see also **soldier**

---

rank² *adj* 1 of a plant: growing too plentifully 2 having a strong, unpleasant taste or smell 3 absolute: *rank nonsense*

rankle *verb* cause lasting annoyance, bitterness *etc*

ransack *verb* search thoroughly; plunder

■ search, scour, comb, rummage, rifle, raid, sack, strip, despoil, ravage, loot, plunder, pillage

ransom *noun* the price paid for the freeing of a captive ◇ *verb* pay money to free (a captive)

■ *noun* price, money, payment, pay-off, redemption, deliverance, rescue, liberation, release ◇ *verb* buy off, redeem, deliver, rescue, liberate, free

rant *verb* talk foolishly and angrily for a long time

rap noun **1** a sharp blow or knock **2** slang a criminal charge **3** a style of music accompanied by a rhythmic monologue ◇ verb (**raps**, **rapping**, **rapped**) **1** (often with **on**) strike with a quick, sharp blow **2** (with **out**) speak sharply ◇ **take the rap** take the blame or punishment

■ noun **1** knock, blow, tap, thump ◇ verb **1** knock, hit, strike, tap, thump

rapacious adj greedy, eager to seize as much as possible

rape[1] verb have sexual intercourse with (someone) against their will, usually by force ◇ noun **1** the act of raping **2** the act of seizing and carrying off by force ◇ **rapist** noun someone who commits rape

■ verb violate, assault, abuse, maltreat ◇ noun **1** violation, assault, abuse, maltreatment

rape[2] noun a type of plant like the turnip whose seeds give oil

rapid adj quick, fast: a rapid rise to fame ◇ **rapidity** noun swiftness ◇ **rapidly** adv ◇ **rapids** noun plural a part in a river where the current flows swiftly

■ swift, speedy, quick, fast, express, lightning, prompt, brisk, hurried, hasty, precipitate

▣ slow, leisurely, sluggish

rapier noun a type of light sword with a narrow blade

rapport /ra'pɔː(r)/ noun a good relationship, sympathy

■ bond, link, affinity, relationship, empathy, sympathy, understanding, harmony

rapprochement /ra'prɒʃmã/ noun a drawing together; a renewal of contact

rapt adj having the mind fully occupied, engrossed: rapt attention

■ engrossed, absorbed, preoccupied, intent, gripped, spellbound, enthralled, captivated, fascinated, entranced

rapture noun great delight ◇ **rapturous** adj

rare adj **1** seldom found, uncommon **2** of meat: lightly cooked ◇ **rarely** adv

■ **1** uncommon, unusual, scarce, sparse, sporadic, infrequent

🔢 Do not confuse with: **unique**

rarefied or **rarified** adj **1** of the air: thin or less dense **2** refined, select, exclusive

raring adj: **raring to go** very keen to go, start etc

■ eager, keen, enthusiastic, ready, willing, impatient, longing, itching

rarity noun (plural **rarities**) **1** something uncommon **2** uncommonness

rascal noun a naughty or wicked person

■ rogue, scoundrel, scamp, scallywag, imp, devil, villain, good-for-nothing

rash[1] adj acting, or done, without thought ◇ **rashly** adv ◇ **rashness** noun the state of being rash

■ reckless, ill-considered, foolhardy, ill-advised, madcap, hare-brained, hot-headed, headstrong, impulsive, impetuous, hasty, headlong, unguarded, imprudent, careless, heedless, unthinking

rash[2] noun a redness or outbreak of spots on the skin

■ eruption, outbreak

rasher noun a thin slice (of bacon or ham)

rasp noun **1** a coarse file **2** a rough, grating sound ◇ verb **1** rub with a file **2** make a rough, grating noise **3** say in a rough voice ◇ **rasping** adj of a sound: rough and unpleasant

■ noun **2** grating, scrape, grinding, scratch, harshness, hoarseness, croak ◇ verb **1** grind, file, sand, scour, abrade, rub **2** grate, scrape

raspberry noun **1** a type of red berry similar to a blackberry **2** the bush which bears this fruit

rat noun a gnawing animal, similar to but larger than a mouse ◇ verb (**rats**, **ratting**, **ratted**) hunt or kill rats ◇ **rat on** informal inform against

ratatouille /ratə'tuːɪ/ noun a Mediterranean vegetable stew

ratchet noun a toothed wheel, eg in a mechanism

rate noun **1** the frequency with which

something happens or is done: *a high rate of road accidents* **2** speed: *speak at a tremendous rate* **3** level of cost, price *etc*: *paid at a higher rate* **4** (**rates**) the sum of money to be paid by the owner of a shop *etc* to pay for local public services ◊ *verb* **1** work out the value of for taxation *etc* **2** value: *I don't rate his work very highly* ◊ **rateable value** a value of a shop *etc* used to work out the rates to be paid on it

■ *noun* **2** speed, velocity, tempo **3** charge, fee, hire, toll, tariff, price, cost, value, worth, tax, duty, amount, figure, percentage ◊ *verb* **2** judge, regard, consider, deem, count, reckon, figure, estimate, evaluate, assess, measure, grade, rank, class, classify

rather *adv* **1** somewhat, fairly: *It's rather cold today* **2** more willingly: *I'd rather talk about it now than later* **3** more correctly speaking: *he agreed, or rather he didn't say no*

ratify *verb* (**ratifies, ratifying, ratified**) approve officially and formally: *ratified the treaty* ◊ **ratification** *noun*

■ approve, uphold, endorse, sign, legalize, sanction, authorize, establish, affirm, confirm, certify, validate, authenticate

■ repudiate, reject

rating *noun* a sailor below the rank of an officer

ratio *noun* (*plural* **ratios**) the proportion of one thing to another: *a ratio of two parts flour to one of sugar*

■ percentage, fraction, proportion, relation, relationship, correspondence, correlation

ration *noun* a measured amount or allowance of food *etc* at a time of shortage ◊ *verb* **1** deal out (*eg* food) in measured amounts **2** allow only a certain amount to (someone)

■ *noun* quota, allowance, allocation, allotment, share, portion, helping, part, measure, amount ◊ *verb* **1** apportion, allot, allocate, share, deal out, distribute, dole out, dispense, supply, issue

rational *adj* **1** able to reason **2** sensible; based on reason: *rational argu-*

ments ◊ **rationality** *noun* ◊ **rationally** *adv*

■ **1** clear-headed, judicious, wise, sane, normal, balanced, lucid, reasoning, thinking, intelligent, enlightened **2** sound, well-founded, logical, reasonable, realistic, sensible, practical

rationalize *verb* think up a good reason for (an action or feeling) so as not to feel guilty about it ◊ **rationalization** *noun*

rat race a fierce, unending competition for success or wealth

rattle *verb* **1** give out short, sharp, repeated sounds: *the coins rattled in the tin* **2** fluster or irritate (someone) ◊ *noun* **1** a sharp noise, quickly repeated **2** a toy or instrument which makes such a sound ◊ **rattle off** go through (a list of names *etc*) quickly

■ *verb* **1** clatter, jingle, jangle, clank ◊ **rattle off** reel off, list, run through, recite, repeat

rattlesnake *noun* a poisonous snake with bony rings on its tail which rattle when shaken

ratty *adj* irritable

raucous *adj* hoarse, harsh: *a raucous voice*

■ harsh, rough, hoarse, husky, rasping, grating, jarring, strident, noisy, loud

raunchy *adj* sexually suggestive, lewd

ravage *verb* cause destruction or damage to; plunder ◊ **ravages** *noun plural* damaging effects: *the ravages of time*

■ *verb* destroy, devastate, lay waste, demolish, raze, wreck, ruin, spoil, damage, loot, pillage, plunder, sack, despoil

rave *verb* **1** talk wildly, as if mad **2** *informal* talk very enthusiastically (about) ◊ *noun* a large party held in a warehouse *etc* with electronic music ◊ **raver** *noun* **1** someone who attends a rave party **2** someone who has a lively social life ◊ **raving** *adj* mad, crazy

■ *verb* **1** rage, storm, thunder, roar, rant, ramble, babble, splutter

raven *noun* a type of large black bird of the crow family ◊ *adj* of hair: black and glossy

ravenous *adj* very hungry

■ hungry, starving, starved, famished, greedy

ravine *noun* a deep, narrow valley between hills

ravioli *noun plural* little pasta cases with savoury fillings

ravish *verb* **1** delight, enrapture **2** rape **3** plunder ◇ **ravishing** *adj* delightful, lovely

■ **1** enrapture, delight, overjoy, enchant, charm, captivate, entrance, fascinate, spellbind

raw *adj* **1** not cooked **2** not prepared or refined, in its natural state: *raw cotton/ raw text* **3** of weather: cold **4** sore ◇ **a raw deal** unjust treatment

■ **2** unrefined, untreated, crude, natural **3** cold, chilly, bitter, biting, piercing, freezing, bleak **4** sore, tender, sensitive

◪ **1** cooked, done **2** processed, refined **3** warm

ray¹ *noun* **1** a line of light, heat *etc* **2** a small degree or amount: *a ray of hope* **3** one of several lines going outwards from a centre

ray² *noun* a kind of flat-bodied fish

rayon *noun* a type of artificial silk

raze *verb* destroy, knock flat (a town, house *etc*)

■ demolish, pull down, tear down, bulldoze, flatten, level, destroy

> ⚠ Do not confuse with: **raise**

razor *noun* a sharp-edged instrument for shaving

razorbill *noun* a type of seabird of the auk family

razorfish *noun* a type of long narrow shellfish

razzmatazz *noun* showiness, glamorous or extravagant show

RC *abbrev* Roman Catholic

re *prep* concerning, about

re- *prefix* **1** again, once more: *recreate* **2** back: *reclaim*

reach *verb* **1** arrive at: *reach the summit/your message never reached me* **2** stretch out (the hand) so as to touch: *I couldn't reach the top shelf* **3** extend ◇ *noun* **1** a distance that can be travelled easily: *within reach of home* **2** the distance someone can stretch their arm **3** a straight part of a stream or river between bends

■ *verb* **1** arrive at, get to, attain, achieve, make **2** touch, contact, grasp **3** stretch, extend

react *verb* **1** act or behave in response to something done or said **2** undergo a chemical change: *metals react with sulphuric acid*

■ **1** respond, retaliate, reciprocate, reply, answer, acknowledge

reaction *noun* **1** behaviour as a response to action **2** a chemical change **3** a movement against a situation or belief: *a reaction against Victorian morality*

■ **1** response, effect, reply, answer, acknowledgement, feedback, counteraction, reflex, recoil

reactionary *adj* favouring a return to old ways, laws *etc* ◇ *noun* (*plural* **reactionaries**) someone who holds reactionary views

■ *adj* conservative, right-wing, rightist, diehard, counter-revolutionary ◇ *noun* conservative, right-winger, rightist, diehard, counter-revolutionary

◪ *adj & noun* progressive, revolutionary

read *verb* (**reads**, **reading**, **read**) **1** look at and understand or say aloud written or printed words **2** study a subject in a university or college: *reading law* ◇ **readable** *adj* **1** able to be read **2** quite interesting ◇ **read-only memory** *comput* a memory device that can only be read, not written to ◇ **read-out** *noun* **1** data from a computer; output **2** data from a radio transmitter

reader *noun* **1** someone who reads books *etc* **2** someone who reads manuscripts for a publisher **3** a senior university lecturer **4** a reading book for children

ready *adj* **1** prepared: *packed and ready to go* **2** willing: *always ready to help* **3** quick: *too ready to find fault* **4** available for use: *your coat is ready for collection* ◇ **readily** *adv* easily; willingly

◇ **readiness** noun ◇ **ready-made** adj of clothes: made for general sale, not made specially for one person

■ **1** prepared, waiting, set, fit, arranged, organized, completed, finished **2** willing, inclined, disposed, happy, informal game, eager, keen **4** available, to hand, present, near, accessible, convenient, handy

real adj **1** actually existing, not imagined (contrasted with: **ideal**) **2** not imitation, genuine: real leather **3** sincere: a real love of music ◇ **real estate** US the ownership of lands or properties on it ◇ **the real McCoy** the genuine article, the real thing

■ **1** actual, existing, physical, material, substantial, tangible **2** genuine, authentic, bona fide, veritable **3** honest, sincere, heartfelt, unfeigned, unaffected

1 unreal, imaginary **2** false

really adv **1** in fact **2** very: really dark hair

realism noun the representation or acceptance of things as they really are ◇ **realist** noun someone who claims to see life as it really is

realistic adj **1** lifelike **2** viewing or accepting things as they really are ◇ **realistically** adv

■ **1** lifelike, faithful, truthful, true, genuine, authentic, natural, real, real-life, graphic, representational **2** practical, down-to-earth, commonsense, sensible, level-headed, clear-sighted, businesslike, hard-headed, pragmatic, matter-of-fact, rational, logical, objective, detached, unsentimental

2 unrealistic, impractical, irrational, idealistic

reality noun (plural **realities**) that which is real and not imaginary; truth

realize verb **1** come to understand, know: I never realized you could sing **2** make real, accomplish: realize an ambition **3** get (money) for: realized £160 000 on the sale of the house ◇ **realization** noun

■ **1** understand, comprehend, grasp, informal get, catch on, informal cotton on, recognize, accept, appreciate **2** achieve, accomplish, fulfil, complete, implement, perform **3** fetch, make, earn, produce, net, clear

realm noun **1** a kingdom, a country **2** an area of activity or interest

realpolitik noun politics based on practical realities, not idealism

realty noun property such as land and houses ◇ **realtor** noun an estate agent

ream noun **1** a measure for paper, 20 quires **2** (**reams**) a large quantity, esp of paper: she wrote reams in her English exam

reap verb **1** cut and gather (corn etc) **2** gain: reap the benefits of hard work ◇ **reaper** noun **1** someone who reaps **2** a machine for reaping

rear[1] noun **1** the back part of anything **2** the last part of an army or fleet ◇ **bring up the rear** come or be last in a series

■ **1** back, stern, end, tail, rump, buttocks, posterior, behind, bottom, informal backside

1 front

rear[2] verb **1** bring up (children) **2** breed (animals) **3** of an animal: stand on its hindlegs

■ **1** bring up, raise, foster, nurse, nurture, train, educate

rear-admiral noun an officer who commands the rear division of the fleet

rearguard noun troops which protect the rear of an army

reason noun **1** cause, excuse: what is the reason for this noise? **2** purpose: what is your reason for visiting America? **3** the power of the mind to form opinions, judge right and truth etc **4** common sense ◇ verb **1** think out (opinions, conclusions etc) **2** (with **with**) try to persuade (someone) by arguing ◇ **reasonable** adj **1** sensible **2** fair

■ noun **1** cause, rationale, explanation, excuse, justification, defence, warrant, ground, basis **2** aim, intention, motive, incentive, purpose, object, end, goal **3** sense, logic, reasoning, rationality, sanity, mind, wit, brain, intellect, understanding, wisdom, judgement ◇ verb **1** work out, solve, resolve, conclude, deduce, infer, think **2** urge, persuade, move, remonstrate with, argue with, debate with, discuss with

reassure *verb* take away (someone's) doubts or fears ◇ **reassurance** *noun* ◇ **reassuring** *adj*

▤ comfort, cheer, encourage, hearten, brace, bolster

▣ alarm

rebarbative *adj* repellent

rebate *noun* a part of a payment or tax which is given back to the payer

rebel *noun* someone who opposes or fights against those in power ◇ *verb* (**rebels, rebelling, rebelled**) take up arms against or oppose those in power ◇ **rebellious** *adj* ◇ **rebelliousness** *noun*

▤ *noun* revolutionary, insurrectionary, mutineer, dissenter, nonconformist ◇ *verb* revolt, mutiny, rise up, run riot, dissent, disobey, defy, resist

rebellion *noun* **1** an open or armed fight against those in power **2** a refusal to obey

▤ **1** revolt, revolution, rising, uprising, insurrection, insurgence, mutiny, coup **2** resistance, opposition, defiance, disobedience, insubordination, dissent

reboot *verb* restart (a computer) using its start-up programs

rebound *verb* bounce back: *the ball rebounded off the wall* ◇ *noun* **1** the act of rebounding **2** a reaction following an emotional situation or crisis: *married him on the rebound*

rebuff *noun* a blunt refusal or rejection ◇ *verb* reject bluntly

▤ *noun* rejection, refusal, discouragement, snub, *informal* brush-off, slight, put-down, cold shoulder ◇ *verb* spurn, reject, refuse, decline, turn down, repulse, discourage, snub, slight, cut, cold-shoulder

rebuke *verb* scold, blame ◇ *noun* a scolding

▤ *verb* reprove, castigate, chide, scold, *informal* tell off, admonish, *informal* tick off, reprimand, upbraid, rate, censure, blame, reproach ◇ *noun* reproach, re-

proof, reprimand, lecture, *informal* dressing-down, *informal* telling-off, *informal* ticking-off, admonition, censure, blame

▣ *verb* praise, compliment ◇ *noun* praise, commendation

rebut *verb* (**rebuts, rebutting, rebutted**) deny (what has been said) ◇ **rebuttal** *noun*

recalcitrant *adj* stubborn; disobedient ◇ **recalcitrance** *noun*

recall *verb* **1** call back: *recalled to headquarters* **2** remember ◇ *noun* **1** a signal or message to return **2** the act of recalling or remembering

▤ *verb* **2** remember, recollect, cast one's mind back, evoke, bring back

recant *verb* **1** take back what you have said **2** reject publicly your beliefs ◇ **recantation** *noun*

recap *verb* (**recaps, recapping, recapped**) *informal* recapitulate ◇ *noun*, *informal* recapitulation

recapitulate *verb* go over again quickly the chief points of anything (*eg* a discussion) ◇ **recapitulation** *noun*

recapture *verb* capture (what has escaped or been lost)

recast *verb* (**recasts, recasting, recast**) shape in a new form

recede *verb* **1** go back **2** become more distant **3** slope backwards ◇ **receding** *adj* **1** going or sloping backwards **2** becoming more distant

▤ *verb* **1** go back, return, retire, withdraw, retreat, ebb

▣ *verb* **1** advance

receipt *noun* **1** the act of receiving (*esp* money or goods) **2** a written note saying that money *etc* has been received

▤ **1** receiving, reception, acceptance **2** voucher, ticket, slip, counterfoil, stub, acknowledgement

receive *verb* **1** have something given or brought to you: *receive a gift/receive a letter* **2** meet and welcome: *receiving visitors* **3** take goods, knowing them to be stolen

▤ **1** take, accept, get, obtain, derive, acquire, pick up, collect, inherit **2** admit, let in, greet, welcome, entertain, accommodate

🔳 **1** give, donate

receiver *noun* **1** someone who receives stolen goods **2** the part of a telephone through which words are heard and into which they are spoken **3** an apparatus through which television or radio broadcasts are received

recent *adj* happening, done or made only a short time ago ◇ **recently** *adv*

🔳 late, latest, current, present-day, contemporary, modern, up-to-date, new, novel, fresh, young

receptacle *noun* an object to receive or hold things, a container

reception *noun* **1** the way in which something or someone is received: *a warm reception* **2** a large meeting to welcome guests **3** the quality of radio or television signals **4** an office or desk where visitors are dealt with on arrival

receptionist *noun* someone employed in an office or hotel to greet clients, answer the telephone *etc*

receptive *adj* quick to take in or accept ideas *etc* ◇ **receptivity** *noun*

🔳 open-minded, amenable, accommodating, suggestible, susceptible, sensitive, responsive, open, accessible, approachable, sympathetic, favourable, interested

🔳 narrow-minded, resistant, unresponsive

recess *noun* (*plural* **recesses**) **1** part of a wall or room set back from the rest, an alcove **2** the time during which parliament or the law courts do not work **3** a remote part: *in the recesses of my memory*

recession *noun* **1** the act of moving back **2** a temporary fall in a country's or world business activities ◇ **recessive** *adj*

🔳 **2** slump, depression, downturn, decline

🔳 **2** boom, upturn

recherché /rəˈʃeəʃeɪ/ *adj* carefully chosen, choice

recidivism *noun* the habit of relapsing into crime ◇ **recidivist** *noun* & *adj*

recipe *noun* instructions on how to prepare or cook a certain kind of food

recipient *noun* someone who receives

reciprocal *adj* both given and received: *reciprocal affection*

🔳 mutual, joint, shared, give-and-take, complementary, alternating, corresponding, equivalent, interchangeable

reciprocate *verb* feel or do the same in return: *I reciprocate his dislike of me*

🔳 respond, reply, requite, return, exchange, swap, trade, match, equal

recite *verb* repeat aloud from memory ◇ **recitation** *noun* a poem *etc* recited

🔳 repeat, tell, narrate, relate, recount, speak, deliver, declaim, perform, reel off

recital *noun* **1** the act of reciting **2** a musical performance **3** the facts of a story told one after the other

reckless *adj* rash, careless ◇ **recklessly** *adj* ◇ **recklessness** *noun*

🔳 heedless, thoughtless, mindless, careless, negligent, irresponsible, imprudent, ill-advised, indiscreet, rash, hasty, foolhardy, daredevil, wild

🔳 cautious, wary, careful, prudent

reckon *verb* **1** count **2** consider, believe: *I reckon it's worth a try* ◇ **reckoning** *noun* **1** the settling of debts, grievances *etc* **2** payment for sins **3** a bill **4** a sum, calculation

🔳 **1** calculate, compute, figure out, work out, add up, total, tally, count, number, enumerate **2** deem, regard, consider, esteem, value, rate, judge, evaluate, assess, estimate, gauge

reclaim *verb* **1** claim back **2** regain (land from the sea) by draining, building banks *etc* **3** make waste land, materials *etc* fit for use ◇ **reclamation** *noun*

🔳 **1** recover, regain, recapture, retrieve, salvage, rescue, redeem, restore, reinstate

recline *verb* lean or lie on your back or side ◇ **reclining** *adj*

recluse *noun* someone who lives alone and avoids other people ◇ **reclusive** *adj*

recognize *verb* **1** know from a previous meeting *etc* **2** admit, acknowledge: *everyone recognized his talent* **3** show appreciation of: *they recognized his courage by giving him a medal* ◇ **recognizable** *adj* ◇ **recognition** *noun* the act of recognizing

☰ **1** identify, know, remember, recollect, recall, place, see, notice, spot, perceive **2** acknowledge, accept, admit, grant, concede, allow, appreciate, understand, realize

recoil *verb* **1** shrink back in horror or fear **2** of a gun: jump back after a shot is fired ◇ *noun* a shrinking or jumping back

recollect *verb* remember ◇ **recollection** *noun* **1** the act or power of remembering **2** a memory, something remembered

recommend *verb* **1** urge, advise: *I recommend that you take a long holiday* **2** speak highly of ◇ **recommendation** *noun* **1** the act of recommending **2** a point in favour of someone or something

☰ **1** advocate, urge, exhort, advise, counsel, suggest, propose **2** praise, commend, *informal* plug, endorse, approve, vouch for

recompense *verb* pay money to or reward (a person) to make up for loss, inconvenience *etc* ◇ *noun* payment in compensation

reconcile *verb* **1** bring together in friendship, after a quarrel **2** show that two statements, facts *etc* do not contradict each other **3** (with **to**) cause to accept patiently: *I became reconciled to her absence* ◇ **reconciliation** *noun*

☰ **1** reunite, conciliate, pacify, appease, placate **2** resolve, settle, square

☲ **1** estrange, alienate

recondite *adj* secret, little-known

reconnaissance *noun* a survey to obtain information, *esp* before a battle

reconnoitre *verb* make a reconnaissance of

☰ explore, survey, scan, spy out, *slang* recce, inspect, examine, scrutinize, investigate, patrol

reconstitute *verb* **1** put back into its original form: *reconstitute the milk* **2** make up or form in a different way

record *verb* /rɪˈkɔːd/ **1** write down for future reference **2** put (music, speech *etc*) on tape or disc so that it can be listened to later **3** show, register: *the thermometer recorded 30°C yesterday* ◇ *noun* /ˈrekɔːd/ **1** a written report of facts **2** a round, flat piece of plastic on which sounds are recorded for playing on a record-player **3** the best known performance: *John holds the school record for the mile* ◇ **break** or **beat the record** do better than any previous performance ◇ **off the record** of a remark *etc*: not to be made public

☰ *verb* **1** note, enter, inscribe, write down, transcribe, register, log, put down, document **2** tape-record, tape, videotape, video, burn ◇ *noun* **1** register, log, report, account, minutes, memorandum, note, entry, document, file, dossier, diary, journal, memoir, history, annals, archives, documentation **2** disc, single, album, LP

recorder *noun* **1** someone who records **2** a type of simple musical wind instrument **3** a judge in certain courts

recording *noun* **1** the act of recording **2** a piece of recorded music, speech *etc*

record-player *noun* a machine for playing records

recount *verb* tell (the story of)

☰ tell, relate, impart, communicate, report, narrate, describe, depict, portray, detail, repeat, rehearse, recite

re-count *verb* count again ◇ *noun* a second count, *esp* of votes in an election

recoup *verb* make good, recover (expenses, losses *etc*)

🛇 Do not confuse with: **recuperate**

recourse *noun*: **have recourse to** make use of in an emergency

recover *verb* **1** get possession of again **2** become well again after an illness ◇ **recoverable** *adj* able to be recovered

☰ **1** regain, get back, recoup, retrieve, retake, recapture, repossess, reclaim, restore **2** get better, improve, pick up, rally, mend, heal, pull through, get over, recuperate, revive, convalesce, come round

re-cover *verb* cover again

recovery *noun* (*plural* **recoveries**) **1** a return to health **2** the regaining of something lost *etc*

recreate *verb* describe or create again (something past)

recreation *noun* a sport, hobby *etc* done in your spare time

■ diversion, distraction, entertainment, hobby, pastime, game, sport, play, leisure, relaxation

recriminate *verb* accuse your accuser in return ◇ **recriminations** *noun plural* accusations made by someone who is themselves accused ◇ **recriminatory** *adj*

recruit *noun* a newly enlisted soldier, member, employee *etc* ◇ *verb* enlist (someone) in an army, political party, job *etc* ◇ **recruitment** *noun*

■ *noun* beginner, novice, initiate, learner, trainee, apprentice, conscript, convert ◇ *verb* enlist, draft, conscript, enrol, sign up, engage, take on

rectangle *noun* a four-sided figure with all its angles right angles and its opposite sides equal in length, an oblong ◇ **rectangular** *adj*

rectify *verb* (**rectifies**, **rectifying**, **rectified**) put right ◇ **rectifiable** *adj*

■ correct, put right, right, remedy, cure, repair, fix, mend, improve, amend, adjust

rectilineal or **rectilinear** *adj* in a straight line or lines

rectitude *noun* honesty; correctness of behaviour

recto *noun* the right-hand page of an open book (*compare with* **verso**)

rector *noun* **1** a member of the Anglican clergy in charge of a parish **2** the headmaster of some Scottish secondary schools **3** a Scottish university official elected by the students ◇ **rectory** *noun* (*plural* **rectories**) the house of an Anglican rector

rectum *noun* the lower part of the alimentary canal

recumbent *adj* lying down

recuperate *verb* recover strength or health ◇ **recuperation** *noun*

■ recover, get better, improve, pick up, rally, revive, mend, convalesce

☒ worsen

⚠ Do not confuse with: **recoup**

recur *verb* (**recurs**, **recurring**, **recurred**) happen again ◇ **recurrence** *noun* ◇ **recurrent** *adj* happening every so often

■ repeat, persist, return, reappear

recycle *verb* **1** remake into something different **2** treat (material) by some process in order to use it again ◇ **recyclable** *adj* ◇ **recycling** *noun*

red *adj* **1** of the colour of blood ◇ *noun* this colour ◇ **redness** *noun* ◇ **red deer** a type of reddish-brown deer ◇ **red-handed** *adv* in the act of doing wrong: *caught red-handed* ◇ **red herring** something mentioned to lead a discussion away from the main subject; a false clue ◇ **red-letter day** a day which is especially important or happy for some reason ◇ **red light 1** a danger signal **2** a signal to stop ◇ **red tape** unnecessary and troublesome rules; bureaucracy ◇ **see red** become very angry

■ *adj* **1** scarlet, vermilion, cherry, ruby, crimson, maroon, pink, reddish, bloodshot, inflamed

redden *verb* make or grow red

■ blush, flush, colour, go red

redeem *verb* **1** buy back (*eg* articles from a pawnbroker) **2** save from sin or condemnation **3** make amends for ◇ **redeemer** *noun* ◇ **the Redeemer** *noun* Jesus Christ ◇ **redeeming** *adj* making up for other faults: *a redeeming feature* ◇ **redemption** *noun*

■ **1** buy back, repurchase, cash (in), exchange, trade, reclaim, regain, repossess, recoup, recover, recuperate, retrieve, salvage **3** compensate for, make up for, offset, outweigh, atone for, expiate

redeploy *verb* move (*eg* soldiers,

workers) to a different place where they will be more useful

redolent *adj* **1** sweet-smelling **2** smelling (of) **3** suggestive, making one think (of): *redolent of earlier times*

redouble *verb* make twice as great: *redouble your efforts*

redoubtable *adj* brave, bold

redress *verb* set right, make up for (a wrong *etc*) ◇ *noun* something done or given to make up for a loss or wrong, compensation

reduce *verb* **1** make smaller **2** lessen **3** bring to the point of by force of circumstances: *reduced to begging in the streets* **4** bring to a lower rank or state **5** change into other terms: *reduce pounds to pence* ◇ **reducible** *adj* ◇ **reduction** *noun*

■ **1** contract, shrink, slim, shorten, curtail, trim, cut, slash, discount, rebate **2** lessen, decrease, lower, moderate, weaken, diminish, impair

⊟ **2** increase

redundant *adj* **1** more than what is needed **2** of a worker: no longer needed because of the lack of a suitable job ◇ **redundancy** *noun* (*plural* **redundancies**)

■ **1** superfluous, surplus, excess, extra, unneeded, unnecessary, unwanted **2** unemployed, out of work, laid off, dismissed, paid off

⊟ **1** necessary, essential

reduplicate *verb* double, repeat

redwood *noun* a North American tree which grows to a great height

reed *noun* **1** a tall stiff grass growing in moist or marshy places **2** a part (originally made of reed) of certain wind instruments which vibrates when the instrument is played ◇ **reedy** *adj* **1** full of reeds **2** like a reed **3** sounding like a reed instrument: *a reedy voice*

reef *noun* a chain of rocks lying at or near the surface of the sea

reefer *noun* **1** a short coat, as worn by sailors **2** *slang* a marijuana cigarette

reef knot a square, very secure knot

reek *noun* **1** a strong, unpleasant smell

2 smoke ◇ *verb* **1** smell strongly **2** send out smoke

reel *noun* **1** a cylinder of plastic, metal or wood on which thread, film, fishing line *etc* may be wound **2** a length of cinema film **3** a lively Scottish or Irish dance ◇ *verb* **1** wind on a reel **2** (with **in**) draw, pull in (a fish on a line) **3** stagger ◇ **reel off** repeat or recite quickly, without pausing

■ *verb* **3** stagger, totter, wobble, rock, sway, waver, falter, stumble, lurch

reeve *noun*, *hist* a chief magistrate, a bailiff

ref *abbrev* **1** referee **2** reference

refectory *noun* (*plural* **refectories**) a communal dining hall for monks, students *etc*

refer *verb* (**refers, referring, referred**) **1** (with **to**) mention **2** turn (to) for information **3** relate, apply (to) **4** direct (to) for information, consideration *etc*: *I referred them to the managing director*

■ **1** allude to, mention, touch on, speak of, bring up **2** consult, look up, turn to, resort to **3** apply, concern, relate, belong, pertain **4** send, direct, point, guide, pass on, transfer

referee *noun* **1** someone to whom a matter is taken for settlement **2** a judge in a sports match **3** someone willing to provide a note about someone's character, work record *etc*

reference *noun* **1** the act of referring **2** a mention **3** a note about a person's character, work *etc* ◇ **reference book** a book to be consulted for information, *eg* an encyclopedia ◇ **reference library** a library of books to be looked at for information but not taken away

■ **2** allusion, remark, mention **3** testimonial, recommendation, endorsement, character

referendum *noun* (*plural* **referenda** or **referendums**) a vote given by the people of a country about some important matter

refine *verb* **1** purify **2** improve, make more exact *etc* ◇ **refined** *adj* **1** purified **2** polite in manners, free of vulgarity

◇**refinement** *noun* **1** good manners, taste, learning **2** an improvement

■ *verb* **1** process, treat, purify, clarify, filter, distil **2** polish, hone, improve, perfect ◇**refined 2** civilized, cultured, cultivated, polished, sophisticated, urbane, genteel, gentlemanly, ladylike, well-bred, well-mannered, polite, civil

refinery *noun* (*plural* **refineries**) a place where sugar, oil *etc* are refined

refit *verb* (**refits**, **refitting**, **refitted**) repair damages (*esp* to a ship)

reflation *noun* an increase in the amount of currency, economic activity *etc* after deflation

reflect *verb* **1** throw back (light or heat): *reflecting the sun's heat* **2** give an image of: *reflected in the mirror* **3** (with **on**) throw blame: *her behaviour reflects on her mother* **4** (often with **on**) think over something carefully

■ **4** think, ponder, consider, mull (over), deliberate, contemplate, meditate, muse

reflection *noun* **1** the act of reflecting **2** the image of someone or something reflected in a mirror *etc* **3** thought, consideration **4** blame, unfavourable criticism: *a reflection on her upbringing*

■ **2** image, likeness **3** thinking, thought, study, consideration, deliberation, contemplation, meditation, musing

reflective *adj* thoughtful

reflector *noun* something (*eg* a piece of shiny metal) which throws back light

reflex *noun* (*plural* **reflexes**) an action which is automatic, not intended, *eg* jerking the leg when the kneecap is struck ◇*adj* done as a reflex, unthinking

reflexive *adj*, *grammar* showing that the object of the verb is the same as its subject, *eg* in 'he cut himself', *himself* is a *reflexive pronoun* and *cut* a *reflexive verb*

reflexology *noun* a way of treating illness or stress by massaging particular areas on the soles of the feet ◇**reflexologist** *noun* a practitioner of reflexology

reform *verb* **1** improve, remove faults from **2** give up bad habits, evil *etc* ◇ *noun* an improvement: *educational reform* ◇**reformer** *noun* someone who wishes to bring about improvements

■ *verb* **1** rebuild, reconstruct, remodel, revamp, renovate, restore, regenerate, reconstitute, reorganize, *informal* shake up, revolutionize, purge ◇ *noun* change, amendment, improvement, rectification, correction, rehabilitation, renovation, reorganization, *informal* shake-up, purge

re-form *verb* form again or in a different way

reformation *noun* a change for the better ◇**the Reformation** the religious movement in the Christian Church in the 16th century from which the Protestant Church arose

refract *verb* change the direction of (a ray of light) ◇**refraction** *noun*

refractory *adj* unruly, not easily controlled

refrain[1] *noun* a chorus coming at the end of each verse of a song

refrain[2] *verb* hold yourself back (from doing something): *please refrain from smoking*

■ stop, cease, quit, leave off, renounce, desist, abstain, forbear, avoid

refresh *verb* give new strength, power or life to ◇**refresher course** a course of study intended to update or increase existing knowledge of a subject ◇**refresh your memory** go over facts again so that they are clear in your mind

■ enliven, invigorate, fortify, revive, restore, renew, rejuvenate, revitalize, reinvigorate

refreshing *adj* **1** bringing back strength **2** cooling

■ **1** bracing, invigorating, energizing, stimulating **2** cool, thirst-quenching, fresh

refreshments *noun plural* food and drink

refrigerator *noun* a storage machine which keeps food cold and so prevents it from going bad ◇**refrigerate** *verb* ◇**refrigeration** *noun*

refuel *verb* (**refuels**, **refuelling**, **refuelled**) supply with, or take in, fresh fuel

refuge *noun* a place of safety (from attack, danger *etc*)

▣ sanctuary, asylum, shelter, protection, security, retreat, hideout, hide-away, resort, harbour, haven

refugee *noun* someone who seeks shelter from persecution in another country

refulgent *adj* beaming, giving off light

refund *verb* pay back: *will they refund the deposit?* ◇ *noun* a payment returned, *eg* for unsatisfactory goods

refuse¹ /rɪˈfjuːz/ *verb* **1** say that you will not do something: *he refused to leave the room* **2** say that you will not accept something: *she refused the prize* **3** withhold, not give (*eg* permission) ◇ **refusal** *noun*

▣ **2** reject, turn down, decline, spurn, repudiate, rebuff, repel **3** deny, withhold

refuse² /ˈrefjuːs/ *noun* something which is thrown aside as worthless, rubbish

▣ rubbish, waste, trash, garbage, junk, litter

refusenik *noun* someone who refuses to comply with a political *etc* regime

refute *verb* prove wrong (something that has been said or written) ◇ **refutation** *noun*

▣ disprove, rebut, confute, give the lie to, discredit, counter, negate

regain *verb* **1** win back again **2** get back to: *regain the shore*

regal *adj* kingly, royal

▣ majestic, kingly, queenly, princely, imperial, royal, sovereign, stately, magnificent, noble

regale *verb* entertain (with stories *etc*)

regalia *noun plural* symbols of royalty, *eg* a crown and sceptre

regard *verb* **1** look upon, consider: *I regard you as a friend* **2** look at carefully **3** pay attention to ◇ *noun* **1** concern: *without regard for her own safety* **2** affec-

tion **3** respect **4** (**regards**) good wishes ◇ **regardless of** paying no care or attention to ◇ **with regard to** or **in regard to** concerning

▣ *verb* **1** consider, deem, judge, rate, think, believe, suppose, imagine, look upon **2** view, observe, watch ◇ *noun* **1** care, concern, consideration, attention, notice, heed **2** affection, love, sympathy **3** respect, deference, honour, esteem, admiration

regarding *prep* concerning, to do with: *a reply regarding his application*

▣ with regard to, as regards, concerning, with reference to, re, about, as to

regatta *noun* a meeting for yacht or boat races

From the name of a gondola race held on the Grand Canal in Venice

regency *see* regent

regenerate *verb* make new and good again ◇ **regeneration** *noun*

regent *noun* someone who governs in place of a king or queen ◇ **regency** *noun* (*plural* **regencies**) **1** rule by a regent **2** the period of a regent's rule **3** *Brit hist* the period during which George IV was regent, 1715–1723

reggae *noun* a strongly rhythmic type of rock music, originally from the West Indies

regicide *noun* **1** the killing of a monarch **2** someone who kills a monarch

régime or **regime** *noun* a method or system of government or administration

▣ government, rule, administration, management, leadership, command, control, establishment, system

regimen *noun* diet and habits to be followed

regiment *noun* a body of soldiers, commanded by a colonel ◇ *verb* organize or control too strictly ◇ **regimental** *adj* of a regiment ◇ **regimentation** *noun* too strict control ◇ **regimented** *adj*

▣ **regimented** strict, disciplined, controlled, regulated, standardized, ordered, methodical, systematic, organized

🔲 **regimented** free, lax, disorganized

region *noun* an area, a district ◇ **regional** *adj* ◇ **in the region of** somewhere near: *offers in the region of £100*
🔲 land, terrain, territory, country, province, area, district, zone, sector, neighbourhood, place

register *noun* **1** a written list (*eg* of attendances at school, of those eligible to vote *etc*) **2** the distance between the highest and lowest notes of a voice or instrument ◇ *verb* **1** write down or be entered in a register: *register for an evening class* **2** record, cast (a vote *etc*) **3** show, record: *a thermometer registers temperature* ◇ **register office** one where records of births, marriages and deaths are kept and where marriages may be performed
🔲 *noun* **1** roll, roster, list, index, catalogue, directory, file, ledger, schedule ◇ *verb* **1** record, note, log, enter, inscribe, mark, list, catalogue, enrol, enlist, sign on, check in **3** show, reveal, betray, display, exhibit, manifest, express, say, read, indicate

registrar *noun* a public official who keeps a register of births, deaths and marriages

registry *noun* (*plural* **registries**) an office where a register is kept

regress *verb* go back to an earlier state

regret *verb* (**regrets, regretting, regretted**) **1** be sorry about: *I regret any inconvenience you have suffered* **2** be sorry (to have to say something): *we regret to inform you* **3** wish that you had not done something: *I regret selling the car* ◇ *noun* sorrow for anything ◇ **regretful** *adj* ◇ **regretfully** *adv*
🔲 *verb* **1** repent, lament, mourn, grieve, deplore **3** rue ◇ *noun* remorse, contrition, compunction, self-reproach, shame, sorrow, grief, disappointment, bitterness

regrettable *adj* to be regretted, unwelcome ◇ **regrettably** *adv*
🔲 unfortunate, unlucky, unhappy, sad,

disappointing, upsetting, distressing, lamentable, deplorable, shameful, wrong, ill-advised
🔲 fortunate, happy

regular *adj* **1** done according to rule or habit; usual **2** arranged in order; even: *regular teeth* **3** happening at certain fixed times **4** having normal bowel movements ◇ *noun* a soldier of the regular army ◇ **regularity** *noun* ◇ **regularly** *adv* ◇ **regular army** the part of the army which is kept always in training, even in peacetime
🔲 **1** routine, habitual, typical, usual, customary, time-honoured, conventional, orthodox, correct, official, standard, normal, ordinary, common, commonplace, everyday **2** uniform, even, level, balanced, symmetrical, orderly **3** periodic, rhythmic, steady, constant, fixed, set, unvarying
🔳 **1** unusual, unconventional **2** irregular

regulate *verb* **1** control by rules **2** adjust to a certain order or rate ◇ **regulator** *noun* someone or something that regulates
🔲 **1** control, direct, guide, govern, rule, administer, manage, handle, conduct, run, organize **2** set, adjust, tune, moderate, balance

regulation *noun* a rule, an order
🔲 rule, statute, law, ordinance, edict, decree, order, commandment, precept, dictate, requirement, procedure

regurgitate *verb* bring back into the mouth after swallowing ◇ **regurgitation** *noun*

rehabilitate *verb* **1** give back rights, powers or health to **2** train or accustom (a disabled person *etc*) to live a normal life again ◇ **rehabilitation** *noun*

rehash *verb* express in different words, do again

rehearsal *noun* **1** a private practice of a play, concert *etc* before performance in public **2** a practice for a future event or action
🔲 **2** practice, drill, exercise, dry run, run-through, preparation

rehearse *verb* **1** practise beforehand **2** recount (facts, events *etc*) in order

reign *noun* **1** the rule of a king or queen **2** the time during which a king or queen rules ◇ *verb* **1** the rule of a king or queen **2** prevail: *silence reigned at last*

reimburse *verb* pay (someone) an amount to cover expenses ◇ **reimbursement** *noun*

■ refund, repay, recompense, compensate, indemnify, remunerate

rein *noun* **1** one of two straps attached to a bridle for guiding a horse **2** (**reins**) a simple device for controlling a child when walking ◇ *verb* control with reins

reincarnation *noun* the rebirth of the soul in another body after death

reindeer *noun* (*plural* **reindeer**) a type of deer found in the far North

reinforce *verb* strengthen with additional people, support *etc*: *reinforced concrete*

■ strengthen, fortify, toughen, harden, stiffen, steel, brace, support, buttress, shore, prop, stay, supplement, augment, increase, emphasize, stress, underline

◘ weaken, undermine

reinforcement *noun* **1** the act of reinforcing **2** something which strengthens **3** (**reinforcements**) additional troops

reinstate *verb* put back in a former position: *he was reinstated as captain of the team* ◇ **reinstatement** *noun*

reiterate *verb* repeat several times ◇ **reiteration** *noun*

reject *verb* **1** throw away, cast aside **2** refuse to accept (*eg* an application, offer, request) ◇ *noun* something discarded or refused ◇ **rejection** *noun*

■ *verb* **1** eliminate, scrap, discard, jettison, cast off **2** refuse, deny, decline, turn down, veto, disallow ◇ **rejection** refusal, denial, veto, dismissal, rebuff, brush-off, *informal* knockback, exclusion, repudiation, renunciation, elimination

◘ *verb* **2** accept ◇ **rejection** acceptance, choice, selection

rejig *verb* (**rejigs**, **rejigging**, **rejigged**) rearrange

rejoice *verb* feel or show joy ◇ **rejoicing** *noun*

■ celebrate, revel, delight, glory, exult, triumph

rejoinder *noun* an answer to a reply

rejuvenate *verb* make young again ◇ **rejuvenation** *noun*

relapse *verb* fall back (*eg* into ill health, bad habits) ◇ *noun* a falling back

■ *verb* worsen, deteriorate, degenerate, weaken, sink, fail, lapse, revert, regress, backslide ◇ *noun* worsening, deterioration, setback, recurrence, weakening, lapse, reversion, regression, backsliding

relate *verb* **1** show a connection between (two or more things) **2** tell (a story) ◇ **related** *adj* **1** (often with **to**) of the same family (as): *I'm related to him/we are not related* **2** connected

■ **1** link, connect, join, couple, ally, associate, correlate **2** tell, recount, narrate, report, describe, recite

relation *noun* **1** someone who is of the same family, either by birth or marriage **2** a connection between two or more things ◇ **relationship** *noun*

■ **1** relative, family, kin, kindred **2** link, connection, bond, relationship, correlation, comparison, similarity, affiliation, interrelation, interconnection, interdependence, regard, reference ◇ **relationship** bond, link, connection, association, liaison, rapport, affinity, closeness, similarity, parallel, correlation, ratio, proportion

relative *noun* someone who is of the same family ◇ *adj* comparative: *relative merits* ◇ **relatively** *adv* more or less: *relatively happy* ◇ **relativity** *noun* **1** the condition of being relative **2** a scientific theory of motion

relax *verb* **1** become or make less tense **2** slacken (*eg* your grip or control) **3** make (laws or rules) less severe ◇ **relaxation** *noun* **1** a slackening **2** rest from work, leisure

■ **1** ease, rest, unwind, calm, tranquillize, sedate **2** slacken, loosen, lessen **3** soften, moderate, abate, remit, relieve ◇ **relaxation 1** slackening, lessening, reduction, moderation, abatement, *informal* let-up, détente, easing **2** rest, repose, refreshment, leisure, recreation, fun, amusement, entertainment, enjoyment, pleasure

relay verb /rɪ'leɪ/ (**relays**, **relaying**, **relayed**) receive and pass on (*eg* a message, a television programme) ◇ *noun* /'ri:leɪ/ **1** the sending out of a radio or television broadcast received from another station **2** a fresh set of people to replace others at a job *etc* ◇ **in relays** in groups which take over from one another in series ◇ **relay race** a race in which members of each team take over from one another, each running a set distance

■ *verb* broadcast, transmit, communicate, send, spread, carry, supply ◇ *noun* **1** broadcast, transmission, programme, communication, message, dispatch **2** shift, turn

release *verb* **1** set free; let go **2** allow (news *etc*) to be made public ◇ *noun* a setting free

■ *verb* **1** loose, unloose, unleash, unfasten, extricate, free, liberate, deliver, emancipate, acquit **2** discharge, issue, publish, circulate, distribute, unveil

◼ *verb* **1** imprison, detain

relegate *verb* put down (to a lower position, group *etc*) ◇ **relegation** *noun*

relent *verb* become less severe or strict; change your mind and agree

■ give in, give way, yield, capitulate, relax, slacken, soften, weaken

relentless *adj* **1** without pity **2** refusing to be turned from a purpose ◇ **relentlessly** *adv*

■ **1** ruthless, remorseless, implacable, merciless, pitiless, unforgiving, cruel, harsh, fierce, grim, hard, punishing **2** uncompromising, inflexible, unyielding, inexorable, unrelenting, persistent, unflagging

◼ **1** merciful **2** yielding

relevant *adj* having to do with the matter in hand ◇ **relevance** *noun*

■ pertinent, material, significant, germane, related, applicable, apposite, apt, appropriate

◼ irrelevant, inapplicable, inappropriate

reliable *adj* able to be trusted or counted on ◇ **reliability** *noun*

■ unfailing, certain, sure, dependable, responsible, trusty, trustworthy, honest, true, faithful, constant, staunch, solid, safe, sound, stable, predictable, regular

◼ unreliable, doubtful, untrustworthy

relic *noun* something left over from a past time; an antiquity

■ memento, souvenir, keepsake, token, survival, remains, remnant, scrap, fragment, vestige, trace

relief *noun* **1** a lessening of pain or anxiety **2** release from a post or duty **3** people taking over someone's duty *etc* **4** help given to those in need: *famine relief* **5** the act of freeing (a town *etc*) from a siege **6** a way of carving or moulding in which the design stands out from its background

relieve *verb* **1** lessen (pain or anxiety) **2** take over a duty from (someone else) **3** come to the help of (a town *etc* under attack)

■ **1** reassure, console, comfort, ease, soothe, alleviate

◼ **1** aggravate, intensify

religion *noun* belief in, or worship of, a god ◇ **religious** *adj*

Religions include:
Christianity, Church of England (C of E), Church of Scotland, Baptists, Catholicism, Methodism, Protestantism, Presbyterianism, Anglicanism, Congregationalism, Calvinism, evangelicalism, Free Church, Jehovah's Witnesses, Mormonism, Quakerism, Amish; Baha'ism, Buddhism, Confucianism, Hinduism, Islam, Jainism, Judaism, Sikhism, Taoism, Shintoism, Zen, Zoroastrianism, voodoo, druidism, paganism

---

relinquish *verb* give up, abandon: *relinquish control*

■ let go, release, hand over, surrender, yield, cede, give up, resign, renounce, repudiate, waive, forgo, abandon, desert, forsake, drop, discard

◪ keep, retain

reliquary *noun* a container for religious relics

relish *verb* **1** enjoy **2** look forward to: *I don't relish the prospect* **3** like the taste of ◇ *noun* (*plural* **relishes**) **1** enjoyment **2** flavour **3** something which adds flavour

◪ *verb* **1** like, enjoy, savour, appreciate, revel in, delight in ◇ *noun* **1** enjoyment, pleasure, delight, gusto, zest **3** seasoning, condiment, sauce, pickle, spice, piquancy, tang

relocate *verb* move to another position, residence *etc* ◇ **relocation** *noun*

reluctant *adj* unwilling ◇ **reluctance** *noun* ◇ **reluctantly** *adv*

◪ unwilling, disinclined, indisposed, hesitant, slow, backward, loth, averse, unenthusiastic, grudging

◪ willing, ready, eager

rely *verb* (**relies**, **relying**, **relied**) have full trust in, depend (on) ◇ **reliance** *noun* ◇ **reliant** *adj*

◪ depend on, lean on, count on, bank on, reckon on, trust, swear by

REM *abbrev* rapid-eye movement, the movement of the eyes behind the eyelids during dreaming

remain *verb* **1** stay, not leave **2** be left: *only two tins of soup remained* **3** be still the same: *the problem remains unsolved* ◇ **remains** *noun plural* **1** that which is left **2** a dead body

◪ **1** stay, rest, dwell, abide, last, endure, survive, prevail, linger, wait **3** stand, persist, continue ◇ **remains 1** rest, remainder, residue, dregs, leavings, leftovers, scraps, crumbs, fragments, remnants, oddments, traces, vestiges, relics **2** body, corpse, carcase

remainder *noun* **1** something which is left behind after removal of the rest **2** *maths* the number left after subtraction or division

remake *noun* a second making of a film *etc* ◇ *verb* make again

remand *verb* put (someone) back in prison until more evidence is found ◇ **on remand** having been remanded

remark *verb* **1** say **2** comment (on) **3** notice ◇ *noun* something said

◪ *verb* **1** mention, say, state, declare **2** comment, observe, note ◇ *noun* comment, observation, opinion, reflection, mention, utterance, statement, assertion, declaration

remarkable *adj* deserving notice, unusual ◇ **remarkably** *adv*

◪ striking, impressive, noteworthy, surprising, amazing, strange, odd, unusual, uncommon, extraordinary, phenomenal, exceptional, outstanding, notable, conspicuous, prominent, distinguished

◪ average, ordinary, commonplace, usual

remedial *adj* **1** remedying **2** relating to the teaching of slow-learning children ◇ **remedially** *adv*

remedy *noun* (*plural* **remedies**) a cure for an illness, problem *etc* ◇ *verb* (**remedies**, **remedying**, **remedied**) **1** cure **2** put right

◪ *noun* cure, antidote, countermeasure, corrective, restorative, medicine, treatment, therapy, relief, solution, answer, panacea, elixir ◇ *verb* **1** cure, heal, restore, treat, help, relieve, soothe, ease **2** correct, rectify, put right, redress, mend, repair, fix, solve

remember *verb* **1** keep in mind **2** recall after having forgotten **3** pass on best wishes from: *remember me to your mother* **4** reward, give a present to: *he remembered her in his will*

◪ **1** memorize, learn, retain **2** recall, recollect, summon up, think back, reminisce, recognize, place

remembrance *noun* **1** the act of remembering **2** a memory **3** something given to remind someone of a person or event, a keepsake

remind *verb* **1** bring (something) back to a person's mind: *remind me to post that letter* **2** cause (someone) to think about someone or something by resemblance: *she reminds me of her sister* ◇ **reminder** *noun* something which reminds

◪ **1** prompt, nudge, hint, jog one's memory, refresh one's memory **2** bring to mind, call to mind

reminisce *verb* think and talk about things remembered from the past

reminiscence *noun* **1** something remembered from the past **2** (**reminiscences**) memories, *esp* told or written

■ **1** memory, remembrance, recollection **2** memoirs, anecdotes, reflections

reminiscent *adj* **1** reminding (of): *reminiscent of Paris* **2** in a mood to remember and think about past events *etc*

remiss *adj* careless, unthinking

remission *noun* **1** a shortening of a prison sentence **2** a lessening of a disease or illness

remit *verb* (**remits, remitting, remitted**) **1** pardon, excuse (a crime *etc*) **2** wipe out, cancel (a debt *etc*) **3** lessen, become less intense **4** send (money) **5** hand over (*eg* a prisoner to a higher court) ◇ **remittance** *noun* payment

remnant *noun* a small piece or number left over

■ scrap, piece, bit, fragment, end, offcut, leftover, remainder, residue, shred, trace, vestige

remonstrate *verb* protest (about) ◇ **remonstrance** *noun*

remorse *noun* regret about something done in the past ◇ **remorseful** *adj* ◇ **remorseless** *adj* having no remorse; cruel

■ regret, compunction, ruefulness, repentance, penitence, contrition, self-reproach, shame, guilt, bad conscience, sorrow, grief

remote *adj* **1** far away in time or place **2** isolated, far from other people **3** slight: *a remote chance*

■ **1** distant, far, faraway, far-off, outlying, out-of-the-way, inaccessible, godforsaken **2** isolated, secluded, lonely **3** slight, small, slim, slender, faint, negligible

▣ **1** close, nearby, accessible

removal *noun* the act of removing, *esp* of moving furniture to a new home

remove *verb* **1** take (something) from its place **2** dismiss from a job **3** take off (clothes *etc*) **4** get rid of: *remove a stain* ◇ *noun* a stage away (from): *one remove*

from anarchy ◇ **removed** *adj* **1** distant (from) **2** of cousins: separated by a generation: *first cousin once removed* (a cousin's child)

■ *verb* **1** detach, pull off, amputate, cut off, extract, pull out, withdraw, take away **2** dismiss, discharge, eject, throw out, oust, depose **3** take off, strip, shed, doff **4** efface, erase, delete, strike out, get rid of, shift

remunerate *verb* pay (someone) for something done ◇ **remuneration** *noun* pay, salary ◇ **remunerative** *adj* profitable

■ **remuneration** pay, wages, salary, emolument, stipend, fee, earnings, income, reward, recompense, payment

renaissance *noun* **1** a rebirth **2** a period of cultural revival and growth

renal *adj* of the kidneys

rend *verb* (**rends, rending, rent**) tear (apart), divide

render *verb* **1** give (*eg* thanks) **2** translate into another language **3** perform (music *etc*) **4** cause to be: *his words rendered me speechless* ◇ **rendering** *noun* **1** a translation **2** a performance

■ **1** give, provide, supply, tender, present, submit, hand over, deliver **2** translate, transcribe, interpret, explain **4** make, cause to be

rendezvous /'rādeɪvuː/ or /'rɒndeɪvuː/ *noun* (*plural* **rendezvous**) **1** a meeting place fixed beforehand **2** an arranged meeting

renegade *noun* someone who deserts their own side, religion or beliefs

renew *verb* **1** make as if new again **2** begin again: *renew your efforts* **3** make valid for a further period (*eg* a driving licence) **4** replace: *renew the water in the tank* ◇ **renewal** *noun*

■ **1** renovate, modernize, regenerate, revive, resuscitate, refresh, rejuvenate, revitalize, restore **2** repeat, recommence, restart, resume **3** extend, prolong **4** replace, replenish, restock

rennet *noun* a substance used in curdling milk for making cheeses *etc*

renounce *verb* give up publicly or formally ◇ **renunciation** *noun*

▤ abandon, forsake, give up, resign, relinquish, surrender

renovate *verb* make (something) like new again ◇ **renovation** *noun*

▤ restore, renew, recondition, repair, overhaul, modernize, refurbish, refit, redecorate, do up, remodel, reform, revamp, improve

renown *noun* fame ◇ **renowned** *adj* famous

rent[1] *noun* payment made for the use of property or land ◇ *verb* (also with **out**) pay or receive rent for (a house *etc*)

▤ *verb* let, sublet, lease, hire, charter

rent[2] *noun* a tear, a split ◇ *verb* past form of **rend**

rental *noun* money paid as rent

rent-boy *noun* a young male homosexual prostitute

renunciation *see* **renounce**

reorganize *verb* put in a different order or arrangement ◇ **reorganization** *noun*

rep *noun, short for* **1** representative: *sales rep* **2** repertory

repair *verb* **1** mend **2** make up for (a wrong) **3** *old* go, move: *repair to the drawing room* ◇ *noun* **1** state, condition: *in bad repair* **2** mending: *in need of repair* **3** a mend ◇ **reparation** *noun* compensation for a wrong

▤ *verb* **1** mend, fix, patch up, overhaul **2** rectify, redress ◇ *noun* **2** overhaul, service, maintenance, restoration, adjustment, improvement **3** mend, patch, darn

repartee *noun* **1** an exchange of witty remarks **2** skill in witty conversation

repast *noun, old* a meal

repatriate *verb* send (someone) back to their own country ◇ **repatriation** *noun*

repay *verb* (**repays**, **repaying**, **repaid**) **1** pay back **2** give or do something in return: *he repaid her kindness with a gift* ◇ **repayment** *noun*

▤ **1** refund, reimburse, compensate, recompense, remunerate, pay **2** reward, get even with, retaliate, reciprocate, revenge, avenge

repeal *verb* do away with, cancel (*esp* a law) ◇ *noun* a cancellation of a law *etc*

▤ *verb* revoke, rescind, abrogate, quash, annul, nullify, void, invalidate, cancel, countermand, reverse, abolish

repeat *verb* **1** say or do over again **2** say from memory **3** pass on (someone's words) ◇ *noun* a musical passage, television programme *etc* played or shown for a second time ◇ **repeatedly** *adv* again and again ◇ **repeater** *noun* a gun which fires several shots

▤ *verb* **1** restate, reiterate, recapitulate **2** quote, recite **3** relate, retell, reproduce

repel *verb* (**repels**, **repelling**, **repelled**) **1** drive back or away **2** disgust ◇ **repellent** *adj* disgusting ◇ *noun* something that repels: *insect repellent*

▤ **1** drive back, repulse, check, hold off, ward off, parry, resist, oppose, fight, refuse, decline, reject, rebuff **2** disgust, revolt, nauseate, sicken, offend

repent *verb* **1** be sorry for your actions **2** (with **of**) regret ◇ **repentance** *noun* ◇ **repentant** *adj* repenting

repercussion *noun* an indirect or resultant effect of something which has happened

▤ result, consequence, upshot, backlash, reverberation, echo

repertoire *noun* the range of works performed by a musician, theatre company *etc*

repertory *noun* (*plural* **repertories**) repertoire ◇ **repertory theatre** a theatre with a permanent company which performs a series of plays

repetition *noun* **1** repeating **2** something repeated ◇ **repetitious** *adj*

▤ **1** restatement, reiteration, recapitulation, echo, return, duplication, tautology **2** echo, return, reappearance, recurrence

repetitive *adj* repeating too often, predictable

▤ recurrent, monotonous, tedious, boring, dull, mechanical, unchanging, unvaried

rephrase *verb* express in different words

replace *verb* **1** put (something) back

where it was **2** put or be in place of (another)

■ **1** put back, return, restore, make good, reinstate, re-establish **2** supersede, succeed, supplant, oust, deputize, substitute

replenish *verb* refill (a stock, supply)

replete *adj* full

replica *noun* an exact copy, *esp* of a work of art

reply *verb* (**replies, replying, replied**) speak or act in answer ◇ *noun* (*plural* **replies**) an answer

■ *verb* answer, respond, retort, rejoin, react, acknowledge, return, echo, reciprocate, counter, retaliate ◇ *noun* answer, response, retort, rejoinder, riposte, repartee, reaction, comeback, acknowledgement, return, echo, retaliation

report *verb* **1** pass on news **2** give a description of (an event) **3** give information about events for a newspaper **4** make a formal complaint against ◇ *noun* **1** a statement of facts **2** an account, a description **3** a news article **4** a rumour **5** a written description of a school pupil's work **6** a loud noise

■ *verb* **1** broadcast, relay, publish, circulate, communicate, notify **2** tell, recount, relate, narrate, describe, detail, cover, document, record, note ◇ *noun* **1** statement, communiqué, declaration, announcement, communication, information **2** account, relation, narrative, description, story, tale **3** article, piece, write-up

reporter *noun* a news journalist

■ journalist, correspondent, columnist, newspaperman, newspaperwoman, hack, newscaster

repose *noun, formal* sleep, rest ◇ *verb* **1** rest **2** place (*eg* trust in a person)

repository *noun* (*plural* **repositories**) a storage place for safe keeping

repossess *verb* take back (goods, a house *etc*), *esp* because of non-payment ◇ **repossession** *noun*

reprehensible *adj* deserving blame ◇ **reprehension** *noun* reprimand, censure

represent *verb* **1** speak or act on behalf of others: *representing the tenants' association* **2** stand for, be a symbol of: *each letter represents a sound* **3** portray or describe (as): *she represented herself as an expert* **4** explain, point out ◇ **representation** *noun* **1** an image, a picture **2** a strong claim or appeal

representative *adj* **1** typical, characteristic: *a representative specimen* **2** standing or acting for others ◇ *noun* **1** someone who acts or speaks on behalf of others **2** a travelling salesman for a company

■ *adj* **1** typical, illustrative, exemplary, archetypal, characteristic, usual, normal ◇ *noun* **1** delegate, deputy, proxy, stand-in, spokesperson, spokesman, spokeswoman, ambassador, commissioner **2** agent, salesman, saleswoman, rep

repress *verb* keep down or under control, often by force ◇ **repression** *noun* ◇ **repressive** *adj*

■ restrain, suppress, bottle up, hold back, inhibit, check, control, curb, stifle, smother, muffle, silence, quell, crush, quash, subdue, overpower, overcome, master, subjugate, oppress

reprieve *verb* **1** pardon (a criminal) **2** relieve from trouble or difficulty ◇ *noun* a pardon, a relief

reprimand *verb* scold severely, censure ◇ *noun* a rebuke, censure

■ *verb* rebuke, reprove, reproach, admonish, scold, chide, *informal* tell off, *informal* tick off, lecture, criticize, *informal* slate, censure, *informal* carpet, blame ◇ *noun* rebuke, reproof, reproach, admonition, *informal* telling-off, *informal* ticking-off, lecture, *informal* talking-to, *informal* dressing-down, censure, blame

reprint *verb* print more copies of (a book *etc*) ◇ *noun* **1** another printing of a book **2** a reprinted copy of a book

reprisal *noun* a return of wrong for wrong, a repayment in kind

reproach *verb* scold, blame ◇ *noun* **1** blame, discredit **2** a cause of blame or censure ◇ **reproachful** *adj*

■ *verb* rebuke, reprove, reprimand, upbraid, scold, chide, reprehend, blame, censure, condemn, criticize, disparage, defame ◇ *noun* **1** rebuke, reproof, reprimand, scolding, blame, censure, condemnation, criticism, disapproval

reprobate *noun* someone of evil or immoral habits ◇ *adj* immoral

reproduce *verb* **1** produce a copy of **2** produce (children or young) ◇ **reproduction** *noun* ◇ **reproductive** *adj* involved in producing children or young

■ **1** copy, transcribe, print, duplicate, mirror, echo, repeat, imitate, emulate, match, simulate, recreate, reconstruct **2** breed, spawn, procreate, generate, propagate, multiply

reprography *noun* reproduction by photocopying

reproof *noun* a scolding, criticism for a fault

■ rebuke, reproach, reprimand, admonition, upbraiding, *informal* dressing-down, scolding, *informal* telling-off, *informal* ticking-off, censure, condemnation, criticism

🖪 praise

reprove *verb* scold, blame ◇ **reproving** *adj*

reptile *noun* a creeping, cold-blooded animal, such as a snake, lizard *etc* ◇ **reptilian** *adj*

> *Reptiles include*:
> adder, puff adder, grass snake, tree snake, asp, viper, rattlesnake, sidewinder, anaconda, boa constrictor, cobra, king cobra, mamba, python; lizard, frilled lizard, chameleon, gecko, iguana, skink, slow-worm; turtle, green turtle, hawksbill turtle, terrapin, tortoise, giant tortoise; alligator, crocodile

republic *noun* a form of government in which power is in the hands of elected representatives with a president at its head ◇ **Republican** *adj* belonging to the more conservative of the two chief political parties in the United States

repudiate *verb* refuse to acknowl-

edge or accept: *repudiate a suggestion* ◇ **repudiation** *noun*

repugnant *adj* hateful, distasteful ◇ **repugnance** *noun*

■ **repugnance** reluctance, distaste, dislike, aversion, hatred, loathing, detestation, abhorrence, horror, repulsion, revulsion, disgust

🖪 liking, pleasure, delight

repulse *verb* **1** drive back **2** reject, snub ◇ **repulsion** *noun* disgust

repulsive *adj* causing disgust, loathsome ◇ **repulsiveness** *noun*

■ repellent, repugnant, revolting, disgusting, nauseating, sickening, offensive, distasteful, objectionable, obnoxious, foul, vile, loathsome, abominable, abhorrent, hateful, horrid, unpleasant, disagreeable, ugly, hideous, forbidding

🖪 attractive, pleasant, delightful

reputation *noun* **1** the opinion held by people in general of a particular person or thing **2** good name ◇ **reputable** *adj* having a good reputation, well thought of

■ **2** honour, character, standing, stature, esteem, credit, repute, fame, renown, celebrity, distinction, name, good name

repute *noun* reputation ◇ **reputed** *adj* **1** considered, said (to be something): *reputed to be dangerous* **2** supposed: *the reputed author of the book* ◇ **reputedly** *adv* in the opinion of most people

request *verb* ask for ◇ *noun* **1** an asking for something **2** something asked for

■ *verb* ask for, solicit, demand, require, seek, desire, beg, entreat, supplicate, petition, appeal ◇ *noun* **1** appeal, call, demand, requisition, desire, application, solicitation, suit, petition, entreaty, supplication, prayer

requiem *noun* a hymn or mass sung for the dead

require *verb* **1** need **2** demand, order: *required by law to wear a crash helmet* ◇ **requirement** *noun* **1** something needed **2** a demand: *a legal requirement*

■ **1** need, want, wish, desire, lack, miss **2**

oblige, force, compel, constrain, make, ask, request, instruct, direct, order, demand ◇ **requirement 1** need, necessity, essential, must, requisite, prerequisite **2** demand, stipulation, condition, term, specification, proviso

requisite adj required; necessary ◇ noun something needed or necessary ◇ **requisition** noun a formal request for supplies, eg for a school or army ◇ verb put in a formal request for

■ adj required, needed, necessary, essential, obligatory, compulsory, set, prescribed

requite verb **1** repay, give back in return **2** avenge (one action) by another ◇ **requital** noun payment in return

rerun verb (**reruns, rerunning, reran, rerun**) run again ◇ noun a repeated television programme

rescind verb do away with, repeal (a law)

rescue verb **1** save from danger etc **2** free from capture ◇ noun an act of saving from danger or freeing from capture

■ verb **1** save, recover, salvage **2** deliver, free, liberate, release ◇ noun saving, recovery, salvage, deliverance, liberation, release, redemption, salvation

research noun (plural **researches**) close and careful scientific study to try to find out new facts: cancer research ◇ verb study carefully, do research ◇ **researcher** noun someone who does research

■ noun investigation, inquiry, fact-finding, groundwork, examination, analysis, scrutiny, study, search, probe, exploration, experimentation ◇ verb investigate, examine, analyse, scrutinize, study, search, probe, explore, experiment

resemble verb look like or be like: he doesn't resemble his sister ◇ **resemblance** noun likeness

■ be like, look like, take after, mirror, echo, duplicate, parallel

☒ differ from

resent verb feel injured, annoyed or insulted by ◇ **resentful** adj ◇ **resentment** noun annoyance

■ **resentful** grudging, envious, jealous, bitter, embittered, hurt, wounded, offended, aggrieved, put out, informal miffed, informal peeved, indignant, angry, vindictive

reservation noun **1** the act of reserving, a booking **2** an exception or condition: she agreed to the plan, but with certain reservations **3** doubt, objection: I had reservations about his appointment **4** an area of land set aside by treaty for Native American people in the United States

■ **1** booking, engagement, appointment **3** doubt, scepticism, misgiving, qualm, scruple, hesitation

reserve verb **1** set aside for future use **2** book, have kept for you (eg a seat, a table) ◇ noun **1** something reserved: a reserve of strength **2** (**reserves**) troops outside the regular army kept ready to help those already fighting **3** a piece of land set apart for some reason: nature reserve **4** shyness, reluctance to speak or act openly ◇ **reservist** noun a member of a military reserve

■ verb **1** set apart, earmark, keep, retain, hold back, save, store, stockpile **2** book, engage, order, secure ◇ noun **1** store, stock, supply, fund, stockpile, cache, hoard, savings **3** reservation, preserve, park, sanctuary **4** shyness, reticence, secretiveness, coolness, aloofness, modesty, restraint

☒ noun **4** friendliness, openness

reserved adj **1** shy, reluctant to speak openly **2** kept back for a particular person or purpose

■ **1** shy, retiring, reticent, unforthcoming, uncommunicative, secretive, silent, taciturn, unsociable, unapproachable, modest, restrained **2** booked, engaged, taken, spoken for, set aside, earmarked, meant, intended, designated, destined, saved, held, kept, retained

☒ **1** friendly, open **2** unreserved, free, available

reservoir noun an artificial lake where water is kept in store

reshuffle verb rearrange ministerial posts within (a government cabinet)

◇*noun* a rearrangement of a government cabinet

reside *verb* **1** live, stay (in) **2** of authority *etc*: be placed (in)

residence *noun* **1** the building where someone lives **2** living, or time of living, in a place

▣ **1** dwelling, habitation, domicile, abode, seat, place, home, house, lodgings, quarters, hall, manor, mansion, palace, villa, country house, country seat

resident *noun* someone who lives in a particular place: *a resident of Dublin* ◇*adj* **1** living (in a place) **2** living in a place of work: *resident caretaker* ◇**residential** *adj* **1** of an area: containing houses rather than shops, offices *etc* **2** providing accommodation: *a residential course*

residue *noun* what is left over ◇**residual** *adj*

resign *verb* give up (a job, position *etc*) ◇**resigned** *adj* patient, not actively complaining ◇**resignedly** *adv* ◇**resign yourself** to accept (a situation) patiently and calmly

▣ stand down, leave, quit, abdicate, vacate, renounce, relinquish, forgo, waive, surrender, yield, abandon, forsake ◇ **resign yourself to** reconcile yourself to, accept, bow, submit, yield, comply, acquiesce

resignation *noun* **1** the act of resigning **2** a letter to say you are resigning **3** patient, calm acceptance of a situation

resilient *adj* **1** able to recover easily from misfortune, hurt *etc* **2** of an object: readily recovering its original shape after being bent, twisted *etc* ◇**resilience** *noun*

▣ **1** strong, tough, hardy, adaptable, buoyant **2** flexible, pliable, supple, plastic, elastic, springy, bouncy

resin *noun* a sticky substance produced by certain plants (*eg* firs, pines) ◇**resinous** *adj*

resist *verb* **1** struggle against, oppose **2** stop yourself from (doing something): *I couldn't resist teasing him about it*

▣ **1** oppose, defy, confront, fight, combat, withstand, repel, counteract **2** avoid, refuse

resistance *noun* **1** the act of resisting **2** an organized opposition, *esp* to an occupying force **3** ability not to be affected by something: *resistance to disease* ◇**resistant** *adj*

resit *verb* (**resits, resitting, resat**) sit (an examination) again ◇*noun* a retaking of an examination

resolute *adj* determined, with mind made up ◇**resolutely** *adv*

▣ determined, resolved, set, fixed, unwavering, staunch, firm, steadfast, relentless, single-minded, persevering, dogged, tenacious, stubborn, obstinate, strong-willed, undaunted, unflinching

▣ irresolute, weak-willed, half-hearted

resolution *noun* **1** determination of mind or purpose **2** a firm decision (to do something) **3** a proposal put before a meeting **4** a decision expressed by a public meeting

resolve *verb* **1** decide firmly (to do something) **2** solve (a difficulty) **3** break up into parts ◇*noun* firmness of purpose

▣ *verb* **1** decide, make up one's mind, determine **2** fix, settle, sort out, work out, solve

resonate *verb* echo ◇**resonance** *noun* a deep, echoing tone ◇**resonant** *adj* echoing, resounding

resort *verb* begin to use, turn (to) in a difficulty: *resorting to bribery* ◇*noun* a popular holiday destination ◇**in the last resort** when all else fails

resound *verb* **1** sound loudly **2** echo ◇**resounding** *adj* **1** echoing **2** thorough: *a resounding victory*

▣ **resounding 1** resonant, reverberating, echoing, ringing, sonorous, booming, thunderous, full, rich, vibrant **2** decisive, conclusive, crushing, thorough

resource *noun* **1** a source of supplying what is required **2** (**resources**) the natural sources of wealth in a country *etc* **3** (**resources**) money or other property **4** an ability to handle situations skilfully and cleverly

resourceful *adj* good at finding ways out of difficulties

📧 ingenious, imaginative, creative, inventive, innovative, original, clever, bright, sharp, quick-witted, able, capable, talented

respect *verb* 1 feel a high regard for 2 treat with consideration; pay proper attention to: *respect his wishes* ◇ *noun* 1 high regard, esteem 2 consideration 3 a detail, a way: *alike in some respects* 4 (**respects**) good wishes ◇ **respectful** *adj* showing respect ◇ **in respect of** concerning, as regards ◇ **with respect to** with reference to

📧 *verb* 1 admire, esteem, regard, appreciate, value 2 obey, observe, heed, follow, honour, fulfil ◇ *noun* 1 admiration, esteem, appreciation, recognition, honour, deference, reverence, veneration 2 politeness, courtesy, consideration, thoughtfulness, heed, regard 3 point, aspect, facet, feature, characteristic, particular, detail, sense, way, regard

🔁 *verb* 1 despise, scorn 2 ignore, disobey ◇ *noun* 1 disrespect

respectable *adj* 1 worthy of respect 2 having a good reputation 3 considerable, fairly good: *a respectable score* ◇ **respectability** *noun*

📧 1 honourable, worthy, dignified 3 acceptable, tolerable, passable, adequate, fair, reasonable

respective *adj* belonging to each (person or thing mentioned) separately: *my brother and his friends went to their respective homes* (*ie* each went to their own home) ◇ **respectively** *adv* in the order given: *James, Andrew and Ian were first, second and third respectively*

respire *verb* breathe ◇ **respiration** *noun* breathing ◇ **respirator** *noun* 1 a mask worn over the mouth and nose to purify the air taken in 2 a device to help people breathe when they are too ill to do so naturally

respite *noun* a pause, a rest: *no respite from work*

resplendent *adj* very bright or splendid in appearance

respond *verb* 1 answer 2 react in response to: *I waved but he didn't respond* 3 show a positive reaction to: *responding to treatment*

📧 1 answer, reply, retort, acknowledge 2 react, return, reciprocate

respondent *see* co-respondent

response *noun* 1 a reply 2 an action, feeling *etc* in answer to or return for another 3 an answer made during a church service

📧 1 answer, reply, retort, comeback, acknowledgement 2 reaction, feedback

responsible *adj* 1 (sometimes with **for**) being the cause of: *responsible for this mess* 2 liable to be blamed (for): *responsible for the conduct of his staff* 3 involving making important decisions *etc*: *a responsible post* 4 trustworthy ◇ **responsibility** *noun* (*plural* **responsibilities**)

📧 1 guilty, culpable, at fault, to blame, liable 2 answerable, accountable 3 important, authoritative, executive, decision-making 4 dependable, reliable, conscientious, trustworthy, honest, sound

🔁 4 irresponsible, unreliable, untrustworthy

responsive *adj* quick to react, to show sympathy *etc* ◇ **responsiveness** *noun*

rest¹ *noun* 1 a break in work 2 a sleep 3 *music* a pause in playing or singing for a given number of beats 4 a support, a prop: *book rest* ◇ *verb* 1 stop working for a time 2 be still 3 sleep 4 depend (on), be based (on): *the case rests on your evidence* 5 stop, develop no further: *I can't let the matter rest there* 6 lean or place on a support ◇ **rest with** be the responsibility of: *the choice rests with you*

📧 *noun* 1 break, pause, breathing-space, *informal* breather, relaxation, holiday, vacation 2 lie-down, sleep, snooze, nap, siesta 4 support, prop, stand, base ◇ *verb* 1 pause, halt, relax, repose, sit, recline, lounge, laze 3 lie down, sleep, snooze, doze **6** lean, prop, support, stand

▣ *noun* **1** work, action, activity ◇ *verb* **1** continue, work

rest² *noun* **1** what is left, the remainder **2** the others, those not mentioned: *I went home but the rest went to the cinema*

◼ **1** remainder, balance, surplus, excess, residue, remains, leftovers, remnants

restaurant *noun* a place where meals may be bought and eaten ◇ **restaurateur** *noun* the owner or manager of a restaurant

restful *adj* **1** relaxing **2** relaxed

restitution *noun* **1** the return of what has been lost or taken away **2** compensation for harm or injury done

restive *adj* restless, impatient

restless *adj* **1** unable to keep still **2** agitated

◼ **1** fidgety, unsettled **2** disturbed, troubled, agitated, nervous, anxious, worried, uneasy, fretful, edgy, jumpy, restive, unruly, turbulent, sleepless

▣ **2** calm, relaxed

restore *verb* **1** put or give back **2** repair (a building, a painting *etc*) so that it looks as it used to **3** cure (a person) ◇ **restoration** *noun* ◇ **restorative** *adj* curing, giving strength

◼ **1** replace, return, reinstate, rehabilitate, re-establish **2** renovate, renew, rebuild, reconstruct, refurbish, retouch, recondition, repair, mend, fix

restrain *verb* hold back or keep under control

◼ hold back, keep back, suppress, subdue, repress, inhibit, check, curb, bridle, stop, arrest, prevent, bind, tie, chain, fetter, manacle, imprison, jail, confine, restrict, regulate, control, govern

restraint *noun* **1** the act of restraining **2** self-control **3** a tie or bond used to restrain

restrict *verb* **1** limit, keep within certain bounds: *restrict their movements/restricted space for parking* **2** open or permit only to certain people: *restrict the use of the photocopier to library staff/a restricted area* ◇ **restriction** *noun* ◇ **restrictive** *adj* restricting

◼ **1** limit, bound, demarcate, control, regulate, confine, contain, cramp, constrain, impede, hinder, hamper, handicap, tie, restrain, curtail

result *noun* **1** a consequence of something already done or said **2** the answer to a sum **3** a score in a game ◇ *verb* **1** (with **from**) be the result or effect of **2** (with **in**) have as a result: *result in a draw* ◇ **resultant** *adj* happening as a result

◼ *noun* **1** effect, consequence, sequel, repercussion, reaction, outcome, upshot ◇ *verb* **1** follow, ensue, happen, occur, issue, emerge, arise, spring, derive, stem, flow, proceed, develop **2** end, finish, terminate, culminate

▣ *noun* **1** cause ◇ *verb* **1** cause

resume *verb* **1** begin again after an interruption: *resume a discussion* **2** take again: *he resumed his seat* ◇ **resumption** *noun*

résumé /ˈrɛzjʊmeɪ/ *noun* **1** a summary **2** *US* a curriculum vitae

resurgent *adj* rising again, becoming prominent again ◇ **resurgence** *noun*

resurrect *verb* bring back to life or into use ◇ **resurrection** *noun* **1** a rising from the dead **2** the act of bringing back into use ◇ **the Resurrection** the rising of Christ from the dead

◼ restore, revive, resuscitate, reactivate, bring back, reintroduce, renew

resuscitate *verb* bring back to consciousness, revive ◇ **resuscitation** *noun*

retail *verb* **1** sell goods to someone who is going to use them (not to another seller) **2** tell (*eg* a story) fully and in detail ◇ *noun* the sale of goods to the actual user ◇ **retailer** *noun* a shopkeeper, a trader

retain *verb* **1** keep possession of **2** keep (something) in your mind **3** reserve (someone's services) by paying a fee in advance **4** hold back, keep in place: *a retaining wall* ◇ **retainer** *noun* **1** a fee for services paid in advance **2** *old* a servant (to a family)

◼ **1** keep, hold, reserve, save, preserve **2**

remember, memorize

▣ 1 release 2 forget

retake *verb* take or capture again ◇ *noun* the filming of part of a film again

retaliate *verb* return like for like, hit back ◇ **retaliation** *noun*

▣ reciprocate, counter, counter-attack, hit back, strike back, fight back, get one's own back, get even, take revenge

retard *verb* **1** keep back, hinder **2** make slow or late ◇ **retardation** *noun* ◇ **retarded** *adj* slow in mental or physical growth

retch *verb* make the actions and sound of vomiting, without actually vomiting

retd *abbrev* retired

retention *noun* **1** the act of holding in or keeping **2** the act of retaining the services of (*eg* a lawyer) ◇ **retentive** *adj* able to hold or retain well: *retentive memory*

reticent *adj* unwilling to speak openly and freely, reserved ◇ **reticence** *noun*

▣ reserved, shy, inhibited, uncommunicative, unforthcoming, tight-lipped, secretive, taciturn, silent, quiet

▣ communicative, forward, frank

retina *noun* (*plural* **retinas** or **retinae**) the part of the back of the eye that receives the image of what is seen

retinue *noun* the attendants of someone important

retire *verb* **1** give up work permanently, usually because of age **2** go to bed **3** draw back, retreat ◇ **retiral** *noun* retirement ◇ **retired** *adj* **1** having given up work **2** out-of-the-way, quiet, secluded

retirement *noun* **1** the act of retiring from work **2** someone's life after they have given up work

retiring *adj* shy, avoiding being noticed

▣ shy, bashful, timid, inhibited, shrinking, quiet, reticent, reserved, self-effacing, unassertive

▣ bold, forward, assertive

retort *verb* make a quick and witty or

angry reply ◇ *noun* a quick and witty or angry reply

▣ *verb* answer, reply, respond, rejoin, return, counter, retaliate ◇ *noun* answer, reply, response, rejoinder, riposte, repartee, quip

retouch *verb* improve or repair with artwork

retrace *verb* go over again: *retrace your steps*

retract *verb* **1** take back (something said or given) **2** draw back: *the cat retracted its claws* ◇ **retractable** *adj* able to be retracted ◇ **retraction** *noun*

▣ **1** take back, withdraw, recant, reverse, revoke, rescind, cancel, repeal, repudiate

retread *noun* a remoulded tyre

retreat *verb* **1** draw back, withdraw **2** go away ◇ *noun* **1** a movement backwards before the advance of an enemy **2** a withdrawal **3** a quiet, peaceful place

▣ *verb* **1** draw back, recoil, shrink, *informal* turn tail, withdraw **2** leave, depart, quit ◇ *noun* **1** withdrawal, evacuation, flight **3** hideaway, den, refuge, asylum, sanctuary, shelter, haven

retrenchment *noun* economizing in spending

retrial *noun* a new hearing of a law case

retribution *noun* punishment

retrieve *verb* **1** get back, recover (something lost) **2** search for and fetch ◇ **retriever** *noun* a breed of dog trained to find and fetch shot birds

▣ **1** recoup, recover, salvage, save, rescue, redeem, restore, regain, get back, recapture, repossess **2** fetch, bring back

retro *adj* recreating or imitating a style *etc* from the past

retroflex *adj* bent backwards

retrograde *adj* **1** going backward **2** going from a better to a worse stage

▣ **1** reverse **2** retrogressive, backward, negative, downward, declining, deteriorating

retrospect *noun*: **in restrospect** considering or looking back on the past

retrospective *adj* **1** looking back on past events **2** of a law: applying to the past as well as the present and the future

retroussé *adj* of a nose: turned up

retsina *noun* a Greek wine flavoured with resin

return *verb* **1** go or come back **2** give, send, pay *etc* back **3** elect to parliament ◇ *noun* **1** the act of returning **2** a profit: *return on your investment* **3** a statement of income for calculating income tax **4** a return ticket ◇ **by return** (**of post**) sent by the first post back ◇ **return match** a second match played between the same team or players ◇ **return ticket** a ticket which covers a journey both to and from a place

▤ *verb* **1** come back, reappear, recur, go back, backtrack, regress **2** give back, hand back, send back, deliver, put back, replace, restore, repay, refund, reimburse, recompense ◇ *noun* **1** reappearance, recurrence, comeback, homecoming **2** revenue, income, proceeds, takings, yield, gain, profit, reward, advantage, benefit

▣ *verb* **1** leave, depart **2** take ◇ *noun* **1** departure, disappearance **2** payment, expense, loss

reunion *noun* a meeting of people who have been apart for some time

reunite *verb* join after having been separated

Rev or **Revd** *abbrev* Reverend

rev *noun* a revolution of an engine ◇ *verb* (**revs, revving, revved**) (often with **up**) increase the speed of (an engine)

revamp *verb* renovate, renew the appearance of

reveal *verb* **1** make known **2** show

▤ **1** disclose, divulge, betray, leak, tell, impart, communicate, broadcast, publish, announce, proclaim **2** expose, uncover, unveil, unmask, show, display, exhibit

reveille /rɪˈvælɪ/ *noun* a bugle call at daybreak to waken soldiers

revel *verb* (**revels, revelling, revelled**) **1** take great delight (in) **2** celebrate ◇ **reveller** *noun* ◇ **revelry** *noun* ◇ **revels** *noun plural* festivities

▤ **1** enjoy, relish, savour, delight in, thrive on, bask in, glory in, lap up, indulge in, wallow in, luxuriate in

revelation *noun* **1** the act of revealing **2** something unexpected which is made known

▤ **1** uncovering, unveiling, exposure, unmasking, exhibition, manifestation, disclosure

revenge *noun* **1** harm done to someone in return for harm they themselves have committed **2** the desire to do such harm ◇ *verb* inflict punishment in return for harm done: *revenging his father's murder* ◇ **revenge yourself** take revenge: *he revenged himself on his enemies*

▤ *noun* **1** vengeance, satisfaction, reprisal, retaliation, requital, payback, retribution

revenue *noun* **1** money received as payment **2** a country's total income

▤ **1** income, return, yield, interest, profit, gain, proceeds, receipts, takings

▣ **1** expenditure

reverberate *verb* echo and re-echo, resound ◇ **reverberation** *noun*

revere *verb* look upon with great respect ◇ **reverence** *noun* great respect or veneration ◇ **reverent** or **reverential** *adj* showing respect

▤ respect, esteem, honour, pay homage to, venerate, worship, adore, exalt

▣ despise, scorn

reverend *adj* **1** worthy of respect **2** (**Reverend**) a title given to a member of the clergy

❗Do not confuse: **reverend** and **reverent** (*see* **revere**)

reverie *noun* a daydream

reversal *noun* the act of reversing or being reversed

reverse *verb* **1** turn upside down or the other way round **2** move backwards: *she reversed into the parking space* **3** undo (a decision, policy *etc*) ◇ *noun* **1** the opposite (of) **2** the other side (of a coin *etc*) **3** a defeat ◇ **reversible** *adj* of clothes: able to be worn with either side out

■ *verb* **1** transpose, turn round, invert, upend, overturn, upset **2** back, retreat, backtrack **3** annul, invalidate, countermand, overrule, revoke, rescind, repeal, retract, quash, overthrow ◇ *noun* **1** inverse, converse, contrary, opposite, antithesis **2** underside, back, rear

revert *verb* **1** go back to an earlier topic, state *etc* **2** return to a previous owner ◇ **reversion** *noun*

review *verb* **1** give an opinion or criticism of (an artistic work) **2** consider again: *review the facts* **3** inspect (*eg* troops) ◇ *noun* **1** an article *etc* giving a critical opinion of a book *etc* **2** a magazine consisting of reviews **3** a second look, a reconsideration **4** an inspection of troops *etc* ◇ **reviewer** *noun* someone who reviews, a critic

■ *verb* **1** criticize, assess, evaluate, judge, weigh, discuss **2** reassess, re-evaluate, re-examine, reconsider, rethink, revise **3** examine, inspect, scrutinize, study, survey ◇ *noun* **1** criticism, critique, assessment, evaluation, judgement, report, commentary **2** magazine, periodical, journal **3** reassessment, re-evaluation, re-examination, revision

⚠ Do not confuse with: **revue**

revile *verb* say harsh things about

revise *verb* **1** correct faults in and make improvements to **2** study notes *etc* in preparation for an examination **3** change (*eg* an opinion) ◇ **revision** *noun* **1** the act of revising **2** a revised version of a book *etc*

■ **1** correct, update, edit, rewrite, reword, recast **2** study, learn, *informal* swot up, *informal* cram **3** change, alter, modify, amend, reconsider, re-examine, review

revival *noun* **1** a return to life, use *etc* **2** a fresh show of interest: *a religious revival* ◇ **revivalist** *noun* someone who helps to create a religious revival

revive *verb* bring or come back to life, use or fame: *revive an ancient custom*

■ resuscitate, reanimate, revitalize, re-

store, renew, refresh, animate, invigorate, rouse, awaken, recover, reawaken, rekindle, reactivate

☒ weary

revivify *verb* put new life into

revoke *verb* **1** cancel (a decision *etc*) **2** fail to follow suit in a card game ◇ **revocation** *noun*

■ **1** repeal, rescind, quash, abrogate, annul, nullify, invalidate, negate, cancel, countermand, reverse, retract, withdraw

revolt *verb* **1** rise up (against), rebel **2** disgust ◇ *noun* a rising, a rebellion ◇ **revolting** *adj* causing disgust

■ *verb* **1** rebel, mutiny, rise up, riot, resist, dissent, disobey, defect **2** disgust, sicken, nauseate, repel, offend, shock, outrage, scandalize ◇ *noun* revolution, rebellion, mutiny, rising, uprising, insurrection, putsch, coup (d'état), secession, defection

revolution *noun* **1** a full turn round a centre **2** the act of turning round a centre **3** a general uprising against those in power **4** a complete change in ideas, way of doing things *etc* ◇ **revolutionize** *verb* bring about a complete change in

■ **1** rotation, turn, spin, cycle, circuit, round, circle, orbit, gyration **2** rotation, gyration **3** revolt, rebellion, mutiny, rising, uprising, insurrection, putsch, coup (d'état) **4** change, transformation, innovation, upheaval

revolutionary *adj* **1** relating to a revolution **2** bringing about great changes **3** turning ◇ *noun* (*plural* **revolutionaries**) someone who is involved in, or is in favour of, revolution

revolve *verb* roll or turn round

revolver *noun* a kind of pistol

revue *noun* a light theatre show, with short topical plays or sketches

⚠ Do not confuse with: **review**

revulsion *noun* **1** disgust **2** a sudden change of feeling

■ **1** repugnance, disgust, distaste, dislike, aversion, hatred, loathing, detestation, abhorrence, abomination

reward *noun* **1** something given in return for work done or for good behaviour *etc* **2** a sum of money offered for helping to find a criminal, lost property *etc* ◇ *verb* **1** give a reward to **2** give a reward for (a service) ◇ **rewarding** *adj* giving pleasure or satisfaction

▤ *noun* **1** prize, honour, medal, decoration, bounty, pay-off, bonus, premium, payment, remuneration, recompense ◇ *verb* **1** pay, remunerate, recompense, repay, requite, compensate, honour, decorate

rewind *verb* wind back (a spool, cassette *etc*) to the beginning

rewrite *verb* (**rewrites, rewriting, rewrote, rewritten**) write again

Rh *abbrev* rhesus

rhapsody *noun* music or poetry which expresses strong feeling ◇ **rhapsodize** *verb* talk or write enthusiastically (about) ◇ **go into rhapsodies over** show wild enthusiasm for

rhesus factor a substance normally present in human blood ◇ **rhesus-negative** *adj* not having this substance in the blood ◇ **rhesus-positive** *adj* having this substance

rhetoric *noun* **1** the art of good speaking or writing **2** language which is too showy, consisting of unnecessarily long or difficult words *etc* ◇ **rhetorical** *adj* ◇ **rhetorical question** one which the asker answers, or which is asked for effect rather than for information

rheumatism *noun* a disease which causes stiffness and pain in the joints ◇ **rheumatic** *adj*

rhinestone *noun* an artificial paste diamond

rhino (*plural* **rhinos**) *short for* rhinoceros

rhinoceros (*plural* **rhinoceros** or **rhinoceroses**) a large, thick-skinned animal, with one or two horns on its nose

rhinoplasty *noun* plastic surgery on the nose

rhizome *noun* an underground plant stem producing roots and shoots

rhododendron *noun* a flowering shrub with thick evergreen leaves and large flowers

rhomboid *noun* a parallelogram with touching sides unequal in length

rhombus *noun* (*plural* **rhombi** or **rhombuses**) a geometrical figure with four equal straight sides

rhubarb *noun* a plant with long red-skinned stalks, edible when cooked

rhyme *noun* **1** a similarity in sound between words or their endings, *eg* humble and *crumble*, or *convention* and *prevention* **2** a word which sounds like another **3** a short poem ◇ *verb* (sometimes with **with**) sound like, be rhymes: *harp rhymes with carp/harp and corn don't rhyme*

rhythm *noun* **1** a regular repeated pattern of sounds or beats in music or poetry **2** a regularly repeated pattern of movements ◇ **rhythmic** or **rhythmical** *adj* ◇ **rhythm and blues** a type of music combining the styles of rock-and-roll and the blues ◇ **rhythm method** a method of contraception by abstaining from intercourse when a woman is most fertile

rib *noun* **1** any of the bones which curve round and forward from the backbone, enclosing the heart and lungs **2** a spar of wood in the framework of a boat, curving up from the keel **3** a ridged knitting pattern ◇ **ribbed** *adj* arranged in ridges and furrows

ribald *adj* of a joke *etc*: coarse, vulgar

ribbon *noun* a narrow strip of silk or other material, used for decoration, tying hair *etc*

riboflavin *noun* a vitamin found in milk, liver *etc*

rice *noun* the seeds of a cereal plant, grown for food in well-watered ground in tropical countries ◇ **rice paper** thin edible paper often put under baking to prevent it sticking

rich *adj* **1** having a lot of money or valuables, wealthy **2** valuable: *a rich reward* **3** (with **in**) having a lot of: *rich in natural resources* **4** of food: containing a lot of fat, eggs *etc* **5** of material: heavily decorated or textured, lavish **6** of a colour: deep in tone ◇**riches** *noun plural* wealth ◇**richly** *adv* ◇**richness** *noun*

■ **1** wealthy, affluent, moneyed, prosperous, well-to-do, well-off, *slang* loaded **3** plentiful, abundant, copious, profuse, prolific, full **4** creamy, fatty, full-bodied, heavy **6** deep, intense, vivid, bright, vibrant, warm

☒ **1** poor, impoverished

Richter scale /ˈrɪxtə-/ a scale for measuring the intensity of earthquakes

rickets *noun sing* a children's disease caused by lack of calcium, with softening and bending of the bones

rickety *adj* unsteady: *a rickety table*

■ unsteady, wobbly, shaky, unstable, insecure, flimsy, jerry-built, decrepit

☒ stable, strong

rickshaw *noun* a two-wheeled carriage pulled by a person on foot, used in Japan *etc*

ricochet /ˈrɪkəʃeɪ/ *verb* (**ricochets, ricocheting, ricocheted** or **ricochetted**) of a bullet: rebound at an angle from a surface

ricotta *noun* a soft Italian sheep's-milk cheese

rictus *noun* a gaping of the mouth, *eg* in horror

rid *verb* (**rids, ridding, rid**) free from, clear of: *rid the city of rats* ◇**get rid of** free yourself of ◇**good riddance to** I am happy to have got rid of

■ clear, purge, free, deliver, relieve, unburden

riddle[1] *noun* **1** a puzzle in the form of a question which describes something in an indirect or misleading way **2** something difficult to understand

■ **1** enigma, mystery, conundrum, brain-teaser, puzzle **2** poser, problem

riddle[2] *noun* a large, coarse sieve for sifting soil *etc* ◇**riddled with 1** pierced with many holes: *riddled with bullets* **2** spread with, filled with: *riddled with corruption*

ride *verb* (**rides, riding, rode, ridden**) **1** travel on a horse or bicycle, or in a vehicle **2** travel on and control (a horse or bicycle) **3** of a ship: float at anchor ◇*noun* **1** a journey on horseback, bicycle *etc* **2** a path through a wood, for riding horses ◇**rider** *noun* **1** someone who rides **2** something added to what has already been said ◇**ride up** of a skirt *etc*: work itself up out of position

ridge *noun* **1** a raised part between furrows **2** a long crest on high ground **3** the edge where two sloping surfaces meet **4** a narrow area of pressure in the atmosphere

ridicule *verb* laugh at, mock ◇*noun* mockery

■ *verb* satirize, send up, caricature, lampoon, parody, mock, make fun of, jeer, scoff, deride, sneer, humiliate, taunt ◇*noun* satire, sarcasm, mockery, jeering, scorn, derision, taunting

ridiculous *adj* deserving to be laughed at, very silly

■ ludicrous, absurd, nonsensical, silly, foolish, contemptible, derisory, laughable, farcical, outrageous

rife *adj* very common: *disease was rife in the country*

riff-raff *noun* worthless people

rifle[1] *verb* **1** search through and rob **2** steal

rifle[2] *noun* a gun fired from the shoulder

rift *noun* **1** a crack **2** a disagreement between friends ◇**rift valley** a long valley formed by the fall of part of the earth's crust

■ **1** split, breach, break, fracture, crack, fault, chink, cleft, cranny, crevice, gap, space, opening **2** disagreement, difference, separation, division, alienation

rig *verb* (**rigs, rigging, rigged**) **1** fit, equip **2** fix (an election result) illegally or dishonestly ◇**rigging** *noun* ship's spars, ropes *etc* ◇**rig out** clothe, dress ◇**rig up** make or build hastily

right *adj* **1** on or belonging to the side of the body which in most people has the more skilful hand (*contrasted with*: **left**) **2** correct, true **3** just, good **4** straight ◇*adv* **1** to or on the right side **2** correctly **3** straight **4** all the way: *right* *along the pier and back* ◇ *noun* **1** something good which ought to be done **2** something you are entitled to: *a right to a fair trial* **3** the right-hand side, direction *etc* **4** the conservative side in politics ◇ *verb* mend, set in order ◇ **rightful** *adj* by right, proper: *the rightful owner* ◇ **by right** because you have the right ◇ **in your own right** not because of anyone else, independently: *famous in her own right* ◇ **right angle** an angle like one of those in a square, an angle of 90° ◇ **right-click** *verb* press the right-hand button on a computer mouse ◇ **right-handed** *adj* using the right hand more easily than the left ◇ **Right Honourable** *adj* used before the names of cabinet ministers in the British government ◇ **right of way** a road or path over private land along which people may go as a right ◇ **right-wing** *adj* of conservative views in politics

◼ *adj* **2** correct, accurate, exact, precise, true **3** proper, fitting, seemly, becoming, appropriate, suitable, fit, admissible, satisfactory, reasonable, fair, just, equitable, lawful, honest, upright, good, righteous, moral, ethical, honourable ◇ *adv* **2** correctly, accurately, exactly, precisely, factually, properly ◇ *verb* rectify, correct, put right, fix, repair, redress, vindicate, avenge, settle, straighten

◼ *adj* **2** wrong, incorrect **3** unfair, wrong, improper, unsuitable ◇ *adv* **2** wrongly, incorrectly, unfairly

righteous *adj* living a good life; just ◇ **righteousness** *noun*

rigid *adj* **1** not easily bent, stiff **2** strict ◇ **rigidity** *noun*

◼ **1** stiff, inflexible, unbending, cast-iron, hard, firm, set, fixed, unalterable, invariable **2** austere, harsh, severe, unrelenting, strict, rigorous, stringent, stern, uncompromising, unyielding

rigmarole *noun* a long, rambling speech

Originally *ragman roll*, a Scots term for a long list or catalogue

rigor mortis stiffening of the body after death

rigorous *adj* very strict

◼ strict, stringent, rigid, firm, exact, precise, accurate, meticulous, painstaking, scrupulous, conscientious, thorough

◼ lax, superficial

rigour *noun* strictness; harshness

rill *noun* a small stream

rim *noun* an edge or border, *eg* the top edge of a cup

rime *noun* thick white frost

rind /raɪnd/ *noun* a thick firm covering, *eg* fruit peel, bacon skin, the outer covering of cheese

ring[1] *noun* **1** a small hoop worn on the finger, on the ear *etc* **2** a hollow circle **3** an enclosed space for boxing, circus performances *etc* **4** a small group of people formed for business or criminal purposes: *a drug ring* ◇ *verb* (**rings, ringing, ringed**) **1** encircle, go round **2** mark (a bird *etc*) by putting on a ring ◇ **ring road** a road that circles a town *etc* avoiding the centre

◼ *noun* **2** circle, round, loop, hoop, halo, band **3** circuit, arena, enclosure **4** group, cartel, syndicate, association, organization, gang ◇ *verb* **1** surround, encircle, gird, circumscribe, encompass, enclose

ring[2] *verb* (**rings, ringing, rang, rung**) **1** (cause to) make the sound of a bell **2** telephone ◇ *noun* the sound of a bell

◼ *verb* **1** chime, peal, toll, tinkle, clink, jingle, clang, sound, resound, resonate, reverberate **2** telephone, phone, call, ring up ◇ *noun* chime, peal, toll, tinkle, clink, jingle, clang

ringleader *noun* someone who takes the lead in mischief *etc*

ringlet *noun* a long curl of hair

ringmaster *noun* someone who is in charge of the performance in a circus ring

ringworm *noun* a skin disease causing circular red patches

rink *noun* a sheet of ice, often artificial, for skating or curling

rinse *verb* **1** wash lightly to remove soap *etc* **2** clean (a cup, your mouth *etc*) by swilling with water ◇ *noun* **1** the act of rinsing **2** liquid colour for the hair

riot *noun* **1** a noisy disturbance or protest by a crowd **2** a striking display: *a riot of colour* **3** a hilarious event ◇ *verb* take part in a riot ◇ **riotous** *adj* noisy, uncontrolled

■ *noun* **1** insurrection, rising, uprising, revolt, rebellion, anarchy, lawlessness, affray, disturbance, turbulence, disorder, confusion, commotion, tumult, turmoil, uproar, row

RIP *abbrev* (may he or she) rest in peace

rip *verb* (**rips, ripping, ripped**) tear or be torn apart or off ◇ *noun* a tear ◇ **let rip** express yourself fully, without restraint ◇ **rip-off** *noun, slang* a cheat, a swindle

■ *verb* tear, rend, split, separate, rupture, burst, cut, slit, slash, gash, lacerate, hack ◇ *noun* tear, rent, split, cleavage, rupture, cut, slit, slash, gash, hole

ripe *adj* **1** of fruit *etc*: ready to be picked or eaten **2** fully developed, mature ◇ **ripeness** *noun*

■ **1** ripened, mature, mellow, seasoned **2** grown, developed, complete, finished

ripen *verb* make or become ripe

riposte *noun* a quick return or reply

ripple *noun* **1** a little wave or movement on the surface of water **2** a soft sound *etc* that rises and falls quickly and gently: *a ripple of laughter*

rise *verb* (**rises, rising, rose, risen**) **1** get up from bed **2** stand up **3** move upwards **4** increase **5** of a river: have its source (in): *the Rhone rises in the Alps* **6** rebel (against) ◇ *noun* **1** a slope upwards **2** an increase in wages, prices *etc* ◇ **rising** *noun* **1** the act of rising **2** a rebellion ◇ **give rise to** cause

■ *verb* **2** stand up, get up, arise, jump up, spring up **3** go up, ascend, climb, mount, slope (up), soar, tower **4** increase, mount, soar, grow **5** originate, spring, flow, issue ◇ *noun* **1** ascent, climb, slope, incline, hill, elevation **2** increase, increment

🞂 *verb* **2** sit down **3** fall, descend ◇ *noun* **1** descent **2** fall

risible *adj* laughable

risk *noun* a chance of loss or injury; a danger ◇ *verb* **1** take the chance of: *risk death* **2** take the chance of losing: *risk one's life*

■ *noun* danger, peril, jeopardy, hazard, chance, possibility, uncertainty, gamble, speculation, venture ◇ *verb* **2** endanger, imperil, jeopardize

risky *adj* possibly resulting in loss or injury

■ dangerous, unsafe, perilous, hazardous, chancy, uncertain, touch-and-go, *informal* dicey, tricky, precarious

🞂 safe

risotto *noun* a dish made with rice

risqué /'rɪskeɪ/ *adj* slightly lewd or suggestive

■ indecent, improper, indelicate, suggestive, coarse, crude, earthy, bawdy, racy, naughty, *informal* saucy, blue

🞂 decent, proper

rissole *noun* a fried cake or ball of minced meat, fish *etc*

rite *noun* a solemn ceremony, *esp* a religious one

ritual *noun* a traditional way of carrying out religious worship *etc* ◇ *adj* relating to a rite or ceremony ◇ **ritualistic** *adj* done in a set, unchanging way

■ *noun* custom, tradition, convention, procedure, rite, sacrament, service, liturgy, observance, ceremony

rival *noun* someone who tries to equal or beat another ◇ *verb* (**rivals, rivalling, rivalled**) (try to) equal ◇ **rivalry** *noun* (*plural* **rivalries**)

■ *noun* competitor, contestant, contender, challenger, opponent, adversary, antagonist, match ◇ *verb* compete with, contend with, vie with, oppose, emulate, match

riven *adj, old* split

river *noun* a large stream of water flowing across land

■ waterway, watercourse, tributary, stream, brook, beck, creek

rivet *noun* a bolt for fastening plates of metal together ◇ *verb* **1** fasten with a rivet **2** fix firmly (someone's attention *etc*): *riveted to the spot* ◇ **riveting** *adj* fascinating

riviera *noun* a warm coastal area

rivulet *noun* a small stream

RN *abbrev* Royal Navy

RNIB *abbrev* Royal National Institute for the Blind

RNLI *abbrev* Royal National Lifeboat Institution

roach *noun* (*plural* **roaches**) a type of freshwater fish

road *noun* **1** a hard, level surface for vehicles and people to travel on **2** a way of getting to somewhere, a route **3** (**roads**) a place where ships may lie at anchor ◇ **road hog** a reckless or selfish driver ◇ **road movie** a film showing the travels of a character or characters

 ▤ **1** roadway, motorway, bypass, highway, thoroughfare, street, avenue, boulevard, crescent, drive, lane, track **2** route, course, way, direction

roadie *noun* a member of the crew who transport, set up and dismantle equipment for rock, jazz *etc* musicians

roadway *noun* the part of a road used by cars *etc*

roadworthy *adj* (of a vehicle) fit to be used on the road

roam *verb* wander about

 ▤ wander, rove, range, travel, walk, ramble, stroll, amble, prowl, drift, stray

 ▤ stay

roan *noun* a horse with a dark-brown coat spotted with grey or white

roar *verb* **1** give a loud, deep sound **2** laugh loudly **3** say (something) loudly ◇ *noun* a loud, deep sound or laugh

roast *verb* cook or be cooked in an oven or over a fire ◇ *adj* roasted: *roast beef* ◇ *noun* **1** roasted meat **2** meat for roasting

rob *verb* (**robs**, **robbing**, **robbed**) steal from ◇ **robber** *noun*

 ▤ steal from, hold up, raid, burgle, loot, pillage, plunder, sack, rifle, ransack, swindle, *slang* rip off, *informal* do, cheat, defraud

robbery *noun* (*plural* **robberies**) the act of robbing or stealing

robe *noun* **1** a long loose garment **2** *US* a dressing-gown **3** (**robes**) the official dress of a judge *etc* ◇ *verb, formal* dress

robin *noun* a type of small bird, known by its red breast

robot *noun* **1** a machine that resembles a human being **2** a machine that can do the work of a person ◇ **robotic** *adj*

robust *adj* strong, healthy ◇ **robustness** *noun*

 ▤ strong, sturdy, tough, hardy, vigorous, powerful, muscular, athletic, fit, healthy, well

 ▤ weak, feeble, unhealthy

rock¹ *noun* **1** a large lump of stone **2** a hard sweet made in sticks ◇ **rocky** *adj* full of rocks ◇ **rock cake** a small rough-textured cake

 ▤ **1** boulder, stone, pebble, crag, outcrop ◇ **rocky** stony, pebbly, craggy, rugged, rough, hard, flinty

---

Rocks include:
basalt, breccia, chalk, coal, conglomerate, flint, gabbro, gneiss, granite, gravel, lava, limestone, marble, marl, obsidian, ore, porphyry, pumice stone, sandstone, schist, serpentine, shale, slate

---

rock² *verb* sway backwards and forwards or from side to side ◇ *noun (also called* **rock music**) music with a heavy beat and simple melody ◇ **rocker** *noun* a curved support on which a chair, cradle *etc* rocks ◇ **rocky** *adj* inclined to rock, unsteady ◇ **rock-and-roll** or **rock'n'roll** *noun* a simpler, earlier form of rock music ◇ **rocking-chair** or **rocking-horse** *noun* a chair or a toy horse which rocks backwards and forwards on rockers

 ▤ *verb* sway, swing, tilt, tip, shake, wobble, roll, pitch, toss, lurch, reel ◇ **rocky** unsteady, shaky, wobbly, staggering, tottering, unstable

rockery *noun* (*plural* **rockeries**) a collection of stones amongst which small plants are grown

rocket *noun* **1** a tube containing inflammable materials, used for signalling and as a firework **2** a spacecraft ◇ *verb* **1** rise or move upwards rapidly: *prices are rocketing*

rococo *adj* extravagantly ornamented

rod *noun* **1** a long thin stick **2** a fishing rod **3** *hist* a measure of distance, about 5 metres

■ **1** bar, shaft, strut, pole, stick, baton, wand, cane, switch, staff, mace, sceptre

rode *past form* of **ride**

rodent *noun* a gnawing animal, such as a rat, beaver *etc*

Rodents include:
agouti, bandicoot, beaver, black rat, brown rat, cane rat, capybara, cavy, chinchilla, chipmunk, cony, coypu, dormouse, fieldmouse, ferret, gerbil, gopher, grey squirrel, groundhog, guinea pig, hamster, hare, harvest mouse, hedgehog, jerboa, kangaroo rat, lemming, marmot, meerkat, mouse, muskrat, musquash, pika, porcupine, prairie dog, rabbit, rat, red squirrel, sewer rat, squirrel, vole, water rat, water vole, woodchuck

---

rodeo *noun* (*plural* **rodeos**) **1** a round-up of cattle for marking **2** a show of riding by cowboys

roe¹ *noun* the eggs of fishes

roe² *noun* **1** (also **roe deer**) a small kind of deer **2** a female red deer ◇ **roe-buck** *noun* the male roe deer

rogue *noun* a dishonest or mischievous person, a rascal ◇ **roguery** *noun* dishonesty; mischief ◇ **roguish** *adj*

■ scoundrel, rascal, scamp, villain, miscreant, *informal* crook, swindler, fraud, cheat, *informal* con man, reprobate, wastrel, ne'er-do-well

roisterer *noun* a reveller

role or **rôle** *noun* a part played by someone, *esp* an actor

roll *verb* **1** move along by turning over like a wheel **2** of a ship: rock from side to side **3** of thunder *etc*: rumble **4** wrap round and round: *roll up a carpet* **5** flatten with a roller: *roll the lawn* ◇ *noun* **1** a

sheet of paper, length of cloth *etc* rolled into a cylinder **2** a very small loaf of bread **3** a rocking movement **4** a list of names **5** a long, rumbling sound: *a roll on the drums* ◇ **rolling pin** a roller for flattening dough ◇ **rolling stock** the trains, engines, carriages *etc* that run on a railway

■ *verb* **2** rock, sway, swing, pitch, toss, lurch **3** rumble, roar, thunder, boom, resound, reverberate **4** wind, coil, furl, twist, curl, wrap, envelop, enfold, bind **5** press, flatten, smooth, level

roller *noun* **1** a cylindrical tool for flattening **2** a tube over which hair is rolled and styled **3** a small solid wheel **4** a long heavy wave on the sea ◇ **roller skates** skates with wheels at each corner of the shoe

Rollerblades *noun plural*, *trademark* roller skates with the wheels in a single line

rollicking *adj* noisy and full of fun

rollmop *noun* a rolled fillet of herring, pickled in vinegar

ROM *abbrev*, *comput* read-only memory

Roman *adj* of a number: written in letters, as I, II, III, IV *etc* for 1, 2, 3, 4 *etc* ◇ **Roman Catholic Church** the Church whose head is the Pope, the Bishop of Rome

romance *noun* **1** a love affair **2** a love story **3** a story about heroic events not likely to happen in real life ◇ *verb* write or tell imaginative stories

romantic *adj* **1** of love or romance **2** full of feeling and imagination **3** of heroic imaginary tales ◇ **romantically** *adv*

■ **1** sentimental, loving, amorous, passionate, tender, fond, *informal* lovey-dovey, soppy, mushy, sloppy **2** dreamy, unrealistic, wild, extravagant, exciting, fascinating **3** imaginary, fictitious, fanciful, fantastic, legendary, fairy-tale, idyllic, utopian, idealistic, quixotic, visionary

Romanesque *adj* of architecture: in a style of the 9th–12th centuries

Romany *noun* (*plural* **Romanies**) **1** a

gypsy **2** the gypsy language

romp *verb* **1** play in a lively way **2** move quickly and easily: *romped through the work* ◇ *noun* a lively game ◇ **rompers** *noun plural* a short suit for a baby

rondo *noun* (*plural* **rondos**) a musical composition with a recurring section

rood *noun, old* **1** a measure of area, equal to a quarter of an acre **2** a cross carrying an image of Christ

roof *noun* (*plural* **roofs**) **1** the top covering of a building, car *etc* **2** the upper part of the mouth ◇ *verb* cover with a roof

rook *noun* **1** a kind of crow **2** *chess* the castle ◇ **rookery** *noun* (*plural* **rookeries**) **1** a nesting place of rooks **2** a breeding place of penguins or seals ◇ **rookie** *noun, informal* a new recruit

room *noun* **1** an inside compartment in a house **2** space: *room for everybody* **3** (**rooms**) lodgings

roomy *adv* having plenty of space

▤ spacious, capacious, large, sizable, broad, wide, extensive, ample, generous

▣ cramped, small, tiny

roost *noun* a perch on which a bird rests at night ◇ *verb* sit or sleep on a roost ◇ **rooster** *noun* a farmyard cock

root *noun* **1** the underground part of a plant **2** the base of anything, *eg* a tooth **3** a cause, a source **4** a word from which other words have developed ◇ *verb* **1** form roots and begin to grow **2** fix or be fixed: *rooted to the spot* **3** of an animal: turn up ground in a search for food **4** search (about): *rooting in her handbag for a comb* ◇ **root-and-branch** *adj* & *adv* thorough(ly), complete(ly) ◇ **root out** or **root up 1** tear up by the roots **2** get rid of completely ◇ **take root 1** form roots and grow firmly **2** become firmly fixed

▤ *noun* **3** origin, source, derivation, cause, starting point, fount, fountainhead, seed, germ ◇ *verb* **3** dig, delve, burrow, forage **4** hunt, rummage, ferret, poke ◇ **root out 1** unearth, dig out, uproot **2** eradicate, extirpate, eliminate, exterminate, destroy, abolish, clear away, remove

rope *noun* **1** a thick cord, made by twisting strands together **2** anything resembling a thick cord: *a rope of hair* ◇ *verb* **1** fasten or catch with a rope **2** enclose, mark off with a rope ◇ **ropy** *adj* **1** like ropes, stringy **2** *informal* bad, unwell ◇ **rope in** persuade to take part

▤ *noun* **1** line, cable, cord, string ◇ *verb* **1** tie, bind, lash, fasten, hitch, moor, tether

rorqual *noun* a fin-backed whale

Rorschach test /ˈrɔːʃak-/ a psychological test in which someone must interpret the shapes made by ink-blots

rosary *noun* (*plural* **rosaries**) **1** a set of prayers **2** a string of beads used in saying prayers

rosé *noun* a pink-coloured wine produced by removing red grape-skins during fermentation

rose[1] *past form* of **rise**

rose[2] *noun* **1** a type of flower, often scented, growing on a *usu* prickly bush **2** a deep pink colour ◇ **rosy** *adj* **1** deep pink **2** of the future *etc*: bright, hopeful ◇ **rosehip** *noun* the fruit of the rose ◇ **rosewood** *noun* a dark Brazilian or Indian wood, which smells of roses when cut

rosemary *noun* an evergreen sweet-smelling shrub, used as a cooking herb

rosette *noun* a badge shaped like a rose, made of ribbons

roster *noun* a list showing a repeated order of duties *etc*

▤ rota, schedule, register, roll, list

rostrum *noun* (*plural* **rostrums** or **rostra**) a platform for public speaking

rot *verb* (**rots**, **rotting**, **rotted**) go bad, decay ◇ *noun* **1** decay **2** *informal* nonsense

▤ *verb* decay, decompose, putrefy, fester, perish, spoil, go bad, go off ◇ *noun* **1** decay, decomposition, putrefaction, mould **2** nonsense, rubbish, *informal* poppycock, drivel, claptrap, twaddle

rota *noun* a list of duties *etc* to be repeated in a set order

rotary *adj* turning round like a wheel

rotate *verb* **1** turn round like a wheel **2** go through a repeating series of changes ◊**rotation** *noun*
■ **1** revolve, turn, spin, wheel, gyrate, pivot, swivel, roll

rotavator *noun, trademark* a machine for tilling soil

rote *noun*: **by rote** off by heart, automatically

rotisserie *noun* a spit for roasting meat

rotor a turning part of a motor, dynamo *etc*

rotten *adj* **1** decayed, bad **2** worthless, disgraceful
■ **1** decayed, decomposed, putrid, addled, bad, off, mouldy, fetid, rancid, stinking, rank, foul, rotting, decaying, disintegrating **2** inferior, bad, poor, inadequate, low-grade, lousy, *slang* crummy, *slang* ropy, mean, nasty, beastly, dirty, despicable, contemptible, dishonourable, wicked
1 fresh **2** good

rotter *noun, informal* a very bad, worthless person

rottweiler *noun* a large, powerful German dog with a smooth coat

rotund *adj* round; plump ◊**rotundity** *noun*

rouble or **ruble** *noun* a standard unit of Russian coinage

roué /'ruːeɪ/ *noun* a debauched person

rouge *noun* a powder or cream used to add colour to the cheeks

rough *adj* **1** not smooth; uneven **2** coarse, harsh **3** boisterous, wild **4** not exact: *a rough guess* **5** stormy ◊*noun* **1** a hooligan, a bully **2** rough ground ◊**rough and ready** not fine or carefully made, but effective ◊**rough out** sketch or shape roughly
■ *adj* **1** uneven, bumpy, lumpy, rugged, craggy, jagged, irregular **2** coarse, bristly, scratchy, harsh, severe, tough, hard, cruel, brutal **4** approximate, estimated, imprecise, inexact, vague, general **5** stormy, tempestuous, violent, wild

1 smooth **2** soft, mild **4** accurate **5** calm

roughage *noun* bran or fibre in food

roughen *verb* make rough

roulade *noun* a meat or vegetable dish shaped into a long roll

roulette *noun* a gambling game, played with a ball which is placed on a wheel

round *adj* **1** shaped like a circle or sphere **2** plump **3** even, exact: *a round dozen* ◊*adv* & *prep* **1** on all sides (of), around: *look round the room* **2** in a circle (about): *the earth moves round the sun* **3** from one (person, place *etc*) to another: *the news went round* ◊*noun* **1** a circle, something round in shape **2** a single bullet or shell **3** a burst of firing, cheering *etc* **4** a song in which the singers take up the tune in turn **5** a usual route: *a postman's round* **6** a series of calls or deliveries: *the doctor on her rounds* **7** each stage of a contest ◊*verb* **1** make or become round **2** of a ship: go round (*eg* a headland) ◊**roundly** *adv* boldly, plainly ◊**round on** make a sudden attack on ◊**round trip** *US* a journey to a place and back ◊**round up** gather or drive together
■ *adj* **1** spherical, globular, ball-shaped, circular, ring-shaped, disc-shaped, rounded, curved **2** rotund, plump, stout, portly ◊**round on** turn on, attack, lay into, abuse ◊**round up** herd, marshal, assemble, gather, rally, collect, group

rounders *noun sing* a ball game played with a bat in which players run around a series of stations

roundabout *noun* **1** a revolving machine for children to ride on in a park *etc* **2** a meeting-place of roads, where traffic must move in a circle ◊*adj* not straight or direct: *a roundabout route*
■ *adj* circuitous, tortuous, twisting, winding, indirect, oblique, devious, evasive
adj straight, direct

roundel *noun* a round painting, glass panel *etc*

roundelay *noun* a song with a refrain

rouse *verb* **1** awaken **2** stir up, excite

◇ **rousing** *adj* stirring, exciting

▤ **1** wake (up), awaken, arouse **2** arouse, stir, anger, provoke, stimulate, incite, inflame, excite, galvanize, whip up

rout *noun* a complete defeat ◇ *verb* defeat utterly

route *noun* the course to be followed, a way of getting to somewhere ◇ *verb* fix the route of

routine *noun* a fixed, unchanging order of doing things ◇ *adj* regular, usual: *routine enquiries*

▤ *noun* procedure, way, method, system, order, pattern, formula, practice, usage, custom, habit

roux /ruː/ *noun* a paste of flour and water used to thicken sauces *etc*

rove *verb* wander or roam ◇ **rover 1** a wanderer; an unsettled person **2** *hist* a pirate ◇ **Rover Scout** an older member of the Scout Association

row¹ /rəʊ/ *noun* a line of people or things

▤ *noun* line, tier, bank, rank, range, column, file, queue, string, series, sequence

row² /rəʊ/ *verb* drive (a boat) by oars ◇ *noun* a trip in a rowing boat ◇ **rower** *noun* someone who rows ◇ **rowing boat** a boat rowed by oars

row³ /raʊ/ *noun* **1** an argument **2** a noise **3** *informal* a scolding

▤ **1** argument, quarrel, dispute, controversy, squabble, tiff, *informal* slanging match, fight, brawl **2** noise, racket, din, uproar, commotion, disturbance, rumpus, fracas

rowan *noun* (*also called* **mountain ash**) a tree with clusters of bright red berries

rowdy *adj* noisy, disorderly

▤ noisy, loud, rough, boisterous, disorderly, unruly, riotous, wild

rowlock *noun* a place to rest an oar on the side of a rowing boat

royal *adj* **1** relating to a king or queen **2** splendid, magnificent: *royal welcome* ◇ **royal blue** a deep, bright blue ◇ **royal icing** stiff cake icing made with egg-white ◇ **royal jelly** a jelly secreted

by worker bees to feed developing larvae

▤ **1** regal, majestic, kingly, queenly, princely, imperial, monarchical, sovereign **2** august, grand, stately, magnificent, splendid, superb

royalist *noun* someone who supports a king or queen

royalty *noun* (*plural* **royalties**) **1** the state of being royal **2** royal people as a whole **3** a sum paid to the author of a book for each copy sold

RP *abbrev* Received Pronunciation, the accepted accent of standard English

rpm *abbrev* revolutions per minute

rps *abbrev* revolutions per second

RSA *abbrev* **1** Royal Society of Arts **2** Royal Scottish Academy

RSI *abbrev* repetitive strain injury

RSPB *abbrev* Royal Society for the Protection of Birds

RSPCA *abbrev* Royal Society for the Prevention of Cruelty to Animals

RSVP *abbrev* please reply (from French *répondez, s'il vous plaît*)

Rt Hon *abbrev* Right Honourable

Rt Rev *abbrev* Right Reverend

rub *verb* (**rubs, rubbing, rubbed**) **1** move one thing against the surface of another **2** clean, polish **3** (with **out**) remove (a mark), *esp* with an eraser ◇ *noun* **1** the act of rubbing **2** a wipe ◇ **rub in** work into (a surface) by rubbing **2** keep reminding someone of (something unpleasant)

▤ *verb* **1** chafe, grate, scrape, abrade **2** clean, wipe, scour, scrub, smooth, polish, buff, shine **3** erase, efface, obliterate, delete

rubber *noun* **1** a tough elastic substance made from plant juices **2** a piece of rubber used for erasing pencil marks **3** an odd number (three or five) of games in cards, cricket *etc* ◇ **rubber bullet** a hard rubber pellet fired by police in riot control ◇ **rubber stamp** an instrument with rubber figures or letters for stamping dates *etc* on paper ◇ **rubber-stamp** *verb* authorize, approve

rubbish noun 1 waste material, litter 2 nonsense
■ 1 refuse, garbage, trash, junk, litter, waste, dross, debris, flotsam and jetsam 2 nonsense, drivel, claptrap, twaddle, gibberish, gobbledygook, balderdash, informal poppycock, informal rot, slang cobblers
■ 2 sense

rubble noun small rough stones, bricks etc left from a building

rubella noun German measles

Rubicon noun: **cross the Rubicon** take a decisive step

After Caesar's crossing of the Rubicon river which meant declaring war on his neighbouring province

rubicund adj red or rosy-faced

ruble another spelling of **rouble**

rubric noun 1 a heading 2 a guiding rule

From a Latin word for red ink, originally an entry in a Biblical text written in red ink

ruby noun (plural **rubies**) a type of red, precious stone

ruche noun a frill

ruck noun a wrinkle, a crease

rucksack noun a bag carried on the back by walkers, climbers etc

ruckus noun, US an uproar, a rumpus

ructions noun plural a row, a disturbance

rudder noun a device fixed to the stern of a boat, or tail of an aeroplane, for steering

ruddy adj 1 red 2 of the face: rosy, in good health

rude adj 1 showing bad manners, not polite 2 roughly made: a rude shelter 3 rough, not refined 4 startling and sudden: a rude awakening 5 coarse, vulgar, lewd ◇ **rudely** adv ◇ **rudeness** noun
■ 1 impolite, discourteous, disrespectful, impertinent, impudent, informal cheeky, insolent, offensive, insulting, abusive, ill-mannered, ill-bred, uncouth,

uncivilized, unrefined, unpolished, un-educated, untutored, uncivil, curt, brusque, abrupt, sharp, short 5 obscene, vulgar, coarse, dirty, naughty, gross
■ 1 polite, courteous, civil 5 clean, decent

rudiments noun plural the first simple rules or facts of anything ◇ **rudimentary** adj in an early stage of development
■ **rudimentary** primary, initial, introductory, elementary, basic, fundamental, primitive, undeveloped, embryonic
■ **rudimentary** advanced, developed

rue[1] noun a shrub with bitter-tasting leaves

rue[2] verb be sorry for, regret ◇ **rueful** adj sorrowful, regretful

ruff noun 1 hist a pleated frill worn round the neck 2 a band of feathers round a bird's neck

ruffian noun a rough, brutal person ◇ **ruffianly** adj

ruffle verb 1 make uneven or disordered (eg hair, a bird's feathers) 2 annoy, offend 3 wrinkle or gather

rug noun 1 a floor mat 2 a blanket

rugby noun a form of football using an oval ball which can be handled

Named after Rugby School in Warwickshire, where the game was supposedly invented

rugged adj 1 having a rough, uneven appearance 2 strong, robust 3 stern, harsh
■ 1 rough, bumpy, uneven, irregular, jagged, rocky, craggy, stark 2 strong, robust, hardy, tough, muscular
■ 1 smooth

ruin noun 1 complete loss of money etc 2 a downfall 3 (**ruins**) broken-down remains of buildings ◇ verb 1 destroy 2 spoil completely: ruin your chances 3 make very poor ◇ **ruination** noun ◇ **ruined** adj in ruins, destroyed ◇ **ruinous** adj 1 ruined 2 likely to cause ruin
■ noun 1 insolvency, bankruptcy, crash 2 disintegration, breakdown, collapse, fall, downfall, failure, defeat, overthrow,

ruination, undoing ◇ *verb* **1** damage, break, smash, shatter, wreck, destroy, demolish, raze, devastate **2** spoil, mar, botch, *informal* mess up, *slang* screw up **3** impoverish, bankrupt

rule *noun* **1** government: *under military rule* **2** a regulation: *school rules* **3** what usually happens **4** a guiding principle **5** a measuring ruler ◇ *verb* **1** govern, be in power **2** decide (that) **3** draw (a line) **4** mark with lines: *ruled paper* ◇ **as a rule** usually ◇ **rule out** leave out, not consider

▤ *noun* **1** power, authority, command, control, influence, regime, government, leadership **2** regulation, law, statute, ordinance, decree, order, principle, formula, guideline **3** custom, convention, practice, routine, habit, wont **4** guide, precept, tenet, canon, maxim, axiom, principle ◇ *verb* **1** reign, govern, command, lead, administer, manage, direct, guide, control, regulate, prevail, dominate **2** decide, find, determine, resolve, establish, decree ◇ **rule out** exclude, eliminate, reject, dismiss

ruler *noun* **1** someone who rules **2** a marked tool for measuring length and drawing straight lines

Titles of rulers include:
Aga, begum, caesar, caliph, consul, duce, emir, emperor, empress, Führer, governor, governor-general, head of state, Kaiser, khan, king, maharajah, maharani, mikado, monarch, nawab, nizam, pharaoh, president, prince, princess, queen, rajah, rani, regent, shah, sheikh, shogun, sovereign, sultan, sultana, suzerain, tsar, viceroy

ruling *adj* governing; most important ◇ *noun* a decision, a rule

▤ *adj* reigning, sovereign, supreme, governing, commanding, leading, main, chief, principal, dominant, predominant, controlling ◇ *noun* judgement, adjudication, verdict, decision, resolution, decree, pronouncement

rum[1] *noun* an alcoholic spirit made from sugar-cane

rum[2] *adj*, *informal* strange, odd

rumba *noun* an Afro-Cuban dance in a square pattern

rumble *verb* make a low rolling noise like that of thunder *etc* ◇ *noun* a low rolling noise

rumbustious *noun* boisterous ◇ **rumbustiousness** *noun*

ruminant *noun* an animal, such as a cow, which chews the cud ◇ **ruminate** *verb* **1** chew the cud **2** be deep in thought ◇ **rumination** *noun* deep thought

rummage *verb* turn things over in search: *rummaging through the contents of the drawer* ◇ *noun* a thorough search

rummy *noun* a card game played with hands of seven cards

rumour *noun* a story passed from person to person which may not be true ◇ *verb* spread a rumour of

▤ *noun* talk, word, news, report, hearsay, gossip, whisper, story, grapevine, bush telegraph

rump *noun* **1** the hind part of an animal **2** the meat from this part

rumple *verb* **1** make untidy **2** crease

rumpus *noun* an uproar, a clamour

run *verb* (**runs**, **running**, **ran**, **run**) **1** move swiftly using very wide strides **2** enter in a race or as a candidate: *run for the presidency* **3** travel: *the train runs every day* **4** of water: flow **5** of a machine: work **6** spread (rapidly): *this colour is running* **7** continue, extend: *the programme runs for two hours* **8** operate (machinery *etc*) **9** organize, conduct (a business *etc*) **10** of the nose or eyes: discharge liquid or mucus ◇ *noun* **1** a trip in a vehicle **2** a spell of running **3** a continuous period: *a run of good luck* **4** a ladder in a stocking *etc* **5** free use (of): *the run of the house* **6** a single score in cricket **7** an enclosure for hens *etc* ◇ **run a risk** take a chance of loss, failure *etc* ◇ **run down 1** knock (someone) down with a vehicle **2** speak ill of ◇ **run-down** *adj* in poor health or condition ◇ **run into 1** bump into, collide with **2** meet accidentally ◇ **run-of-the-mill**

adj ordinary ◇**run out of** become short of, have no more of ◇**run over** knock down or pass over with a vehicle ◇**run up** accumulate (debts *etc*)

■ *verb* **1** career, tear, dash, hurry, rush, speed, bolt, dart, scoot, sprint, race **3** go, pass, move, proceed **4** flow, stream, pour, gush **5** function, work, operate, perform **7** last, continue, extend, reach, stretch, spread, range **9** head, lead, administer, direct, manage, superintend, supervise, oversee, control, regulate ◇ *noun* **1** drive, ride, spin, jaunt, excursion, outing, trip, journey **2** jog, gallop, race, sprint, spurt, dash, rush **3** sequence, series, string, chain, course ◇**run down 1** run over, knock over, hit, strike **2** criticize, belittle, disparage, denigrate, defame

runaway *noun* a person, animal or vehicle which runs away

■ escaper, escapee, fugitive, absconder, deserter, refugee

rune *noun* a letter of an early alphabet used in ancient writings ◇**runic** *adj* written in runes

rung[1] *noun* a step of a ladder

rung[2] *past participle* of **ring**

runnel *noun* a small stream

runner *noun* **1** someone who runs **2** a messenger **3** a rooting stem of a plant **4** a blade of a skate or sledge ◇**do a runner** *slang* leave without paying a bill ◇**runner-up** *noun* (*plural* **runners-up**) someone who comes second in a race or competition

■ **1** jogger, sprinter, athlete, competitor, participant **2** courier, messenger

running *noun* **1** the act of moving fast **2** management, control ◇*adj* **1** for use in running **2** giving out fluid: *running sore* **3** carried on continuously: *running commentary* ◇*adv* one after another: *three days running* ◇**in** (**out of**) **the running** having (or not having) a chance of success

■ *adj* **3** unbroken, uninterrupted, continuous, constant, perpetual, incessant, unceasing ◇ *adv* consecutively, in succession

runway *noun* a path for aircraft to take off from or land on

rupee *noun* the standard currency of India, Pakistan and Sri Lanka

rupture *noun* **1** a breaking, *eg* of a friendship **2** a tear in a part of the body ◇ *verb* break, burst

■ *noun* **1** separation, division, estrangement, schism, rift, disagreement, quarrel, falling-out **2** split, tear, burst, puncture, break, fracture, crack

rural *adj* of the country (*contrasted with*: **urban**)

■ country, rustic, pastoral, agricultural, agrarian

◪ urban

ruse *noun* a trick, a cunning plan

rush[1] *verb* **1** move quickly, hurry **2** make (someone) hurry **3** take (a fort *etc*) by a sudden attack ◇*noun* (*plural* **rushes**) **1** a quick, forward movement **2** a hurry

■ *verb* **1** hurry, hasten, bolt, dart, shoot, fly, tear, career, dash, race, run, sprint, scramble **2** press, push **3** stampede, charge ◇ *noun* **1** stampede, charge, dash, race, scramble, flow, surge **2** hurry, haste, urgency, speed, swiftness

rush[2] *noun* (*plural* **rushes**) a tall grass-like plant growing near water

rusk *noun* a hard dry biscuit like toast

russet *adj* reddish-brown ◇*noun* a type of apple of russet colour

rust *noun* a reddish-brown coating on metal, caused by air and moisture ◇*verb* form rust ◇**rustproof** *adj* resistant to rust

rustic *adj* **1** relating to the country **2** roughly made **3** simple, unsophisticated ◇*noun* someone who lives in the country ◇**rusticate** *verb* **1** live in the country **2** suspend (a student) from college or university ◇**rusticity** *noun* **1** country living **2** simplicity

■ *adj* **1** pastoral, sylvan, bucolic, countrified, country, rural **2** rough, crude, coarse, rude, unsophisticated, unrefined **3** plain, simple, unsophisticated, unrefined

◪ *adj* **1** urban **3** sophisticated, cultivated, polished

rustle *verb* **1** of silk *etc*: make a soft, whispering sound **2** steal (cattle) ◇ *noun* a soft, whispering sound ◇ **rustler** *noun* someone who steals cattle ◇ **rustle up** *informal* prepare quickly: *rustle up a meal*

rusty *adj* **1** covered with rust **2** *informal* showing lack of practice: *my French is rusty*

▤ **1** corroded, rusted, rust-covered, oxidized, tarnished **2** unpractised, weak, poor, deficient, dated, old-fashioned, outmoded, antiquated, stale

rut *noun* a deep track made by a wheel *etc* ◇ **rutted** *adj* full of ruts ◇ **in a rut** having a dull, routine way of life

ruthless *adj* without pity, cruel ◇ **ruthlessly** *adv* ◇ **ruthlessness** *noun*

▤ merciless, pitiless, hard-hearted, hard, heartless, unfeeling, callous, cruel, inhuman, brutal, savage, cut-throat, fierce, ferocious, vicious, relentless, unrelenting, inexorable, implacable, harsh, severe

▤ merciful, compassionate

RV *abbrev*, *US* recreational vehicle

rye *noun* a kind of grain, similar to barley ◇ **rye bread** bread made with flour from this grain ◇ **rye grass** a grass grown for cattle-feeding

Ss

S *abbrev* south; southern

s *abbrev* second(s)

Sabbath *noun* the day of the week regularly set aside for religious services and rest (among Muslims, Friday; Jews, Saturday; and Christians, Sunday)

sabbatical *noun* a period of paid leave from work

sable (*plural* **sable** or **sables**) *noun* a small weasel-like animal with dark brown or blackish fur ◇*adj* black or dark brown in colour

sabotage *noun* deliberate destruction of machinery, an organization *etc* by enemies or dissatisfied workers ◇*verb* destroy or damage deliberately

▣ *noun* vandalism, damage, impairment, disruption, wrecking, destruction ◇ *verb* damage, spoil, mar, disrupt, vandalize, wreck, destroy, thwart, scupper, cripple, incapacitate, disable, undermine, weaken

> Originally meaning the destruction of machinery by factory workers, from French *sabot* 'clog'

saboteur *noun* someone who carries out sabotage

sabre *noun*, *hist* a curved sword used by cavalry ◇**sabre-rattling** *noun* an obvious display of force to frighten an enemy

sac *noun* a bag containing a liquid, part of a plant or animal body

saccharin *noun* a very sweet substance used as a sugar substitute

saccharine *adj* over-sentimental or cloying

sacerdotal *noun* of a priest; priestly

sachet /'saʃeɪ/ *noun* 1 a small sealed packet containing powder or liquid, *eg* shampoo 2 a small bag to hold handkerchiefs *etc*

sack¹ *noun* 1 a large bag of coarse cloth for holding flour *etc* 2 (**the sack**) *informal* dismissal from your job ◇*verb*, *informal* dismiss from a job ◇**sackcloth** *noun* 1 coarse cloth for making sacks 2 a garment made of this worn as a sign of repentance ◇**sacking** *noun* sackcloth ◇**get the sack** *informal* be dismissed from a job

▣ *noun* 2 dismissal, discharge, one's cards, notice, *informal* the boot, *informal* the push, *informal* the elbow, *informal* the axe, *informal* the chop ◇ *verb* dismiss, fire, discharge, *informal* axe, lay off, make redundant

sack² *noun* the plundering of a captured town ◇*verb* plunder

sackbut *noun* an early wind instrument with a slide like a trombone

sacral *adj* of the sacrum

> ❗ Do not confuse with: **sacred**

sacrament *noun* a religious ceremony, *eg* baptism or communion ◇**sacramental** *adj*

sacred *adj* 1 holy 2 religious: *sacred music* 3 not to be challenged or breached: *sacred laws*

▣ 1 holy, divine, heavenly, blessed, hallowed, sanctified, consecrated 3 religious, devotional, ecclesiastical, priestly, saintly, godly, revered

> ❗ Do not confuse with: **sacral**

sacrifice *noun* 1 the offering of an animal killed for the purpose to a god 2 an animal *etc* offered to a god 3 the giving up of something for the benefit of another person, or to gain something more important 4 something given up for this purpose ◇*verb* 1 offer (an animal *etc*) as a sacrifice to a god 2 give up (something) for someone or something else ◇**sacrificial** *adj* of or for sacrifice ◇**sacrificially** *adv*

▣ *verb* 2 surrender, forfeit, relinquish, let

go, abandon, renounce, give up, forgo, offer

sacrilege *noun* the use of something holy in a blasphemous way ◇ **sacrilegious** *adj* ◇ **sacrilegiously** *adv*

■ blasphemy, profanity, heresy, desecration, profanation, violation, outrage, irreverence, disrespect

sacrosanct *adj* **1** very sacred **2** not to be harmed or touched

sacrum /ˈseɪkrəm/ *noun* a triangular bone forming part of the human pelvis

SAD *abbrev* seasonal affective disorder, a form of depression thought to be caused by lack of sunlight in winter

sad *adj* **1** sorrowful, unhappy **2** causing sorrow: *sad story* **3** *informal* pitiful, feeble ◇ **sadly** *adv*

■ **1** unhappy, sorrowful, tearful, grief-stricken, heavy-hearted, upset, distressed, miserable, low-spirited, downhearted, glum, long-faced, crestfallen, dejected, despondent, melancholy, depressed, low, gloomy **2** upsetting, distressing, painful, depressing, touching, poignant, heart-rending, tragic, grievous, lamentable, regrettable, unfortunate

Ea **1** happy, cheerful **2** fortunate, lucky

sadden *verb* make or become sad

■ upset, distress, grieve, depress, dismay, discourage, dishearten

Ea cheer, please, gratify, delight

saddle *noun* **1** a seat for a rider on the back of a horse or bicycle **2** a cut or joint of meat from the back of an animal ◇ *verb* put a saddle on (an animal) ◇ **saddle with** burden with: *saddled with debts*

■ **saddle with** burden, encumber, lumber, impose, tax, charge, *informal* load

saddlebag *noun* a bag attached to a horse or bicycle saddle

saddler *noun* a maker of saddles and harnesses

sadhu /ˈsɑːduː/ *noun* (*plural* **sadhus**) a Hindu ascetic

sadism /ˈseɪdɪzəm/ *noun* taking pleasure in cruelty to others ◇ **sadist** *noun* ◇ **sadistic** *adj*

■ **sadistic** cruel, inhuman, brutal, savage, vicious, merciless, pitiless, barbarous, bestial, unnatural, perverted

SAE or **sae** *abbrev* stamped addressed envelope

safari *noun* an expedition for observing or hunting wild animals ◇ **safari park** an enclosed area where wild animals are kept outdoors and on view to visitors

safe *adj* **1** unharmed **2** free from harm or danger **3** reliable, trustworthy ◇ *noun* a lockable box or cabinet for keeping money and valuables ◇ **safe and sound** unharmed

■ *adj* **1** unharmed, undamaged, unscathed, uninjured, unhurt, intact **2** secure, protected, guarded, impregnable, invulnerable, immune **3** tried, tested, sound, dependable, reliable, trustworthy

Ea *adj* **2** vulnerable, exposed **3** risky

safeguard *noun* anything that gives protection or security ◇ *verb* protect

■ *verb* protect, preserve, defend, guard, shield, screen, shelter, secure

Ea *verb* endanger, jeopardize

safety *noun* freedom from harm or danger ◇ *adj* giving protection or safety: *safety belt* ◇ **safety belt** a seatbelt ◇ **safety-pin** *noun* a curved pin in the shape of a clasp, with a guard covering its point

■ *noun* protection, refuge, sanctuary, shelter, cover, security, safeguard, immunity, impregnability, safeness

safflower *noun* an Indian thistle-like plant whose dried leaves produce a red dye

saffron *noun* a type of crocus from which is obtained a yellow food dye and flavouring agent

sag *verb* (**sags**, **sagging**, **sagged**) droop or sink in the middle

■ bend, give, bag, droop, hang, fall, drop, sink, dip, slump, flop, fail, flag, weaken, wilt

Ea bulge, rise

saga *noun* **1** an ancient story about heroes *etc* **2** a novel or series of novels about several generations of a family **3**

informal a long detailed story

sagacious *adj* very wise, quick at understanding ◇ **sagaciously** *adv* ◇ **sagacity** *noun*

sage[1] *noun* a type of herb with grey-green leaves which are used for flavouring

sage[2] *noun* a wise man ◇ *adj* wise ◇ **sagely** *adv*

sago *noun* a white starchy substance obtained from a palm-tree, often used in puddings

sahib /saːɪb/ *noun* a term of respect used in India

said *adj, formal* mentioned before: *the said shopkeeper* ◇ *past form* of **say**

sail *noun* **1** a sheet of canvas spread out to catch the wind and drive forward a ship or boat **2** a journey in a ship or boat **3** an arm of a windmill ◇ *verb* **1** travel in a ship or boat (with or without sails) **2** navigate or steer a ship or boat **3** begin a sea voyage **4** glide along easily ◇ **sailboard** *noun* a surfboard fitted with a mast and sail ◇ **set sail** set out on a sea voyage

🔲 *verb* **1** cruise, voyage **2** captain, skipper, pilot, navigate, steer **3** embark, set sail, weigh anchor, put to sea **4** glide, plane, sweep, float, skim, scud, fly

sailor *noun* **1** someone who sails **2** a member of a ship's crew

saint *noun* **1** a title conferred after death on a holy person by the Roman Catholic Church (*short form*: **St**) **2** a very good or kind person ◇ **saintly** *adj* very holy or very good

🔲 **saintly** godly, pious, devout, God-fearing, holy, religious, blessed, angelic, pure, spotless, innocent, blameless, sinless, virtuous, upright, worthy, righteous

🔳 **saintly** godless, unholy, wicked

Saint Bernard or **St Bernard** a breed of large dog, famous for its use in mountain rescues

sake[1] *noun* **1** cause, purpose: *for the sake of making money* **2** benefit, advantage: *for my sake*

🔲 **1** cause, reason **2** benefit, advantage,

good, welfare, wellbeing, gain, profit, behalf, interest, account, regard, respect

sake[2] /saːkɪ/ *noun* a Japanese alcoholic drink made from fermented rice

salaam *noun* a low bow with the right palm on the forehead, a form of Eastern greeting ◇ *verb* perform this greeting

salacious *adj* lustful, lecherous ◇ **salaciously** *adv* ◇ **salaciousness** *noun*

salad *noun* a dish of raw vegetables, *eg* lettuce, cucumber *etc* ◇ **salad cream** or **salad dressing** sauce for putting on salad ◇ **salad days** youth, early days

salamander *noun* a kind of small lizard-like animal

salami *noun* a type of highly seasoned sausage

salary *noun* (*plural* **salaries**) fixed wages regularly paid for work

🔲 pay, remuneration, emolument, *formal* stipend, wages, earnings, income

> Based on Latin *salarium*, ration money given to Roman legionaries for buying salt

sale *noun* **1** the exchange of anything for money **2** a selling of goods at reduced prices **3** an auction ◇ **saleroom** *noun* an auction room

🔲 **1** selling, marketing, vending, trade, traffic, dealing

salesman, saleswoman *noun* someone who sells or shows goods to customers

salient *adj* **1** outstanding, chief: *salient points of the speech* **2** pointing outwards: *salient angle*

🔲 **1** important, significant, chief, main, principal, striking, conspicuous, noticeable, obvious, prominent, outstanding, remarkable

saline *adj* containing salt, salty: *saline solution*

saliva *noun* the liquid that forms in the mouth to help digestion; spittle ◇ **salivary** *adj* of or producing saliva ◇ **salivate** *verb* **1** produce saliva **2** anticipate keenly

sallow *adj* of complexion: pale, yellowish

▣ yellowish, pale, pallid, wan, pasty, sickly, unhealthy, anaemic, colourless

sally *noun* (*plural* **sallies**) **1** a sudden rush forward **2** a trip, an excursion **3** a witty remark or retort ◇ *verb* (**sallies**, **sallying**, **sallied**) rush out suddenly ◇ **sally forth** go out, emerge

salmon *noun* (*plural* **salmon**) a large fish with yellowish-pink flesh

salmonella *noun* **1** a bacterium which causes food poisoning **2** food poisoning caused by these bacteria

salon *noun* **1** a shop in which hairdressing *etc* is done **2** a large room for receiving important guests **3** a gathering of such people

saloon *noun* **1** a covered-in motor-car **2** a passengers' dining-room in a ship **3** a public-house, a bar

salopettes *noun plural* quilted trousers held up by shoulder-straps, worn for skiing

salsa *noun* **1** a type of Latin American dance music **2** a spicy sauce made from tomatoes, chillies *etc*

salsify *noun* (*plural* **salsifies**) a plant with an edible root which tastes of oysters

salt *noun* **1** a substance used for seasoning, either mined from the earth or obtained from sea water **2** a substance formed from a metal and an acid **3** *informal* (also **old salt**) a sailor ◇ *adj* **1** containing salt: *salt water* **2** tasting of salt **3** preserved in salt: *salt herring* ◇ *verb* **1** sprinkle with salt **2** preserve with salt ◇ **salt cellar** a small container for salt

saltire /ˈsɔːltaɪə(r)/ *noun* the flag of Scotland, a white cross on a blue background

saltpetre or *US* **saltpeter** *noun* potassium nitrate

salty *adj* tasting of salt

▣ salt, salted, saline, briny, brackish, savoury, spicy, piquant, tangy

salubrious *adj* **1** clean, health-giving **2** pleasant, respectable

▣ **1** sanitary, hygienic, health-giving, healthy, wholesome

salutary *adj* **1** giving health or safety **2** beneficial, useful: *salutary lesson*

▣ **2** good, beneficial, advantageous, profitable, valuable, helpful, useful, practical, timely

salute *verb* **1** greet with words, an embrace *etc* **2** *military* raise the hand to the forehead to show respect to **3** honour or pay tribute to someone ◇ *noun* an act or way of saluting ◇ **salutation** *noun* an act of greeting

▣ *verb* **1** greet, acknowledge, recognize, wave, hail, address, nod, bow ◇ *noun* greeting, acknowledgement, recognition, wave, gesture, hail, address, handshake, nod, bow, tribute

salvage *noun* **1** goods saved from destruction or waste **2** the act of saving a ship's cargo, goods from a fire *etc* **3** payment made for this act ◇ *verb* save from loss or ruin

▣ *verb* save, preserve, conserve, rescue, recover, recuperate, retrieve, reclaim, redeem, repair, restore

▣ *verb* waste, abandon

salvation *noun* **1** an act, means or cause of saving: *the arrival of the police was his salvation* **2** the saving of humanity from sin

salve *noun* an ointment for healing or soothing ◇ *verb* soothe (pride, conscience *etc*)

▣ *noun* ointment, lotion, cream, balm, liniment, embrocation, medication, preparation, application

salver *noun* a small tray, often of silver

salvo *noun* (*plural* **salvos**) a great burst of gunfire, clapping etc

Samaritans *noun plural* an organization that provides a telephone helpline for people in distress

same *adj* **1** exactly alike, identical: *we both had the same feeling* **2** not different, unchanged: *he still looks the same* **3** mentioned before: *the same person came again* ◇ *pronoun* the thing just mentioned: *he drank lemonade and I drank the same* ◇ **sameness** *noun* lack of change or variety ◇ **samey** *adj* boringly similar ◇ **all the same** or **just the same** in spite of that ◇ **at the same time** still, however

■ *adj* **1** identical, comparable, matching, corresponding, unvarying, selfsame

◨ *adj* **1**, **2**, **3** different

samizdat *noun* underground literature, forbidden by *eg* the former Soviet Union

samosa *noun* a fried Indian pastry with a spicy filling

samovar *noun* a Russian tea-urn

sampan *noun* a kind of small boat used in Far Eastern countries

sample *noun* a small part extracted to show what the whole is like ◇ *verb* **1** test a sample of: *sample a cake* **2** mix an extract from one recording onto a different backing track

■ *noun* specimen, example, cross-section, model, pattern, swatch, piece, demonstration, *informal* demo, illustration, instance, sign, indication, foretaste ◇ *verb* **1** try, test, taste, sip, inspect, experience

sampler *noun* **1** someone who samples **2** a piece of needlework *etc* showing skill in different techniques

samurai *noun*, *hist* a member of the military caste in feudal Japan

sanatorium *noun* **1** a hospital, *esp* for people suffering from respiratory diseases **2** a sick room in a school *etc*

sanctify *verb* (**sanctifies**, **sanctifying**, **sanctified**) make holy or sacred ◇ **sanctification** *noun*

■ hallow, consecrate, bless, venerate, anoint, dedicate, cleanse, purify, exalt, canonize

◨ desecrate, defile

sanctimonious *adj* self-righteous, priggish

sanction *noun* **1** permission, approval **2** a penalty for breaking a law or rule **3** (**sanctions**) measures applied to force another country *etc* to stop a course of action ◇ *verb* approve, authorize

■ *noun* **1** authorization, permission, agreement, *informal* OK, approval, go-

ahead, *informal* green light, ratification, confirmation, support, backing, endorsement, licence, authority ◇ *verb* authorize, allow, permit, approve, ratify, confirm, support, back, endorse, underwrite, accredit, license, warrant

◨ *noun* **1** veto, disapproval ◇ *verb* veto, forbid, disapprove

sanctity *noun* holiness; sacredness

sanctuary *noun* (*plural* **sanctuaries**) **1** a sacred place **2** a place of safety from arrest or violence **3** a protected reserve for birds or animals

■ **1** church, temple, tabernacle, shrine, altar **2** asylum, refuge, protection, shelter, haven, retreat

sanctum *noun*: **inner sanctum** a very sacred or private room *etc*

sand *noun* **1** a mass of tiny particles of crushed rocks *etc* **2** (**sands**) a stretch of sand on the seashore ◇ *verb* **1** smooth or polish with sandpaper **2** sprinkle or mix with sand ◇ **sander** *noun* a power tool fitted with an abrasive disc, used for sanding wood *etc* ◇ **sand dune** a ridge of sand blown up by the wind ◇ **sand martin** a small bird which nests in sandy banks

sandal *noun* a shoe with straps to hold the sole onto the foot ◇ **sandalwood** *noun* a fragrant E Indian wood

sandbag *noun* a bag filled with sand, used as a protective barrier

sandpaper *noun* paper with a layer of sand glued to it for smoothing and polishing

sandshoe *noun* a light shoe with a rubber sole

sandstone *noun* a soft rock made of layers of sand pressed together

sandwich *noun* (*plural* **sandwiches**) two slices of bread, or a split roll, stuffed with a filling ◇ *verb* fit between two other objects

After the 18th-century Earl of *Sandwich*, said to have invented it to allow him to gamble without interruption for meals

sandy *adj* **1** covered with sand **2** like

sand **3** of hair: yellowish-red in colour

sane *adj* **1** of sound mind, not mad **2** sensible ◇ **sanely** *adv* ◇ **sanity** *noun*

■ **1** normal, rational, right-minded, *informal* all there, balanced, stable, sound **2** sober, level-headed, sensible, judicious, reasonable, moderate

🞱 **1** insane, mad, crazy, foolish

sang *past form* of sing

sangfroid /sɒŋ'frwɑ:/ *noun* coolness, composure

sanguinary *adj* bloodthirsty, bloody

> 🛈 Do not confuse: **sanguinary** and **sanguine**

sanguine *adj* **1** hopeful, cheerful **2** of a complexion: red, ruddy

sanitary *adj* **1** promoting good health, *esp* by having good drainage and sewage disposal **2** free from dirt, infection *etc* ◇ **sanitary towel** a pad of absorbent material worn to soak up menstrual blood

■ **1** hygienic, salubrious, healthy, wholesome **2** clean, pure, uncontaminated, unpolluted, aseptic, germ-free, disinfected, hygienic

sanitation *noun* arrangements for protecting health, *esp* drainage and sewage disposal

sanity *noun* **1** soundness of mind **2** mental health **3** good sense or judgement

■ **1** normality, rationality, reason, balance of mind, stability **3** soundness, level-headedness, judiciousness, sense, common sense

sank *past form* of sink

sanserif /san'serɪf/ *noun* a printing type without serifs

Sanskrit *noun* the ancient literary language of India

sap *noun* **1** the juice in plants, trees *etc* **2** *slang* a weakling, a fool **3** energy, vitality ◇ *verb* (**saps, sapping, sapped**) weaken (someone's strength *etc*)

■ *verb* bleed, drain, exhaust, weaken, undermine, deplete, reduce, diminish, impair

🞱 *verb* strengthen, build up, increase

sapling *noun* a young tree

saponify *verb* convert fats into soap

sapphire *noun* a precious stone of a deep blue colour

sappy *adj* **1** of a plant: full of sap **2** full of energy **3** *slang* foolishly weak or sentimental

Saracen *noun, hist* an Islamic opponent of the Crusaders; a Moor

sarcasm *noun* **1** a hurtful remark made in scorn **2** the use of such remarks

■ **2** irony, satire, mockery, sneering, derision, scorn, contempt, cynicism, bitterness

sarcastic *adj* **1** containing sarcasm **2** often using sarcasm, scornful ◇ **sarcastically** *adv*

■ **1, 2** ironical, satirical, mocking, taunting, sneering, derisive, scathing, disparaging, cynical, incisive, cutting, biting, caustic, mordant

sarcoma *noun* (*plural* **sarcomas** or **sarcomata**) a tumour

sarcophagus *noun* (*plural* **sarcophaguses** or **sarcophagi**) a stone coffin

sardine *noun* a young pilchard, often tinned in oil

sardonic *adj* bitter, mocking, scornful ◇ **sardonically** *adv*

■ mocking, jeering, sneering, derisive, scornful, sarcastic, biting, cruel, heartless, malicious, cynical, bitter

sari *noun* a long cloth wrapped round the waist and brought over the shoulder, traditionally worn by Indian women

sarky *adj, informal* sarcastic

sarnie *noun, informal* a sandwich

sarong *noun* a skirt traditionally worn by Malay men and women

sarsaparilla /sɑ:spə'rɪlə/ *noun* **1** a tropical American plant whose root is used in medicine **2** a soft drink flavoured with its root

sartorial *adj* relating to dress or clothes: *sartorial elegance*

SAS *abbrev* Special Air Service

sash[1] *noun* (*plural* **sashes**) a decorative band worn round the waist or over the shoulder

◨ belt, girdle, cummerbund, waistband

sash[2] *noun* (*plural* **sashes**) a sliding frame for window panes

sashimi *noun* a Japanese dish of thin slices of raw fish

sassafras *noun* a N American laurel tree whose bark is used as a stimulant

Sassenach *noun*, *Scot derog* an English person

sat *past form* of **sit**

Satan *noun* the Devil ◇ **satanic** *adj* of Satan, devilish ◇ **satanism** *noun* devil worship ◇ **satanist** *noun*

◨ **satanic** satanical, diabolical, devilish, demonic, fiendish, hellish, infernal, inhuman, malevolent, wicked, evil, black

◪ **satanic** holy, divine, godly, saintly, benevolent

satchel *noun* a small bag for carrying schoolbooks *etc*

sate *verb* satisfy fully; give more than enough to ◇ **sated** *adj*

satellite *noun* **1** a moon orbiting a planet **2** a man-made object fired into space to orbit a planet and aid communication *etc* **3** a state controlled by a more powerful neighbour ◇ **satellite television** the broadcasting of television programmes via satellite

satiate *verb* satisfy fully; to give more than enough to ◇ **satiety** *noun*

satin *noun* a closely woven silk with a glossy surface

satinwood *noun* a smooth kind of wood

satire *noun* **1** a piece of writing *etc* which makes fun of particular people or events **2** ridicule, scorn ◇ **satirical** *adj* ◇ **satirist** *noun* a writer of satire

◨ **1** skit, send-up, spoof, *informal* take-off, parody, caricature, travesty **2** ridicule, irony, sarcasm, wit, burlesque

satisfaction *noun* **1** the act of satisfying or being satisfied **2** a feeling of pleasure or comfort **3** something that satisfies **4** compensation for damage *etc*

◨ **2** gratification, contentment, happiness, pleasure, enjoyment, comfort, ease, well-being, fulfilment, self-satisfaction, pride **4** settlement, compensation, reimbursement, indemnification, damages, reparation, amends, redress, recompense, requital, payback, vindication

satisfactory *adj* **1** satisfying **2** fulfilling the necessary requirements ◇ **satisfactorily** *adv*

◨ **2** acceptable, passable, up to the mark, all right, *informal* OK, fair, average, competent, adequate, sufficient

satisfy *verb* (**satisfies**, **satisfying**, **satisfied**) **1** give enough (of something) to **2** please, make content **3** convince: *satisfied that he was innocent* **4** fulfil: *satisfy all our requirements*

◨ **1** quench, slake, sate, satiate, surfeit **2** gratify, indulge, appease, content, please, delight **3** assure, convince, persuade **4** meet, fulfil, discharge, settle, answer, fill

satsuma *noun* a small seedless orange

saturate *verb* **1** soak or immerse in water **2** cover or fill completely (with): *saturated with information* ◇ **saturation** *noun*

◨ **1** soak, steep, souse, drench, waterlog **2** impregnate, permeate, imbue, suffuse, fill

Saturday *noun* the seventh day of the week

saturnine *adj* gloomy, sullen

satyr /ˈsatə(r)/ *noun* a mythological creature, half man, half goat, living in the woods

sauce *noun* **1** a liquid seasoning added to food to improve flavour **2** *informal* cheek, impudence

saucepan *noun* a deep-sided cooking pan with a long handle

saucer *noun* a small, shallow dish for placing under a cup

saucy *adj* impudent, cheeky

◨ cheeky, impertinent, impudent, insolent, disrespectful, pert, forward, presumptuous, flippant

◪ polite, respectful

sauerkraut *noun* a dish of finely-cut cabbage pickled in salt *etc*

sauna *noun* a room filled with dry steam to induce sweating

saunter *verb* stroll about without hurrying ◊ *noun* a leisurely stroll

◨ *verb* stroll, amble, *informal* mosey, *informal* mooch, wander, *slang* ramble, meander

sausage *noun* minced meat seasoned and stuffed into a tube of animal gut *etc* ◊ **sausage roll** meat baked in a roll of pastry

sauté /'soʊteɪ/ *verb* (**sautés** or **sautées**, **sautéing** or **sautéeing**, **sautéed**) fry quickly in a small amount of oil or butter

savage *adj* **1** wild, untamed **2** fierce or furious: *a savage temper* **3** uncivilized **4** cruel ◊ *noun* **1** an uncivilized person **2** someone fierce or cruel ◊ *verb* attack very fiercely ◊ **savagely** *adv* ◊ **savagery** *noun*

◨ *adj* **1** wild, untamed, undomesticated, uncivilized, primitive **4** barbaric, barbarous, fierce, ferocious, vicious, beastly, cruel, inhuman, brutal, bloodthirsty, bloody, murderous, pitiless, merciless, ruthless, harsh ◊ *noun* **2** brute, beast, barbarian ◊ *verb* attack, bite, claw, tear, maul, mangle

savanna or **savannah** *noun* a grassy, treeless plain

save *verb* **1** bring out of danger, rescue **2** protect from harm, damage or loss **3** keep from spending or using: *saving money/saves time* **4** put money aside for the future ◊ *prep* except (for): *all the records were scratched save this one* ◊ **saving grace** a good quality that makes up for faults ◊ **save up** put money aside for future use

◨ *verb* **1** rescue, deliver, liberate, free, salvage, recover, reclaim **2** protect, guard, screen, shield, safeguard, spare, prevent, hinder **3** economize, cut back, conserve, preserve, keep, retain, hold, reserve, store, set aside, put by, hoard, *informal* stash

◨ *verb* **3** spend, squander, waste, discard

savings *noun plural* money put aside for the future

saviour *noun* **1** someone who saves others from harm or evil **2** (**the Saviour**) *Christianity* Christ

◨ **1** rescuer, deliverer, redeemer, liberator, emancipator, guardian, protector, defender, champion

savour or *US* **savor** *noun* **1** characteristic taste or flavour **2** an interesting quality ◊ *verb* **1** taste or smell of **2** taste with enjoyment **3** have a trace or suggestion (of): *his reaction savours of jealousy* **4** experience, relish

savoury or *US* **savory** *adj* **1** having a pleasant taste or smell **2** salt or sharp in flavour; not sweet ◊ *noun* (*plural* **savouries**) a savoury dish or snack

◨ *adj* **1** tasty, appetizing, delicious, mouthwatering, luscious, palatable **2** salty, spicy, aromatic, piquant, tangy

savoy *noun* a type of winter cabbage

savvy *adj*, *slang* wise, shrewd ◊ *verb* (**savvies**, **savvying**, **savvied**) understand or know

saw[1] *past form* of **see**

saw[2] *noun* a tool with a toothed edge for cutting wood *etc* ◊ *verb* (**saws, sawing, sawn, sawed**) cut with a saw ◊ **sawdust** *noun* a dust of fine fragments of wood, made in sawing ◊ **sawmill** *noun* a mill where wood is sawn up

sax *noun*, *informal* a saxophone

saxifrage *noun* a type of rock plant

Saxon *noun*, *hist* one of a Germanic people who invaded Britain in the 5th century

saxophone *noun* a wind instrument with a curved metal tube and keys for the fingers ◊ **saxophonist** *noun* a player of the saxophone

say *verb* (**says, saying, said**) **1** speak, utter: *why don't you say 'Yes'?* **2** express in words, state: *they said they knew him* ◊ *noun* **1** the right to speak: *no say in the matter* **2** the opportunity to speak: *I've had my say* ◊ **I say!** *interj* **1** expressing surprise or protest **2** used to try to attract attention ◇ **that is to say** in other words

■ *verb* **1** express, utter, voice, pronounce, indicate **2** tell, instruct, order, communicate, convey, intimate, announce, declare, state, assert, affirm, maintain, claim, allege, suggest, signify, reveal, disclose, divulge

saying *noun* something often said; a proverb

■ adage, proverb, dictum, precept, axiom, aphorism, maxim, motto, slogan, phrase, expression, quotation

scab *noun* **1** a crust formed over a sore **2** any of several diseases of animals or plants **3** *informal* a blackleg

scabbard *noun* the sheath in which the blade of a sword is kept

scabby *adj* **1** covered in scabs **2** *informal* disgusting, revolting

scabies *noun* an itchy skin disease caused by a mite which bores under the skin

scabrous *adj* **1** rough, harsh **2** indecent, rude

scaffold *noun* **1** a temporary platform for *eg* performers **2** (**the scaffold**) a platform on which people are put to death

scaffolding *noun* a framework of poles and platforms used by people doing repairs on a building *etc*

scald *verb* **1** burn with hot liquid or steam **2** heat (milk *etc*) just short of boiling point ◇ *noun* a burn caused by hot liquid or steam

scale¹ *noun* **1** a set of regularly spaced marks for measurement on a thermometer *etc* **2** a series or system of increasing values: *salary scale* **3** *music* a group of notes going up or down in order **4** the measurements of a map compared with the actual size of the area shown: *drawn to the scale 1:50000* **5** size or extent: *manufacture on a small scale* ◇ *verb* **1** climb up **2** (**scale up** or **scale down**) change something's size according to scale

■ *noun* **2** progression, order, hierarchy, ranking **5** proportion, measure, degree, extent ◇ *verb* **1** climb, ascend,

mount, clamber, scramble, shin up

scale² *noun* **1** one of a number of small, thin flakes forming a covering on the skin of a fish or snake **2** a crusty white deposit caused by hard water ◇ *verb* **1** clear of scales **2** remove in thin layers **3** become covered in scale ◇ **scaly** *adj*

scale³ *noun*: **scales** a weighing machine or device

scallion *noun* a spring onion

scallop *noun* a shellfish with a pair of hinged fan-shaped shells ◇ **scalloped** *adj* of an edge: cut into curves or notches

scallywag *noun*, *informal* a rogue

scalp *noun* **1** the outer covering of the skull **2** the skin and hair on top of the head ◇ *verb* cut the scalp from

scalpel *noun* a small, thin-bladed knife, used in surgery

scam *noun*, *informal* a swindle, a trick

scamp *noun* a rascal

■ rogue, rascal, *informal* scallywag, monkey, imp, devil

scamper *verb* **1** run about playfully **2** run off in haste

■ **1** romp, frolic, gambol **2** scuttle, scurry, scoot, dart, dash, run, sprint, rush, hurry, hasten, fly

scampi *noun plural* large prawns cooked for eating

scan *verb* (**scans**, **scanning**, **scanned**) **1** examine carefully **2** read quickly, skim over **3** count the beats in a line of poetry **4** of poetry: have the correct number of beats **5** pass an X-ray, ultrasonic wave *etc* over ◇ *noun* an act of scanning

■ *verb* **1** examine, scrutinize, study, search, survey, sweep, investigate, check **2** skim, glance at, flick through, thumb through ◇ *noun* screening, examination, scrutiny, search, probe, check, investigation

scandal *noun* **1** something disgraceful or shocking **2** talk or gossip about people's (supposed) misdeeds

■ **1** discredit, dishonour, disgrace, sleaze, shame, embarrassment, ignominy **2** outcry, uproar, furore, gossip, rumours, smear, dirt

scandalize *verb* shock, horrify

▣ shock, horrify, appal, dismay, disgust, repel, revolt, offend, affront, outrage

scandalmonger *noun* someone who spreads gossip or scandal

scandalous *adj* 1 shameful, disgraceful 2 containing scandal ◇ **scandalously** *adv*

▣ 1 shocking, appalling, atrocious, abominable, monstrous, unspeakable, outrageous, disgraceful, shameful 2 defamatory, scurrilous, slanderous, libellous

scanner *noun* a machine which scans

scansion *noun* 1 scanning of poetry 2 division of verse into metrical feet

scant *adj* not plentiful, hardly enough: *pay scant attention*

scanty *adj* little or not enough in amount: *scanty clothing* ◇ **scantily** *adv*

▣ deficient, short, inadequate, insufficient, scant, little, limited, restricted, narrow, poor, meagre, insubstantial, thin, skimpy, sparse, bare

▣ adequate, sufficient, ample, plentiful, substantial

scapegoat *noun* someone who takes the blame for the wrongdoing of others

> Literally 'escape goat', after an ancient Jewish ritual of transferring the people's sins to a goat which was afterwards let free in the wilderness

scapula *noun* (*plural* **scapulas** or **scapulae**) the shoulderblade

scar *noun* 1 the mark left by a wound or sore 2 a mark, a blemish ◇ *verb* (**scars**, **scarring**, **scarred**) mark with a scar

▣ *noun* 2 mark, lesion, wound, injury, blemish, stigma ◇ *verb* mark, disfigure, spoil, damage, brand, stigmatize

scarab *noun* a beetle regarded as sacred by the ancient Egyptians

scarce *adj* 1 not plentiful, not enough 2 rare, seldom found ◇ **make yourself scarce** go, run away

▣ 1 sparse, scanty, insufficient, deficient, lacking 2 few, rare, infrequent, uncommon, unusual

scarcely *adv* 1 only just, barely: *could scarcely hear* 2 hardly ever: *he's scarcely ever ill* 3 not really: *you can scarcely expect me to eat that*

scarcity *noun* (*plural* **scarcities**) want, shortage

▣ lack, shortage, dearth, deficiency, insufficiency, paucity, sparseness, scantiness

scare *verb* 1 drive away with fear 2 startle, frighten ◇ *noun* a sudden fright or alarm

▣ *verb* 2 frighten, startle, alarm, dismay, daunt, intimidate, unnerve, threaten, menace, terrorize, shock, panic, terrify

scarecrow *noun* a figure set up to scare birds away from crops

scaremonger *noun* someone who spreads (unnecessary) panic or alarm ◇ **scaremongering** *noun*

scarey *another spelling* of **scary**

scarf *noun* (*plural* **scarves** or **scarfs**) a strip of material worn round the neck, shoulders or head

scarlatina *noun* a mild form of scarlet fever

scarlet *noun* a bright red colour ◇ *adj* bright red ◇ **scarlet fever** an infectious illness, causing a rash and fever

scarper *verb, slang* run away

scary or **scarey** *adj, informal* frightening

▣ frightening, alarming, daunting, intimidating, disturbing, shocking, horrifying, terrifying, hair-raising, bloodcurdling, spine-chilling, chilling, creepy, eerie, *informal* spooky

scat *interj, informal* go away!

scathing *adj* cruel, hurtful: *scathing remark*

▣ sarcastic, scornful, critical, trenchant, mordant, cutting, biting, caustic, acid, vitriolic, bitter, harsh, brutal, savage, unsparing

▣ complimentary

scatological *adj* full of references to faeces or defecation: *scatological humour*

scatter *verb* 1 throw loosely about; sprinkle 2 spread widely 3 flee in all directions ◊ **scattered** adj thrown or spread about widely ◊ **scattering** noun a small amount thinly spread or scattered

▤ **1** sprinkle, sow, strew, fling, shower **2** broadcast, disseminate, spread, disperse, dispel, dissipate

scatterbrain noun, informal someone who is disorganized or frequently forgets things

scatty adj, informal forgetful or disorganized

scavenge verb forage, esp for food ◊ **scavenger** noun an animal which feeds on dead flesh

SCE abbrev Scottish Certificate of Education

scenario noun (plural **scenarios**) **1** a scene-by-scene outline of a play, film etc **2** a possible series of events

▤ **1** outline, synopsis, summary, résumé, storyline, plot **2** projection, hypothesis

> **❗** Do not confuse with: **scene**

scene noun **1** the place where something happens: scene of the accident **2** a view, a landscape **3** a division of a play or opera **4** an area of activity: the music scene **5** an embarrassing public show of emotion: don't create a scene

▤ **1** place, area, spot, locale, site, situation, position, whereabouts, location, locality, environment, milieu, setting **2** landscape, panorama, view, vista **3** episode, incident, part, division, act **5** fuss, commotion, informal to-do, performance, drama, exhibition

scenery noun **1** the general appearance of a stretch of country **2** items making up a theatre or film set

▤ **1** landscape, terrain, panorama, view, vista, outlook **2** scene, background, setting, backdrop, set

scenic adj **1** of scenery **2** picturesque

▤ **2** picturesque, attractive, pretty, beautiful, grand, striking, impressive, spectacular, breathtaking, awe-inspiring

▰ **2** dull, dreary

scent verb **1** discover by the smell **2** have a suspicion of, sense: scent danger **3** give a pleasant smell to: roses scented

the air ◊ noun **1** an odour, a smell **2** the trail of smell used to track an animal etc **3** perfume

sceptic or US **skeptic** /'skɛptɪk/ noun someone who doubts what they are told ◊ **sceptical** adj unwilling to believe, doubtful ◊ **sceptically** adv ◊ **scepticism** noun

▤ **sceptical** doubting, doubtful, unconvinced, unbelieving, disbelieving, questioning, distrustful, mistrustful, hesitating, dubious, suspicious, scoffing, cynical, pessimistic

> **❗** Do not confuse with: **septic**

sceptre /'sɛptə(r)/ noun an ornamental rod carried by a monarch on ceremonial occasions

schadenfreude /'ʃɑːdənfrɔɪdə/ noun pleasure in the misfortunes of others

schedule /'ʃɛdʒuːl/ or /'skɛdʒuːl/ noun **1** the time set for doing something: I'm two weeks behind schedule **2** a list of planned events ◊ verb **1** put into a schedule **2** plan, arrange

▤ noun **1** itinerary, plan, scheme, list, inventory, catalogue **2** timetable, programme, agenda, diary, calendar ◊ verb **1** timetable, time, table, programme **2** plan, organize, arrange, appoint, assign

schema /'skiːmə/ noun (plural **schemata**) a scheme, a plan

schematic adj according to a plan ◊ **schematically** adv

▤ diagrammatic, representational, symbolic, illustrative, graphic

scheme /skiːm/ noun **1** a plan, a systematic arrangement **2** a dishonest or crafty plan ◊ verb make schemes, plot ◊ **scheming** adj crafty, cunning

▤ noun **1** programme, schedule, plan, project, idea, proposal, proposition, suggestion, draft, outline **2** intrigue, plot, conspiracy, device, stratagem, ruse, ploy ◊ verb plot, conspire, connive, collude, intrigue, machinate, manipulate, pull strings, mastermind, plan, contrive

scherzo /'skɛətsoʊ/ noun (plural **scherzi** or **scherzos**) music a lively movement in triple time

schism /'skɪzəm/ *noun* a breaking away from the main group

schist /ʃɪst/ *noun* a type of rock that splits easily into layers

schizo /'skɪtsoʊ/ *noun* (*plural* **schizos**) *adj*, *slang* (a) schizophrenic

schizophrenia /skɪtsə'friːnɪə/ *noun* a mental illness involving a complete change in personality and behaviour ◇ **schizophrenic** *noun* & *adj* (someone) suffering from schizophrenia

schlock *noun*, *informal* tacky or shoddy goods ◇ **schlocky** *adj*

schmaltz *noun*, *informal* sentimentality ◇ **schmaltzy** *adj*

schmuck *noun*, *informal* an idiot, a fool

schnapps *noun* a German liqueur

schnitzel *noun* a veal cutlet

scholar *noun* **1** someone of great learning **2** a pupil, a student **3** someone who has been awarded a scholarship ◇ **scholastic** *adj* of schools or scholars
▤ **1** academic, intellectual, *informal* egghead, authority, expert, *informal* boffin

scholarly *adj* showing or having knowledge and high intelligence ◇ **scholarliness** *noun*
▤ learned, erudite, lettered, academic, scholastic, school, intellectual, highbrow, bookish, studious, knowledgeable, well-read, analytical, scientific

scholarship *noun* **1** learning **2** a sum of money given to help an outstanding student to carry on further studies

school[1] *noun* **1** a place for teaching, *esp* children **2** a group of artists *etc* who share the same ideas ◇ *verb* **1** educate in a school **2** train by practice ◇ **schooling** *noun* **1** education in a school **2** training
▤ *verb* **1** educate, teach, instruct, tutor, coach, train, discipline, drill, verse, prime

school[2] *noun* a group of fish, whales *etc* swimming together

schoolteacher *noun* a teacher at a school

schooner *noun* **1** a two-masted sailing ship **2** a large sherry glass **3** *US* & *Austral* a large beer glass

schwa *noun* an unstressed vowel sound, written (ə)

sciatic /saɪ'atɪk/ *adj* relating to the hip

sciatica /saɪ'atɪkə/ *noun* severe pain in the upper part of the leg

science *noun* **1** knowledge obtained by observation of, and experiment with, natural phenomena **2** a branch of this knowledge, *eg* chemistry, physics, biology *etc* **3** an area of knowledge obtained by formal principles: *political science* ◇ **science fiction** stories dealing with future life on earth, space travel, other planets *etc*

Sciences include:
acoustics, aerodynamics, aeronautics, agricultural science, agriscience, anatomy, anthropology, archaeology, astronomy, astrophysics, behavioural science, biochemistry, biology, biophysics, botany, chemistry, chemurgy, climatology, computer science, cybernetics, diagnostics, dietetics, domestic science, dynamics, earth science, ecology, economics, electrodynamics, electronics, engineering, entomology, environmental science, food science, genetics, geochemistry, geographical science, geology, geophysics, graphology, hydraulics, information technology, inorganic chemistry, life science, linguistics, macrobiotics, materials science, mathematics, mechanical engineering, mechanics, medical science, metallurgy, meteorology, microbiology, mineralogy, morphology, natural science, nuclear physics, organic chemistry, ornithology, pathology, pharmacology, physics, physiology, political science, psychology, radiochemistry, robotics, sociology, space technology, telecommunications, thermodynamics, toxicology, ultrasonics, veterinary science, zoology

scientific adj **1** of science **2** done according to the methods of science ◇ **scientifically** adv

■ **2** methodical, systematic, controlled, regulated, analytical, mathematical, exact, precise, accurate

scientist noun someone who studies one or more branches of science

sci fi abbrev, informal science fiction

scimitar noun a sword with a short curved blade

scintillate verb **1** sparkle **2** show brilliant wit etc ◇ **scintillating** adj

■ **scintillating** sparkling, glittering, flashing, bright, shining, brilliant, dazzling, exciting, stimulating, lively, animated, vivacious, ebullient, witty

ᴇᴀ **scintillating** dull

scion /'saɪən/ noun **1** a cutting for grafting on another plant **2** a young member of a family **3** a descendant

scissors noun plural a cutting instrument with two hinged blades

sclerosis noun hardening, esp of the arteries

scoff verb **1** express scorn **2** (**scoff at**) make fun of, mock

■ **2** mock, ridicule, poke fun, taunt, tease, slang rib, jeer

scold verb blame or rebuke with angry words ◇ noun a bad-tempered person ◇ **scolding** noun

■ verb chide, informal tell off, informal tick off, reprimand, reprove, rebuke, take to task, admonish, upbraid, reproach, blame, censure, lecture, nag

ᴇᴀ verb praise, commend

scone noun a small plain cake made with flour and water

scoop noun **1** a hollow instrument used for lifting loose material, water etc **2** an exclusive news story ◇ verb lift or dig out with a scoop

■ noun **1** ladle, spoon, dipper, bailer, bucket, shovel **2** exclusive, coup, inside story, revelation, exposé, sensation, informal latest

scoosh or **skoosh** verb squirt ◇ noun **1** a squirt **2** a fizzy drink

scooter noun **1** a two-wheeled toy vehicle pushed along by foot **2** a low-powered motor-cycle

scope noun **1** opportunity or room to do something: scope for improvement **2** extent, range: outside the scope of this dictionary

■ **1** room, space, capacity, latitude, leeway, freedom, liberty, opportunity **2** range, compass, field, area, sphere, ambit, terms of reference, confines, reach, extent, span, breadth

scorch verb **1** burn slightly, singe **2** dry up with heat

scorching adj **1** burning, singeing **2** very hot **3** harsh, severe: scorching criticism

■ **2** burning, boiling, baking, roasting, sizzling, blistering, sweltering, torrid, tropical, searing

score noun **1** the total number of points gained in a game **2** a gash, a notch **3** a set of twenty **4** (**scores**) a great many: scores of people **5** a reason, account: don't worry on that score **6** a written piece of music showing separate parts for voices and instruments **7** the music from a film or play **8** an account, a debt: settle old scores ◇ verb **1** gain (points) **2** keep a note of points gained in a game **3** mark with lines or notches **4** compose music for a film or play ◇ **score out** cross out

■ noun **1** result, total, sum, tally, points, marks **2** scratch, line, groove, mark, nick, notch ◇ verb **1** notch up, make **2** record, register, chalk up, notch up, count, total **3** scratch, scrape, graze, mark, groove, gouge, cut, incise, engrave, indent, nick, slash

scorn verb **1** look down on, despise **2** refuse (help etc) because of pride ◇ noun despisal, contempt

■ noun contempt, scornfulness, disdain, sneering, derision, mockery, ridicule, sarcasm, disparagement, disgust

ᴇᴀ noun admiration, respect

scornful adj full of scorn and contempt ◇ **scornfully** adv

■ contemptuous, disdainful, supercilious, haughty, arrogant, sneering, scoffing, derisive, mocking, jeering, sarcastic, scathing, disparaging, insulting, slighting, dismissive

scorpion *noun* a spider-like invertebrate with a poisonous sting in its tail

scotch *verb* stamp out, suppress

Scotch *adj* of things (but not *usu* people): Scottish ◊ *noun* whisky ◊ **Scotch tape** *US, trademark* adhesive tape ◊ **Scotch terrier** a breed of small rough-coated dog

scot-free *adj* unhurt; unpunished

scoundrel *noun* a rascal

scour *verb* **1** clean by hard rubbing; scrub **2** search thoroughly
■ **1** scrape, abrade, rub, polish, burnish, scrub **2** search, hunt, comb, drag, ransack, rummage, forage, rake

scourge *noun* **1** a whip **2** a cause of great suffering ◊ *verb* **1** whip, lash **2** afflict, cause to suffer
■ *noun* **2** affliction, misfortune, torment, terror, bane, evil, curse, plague, penalty, punishment

Scouse *noun, Brit* a native or inhabitant of Liverpool

scout *noun* **1** a guide or spy sent ahead to bring back information **2** (**Scout**) a member of the Scout Association ◊ *verb* investigate or act as a spy
■ *noun* **1** spy, reconnoitre, vanguard, outrider, escort, lookout, recruiter, spotter ◊ *verb* spy out, reconnoitre, explore, investigate, check out, survey, *slang* case, spy, snoop, search, seek, hunt, probe, look, watch, observe

scowl *verb* wrinkle the brows in displeasure or anger ◊ *noun* a frown

Scrabble *noun, trademark* a word-building game

scrabble *verb* scratch or grope about

scraggy *adj* **1** long and thin **2** uneven, rugged
■ **1** scrawny, skinny, thin, lean, lanky, bony, angular, gaunt, undernourished, emaciated, wasted

scram *exclam* go away!

scramble *verb* **1** struggle to seize something before others **2** crawl or climb on hands and knees **3** mix or toss together: *scramble eggs* **4** jumble up (a message) to make it unintelligible without decoding ◊ *noun* **1** a rush and struggle to get something **2** a motorcycle race over rough country
■ *verb* **1** rush, hurry, hasten, run, push, jostle, struggle, strive, vie, contend **2** clamber, crawl, shuffle, scrabble, grope ◊ *noun* **1** rush, hurry, race, dash, hustle, bustle, commotion, confusion, muddle, struggle, free-for-all, mêlée

scrap *noun* (**scraps**, **scrapping**, **scrapped**) **1** a small piece, a fragment **2** *informal* a fight **3** parts of a car *etc* no longer required: *sold as scrap* **4** (**scraps**) small pieces, odds and ends ◊ *verb* **1** abandon as useless **2** *informal* fight, quarrel ◊ **scrapbook** *noun* a blank book in which to stick pictures *etc* ◊ **scrap metal** metal for melting and re-using
■ *noun* **1** bit, piece, fragment, part, fraction, crumb, morsel, bite, mouthful, sliver, shred, snippet, grain, particle, mite, trace, vestige, remnant **2** fight, scuffle, brawl, *informal* dust-up ◊ *verb* **1** discard, throw away, jettison, shed, abandon, drop, dump, *slang* ditch, write off

scrape *verb* **1** rub and mark with something sharp **2** drag or rub against or across a surface with a harsh grating sound **3** (with **up** or **together**) collect (money *etc*) with difficulty ◊ *noun* **1** an act of scraping **2** a mark or sound made by scraping **3** *informal* a difficult situation ◊ **scrape through** only just avoid failure
■ *verb* **1** grate, grind, rasp, file, abrade, scour, rub, clean, remove, erase, scrabble, claw, scratch, graze, skin, bark, scuff

scrapheap *noun* a heap of old metal *etc*, a rubbish heap ◊ **on the scrapheap** no longer needed

scrapie *noun* a disease of sheep

scrappy *adj* made up of odd scraps, not well put together ◊ **scrappily** *adv*
■ bitty, disjointed, piecemeal, fragmentary, incomplete, sketchy, superficial, slapdash, slipshod

scratch *verb* **1** draw a sharp point across the surface of **2** mark by doing this **3** tear or dig with claws, nails *etc* **4** rub with the nails to relieve or stop itching **5** withdraw from a competition ◇ *noun* (*plural* **scratches**) **1** an act of scratching **2** a mark or sound made by scratching **3** a slight wound ◇ *adj* **1** *golf* too good to be allowed a handicap **2** of a team: made up of players hastily put together ◇ **scratch the surface** deal with the superficial aspects of an issue ◇ **come up to scratch** be satisfactory ◇ **start from scratch** start from nothing, right at the beginning

■ *verb* **1** claw, scrape **2** score, mark, cut, incise, etch, engrave **3** claw, gouge, graze, gash, lacerate ◇ *noun* **2** mark, line **3** scrape, abrasion, graze

scrawl *verb* write or draw untidily or hastily ◇ *noun* **1** untidy, hasty or bad writing **2** something scrawled

scrawny *adj* thin, skinny

■ scraggy, skinny, thin, lean, lanky, angular, bony, underfed, undernourished, emaciated, wasted

◫ fat, plump

scream *verb* utter a shrill, piercing cry as in pain, fear *etc*; shriek ◇ *noun* a shrill cry

■ *verb & noun* shriek, screech, cry, shout, yell, bawl, roar, howl, wail, squeal, yelp

scree *noun* loose stones covering a steep mountain side

screech *verb* utter a harsh, shrill and sudden cry ◇ *noun* a harsh shrill cry

screed *noun* a long boring speech or letter

screen *noun* **1** a flat covered framework to shelter from view or protect from heat, cold *etc* **2** something that shelters from wind, danger, difficulties *etc* **3** the surface on which cinema films are projected **4** the surface on which a television picture, or computer data, appears ◇ *verb* **1** shelter, hide **2** sort out (the good from the bad) by testing **3** conduct examinations on someone to test for disease **4** show on a screen ◇ **screen off** hide behind, or separate by, a screen

■ *noun* **1** partition, divider, shield, guard, cover, shelter, shade, awning, canopy ◇ *verb* **1** shield, protect, safeguard, defend, guard, cover, mask, veil, cloak, shroud, hide, conceal, shelter, shade **4** show, present, broadcast

screensaver *noun* a (moving) image displayed on the screen when a computer is not in use

screw *noun* **1** a nail with a slotted head and a winding groove or ridge (called the **thread**) on its surface **2** a kind of propeller (a **screw-propeller**) with spiral blades, used in ships and aircraft **3** a turn or twist (of a screw *etc*) **4** *slang* a prison officer **5** *coarse slang* an act of sexual intercourse ◇ *verb* **1** fasten or tighten with a screw **2** fix (*eg* a stopper) in place with a twisting movement **3** twist, turn round *etc* **4** twist up, crumple, pucker **5** *informal* swindle, cheat **6** *coarse slang* have sexual intercourse (with) ◇ **screwdriver** *noun* a tool for turning screws

scribble *verb* **1** write carelessly **2** make untidy or meaningless marks with a pencil *etc* ◇ *noun* **1** careless writing **2** meaningless marks, a doodle

■ *verb* **1** write, pen, jot, dash off, scrawl **2** doodle

scribe *noun*, *hist* **1** a clerk who copied out manuscripts **2** a Jewish teacher of law

scrimp *verb* be sparing or stingy with money: *scrimping and saving for a holiday*

script *noun* **1** the text of a play, talk *etc* **2** handwriting like print **3** a simple program used *esp* on web pages

■ **1** text, lines, words, dialogue, screenplay, libretto, book **2** writing, handwriting, hand, longhand, calligraphy, letters, manuscript, copy

scripture *noun* **1** sacred writings **2** (**Scripture**) the Christian Bible

scrofula *noun* a disease of the lymph nodes in the neck

scroll *noun* **1** a piece of paper containing text, rolled up **2** a decorative spiral shape

scrotum *noun* (*plural* **scrotums** or **scrota**) the bag of skin enclosing the testicles

scrounge *verb, slang* **1** cadge **2** get by begging ◇ *noun* an attempt to beg or cadge: *on the scrounge* ◇ **scrounger** *noun*

◼ *verb* **1** cadge, beg, sponge

scrub[1] *verb* (**scrubs, scrubbing, scrubbed**) rub hard in order to clean

◼ *verb* rub, brush, clean, wash, cleanse, scour

scrub[2] *noun* countryside covered with low bushes

scruff *noun* **1** the back of the neck **2** a dirty, untidy person

scruffy *adj* untidy

◼ untidy, messy, unkempt, dishevelled, bedraggled, tattered, shabby, worn-out, ragged, slovenly

◼ tidy, well-dressed

scrum *noun, rugby* a struggle for the ball by the forwards of the opposing sides bunched together

scrumple *verb* crush, crumple

scrumptious *adj, informal* delicious

scrunch *verb* crumple

scruple *noun* **1** doubt over what is right or wrong that keeps someone from doing something **2** (**scruples**) standards, morals ◇ *verb* hesitate because of a scruple

◼ *noun* **1** reluctance, hesitation, doubt, qualm, misgiving, uneasiness, difficulty, perplexity

scrupulous *adj* **1** careful over the smallest details **2** principled, having morals

◼ **1** painstaking, meticulous, conscientious, careful, rigorous, strict, exact, precise, minute, nice **2** principled, moral, ethical, honourable, upright

scrutinize *verb* examine very closely

◼ examine, inspect, study, scan, analyse, sift, investigate, probe, search, explore

scrutiny *noun* (*plural* **scrutinies**) careful examination, a close look

SCSI /ˈskʌzɪ/ *abbrev, comput* small computer systems interface, a method of connecting a PC to peripheral devices

scuba *noun* breathing apparatus used by skin-divers in **scuba diving**

scud *verb* (**scuds, scudding, scudded**) move or sweep along quickly: *scudding waves*

scuff *verb* mark or graze by dragging

◼ scrape, scratch, graze, abrade, rub, brush, drag

scuffle *noun* a confused fight

◼ fight, *informal* scrap, tussle, brawl, fray, set-to, disturbance, affray

scull *noun* a short oar ◇ *verb* move (a boat) with a pair of these or with one oar worked at the back of the boat

scullery *noun* (*plural* **sculleries**) a room for rough kitchen work

sculpt *verb* form by carving or modelling

◼ sculpture, carve, chisel, hew, cut, model, mould, cast, form, shape, fashion

sculptor, sculptress *noun* an artist who carves or models figures in wood, stone, clay *etc* ◇ **sculpture** *noun* **1** the art of the sculptor or sculptress **2** a piece of their work

scum *noun* **1** foam that rises to the surface of liquids **2** the most worthless part of anything: *the scum of the earth*

◼ **1** froth, foam, film **2** dross, dregs, rubbish, trash

scunner *noun, Scot* a nuisance, a pest

scupper *verb* put an end to, ruin: *scupper his chances* ◇ *noun* a hole in the side of a ship to drain water from the deck

scurf *noun* small flakes of dead skin (*esp* on the scalp)

scurrilous *adj* insulting, abusive: *a scurrilous attack*

◼ rude, vulgar, coarse, foul, obscene, indecent, salacious, offensive, abusive, insulting, disparaging, defamatory, slanderous, libellous, scandalous

◼ polite, courteous, complimentary

scurry *verb* (**scurries, scurrying, scurried**) hurry along, scamper

◼ dash, rush, hurry, hasten, bustle, scramble, scuttle, scamper, scoot, dart, run, sprint, trot, race, fly

scurvy *noun* a type of disease caused by a lack of vitamin C

scuttle *noun* **1** a fireside container for

coal **2** an opening with a lid in a ship's deck or side ◇ *verb* **1** make a hole in (a ship) in order to sink it **2** hurry along, scamper

scuzzy *adj, slang* seedy, sleazy; grubby

scythe /saɪð/ *noun* a large curved blade, on a long handle, for cutting grass *etc* by hand ◇ *verb* cut with a scythe

SE *abbrev* south-east; south-eastern

sea *noun* **1** the mass of salt water covering most of the earth's surface **2** a great stretch of water of less size than an ocean **3** a great expanse or number: *a sea of faces* ◇ **sea anemone** a type of small plant-like animal found on rocks at the seashore ◇ **sea dog** an old sailor; a pirate ◇ **sea horse** a type of small fish with a horse-like head and neck ◇ **sea level** the level of the surface of the sea ◇ **sea-lion** *noun* a large kind of seal the male of which has a mane ◇ **sea urchin** a type of small sea creature with a spiny shell ◇ **at sea 1** on the sea **2** completely puzzled

■ **1** ocean, main, deep, *informal* briny **3** multitude, abundance, profusion, mass ◇ **at sea 2** lost, confused, bewildered, baffled, puzzled, *informal* flummoxed, perplexed, mystified

seaboard *noun* land along the edge of the sea

seafarer *noun* a traveller by sea, a sailor ◇ **seafaring** *adj*

seafront *noun* a promenade with its buildings facing the sea

seagoing *adj* (of a ship) sailing on the ocean

seagull *noun* a type of web-footed sea bird

seal¹ *noun* a furry sea animal living partly on land

seal² *noun* **1** a piece of wax with a design pressed into it, attached to a document to show that it is legal or official **2** a piece of wax used to keep a parcel closed **3** anything that closes tightly ◇ *verb* **1** mark or fasten with a seal **2** close up completely **3** make (legally) binding and definite: *seal a bargain*

◇ **sealing wax** a hard kind of wax for sealing letters, documents *etc*

■ *noun* **1** stamp, signet, insignia ◇ *verb* **2** close, shut, stop, plug, cork, waterproof, fasten, secure **3** settle, conclude, finalize

seam *noun* **1** the line formed by the sewing together of two pieces of cloth **2** a line or layer of metal, coal *etc* in the earth ◇ **seamless** *adj* **1** having no seams **2** continuous or consistently good: *a seamless performance* ◇ **seamstress** *noun* a woman who sews for a living

seaman *noun* (*plural* **seamen**) a sailor, *esp* a member of a ship's crew who is not an officer ◇ **seamanship** *noun* the art of steering and looking after ships at sea

seamy *adj* sordid and unpleasant

■ disreputable, sleazy, sordid, squalid, unsavoury, rough, dark, low, nasty, unpleasant

🡆 respectable, wholesome, pleasant

Seanad /ˈʃanəθ/ *noun* the upper house of parliament in the Republic of Ireland

séance /ˈseɪɑns/ *noun* a meeting of people to receive messages from the spirits of the dead

seaplane *noun* an aeroplane which can take off from and land on the water

sear *verb* **1** scorch, burn **2** hurt severely

■ **1** burn, scorch, brown, fry, sizzle, seal, cauterize, brand

search *verb* **1** look over in order to find something **2** (with **for**) look for, seek ◇ *noun* (*plural* **searches**) **1** an act of searching **2** an attempt to find ◇ **search warrant** permission given to the police to search a house *etc* for stolen goods *etc*

■ *verb* **1** scour, comb, sift, probe, explore, *slang* frisk, examine, scrutinize, inspect, check **2** seek, look for, hunt for

searching *adj* examining closely and carefully: *searching question*

■ penetrating, piercing, keen, sharp, close, intent, probing, thorough, minute

🡆 vague, superficial

searchlight *noun* a strong beam of light used for picking out objects at night

seashore *noun* the land next to the sea

seasick *adj* made ill by the rocking movement of a ship

seaside *noun* the land beside the sea
■ coast, shore, front, strand, beach, sands

season *noun* **1** one of the four divisions of the year (spring, summer, autumn, winter) **2** a time with particular characteristics: *our busy season* **3** a time associated with a particular activity: *football season* ◇ *verb* **1** add (salt *etc*) to improve the flavour of (food) **2** dry (wood) till it is ready for use ◇ **in season** of a particular food: readily available at the given time of year ◇ **out of season** of a particular food: not yet available ◇ **season ticket** a ticket that can be used repeatedly for a certain period of time
■ *noun* **3** period, spell, phase, term ◇ *verb* **1** flavour, spice, salt **2** age, mature, ripen, harden, toughen, prepare, condition

seasonable *adj* **1** happening at the proper time **2** of weather: suitable for the season

seasonal *adj* **1** of the seasons or a season **2** of work *etc*: taking place in one particular season only

seasoned *adj* **1** of food: flavoured **2** of wood: ready to be used **3** trained, experienced: *a seasoned traveller*
■ **3** mature, experienced, practised, well-versed, veteran, old, hardened, toughened, conditioned, acclimatized, weathered

seasoning *noun* something (eg salt, pepper) added to food to give it more taste
■ flavouring, spice, condiment, salt, pepper, relish, sauce, dressing

seat *noun* **1** a piece of furniture for sitting on **2** the part of a chair on which you sit **3** the buttocks **4** a mansion **5** a place in parliament, on a council *etc* **6** the centre of some activity: *the seat of government* ◇ *verb* **1** make to sit down **2** have seats for (a certain number): *the room seats forty*
■ *noun* **1** chair, bench, pew, stool, throne **4** residence, mansion **6** headquarters, centre, heart, hub, axis, source, cause, bottom, base, foundation ◇ *verb* **1** sit, place, set, locate, install, settle **2** accommodate, hold, contain, take

seatbelt *noun* a belt fixed to a seat in a car *etc* to prevent a passenger from being thrown out of the seat

seaward *adj* & *adv* towards the sea

seaweed *noun* any of many kinds of plants growing in the sea

seaworthy *adj* in a good enough condition to go to sea

sebaceous *adj* secreting sebum

sebum *noun* an oily substance secreted by the skin and hair

sec *short for* **1** second **2** secretary

secateurs *noun plural* a tool like scissors, for trimming bushes *etc*

secede *verb* break away from a group, society *etc* ◇ **secession** *noun*

seclude *verb* keep (yourself) apart from people's notice or company ◇ **secluded** private, isolated ◇ **seclusion** *noun*
■ **secluded** private, cloistered, sequestered, shut away, cut off, isolated, lonely, solitary, remote, out-of-the-way, sheltered, hidden, concealed

second¹ /ˈsɛkənd/ *adj* **1** next after the first in time, place *etc* **2** other, alternate: *every second week* **3** another of the same kind as: *they thought him a second Mozart* ◇ *noun* **1** someone or something that is second **2** an attendant to someone who boxes or fights a duel **3** an article not quite perfectly made: *these gloves are seconds* ◇ *verb* support, back up ◇ **second-best** *adj* next to the best, not the best ◇ **second nature** a firmly fixed habit: *organizing people is second nature to her*
■ *verb* approve, agree with, endorse, back, support, help, assist, aid

second² /ˈsɛkənd/ *noun* **1** $\frac{1}{60}$ of a minute of time **2** $\frac{1}{60}$ of a degree, used in measuring angles **3** a moment: *wait a second*

second³ /sə'kɒnd/ *verb* transfer (someone) temporarily to another job or location ◇ **secondment** *noun*

secondary *adj* **1** second in position or importance **2** developed from something earlier: *a secondary infection* ◇ **secondary school** a school between primary school and university *etc*
■ subsidiary, subordinate, lower, inferior, lesser, minor, unimportant, ancillary, auxiliary, supporting, relief, back-up, reserve, spare, extra, second, alternative, indirect, derived, resulting

second-hand *adj* **1** not new; having been used by another: *second-hand clothes* **2** of a shop: dealing in second-hand goods
■ **1** used, old, worn, hand-me-down, pre-owned
■ **1** new

secondly *adv* in the second place

second-rate *adj* not of the best quality, inferior
■ inferior, substandard, second-class, second-best, poor, low-grade, *informal* low-rent, shoddy, cheap, tawdry, mediocre, undistinguished, uninspired, uninspiring
■ first-rate

secrecy *noun* the state of being secret, mystery
■ confidentiality, covertness, concealment, furtiveness, surreptitiousness, stealthiness, stealth, mystery

secret *adj* **1** hidden from, or not known by, others **2** secretive ◇ *noun* a fact, plan *etc* that is not told or known ◇ **secretive** *adj* inclined to hide or conceal your feelings, activities *etc* ◇ **secret service** a government department dealing with spying
■ *adj* **1** private, discreet, covert, hidden, concealed, unseen, shrouded, covered, disguised, camouflaged, undercover **2** furtive, surreptitious, stealthy, sly, underhand, clandestine

secretary *noun* (*plural* **secretaries**) **1** someone employed to write letters, keep records *etc* in an office **2** someone

elected to deal with the written business of a club *etc* ◇ **secretarial** *adj* of a secretary or their work ◇ **Secretary of State** **1** a government minister in charge of an administrative department **2** *US* the person in charge of foreign affairs

secrete¹ *verb* hide, conceal in a secret place
■ hide, conceal, *informal* stash away, bury, cover, screen, shroud, veil, disguise, take, appropriate

secrete² *verb* of a part of the body: store up and give out (a fluid) ◇ **secretion** *noun*
■ exude, discharge, release, give off, emit, emanate, produce

sect *noun* a group of people who hold certain views *esp* in religious matters ◇ **sectarian** *adj* **1** of a sect **2** loyal to a sect **3** narrow-minded

section *noun* **1** a part, a division: *a section of the community* **2** a thin slice of a specimen for examination under a microscope **3** the view of the inside of anything when it is cut right through or across: *a section of a plant*
■ **1** division, subdivision, part, sector, zone, district, area, region, department, branch, wing, component, fraction, fragment, bit, piece, slice, portion, segment

sector *noun* **1** a three-sided part of a circle whose sides are two radii and a part of the circumference **2** a part, a section, a division

secular *adj* **1** of worldly, not spiritual or religious things **2** of music *etc*: not sacred or religious

secure *adj* **1** safe, free from danger or fear **2** confident: *secure in the knowledge that she had no rivals* **3** firmly fixed or fastened: *the lock is secure* ◇ *verb* **1** make safe, firm or established: *secure your position* **2** seize, get hold of: *secure the diamonds* **3** fasten: *secure the lock*
■ *adj* **1** safe, unharmed, undamaged, protected, sheltered, shielded, immune **2** confident, assured, reassured **3** impregnable, fortified, fast, tight, fastened, locked, fixed ◇ *verb* **2** obtain,

acquire, gain, get **3** fasten, attach, fix, make fast, tie, moor, lash, chain, lock (up), padlock, bolt, batten down, nail, rivet

security noun **1** safety **2** (**securities**) property or goods which a lender may keep until the loan is paid back ◇adj providing security: security guard

⬛ **1** safety, immunity, asylum, sanctuary, refuge, cover, protection, defence, surveillance, safekeeping, preservation, care, custody

secy abbrev secretary

sedan noun **1** an enclosed chair for one person, carried on two poles by two bearers (also called **sedan chair**) **2** US a saloon car

sedate adj calm, serious, dignified ◇**sedateness** noun

⬛ dignified, solemn, grave, serious, sober, decorous, proper, seemly, demure, composed, unruffled, serene, tranquil, calm, quiet, cool, collected, imperturbable, informal unflappable

🔲 undignified, lively, agitated

sedative adj calming, soothing ◇noun a medicine with this effect ◇**sedation** noun the use of sedatives to calm a patient

⬛ adj calming, soothing, anodyne, lenitive, tranquillizing, relaxing, soporific, depressant ◇ noun tranquillizer, sleeping pill, narcotic, barbiturate

sedentary adj of a job etc: requiring much sitting

sedge noun a type of coarse grass growing in swamps and rivers

sediment noun the grains or solid parts which settle at the bottom of a liquid

⬛ deposit, residue, grounds, lees, dregs

sedition noun the stirring up of rebellion against the government ◇**seditious** adj encouraging rebellion, rebellious

seduce verb **1** tempt (someone) away from right or moral behaviour **2** persuade (someone) to have sexual intercourse **3** attract ◇**seducer** noun ◇**seduction** noun ◇**seductive** adj attractive, tempting ◇**seductress** noun

⬛ **1** ensnare, entice, lead astray, mislead, corrupt, dishonour, ruin **3** lure, attract, tempt, charm, beguile

sedulous adj diligent, painstaking

see verb (**sees, seeing, saw, seen**) **1** have sight **2** be aware of, notice by means of the eye: he can see us coming **3** form a picture of in the mind **4** understand: I see what you mean **5** find out: I'll see what is happening **6** predict: I can't see him agreeing **7** make sure: see that he finishes his homework **8** accompany: I'll see you home **9** meet: I'll see you at the usual time **10** watch: go to see a play ◇noun the district over which a bishop or archbishop has authority ◇**seeing that** since, because ◇**see off 1** accompany (someone) to their place of departure **2** get rid of (someone) ◇**see through 1** take part in to the end **2** not be deceived by (a person, trick etc) ◇**see to** attend to (the preparation of): see to a meal

⬛ verb **2** perceive, glimpse, discern, spot, make out, distinguish, identify, sight, notice **3** imagine, picture, visualize, envisage, foresee, anticipate **4** understand, comprehend, grasp, follow, realize, recognize, appreciate **5** discover, find out, learn, ascertain, determine **8** accompany, escort ◇ **see to** attend to, deal with, take care of, look after, arrange, organize, manage, do, fix, repair, sort out

seed noun **1** the part of a tree, plant etc from which a new plant may grow **2** a seed-like part of a grain or a nut **3** the beginning from which anything grows: the seeds of rebellion **4** a seeded player in a tournament **5** old children, descendants ◇verb **1** of a plant: produce seed **2** sow **3** remove the seeds from (eg a fruit) **4** arrange (good players) in a tournament so that they do not compete against each other till the later rounds ◇**go to seed** or **run to seed 1** of a plant: develop seeds **2** of a person, area etc: deteriorate, become run down

seedling noun a young plant just sprung from a seed

seedy adj **1** full of seeds **2** shabby **3** sickly, not very well

■ **2** shabby, scruffy, tatty, mangy, sleazy, squalid, *informal* grotty, *slang* crummy, run-down, dilapidated, decaying **3** unwell, ill, sick, poorly, ailing, off-colour, *informal* under the weather

seek *verb* (**seeks, seeking, sought**) **1** look or search for **2** try (to do something): *seek to establish proof* **3** try to get (advice *etc*)

■ **1** look for, search for, hunt for **2** want, desire, aim, aspire, try, attempt, endeavour, strive **3** pursue, inquire, ask, request, solicit, petition

seem *verb* **1** appear to be: *he seems kind* **2** appear: *she seems to like it* ◇ **seeming** *adj* apparent but not actual or real: *a seeming success* ◇ **seemly** *adj* suitable; decent

seen *past participle* of **see**

seep *verb* flow slowly through a small opening, leak ◇ **seepage** *noun*

■ ooze, leak, exude, well, trickle, dribble, percolate, permeate, soak

seer *noun* a prophet

seersucker *noun* a lightweight ribbed cotton fabric

seesaw *noun* **1** a plank balanced across a stand so that one end of it goes up when the other goes down **2** an up-and-down movement like that of a seesaw ◇ *verb* move with a seesaw-like movement

seethe *verb* **1** be very angry **2** boil or churn ◇ **seething** *adj*

■ **1** rage, fume, smoulder, storm **2** boil, simmer, bubble, effervesce, fizz, foam, froth, ferment, rise, swell, surge, teem, swarm

segment *noun* **1** a part or portion **2** a part of a circle cut off by a straight line

segregate *verb* separate (someone or a group) from others ◇ **segregation** *noun*

■ separate, keep apart, cut off, isolate, quarantine, set apart, exclude
▣ unite, join

seismic /'saɪzmɪk/ *adj* of earthquakes ◇ **seismograph** *noun* an instrument that records earthquake shocks and measures their force

seize *verb* **1** take suddenly by force **2** overcome: *seized with fury* **3** take legal possession of (something) ◇ **seize up 1** of machinery: become stuck, break down **2** of a body part: become stiff through exertion

■ grab, snatch, grasp, clutch, grip, hold, take, confiscate, impound, appropriate, commandeer, hijack, annex, abduct, catch, capture, arrest, apprehend, *informal* nab, *slang* nick

seizure *noun* **1** sudden capture **2** a sudden attack of illness, rage *etc*

seldom *adv* not often, rarely: *you seldom see an owl during the day*

select *verb* pick out from several according to your preference, choose ◇ *adj* **1** picked out, chosen above all others **2** exclusive, allowing only certain people in

■ *verb* choose, pick, single out, decide on, appoint, elect, prefer, opt for ◇ *adj* **1** selected, choice, prime, superior **2** élite, exclusive, limited, special, *informal* posh, up-market
▣ *adj* **1** second-rate, ordinary **2** general

selection *noun* **1** the act of choosing **2** things chosen **3** a number of things from which to choose

selective *adj* **1** selecting carefully, discriminating **2** exclusive

selector *noun* someone who chooses (*eg* members for a national team)

self *noun* (*plural* **selves**) **1** personality, or an aspect of it **2** someone's personality, character ◇ *adj* of the same material or colour

self-assured *adj* trusting in your own power or ability, confident

self-centred *adj* concerned with your own affairs, selfish

■ selfish, self-seeking, self-serving, self-interested, egotistic(al), narcissistic, self-absorbed, egocentric
▣ altruistic

self-confident *adj* believing in your own powers or abilities

■ confident, self-reliant, self-assured, assured, self-possessed, cool, fearless
▣ unsure, self-conscious

self-conscious *adj* too aware of your faults *etc* and therefore embarrassed in the company of others

▣ uncomfortable, ill at ease, awkward, embarrassed, shamefaced, sheepish, shy, bashful, coy, retiring, shrinking, self-effacing, nervous, insecure

▣ natural, unaffected, confident

self-contained *adj* **1** of accommodation: complete in itself, not sharing any part **2** of a person: self-reliant

self-control *noun* control over yourself, your feelings *etc*

▣ calmness, composure, cool, patience, self-restraint, restraint, self-denial, temperance, self-discipline, self-mastery, will-power

self-defence *noun* the defence of your own person, property *etc*

self-denial *noun* doing without something, *esp* in order to give to others

▣ moderation, temperance, abstemiousness, asceticism, self-sacrifice, unselfishness, selflessness

▣ self-indulgence

self-effacing *adj* keeping yourself from being noticed, modest

self-esteem *noun* good opinion of yourself

self-evident *adj* clear enough to need no proof

▣ obvious, manifest, clear, plain, undeniable, axiomatic, unquestionable, incontrovertible, inescapable

self-expression *noun* expressing your own personality in your activities

self-important *adj* having a mistakenly high sense of your importance

self-indulgent *adj* too ready to satisfy your own inclinations and desires

▣ hedonistic, dissolute, dissipated, profligate, extravagant, intemperate, immoderate

▣ abstemious

self-interest *noun* a selfish desire to consider only your own interests or advantage

selfish *adj* caring only for your own pleasure or advantage ◇ **selfishly** *adv* ◇ **selfishness** *noun*

▣ self-interested, self-seeking, self-serving, mean, miserly, mercenary, greedy, covetous, self-centred, egocentric, egotistic(al)

▣ unselfish, selfless, generous, considerate

selfless *adj* thinking of others before yourself, unselfish ◇ **selflessly** *adv* ◇ **selflessness** *noun*

▣ unselfish, altruistic, self-denying, self-sacrificing, generous, philanthropic

▣ selfish, self-centred

self-made *adj* owing success *etc* to your own efforts: *a self-made man*

self-portrait *noun* an artist's portrait of themselves

self-possessed *adj* calm in mind or manner, quietly confident

self-raising *adj* of flour: containing an ingredient to make dough rise

self-reliant *adj* trusting in your own abilities *etc*

self-respect *noun* respect for yourself and concern for your own character and reputation

▣ pride, dignity, self-esteem, self-assurance, self-confidence

self-righteous *adj* thinking highly of your own goodness and virtue

▣ smug, complacent, superior, *informal* goody-goody, pious, sanctimonious, holier-than-thou

self-sacrifice *noun* the act of giving up your own life, possessions *etc* in order to do good to others

▣ self-denial, selflessness, generosity

selfsame *adj* the very same

self-satisfied *adj* pleased, smug, satisfied with yourself

▣ smug, complacent, self-congratulatory, self-righteous

▣ humble

self-service *adj* of a restaurant, petrol station *etc*: where customers help or serve themselves

self-sufficient *adj* needing no help or support from anyone else

self-willed *adj* determined to have your own way, obstinate

sell *verb* (**sells**, **selling**, **sold**) **1** give or hand over (something) for money **2** have or keep for sale: *he sells newspapers* **3** be sold for, cost: *this book sells for £20* **4** betray (*eg* your principles) to get something ◇ **sell off** dispose of by selling cheaply ◇ **sell out 1** sell your entire stock **2** betray (*eg* your principles) to another party ◇ **sell up** sell your home or business

■ **2** auction, vend, retail, stock, handle, deal in, trade in, merchandise, peddle

seller *noun* someone who sells

■ vendor, merchant, trader, dealer, supplier, stockist, retailer, shopkeeper, salesman, saleswoman, agent, representative, *informal* rep

Sellotape *noun, trademark* transparent adhesive tape, used for sticking pieces of paper together

selvage or **selvedge** *noun* the firm edge of a piece of cloth, that does not fray

semantic *adj* relating to the meaning of words *etc*

semaphore *noun* a form of signalling using the arms to form different positions for each letter

semblance *noun* an outward, often false, appearance: *a semblance of listening*

■ appearance, air, show, pretence, guise, mask, front, façade, veneer, apparition, image

semen *noun* the liquid that carries sperm

semester *noun, US* a term at a university *etc*

semi *noun* **1** *informal* a semi-detached house **2** a semi-final

semi- *prefix* **1** half **2** *informal* partly

semibreve *noun, music* a whole-note (○), equal to four crotchets in length

semicircle *noun* half of a circle

semicolon *noun* the punctuation mark (;)

semi-detached *adj* of a house: joined to another house on one side but not on the other

semi-final *noun* the stage or match of a contest immediately before the final

seminal *adj* influential, important

seminar *noun* a group of students working on, or meeting to discuss, a particular subject

seminary *noun* (*plural* **seminaries**) a school or college

semiotics *noun plural* the study of signs and symbols ◇ **semiotician** *noun* someone who studies semiotics

semi-precious *adj* of a stone: having some value, but not considered a gem

semi-professional *adj* **1** engaging part-time in a professional activity **2** engaged in by semi-professionals

semolina *noun* the hard particles of wheat sifted from flour, used for puddings *etc*

Semtex *noun, trademark* a material used to make explosives

senate *noun* **1** the upper house of parliament in the USA, Australia *etc* **2** the governing council of some universities **3** *hist* the law-making body in ancient Rome ◇ **senator** *noun* a member of a senate

send *verb* (**sends**, **sending**, **sent**) **1** cause to go **2** have (something) carried or delivered to a place ◇ **sender** *noun* ◇ **send-off** *noun* **1** a start **2** a friendly farewell for someone going on a journey *etc* ◇ **send for** order to be brought ◇ **send off 1** dispatch, *esp* by post **2** dismiss (a sports player) from the field of play ◇ **send up** *informal* make fun of, parody

■ **1** propel, drive, move, throw, fling, hurl, launch, fire, shoot, discharge, emit, direct **2** post, mail, dispatch, consign, remit, forward ◇ **send for** summon, call for, request, order, command

■ **send for** dismiss

senile *adj* **1** of old age **2** showing the mental feebleness of old age ◇ **senility** *noun*

senior *adj* older in age or higher in rank ◇ *noun* someone in a senior position ◇ **seniority** *noun* the fact of being senior

▣ *adj* older, elder, higher, superior, high-ranking, major, chief

▣ *adj* junior

senna *noun* the dried leaves of certain plants, used as a laxative

sensation *noun* **1** a feeling through any of the five senses **2** a vague effect: *a floating sensation* **3** a state of excitement: *causing a sensation* ◇ **sensational** *adj* causing great excitement, horror *etc* ◇ **sensationalize** *verb* make something appear more exciting or shocking than it really is

▣ **1** feeling, sense, impression, perception **3** commotion, stir, agitation, excitement, thrill, furore, outrage, scandal ◇ **sensational** exciting, thrilling, electrifying, breathtaking, startling, *informal* jaw-dropping, amazing, astounding, staggering, dramatic, spectacular, impressive

sense *noun* **1** one of the five powers by which humans feel or notice (hearing, taste, sight, smell, touch) **2** a feeling: *a sense of loss* **3** an ability to understand or appreciate: *a sense of humour* **4** (**senses**) right mind, common sense: *to take leave of your senses* **5** wisdom, ability to act in a reasonable way **6** ability to be understood: *your sentence does not make sense* **7** meaning: *to what sense of this word are your referring?* ◇ *verb* feel, realize: *sense disapproval* ◇ **make sense 1** be understandable **2** be wise or reasonable

▣ *noun* **2** feeling, sensation, impression, perception, awareness **5** reason, logic, intelligence, cleverness, understanding, discernment, judgement, intuition, nous **7** meaning, significance, definition, interpretation, implication ◇ *verb* feel, suspect, intuit, perceive, detect, notice, observe, realize

▣ *noun* **5** foolishness **6** nonsense

senseless *adj* stunned, unconscious; foolish

sensible *adj* **1** wise **2** able to be felt or noticed **3** (with **to**) aware of, sensitive to ◇ **sensibility** *noun* (*plural* **sensibilities**) ability to feel, sensitivity

▣ **1** wise, prudent, judicious, well-advised, shrewd, far-sighted, intelligent, level-headed, down-to-earth, commonsense, sober, sane, rational, logical, reasonable, realistic, practical, functional, sound

▣ **1** senseless, foolish, unwise

sensitive *adj* **1** feeling, *esp* strongly or painfully **2** easily upset or offended **3** stimulating strong feeling: *a sensitive issue* **4** of documents *etc*: containing confidential information **5** of scientific instruments *etc*: responding to small changes ◇ **sensitivity** *noun* ◇ **sensitize** *verb* make sensitive (*esp* to light)

sensor *noun* a device that detects and measures physical changes ◇ **sensory** *adj* of the senses

sensual *adj* **1** of the senses rather than the mind **2** indulging in bodily pleasures ◇ **sensuality** *noun* ◇ **sensually** *adv*

▣ **2** self-indulgent, voluptuous, worldly, physical, animal, carnal, fleshly, bodily, sexual, erotic, sexy, lustful

🛈 Do not confuse: **sensual** and **sensuous**

sensuous *adj* **1** pleasing to the senses **2** aware of what is felt through the senses ◇ **sensuosity** *noun* ◇ **sensuously** *adv*

▣ **1** pleasurable, gratifying, voluptuous, rich, lush, luxurious, sumptuous

▣ **1** ascetic, plain, simple

sent *past form* of **send**

sentence *noun* **1** a number of words which together make a complete statement **2** a judgement announced by a judge or court ◇ *verb* condemn to a particular punishment

▣ *noun* **2** judgement, decision, verdict, condemnation, pronouncement, ruling, decree, order ◇ *verb* condemn, doom, punish, penalize

sentient *adj* thinking, reasoning

sentiment *noun* **1** a thought expressed in words **2** a show of feeling or emotion, often excessive

▣ **1** thought, idea, feeling, opinion, view, judgement, belief, persuasion, attitude **2** emotion, sensibility, tenderness, softheartedness, romanticism, sentimentality

sentimental *adj* having or showing feeling or emotion ◇ **sentimentality** *noun*

■ tender, soft-hearted, emotional, gushing, *informal* touchy-feely, touching, pathetic, tear-jerking, *informal* weepy, maudlin, mawkish, nostalgic, romantic, *informal* lovey-dovey, slushy, mushy, sloppy, schmaltzy, soppy, *informal* corny

◪ unsentimental, realistic, cynical

sentinel *noun* a soldier on guard

sepal *noun* one of the green leaves beneath the petals of a flower

separate *verb* /ˈsɛpəreɪt/ **1** set or keep apart **2** divide into parts **3** disconnect **4** go different ways **5** move and live apart by choice ◇ *adj* /ˈsɛpərət/ **1** placed, kept *etc* apart **2** divided **3** different: *that's a separate issue* ◇ **separation** *noun* a dividing or putting apart

■ *verb* **1** disaffiliate, disentangle, segregate, isolate, cut off, abstract, remove, detach **2** divide, sever **3** disunite, disconnect, uncouple **4** split (up), part company, diverge ◇ *adj* **1** single, individual, particular, independent, alone, solitary, segregated, isolated **2** divided, disjointed, detached, disunited, unattached, unconnected, unrelated **3** different, disparate, distinct, discrete, several, sundry

◪ *verb* **2** join, unite, combine

separatist *noun* someone who withdraws or urges separation from an established church, state *etc* ◇ **separatism** *noun*

Sephardic *adj* relating to the Jewish people of Spain, Portugal or N Africa

sepia *noun* a brown colour

sept *noun* a division of a clan

sept- *prefix* seven

September *noun* the ninth month of the year

septet *noun* a group of seven musicians *etc*

septic *adj* of a wound: full of germs poisoning the blood ◇ **septic tank** a tank in which sewage is partially purified

■ infected, poisoned, festering, putrefying, putrid

> ⚠ Do not confuse with: **sceptic**

septuagenarian *noun* someone from seventy to seventy-nine years old

sepulchre *noun* a tomb ◇ **sepulchral** *adj* **1** of sepulchres **2** dismal, gloomy **3** of a voice: deep, hollow in tone

sequel *noun* **1** a story that is a continuation of an earlier story **2** an event following on from an earlier one

sequence *noun* **1** the order (of events) in time **2** a number of things following in order, a connected series ◇ **sequential** *adj*

■ **1** order, arrangement **2** course, track, cycle, set, succession, series, run, progression, chain, string, train, line, procession

sequestered *adj* of a place: lonely, quiet

sequestrate *verb* keep apart, isolate

sequin *noun* a small round sparkling ornament sewn on a dress *etc*

sequoia *noun* a giant N American redwood tree

seraglio *noun* (*plural* **seraglios**) a harem

seraph *noun* (*plural* **seraphs** or **seraphim**) an angel of the highest rank ◇ **seraphic** *adj* like an angel

sere *adj*, *formal* dry, withered

serenade *noun* music played or sung in the open air at night, *esp* under a woman's window ◇ *verb* sing or play a serenade (to)

serendipity *noun* happy chance, luck ◇ **serendipitous** *adj*

serene *adj* **1** calm **2** not worried, happy, peaceful ◇ **serenity** *noun* calmness, peacefulness

■ **1** calm, tranquil, cool, composed, placid, still, quiet, peaceful **2** untroubled, undisturbed

◪ **2** troubled, disturbed

serf *noun*, *hist* a slave bought and sold with the land on which he worked ◇ **serfdom** *noun* slavery

serge *noun* a strong type of cloth

sergeant *noun* **1** an army rank above corporal **2** a rank in the police force above a constable ◇ **sergeant-major** *noun* an army rank above sergeant

series *noun* (*plural* **series**) **1** a number of things following each other in order **2** a set of things of the same kind: *a series of books on art*

■ **1** cycle, succession, sequence, run, progression, chain, string, line, train, order, arrangement, course

serial *noun* a story which is published, broadcast or televised in instalments

serif *noun* a short line or stroke on the end of a printed letter

serious *adj* **1** grave, thoughtful: *serious expression on her face* **2** not joking, in earnest: *serious remark* **3** important, needing careful thought: *a serious matter* **4** likely to have dangerous results: *serious accident* ◇ **seriously** *adv* ◇ **seriousness** *noun*

■ **1** unsmiling, long-faced, humourless, solemn, sober, stern, thoughtful, pensive, earnest, sincere **3** important, significant, weighty, momentous, crucial, critical, urgent, pressing, acute, grave

■ **1** smiling, facetious, frivolous **3** trivial, slight

sermon *noun* a serious talk, *esp* one given in church

serpent *noun*, *old* a snake ◇ **serpentine** *adj* like a serpent; winding, full of twists

SERPS *abbrev* state earnings-related pension scheme

serrated *adj* having notches or teeth like a saw

■ toothed, notched, indented, jagged
■ smooth

serried *adj* crowded together: *serried ranks*

serum *noun* (*plural* **serums** or **sera**) **1** a yellowish fluid in blood that helps fight disease **2** the watery part of plant fluid

servant *noun* **1** someone paid to work for another, *esp* in helping to run a house **2** a government employee: *civil servant/public servant*

■ **1** domestic, maid, valet, steward, attendant, lackey, menial, *informal* skivvy, help, helper, assistant

serve *verb* **1** work for and obey **2** attend or wait upon at table **3** give out food, goods *etc* **4** be able to be used (as): *the cave will serve as a shelter* **5** be suitable for: *serve a purpose* **6** carry out duties as a member of the armed forces **7** undergo (a sentence in prison *etc*) **8** *tennis etc* throw up the ball and hit it with the racket to start play ◇ **serve someone right** be deserved by them

■ **1** wait on, attend, minister to, work for, help, aid, assist **3** distribute, dole out, mete out, present, deliver, provide, supply **4** perform, act, function

server *noun* **1** someone who attends to customers *esp* in a restaurant **2** a computer that stores and manages data from other smaller ones

service *noun* **1** an act of serving **2** the duty required of a servant or other employee **3** a performance of (public) worship **4** use: *bring the new machine into service* **5** an overhaul **6** time spent in the armed forces **7** (**services**) the armed forces **8** (**services**) help: *services to refugees* **9** a regular supply: *bus service* **10** (**services**) public supply of water, gas, electricity *etc* **11** a set of dishes: *dinner service* ◇ *verb* keep (a car, machine *etc*) in good working order by regular repairs ◇ **service charge** a percentage of a bill added on to cover service cost ◇ **service station** a petrol station with facilities such as a shop *etc* ◇ **active service** service in battle ◇ **at your service** ready to help or be of use

■ *noun* **2** work, labour, business, duty, function, performance **3** worship, observance, ceremony, rite **4** use, usefulness, utility, benefit, help, assistance **5** maintenance, overhaul, check ◇ *verb* maintain, overhaul, check, repair, recondition, tune

serviceable *adj* useful; lasting a long time: *serviceable clothes*

serviette *noun* a table napkin

servile *adj* slave-like; fawning or sub-

missive: *a servile attitude to his employer*
◊ **servility** *noun* ◊ **servitude** *noun*
slavery; the state of being under strict
control

■ obsequious, sycophantic, toadying, cringing, fawning, grovelling, bootlicking, slavish, subservient, subject, submissive, humble, abject

◼ assertive, aggressive

sesame *noun* a SE Asian plant whose seeds produce an edible oil

sesquicentenary or **sesquicentennial** *noun* a hundred and fiftieth anniversary

session *noun* **1** a meeting of a court, council *etc* **2** the period of the year when classes are held in a school *etc* **3** a period of time spent on a particular activity

■ **1** sitting, hearing, meeting, assembly, convention, conference, discussion **2** term, semester, year **3** period, time

sestet *noun* a group of six musicians *etc*

set¹ *verb* (**sets**, **setting**, **set**) **1** place or put in a specified position or condition: *set them straight* **2** fix in the proper place (*eg* broken bones) **3** arrange (a table for a meal *etc*) **4** fix (a date, a price *etc*) **5** adjust (a clock or a machine *etc*) so that it is ready to work or perform some function **6** give (a task *etc*): *set him three problems* **7** (with **off** or **out** or **forth**) start (on a journey *etc*) **8** of a jelly *etc*: become firm or solid **9** place (a film *etc*) in a specified period or location **10** compose music for: *he set the poem to music* **11** of the sun: go out of sight below the horizon ◊ *adj* **1** fixed or rigid: *a set menu/set expression on his face* **2** established: *set phrases/set in her ways* **3** prepared: *all set to go* ◊ *noun* **1** pose, position: *the set of his head* **2** scenery made ready for a play *etc* **3** a fixing of hair in waves or curls ◊ **set about 1** begin (doing something) **2** attack ◊ **set in** begin: *winter has set in* ◊ **set off 1** detonate (an explosive) **2** show off to good advantage ◊ **set on** attack ◊ **set up 1** put (someone) in a position of security **2** trick (someone) *esp* into taking the blame for something **3** establish **4** erect

◊ *verb* **1** put, place, locate, situate, position, arrange, park, deposit **2** lodge, fix, stick **4** schedule, appoint, designate, specify, name, prescribe, ordain, assign, allocate, impose, fix, establish, determine, decide **5** adjust, regulate, synchronize, co-ordinate **8** congeal, thicken, gel, stiffen, solidify, harden, crystallize ◊ *adj* **1** firm, strict, rigid, inflexible **2** scheduled, appointed, arranged, prepared, prearranged, fixed, established, definite, decided, agreed, settled, firm

◼ *adj* **1** movable, free **2** spontaneous, undecided

set² *noun* **1** a group of related people **2** a collection of related things or pieces to be used together: *a chess set* **3** the songs or tunes played by a singer or band at a concert **4** a series of games in tennis, darts *etc* **5** an apparatus: *a television set*

■ **1** group, band, gang, crowd, circle, clique, faction **2** batch, series, kit, outfit, compendium

set³ or **sett** *noun* a badger's burrow

setback *noun* a movement in the wrong direction, a failure

■ delay, hold-up, problem, snag, hitch, hiccup, reverse, misfortune, upset, disappointment, defeat

set-square *noun* a triangular drawing instrument, with one right angle

sett *another spelling of* **set³**

settee *noun* a sofa

setter *noun* a dog trained to point out game in hunting

setting *noun* **1** the way in which something is set **2** an arrangement **3** a background: *against a setting of hills and lochs*

■ **3** surroundings, milieu, environment, background, context, perspective, position, location, locale, site, scene, scenery

settle¹ *verb* **1** place in a position or at rest **2** come to rest **3** agree over (a matter): *settle the price* **4** (sometimes with **down**) become calm or quiet **5** (sometimes with **down**) make your home in a place **6** pay (a bill) **7** fix, decide (on) **8**

bring (a quarrel *etc*) to an end **9** sink to the bottom

■ *verb* **1** arrange, order, adjust **2** descend, land, alight **3** fix, establish, determine, decide, agree, confirm **5** colonize, occupy, populate, people, inhabit, live, reside **6** pay, clear, discharge **7** choose, appoint, fix, establish, determine, decide **9** sink, subside, drop, fall, descend

settle[2] *noun* a long high-backed bench

settlement *noun* **1** the act of settling **2** a decision, an agreement **3** payment for a bill or compensation **4** a number of people who have come to live in a country

■ **2** resolution, agreement, arrangement, decision, conclusion **3** payment, clearance, clearing, discharge

settler *noun* someone who goes to live in a new country

seven *noun* the number 7 ◇ *adj* 7 in number ◇ **seventh** *adj* the last of a series of seven ◇ *noun* one of seven equal parts

seventeen *noun* the number 17 ◇ *adj* 17 in number ◇ **seventeenth** *adj* the last of a series of seventeen ◇ *noun* one of seventeen equal parts

seventy *noun* the number 70 ◇ *adj* 70 in number ◇ **seventieth** *adj* the last of a series of seventy ◇ *noun* one of seventy equal parts

sever *verb* **1** cut apart or away, break off **2** separate, part ◇ **severance** *noun*

■ **1** cut, cleave, split, rend, cut off, amputate, detach **2** part, separate, divide

several *adj* **1** more than one or two, but not many **2** various **3** different: *going their several ways* ◇ *pronoun* more than one or two people, things *etc*, but not a great many

severe *adj* **1** serious: *a severe illness* **2** harsh, strict **3** very plain and simple, not fancy ◇ **severity** *noun*

■ **1** serious, grave, critical, dangerous **2** stern, disapproving, sober, strait-laced, strict, rigid, unbending, harsh, tough, hard, difficult, demanding, arduous, punishing, rigorous, merciless, oppressive **3** plain, simple, unadorned, un-

embellished, functional, restrained, austere, ascetic

■ **2** kind, compassionate, sympathetic, lenient, mild **3** decorated, ornate

sew *verb* (**sews**, **sewing**, **sewed**, **sewn**) **1** join together with a needle and thread **2** make or mend in this way ◇ **sewer** *noun*

sewage *noun* water and waste matter

sewer *noun* an underground drain for carrying off water and waste matter ◇ **sewerage** *noun* **1** a system of sewers **2** drainage of sewage using sewers

sex *noun* **1** either of the two classes (male or female) into which animals are divided according to the part they play in producing children or young **2** sexual intercourse

■ **1** gender **2** intercourse, sexual relations, copulation, coitus, lovemaking, fornication, reproduction, union, intimacy

sex- *prefix* six

sexagenarian *noun* someone from sixty to sixty-nine years old

sexism *noun* discrimination against someone on the grounds of their sex ◇ **sexist** *noun* & *adj*

sexology *noun* the study of human sexual behaviour ◇ **sexologist** *noun*

sextant *noun* an instrument used for calculating distances by means of measuring angles *eg* the distance between two stars

sextet *noun* a group of six musicians *etc*

sexton *noun* someone who has various responsibilities in a church, *eg* bellringing, gravedigging *etc*

sexual *adj* **1** of sex or gender **2** relating to sexual intercourse ◇ **sexuality** *noun* ◇ **sexually** *adv* ◇ **sexual intercourse** physical union between a man and a woman involving the insertion of the penis into the vagina

sexy *adj* sexually attractive

■ sensual, voluptuous, nubile, *informal* beddable, seductive, inviting, flirtatious, arousing, provoking, provocative, titillating, pornographic, erotic, *slang* horny

SF *abbrev* science fiction

SFA *abbrev* Scottish Football Association

SFX *abbrev* special effects

SGML *abbrev, comput* standard generalized mark-up language

sgraffito *noun* decorative artwork in which layers are scraped away to reveal different colours

shabby *adj* **1** worn-looking **2** poorly dressed **3** of behaviour: mean, unfair ◇ **shabbily** *adv*
≣ **1** ragged, tattered, frayed, worn, worn-out, mangy, moth-eaten, scruffy, tatty **2** scruffy, tatty **3** contemptible, despicable, rotten, mean, low, cheap, shoddy, shameful, dishonourable
ⓔ **1** smart **3** honourable, fair

shack *noun* a roughly-built hut

shackle *verb* **1** fasten with a chain **2** hold back, prevent, hinder ◇ **shackles** *noun plural* chains fastening a prisoner's legs or arms

shade *noun* **1** slight darkness caused by cutting off some light **2** a place not in full sunlight **3** a screen from the heat or light **4** (**shades**) *informal* sunglasses **5** the deepness or a variation of a colour **6** the dark parts in a picture **7** a very small amount or difference: *a shade larger* ◇ *verb* **1** shelter from the sun or light **2** make parts of a picture darker **3** change gradually, *eg* from one colour into another ◇ **shading** *noun* the marking of the darker places in a picture
≣ *noun* **1** shadow, darkness, obscurity, semi-darkness, dimness, gloom, gloominess, twilight, dusk, gloaming **3** awning, canopy, cover, shelter, screen, blind, curtain, shield, visor, umbrella, parasol **5** colour, hue, tint, tone, tinge **7** trace, dash, hint, suggestion, suspicion, soupçon, nuance, degree ◇ *verb* **1** shield, screen, protect, cover, shroud

shadow *noun* **1** shade caused by some object coming in the way of a light **2** the dark shape of that object on the ground **3** a dark part in a picture **4** a very small amount: *a shadow of doubt* ◇ *verb* **1** shade, darken **2** follow someone about secretly and watch them

closely ◇ **shadow cabinet** leading members of the opposition in parliament
≣ *noun* **1** shade **4** trace, hint, suggestion, suspicion, vestige, remnant ◇ *verb* **1** shade, shield, screen, obscure, darken **2** follow, tail, stalk, trail, watch

shady *adj* **1** sheltered from light or heat **2** *informal* dishonest, underhand: *a shady character*
≣ **1** shaded, shadowy, dim, dark, cool, leafy **2** dubious, questionable, suspect, suspicious, *informal* fishy, dishonest, crooked, unreliable, untrustworthy, disreputable, unscrupulous, unethical, underhand
ⓔ **1** sunny, sunlit, bright **2** honest, trustworthy, honourable

shaft *noun* **1** anything long and straight **2** the rod on which the head of an axe, arrow *etc* is fixed **3** an arrow **4** a revolving rod which turns a machine or engine **5** the pole of a cart to which the horses are tied **6** the deep, narrow passageway leading to a mine **7** a deep vertical hole for a lift **8** a ray (of light)

shag[1] *noun* **1** a ragged mass of hair **2** a coarse pile on fabric **3** tobacco cut into coarse shreds

shag[2] *verb, slang* (**shags, shagging, shagged**) **1** have sexual intercourse **2** have sexual intercourse with ◇ *noun* an act of sexual intercourse

shaggy *adj* rough, hairy, or woolly

shagpile *adj* of a carpet: having a thick pile

shake *verb* (**shakes, shaking, shaken, shook**) **1** move backwards and forwards or up and down with quick, jerky movements **2** make or be made unsteady **3** shock, disturb: *his parting words shook me* ◇ *noun* **1** the act of shaking or trembling **2** a shock **3** a drink mixed by shaking or stirring quickly: *milk shake*
≣ *verb* **1** wave, flourish, brandish, wag, waggle, agitate, rattle, joggle, jolt, jerk, twitch, convulse **2** waver, wobble, totter, sway, rock, tremble, quiver, quake, shiver, shudder **3** upset, distress, shock, frighten, unnerve, intimidate,

disturb, discompose, unsettle, agitate, stir

shaky *adj* unsteady; trembling ◇ **shakily** *adv*

≡ trembling, quivering, faltering, tentative, uncertain, unstable, unsteady, unsafe, insecure, precarious, wobbly, rocky, tottery, rickety, weak

shale *noun* a kind of rock from which oil can be obtained

shall *verb* 1 used to form future tenses of other verbs when the subject is *I* or *we*: *I shall tell you later* 2 used for emphasis, or to express a promise, when the subject is *you, he, she, it* or *they*: *you shall go if I say you must/you shall go if you want to; see also* **should**

shallot *noun* a kind of onion

shallow *adj* 1 not deep 2 not capable of thinking or feeling deeply ◇ *noun* (often **shallows**) a place where the water is not deep

≡ *adj* 2 superficial, frivolous, foolish, idle, empty, meaningless, unscholarly, ignorant, simple

shalom *exclam* peace be with you, a Jewish greeting

sham *noun* something which is not what it appears to be, a pretence ◇ *adj* false, imitation, pretended: *a sham fight* ◇ *verb* (**shams, shamming, shammed**) pretend, feign: *shamming sleep*

≡ *noun* pretence, fraud, counterfeit, forgery, fake, imitation, simulation, hoax, humbug ◇ *adj* false, fake, counterfeit, spurious, bogus, *informal* phoney, pretended, feigned, put-on, simulated, artificial, mock, imitation, synthetic ◇ *verb* pretend, feign, affect, put on, simulate, imitate, fake, counterfeit

▣ *adj* genuine, authentic, real

shaman *noun* a tribal healer or medicine man

shamble *verb* walk in a shuffling or awkward manner ◇ **shambles** *noun plural, informal* a mess, confused disorder

shambolic *adj, slang* chaotic, messy

shame *noun* 1 an uncomfortable feeling caused by realization of guilt or failure 2 disgrace, dishonour 3 *informal* bad luck, a pity: *it's a shame that you can't go* ◇ *verb* 1 make to feel shame or ashamed 2 (with **into**) cause (someone to do something) by making them ashamed: *they shamed him into paying his share* ◇ **put to shame** cause to feel ashamed

≡ *noun* 1 shamefacedness, remorse, guilt, embarrassment, mortification 2 disgrace, dishonour, discredit, stain, stigma, disrepute, infamy, scandal, ignominy, humiliation, degradation ◇ *verb* 1 embarrass, mortify, abash, confound, humiliate, ridicule, humble, put to shame, show up, disgrace, dishonour, discredit

shamefaced *adj* showing shame or embarrassment

shameful *adj* disgraceful

≡ disgraceful, outrageous, scandalous, indecent, abominable, atrocious, wicked, mean, low, vile, reprehensible, contemptible, unworthy, ignoble

shameless *adj* feeling or showing no shame

≡ unashamed, unabashed, unrepentant, impenitent, barefaced, flagrant, blatant, brazen, brash, audacious, insolent, defiant, hardened, incorrigible

▣ ashamed, shamefaced, contrite

shammy *another spelling of* **chamois**

shampoo *noun* 1 an act of shampooing 2 a soapy liquid used for cleaning the hair 3 a similar liquid used for cleaning carpets or upholstery ◇ *verb* wash or clean with shampoo

shamrock *noun* a plant like clover with leaves divided in three

shanghai *verb* 1 drug and send to sea as a sailor 2 trick into doing something unpleasant

Shangri-la *noun* an imaginary paradise

shank *noun* 1 the part of the leg between the knee and the foot 2 a long straight part (of a tool *etc*)

shank's pony *informal* walking, on foot

shan't *short for* shall not

shanty[1] *noun* (*plural* **shanties**) a roughly-made hut

shanty[2] *noun* a sailors' song

shantytown *noun* an area of makeshift, squalid housing

shape *noun* 1 the form or outline of anything 2 a person's form or figure 3 a form, person *etc*: *an assistant in the shape of my brother* 4 condition: *in good shape* ◇ *verb* 1 make into a certain form 2 model, mould 3 develop (in a particular way): *our plans are shaping well* ◇ **shapeless** *adj* having no shape or regular form ◇ **shapely** *adj* having an attractive shape

■ *noun* 1 form, outline, silhouette, profile, model, mould, pattern, cut, lines, contours, format, configuration 3 form, contours, figure, physique, build, frame 4 condition, state, form, health, trim, fettle ◇ *verb* 1, 2 fashion, model, mould, cast, forge, sculpt, carve, whittle

> *Geometrical shapes include*:
> polygon, circle, semicircle,
> quadrant, oval, ellipse, crescent,
> triangle, equilateral triangle,
> isosceles triangle, scalene triangle,
> quadrilateral, square, rectangle,
> oblong, rhombus, diamond, kite,
> trapezium, parallelogram,
> pentagon, hexagon, heptagon,
> octagon, nonagon, decagon;
> polyhedron, cube, cuboid, prism,
> pyramid, tetrahedron, pentahedron,
> octahedron, cylinder, cone, sphere,
> hemisphere

share *noun* 1 one part of something that is divided among several people 2 one of the parts into which the money of a business firm is divided ◇ *verb* 1 divide out among a number of people 2 allow others to use (your possessions *etc*) 3 have or use in common with someone else: *we share a liking for music*

■ *noun* 1 portion, ration, quota, allowance, allocation, allotment, lot, part, division, proportion, percentage, cut ◇ *verb* 1 divide, split, go halves, share out, distribute, dole out, mete out, give

out, deal out, apportion, allot, allocate, assign

shareholder *noun* someone who owns shares in a business company

shareware *noun* computer software that is made available for a small fee

shark *noun* 1 a large, very fierce, flesh-eating fish 2 *informal* a swindler

sharp *adj* 1 cutting, piercing 2 having a thin edge or fine point 3 hurting, stinging, biting: *sharp wind/sharp words* 4 alert, quick-witted 5 severe, inclined to scold 6 *music* of a note: raised half a tone in pitch 7 of a voice: shrill 8 of an outline: clear ◇ *adv* punctually: *come at ten o'clock sharp* ◇ *noun, music* a sign (♯) showing that a note is to be raised half a tone ◇ **sharp practice** cheating ◇ **sharp-witted** *adj* alert, intelligent ◇ **look sharp** hurry

■ *adj* 2 pointed, keen, edged, knife-edged, razor-sharp, cutting, serrated, jagged, barbed, spiky 4 quick-witted, alert, shrewd, astute, perceptive, observant, discerning, penetrating, clever 5 cutting, caustic, sarcastic, sardonic, scathing, vitriolic, mordant ◇ *adv* punctually, promptly, on the dot, exactly, precisely

◪ *adj* 2 blunt 4 slow, stupid 5 gentle

sharpen *verb* make or grow sharp

sharpener *noun* an instrument for sharpening: *pencil sharpener*

sharper *noun* a cheat, *esp* at cards

shatter *verb* 1 break in pieces 2 to upset, ruin (hopes, health *etc*)

■ 1 break, smash, splinter, shiver, crack, split, burst, explode, blast, crush, demolish, destroy, devastate 2 wreck, ruin, overturn, upset

shave *verb* 1 cut away hair with a razor 2 scrape away the surface of (wood *etc*) 3 touch lightly, or just avoid touching, in passing ◇ *noun* 1 the act of shaving 2 a narrow escape: *a close shave* ◇ **shaven** *adj* shaved

shavings *noun plural* very thin slices of wood *etc*

shawl *noun* a loose covering for the shoulders

she *pronoun* a woman, girl or female animal *etc* already spoken about (used only as the subject of a verb): *when the girl saw us, she waved*

sheaf *noun* (*plural* **sheaves**) a bundle (*eg* of corn, papers) tied together

shear *verb* (**shears**, **shearing**, **shorn**, **sheared**) **1** clip, cut (*esp* wool from a sheep) **2** cut through, cut off ◇ **shears** *noun plural* large scissors

⚠ Do not confuse with: **sheer**

sheath *noun* **1** a case for a sword or dagger **2** a long close-fitting covering **3** a condom ◇ **sheathe** *verb* put into a sheath

▤ **1** scabbard **2** case, sleeve, envelope, shell, casing, covering **3** condom, *slang* rubber, *slang* French letter, *slang* johnnie

shebang *noun*, *informal* a matter, an affair

shed[1] *noun* **1** a building for storage or shelter: *coalshed/bicycle shed* **2** an outhouse

▤ **2** outhouse, lean-to, hut, shack

shed[2] *verb* (**sheds**, **shedding**, **shedded**) **1** throw or cast off (leaves, a skin, clothing) **2** pour out (tears, blood) **3** give out (light *etc*)

▤ **1** cast (off), moult, slough, discard **2** drop, spill, pour, shower **3** diffuse, emit, radiate, shine, throw

sheen *noun* brightness, gloss

▤ lustre, gloss, shine, shimmer, brightness, brilliance, shininess, polish, burnish

sheep *noun* (*plural* **sheep**) **1** an animal whose flesh is used as food and whose fleece is used for wool **2** a very meek person who lacks confidence ◇ **sheep-dip** *noun* a liquid for disinfecting sheep

sheepdog *noun* a dog trained to look after sheep

sheepish *adj* shy; embarrassed, shamefaced

▤ ashamed, shamefaced, embarrassed, mortified, chastened, abashed, uncomfortable, self-conscious, silly, foolish

▤ unabashed, brazen, bold

sheepshank *noun* a kind of knot, used for shortening a rope

sheepskin *noun* **1** the skin of a sheep **2** a kind of leather made from this

sheer[1] *adj* **1** very steep: *sheer drop from the cliff* **2** pure, not mixed: *sheer delight/sheer nonsense* **3** of cloth: very thin or fine ◇ *adv* straight up and down, very steeply

▤ *adj* **1** vertical, perpendicular, precipitous, abrupt, steep **2** utter, complete, total, absolute, thorough, mere, pure, unadulterated, downright, out-and-out, rank **3** thin, fine, flimsy, gauzy, gossamer, translucent, transparent, seethrough

▤ *adj* **1** gentle, gradual **3** thick, heavy

⚠ Do not confuse with: **shear**

sheer[2] *verb* turn aside from a straight line, deviate

sheet *noun* **1** a large piece of linen, cotton, nylon *etc* for a bed **2** a large thin piece of metal, glass, ice *etc* **3** a piece of paper **4** a sail ◇ **sheet-anchor** *noun* a large anchor for use in emergencies ◇ **sheeting** *noun* any material from which sheets are made ◇ **sheet lightning** lightning which appears in great sheets or flashes

▤ **2** piece, panel, slab, pane, expanse **3** leaf, page, folio, piece

sheikh or **sheik** *noun* an Arab chief

shekel *noun*, *hist* an ancient Jewish weight and coin

shelf *noun* (*plural* **shelves**) **1** a board fixed on a wall, for laying things on **2** a flat layer of rock, a ledge **3** a sandbank

shell *noun* **1** a hard outer covering (of a shellfish, egg, nut *etc*) **2** a husk or pod (*eg* of peas) **3** a metal case filled with explosive fired from a gun **4** a framework, *eg* of a building not yet completed or burnt out: *only the shell of the warehouse was left* ◇ *verb* **1** take the shell from (a nut, egg *etc*) **2** fire shells at

▤ *noun* **1** covering, hull, husk, pod, rind, crust, case, casing **4** frame, framework, structure, skeleton ◇ *verb* **2** bomb, bombard, barrage, blitz, attack

she'll *short for* **she will**

shellac *noun* a type of resin once used to make gramophone records

shellfish *noun* a water creature covered with a shell, *eg* an oyster, limpet or mussel

shelter *noun* **1** a building which acts as a protection from harm, rain, wind *etc* **2** the state of being protected from any of these ◊ *verb* **1** give protection to **2** put in a place of shelter or protection **3** go to, or stay in, a place of shelter ◊ **take shelter** go to a place of shelter

≡ *noun* **1** haven, refuge, retreat **2** security, safety, sanctuary, asylum ◊ *verb* **1** protect, safeguard, defend, guard, shield, harbour, hide, accommodate, put up **2** cover, shroud, screen, shade

⊟ *verb* **2** expose

shelve *verb* **1** put up shelves in **2** put aside (a problem *etc*) for later consideration

≡ **2** postpone, defer, put off, suspend, halt, put aside, pigeonhole, put on ice, mothball

shenanigans *noun plural, informal* trickery, mischief

shepherd, shepherdess *noun* someone who looks after sheep ◊ *verb* watch over carefully, guide ◊ **shepherd's pie** a dish of minced meat covered with mashed potatoes

sherbet *noun* a sweet powder eaten as confectionery or made into a fizzy drink

sheriff *noun* **1** the chief representative of a monarch in a county, whose duties include keeping the peace **2** in Scotland, the chief judge of a county **3** *US* the chief law-enforcement officer of a county

sherry *noun* a strong kind of wine, often drunk before a meal

shiatsu /ʃɪˈatsuː/ *noun* a Japanese therapy which treats illness by applying pressure to certain points of the body

shibboleth *noun* **1** a common saying **2** an outdated catchphrase, custom *etc* **3** a word or attribute which identifies members of a group

Originally a word giving membership to a group, after a Biblical story in which its correct pronunciation was used as a password

shied *past form* of **shy**

shield *noun* **1** anything that protects from harm **2** a broad piece of metal carried by a soldier *etc* as a defence against weapons **3** a shield-shaped trophy won in a competition **4** a shield-shaped plaque bearing a coat-of-arms ◊ *verb* protect, defend, shelter

≡ *noun* **1** defence, bulwark, rampart, screen, guard, cover, shelter, protection, safeguard **2** buckler, escutcheon ◊ *verb* defend, guard, protect, safeguard, screen, shade, shadow, cover, shelter

⊟ *verb* expose

shift *verb* **1** move, change the position of: *shift the furniture/trying to shift the blame* **2** change position or direction: *the wind shifted* **3** get rid of **4** in a vehicle: change (gear) ◊ *noun* **1** a change: *shift of emphasis* **2** a change of position, transfer **3** a group of workers on duty at the same time: *day shift/night shift* **4** a specified period of work or duty **5** a loose-fitting lightweight dress

≡ *verb* **1** move, budge, dislodge, displace, relocate, reposition, rearrange **2** transfer, switch, swerve, veer

shifty *adj* not to be trusted, looking dishonest

≡ untrustworthy, dishonest, deceitful, scheming, contriving, artful, tricky, wily, crafty, cunning, sly, devious, evasive, slippery, furtive, underhand, dubious, *informal* shady

shiitake *noun* a dark brown Japanese mushroom

shilling *noun, Brit hist* a silver-coloured coin in use before decimalization, worth of £1 (now the 5 pence piece)

shillyshally *verb* (**shillyshallies, shillyshallying, shillyshallied**) hesitate in making up your mind, waver

shimmer *verb* shine with a quivering

or unsteady light ◇*noun* a quivering light

▤ *verb* glisten, gleam, glimmer, glitter, scintillate, twinkle ◇ *noun* lustre, gleam, glimmer, glitter, glow

shin *noun* the front part of the leg below the knee ◇ **shin up** climb

shindig *noun*, *informal* a party, a celebration

shindy *noun* (*plural* **shindies**) *informal* a noise, uproar

shine *verb* (**shines**, **shining**, **shone**) **1** give out or reflect light **2** be bright **3** polish (shoes etc) **4** be very good at: *he shines at arithmetic* ◇ *noun* **1** brightness **2** an act of polishing ◇ **shining** *adj* **1** very bright and clear **2** admired, distinguished: *a shining example*

▤ *verb* **1** beam, radiate, glow, flash, glare, gleam, glint, glitter, sparkle, twinkle, shimmer, glisten, glimmer **3** polish, burnish, buff, brush, rub **4** excel, stand out

shingle *noun* coarse gravel of rounded stones on the shores of rivers or of the sea ◇ **shingles** *noun plural* an infectious disease causing a painful rash

shinty *noun* a Scottish ball-game resembling hockey

shiny *adj* glossy, polished ◇ **shininess** *noun*

▤ polished, burnished, sheeny, lustrous, glossy, sleek, bright, gleaming, glistening

▨ dull, matt

ship *noun* a large vessel for journeys across water ◇ *verb* (**ships**, **shipping**, **shipped**) **1** take onto a ship **2** send by ship **3** go by ship

▤ *noun* vessel, craft, liner, steamer, tanker, trawler, ferry, boat, yacht

shipment *noun* **1** an act of putting on board ship **2** a load of goods sent by ship

shipshape *adj* in good order, neat, trim

shipwreck *noun* **1** the sinking or destruction of a ship (*esp* by accident) **2** a wrecked ship **3** ruin ◇ **shipwrecked** *adj* involved in a shipwreck

shipwright *noun* someone who is employed to build or repair ships

shipyard *noun* the yard in which ships are built or repaired

shire *noun* a county

shirk *verb* avoid or evade (doing your duty *etc*) ◇ **shirker** *noun*

▤ dodge, evade, avoid, *informal* duck, shun, slack, *informal* skive

shirt *noun* a garment worn on the upper part of the body, having a collar, sleeves and buttons down the front

shish kebab pieces of meat and vegetables grilled on a skewer

shit *noun*, *taboo slang* **1** excrement, faeces **2** an unpleasant or worthless person ◇ *verb* (**shits**, **shitting**, **shitted** or **shat**) empty the bowels ◇ *exclam* expressing anger, annoyance, displeasure *etc* ◇ **shitty** *adj* very disagreeable, unpleasant

shiver *verb* tremble with cold or fear ◇ *noun* **1** the act of shivering **2** a small broken piece: *shivers of glass*

▤ *verb* **1** shudder, tremble, quiver, quake, shake, palpitate

shoal¹ *noun* a group of fishes, moving and feeding together

shoal² *noun* a shallow place, a sandbank

shock *noun* **1** a sudden forceful blow **2** a feeling of fright, horror, dismay *etc* **3** a state of weakness or illness following such feelings **4** the cause of such feelings **5** the effect on the body of an electric current passing through it **6** a state of physical collapse caused by *eg* a drug overdose **7** an earthquake **8** a bushy mass (of hair) ◇ *verb* **1** give a shock to **2** upset or horrify ◇ **shock-absorber** *noun* a device in an aircraft, car *etc* for lessening the impact or force of bumps ◇ **shocker** *noun*, *informal* **1** a sensational tale **2** an offensive person or thing ◇ **shocking** *adj* causing horror or dismay; disgusting

▤ *noun* **2** fright, start, jolt, impact, collision, surprise, bombshell, *informal* whammy, dismay, consternation, disgust, outrage **3** trauma, upset, distress ◇ *verb* **1** jolt, jar, shake, agitate **2** disquiet, unnerve, confound, dismay, disgust, revolt, sicken, offend, appal, outrage, scandalize, horrify, astound, stagger, stun, stupefy

◼ *noun* **2** delight, pleasure, reassurance ◇ *verb* delight, please, reassure

shod *adj* wearing shoes ◇ *verb, past form* of **shoe**

shoddy *adj* **1** of poor material or quality: *shoddy goods* **2** mean, low: *a shoddy trick*

◼ 1 inferior, second-rate, cheap, tawdry, tatty, trashy, rubbishy, poor, careless, slipshod, slapdash

◰ 1 superior, well-made

shoe *noun* **1** a stiff outer covering for the foot, not reaching above the ankle **2** a rim of iron nailed to the hoof of a horse ◇ *verb* (**shoes, shoeing, shod**) put shoes on (a horse)

shoehorn *noun* a curved piece of horn, metal *etc* for making a shoe slip easily over your heel

shoelace *noun* a cord or string used for fastening a shoe

shoemaker *noun* someone who makes and mends shoes

shoestring *noun*: **on a shoestring** with very little money

shone *past form* of **shine**

shoo *exclam* used to scare away birds, animals *etc* ◇ *verb* (**shoos, shooing, shooed**) drive or scare away

shook *past form* of **shake**

shoot *verb* (**shoots, shooting, shot**) **1** send a bullet from a gun, or an arrow from a bow **2** hit or kill with an arrow, bullet *etc* **3** let fly swiftly and with force **4** kick for a goal **5** score (a goal) **6** of a plant: grow new buds **7** photograph, film **8** move very swiftly or suddenly **9** slide (a bolt) ◇ *noun* **1** a new sprout on a plant **2** an expedition to shoot game **3** land where game is shot **4** the shooting of a film or photographic session ◇ **shooting-brake** *noun, old* an estate car ◇ **shooting star** a meteor

◼ *verb* **1** fire, discharge **2** hit, kill, blast, bombard, gun down, snipe at, pick off **3** propel, hurl, fling, project **8** dart, bolt,

dash, tear, rush, race, sprint, speed, charge, hurtle ◇ *noun* **1** sprout, bud, offshoot, branch, twig, sprig

shop *noun* **1** a place where goods are sold **2** a workshop ◇ *verb* (**shops, shopping, shopped**) **1** visit shops and buy goods **2** *slang* betray (someone) to the police ◇ **shop steward** a worker elected by the other workers as their representative ◇ **talk shop** *informal* talk about work when off duty

shopkeeper *noun* someone who owns and keeps a shop

shoplifter *noun* someone who steals goods from a shop

shopper *noun* someone who shops, a customer

shore¹ *noun* the land bordering on a sea or lake

◼ *noun* seashore, beach, sand(s), shingle, strand, waterfront, front, promenade, coast, seaboard, lakeside, bank

shore² *verb* prop (up), support: *shoring up an unprofitable organization*

◼ support, hold, prop, stay, underpin, buttress, brace, strengthen, reinforce

shorn *past participle* of **shear**

short *adj* **1** not long: *short skirt* **2** not tall **3** brief, not lasting long: *short talk* **4** not enough, less than it should be **5** rude, sharp, abrupt **6** *informal* lacking money **7** of pastry: crisp and crumbling easily ◇ *adv* **1** suddenly, abruptly: *stop short* **2** not as far as intended: *the shot fell short* ◇ *noun* **1** a short film **2** a short-circuit **3** (**shorts**) short trousers ◇ *verb* short-circuit ◇ **short cut** a short way of going somewhere or doing something ◇ **short-handed** *adj* having fewer workers than usual ◇ **short list** a list of candidates selected from the total number of applicants or contestants ◇ **short-sighted** *adj* **1** seeing clearly only things which are near **2** taking no account of what may happen in the future ◇ **short-tempered** *adj* easily made angry ◇ **short-term** *adj* intended to last only a short time ◇ **give short shrift to** waste little time or consideration on ◇ **in short** in a few words ◇ **short for** an abbreviated form of: *Jen* *is short for Jennifer* ◇ **short of 1** not having enough: *short of money* **2** less than, not as much or as far as: *5 miles short of Inverness/£5 short of the price* **3** without going as far as: *he didn't know how to get the money, short of stealing it*

■ *adj* **2** small, little, low, petite, diminutive, squat **3** brief, concise, succinct, terse, pithy, compact **4** inadequate, insufficient, deficient, lacking, wanting, low, poor, meagre, scant, sparse **5** brusque, curt, gruff, snappy, sharp, abrupt, laconic, blunt, direct, rude, impolite, discourteous, uncivil

☒ *adj* **2** tall **3** long, lasting **4** adequate, ample **5** polite

shortage *noun* a lack

■ inadequacy, insufficiency, deficiency, shortfall, deficit, lack, want, need, scarcity, paucity, poverty, dearth, absence

☒ sufficiency, abundance, surplus

shortbread *noun* a thick biscuit made of butter and flour *etc*

shortcoming *noun* a fault, a defect

■ defect, imperfection, fault, flaw, drawback, failing, weakness, foible

shorten *verb* make less in length

■ cut, trim, prune, crop, dock, curtail, truncate, abbreviate, abridge, reduce, lessen, decrease, diminish, take up

☒ lengthen

shorthand *noun* a method of swift writing using strokes and dots to show sounds (*contrasted with* **longhand**)

shortlived *adj* living or lasting only a short time

shortly *adv* **1** soon **2** curtly, abruptly **3** briefly

■ **1** soon, before long, presently, by and by

short-circuit *noun* the missing out of a major part of an intended electric circuit, sometimes causing blowing of fuses ◇ *verb* **1** of an electrical appliance: have a short-circuit **2** bypass (a difficulty *etc*)

shot *noun* **1** something which is shot or fired **2** small lead bullets, used in cartridges **3** a single act of shooting **4** the sound of a gun being fired **5** the distance covered by a bullet, arrow *etc* **6** a

marksman **7** a throw or turn in a game **8** an attempt at doing something, guessing *etc* **9** a photograph **10** a scene in a motion picture ◇ *adj* **1** of silk: showing changing colours **2** streaked or mixed with (a colour *etc*) ◇ *past form of* **shoot** ◇ **shotgun** *noun* a light type of gun which fires shot ◇ **a shot in the dark** a guess

■ *noun* **1** bullet, missile, projectile, ball, pellet, *informal* slug, discharge, blast **8** attempt, try, effort, endeavour, *informal* go, *informal* bash, *informal* crack, *informal* stab, guess, turn

should *verb* **1** the form of the verb **shall** used to express a condition: *I should go if I had time* **2** used to mean 'ought to': *you should know that already*

shoulder *noun* **1** the part of the body between the neck and upper arm **2** the upper part of an animal's foreleg **3** a hump, a ridge: *the shoulder of the hill* ◇ *verb* **1** carry on the shoulders **2** bear the full weight of (a burden *etc*) **3** push with the shoulder ◇ **shoulderblade** *noun* the broad flat bone of the shoulder

shout *noun* **1** a loud cry or call **2** a loud burst (of laughter *etc*) ◇ *verb* make a loud cry

■ *noun & verb* call, cry, scream, shriek, yell, roar, bellow, bawl, howl, bay, cheer

shove *verb* push roughly, thrust, push aside ◇ *noun* a rough push

■ *verb* push, thrust, drive, propel, force, barge, jostle, elbow, shoulder, press, crowd

shovel *noun* a spade-like tool used for lifting coal, gravel *etc* ◇ *verb* (**shovels**, **shovelling**, **shovelled**) lift or move with a shovel

show *verb* (**shows**, **showing**, **showed**, **shown** or **showed**) **1** allow, or cause, to be seen: *show me your new dress* **2** be able to be seen: *your underskirt is showing* **3** exhibit, display (an art collection *etc*) **4** point out (the way *etc*) **5** direct, guide: *show her to a seat* **6** make clear, demonstrate: *that shows that I was right* ◇ *noun* **1** the act of showing **2** a display, an exhibition **3** a performance, an entertainment ◊ **show business** the branch of the theatre concerned with variety entertainments ◊ **show off 1** show or display (something) **2** try to impress others with your talents *etc* ◊ **show up 1** make to stand out clearly **2** expose, make obvious (*esp* someone's faults)

◼ *verb* **1** reveal, expose, uncover, disclose, present, offer **3** exhibit, display **5** lead, guide, conduct, usher, escort, accompany **6** prove, illustrate, manifest, exemplify, explain, clarify, elucidate ◊ *noun* **2** presentation, exhibition, exposition, fair, display **3** pageant, extravaganza, spectacle, entertainment, performance, production, staging, showing ◊ **show off 1** display, flaunt, exhibit, demonstrate, advertise **2** swagger, brag, boast, *informal* swank ◊ **show up 1** show, expose, unmask, lay bare, highlight, pinpoint **2** humiliate, embarrass, mortify, shame, disgrace

shower *noun* **1** a short fall of rain **2** a large quantity: *a shower of questions* **3** a device in which water is sprayed from above **4** a cubicle or room containing this device **5** *US* a party at which gifts are given to someone about to be married or for a baby ◊ *verb* **1** pour (something) down on **2** bathe under a shower ◊ **showerproof** *adj* of material, a coat *etc*: able to withstand light rain ◊ **showery** *adj* raining from time to time

◼ *noun* **2** stream, torrent, deluge, hail, volley, barrage

showjumping *noun* a sport in which riders on horseback jump a variety of obstacles ◊ **showjumper** *noun*

shown *past participle* of **show**

showpiece *noun* **1** an item on display **2** an item presented as an excellent example of its type

showroom *noun* a room where goods are laid out for people to see

showy *adj* bright, gaudy; (too) obvious, striking

◼ flashy, flamboyant, ostentatious, *informal* glitzy, gaudy, garish, loud, tawdry, fancy, ornate, pretentious, pompous,

informal swanky, *informal* flash

◼ quiet, restrained

shrank *see* **shrink**

shrapnel *noun* **1** a shell containing bullets *etc* which scatter on explosion **2** splinters of metal, a bomb *etc*

After Henry *Shrapnel*, 18th-century British general who invented the shell

shred *noun* **1** a long, narrow piece, cut or torn off **2** a scrap, a very small amount: *not a shred of evidence* ◊ *verb* (**shreds**, **shredding**, **shredded**) cut or tear into shreds

◼ *noun* **1** ribbon, tatter, rag, scrap, snippet, sliver **2** bit, piece, fragment, jot, iota, atom, grain, mite, whit, trace

shrew *noun* **1** a small mouse-like type of animal with a long nose **2** a quarrelsome or scolding woman ◊ **shrewish** *adj* quarrelsome, ill-tempered

shrewd *adj* clever, cunning

◼ astute, judicious, well-advised, calculated, far-sighted, smart, clever, intelligent, sharp, keen, acute, alert, perceptive, observant, discerning, discriminating, knowing, *informal* clued-up, calculating, cunning, crafty, artful, wily, sly

◼ unwise, obtuse, nave, unsophisticated

shriek *verb* make a shrill scream or laugh ◊ *noun* a shrill scream or laugh

◼ *verb & noun* scream, screech, squawk, squeal, cry, shout, yell, wail, howl

shrift *noun*: **give someone short shrift** dismiss them quickly

Originally a short confession made before being executed

shrike *noun* a bird which preys on smaller birds

shrill *adj* of a sound or voice: high in tone, piercing ◊ **shrilly** *adv*

◼ high, high-pitched, treble, sharp, acute, piercing, penetrating, screaming, screeching, strident, ear-splitting

◼ deep, low, soft, gentle

shrimp *noun* **1** a small, long-tailed edible shellfish **2** *informal* a small person

shrine noun a holy or sacred place

shrink verb (**shrinks**, **shrinking**, **shrank** or **shrunk**, **shrunk**) **1** make or become smaller **2** draw back in fear and disgust (from) ◇ noun, informal a psychiatrist ◇ **shrink-wrap** noun clear plastic film for wrapping, heated so that it shrinks to fit tightly ◇ verb wrap with this type of film

■ verb **1** contract, shorten, narrow, decrease, lessen, diminish, dwindle, shrivel, wrinkle, wither **2** recoil, back away, shy away, withdraw, retire, balk, quail, cower, cringe, wince, flinch

▨ verb **1** expand, stretch **2** accept, embrace

shrinkage noun the amount by which something grows smaller

shrivel verb (**shrivels**, **shrivelling**, **shrivelled**) dry up, wrinkle, wither

■ wrinkle, pucker, wither, wilt, shrink, dwindle, parch, dehydrate, desiccate, scorch, sear, burn, frizzle

shroud noun **1** a cloth covering a dead body **2** something which covers: *a shroud of mist* ◇ verb wrap up, cover

■ verb wrap, envelop, swathe, cloak, veil, screen, hide, conceal, blanket, cover

Shrove Tuesday the day before Ash Wednesday

shrub noun a small bush or plant ◇ **shrubbery** noun (plural **shrubberies**) a place where shrubs grow

---

Shrubs include:
azalea, berberis, broom, buddleia, camellia, carabana, clematis, cotoneaster, daphne, dogwood, eucryphia, euonymus, firethorn, flowering currant, forsythia, fuchsia, heather, hebe, holly, honeysuckle, hydrangea, ivy, japonica, jasmine, laburnum, laurel, lavender, lilac, magnolia, mallow, mimosa, mock orange, peony, privet, musk rose, rhododendron, rose, spiraea, viburnum, weigela, witch hazel, wisteria
see also **flower**; **plant**

---

shrug verb (**shrugs**, **shrugging**, **shrugged**) show doubt, lack of interest etc by drawing up the shoulders ◇ noun a movement of the shoulders to show lack of interest ◇ **shrug off** dismiss, treat as being unimportant

shrunk past form of **shrink**

shrunken adj made smaller

shtook adj, slang trouble, bother

shtoom adj, slang quiet, silent: *keeping shtoom*

shudder verb tremble from fear, cold, disgust ◇ noun a trembling

■ verb shiver, shake, tremble, quiver, quake, heave, convulse ◇ noun shiver, quiver, tremor, spasm, convulsion

shuffle verb **1** mix, rearrange (eg playing-cards) **2** move by dragging or sliding the feet along the ground without lifting them **3** move (the feet) in this way ◇ noun **1** a rearranging **2** a dragging movement of the feet

■ verb **1** mix (up), intermix, jumble, confuse, disorder, rearrange, reorganize, shift around, switch **2** shamble, scuffle, scrape, drag, limp, hobble

shun verb (**shuns**, **shunning**, **shunned**) avoid, keep clear of

■ avoid, evade, elude, steer clear of, shy away from, spurn, ignore, cold-shoulder, ostracize

▨ accept, embrace

shunt verb move (railway trains, engines etc) onto a side track

shut verb (**shuts**, **shutting**, **shut**) **1** move (a door, window, lid etc) so that it covers an opening **2** close, lock (a building etc) **3** become closed: *the door shut with a bang* **4** confine, restrain in a building etc: *shut the dog in his kennel* ◇ **shut down** close (a factory etc) ◇ **shut up 1** close completely **2** informal stop speaking or making other noise

■ **1** close, slam, seal **2** fasten, secure, lock, latch, bolt, bar ◇ **shut up 2** pipe down, hold one's tongue, informal clam up

shutter noun **1** a cover for a window **2** a cover which closes over a camera lens as it takes a picture

shuttle noun the part of a weaving

loom which carries the cross thread from side to side ◇ *adj* of a transport service: going frequently and directly between two places

shuttlecock *noun* a rounded cork stuck with feathers, used in the game of badminton

shy¹ *adj* **1** of a wild animal: easily frightened, timid **2** lacking confidence in the presence of others **3** not wanting to attract attention ◇ *verb* (**shies, shying, shied**) jump or turn suddenly aside in fear ◇ **shyly** *adv* ◇ **shyness** *noun* ◇ **fight shy of** avoid, keep away from

■ *adj* **2** timid, bashful, diffident, coy, self-conscious, hesitant, nervous **3** modest, self-effacing, shrinking, cautious, reticent, reserved, retiring

◪ *adj* **2** assertive, confident **3** bold

shy² *verb* throw, toss ◇ *noun* a throw, toss

shyster *noun, slang* a swindler

SI *abbrev, French* Système International (d'Unités), the metric unit system

Siamese *adj*: **Siamese cat** a fawn-coloured domestic cat ◇ **Siamese twins** conjoined twins

sibilant *adj* of a sound: hissing

sibling *noun* a brother or sister

sibyl *noun* a prophetess

sic *adv* so, thus (written in brackets after a word to show that it is meant to be spelt as given)

sick *adj* **1** wanting to vomit **2** vomiting **3** not well, ill **4** (with **of**) tired of ◇ **sickness** *noun* ◇ **sick bed** or **sick room** a bed or room for people to rest in when ill ◇ **sick leave** time off work for illness

■ **1** queasy, bilious, nauseous, seasick, airsick **3** ill, unwell, indisposed, laid up, poorly, ailing, sickly, off-colour, *informal* under the weather, weak, feeble **4** bored, *informal* fed up, tired, weary, disgusted, nauseated

◪ **3** well, healthy

sicken *verb* make or become sick ◇ **sickening** *adj* **1** causing sickness **2** disgusting, revolting

■ nauseate, revolt, disgust, repel, put off,

slang turn off ◇ **sickening 2** nauseating, revolting, *informal* stomach-turning, disgusting, offensive, distasteful, foul, vile, loathsome, repulsive

◪ delight, attract ◇ **sickening 2** delightful, pleasing, attractive

sickle *noun* a hooked knife for cutting or reaping grain, hay *etc* ◇ **sickle-cell anaemia** a hereditary disease in which the red blood cells are distorted in a sickle shape

sickly *adj* **1** unhealthy **2** causing a feeling of sickness; too sweet

■ **1** unhealthy, infirm, delicate, weak, feeble, frail, wan, pallid, ailing, indisposed, sick, bilious, faint, languid **2** nauseating, revolting, sweet, syrupy, cloying

side *noun* **1** an edge, border or boundary line **2** a surface that is not the top, bottom, front or back **3** either surface of a piece of paper, cloth *etc* **4** the right or left part of the body **5** a division, a part: *the north side of the town* **6** an aspect, point of view: *all sides of the problem* **7** a slope (of a hill) **8** a team or party which is opposing another ◇ *adj* **1** on or towards the side: *side door* **2** indirect, additional but less important: *side issue* ◇ *verb* (with **with**) support (one person, group *etc* against another) ◇ **side effect** an additional (often bad) effect of a drug ◇ **take sides** choose to support (a party, person) against another

■ *noun* **1** edge, margin, fringe, periphery, border, boundary, limit, verge, brink, bank, shore **6** standpoint, viewpoint, view, aspect, angle, slant **8** team, party, faction, camp ◇ *adj* **1** lateral, flanking **2** secondary, subsidiary, subordinate, lesser, minor

sideboard *noun* a piece of furniture in a dining-room for holding dishes *etc*

sidecar *noun* a small car for a passenger, attached to a motorcycle

sideline *noun* an extra bit of business outside regular work

sidelong *adj & adv* from or to the side: *sidelong glance*

sidereal *adj* relating to the stars

sideshow *noun* a less important

show that is part of a larger one

sidestep *verb* avoid

■ avoid, dodge, duck, evade, elude, skirt, bypass

◨ tackle, deal with

sidetrack *verb* turn (someone) away from what they were going to do or say

sidewalk *noun*, *US* a pavement

sideways *adv* 1 with the side foremost 2 towards the side

■ 2 sidewards, edgeways, laterally, obliquely

siding *noun* a short line of rails on which trucks are shunted off the main line

sidle *verb* 1 go or move sideways 2 move stealthily, sneak

■ 2 slink, edge, inch, creep, sneak

siege /siːdʒ/ *noun* 1 an attempt to capture a town *etc* by keeping it surrounded by an armed force 2 a constant attempt to gain control ◇ **lay siege to** besiege

siemens unit a unit of electrical conductance

sienna *noun* a reddish-brown, or yellowish-brown, pigment used in paints

sierra *noun* a range of mountains with jagged peaks

siesta *noun* a short sleep or rest taken in the afternoon

sieve /sɪv/ *noun* a container with a mesh used to separate liquids from solids, or fine pieces from coarse pieces *etc* ◇ *verb* put through a sieve

■ *noun* colander, strainer, sifter, riddle ◇ *verb* sift, strain, separate

sift *verb* 1 separate by passing through a sieve 2 consider and examine closely: *sifting all the evidence*

■ 1 sieve, strain, filter, riddle, screen, winnow, separate, sort 2 examine, scrutinize, investigate, analyse, probe, review

sigh *noun* a long, deep-sounding breath, showing tiredness, longing *etc* ◇ *verb* give out a sigh

■ *verb* breathe, exhale, moan, complain, lament, grieve

sight *noun* 1 the act or power of seeing 2 a view, a glimpse: *catch sight of her* 3 (often **sights**) something worth seeing: *the sights of London* 4 something or someone unusual, ridiculous, shocking *etc*: *she's quite a sight in that hat* 5 a guide on a gun for taking aim ◇ *verb* 1 get a view of, see suddenly 2 look at through the sight of a gun ◇ **sight-reading** *noun* playing or singing from music that has not been seen previously

■ *noun* 1 vision, eyesight, seeing, observation, perception 2 view, look, glance, glimpse 4 eyesore, monstrosity, *informal* fright ◇ *verb* 1 see, observe, spot, notice, glimpse, perceive, discern, distinguish, make out

⚠ Do not confuse with: **site** and **cite**

sightseeing *noun* visiting the chief buildings, monuments *etc* of a place

sign *noun* 1 a mark with a special meaning, a symbol 2 a gesture (*eg* a nod, wave of the hand) to show your meaning 3 an advertisement or notice giving information 4 something which shows what is happening or is going to happen: *signs of irritation/a sign of good weather* ◇ *verb* 1 write your name on (a document, cheque *etc*) 2 make a sign or gesture to 3 show (your meaning) by a sign or gesture 4 become employed by signing a contract: *United have signed Veron* 5 use sign language ◇ **sign language** communication using gestures to represent words and ideas ◇ **sign on** *informal* claim state benefits for the unemployed ◇ **sign up** enter your name on a list for work, the army *etc*

■ *noun* 1 symbol, token, character, figure, representation, emblem, badge, insignia, logo 2 indication, signal, gesture 3 notice, poster, board, placard 4 evidence, manifestation, clue, pointer, hint, suggestion, trace, portent, omen, forewarning ◇ *verb* 1 autograph, initial, endorse

signal *noun* 1 a gesture, light or sound giving a command, warning etc: *air-raid signal* 2 something used for this purpose: *railway signals* 3 the wave of sound received or sent out by a radio *etc* set ◇ *verb* (**signals, signalling, signalled**) **1** make signals (to) **2** send (information) by signal ◇ *adj* remarkable: *a signal success* ◇ **signalman** *noun* someone who works railway signals, or who sends signals

▣ *noun* **1** sign, indication, mark, gesture, cue, go-ahead, password, alert, warning, tip-off **2** light, indicator, beacon, flare, rocket, alarm

signature *noun* **1** a signed name **2** an act of signing **3** *music* the flats or sharps at the beginning of a piece which show its key, or figures showing its timing ◇ **signature tune** a tune used to identify a particular radio or television series *etc* played at the beginning or end of the programme

signatory *noun* (*plural* **signatories**) someone who has signed an agreement *etc*

signet *noun* a small seal, usually bearing someone's initials ◇ **signet ring** a ring imprinted with a signet

⚠ Do not confuse with: **cygnet**

significance *noun* **1** meaning **2** importance ◇ **significant** *adj* meaning much; important: *no significant change* ◇ **significantly** *adv*

▣ **1** meaning, implication, sense, point, message **2** importance, relevance, consequence, matter, interest, consideration, weight, force ◇ **significant** important, relevant, consequential, momentous, weighty, serious, noteworthy, critical, vital, marked, considerable, appreciable

signify *verb* (**signifies, signifying, signified**) **1** mean, be a sign of **2** show, make known by a gesture: *signifying disapproval* **3** have meaning or importance

signpost *noun* a post with a sign, *esp* one showing direction and distances to certain places

silage *noun* green fodder preserved in a silo

silence *noun* **1** absence of sound or speech **2** a time of quietness ◇ *verb* cause to be silent

▣ *noun* **1** lull, noiselessness, soundlessness, muteness, dumbness, speechlessness, taciturnity **2** quiet, quietness, hush, peace, stillness, calm ◇ *verb* quiet, quieten, hush, mute, deaden, muffle, stifle, gag, muzzle, suppress, subdue, quell, still, dumbfound

silencer *noun* a device (on a car engine, gun *etc*) for making noise less

silent *adj* **1** free from noise **2** not speaking ◇ **silently** *adv*

▣ **1** inaudible, noiseless, soundless, quiet, peaceful, still, hushed **2** mute, dumb, speechless, tongue-tied, taciturn, mum, reticent, reserved

silhouette *noun* **1** an outline drawing of someone, often in profile, filled in with black **2** a dark outline seen against the light

After the 18th-century French finance minister, Etienne de *Silhouette*, possibly because of his notorious stinginess

silica *noun* a white or colourless substance, of which flint, sandstone, quartz *etc* are mostly made up

silk *noun* **1** very fine, soft fibres spun by silkworms **2** thread or cloth made from this ◇ *adj* **1** made of silk **2** soft, smooth ◇ **silky** *adj* like silk

▣ **silky** silken, fine, sleek, lustrous, glossy, satiny, smooth, soft, velvety

silken *adj* **1** made of silk **2** smooth like silk

silkworm *noun* the caterpillar of certain moths which spins silk

sill *noun* a ledge of wood, stone *etc* below a window or a door

silly *adj* foolish, not sensible

▣ foolish, stupid, imprudent, senseless, pointless, idiotic, *informal* daft, ridiculous, ludicrous, preposterous, absurd, meaningless, irrational, illogical, childish, puerile, immature, irresponsible, scatterbrained, *informal* dizzy, *informal* air-headed

▣ wise, sensible, sane, mature, clever, intelligent

silo *noun* (*plural* **silos**) **1** a tower for

storing grain *etc* **2** a pit or airtight chamber for holding silage **3** an underground chamber built to contain a guided missile

silt *noun* sand or mud left behind by flowing water ◇**silt up** become blocked by mud

■ sediment, deposit, alluvium, sludge, mud, ooze ◇ **silt up** block, clog, choke

silver *noun* **1** a white precious metal, used in ornaments and jewellery, and to conduct electricity **2** money made of silver or of a metal alloy resembling it **3** objects (*esp* cutlery) made of, or plated with, silver **4** a silver medal ◇*adj* made of, or looking like, silver ◇*verb* **1** cover with silver **2** become like silver ◇**silvery** *adj* **1** like silver **2** of sound: ringing and musical ◇**silver foil** or **silver leaf** silver beaten to paper-thinness, used for decoration ◇**silver medal** in sports competitions: a medal of silver awarded for second place ◇**silver wedding** a 25th anniversary of a wedding

silverfish *noun* a wingless, silvery insect, sometimes found in houses

silversmith *noun* someone who makes or sells articles of silver

SIM *abbrev* subscriber identity module ◇**SIM card** a small flat device placed in a mobile phone to allow user identification

simian *adj* ape-like

similar *adj* alike, almost the same ◇**similarly** *adv* **1** in the same, or a similar, way **2** likewise, also

■ alike, close, related, akin, corresponding, equivalent, analogous, comparable, uniform, homogeneous

ⓔ dissimilar, different

similarity *noun* (*plural* **similarities**) a likeness

■ likeness, resemblance, similitude, closeness, relation, correspondence, congruence, equivalence, analogy, comparability, compatibility, agreement, affinity, homogeneity, uniformity

ⓔ dissimilarity, difference

simile *noun* an expression using 'like' or 'as', in which one thing is likened to

another that is well-known for a particular quality (*eg* 'as black as night', 'to swim like a fish')

simmer *verb* cook gently just below or at boiling-point

simnel cake a fruit cake covered with marzipan, traditionally eaten at Easter

simper *verb* **1** smile in a silly manner **2** say with a simper ◇*noun* a silly smile

simple *adj* **1** easy, not difficult or complicated **2** plain, not fancy: *simple hairstyle* **3** ordinary: *simple, everyday objects* **4** of humble rank: *a simple peasant* **5** mere, nothing but: *the simple truth* **6** too trusting, easily cheated **7** foolish, half-witted

■ **1** easy, elementary, straightforward, uncomplicated, uninvolved, clear, lucid, plain, understandable, comprehensible **6** innocent, artless, guileless, ingenuous, naive, green **7** foolish, stupid, silly, idiotic, half-witted, simple-minded, feeble-minded, backward

ⓔ **1** difficult, hard, complicated, intricate **6** sophisticated, worldly, artful **7** clever

simpleton *noun* a foolish person

simplicity *noun* the state of being simple

simplistic *adj* oversimplified

simplify *verb* (**simplifies, simplifying, simplified**) make simpler ◇**simplification** *noun* **1** an act of making simpler **2** a simple form of anything

■ decipher, clarify, paraphrase, abridge, reduce, streamline

simply *adv* **1** in a simple manner **2** merely: *I do it simply for the money* **3** absolutely: *simply beautiful* **4** just: *simply not good enough*

simulacrum *noun* (*plural* **simulacra**) a resemblance, an image

simulate *verb* **1** pretend, feign: *she simulated illness* **2** have the appearance of, look like ◇**simulated** *adj* **1** pretended **2** having the appearance of: *simulated leather* ◇**simulation** *noun*

■ **1** pretend, affect, assume, put on, act, feign, sham, fake, counterfeit

simulcast *noun* a simultaneous television and radio broadcast of the same event

simultaneous *adj* happening, or done, at the same time ◇**simultaneously** *adv*

■ synchronous, synchronic, concurrent, contemporaneous, coinciding, parallel

sin *noun* **1** a wicked act, *esp* one which breaks religious laws **2** wrongdoing **3** *informal* a shame, pity ◇*verb* (**sins, sinning, sinned**) commit a sin, do wrong ◇**sinner** *noun* one who sins

since *adv* **1** (often with **ever**) from that time onwards: *I have avoided him ever since* **2** at a later time: *we have since become friends* **3** ago: *long since* **4** from the time of: *since his arrival* ◇*conj* **1** after the time when: *I have been at home since I returned from Italy* **2** because: *since you are going, I will go too*

sincere *adj* **1** honest, meaning what you say or do: *a sincere friend* **2** truly felt, genuine: *a sincere desire* ◇**sincerely** *adv* ◇**sincerity** *noun*

■ **1** honest, truthful, candid, frank, open, direct, straightforward, plain-spoken, serious, earnest **2** heartfelt, whole-hearted, real, true, genuine, pure, unadulterated

☒ **1** insincere, hypocritical **2** affected

sinecure *noun* a job for which someone receives money but has little or no work to do

Literally 'without cure', originally a paid church position which carried no responsibility for curing souls

sine qua non an indispensable condition

sinew *noun* **1** a tough cord that joins a muscle to a bone **2** (**sinews**) physical strength ◇**sinewy** *adj* having strong sinews, tough

sinful *adj* wicked

■ wrong, wrongful, criminal, bad, wicked, iniquitous, erring, fallen, immoral, corrupt, depraved, impious, ungodly, unholy, irreligious, guilty

sing *verb* (**sings, singing, sang, sung**) **1** make musical sounds with the voice **2** utter (words, a song *etc*) by

doing this ◇**singer** *noun* ◇**sing-song** *noun* **1** a gathering of people singing informally together **2** an up-and-down tone of voice ◇*adj* in an up-and-down voice

singe *verb* burn slightly on the surface, scorch ◇*noun* a surface burn

■ *verb* scorch, char, blacken, burn, sear

single *adj* **1** one only **2** not married or without a partner **3** for one person: *a single bed* **4** for one direction of a journey: *a single ticket* **5** even one: *not a single person turned up* ◇**singleness** *noun* the state of being single ◇**singly** *adv* one by one, separately ◇**single-handed** *adj* working *etc* by yourself ◇**single-minded** *adj* having one aim only ◇**single out** pick out, treat differently in some way

■ **1** one, unique, singular, individual, particular, exclusive, sole, only, lone, solitary **2** free, unattached, unmarried, celibate ◇**single-minded** determined, resolute, dogged, persevering, tireless, unwavering, fixed, unswerving, undeviating, steadfast, dedicated, devoted

singlet *noun* a vest, an undershirt

singular *adj* **1** *grammar* the opposite of **plural**, showing one person, thing *etc* **2** exceptional: *singular success* **3** unusual, strange: *a singular sight* ◇**singularly** *adv* strangely, exceptionally: *singularly ugly*

sinister *adj* suggesting evil, evil-looking

■ ominous, menacing, threatening, disturbing, disquieting, unlucky, inauspicious, malevolent, evil

☒ auspicious, harmless, innocent

sink *verb* (**sinks, sinking, sank, sunk**) **1** go down below the surface of the water *etc* **2** go down or become less: *my hopes sank* **3** of a very ill person: become weaker **4** lower yourself (into): *sink into a chair* **5** push (your teeth *etc*) deep into (something) **6** invest (money *etc*) into a business **7** ruin: *we are sunk* ◇*noun* a basin in a kitchen, bathroom *etc*, with a water supply connected to it and a drain for carrying off dirty water *etc* ◊ **sinker** *noun* a weight fixed to a fishing line *etc*

◼ *verb* **1** descend, slip, fall, disappear, vanish **2** decrease, lessen, subside, abate, dwindle, diminish, ebb, fade, flag, weaken, fail, decline

◼ *verb* **1** rise **2** increase

Sino- *prefix* relating to China or the Chinese

sinuous *adj* bending in and out, winding ◊ **sinuosity** *noun*

sinus *noun* (*plural* **sinuses**) an air cavity in the head connected with the nose ◊ **sinusitis** *noun* inflammation of (one of) the sinuses

sip *verb* (**sips**, **sipping**, **sipped**) drink in very small quantities ◊ *noun* a taste of a drink, a swallow

◼ *verb* taste, sample, drink, sup ◊ *noun* taste, drop, spoonful, mouthful

siphon or **syphon** *noun* **1** a bent tube for drawing off liquids from one container into another **2** a glass bottle, for soda water *etc*, containing such a tube ◊ *verb* **1** draw (off) through a siphon **2** (with **off**) take (part of something) away gradually: *he siphoned off some of the club's funds*

sir *noun* **1** a polite form of address used to a man **2** (**Sir**) the title of a knight or baronet

sire *noun* **1** a male parent, *esp* of a horse **2** *hist* a title used in speaking to a king ◊ *verb* of an animal: to be the male parent of

siren *noun* **1** an instrument that gives out a loud hooting noise as a warning **2** a mythical sea nymph whose singing enchanted sailors and tempted them into danger **3** an attractive but dangerous woman

sirloin *noun* the upper part of the loin of beef

sirocco *noun* a hot dry wind blowing from N Africa to the Mediterranean coast

sirrah *noun, old* sir

sisal *noun* a fibre from a W Indian plant, used for making ropes

sister *noun* **1** a female born of the same parents as yourself **2** a senior nurse, often in charge of a hospital ward **3** a nun ◊ *adj* **1** closely related **2** of similar design or structure ◊ **sisterhood** *noun* **1** the state of being a sister **2** a religious community of women ◊ **sister-in-law** *noun* **1** the sister of your husband or wife **2** the wife of your brother or of your brother-in-law ◊ **sisterly** *adj* like a sister

sit *verb* (**sits**, **sitting**, **sat**) **1** rest on the buttocks, be seated **2** of a bird: perch **3** rest on eggs in order to hatch them **4** be an official member: *sit in parliament/sit on a committee* **5** of a court *etc*: meet officially **6** pose (for) a photographer, painter *etc* **7** take (an examination *etc*) ◊ **sitter** *noun* **1** someone who poses for a portrait *etc* **2** a babysitter **3** a bird sitting on eggs ◊ **sit-in** *noun* an occupation of a building *etc* by protestors ◊ **sit in 1** (with **for**) act as a substitute (for) **2** (with **on**) be present as an observer ◊ **sit tight** be unwilling to move ◊ **sit-up** *noun* an exercise in which the head and torso are raised from a lying position ◊ **sit up 1** sit with your back straight **2** take sudden interest

sitar *noun* a guitar-like instrument of Indian origin with a long neck

sitcom *noun* a television comedy series with a running theme

site *noun* **1** a place where a building, town *etc* is or is to be placed **2** an area set aside for an activity: *a caravan site* ◊ *verb* select a place for (a building *etc*)

◼ *noun* location, place, spot, position, situation, station, setting, scene, plot, lot, ground, area ◊ *verb* locate, place, position, situate, station, set, install

❚ Do not confuse with: **sight** and **cite**

sitting *noun* the state or time of sitting ◊ *adj* **1** seated **2** for sitting in or on **3** in office: *sitting member of parliament* **4** in possession: *sitting tenant* ◊ **sitting duck** someone in an exposed position ◊ **sitting pretty** *informal* in an advantageous situation ◊ **sitting-room** *noun* a room chiefly for sitting in

situated *adj* placed

situation *noun* **1** the place where anything stands **2** a job, employment **3** a state of affairs, circumstances: *in an awkward situation*

▣ **1** site, location, position, place, spot, seat, locality, locale, setting, scenario **2** post, office, job, employment **3** case, circumstances, predicament, state, condition, status, rank, station,

six *noun* the number 6 ◇ *adj* 6 in number ◇ **six-pack** *noun* a package of six cans of beer *etc* sold together ◇ **at sixes and sevens** in confusion ◇ **sixth** *adj* the last of a series of six ◇ *noun* one of six equal parts ◇ **sixth sense** the ability to sense things that cannot be perceived by sight, hearing *etc*

sixpence *noun*, *old* a silvercoloured coin worth of £1

sixteen *noun* the number 16 ◇ *adj* 16 in number ◇ **sixteenth** *adj* the last of a series of sixteen ◇ *noun* one of sixteen equal parts

sixty *noun* the number 60 ◇ *adj* 60 in number ◇ **sixtieth** *adj* the last of a series of sixty ◇ *noun* one of sixty equal parts

size *noun* **1** space taken up by anything; measurements, dimensions **2** largeness a class into which shoes and clothes are grouped according to size: *she takes size 4 in shoes* ◇ **sizeable** or **sizable** *adj* fairly large ◇ **size up** form an opinion of a person, situation *etc*

▣ **1** volume, bulk, mass, height, length, extent, measurement(s), dimensions, proportions, range, scale, amount **2** magnitude, greatness, largeness, bigness, vastness, immensity

sizzle *verb* **1** make a hissing sound **2** fry, scorch

ska *noun* a style of Jamaican music similar to reggae

skate¹ *noun* **1** a steel blade attached to a boot for gliding on ice **2** a rollerskate ◇ *verb* move on skates or a skateboard ◇ **skateboard** *noun* a narrow board on four rollerskate wheels ◇ **skateboard-**

ing *noun* the activity of going on a skateboard

skate² *noun* a type of large flatfish

skedaddle *verb*, *informal* run off in a hurry

skein *noun* a coil of thread or yarn, loosely tied in a knot

skeleton *noun* **1** the bony framework of an animal or person, without the flesh **2** any framework or outline ◇ *adj* of staff *etc*: reduced to a very small or minimum number **3** a type of metal toboggan ◇ **skeletal** *adj* of or like a skeleton ◇ **skeleton key** a key from which the inner part has been cut away so that it can open many different locks

▣ *noun* **1** bones, frame **2** structure, framework, bare bones, outline, draft, sketch

skerry *noun* a reef of rock

sketch *noun* (*plural* **sketches**) **1** a rough plan or drawing **2** a short or rough account **3** a short play, dramatic scene *etc* ◇ *verb* **1** draw roughly **2** give the chief points of ◇ **sketchy** *adj* **1** roughly done **2** not thorough, incomplete: *my knowledge of geography is rather sketchy*

▣ *noun* **1** drawing, vignette, design, plan, diagram, draft **2** outline ◇ *verb* **1** draw, pencil, outline, delineate, draft **2** outline ◇ **sketchy 1** rough, vague, scrappy, bitty, imperfect, cursory, hasty **2** incomplete, unfinished, inadequate, insufficient, slight, superficial

skew *adj* & *adv* off the straight, slanting ◇ *verb* set at a slant

skewer *noun* a long pin of wood or metal for holding meat together while roasting *etc* ◇ *verb* fix with a skewer or with something sharp

ski *noun* (*plural* **skis**) one of a pair of long narrow strips of wood or metal that are attached to boots for gliding over snow ◇ *verb* (**skis, skiing, skied**) move or travel on skis

skid *noun* a slide sideways: *the car went into a skid* ◇ *verb* **1** slip sideways, *esp* out of control ◇ **on the skids** on the way down ◇ **skid row** *informal* the poorest part of a town *etc*

skiff *noun* a small light boat

skilful or *US* **skillfull** *adj* having or showing skill ◇ **skilfully** *adv*

▣ able, capable, adept, competent, proficient, deft, adroit, handy, expert, masterly, accomplished, skilled, practised, experienced, professional, clever, tactical, cunning

▣ inept, clumsy, awkward

skill *noun* cleverness at doing a thing, either from practice or as a natural gift ◇ **skilled** *adj* **1** having skill, *esp* through training **2** of a job: requiring skill

▣ skilfulness, ability, aptitude, facility, handiness, talent, knack, art, technique, training, experience, expertise, *informal* know-how, expertness, mastery, proficiency, competence, accomplishment, cleverness, intelligence

skillet *noun* a small metal pan with a long handle for frying food

skim *verb* (**skims**, **skimming**, **skimmed**) **1** remove cream, scum *etc* from the surface of (something) **2** move lightly and quickly over (a surface) **3** read quickly, missing parts ◇ **skimmed milk** *noun* milk from which some of the fat has been skimmed

skimp *verb* **1** give (someone) hardly enough **2** do (a job) imperfectly **3** spend too little money (on): *skimping on clothes* ◇ **skimpy** *adj* **1** too small **2** of clothes: very short or tight

▣ **1** scrimp, pinch, stint, withhold **2** cut corners **3** economize, scrimp, stint

skin *noun* **1** the natural outer covering of an animal or person **2** a thin outer layer on a fruit **3** a thin film that forms on a liquid ◇ *verb* (**skins**, **skinning**, **skinned**) strip the skin from ◇ **skin-deep** *adj* as deep as the skin only, on the surface ◇ **skin-diver** *noun* a diver who wears simple equipment ◇ **by the skin of your teeth** very narrowly

▣ *noun* **1** hide, pelt **2** peel, rind, husk **3** membrane, film, coating, surface

skinflint *noun* a very mean person

skinny *adj* very thin

▣ thin, lean, scrawny, scraggy, skeletal, bony, skin-and-bone, emaciated, wasted, underfed, undernourished

▣ fat, plump

skint *adj*, *Brit informal* broke, without much money

skip¹ *verb* (**skips**, **skipping**, **skipped**) **1** go along with a rhythmic step and hop **2** jump over a turning rope **3** leap, *esp* lightly or joyfully **4** leave out (parts of a book, a meal *etc*) **5** *informal* fail to attend, *eg* school ◇ *noun* an act of skipping ◇ **skipping rope** a rope used in skipping

▣ *verb* **1** dance, gambol, frisk, caper, prance **3** hop, jump, leap **4** miss, omit, leave out, cut

skip² *noun* a large metal container for collecting rubbish *eg* from building work

skipper *noun* the captain of a ship, aeroplane or team ◇ *verb* act as captain for (a ship, team *etc*)

skirl *noun* a shrill sound, *esp* that made by bagpipes

skirmish *noun* (*plural* **skirmishes**) **1** a fight between small parties of soldiers **2** a short sharp contest or disagreement ◇ *verb* fight briefly or informally

▣ *noun* **1** combat, battle, conflict **2** fight, clash, brush, *informal* scrap, tussle, set-to, *informal* dust-up, *informal* scuffle

skirt *noun* **1** a garment, worn by women, that hangs from the waist **2** the lower part of a dress ◇ *verb* pass along, or lie along, the edge of ◇ **skirting** or **skirting-board** *noun* the narrow board next to the floor round the walls of a room (*also called* **wainscot**)

▣ *verb* circle, circumnavigate, border, edge, flank, bypass, avoid, evade, circumvent

skit *noun* a piece of writing, short play *etc* that makes fun of a person or event *etc*

▣ satire, parody, caricature, spoof, take-off, sketch

skittish *adj* frivolous, light-headed

skittle *noun* **1** a bottle-shaped object used as a target in bowling, a ninepin **2** (**skittles**) a game in which skittles are knocked over by a ball

skive verb, informal (often with **off**) avoid doing a duty ◇ **skiver** noun a shirker

skivvy noun, informal a domestic servant, a cleaner

skua noun a type of seagull

skulduggery or US **skullduggery** noun trickery, underhand practices

skulk verb **1** wait about, stay hidden **2** move stealthily away, sneak

▪ **1** lurk, hide **2** prowl, sneak, creep, slink

skull noun **1** the bony case which encloses the brain **2** the head ◇ **skullcap** noun a cap which fits closely to the head ◇ **skull and crossbones** the sign on a pirate's flag, now used as a symbol of death and danger

skunk noun **1** a small American animal which defends itself by giving off a bad smell **2** a contemptible person

sky noun (plural **skies**) **1** the upper atmosphere, the heavens **2** the weather, the climate ◇ **sky-high** adj of prices: very high

skydiving noun jumping with a parachute as a sport

skylark noun the common lark which sings while hovering far overhead

skylight noun a window in a roof or ceiling

skyline noun the horizon

skyscraper noun a high building of very many storeys

slab noun **1** a thick flat piece of stone **2** any thick piece of anything: a slab of cake

▪ **2** piece, block, lump, chunk, hunk, informal wodge, wedge, slice, portion

slack adj **1** not tightly stretched; not firmly in position **2** not strict or diligent: slack discipline **3** lazy or careless **4** not busy: slack holiday season ◇ noun **1** the loosely hanging part of a rope **2** (**slacks**) loose, casual trousers ◇ verb **1** do less work than you should, be lazy **2** loosen

▪ adj **1** loose, limp, sagging, baggy **2** permissive, lax, relaxed, informal easygoing **3** lazy, sluggish, slow, quiet, idle, inactive, neglectful, negligent, careless,

inattentive, remiss ◇ verb **1** idle, shirk, informal skive, neglect

slacken verb **1** make or become looser **2** make or become less active, less busy or less fast etc

slag[1] noun waste left from metal-smelting

slag[2] verb, slang (**slags**, **slagging**, **slagged**) criticize, make fun of cruelly

slag[3] noun, derogatory a promiscuous woman

slain past participle of **slay**

slake verb **1** quench, satisfy (thirst, longing etc) **2** put out (fire) **3** mix (lime) with water

slalom noun **1** a downhill, zigzag ski run among posts or trees **2** an obstacle race in canoes

slam verb (**slams**, **slamming**, **slammed**) **1** shut (a door, lid etc) with a loud noise **2** put down with a loud noise **3** slang criticize severely ◇ noun **1** the act or sound of slamming **2** (also **grand slam**) a winning of every trick in cards or every contest in a competition etc

▪ verb **2** bang, crash, dash, smash, throw

slander noun an untrue statement aimed at harming someone's reputation ◇ verb speak slander against (someone) ◇ **slanderous** adj

▪ noun defamation, calumny, misrepresentation, libel, scandal, smear, slur, aspersion ◇ verb defame, vilify, malign, denigrate, disparage, libel, smear, slur, cast aspersions

slang noun **1** popular words and phrases that are used in informal, everyday speech or writing **2** the special language of a particular group: Cockney slang ◇ verb scold, abuse

slant verb **1** slope **2** lie or move diagonally or in a sloping position **3** give or present (facts or information) in a distorted way that suits your own purpose ◇ noun **1** a slope **2** a diagonal direction **3** a point of view

▪ verb **1** tilt, slope, incline, lean, list **3** distort, twist, warp, bend, weight, bias, colour

slap noun a blow with the palm of the

hand or anything flat ◇ *verb* (**slaps, slapping, slapped**) give a slap to

■ *noun* smack, spank, cuff, blow, *informal* clout, bang, clap ◇ *verb* smack, spank, hit, strike, cuff, *informal* clout, bang, clap

slapdash *adj* hasty, careless

slapstick *adj* of comedy: boisterous, funny in a very obvious way ◇ *noun* comedy in this style

slash *verb* **1** make long cuts in **2** strike at violently ◇ *noun* (*plural* **slashes**) **1** a long cut **2** a sweeping blow

■ *verb* **1** cut, slit, gash, lacerate, rip, tear, rend ◇ *noun* **1** cut, incision, slit, gash, laceration, rip, tear, rent

slat *noun* a thin strip of wood, metal or other material ◇ **slatted** *adj* having slats

slate[1] *noun* an easily split blue-grey rock, used for roofing, or at one time for writing upon ◇ *adj* **1** made of slate **2** slate-coloured ◇ *verb* cover with slate

slate[2] *verb* say or write harsh things to or about: *the play was slated*

■ scold, rebuke, reprimand, berate, censure, blame, criticize, *informal* knock, *informal* slam

slattern *noun* a woman of untidy appearance or habits

slaughter *noun* **1** the killing of animals, *esp* for food **2** cruel killing of great numbers of people ◇ *verb* **1** kill (an animal) for food **2** kill brutally

slaughterhouse *noun* a place where animals are killed in order to be sold for food

slave *noun* **1** someone forced to work for a master and owner **2** someone who serves another devotedly **3** someone who works very hard for another **4** someone who is addicted to something: *a slave to fashion* ◇ *verb* work very hard ◇ **slavish** *adj* thinking or acting exactly according to rules or instructions

■ *verb* toil, labour, drudge, sweat, grind, slog, *informal* skivvy ◇ **slavish** imitative, unimaginative, uninspired, literal, strict, servile, abject, submissive, sycophantic

slaver *noun* saliva running from the mouth ◇ *verb* let saliva run out of the mouth

slavery *noun* **1** the state of being a slave **2** the system of owning slaves

■ **1** servitude, bondage, captivity, enslavement, serfdom, thraldom, subjugation

◨ **1** freedom, liberty

Slavic *adj* relating to a group of E European people or their languages, including Russian, Polish *etc*

slay *verb, formal* (**slays, slaying, slew, slain**) kill

sleazy *adj* squalid, disreputable ◇ **sleaze** or **sleaziness** *noun*

sled or **sledge** *noun* a vehicle with runners, made for sliding upon snow ◇ *verb* ride on a sledge ◇ **sledgehammer** *noun* a large, heavy hammer

sleek *adj* **1** smooth, glossy **2** of an animal: well-fed and well-cared for **3** elegant, well-groomed

■ **1** shiny, glossy, lustrous, smooth, silky

sleep *verb* (**sleeps, sleeping, slept**) rest with your eyes closed in a state of natural unconsciousness ◇ *noun* a rest taken in this way ◇ **sleeping bag** a large warm bag for sleeping in, used by campers *etc* ◇ **sleeping car** a railway coach with beds or berths ◇ **go to sleep 1** pass into the state of being asleep **2** of a limb: become numb, tingle ◇ **put to sleep 1** make to go to sleep, make unconscious **2** put (an animal) to death painlessly, *eg* by an injection of a drug ◇ **sleep with** *informal* have sexual intercourse with

■ *verb* doze, snooze, slumber, *slang* kip, *slang* doss (down), hibernate, drop off, nod off, rest, repose ◇ *noun* doze, snooze, nap, *informal* forty winks, *informal* shut-eye, *slang* kip, slumber, hibernation, rest, repose, siesta

sleeper *noun* **1** someone who sleeps **2** a beam of wood or metal supporting railway lines **3** a sleeping car or sleeping berth on a railway train

sleepless *adj* unable to sleep, without sleep ◇ **sleeplessly** *adv* ◇ **sleeplessness** *noun*

sleepwalker *noun* someone who walks *etc* while asleep

sleepy *adj* **1** drowsy, wanting to sleep **2** looking as if needing sleep **3** quiet, not bustling: *sleepy town* ◇ **sleepily** *adv* ◇ **sleepiness** *noun*

■ **1** drowsy, somnolent, tired, weary, heavy, slow, sluggish, torpid, lethargic **3** inactive, quiet, dull

🗷 **1** awake, alert, wakeful, restless

sleet *noun* rain mixed with snow or hail

sleeve *noun* **1** the part of a garment which covers the arm **2** a cover for a record ◇ **sleeveless** *adj* without sleeves

sleigh *noun* a large horse-drawn sledge

sleight-of-hand *noun* skill and quickness of hand movement in performing card tricks *etc*

slender *adj* **1** thin, narrow **2** slim **3** small in amount: *by a slender margin*

■ **2** slim, thin, lean, slight, svelte, graceful **3** faint, remote, slight, feeble, inadequate, insufficient, meagre, scanty

slept *past form* of **sleep**

sleuth *noun* someone who tracks down criminals, a detective

slew¹ *verb* (**slews, slewing, slewed**) swing round

slew² *past form* of **slay**

slice *noun* **1** a thin, broad piece of something: *slice of toast* **2** a broad-bladed utensil for serving fish *etc* ◇ *verb* **1** cut into slices **2** cut through **3** cut (off from *etc*) **4** *golf* hit (a ball) in such a way that it curves away to the right

■ *noun* **1** piece, sliver, wafer, rasher, tranche, slab, wedge, segment, section ◇ *verb* **1** carve, cut, chop, divide, segment **2** cut

slick *adj* **1** smart, clever, often too much so **2** smooth ◇ *noun* a thin layer of spilt oil

■ *adj* **1** glib, plausible, deft, adroit, dexterous, skilful, professional **2** smooth, sleek, glossy, shiny, polished

slide *verb* (**slides, sliding, slid**) **1** move smoothly over a surface **2** slip **3** pass quietly or secretly ◇ *noun* **1** an act of sliding **2** a smooth, slippery slope or track **3** a chute **4** a groove or rail on which a thing slides **5** a fastening for the hair **6** a picture for showing on a screen **7** a piece of glass on which to place objects to be examined under a microscope ◇ **slide-rule** *noun* an instrument used for calculating, made up of one ruler sliding against another ◇ **sliding scale** a scale of wages, charges *etc* which can be changed according to outside conditions

■ *verb* **1** skate, glide, plane, coast, skim **2** slip, slither, skid

slight *adj* **1** of little amount or importance: *slight breeze/slight quarrel* **2** small, slender ◇ *verb* treat as unimportant, insult by ignoring ◇ *noun* an insult, an offence

■ *adj* **1** minor, unimportant, insignificant, negligible, trivial, paltry, modest, small, little **2** slender, slim, diminutive, petite, delicate ◇ *verb* scorn, despise, disdain, disparage, insult, affront, offend, snub, cut, cold-shoulder, ignore, disregard ◇ *noun* insult, affront, slur, snub, rebuff, rudeness, discourtesy, disrespect

🗷 *adj* **1** major, significant, noticeable, considerable **2** large, muscular ◇ *verb* respect, praise, compliment, flatter

slim *adj* **1** slender, thin **2** small, slight: *slim chance* ◇ *verb* (**slims, slimming, slimmed**) **1** make slender **2** use means (such as eating less) to become slender

■ *adj* **1** slender, thin, lean, svelte, trim **2** slight, remote, faint, poor ◇ *verb* **1** reduce **2** lose weight, diet

slime *noun* sticky, half-liquid material, *esp* thin, slippery mud ◇ **slimy** *adj* **1** covered with slime **2** oily, greasy

sling *noun* **1** a bandage hanging from the neck or shoulders to support an injured arm **2** a strap with a string attached to each end, for flinging stones **3** a net of ropes *etc* for hoisting and carrying heavy objects ◇ *verb* (**slings, slinging, slung**) **1** throw with a sling **2** move or swing by means of a sling **3** *informal* throw

■ *verb* **3** throw, hurl, fling, catapult, heave, pitch, lob, toss, *informal* chuck

slink *verb* (**slinks, slinking, slunk**) sneak away, move stealthily

slinky *adj* attractively close-fitting: *a slinky dress*

slip *verb* (**slips, slipping, slipped**) **1** slide accidentally and lose footing or balance: *slip on the ice* **2** fall out of place, or out of your control: *the plate slipped from my grasp* **3** move quickly and easily **4** move quietly, quickly and secretly **5** escape from: *slip your mind* **6** make a slight mistake ◇ *noun* **1** the act of slipping **2** an error, a slight mistake **3** a cutting from a plant **4** a strip or narrow piece of anything (*eg* paper) **5** a slim, slight person: *a slip of a girl* **6** a thin undergarment worn under a dress, an underskirt **7** a cover for a pillow **8** a slipway ◇ **slippy** *informal* slippery ◇ **slipped disc** displacement of one of the discs between the vertebrae causing severe back pain ◇ **slip road** a road by which vehicles join or leave a motorway ◇ **slip up** make a mistake ◇ **slip-up** *noun* a mistake

■ *verb* **1** skid, stumble, trip, fall **2** slide, fall **3** glide, slither, slink **4** slink, sneak, steal, creep ◇ *noun* **2** mistake, error, *informal* slip-up, *informal* bloomer, blunder, fault, indiscretion, gaffe, *informal* boob, omission, oversight

slipknot *noun* a knot made with a loop so that it can slip

slipper *noun* a loose indoor shoe

slippery *adj* **1** causing skidding or slipping **2** not trustworthy

■ **1** slippy, icy, greasy, glassy, smooth, dangerous, treacherous, perilous **2** dishonest, untrustworthy, false, duplicitous, two-faced, crafty, cunning, devious, evasive, *informal* shifty, smooth, smarmy

slipshod *adj* untidy, careless

■ careless, slap-dash, sloppy, slovenly, untidy, negligent, lax, casual
🖪 careful, fastidious, neat, tidy

slipstream *noun* the stream of air driven back by an aircraft propeller *etc*

slipway *noun* a smooth slope on which a ship is built

slit *verb* (**slits, slitting, slit**) **1** make a long narrow cut in **2** cut into strips ◇ *noun* a long narrow cut or opening

■ *verb* **1** cut, gash, slash, slice, split, rip, tear ◇ *noun* opening, aperture, vent, cut, incision, gash, slash, split, tear, rent

slither *verb* **1** slide or slip about (*eg* on mud) **2** move with a gliding motion ◇ **slithery** *adj* slippery

sliver *noun* a thin strip or slice

slobber *verb* let saliva dribble from the mouth, slaver

sloe *noun* the small black fruit of a blackthorn shrub, often used to flavour gin

slog *verb* (**slogs, slogging, slogged**) work or plod on steadily, *esp* against difficulty ◇ *noun* a difficult spell of work

slogan *noun* an easily remembered and frequently repeated phrase, used in advertising *etc*

■ jingle, motto, catchphrase, catchword, watchword

sloop *noun* a one-masted sailing ship

slop *verb* (**slops, slopping, slopped**) **1** flow over, spill **2** splash ◇ *noun* **1** spilt liquid **2** (**slops**) dirty water **3** (**slops**) thin, tasteless food ◇ **sloppy** *adj* **1** wet, muddy **2** careless, untidy **3** silly, sentimental

■ *verb* **1** spill, overflow **2** slosh, splash, splatter, spatter

slope *noun* **1** a position or direction that is neither level nor upright, a slant **2** a surface with one end higher than the other, *eg* a hillside ◇ *verb* be in a slanting, sloping position ◇ **slope off** leave furtively

■ *noun* **1** slant, tilt, pitch, inclination **2** incline, gradient, ramp, hill ◇ *verb* slant, lean, tilt, tip, pitch, incline, rise, fall

slosh *verb* **1** splash **2** *informal* hit

slot *noun* **1** a small, narrow opening, *eg* to insert coins **2** a position ◇ *verb* (**slots, slotting, slotted**) **1** make a slot in **2** (sometimes with **into**) find a position or place for ◇ **slot machine** a vending machine worked by putting a coin in a slot

■ *noun* **1** hole, opening, aperture, slit,

vent, groove, channel, gap, space **2** vacancy, place, spot, position, niche ◇ *verb* **2** insert, fit, place, position, assign, pigeonhole

sloth *noun* **1** laziness **2** a slow-moving S American animal that lives in trees ◇ **slothful** *adj* lazy

slouch *noun* a hunched-up body position ◇ *verb* walk with shoulders rounded and head hanging

■ *verb* stoop, hunch, droop, slump, lounge, loll, shuffle, shamble

slough[1] /slaʊ/ *noun* a bog, a marsh

slough[2] /slʌf/ *noun* the cast-off skin of a snake ◇ *verb* **1** cast off (*eg* a skin) **2** of skin: come (off)

slovenly *adj* untidy, careless, dirty

■ sloppy, careless, slipshod, untidy, scruffy, slatternly, sluttish

☒ neat, smart

slow *adj* **1** not fast **2** not hasty or hurrying **3** of a clock: behind in time **4** not quick in learning, dull ◇ *verb* (often with **down**) make or become slower ◇ **slowly** *adv* ◇ **slow-motion** *adj* **1** slower than normal movement **2** of a film: slower than actual motion ◇ **slowness** *noun*

■ *adj* **2** leisurely, unhurried, lingering, loitering, dawdling, lazy, sluggish, slow-moving, creeping, plodding **4** stupid, slow-witted, dim, *informal* thick, dense ◇ *verb* brake, decelerate, delay, hold up, retard, handicap, check, curb

☒ *adj* **1** quick, fast, swift, rapid, speedy **4** clever, intelligent ◇ *verb* speed up, accelerate

slowcoach *noun* someone who moves, works *etc* slowly

slow-worm *noun* a snake-like, legless lizard

sludge *noun* soft, slimy mud

slug[1] *noun* a snail-like animal with no shell

slug[2] *noun* a small piece of metal used as a bullet

slug[3] *noun* a heavy blow

sluggard *noun* someone who has slow and lazy habits

sluggish *adj* moving slowly ◇ **sluggishly** *adv*

■ lethargic, listless, torpid, heavy, dull, slow, slow-moving, slothful, lazy, idle, inactive, lifeless, unresponsive

☒ brisk, vigorous, lively, dynamic

sluice *noun* **1** a sliding gate for controlling a flow of water in an artificial channel (*also called* **sluicegate**) **2** the stream which flows through this ◇ *verb* clean out with a strong flow of water

slum *noun* **1** an overcrowded part of a town where the houses are dirty and unhealthy **2** a house in a slum

slumber *verb* sleep ◇ *noun* sleep

slump *verb* **1** fall or sink suddenly and heavily **2** lose value suddenly ◇ *noun* a sudden fall in values, prices *etc*

■ *verb* **1** collapse, fall, drop, plunge, plummet, sink, crash, droop, sag, slouch, loll, flop **2** collapse, drop, plunge, plummet, sink, decline, crash ◇ *noun* recession, depression, stagnation, downturn, low, trough, decline, collapse, crash

☒ *noun* boom

slung *past form of* **sling**

slunk *past form of* **slink**

slur *verb* (**slurs**, **slurring**, **slurred**) **1** pronounce indistinctly **2** damage (a reputation *etc*), speak ill of ◇ *noun* **1** a blot or stain (on someone's reputation) **2** a criticism, an insult

slurp *verb* drink or gulp noisily ◇ *noun* a noisy gulp

slurry *noun* **1** thin, liquid cement **2** liquid waste

slush *noun* **1** melting snow **2** watery mud **3** sentimentality ◇ **slushy** *adj* **1** covered with, or like, slush **2** sentimental

slut *noun, derogatory* a promiscuous woman ◇ **sluttish** *adj*

sly *adj* cunning; wily; deceitful ◇ **slyly** or **slily** *adv* ◇ **slyness** *noun* ◇ **on the sly** secretly, surreptitiously

■ wily, foxy, crafty, cunning, artful, guileful, clever, canny, shrewd, astute, knowing, subtle, devious, shifty, tricky, furtive, stealthy, surreptitious, underhand, covert, secretive, scheming, conniving, mischievous, roguish

🖪 honest, frank, candid, open

smack[1] *verb* strike smartly, slap ◇ *noun* **1** an act of smacking **2** the sound made by smacking **3** a boisterous kiss ◇ *adv* with sudden violence: *run smack into the door*

🔳 *verb* **1** hit, strike, slap, spank, *informal* whack, *informal* thwack, clap, box, cuff, pat, tap ◇ *noun* **1** blow, slap, spank, *informal* whack, *informal* thwack, box, cuff, pat, tap

smack[2] *verb* have a trace or suggestion of: *this smacks of treason* ◇ *noun* **1** a trace, suggestion **2** a taste, flavour

smack[3] *noun* a small fishing vessel

small *adj* **1** little, not big or much **2** not important or great: *a small matter* **3** humiliated: *feel small* ◇ *noun* **1** the most slender or narrow part: *the small of the back* **2** (**smalls**) *informal* underwear ◇ *adv* into small pieces: *cut up small* ◇ **small beer** something trivial or unimportant ◇ **small fry** someone or something of little importance ◇ **small hours** the hours just after midnight ◇ **small-minded** *adj* having narrow opinions, ungenerous ◇ **small talk** polite conversation about nothing very important

🔳 **1** little, tiny, minute, minuscule, short, slight, puny, petite, diminutive, *informal* pint-size(d), miniature, mini, pocket, pocket-sized, young **2** petty, trifling, trivial, unimportant, insignificant, minor, inconsiderable, negligible

🖪 **1** large, big, huge **2** great, considerable

smallpox *noun* a serious infectious illness, causing a rash of large pimples (**pocks**)

smarmy *adj* smooth in manner, unctuous, ingratiating

🔳 smooth, oily, unctuous, servile, obsequious, sycophantic, toadying, ingratiating, crawling, fawning

smart *adj* **1** clever and quick in thought or action **2** well-dressed **3** brisk **4** sharp, stinging ◇ *noun* a sharp, stinging pain ◇ *verb* **1** feel a sharp, stinging pain **2** feel annoyed, resentful *etc* after being insulted ◇ **smartly** *adv*

🔳 *adj* **1** clever, intelligent, bright, sharp, acute, shrewd, astute **2** elegant, stylish, chic, fashionable, modish, neat, tidy, spruce, trim, well-groomed ◇ *verb* **1** sting, hurt, prick, burn, tingle, twinge, throb

smash *verb* **1** break in pieces, shatter **2** strike with force: *smash a ball with a racket* **3** crash (into *etc*): *the car smashed into the wall* ◇ *noun* (*plural* **smashes**) **1** an act of smashing **2** a crash, a collision (of vehicles) **3** *sport* a forceful strike with a racket **4** *informal* a big hit ◇ **smashed** *adj*, *slang* drunk

smattering *noun* a very slight knowledge of a subject

🔳 bit, modicum, dash, sprinkling, basics, rudiments, elements

smear *verb* **1** spread (something sticky or oily) **2** spread, smudge with (something sticky *etc*) **3** become smeared or smudged **4** slander, insult ◇ *noun* a smudge of something sticky ◇ **smear test** the taking of a sample of cells from a woman's cervix for examination

🔳 *verb* **1** daub, plaster, spread **2** daub, plaster, spread, cover, coat, rub, smudge, streak **4** defame, malign, vilify, blacken, sully, stain, tarnish ◇ *noun* streak, smudge, blot, blotch, splodge, daub

smell *noun* **1** the sense or power of being aware of things through your nose **2** an act of using this sense **3** something sensed through the nose, a scent ◇ *verb* (**smells**, **smelling**, **smelt** or **smelled**) **1** notice by the sense of smell: *I smell gas* **2** use your sense of smell on: *smell this fish* **3** give off a smell: *this room smells* ◇ **smelling-salts** *noun plural* strong-smelling chemicals in a bottle, used to revive fainting people ◇ **smelly** *adj* having a bad smell ◇ **smell out** find out by prying or inquiring closely

🔳 *noun* **3** odour, whiff, scent, perfume, fragrance, bouquet, aroma, stench, stink, *informal* pong ◇ *verb* **2** sniff, nose, scent **3** stink, reek, *informal* pong

smelt[1] *verb* **1** melt (ore) in order to separate the metal from other material **2** *past form* of **smell**

smelt² *noun* a fish related to the salmon

smile *verb* **1** show pleasure by drawing up the corners of the lips **2** (sometimes with **on**) be favourable to: *fortune smiled on him* ◇ *noun* an act of smiling

■ *verb* **1** grin, beam, simper, smirk, leer
◇ *noun* grin, beam, simper, smirk, leer

smiley *noun*, *comput* a stylized representation on screen of a smiling face, *eg* :-)

smirch *verb* stain, soil ◇ *noun* a stain

smirk *verb* smile in a self-satisfied or foolish manner ◇ *noun* a self-satisfied smile

smite *verb* (**smites**, **smiting**, **smote**, **smitten**) strike, hit hard ◇ **smitten with** affected by; strongly attracted by

smith *noun* a worker in metals; a blacksmith ◇ **smithy** *noun* (*plural* **smithies**) the workshop of a smith

smithereens *noun plural* fragments

smitten *past participle* of **smite**

smock *noun* a loose shirt-like garment, sometimes worn over other clothes as a protection

smog *noun* thick, smoky fog ◇ **smoggy** *adj*

smoke *noun* **1** the cloud-like gases and particles of soot given off by anything burning **2** an act of smoking (a cigarette *etc*) ◇ *verb* **1** give off smoke **2** inhale and exhale tobacco smoke from a cigarette, pipe *etc* **3** cure or preserve (ham, fish *etc*) by applying smoke **4** darken (*eg* glass) by applying smoke ◇ **smoker** *noun* someone who smokes ◇ **smoky** *adj* **1** full of smoke **2** tasting of smoke

■ *noun* **1** fumes, exhaust, gas, vapour, smog ◇ *verb* **1** fume, smoulder **3** cure, dry

smokeless *adj* **1** burning without smoke **2** where the emission of smoke is prohibited: *a smokeless zone*

smokescreen *noun* anything (*orig* smoke) meant to confuse or mislead

smolt *noun* a young salmon

smooch *verb*, *informal* kiss, pet

smooth *adj* **1** not rough **2** having an even surface **3** without lumps: *a smooth sauce* **4** hairless **5** without breaks, stops or jolts: *smooth journey* **6** too charming in manner ◇ *verb* **1** make smooth **2** calm, soothe **3** free from difficulty

■ *adj* **1** shiny, polished, glossy, silky, glassy, calm, undisturbed, serene, tranquil, peaceful **2** level, plane, even, flat, horizontal, flush **5** steady, unbroken, flowing, regular, uniform, rhythmic, easy **6** suave, smooth-talking, glib, plausible, persuasive, slick, smarmy, unctuous, ingratiating ◇ *verb* **1** iron, press, roll, flatten, level, plane, file, sand, polish **2** ease, alleviate, assuage, allay, mitigate, calm, mollify

■ *adj* **1** rough, choppy **2** rough **3** lumpy **5** irregular, erratic, unsteady ◇ *verb* **1** wrinkle, crease

smorgasbord *noun* a selection of Swedish hors d'oeuvres

smote *past form* of **smite**

smother *verb* **1** kill by keeping air from, *eg* by covering the nose and mouth **2** die by this means **3** cover up, conceal (feelings *etc*) **4** put down, suppress (a rebellion *etc*)

■ **1** suffocate, asphyxiate, strangle, throttle, choke, stifle **3** repress, hide, conceal, cover, shroud

smoulder *verb* **1** burn slowly without bursting into flame **2** exist in a hidden state **3** harbour hidden emotion, *eg* anger, hate

SMS *abbrev* short message service

smudge a smear ◇ *verb* make dirty with spots or smears

■ *noun* blot, stain, spot, blemish, blur, smear, streak ◇ *verb* blur, smear, daub, mark, spot, stain, dirty, soil

smug *adj* well-satisfied, too obviously pleased with oneself

■ self-satisfied, superior, self-righteous, conceited

■ humble, modest

smuggle *verb* **1** take (goods) into, or out of, a country without paying the required taxes **2** send or take secretly ◇ **smuggler** *noun* someone who smuggles goods ◇ **smuggling** *noun*

smut *noun* **1** a spot of dirt or soot **2** vulgar or indecent talk *etc* ◇ **smutty** *adj* **1** dirty, grimy **2** indecent, vulgar

snack *noun* a light, hasty meal

■ refreshment(s), bite, nibble, titbit, *informal* elevenses

snaffle *verb*, *slang* steal

snafu /sna'fu:/ *noun, US slang* chaos (*abbrev* of 'situation *n*ormal - *a*ll *f*ucked *u*p')

snag *noun* a difficulty, an obstacle ◇ *verb* (**snags**, **snagging**, **snagged**) catch or tear on something sharp

■ *noun* disadvantage, inconvenience, drawback, catch, problem, difficulty, complication, setback, hitch, obstacle, stumbling-block ◇ *verb* catch, rip, tear, hole, ladder

snail *noun* **1** a soft-bodied, small, crawling animal with a shell **2** someone who is very slow

snake *noun* **1** a legless reptile with a long body, which moves along the ground with a winding movement **2** anything snake-like in form or movement **3** a cunning, deceitful person

snap *verb* (**snaps**, **snapping**, **snapped**) **1** make a sudden bite **2** (with **up**) eat up, or grab, eagerly **3** break suddenly with a sharp noise **4** cause (the fingers) to make a sharp noise **5** speak sharply **6** take a photograph of ◇ *noun* **1** the noise made by snapping **2** a sudden spell (*eg* of cold weather) **3** a card-game in which players try to match cards **4** a photograph

■ *verb* **1** bite, nip **2** snatch, seize, catch, grasp **3** break, crack, split, separate ◇ *noun* **1** crack, crackle, pop

snapdragon *noun* a garden plant whose flower, when pinched, opens and shuts like a mouth

snappy *adj* irritable, inclined to speak sharply ◇ **snappily** *adv*

■ cross, irritable, edgy, touchy, brusque, quick-tempered, ill-natured, crabbed, testy, *informal* grouchy

snapshot *noun* a quickly taken photograph

snare *noun* **1** a noose or loop that draws tight when pulled, for catching an animal **2** a trap **3** a hidden danger or temptation ◇ *verb* catch in or with a snare

■ *noun* **1** wire, net, noose **2** catch, pitfall, trap ◇ *verb* trap, ensnare, entrap, catch, net

snarl¹ *verb* **1** growl, showing the teeth **2** speak in a furious, spiteful tone ◇ *noun* a growl, a furious noise

snarl² *verb* become tangled ◇ *noun* **1** a tangle, a knot **2** a muddled or confused state

snatch *verb* **1** seize or grab suddenly **2** take quickly when you have time: *snatch an hour's sleep* ◇ *noun* (*plural* **snatches**) **1** an attempt to seize **2** a small piece or quantity: *a snatch of music*

■ *verb* **1** grab, seize, kidnap, take, *informal* nab, pluck, pull, wrench, wrest **2** gain, win

snazzy *adj, informal* smart, stylish

sneak *verb* **1** creep or move in a stealthy, secretive way **2** tell tales, tell on others ◇ *noun* **1** someone who tells tales **2** a deceitful, underhand person

■ *verb* **1** creep, steal, slip, slink, sidle, skulk, lurk, prowl, smuggle, spirit **2** tell tales, *slang* split, inform on, *slang* grass on ◇ *noun* **1** tell-tale, informer, *slang* grass

sneaker *noun, US* a sports shoe

sneaky *adj* underhand, deceitful ◇ **sneakily** *adv*

sneer *verb* show contempt by a scornful expression, words *etc* ◇ *noun* a scornful expression or remark

■ *verb* scorn, disdain, look down on, deride, scoff, jeer, mock, ridicule, gibe, laugh, snigger ◇ *noun* scorn, disdain, jeer, mockery, ridicule, gibe, snigger

sneeze *verb* make a sudden, unintentional and violent blowing noise through the nose and mouth ◇ *noun* an involuntary blow through the nose

snicker *verb* **1** snigger **2** of a horse: neigh

snide *adj* mean, malicious: *a snide remark*
- derogatory, disparaging, sarcastic, cynical, scornful, sneering, hurtful, unkind, nasty, mean, spiteful, malicious, ill-natured
- complimentary

sniff *verb* **1** draw in air through the nose with a slight noise, *eg* when having a cold, or showing disapproval **2** smell (a scent *etc*) **3** (with **at**) treat with scorn or suspicion ◇ *noun* a quick drawing in of air through the nose

sniffle *noun* a light sniff, a snuffle ◇ *verb* sniff lightly

snifter *noun* **1** *informal* a short drink, a dram **2** a bulbous glass for drinking brandy *etc*

snigger *verb* laugh in a quiet, sly manner ◇ *noun* a quiet, sly laugh
- *verb & noun* laugh, giggle, titter, chuckle, chortle

snip *verb* (**snips**, **snipping**, **snipped**) cut off sharply, *esp* with a single cut ◇ *noun* **1** a cut with scissors **2** a small piece snipped off **3** *informal* a bargain: *a snip at the price*
- *verb* cut, clip, trim, crop, dock, slit, nick, notch

snipe *noun* a bird with a long straight beak, found in marshy places ◇ *verb* **1** (with **at**) shoot at from a place of hiding **2** (with **at**) attack with critical remarks ◇ **sniper** *noun* someone who shoots at a single person from cover

snippet *noun* a little piece, *esp* of information or gossip
- piece, scrap, cutting, clipping, fragment, particle, shred, snatch

snitch *noun*, *informal* an informer, a tell-tale ◇ *verb* inform (on)

snivel *verb* (**snivels**, **snivelling**, **snivelled**) **1** whine or complain tearfully **2** have a running nose, *eg* because of a cold ◇ *noun* an act of snivelling ◇ **snivelly** *adj*

snob *noun* someone who looks down on those in a lower social class ◇ **snobbish** *adj* ◇ **snobbishness** *noun*
- snobbish supericilous, disdainful, *informal* snooty, *informal* stuck-up, *informal* toffee-nosed, superior, lofty, high and mighty, arrogant, pretentious, affected, condescending, patronizing

> Originally a slang term for 'shoemaker' which changed its meaning to someone of low social class, and later to an ostentatious vulgarian

snobbery *noun* being a snob
- snobbishness, superciliousness, *informal* snootiness, airs, loftiness, arrogance, pride, pretension, condescension

snog *verb*, *slang* (**snogs**, **snogging**, **snogged**) kiss, pet

snood *noun* a decorative pouch worn on the back of the head

snooker *noun* a game like billiards, using twenty-two coloured balls

snoop *verb* spy or pry in a sneaking secretive way ◇ *noun* someone who pries

snooty *adj* haughty, snobbish

snooze *verb* sleep lightly, doze ◇ *noun* a light sleep
- *verb* nap, doze, sleep, *slang* kip ◇ *noun* nap, catnap, *informal* forty winks, doze, siesta, sleep, *slang* kip

snore *verb* make a snorting noise in your sleep while breathing ◇ *noun* a snorting sound made in sleep

snorkel *noun* **1** a tube with one end above the water, to enable an underwater swimmer to breathe **2** a similar device for bringing air into a submarine

snort *verb* **1** force air noisily through the nostrils **2** make such a noise to express disapproval, anger, laughter *etc* ◇ *noun* a loud noise made through the nostrils

snot *noun* mucus of the nose

snotty *adj* supercilious

snout *noun* the projecting nose and mouth of an animal, *eg* of a pig

snow *noun* frozen water vapour which falls in light white flakes ◇ *verb* fall down in, or like, flakes of snow ◇ **snow blindness** dimness of sight caused by the brightness of light reflected from the snow ◇ **snowed**

under overwhelmed

snowball *noun* a ball made of snow pressed hard together ◇*verb* **1** throw snowballs **2** grow increasingly quickly: *unemployment has snowballed recently*

snowboard *noun* a single board used as a ski on snow

snowdrift *noun* a bank of snow blown together by the wind

snowdrop *noun* a small white flower growing from a bulb in early spring

snowflake *noun* a flake of snow

snowline *noun* the height up a mountain above which there is always snow

snowman *noun* a figure shaped like a human being, made of snow

snowplough *noun* a large vehicle for clearing snow from roads *etc*

snowshoe *noun* a long broad frame with a mesh, one of a pair for walking on top of snow

snowy *adj* **1** covered with snow **2** white, pure

SNP *abbrev* Scottish National Party

snub *verb* (**snubs**, **snubbing**, **snubbed**) treat or speak to in an abrupt, scornful way, insult ◇*noun* an act of snubbing ◇*adj* of a nose: short and turned up at the end

▣ *verb* rebuff, brush off, cut, cold-shoulder, slight, rebuke, put down, squash, humble, shame, humiliate, mortify ◇ *noun* rebuff, brush-off, slight, affront, insult, rebuke, put-down, humiliation

snuck *US past form of* **sneak**

snuff *verb* put out or trim the wick of (a candle) ◇*noun* powdered tobacco for drawing up into the nose ◇**snuffbox** *noun* a box for holding snuff

snuffle *verb* make a sniffing noise through the nose, *eg* because of a cold ◇*noun* a sniffing through the nose

snug *adj* **1** lying close and warm **2** cosy, comfortable **3** closely fitting; neat and trim

▣ **2** cosy, warm, comfortable, homely, friendly, intimate **3** tight, close-fitting

snuggle *verb* **1** curl up comfortably **2** draw close to for warmth, affection *etc*

so *adv* **1** to such an extent, to a great extent: *so heavy/you look so happy* **2** as shown, *eg* by a hand gesture: *so high* **3** extremely: *she is so talented* **4** in this or that way: *he promised to behave and has done so* **5** correct: *is that so?* **6** also: *she's my friend and so are you* **7** used to avoid repeating a statement: *you will go because I say so* ◇*conj* therefore: *you don't need it, so don't buy it* ◇**so as to** in order to ◇**so far** up to this or that point ◇**so forth** more of the same sort of thing: *pots, pans and so forth* ◇**so much for** that is the end of: *so much for that idea!* ◇**so that** with the purpose or result that ◇**so what?** what difference does it make? does it matter?

soak *verb* **1** let stand in a liquid until wet through **2** drench (with) **3** (with **up**) suck up, absorb

▣ **1** bathe, marinate, souse, steep, submerge, immerse **2** wet, drench, saturate, penetrate, permeate, infuse

soaking *adj* wet through ◇*noun* a wetting, drenching ◇**soaking wet** thoroughly wet, drenched

▣ *adj* soaked, drenched, sodden, waterlogged, saturated, sopping, wringing, dripping

so-and-so *noun*, *informal* **1** this or that person or thing **2** *euphem* used instead of a stronger insult: *she's a real so-and-so, saying that to you!*

soap *noun* **1** a mixture containing oils or fats and other substances, used in washing **2** *informal* a soap opera ◇*verb* use soap on ◇**soap opera** a television series about a group of characters and their daily lives

soap-box *noun* **1** a small box for holding soap **2** a makeshift platform for standing on when speaking to a crowd out of doors

soapsuds *noun plural* soapy water worked into a froth

soapy *adj* **1** like soap **2** full of soap

soar *verb* **1** fly high into the air **2** of prices: rise high and quickly

▣ **1** fly, wing, glide, plane, tower, rise, ascend, climb **2** climb, mount, escalate, rocket

◼ **1, 2** fall, plummet

sob verb (**sobs, sobbing, sobbed**) weep noisily ◇ noun a noisy weeping ◇ **sob story** a story told to arouse sympathy

◼ verb cry, weep, bawl, howl, blubber, snivel

sober adj **1** not drunk **2** serious, staid **3** not florid, unelaborate ◇ verb (sometimes with **up**) make or become sober ◇ **soberly** adv ◇ **soberness** or **sobriety** noun the state of being sober

◼ adj **2** solemn, dignified, serious, staid, steady, sedate, quiet, serene, calm, composed, unruffled, unexcited, cool, level-headed, practical, pragmatic, realistic, reasonable, rational, clear-headed **3** sombre, drab, dull, plain, subdued, restrained

◼ adj **1** drunk **2** frivolous, excited, irrational **3** flashy, garish

sobriquet noun a nickname

From a French phrase meaning literally an affectionate chuck under the chin

so-called adj called by such a name, often mistakenly: a so-called expert

◼ alleged, supposed, purported, ostensible, nominal, self-styled, professed, would-be, pretended

soccer noun association football

sociable adj fond of the company of others, friendly ◇ **sociability** or **sociableness** noun

◼ outgoing, gregarious, friendly, affable, companionable, genial, convivial, cordial, warm, hospitable, neighbourly, approachable, accessible, familiar

◼ unsociable, withdrawn, unfriendly, hostile

social adj **1** relating to society, or to a community: social history **2** living in communities: social insects **3** of companionship: social gathering **4** of rank or level in society: social class ◇ noun a social gathering, esp organized by a club or group ◇ **socially** adv ◇ **social security** the system, paid for by taxes, of providing insurance against old age, illness, unemployment etc ◇ **social work** work which deals with the care of the people in a community, esp of the poor or underprivileged ◇ **social worker**

socialism noun the belief that a country's wealth should belong to the people as a whole, not to private owners ◇ **socialist** noun & adj

socialize verb behave sociably

◼ mix, mingle, fraternize, get together, go out, entertain

society noun **1** humanity considered as a whole **2** a community of people **3** a social club, an association **4** the class of people who are wealthy, fashionable etc **5** company, companionship: I enjoy his society

◼ **1** people, mankind, humanity **2** community, population, culture **3** club, circle, group, association, organization, league **4** upper classes, aristocracy, gentry, nobility, elite **5** friendship, companionship, camaraderie, fellowship, company

sociology noun the study of human society ◇ **sociological** adj ◇ **sociologist** noun

sociopath noun someone who hates the company of others

sock[1] noun a short stocking ◇ **pull your socks up** make an effort to do better

sock[2] slang, verb to hit with a powerful blow ◇ noun a powerful blow

socket noun a hollow into which something is fitted: an electric socket

sod[1] noun a piece of earth with grass growing on it, a turf

sod[2] noun, Brit slang an obnoxious person ◇ **sod off** go away ◇ **Sod's Law** the law that the most inconvenient thing is the most likely to happen

soda noun **1** the name of several substances formed from sodium **2** soda-water ◇ **baking soda** sodium bicarbonate, a powder used as a raising agent in baking

soda-water noun water through

which gas has been passed, making it fizzy

sodden *adj* soaked through and through

sodium *noun* a metallic element from which many substances are formed, including common salt

sofa *noun* a kind of long, stuffed seat with back and arms ◇ **sofa bed** a sofa incorporating a fold-away bed

soft *adj* **1** easily put out of shape when pressed **2** not rough **3** not loud **4** of a colour: not bright or glaring **5** not strict enough **6** lacking strength or courage **7** lacking common sense, weak in the mind **8** of a drink: not alcoholic **9** of water: containing little calcium *etc* ◇ *adv* gently, quietly ◇ **soft furnishings** rugs, curtains, cushions *etc* ◇ **soft option** the easiest of two alternatives ◇ **soft spot** *informal* a special affection ◇ **softy** *noun*, *informal* **1** someone who is easily upset **2** a sentimental person

■ *adj* **1** yielding, pliable, flexible, elastic, plastic, malleable, spongy, squashy, pulpy **2** furry, downy, velvety, silky, smooth **3** muted, quiet, low, soothing, sweet, mellow, melodious, dulcet, pleasant **4** pale, light, pastel, delicate **5** lenient, lax, permissive, indulgent, tolerant, *informal* easy-going, kind, generous, gentle, soft-hearted **6** sensitive, weak, spineless, *informal* wimpish

E3 *adj* **1** hard, rigid **2** rough, coarse **4** harsh, strong **5** strict, severe

soften *verb* make or grow soft

■ moderate, temper, mitigate, lessen, diminish, abate, alleviate, ease, soothe, subdue, mollify, appease, calm, still, relax, melt, liquefy, dissolve, reduce, cushion, pad, muffle

soft-hearted *adj* kind and generous

■ sympathetic, compassionate, kind, benevolent, charitable, generous, warm-hearted, tender, sentimental

E3 hard-hearted, callous

software *noun*, *comput* programs *etc* as opposed to the machines (*contrasted with*: **hardware**)

softwood *noun* the wood of a cone-

bearing tree (*eg* fir, larch)

soggy *adj* **1** soaked **2** soft and wet

■ **1** soaked, drenched, sodden, waterlogged, saturated, sopping, dripping **2** wet, damp, moist, heavy, boggy, spongy, pulpy

soi-disant *adj* pretended, would be

soil[1] *noun* **1** the upper layer of the earth in which plants grow **2** loose earth; dirt

soil[2] *verb* make dirty

■ *verb* dirty, begrime, stain, spot, smudge, smear, foul, muddy, pollute, defile, sully, tarnish

soirée /'swɑːreɪ/ *noun* an evening get-together

sojourn *verb* stay for a time ◇ *noun* a short stay

solace *noun* something which makes pain or sorrow easier to bear, comfort ◇ *verb* comfort

■ *noun* comfort, consolation, relief, alleviation, support, cheer

solar *adj* **1** relating to the sun **2** influenced by the sun **3** powered by energy from the sun's rays ◇ **solar system** the sun with the planets (including the earth) going round it

sold *past form* of **sell**

solder *noun* melted metal used for joining metal surfaces ◇ *verb* join (two pieces of metal) with solder

soldering-iron *noun* an electric tool for soldering joints

soldier *noun* someone in military service, *esp* someone who is not an officer ◇ **soldier on** continue determinedly

---

Types of soldier include:
cadet, private, sapper, NCO, orderly, officer, gunner, infantryman, trooper, fusilier, rifleman, paratrooper, sentry, guardsman, marine, commando, tommy, dragoon, cavalryman, lancer, hussar, conscript, recruit, regular, Territorial, (*US*) GI, warrior, mercenary, legionnaire, guerrilla, partisan, centurion; troops; serviceman, servicewoman
see also **rank**

sole[1] *noun* **1** the underside of the foot **2** the underside of a shoe *etc* ◇ *verb* put a sole on (a shoe etc)

sole[2] *adj* **1** only: *the sole survivor* **2** belonging to one person or group only: *the sole right* ◇ **solely** *adv* only, alone

■ **1** only, unique, exclusive, individual, single, singular, one, lone, solitary, alone

🆎 **1** shared, multiple

sole[3] *noun* a small type of flat fish

solecism *noun* **1** *grammar* an improper or non-standard usage **2** a breach of good manners ◇ **solecistic** or **solecistical** *adj*

solemn *adj* **1** serious, earnest **2** of an occasion: celebrated with special ceremonies ◇ **solemnity** *noun*

■ **1** serious, grave, sober, sedate, sombre, glum, thoughtful, earnest, awed, reverential **2** grand, stately, majestic, ceremonial, ritual, formal, ceremonious, pompous, dignified, awe-inspiring, impressive, imposing, momentous

🆎 **1** light-hearted **2** frivolous

solemnize *verb* carry out (a wedding *etc*) with religious ceremonies

sol-fa *noun, music* a system of syllables (do, ray, me *etc*) to be sung to the notes of a scale

solicit *verb* **1** ask for (something, or something from someone): *solicit advice* **2** of a prostitute: approach people with offers of sex for money

■ **1** ask, request, seek, crave, beg, beseech, entreat, implore

solicitor *noun* a lawyer who advises people about legal matters

solicitous *adj* **1** anxious **2** considerate, careful ◇ **solicitously** *adv*

solicitude *noun* care or anxiety about someone or something

solid *adj* **1** fixed in shape, not in the form of gas or liquid **2** in three dimensions, with length, breadth and height **3** not hollow **4** firm, strongly made **5** made or formed completely of one substance: *solid silver* **6** reliable, sound: *solid business* **7** *informal* without a break: *three solid hours' work* ◇ *noun* **1** a substance that is solid **2** a figure that has three dimensions

■ *adj* **1** hard, firm, dense, compact **4** hard, firm, strong, sturdy, substantial, sound, unshakable **6** reliable, dependable, trusty, worthy, decent, upright, sensible, level-headed, stable, serious **7** unbroken, continuous, uninterrupted

🆎 *adj* **1** liquid, gaseous, hollow **6** unreliable, unstable

solidarity *noun* unity of interests *etc*

■ unity, agreement, accord, unanimity, consensus, harmony, concord, cohesion, like-mindedness, camaraderie, team spirit, esprit de corps, soundness, stability

🆎 discord, division, schism

solidify *verb* (**solidifies, solidifying, solidified**) make or become firm or solid

■ harden, set, jell, congeal, coagulate, clot, cake, crystallize

🆎 soften, liquefy, dissolve

solidity *noun* the state of being solid

solidus *noun* a slanting stroke, a slash (/)

soliloquize *verb* speak to yourself, *esp* on the stage

soliloquy *noun* (*plural* **soliloquies**) a speech made by an actor *etc* to themselves

solipsism *noun* the belief that nothing is knowable except the self ◇ **solipsistic** *adj*

solitaire *noun* a card game for one player (*also called*: **patience**)

solitary *adj* **1** lone, alone **2** single: *not a solitary crumb remained*

■ **1** alone, lonely, lonesome, friendless, unsociable, reclusive, withdrawn, retired, secluded, separate, isolated, remote, inaccessible, unfrequented

🆎 **1** accompanied, gregarious, busy

solitude *noun* the state of being alone; lack of company

■ aloneness, loneliness, reclusiveness, retirement, privacy, seclusion, isolation, remoteness

🆎 companionship

solo *noun* (*plural* **solos**) a musical piece for one singer or player ◇ *adj* performed by one person alone: *solo flight* ◇**soloist** *noun* someone who plays or sings a solo

solstice *noun* the time of longest daylight (**summer solstice** about 21 June) or longest dark (**winter solstice** about 21 December)

soluble *adj* **1** able to be dissolved or made liquid **2** of a problem *etc*: able to be solved ◇**solubility** *noun*

solution *noun* **1** a liquid with something dissolved in it **2** the act of solving a problem *etc* **3** an answer to a problem, puzzle *etc*

☰ **3** answer, result, explanation, resolution, key, remedy

solve *verb* **1** clear up or explain (a mystery) **2** discover the answer or solution to

☰ **1** resolve, settle, clear up, clarify, explain **2** work out, figure out, puzzle out, decipher, crack, disentangle, unravel, answer

solvent *adj* able to pay all debts ◇ *noun* anything that dissolves another substance ◇**solvency** *noun* the state of being able to pay all debts

somatic *adj* relating to sleep

sombre *adj* gloomy, dark, dismal

☰ dark, funereal, drab, dull, dim, obscure, shady, shadowy, gloomy, dismal, melancholy, mournful, sad, joyless, sober, serious, grave

☲ bright, cheerful, happy

sombrero *noun* (*plural* **sombreros**) a broad-brimmed Mexican hat

some *adj* **1** an unspecified amount: *she owns some shares* **2** a few: *some oranges, but not many* **3** a little: *some bread, but not much* **4** certain: *some people are rich* **5** having an unknown nature: *some problem with the engine* **6** quite a lot of: *we have waited some time for this* ◇ *pronoun* **1** a number or part out of a quantity: *please try some* **2** certain people: *some won't be happy*

somebody or **someone** *noun* **1** an unknown or unnamed person: *somebody I'd never seen before* **2** an important person: *he really is somebody now*

somehow *adv* in some way or other

somersault *noun* a forward or backward roll in which the heels go over the head ◇ *verb* perform a somersault

something *pronoun* **1** a thing not known or not stated **2** a thing of importance **3** a slight amount, a degree: *he has something of his father's looks*

sometime *adv* at a time not known or stated definitely

sometimes *adv* at times, now and then

☰ occasionally, now and again, now and then, once in a while, from time to time

☲ always, never

somewhat *adv* rather: *somewhat boring*

somewhere *adv* in some place

somnambulist *noun* a sleepwalker ◇**somnambulism** *noun*

somnolence *noun* sleepiness ◇ **somnolent** *adj* sleepy; causing sleepiness

son *noun* a male child

sonata *noun* a piece of music with three or more movements, usually for one instrument

son et lumière a display of lights and sound effects, often describing a historical event

song *noun* **1** singing **2** a piece of music to be sung ◇**for a song** (bought, sold *etc*) very cheaply

songbird *noun* a bird that sings

songster, songstress *noun, old* a singer

sonic *adj* of sound waves ◇**sonic boom** an explosive sound that can be heard when an aircraft travels faster than the speed of sound

son-in-law *noun* a daughter's husband

sonnet *noun* a type of poem in fourteen lines

sonorous *adj* giving a clear, loud sound ◇**sonority** *noun*

soon *adv* **1** in a short time from now or from the time mentioned: *he will come soon* **2** early: *too soon to tell* **3** (with **as**) as readily, as willingly: *I would as soon stand as sit* ◊ **as soon as** at the moment when: *leave as soon as you are ready*

■ **1** shortly, presently, in a minute, before long, in the near future

sooner *adv* more willingly, rather: *I would sooner stand than sit* ◊ **sooner or later** at some time in the future

soot *noun* the black powder left by smoke ◊ **sooty** *adj* like, or covered with, soot

soothe *verb* **1** calm or comfort (a person, feelings *etc*) **2** help or ease (a pain *etc*) ◊ **soothing** *adj*

■ **1** allay, calm, compose, settle, still, quiet, hush, lull, pacify, appease, mollify, assuage, mitigate, soften **2** alleviate, relieve, ease, salve, comfort

🖭 **1** annoy, vex **2** aggravate, irritate

soothsayer *noun* someone who predicts the future

sop *noun* **1** bread dipped in soup *etc* **2** a bribe given to keep someone quiet ◊ *verb* (**sops, sopping, sopped**) soak (up)

sophism *noun* a plausible fallacy ◊ **sophist** *noun* ◊ **sophistic** *adj*

sophisticated *adj* **1** of a person: full of experience **2** accustomed to an elegant, cultured way of life **3** of ways of thought, or machinery *etc*: highly developed, complicated, elaborate

■ **1** urbane, cosmopolitan, worldly, worldly-wise, cultured, cultivated, refined, polished **3** advanced, highly-developed, complicated, complex, intricate, elaborate

🖭 **1** unsophisticated, naive **2** primitive, simple

sophomore *noun*, *US* a second-year college student

soporific *adj* causing sleep ◊ *noun* something which causes sleep

■ *adj* sleep-inducing, hypnotic, sedative, tranquillizing, sleepy, somnolent

🖭 *adj* stimulating, invigorating

sopping *adj* wet through

soppy *adj* overly sentimental

■ sentimental, *informal* lovey-dovey, *informal* touchy-feely, *informal* weepy,

sloppy, slushy, mushy, *informal* corny, cloying, soft, silly, *informal* daft

soprano *noun* (*plural* **sopranos**) **1** a singing voice of high pitch **2** a singer with this voice

sorcerer, sorceress *noun* someone who works magic spells; a witch or wizard

sorcery *noun* magic, witchcraft

■ magic, black magic, witchcraft, wicca, wizardry, necromancy, voodoo, spell, incantation, charm, enchantment

sordid *adj* **1** dirty, filthy **2** mean, selfish **3** contemptible

■ **1** dirty, filthy, unclean, foul, vile, squalid, sleazy, seamy, seedy, disreputable, shabby, tawdry **2** mean, miserly, niggardly, grasping, mercenary **3** disreputable, shabby, tawdry, corrupt, degraded, degenerate, debauched, low, base, despicable, shameful

sore *adj* painful ◊ *noun* a painful, inflamed spot on the skin ◊ **soreness** *noun*

■ *adj* painful, hurting, aching, smarting, stinging, tender, sensitive, inflamed, red, raw ◊ *noun* wound, lesion, swelling, inflammation, boil, abscess, ulcer

sorely *adv* very greatly: *sorely in need*

sorghum *noun* a grass similar to sugar-cane

sorority *noun* (*plural* **sororities**) a society of female students (*compare with*: **fraternity**)

sorrel *noun* a type of plant with sour-tasting leaves

sorrow *noun* sadness caused by a loss, disappointment *etc* ◊ *verb* be sad ◊ **sorrowful** *adj*

■ *noun* sadness, unhappiness, grief, mourning, misery, woe, distress, affliction, anguish, heartache, heartbreak, misfortune, hardship, trouble, worry, trial, tribulation, regret, remorse

🖭 *noun* happiness, joy

sorry *adj* **1** feeling regret for something you have done: *I'm sorry I mentioned it* **2** feeling sympathy or pity (for): *sorry for you* **3** miserable: *in a sorry state*

■ **1** apologetic, regretful, remorseful, contrite, penitent, repentant, conscience-stricken, guilt-ridden, shamefaced **2** sympathetic, compassionate, understanding, pitying, concerned, moved **3** pathetic, pitiful, poor, wretched, miserable, sad, unhappy, dismal

Ea **1** impenitent, unashamed **2** uncaring **3** happy, cheerful

sort *noun* a kind of (person or thing): *the sort of sweets I like* ◇ *verb* **1** separate things, putting each in its place: *sort letters* **2** *informal* fix or mend: *the problem is sorted* ◇ **a sort of** a thing like a: *he wore a sort of crown* ◇ **sort out 1** separate (things) out from a collection **2** arrange in order **3** *informal* deal with (someone or something) firmly ◇ **of a sort** or **of sorts** of a kind, usually inadequate: *a party of sorts* ◇ **out of sorts** not feeling very well

■ *noun* kind, type, genre, family, race, breed, species, genus, variety, order, class, category, group, denomination, style, make, brand, stamp, quality, nature ◇ *verb* class, group, categorize, distribute, divide, separate, segregate, sift, grade, rank, order, classify, catalogue, arrange, organize, systematize

sortie *noun* a sudden attack made by the defenders of a place on those who are trying to capture it

SOS *noun* **1** a code signal calling for help **2** any call for help

so-so *adj* not particularly good

sot *noun* a drunkard ◇ **sottish** *adj* stupid with drink

sotto voce *adv* in a low voice, so as not to be overheard

soufflé /'suːfleɪ/ *noun* a light, cooked dish, made of whisked egg-whites *etc*

sough *verb* of the wind: make a sighing sound

sought *past form* of **seek** ◇ **sought after** popular, much in demand

soul *noun* **1** the spirit, the part of someone which is not the body **2** a person: *a dear old soul* **3** a perfect example (of): *the soul of kindness*

■ **1** spirit, psyche, mind, reason, intellect, character, inner being, essence, life, vital force **2** individual, person, man, woman, creature

soulful *adj* full of feeling

soulless *adj* **1** having no soul or atmosphere **2** dull, very boring

sound¹ *noun* **1** anything that can be heard, a noise **2** a distance from which something may be heard: *within the sound of Bow Bells* ◇ *verb* **1** strike you as being: *that sounds awful* **2** (with **like**) resemble in sound: *that sounds like Henry's voice* **3** make a noise with: *sound a horn* **4** examine by listening carefully to: *sound a patient's chest* ◇ **sound card** a device enabling a computer to record and play sound

■ *noun* **1** noise, din, report, resonance, reverberation, tone

sound² *adj* **1** healthy, strong **2** reliable: *sound opinions* **3** thorough: *a sound beating* **4** of sleep: deep

■ **1** fit, well, healthy, vigorous, robust, sturdy, firm, solid, whole, complete, intact, perfect, unbroken, undamaged, unimpaired, unhurt, uninjured **2** valid, well-founded, reasonable, rational, true, proven, reliable, trustworthy, secure

Ea *adj* **1** unfit, ill, shaky **2** unsound, unreliable, poor

sound³ *verb* measure (the depth of water) ◇ **sound out** try to find out someone's opinions: *I'll sound him out tomorrow*

sound⁴ *noun* a narrow passage of water

soundproof *adj* built or made so that sound cannot pass in or out ◇ *verb* make soundproof

soundtrack *noun* the strip on a film where the speech and music are recorded

soup *noun* a liquid food made from meat, vegetables *etc* boiled in water or stock

soupçon /'suːpsɒn/ *noun* a taste, a morsel

sour *adj* **1** having an acid or bitter taste, often as a stage in going bad: *sour* *milk* **2** bad-tempered ◇ *verb* make sour

■ *adj* **1** tart, sharp, acid, pungent, vinegary, bitter, rancid **2** embittered, acrimonious, ill-tempered, peevish, crabbed, crusty, disagreeable

◨ *adj* **1** sweet, sugary **2** good-natured, generous

source *noun* **1** the place where something has its beginning or is found **2** a spring, *esp* one from which a river flows

■ **1** origin, derivation, beginning, start, commencement, cause, root

souse *verb* soak (*eg* herrings) in salted water

south *noun* one of the four chief directions, that to one's left as one faces the setting sun ◇ *adj & adv* to or in the south ◇ *adj* in the south-east or south-west ◇ **south pole** the southern end of the imaginary axis on which the earth turns

south-east *noun* the point of the compass midway between south and east

southerly *adj* **1** towards the south **2** of wind: from the south

southern *adj* of, from or in the south

southerner *noun* someone from a southern region or country

southward or **southwards** *adj & adv* towards the south

south-west *noun* the point of the compass midway between south and west

souvenir *noun* something bought or given as a reminder of a person, place or occasion

■ memento, reminder, remembrance, keepsake, relic, token

sovereign *noun* **1** a king or queen **2** *hist* a British gold coin worth £1 ◇ *adj* **1** supreme, highest: *sovereign lord* **2** having its own government: *sovereign state* ◇ **sovereignty** *noun* highest power

■ *noun* **1** ruler, monarch, king, queen, emperor, empress, potentate, chief ◇ *adj* **1** ruling, royal, imperial, absolute, unlimited, supreme, paramount, predominant, principal, chief, dominant **2** independent, autonomous

sou'wester *noun* a kind of waterproof hat

sow[1] /soʊ/ *verb* (**sows**, **sowing**, **sown** or **sowed**, **sowed**) **1** scatter (seeds) so that they may grow **2** cover (an area) with seeds ◇ **sower** *noun*

■ **1** plant, seed, scatter, strew, spread, disseminate, lodge, implant

sow[2] /saʊ/ *noun* a female pig

soya bean or **soy bean** a kind of bean, rich in protein, used as a substitute for meat

soya sauce or **soy sauce** a sauce made from soya beans used in Chinese cooking

spa *noun* a place where people go to drink or bathe in the water from a natural spring

space *noun* **1** the empty region in which all stars, planets *etc* are situated **2** extent, area: *no space for a pool* **3** a gap **4** length of time: *in the space of a day* **5** one of a restricted number of places, seat *etc* ◇ *verb* put things apart from each other, leaving room between them

■ *noun* **2** room, accommodation, capacity, volume, extent, expansion, scope, range, play, elbow-room **3** blank, omission, gap, opening, lacuna, interval, intermission, chasm

spacecraft *noun* a machine for travelling in space

spaceman, spacewoman *noun* a traveller in space

spaceship *noun* a manned spacecraft

spacious *adj* having plenty of room ◇ **spaciousness** *noun*

■ roomy, capacious, ample, big, large, sizable, broad, wide, huge, vast, extensive, open, uncrowded

◨ small, narrow, cramped, confined

spade *noun* **1** a tool with a broad blade for digging in the earth **2** one of the four suits of playing-cards ◇ **call a spade a spade** say plainly and clearly what you mean

spaghetti *noun* a type of pasta made into long sticks

spake *verb, old* spoke

span *noun* **1** the distance between the tips of the little finger and the thumb when the hand is spread out (about 23 centimetres, 9 inches) **2** the full time anything lasts **3** an arch of a bridge ◇ *verb* (**spans, spanning, spanned**) stretch across: *the bridge spans the river*
▣ *noun* **2** spread, stretch, duration, term, period, spell ◇ *verb* arch, vault, bridge, link, cross, traverse, extend, cover

spangle *noun* a thin sparkling piece of metal used as an ornament ◇ **spangled** *adj* ◇ **spangly** *adj*

spaniel *noun* a breed of dog with large, hanging ears

spank *verb* strike with the flat of the hand ◇ *noun* a slap with the hand, *esp* on the buttocks

spanking *noun* a beating with the hand ◇ *adj* fast: *a spanking pace*

spanner *noun* a tool used to tighten or loosen nuts, screws *etc*

spar¹ *noun* a long piece of wood or metal used as a ship's mast or its crosspiece

spar² *verb* (**spars, sparring, sparred**) **1** fight with the fists **2** engage in an argument

spare *verb* **1** do without: *I can't spare you today* **2** afford, set aside: *I can't spare the time to do it* **3** treat with mercy, hold back from injuring **4** avoid causing (trouble *etc*) to ◇ *adj* **1** extra, not yet in use: *spare tyre* **2** thin, small: *spare but strong* ◇ *noun* another of the same kind (*eg* a tyre, part of a machine) kept for emergencies ◇ **to spare** over and above what is needed
▣ *adj* **1** reserve, emergency, extra, additional, surplus, superfluous, free, unoccupied
▣ *adj* **1** necessary, vital, used

sparing *adj* careful, economical
▣ economical, thrifty, careful, prudent, frugal, meagre, miserly
▣ unsparing, liberal, lavish

spark *noun* **1** a small red-hot part thrown off from something burning **2** a trace: *a spark of humanity* ◇ *verb* make sparks ◇ **spark off** stimulate or start

sparking-plug or **spark-plug** *noun* a device in a car engine that produces a spark to set on fire explosive gases

sparkle *noun* **1** a point of shiny light **2** brightness, liveliness **3** bubbles, as in wine ◇ *verb* **1** shine in a glittering way **2** be lively or witty **3** bubble
▣ *noun* **1** twinkle, glitter, flash, gleam, glint, flicker **2** radiance, brilliance, dazzle, spirit, vitality, life, animation ◇ *verb* **1** twinkle glitter, scintillate, flash, gleam, glint, glisten, shimmer, shine, beam **3** effervesce, fizz, bubble

sparkling *adj* **1** glittering **2** witty **3** of a drink: bubbling, fizzy

sparrow *noun* a type of small dull-coloured bird

sparrowhawk *noun* a type of short-winged hawk

sparse *adj* **1** thinly scattered **2** not much, not enough
▣ **1** scattered, infrequent, sporadic **2** scarce, scanty, meagre
▣ **1** thick, dense **2** plentiful

spartan *adj* of conditions *etc*: hard, without luxury
▣ austere, harsh, severe, rigorous, strict, disciplined, ascetic, abstemious, temperate, frugal, plain, simple, bleak, joyless
▣ luxurious, self-indulgent

spasm *noun* **1** a sudden involuntary jerk of the muscles **2** a strong, short burst (*eg* of anger, work)
▣ **1** convulsion, seizure, attack, contraction, jerk, twitch **2** burst, eruption, outburst, frenzy, fit

spasmodic *adj* **1** occurring in spasms **2** coming now and again, not regularly ◇ **spasmodically** *adv*

spastic *adj* suffering from brain damage which has resulted in extreme muscle spasm and paralysis

spat¹ *past form* of **spit**

spat² *noun, informal* a petty fight or quarrel

spate *noun* **1** flood: *the river is in spate* **2** a sudden rush: *a spate of new books*

■ **2** flood, deluge, torrent, rush, outpouring, flow

spatial *adj* of or relating to space ◇ **spatially** *adv*

spats *noun plural* short gaiters reaching just above the ankle

spatter *verb* splash (*eg* with mud)

spatula *noun* a tool with a broad, blunt blade

spawn *noun* a mass of eggs of fish, frogs *etc* ◇ *verb* **1** of fish *etc*: lay eggs **2** cause, produce

spay *verb* remove the ovaries of (a female animal)

speak *verb* (**speaks**, **speaking**, **spoke**, **spoken**) **1** say words, talk **2** hold a conversation (with) **3** make a speech **4** be able to talk (a certain language) ◇ **speak your mind** give your opinion openly ◇ **speak out, speak up 1** speak more loudly or clearly **2** give your opinion openly

■ **1** talk, say, express, utter, voice, articulate, enunciate, pronounce, tell, communicate **2** talk, converse **3** address, lecture

spear *noun* **1** a long weapon, with an iron or steel point **2** a long, pointed shoot or leaf (*esp* of grass) ◇ *verb* pierce with a spear ◇ **the spear side** the male side or line of descent (*contrasted with:* **distaff side**)

special *adj* **1** distinct from others, exceptional: *special occasion/special friend* **2** for a particular purpose: *you can get a special program to do that* **3** not ordinary or common: *special skills* ◇ **specially** *adv*

■ **1** important, significant, momentous, major, noteworthy, distinguished, memorable, remarkable, extraordinary, exceptional, different, distinctive, characteristic, peculiar, singular, individual, unique **3** particular, specific

🡒 **1** normal, ordinary, usual

specialist *noun* someone who studies one branch of a subject or field: *heart specialist*

■ consultant, authority, expert, master, professional, connoisseur

speciality *noun* (*plural* **specialities**) an activity or skill in which someone specializes

■ strength, forte, talent, field, specialty, pièce de résistance

specialize *verb* work in, or study, a particular job, subject *etc* ◇ **specialization** *noun*

specialized *adj* of knowledge: obtained by specializing

specialty *noun* (*plural* **specialties**) a branch of work in which someone specializes

specie /ˈspiːʃiː/ *noun* gold and silver coins

species *noun* (*plural* **species**) **1** a group of plants or animals which are alike in most ways **2** a kind (of anything)

specific *adj* giving all the details clearly; particular, exactly stated: *a specific purpose* ◇ **specifically** *adv*

■ precise, exact, fixed, limited, particular, special, definite, unequivocal, clear-cut, explicit, express, unambiguous

🡒 vague, approximate

specification *noun* **1** the act of specifying **2** (often **specifications**) a full description of details (*eg* in a plan or contract)

■ **2** requirements, conditions, qualifications, description, listing, items, particulars, details

specify *verb* (**specifies**, **specifying**, **specified**) **1** set down or say clearly (what is wanted) **2** make particular mention of

■ **1** stipulate, spell out, define, particularize, detail, itemize, enumerate, list **2** mention, cite, name, designate, indicate, describe

specimen *noun* something used as a sample of a group or kind of anything, *esp* for study or for putting in a collection

■ sample, example, instance, illustration, model, pattern, paradigm, exemplar, representative, copy, exhibit

specious *adj* looking or seeming good but really not so good

speck *noun* **1** a small spot **2** a tiny piece (*eg* of dust)

speckle *noun* a spot on a different-coloured background ◇ **speckled** *adj* dotted with speckles

spectacle *noun* **1** a striking or wonderful sight **2** (**spectacles**) glasses worn to improve eyesight
▣ **1** scene, sight, curiosity, wonder, marvel, phenomenon

spectacular *adj* making a great show or display; impressive ◇ **spectacularly** *adv*
▣ grand, splendid, magnificent, sensational, impressive, striking, stunning, staggering, amazing, remarkable, dramatic, daring, breathtaking, dazzling, eye-catching, colourful
▣ unimpressive, ordinary

spectator *noun* someone who watches (an event *eg* a football match)

spectre *noun* a ghost ◇ **spectral** *adj* ghostly

spectrum *noun* (*plural* **spectra** or **spectrums**) **1** the band of colours as seen in a rainbow, sometimes formed when light passes through water or glass **2** the range or extent of anything

speculate *verb* **1** guess **2** wonder (about) **3** buy goods, shares *etc* in order to sell them again at a profit ◇ **speculation** *noun* ◇ **speculative** *adj* ◇ **speculator** *noun*
▣ **1** suppose, guess, conjecture **2** wonder, contemplate, meditate, muse, reflect, consider, deliberate ◇ **speculative** conjectural, hypothetical, theoretical, notional, abstract, academic, tentative, risky, hazardous, uncertain, unpredictable

speculum *noun* (*plural* **specula** or **speculums**) an instrument inserted in a woman's vagina to help a doctor view her cervix *etc*

sped *past form* of **speed**

speech *noun* **1** the power of making sounds which have meaning for other people **2** a way of speaking: *his speech is always clear* **3** (*plural* **speeches**) a (formal) talk given to an audience
▣ **2** diction, articulation, enunciation, elo-cution, delivery **3** oration, address, discourse, talk, lecture, monologue

speechless *adj* so surprised *etc* that you cannot speak
▣ dumbfounded, thunderstruck, amazed, aghast, tongue-tied, inarticulate, mute, dumb, silent, mum
▣ talkative

speed *noun* **1** quickness of, or rate of, movement or action **2** *slang* amphetamine ◇ *verb* (**speeds**, **speeding**, **sped** or **speeded**) **1** (*past* **sped**) (cause to) move along quickly, hurry **2** (*past* **speeded**) drive very fast in a car *etc* (*esp* faster than is allowed by law) ◇ **speed limit** the greatest speed permitted on a particular road
▣ *noun* **1** velocity, rate, pace, tempo, quickness, swiftness, rapidity, celerity, rush, acceleration, haste, hurry ◇ *verb* **1** race, tear, *informal* belt, zoom, career, sprint, gallop, hurry, rush, hasten, accelerate, quicken
▣ *noun* **1** slowness, delay

speeding *noun* driving at (an illegally) high speed

speedometer *noun* an instrument that shows how fast you are travelling

speedway *noun* a motorcycle racing track

speedwell *noun* a type of small plant with blue flowers

speedy *adj* going quickly
▣ fast, quick, swift, rapid, nimble, express, prompt, immediate, hurried, hasty, precipitate, cursory
▣ slow, leisurely

speleologist *noun* someone who studies or explores caves ◇ **speleology** *noun*

spell¹ *verb* (**spells**, **spelling**, **spelt** or **spelled**) **1** give or write correctly the letters which make up a word **2** mean, imply: *this defeat spells disaster for us all* ◇ **spell out** say (something) very frankly or clearly

spell² *noun* words which, when spoken, are supposed to have magic power
▣ charm, incantation

spell³ *noun* **1** a (short) space of time

2 a period of work *etc*

■ **1** period, time, stretch, patch **2** session, term, season, interval, turn, stint

spellbound *adj* charmed, held by a spell

■ transfixed, hypnotized, mesmerized, fascinated, enthralled, gripped, entranced, captivated, bewitched, enchanted, charmed

spellchecker *noun*, *comput* a program in a word processor identifying spelling errors

spelling *noun* **1** the ability to spell words **2** the study of spelling words correctly

spelt *see* spell¹

spelunking *noun* exploring in caves as a hobby

spend *verb* (**spends**, **spending**, **spent**) **1** use (money) for buying **2** use (energy *etc*) **3** pass (time): *I spent a week there* **4** use up energy, force *etc* completely: *the storm spent itself and the sun shone*

■ **1** pay out, *informal* fork out, *informal* shell out, invest, lay out, *informal* splash out, waste, squander **3** pass, fill, occupy **4** expend, consume, use up, exhaust

■ **1** save, hoard

spendthrift *noun* someone who spends money freely and carelessly

■ squanderer, prodigal, profligate, wastrel

■ miser

spent *adj* exhausted; having lost force or power: *a spent bullet*

sperm *noun* (the fluid in a male carrying) the male sex-cell that fertilizes the female egg ◇ **sperm bank** a store of semen for use in artificial insemination

spermatozoon *noun* (*plural* **spermatozoa**) a male sex cell contained in sperm

spermicide *noun* a substance which kills spermatozoa

sperm whale a large whale from the head of which 'spermaceti', a waxy substance, is obtained

spew *verb* **1** vomit **2** pour out

sphagnum *noun* a kind of moss

sphere *noun* **1** a ball or similar perfectly round object **2** a position or level in society: *he moves in the highest spheres* **3** range (of influence or action) ◇ **spherical** *adj* having the shape of a sphere

■ **1** ball, globe, orb, round **3** domain, realm, province, department, territory, field, range, scope, compass, rank, function, capacity

sphincter *noun* a ring-like muscle which narrows an opening (*eg* the anus)

Sphinx *noun* **1** a mythological monster with the head of a woman and the body of a lioness **2** the large stone model of the Sphinx in Egypt **3** (**sphinx**) someone whose real thoughts you cannot guess

spice *noun* **1** any substance used for flavouring *eg* pepper, nutmeg **2** anything that adds liveliness, interest ◇ *verb* flavour with spice

spick-and-span *adj* neat, clean and tidy

spicy *adj* **1** full of spices **2** lively and sometimes slightly indecent: *a spicy tale* ◇ **spiciness** *noun*

■ **1** piquant, hot, pungent, tangy, seasoned, aromatic, fragrant **2** racy, risqué, ribald, suggestive, *informal* saucy, indelicate, improper, indecorous, unseemly, scandalous, sensational

■ **1** bland, insipid **2** decent

spider *noun* a kind of small, insect-like creature with eight legs, that spins a web

spidery *adj* **1** like a spider **2** of handwriting: having fine, sprawling strokes

spiel /ʃpiːl/ or /spiːl/ *noun*, *informal* a (long or often repeated) story or speech

spigot *noun* **1** a peg for sealing a hole **2** *US* a tap

spike *noun* **1** a pointed piece of rod (of wood, metal *etc*) **2** a type of large nail **3** an ear of corn or a head of flowers **4** (**spikes**) running shoes with spiked soles ◇ *verb* **1** pierce with a spike **2** make useless **3** *informal* add an alcoholic drink *esp* to a soft drink ◇ **spiky**

adj having spikes or a sharp point

■ *noun* **1** point, prong, tine, spine, barb, nail, stake ◇ *verb* **1** impale, stick, spear, skewer, spit

spill[1] *verb* (**spills**, **spilling**, **spilt** or **spilled**) (allow liquid to) run out or overflow ◇ *noun* **1** an instance of spilling: *an oil spill* **2** *informal* a fall ◇ **spill the beans** *informal* give away a secret, *esp* unintentionally

■ *verb* overturn, upset, slop, overflow, disgorge, pour, tip, discharge, shed, scatter

spill[2] *noun* a thin strip of wood or twisted paper for lighting a candle *etc*

spillage *noun* an act of spilling or what is spilt

spin *verb* (**spins**, **spinning**, **spun**) **1** (cause to) whirl round quickly **2** draw out (cotton, wood, silk *etc*) and twist into threads **3** produce a fine thread as a spider does **4** propel (a ball) so that it rotates as it moves ◇ *noun* **1** a whirling motion **2** rotation in a ball **3** *informal* a ride (*esp* on wheels) **4** of information *etc*: a favourable bias ◇ **spinner** *noun* ◇ **spin a yarn** tell a long story ◇ **spin out** make to last a long or longer time

■ *verb* **1** turn, revolve, rotate, twist, gyrate, twirl, pirouette, wheel, whirl, swirl, reel ◇ *noun* **1** turn, revolution, twist, gyration, twirl, pirouette, whirl, swirl **3** drive, ride, run ◇ **spin out** prolong, protract, extend, lengthen, amplify, pad out

spina bifida a birth defect which leaves part of the spinal cord exposed

spinach *noun* a type of plant whose leaves are eaten as vegetables

spinal *adj* of the spine ◇ **spinal cord** a cord of nerve cells in the spine

spindle *noun* **1** the pin from which the thread is twisted in spinning wool or cotton **2** a pin on which anything turns round

spindly *adj* long and thin

spin doctor someone employed by a public figure to speak to the media *etc* on their behalf

spindrier or **spin dryer** *noun* a machine for taking water out of clothes by whirling them round

spindrift *noun* the spray blown from the tops of waves

spine *noun* **1** the line of linked bones running down the back in animals and humans, the backbone **2** a ridge **3** a stiff, pointed spike which is part of an animal's body (*eg* a porcupine) **4** a thorn

spineless *adj* **1** having no spine **2** weak

■ **2** weak, feeble, irresolute, ineffective, cowardly, faint-hearted, lily-livered, *slang* yellow, soft, wet, submissive, weak-kneed, *informal* wimpish

◼ **2** strong, brave

spinnaker *noun* a light triangular sail

spinneret *noun* in a spider *etc*, the organ for producing thread

spinney *noun* (*plural* **spinneys**) a small clump of trees

spinning wheel a machine for spinning thread, consisting of a wheel which drives spindles

spinster *noun* a woman who is not married

spiral *adj* **1** coiled round like a spring **2** winding round and round, getting further and further away from the centre ◇ *noun* **1** anything with a spiral shape **2** a spiral movement **3** an increase which gets ever more rapid ◇ *verb* (**spirals**, **spiralling**, **spiralled**) **1** move in a spiral **2** increase ever more rapidly

■ *adj* **1** winding, coiled, corkscrew, helical **2** winding, whorled, scrolled

spire *noun* a tall, sharp-pointed tower (*esp* on the roof of a church)

spirit *noun* **1** the soul **2** a being without a body, a ghost: *an evil spirit* **3** liveliness, boldness: *he acted with spirit* **4** a feeling or attitude: *a spirit of kindness* **5** the intended meaning: *the spirit of the laws* **6** a distilled liquid, *esp* alcohol **7** (**spirits**) strong alcoholic drinks in general (*eg* whisky) **8** (**spirits**) state of mind, mood: *in high spirits* ◇ *verb* (*esp* with **away**) remove, as if by magic

■ *noun* **1** soul, psyche, mind, breath, life **2**

ghost, spectre, phantom, apparition, angel, demon **3** liveliness, vivacity, animation, sparkle, vigour, energy, zest, fire, ardour, motivation, enthusiasm, zeal **5** meaning, sense, substance, essence, gist, tenor, character, quality **8** mood, humour, temper, disposition, temperament, feeling, morale, attitude, outlook

spirited *adj* lively

▣ lively, vivacious, animated, sparkling, high-spirited, vigorous, energetic, active, ardent, zealous, bold, courageous, mettlesome, plucky, feisty

▣ spiritless, lethargic, cowardly

spiritual *adj* having to do with the soul or with ghosts ◇ *noun* an emotional, religious song of a kind originally sung by African American slaves

▣ *adj* unworldly, immaterial, otherworldly, heavenly, divine, holy, sacred, religious, ecclesiastical

▣ *adj* physical, material

spiritualism *noun* the belief that living people can communicate with the souls of dead people ◇ **spiritualist** *noun* someone who holds this belief

spit¹ *noun* the liquid which forms in a person's mouth ◇ *verb* (**spits**, **spitting**, **spat** or **spitted**) (*past form* **spat**) **1** throw liquid out from the mouth **2** rain slightly **3** (*past form* **spitted**) pierce with something sharp ◇ **spitting image** an exact likeness

spit² *noun* **1** a metal rod on which meat is skewered and roasted **2** a long piece of land running into the sea

spite *noun* the wish to hurt (*esp* feelings) ◇ *verb* annoy out of spite ◇ **spiteful** *adj* ◇ **in spite of** regardless, notwithstanding: *the ground was dry in spite of all the rain*

▣ *noun* spitefulness, malice, venom, gall, bitterness, rancour, animosity, ill feeling, grudge, malevolence, malignity, hate, hatred ◇ *verb* annoy, irritate, irk, vex, provoke, gall, hurt, injure, offend, put out ◇ **spiteful** malicious, catty, bitchy, snide, cruel, vindictive, vengeful, malevolent, malignant, ill-natured, ill-disposed, nasty

▣ *noun* goodwill, compassion, affection ◇ **spiteful** charitable, affectionate

spittle *noun* spit

spittoon *noun* a kind of dish into which people may spit

splash *verb* **1** spatter with water, mud *etc* **2** move or fall with a splash or splashes ◇ *noun* (*plural* **splashes**) **1** the sound made by, or the scattering of liquid caused by, something hitting water *etc* **2** a mark made by splashing (*eg* on your clothes) **3** a bright patch: *a splash of colour* ◇ **make a splash** attract a lot of attention

▣ *verb* **1** spray, squirt, sprinkle, spatter, splatter, splodge, plaster, slop, slosh, splosh

splay *verb* turn out at an angle ◇ **splay-footed** *adj* with flat feet turned outwards

spleen *noun* **1** a spongy, blood-filled organ inside the body, near the stomach **2** bad temper

splendid *adj* **1** magnificent, brilliant **2** *informal* excellent ◇ **splendidly** *adv*

▣ **1** brilliant, dazzling, glittering, lustrous, bright, radiant, glowing, glorious, magnificent, gorgeous, resplendent, sumptuous, luxurious, lavish, rich, fine, grand, stately, imposing **2** superb, excellent, first-class, wonderful, marvellous

▣ **1** drab, ordinary, run-of-the-mill

splendour *noun* magnificence

▣ brightness, radiance, brilliance, dazzle, lustre, glory, resplendence, magnificence, richness, grandeur, ceremony, display, show, spectacle

▣ drabness, squalor

splenetic *adj* irritable

splice *verb* **1** join (two ends of a rope) by twining the threads together **2** join the ends of (two pieces of film, wire *etc*) ◇ *noun* a joint so made

splint *noun* a piece of wood *etc* tied to a broken limb to keep it in a fixed position

splinter *noun* a sharp, thin, broken piece of wood, glass *etc* ◇ *verb* split into splinters ◇ **splinter group** a group which breaks away from a larger one

split *verb* **1** cut or break lengthways **2** crack, break **3** divide into pieces or groups *etc* ◇ *noun* a crack, a break ◇ **the splits** the feat of going down on the floor with one leg stretched forward and the other back ◇ **a split second** a fraction of a second ◇ **split your sides** laugh heartily

▣ *verb* **2** gape, fork, diverge, break, splinter, shiver, snap, crack, burst, rupture, tear, rend, rip, slit, slash, cleave **3** divide, separate, partition, part, share, distribute, parcel out ◇ *noun* division, separation, partition, break, cleft, crevice, crack, fissure, rupture, tear, rent, rip, rift, slit, slash

splitting *adj* of a headache: severe, intense

splutter *verb* **1** make spitting noises **2** speak hastily and unclearly

spoil *verb* (**spoils, spoiling, spoiled**) **1** make useless; damage, ruin **2** give in to the wishes of (a child *etc*) and so ruin its character **3** of food: become bad or useless **4** (*past form* **spoiled**) rob, plunder ◇ *noun* (often **spoils**) plunder ◇ **spoiling for** eager for (*esp* a fight)

▣ *verb* **1** mar, wreck, ruin, destroy, damage, impair, harm, hurt, injure, deface, disfigure, blemish **2** indulge, pamper, cosset, coddle, mollycoddle, spoonfeed **3** deteriorate, go bad, go off, sour, turn, curdle, decay, decompose

spoilsport *noun* someone who won't join in other people's fun

spoke *noun* one of the ribs or bars from the centre to the rim of a wheel ◇ *verb, past form* of **speak**

spoken *past participle* of **speak**

spokesman, spokeswoman *noun* someone who speaks on behalf of others

spoliation *noun* plundering

sponge *noun* **1** a sea animal **2** its soft, elastic skeleton which can soak up water and is used for washing **3** an artificial object like this used for washing **4** a light cake or pudding ◇ *verb* **1** wipe with a sponge **2** *informal* live off money *etc* given by others ◇ **sponger** *noun, in-*

formal someone who lives at others' expense ◇ **spongy** *adj* soft like a sponge ◇ **throw in the sponge** give up a fight or struggle

▣ **spongy** soft, cushioned, yielding, elastic, springy, porous, absorbent, light

sponsor *noun* **1** someone who takes responsibility for introducing something, a promoter **2** someone who promises to pay a sum of money if another person completes a set task (*eg* a walk, swim *etc*) **3** a business firm which pays for a radio or television programme and advertises its products during it ◇ *verb* act as a sponsor to ◇ **sponsorship** *noun* the act of sponsoring

spontaneous *adj* **1** not planned beforehand **2** natural, not forced ◇ **spontaneity** *noun*

▣ **1** unpremeditated, free, willing, unhesitating, voluntary, unprompted, impromptu, ad-lib **2** natural, unforced, untaught, instinctive, impulsive

▣ **1** planned, deliberate **2** forced, studied

spoof *noun* **1** a satirical imitation **2** a trick played as a joke, a hoax

spook *noun* a ghost ◇ **spooky** *adj* frightening

spool *noun* a reel for thread, film *etc*

spoon *noun* a piece of metal *etc* with a hollow bowl at one end, used for lifting food to the mouth ◇ *verb* lift with a spoon

spoonerism *noun* a mistake in speaking in which the first sounds of words change position, as in *every crook and nanny* for *every nook and cranny*

spoonfeed *verb* **1** feed (a baby) using a spoon **2** teach without encouraging independent thought

spoor *noun* the footmarks or trail left by an animal

sporadic *adj* happening here and there, or now and again ◇ **sporadically** *adv*

▣ occasional, intermittent, infrequent, isolated, spasmodic, erratic, irregular, uneven, random, scattered

▣ frequent, regular

spore *noun* the seed of certain plants (*eg* ferns, fungi)

sporran *noun* a small pouch worn hanging in front of a kilt

sport *noun* **1** games such as football, tennis, skiing *etc* in general **2** any one game of this type **3** a good-natured, obliging person ◇ *verb* **1** have fun, play **2** wear: *sporting a pink tie* ◇ **sports car** a small, fast car with only two seats

■ *noun* **2** game, exercise, activity ◇ *verb* **2** wear, display, exhibit, show off

Sports include: badminton, fives, lacrosse, squash, table-tennis, *informal* ping-pong, tennis; American football, Australian Rules football, baseball, basketball, billiards, boules, bowls, Canadian football, cricket, croquet, football, futsal, Gaelic football, golf, handball, hockey, netball, pétanque, pitch and putt, polo, pool, putting, rounders, rugby, shinty, snooker, soccer, tenpin bowling, volleyball; athletics, cross-country, decathlon, discus, high jump, hurdling, javelin, long jump, marathon, pentathlon, pole vault, running, shot put, triple jump; angling, aqua aerobics, canoeing, diving, fishing, rowing, sailing, skin-diving, surfing, swimming, synchronized swimming, water polo, water-skiing, windsurfing, yachting; bobsleigh, cross-country skiing, curling, downhill skiing, ice hockey, ice-skating, skeleton bob, skiing, slalom, snowboarding, speed skating, tobogganing (luging); aerobics, fencing, gymnastics, in-line skating, jogging, keep-fit, roller-skating, skateboarding, trampolining; archery, darts, quoits; boxing, judo, jujitsu, karate, tae kwon do, weightlifting, wrestling; climbing, mountaineering, rock climbing, walking, orienteering, pot-holing; cycle racing, drag racing, go-karting, motor racing, speedway racing, stock-car racing, greyhound racing, horse racing, showjumping, trotting, hunting, shooting, clay pigeon shooting; gliding, paragliding, skydiving

sporting *adj* **1** to do with sport: *sporting activities* **2** believing in fair play, good-natured ◇ **sporting chance** a reasonably good chance

■ **2** sportsmanlike, gentlemanly, decent, considerate, fair

✸ **2** unsporting, ungentlemanly, unfair

sportsman, sportswoman *noun* **1** someone who plays sports **2** someone who shows fair play in sports ◇ **sportsmanlike** *adj*

spot *noun* **1** a small mark or stain (of mud, paint *etc*) **2** a round mark as part of a pattern on material *etc* **3** a pimple **4** a place (**spots**, **spotting**, **spotted**) **1** mark with spots **2** catch sight of ◇ **spot check** a random inspection ◇ **in a spot** in trouble ◇ **on the spot 1** in the place where someone is most needed **2** right away, immediately **3** in an embarrassing or difficult position

■ *noun* **1** mark, speck, blotch, blot, smudge, daub, splash, stain, discoloration, blemish **2** dot, speckle, fleck **3** blemish, flaw, pimple **4** place, point, position, situation, location, site, scene, locality ◇ *verb* **2** see, notice, observe, detect, discern, identify, recognize

spotless *adj* very clean

■ immaculate, clean, white, gleaming, spick and span, unmarked, unstained, unblemished, unsullied, pure, untouched, innocent, blameless, faultless, irreproachable

✸ dirty, impure

spotlight *noun* a bright light that is shone on an actor on the stage ◇ *verb* **1** show up clearly **2** draw attention to

spotty or **spotted** *adj* covered with spots

spouse *noun* a husband or wife

spout *noun* **1** the part of a kettle, teapot *etc* through which liquid is poured out **2** a strong jet of liquid ◇ *verb* pour or spurt out

■ *noun* **2** jet, fountain, outlet, nozzle, rose, spray ◇ *verb* jet, spurt, squirt, spray, shoot, gush, stream, surge, erupt, emit, discharge

sprain noun a painful twisting (eg of an ankle) ◇ verb twist painfully

sprang past form of **spring**

sprat noun a small fish similar to a herring

sprawl verb **1** sit, lie or fall with the limbs spread out widely **2** of a town etc: spread out in an untidy, irregular way

▣ **1** spread, flop, slump, slouch, loll, lounge **2** spread, straggle, trail, ramble

spray noun **1** a fine mist of liquid like that made by a waterfall **2** a device with many small holes (eg on a watering-can or shower) for producing spray **3** a liquid for spraying **4** a shoot spreading out in flowers ◇ verb cover with a mist or fine jets of liquid

▣ noun **1** moisture, drizzle, mist, foam, froth ◇ verb shower, spatter, sprinkle, scatter, diffuse, wet, drench

spread verb (**spreads, spreading, spread**) **1** put more widely or thinly over an area: spread the butter on the bread **2** cover: spread the bread with jam **3** (often with **out**) open out (eg your arms, a map) **4** (sometimes with **out**) scatter or distribute over a wide area, length of time etc ◇ noun **1** the act of spreading **2** the extent or range (of something) **3** a food which is spread on bread: sandwich spread **4** informal a large meal laid out on a table

▣ verb **3** stretch, extend, sprawl, broaden, widen, open **4** scatter, strew, diffuse, radiate, broadcast, transmit, communicate, publicize, advertise, publish, circulate, distribute ◇ noun **2** stretch, reach, span, extent, expanse, sweep, compass

▣ verb **3** close, fold **4** suppress

spread-eagled adj with limbs spread out

spreadsheet noun a computer program with which data can be viewed on screen and manipulated

spree noun a careless spell of some activity: a spending spree

sprig noun a small twig or shoot

sprightly adj lively, brisk ◇ **sprightliness** noun

▣ agile, nimble, spry, active, energetic, lively, spirited, vivacious, hearty, brisk, jaunty, cheerful, blithe, airy

▤ doddering, inactive, lifeless

spring verb (**springs, springing, sprang** or **sprung, sprung**) **1** jump, leap **2** move swiftly **3** set off (a trap etc) **4** give, reveal unexpectedly: he sprang the news on me **5** come from: his bravery springs from his love of adventure ◇ noun **1** a leap **2** a coil of wire used eg in a mattress **3** the ability to stretch and spring back **4** bounce, energy **5** a small stream flowing out from the ground **6** the season which follows winter, when plants begin to grow again ◇ **spring a leak** begin to leak ◇ **spring up** appear suddenly

▣ verb **1** jump, leap, vault, bound, hop, bounce **5** originate, derive, come, stem, arise, start, proceed, issue, emanate ◇ noun **1** jump, leap, vault, bound **3** springiness, resilience, give, flexibility, elasticity, buoyancy

springboard noun a springy board from which swimmers may dive

springbok noun a type of deer found in S Africa

spring-cleaning noun a thorough cleaning of a house, esp in the spring

springy adj able to spring back into its former position etc, elastic

▣ bouncy, resilient, flexible, elastic, stretchy, rubbery, spongy, buoyant

▤ hard, stiff

sprinkle verb scatter or cover in small drops or pieces ◇ **sprinkler** noun something which sprinkles water

▣ shower, spray, spatter, scatter, strew, dot, pepper, dust, powder

sprinkling noun a small number

sprint verb run at full speed ◇ noun a short running race at high speed ◇ **sprinter** noun

▣ verb run, race, dash, tear, informal belt, dart, shoot

sprite noun **1** a supernatural spirit **2** comput an icon which can be moved about a screen

sprocket noun one of a set of teeth on the rim of a wheel

sprog noun, slang a child

sprout verb 1 begin to grow 2 put out new shoots ◇ noun 1 a young bud 2 (**sprouts**) Brussels sprouts

spruce[1] adj neat, smart
■ adj smart, elegant, neat, trim, dapper, well-dressed, well-turned-out, well-groomed, sleek
✷ adj scruffy, untidy

spruce[2] noun a kind of fir-tree

sprung past form of **spring**

spry adj lively, active

spud noun, informal a potato

spume noun froth, foam

spun past form of **spin**

spunk noun 1 pluck, spirit 2 slang ejaculated semen

spur noun 1 a sharp point worn by a horse-rider on the heel and used to urge on a horse 2 anything that urges someone on 3 a claw-like point at the back of a bird's leg 4 a small line of mountains running off from a larger range ◇ verb (**spurs**, **spurring**, **spurred**) 1 use spurs on (a horse) 2 urge on ◇ **on the spur of the moment** without thinking beforehand
■ noun 2 incentive, encouragement, inducement, motive, stimulus, incitement, impetus ◇ verb 2 goad, prod, poke, prick, stimulate, prompt, incite, drive, propel, impel, urge, encourage, motivate
✷ verb 2 curb, discourage

spurious adj not genuine, false ◇ **spuriousness** noun
■ false, fake, counterfeit, forged, bogus, informal phoney, mock, sham, feigned, pretended, simulated, imitation, artificial
✷ genuine, authentic, real

spurn verb cast aside, reject with scorn
■ reject, turn down, informal knock back, scorn, despise, disdain, rebuff, repulse, slight, snub, cold-shoulder, ignore, disregard
✷ accept, embrace

spurt verb pour out in a sudden stream ◇ noun 1 a sudden stream pouring or squirting out 2 a sudden increase of effort: put a spurt on
■ verb gush, squirt, jet, shoot, burst, erupt, surge

sputnik noun a small spacecraft orbiting the earth, orig Russian

sputter verb make a noise as of spitting and throw out moisture in drops

sputum noun mucus and spittle from the nose, throat etc

spy noun (plural **spies**) someone who secretly collects (and reports) information about another person, country, firm etc ◇ verb (**spies**, **spying**, **spied**) 1 catch sight of 2 (with **on**) watch secretly
■ noun secret agent, undercover agent, double agent, informal mole, scout, snooper ◇ verb 1 spot, glimpse, notice, observe, discover

spyglass noun a small telescope

sq abbrev square

squabble verb quarrel noisily ◇ noun a noisy quarrel
■ verb bicker, wrangle, quarrel, row, argue, dispute, clash, brawl, informal scrap, fight

squad noun 1 a group of soldiers, workmen etc doing a particular job 2 a group of people

squaddie noun, informal a private, an ordinary soldier

squadron noun a division of a regiment, section of a fleet or group of aeroplanes ◇ **squadron leader** in the air force, an officer below a wing commander

squalid adj 1 very dirty, filthy 2 contemptible
■ 1 dirty, filthy, unclean, foul, disgusting, repulsive, sordid, seedy, dingy, untidy, slovenly, unkempt, broken-down, run-down, neglected 2 low, mean, nasty
✷ 1 clean, pleasant, attractive

squall noun a sudden violent storm ◇ **squally** adj stormy

squalor noun dirty or squalid living conditions

squander verb waste (money, goods, strength etc) ◊ **squanderer** noun

▪ waste, misspend, misuse, lavish, slang blow, fritter away, throw away, dissipate, scatter, spend, expend, consume

square noun **1** a figure with four equal sides and four right angles (□) **2** an open space enclosed by buildings in a town **3** the answer when a number is multiplied by itself (eg the square of 3 is 9) ◊ adj **1** shaped like a square **2** angular: a square jaw **3** of two or more people: not owing one another anything **4** straight, level ◊ verb **1** make like a square **2** straighten (the shoulders) **3** multiply a number by itself **4** fit, agree: that doesn't square with what you said earlier **5** (with **up**) settle (a debt) ◊ adv **1** in a straight or level position **2** directly; exactly: hit square on the nose ◊ **square deal** fair treatment ◊ **square foot** or **square metre** etc an area equal to that of a square each side of which is one foot or one metre etc long ◊ **square meal** a large, satisfying meal ◊ **square root** the number which, multiplied by itself, gives a certain other number (eg 3 is the square root of 9)

▪ verb **4** tally, agree, accord, harmonize, correspond, match, balance, straighten, level

squash¹ verb **1** crush flat or to a pulp **2** put down, defeat (rebellion etc) ◊ noun **1** a crushing or crowding **2** a mass of people crowded together **3** a drink made from the juice of crushed fruit **4** a game with rackets and a rubber ball played in a walled court ◊ **squashy** adj soft or easily squashed

▪ verb **1** crush, flatten, press, squeeze, compress, trample, stamp, pound, pulp, smash **2** suppress, silence, quell, quash, annihilate, put down, snub, humiliate

🔁 adj stretch, expand

squash² noun **1** a trailing plant cultivated for its marrow-like fruit **2** this fruit eaten as a vegetable

squat verb (**squats, squatting, squatted**) **1** sit down on the heels **2** settle without permission in property which you do not pay rent for ◊ adj short and thick

▪ verb **1** crouch, stoop, bend, sit ◊ adj short, stocky, thickset, dumpy, chunky, stubby

🔁 adj slim, lanky

squatter noun someone who squats in a building, on land etc

squaw noun, derogatory **1** a Native American woman or wife **2** a woman

squawk verb give a harsh cry ◊ noun a harsh cry

squeak verb give a short, high-pitched sound ◊ noun a high-pitched noise ◊ **squeaky** adj

squeal verb **1** give a loud, shrill cry **2** informal inform on ◊ **squealer** noun

▪ **1** cry, shout, yell, yelp, wail, scream, screech, shriek, squawk

squeamish adj **1** easily sickened or shocked **2** feeling sick

squeegee noun a sponge for washing windows etc

squeeze verb **1** press together **2** grasp tightly **3** force out (liquid or juice from) by pressing **4** force a way: squeeze through the hole in the wall ◊ noun **1** a squeezing or pressing **2** a few drops got by squeezing: a squeeze of lemon juice **3** a crowd of people crushed together

▪ verb **1** press, squash, crush, pinch, nip, compress, cram, stuff, pack, crowd, wedge, jam **2** clasp, clutch, hug, embrace, enfold, cuddle **3** wring, wrest, extort, milk **4** force, ram, push, thrust, shove, jostle ◊ noun **1** press, squash, crush, crowd, congestion, jam

squelch noun a sound made eg by walking through marshy ground ◊ verb make this sound

squib noun a type of small firework

squid noun a sea animal with tentacles, related to the cuttlefish

squiggle noun a curly or wavy mark ◊ adj **squiggly** curly

squillions noun plural, informal a great many; millions

squint verb **1** screw up the eyes in looking at something **2** have the eyes looking in different directions ◊ noun **1** a fault in eyesight which causes squinting **2** *informal* a quick, close glance

squire *noun, hist* **1** a country land-owner **2** a knight's servant

squirm *verb* wriggle or twist the body, *esp* in pain or embarrassment

squirrel *noun* a small gnawing animal, either reddish-brown or grey, with a bushy tail

squirt *verb* shoot out a narrow jet of liquid ◇ *noun* a narrow jet of liquid
∎ *verb* spray, spurt, jet, shoot, spout, discharge, emit, eject, expel ◇ *noun* spray, spurt, jet

Sr *abbrev* senior

St *abbrev* **1** saint **2** street **3** strait

st *abbrev* stone (in weight)

stab *verb* (**stabs**, **stabbing**, **stabbed**) **1** wound or pierce with a pointed weapon **2** poke (at) ◇ *noun* **1** the act of stabbing **2** a wound made by stabbing **3** a sharp pain ◇ **have a stab at** make an attempt at
∎ *verb* **1** pierce, puncture, cut, wound, injure, gore, knife, spear, stick, jab, thrust ◇ *noun* **3** ache, pang, twinge, prick

stability *noun* steadiness
∎ steadiness, firmness, soundness, constancy, steadfastness, strength, sturdiness, solidity, durability, permanence
⊠ instability, unsteadiness, insecurity, weakness

stabilize *verb* make steady

stable *noun* a building for keeping horses ◇ *verb* put or keep (horses) in a stable ◇ *adj* firm, steady
∎ *adj* steady, firm, secure, fast, sound, sure, constant, steadfast, reliable, established, strong, sturdy, durable, lasting, enduring, permanent, unchangeable, unalterable, invariable, fixed, balanced
⊠ *adj* unstable, wobbly, shaky, weak

staccato *adj* **1** of sounds: sharp and separate, like the sound of tapping **2** *also adv, music* (with each note) sounded separately and clearly

stack *noun* a large pile (of straw, hay, wood *etc*) ◇ *verb* pile in a stack
∎ *noun* heap, pile, mound, mass, load, accumulation, hoard, stockpile, cache, in-

formal stash ◇ *verb* heap, pile, load, amass, accumulate, assemble, gather, save, hoard, stockpile

stadium *noun* (*plural* **stadiums** or **stadia**) a large sports-ground or race-course with seats for spectators

staff *noun* **1** workers employed in a business, school **2** a group of army officers who assist a commanding officer **3** (*plural* **staffs** or **staves**) a stick or pole carried in the hand **4** (*plural* **staffs** or **staves**) *music* a stave *etc* ◇ *verb* supply (a school *etc*) with staff
∎ *noun* **1** personnel, workforce, employees, workers, crew, team, teachers, officers **3** stick, cane, rod, baton, wand, pole, prop

stag *noun* a male deer ◇ **stag party** a party for men only held before one of them gets married

stage *noun* **1** a platform for performing or acting on **2** (with **the**) the theatre; the job of working as an actor **3** a step in development: *the first stage of the plan* **4** a landing place (*eg* for boats) **5** a part of a journey **6** a stopping place on a journey ◇ *verb* **1** prepare and put on a performance of (a play *etc*) **2** arrange (an event, *eg* an exhibition) ◇ **stagefright** *noun* an actor's fear when acting in public *esp* for the first time ◇ **stage whisper** a loud whisper ◇ **on the stage** in the theatre-world
∎ *noun* **3** point, juncture, step, phase ◇ *verb* **2** mount, put on, present, produce, give, do, arrange, organize

stagecoach *noun, hist* a coach running every day with passengers

stagger *verb* **1** walk unsteadily, totter **2** astonish **3** arrange (people's hours of work *etc*) so that they do not begin or end together ◇ **staggered** *adj* ◇ **staggering** *adj* astonishing
∎ **1** lurch, totter, teeter, wobble, sway, rock, reel, falter, hesitate, waver **2** surprise, amaze, astound, astonish, stun, stupefy, dumbfound, *informal* flabbergast, shake, shock, confound, overwhelm

staging *noun* **1** scaffolding **2** putting on the stage

stagnant *adj* **1** of water: standing still, not flowing and therefore not pure **2** not developing, inactive: *a stagnant market*

▤ still, motionless, standing, stale, sluggish, torpid, lethargic

▰ fresh, moving

stagnate *verb* **1** of water: remain still and so become impure **2** remain for a long time in the same situation and so become bored, inactive *etc* ◇ **stagnation** *noun*

staid *adj* set in your ways, sedate

▤ sedate, calm, composed, sober, demure, solemn, serious, grave, quiet, steady

▰ jaunty, debonair, frivolous, adventurous

stain *verb* **1** give a different colour to (wood *etc*) **2** mark or make dirty by accident ◇ *noun* **1** a liquid which dyes or colours something **2** a mark which is not easily removed **3** something shameful in someone's character or reputation ◇ **stained glass** coloured glass cut in shapes and leaded together ◇ **stainless steel** a mixture of steel and chromium which does not rust

▤ *verb* **1** dye, tint, tinge, colour, paint, varnish **2** mark, spot, blemish, blot, smudge, discolour, dirty, soil, taint, contaminate, sully, tarnish, blacken ◇ *noun* **2** mark, spot, blemish, blot, smudge, discoloration, smear **3** slur, disgrace, shame, dishonour

stair *noun* **1** one or all of a number of steps one after the other **2** (**stairs**) a series or flight of steps

staircase *noun* a stretch of stairs with rails on one or both sides

stake¹ *noun* **1** a strong stick pointed at one end **2** *hist* a post to which people were tied to be burned ◇ *verb* mark the limits or boundaries (of a field *etc*) with stakes ◇ **stake a claim** establish ownership or right (to something)

▤ *noun* **1** post, pole, standard, picket, pale, paling, spike, stick

stake² *noun* money put down as a bet ◇ *verb* **1** bet (money) **2** risk ◇ **at stake 1** be won or lost **2** in great danger: *his life*

is at stake ◇ **have a stake in** be concerned in (because you have something to gain or lose)

▤ bet, wager, pledge, interest, concern, involvement, share, investment, claim ◇ *verb* **1** gamble, bet, wager, pledge **2** risk, chance, hazard, venture

stalactite *noun* a spike of limestone hanging from the roof of a cave, formed by the dripping of water containing lime

stalagmite *noun* a spike of limestone, like a stalactite, rising from the floor of a cave

stale *adj* **1** of food: no longer fresh **2** no longer interesting because heard, done *etc* too often before **3** not able to do your best (because of overworking, boredom *etc*)

▤ **1** dry, hard, old, musty, insipid, tasteless **2** overused, hackneyed, clichéd, stereotyped, jaded, unoriginal, trite, banal, commonplace

stalemate *noun* **1** *chess* a position in which a player cannot move without putting their king in danger **2** a position in an argument in which neither side can win

stalk *noun* the stem of a plant or of a leaf or flower ◇ *verb* **1** quietly follow a hunted animal to shoot at close range **2** follow (someone) persistently **3** walk stiffly or proudly ◇ **stalker** *noun*

▤ *verb* **2** track, trail, hunt, follow, pursue, shadow, tail, haunt

stall¹ *noun* **1** a division for one animal in a cowshed *etc* **2** a table on which things are laid out for sale **3** an openfronted shop **4** a seat in a church (*esp* for choir or clergy) **5** (**stalls**) theatre seats on the ground floor

stall² *verb* **1** of a car engine: come to a halt without the driver intending it to do so **2** of an aircraft: lose flying speed and so fall out of control **3** *informal* avoid action or decision for the time being

▤ *verb* **3** temporize, play for time, delay, hedge, equivocate, obstruct

stallion *noun* a male horse, *esp* one kept for breeding purposes

stalwart *adj* brave, stout-hearted

◇ *noun* a brave, stout-hearted person

∎ *adj* strong, sturdy, robust, stout, strapping, muscular, athletic, vigorous, valiant, daring, intrepid, indomitable, determined, resolute, staunch, steadfast, reliable, dependable

🗦 *adj* weak, feeble, timid

stamen *noun* one of the thread-like spikes in the middle of a flower which bear the pollen

stamina *noun* strength, power to keep going

∎ energy, vigour, strength, power, force, grit, resilience, resistance, endurance

🗦 weakness

stammer *verb* 1 have difficulty in saying the first letter of words in speaking 2 stumble over words ◇ *noun* a speech difficulty of this kind

stamp *verb* 1 bring the foot down firmly on the ground 2 stick a (postage stamp) on 3 mark with a design cut into a mould and inked 4 fix or mark deeply: *forever stamped in my memory* ◇ *noun* 1 the act of stamping 2 a design *etc* made by stamping 3 a cut or moulded design for stamping 4 a characteristic mark: *this bears the stamp of a criminal* 5 a small piece of gummed paper indicating a fee has been paid, or which can be collected in exchange for goods ◇ **stamping ground** someone's favourite or habitual place to be ◇ **stamp out** 1 put out (a fire) by stamping 2 suppress, crush

∎ *verb* 1 beat, pound 3 imprint, impress, print, inscribe, engrave, emboss, mark, brand, label, categorize, identify, characterize ◇ *noun* 2 print, imprint, impression, seal, signature, authorization, mark, hallmark 3 brand, cast, mould, cut

stampede *noun* 1 a wild rush of frightened animals 2 a sudden, wild rush of people ◇ *verb* rush wildly

∎ *noun* 1, 2 charge, rush, dash, sprint, flight ◇ *verb* charge, rush, dash, tear, run, sprint, gallop, shoot, fly, flee, scatter

stance *noun* someone's manner of standing

stanchion *noun* an upright iron bar used as a support (*eg* in windows, ships)

stand *verb* (**stands**, **standing**, **stood**) 1 be on your feet (not lying or sitting down) 2 (often with **up**) rise to your feet 3 of an object: (cause to) be in a particular place: *it stood by the door/stood the case in the corner* 4 bear: *I cannot stand this heat* 5 treat (someone) to: *stand you tea* 6 remain: *this law still stands* 7 be a candidate (for): *he stood for parliament* 8 be short (for): *PO stands for Post Office* ◇ *noun* 1 something on which anything is placed 2 an object made to hold, or for hanging, things: *a hat-stand* 3 lines of raised seats from which people may watch games *etc* 4 an effort made to support, defend, resist *etc*: *a stand against violence* 5 *US* a witness box in a law court ◇ **stand by** be ready or available to be used or help in an emergency *etc* (**standby** *noun*) ◇ **stand down** withdraw (from a contest) or resign (from a job) ◇ **stand fast** refuse to give in ◇ **stand in** (**for**) take another's place, job *etc* for a time (**stand-in** *noun*) ◇ **stand out** stick out, be noticeable ◇ **stand to reason** be likely or reasonable ◇ **stand up for** defend strongly ◇ **stand up to** face or oppose bravely

∎ *verb* 2 rise, get up, stand up 3 put, place, set, erect, position, station 4 bear, tolerate, abide, endure, *informal* hack, suffer, experience, undergo, withstand ◇ *noun* 2 frame, rack ◇ **stand down** step down, resign, abdicate, quit, give up, retire, withdraw ◇ **stand out** show, catch the eye, stick out, jut out, protrude, project ◇ **stand up for** defend, stick up for, side with, fight for, support, protect, champion, uphold ◇ **stand up to** defy, oppose, resist, withstand, face, confront, brave

🗦 **stand up for** attack ◇ **stand up to** give in to

standard *noun* 1 a model against which things may be judged 2 a level of excellence aimed at: *artistic standards* 3 a large flag *etc* on a pole ◇ *adj* 1 normal, usual: *standard charge* 2 ordin-

ary, without extras: *standard model*
◇ **standard bearer** an outstanding
leader ◇ **standard lamp** a kind of tall
lamp which stands on the floor of a
room *etc* ◇ **standard of living** a level
of material comfort considered necessary by a particular group of society *etc*

◼ *noun* **1** norm, average, type, model,
pattern, example, sample, guideline,
benchmark, touchstone, yardstick,
rule, measure, gauge, level, criterion,
requirement, specification, grade, quality ◇ *adj* **1** normal, average, typical **2**
basic, staple, usual, regular

standardize *verb* make all of one
kind or size ◇ **standardization** *noun*

standing *noun* position, status or reputation ◇ *adj* **1** on your feet **2** placed
on end **3** not moving **4** lasting, permanent: *a standing joke* ◇ **standing order**
an instruction to a bank to make regular payments from your account to another

standoffish *adj* unfriendly

◼ aloof, remote, distant, unapproachable, unsociable, uncommunicative,
reserved, cold

◪ friendly

standpoint *noun* the position from
which you look at something (*eg* a
question, problem), point of view

◼ position, station, vantage point, stance,
viewpoint, angle, point of view

standstill *noun* a complete stop

◼ stop, halt, pause, lull, rest, stoppage,
jam, log-jam, hold-up, impasse, deadlock, gridlock, stalemate

◪ advance, progress

stand-up *adj* **1** of a fight: earnest, fervent **2** of comedy: performed solo before a live audience

stank *past form* of **stink**

stanza *noun* a group of lines making
up a part of a poem, a verse

staple¹ *noun* **1** a U-shaped iron nail **2**
a piece of wire driven through sheets of
paper to fasten them together ◇ *verb*
fasten with a staple

staple² the main item in a country's
production, a person's diet *etc* ◇ *adj*
chief, main

◼ *adj* basic, fundamental, primary, key,
main, chief, major, principal, essential,
necessary, standard

◪ *adj* minor

star *noun* **1** any of the bodies in the sky
appearing as points of light **2** the fixed
bodies which are really distant suns,
not the planets **3** an object, shape or
figure with a number of pointed rays
(often five) **4** a leading actor or actress
or other well-known performer ◇ *adj*
for or of a star (in a film *etc*) ◇ *verb*
(**stars**, **starring**, **starred**) **1** act the
chief part (in a play or film) **2** of a play
etc: have as its star ◇ **Stars and Stripes**
the flag of the United States of America

starboard *noun* the right side of a
ship, as you look towards the bow (or
front) ◇ *adj* of this side of a ship

starch *noun* (*plural* **starches**) **1** a
white carbohydrate (found in flour, potatoes, bread, biscuits *etc*) **2** a form of
this used for stiffening clothes ◇ **starchy** *adj* **1** of food: containing starch **2**
stiff and unfriendly

stardom *noun* the state of being a
leading performer

stare *verb* look with a fixed gaze
◇ *noun* a fixed gaze

◼ *verb* gaze, look, watch, gape, gawp,
gawk, goggle, glare

starfish *noun* a type of small sea creature with five points or arms

stark *adj* **1** barren, bare **2** harsh, severe **3** sheer: *stark idiocy* ◇ *adv* completely: *stark naked*

◼ *adj* **1** bare, barren, bleak, bald, plain,
simple **2** austere, harsh, severe, grim,
dreary, gloomy, depressing **3** utter, unmitigated, total, complete, absolute,
sheer, downright, out-and-out

starling *noun* a common bird with
dark, glossy feathers

starry *adj* full of stars; shining like
stars

start *verb* **1** begin, establish **2** get (a
machine *etc*) working: *he started the car*
3 begin a journey: *he started for home* **4**
jump or jerk (*eg* in surprise) ◇ *noun* **1**
the act of starting **2** a sudden movement of the body **3** a sudden shock:

you gave me a start **4** in a race *etc*: the advantage of beginning before, or farther forward than, others, or the amount of this: *a start of five metres* ◇ **start-up** *noun* a recently established company

■ *verb* **1** begin, commence, originate, initiate, introduce, pioneer, create, found, establish, set up, institute, inaugurate, launch, open **2** activate, trigger **3** set out **4** jump, jerk, twitch, flinch, recoil ◇ *noun* **1** beginning, commencement, outset, inception, initiation, introduction **2** jump, jerk, twitch, spasm, convulsion, fit

◨ *verb* **1** stop, finish, end

startle *verb* give a shock or fright to ◇ **startled** *adj* ◇ **startling** *adj*

■ surprise, amaze, astonish, astound, shock, scare, frighten, alarm, agitate, upset, disturb

◨ calm

starve *verb* **1** die for want of food **2** suffer greatly from hunger **3** deprive (of something needed or wanted badly): *starved of company here* ◇ **starvation** *noun*

stash *verb, informal* store in a hidden place ◇ *noun* a hidden supply of something

state *noun* **1** the condition (of something or someone): *the bad state of the roads* **2** *informal* an agitated or untidy condition: *look at the state you're in!* **3** the people of a country under a government **4** *US* an area and its people with its own laws forming part of the whole country **5** a government and its officials ◇ *adj* **1** of the government **2** national and ceremonial: *state occasions* **3** *US* of a certain state of America: *the state capital of Texas is Austin* ◇ *verb* tell, say or write (*esp* clearly and fully)

■ *noun* **1** condition, shape, situation, position, circumstances, case ◇ *adj* **2** national, public, official, formal, ceremonial, pompous, stately ◇ *verb* say, declare, announce, report, communicate, assert, affirm, specify, present, express, put, formulate, articulate, voice

stately *adj* noble-looking; dignified

◇ **stateliness** *noun*

■ grand, imposing, impressive, elegant, majestic, regal, royal, imperial, noble, august, lofty, pompous, dignified, measured, deliberate, solemn, ceremonious

◨ informal, unimpressive

statement *noun* that which is said or written

■ account, report, bulletin, announcement, declaration, proclamation, communication, utterance, testimony

state-of-the-art *adj* most up-to-date

stateside *adj & adv, informal* of or in the United States

statesman *noun* someone skilled in government ◇ **statesmanlike** *adj*

static *adj* not moving ◇ *noun* **1** electricity on the surface of objects which will not conduct it *eg* hair, nylons *etc* (*also called*: **static electricity**) **2** atmospheric disturbances causing poor reception of radio or television programmes

■ *adj* stationary, motionless, immobile, unmoving, still, inert, resting, fixed, constant, unvarying, stable

◨ *adj* dynamic, mobile, varying

station *noun* **1** a building with a ticket office, waiting rooms *etc* where trains, buses or coaches stop to pick up or set down passengers **2** a place which is the centre for work or duty of any kind: *fire station/police station* **3** a building equipped for a particular purpose: *petrol station* **4** rank, position: *lowly station* ◇ *verb* assign to a position or place

stationary *adj* standing still, not moving

■ motionless, immobile, unmoving, still, static, inert, standing, resting, parked, moored, fixed

◨ mobile, moving, active

❚ Do not confuse: **stationary** and **stationery**

stationery *noun* writing paper, envelopes, pens *etc* ◇ **stationer** *noun* someone who sells these

statistics *noun* **1** (*noun plural*) figures and facts set out in order: *statistics of* *road accidents for last year* **2** (*noun sing*) the study of these: *statistics is not an easy subject* ◇ **statistical** *adj* ◇ **statistician** *noun* someone who produces or studies statistics

statue *noun* a likeness of someone or an animal carved in stone, metal *etc*

statuesque *adj* like a statue in dignity *etc*

statuette *noun* a small statue

stature *noun* **1** height **2** importance, reputation

status *noun* position, rank (of a person) in the eyes of others ◇ **status quo** the state of affairs now existing, or existing before a certain time or event ◇ **status symbol** a possession which is thought to show the high status of the owner (*eg* a powerful car)

 ▤ rank, grade, degree, level, class, station, standing, position, state, condition, prestige, eminence, distinction, importance, consequence, weight

 ▨ unimportance, insignificance

statute *noun* a written law of a country ◇ **statutory** *adj* according to law

staunch[1] *adj* firm, loyal; trustworthy

 ▤ *adj* loyal, faithful, hearty, strong, stout, firm, sound, sure, true, trusty, reliable, dependable, steadfast

 ▨ *adj* unfaithful, weak, unreliable

staunch[2] *verb* stop from flowing (*esp* blood from a wound)

stave *noun* **1** a set of spaced lines on which music is written **2** one of the strips making the side of a barrel ◇ *verb* (**staves**, **staving**, **stove** or **staved**, **staved**) **1** (with **in**) crush in **2** (*past form* **staved**) (with **off**) keep away, delay

stay[1] *verb* **1** continue to be: *stayed calm/stay here while I go for help* **2** live (for a time): *staying in a hotel* ◇ *noun* **1** time spent in a place **2** suspension of legal proceedings or postponement of a punishment ◇ **stay put** remain in the same place

 ▤ *verb* **1** last, continue, endure, abide, remain, linger, persist **2** reside, dwell, live, settle, stop, halt, pause, wait

 ▨ *verb* **1** go, leave

stay[2] *noun* **1** a prop or support **2** (**stays**) *old* corsets

St Bernard *see* **Saint Bernard**

stead *noun* place: *she went in my stead* ◇ **stand you in good stead** turn out to be helpful to you: *his German stood him in good stead*

steadfast *adj* **1** unwavering, resolute **2** faithful, loyal ◇ **steadfastly** *adv* ◇ **steadfastness** *noun*

steading *noun* farm buildings

steady *adj* **1** firmly fixed **2** not moving or changing **3** stable, not easily undermined **4** having a sober character ◇ *verb* (**steadies**, **steadying**, **steadied**) make or become steady ◇ **steadily** *adv* ◇ **steadiness** *noun*

 ▤ *adj* **1** stable, balanced, poised, fixed, immovable, firm **2** even, uniform, consistent, unvarying, unchanging, constant, persistent, uninterrupted, unbroken, regular, rhythmic, steadfast, unwavering ◇ *verb* balance, stabilize, fix, secure, brace, support

 ▨ *adj* **1** unsteady, unstable **3** variable, wavering

steak *noun* a thick slice of meat *etc* for cooking

steal *verb* (**steals**, **stealing**, **stole**, **stolen**) **1** take (something not belonging to you) without permission **2** move quietly **3** take quickly or secretly: *stole a look at him*

 ▤ **1** thieve, pilfer, filch, *informal* pinch, *slang* nick, take, appropriate, snatch, swipe, shoplift, poach, embezzle, lift **2** creep, tiptoe, slip, slink, sneak

 ▨ **1** return, give back

stealth *noun* a secret way of doing, acting *etc* ◇ **stealthily** *adv* ◇ **stealthy** *adj*

 ▤ **stealthy** surreptitious, clandestine, covert, secret, unobtrusive, secretive, quiet, furtive, sly, cunning, sneaky, underhand

 ▨ **stealthy** open

steam *noun* **1** vapour from hot liquid, *esp* from boiling water **2** power produced by steam: *in the days of steam* ◇ *verb* **1** give off steam **2** cook by steam **3** open or loosen by putting into steam:

steam open the envelope **4** move or travel by steam ◇ **steam up** of glass: become covered with condensed steam in the form of small drops of water

steamboat *noun* a steamer

steam-engine *noun* an engine (*esp* a railway engine) worked by steam

steamer *noun* a ship driven by steam

steamroller *noun* a steam-driven engine with large and very heavy wheels, used for flattening the surfaces of roads

steamship *noun* a steamer

steamy *adj* **1** full of steam: *steamy atmosphere* **2** *informal* passionate, erotic

steed *noun*, *old* a horse

steel *noun* **1** a very hard mixture of iron and carbon **2** a bar of steel for sharpening knife blades ◇ **of steel** hard, strong: *a grip of steel* ◇ **steel yourself** get up courage (to) ◇ **steely** *adj* hard, cold, strong like steel

steep *adj* **1** of a slope: rising nearly straight up **2** *informal* of a price: too great ◇ *verb* **1** soak in a liquid **2** fill with knowledge of: *steeped in French literature*

steeple *noun* a tower of a church *etc* rising to a point, a spire

steeplechase *noun* **1** a race run across open country, over hedges *etc* **2** a race over a course on which obstacles (*eg* walls) have been made

steeplejack *noun* someone who climbs steeples or other high buildings to make repairs

steer *noun* a young ox raised for its beef ◇ *verb* **1** control the course of (a car, ship, discussion *etc*) **2** follow (a course) ◇ **steer clear of** keep away from

▣ *verb* **1** pilot, guide, direct, control

steerage *noun*, *old* the part of a ship set aside for the passengers who pay the lowest fares

steering *noun* the parts of a ship, motor-car *etc* which have to do with controlling its course ◇ **steering-wheel** *noun* the wheel in a car used by the driver to steer it

stellar *adj* of the stars

stem *noun* **1** the part of a plant from which the leaves and flowers grow **2** the thin support of a wine-glass ◇ *verb* (**stems, stemming, stemmed**) **1** stop, halt: *stem the bleeding* **2** start, spring (from): *hate stems from envy*

▣ *verb* **1** stop, halt, arrest, stanch, staunch, block, dam, check, curb, restrain, contain, resist, oppose

▣ *verb* **1** encourage

stench *noun* a strong unpleasant smell

▣ stink, reek, *informal* pong, *slang* niff, smell, odour

stencil *noun* **1** a sheet of metal, cardboard *etc* with a pattern cut out **2** the drawing or design made by rubbing ink or brushing paint *etc* over a cut-out pattern **3** a piece of waxed paper on which words are cut with a typewriter, and which is then used to make copies ◇ *verb* (**stencils, stencilling, stencilled**) make a design or copy in one of these ways

stenographer *noun*, *US* a shorthand typist ◇ **stenography** *noun*, *US* shorthand

stentorian *adj* **1** of the voice: loud **2** loud-voiced

Named after *Stentor*, a loud-voiced Greek herald in the *Iliad*

⚠ Do not confuse with: **stertorous**

step *noun* **1** a movement of the leg in walking, running *etc* **2** the distance covered by this **3** a particular movement of the feet, as in dancing: **4** the sound made by the foot in walking *etc*: *heard a step outside* **5** a riser on a stair, or rung on a ladder **6** one of a series of moves in a plan, career *etc*: *take the first step* **7** a way of walking: *springy step* **8** (**steps**) a flight of stairs **9** (**steps**) a stepladder ◇ *verb* (**steps, stepping, stepped**) **1** take a step **2** walk, move: *step this way, please* ◇ **in step 1** walking in time with music or with others **2** acting *etc* in agreement (with) ◇ **out of step 1** not walking in time with music or with others **2** not in agreement ◇ **step down** resign ◇ **step in 1** do a job in place of someone **2** intervene ◇ **step on it** *informal* hurry up ◇ **step out 1** walk confidently **2** *informal* go out socially ◇ **step up** increase (*eg* production) ◇ **take steps** begin to do something for a certain purpose

◼ *noun* **2** pace, stride, footstep **6** move, act, action, deed, measure, procedure, process, proceeding, progression, movement, stage, phase, degree ◇ *verb* **1** pace, stride, tread, stamp, walk, move ◇ **step up** increase, raise, augment, boost, build up, intensify, escalate, accelerate, speed up

◨ **step up** decrease

step- *prefix* related as the result of a second marriage: *stepfather/stepdaughter*

stepladder *noun* a ladder with a support on which it rests

steppe *noun* a dry, grassy treeless plain in SE Europe and Asia

stepping-stone *noun* **1** a stone rising above water or mud, used to cross on **2** anything that helps you to advance

stereo *adj, short for* **stereophonic** ◇ *noun* (*plural* **stereos**) stereophonic equipment, *eg* a CD player, record-player or tape recorder, with amplifier and loudspeakers

stereo- *prefix* in three dimensions

stereophonic *adj* of sound: giving a life-like effect, with different instruments, voices *etc* coming from different directions

stereotype *noun* **1** a generalized and preconceived notion of what characterizes someone or something **2** a characteristic type of person or thing ◇ **stereotypical** *adj*

Originally a printing term for a fixed block of type

sterile *adj* **1** unable to produce offspring, fruit or seeds **2** producing no ideas *etc*: *sterile imagination* **3** free from germs ◇ **sterility** *noun* the state of being sterile

◼ **1** infertile, barren **2** unproductive, fruitless **3** germ-free, aseptic, sterilized, disinfected, sanitized, antiseptic, uncontaminated

◨ **1** fertile **2** fruitful **3** septic

sterilize *verb* **1** make sterile **2** free from germs by boiling *etc* ◇ **sterilization** *noun*

sterling *noun* British money, when used in international trading: *one pound sterling* ◇ *adj* **1** of silver: of a certain standard of purity **2** worthy, good: *sterling qualities*

So called after the image of a small star that was impressed on medieval silver pennies

stern[1] *adj* **1** looking or sounding angry or displeased **2** severe, strict, harsh: *stern prison sentence* ◇ **sternly** *adv* ◇ **sternness** *noun* the state or quality of being stern

◼ **1** grim, forbidding, stark, austere **2** strict, severe, authoritarian, rigid, inflexible, unyielding, hard, tough, rigorous, stringent, harsh, cruel, relentless

◨ **1** kind, gentle **2** mild, lenient

stern[2] *noun* the back part of a ship

steroid *noun* any of a number of substances, including certain hormones; *see also* **anabolic steroids**

stertorous *adj* making a snoring noise

🅷 Do not confuse with: **stentorian**

stethoscope *noun* an instrument by means of which a doctor listens to someone's heartbeats, breathing *etc*

stetson *noun* a soft, wide-brimmed hat worn traditionally by cowboys

stevedore *noun* someone employed to load and unload ships

stew *verb* cook by boiling slowly ◇ *noun* **1** a dish of stewed food, often containing meat and vegetables **2** *informal* a state of worry; a flap

steward *noun* **1** an attendant on an aircraft or ship **2** someone who guides people and supervises crowds at a sporting event, concert *etc* **3** an official at a race meeting *etc* **4** *old* someone who manages an estate or farm for someone else

stewardess *noun, old* a female attendant on a ship or aeroplane

stick[1] *noun* **1** a long thin piece of wood; a branch or twig from a tree **2** a piece of wood shaped for a special purpose: *hockey-stick/drumstick* **3** a long piece (*eg* of rhubarb) **4** *informal* criticism or mockery ◇ **the sticks** *informal* a rural area considered remote

stick[2] *verb* (**sticks, sticking, stuck**) **1** push or thrust (something): *stick the knife in your belt* **2** fix with glue *etc*: *I'll stick the pieces back together* **3** be or become caught, fixed or held back: *stuck in the ditch* **4** hold fast to, keep to (*eg* a decision) **5** *informal* place or put **5** *informal* bear or tolerate ◇ **stick up for** speak in defence of

■ *verb* **1** thrust, poke, stab, jab, pierce, penetrate, puncture, spear **2** glue, gum, paste, cement, bond, fuse, weld, solder, adhere ◇ **stick up for** stand up for, speak up for, defend, champion, support, uphold

sticking-plaster *noun* a kind of tape with a sticky surface, used to protect slight cuts *etc*

stick-in-the-mud *noun* someone who is against new ideas, change *etc*

stickleback *noun* a type of small river-fish with prickles on its back

stickler *noun* someone who attaches great importance to a particular (often small) matter: *stickler for punctuality*

sticky *adj* **1** clinging closely (like glue, treacle *etc*) **2** covered with something sticky **3** difficult: *a sticky problem* ◇ **stickiness** *noun*

■ **1** viscous, glutinous, *informal* gooey **2** adhesive, gummed, tacky, gluey, gummy **3** difficult, tricky, thorny, unpleasant, awkward, embarrassing, delicate
🖅 **3** easy

stiff *adj* **1** not easily bent or moved **2** of a mixture, dough *etc*: thick, not easily stirred **3** cold and distant in manner **4** hard, difficult: *stiff examination* **5** severe: *stiff penalty* **6** strong: *stiff drink*

■ **1** rigid, inflexible, unbending, unyielding, hard, solid, hardened, solidified, firm, tight, taut **3** formal, pompous, stand-offish, cold, prim **4** difficult, hard, tough **5** austere, strict, severe, harsh
🖅 **1** flexible **3** informal **4** easy

stiffen *verb* **1** make or become stiff **2** become tense

■ **1** harden, solidify, tighten, tense, brace, reinforce, starch, thicken, congeal, coagulate, set

stiff-necked *adj* proud, obstinate

stifle *verb* **1** suffocate **2** put out (flames) **3** keep back (tears, a yawn *etc*)

■ **1** smother, suffocate, asphyxiate, strangle, choke **3** suppress, quell, check, curb, restrain, repress

stifling *adj* very hot and stuffy

stigma *noun* **1** (*plural* **stigmata**) a mark of disgrace **2** (*plural* **stigmas**) in a flower, the top of the pistil ◇ **stigmatize** *verb* mark, describe as something bad: *stigmatized for life*

stile *noun* a step or set of steps for climbing over a wall or fence

stiletto *noun* (*plural* **stilettos**) **1** a dagger, or a type of instrument, with a narrow blade **2** (a shoe with) a stiletto heel ◇ **stiletto heel** a high, thin heel on a shoe

still[1] *adj* **1** not moving **2** calm, without wind; quiet **3** of drinks: not fizzy ◇ *verb* make calm or quiet ◇ *adv* **1** up to the present time or the time spoken of: *it was still there* **2** even so, nevertheless: *it's difficult but we must still try* **3** even: *still more people* **4** without moving: *sit still* ◇ **stillness** *noun* the state of being still ◇ **still life** a picture of something that is not living (as a bowl of fruit *etc*)

■ *adj* **1** stationary, motionless, lifeless, stagnant **2** undisturbed, unruffled, calm, tranquil, serene, restful, peaceful, hushed, quiet, silent, noiseless ◇ *verb* calm, soothe, allay, tranquillize, subdue, restrain, hush, quieten, silence, pacify, settle, smooth ◇ *adv* **2** yet, even so, nevertheless, nonetheless, notwithstanding, however
🖅 *adj* **1** active **2** disturbed, agitated, noisy ◇ *verb* agitate, stir up

still² _noun_ an apparatus for distilling alcoholic spirit

stillborn _adj_ of a child: dead at birth

stilted _adj_ stiff, not natural
- artificial, unnatural, stiff, wooden, forced, constrained
- fluent, flowing

stilts _noun plural_ **1** long poles with footrests on which someone may walk clear of the ground **2** tall poles (_eg_ to support a house built above water)

stimulant _noun_ something which makes a part of the body more active or which makes you feel livelier

stimulate _verb_ **1** make more active **2** encourage **3** excite
- **1** rouse, arouse, animate, quicken, fire, inflame, provoke, incite, instigate, trigger off **2** inspire, motivate, encourage, induce
- **2** discourage, hinder, prevent

stimulus _noun_ (_plural_ **stimuli**) **1** something that brings on a reaction in a living thing **2** something that rouses (someone _etc_) to action or greater effort
- **2** incentive, encouragement, inducement, spur, goad, provocation, incitement
- **2** discouragement

sting _noun_ **1** the part of some animals and plants (as the wasp, the nettle) which can prick the skin and cause pain or irritation **2** the act of piercing with a sting **3** the wound, swelling or pain caused by a sting **4** _slang_ a trick or swindle ◇ _verb_ (**stings**, **stinging**, **stung**) **1** pierce with a sting or cause pain like that of a sting **2** be painful, smart: _made his eyes sting_ **3** hurt the feelings of: _stung by his words_ **4** _slang_ cheat or swindle
- _verb_ **1** bite, prick, hurt, injure, wound **2** smart, tingle, burn, pain

stingy _adj_ mean, not generous ◇ **stinginess** _noun_
- mean, miserly, niggardly, _informal_ tight-fisted, parsimonious, penny-pinching
- generous, liberal

stink _noun_ a bad smell ◇ _verb_ (**stinks**, **stinking**, **stank** or **stunk**, **stunk**) give out a bad smell

stint _verb_ allow (someone) very little: _don't stint on ..._ ◇ _noun_ **1** limit: _praise without stint_ **2** a fixed amount of work: _my daily stint_
- _noun_ **2** spell, stretch, period, time, shift, turn, bit, share, quota

stipend _noun_ pay, salary, _esp_ of a parish minister ◇ **stipendiary** _adj_

stipple _verb_ paint or mark with tiny dots from a brush

stipulate _verb_ state as a condition (of doing something)
- specify, lay down, require, demand, insist on

stipulation _noun_ something stipulated, a condition
- specification, requirement, demand, condition, proviso

stir _verb_ (**stirs**, **stirring**, **stirred**) **1** set (liquid) in motion, _esp_ with a spoon _etc_ moved circularly **2** move slightly: _he stirred in his sleep_ **3** arouse (a person, a feeling _etc_) ◇ _noun_ disturbance, fuss ◇ **stir up** rouse, cause (_eg_ trouble)
- _verb_ **3** excite, thrill, disturb, agitate, shake ◇ _noun_ activity, movement, bustle, flurry, commotion, ado, _informal_ fuss, to-do, uproar, tumult, disturbance, disorder, agitation, excitement, ferment ◇ **stir up** rouse, arouse, awaken, animate, quicken, fire, inflame, stimulate, spur, prompt, provoke, incite, instigate, agitate
- _verb_ **3** calm

stirring _adj_ exciting

stirrup _noun_ a metal loop hung from a horse's saddle as a support for the rider's foot

stitch _noun_ (_plural_ **stitches**) **1** the loop made in a thread, wool _etc_ by a needle in sewing or knitting **2** a sharp, sudden pain in your side ◇ _verb_ put stitches in, sew

stoat _noun_ a type of small fierce animal similar to a weasel, sometimes called an ermine when in its white winter fur

stock _noun_ **1** goods in a shop, warehouse _etc_ **2** a supply of something **3** liquid (used for soup) obtained by boiling meat, bones _etc_ **4** the handle of a whip, rifle *etc* **5** the animals of a farm (*also called:* **livestock**) **6** the capital of a business company divided into shares **7** family, race: *of ancient stock* **8** a type of scented garden flower **9** (**stocks**) *hist* a wooden frame, with holes for the ankles and wrists, in which criminals *etc* were fastened as a punishment **10** (**stocks**) the wooden framework upon which a ship is supported when being built ◇ *verb* **1** keep a supply of (for sale) **2** supply (a farm with animals *etc*) ◇ *adj* **1** usual, known by everyone: *a stock joke* **2** usually stocked (by a shop *etc*) ◇ **stock exchange 1** a place where stocks and shares are bought and sold **2** an association of people who do this ◇ **stock-in-trade** *noun* **1** the necessary equipment *etc* for a particular trade *etc* **2** someone's usual ways of speaking, acting *etc*: *sarcasm is part of his stock-in-trade* ◇ **stock market** the stock exchange; dealings in stocks and shares ◇ **stock up on** gather a supply ◇ **take stock of** form an opinion or estimation about (a situation *etc*)

■ *noun* **1** goods, merchandise, wares, commodities, capital, assets, inventory, range, supply, store, reserve, stockpile, hoard **5** livestock, animals, cattle, horses, sheep, herds, flocks **7** parentage, ancestry, descent, extraction, family, line, lineage, pedigree, race, blood ◇ *verb* **1** keep, carry, sell, trade in, deal in, handle **2** supply, provide ◇ *adj* **1** standard, basic, regular, routine, ordinary, run-of-the-mill, usual, customary, traditional, conventional, set, stereotyped, hackneyed, banal, trite
☒ *adj* **1** original, unusual

stockade *noun* a fence of strong posts set up round an area or building for defence

stockbroker *noun* someone who buys and sell shares in business companies on behalf of others

stocking *noun* a close-fitting covering in a knitted fabric (wool, nylon *etc*) for the leg and foot

stockpile *noun* a store, a reserve supply ◇ *verb* build up a store

stock-still *adj* perfectly still

stocktaking *noun* a regular check of the goods in a shop or warehouse

stocky *adj* short and stout ◇ **stocki-ness** *noun*

■ sturdy, solid, thickset, chunky, short, squat, dumpy, stubby, stumpy
☒ tall, skinny

stodgy *adj* **1** of food: heavy, not easily digested **2** of a person, book *etc*: dull ◇ **stodginess** *noun*

stoic *noun* someone who bears pain, hardship *etc* without showing any sign of feeling it ◇ **stoical** *adj* ◇ **stoicism** *noun* the bearing of pain *etc* patiently

■ **stoical** patient, long-suffering, uncomplaining, resigned, philosophical, indifferent, impassive, unemotional, cool, calm, imperturbable
☒ **stoical** excitable, anxious

stoke *verb* put coal, wood, or other fuel on (a fire) ◇ **stoker** *noun* someone who looks after a furnace

stole[1] *noun* a length of silk, linen or fur worn over the shoulders

stole[2] *past form* of **steal**

stolen *past participle* of **steal**

stolid *adj* dull, not easily excited ◇ **stolidity** *noun* ◇ **stolidly** *adv*

■ slow, heavy, dull, wooden, impassive, unemotional
☒ lively, interested

stomach *noun* **1** the bag-like part of the body into which the food passes when swallowed **2** desire or courage (for something): *no stomach for a fight* ◇ *verb* put up with, bear: *can't stomach her rudeness*

■ *verb* tolerate, bear, stand, abide, *informal* hack, endure, suffer, submit to, take

stomp *verb* stamp the feet, *esp* noisily

stone *noun* **1** the material of which rocks are composed **2** a (small) loose piece of this **3** a piece of this shaped for a certain purpose: *tombstone* **4** a precious stone (*eg* a diamond) **5** the hard shell around the seed of some fruits (*eg* peach, cherry) **6** a measure of weight (14 pounds, 6.35 kilograms) **7** a piece of hard material that forms in the kidney, bladder *etc*, causing pain

◇*verb* **1** throw stones at **2** take the stones out of fruit ◇*adj* made of stone ◇**Stone Age** human culture before the use of metal ◇**a stone's throw** a very short distance ◇**leave no stone unturned** do everything possible

stone-cold *adj* very cold

stone-dead *adj* completely dead

stone-deaf *adj* completely deaf

stoneware *noun* a kind of pottery made out of coarse clay

stonework *noun* something that is built of stone *esp* the stone parts of a building

stony *adj* **1** like stone **2** covered with stones **3** hard, cold in manner: *stony look*
- ▣ **2** pebbly, shingly, rocky **3** blank, expressionless, hard, cold, frigid, icy, indifferent, unfeeling, heartless, callous, merciless, pitiless, hostile
- ▣ **3** warm, soft-hearted, friendly

stood *past form* of **stand**

stooge *noun* someone who is used by another to do a (*usu* humble or unpleasant) job

stool *noun* a seat without a back

stool-pigeon *slang* a police informer

stoop *verb* **1** bend the body forward and downward **2** be low or wicked enough to do a certain thing: *I wouldn't stoop to stealing* ◇*noun* **1** the act of stooping **2** a forward bend of the body
- ▣ *verb* **1** hunch, bow, bend, incline, lean, duck, squat, crouch, kneel **2** descend, sink, lower oneself, resort, go so far as

stop *verb* (**stops**, **stopping**, **stopped**) **1** bring or come to a halt or end: *stop the car/the rain has stopped* **2** prevent from doing: *stop him from working* **3** (with **up**) block (a hole *etc*) ◇*noun* **1** the state of being stopped **2** a place where something stops **3** a full stop **4** a knob on an organ which brings certain pipes into use ◇**stop off, in** or **by** visit while on the way to somewhere else ◇**stop press** a space in a newspa-

per for news put in at the last minute
- ▣ *verb* **1** finish, conclude, terminate, discontinue, suspend, interrupt, pause, quit, refrain, desist, halt, cease, end **2** prevent, bar, frustrate, thwart, intercept, hinder, impede, check, restrain **3** seal, close, plug, block, obstruct ◇*noun* **1** halt, standstill, cessation, end, finish, conclusion, termination, discontinuation **2** station, terminus, destination
- ▣ *noun* **1** start, beginning, continuation

stopcock *noun* a tap for controlling the flow of liquid through a pipe

stopgap *noun* something which is used in an emergency until something better is found

stoppage *noun* **1** something which blocks up (*eg* a tube or a passage in the body) **2** a halt (*eg* in work in a factory)
- ▣ **1** blockage, obstruction, check, hindrance **2** stop, halt, standstill, interruption, shutdown, closure, strike, walkout, sit-in
- ▣ **2** start, continuation

stopper *noun* something that stops up an opening (*esp* in the neck of a bottle, jar *etc*)

stopwatch *noun* a watch that can be stopped and started, used in timing races

storage *noun* **1** the act of storing **2** the state of being stored: *our furniture is in storage*

store *noun* **1** a supply (*eg* of goods) from which things are taken when needed **2** a place where goods are kept **3** a shop **4** a collected amount or number ◇*verb* put aside for future use ◇**in store for** awaiting: *trouble in store* ◇**set** (**great**) **store by** value highly
- ▣ *noun* **1** stock, supply, provision, fund, reserve, hoard, cache, stockpile, accumulation **2** storeroom, storehouse, warehouse, repository, depository ◇*verb* save, keep, put aside, lay by, reserve, stock, deposit, lay up, accumulate, hoard, salt away, stockpile, *informal* stash
- ▣ *noun* **1** scarcity

storehouse or **storeroom** *noun* a building or room where goods are stored

storey *noun* (*plural* **storeys**) all that part of a building on the same floor

> ❗ Do not confuse with: **story**

stork *noun* a wading bird with a long bill, neck and legs

storm *noun* **1** a sudden burst of bad weather (*esp* with heavy rain, lightning, thunder, high wind) **2** a violent outbreak (*eg* of anger) ◇ *verb* **1** be in a fury **2** rain, blow *etc* violently **3** attack (a stronghold *etc*) violently ◇ **go down a storm** be popular or well received ◇ **take by storm** enthral or captivate instantly ◇ **storm in a teacup** a great fuss over nothing

☰ *noun* **1** tempest, thunderstorm, blizzard, gale, hurricane, whirlwind, tornado, cyclone **2** outburst, uproar, furore, outcry, row, rumpus, commotion, tumult, disturbance, turmoil, stir, agitation, rage, outbreak, attack, assault ◇ *verb* **1** rage, rant, rave, fume **3** charge, rush, attack, assault, assail

🔁 *noun* **2** calm

story *noun* (*plural* **stories**) an account of an event or events, real or imaginary

☰ tale, fairy-tale, fable, myth, legend, novel, romance, fiction, yarn, anecdote, episode, plot, narrative, history, chronicle, record, account, relation, recital, report, article, feature

> ❗ Do not confuse with: **storey**

storyboard *noun* a series of drawings forming an outline for shooting a scene in a film

storyline *noun* the plot of a novel, film *etc*

stout *adj* **1** fat, stocky **2** brave: *stout resistance* **3** strong: *stout walking-stick* ◇ *noun* a strong, dark-coloured beer ◇ **stoutness** *noun*

☰ *adj* **1** fat, plump, fleshy, portly, corpulent, overweight, heavy, bulky, big, brawny, beefy, hulking, burly, muscular, athletic **2** brave, courageous, valiant, plucky, fearless, bold, dauntless, reso-

lute **3** strong, tough, durable, thick, sturdy, robust, hardy

🔁 **1** thin, lean, slim **2** cowardly, timid **3** weak

stout-hearted *adj* having a brave heart

stove *noun* an apparatus using coal, gas or electricity *etc*, used for heating, cooking *etc* ◇ *verb*, *past form* of **stave**

stow *verb* **1** pack or put away **2** fill, pack

stowaway *noun* someone who hides in a ship in order to travel without paying a fare

straddle *verb* **1** stand or walk with legs apart **2** sit with one leg on each side of (*eg* a chair or horse)

straggle *verb* **1** wander from the line of a march *etc* **2** lag behind **3** grow or spread beyond the intended limits: *his long beard straggled over his chest* ◇ **straggler** *noun* someone who lags behind ◇ **straggly** *adj* spread out untidily

straight *adj* **1** not bent or curved: *a straight line* **2** level; not leaning or twisted: *is the picture straight?* **3** in the proper position or order: *your tie isn't straight* **4** direct, frank, honest: *a straight answer* **5** respectable, legitimate **6** in a row: *we won three straight sets* **7** not comic, serious **8** expressionless: *he kept a straight face* **9** without anything added: *a straight vodka* **10** *informal* heterosexual ◇ *adv* **1** in a level, upright *etc* position **2** by the shortest way, directly: *straight across the desert* **3** at once, without delay: *I came straight here after work* **4** fairly, frankly: *he's not playing straight with you* ◇ *noun* (with **the**) the straight part of a racecourse *etc* ◇ **straightness** *noun* the state of being straight ◇ **straight fight** a contest between two people only ◇ **straight away** immediately

☰ *adj* **1** level, even, flat, horizontal, upright, vertical, aligned, direct, undeviating **3** tidy, neat, orderly **4** frank, candid, blunt, forthright, direct **9** undiluted, neat, unadulterated, unmixed ◇ *adv* **4** directly, point-blank, honestly, frankly, candidly ◇ **straight away** at once, immediately, instantly, right away, directly, now, there and then

☲ *adj* **1** bent, crooked **2** evasive ◇ **straight away** later, eventually

⚠ Do not confuse with: **strait**

straighten *verb* make straight

☰ unbend, align, tidy, neaten, order, arrange

☲ bend, twist

straightforward *adj* **1** without any difficulties **2** honest, frank

☰ **1** easy, simple, uncomplicated, clear, elementary **2** honest, truthful, sincere, genuine, open, frank, candid, direct, forthright

☲ **1** complicated, difficult **2** evasive, devious

strain¹ *verb* **1** hurt (a muscle or other part of the body) by overworking or misusing it **2** work or use to the fullest: *he strained his ears to hear the whisper* **3** make a great effort: *he strained to reach the rope* **4** stretch too far, to the point of breaking (a person's patience *etc*) **5** separate liquid from a mixture of liquids and solids by passing it through a sieve ◇ *noun* **1** the act of straining **2** a hurt to a muscle *etc* caused by straining it **3** (the effect of) too much work, worry *etc*: *suffering from strain* **4** too great a demand: *a strain on my patience* **5** a tune

☰ *verb* **1** pull, wrench, twist, sprain, tear **3** labour, try, endeavour, struggle, strive, exert, force, drive **5** sieve, sift, screen, separate, filter, purify, drain ◇ *noun* **2** pull, sprain, injury **3** stress, anxiety, burden, pressure, tension

strain² *noun* **1** a kind, breed that is maintained by inbreeding **2** an inherited tendency or streak: *a strain of madness in the family*

strained *adj* **1** not natural, done with effort: *a strained conversation* **2** unfriendly: *strained relations*

☰ **1** forced, constrained, laboured, false, artificial, unnatural, stiff, tense, unrelaxed, uneasy, uncomfortable, awkward, embarrassed, self-conscious

☲ **1** natural, relaxed

strainer *noun* a sieve

strait *noun* **1** a narrow strip of sea between two pieces of land **2** (**straits**) difficulties, hardships: *dire straits*

⚠ Do not confuse with: **straight**

straitened *adj* poor and needy

straitjacket *noun* a jacket with long sleeves tied behind to prevent a violent or insane person from using their arms

straitlaced *adj* strict in attitude and behaviour

☰ prudish, stuffy, starchy, prim, proper, strict, narrow, narrow-minded, puritanical, moralistic

☲ broad-minded

strand¹ *noun* **1** a length of something soft and fine (*eg* hair, thread) **2** a single element: *the strands of the argument*

strand² *verb* **1** run (a ship) aground **2** leave in a helpless position ◇ *noun*, *old* the shore of a sea or lake

stranded *adj* **1** of a ship: run aground on the shore **2** left helpless without money or friends

☰ **1** marooned, high and dry, grounded, beached, shipwrecked, wrecked **2** high and dry, abandoned, forsaken, in the lurch, helpless

strange *adj* **1** unusual, odd: *a strange look on his face* **2** not known, seen, heard *etc* before, unfamiliar: *the method was strange to me* **3** not accustomed (to) **4** foreign: *a strange country* ◇ **strangely** *adv* ◇ **strangeness** *noun*

☰ **1** odd, peculiar, *informal* funny, curious, queer, weird, bizarre, eccentric, abnormal, irregular, uncommon, unusual, exceptional, remarkable, extraordinary, mystifying, perplexing, unexplained **2** new, novel, untried, unknown, unheard-of, unfamiliar, foreign, alien, exotic

☲ **1** ordinary, common **2** well-known, familiar

stranger *noun* **1** someone who is unknown to you **2** a visitor ◇ **a stranger to** someone who is quite unfamiliar with: *a stranger to hard work*

strangle *verb* **1** kill by gripping or

squeezing the throat tightly **2** keep in, prevent oneself from giving (*eg* a scream, a sigh) **3** stop the growth of

■ **1** throttle, choke, asphyxiate, suffocate, stifle, smother

stranglehold *noun* a tight control over something which prevents it from escaping, growing *etc*

strangulate *verb* strangle, constrict ◇ **strangulation** *noun*

strap *noun* a narrow strip of leather, cloth *etc* used to hold things in place or together *etc* ◇ *verb* (**straps, strapping, strapped**) **1** bind or fasten with a strap *etc* **2** beat with a strap

■ *noun* thong, tie, band, belt, leash ◇ *verb* **1** fasten, secure, tie, bind **2** beat, lash, whip, flog, belt

strapping *adj* tall and strong: *strapping young man*

stratagem *noun* a cunning act, meant to deceive and outwit an enemy

strategic *adj* **1** of strategy **2** done according to a strategy: *a strategic retreat* **3** giving an advantage: *a strategic position*

■ **2** important, key, critical, decisive, crucial, vital, tactical, planned, calculated, deliberate, politic, diplomatic

◨ **2** unimportant

strategy *noun* (*plural* **strategies**) **1** the art of guiding, forming or carrying out a plan **2** a plan or policy ◇ **strategist** *noun* someone who plans military operations

■ **2** tactics, plan, policy, approach, procedure, plan, programme, design, scheme

stratify *verb* (**stratifies, stratifying, stratified**) form layers or levels ◇ **stratification** *noun*

stratosphere *noun* the layer of the earth's atmosphere between 10 and 60 kilometres above the earth ◇ **stratospheric** *adj*

stratum *noun* (*plural* **strata**) **1** a layer of rock or soil **2** a level of society

stratus *noun* low, spread-out clouds

straw *noun* **1** the stalk on which corn grows **2** a paper or plastic tube for sucking up a drink

strawberry *noun* (*plural* **strawber-**ries) a type of small, juicy, red fruit or the low creeping plant which bears it ◇ **strawberry blonde** a woman with reddish blond hair

stray *verb* **1** wander **2** lose your way, become separated (from companions *etc*) ◇ *adj* **1** wandering, lost **2** happening *etc* here and there: *a stray example* ◇ *noun* a wandering animal which has been abandoned or lost

■ *verb* **1** wander (off), ramble, roam, rove, range, meander, straggle, drift, diverge, deviate, digress ◇ *adj* **1** lost, abandoned, homeless, wandering, roaming **2** random, chance, accidental, freak, odd, erratic

streak *noun* **1** a line or strip different in colour from that which surrounds it **2** a smear of dirt, polish *etc* **3** a flash (*eg* of lightning) **4** a trace of some quality in one's character: *a streak of selfishness* ◇ *verb* **1** mark with streaks **2** *informal* move very fast ◇ **streaked** *adj*

■ *noun* **1** line, stripe, strip **2** line, stroke, smear, band **4** vein, trace, dash, touch, element, strain ◇ *verb* **1** band, stripe, striate, smear **2** speed, tear, hurtle, sprint, gallop, fly, dart, flash, whistle, zoom, whizz, sweep

streaker *noun, informal* someone who runs naked in public

streaky *adj* marked with streaks ◇ **streakiness** *noun* ◇ **streaky bacon** bacon with streaks of fat and lean

stream *noun* **1** a flow (of water, air, light *etc*) **2** a small river, a brook **3** any steady flow of people or things: *a stream of traffic* ◇ *verb* flow or pour out

■ *noun* **2** river, creek, brook, burn, rivulet, tributary **3** current, drift, flow, run, gush, flood, deluge, cascade, torrent ◇ *verb* issue, well, surge, run, flow, course, pour, spout, gush, flood, cascade

streamer *noun* **1** a long strip *usu* of paper, used for decorating rooms *etc* (*esp* at Christmas) **2** a narrow flag blowing in the wind

streamline *verb* **1** shape (a vehicle *etc*) so that it may cut through the air or water as easily as possible **2** make more efficient: *we've streamlined our methods of paying* ◇ **streamlined** *adj*

street *noun* a road lined with houses *etc* ◇ **street cred** knowledge of current fashion, speech *etc* ◇ **street value** the price something, *esp* illegal drugs, is likely to be sold for ◇ **streets ahead of** much better *etc* than ◇ **up someone's street** relating to their interests or abilities

streetwalker *noun, informal* a prostitute

strength *noun* **1** the state of being strong **2** an available number or force (of soldiers, volunteers *etc*) ◇ **on the strength of** encouraged by or counting on

- toughness, robustness, sturdiness, brawn, muscle, power, might, force, vigour, energy, stamina, health, fitness, courage, fortitude, spirit, resolution, firmness, effectiveness, potency

☲ weakness, feebleness, impotence

strengthen *verb* make, or become, strong or stronger

- reinforce, brace, steel, fortify, bolster, support, toughen, harden, stiffen, corroborate, confirm, encourage, hearten, refresh, restore, invigorate, nourish, increase, heighten, intensify

☲ weaken, undermine

strenuous *adj* making or needing great effort: *the plans met strenuous resistance/squash is a strenuous game* ◇ **strenuously** *adv* ◇ **strenuousness** *noun*

- hard, tough, demanding, gruelling, taxing, laborious, arduous, tiring, exhausting, active, energetic, vigorous, eager, earnest, determined, resolute, spirited, tireless

☲ easy, effortless

stress *noun* (*plural* **stresses**) **1** force, pressure, pull *etc* of one thing on another **2** physical or nervous pressure or strain: *the stress of modern life* **3** emphasis, importance **4** extra weight laid on a part of a word (as in *but* ter) ◇ *verb* put stress, pressure, emphasis or strain on

☲ *noun* **2** pressure, strain, tension, worry,

anxiety, weight, burden, trauma, *informal* hassle **3** emphasis, accent, accentuation, beat, force, weight, importance, significance ◇ *verb* emphasize, accentuate, highlight, underline, repeat

☲ *noun* **2** relaxation ◇ *verb* understate, downplay

stretch *verb* **1** draw out to greater length, or too far, or from one point to another: *don't stretch that elastic too far/ stretch a rope from post to post* **2** be able to be drawn out to a greater length or width: *that material stretches* **3** extend in space or time **4** extend the body or part of the body **5** (cause to) exert (yourself): *the work stretched him to the full* **6** make (something, *eg* words, the law) appear to mean more than it does ◇ *noun* (*plural* **stretches**) **1** the act of stretching **2** the state of being stretched **3** a length in distance or time: *a stretch of bad road* ◇ **stretch limo** a luxurious extra-long limousine ◇ **at a stretch** continuously: *working three hours at a stretch* ◇ **at full stretch** at the limit, using all resources

☲ *verb* **1** pull, tighten, tauten, extend **2** lengthen, elongate, expand, spread **4** extend, hold out, put out, reach **5** strain, tax ◇ *noun* **3** expanse, spread, sweep, reach, extent, distance, space, area, tract, period, time, term, spell, stint, run

☲ *verb* **4** draw back

stretcher *noun* a light folding bed with handles for carrying the sick or wounded

strew *verb* (**strews**, **strewing**, **strewed**, **strewn** or **strewed**) **1** scatter: *papers strewn over the floor* **2** cover, sprinkle (with): *the floor was strewn with papers*

striated *adj* streaked

stricken *adj* **1** wounded **2** deeply affected (*eg* by illness) **3** struck

strict *adj* **1** insisting on exact obedience to rules **2** exact: *the strict meaning of a word* **3** allowing no exception, complete: *strict orders* ◇ **strictly** *adv* ◇ **strictness** *noun*

■ **1** stern, authoritarian, no-nonsense, firm, rigid, inflexible, stringent, rigorous, harsh, severe, austere **2** exact, precise, accurate, literal, faithful, true, absolute, utter, total, complete, meticulous, scrupulous, particular

☲ **1** *informal*, easy-going, flexible **2** loose

stricture *noun* criticism, blame

stride *verb* (**strides**, **striding**, **strode**, **stridden**) **1** walk with long steps **2** take a long step **3** move or extend over, along *etc* ◇ *noun* **1** a long step **2** the distance covered by a step **3** a step forward ◇ **take in your stride** manage to do easily

strident *adj* of a sound: harsh, grating ◇ **stridency** *noun*

■ loud, blaring, clamorous, vociferous, harsh, raucous, grating, rasping, shrill, screeching, discordant, jarring, jangling

☲ quiet, soft

strife *noun* quarrelling; fighting

■ conflict, discord, controversy, animosity, friction, rivalry, contention, quarrel, row, wrangling, struggle, fighting, combat, battle, warfare

☲ peace

strike *verb* (**strikes**, **striking**, **struck**) **1** hit with force **2** strike, deliver (a blow) **3** happen suddenly: *disaster struck* **4** attack: *the enemy struck at dawn* **5** hit or discover suddenly: *strike oil* **6** affect suddenly: *I am struck by her beauty* **7** give (someone) the impression of being: *did he strike you as lazy?* **8** light (a match) **9** of a clock: sound (*eg* at ten o'clock with ten chimes) **10** make (a musical note) sound **11** make (an agreement *etc*) **12** stop working (in support of a claim for more pay *etc*) ◇ *noun* **1** the act of stopping work as a protest **2** a find, *eg* of oil ◇ **strike camp** take down tents ◇ **strike home 1** of a blow: hit the point aimed at **2** of a remark: have the intended effect ◇ **strike off** remove from a register of professionals due to misconduct *etc* ◇ **strike out 1** draw a line through **2** make a move ◇ **strike up 1** begin to play or sing (a tune) **2** begin (a friendship, conversation *etc*)

■ *verb* **1** beat, pound, hammer, buffet, *informal* wallop, hit, knock, collide with, slap, smack, cuff, clout, thump, *informal* wallop **4** raid, attack, pounce **5** find, discover, unearth, uncover, encounter, reach **6** impress, affect, touch **12** stop work, down tools, work to rule, walk out, protest, mutiny, revolt ◇ **strike out 1** cross out, delete, strike through, cancel

striking *adj* **1** noticeable: *a striking resemblance* **2** impressive

■ **1** noticeable, conspicuous, salient **2** remarkable, extraordinary, memorable, impressive, dazzling, arresting, astonishing, stunning

☲ **2** unimpressive

string *noun* **1** a long narrow cord for binding, tying *etc* made of threads twisted together **2** a piece of wire or gut producing a note on a musical instrument **3** (**strings**) the stringed instruments in an orchestra **4** a line of objects threaded together: *string of pearls* **5** a number of things coming one after another: *string of abuse* ◇ *verb* (**strings**, **stringing**, **strung**) **1** put on a string **2** stretch out in a line ◇ **stringed** *adj* having strings ◇ **string along** give false expectations to, deceive ◇ **string up** hang

stringent *adj* strictly enforced: *stringent rules* ◇ **stringency** *noun* strictness

■ binding, strict, severe, rigorous, tough, rigid, inflexible, tight

☲ lax, flexible

stringy *adj* **1** like string **2** of meat: tough and fibrous

strip *noun* a long narrow piece (*eg* of paper) ◇ *verb* (**strips**, **stripping**, **stripped**) **1** pull (off) in strips **2** remove (*eg* leaves, fruit) from **3** remove the clothes from **4** deprive: *stripped of his disguise* **5** make bare or empty: *strip the bed* ◇ **strip search** a body search of someone who had been asked to strip

■ *noun* ribbon, thong, strap, belt, sash, band, stripe, slat, piece, slip, shred ◇ *verb* **1** peel, skin, flay **3** undress, disrobe, unclothe **5** lay bare, bare, empty, clear, gut

strip-cartoon *noun* a line of drawings which tell a story

stripe *noun* **1** a band of colour different from the background on which it lies **2** a blow with a whip or rod ◇*verb* make stripes on ◇**stripy** *adj* patterned with stripes

stripling *noun* a growing youth

striptease *noun* an act in which a performer strips naked

strive *verb* (**strives**, **striving**, **strove**, **striven**) **1** try hard **2** *old* fight

　▤ **1** try, attempt, endeavour, struggle, strain, work, toil, labour

strobe *noun* a light which produces a flickering beam

strode *past form* of **stride**

stroganoff *noun* a rich stew in a cream sauce

stroke *noun* **1** the act of striking **2** a blow (*eg* with a sword, whip) **3** something unexpected: *a stroke of good luck* **4** one movement (of a pen, an oar) **5** one chime of a clock **6** one complete movement of the arms and legs in swimming **7** a particular style of swimming: *breast stroke* **8** a way of striking the ball (*eg* in tennis, cricket) **9** an achievement **10** a sudden attack of illness causing paralysis ◇*verb* rub gently, *esp* as a sign of affection ◇**at a stroke** in a single action or effort

　▤ *noun* **2** blow, hit, knock, swipe **4** sweep, flourish, movement, action, move, line ◇ *verb* caress, fondle, pet, touch, pat, rub, massage

stroll *verb* walk slowly in a leisurely way ◇*noun* a leisurely walk; an amble

strong *adj* **1** healthy, robust; having great muscular strength **2** not easily worn away: *strong cloth* **3** not easily resisted: *strong wind* **4** forceful, convincing, commanding respect or obedience **5** of a smell, colour *etc*: striking, very noticeable **6** of a feeling: intense: *strong dislike* **7** in number: *a workforce 500 strong* ◇**strongly** *adv* ◇**strong point** something in which a person excels

　▤ **1** strapping, stout, burly, well-built, beefy, brawny, muscular, sinewy, athletic, fit, healthy, hardy, powerful, mighty, potent **2** tough, resilient, dur-
able, hard-wearing, heavy-duty, robust **4** convincing, persuasive, cogent, effective, forceful, weighty, compelling **5** highly-flavoured, piquant, hot, spicy, highly-seasoned, sharp, pungent, undiluted, concentrated **6** intense, deep, vivid, fierce, violent, vehement, keen, eager, zealous, fervent, ardent, dedicated, staunch

　▣ **1**, **2** weak, feeble **4** unconvincing, indecisive **5** mild, bland

strongbox *noun* a box for storing valuable objects or money

stronghold *noun* a place built to withstand attack, a fortress

strongroom *noun* a room for storing valuable objects or money

strop *noun* a strip of leather on which a razor is sharpened ◇*verb* (**strops**, **stropping**, **stropped**) sharpen a razor

stroppy *adj*, *informal* quarrelsome, disobedient, rowdy

strove *past form* of **strive**

struck *past form* of **strike**

structure *noun* **1** a building; a framework **2** the way the parts of anything are arranged: *the structure of the story* ◇**structural** *adj* ◇**structurally** *adv*

　▤ **1** construction, erection, building, edifice, fabric, framework, form, shape, design **2** configuration, make-up, formation, arrangement, organization, set-up

strudel *noun* a thin pastry filled with fruit and spices

struggle *verb* **1** try hard (to do something) **2** twist and fight to escape **3** fight (with or against someone) **4** move with difficulty: *struggling through the mud* ◇*noun* **1** a great effort **2** a fight

　▤ *verb* **1** strive, work, toil, labour, strain **3** agonize, fight, battle, wrestle, grapple ◇ *noun* **1** difficulty, problem, effort, exertion, pains, agony, work, labour, toil **2** clash, conflict, strife, fight, battle, encounter, combat, hostilities, contest

　▣ *verb* **3** yield, give in ◇ *noun* **1** ease **2** submission, co-operation

strum *verb* (**strums**, **strumming**,

strummed) play (a guitar *etc*) in a relaxed way

strung *past form of* **string** ◇ **highly strung** easily excited or agitated

strut *verb* (**struts**, **strutting**, **strutted**) walk in a proud manner ◇ *noun* **1** a proud way of walking **2** a bar *etc* which supports something

strychnine *noun* a bitter, poisonous drug

stub *noun* a small stump (*eg* of a pencil, cigarette) ◇ *verb* (**stubs**, **stubbing**, **stubbed**) **1** put out, (*eg* a cigarette) by pressure against something **2** knock (your toe) painfully against something

stubble *noun* **1** the short ends of the stalks of corn left after it is cut **2** a short growth of beard

stubborn *adj* **1** unwilling to give way, obstinate **2** of resistance *etc*: strong, determined **3** difficult to manage or deal with: *stubborn stains* ◇ **stubbornly** *adv* ◇ **stubbornness** *noun*

▣ **1** obstinate, pig-headed, obdurate, intransigent, rigid, inflexible, unbending, unyielding, persistent, tenacious, headstrong, self-willed, wilful, difficult, unmanageable

▨ **1** compliant, flexible, yielding

stubby *adj* short, thick and strong: *stubby fingers*

stucco *noun* (*plural* **stuccos**) **1** a kind of plaster used for covering walls, moulding ornaments *etc* **2** work done in stucco

stuck *past form of* **stick**

stud¹ *noun* **1** a decorative knob on a surface **2** a projection on the sole of a boot or shoe to give added grip **3** a button with two heads for fastening a collar **4** a small round earring or nose-ring ◇ *verb* (**studs**, **studding**, **studded**) **1** cover or fit with studs **2** sprinkle thickly (with): *the meadow is studded with flowers*

stud² *noun* **1** a male animal kept for breeding **2** a collection of animals kept for breeding **3** *informal* a man with great sexual energy

student *noun* someone who studies,

esp at college, university *etc*

▣ undergraduate, postgraduate, scholar, schoolboy, schoolgirl, pupil, learner, trainee

studied *adj* **1** done on purpose, intentional: *a studied insult* **2** too careful, not natural: *a studied smile*

studio *noun* (*plural* **studios**) **1** the workshop of an artist or photographer **2** a building or place in which cinema films are made **3** a room from which television or radio programmes are broadcast ◇ **studio flat** a small flat with a single open-plan room

studious *adj* **1** studying carefully and much **2** careful: *his studious avoidance of quarrels* ◇ **studiously** *adv* ◇ **studiousness** *noun*

▣ **1** scholarly, academic, intellectual, diligent, hard-working, bookish **2** careful, attentive, earnest, eager

▨ **1** lazy, idle, negligent

study *verb* (**studies**, **studying**, **studied**) **1** gain knowledge of (a subject) by reading, experiment *etc* **2** take an educational course in a subject **3** consider carefully (*eg* a problem) ◇ *noun* (*plural* **studies**) **1** the gaining of knowledge of a subject: *the study of history* **2** a detailed examination **3** a room where someone reads and writes **4** a piece of music which is meant to develop the skill of the player **5** a work of art done as an exercise, or to try out ideas for a later work

▣ *verb* **1** read, learn, revise, cram, *informal* swot, read up, research **2** analyse, survey, scan, examine, scrutinize **3** pore over, contemplate, meditate, ponder, consider, deliberate ◇ *noun* **1** reading, homework, preparation, learning, revision, cramming, *informal* swotting, research, investigation

Subjects of study include:
accountancy, agriculture, anatomy, anthropology, archaeology, architecture, art, astrology, astronomy, biology, botany, building studies, business studies, calligraphy, chemistry, CDT (craft, design and technology), civil

engineering, the Classics, commerce, computer studies, cosmology, craft, dance, design, domestic science, drama, dressmaking, driving, ecology, economics, education, electronics, engineering, environmental studies, erotology, ethnology, eugenics, fashion, fitness, food technology, forensics, gender studies, genetics, geography, geology, heraldry, history, home economics, horticulture, hospitality management, hotel management, information and communication technology (ICT), information technology (IT), journalism, languages, law, leisure studies, lexicography, lexicology, librarianship, linguistics, literature, logistics, management studies, marine studies, marketing, mathematics, mechanics, media studies, medicine, metallurgy, metaphysics, meteorology, music, mythology, natural history, oceanography, ornithology, pathology, penology, personal and social education (PSE); personal, health and social education (PHSE), pharmacology, pharmacy, philosophy, photography, physics, physiology, politics, pottery, psychology, religious studies, science, shorthand, social sciences, sociology, sport, statistics, surveying, technology, theology, visual arts, web design, women's studies, word processing, writing, zoology

stuff *noun* **1** substance or material of any kind: *what is that stuff all over the wall?* **2** belongings **3** positive characteristics: *made of stern stuff* ◇ *verb* **1** pack full **2** thrust or put away **3** fill the skin of (a dead animal) to preserve it **4** fill (a foodstuff) with stuffing before cooking ◇ **do your stuff** *informal* display talent or skill ◇ **know your stuff** *informal* have a thorough understanding of your subject ◇ **stuffed shirt** an inflexible, old-fashioned person ◇ **get**

stuffed *slang* get lost, go away
▪ *noun* **1** matter, substance, essence **2** belongings, possessions, things, objects, articles, goods, *informal* gear, *informal* clobber, kit ◇ *verb* **1** pack, stow, load, fill, cram, crowd, force, push, shove, ram, wedge, jam, squeeze, compress
▪ *verb* **1** unload, empty

stuffing *noun* **1** feathers, scraps of material *etc* used to stuff a cushion, chair *etc* **2** breadcrumbs, onions *etc* packed inside a fowl or other foodstuff and cooked with it

stuffy *adj* **1** full of stale air, badly ventilated **2** *informal* dull, having old-fashioned ideas ◇ **stuffily** *adv* ◇ **stuffiness** *noun*
▪ **1** musty, stale, airless, unventilated, suffocating, stifling, oppressive, heavy, close, muggy, sultry **2** staid, straitlaced, prim, conservative, conventional, old-fashioned, *informal* buttoned-down, pompous, dull, dreary
▪ **1** airy, well-ventilated **2** modern, lively

stultify *verb* (**stultifies, stultifying, stultified**) dull the mind, make stupid

stumble *verb* **1** trip while walking **2** walk unsteadily, as if blind **3** make mistakes or hesitate in speaking **4** (with **on**) find by chance ◇ *noun* the act of stumbling ◇ **stumbling block** a difficulty in the way of a plan or of progress
▪ *verb* **1** trip, slip, fall, lurch **2** stagger, flounder, reel **3** stammer, stutter, hesitate, falter **4** come across, chance upon, happen upon, find, discover, encounter ◇ **stumbling block** obstacle, hurdle, barrier, bar, obstruction, hindrance, impediment, difficulty, problem, snag

stump *noun* **1** the part of a tree, leg, tooth *etc* left after the main part has been cut away **2** *cricket* one of the three wooden stakes which make up a wicket ◇ *verb*, *cricket* **1** put out (a batsman) by touching the stumps with the ball **2** puzzle completely **3** walk stiffly or heavily ◇ **stump up** *informal* pay up
▪ *verb* **2** outwit, confound, perplex, puzzle, baffle, mystify, confuse, bewilder, *informal* flummox, *informal* bamboozle,

dumbfound ◇ **stump up** *informal* pay, hand over, *informal* fork out, *informal* shell out, donate, contribute, *informal* cough up

☒ **stump up** receive

stumpy *adj* short and thick

stun *verb* (**stuns, stunning, stunned**) 1 knock senseless (by a blow *etc*) 2 surprise or shock very greatly: *stunned by the news*

☐ 2 amaze, astonish, astound, stagger, shock, daze, stupefy, dumbfound, *informal* flabbergast, overcome, confound, confuse, bewilder

stung *past form* of **sting**

stunk *past form* of **stink**

stunning *adj* 1 extraordinarily beautiful, attractive, *etc* 2 impressive

☐ 1 beautiful, lovely, gorgeous, ravishing, dazzling, brilliant, striking 2 impressive, spectacular, remarkable, wonderful, marvellous, great, sensational

☒ 1 ugly 2 awful

stunt¹ *noun* 1 a daring trick 2 something done to attract attention: *a publicity stunt*

stunt² *verb* stop the growth of ◇ **stunted** *adj* small and badly shaped

stupefy *verb* (**stupefies, stupefying, stupefied**) 1 make stupid, deaden the feelings of 2 astonish ◇ **stupefaction** *noun*

☐ 2 daze, stun, numb, dumbfound, *informal* flabbergast, shock, stagger, amaze, astound

stupendous *adj* wonderful, amazing (*eg* because of size and power)

☐ huge, enormous, gigantic, colossal, vast, prodigious, phenomenal, tremendous, breathtaking, overwhelming, staggering, stunning, amazing, astounding, fabulous, fantastic, superb, wonderful, marvellous

☒ ordinary, unimpressive

stupid *adj* 1 foolish: *a stupid thing to do* 2 dull, slow at learning 3 stupefied (*eg* from lack of sleep) ◇ **stupidity** *noun*

☐ 1 silly, foolish, irresponsible, foolhardy, rash, senseless, mad, lunatic, brainless, half-witted, idiotic, imbecilic, puerile, nonsensical, absurd, ludicrous, ridicu-

lous 2 simple-minded, slow, dim, dull, dense, thick, dumb, dopey 3 dazed, groggy, stupefied, stunned, sluggish, semiconscious

☒ 1 sensible, wise 2 clever, intelligent 3 alert

stupor *noun* the state of being only partly conscious

sturdy *adj* strong, well built; healthy ◇ **sturdily** *adv* ◇ **sturdiness** *noun*

☐ strong, robust, durable, well-made, stout, substantial, solid, well-built, powerful, muscular, athletic, steadfast, firm, resolute, determined

☒ weak, flimsy, puny

sturgeon *noun* a type of large fish from which caviare is taken

stutter *verb* speak in a halting, jerky way; stammer ◇ *noun* a stammer

sty or **stye** *noun* (*plural* **sties** or **styes**) an inflamed swelling on the eyelid

Stygian *adj* hellish, infernal

style *noun* 1 manner of acting, writing, speaking *etc* 2 fashion: *in the style of the late 19th century* 3 an air of elegance 4 the middle part of the pistil of a flower ◇ *verb* 1 design, shape *etc* in a particular way 2 call, name: *styling himself 'Lord John'* ◇ **stylized** *adj* ◇ **in style** with no expense or effort spared

☐ *noun* 1 technique, approach, method, manner, mode, fashion, way, custom 2 fashion, vogue, trend, mode, cut, design, pattern, shape, form, genre 3 elegance, smartness, chic, flair, panache, stylishness, taste, polish, refinement, sophistication ◇ *verb* 2 designate, term, name, call, address, title, dub, label

☒ *noun* 3 inelegance, tastelessness

stylish *adj* smart, elegant, fashionable

☐ chic, fashionable, modish, in vogue, voguish, *informal* trendy, *informal* snazzy, dressy, smart, elegant, *informal* classy, polished, refined, sophisticated

☒ old-fashioned, shabby

stylus *noun* (*plural* **styluses**) a needle for a record-player

stymie *verb* block, impede

Originally a golfing term for an opponent's ball in the way of your own

suave /swaːv/ adj superficially polite and pleasant, smooth

🔳 polite, courteous, charming, agreeable, affable, soft-spoken, smooth, sophisticated

🔲 rude, unsophisticated

sub- prefix **1** under, below **2** less than **3** lower in rank or importance

subaltern noun an officer in the army under the rank of captain

subconscious noun that part of one's mind of which one is not aware ◇ adj of the subconscious, not conscious or aware: a subconscious desire for fame

🔳 adj subliminal, unconscious, intuitive, inner, innermost, hidden, latent, repressed, suppressed

🔲 adj conscious

subcontract verb give a contract for (work forming part of a larger contract) to another company

subculture noun an identifiable group within a larger culture or group

subcutaneous adj beneath the skin

subdirectory noun, comput a directory contained within another

subdivide verb divide into smaller parts ◇ **subdivision** noun a part made by subdividing

subdue verb **1** conquer (an enemy etc) **2** keep under control (eg a desire) **3** make less bright (eg a colour, a light) **4** make quieter: he seemed subdued after the fight

🔳 **1** overcome, quell, suppress, repress, overpower, crush, defeat, conquer, vanquish **2** tame, master, discipline, control, check **4** soften, quieten

subedit verb edit (text) at a secondary or later stage

subject adj /'sʌbdʒɪkt/ **1** under the power of another: a subject nation **2** (with **to**) liable to suffer from (eg colds) **3** (with **to**) depending on: subject to your approval ◇ noun /'sʌbdʒɪkt/ **1** someone under the power of another: the king's subjects **2** something or some-

one spoken about, studied etc **3** someone who undergoes an experiment, treatment etc **4** grammar the word in a sentence or clause which stands for the person or thing doing the action of the verb (eg cat is the subject in 'the cat drank the milk') ◇ verb /sʌb'dʒɛkt/ (often with **to**) force to submit (to)

🔳 adj **1** subjugated, captive, bound, answerable, subordinate, inferior, subservient, submissive **2** liable, disposed, prone, susceptible, vulnerable ◇ noun **2** topic, theme, matter, issue, question, point, case, affair, business, discipline, field ◇ verb expose, lay open, submit, subjugate

🔲 adj **1** free, superior **2** immune

subjection noun the act of subjecting or the state of being subjected

🔳 subjugation, defeat, captivity, bondage, chains, slavery, enslavement, oppression, domination, mastery

subjective adj based on personal feelings, thoughts etc, not impartial ◇ **subjectivity** noun

🔳 biased, prejudiced, personal, individual, idiosyncratic, emotional, intuitive, instinctive

🔲 objective, unbiased, impartial

subjoin verb, formal add at the end, append

subjugate verb bring under your power; make obedient

subjunctive adj, grammar of a verb: in a form which indicates possibility, contingency etc ◇ noun a subjunctive form of a verb

sublet verb let out (rented property) to another person, eg while the original tenant is away

sublieutenant noun an officer in the navy below the rank of lieutenant

sublime adj very noble, great or grand ◇ **sublimity** noun

🔳 exalted, elevated, high, lofty, noble, majestic, great, grand, imposing, magnificent, glorious

🔲 lowly, base

subliminal adj working below the level of consciousness: subliminal messages ◇ **subliminally** adv

submachine-gun *noun* a light machine-gun fired from the hip or shoulder

submarine *noun* a type of ship which can travel under water ◇ *adj* under the surface of the sea

submerge *verb* cover with water; sink ◇ **submergence** or **submersion** *noun* ◇ **submersible** *noun* a boat that can operate under water

▭ submerse, immerse, plunge, duck, dip, sink, drown, engulf, overwhelm, swamp, flood, inundate, deluge

▣ surface

submission *noun* **1** the act of submitting **2** readiness to yield, meekness **3** an idea, statement *etc* offered for consideration

▭ **2** surrender, capitulation, resignation, acquiescence, assent, compliance, obedience, deference, submissiveness, meekness, passivity **3** offering, contribution, entry, suggestion, proposal

▣ **2** intransigence, intractability

submissive *adj* meek, yielding easily ◇ **submissively** *adv*

▭ yielding, unresisting, resigned, patient, uncomplaining, accommodating, obedient, compliant, deferential, ingratiating, subservient, humble, meek, docile, subdued, passive

▣ intransigent, intractable

submit *verb* (**submits**, **submitting**, **submitted**) **1** give in, yield **2** place (a matter) before someone for making a judgement

▭ **1** yield, give in, surrender, bow, bend, stoop, succumb, agree, comply **2** present, tender, offer, put forward, suggest, propose, table, state

▣ **1** resist **2** withdraw

subordinate *adj* (often with **to**) lower in rank or importance (than) ◇ *noun* someone who is subordinate ◇ *verb* (with **to**) consider as of less importance than ◇ **subordination** *noun*

▭ *adj* secondary, auxiliary, ancillary, subsidiary, dependent, inferior, lower, junior, minor, lesser ◇ *noun* inferior, junior, assistant, attendant, second, aide, dependant

▭ *adj* superior, senior ◇ *noun* superior, boss

suborn *verb* persuade (someone) to do something illegal, *esp* by bribery

subpoena *noun* an order for someone to appear in court ◇ *verb* order to appear in court

subscribe *verb* **1** make a contribution (*esp* of money) towards a charity **2** promise to take and pay for a number of issues of a magazine *etc* **3** (with **to**) agree with (an idea, statement *etc*) ◇ **subscription** *noun*

▭ **3** support, endorse, back, advocate, approve, agree

subsequent *adj* following, coming after

▭ following, later, future, next, succeeding, consequent, resulting, ensuing

▣ previous, earlier

subservient *adj* weak-willed, ready to do as you are told ◇ **subservience** *noun*

subside *verb* **1** settle down, sink lower **2** of noise *etc*: get less and less

▭ **1** sink, collapse, settle, descend, fall, drop, lower **2** lessen, diminish, dwindle, decline, die down, quieten

▣ **2** rise, increase

subsidence *noun* a sinking down, *esp* into the ground

subsidiary *adj* **1** acting as a help **2** of less importance **3** of a company: controlled by another company ◇ *noun* (*plural* **subsidiaries**) a subsidiary person or thing

subsidize *verb* give money as a help

▭ support, back, underwrite, sponsor, finance, fund, aid, promote

subsidy *noun* (*plural* **subsidies**) money paid by a government *etc* to help an industry

▭ grant, allowance, assistance, help, aid, contribution, sponsorship, finance, support, backing

subsist *verb* **1** exist **2** (with **on**) live on (a kind of food *etc*)

subsistence *noun* **1** existence **2** means or necessities for survival

▭ **1** living, survival, existence, livelihood **2**

support, keep, sustenance, nourishment, food, provisions, rations

subsoil *noun* the layer of the earth just below the surface soil

substance *noun* **1** a material that can be seen and felt: *glue is a sticky substance* **2** general meaning (of a talk, essay *etc*) **3** thickness, solidity **4** wealth, property: *a woman of substance* **5** foundation, truth
- **1** matter, material, stuff, fabric, essence **2** subject, subject-matter, theme, gist, meaning, significance **3** solidity, concreteness **5** reality, actuality, ground, foundation

substantial *adj* **1** solid, strong **2** large: *a substantial building* **3** able to be seen and felt **4** in the main, but not in detail: *substantial agreement* ◇ **substantially** *adv* for the most part: *substantially the same*
- **1** hefty, well-built, stout, sturdy, strong, sound, durable **2** large, big, sizable, ample, great, considerable
- **1** weak **2** small, insignificant

substantiate *verb* give proof of, or evidence for

substantive *noun*, *grammar* a noun

substitute *verb* (with **for**) put in place or instead of ◇ *noun* a person or thing used instead of another ◇ **substitution** *noun*
- *verb* change, exchange, swap, switch, interchange, replace ◇ *noun* reserve, standby, stand-in, replacement, relief, agent, deputy, stopgap

substratum *noun* (*plural* **substrata**) **1** a layer lying underneath **2** a foundation

subsume *verb* include in something larger

subterfuge *noun* a cunning trick to get out of a difficulty *etc*

subterranean *adj* found under the ground

subtitle *noun* **1** a second additional title of a book *etc* **2** a translation of *eg* the dialogue in a foreign-language film, appearing at the bottom of the screen

subtle *adj* **1** difficult to describe or explain: *a subtle difference* **2** cunning: *by a subtle means* ◇ **subtly** *adv* ◇ **subtlety** *noun* (*plural* **subtleties**)
- **1** delicate, understated, implied, indirect, slight, tenuous, faint, mild, fine **2** artful, cunning, crafty, sly, devious, shrewd, astute
- **1** blatant, obvious **2** artless, open

subtotal *noun* a total of one set of figures within a larger group

subtract *verb* **1** take away (a part from) **2** take away (one number from another) ◇ **subtraction** *noun*

suburb *noun* a residential area on the outskirts of a town ◇ **suburban** *adj* of suburbs

suburbia *noun* the suburbs

subversive *adj* likely to overthrow (government, discipline *etc*)
- seditious, treasonous, treacherous, traitorous, inflammatory, incendiary, disruptive, riotous, weakening, undermining, destructive
- loyal

subvert *verb* undermine or overthrow (a government, discipline *etc*)

subway *noun* **1** an underground crossing for pedestrians *etc* **2** an underground railway

succeed *verb* **1** (with **in**) manage to do what you have been trying to do **2** get on well **3** take the place of, follow **4** (often with **to**) follow in order (to the throne *etc*)
- **1** triumph, make it, get on, thrive, flourish, prosper, make good, manage, work **3** follow, replace, result, ensue

success *noun* (*plural* **successes**) **1** the achievement of something worked for **2** someone who succeeds **3** something that turns out well
- **1** triumph, victory, luck, fortune, prosperity, fame, happiness **2** celebrity, star, somebody, winner, bestseller, hit, sensation
- **1** failure, disaster

successful *adj* **1** having achieved what was aimed at **2** having achieved wealth, importance *etc* **3** turning out as planned
- **1** victorious, winning, lucky, fortunate,

prosperous, wealthy, thriving, flourishing, fruitful, productive **2** famous, well-known, popular, leading, bestselling, top, unbeaten

☒ **1** unsuccessful, unprofitable, fruitless **2** unknown

succession *noun* **1** the act of following after **2** the right of becoming the next holder (of a throne *etc*) **3** a number of things coming one after the other: *a succession of failures* ◇ **in succession** one after another

successive *adj* following one after the other

successor *noun* someone who comes after, follows in a post *etc*

succinct *adj* in a few words, brief, concise: *a succinct reply*

☐ short, brief, terse, pithy, epigrammatic, concise, compact, condensed, summary

☒ long, lengthy, wordy, verbose

succour *verb* help in time of distress ◇ *noun* help

succulent *adj* **1** juicy **2** of a plant: having thick, juicy leaves or stems

☐ **1** fleshy, juicy, moist, luscious, mouthwatering, lush

☒ **1** dry

succumb *verb* yield (to): *succumbed to temptation*

☐ give way, yield, give in, submit, knuckle under, surrender, capitulate, collapse, fall

☒ overcome, master

such *adj* **1** of a kind previously mentioned: *such things are difficult to find* **2** of a similar type: *doctors, nurses and such people* **3** so great: *his excitement was such that he shouted out loud* **4** used for emphasis: *it's such a disappointment!* ◇ *pronoun* thing, people *etc* of a kind already mentioned: *such as these are not to be trusted* ◇ **as such** by itself ◇ **such as** of the same kind as

such-and-such *adj* & *pronoun* any given (person or thing): *such-and-such a book*

suck *verb* **1** draw into the mouth **2** draw milk from with the mouth **3** hold in the mouth and lick hard (*eg* a sweet)

4 (often with **up** or **in**) draw in, absorb ◇ *noun* the act of sucking ◇ **suck up to** *informal* flatter or toady

sucker *noun* **1** a side shoot rising from the root of a plant **2** a part of an animal's body by which it sticks to objects **3** a pad (of rubber *etc*) which can stick to a surface **4** *informal* someone easily fooled

suckle *verb* of a woman or female animal: give milk from the breast or teat

suckling *noun* a baby or young animal which still sucks its mother's milk

sucrose *noun* a sugar found in sugarbeet

suction *noun* **1** the act of sucking **2** the process of reducing the air pressure, and so producing a vacuum, on the surface or between surfaces

sudden *adj* happening all at once without being expected: *a sudden attack* ◇ **suddenly** *adv* ◇ **suddenness** *noun*

☐ unexpected, unforeseen, surprising, startling, abrupt, sharp, quick, swift, rapid, prompt, hurried, hasty, rash, impetuous, impulsive, *informal* snap

☒ expected, predictable, gradual, slow

suds *noun plural* frothy, soapy water

sue *verb* start a law case against

suede /sweɪd/ *noun* a kind of leather with a soft, dull surface

suet *noun* a kind of hard animal fat

suffer *verb* **1** feel pain or punishment **2** bear, endure **3** tolerate **4** *old* allow ◇ **suffering** *noun* ◇ **on sufferance** allowed or tolerated but not really wanted

☐ **1** hurt, ache, agonize, grieve, sorrow **2** bear, support, tolerate, endure, sustain, undergo, go through, feel ◇ **suffering** pain, discomfort, agony, anguish, affliction, distress, misery, hardship, ordeal, torment, torture

☒ **suffering** ease, comfort

suffice *verb* be enough, or good enough

sufficient *adj* enough ◇ **sufficiently** *adv*

☐ enough, adequate, satisfactory, effective

▣ insufficient, inadequate

suffix noun (plural **suffixes**) a small part added to the end of a word to make another word, such as -ness to good to make goodness, -ly to quick to make quickly etc

suffocate verb **1** kill by preventing the breathing of **2** die from lack of air **3** feel unable to breathe freely: suffocating in this heat ◇ **suffocation** noun

suffrage noun **1** a vote **2** the right to vote

suffuse verb spread over ◇ **suffusion** noun

sugar noun a sweet substance obtained mostly from sugar-cane and sugar-beet ◇ verb mix or sprinkle with sugar ◇ **sugar daddy** an older man who lavishes money on a younger woman in exchange for companionship and often sex

sugar-beet noun a vegetable whose root yields sugar

sugar-cane noun a tall grass from whose juice sugar is obtained

sugary adj **1** tasting of sugar **2** too sweet

suggest verb **1** put forward, propose (an idea etc) **2** put into the mind, hint

■ **1** propose, put forward, advocate, recommend, advise, counsel **2** imply, insinuate, hint, intimate, evoke, indicate

suggestible adj easily influenced by suggestions

suggestion noun **1** an act of suggesting **2** an idea put forward **3** a slight trace: a suggestion of anger in her voice

■ **2** proposal, proposition, motion, recommendation, idea, plan **3** implication, hint, intimation, suspicion, trace, indication

suggestive adj **1** that suggests something particular, esp sexually improper: suggestive remarks **2** (with **of**) giving the idea of: suggestive of mental illness

■ **1** indecent, improper, indelicate, immodest, risqué, bawdy, dirty, smutty, provocative **2** reminiscent, expressive, meaning, indicative

▣ **1** decent, clean

suicidal adj **1** of or considering suicide **2** likely to cause death or ruin: suicidal action

suicide noun **1** the taking of your own life **2** someone who kills themselves

suit noun **1** a set of clothes to be worn together **2** a case in a law court **3** one of the four divisions (spades, hearts, diamonds, clubs) of playing-cards ◇ verb **1** be convenient or suitable for: the climate suits me **2** look well on: that dress suits you **3** (with **to**) make fitting or suitable for: suited his words to the occasion ◇ **follow suit** do just as someone else has done

■ verb **1** satisfy, gratify, please, answer, match, tally, agree, correspond, harmonize

▣ verb **1** displease, clash

suitable adj fitting the purpose or occasion ◇ **suitability** noun

■ appropriate, fitting, convenient, suited, due, apt, apposite, relevant, applicable, fit, adequate, satisfactory, acceptable, befitting, becoming, seemly, proper, right

▣ unsuitable, inappropriate

suitcase noun a travelling case for carrying clothes etc

suite noun **1** a number of things in a set, eg rooms, furniture, pieces of music **2** a group of attendants for an important person

suitor noun a man who tries to gain the love of a woman

sulk verb keep silent because of being displeased ◇ **sulky** adj ◇ **the sulks** a fit of sulking

■ **sulky** brooding, moody, morose, resentful, grudging, disgruntled, put out, cross, bad-tempered, sullen, aloof, unsociable

▣ **sulky** cheerful, good-tempered, sociable

sullen adj angry and silent, sulky ◇ **sullenness** noun

■ sulky, moody, morose, glum, gloomy, silent, surly, sour

▣ cheerful, happy

sully verb (**sullies**, **sullying**, **sullied**) make less pure, dirty

■ dirty, soil, defile, pollute, contaminate, taint, spoil, mar, spot, blemish, stain, tarnish, disgrace, dishonour

🔁 cleanse, honour

sulphur *noun* a yellow substance found in the ground which gives off a choking smell when burnt, used in matches, gunpowder *etc* ◇ **sulphuric acid** a powerful acid much used in industry

sultan *noun* **1** *hist* the head of the Turkish Ottoman empire **2** an Islamic ruler

sultana *noun* **1** a sultan's wife **2** a light-coloured raisin

sultry *adj* **1** of weather: very hot and close **2** passionate, steamy

■ **1** hot, sweltering, stifling, stuffy, oppressive, close, humid, muggy, sticky

🔁 **1** cool, cold

sum *noun* **1** the amount made by two or more things added together **2** a quantity of money **3** a problem in arithmetic **4** the general meaning (of something said or written) ◇ **summing-up** *noun* a review of the main points (of a discussion, trial *etc*) ◇ **sum total 1** the sum of several smaller sums **2** the main point, total effect ◇ **sum up 1** give the main points of (a discussion, evidence in a trial *etc*) **2** make a quick assessment of (a person, situation *etc*)

■ **1** total, sum total, aggregate, whole, entirety ◇ **sum up** summarize, review, recapitulate, recap, conclude, close

summarize *verb* state briefly, make a summary of

■ outline, précis, condense, abbreviate, shorten, sum up, encapsulate, review

🔁 expand (on)

summary *noun* (*plural* **summaries**) a shortened form (of a story, statement *etc*) giving only the main points ◇ *adj* **1** short, brief **2** done without wasting time or words ◇ **summarily** *adv*

■ *noun* synopsis, résumé, outline, abstract, précis, condensation, abridgement, summing-up, review, recap ◇ *adj* **1** short, succinct, brief, cursory **2** hasty, prompt, direct, unceremonious, arbitrary

🔁 *adj* **1, 2** lengthy, careful

summer *noun* the warmest season of the year ◇ *adj* of or in summer

summerhouse *noun* a small house in a garden for sitting in

summit *noun* the highest point of a hill *etc* ◇ **summit conference** a conference between heads of governments

■ top, peak, pinnacle, apex, point, crown, head, zenith, acme, culmination, height

🔁 bottom, foot

summon *verb* **1** order (someone) to come to you, appear in a court of law *etc* (with **up**) gather up (courage, strength *etc*)

■ **1** call, send for, invite, bid, beckon, gather, assemble **2** muster, mobilize, rouse, arouse

summons *noun* (*plural* **summonses**) **1** an order to appear in court **2** any authoritative order to attend a meeting *etc*

sumo *noun* a Japanese form of wrestling

sump *noun* **1** part of a motor-engine which contains the oil **2** a small drainage pit

sumptuous *adj* costly, splendid

■ luxurious, plush, lavish, extravagant, rich, costly, expensive, dear, splendid, magnificent, gorgeous, superb, grand

🔁 plain, poor

sun *noun* **1** the round body in the sky which gives light and heat to the earth **2** sunshine ◇ *verb* (**suns, sunning, sunned**) (with **yourself**) lie in the sunshine, sunbathe

sunbathe *verb* lie or sit in the sun to acquire a suntan

sunbeam *noun* a ray of light from the sun

sunburn *noun* a burning or redness caused by over-exposure to the sun ◇ **sunburned** or **sunburnt** *adj* affected by sunburn

sundae *noun* a sweet dish of ice-cream served with fruit, syrup *etc*

Sunday *noun* the first day of the week, the Christian Sabbath

sunder *verb*, *old* separate, part

sundial *noun* an instrument for telling

the time from the shadow of a rod on its surface cast by the sun

sundries *noun plural* odds and ends

sundry *adj* several, various: *sundry articles for sale*
- various, diverse, miscellaneous, assorted, varied, different, several, some, a few

sunflower *noun* a large yellow flower with petals like rays of the sun

sung *past participle* of **sing**

sunglasses *noun plural* spectacles with tinted lenses that shield the eyes from sunlight

sunk *adj* 1 on a lower level than the surroundings; sunken 2 *informal* defeated, done for ◇ *past participle* of **sink**

sunken *adj* 1 that has been sunk 2 of cheeks *etc*: hollow
- 1 submerged, buried, recessed, lower 2 depressed, concave, hollow, haggard, drawn

sunlight *noun* the light from the sun ◇ **sunlit** *adj*

sunny *adj* 1 full of sunshine 2 cheerful: *sunny nature*
- 1 fine, cloudless, clear, summery, sunlit, bright, brilliant 2 cheerful, happy, joyful, smiling, beaming, radiant, light-hearted, buoyant, optimistic, pleasant
- 1 sunless, dull 2 gloomy

sunrise *noun* the rising of the sun in the morning

sunset *noun* the setting of the sun in the evening

sunshine *noun* 1 bright sunlight 2 cheerfulness

sunstroke *noun* a serious illness caused by over-exposure to very hot sunshine

suntan *noun* a browning of the skin caused by exposure to the sun

sup *verb* (**sups**, **supping**, **supped**) eat or drink in small mouthfuls

super *adj*, *informal* extremely good

super- *prefix* above, beyond, very, too

superannuate *verb* make (someone) retire from their job because of old age

superannuation *noun* a pension given to someone retired

superb *adj* magnificent, very fine, excellent: *a superb view*
- excellent, first-rate, first-class, superior, choice, fine, exquisite, gorgeous, magnificent, splendid, grand, wonderful, marvellous, admirable, impressive, breathtaking
- bad, poor, inferior

supercilious *adj* looking down on others, haughty ◇ **superciliousness** *noun*

superficial *adj* 1 of a wound: affecting the surface of the skin only, not deep 2 not thorough or detailed: *superficial interest* 3 apparent at first glance, not actual: *superficial likeness* 4 of a person: not capable of deep thoughts or feelings ◇ **superficiality** *noun* ◇ **superficially** *adv*
- 1 surface, external, exterior 4 shallow, lightweight, frivolous, casual

> **!** Do not confuse: **superficial** and **superfluous**

superfluous *adj* beyond what is enough or necessary ◇ **superfluity** *noun*
- extra, spare, excess, surplus, remaining, left-over, redundant, unnecessary, needless, unwanted, uncalled-for, excessive
- necessary, needed, wanted

superhuman *adj* 1 divine, godly 2 greater than would be expected of an ordinary person: *superhuman effort*

superimpose *verb* lay or place (one thing on another)

superintend *verb* be in charge or control, manage

superintendent *noun* 1 someone who is in charge of an institution, building *etc* 2 a police officer above a chief inspector

superior *adj* 1 higher in place or rank 2 better or greater than others: *superior forces/superior goods* 3 having an air of being better than others ◇ *noun* someone better than, or higher in rank than, others ◇ **superiority** *noun*
- *adj* 2 excellent, first-class, first-rate, select, fine, exceptional, unrivalled 3

haughty, lordly, pretentious, snobbish, *informal* snooty, lofty, supercilious, disdainful, condescending, patronizing ◊ *noun* senior, elder, better, boss, chief, principal, director, manager, foreman, supervisor

ᴇꜰ *adj* **2** inferior, average **3** humble ◊ *noun* inferior, junior, assistant

superlative *adj* **1** better than, or going beyond, all others: *superlative skill* **2** *grammar* an adjective or adverb of the highest degree of comparison, *eg* kindest, worst, most boringly

ᴇ **1** best, greatest, highest, supreme, unbeatable, unrivalled, unparalleled, unsurpassed, unbeaten, consummate, excellent, outstanding, *informal* top-drawer

ᴇꜰ **1** poor, average

supermarket *noun* a large self-service store selling food *etc*

supernatural *adj* not happening in the ordinary course of nature ◊ **supernaturally** *adv*

ᴇ paranormal, unnatural, abnormal, metaphysical, spiritual, psychic, mystic, occult, hidden, mysterious, miraculous, magical, phantom, ghostly

ᴇꜰ natural, normal

supernova *noun* an exploding star surrounded by a bright cloud of gas

supernumerary *adj* above the usual or required number ◊ *noun* (*plural* **supernumeraries**) someone beyond the required number, an extra

supersede *verb* **1** take the place of: *he superseded his brother as headmaster* **2** replace (something with something else)

supersonic *adj* faster than the speed of sound: *supersonic flight*

superstition *noun* **1** belief in magic and in things that cannot be explained by reason **2** an example of such belief (*eg* not walking under ladders)

superstitious *adj* having superstitions

ᴇ mythical, false, fallacious, irrational, groundless, delusive, illusory

ᴇꜰ rational, logical

supervene *verb* come after or in addition

supervise *verb* be in charge of work and see that it is properly done ◊ **supervisor** *noun*

ᴇ oversee, watch over, look after, superintend, run, manage, administer, direct, conduct, preside over, control, handle

supervision *noun* the act of supervising; control, inspection

ᴇ surveillance, care, charge, running, management, administration, direction, control, guidance, instruction

supine *adj* **1** lying on the back **2** not showing any interest or energy

supper *noun* a meal taken in the evening

supplant *verb* take the place of somebody or of something: *the baby supplanted the dog in her affections*

ᴇ replace, supersede, usurp, oust, displace, remove, overthrow, topple, unseat

supple *adj* bending easily, flexible ◊ **suppleness** *noun* ◊ **supply** *adv*

ᴇ flexible, bending, pliant, pliable, plastic, lithe, graceful, loose-limbed, double-jointed, elastic

ᴇꜰ stiff, rigid, inflexible

supplement *noun* **1** something added to supply a need or lack **2** a special section added to the main part of a newspaper or magazine ◊ *verb* make or be an addition to: *her earnings supplemented his income*

ᴇ *verb* add to, augment, boost, reinforce, fill up, top up, complement, extend

ᴇꜰ *verb* deplete, use up

supplementary *adj* added to supply a need; additional

ᴇ additional, extra, auxiliary, secondary, complementary, accompanying

suppliant *adj* asking earnestly and humbly ◊ *noun* someone who asks in this way

supplicate *verb* ask earnestly, beg ◊ **supplicant** *noun* ◊ **supplication** *noun* a humble, earnest request

supply *verb* (**supplies**, **supplying**, **supplied**) **1** provide (what is wanted or needed) **2** provide (someone with something) ◇ *noun* (*plural* **supplies**) **1** an act of supplying **2** something supplied **3** a stock or store **4** (**supplies**) a stock of essentials, *eg* food, equipment, money *etc* ◇ *adj* of a teacher: filling another's place or position for a time

■ *verb* **1** provide, give, donate, grant, contribute, produce, sell **2** provide, furnish, equip, outfit, endow, stock ◇ *noun* **3** source, amount, quantity, stock, fund, reservoir, store, reserve, stockpile, hoard, cache

🗷 *verb* **1** take, receive

support *verb* **1** hold up, take part of the weight of **2** help, encourage; back **3** supply with a means of living: *support a family* **4** bear, put up with: *I can't support lies* **5** reinforce the truth of (a claim *etc*) ◇ *noun* **1** an act of supporting **2** something that supports

■ *verb* **1** hold up, bear, carry, sustain, reinforce, strengthen, prop, buttress, bolster **2** back, second, defend, help, aid, assist, rally round, finance, fund **3** maintain, keep, provide for, feed, nourish ◇ *noun* **2** prop, stay, post, pillar, brace, crutch, foundation

🗷 *verb* **2** oppose **3** live off

supporter *noun* someone who supports (*esp* a football club)

■ fan, follower, adherent, advocate, champion, defender, seconder, patron, sponsor, helper, ally, friend

🗷 opponent

suppose *verb* **1** take as true, assume for the sake of argument: *suppose that we have £100 to spend* **2** believe, think probable: *I suppose you know*

■ **1** assume, presume, expect, conclude, guess **2** believe, think, consider, judge, imagine, conceive, fancy, pretend, postulate, hypothesize

supposed *adj* believed (often mistakenly) to be so: *her supposed generosity* ◇ **be supposed to** be required or expected to (do)

■ alleged, reported, rumoured, assumed, presumed, reputed, imagined, hypothetical

🗷 known, certain

supposedly *adv* according to what is supposed

supposing *conj* in the event that: *supposing it rains – what will we do?*

supposition *noun* **1** the act of supposing **2** something supposed

■ **2** assumption, presumption, guess, conjecture, speculation, theory, hypothesis, idea, notion

🗷 **2** knowledge

suppository *noun* (*plural* **suppositories**) a medicated swab inserted into the rectum or vagina

suppress *verb* **1** crush, put down (a rebellion *etc*) **2** keep back (a yawn, a piece of news *etc*) ◇ **suppression** *noun* the act of suppressing

■ **1** crush, stamp out, quash **2** quell, stop, silence, censor, stifle, smother, strangle, conceal, withhold, hold back, contain, restrain, check, repress, inhibit

🗷 **1** encourage, incite

suppurate *verb* of a wound: be full of, or discharge, pus

supremacist *noun* someone who believes in the supremacy of their own race *etc*: *white supremacist*

supremacy *noun* highest power or authority

supreme *adj* **1** highest, most powerful: *supreme ruler* **2** greatest: *supreme courage*

■ **1** top, crowning, culminating, first, leading, foremost, chief, principal, head, sovereign **2** best, greatest, highest, prevailing, world-beating, unsurpassed, second-to-none, incomparable, matchless, consummate, transcendent, superlative, prime, ultimate, extreme, final

supremo *noun* (*plural* **supremos**) *informal* a chief, a boss

surcharge *noun* an extra charge or tax

sure *adj* **1** having no doubt; confident: *I'm sure that I can come* **2** certain (to do, happen *etc*): *he is sure to be there* **3** reliable, secure: *a sure method* ◇ **be sure** see to it that: *be sure that he does it* ◇ **make sure** act so that, or check that, something is sure ◊ **sure of yourself** confident ◊ **to be sure 1** certainly! **2** undoubtedly: *to be sure, you are correct*

■ **1** certain, convinced, confident, decided, positive **2** assured, definite, clear, accurate, unquestionable, indisputable, undoubted, undeniable, inevitable, bound **3** safe, secure, fast, solid, firm, steady, stable, guaranteed, reliable, dependable, trustworthy, unerring, unfailing, infallible, effective

✷ **1** unsure, uncertain, doubtful **3** unsafe, insecure

sure-footed *adj* unlikely to slip or stumble

surely *adv* **1** certainly, without doubt **2** sometimes expressing a little doubt: *surely you won't tell him?* **3** without hesitation, mistake *etc*

surety *noun* (*plural* **sureties**) **1** someone who promises that another person will do something (*esp* appear in court) **2** a pledge, a guarantee

surf *noun* the foam made by the breaking of waves ◊ *verb* ride on a surfboard ◊ **surfboard** *noun* a long, narrow board on which someone can ride over the surf ◊ **surfer** *noun* someone who surfs ◊ **surfing** *noun* the sport of riding on a surfboard

surface *noun* the outside or top part of anything (*eg* of the earth, of a road *etc*) ◊ *verb* **1** come up to the surface of (water *etc*) **2** put a (smooth) surface on ◊ *adj* **1** on the surface **2** travelling on the surface of land or water: *surface mail*

■ *noun* outside, exterior, façade, veneer, covering, skin, top, side, face, plane ◊ *verb* **1** rise, arise, come up, emerge, appear

✷ *noun* inside, interior ◊ *verb* **1** sink, disappear, vanish

surfeit *noun* too much of anything

surge *verb* **1** move (forward) like waves **2** rise suddenly or excessively ◊ *noun* **1** the swelling of a large wave **2** a swelling or rising movement like this **3** a sudden rise or increase (of pain *etc*)

surgeon *noun* a doctor who performs operations, often cutting the body

open to examine or remove a diseased part

surgery *noun* (*plural* **surgeries**) **1** treatment of diseases *etc* by operation **2** a doctor's or dentist's consulting room ◊ **surgical** *adj* ◊ **surgically** *adv*

surly *adj* gruff, rude, ill-mannered ◊ **surliness** *noun*

■ gruff, brusque, churlish, ungracious, bad-tempered, cross, crabbed, grouchy, crusty, sullen, sulky, morose

✷ friendly, polite

surmise *verb* suppose, guess ◊ *noun* a supposition

surmount *verb* **1** overcome (a difficulty *etc*) **2** climb over, get over ◊ **surmountable** *adj*

surname *noun* a person's last name or family name

surpass *verb* go beyond, be more or better than: *his work surpassed my expectations*

■ beat, outdo, exceed, outstrip, better, excel, transcend, outshine, eclipse

surplice *noun* a loose white gown worn by members of the clergy

❗ Do not confuse: **surplice** and **surplus**

surplus *noun* the amount left over after what is needed has been used up ◊ *adj* left over, extra

■ *noun* excess, residue, remainder, balance, superfluity, glut, surfeit ◊ *adj* excess, superfluous, redundant, extra, spare, remaining, left-over, unused

✷ *noun* lack, shortage

surprise *noun* **1** the feeling caused by an unexpected happening **2** an unexpected happening ◊ *verb* **1** cause someone to feel surprise **2** come upon (someone) suddenly and without warning ◊ **surprising** *adj* ◊ **take by surprise** come upon, or capture, without warning

■ *noun* **1** amazement, astonishment, incredulity, wonder, bewilderment, dismay, shock, start **2** shock, bombshell, revelation ◊ *verb* **1** startle, amaze, astonish, astound, stagger, *informal* flabbergast, bewilder, confuse, nonplus,

disconcert, dismay
■ *noun* **1** composure

surreal *adj* dreamlike, using images from the subconscious ◇ **surrealism** *noun* the use of surreal images in art ◇ **surrealist** *noun* & *adj*

surrender *verb* **1** give up, give in, yield: *surrender to the enemy* **2** hand over: *she surrendered the note to the teacher* ◇ *noun* an act of surrender, *esp* in a war

■ *verb* **1** resign, concede, yield, give in, cede, give up, quit **2** relinquish, abandon, renounce ◇ *noun* capitulation, resignation, submission, yielding, relinquishment, renunciation

surreptitious *adj* done in a secret, underhand way

■ furtive, stealthy, sly, covert, veiled, hidden, secret, clandestine, underhand, unauthorized
■ open, obvious

surrogate *noun* a substitute ◇ **surrogacy** *noun*

surround *verb* **1** be all round (someone or something) **2** enclose, put round ◇ *noun* a border

surroundings *noun plural* **1** the country lying round a place **2** the things, people and places around you

■ **2** neighbourhood, vicinity, locality, setting, environment, background, milieu, ambience

surtax *noun* an extra tax *esp* on income

surtitles *noun plural* a translation of an opera libretto projected on a screen above the audience

surveillance *noun* a close watch or constant guard

survey *verb* (**surveys**, **surveying**, **surveyed**) **1** look over or examine **2** inspect, examine (a building) to assess its value **3** make careful measurements of (a piece of land *etc*) ◇ *noun* (*plural* **surveys**) **1** a detailed examination or inspection, *esp* to find out public or customer opinion **2** an inspection of a building to assess its value **3** a careful measuring of land *etc* **4** a map made with the measurements obtained

■ *verb* **1** view, contemplate, observe, scan, scrutinize, examine, inspect, study, research, review, consider ◇ *noun* **1** review, overview, scrutiny, examination, inspection, study, pull, appraisal, assessment, measurement

surveyor *noun* someone who makes surveys of land, buildings *etc*

survival *noun* **1** the state of surviving **2** a custom, relic *etc* that remains from earlier times

survive *verb* **1** remain alive, continue to exist (after an event *etc*) **2** live longer than: *he survived his wife*

■ **1** stay, remain, live, exist, withstand, weather **2** outlive, outlast

survivor *noun* someone who remains alive: *the only survivor of the crash*

susceptible *adj* **1** (with **to**) liable to be affected by: *susceptible to colds* **2** easily affected or moved ◇ **susceptibility** *noun* (*plural* **susceptibilities**)

■ **1** liable, prone, inclined, disposed, given **2** receptive, responsive, impressionable, suggestible, weak, vulnerable, open, sensitive, tender
■ **1** resistant, immune

sushi *noun* a Japanese dish of cakes of cold rice, slices of raw fish *etc*

suspect *verb* **1** be inclined to think (someone) guilty: *I suspect her of the crime* **2** distrust, have doubts about: *I suspected his air of frankness* **3** guess: *I suspect that we're wrong* ◇ *noun* someone thought to be guilty of a crime *etc* ◇ *adj* arousing doubt, suspected

■ *verb* **2** doubt, distrust, mistrust, call into question **3** believe, fancy, feel, guess, conjecture, speculate, surmise, suppose, consider, conclude, infer ◇ *adj* suspicious, doubtful, dubious, questionable, debatable, unreliable, *informal* dodgy, *informal* fishy
■ *adj* acceptable, reliable

suspend *verb* **1** hang **2** keep from falling or sinking: *particles suspended in a liquid* **3** stop for a time: *suspend business* **4** take away a job, privilege *etc* from for a time: *they suspended the student from classes*

■ **1** hang, dangle, swing **3** adjourn, interrupt, discontinue, cease, delay, defer, postpone, put off, shelve **4** expel, dismiss, exclude

▣ **4** restore, reinstate

suspender *noun* **1** an elastic strap to keep up socks or stockings **2** (**suspenders**) *US* braces

suspense *noun* **1** tension caused by the desire to know the outcome of something **2** a state of uncertainty or worry

▣ **2** uncertainty, insecurity, anxiety, tension, apprehension

▣ **2** certainty, knowledge

suspension *noun* **1** the act of suspending **2** the state of being suspended **3** temporary exclusion from a school, job *etc* **4** temporary cessation **5** in a vehicle: a system that absorbs some unwanted vibrations caused by the road surface **6** the state of a solid which is mixed with a liquid or gas and does not sink or dissolve in it ◇ **suspension bridge** a bridge which is suspended from cables hanging from towers

suspicion *noun* **1** a feeling of doubt or mistrust **2** an opinion, a guess **3** a small amount

▣ **1** doubt, scepticism, distrust, mistrust, wariness, caution, misgiving **2** idea, notion, hunch

suspicious *adj* **1** inclined to suspect or distrust **2** arousing suspicion ◇ **suspiciously** *adv*

▣ **1** doubtful, sceptical, unbelieving, suspecting, distrustful, mistrustful, wary, chary, apprehensive, uneasy **2** dubious, questionable, suspect, irregular, shifty, *informal* shady, *informal* dodgy, *informal* fishy, *informal* iffy

▣ **1** trustful, confident **2** trustworthy, innocent

suss or **sus** *verb, slang* (often with **out**) investigate, find out ◇ **have someone sussed** understand their character, motives *etc*

sustain *verb* **1** hold up, support **2** bear (an attack *etc*) without giving way **3** suffer (an injury *etc*) **4** give strength to: *the food will sustain you* **5** keep up, keep going: *sustain a conversation*

▣ **1** support, uphold, endorse, bear, carry **4** nourish, provide for, nurture **5** maintain, keep going, keep up, continue, prolong, hold

sustenance *noun* food, nourishment

▣ nourishment, food, provisions, fare, maintenance, subsistence, livelihood

SUV *abbrev* Sport Utility Vehicle

svelte *adj* slender, trim

SW *abbrev* south-west; south-western

swab *noun* **1** a piece of cottonwool used for cleaning, absorbing blood *etc* **2** a specimen of bodily fluid *etc* taken for examination ◇ *verb* (**swabs, swabbing, swabbed**) clean with a swab

swaddle *verb* wrap up (a young baby) tightly ◇ **swaddling clothes** *old* strips of cloth used to wrap up a young baby

swag *noun, Austral informal* a bundle of possessions

swagger *verb* **1** walk proudly, swinging the arms and body **2** boast ◇ *noun* a proud walk or attitude

▣ *verb* **1** parade, strut **2** bluster, boast, crow, brag, *informal* swank ◇ *noun* bluster, show, ostentation, arrogance

swain *noun, old* a young man

swallow¹ *verb* **1** pass (food or drink) down the throat into the stomach **2** (with **up**) make disappear **3** receive (an insult *etc*) without objection **4** keep back (tears, a laugh *etc*) ◇ *noun* an act of swallowing

▣ *verb* **1** consume, devour, eat, gobble up, guzzle, *informal* snarf, drink, *informal* knock back, gulp, *informal* down **2** engulf, enfold, envelop, absorb

swallow² *noun* a bird with pointed wings and a forked tail

swam *past form* of **swim**

swamp *noun* permanently wet, marshy ground ◇ *verb* **1** fill (a boat) with water **2** overwhelm: *swamped with work*

▣ *verb* **1** flood, inundate, deluge, engulf, submerge, drench, saturate, waterlog **2** overload, overwhelm

swan *noun* a large, stately water bird, with white feathers and a long neck

◇ **swan song** the last work of a musician, writer *etc*

swank *verb*, *informal* show off ◇ **swanky** *adj*

swap or **swop** *verb* (**swaps** or **swops**, **swapping** or **swopping**, **swapped** or **swopped**) give one thing in exchange for another: *swap addresses*

swarm *noun* 1 a large number of insects flying or moving together 2 a dense moving crowd ◇ *verb* 1 of insects: gather together in great numbers 2 move in crowds 3 be crowded with: *swarming with tourists*
∎ *noun* 2 crowd, throng, mob, mass, multitude ◇ *verb* 2 flock, flood, stream, mass, congregate, crowd, throng 3 teem, crawl, bristle, abound

swarthy *adj* dark-skinned

swashbuckling *adj* bold, swaggering

swastika *noun* an ancient design of a cross with bent arms, taken up as a symbol of Nazism

swat *verb* (**swats**, **swatting**, **swatted**) squash (a fly *etc*) ◇ *noun* an instrument for squashing insects

swatch *noun* a piece of fabric, carpet *etc* used as a sample

swath or **swathe** *noun* 1 a line of corn or grass cut by a scythe 2 a strip

swathe *verb* wrap round with clothes or bandages

sway *verb* 1 swing or rock to and fro 2 bend in one direction or to one side 3 influence: *sway opinion* ◇ *noun* 1 a swaying movement 2 rule, power: *hold sway over*
∎ *verb* 1 rock, roll, lurch, swing, wave, oscillate, fluctuate 2 bend, incline, lean 3 influence, affect, persuade, convince, convert, overrule, dominate, govern

swear *verb* (**swears**, **swearing**, **swore**, **sworn**) 1 curse, using the name of God or other sacred things without respect 2 promise or declare solemnly 3 make (someone) take an oath: *to swear someone to secrecy* ◇ **swear word** a word used in swearing or cursing ◇ **swear by** rely on, have complete faith in

sweat *noun* 1 moisture secreted by the skin, perspiration 2 a laborious activity 3 a period of anxiety or fear ◇ *verb* 1 give out sweat 2 be anxious or afraid ◇ **sweat blood** work very hard ◇ **sweat it out** *informal* endure a difficult situation to the end

sweater *noun* a jersey, a pullover

sweaty *adj* wet, or stained with, sweat
∎ damp, moist, clammy, sticky, sweating, perspiring
Ⓔ dry, cool

swede *noun* a kind of large yellow turnip

sweep *verb* (**sweeps**, **sweeping**, **swept**) 1 clean (a floor *etc*) with a brush or broom 2 (often with **up**) gather up (dust *etc*) by sweeping 3 carry (away, along, off) with a long brushing movement 4 travel over quickly, move with speed: *a new fad which is sweeping the country* 5 move quickly in a proud manner (*eg* from a room) 6 search: *sweep the sea for enemy mines* 7 curve widely or stretch far ◇ *noun* 1 a sweeping movement 2 a curve, a stretch 3 a chimney sweeper 4 a sweepstake
∎ *verb* 1 brush, dust, clean, clear ◇ *noun* 1 swing, stroke, movement, gesture 2 arc, curve, bend

sweeping *adj* 1 of a search, change *etc*: thorough and wide-ranging 2 of a victory *etc*: great, overwhelming 3 of a statement *etc*: too general, allowing no exceptions, rash
∎ 3 general, global, universal, all-inclusive, blanket, across-the-board, broad, wide-ranging, extensive, far-reaching, comprehensive, indiscriminate
Ⓔ 3 specific, narrow

sweepstake *noun* a gambling system in which those who take part stake money which goes to the holder of the winning ticket

sweet *adj* 1 having the taste of sugar, not salty, sour or bitter 2 pleasing to taste, hear or smell 3 kindly, agreeable, charming ◇ *noun* 1 a small piece of sweet substance, *eg* chocolate, toffee *etc* **2** something sweet served towards the end of a meal, a pudding ◇ **sweetly** *adv* ◇ **sweetness** *noun* ◇ **sweet nothings** endearments between lovers ◇ **sweet pea** a sweet-smelling climbing flower grown in gardens ◇ **sweet potato** the swollen root of a climbing plant, eaten as a vegetable ◇ **sweet talk** flattery, persuasion ◇ **sweet tooth** a liking for sweet-tasting things ◇ **sweet william** a sweet-smelling type of garden flower

◼ *adj* **1** sugary, syrupy, sweetened, honeyed, saccharine **2** luscious, delicious, pleasant, delightful, melodious, tuneful, harmonious, musical, dulcet, soft, mellow, fresh, clean, wholesome, pure, clear, perfumed, fragrant, aromatic **3** winsome, cute, appealing, lovable, charming, agreeable, amiable, affectionate, tender, kind, treasured, precious, dear

◼ *adj* **1** savoury, salty, sour, bitter **2** unpleasant, nasty, discordant

sweetbreads *noun plural* an animal's pancreas used for food

sweetcorn *noun* maize

sweeten *verb* **1** make or become sweet **2** *informal* make (someone) more agreeable by flattery *etc* **3** *informal* make (an offer) more inviting by making additions

◼ **1** sugar, honey, mellow, soften, soothe, appease, temper, cushion

◼ sour, embitter

sweetener *noun* **1** an artificial substance used to sweeten food or drinks **2** *informal* a bribe

sweetheart *noun* a lover

sweetmeat *noun, old* a sweet, a confection

swell *verb* (**swells**, **swelling**, **swelled**, **swollen**) **1** increase in size or volume **2** of the sea: rise into waves **3** of a person: visibly fill with emotion ◇ *noun* **1** an increase in size or volume **2** large, heaving waves **3** *old* a dandy ◇ *adj, US informal* fine, splendid

◼ *verb* **1** expand, dilate, inflate, blow up, puff up, bloat, fatten, bulge, balloon, billow, surge, rise, mount, increase, enlarge, extend, grow, augment, heighten, intensify

◼ *verb* **1** shrink, contract, decrease, dwindle

swelling *noun* a swollen part of the body, a lump

◼ lump, tumour, bump, bruise, blister, boil, inflammation, bulge, protuberance, puffiness, distension, enlargement

swelter *verb* be too hot ◇ **sweltering** *adj* very hot

◼ **sweltering** hot, tropical, baking, scorching, stifling, suffocating, airless, oppressive, sultry, steamy, sticky, humid

◼ **sweltering** cold, cool, fresh, breezy, airy

swept *past form* of **sweep**

swerve *verb* turn quickly to one side ◇ *noun* a quick turn aside

◼ *verb* turn, bend, incline, veer, swing, shift, deviate, stray, wander, diverge, deflect, sheer

swift *adj* moving quickly; rapid ◇ *noun* a bird rather like the swallow ◇ **swiftly** *adv* ◇ **swiftness** *noun*

◼ *adj* fast, quick, rapid, speedy, express, flying, hurried, hasty, short, brief, sudden, prompt, ready, agile, nimble, *informal* nippy

◼ *adj* slow, sluggish, unhurried

swig *noun, informal* a mouthful of liquid, a large drink ◇ *verb* (**swigs**, **swigging**, **swigged**) *informal* gulp down

swill *verb* **1** wash out **2** *informal* drink a great deal ◇ *noun* **1** partly liquid food given to pigs **2** disgusting food or drink

swim *verb* (**swims**, **swimming**, **swam**, **swum**) **1** move on or in water, using arms, legs, fins *etc* **2** cross by swimming: *swim the Channel* **3** float, not sink **4** be dizzy **5** be covered (with liquid): *meat swimming in grease* ◇ *noun* an act of swimming ◇ **swimmer** *noun* ◇ **swimming bath** or **swimming pool** a large water-filled tank designed for swimming, diving in *etc* ◇ **swimming costume** or **swimsuit** *noun* a brief close-fitting garment for swimming in

swimmingly *adv* smoothly, easily, successfully

swindle *verb* **1** cheat, defraud **2** get money *etc* (from someone) by cheating ◇ *noun* a fraud, a deception ◇ **swindler** *noun*
 ▣ *verb* **1** cheat, defraud, diddle, trick, deceive, dupe, *informal* con, *slang* sting **2** *informal* do, overcharge, fleece, *slang* rip off, *informal* clean out ◇ *noun* fraud, fiddle, racket, *informal* scam, double-dealing, trickery, deception, *informal* con, *slang* sting, *slang* rip-off, *informal* clean-out

swine *noun* (*plural* **swine**) **1** *old* a pig **2** *informal* a contemptible person

swineherd *noun*, *old* someone who looks after pigs

swing *verb* (**swings**, **swinging**, **swung**) **1** move to and fro, sway **2** turn or whirl round **3** to change opinion, mood, direction *etc* **4** arrange or achieve: *his sales pitch could swing the sale* ◇ *noun* **1** a swinging movement **2** a seat for swinging, hung on ropes *etc* from a support **3** a (sudden or sharp) change ◇ **swing bridge** a kind of bridge that swings open to let ships pass ◇ **in full swing** going on busily
 ▣ *verb* **1** sway, rock, oscillate, vibrate, fluctuate **2** turn, whirl, twirl, spin, rotate ◇ *noun* **1** sway, rock, oscillation, vibration, fluctuation, variation, change, shift, movement, motion, rhythm

swingeing *adj* very great, severe: *swingeing cuts in taxation*

⚠ Do not confuse with: **swinging**

swipe *verb* **1** strike with a sweeping blow **2** pass (a plastic card) through a device that decodes the information on it ◇ *noun* a sweeping blow
 ▣ *verb* hit, strike, lunge, lash out, slap, *informal* whack, *informal* wallop, *slang* sock ◇ *noun* stroke, blow, slap, smack, clout, whack *informal*, wallop *informal*

swirl *verb* sweep along with a whirling motion ◇ *noun* a whirling movement

swish¹ *verb* move with a rustling sound: *swishing out of the room in her* long dress ◇ *noun* a rustling sound or movement

swish² *adj*, *informal* stylish

switch *noun* (*plural* **switches**) **1** a small lever or handle *eg* for turning an electric current on and off **2** an act of switching **3** a change: *a switch of loyalty* **4** a thin stick ◇ *verb* **1** change, turn: *switch jobs/hastily switching the conversation* **2** reverse the positions of ◇ **switch on** or **switch off** turn (on or off) by means of a switch
 ▣ *noun* **3** change, alteration, shift, exchange, swap, interchange, substitution, replacement ◇ *verb* **1** change, turn, veer, deviate, divert, deflect **2** exchange, swap, trade, interchange, transpose, substitute, replace, shift, rearrange

switchback *noun* a road or railway with steep ups and downs or sharp turns

switchblade *noun* a flick-knife

switchboard *noun* a board with equipment for making telephone connections

swither *verb* waver, oscillate

swivel *noun* a joint that turns on a pin or pivot ◇ *verb* (**swivels**, **swivelling**, **swivelled**) turn on a swivel, pivot
 ▣ *verb* pivot, spin, rotate, revolve, turn, twirl, pirouette, gyrate, wheel

swiz or **swizzle** *noun*, *informal* a cheat, a swindle

swizzle stick a small stick used to stir drinks, *esp* cocktails

swollen *adj* increased in size by swelling ◇ *past form* of **swell**
 ▣ *adj* bloated, distended, inflated, tumid, puffed up, puffy, inflamed, enlarged, bulbous, bulging
 ▣ *adj* shrunken, shrivelled

swoon *verb*, *old* faint ◇ *noun* a fainting fit

swoop *verb* come down with a sweep, like a bird of prey ◇ *noun* a sudden downward rush ◇ **at one fell swoop** all at one time, at a stroke
 ▣ *verb* dive, plunge, drop, fall, descend, stoop, pounce, lunge, rush ◇ *noun* dive,

plunge, drop, descent, pounce, lunge, rush, attack, onslaught

swop *another spelling of* **swap**

sword *noun* a type of weapon with a long blade for cutting or piercing

swordfish *noun* a large type of fish with a long pointed upper jaw like a sword

swore *past form of* **swear**

sworn *adj* holding steadily to an attitude *etc*: *they had been sworn friends since childhood/the two rivals became sworn enemies*

swot *verb, informal* study hard ◇ *noun* someone who studies hard
■ study, work, learn, memorize, revise, cram, *slang* bone up

swum *past participle of* **swim**

swung *past form of* **swing**

sybaritic *adj* **1** luxurious **2** fond of luxury

> After the ancient Greek city of *Sybaris* in Italy, noted for its luxury

sycamore *noun* a name given to several different types of tree, the maple, plane, and a kind of fig tree

sycophant *noun* someone who flatters others in order to gain favour or personal advantage ◇ **sycophancy** *noun* ◇ **sycophantic** *adj*

syllable *noun* a word or part of a word spoken with one breath (*cheese* has one syllable, *but-ter* two, *mar-gar-ine* three) ◇ **syllabic** *adj*

syllabus *noun* (*plural* **syllabuses** or **syllabi**) a programme or list of lectures, classes *etc*
■ curriculum, course, programme, schedule, plan

syllogism *noun* a combination of two propositions which lead to a third conclusion ◇ **syllogistic** *adj*

sylph *noun* **1** a type of fairy supposed to inhabit the air **2** a slender, graceful woman ◇ **sylphlike** *adj*

symbiosis *noun* (*plural* **symbioses**) a mutually beneficial partnership ◇ **symbiotic** *adj*

symbol *noun* **1** something that stands for or represents another thing, *eg* the red cross, which stands for first aid **2** a character used as a short form of something, *eg* the signs + meaning plus, and O meaning oxygen ◇ **symbolist** *noun* & *adj*
■ **1** sign, token, representation, mark, emblem, badge, logo, character, figure, image

symbolic or **symbolical** *adj* standing as a symbol of
■ representative, emblematic, token, figurative, metaphorical, allegorical, meaningful, significant

symbolism *noun* the use of symbols to express ideas *esp* in art and literature

symbolize *verb* be a symbol of
■ represent, stand for, denote, mean, signify, typify, exemplify, epitomize, personify

symmetrical *adj* having symmetry; not lopsided in appearance ◇ **symmetrically** *adv*

symmetry *noun* the equality in size, shape and position of two halves on either side of a dividing line: *spoiling the symmetry of the building*
■ balance, evenness, regularity, parallelism, correspondence, proportion, harmony, agreement
⊟ asymmetry, irregularity

sympathetic *adj* feeling or showing sympathy ◇ **sympathetically** *adv* ◇ **sympathetic to** or **towards** inclined to be in favour of: *sympathetic to the scheme*
■ understanding, appreciative, supportive, comforting, consoling, commiserating, pitying, interested, concerned, caring, compassionate, tender, kind, warm-hearted, affectionate, agreeable, friendly, congenial, like-minded, compatible
⊟ unsympathetic, indifferent, callous, antipathetic

sympathize *verb*: **sympathize with** express or feel sympathy (for)
■ understand, comfort, commiserate, pity, feel for, empathize, identify

with, respond to
◨ ignore, disregard

sympathy noun (plural **sympathies**)
1 a feeling of pity or sorrow for someone in trouble **2** agreement with, or understanding of, the feelings, attitudes
etc of others
▣ **1** condolences, commiseration, pity,
compassion, comfort, consolation **2**
agreement, accord, correspondence,
harmony, understanding, tenderness,
kindness, warmth, thoughtfulness, empathy, affinity
◨ **1** indifference, insensitivity, callousness
2 disagreement

symphony noun (plural **sympho-
nies**) a long piece of music written for
an orchestra of many different instruments

symposium noun (plual **symposia**
or **symposiums**) **1** a meeting or conference for the discussion of some subject
2 a collection of essays dealing with a
single subject

symptom noun **1** an outward sign indicating the presence of a disease etc:
symptoms of measles **2** an indication of
a state or condition: a symptom of moral
decline ◇ **symptomatic** adj
▣ **1**, **2** sign, indication, evidence, manifestation, expression, feature, characteristic, mark, token, warning
◇ **symptomatic** indicative, typical,
characteristic, associated, suggestive

synagogue noun a Jewish place of
worship

synchronize verb **1** happen at the
same time **2** agree in time: synchronize
watches

syncopate verb, music change the
beat by accenting beats not usually ac-
cented ◇ **syncopation** noun

syndicate noun a number of persons
or groups who join together to manage
some piece of business ◇ verb form into
a syndicate

syndrome noun a pattern of behaviour, events etc characteristic of some
problem or condition

synod noun a meeting of members of
the clergy

synonym noun a word which has the
same, or nearly the same, meaning as
another, eg 'ass' and 'donkey', or 'brave'
and 'courageous' ◇ **synonymous** adj
having the same meaning
▣ **synonymous** interchangeable, sub-
stitutable, the same, identical, similar,
comparable, tantamount, equivalent,
corresponding
◨ **synonymous** antonymous, opposite

synopsis noun (plural **synopses**) a
short summary of the main points of a
book, speech etc

syntax noun rules for the correct combination of words to form sentences
◇ **syntactic** or **syntactical** adj

synthesis noun (plural **syntheses**) **1**
the act of making a whole by putting together its separate parts **2** the result of
this process **3** the making of a substance by combining chemical elements

synthesize verb make (eg a drug) by
synthesis

synthesizer noun a computerized instrument which creates electronic musical sounds

synthetic adj **1** made artificially to
look like a natural product: synthetic
leather **2** not natural, pretended: synthetic charm ◇ **synthetically** adv
▣ **1** manufactured, man-made, simulated,
artificial, imitation, fake **2** fake, mock,
sham, pseudo, bogus
◨ **1**, **2** genuine, real, natural

syphilis noun an infectious disease,
transmitted sexually ◇ **syphilitic** adj

syphon another spelling of **siphon**

syringe noun a tubular instrument
with a needle and plunger, used to extract blood, inject drugs etc ◇ verb clean
out, inject etc with a syringe: needing his
ears syringed

syrup noun **1** a thick sticky liquid
made by boiling water or fruit juice
with sugar **2** a purified form of treacle
◇ **syrupy** adj

system noun **1** an arrangement of several parts which work together: railway
system/solar system **2** a way of organiz-

ing: *democratic system of government* **3** a regular method of doing something **4** the body, or its parts, considered as a whole: *my system is run down* ◇**systemic** *adj* affecting the whole body

■ **1** structure, set-up, co-ordination, methodology, classification, arrangement, order **2** organization, systematization, plan, scheme **3** method, mode, technique, procedure, process, routine, practice, usage, rule

systematic *adj* following a system; methodical ◇**systematically** *adv*

■ methodical, logical, ordered, well-ordered, planned, well-planned, organized, well-organized, structured, systematized, standardized, orderly, businesslike, efficient

☒ unsystematic, arbitrary, disorderly, inefficient

t *abbrev* ton

ta *exclam, Brit informal* thanks

tab *noun* **1** a small tag or flap attached to something **2** a bill in a bar, restaurant *etc*

tabard *noun* a short sleeveless tunic

tabby *noun* (*plural* **tabbies**) or **tabby-cat** a striped (usually female) cat

tabernacle *noun* **1** in the Roman Catholic Church: a receptacle where consecrated bread and wine are kept **2** a place of worship

table *noun* **1** a flat-topped piece of furniture, supported by legs **2** a flat surface, a plateau **3** facts or figures set out in columns: *multiplication tables* ◇ *verb* **1** make into a list or table **2** put forward for discussion: *table a motion* ◇ **table linen** tablecloths, napkins *etc* ◇ **table tennis** a form of tennis played across a table with small bats and a light ball ◇ **turn the tables** reverse a situation

■ *noun* **3** chart, timetable, schedule, programme, list, inventory, catalogue, index, register, record ◇ *verb* **2** propose, suggest, submit, put forward

tableau *noun* (*plural* **tableaux**) a striking group or scene

tablecloth *noun* a cloth for covering a table

table d'hôte a meal of several courses at a fixed price

tableland *noun* a raised stretch of land with a level surface

tablespoon *noun* a large size of spoon ◇ **tablespoonful** *noun* (*plural* **tablespoonfuls**) the amount held in a tablespoon

tablet *noun* **1** a pill **2** a small flat piece, *eg* of soap or chocolate **3** a small flat plate on which to write, paint *etc*

tabloid *noun* a small-sized newspaper giving news in shortened and often simplified form

taboo *adj* forbidden by common consent; not approved by social custom ◇ *noun* a taboo subject or behaviour

■ *adj* forbidden, prohibited, banned, proscribed, unacceptable, unmentionable, unthinkable

☒ *adj* permitted, acceptable

tabor /'teɪbə(r)/ *noun* a small kind of drum

tabular *adj* set in the form of a table

tabulate *verb* set out (information *etc*) in columns or rows

tachograph *noun* an instrument showing a vehicle's mileage, number of stops *etc*

tachometer *noun* an instrument showing speed

tacit /'tasɪt/ *adj* understood but not spoken aloud, silent: *tacit agreement* ◇ **tacitly** *adv*

■ unspoken, unexpressed, unvoiced, silent, understood, implicit, implied, inferred

☒ express, explicit

taciturn *adj* not inclined to talk ◇ **taciturnity** *noun* ◇ **taciturnly** *adv*

■ silent, quiet, uncommunicative, unforthcoming, reticent, reserved, withdrawn, aloof, distant, cold

☒ talkative, communicative, forthcoming

tack *noun* **1** a short sharp nail with a broad head **2** a sideways movement allowing a yacht *etc* to sail against the wind **3** a direction, a course **4** a rough stitch to keep material in place while sewing ◇ *verb* **1** fasten with tacks **2** sew with tacks **3** of a yacht *etc*: move from side to side across the face of the wind ◇ **tack on** add (something) ◇ **change tack** change course or direction ◇ **on the wrong tack** following the wrong train of thought

■ *noun* **3** course, path, bearing, heading, direction, line, approach ◇ *verb* **1** attach, affix, fasten, fix, nail, pin, staple

tackle *verb* **1** try to come to grips with, deal with **2** *football etc* try to stop, or take the ball from, another player ◇ *noun* **1** the ropes and rigging of a ship **2** equipment, gear: *fishing tackle* **3** ropes and pulleys for raising heavy weights **4** *football etc* an act of tackling
■ *verb* **1** embark on, take on, confront, encounter, face up to, grapple with, deal with, attend to, handle **2** intercept, block, halt, stop, check, challenge ◇ *noun* **2** equipment, tools, implements, apparatus, rig, outfit, gear, trappings, paraphernalia
☒ *verb* **1** avoid, sidestep

tacky *adj* **1** sticky, gluey **2** *informal* shabby; vulgar, in bad taste

tact *noun* skill in dealing with people so as to avoid giving offence
■ tactfulness, diplomacy, discretion, prudence, delicacy, sensitivity, perception, discernment, judgement, understanding, thoughtfulness, consideration, skill
☒ tactlessness, indiscretion

tactful *adj* using tact; avoiding giving offence ◇ **tactfully** *adv* ◇ **tactfulness** *noun*
■ diplomatic, discreet, prudent, careful, delicate, subtle, sensitive, perceptive, discerning, understanding, thoughtful, considerate, polite, skilful, adroit.
☒ tactless, indiscreet, thoughtless, rude

tactical *adj* **1** involving clever and successful planning **2** diplomatic, politic: *tactical withdrawal* ◇ **tactically** *adv*

tactics *noun plural* **1** a way of acting in order to gain advantage **2** the art of co-ordinating military forces in action ◇ **tactician** *noun* someone who uses tactics skilfully
■ **1** strategy, plan, scheme, policy, approach, line of attack, moves, manoeuvres

tactile *adj* of or perceived through touch

tactless *adj* giving offence through lack of thought ◇ **tactlessly** *adv* ◇ **tactlessness** *noun*
■ undiplomatic, indiscreet, indelicate, inappropriate, imprudent, careless, clumsy, blundering, insensitive, unfeel-ing, hurtful, unkind, thoughtless, inconsiderate, rude, impolite, discourteous
☒ tactful, diplomatic, discreet

tadpole *noun* a young frog or toad in its first stage of life

tae kwon do a Korean martial art similar to karate

taffeta *noun* a thin, glossy fabric made mainly of silk

tag *noun* **1** a label carrying information: *price tag* **2** an electronic device attached to a person or animal to supervise their movements **3** a chasing game played by children (*also called* **tig**) ◇ *verb* (**tags**, **tagging**, **tagged**) put a tag or tags on ◇ **tag on** or **tag along** follow or accompany, *esp* uninvited
■ *noun* **1** label, sticker, tab, ticket, mark, identification, note, slip ◇ *verb* label, mark, identify, designate

tagliatelle *noun* pasta made in long ribbons

t'ai chi a Chinese system of exercise and self-defence stressing the importance of balance and coordination

tail *noun* **1** an appendage sticking out from the end of the spine on an animal, bird or fish **2** something similar in form or position to a creature's tail: *tail of an aeroplane/shirt tail* **3** a final or rear part: *the tail of the storm* **4** (**tails**) the side of a coin opposite to the head **5** (**tails**) a tailcoat ◇ *verb* **1** follow closely **2** remove the tails from (fruit *etc*) ◇ **tail off** become less, fewer or worse ◇ **turn tail** run away
■ *verb* **1** follow, pursue, shadow, dog, stalk, track, trail ◇ **tail off** decrease, decline, drop, fall away, fade, wane, dwindle, taper off, peter out, die (out)
☒ **tail off** increase, grow

tailback *noun* a line of traffic stretching back from an obstruction

tailboard *noun* a movable board at the back end of a lorry *etc*

tailcoat *noun* a coat with a divided tail, part of a man's evening dress

tail-end *noun* the very end of a procession *etc*

tailgate *noun* a door at the back of a car that opens upwards ◇*verb* drive very closely behind (someone)

tail-light *noun* a rear light on a vehicle

tailor *noun* someone who cuts out and makes clothes ◇*verb* **1** make and fit (clothes) **2** make to fit the circumstances, adapt: *tailored to your needs* ◇**tailored** *adj* of clothes: fitting the wearer exactly ◇**tailor-made** *adj* exactly suited to requirements

■ *verb* **1** fit, suit, cut, trim, style, fashion, shape **2** alter, modify, adapt, adjust, accommodate

tailspin *noun* a steep, spinning, downward dive of an aeroplane

tail-wind *noun* a wind blowing from behind

taint *verb* **1** spoil by contact with something bad or rotten **2** corrupt ◇*noun* a trace of decay or evil

■ *verb* **1** contaminate, infect, pollute, dirty, soil, muddy, defile, sully, harm, damage, blight, spoil, ruin **2** corrupt, deprave, shame, disgrace, dishonour ◇*noun* contamination, infection, pollution, corruption, stain, blemish, fault, flaw, defect, spot, blot, smear, stigma, shame, disgrace, dishonour

tajine or **tagine** /ta'ʒiːn/ *noun* a North African stew traditionally cooked in a clay pot

take *verb* (**takes, taking, taken, took**) **1** lay hold of, grasp **2** do or perform: *take revenge* **3** obtain or buy **4** lead, carry, drive: *take the children to school* **5** accept, agree to have: *do you take credit cards?/please take a biscuit* **6** commit to: *take a decision* **7** endure or put up with **8** require: *it'll take too much time* **9** use, make use of: *take a train* **10** photograph: *took some shots inside the house* **11** occupy (a seat, country *etc*) **12** have room for: *my car only takes four people* **13** understand, perceive: *took what I said the wrong way* **14** eat, swallow: *take a pill/doesn't take sugar* **15** be in charge of: *take a meeting* **16** experience, feel: *takes great pride in his work* **17** subtract: *take two from eight* **18** have

an effect: *the medicine didn't take* **19** of a plant: root successfully ◇**take after** be like in appearance or behaviour ◇**take back 1** make (someone) remember the past **2** withdraw (a statement) ◇**take down** write, note down ◇**take for** believe (mistakenly) to be: *I took him for his brother* ◇**take in 1** include: *the tour takes in many cities* **2** receive: *take in guests* **3** understand: *didn't take in what you said* **4** make smaller: *take in a dress* **5** cheat, deceive ◇**take off 1** remove (clothes *etc*) **2** imitate unkindly **3** of an aircraft: leave the ground **4** (of a product *etc*) be successful ◇**take-off** *noun* ◇**take on 1** undertake (work *etc*) **2** accept (as an opponent): *take you on at tennis* **3** acquire (a new meaning, quality *etc*) **4** give (someone) employment ◇**take over** take control of ◇**takeover** *noun* ◇**take part in** share or help in ◇**take out 1** go out with **2** remove **3** *slang* kill or destroy **4** obtain on application: *take out a warrant* ◇**take place** happen ◇**take to 1** be attracted by **2** begin to do or use regularly: *took to rising early* ◇**take up 1** lift, raise **2** occupy (space, time *etc*) **3** begin to learn, show interest in: *take up playing the harp* **4** resume (a story *etc*) after a pause **5** accept (an offer *etc*)

■ **1** seize, grab, snatch, grasp, hold, catch, capture, get, obtain, acquire, secure, gain **4** convey, carry, bring, transport, ferry, accompany, escort, lead, guide **7** bear, tolerate, stand, stomach, abide, endure, *informal* hack, suffer, undergo, withstand **8** need, necessitate, require, demand, call for **17** remove, eliminate, take away, subtract, deduct ◇**take down** note, record, write down, put down, set down, transcribe ◇**take in 1** contain, include, comprise, incorporate **3** realize, appreciate, understand, comprehend, grasp ◇**take off 2** imitate, mimic, parody, caricature, satirize, mock, send up ◇**take up 2** occupy, fill, engage, engross, absorb, monopolize, use up **3** start, begin, embark on, pursue, carry on, continue

▨ **1** leave, refuse **8** replace, put back

takeaway *noun* **1** a meal prepared and bought in a restaurant or shop but taken away and eaten somewhere else **2** a restaurant or shop providing such meals

taking *adj* pleasing, attractive ◇ *noun* **1** an act of taking **2** (**takings**) money received from things sold

talc *noun* **1** a soft mineral, soapy to the touch **2** *informal* talcum powder ◇ **talcum powder** or **talcum** a fine, often perfumed, powder made from talc, used for rubbing on the body

tale *noun* **1** a story **2** an untrue story, a lie
▄ **1** story, yarn, anecdote, *informal* spiel, narrative, account, report, fable, myth, legend, saga **2** lie, fib, falsehood, untruth, fabrication

talent *noun* **1** a special ability or skill: *a talent for music* **2** high ability
▄ **1** gift, endowment, genius, flair, feel, knack, bent, aptitude, faculty, skill, ability, capacity, strength, forte
▨ **1**, **2** inability, weakness

talented *adj* skilled, gifted
▄ gifted, brilliant, well-endowed, versatile, accomplished, able, capable, proficient, adept, adroit, deft, clever, skilful
▨ inept

talisman *noun* an object believed to have magic powers; a charm

talk *verb* **1** speak; convey ideas using the voice, sign language *etc* **2** gossip **3** discuss: *talk business* ◇ *noun* **1** conversation **2** gossip **3** the subject of conversation: *the talk is of revolution* **4** a discussion or lecture: *gave a talk on stained glass* ◇ **talk back** answer impudently ◇ **talk down 1** silence by speaking aggressively **2** (with **to**) speak condescendingly (to) ◇ **talk over 1** discuss **2** persuade ◇ **talk round 1** discuss without coming to the main point **2** persuade ◇ **talk shop** *see* **shop**
▄ *verb* **1** speak, utter, articulate, say **2** chat, gossip, *informal* natter, chatter ◇ *noun* **1** conversation, dialogue, discussion, meeting, consultation **2** chat, chatter, *informal* natter, gossip, hearsay, rumour, tittle-tattle **4** lecture, seminar, speech, address, discourse

talkative *adj* inclined to chatter
▄ garrulous, voluble, vocal, communicative, forthcoming, unreserved, expansive, chatty, gossipy, verbose, wordy
▨ taciturn, quiet, reserved

talking-to *noun* a scolding
▄ lecture, *informal* dressing-down, *informal* telling-off, *informal* ticking-off, scolding, reprimand, rebuke, reproof, reproach, criticism
▨ praise, commendation

tall *adj* **1** high or higher than average **2** hard to believe: *tall story* ◇ **tallness** *noun* ◇ **tall order** a request to do something awkward or unreasonable
▄ **1** high, lofty, elevated, soaring, towering, big, great, giant, gigantic
▨ **1** short, low, small

tallboy *noun* a tall kind of chest of drawers

tallow *noun* animal fat melted down to make soap, candles *etc*

tally *noun* (*plural* **tallies**) **1** a counting up (of scores, work done *etc*) **2** a ticket, a label **3** *old* a notched stick for keeping a score ◇ *verb* (**tallies**, **tallying**, **tallied**) agree (with): *his story doesn't tally with yours*
▄ *noun* **1** record, count, total, score, reckoning, account ◇ *verb* agree, concur, tie in, square, accord, harmonize, coincide, correspond, match, conform, suit, fit
▨ *verb* disagree, differ

tally-ho *exclam* a cry used by fox-hunters

Talmud *noun* the basic code of Jewish civil and canon law ◇ **Talmudic** or **Talmudical** *adj*

tamarind *noun* a tropical tree which produces long brown seed pods filled with a sweet-tasting pulp

tambourine *noun* a small one-sided drum with tinkling metal discs set into the sides

tame *adj* **1** of an animal: not wild, used to living with humans **2** docile, submissive **3** dull, not exciting ◇ *verb* **1** make (an animal) used to living with humans **2** make meek, subdue

■ *adj* **1** domesticated, broken in, trained, disciplined, manageable, tractable **2** amenable, gentle, docile, meek, submissive, obedient **3** dull, boring, tedious, uninteresting, flat, bland, insipid, weak, feeble, uninspired, unadventurous, unenterprising, lifeless, spiritless ◇ *verb* **1** domesticate, housetrain, break in, train, discipline **2** master, conquer, repress, suppress, subdue, temper, soften, mellow, calm, pacify, humble

■ *adj* **1, 2** wild, unmanageable, rebellious **3** exciting, lively

tamper *verb*: **tamper with** meddle with so as to damage or alter

■ interfere, meddle, *informal* mess, tinker, fiddle, fix, rig, manipulate, alter, damage

tampon *noun* a plug of cotton-wool inserted into the vagina to absorb blood during menstruation

tan *verb* (**tans, tanning, tanned**) **1** make or become brown, *eg* by exposure to the sun **2** make (animal skin) into leather by treating with tannin ◇ *noun* **1** a yellowish-brown colour **2** a suntan

tandem *noun* a long bicycle with two seats and two sets of pedals one behind the other ◇ *adv* one behind the other ◇ **in tandem** together, in conjunction

tandoori *noun* a style of Indian cookery in which food is baked over charcoal in a clay oven

tang *noun* a strong taste, flavour or smell: *the tang of lemons* ◇ **tangy** *adj*

tangent *noun* a straight line which touches a circle or curve without crossing it ◇ **go off at a tangent** go off suddenly in another direction or line of thought

tangential *adj* **1** of a tangent **2** peripheral, irrelevant

tangerine *noun* a small type of orange

Originally meaning 'from Tangiers', from where the fruit was exported in the 19th century

tangible *adj* **1** able to be felt by touching **2** real, definite: *tangible profits* ◇ **tangibly** *adv*

■ **1** touchable, tactile, palpable, solid, concrete, material, substantial, physical **2** real, actual, perceptible, discernible, evident, manifest, definite, positive

■ **1, 2** intangible, abstract, unreal

tangle *verb* **1** twist together in knots **2** make or become difficult or confusing **3** (with **with**) become involved in an argument *etc* (with) ◇ *noun* **1** a twisted mass of knots **2** a confused situation ◇ **tangled** *adj*

■ *verb* **1** entangle, knot, snarl, ravel, twist, coil, interweave, interlace, intertwine, ensnare **2** embroil, implicate, muddle, confuse ◇ *noun* **1** knot, snarl-up, twist, coil, convolution, mesh, web **2** mix-up, confusion, entanglement, embroilment, complication

■ *verb* **1** disentangle

tango *noun* (*plural* **tangos**) a ballroom dance with long steps and pauses, originally from South America

tank *noun* **1** a large container for water, petrol *etc* **2** a heavy armoured vehicle which moves on caterpillar wheels

tankard *noun* a large drinking mug

tanker *noun* **1** a ship or large lorry for carrying liquids, *eg* oil **2** an aircraft carrying fuel

tanner *noun* someone who works at tanning leather ◇ **tannery** *noun* (*plural* **tanneries**) a place where leather is made

tannin *noun* a bitter-tasting substance found in tea, red wine *etc*, also used in tanning and dyeing

tantalize *verb* torment by offering something and keeping it out of reach ◇ **tantalizing** *adj*

■ tease, taunt, torment, torture, provoke, lead on, titillate, tempt, entice, bait, frustrate

■ gratify, satisfy, fulfil

tantamount *adj*: **tantamount to** coming to the same thing as, equivalent to: *tantamount to stealing*

■ as good as, equivalent, commensurate,

equal, synonymous, the same as

tantrum *noun* a fit of rage or bad temper

Taoism *noun* an ancient Chinese philosophy emphasizing unity underlying all things ◇**Taoist** *noun & adj*

tap¹ *noun* **1** a light touch or knock **2** tapdancing ◇*verb* (**taps, tapping, tapped**) knock or strike lightly
■ *noun* **1** knock, rap, beat, pat, touch ◇ *verb* hit, strike, knock, rap, beat, drum, pat, touch

tap² *noun* a device with a valve for controlling the flow of liquid, gas *etc* ◇ *verb* **1** draw on **2** start using (a supply *etc*) **3** attach a listening device secretly to (a telephone) **4** *informal* obtain money from
■ **1** siphon, milk, drain, mine, quarry **2** use, utilize, exploit

tapas *noun, plural* savoury snacks, *orig* Spanish style

tapdance *noun* a dance done with special shoes that make a tapping sound ◇*verb* perform a tapdance ◇**tapdancing** *noun*

tape *noun* **1** a narrow band or strip used for tying **2** a strip of magnetic material for recording sound or pictures **3** a length of tape with sound or pictures recorded on it **4** a strip of thin plastic with a sticky surface, used for fastening *etc* **5** a piece of string over the finishing line on a racetrack **6** a tape-measure ◇*verb* **1** fasten with tape **2** record on tape ◇**have someone taped** have a good understanding of their character or worth

tape-measure *noun* a narrow strip of paper, plastic *etc* used for measuring distance

taper *noun* **1** a long, thin kind of candle **2** a long waxed wick used for lighting oil lamps *etc* ◇ *verb* make or become thinner at one end ◇**tapering** *adj* ◇**taper off** become gradually less
■ *verb* less, narrow, attenuate, thin, slim ◇ **taper off** decrease, reduce, lessen, dwindle, fade, wane, peter out, tail off, die away
🗷 *verb* widen, flare

tape-recorder *noun* an instrument for recording sound *etc* on magnetic tape

tapestry *noun* (*plural* **tapestries**) a cloth with designs or figures woven into it, used to decorate walls or cover furniture

tapeworm *noun* a type of long worm sometimes found in the intestines of humans and animals

tapioca *noun* a starchy food obtained from the root of the cassava plant

tapir *noun* a kind of wild animal something like a large pig

tar *noun* **1** a thick, black, sticky liquid derived from wood or coal, used in roadmaking *etc* **2** a similar substance *esp* the residue from tobacco ◇ *verb* (**tars, tarring, tarred**) smear with tar ◇**tarry** *adj* ◇**tarred with the same brush** (**as**) having the same faults (as)

taramasalata *noun* a Middle Eastern paste made from smoked cod's roe

tarantella *noun* a lively dance for pairs, originally from Naples

tarantula *noun* a type of large, poisonous spider

tardy *adj* slow; late ◇**tardiness** *noun*

tare¹ *noun* the weight of a vehicle *etc* when empty

tare² *noun* a weed

target *noun* **1** a mark to aim at in shooting, darts *etc* **2** a result or sum that is aimed at: *a target of £3000* **3** someone at whom unfriendly remarks are aimed: *the target of her criticism* ◇ *verb* aim at
■ *noun* **2** aim, object, end, purpose, intention, ambition, goal, destination, objective **3** butt, mark, victim, prey, quarry

tariff *noun* **1** a list of prices **2** a list of taxes payable on goods brought into a country

tarmac *noun* the surface of a road or airport runway, made of tarmacadam ◇*verb* (**tarmacs, tarmacking, tarmacked**) surface with tarmacadam

tarmacadam *noun* a mixture of small stones and tar used to make road surfaces *etc*

tarnish *verb* **1** of metal: (cause to) become dull or discoloured **2** spoil (a reputation *etc*)

▣ **1** discolour, corrode, rust, dull, dim, darken, blacken, sully, taint, stain **2** taint, blemish, spot, blot, mar, spoil

▣ **1** polish, brighten

tarot /'taroʊ/ *noun* a system of fortune-telling using special cards divided into suits

tarpaulin *noun* **1** strong waterproof cloth **2** a sheet of this material

tarragon *noun* a herb used in cooking

tarry *verb* (**tarries, tarrying, tarried**) **1** stay behind, linger **2** be slow or late

tart[1] *noun* a small pie containing fruit, vegetables *etc*

tart[2] *adj* **1** sharp, sour **2** sarcastic, cutting ◇ **tartness** *noun*

▣ *adj* **1** sharp, acid, sour, bitter, tangy, piquant, pungent, biting, caustic, astringent

▣ *adj* **1** bland, sweet

tart[3] *noun, slang* a promiscuous woman or a prostitute ◇ **tarty** *adj* ◇ **tart up** dress up or decorate

tartan *noun* **1** fabric patterned with squares of different colours, traditionally used by Scottish Highland clans **2** one of these patterns: *Macdonald tartan* ◇ *adj* with a pattern of tartan

tartar *noun* **1** a substance that gathers on the teeth **2** a difficult or demanding person

task *noun* a set piece of work to be done ◇ **task force** a group of people gathered together with the purpose of performing a special or specific task ◇ **take to task** scold, find fault with

▣ job, chore, duty, charge, assignment, exercise, mission, errand, undertaking, enterprise, business, occupation, activity, employment, work, labour, toil, burden

taskmaster *noun* someone who sets and supervises tasks

tassel *noun* a hanging bunch of threads, used to decorate a hat *etc*

taste *verb* **1** perceive flavour in the mouth **2** try by eating or drinking a sample **3** recognize (a flavour): *can you taste the chilli in it?* **4** have a particular flavour: *tasting of garlic* **5** experience: *taste success* ◇ *noun* **1** the act or sense of tasting **2** a flavour **3** a small quantity of something **4** a liking: *taste for literature* **5** ability to judge what is suitable in behaviour, dress *etc*, or what is fine or beautiful

▣ *verb* **2** nibble, sip, try, test **3** distinguish, discern, perceive **5** experience, undergo, feel, encounter, meet, know ◇ *noun* **2** flavour, savour, relish, smack, tang **3** sample, bit, piece, morsel, titbit, bite, nibble, mouthful, sip, drop, dash, soupçon **4** liking, fondness, partiality, preference, inclination, leaning, penchant, desire, appetite **5** discrimination, discernment, judgement, perception, appreciation, sensitivity, refinement, polish, culture, cultivation, breeding, decorum, finesse, style, elegance, tastefulness

▣ *noun* **2** blandness **4** distaste **5** tastelessness

tasteful *adj* showing good taste and judgement ◇ **tastefully** *adv* ◇ **tastefulness** *noun*

▣ refined, polished, cultured, cultivated, elegant, smart, stylish, artistic, harmonious, beautiful, exquisite, delicate, graceful, correct, fastidious, discriminating

▣ tasteless, garish, tawdry

tasteless *adj* **1** without flavour **2** not tasteful; vulgar ◇ **tastelessly** *adv* ◇ **tastelessness** *noun*

▣ **1** flavourless, insipid, bland, mild, weak, watery, flat, stale, dull, boring, uninteresting, *informal* vanilla, vapid **2** inelegant, graceless, unseemly, improper, indiscreet, crass, rude, crude, vulgar, *slang* naff, cheesy, cheap, flashy, gaudy, garish, loud

▣ **1** tasty **2** tasteful, elegant

tasty *adj* having a good flavour

▣ luscious, palatable, appetizing, mouth-watering, delicious, flavoursome, succulent, *informal* scrumptious, *informal* yummy, piquant, savoury, sweet

▣ tasteless, insipid

tat *noun* shabby articles; rubbish ◇ **tatty** *adj* shabby, tawdry

tatters *noun plural* torn, ragged pieces ◇ **tattered** *adj* ragged

tattie *noun*, *Scot* a potato

tattle *noun* gossip

tattoo¹ *noun* a coloured design on the skin, made by pricking with needles and inserting dyes ◇ *verb* prick coloured designs into the skin ◇ **tattooed** *adj* marked with tattoos

tattoo² *noun* 1 a drumbeat 2 an outdoor military display with music *etc*

From a Dutch term meaning to shut off beer taps at closing time, later applied to a military drumbeat at the end of the day

taught *past form* of **teach**

taunt *verb* tease or jeer at unkindly ◇ *noun* a jeer

▤ *verb* tease, torment, provoke, bait, goad, jeer, mock, ridicule, gibe, *slang* rib, deride, sneer, insult, revile, reproach ◇ *noun* jeer, gibe, dig, sneer, insult, reproach, taunting, teasing, provocation, ridicule, sarcasm, derision, censure

Originally a phrase *taunt for taunt*, based on the French *tant pour tant* meaning 'tit for tat'

taut *adj* 1 pulled tight 2 tense, strained ◇ **tauten** *verb* make or become tight

▤ 1 tight, stretched, contracted 2 strained, tense, unrelaxed, stiff, rigid

▨ 1 slack, loose 2 relaxed

tautology *noun* a form of repetition in which the same thing is said in different ways, *eg* 'he looked *anxious* and *worried*' ◇ **tautological** *adj*

tavern *noun*, *old* a public house, an inn

tawdry *adj* cheap-looking and gaudy

▤ cheap, vulgar, tasteless, fancy, showy, flashy, gaudy, garish, tinselly, glittering

▨ fine, tasteful

From *St Audrey's lace*, once used to make cheap lace neckties

tawny *adj* yellowish-brown

tax *noun* (*plural* **taxes**) 1 a charge made by the government on income, certain types of goods *etc* 2 a strain, a burden: *severe tax on my patience* ◇ *verb* 1 make to pay a tax 2 to put a strain on: *taxing her strength* ◇ **tax with** accuse of

▣ *noun* 1 levy, charge, rate, tariff, customs 2 imposition, burden, load ◇ *verb* 2 burden, load, strain, stretch, try, tire, weary, exhaust, drain, sap, weaken

Taxes include:
airport tax, capital gains tax, capital transfer tax, community charge, corporation tax, council tax, customs, death duty, estate duty, excise, income tax, inheritance tax, PAYE, poll tax, property tax, rates, surtax, tithe, toll, value added tax (VAT)

taxation *noun* 1 the act or system of taxing 2 taxes

taxi *noun* (*plural* **taxis**) a vehicle which may be hired, with a driver (*also called*: **taxi-cab**) ◇ *verb* (**taxies**, **taxiing**, **taxied**) 1 travel in a taxi 2 of an aeroplane: travel on the runway before or after take-off ◇ **taxi rank** a place where taxis park to wait for hire

taxidermy *noun* the art of preparing and stuffing the skins of animals to make them lifelike ◇ **taxidermist** *noun* someone who does this work

taxpayer *noun* someone who pays taxes

TB *abbrev* tuberculosis

tea *noun* 1 a plant grown in India, China *etc*, or its dried and prepared leaves 2 a drink made by infusing its dried leaves 3 a hot drink, an infusion: *beef tea/camomile tea* 4 an afternoon or early evening meal ◇ **tea chest** a tall box of thin wood used to pack tea for export, often used as a packing case when empty

teacake *noun* a light, flat bun

teach *verb* (**teaches**, **teaching**, **taught**) 1 give (someone) skill or knowledge 2 give knowledge of, or training in (a subject): *she teaches*

French **3** be a teacher: *decide to teach*

🔳 **1** instruct, train, coach, tutor, lecture, ground, verse, school, educate, enlighten, edify, inform, advise, counsel, guide

teacher *noun* someone employed to teach others in a school, or in a particular subject: *guitar teacher*

🔳 schoolteacher, schoolmaster, master, schoolmistress, mistress, educator, pedagogue, tutor, lecturer, professor, don, instructor, trainer, coach, mentor

teaching *noun* **1** the work of a teacher **2** guidance, instruction **3** (**teachings**) beliefs or rules of conduct that are preached or taught

teacup *noun* a medium-sized cup for drinking tea ◇ **storm in a teacup** *see* **storm**

teak *noun* **1** a hardwood tree from the East Indies **2** its very hard wood

teal *noun* **1** a small water-bird like a duck **2** a greenish-blue colour

team *noun* **1** a group of people working together **2** a side in a game: *a football team* **3** two or more animals working together: *team of oxen* ◇ **team spirit** willingness to work as part of a team ◇ **team up with** join together with, join forces with

🔳 **1** squad, shift, crew, gang, band, group, company **2** side, line-up, squad ◇ **team up with** join, unite, combine, band together, co-operate, collaborate, work together

⚠ Do not confuse with: **teem**

teapot *noun* a pot with a spout, for making and pouring tea

tear[1] /tɪə(r)/ *noun* **1** a drop of liquid from the eye **2** (**tears**) grief ◇ **tear gas** gas which causes the eyes to stream with tears ◇ **in tears** weeping

tear[2] /tɛə(r)/ *verb* (**tears**, **tearing**, **torn**, **tore**) **1** pull with force: *tear apart/tear down* **2** make a hole or split in (material *etc*) **3** come apart **4** *informal* rush: *tearing off down the road* ◇ *noun* a hole or split made by tearing

🔳 *verb* **1** pull, snatch, grab, seize, wrest **2** rip, rend, divide, rupture, sever, shred, scratch, gash, lacerate, mutilate, man-gle **4** dash, rush, hurry, speed, race, run, sprint, fly, shoot, dart, bolt, *informal* belt, career, charge ◇ *noun* rip, rent, slit, hole, split, rupture, scratch, gash, laceration

tearful *adj* **1** inclined to weep **2** in tears, crying ◇ **tearfully** *adv*

🔳 **1** emotional, *informal* weepy **2** crying, weeping, sobbing, whimpering, blubbering, sad, sorrowful, upset, distressed

🔳 **2** happy, smiling, laughing

tease *verb* **1** annoy, irritate on purpose **2** pretend to upset or annoy for fun: *I'm only teasing* **3** untangle (wool *etc*) with a comb **4** sort out (a problem or puzzle) ◇ *noun* someone who teases

🔳 *verb* **1** taunt, provoke, bait, annoy, irritate, *informal* aggravate, *informal* needle, badger, worry, pester, plague, harass, torment, tantalize, mock, ridicule **2** gibe, banter, *slang* rag, *slang* rib

teasel *noun* a type of prickly plant

teaser *noun* a problem, a puzzle

teaspoon *noun* a small spoon

teat *noun* **1** the part of an animal through which milk passes to its young **2** a rubber object shaped like this attached to a baby's feeding bottle

tea-towel *noun* a cloth for drying dishes

technical *adj* **1** relating to a particular art or skill, *esp* a mechanical or industrial one: *what is the technical term for this?/a technical expert* **2** according to strict laws or rules: *technical defeat*

🔳 **1** scientific, specialized, expert, professional

technicality *noun* (*plural* **technicalities**) a technical detail or point

technically *adv* according to the rules, strictly speaking

technician *noun* someone trained in the practical side of an art

technique *noun* the way in which a process is carried out; a method

🔳 method, system, procedure, manner, fashion, style, mode, way, means, approach, course, performance, delivery, artistry, craftsmanship, skill, proficiency, expertise, *informal* know-how, art, craft, knack, touch

technology *noun* **1** science applied to practical (*esp* industrial) purposes **2** the practical skills of a particular civilization, period *etc* ◇ **technological** *adj* ◇ **technologically** *adv* ◇ **technologist** *noun*

teddy or **teddybear** *noun* (*plural* **teddies** or **teddybears**) **1** a stuffed toy bear **2** (**teddy**) a one-piece woman's undergarment

tedious *adj* long and tiresome ◇ **tediously** *adv* ◇ **tedium** *noun*

▣ boring, monotonous, uninteresting, unexciting, dull, dreary, drab, banal, humdrum, tiresome, tiring, laborious, long-winded, long-drawn-out

▨ lively, interesting, exciting

tee *noun* **1** the square of level ground from which a golfball is driven **2** the peg or sand heap on which the ball is placed for driving ◇ **tee up** place (a ball) on a tee

teem *verb* **1** be full: *teeming with people* **2** rain heavily

> ⚠ Do not confuse with: **team**

teenage *adj* suitable for, or typical of, those in their teens ◇ **teenager** *noun* someone in their teens ◇ **teens** *noun plural* the years of age from thir*teen* to nine*teen*

teeny *adj*, *informal* tiny, minute

tee-shirt or **T-shirt** *noun* a short-sleeved shirt pulled on over the head

teeth *plural* of **tooth**

teethe *verb* of a baby: grow its first teeth ◇ **teething troubles 1** pain caused by growing teeth **2** difficulties encountered at the beginning of an undertaking

teetotal *adj* never drinking alcohol ◇ **teetotaller** *noun*

▣ temperate, abstinent, abstemious, sober, *slang* on the wagon

telecommunications *noun plural* the sending of information by telephone, radio, television *etc*

telecommuter *noun* someone who works at home and communicates with the office by phone, computer *etc*

telegram *noun* a message sent by telegraph

telegraph *noun* an instrument for sending messages to a distance using electrical impulses ◇ *verb* send (a message) by telegraph ◇ **telegraphic** *adj* **1** of a telegraph **2** short, brief, concise

telekinesis *noun* the movement of objects from a distance through will-power not touch

teleology *noun* the philosophy of viewing things in terms of their purpose, not their cause ◇ **teleologist** *noun*

telepathy *noun* communication between people without using sight, hearing *etc* ◇ **telepathic** *adj*

▣ mind-reading, thought transference, sixth sense, clairvoyance

telephone *noun* an instrument for speaking over distances, which uses an electric current travelling along a wire, or radio waves ◇ *verb* send (a message) by telephone

▣ *verb* phone, ring (up), call (up), dial, *informal* buzz, contact, get in touch

telephonist *noun* an operator on a telephone switchboard

telephoto *adj* of a lens: used to photograph enlarged images of distant objects

teleprinter *noun* a typewriter which receives and prints out messages sent by telegraph

telescope *noun* a tubular instrument fitted with lenses which magnify distant objects ◇ *verb* **1** push or fit together so that one thing slides inside another **2** force together, compress

teletext *noun* news and general information transmitted by television companies, viewable only on special television sets

televise *verb* broadcast on television: *are they televising the football match?*

television *noun* **1** the reproduction on a small screen of pictures sent from a distance **2** an apparatus for receiving these pictures

▣ **2** TV, receiver, set, *informal* telly, *informal* the box, *informal* goggle-box, *informal* idiot box, small screen

teleworker *noun* someone who works from home and communicates with their employer by computer, fax *etc*

telex *noun* **1** the sending of messages by means of teleprinters **2** a message sent in this way

tell *verb* (**tells**, **telling**, **told**) **1** say or express in words: *she's telling the truth* **2** give the facts of (a story) **3** inform, give information: *can you tell me when it's 9 o'clock* **4** order, command: *tell him to go away!* **5** make out, distinguish: *I can't tell one wine from the other* **6** give away a secret: *promise not to tell* **7** be effective, produce results: *training will tell in the end* ◇ **all told** altogether, counting all ◇ **tell off** *informal* scold ◇ **tell on 1** have an effect on **2** give information about ◇ **tell tales** give away information about the misdeeds of others

▣ **1** speak, utter, say **2** narrate, recount, relate, report, announce, describe **3** inform, notify, let know, acquaint, impart, communicate **4** order, command, direct, instruct **5** differentiate, distinguish, discriminate, discern, recognize, identify, discover, see, understand, comprehend **6** divulge, disclose, reveal ◇ **tell off** *informal* scold, chide, *informal* tick off, reprimand, rebuke, reprove, lecture, berate, *informal* dress down, *informal* carpet

teller *noun* **1** a bank clerk who receives and pays out money **2** someone who counts votes at an election

telling *adj* having a marked effect: *telling remark*

temerity *noun* rashness, boldness

▣ impudence, impertinence, *informal* cheek, gall, *informal* nerve, audacity, boldness, chutzpah, daring, rashness, recklessness, impulsiveness

▣ caution, prudence

temp *abbrev* **1** temperature **2** temporary ◇ *noun*, *informal* a temporarily employed secretarial worker ◇ *verb*, *informal* work as a temp

temper *noun* **1** habitual state of mind: *of an even temper* **2** a passing mood: *in a good temper* **3** a tendency to get angry easily **4** a fit of anger **5** the amount of hardness in metal, glass *etc* ◇ *verb* **1** make less severe **2** bring (metal *etc*) to the right degree of hardness by heating and cooling ◇ **lose your temper** show anger

▣ *noun* **1** temperament, character, disposition, constitution, nature **2** mood, humour **3** annoyance, irritability, ill-humour **4** rage, fury, passion, tantrum ◇ *verb* **2** modify, lessen, reduce, calm, soothe, allay, assuage, mitigate, modify, soften, sweeten

▣ *noun* **3** calmness, self-control

temperament *noun* someone's nature as it affects the way they feel and act; disposition

▣ nature, character, personality, disposition, tendency, constitution, make-up, spirit, mood, humour, temper, state of mind, attitude, mindset

temperamental *adj* **1** excitable, emotional **2** of a machine *etc*: not working consistently

▣ **1** moody, emotional, neurotic, highly-strung, sensitive, touchy, irritable, impatient, passionate, fiery, excitable, explosive, volatile **2** unpredictable, unreliable

▣ **1** calm, level-headed, steady

temperance *noun* the habit of not drinking much (or any) alcohol

temperate *adj* **1** moderate in temper, eating or drinking *etc* **2** of climate: neither very hot nor very cold

▣ **1** teetotal, abstinent, abstemious, sober, continent, moderate, restrained, controlled, even-tempered, calm, composed, reasonable, sensible **2** mild, clement, balmy, fair, equable, balanced, stable, gentle, pleasant, agreeable

▣ **1** intemperate, extreme, excessive

temperature *noun* **1** degree of heat or cold: *today's temperature* **2** a body heat higher than normal

tempest *noun* a storm, with great wind

tempestuous adj 1 very stormy and windy 2 passionate, violently emotional

■ 1 stormy, windy, gusty, blustery, turbulent, tumultuous 2 wild, violent, furious, raging, heated, passionate, intense

🖙 1, 2 calm

template noun a thin plate cut in a design for drawing round

temple¹ noun a building used for public worship; a church

temple² noun a small flat area on each side of the forehead

tempo noun (plural **tempos** or **tempi**) 1 the speed at which music is played 2 the speed or rate of an activity

temporal adj 1 relating to this world or this life only, not eternal or spiritual 2 relating to time

■ 1 secular, profane, worldly, earthly, terrestrial, material, carnal, fleshly, bodily, mortal

🖙 1 spiritual

temporary adj lasting only for a time, not permanent ◇ **temporarily** adv

■ impermanent, provisional, stopgap, transient, transitory, passing, ephemeral, fleeting, brief, short-lived, momentary

🖙 permanent, everlasting

temporize verb avoid or delay taking action in order to gain time

tempt verb 1 try to persuade or entice 2 attract 3 make inclined (to): tempted to phone him up

■ 1 entice, coax, persuade, woo 2 lure, allure, attract, draw, seduce 3 invite, tantalize, provoke, incite

🖙 1 discourage 2 dissuade, repel

temptation noun 1 the act of tempting 2 the feeling of being tempted 3 something which tempts

■ 2 enticement, inducement, coaxing, persuasion, bait, lure, allure, appeal 3 attraction, draw, pull, seduction, invitation

tempting adj attractive

tempura noun a Japanese dish of fish, vegetables etc fried quickly in batter

ten noun the number 10 ◇ adj 10 in number

tenable adj able to be defended; justifiable

■ credible, defensible, justifiable, reasonable, rational, sound, arguable, believable, defendable, plausible, viable, feasible

🖙 untenable, indefensible, unjustifiable

tenacious adj 1 keeping a firm hold or grip 2 obstinate, persistent, determined ◇ **tenaciously** adv ◇ **tenacity** noun

tenancy noun (plural **tenancies**) 1 the holding of a house, farm etc by a tenant 2 the period of this holding

tenant noun someone who pays rent for the use of a house, land etc

tend verb 1 be likely or inclined to do something: these flowers tend to wilt 2 move or slope in a certain direction 3 take care of, look after

■ 2 incline, lean, bend, bear, head, aim, lead, go, move, gravitate 3 look after, care for, cultivate, keep, maintain, manage, handle, guard, protect, watch, mind, nurture, nurse, minister to, serve, attend

🖙 3 neglect, ignore

tendency noun (plural **tendencies**) a leaning or inclination (towards): tendency to daydream

■ trend, drift, movement, course, direction, bearing, heading, bias, partiality, predisposition, propensity, susceptibility, proneness, inclination

tender¹ adj 1 soft, not hard or tough 2 easily hurt or damaged 3 hurting when touched 4 loving, gentle ◇ **tenderly** adv ◇ **of tender years** very young

■ adj 1 soft, succulent, fleshy, dainty 2 delicate, fragile, frail, weak, feeble 3 sore, painful, aching, smarting, bruised, inflamed, raw 4 kind, gentle, caring, humane, considerate, compassionate, sympathetic, warm, fond, affectionate, loving, amorous, romantic, sentimental, emotional, sensitive, tender-hearted, soft-hearted

▣ *adj* **1** tough, hard **4** hard-hearted, callous

tender² *verb* **1** offer (a resignation, money *etc*) formally **2** (*usu* with **for**) make a formal offer for a job ◊ *noun* an offer to take on work, supply goods *etc* for a fixed price ◊ **legal tender** coins or notes which must be accepted when offered

▣ *verb* **1** offer, proffer, extend, give, present, submit, propose, suggest, advance, volunteer **2** propose, suggest, advance ◊ *noun* offer, bid, estimate, quotation, proposal, proposition, suggestion

tender³ *noun* **1** a person who looks after something **2** a small boat that carries stores for a large one **3** a truck for coal and water attached to a steam engine

tenderfoot *noun* an inexperienced person

tender-hearted *adj* kind, sympathetic

tenderize *verb* soften (meat) before cooking

tendon *noun* a tough cord joining a muscle to a bone

tendril *noun* **1** a thin curling stem of a climbing plant which attaches itself to a support **2** a curling strand of hair *etc*

tenement *noun* a block of flats

tenet *noun* a belief, opinion

tenner *noun*, *informal* a ten-pound note; ten pounds

tennis *noun* a game for two or four players using rackets to hit a ball to each other over a net ◊ **tennis court** a place made level and prepared for tennis

tenon *noun* a projecting part at the end of a piece of wood made to fit a **mortise**

tenor *noun* **1** a singing voice of the highest normal range for an adult male **2** a singer with this voice **3** an instrument, *eg* a viola, with a similar range **4** general course or meaning: *the tenor of the speech*

tenpin bowling a game like skittles played by bowling a ball at ten pins standing at the end of a bowling lane

tense¹ *noun* the form of a verb that shows time of action, *eg* '*I was*' (**past tense**), '*I am*' (**present tense**), '*I shall be*' (**future tense**)

tense² *adj* **1** tightly stretched **2** nervous, strained: *feeling tense/tense with excitement*

▣ **1** tight, taut, stretched, strained, stiff, rigid **2** nervous, anxious, worried, jittery, uneasy, apprehensive, edgy, fidgety, restless, jumpy, overwrought, keyed up, *informal* wired

▣ **1** loose, slack **2** calm, relaxed

tensile *adj* relating to stretching

tension *noun* **1** the state of being stretched **2** strain, anxiety

▣ **1** tightness, tautness, stiffness, strain, stress, pressure **2** nervousness, anxiety, worry, uneasiness, apprehension, edginess, restlessness, suspense

▣ **1** looseness **2** calm(ness), relaxation

tent *noun* a movable shelter of canvas or other material, supported by poles and pegged to the ground

tentacle *noun* a long thin flexible part of an animal used to feel or grasp, *eg* the arm of an octopus ◊ **tentacular** *adj*

tentative *adj* **1** experimental, initial: *a tentative offer* **2** uncertain, hesitating: *tentative smile* ◊ **tentatively** *adv*

▣ **1** experimental, exploratory, speculative, provisional **2** hesitant, faltering, cautious, unsure, uncertain, doubtful, undecided, indefinite, unconfirmed

▣ **1** definite, decisive **2** conclusive, final

tenterhooks *noun plural*: **on tenterhooks** uncertain and very anxious about what will happen

tenth *adj* the last of ten items ◊ *noun* one of ten equal parts

tenuous *adj* slight, weak: *tenuous connection* ◊ **tenuously** *adv*

▣ thin, slim, slender, fine, slight, flimsy, fragile, delicate, weak, shaky, doubtful, dubious, questionable

▣ strong, substantial

tenure *noun* **1** the holding of property

or a position of employment **2** the period, or terms or conditions, of this

tepee *noun* a traditional Native American tent made of animal skins

tepid *adj* **1** lukewarm **2** unenthusiastic

■ **1, 2** lukewarm, cool **2** half-hearted, unenthusiastic, apathetic

🗷 **1, 2** cold, hot **2** passionate

tequila /təˈkiːlə/ *noun* a Mexican alcoholic drink made from the agave plant

tercentenary *noun* the 300th anniversary of an event

term *noun* **1** a length of time: *term of imprisonment* **2** a division of an academic or school year: *autumn term* **3** a word, an expression: *dictionary of computing terms* **4** (**terms**) the rules or conditions of an agreement: *what are their terms?* **5** (**terms**) fixed charges **6** (**terms**) relationship: *on good terms with his neighbours* ◇ *verb* name, call ◇ **come to terms** reach an agreement or understanding ◇ **come to terms with** accept, be able to live with ◇ **in terms of** from the point of view of

■ *noun* **1** time, period, course, duration, spell, span, stretch, interval, space **2** semester, session, season **3** word, name, designation, appellation, title, epithet, phrase, expression **4** conditions, specifications, stipulations, provisos, provisions, qualifications, particulars **5** rates, charges, fees, prices, tariff **6** relations, relationship, footing, standing, position ◇ *verb* call, name, dub, style, designate, label, tag, title, entitle

termagant *noun* a bad-tempered, noisy woman

terminal *adj* **1** of or growing at the end: *terminal bud* **2** of an illness: fatal, incurable ◇ *noun* **1** an end **2** a point of connection in an electric circuit **3** a computer monitor connected to a network **4** an airport building containing arrival and departure areas **5** a bus station in a town centre running a service to a nearby airport ◇ **terminally** *adv*

terminate *verb* bring or come to an end ◇ **termination** *noun*

■ finish, complete, conclude, cease, end,

stop, close, discontinue, wind up, cut off, abort, lapse, expire

🗷 begin, start, initiate

terminology *noun* the special words or expressions used in a particular art, science *etc*

terminus *noun* (*plural* **termini** or **terminuses**) **1** the end **2** an end point on a railway, bus route *etc*

termite *noun* a pale-coloured wood-eating insect, like an ant

tern *noun* a type of sea bird like a small gull

terrace *noun* **1** a raised level bank of earth **2** a raised flat place **3** a connected row of houses **4** (**terraces**) tiered areas in a sports ground, where spectators stand ◇ *verb* form into a terrace or terraces

terracotta *noun* a brownish-red mixture of clay and sand used for tiles, pottery *etc*

terra firma land as opposed to water

terrain *noun* an area of land considered in terms of its physical features: *the terrain is a bit rocky*

■ land, ground, territory, country, countryside, landscape, topography

terrapin *noun* a small turtle living in ponds or rivers

terrarium *noun* (*plural* **terraria** or **terrariums**) an ornamental glass jar containing living plants *etc*

terrestrial *adj* of or living on the earth

terrible *adj* **1** causing great fear: *terrible sight* **2** causing great hardship or distress: *terrible disaster* **3** *informal* very bad: *a terrible writer/a terrible smell*

■ **1** dreadful, shocking, appalling, horrible, gruesome, horrific, harrowing, distressing **2** dreadful, appalling, grave, serious, severe, extreme, desperate **3** bad, awful, frightful, dreadful, disgusting, revolting, repulsive, offensive, unpleasant, vile, hideous

🗷 **3** excellent, wonderful, superb

terribly *adv, informal* **1** badly: *sang terribly* **2** extremely: *terribly tired*

■ **2** very, much, greatly, extremely, exceedingly, awfully, frightfully, decidedly, seriously

terrier *noun* a breed of small dog

terrific *adj* **1** powerful, dreadful **2** huge, amazing **3** *informal* attractive, enjoyable *etc*: *a terrific party*
- **2** huge, enormous, gigantic, tremendous, great, intense, extreme, excessive **3** excellent, wonderful, marvellous, super, *informal* smashing, outstanding, brilliant, magnificent, superb, *informal* fabulous, *informal* fantastic, *slang* mega, sensational, amazing, stupendous, breathtaking

terrify *verb* (**terrifies**, **terrifying**, **terrified**) frighten greatly
- petrify, horrify, appal, shock, terrorize, intimidate, frighten, scare, alarm, dismay

territorial *adj* of, belonging to a territory ◇ **territorial waters** seas close to, and considered to belong to, a country

territory *noun* (*plural* **territories**) **1** an area of land, a region **2** land under the control of a ruler or state **3** an area allocated to a salesman *etc* **4** an area which a bird or animal treats as its own **5** a field of activity or interest

terror *noun* **1** very great fear **2** something which causes great fear **3** *informal* an uncontrollable child
- **1** fear, panic, dread, trepidation, horror, shock, fright, alarm

terrorism *noun* the organized use of violence or intimidation for political or other ends ◇ **terrorist** *noun* someone who practises terrorism

terrorize *verb* frighten very greatly
- threaten, menace, intimidate, oppress, coerce, bully, browbeat, frighten, scare, alarm, terrify, petrify, horrify, shock

terse *adj* using few words; curt, brusque ◇ **tersely** *adv* ◇ **terseness** *noun*
- short, brief, succinct, concise, compact, condensed, epigrammatic, pithy, incisive, snappy, curt, brusque, abrupt
- ⊠ long-winded, verbose

tertiary *adj* third in position or order ◇ **tertiary education** education at university or college level

tessera *noun* (*plural* **tesserae**) one of the small pieces making up a mosaic

test *noun* **1** an examination **2** something done to check soundness, reliability *etc*: *ran tests on the new model* **3** a means of finding the presence of: *test for radioactivity* **4** an event that shows up a good or bad quality: *a test of courage* ◇ *verb* carry out tests on ◇ **test match** *cricket* one of a series of matches between two countries ◇ **test pilot** a pilot who tests new aircraft ◇ **test tube** a glass tube closed at one end, used in chemical tests
- *noun* **1** examination, assessment **2** trial, try-out, experiment, evaluation, check, investigation, analysis ◇ *verb* try, experiment, examine, assess, evaluate, check, investigate, analyse, screen, prove, verify

testament *noun* **1** a written statement **2** a will ◇ **Old Testament** and **New Testament** the two main divisions of the Christian Bible

testate *adj* having left a valid will

testator *noun* the writer of a will ◇ **testatory** *adj* of a will or testament

testicle *noun* one of two sperm-producing glands enclosed in the male scrotum

testify *verb* (**testifies**, **testifying**, **testified**) **1** give evidence in a law court **2** make a solemn declaration of **3** (**testify to**) show, give evidence of: *testifies to his ignorance*
- **2** declare, assert, swear, avow, attest, vouch, certify, corroborate

testimonial *noun* **1** a personal statement about someone's character, abilities *etc* **2** a gift given in thanks for services given **3** *sport* a match held in honour of a player, who receives the proceeds

testimony *noun* (*plural* **testimonies**) **1** the statement made by someone who testifies **2** evidence

testis *noun* (*plural* **testes**) *formal* a testicle

testosterone *noun* the chief male sex hormone, secreted by the testicles

testy *adj* easily angered, irritable ◇ **testily** *adv* ◇ **testiness** *noun*

tetanus *noun* a disease, caused *esp* by an infected wound, causing stiffening and spasms in the jaw muscles (*also called*: **lockjaw**)

tetchy *adj* irritable, testy ◇ **tetchily** *adv* ◇ **tetchiness** *noun*

tête-à-tête /teɪtəˈteɪt/ or /tɛtəˈtɛt/ *noun* a private talk between two people

tether *noun* a rope or chain for tying an animal to restrict its movement ◇ *verb* **1** tie with a tether **2** limit the freedom of ◇ **at the end of your tether** having reached the limit of your patience *etc*

☒ *noun* chain, rope, cord, line, lead, leash, bond, fetter, shackle, restraint, fastening ◇ *verb* **1** tie, fasten, secure, restrain, chain, rope, leash, bind, lash

Teutonic *adj* Germanic

text *noun* **1** the written or printed part of a book, not the pictures, notes *etc* **2** a printed or written version of a speech, play *etc* **3** a Biblical passage used as the basis for a sermon **4** the subject matter of a speech, essay *etc*

☒ **1** words, wording **2** passage, paragraph, sentence, book **4** subject, topic, theme

textbook *noun* a book used for teaching, giving the main facts about a subject

textile *noun* a woven cloth or fabric ◇ *adj* of weaving; woven

textual *adj* of or in a text ◇ **textually** *adv*

texture *noun* **1** the quality of cloth resulting from weaving: *loose texture* **2** the quality of a substance in terms of how it looks or feels: *rough texture/lumpy texture*

☒ **1** grain, weave, tissue, fabric **2** consistency, feel, surface, composition

than *conj & prep* used in comparisons: *easier than I expected/better than usual* ◇ *conj* used to introduce an alternative: *would rather walk than drive*

thane *noun*, *hist* a noble who held land from the crown

thank *verb* express gratitude to (someone) for a favour, gift *etc* ◇ **thanks** *noun plural* gratitude; appreciation: *you'll get no thanks for it* ◇ **thanks to 1** with the help of: *we arrived on time, thanks to our friends* **2** owing to: *we were late, thanks to our car breaking down* ◇ **thank you** or **thanks** a polite expression used to thank someone

☒ say thank you, be grateful, appreciate, acknowledge, recognize, credit ◇ **thanks** gratitude, gratefulness, appreciation, acknowledgment, recognition, credit

thankful *adj* grateful; relieved and glad ◇ **thankfully** *adv* ◇ **thankfulness** *noun*

☒ grateful, appreciative, obliged, indebted, pleased, contented, relieved

☒ ungrateful, unappreciative

thankless *adj* neither worthwhile nor appreciated: *thankless task*

☒ unrecognized, unappreciated, unrequited, unrewarding, unprofitable, fruitless

☒ rewarding, worthwhile

thanksgiving *noun* **1** a church service giving thanks to God **2** (**Thanksgiving**) *US* the fourth Thursday of November, a national holiday commemorating the first harvest of the Puritan settlers

that *adj & pronoun* (*plural* **those**) used to point out a thing or person *etc* (*contrasted with*: **this**): *that woman over there/don't say that* ◇ *relative pronoun* used to introduce a relative clause that distinguishes or restricts the person or thing mentioned in the previous clause: *those are the colours that he chose/the man that I spoke to* ◇ *adv* to such an extent or degree: *why were you that late?* ◇ *conj* **1** used in reporting speech: *she said that she was there* **2** used to connect clauses: *I heard that you were ill*

thatch *noun* straw *etc* used to make the roof of a house ◇ *verb* cover with thatch

thaw *verb* **1** melt **2** of frozen food: defrost, become unfrozen **3** become friendly ◇ *noun* **1** the melting of ice and snow by heat **2** a change in the weather that causes this

■ *verb* **1** melt, soften, liquefy, dissolve **2** melt, defrost, defreeze, de-ice

the *adj* **1** referring to a particular person or thing: *the boy in the park/I like the jacket I'm wearing* **2** referring to all or any of a general group: *the horse is of great use to man*

theatre or *US* **theater** *noun* **1** a place for the public performance of plays, lectures *etc* **2** the acting profession **3** a room in a hospital for surgical operations

theatrical *adj* **1** of theatres or acting **2** over-dramatic, overdone ◇ **theatricality** *noun*

■ **2** melodramatic, histrionic, mannered, affected, artificial, ostentatious, showy, extravagant, exaggerated, over the top, *informal* OTT, overdone

Theatrical forms include:
ballet, burlesque, cabaret, circus, comedy, black comedy, comedy of humours, comedy of manners, comedy of menace, commedia dell'arte, duologue, farce, fringe theatre, Grand Guignol, kabuki, Kensington gore, Kitchen-Sink, legitimate drama, masque, melodrama, mime, miracle play, monologue, morality play, mummery, musical, musical comedy, music hall, mystery play, Noh, opera, operetta, pageant, pantomime, play, Punch and Judy, puppet theatre, revue, street theatre, tableau, theatre-in-the-round, Theatre of the Absurd, Theatre of Cruelty, tragedy

thee *pronoun, old* you (*sing*) as the object of a sentence

theft *noun* stealing

■ robbery, thieving, stealing, pilfering, shoplifting, kleptomania, fraud, embezzlement

their *adj* belonging to them: *their car* ◇ **theirs** *pronoun*: *the red car is theirs*

🚫 Do not confuse with: **there**

theism *noun* belief in the existence of God ◇ **theistic** or **theistical** *adj*

them *pronoun plural* **1** people or things already spoken about (as the object of a verb): *we've seen them* **2** *informal* those: *one of them over in the corner* ◇ *pronoun sing* used to avoid giving the gender of the person being referred to: *if anyone phones, ask them to leave their number*

theme *noun* **1** the subject of a discussion, essay *etc* **2** *music* a main melody which is often repeated ◇ **theme park** a public display in an open area, related to a single theme ◇ **theme song** or **theme tune** a tune that is repeated often in a film, television series *etc*

■ **1** subject, topic, thread, motif, idea, gist, essence, argument, thesis

themselves *pronoun plural* **1** used reflexively: *they tired themselves out walking* **2** used for emphasis: *they'll have to do it by themselves*

then *adv* **1** at that time: *I didn't know you then* **2** after that: *and then where did you go?* ◇ *conj* in that case, therefore: *if you're busy, then don't come*

thence *adv, old* from that time or place

thenceforth *adv* from that time onward

theocracy *noun* government of a state according to religious laws ◇ **theocratic** *adj*

theodolite *noun* an instrument for measuring angles, used in surveying

theology *noun* the study of God and religion ◇ **theologian** *noun* someone who studies theology ◇ **theological** *adj*

theorem *noun* a proposition to be proved in mathematics *etc*

theoretical *adj* of theory, not experience or practice ◇ **theoretically** *adv*

■ hypothetical, conjectural, speculative, abstract, academic, doctrinaire, pure, ideal

🔁 practical, applied, concrete

theorize *verb* form theories

theory *noun* (*plural* **theories**) **1** an explanation that has not been proved or tested **2** the underlying ideas in an art, science *etc*, compared to practice or performance

therapeutic *adj* **1** of therapy **2** healing, curing
- **2** remedial, curative, healing, restorative, tonic, medicinal, corrective, good, beneficial
- **2** harmful, detrimental

therapist *noun* someone who gives therapeutic treatment: *speech therapist*

therapy *noun* (*plural* **therapies**) treatment of disease or disorders

there *adv* at, in or to that place: *what did you do there?* ◇ *pronoun* used (with *be*) as a subject of a sentence or clause when the real subject follows the verb: *there is nobody at home*

⚠ Do not confuse with: **their**

thereabouts *adv* approximately

thereafter *adv* after that

thereby *adv* by that means

therefore *adv* for this or that reason
- so, then, consequently, as a result

theremin *noun* an electronic device which produces vibrating synthetic sounds, used in film special effects *etc*

thereof *adv* of that

thereupon *adv* **1** because of this or that **2** immediately

therm *noun* a unit of heat used in measuring gas

thermal *adj* **1** of heat **2** of clothing: designed to prevent loss of body heat

thermodynamics *noun sing* the science of the relation between heat and mechanical energy

thermometer *noun* an instrument for measuring temperature

thermonuclear *adj* relating to the fusion of nuclei at high temperatures

Thermos *noun*, *trademark* a kind of vacuum flask

thermostat *noun* a device for automatically controlling temperature in a room

thesaurus *noun* (*plural* **thesauri** or **thesauruses**) a reference book or word processing facility listing words and their synonyms

thesis *noun* (*plural* **theses**) **1** a long piece of written work on a topic, often part of a university degree **2** a statement of a point of view
- **1** dissertation, essay, composition, paper **2** idea, opinion, view, theory, hypothesis, proposal, proposition, premise, statement, argument

thespian *noun*, *formal* an actor

Named after *Thespis*, founder of ancient Greek tragedy

they *pronoun plural* some people or things already mentioned (used only as the subject of a verb): *they followed the others* ◇ *pronoun sing* used to avoid giving the gender of the person being referred to: *anyone can come if they like*

thick *adj* **1** not thin, of reasonable distance between sides: *a thick slice/two metres thick* **2** having a specified distance between sides **3** of a mixture: containing solid matter, stiff: *a thick soup* **4** dense, difficult to see or pass through: *thick fog/thick woods* **5** of speech: not clear **6** *informal* stupid **7** *informal* very friendly ◇ *noun* the thickest, most crowded or active part: *in the thick of the fight* ◇ **thick as thieves** very close ◇ **through thick and thin** whatever happens
- *adj* **1** wide, broad **3** viscous, coagulated, clotted **4** heavy, solid, dense, impenetrable, close **6** *informal* stupid, foolish, slow, dull, dim-witted, brainless, simple

thicken *verb* **1** make or become thick **2** become more complicated
- **1** condense, stiffen, congeal, coagulate, clot, cake, gel, set
- thin

thicket *noun* a group of close-set trees and bushes

thickness *noun* **1** the quality of being thick **2** the distance between opposite sides **3** a layer
- **1** density, viscosity **2** width, breadth,

diameter, bulk, body **3** layer, stratum, ply, sheet, coat

▣ 1 thinness

thickset *adj* **1** closely set or planted **2** having a thick sturdy body

thick-skinned *adj* not sensitive or easily hurt

thief *noun* (*plural* **thieves**) someone who steals

▤ robber, bandit, mugger, pickpocket, shoplifter, burglar, housebreaker, poacher, stealer, pilferer, filcher, kleptomaniac, swindler

thieve *verb* steal ◇**thieving** *noun* ◇**thievish** *adj* inclined to stealing

thigh *noun* the thick, fleshy part of the leg between the knee and the hip

thimble *noun* a small cap worn over a fingertip, used to push a needle while sewing

thin *adj* **1** not very wide between its two sides: *thin paper/thin slice* **2** slim, not fat **3** not dense or crowded: *thin population* **4** lacking in body, weak: *thin wine* **5** of a voice: weak, not resonating **6** of a mixture: not stiff, watery: *a thin soup* ◇*verb* (**thins**, **thinning**, **thinned**) make or become thin or thinner ◇**thinness** *noun*

▤ *adj* **1** fine, delicate, light, flimsy, filmy, gauzy, narrow **2** lean, slim, slender, slight, skinny, bony, scrawny, lanky, gaunt, underweight, emaciated **3** sparse, scarce, scattered, scant, meagre, poor, inadequate, deficient **5** weak, feeble **6** runny, watery, diluted ◇ *verb* narrow, diminish, reduce, trim, weaken, dilute, water down

▣ *adj* **1** thick, dense, solid **2** fat, broad **3** plentiful, abundant

thine *adj*, *old* belonging to you (used before words beginning with a vowel or a vowel sound): *thine enemies* ◇*pronoun*, *old* something belonging to you: *my heart is thine*

thing *noun* **1** an object that is not living **2** (**things**) belongings **3** an individual event, quality, idea *etc* that may be referred to: *several things must be taken into consideration* **4** (**things**) affairs in general: *how are things?* **5** a preoccupa-

tion: *she's got a thing about cats* **6** *informal* a person or animal: *a nice old thing*

▣ 1 article, object, entity, item **2** belongings, possessions, *informal* stuff, goods, luggage, baggage, equipment, *informal* gear, *informal* clobber, odds and ends, bits and pieces **3** factor, element, point, fact, concept

think *verb* (**thinks**, **thinking**, **thought**) **1** form ideas in the mind **2** work things out, reason **3** believe, judge or consider: *I think that we should go* **4** plan, intend: *she is thinking of resigning* **5** expect: *I think he will leave* **6** keep in mind: *think of the children* ◇**thinker** *noun* ◇**think tank** a group of people who give expert advice and come up with ideas ◇**think highly of** or **think much of** have a good opinion of ◇**think nothing of 1** have a poor opinion of **2** consider as easy ◇**think out** work out in the mind ◇**think over** or **through** consider all the advantages, disadvantages or consequences of (a plan *etc*) ◇**think twice** hesitate ◇**think up** invent

▤ 2 ponder, mull over, chew over, ruminate, meditate, contemplate, muse, cogitate, reflect, deliberate, weigh up **3** believe, hold, consider, regard, esteem, deem, judge, estimate, reckon **5** conceive, imagine, suppose, presume, surmise, expect, foresee, envisage

thin-skinned *adj* sensitive, easily hurt

third *adj* the last of a series of three ◇*noun* one of three equal parts ◇**third age** the age after retirement, early old age

third-rate *adj* of very poor quality

▤ low-grade, poor, bad, inferior, mediocre, indifferent, shoddy, cheap and nasty, *slang* low-rent

▣ first-rate

thirst *noun* **1** a dry feeling in the mouth caused by lack of fluid **2** an eager desire (for): *thirst for knowledge* ◇*verb* **1** feel thirsty **2** (with **for**) desire eagerly

▤ *noun* **2** desire, longing, yearning, hankering, craving, hunger, appetite, lust, passion, eagerness, keenness

thirsty *adj* 1 having thirst 2 of earth: parched, dry 3 eager (for)

▣ 1 dry, *informal* parched, *informal* gasping 3 desirous, longing, yearning, hankering, craving, hungry, burning, itching, dying, eager, avid, greedy

thirteen *noun* the number 13 ◇ *adj* thirteen in number

thirteenth *adj* the last of a series of thirteen ◇ *noun* one of thirteen equal parts

thirtieth *adj* the last of a series of thirty ◇ *noun* one of thirty equal parts

thirty *noun* the number 30 ◇ *adj* thirty in number

this *adj & pronoun* (*plural* these) used to point out someone or something, *esp* one nearby (*contrasted with*: that): *look at this letter/take this instead* ◇ *adv* to such an extent or degree: *this early*

thistle *noun* a prickly plant with purple flowers ◇ **thistledown** *noun* the feathery bristles of the seeds of the thistle

thither *adv* to that place

thong *noun* 1 a thin strap of leather to fasten anything 2 the lash of a whip

thorax *noun* (*plural* **thoraxes** or **thoraces**) 1 the chest in the human or animal body 2 the middle section of an insect's body

thorn *noun* 1 a sharp prickle sticking out from the stem of a plant 2 a bush with thorns, *esp* the hawthorn ◇ **thorn in the flesh** a cause of constant irritation

thorny *adj* 1 full of thorns; prickly 2 difficult, causing arguments: *a thorny problem*

thorough *adj* 1 complete, absolute: *a thorough muddle* 2 very careful, attending to every detail ◇ **thoroughly** *adv*

▣ 1 full, complete, total, entire, utter, absolute, perfect, pure, sheer, unmitigated, downright 2 exhaustive, thoroughgoing, intensive, in-depth, conscientious, efficient, painstaking, scrupulous, meticulous, careful

▣ 1 partial, superficial 2 careless

thoroughbred *noun* an animal of pure breed

thoroughfare *noun* 1 a public street 2 a passage or way through: *no thoroughfare*

thoroughgoing *adj* thorough, complete

those *see* that

thou *pronoun*, *old* you (as the subject of a sentence)

though *conj* despite the fact that, although: *though he disliked it, he ate it all* ◇ *adv*, *informal* however: *I wish I'd never said it, though*

▣ *conj* although, even if, notwithstanding, while, allowing, granted ◇ *adv* however, nevertheless, nonetheless, yet, still, even so, all the same, for all that

thought *noun* 1 the act of thinking 2 something which you think, an idea 3 an opinion 4 consideration: *after much thought* ◇ *past form of* **think**

▣ *noun* 2 idea, notion, concept, conception, plan, design, intention, purpose, aim 3 belief, conviction, opinion, view, judgement, assessment, conclusion 4 thinking, attention, heed, regard, consideration, study, scrutiny, introspection, meditation, contemplation, cogitation, reflection, deliberation

thoughtful *adj* 1 full of thought 2 thinking of others, considerate 3 showing careful thought: *thoughtful answer* ◇ **thoughtfully** *adv* ◇ **thoughtfulness** *noun*

▣ 1 pensive, wistful, dreamy, reflective, contemplative, introspective, thinking, absorbed, studious, serious, solemn 2 considerate, kind, unselfish, helpful, caring, attentive, heedful, mindful 3 careful, prudent, cautious, wary

▣ 2 thoughtless, insensitive, selfish

thoughtless *adj* 1 inconsiderate 2 rash, showing lack of careful thought ◇ **thoughtlessly** *adv* ◇ **thoughtlessness** *noun*

▣ 1 inconsiderate, unthinking, insensitive, unfeeling, tactless, undiplomatic, unkind, selfish, uncaring

▣ 1 thoughtful, considerate

thousand *noun* the number 1000 ◇ *adj* a thousand in number

thousandth *adj* the last of a series of

a thousand ◇ *noun* one of a thousand equal parts

thrall *noun*: **in thrall** enchanted, fascinated

thrash *verb* **1** beat severely **2** *informal* defeat **3** move or toss violently (about) **4** (with **out**) discuss (a problem *etc*) thoroughly **5** thresh (grain) ◇ **thrashing** *noun* a flogging, a beating

▪ **1** punish, beat, whip, lash, flog, scourge, cane, *informal* belt, spank, clobber, *informal* wallop, lay into **2** defeat, beat, trounce, *informal* hammer, *informal* slaughter, crush **4** discuss, debate, negotiate, settle, resolve

thread *noun* **1** a very thin line of cotton, wool, silk etc, often twisted and drawn out **2** the ridge which goes in a spiral round a screw **3** a connected series of details in correct order in a story ◇ *verb* **1** put a thread through a needle *etc* **2** make (your way) in a narrow space

threadbare *adj* of clothes: worn thin

▪ worn, frayed, ragged, moth-eaten, scruffy, shabby, tatty

threadworm *noun* a nematode

threat *noun* **1** a warning that you intend to hurt or punish someone **2** a warning of something bad that may come: *a threat of war* **3** something likely to cause harm: *a threat to our plans*

▪ **2** menace, warning, omen, portent, presage, foreboding **3** danger, risk, hazard, peril

threaten *verb* **1** make a threat: *threatened to kill himself* **2** suggest the approach of something unpleasant: *the clouds threatened rain* **3** be a danger to

▪ **1** menace, intimidate, pressurize, bully, terrorize **2** warn, portend, presage, forebode **3** endanger, jeopardize, imperil

three *noun* the number 3 ◇ *adj* 3 in number

3-D *short for* three-dimensional

threnody *noun* a lament

thresh *verb* beat out (grain) from straw

threshold *noun* **1** a piece of wood or stone under the door of a building **2** a doorway **3** an entry or beginning: *on the threshold of a new era*

▪ **1** doorstep, sill **2** doorway, door, entrance **3** brink, verge, starting-point, dawn, beginning, start, outset, opening

threw *past form* of **throw**

thrice *adv* three times

thrift *noun* careful management of money in order to save ◇ **thrifty** *adj* careful about spending

▪ **thrifty** economical, saving, frugal, sparing, prudent, careful

▣ **thrifty** extravagant, profligate, prodigal, wasteful

thrill *noun* **1** an excited feeling **2** quivering, vibration ◇ *verb* **1** feel excitement **2** make excited

▪ *noun* **1** excitement, adventure, pleasure, stimulation, charge, kick, *slang* buzz, *slang* hit, sensation, glow **2** tingle, throb, shudder, quiver, tremor ◇ *verb* **1** glow, tingle, throb, shudder, tremble, quiver, shake **2** excite, electrify, galvanize, exhilarate, rouse, arouse, move, stir, stimulate

thriller *noun* an exciting story, often about crime and detection

thrilling *adj* very exciting

thrive *verb* (**thrives**, **thriving**, **throve** or **thrives**, **thriven** or **thrived**) **1** grow strong and healthy **2** get on well, be successful

▪ **2** flourish, prosper, boom, grow, increase, advance, develop, bloom, blossom, gain, profit, succeed

▣ **2** languish, stagnate, fail

thro' *short for* **through**

throat *noun* **1** the back part of the mouth **2** the front part of the neck

throb *verb* (**throbs**, **throbbing**, **throbbed**) **1** of pulse *etc*: beat *esp* more strongly than normal **2** beat or vibrate rhythmically and regularly ◇ *noun* a strong regular beat

▪ **1** palpitate, vibrate, pound, thump **2** pulse, pulsate, beat, vibrate

throes *noun plural* great suffering or struggle ◇ **in the throes of** in the middle of (a struggle, doing a task *etc*)

thrombosis *noun* the forming of a clot in a blood vessel

throne *noun* **1** the seat of a monarch or bishop **2** a monarch or their power

throng *noun* a crowd ◊ *verb* **1** move in a crowd **2** crowd, fill (a place)

throttle *noun* the part of an engine through which steam or petrol can be turned on or off ◊ *verb* choke by gripping the throat

■ *verb* strangle, choke, asphyxiate, suffocate, smother, stifle, gag, silence, suppress, inhibit

through *prep* **1** entering from one direction and out in the other: *through the tunnel* **2** from the beginning to the end: *all through the performance* **3** by way of: *related through his grandmother* **4** as a result of: *through his expertise* **5** *US* from (one date) to (another) inclusive: *Monday through Friday is five days* ◊ *adv* **1** into and out, from beginning to end: *go straight through the tunnel* **2** to the end: *got through the exam* ◊ *adj* **1** without break or change: *through train* **2** *informal* finished: *are you through with the newspaper?* **3** of a telephone call: connected: *I couldn't get through this morning* ◊ **through and through** *adv* completely, entirely: *a gentleman through and through*

■ *prep* **1** by, via, by way of, by means of, using **2** throughout, during, in **4** because of, as a result of, thanks to ◊ *adj* **1** direct, express, non-stop **2** finished, ended, completed, done

throughout *prep* **1** in all parts of: *throughout Europe* **2** from start to finish of: *throughout the journey*

throughput *noun* an amount of material put through a process

throw *verb* (**throws, throwing, threw, thrown**) **1** send through the air *usu* with force **2** confuse: *that's thrown you!* **3** move (a switch) **4** *informal* deliberately lose (a contest) **5** give (a party) ◊ *noun* **1** the act of throwing **2** the distance a thing is thrown: *within a stone's throw of the house*

■ *verb* **1** hurl, heave, lob, pitch, *informal*

chuck, sling, cast, fling, toss, launch, propel, send **2** perplex, baffle, confound, confuse, disconcert, astonish, dumbfound ◊ *noun* **1** heave, lob, pitch, sling, fling, toss, cast

throwback *noun* a reversion to an earlier form

thru *US, informal* through

thrush *noun* (*plural* **thrushes**) **1** a type of singing bird with a speckled breast **2** a type of infectious disease of the mouth, throat or vagina

thrust *verb* (**thrusts, thrusting, thrust**) **1** push with force **2** make a sudden push forward with a pointed weapon **3** (with **on, upon**) force (something, yourself) upon ◊ *noun* **1** a stab **2** a pushing force

■ *verb* **1** push, shove, butt, ram, jam, wedge **2** stick, poke, prod, jab, lunge, pierce, stab, plunge

thud *noun* a dull, hollow sound like that made by a heavy body falling ◊ *verb* (**thuds, thudding, thudded**) move or fall with such a sound

■ *noun & verb* thump, clump, knock, clunk, smack, *informal* wallop, crash, bang

thug *noun* a violent, brutal person

■ *noun* ruffian, tough, robber, bandit, mugger, killer, murderer, assassin, gangster, hooligan

thumb *noun* the short, thick finger of the hand ◊ *verb* turn over (the pages of a book) with the thumb or fingers ◊ **rule of thumb** a rough-and-ready practical method ◊ **thumbs down** or **thumbs up** showing disapproval, or approval, of something ◊ **under someone's thumb** under their control

thumbnail *noun* **1** the nail on the thumb **2** *comput* a small version of a picture

thumbscrew *noun, hist* an instrument of torture which worked by squashing the thumbs

thump *noun* a heavy blow ◊ *verb* **1** beat heavily **2** move or fall with a dull, heavy noise

■ *noun* knock, blow, punch, clout, box, cuff, smack, *informal* whack, *informal* wallop, crash, bang, thud ◇ *verb* **1** hit, strike, knock, punch, clout, box, cuff, smack, thrash, *informal* whack, *informal* wallop **2** crash, bang, thud, batter, pound, hammer

thunder *noun* **1** the deep rumbling sound heard after a flash of lightning **2** any loud, rumbling noise ◇ *verb* **1** produce the sound of, or a sound like, thunder **2** shout out angrily ◇ **thundery** *adj* of weather: sultry, bringing thunder

▤ *verb* boom, resound, resonate, reverberate, crash, bang, crack, clap, peal, rumble, roll, roar, blast

thunderbolt *noun* **1** a flash of lightning followed by thunder **2** a very great and sudden surprise

thunderclap *noun* a sudden roar of thunder

thunderous *adj* like thunder; very angry

▤ booming, resounding, reverberating, roaring, loud, noisy, deafening, ear-splitting

thunderstruck *adj* overcome by surprise

Thursday *noun* the fifth day of the week

thus *adv* **1** in this or that manner: *he always talks thus* **2** to this degree or extent: *thus far* **3** because of this, therefore: *thus, we must go on*

thwart *verb* **1** hinder (someone) from carrying out a plan, intention *etc* **2** prevent (an attempt *etc*) ◇ *noun* a cross seat for rowers in a boat

▤ *verb* **1** hinder, impede, obstruct, block **2** frustrate, foil, stop, prevent, oppose

▨ *verb* **1** help, assist, aid

thy *adj*, *old* belonging to you: *thy wife and children*

thyme *noun* a small sweet-smelling herb used for seasoning food

thyroid gland a large gland in the neck which influences the rate at which energy is used by the body

Based on a Greek word meaning 'door-shaped', because of the shape

of the cartilage in the front of the throat

tiara *noun* a jewelled ornament for the head like a crown

tibia *noun* the bone of the shin, the larger of the two bones between knee and ankle (*compare with*: **fibula**)

tic *noun* a twitching motion of certain muscles, *esp* of the face

tick¹ *noun* **1** a light mark (✓) used to mark as correct, or mark off in a list **2** a small quick noise, made regularly by a clock or watch **3** *informal* a moment: *I'll just be a tick* ◇ *verb* **1** mark with a tick **2** of a clock *etc*: produce regular ticks ◇ **ticking** *noun* the noise made by a clock *etc* ◇ **ticker tape** paper tape that prints the latest news of share prices *etc*

tick² *noun* a tiny blood-sucking animal

ticket *noun* **1** a printed piece of paper or card showing that the holder has paid eg a fare to travel, admission to a cinema *etc* **2** an official notice given to someone who has committed a traffic offence **3** a label ◇ *verb* give or attach a ticket or label to someone or something **4** the policies of a particular political party

▤ *noun* **1** pass, card, certificate, token, voucher **3** slip, label, tag, sticker

tickle *verb* **1** excite the surface nerves of a part of the body by touching lightly **2** please or amuse

▤ **1** excite, thrill **2** delight, please, gratify, amuse, entertain, divert

ticklish *adj* **1** sensitive to tickling **2** not easy to deal with: *ticklish problem* ◇ **tickly** *adj* ticklish

▤ **2** sensitive, touchy, delicate, thorny, awkward, difficult, tricky, critical, risky, hazardous, *informal* dodgy

▨ **2** easy, simple

tiddly *adj* **1** slightly drunk **2** tiny

tiddlywinks *noun sing* a game in which small plastic discs (**tiddlywinks**) are flipped into a cup

tidal *adj* of the tide ◇ **tidal wave** an enormous wave in the sea often caused by an earthquake *etc*

tide noun 1 the rise and fall of the sea which happens regularly twice each day 2 old time, season: *Christmastide* ◊ **tide over** help to get over a difficulty for a time

tidemark noun 1 a mark made by the tide at its highest point 2 a mark on the skin showing the furthest point of washing

tidings noun plural news

tidy adj 1 in good order, neat 2 informal fairly big: *a tidy sum of money* ◊ verb (**tidies**, **tidying**, **tidied**) make neat ◊ **tidily** adv ◊ **tidiness** noun

■ adj 1 neat, orderly, methodical, systematic, organized, clean, spick-and-span, shipshape, smart, spruce, trim, well-kept, ordered, uncluttered 2 large, substantial, sizable, considerable, good, generous, ample ◊ verb neaten, straighten, order, arrange, clean, smarten, spruce up, groom

■ adj 1 untidy, messy, disorganized 2 small, insignificant

tie verb (**ties**, **tying**, **tied**) 1 fasten with a cord, string etc 2 knot or put a bow in (string, shoelaces etc) 3 join, unite 4 limit, restrict: *tied to a tight schedule* 5 score the same number of points (in a game etc), draw ◊ noun 1 a band of fabric worn round the neck, tied with a knot or bow 2 something that connects: *ties of friendship* 3 something that restricts or limits 4 an equal score in a competition 5 a game or match to be played

■ verb 1 tether, attach, fasten, moor, secure, rope, lash, strap, bind 2 knot 3 join, connect, link, unite 4 restrain, restrict, confine, limit, hamper, hinder ◊ noun 2 connection, link, liaison, relationship, bond 3 commitment, duty, restraint, restriction, limitation, hindrance

tie-breaker noun an extra question or part of a tied contest to decide a winner

tier /tɪə(r)/ noun a row of seats in a theatre etc, with others above or below it

■ level, stage, stratum, layer, belt, zone, band, echelon, rank, row, line

tiff noun a slight quarrel

tiger noun a large animal of the cat family with a tawny coat striped with black ◊ **tiger lily** a kind of lily with large spotted flowers

tight adj 1 firmly stretched, not loose 2 fitting too closely: *these jeans are a bit tight* 3 close: *a tight result* 4 informal stingy 5 informal drunk ◊ **tight spot** an awkward situation

■ 1 taut, stretched, tense, rigid, stiff, firm 2 snug, close-fitting 4 mean, stingy, miserly, informal tight-fisted

■ 2 loose, slack 4 generous

tighten verb make or become tight or tighter

■ tauten, stretch, tense, stiffen, fix, fasten, secure, narrow, close, cramp, constrict, crush, squeeze

■ loosen, relax

tight-fisted adj, informal stingy

■ mean, stingy, miserly, informal mingy, penny-pinching, sparing, informal tight, grasping

■ generous, charitable

tight-lipped adj uncommunicative

tightrope noun a tightly stretched rope on which acrobats perform

tights noun plural a close-fitting garment covering the feet, legs and body as far as the waist

tigress noun a female tiger

tile noun a piece of baked clay etc used in covering floors or roofs ◊ verb cover with tiles

till¹ noun a container or drawer for money in a shop

till² verb cultivate (land); plough ◊ **tillage** noun 1 the act of tilling 2 tilled land

till³ see until

tiller noun the handle of a boat's rudder

tilt verb 1 fall into, or place in, a sloping position 2 hist joust 3 hist (with **at**) attack on horseback, using a lance ◊ noun 1 a slant 2 a thrust, a jab ◊ **at full tilt** with full speed and force

■ noun 1 slope, incline, angle, inclination, slant, pitch, list

timber noun 1 wood for building etc 2

trees suitable for this **3** a wooden beam in a house or ship

timbre *noun* the quality of a musical sound or voice

time *noun* **1** the continuous passing of seconds, days, years *etc* **2** the hour of the day **3** the period at or during which something happens **4** (often **times**) a particular period: *in modern times* **5** opportunity: *no time to listen* **6** a suitable or right moment: *now is the time to ask* **7** one of a number of occasions: *he won four times* **8** (**times**) multiplied by: *two times four* **9** the rhythm or rate of performance of a piece of music ◇ *adj* **1** of time **2** arranged to go off at a particular time: *a time bomb* ◇ *verb* **1** measure the minutes, seconds *etc* taken to do anything **2** choose the time for (well, badly *etc*): *time your entrance well* ◇ **at times** occasionally ◇ **do time** *slang* serve a prison sentence ◇ **in time** early enough ◇ **on time** or **up to time** punctual ◇ **the time being** the present time

■ *noun* **3** spell, stretch, period, term, season, session, span, duration, interval, space, while **4** age, era, epoch, life, lifetime, generation **6** moment, point, juncture, stage, instance, occasion, date, day, hour **9** tempo, beat, rhythm, metre, measure ◇ *verb* **1** clock, measure, meter, regulate

---

Periods of time include:
eternity, eon, era, age, generation, epoch, millennium, chiliad, century, lifetime, decade, decennium, quinquennium, year, light-year, yesteryear, quarter, month, fortnight, week, midweek, weekend, long weekend, day, today, tonight, yesterday, tomorrow, morrow, weekday, hour, minute, second, moment, instant, millisecond, microsecond, nanosecond; dawn, sunrise, sun-up, the early hours, *informal* wee small hours, morn, a.m., daytime, midday, noon, high noon, p.m., afternoon, tea-time, evening, twilight, dusk, sunset, nightfall, bedtime, night, night-time; season, spring, summer, midsummer, autumn, *US* fall, winter

---

time-honoured *adj* respected because it has lasted a long time

timeless *adj* **1** not belonging to any particular time **2** never ending: *timeless beauty*

■ **2** ageless, immortal, everlasting, eternal, endless, permanent, changeless, unchanging

timely *adj* coming at the right moment: *a timely reminder*

■ well-timed, seasonable, suitable, appropriate, convenient, opportune, propitious, prompt, punctual

◨ ill-timed, unsuitable, inappropriate

timepiece *noun, old* a clock or watch

time-sharing *noun* a scheme by which someone buys the right to use a holiday home for a specified period each year ◇ **timeshare** *noun*

timetable *noun* a list showing times of classes, arrivals or departures of trains *etc*

■ schedule, programme, agenda, calendar, diary, rota, roster, list, listing

timid *adj* easily frightened; shy ◇ **timidity** *noun* ◇ **timidly** *adv*

■ shy, bashful, modest, shrinking, retiring, nervous, apprehensive, afraid, timorous, fearful, cowardly, faint-hearted, *informal* wimpish, spineless, irresolute

◨ brave, bold, audacious

timorous *adj* very timid ◇ **timorously** *adv*

timpani or **tympani** *noun plural* kettledrums ◇ **timpanist** or **tympanist** *noun* someone who plays timpani

tin *noun* **1** a silvery-white kind of metal **2** a box or can made of **tinplate,** thin iron covered with tin or other metal ◇ *verb* (**tins, tinning, tinned**) **1** cover with tin **2** pack (food *etc*) in tins

tincture *noun* **1** a slight tinge of colour **2** a characteristic quality **3** a medicine mixed in alcohol

tinder *noun* dry material easily set alight by a spark ◇ **tinderbox** *noun* a box containing tinder

tinfoil *noun* a very thin sheet of tin, aluminium *etc* used for wrapping

tinge verb **1** tint, colour slightly **2** (with **with**) add a slight amount of (something) to ◇ noun a slight amount; a hint: *tinge of pink/tinge of sadness*
▪ verb **1** tint, dye, stain, colour, shade, suffuse, imbue ◇ noun tint, shade, touch, trace, suggestion, hint, smack, flavour, pinch, drop, dash, bit, sprinkling, smattering

tingle verb **1** feel a sharp prickling sensation **2** feel a thrill of excitement ◇ noun a sharp prickle
▪ verb **1** sting, prickle, tickle, itch, thrill, throb, quiver, vibrate ◇ noun stinging, prickling, pins and needles, tickle, tickling, itch, itching, thrill, throb, quiver, shiver, gooseflesh, goosepimples

tinker noun a mender of kettles, pans *etc* ◇ verb **1** work clumsily or unskilfully **2** meddle (with)
▪ verb **2** fiddle, play, toy, trifle, potter, dabble, meddle, tamper

tinkle verb (cause to) make a light, ringing sound; clink, jingle, ◇ noun a light, ringing sound

tinnitus noun persistent ringing in the ears

tinny adj **1** like tin **2** of sound: thin, high-pitched

tinpot adj of poor quality; feeble

tinsel noun a sparkling, glittering material used for decoration

tint noun a variety or shade of a colour ◇ verb give slight colour to
▪ noun dye, stain, rinse, wash, colour, hue, shade, tincture, tinge, tone, cast, streak, trace, touch ◇ verb dye, colour, tinge, streak, stain, taint

tiny adj very small
▪ minute, microscopic, *informal* teeny, small, little, slight, negligible, insignificant, diminutive, petite, *informal* pint-sized, pocket, miniature, *informal* mini
▪ huge, enormous, immense

tip¹ noun the top or point of something ◇ verb (**tips**, **tipping**, **tipped**) put a tip on
▪ noun end, extremity, point, nib, apex, peak, pinnacle, summit, acme, top, cap, crown, head

tip² verb (**tips**, **tipping**, **tipped**) **1** slant **2** (with **over**) overturn **3** (with **out** or **into**) empty out or into ◇ noun a rubbish dump
▪ verb **1** lean, incline, slant, list, tilt **2** topple over, capsize, upset, overturn **3** spill, pour out, empty, unload, dump ◇ noun dump, rubbish heap, refuse heap

tip³ noun **1** a piece of useful information **2** a small gift of money to a waiter *etc* ◇ verb (**tips**, **tipping**, **tipped**) **1** (also with **off**) give a hint to **2** give a small gift of money
▪ noun **1** clue, pointer, hint, suggestion, advice, warning, tip-off, information, forecast ◇ verb **1** advise, suggest, warn, caution, forewarn, tip off, inform, tell

tipple verb, *informal* drink small amounts of alcohol regularly ◇ noun an alcoholic drink ◇ **tippler** noun

tipster noun someone who gives tips about horse-racing *etc*

tipsy adj rather drunk ◇ **tipsiness** noun

tiptoe verb walk on your toes in order to go very quietly ◇ **on tiptoe** standing or walking on your toes

tirade noun a long, bitter, scolding speech

tire¹ verb **1** make or become weary **2** (with **of**) lose patience or interest in
▪ **1** weary, fatigue, wear out, exhaust, drain, enervate
▪ **1** enliven, invigorate, refresh

tire² *US* spelling of **tyre**

tired adj **1** weary **2** (with **of**) bored with
▪ **1** weary, drowsy, sleepy, flagging, fatigued, worn out, exhausted, dog-tired, drained, *slang* fagged, *informal* bushed, *informal* whacked, *informal* shattered, *informal* beat, *informal* dead-beat, *informal* knackered **2** fed up, bored, sick
▪ **1** lively, energetic, rested, refreshed

tireless adj **1** never becoming weary **2** never resting ◇ **tirelessly** adv
▪ **1** untiring, unwearied, unflagging, indefatigable **2** energetic, vigorous, diligent
▪ **2** tired, lazy

tiresome adj **1** making weary **2** long and dull **3** annoying: a tiresome child ◇ **tiresomely** adv

■ **2** dull, boring, tedious, monotonous, uninteresting **3** troublesome, trying, annoying, irritating, exasperating

🗗 **2** interesting, stimulating

tiring adj causing tiredness or weariness: a tiring journey

■ wearying, fatiguing, exhausting, draining, wearing, demanding, exacting, taxing, arduous, strenuous, laborious

tiro or **tyro** noun (plural **tiros** or **tyros**) a beginner

tissue noun **1** the substance of which body organs are made: muscle tissue **2** a mass, a network (of lies, nonsense etc) **3** a paper handkerchief **4** finely woven cloth ◇ **tissue paper** thin, soft paper used for wrapping

tit[1] noun a type of small bird: blue tit/ great tit

tit[2] noun **1** a teat **2** slang a woman's breast

tit[3] noun: **tit for tat** blow for blow, repayment of injury with injury

titanic adj huge, enormous

titanium noun a light, strong type of metal used in aircraft

titbit noun a tasty piece of food etc

■ morsel, scrap, appetizer, snack, delicacy, dainty, treat

titchy adj, informal tiny

tithe noun, hist a tax paid to the church, a tenth part of someone's income or produce

titillate verb gently stimulate or arouse (often sexually)

■ stimulate, arouse, slang turn on, excite, thrill, tickle, provoke, tease, tantalize, intrigue, interest

⚠ Do not confuse: **titillate** and **titivate**

titivate verb make smarter; improve in appearance

title noun **1** the name of a person, book, poem etc **2** a word in front of a name to show rank or office (eg Sir, Lady, Major), or in addressing anyone formally (eg Mr, Mrs, Ms) **3** right or claim to money, an estate etc **4** (**titles**) written material on film giving credits etc ◇ **title deed** a document that proves a right to ownership (of a house etc) ◇ **title page** the page of a book on which are the title, author's name etc ◇ **title role** the part in a play which is the same as the title eg Hamlet

■ **1** name, appellation, denomination, term, designation, label, epithet, nickname, slang moniker, pseudonym **3** right, prerogative, privilege, claim, entitlement, ownership, deeds

titled adj having a title which shows noble rank

titter verb giggle ◇ noun a giggle

■ verb laugh, chortle, chuckle, giggle, snigger, mock

tittletattle noun gossip, idle chatter

titular adj **1** of or constituting a title **2** having the title without the duties of an office

tizzy noun, informal a state of confusion, a flap

TLA abbrev, comput three-letter acronym

TLC abbrev tender loving care

TNT abbrev trinitrotoluene, a high explosive

to prep **1** showing the place or direction aimed for: going to the cinema/emigrating to New Zealand **2** showing the indirect object in a phrase, sentence etc: show it to me **3** used before a verb to indicate the infinitive: to err is human **4** showing that one thing belongs with another in some way: key to the door **5** compared with: nothing to what happened before **6** about, concerning: what did he say to that? **7** showing a ratio, proportion etc: odds are six to one against **8** showing the purpose or result of an action: tear it to pieces ◇ adv almost closed: pull the door to ◇ **to and fro** backwards and forwards

toad noun a type of amphibian like a frog

toadstool noun a mushroom-like fungus, often poisonous

toady *verb* give way to someone's wishes, or flatter them, to gain favour ◇ *noun* someone who acts in this way

toast *verb* 1 brown (bread) by heating at a fire or grill 2 warm (your feet *etc*) at a fire 3 drink to the success or health of (someone) ◇ *noun* 1 bread toasted 2 the person to whom a toast is drunk 3 the drinking of a toast ◇ **toaster** *noun* an electric machine for toasting bread ◇ **toastmaster** *noun* the announcer of toasts at a public dinner ◇ **toast-rack** *noun* a stand with partitions for slices of toast

■ *noun* 3 drink, pledge, tribute, salute, compliment, health

tobacco *noun* a type of plant whose dried leaves are used for smoking ◇ **tobacconist** *noun* someone who sells tobacco, cigarettes *etc*

toboggan *noun* a long, light sledge ◇ *verb* go in a toboggan

today *adv & noun* 1 (on) this day 2 (at) the present time

toddle *verb* walk unsteadily, with short steps

toddler *noun* a young child just able to walk

toddy *noun* (*plural* **toddies**) a hot drink of whisky and honey

to-do *noun, informal* (*plural* **to-dos**) a bustle, commotion

toe *noun* 1 one of the five finger-like parts of the foot 2 the front part of an animal's foot 3 the front part of a shoe, golf club *etc* ◇ **on your toes** alert, ready for action ◇ **toe the line** do as you are told

toff *noun, informal* an upper-class person

toffee *noun* a kind of sweet made of sugar and butter

toffee-nosed *adj, informal* snobbish, conceited

tofu *noun* a paste of unfermented soya beans

toga *noun, hist* the loose outer garment worn by a citizen of ancient Rome

together *adv* 1 with each other, in place or time: *we must stay together/three buses arrived together* 2 in or into union or connection: *glue the pages together* 3 by joint action: *together we can afford it* 4 *informal* in a suitable order: *get your things together*

■ 1 jointly, simultaneously, at the same time, all at once, collectively, en masse 3 jointly, in unison, as one, hand in hand

⊞ 1 separately 3 individually, alone

toggle *noun* 1 a cylindrical fastening for a coat 2 *comput* a keyboard command allowing switching between modes ◇ *verb* switch quickly between two positions, states *etc* (*esp* between being on and off)

togs *noun plural, informal* clothes

toil *verb* 1 work hard and long 2 walk, move *etc* with effort ◇ *noun* hard work ◇ **toiler** *noun*

■ *verb* 1 labour, work, slave, drudge, sweat, grind, slog, *informal* graft, *informal* plug away, persevere, strive, struggle ◇ *noun* labour, hard work, donkeywork, drudgery, sweat, *informal* graft, industry, effort, exertion

toilet *noun* 1 a receptacle for waste matter from the body, with a water-supply for flushing this away 2 a room containing this 3 the act of washing yourself, tidying your hair ◇ **toiletries** *noun plural* soaps, cosmetics *etc* ◇ **toilet water** a lightly perfumed, spirit-based liquid for the skin

token *noun* 1 a mark, a sign: *a token of my friendship* 2 a stamped piece of plastic *etc*, or a voucher, for use in place of money: *bus token/book token* ◇ *adj* done for show only, insincere: *token gesture*

■ *noun* 1 symbol, emblem, representation, mark, sign, indication, manifestation, demonstration, expression, evidence, proof, clue, reminder, memorial, memento, souvenir, keepsake 2 voucher, coupon, counter, disc ◇ *adj* symbolic, emblematic, nominal, minimal, perfunctory, superficial, cosmetic, hollow, insincere

told *past form* of **tell**

tolerable *adj* 1 bearable, endurable 2

fairly good: *tolerable player* ◇ **tolerably** *adv*

◼ **1** bearable, endurable, sufferable, acceptable, passable **2** adequate, reasonable, fair, average, mediocre, indifferent, *informal* so-so, unexceptional, ordinary, run-of-the-mill

◨ **1** intolerable, unbearable, insufferable

tolerance *noun* **1** putting up with and being fair to people with different beliefs, manners *etc* from your own **2** ability to resist the effects of a drug *etc* ◇ **tolerant** *adj*

◼ **1** toleration, patience, forbearance, open-mindedness, broad-mindedness, magnanimity, sympathy, understanding, lenity, indulgence, permissiveness **2** resistance, resilience, toughness, endurance, stamina

◨ **1** intolerance, prejudice, bigotry, narrow-mindedness

tolerate *verb* **1** bear, endure; put up with **2** allow ◇ **toleration** *noun*

◼ **1** endure, suffer, put up with, bear, stand, abide, *informal* hack, stomach, swallow, take **2** admit, allow, permit, condone

toll[1] *noun* **1** a tax charged for crossing a bridge *etc* **2** cost in loss, damage *etc* ◇ **take toll** cause damage or loss

◼ **1** charge, fee, payment, levy, tax, duty, tariff **2** cost, penalty, loss

toll[2] *verb* **1** sound (a large bell) slowly, as for a funeral **2** of a bell: be sounded slowly

◼ **2** ring, peal, chime, knell, sound, strike, announce, call

tomahawk *noun, hist* a Native American light axe used as a weapon and tool

tomato *noun* (*plural* **tomatoes**) a juicy red-skinned fruit, used in salads, sauces *etc*

tomb *noun* a burial vault or chamber

◼ burial place, vault, crypt, sepulchre, catacomb, mausoleum, cenotaph

tombola *noun* a kind of lottery

tomboy *noun* a high-spirited active girl

tombstone *noun* a stone placed over a grave in memory of the dead person

tomcat *noun* a male cat

tome *noun* a large heavy book

tomfoolery *noun* silly behaviour

tomorrow *adv & noun* **1** (on) the day after today **2** (in) the future: *I'll do it tomorrow/the children of tomorrow*

tomtit *noun* a kind of small bird

tomtom *noun* a type of drum beaten with the hands

ton *noun* **1** a measure of weight equal to 2240 pounds, about 1016 kilograms **2** a unit (100 cubic feet) of space in a ship **3** (also **tonne**) a metric unit of weight equal to 1000 kilograms (*in full:* **metric ton**)

tone *noun* **1** sound **2** quality of sound: *harsh tone* **3** *music* one of the larger intervals in a scale, *eg* between C and D **4** the quality of a voice expressing the mood of the speaker: *a gentle tone* **5** the general character or style of a piece of writing, *etc* **6** a shade of colour **7** muscle firmness or strength ◇ *verb* **1** (sometimes with **in**) blend, fit in well **2** (with **down**) make or become softer **3** (with **up**) give strength to (muscles *etc*)

◼ *noun* **2** note, timbre, pitch, volume, intonation, modulation, inflection, accent, stress, emphasis, force, strength **4, 5** manner, quality, feel **6** tint, tinge, colour, hue, shade, cast ◇ *verb* **1** match, co-ordinate, blend, harmonize **2** moderate, temper, subdue, restrain, soften, dim, dampen, play down, reduce, alleviate, assuage, mitigate

tongs *noun plural* an instrument for lifting and grasping coals, sugar lumps *etc*

tongue *noun* **1** the fleshy organ inside the mouth, used in tasting, speaking, and swallowing **2** a flap in a shoe **3** a long, thin strip of land **4** the tongue of an animal served as food **5** a language: *his mother tongue* ◇ **hold your tongue** say nothing ◇ **tongue in cheek** with ironic intention

◼ **5** language, speech, discourse, talk, utterance, parlance, vernacular, dialect

tongue-tied *adj* not able to speak freely

◼ speechless, dumbstruck, inarticulate,

silent, mute, dumb, voiceless
■ talkative, garrulous, voluble

tongue-twister *noun* a phrase, sentence *etc* not easy to say quickly, *eg* 'she sells sea shells'

tonic *noun* **1** a medicine which gives strength and energy **2** anything invigorating **3** *music* the keynote of a scale **4** tonic water ◇ *adj* **1** increasing strength and wellbeing **2** of tones or sounds ◇ **tonic water** aerated water with quinine

■ *noun* **1** cordial, pick-me-up, restorative, refresher, bracer, stimulant, boost

tonight *adv & noun* (on) the night of the present day

tonnage *noun* the space available in a ship, measured in tons

tonne *another spelling of* **ton** (sense 3)

tonsil *noun* one of a pair of soft, fleshy lumps at the back of the throat

tonsillitis *noun* reddening and pain in the tonsils

tonsure *noun* **1** the shaving of the top of the head of priests and monks **2** the part of the head so shaved

too *adv* **1** to a greater extent, in a greater quantity *etc* than is wanted: *too hot to go outside/too many people in the room* **2** (often with a negative) very, particularly: *not feeling too well/you're too generous!* **3** also, as well: *I'm feeling quite cold, too*

■ **1** excessively, inordinately, unduly, over, overly, ridiculously, extremely, very **3** also, as well, in addition, besides, moreover, likewise

took *past form of* **take**

tool *noun* an instrument for doing work, *esp* by hand ◇ **tool up 1** equip **2** *slang* arm yourself

■ implement, instrument, utensil, gadget, device, contrivance, contraption, apparatus, appliance, machine, means

Types of tool include:
bolster, caulking iron, crowbar, hod, jackhammer, jointer, mattock, pick, pickaxe, plumbline, sledgehammer; chaser, clamp, dividers, dolly, drill, hacksaw, jack, pincers, pliers, protractor, punch, rule, sander, scriber, snips, socket-wrench, soldering iron, spraygun, tommy bar, vice; auger, awl, brace and bit, bradawl, chisel, file, fretsaw, hammer, handsaw, jack plane, jigsaw, level, mallet, plane, rasp, saw, screwdriver, set square, spirit level, tenon saw, T-square; billhook, chainsaw, chopper, dibber, fork, grass rake, hay fork, hoe, pitchfork, plough, pruning knife, pruning shears, rake, scythe, secateurs, shears, shovel, sickle, spade, thresher, trowel; needle, scissors, pinking shears, bodkin, crochet hook, forceps, scalpel, tweezers, tongs, cleaver, steel, gimlet, mace, mortar, pestle, paper-cutter, paper-knife, stapler, pocket-knife, penknife

toolbar *noun* a horizontal strip on a computer screen showing function buttons

toot *noun* the sound of a car horn *etc*

tooth *noun* (*plural* **teeth**) **1** any of the hard, bony objects projecting from the gums, arranged in two rows in the mouth **2** any of the points on a saw, cogwheel, comb *etc* ◇ **tooth and nail** fiercely, determinedly

toothache *noun* pain in a tooth

toothpaste *noun* paste for cleaning the teeth

toothpick *noun* a small sharp instrument for picking out food from between the teeth

toothsome *adj* pleasant to the taste

top[1] *noun* **1** the highest part of anything **2** the upper surface **3** the highest place or rank **4** a lid **5** a garment covering the upper half of the body ◇ *adj* highest, chief ◇ *verb* (**tops**, **topping**, **topped**) **1** cover on the top **2** rise above **3** do better than **4** reach the top of **5** take off the top of ◇ **top dog** *informal* a winner or leader ◇ **top hat** a man's tall silk hat

■ *noun* **1** head, tip, vertex, apex, crest, crown, peak, pinnacle, summit, acme, zenith, culmination, height **4** lid, cap, cover, cork, stopper ◇ *adj* highest, topmost, upmost, uppermost, upper, superior, head, chief, leading, first, foremost, principal, ruling, dominant, prime, greatest, maximum, best, finest, premium, supreme, crowning, culminating ◇ *verb* **3** beat, exceed, outstrip, better, excel, best, surpass, eclipse, outshine, outdo, surmount, transcend

◨ *noun* **1** bottom, base, nadir ◇ *adj* bottom, lowest, inferior

top² *noun* a toy that spins on a pointed base

topaz *noun* a type of precious stone, of various colours

topcoat *noun* an overcoat

top-heavy *adj* having the upper part too heavy for the lower

topi or **topee** *noun* a helmet-like hat used as a protection against the sun

topiary *noun* the art of trimming bushes, hedges *etc* into decorative shapes

topic *noun* a subject spoken or written about

◨ subject, theme, issue, question, matter, point, thesis, text

topical *adj* of current interest, concerned with present events ◇ **topicality** *noun*

◨ current, contemporary, up-to-date, up-to-the-minute, recent, newsworthy, relevant, popular

topmost *adj* highest, uppermost

topnotch *adj* of the highest quality

topography *noun* the description of the features of the land in a certain region ◇ **topographical** *adj*

topple *verb* become unsteady and fall

◨ totter, overbalance, tumble, fall, collapse, upset, overturn, capsize, overthrow, oust

top-secret *adj* (of information *etc*) very secret

topsyturvy *adj* & *adv* turned upside down

torch *noun* (*plural* **torches**) **1** a small hand-held light with a switch and electric battery **2** a flaming piece of wood or

coarse rope carried as a light in processions ◇ *verb*, *slang* set fire to deliberately

tore *past form* of **tear**

toreador *noun* a bullfighter mounted on horseback

torment *verb* **1** treat cruelly and make suffer **2** worry greatly **3** tease ◇ *noun* **1** great pain, suffering **2** a cause of these ◇ **tormentor** *noun*

◨ *verb* **1** provoke, annoy, harass, *informal* hassle, hound, pester, plague, afflict, distress, harrow, pain, torture, persecute **2** vex, trouble, worry, bother ◇ *noun* **1** suffering, pain, agony, ordeal, torture, persecution, anguish, distress, misery, affliction **2** provocation, annoyance, vexation, bane, scourge, trouble, bother, nuisance, *informal* hassle

torn *past participle* of **tear**

tornado *noun* (*plural* **tornadoes**) a violent whirling wind that causes great damage

torpedo *noun* (*plural* **torpedoes**) a large cigar-shaped type of missile fired by ships, planes *etc* ◇ *verb* (**torpedoes**, **torpedoing**, **torpedoed**) hit or sink (a ship) with a torpedo

torpid *adj* slow, dull, stupid ◇ **torpidity** or **torpor** *noun* dullness

torrent *noun* **1** a rushing stream **2** a heavy downpour of rain **3** a violent flow of words *etc*: *torrent of abuse*

◨ **2** flood, spate, deluge, cascade, downpour **3** volley, outburst, gush, rush, flood

◨ **1** trickle

torrential *adj* like a torrent; rushing violently

torrid *adj* **1** parched by heat; very hot **2** very passionate: *torrid love affair*

torsion *noun* twisting; a twist

torso *noun* (*plural* **torsos**) the body, excluding the head and limbs

tortilla *noun* a Mexican flat round cake made from wheat or maize

tortoise *noun* a four-footed, slow-moving kind of reptile, covered with a hard shell

tortoiseshell *noun* the shell of a kind

of sea turtle, used in making ornamental articles ◇ *adj* **1** made of this shell **2** mottled brown, yellow and black: *a tortoiseshell cat*

tortuous *adj* winding, roundabout, not straightforward

■ twisting, winding, meandering, serpentine, zigzag, circuitous, roundabout, indirect, convoluted, complicated, involved

🖃 straight, straightforward

torture *verb* **1** treat someone cruelly as a punishment or to force them to confess something **2** cause to suffer ◇ *noun* **1** the act of torturing **2** great suffering

■ *verb* **1** persecute, torment, afflict, distress **2** agonize, excruciate, pain, rack ◇ *noun* **2** pain, agony, suffering, affliction, distress, misery, anguish, torment

Tory *noun* (*plural* **Tories**) a member of the British Conservative Party

> Originally one of a group of Irish Catholics thrown off their land who waged guerrilla war on British settlers, later applied to any royalist supporter

toss *verb* **1** throw up in the air **2** throw up (a coin) to see which side falls uppermost **3** throw away **4** turn restlessly from side to side **5** jerk (the head) **6** of a ship: be thrown about by rough water ◇ **toss off 1** produce quickly **2** *slang* masturbate ◇ **toss up** toss a coin

■ **1** fling, throw, *informal* chuck, sling, hurl, lob **2** flip, cast **4** agitate, rock, thrash, squirm, wriggle **6** roll, heave, pitch, lurch, jolt, shake

toss-up *noun* an equal choice or chance

tot[1] *noun* **1** a little child **2** a small amount of alcoholic spirits

tot[2] *verb*: **tot up** add up

total *adj* **1** whole: *total number* **2** complete: *total wreck* ◇ *noun* **1** the entire amount **2** the sum of amounts added together ◇ *verb* (**totals, totalling, totalled**) **1** add up **2** amount to **3** *informal* damage irreparably; wreck ◇ **totally** *adv* completely

■ *adj* **1** full, complete, entire, whole, integral **2** utter, absolute, unqualified, outright, undisputed, perfect, sheer, downright, thorough ◇ *noun* **1** whole, entirety, totality, all, lot, mass, **2** sum, aggregate ◇ *verb* **1** add (up), sum (up), tot (up), count (up), **2** amount to, come to, reach

🖃 *adj* **1** partial

totalitarian *adj* governed by a single party that allows no rivals

totem *noun* an image of an animal or plant used as the badge or sign of a Native American tribe ◇ **totem pole** a pole on which totems are carved and painted

totter *verb* **1** shake as if about to fall **2** stagger

■ **1** sway, rock, shake, quiver, tremble **2** stagger, reel, lurch, stumble, falter, waver, teeter

toucan *noun* a type of S American bird with a very big beak ◇ **toucan crossing** a road crossing for cyclists and pedestrians

touch *verb* **1** feel (with the hand) **2** come or be in contact (with): *a leaf touched his cheek* **3** move, affect the feelings of: *the story touched those who heard it* **4** mark slightly with colour: *touched with gold* **5** reach the standard of: *I can't touch him at chess* **6** have anything to do with: *I wouldn't touch a job like that* **7** eat or drink: *he won't touch meat* **8** concern (someone) **9** *informal* persuade (someone) to lend you money: *I touched him for £10* ◇ *noun* **1** the act of touching **2** the physical sense of touch **3** a small quantity or degree: *a touch of salt* **4** a detail which adds to a general appearance: *the flowers are an elegant touch* **5** of an artist, pianist *etc*: individual skill or style **6** *football etc* the ground beyond the edges of the pitch marked off by **touchlines** ◇ **in** (or **out of**) **touch with** in (or not in) communication or contact with ◇ **touch down** of an aircraft: land ◇ **touch off** cause to happen ◇ **touch on** mention briefly ◇ **touch up** improve (a drawing or photograph *etc*) by making details clearer *etc*

■ *verb* **1** feel, handle, finger, brush, graze, stroke, caress, fondle **2** strike, contact, meet **3** move, stir, upset, disturb, impress, inspire **5** reach, attain, equal, match, rival, better **8** affect, concern, regard ◇ *noun* **1** brush, stroke, caress, pat, tap, contact **3** trace, spot, dash, pinch, soupçon, hint, suggestion, speck, jot, tinge, smack **5** skill, art, knack, flair, style, method, manner, technique, approach

touch-and-go *adj* very uncertain: *it's touch-and-go whether we'll get it done on time*

touché /'tuːʃeɪ/ *exclam* acknowledging a point scored in a game or argument

touching *prep* about, concerning ◇ *adj* causing emotion, moving

■ *adj* moving, stirring, affecting, poignant, pitiable, pitiful, pathetic, sad, emotional, tender

touchstone *noun* a test or standard of measurement of quality *etc*

touchy *adj* easily offended ◇ **touchily** *adv* ◇ **touchiness** *noun*

■ irritable, irascible, quick-tempered, bad-tempered, *informal* stroppy, grumpy, grouchy, crabbed, cross, peevish, captious, edgy, over-sensitive

F3 calm, imperturbable

tough *adj* **1** strong, not easily broken **2** of meat *etc*: hard to chew **3** of strong character, able to stand hardship or strain **4** difficult to cope with or overcome: *tough opposition* **5** rough and violent

■ **1** strong, durable, resilient, resistant, hardy, sturdy, solid, rigid, stiff, inflexible, hard **2** hard, leathery **3** firm, resolute, determined, tenacious **4** hard, difficult **5** rough, harsh, violent

F3 **1** fragile, delicate, weak **2** tender **4** easy, simple

toughen *verb* (cause to) become tough

toupee *noun* a small wig or piece of false hair worn to cover a bald spot

tour *noun* a journey in which you visit various places; a pleasure trip ◇ *verb* make a tour (of)

■ *noun* circuit, round, visit, expedition, journey, trip, outing, excursion, drive, ride, course ◇ *verb* visit, go round, sightsee, explore, travel, journey, drive, ride

tour de force an outstanding effort or accomplishment

tourism *noun* the activities of tourists and of those who cater for their needs

tourist *noun* someone who travels for pleasure, and visits places of interest

tournament *noun* **1** a competition involving many contests and players **2** *hist* a meeting at which knights fought together on horseback

■ **1** championship, series, competition, contest, match, event, meeting

tourniquet /'tʊənɪkeɪ/ or /'tɔːnɪkeɪ/ *noun* a bandage tied tightly round a limb to prevent loss of blood from a wound

tousled *adj* of hair: untidy, tangled

tout *verb* go about looking for support, votes, buyers *etc* ◇ *noun* **1** someone who does this **2** someone who gives tips to people who bet on horse races

tow *verb* pull (a car etc) with a rope attached to another vehicle ◇ *noun* **1** the act of towing **2** the rope used for towing ◇ **in tow** following as an escort ◇ **on tow** being towed

■ *verb* pull, draw, trail, haul, transport

towards or **toward** *prep* **1** moving in the direction of (a place, person *etc*): *walking towards the house* **2** to (a person, thing *etc*): *his attitude towards his son* **3** as a help or contribution to: *I gave £5 towards the cost* **4** near, about (a time *etc*): *towards four o'clock*

towel *noun* a cloth for drying or wiping (*eg* the skin after washing) ◇ *verb* (**towels, towelling, towelled**) rub dry with a towel

towelling *noun* a cotton cloth often used for making towels

tower *noun* **1** a high narrow building **2** a high narrow part of a castle *etc* ◇ *verb* rise high (over, above) ◇ **towering** *adj* **1** rising high **2** intense: *a towering rage*

■ *verb* rise, rear, ascend, mount, soar, loom, overlook, dominate, surpass, transcend, exceed, top

town *noun* a place, larger than a village, which includes many buildings, houses, shops *etc* ◇ **town crier** *hist* someone who made public announcements in a town ◇ **town hall** the building where the official business of a town is done ◇ **town planning** planning of the future development of a town ◇ **go to town** *informal* act, work *etc* thoroughly

towpath *noun* a path alongside a canal used by horses which tow barges

toxaemia *noun* poisoning

toxic *adj* **1** poisonous **2** caused by poison

■ **1** poisonous, harmful, noxious, unhealthy, dangerous, deadly, lethal

■ **1** harmless, safe

toxicology *noun* the scientific study of poisons ◇ **toxicologist** *noun*

toxin *noun* a naturally-occurring poison

toy *noun* **1** an object for a child to play with **2** an object for amusement only ◇ **toy with** play or trifle with

toyboy *noun*, *informal* a young male companion of an older woman

trace *noun* **1** a mark or sign left behind **2** a footprint **3** a small amount **4** a line drawn by an instrument recording a change (*eg* in temperature) ◇ *verb* **1** follow the tracks or course of **2** copy (a drawing *etc*) on transparent paper placed over it

■ *noun* **1** trail, track **2** footprint, footmark, mark **3** hint, suggestion, suspicion, soupçon, dash, drop, spot, bit, jot, touch, tinge, smack ◇ *verb* **1** track (down), trail, stalk, hunt, seek, follow, pursue, shadow **2** copy, draw, sketch, outline, delineate, mark, record, map

traceable *adj* able to be traced (to)

tracery *noun* decorated stonework holding the glass in some church windows

trachea /trə'kɪə/ (*plural* **tracheae**) *noun* the windpipe

tracheotomy /trakɪ'ɒtəmɪ/ *noun* a surgical cut in the trachea to make an alternative airway

trachoma *noun* an eye disease

tracing *noun* a traced copy

track *noun* **1** a mark left **2** (**tracks**) footprints **3** a path or rough road **4** a racecourse for runners, cyclists *etc* **5** a railway line **6** a line or course: *the track of his argument* **7** a single song *etc* on an album **8** an endless band on which wheels of a tank *etc* travel ◇ *verb* follow (an animal) by its footprints and other marks left ◇ **keep** or **lose track of** keep or fail to keep aware of the whereabouts or progress of ◇ **make tracks for** set off towards ◇ **track and field** athletic events, including running races and jumping and throwing competitions ◇ **track down** search for (someone or something) until caught or found

■ *noun* **2** footsteps, footprints, footmarks **3** path, way, route ◇ *verb* stalk, trail, hunt, trace, follow, pursue, chase, tail, shadow ◇ **track down** find, discover, trace, hunt down, run to earth, sniff out, ferret out, dig up, unearth, catch, capture

trackball *noun* a rotating ball in a computer keyboard which controls cursor movement

tracksuit *noun* a warm suit worn while jogging, before and after an athletic performance *etc*

tract *noun* **1** a stretch of land **2** a short pamphlet, *esp* on a religious subject **3** a system made up of connected parts of the body: *the digestive tract*

tractable *adj* easily made to do what is wanted

traction *noun* **1** the act of pulling or dragging **2** the state of being pulled ◇ **traction engine** a road steamengine

tractor *noun* a motor vehicle for pulling loads, ploughs *etc*

trade *noun* **1** the buying and selling of goods **2** someone's occupation, craft, job: *a carpenter by trade* ◇ *verb* **1** buy and sell **2** have business dealings (with) **3** exchange, swap: *trade insults* ◇ **trader** *noun* ◇ **trade union** a group of workers of the same trade who join together to bargain with employers for fair wages *etc* ◇ **trade unionist** a member of a trade union ◇ **trade in** give as part-payment for something else (*eg* an old car for a new one) ◇ **trade on** take advantage of, often unfairly

■ *noun* **1** commerce, traffic, business, dealing, buying, selling, shopkeeping, barter, exchange, transactions, custom ◇ *verb* **1** buy, sell, barter, exchange, swap, switch, bargain

trademark *noun* a registered mark or name put on goods to show that they are made by a certain company

■ brand, label, name, sign, symbol, logo, insignia, crest, emblem, badge, hallmark

tradesman *noun* **1** a shopkeeper **2** a workman in a skilled trade

tradewind *noun* a wind which blows towards the equator (from the north-east and south-east)

tradition *noun* **1** the handing-down of customs, beliefs, stories *etc* from generation to generation **2** a custom, belief *etc* handed down in this way ◇ **traditional** *adj* ◇ **traditionalist** *noun* someone who believes in maintaining traditions

■ **2** convention, custom, usage, way, habit, routine, ritual, institution, folklore ◇ **traditional** conventional, customary, habitual, usual, accustomed, established, fixed, long-established, time-honoured, old

■ **traditional** unconventional, innovative, new, modern, contemporary

traffic *noun* **1** the cars, buses, boats *etc* which use roads or waterways **2** trade **3** dishonest dealings (*eg* in drugs) ◇ *verb* (**traffics**, **trafficking**, **trafficked**) **1** trade **2** deal (in) ◇ **traffic island** a platform in the middle of a road for pedestrians to stand on while waiting to cross ◇ **traffic jam** a queue of vehicles at a standstill ◇ **traffic lights** lights of changing colours for controlling traffic at road junctions or street crossings ◇ **traffic warden** someone whose job is to control traffic

tragedy *noun* (*plural* **tragedies**) **1** a very sad event **2** a play about unhappy events and with a sad ending ◇ **tragedian** *noun* an actor or writer specializing in tragedy

■ **1** calamity, disaster, catastrophe, blow, misfortune, unhappiness, affliction

tragic *adj* of tragedy; very sad ◇ **tragically** *adv*

■ sad, sorrowful, miserable, unhappy, unfortunate, unlucky, ill-fated, pitiable, pathetic, heartbreaking, heart-rending, shocking, appalling, dreadful, awful, dire, calamitous, disastrous, catastrophic, deadly, fatal

■ happy, comic, successful

trail *verb* **1** draw along, in or through: *trailing his foot through the water* **2** hang down (from) or be dragged loosely behind **3** hunt (animals) by following footprints *etc* **4** walk wearily **5** to lag behind in a race, contest *etc* **6** of a plant: grow over the ground or a wall ◇ *noun* **1** an animal's track **2** a pathway through a wild region **3** something left stretching behind: *a trail of dust*

■ *verb* **1** drag, pull **2** droop, dangle, extend, straggle ◇ *noun* **2** path, footpath, road, route, way

trailer *noun* **1** a vehicle pulled behind a motorcar **2** a short film advertising a longer film to be shown at a later date

train *noun* **1** a railway engine with carriages or trucks **2** a part of a dress which trails behind the wearer **3** the attendants who follow an important person **4** a line (of thought, events *etc*) ◇ *verb* **1** prepare yourself by practice or exercise for a sporting event, job *etc* **2** educate **3** exercise (animals or people) in preparation for a race *etc* **4** tame and teach (an animal) **5** (with **on** or **at**) aim, point (a gun, telescope *etc*) at **6** make (a tree or plant) grow in a certain direction

■ *noun* **3** retinue, entourage, attendants, court, household, staff, followers, following **4** sequence, succession, series, progression, order, string, chain, line ◇ *verb* **1** exercise, work out, practise, rehearse **2** teach, instruct, coach, tutor, educate, improve, school, discipline, prepare **5** point, direct, aim, level

trainee *noun* someone who is being trained

trainer *noun* someone who trains people or animals for a sport, circus *etc*

training *noun* **1** preparation for a sport **2** experience or learning of the practical side of a job

■ **1** exercise, working-out, practice **2** teaching, instruction, coaching, tuition, education, schooling, discipline, preparation, grounding

trait *noun* a point that stands out in a person's character: *patience is one of his good traits*

■ feature, attribute, quality, characteristic, idiosyncrasy, peculiarity, quirk

traitor *noun* **1** someone who goes over to the enemy's side, or gives away secrets to the enemy **2** someone who betrays trust ◇ **traitorous** *adj*

trajectory *noun* (*plural* **trajectories**) the curved path of something (*eg* a bullet) moving through the air or through space

tram *noun* a long car running on rails and driven by electric power for carrying passengers (*also called*: **tramcar**)

tramline *noun* **1** a rail of tramway **2** (**tramlines**) *tennis* the parallel lines marked at the sides of the court

trammel *noun* something that hinders movement ◇ *verb* (**trammels**, **trammelling**, **trammelled**) hinder

tramp *verb* **1** walk with heavy footsteps **2** walk along, over *esp* wearily: *tramping the streets in search of a job* ◇ *noun* **1** someone with no fixed home and no job, who lives by begging **2** a journey made on foot **3** the sound of heavy footsteps

■ *verb* **1** stamp, stomp, stump, plod **2** walk, march, tread, trudge, traipse, trail, trek, hike, ramble, roam, rove ◇ *noun* **1** vagrant, vagabond, hobo, down-and-out, *slang* dosser

trample *verb* **1** tread under foot, stamp on **2** (*usu* with **on**) treat roughly or unfeelingly **3** tread heavily

trampoline *noun* a bed-like frame-work holding a sheet of elastic material for bouncing on, used by gymnasts *etc*

tramway *noun* a system of tracks on which trams run

trance *noun* a sleep-like or half-conscious state

■ dream, reverie, daze, stupor, unconsciousness, spell, ecstasy, rapture

tranquil *adj* quiet, peaceful ◇ **tranquillity** *noun*

■ calm, composed, cool, unexcited, placid, sedate, relaxed, *informal* laid-back, serene, peaceful, restful, still, undisturbed, untroubled, quiet, hushed, silent

◼ agitated, disturbed, troubled, noisy

tranquillize *verb* make calm

tranquillizer *noun* a drug to calm the nerves or cause sleep

trans- *prefix* across, through

transact *verb* do (a piece of business)

transaction *noun* **1** a piece of business, a deal **2** (**transactions**) the published reports of the meeting of a society

■ **1** deal, bargain, agreement, arrangement, negotiation, business, affair, matter, proceeding, enterprise, undertaking, deed, action, execution, discharge

transatlantic *adj* **1** crossing the Atlantic Ocean: *transatlantic yacht race* **2** across or over the Atlantic: *transatlantic friends*

transcend *verb* **1** be, or rise, above **2** be, or do, better than

■ **2** surpass, excel, outshine, eclipse, outdo, outstrip, beat, surmount, exceed, overstep

transcribe *verb* **1** copy from one book into another or from one form of writing (*eg* shorthand) into another **2** write out (a spoken text) **3** transliterate **4** adapt (a piece of music) for a particular instrument **5** *comput* transfer (data) from one storage device to another

transcript *noun* a written copy

■ transcription, copy, reproduction, duplicate, transliteration, translation, version, note, record, manuscript

transcription *noun* **1** the act of transcribing **2** a written copy

transept *noun* the part of a church which lies across the main part

transexual or **trans-sexual** *noun* someone who is anatomically of one sex, but adopts the characteristics and behaviour of the opposite sex

transfer *verb* /trans'fɜ:(r)/ (**transfers, transferring, transferred**) **1** remove to another place **2** hand over to another person ◇ *noun* /'transfɜ:(r)/ **1** the act of transferring **2** a design or picture which can be transferred from one surface to another ◇ **transferable** or **transferrable** *adj* able to be transferred ◇ **transference** *noun*

▣ *verb* **1** change, transpose, move, shift, remove, relocate, transplant, transport, carry, convey **2** transmit, consign, grant, hand over ◇ *noun* **1** change, changeover, transposition, move, shift, removal, relocation, displacement, transmission, handover, transference

transfigure *verb* change (greatly and for the better) the form or appearance of ◇ **transfiguration** *noun*

transfix *verb* **1** make unable to move or act (*eg* because of surprise): *transfixed by the sight* **2** pierce through (as with a sword)

▣ **1** fascinate, spellbind, mesmerize, hypnotize, paralyse **2** impale, spear, skewer, spike, stick

transform *verb* change in shape or appearance ◇ **transformation** *noun*

▣ change, alter, adapt, convert, remodel, reconstruct, transfigure, revolutionize

▣ preserve, maintain

transformer *noun* an apparatus for changing electrical energy from one voltage to another

transfuse *verb* **1** pass (*eg* liquid) from one thing to another **2** transfer (blood of one person) to the body of another ◇ **transfusion** *noun*

transgress *verb* break a rule, law *etc* ◇ **transgression** *noun* the act of breaking a rule, law *etc*; a sin ◇ **transgressor** *noun* someone who breaks a rule, law *etc*

transient *adj* not lasting, passing ◇ **transience** *noun*

▣ transitory, passing, flying, fleeting, brief, short, momentary, ephemeral, short-lived, temporary, short-term

▣ lasting, permanent

transistor *noun* **1** a small device, made up of a crystal enclosed in plastic or metal, which controls the flow of an electrical current **2** a portable radio set using these

transit *noun* **1** the carrying or movement of goods, passengers *etc* from place to place **2** the passing of a planet between the sun and the earth

▣ **1** passage, travel, movement, transfer, transportation, conveyance, carriage, haulage, shipment

transition *noun* a change from one form, place, appearance *etc* to another ◇ **transitional** *adj*

▣ passage, passing, progress, progression, development, evolution, flux, change, alteration, conversion, transformation, shift ◇ **transitional** provisional, temporary, passing, intermediate, developmental, changing, fluid, unsettled

▣ **transitional** initial, final

transitive *adj*, *grammar* of a verb: having an object, *eg* the verb '*hit*' in 'he *hit* the ball'

transitory *adj* lasting only for a short time

translate *verb* **1** turn (something said or written) into another language **2** interpret: *translated her expression as contempt* **3** convert from one thing to another ◇ **translatable** *adj* able to be translated

▣ **1** interpret, render, paraphrase, decode, decipher, transliterate, transcribe **3** change, alter, convert, transform

translation *noun* **1** the act of translating **2** something translated

translator *noun* someone who translates

transliterate *verb* write (a word) in the letters of another alphabet ◇ **transliteration** *noun*

translucent *adj* allowing light to

pass through, but not transparent
◊ **translucence** noun

transmission noun **1** the act of trans mitting **2** a radio or television broad cast

▣ **1** broadcasting, diffusion, spread, com munication, conveyance, transport, shipment, sending, dispatch, relaying, transfer **2** broadcast, programme, show, signal

▣ **1** reception

transmit verb (**transmits**, **transmit ting**, **transmitted**) **1** pass on (a mes sage, news, heat) **2** send out signals which are received as programmes

▣ **1** communicate, impart, convey, carry, bear, transport, send, dispatch, for ward, relay, transfer **2** broadcast, radio, disseminate, network

transmitter noun an instrument for transmitting (esp radio signals)

transmute verb change the form or nature of ◊ **transmutation** noun

transom noun a beam across a win dow or the top of a door

transparency noun (plural **transpar encies**) **1** the state of being trans parent **2** a photograph printed on transparent material and viewed by shining light through it

transparent adj **1** able to be seen through **2** easily seen to be true or false: a transparent excuse

▣ **1** clear, see-through, translucent, sheer **2** plain, distinct, clear, lucid, explicit, un ambiguous, unequivocal, apparent, visible, obvious, evident, manifest, patent, undisguised, open, candid, straightforward

▣ **1** opaque **2** unclear, ambiguous

transpire verb **1** of a secret: become known **2** happen: tell me what transpired **3** let out (moisture etc) through pores of the skin or through the surface of leaves

transplant verb /trans'plɑ:nt/ **1** lift and plant (a growing plant) in another place **2** remove (skin) and graft it on an other part of the same body **3** remove (an organ) and graft it in another per son or animal ◊ noun /'transplɑ:nt/ **1** the

act of transplanting **2** a transplanted organ, plant etc ◊ **transplantation** noun

transport verb /trans'pɔ:t/ **1** carry from one place to another **2** overcome with strong feeling: transported with de light **3** hist send (a prisoner) to a prison in a different country ◊ noun /'transpɔ:t/ **1** the act of transporting **2** any means of carrying persons or goods: rail transport **3** strong feeling: transports of joy

▣ verb **1** convey, carry, bear, take, fetch, bring, move, shift, transfer, ship, haul, remove, deport ◊ noun **2** transporta tion, shipment, shipping, haulage, re moval

transportation noun **1** the act of transporting **2** means of transport **3** hist punishment of prisoners by send ing them to a prison in a different coun try

transporter noun a large vehicle used to carry other vehicles, heavy ma chinery etc

transpose verb **1** cause (two things) to change places **2** change (a piece of music) from one key to another ◊ **tran sposition** noun

▣ **1** swap, exchange, switch, interchange, transfer, shift, rearrange, reorder, change, alter, move, substitute

transputer noun, comput a chip used in parallel processing

trans-sexual another spelling of transexual

transubstantiate verb change into a different substance

transverse adj lying, placed etc across: transverse beams in the roof

transvestite noun someone who likes to wear clothes intended for the opposite sex ◊ **transvestism** noun

trap noun **1** a device for catching ani mals etc **2** a plan or trick for taking someone by surprise **3** a bend in a pipe which is kept full of water, for prevent ing the escape of air or gas **4** a carriage with two wheels ◊ verb (**traps**, **trap ping**, **trapped**) catch in a trap, or in such a way that escape is not possible

▣ noun **1** snare, net, noose, booby-trap **2**

trick, wile, ruse, stratagem, device, trickery, artifice, deception ◇ *verb* snare, net, entrap, ensnare, catch, take, ambush, corner, trick, deceive, dupe

trapdoor *noun* a door in a floor or ceiling

trapeze *noun* a swing used in performing gymnastic exercises or feats

trapezium *noun* a figure with four sides, two of which are parallel

trapper *noun* someone who makes a living by catching animals for their skins and fur

trappings *noun plural* **1** clothes or ornaments suitable for a particular person or occasion **2** ornaments put on horses

Trappist *noun* a monk of an order whose members have taken a vow of silence

trash *noun* something of little worth, rubbish ◇ **trashy** *adj*

■ rubbish, garbage, refuse, junk, waste, litter, sweepings, scum, dregs

trauma *noun* **1** injury to the body **2** a very violent or distressing experience which has a lasting effect **3** a condition (of a person) caused in this way ◇ **traumatic** *adj*

■ **1** injury, wound, hurt, damage **2** suffering, anguish, agony, torture, ordeal, shock, jolt, upset, disturbance, upheaval, strain, stress ◇ **traumatic** painful, hurtful, injurious, wounding, shocking, upsetting, distressing, disturbing, unpleasant, frightening, stressful

■ *traumatic* healing, relaxing

travail *noun, old* hard work

travel *verb* (**travels, travelling, travelled**) **1** go on a journey **2** move: *light travels in a straight line* **3** go along or across: *travel the country* **4** visit foreign countries ◇ *noun* the act of travelling

■ *verb* **1** journey, voyage **2** proceed, progress **3** move, wander, ramble, roam, rove ◇ *noun* travelling, touring, tourism, globetrotting

■ *verb* **1** stay, remain

traveller *noun* **1** someone who travels **2** a travelling representative of a busi-

ness firm who tries to obtain orders for his firm's products **3** *informal* a gypsy

■ **1** tourist, explorer, voyager, globetrotter, holidaymaker, *informal* tripper, passenger, wanderer, rambler, hiker, migrant, nomad, refugee **2** salesman, saleswoman, representative, *informal* rep, agent **3** gypsy, itinerant, tinker, vagrant

traverse *verb* go across, pass through ◇ *noun* **1** something that crosses or lies across **2** a passage across a rock face *etc*

travesty *noun* (*plural* **travesties**) a poor or ridiculous imitation: *a travesty of justice*

■ mockery, parody, *informal* take-off, send-up, farce, caricature, distortion, sham

trawl *verb* fish by dragging a trawl along the bottom of the sea ◇ *noun* a wide-mouthed, bag-shaped net

trawler *noun* a boat used for trawling

tray *noun* a flat piece of wood, metal *etc* with a low edge, for carrying dishes

treacherous *adj* **1** likely to betray **2** dangerous: *treacherous road conditions* ◇ **treacherously** *adv*

■ **1** traitorous, disloyal, unfaithful, faithless, unreliable, untrustworthy, false, untrue, deceitful, double-crossing **2** dangerous, hazardous, risky, perilous, precarious, icy, slippery

■ **1** loyal, faithful, dependable **2** safe, stable

treachery *noun* (*plural* **treacheries**) the act of betraying those who have trusted you

■ treason, betrayal, disloyalty, infidelity, falseness, duplicity, double-dealing

■ loyalty, dependability

treacle *noun* a thick, dark syrup produced from sugar when it is being refined ◇ **treacly** *adj*

tread *verb* (**treads, treading, trodden, trod**) **1** walk on or along **2** (with **on**) put your foot on **3** crush, trample under foot ◇ *noun* **1** a step **2** a way of walking **3** the part of a tyre which touches the ground ◇ **tread on someone's toes** offend or upset them

◊ **tread water** keep yourself afloat in an upright position by moving your arms and legs

■ *verb* **1** walk, step, pace, stride, march, hike, tramp, trudge, plod **3** stamp, trample, walk on, press, crush, squash

treadle *noun* part of a machine which is worked by the foot

treadmill *noun* **1** *hist* a mill turned by the weight of people who were made to walk on steps fixed round a big wheel **2** a similar piece of equipment used for exercising **3** any tiring, routine work

treason *noun* disloyalty to your own country or its government, *eg* by giving away its secrets to an enemy ◊ **treasonable** *adj* consisting of, or involving, treason

treasure *noun* **1** a store of money, gold *etc* **2** anything of great value or highly prized ◊ *verb* **1** value greatly **2** keep carefully because of personal value: *she treasures the mirror her mother left her*

■ *noun* **1** fortune, wealth, riches, money, cash, gold, jewels, hoard, cache ◊ *verb* **1** prize, value, esteem **2** love, adore, idolize, cherish, preserve, guard

🖪 *verb* **2** disparage, belittle

treasurer *noun* someone who has charge of the money of a club

treasure-trove *noun* treasure or money found hidden, the owner of which is unknown

Treasury or **treasury** *noun* (*plural* **treasuries**) the part of a government which has charge of the country's money

treat *verb* **1** deal with, handle, act towards: *I was treated very well in prison* **2** try to cure (someone) of a disease **3** try to cure (a disease) **4** put (something) through a process *etc* **5** write or speak about **6** buy (someone) a meal, drink *etc* ◊ *noun* something special (*eg* an outing) that gives pleasure: *they went to the theatre as a treat*

■ *verb* **1** deal with, manage, handle **2** tend, nurse, minister to, attend to, look after, care for, heal, cure **6** pay for, buy, stand, give, provide

treatise *noun* a long, detailed essay *etc* on some subject

treatment *noun* **1** the act of treating (*eg* a disease) **2** remedy, medicine: *a new treatment for cancer* **3** the way in which someone or something is dealt with: *rough treatment* **4** a way of presenting something in art, literature *etc*

■ **1** healing, care, nursing **2** cure, remedy, medication, therapy, surgery **3** management, handling, use

treaty *noun* (*plural* **treaties**) an agreement made between countries

■ pact, convention, agreement, covenant, compact, negotiation, contract, bond, alliance

treble *adj* **1** threefold, three times normal: *wood of treble thickness* **2** high in pitch: *treble note* ◊ *verb* make or become three times as great ◊ *noun* **1** the highest part in singing **2** a child who sings the treble part of a song

tree *noun* **1** the largest kind of plant with a thick, firm wooden stem and branches **2** anything like a tree in shape or structure: *a mug tree*

trefoil *noun* a three-part leaf or decoration

trek *noun* **1** a long or wearisome journey **2** *old* a journey by wagon ◊ *verb* (**treks**, **trekking**, **trekked**) **1** make a long hard journey **2** *old* make a journey by wagon

■ *noun* **1** hike, walk, march, tramp, journey, expedition, safari ◊ *verb* **1** hike, walk, march, tramp, trudge, plod, journey, rove, roam

trellis *noun* (*plural* **trellises**) a network of strips for holding up growing plants

tremble *verb* **1** shake with cold, fear, weakness **2** feel fear (for another person's safety *etc*) ◊ *noun* a trembling movement or fit of trembling

■ *verb* **1** shake, shiver, shudder, vibrate, quake, quiver ◊ *noun* shake, vibration, quake, shiver, shudder, quiver, tremor, wobble

🖪 *noun* **2** steadiness

tremendous *adj* **1** very great or strong **2** *informal* very good, excellent

◊ **tremendously** *adv, informal* very

■ **1** huge, immense, vast, colossal, gigantic, towering, formidable **2** wonderful, marvellous, stupendous, sensational, spectacular, extraordinary, amazing, incredible, terrific, *slang* mega

Ⓔ **2** ordinary, unimpressive

tremolo *noun* (*plural* **tremolos**) *music* rapid repetition of the same note giving a trembling sound

tremor *noun* **1** a shaking or quivering **2** a minor earthquake

■ **1** shake, quiver, tremble, shiver, quake, quaver, wobble, vibration, agitation, thrill **2** shock, earthquake

Ⓔ **1** steadiness

tremulous *adj* **1** shaking **2** showing fear: *a tremulous voice*

trench *noun* (*plural* **trenches**) a long narrow ditch dug in the ground (*eg* by soldiers as a protection against enemy fire) ◊ *verb* dig a trench in

trenchant *adj* **1** going deep, hurting: *a trenchant remark* **2** of a policy *etc*: effective, vigorous

trenchcoat *noun* a kind of waterproof overcoat with a belt

trencher *noun*, *old* a wooden plate ◊ **trencherman** *noun* someone able to eat large meals: *a good trencherman*

trend *noun* **1** a general direction: *the trend of events* **2** fashion; craze

■ **1** course, flow, drift, tendency, inclination, leaning **2** craze, *informal* rage, fashion, vogue, mode, style, look

trendy *adj, informal* fashionable

trepan *verb* (**trepans, trepanning, trepanned**) *med* remove a piece of the skull from

trepidation *noun* fear, nervousness

trespass *verb* **1** go illegally on private land *etc* **2** (with **on**) demand too much of: *trespassing on my time* **3** *old* sin ◊ *noun* (*plural* **trespasses**) the act of trespassing ◊ **trespasser** *noun*

■ *verb* **2** invade, intrude, encroach, poach, infringe, violate ◊ *noun* invasion, intrusion, encroachment, poaching, infringement, violation, contravention, offence, misdemeanour

tress *noun* (*plural* **tresses**) **1** a lock of hair **2** (**tresses**) hair, *esp* long

trestle *noun* a wooden support with legs, used for holding up a table, platform *etc*

trews *noun plural* tartan trousers

trial *noun* **1** the act of testing or trying (*eg* something new) **2** the judging (of a prisoner) in a court of law **3** suffering ◊ **on trial 1** being tried (*esp* in a court of law) **2** for the purpose of trying out: *goods sent on trial* **3** being tested: *I'm still on trial with the company* ◊ **trial and error** the trying of various methods or choices until the right one is found

■ **1** experiment, test, examination, check, dry run, dummy run, practice, rehearsal **2** litigation, lawsuit, hearing, inquiry, tribunal **3** affliction, suffering, grief, misery, distress, adversity, hardship, ordeal, trouble, nuisance

Ⓔ **3** relief, happiness

triangle *noun* **1** a figure with three sides and three angles: (△) **2** a triangular metal musical instrument, played by striking with a small rod ◊ **triangular** *adj* having the shape of a triangle

triathlon *noun* a sporting contest consisting of three events, often swimming, running and cycling

tribe *noun* **1** a people who are all descended from the same ancestor **2** a group of families, *esp* of a wandering people ruled by a chief ◊ **tribal** *adj* ◊ **tribesman, tribeswoman** *noun*

tribulation *noun* **1** great hardship or sorrow **2** a source of this

tribunal *noun* **1** a group of people appointed to give judgement, *esp* on an appeal **2** a court of justice

tribune *noun*, *hist* a high official elected by the people in ancient Rome

tributary *noun* (*plural* **tributaries**) **1** a stream that flows into a river or other stream **2** *hist* someone who gives a tribute

tribute *noun* **1** an expression, in word or deed, of praise, thanks *etc*: *a warm tribute to his courage* **2** a sign of something worthy of praise: *her success is a tribute to her hard work* **3** money paid regularly by one nation or ruler to another in return for protection or peace

◼ **1** praise, commendation, compliment, accolade, homage, respect, honour, credit, acknowledgement, recognition, gratitude **2** testimony, indication, evidence **3** payment, levy, charge, tax, duty, offering, contribution

trice *noun*: **in a trice** in a very short time

triceps *noun* a muscle at the back of the arm that straightens the elbow

trick *noun* **1** something done to cheat or fool someone **2** a mischievous act or plan, a prank **3** a cunning or skilful action to puzzle, amuse *etc* **2** in card games, the cards picked up by the winner when each player has played a card ◇ *adj* meant to deceive: *trick photography* ◇ *verb* cheat by some quick or cunning action

◼ *noun* **1** practical joke, joke, jape, *informal* leg-pull, prank, antic, caper, frolic, feat, stunt, ruse, wile, dodge, subterfuge, trap, device, knack, technique, secret ◇ *adj* false, mock, artificial, imitation, fake, forged, counterfeit, sham, bogus ◇ *verb* deceive, delude, dupe, fool, mislead, bluff, hoax, *informal* pull someone's leg, cheat, swindle, *slang* sting, diddle, defraud, *informal* con, trap, outwit

◼ *adj* real, genuine

trickery *noun* cheating

◼ deception, illusion, pretence, guile, deceit, dishonesty, cheating, swindling, fraud, double-dealing, monkey business, *slang* funny business

◼ straightforwardness, honesty

trickle *verb* **1** flow in small amounts **2** arrive or leave slowly and gradually: *replies are trickling in* ◇ *noun* a slow, gradual flow

◼ *verb* **1** dribble, run, leak, seep, ooze, exude, drip, drop, filter, percolate

◼ *verb* **1** stream, gush

trickster *noun* someone who deceives by tricks

tricky *adj* not easy to do

◼ difficult, awkward, problematic, complicated, knotty, thorny, delicate

◼ easy, simple

tricolour or *US* **tricolor** *noun* a three-coloured flag, *esp* with three bands of equal size

tricycle *noun* a three-wheeled bicycle

trident *noun* a three-pronged spear

tried *past form* of **try**

triennial *adj* **1** lasting for three years **2** happening every third year

tries *see* **try**

trifle *noun* **1** anything of little value **2** a small amount **3** a pudding of whipped cream, sponge-cake, wine *etc* ◇ *verb* **1** (with **with**) act towards without sufficient respect: *in no mood to be trifled with* **2** amuse yourself in an idle way (with): *he trifled with her affections* **3** behave in a light, thoughtless manner

◼ *noun* **1** toy, plaything, trinket, bauble, knick-knack, triviality, nothing **2** little, bit, spot, drop, dash, touch, trace, tad ◇ *verb* **1** toy, play, sport, flirt, dally, dabble, fiddle, meddle, fool

trifling *adj* very small in value or amount

◼ small, paltry, slight, negligible, inconsiderable, unimportant, insignificant, minor, trivial, petty, silly, frivolous, idle, empty, worthless

◼ important, significant, serious

trigger *noun* a small lever on a gun which, when pulled with the finger, causes the bullet to be fired ◇ *verb* (with **off**) start, be the cause of, an important event, chain of events *etc*

◼ *verb* cause, start, initiate, activate, set off, spark off, provoke, incite, prompt, elicit, generate, produce

trigonometry *noun* the branch of mathematics which has to do chiefly with the relationship between the sides and angles of triangles ◇ **trigonometric** or **trigonometrical** *adj*

trilby *noun* a man's hat with an indented crown and narrow brim

So called because a hat of this shape was worn by an actress in the original stage version of George du Maurier's novel, *Trilby* (1894)

trill *verb* sing, play or utter in a quivering or bird-like way ◇*noun* a trilled sound; in music, a rapid repeating of two notes several times

trillion *noun* **1** a million million millions **2** (originally *US*) a million millions

trilobite *noun* a fossil whose body forms three long furrows

trilogy *noun* (*plural* **trilogies**) a group of three related plays, novels *etc* by the same author, meant to be seen or read as a whole

trim *verb* (**trims**, **trimming**, **trimmed**) **1** clip the edges or ends of: *trim the hedge* **2** remove by or as if by cutting: *trim ten pounds off the cost* **3** decorate (*eg* a hat) **4** arrange (sails, cargo) so that a boat is ready for sailing ◇*noun* **1** the act of trimming **2** dress: *hunting trim* ◇*adj* **1** tidy, in good order, neat **2** slim

   ◼ *verb* **1** cut, clip, crop, dock, prune **3** decorate, ornament, embellish, garnish, dress, array ◇ *adj* **1** neat, tidy, orderly, shipshape, spick-and-span, spruce, smart, dapper **2** slim, slender, svelte
   ◼ *adj* untidy, scruffy

trimming *noun* **1** a decoration added to a dress, cake *etc* **2** a piece of cloth, hair *etc* cut off while trimming

trinity *noun* **1** a group of three **2** (**Trinity**) in Christianity, the union of Father, Son and Holy Ghost in one God

trinket *noun* a small ornament (*esp* one of little value)

trio *noun* (*plural* **trios**) **1** three performers **2** three people or things

trip *verb* (**trips**, **tripping**, **tripped**) **1** (often with **up**) stumble, fall over **2** move with short, light steps **3** (with **up**) make a mistake ◇*noun* **1** a journey for pleasure or business **2** a light short step ◇**tripper** *noun* someone who goes on a short pleasure trip

   ◼ *verb* **1** stumble, slip, fall, tumble, stagger ◇ *noun* **1** outing, excursion, tour, jaunt, ride, drive, spin, journey, voyage, expedition

tripartite *adj* **1** in or having three parts **2** of an agreement: between three countries

tripe *noun* **1** part of the stomach of the cow or sheep used as food **2** *informal* rubbish, nonsense

triple *adj* **1** made up of three **2** three times as large (as something else) ◇*verb* make or become three times as large

triplet *noun* **1** one of three children or animals born of the same mother at one time **2** three rhyming lines in a poem **3** *music* a group of three notes played in the time of two

triplicate *noun*: **in triplicate** in three copies

tripod *noun* a three-legged stand (*esp* for a camera)

triptych *noun* three painted panels forming a whole work of art

trisect *verb* cut into three ◇**trisection** *noun*

triskaidekaphobia *noun* fear of the number thirteen ◇**triskaidekaphobic** *adj*

trite *adj* of a remark: used so often that it has little force or meaning

   ◼ banal, commonplace, ordinary, run-of-the-mill, humdrum, stale, tired, worn, unoriginal, hackneyed, overused, stereotyped, clichéd, *informal* corny
   ◼ original, new, fresh

triumph *noun* **1** a great success or victory **2** celebration after a success: *ride in triumph through the streets* ◇*verb* **1** (often with **over**) win a victory **2** rejoice openly because of a victory ◇**triumphal** *adj* used in celebrating a triumph

   ◼ *noun* **1** win, victory, conquest, walkover, success, achievement, accomplishment, feat, coup, hit, sensation **2** exultation, jubilation, rejoicing, celebration, elation, joy, happiness ◇ *verb* **1** win, succeed, prosper, conquer, vanquish **2** celebrate, rejoice, glory, gloat
   ◼ *noun* **1** failure, defeat

triumphant *adj* victorious; showing joy because of, or celebrating, triumph

◇ **triumphantly** *adv*

■ winning, victorious, conquering, successful, exultant, jubilant, rejoicing, celebratory, glorious, elated, joyful, proud, boastful, gloating, swaggering

✕ defeated, humble

trivet *noun* a metal tripod for resting a teapot or kettle on

trivia *noun plural* unimportant matters or details

trivial *adj* of very little importance ◇ **triviality** *noun* (*plural* **trivialities**) **1** something unimportant **2** the state of being trivial ◇ **trivially** *adv*

■ unimportant, insignificant, inconsequential, incidental, minor, petty, paltry, trifling, small, little, inconsiderable, negligible, worthless, meaningless, frivolous, banal, trite, commonplace, everyday ◇ **triviality 1** trifle, nothing, detail, technicality **2** unimportance, insignificance, pettiness, smallness, worthlessness, frivolity

✕ important, significant, profound

trivialize *verb* make or treat as unimportant

trod and **trodden** *see* tread

troglodyte *noun* a cave-dweller

troll *noun* a mythological creature, giant or dwarf, who lives in a cave ◇ *verb* send messages on the Internet to provoke other users into responding

trolley *noun* (*plural* **trolleys**) **1** a small cart for conveying luggage *etc* **2** a supermarket basket on wheels **3** a hospital bed on wheels for transporting patients **4** a small wagon or truck ◇ **trolley-bus** *noun* a bus which gets its power from overhead wires

trollop *noun* **1** a careless, untidy woman **2** a sexually promiscuous woman

trombone *noun* a brass wind instrument with a sliding tube which changes the notes ◇ **trombonist** *noun*

trompe l'oeil a painting or decoration which gives the illusion of reality

troop *noun* **1** a collection of people or animals **2** (**troops**) soldiers **3** a unit in cavalry *etc* ◇ *verb* **1** gather in numbers **2** go in a group: *they all trooped out*

◇ **troop the colour** carry a regiment's flag past the lined-up soldiers of the regiment

■ *noun* **1** gang, band, bunch, group, body, pack, herd, flock, horde, crowd, throng, multitude **2** army, military, soldiers, servicemen, servicewomen **3** contingent, squadron, unit, division, company, squad, team, crew ◇ *verb* **2** go, march, parade, stream, flock, swarm, throng

trooper *noun* a cavalry soldier

troopship *noun* a ship for carrying soldiers

trope *noun* a figure of speech

trophy *noun* (*plural* **trophies**) **1** a prize such as a silver cup won in a sports competition *etc* **2** something taken from an enemy and kept in memory of the victory ◇ *adj* of a person's partner *etc*: elevating that person's status: *trophy wife*

tropic *noun* **1** either of two imaginary circles running round the earth at about 23 degrees north (**Tropic of Cancer**) or south (**Tropic of Capricorn**) of the equator **2** (**tropics**) the hot regions near or between these circles ◇ *adj* (also **tropical**) **1** of the tropics **2** growing in hot countries: *tropical fruit* **3** very hot

■ *adj* **3** hot, torrid, sultry, sweltering, stifling, steamy, humid

✕ *adj* **3** arctic, cold, cool, temperate

trot *verb* (**trots, trotting, trotted**) **1** of a horse: run with short, high steps **2** of a person: run slowly with short steps **3** make (a horse) trot ◇ *noun* the pace of a horse or person when trotting ◇ **trot out** produce (a story, article *etc*) without much thought

trotters *noun plural* the feet of pigs or sheep, *esp* when used as food

troubadour *noun*, *hist* a medieval travelling singer-musician, *esp* in France

trouble *verb* **1** cause worry or sorrow to **2** cause inconvenience to **3** make an effort, bother (to): *I didn't trouble to ring him* ◇ *noun* **1** worry, uneasiness **2** difficulty; disturbance **3** something which causes worry, difficulty *etc* **4** illness or disease: *heart trouble* **5** care and effort put into doing something **6** (*usu* **troubles**) public unrest ◇**troubled** *adj* worried or disturbed ◇**in trouble** in difficulty

■ *verb* **1** upset, distress, sadden, pain, afflict, burden, worry, agitate, disconcert, perplex **2** annoy, vex, harass, torment, bother, inconvenience, disturb ◇ *noun* **1** pain, suffering, affliction, distress, grief, woe, heartache, concern, uneasiness, worry, anxiety, agitation **2** problem, difficulty, struggle **3** annoyance, irritation, bother, nuisance, inconvenience, misfortune **4** disorder, complaint, ailment, illness, disease, disability, defect **5** effort, exertion, pains, care, attention, thought

■ *verb* **1** reassure, help ◇ *noun* **1** relief, calm **4** health

troubleshooter *noun* someone whose job is to solve difficulties (*eg* in a firm's business activities)

troublesome *adj* causing difficulty or inconvenience

■ annoying, irritating, vexatious, irksome, bothersome, inconvenient, difficult, hard, tricky, thorny, taxing, demanding, laborious, tiresome, wearisome, unruly, rowdy, turbulent, trying, uncooperative, insubordinate, rebellious

■ easy, simple, helpful

trough /trɒf/ *noun* **1** a long, open container for holding animals' food and water **2** a channel or gutter **3** an area of low atmospheric pressure **4** a dip between two sea waves **5** a low point

trounce *verb* **1** punish or beat severely **2** defeat heavily

troupe /truːp/ *noun* a company of actors, dancers *etc* ◇**trouper** *noun* a member of a troupe

trousers *noun plural* an outer garment for the lower part of the body which covers each leg separately ◇**trouser** *adj* of a pair of trousers: *trouser leg*

trousseau *noun* (*plural* **trousseaux** or **trousseaus**) a bride's outfit for her wedding, and linen for her married life

trout *noun* (*plural* **trout**) a freshwater or sea (**sea-trout**) fish, used as food

trowel *noun* **1** a small spade used in gardening **2** a similar tool with a flat blade, used for spreading mortar

troy weight a system of weights for weighing gold, gems *etc*

truant *noun* someone who stays away from school *etc* without permission ◇**truancy** *noun* ◇**play truant** stay away from school, work *etc* without permission *etc*

■ *noun* absentee, deserter, runaway, idler, shirker, *informal* skiver, dodger ◇**truancy** absence, absenteeism, shirking, *informal* skiving

■ **truancy** attendance

truce *noun* a rest from fighting or quarrelling agreed to by both sides

■ cease-fire, peace, armistice, cessation, moratorium, suspension, stay, respite, *informal* let-up, lull, rest, break, interval, intermission.

■ war, hostilities

truck[1] *noun* **1** a wagon for carrying goods on a railway **2** a strong lorry for carrying heavy loads ◇**trucker** *noun*, *US* a lorry driver

truck[2] *noun*: **have no truck with** refuse to have dealings with

truculent *adj* fierce and threatening, aggressive ◇**truculence** *noun*

trudge *verb* walk with heavy steps, as if tired

true *adj* **1** of a story *etc*: telling of something which really happened **2** correct, not invented or wrong: *it's true that the earth is round* **3** accurate: *a true picture* **4** faithful: *a true friend* **5** real, properly so called: *the spider is not a true insect* **6** rightful: *the true heir* **7** in the correct or intended position ◇**truly** *adv* ◇**come true** be fulfilled

■ **1** real, genuine, authentic, actual **2** correct, right, factual, truthful, sincere, honest, legitimate, valid, rightful, proper **3** exact, precise, accurate **4** faithful, loyal, constant, steadfast, staunch, firm, trustworthy, trusty, honourable, dedicated, devoted ◇**truly** very, greatly, extremely, really, genuinely, sincerely, honestly, truthfully, undeniably, indubitably, indeed, in fact, in reality, exactly, precisely, correctly, rightly, properly

▪ **2** incorrect, false, wrong **3** inaccurate **4** unfaithful ◊ **truly** slightly, falsely, incorrectly

truffle *noun* a round fungus found underground and much valued as a flavouring for food

trug *noun* a shallow basket used in gardening

truism *noun* a statement which is so clearly true that it is not worth making

trump *noun* **1** a suit having a higher value than cards of other suits **2** a card of this suit ◊ *verb* **1** play a card which is a trump **2** win a surprising advantage over (a person, idea *etc*) ◊ **trump card 1** a card which is a trump **2** something kept in reserve as a means of winning an argument *etc* ◊ **trump up** make up, invent ◊ **turn up trumps** be (unexpectedly) useful or helpful

trumpery *noun* (*plural* **trumperies**) something showy but worthless

trumpet *noun* **1** a brass musical instrument with a clear, high-pitched tone **2** the cry of an elephant ◊ *verb* **1** announce (*eg* news) so that all may hear **2** to blow a trumpet ◊ **trumpeter** *noun*

▪ *verb* **1** blare, blast, roar, bellow, shout, proclaim, announce, broadcast, advertise

truncated *adj* **1** cut off at the top or end **2** shortened: *a truncated version*

truncheon *noun* a short heavy staff or baton such as that used by police officers

trundle *verb* wheel or roll along

trunk *noun* **1** the main stem of a tree **2** the body (not counting the head, arms, or legs) of someone or an animal **3** the long nose of an elephant **4** a large box or chest for clothes *etc* **5** *US* the luggage compartment of a motor-car **6** (**trunks**) short pants worn by boys and men for swimming ◊ **trunk road** a main road

▪ **2** torso, body, frame, shaft, stock, stem, stalk **4** case, suitcase, chest, coffer, box, crate

truss *noun* (*plural* **trusses**) **1** a bundle (*eg* of hay, straw) **2** a system of beams to support a bridge **3** a kind of supporting bandage ◊ *verb* **1** bind, tie tightly (up) **2** (often with **up**) prepare (a bird ready for cooking) by tying up the legs and wings

▪ *noun* **2** support, brace, prop, stay, shore, strut, joist **3** binding, bandage, support ◊ *verb* **1** tie, strap, bind, pinion, fasten, secure, bundle, pack

▪ *verb* **1** untie, loosen

trust *noun* **1** belief in the power, truth or goodness of a thing or person **2** a task, a valuable handed over to someone in the belief that they will do it, guard it *etc* **3** charge, keeping: *the child was put in my trust* **4** arrangement by which something (*eg* money) is given to someone to manage for the benefit of someone else **5** a number of business firms working closely together ◊ *verb* **1** have faith or confidence (in) **2** give (someone something) in the belief that they will use it well *etc: I can't trust your sister with my tennis racket* **3** feel confident (that): *I trust that you can find your way here* ◊ **trustful** *adj* ◊ **trustworthy** *adj* ◊ **trust fund** money or property held in trust ◊ **take on trust** believe without checking or testing

▪ *noun* **1** faith, belief, credence, credit, hope, expectation, reliance, confidence, assurance, conviction, certainty **3** care, charge, custody, safekeeping, guardianship, protection, responsibility, duty ◊ *verb* **1** rely on, depend on, count on, bank on, swear by **2** entrust, commit, consign, give, assign, delegate **3** believe, imagine, assume, presume, suppose ◊ **trustworthy** honest, upright, honourable, principled, dependable, reliable, steadfast, true, responsible, sensible

▪ *noun* **1** distrust, mistrust, scepticism, doubt ◊ **trustworthy** untrustworthy, dishonest, unreliable, irresponsible

trustee *noun* someone who manages money or property for another

trusting *adj* ready to trust, not suspicious

🔲 trustful, credulous, gullible, naive, innocent, unquestioning, unsuspecting, unguarded, unwary

🔳 distrustful, suspicious, cautious

trusty *adj* able to be depended on

truth *noun* **1** the state of being true **2** a true statement **3** the facts

🔲 **1** truthfulness, candour, frankness, honesty, sincerity, genuineness, authenticity, exactness, precision, accuracy, validity **2** reality, actuality, fact, axiom, maxim, principle, truism

🔳 **1** deceit, dishonesty, falseness **2** lie, falsehood

truthful *adj* **1** telling the truth, not lying **2** accurate, realistic ◇ **truthfully** *adv* ◇ **truthfulness** *noun*

🔲 **1** frank, candid, straight, honest, sincere, realistic, faithful, trustworthy, reliable **2** true, veritable, exact, precise, accurate, correct

🔳 **1** untruthful, deceitful **2** false, untrue

try *verb* (**tries**, **trying**, **tried**) **1** attempt, make an effort (to do something) **2** test by using: *try this new soap* **3** test severely, strain: *you're trying my patience* **4** attempt to use, open *etc*: *I tried the door but it was locked* **5** judge (a prisoner) in a court of law ◇ *noun* (*plural* **tries**) **1** an effort, an attempt **2** *rugby* an act of carrying the ball over the opponent's goal line and touching it on the ground ◇ **try on** put on (clothing) to see if it fits *etc* ◇ **try out** test by using

🔲 *verb* **1** attempt, endeavour, venture, undertake, seek, strive **2** experiment, test, sample, inspect, examine, investigate, evaluate **5** hear, judge ◇ *noun* **1** attempt, endeavour, effort, *informal* go, *informal* bash, *informal* crack, *informal* shot, *informal* stab

trying *adj* hard to bear; testing

🔲 annoying, irritating, *informal* aggravating, vexatious, exasperating, troublesome, tiresome, wearisome, difficult, hard, tough, arduous, taxing, demanding, testing

🔳 easy

tryst *noun*, *old* an arrangement to meet someone at a certain place

tsar, **tzar** or **czar** /zɑ:(r)/ or /tsɑ:(r)/ *noun*, *hist* the emperor of pre-revolutionary Russia

tsarina, **tzarina** or **czarina** /zɑ:ˈriːnə/ or /tsɑːˈriːnə/ *noun*, *hist* **1** the wife of a tsar **2** an empress of Russia

tsetse /ˈtsɛtsɪ/ *noun* or **tsetse fly** an African biting fly which spreads dangerous diseases

T-shirt *another spelling of* **tee-shirt**

tsunami *noun* a large sea wave caused by an earthquake

TT *abbrev* **1** Tourist Trophy (motorcycle races held on the Isle of Man) **2** tuberculin tested **3** teetotal

tub *noun* **1** a round wooden container used for holding water *etc* **2** a round container for ice-cream *etc* **3** a bath

🔲 **1** bath, basin, vat, tun, butt, cask, barrel, keg

tuba *noun* a large brass musical instrument giving a low note

tubby *adj* fat or plump

tube *noun* **1** a hollow, cylinder-shaped object through which liquid may pass **2** an organ of this kind in humans, animals *etc* **3** a container from which something may be squeezed **4** an underground railway system **5** a cathode ray tube

🔲 **1** hose, pipe, cylinder, duct, conduit, spout, channel

tuber *noun* a swelling on the underground stem of a plant (*eg* a potato)

tuberculosis *noun* an infectious disease affecting the lungs

tubing *noun* a length or lengths of tube

tubular *adj* shaped like a tube

TUC *abbrev* Trades Union Congress

tuck *noun* **1** a fold stitched in a piece of cloth **2** *informal* sweets, cakes *etc* **3** a cosmetic operation to tighten a flabby part ◇ *verb* **1** gather (cloth) together into a fold **2** fold or push (into or under a place) **3** (with **in** or **up**) push bedclothes closely round (someone in bed) ◇ **tuck shop** a shop in a school where sweets, cakes *etc* are sold ◇ **tuck in** *informal* to eat with enjoyment or greedily

◨ *noun* **1** fold, pleat, gather, pucker, crease ◇ *verb* **1** fold, pleat, gather, crease **2** insert, push, thrust, stuff, cram

Tuesday *noun* the third day of the week

tuft *noun* a bunch or clump of grass, hair *etc*

tug *verb* (**tugs**, **tugging**, **tugged**) **1** pull hard **2** pull along ◇ *noun* **1** a strong pull **2** a tugboat

◨ *verb* **1** heave, wrench, jerk, pluck **2** pull, draw, tow, haul, drag, lug ◇ *noun* **1** pull, tow, haul, heave, wrench, jerk, pluck

tugboat *noun* a small but powerful ship used for towing larger ones

tug-of-war *noun* a contest in which two sides, holding the ends of a strong rope, pull against each other

tuition *noun* teaching or coaching, especially private

◨ teaching, instruction, coaching, training, lessons, schooling, education

tulip *noun* a type of flower with cup-shaped flowers grown from a bulb

> Based on a Persian word for 'turban', because of the similarity in shape

tulle *noun* a kind of cloth made of thin silk or rayon net

tumble *verb* **1** fall or come down suddenly and violently **2** roll, toss (about) **3** do acrobatic tricks ◇ *noun* **1** a fall **2** a somersault **3** a confused state ◇ **tumble-drier** *noun* a machine for drying laundry by heating and rotating them ◇ **tumble to** understand suddenly

◨ *verb* **1** fall, stumble, trip, topple **2** pitch, roll, toss ◇ *noun* **1** fall, trip, drop, plunge, roll, toss

tumbledown *adj* falling to pieces

tumbler *noun* **1** a large drinking glass **2** an acrobat

tumbrel or **tumbril** *noun*, *hist* a two-wheeled cart of the kind used to take victims to the guillotine during the French Revolution

tumescent *adj* swollen, enlarged

tummy *noun* (*plural* **tummies**) *informal* the stomach

tumour or *US* **tumor** *noun* an abnormal growth on or in the body

tumult *noun* **1** a great noise made by a crowd **2** excitement, agitation ◇ **tumultuous** *adj*

◨ **1** noise, clamour, din, racket, hubbub **2** commotion, turmoil, disturbance, upheaval, stir, agitation, unrest, disorder, chaos

◪ **2** calm, composure

tumulus *noun* (*plural* **tumuli**) an artificial mound of earth, *esp* over a tomb

tun *noun* a large cask, *esp* for wine

tuna *noun* (*plural* **tuna** or **tunas**) a large sea fish, used as food (*also called*: **tunny**)

tundra *noun* a level treeless plain in Arctic regions

tune *noun* **1** notes put together to form a melody **2** the music of a song ◇ *verb* **1** (sometimes with **up**) put (a musical instrument) in tune **2** (sometimes with **in**) adjust a radio set to a particular station **3** (sometimes with **up**) improve the working of an engine ◇ **tuner** *noun* ◇ **tuning fork** a steel fork which, when struck, gives a note of a certain pitch ◇ **change your tune** change your opinions, attitudes *etc* ◇ **in tune 1** of a musical instrument: having each note adjusted to agree with the others or with the notes of other instruments **2** of a voice: agreeing with the notes of other voices or instruments **3** in agreement (with) ◇ **to the tune of** to the sum of

◨ *noun* **1** melody, theme, motif, song, number, air, strain ◇ *verb* **1** pitch, harmonize, set, regulate, adjust

tuneful *adj* having a pleasant or recognizable tune ◇ **tunefully** *adv*

◨ melodious, melodic, catchy, musical, euphonious, harmonious, pleasant, mellow, sonorous

◪ tuneless, discordant

tungsten *noun* an element, a grey metal

tunic *noun* **1** a soldier's or police officer's jacket **2** *hist* a loose garment reaching to the knees, worn in ancient

Greece and Rome **3** a similar modern garment: *gym tunic*

tunnel *noun* an underground passage (*eg* for a railway train) ◇ *verb* (**tunnels**, **tunnelling**, **tunnelled**) **1** make a tunnel **2** of an animal: burrow

▣ *noun* passage, passageway, gallery, subway, underpass, burrow, hole, mine, shaft

tunny *same as* **tuna**

turban *noun* **1** a long piece of cloth wound round the head, worn by Muslims **2** a kind of hat resembling this

turbid *adj* **1** of liquid: muddy, clouded **2** of writing *etc*: confused, unclear ◇ **turbidity** *noun*

turbine *noun* an engine with curved blades, turned by the action of water, steam, hot air *etc*

turbo- *prefix* using a turbine engine

turbot *noun* a type of large flat sea fish, used as food

turbulence *noun* **1** a disturbed or unruly state **2** stormy weather **3** irregular movement of air currents, *esp* when affecting the flight of aircraft

turbulent *adj* disturbed, in a restless state

▣ rough, choppy, stormy, blustery, tempestuous, raging, furious, violent, wild, tumultuous, boisterous, rowdy, disorderly, unruly, undisciplined, obstreperous, rebellious, mutinous, riotous, agitated, unsettled, unstable, confused, disordered.

🔁 calm, composed

turd *noun* **1** a lump of dung **2** *slang* a despicable person

tureen *noun* a large dish for holding soup at table

turf *noun* (*plural* **turfs** or **turves**) **1** grass and the soil below it **2** a slab of peat used as fuel **3** (used with **the**) the world of horse-racing ◇ *verb* cover with turf ◇ **turf accountant** a bookmaker ◇ **turf out** *informal* to throw out

turgid *adj* **1** swollen **2** of language: sounding grand but meaning little, pompous ◇ **turgidity** *noun*

turkey *noun* (*plural* **turkeys**) **1** a large farmyard bird, used as food **2** a play or film that is a failure ◇ **talk turkey** talk business or money

Turkish bath a type of hot air or steam bath in which someone is made to sweat heavily, is massaged and then slowly cooled

turmeric *noun* the yellow powder made from the root of a ginger-like plant, used as a spice in curries *etc*

turmoil *noun* a state of wild, confused movement or disorder

▣ confusion, disorder, tumult, commotion, disturbance, trouble, disquiet, agitation, turbulence, upheaval, stir, bustle, chaos, pandemonium, bedlam, noise, din, hubbub, row, uproar

🔁 calm, peace, quiet

turn *verb* **1** go round: *wheels turning* **2** face or go in another direction: *turned and walked away/the road turns sharply to the left* **3** direct (*eg* attention) **4** become: *his hair turned white* **5** to change or cause to change colour **6** of milk: go sour **7** shape in a lathe **8** pass (the age of): *she must have turned 40* **9** (with **on**) to move, swing *etc*: *the door turns on its hinges* ◇ *noun* **1** an instance of turning **2** a point where someone may change direction, *eg* a road junction: *take the first turn on the left* **3** a bend (*eg* in a road) **4** a change in character or course: *turn of events* **5** a spell of duty: *your turn to wash the dishes* **6** an act (*eg* in a circus) **7** an act of a specified kind: *a good turn* **8** a short stroll: *a turn along the beach* **9** a fit of dizziness, shock *etc* ◇ **by turns** or **in turn** one after another in a regular order ◇ **to a turn** exactly, perfectly: *cooked to a turn* ◇ **turn against** become hostile to ◇ **turn away** reject or send away ◇ **turn down 1** say no to, refuse (*eg* an offer, a request) **2** reduce, lessen (heat, volume of sound *etc*) ◇ **turn in 1** go to bed **2** hand over to those in authority ◇ **turn off 1** stop the flow of (a tap) **2** switch off the power for (a television *etc*) **3** *informal* make (someone) lose interest ◇ **turn on 1** set running (*eg* water from a tap) **2** switch on power for (a television *etc*) **3** depend (on) **4** become angry with (someone) unexpectedly **5** *informal* arouse sexually ◇ **turn out 1** make to leave, drive out **2** make, produce **3** empty: *turn out your pockets* **4** of a crowd: come out, gather for a special purpose **5** switch off (a light) **6** prove (to be): *he turned out to be right* ◇ **turn to 1** set to work **2** go to for help *etc* ◇ **turn up 1** appear, arrive **2** be found **3** increase (*eg* heat, volume of sound *etc*) ◇ **turn someone's head** fill them with pride or conceit

■ *verb* **1** revolve, circle, spin, twirl, whirl, twist, gyrate, pivot, hinge, swivel, rotate, roll **2** bend, veer, swerve, divert **6** sour, curdle, spoil, go off, go bad ◇ *noun* **1** revolution, cycle, round, circle, rotation, spin, twirl, twist, bend, curve, loop **2** change, alteration, shift, deviation **5** go, chance, opportunity, occasion, stint, period, spell ◇ **turn down 1** reject, decline, refuse, spurn, rebuff, repudiate, *informal* knock back **2** lower, lessen, quieten, soften, mute, muffle ◇ **turn in 1** go to bed, retire **2** hand over, give up, surrender, deliver, hand in, tender, submit, return, give back ◇ **turn on 2** switch on, start (up), activate, connect **3** hinge on, depend on, rest on **4** attack, round on, fall on **5** arouse, stimulate, excite, thrill, please, attract ◇ **turn out 1** evict, throw out, expel, deport, banish, dismiss, discharge, drum out, kick out, *informal* sack **5** switch off, turn off, unplug, disconnect **6** happen, come about, transpire, ensue, result, end up, become, develop, emerge ◇ **turn up 1** attend, come, arrive, appear, *informal* show up **3** amplify, intensify, raise, increase

◨ **turn down 1** accept **2** turn up ◇ **turn in 1** get up **2** keep ◇ **turn out 1** admit

turncoat *noun* someone who betrays their party, principles *etc*

turning *noun* **1** the act of turning **2** a point where a road *etc* joins another **3** the act of shaping in a lathe

◨ **2** turn-off, junction, crossroads, fork, bend, curve, turn

turning-point *noun* a crucial point of change

turnip *noun* a plant with a large round root used as a vegetable

turnover *noun* **1** rate of change or replacement (*eg* of workers in a firm *etc*) **2** the total amount of sales made by a firm during a certain time

turnpike *noun* **1** *hist* a gate across a road which opened when the user paid a toll **2** *US* a road on which a toll is paid

turnstile *noun* a gate which turns, allowing only one person to pass at a time

turntable *noun* **1** a revolving platform for turning a railway engine round **2** the revolving part of a record player on which the record rests

turpentine *noun* an oil from certain trees used for mixing paints, cleaning paint brushes *etc*

turpitude *noun* wickedness, depravity

turquoise *noun* a greenish-blue precious stone

Literally 'Turkish stone', because first found in Turkestan

turret *noun* **1** a small tower on a castle or other building **2** a structure for supporting guns on a warship ◇ **turreted** *adj* having turrets

turtle *noun* a kind of large tortoise which lives in water ◇ **turn turtle** of a boat *etc:* turn upside down, capsize

turtledove *noun* a type of dove noted for its sweet, soft song

turtleneck *noun* a high, round neck

tusk *noun* a large tooth (one of a pair) sticking out from the mouth of certain animals (*eg* an elephant, a walrus)

tussle *noun* a struggle ◇ *verb* struggle, compete

tussock *noun* a tuft of grass

tutelage *noun* the state of being protected by a guardian ◇ **tutelary** *adj* protecting

tutor *noun* **1** a teacher of students in a university *etc* **2** a teacher employed privately to teach individual pupils ◇ *verb* teach

■ *noun* **1** teacher, educator, lecturer,

supervisor, guide, mentor, guru **2** teacher, instructor, coach ◇ *verb* teach, instruct, train, drill, coach, educate, school, lecture, supervise, direct, guide

tutorial *adj* of a tutor ◇ *noun* a meeting for study or discussion between tutor and students

tutti-frutti *noun* an Italian ice-cream containing nuts and various kinds of fruit

tutu *noun* a ballet dancer's short, stiff, spreading skirt

tuxedo *noun* (*plural* **tuxedos** or **tuxedoes**) an evening suit with a dinner-jacket

TV *abbrev* television

twaddle *noun*, *informal* nonsense

twain *noun*, *old* two ◇ **in twain** *old* in two, apart

twang *noun* **1** a sound like that of a tightly-stretched string being plucked **2** a tone of voice in which the words seem to come through the nose ◇ *verb* make such a sound

tweak *verb* **1** pull with a sudden jerk, twitch **2** make fine adjustments to (a machine *etc*) ◇ *noun* **1** a sudden jerk or pull **2** a fine adjustment

■ *verb & noun* **1** twist, pinch, squeeze, nip, pull, tug, jerk, twitch

tweed *noun* **1** a woollen cloth with a rough surface **2** (**tweeds**) clothes made of this cloth ◇ *adj* made of tweed

tweezers *noun plural* small pincers for pulling out hairs, holding small things *etc*

twelfth *adj* the last of a series of twelve ◇ *noun* one of twelve equal parts

twelve *noun* the number 12 ◇ *adj* 12 in number

twentieth *adj* the last of a series of twenty ◇ *noun* one of twenty equal parts

twenty *noun* the number 20 ◇ *adj* 20 in number

twerp *noun*, *informal* an idiot

twice *adv* two times

twiddle *verb* play with, twirl idly ◇ **twiddle your thumbs 1** turn your

thumbs around one another **2** have nothing to do

■ turn, twirl, swivel, twist, wiggle, adjust, fiddle, finger

twig *noun* a small branch of a tree

twilight *noun* **1** the faint light between sunset and night, or before sunrise **2** the time just after the peak of something: *the twilight of the dictatorship*

twill *noun* a kind of strong cloth with a ridged appearance

twin *noun* **1** one of two children or animals born of the same mother at the same birth **2** one of two things exactly the same ◇ *adj* **1** born at the same birth **2** very like another **3** made up of two parts or things which are alike ◇ *verb* (**twin, twinning, twinned**) link (a town) with another in a different country ◇ **twin bed** one of two matching single beds

■ *noun* **2** double, lookalike, likeness, duplicate, clone, match, counterpart ◇ *adj* **2** identical, matching, duplicate, corresponding, symmetrical, parallel, co-ordinating, matched **3** double, dual, twofold

twine *noun* a strong kind of string made of twisted threads ◇ *verb* **1** wind or twist together **2** wind (about or around something)

■ *verb* **1** entwine, plait, braid, knit, weave **2** wind, coil, spiral, loop, curl, bend, twist, wreathe, wrap, surround, encircle

twinge *noun* a sudden, sharp pain

twinkle *verb* **1** of a star *etc*: shine with light which seems to vary in brightness **2** of eyes: shine with amusement *etc* ◇ **twinkle** or **twinkling** *noun* the act or state of twinkling ◇ **in the twinkling of an eye** in an instant ◇ **twinkly** *adj*

■ **1, 2** sparkle, glitter, shimmer, glisten, glimmer, flicker, flash, glint, gleam, shine

twinset *noun* a matching cardigan and jumper

twirl *verb* **1** turn or spin round quickly and lightly **2** turn round and round with the fingers ◇ *noun* a spin

∎ *verb* **1** spin, whirl, pirouette, rotate, gyrate, revolve, swivel, turn, twist **2** spin, whirl, wheel, rotate, revolve, swivel, pivot, turn, twist, wind, coil ◇ *noun* spin, whirl, pirouette, rotation, revolution, turn, twist, gyration, convolution, spiral, coil

twist *verb* **1** wind (threads) together **2** wind round or about something: *twist the knob round/the road twists round the mountain* **3** make (*eg* a rope) into a coil **4** bend out of shape **5** bend or wrench painfully (*eg* your ankle) **6** make (*eg* facts) appear to have a meaning which is really false ◇ *noun* **1** the act of twisting **2** a painful wrench **3** something twisted: *a twist of tissue paper*

∎ *verb* **1** twine, entwine, intertwine, weave, entangle **2** turn, screw, wring, spin, swivel, wind, zigzag, bend, coil, spiral, curl **5** wrench, rick, sprain, strain **6** change, alter, misquote, misrepresent, distort, contort, warp, pervert ◇ *noun* **1** turn, screw, spin, convolution **3** curl, loop, coil, spiral

twisted *adj* **1** full of twists, convoluted **2** of someone or their mind: perverted

twister *noun*, *informal* a dishonest and unreliable person

twitch *verb* **1** pull with a sudden light jerk **2** jerk slightly and suddenly: *a muscle in his face twitched* ◇ *noun* **1** a sudden jerk **2** a muscle spasm

∎ *verb* **1** pull, tug, tweak, snatch, pluck **2** jerk, jump, start, blink, shake ◇ *noun* **1** jerk, jump, start **2** spasm, convulsion, tic, tremor

twitter *noun* **1** high, rapidly repeated sounds, as are made by small birds **2** slight nervous excitement ◇ *verb* **1** of a bird: make a series of high quivering notes **2** of a person: to talk continuously

two *noun* the number 2 ◇ *adj* 2 in number

two-faced *adj* deceitful, insincere

∎ hypocritical, insincere, false, lying, deceitful, treacherous, double-dealing, devious, untrustworthy

Ea honest, candid, frank

twofold *adj* double

two-time *verb* have a love affair with two people at the same time

tycoon *noun* a business man of great wealth and power

> Based on a Japanese title for a warlord

tyke *noun* a dirty, ill-kempt dog

tympani, tympanist *another spelling* of **timpani**, **timpanist**

type *noun* **1** a class of people, animals or things which share characteristics **2** an example which has all the usual characteristics of its kind **3** a small metal block with a raised letter or sign, used for printing **4** a set of these **5** printed lettering ◇ *verb* **1** use a typewriter or word processor **2** identify or classify as a particular type

∎ *noun* **1** sort, kind, form, genre, variety, strain, species, breed, group, class, category, classification, description, designation **2** archetype, embodiment, prototype, original, model, pattern, specimen, example **5** print, printing, characters, letters, lettering, face, fount, font

typecast *verb* give (an actor) parts very similar in character

typeface *noun* a set of letters, characters *etc* of a specified design

typescript *noun* a typed script for a play *etc*

typeset *verb* (**typesets**, **typesetting**, **typeset**) arrange (type) or set (a page *etc*) in type for printing

typewriter *noun* a machine with keys which, when struck, print letters on a sheet of paper

typhoid *noun* an infectious disease caused by germs in infected food or drinking water

typhoon *noun* a violent storm of wind and rain in Eastern seas

typhus *noun* a dangerous fever carried by lice

typical *adj* having or showing the usual characteristics: *a typical Irishman/typical of her to be late* ◇ **typically** *adv*

▭ standard, normal, usual, average, conventional, orthodox, representative, illustrative, indicative, characteristic, distinctive

▣ atypical, unusual

typify *verb* (**typifies**, **typifying**, **typified**) be a good example of: *typifying the English abroad*

▭ embody, epitomize, encapsulate, personify, characterize, exemplify, symbolize, represent, illustrate

typist *noun* someone who works with a typewriter or word processor

typography *noun* the use of type for printing ◇ **typographer** *noun* someone who sets or knows about printing type ◇ **typographical** *adj* ◇ **typographically** *adv*

tyrannical or **tyrannous** *adj* like a tyrant, cruel

▭ dictatorial, despotic, autocratic, absolute, authoritarian, domineering, overbearing, high-handed, imperious, magisterial, ruthless, harsh, severe, strict, oppressive, overpowering, unjust, unreasonable

▣ liberal, tolerant

tyrannize *verb* act as a tyrant; rule over harshly

tyranny *noun* (*plural* **tyrannies**) the rule of a tyrant

▭ dictatorship, despotism, autocracy, absolutism, authoritarianism, imperiousness, ruthlessness, harshness, severity, oppression, injustice

▣ democracy, freedom

tyrant *noun* a ruler who governs cruelly and unjustly

▭ dictator, despot, autocrat, absolutist, authoritarian, bully, oppressor, slavedriver, taskmaster

tyre or *US* **tire** *noun* a thick rubber cover round a motor or cycle wheel

tyro *another spelling of* **tiro**

tzar, tzarina *another spelling of* **tsar, tsarina**

Uu

ubiquitous /jʊbɪkwɪtəs/ *adj* **1** being everywhere at once **2** found everywhere ◇ **ubiquitously** *adv* ◇ **ubiquity** *noun*

▣ **1** omnipresent, ever-present, everywhere, universal, global **2** everywhere, pervasive, common, frequent

▣ **2** rare, scarce

UDA *abbrev* Ulster Defence Association

udder *noun* a bag-like part of a cow, goat *etc* with teats which supply milk

UDI *abbrev* Unilateral Declaration of Independence

UDR *abbrev* Ulster Defence Regiment

UEFA *abbrev* Union of European Football Associations

UFO *abbrev* unidentified flying object

ugli fruit a citrus fruit that is a cross between a grapefruit, a Seville orange and a tangerine

ugly *adj* **1** unpleasant to look at or hear: *ugly sound* **2** threatening, dangerous: *gave me an ugly look* ◇ **ugliness** *noun* ◇ **ugly duckling** an unattractive or disliked person who later turns into a beauty, success *etc*

▣ **1** unattractive, unsightly, plain, unprepossessing, ill-favoured, hideous, monstrous, misshapen, deformed **2** unpleasant, disagreeable, nasty, horrid, disgusting, revolting, repulsive, vile, frightful, terrible

▣ **1** attractive, beautiful, handsome, pretty **2** pleasant

UHF *abbrev* ultra high frequency

UHT *abbrev* **1** ultra-heat treated **2** ultra high temperature

ukulele /jʊkə'leɪlɪ/ *noun* a small, stringed musical instrument played like a banjo

ulcer *noun* an open sore on the inside or the outside of the body ◇ **ulcerated** *adj* having an ulcer or ulcers ◇ **ulcerous** *adj*

ulterior *adj* beyond what is admitted or seen: *ulterior motive*

▣ secondary, hidden, concealed, undisclosed, unexpressed, covert, secret, private, personal, selfish

▣ overt

ultimate *adj* **1** last, final **2** most important, greatest possible

▣ **1** final, last, closing, concluding, eventual, terminal, furthest, remotest **2** extreme, utmost, greatest, perfect, fundamental, primary

ultimately *adv* finally, in the end

▣ finally, eventually, at last, in the end, after all

ultimatum *noun* a final demand sent with a threat to break off discussion, declare war *etc* if it is not met

ultra- *prefix* **1** very: *ultra-careful* **2** beyond: *ultramicroscopic*

ultramarine *adj* of a deep blue colour

ultrasonic *adj* beyond the range of human hearing

ultraviolet *adj* having rays of slightly shorter wavelength than visible light

umber *noun* a mineral substance used to produce a brown paint

umbilical *adj* of the navel ◇ **umbilical cord** a tube connecting an unborn mammal to its mother through the placenta

umbrage *noun* a feeling of offence or hurt: *took umbrage at my suggestion*

umbrella *noun* an object made up of a folding covered framework on a stick which protects against rain

Literally 'little shadow' and originally used to refer to a sunshade

umlaut /'ʊmlaʊt/ *noun* a character (¨) placed over a letter to modify its pronunciation

umpire *noun* **1** a sports official who sees that a game is played according to the rules **2** a judge asked to settle a dispute ◇ *verb* act as an umpire
- ▣ *noun* **1** referee, linesman, judge, adjudicator **2** arbiter, arbitrator, mediator, moderator ◇ *verb* referee, judge, adjudicate, arbitrate, mediate, moderate, control

umpteen *adj* many, lots ◇ **umpteenth** *adj*
- ▣ a good many, numerous, plenty, millions, countless, innumerable
- ▣ few

Originally *umpty*, a signaller's slang term for a dash in Morse code

UN *abbrev* United Nations

un- *prefix* **1** not: *unequal* **2** (with verbs) used to show the reversal of an action: *unfasten*

unabashed *adj* shameless, blatant
- ▣ unashamed, unembarrassed, brazen, blatant, bold, confident, undaunted, unconcerned, undismayed
- ▣ abashed, sheepish

unable *adj* lacking enough strength, power, skill *etc*
- ▣ incapable, powerless, impotent, unequipped, unqualified, unfit, incompetent, inadequate
- ▣ able, capable

unaccountable *adj* not able to be explained ◇ **unaccountably** *adv*
- ▣ inexplicable, unexplainable, unfathomable, incomprehensible, baffling, puzzling, mysterious, astonishing, extraordinary, strange, odd, peculiar, singular, unusual, uncommon
- ▣ explicable, explainable

unaccustomed *adj* not used (to)
- ▣ unused, unacquainted, unfamiliar, unpractised, inexperienced
- ▣ accustomed, familiar

unadulterated *adj* pure, not mixed with anything else

unanimous *adj* **1** all of the same opinion: *we were unanimous* **2** agreed to by all: *a unanimous decision* ◇ **unanimously** *adv* ◇ **unanimity** *noun*
- ▣ **1** united, in agreement, in accord, harmonious, as one **2** concerted, joint, common
- ▣ **1** disunited, divided

unanswerable *adj* not able to be answered

unapproachable *adj* unfriendly and stiff in manner
- ▣ inaccessible, remote, distant, aloof, stand-offish, withdrawn, reserved, unsociable, unfriendly, forbidding
- ▣ approachable, friendly

unarmed *adj* not armed
- ▣ defenceless, unprotected, exposed, open, vulnerable, weak, helpless
- ▣ armed, protected

unassuming *adj* modest
- ▣ unassertive, self-effacing, retiring, modest, humble, meek, unobtrusive, unpretentious, simple, restrained
- ▣ presumptuous, assertive, pretentious

unattached *adj* **1** not attached **2** single, not married, not having a partner
- ▣ **2** unmarried, single, free, available, footloose, fancy-free, independent
- ▣ **2** engaged, committed

unaware *adj* not knowing, ignorant (of): *unaware of the danger* ◇ **unawares** *adv* **1** without warning **2** unintentionally
- ▣ oblivious, unconscious, ignorant, uninformed, unknowing, unsuspecting, unmindful, heedless
- ▣ aware, conscious

unbalanced *adj* mad; lacking balance: *unbalanced view*

unbearable *adj* too painful or bad to be endured
- ▣ intolerable, unacceptable, insupportable, insufferable, unendurable, excruciating
- ▣ bearable, acceptable

unbelievable *adj* too unusual to be believed; astonishing ◇ **unbelievably** *adv*

unbeliever *noun* someone who does not follow a certain religion

unbending *adj* severe

unbounded *adj* not limited, very great: *unbounded enthusiasm*
- ▣ boundless, limitless, unlimited, unre-

stricted, unrestrained, unchecked, unbridled, infinite, endless, immeasurable, vast

Ea limited, restrained

unbridled *adj* not kept under control: *unbridled fury*

≡ immoderate, excessive, uncontrolled, unrestrained, unchecked, *slang* full-on

unburden *verb*: **unburden yourself** tell your secrets or problems to someone else

uncalled *adj*: **uncalled for** quite unnecessary: *your remarks were uncalled for*

≡ gratuitous, unprovoked, unjustified, unwarranted, undeserved, unnecessary, needless

Ea timely

uncanny *adj* strange, mysterious ◇ **uncannily** *adv*

≡ weird, strange, queer, bizarre, mysterious, unaccountable, incredible, remarkable, extraordinary, fantastic, unnatural, unearthly, supernatural, eerie, creepy, *informal* spooky

uncared *adj*: **uncared for** not looked after properly

unceremonious *adj* informal, offhand ◇ **unceremoniously** *adv*

uncertain *adj* 1 not certain, doubtful 2 not definitely known 3 changeable

≡ 1 unsure, unconvinced, doubtful, dubious, undecided, ambivalent, hesitant, wavering, vague, vacillating 2 unconfirmed, indefinite 3 unpredictable, unforeseeable, undetermined, unsettled

Ea 1 certain, sure 3 predictable

uncharted *adj* 1 not shown on a map or chart 2 little known

uncle *noun* 1 the brother of your father or mother 2 the husband of your father's or mother's sister ◇ **Uncle Sam** *informal* the United States

unclean *adj* dirty, impure

≡ dirty, soiled, filthy, foul, polluted, contaminated, tainted, impure, unhygienic, corrupt, defiled, sullied

Ea clean, hygienic

uncoil *verb* unwind

uncomfortable *adj* 1 not comfortable 2 not at ease

≡ 1 cramped, hard, cold, ill-fitting, irritating, painful 2 awkward, embarrassed, self-conscious, uneasy

uncommon *adj* not common, strange ◇ **uncommonly** *adv* very: *uncommonly well*

≡ rare, scarce, infrequent, unusual, abnormal, unfamiliar, strange, odd, curious, bizarre, extraordinary, remarkable, outstanding, exceptional, distinctive, special

Ea common, usual, normal

uncompromising *adj* not willing to give in or make concessions to others

unconditional *adj* with no conditions attached; absolute ◇ **unconditionally** *adv*

≡ unqualified, unreserved, unrestricted, unlimited, absolute, utter, full, total, complete, entire, whole-hearted, downright, outright, positive, categorical, unequivocal

Ea conditional, qualified, limited

unconscionable *adj* more than is reasonable: *unconscionable demands*

unconscious *adj* 1 senseless, stunned (eg by an accident) 2 not aware (of) 3 not done intentionally; involuntary: *an unconscious reaction* ◇ *noun* the deepest level of the mind

≡ *adj* 1 stunned, knocked out, out, out cold, out for the count, concussed, comatose 2 unaware, oblivious, blind, deaf, heedless, unmindful, ignorant 3 involuntary, automatic, reflex, instinctive, impulsive, innate, subconscious, subliminal, repressed, suppressed, latent, unwitting, inadvertent, accidental, unintentional

Ea *adj* 1 conscious 2 aware 3 intentional

uncouth *adj* 1 clumsy, awkward 2 rude

uncover *verb* 1 remove a cover from 2 disclose

≡ 1 unveil, unmask, unwrap, strip, bare, open, expose 2 disclose, divulge, leak, reveal, show

Ea 1 cover 2 suppress, conceal

unction *noun* anointing; anointment ◇ **unctuous** *adj* oily, ingratiating

uncut *adj* not cut; not edited down

undaunted *adj* fearless; not discouraged

▤ undeterred, undiscouraged, unbowed, resolute, steadfast, brave, courageous, fearless, bold, intrepid, dauntless, indomitable

▨ discouraged, timorous

undecided *adj* not yet decided

▤ uncertain, unsure, in two minds, ambivalent, doubtful, hesitant, wavering, irresolute, uncommitted, indefinite, vague, dubious, debatable, moot, unsettled, open

▨ decided, certain, definite

undeniable *adj* not able to be denied, clearly true ◇ **undeniably** *adv*

under *prep* **1** directly below or beneath **2** less than: *costing under £5* **3** within the authority or command of: *under General Montgomery* **4** going through, suffering: *under attack* **5** having, using: *under a false name* **6** in the category of **7** in accordance with: *under our agreement* ◇ *adv* in or to a lower position, condition *etc* ◇ **go under 1** sink beneath the surface of water **2** go bankrupt, go out of business ◇ **under age** younger than the legal or required age ◇ **under way** in motion, started

under- *prefix* **1** below, beneath **2** lower in position or rank **3** too little

underachieve *verb* achieve less than your potential ◇ **underachiever** *noun*

underarm *adv* of bowling *etc*: with the arm kept below the shoulder

undercarriage *noun* the wheels of an aeroplane and their supports

underclothes *noun plural* clothes worn next to the skin under other clothes

undercover *adj* acting or done in secret: *an undercover agent (ie a spy)*

▤ secret, *informal* hush-hush, private, confidential, spy, intelligence, underground, clandestine, surreptitious, furtive, covert, hidden, concealed.

▨ open, unconcealed

undercurrent *noun* **1** a flow or movement under the surface **2** a half-hidden feeling or tendency: *an under-current of despair in her voice*

▤ **2** undertone, overtone, hint, suggestion, tinge, flavour, aura, atmosphere, feeling, sense, movement, tendency, trend, drift

undercut *verb* (**undercuts, undercutting, undercut**) sell at a lower price than someone else

underdeveloped *adj* **1** not fully grown **2** of a country: lacking modern agricultural and industrial systems, and with a low standard of living

underdog *noun* the weaker side, or the loser in any conflict or fight

underdone *adj* of food: not quite cooked

underestimate *verb* estimate at less than the real worth, value *etc*

▤ underrate, undervalue, misjudge, miscalculate, minimize, belittle, disparage, dismiss

▨ overestimate, exaggerate

underfoot *adj* under the feet

undergo *verb* (**undergoes, undergoing, underwent, undergone**) **1** suffer, endure **2** receive (*eg* as medical treatment)

undergraduate *noun* a university student who has not yet passed final examinations

underground *adj* **1** below the surface of the ground **2** secret, covert ◇ *noun* a railway which runs in a tunnel beneath the surface of the ground

▤ *adj* **1** subterranean, buried, sunken, covered, hidden, concealed **2** secret, covert, undercover, revolutionary, subversive, radical, experimental, avant-garde, alternative, unorthodox, unofficial

undergrowth *noun* shrubs or low plants growing amongst trees

underhand *adj* sly, deceitful

▤ unscrupulous, unethical, immoral, improper, sly, crafty, sneaky, stealthy, surreptitious, furtive, clandestine, devious, dishonest, deceitful, deceptive, fraudulent, *informal* crooked, *informal* shady

▨ honest, open, above board

underlay *noun* a protective layer beneath a carpet *etc*

underlie *verb* (**underlies, underlying, underlay, underlain**) be the hidden cause or source of ◇ **underlying** *adj*

▤ **underlying** basic, fundamental, essential, primary, elementary, root, intrinsic, latent, hidden, lurking, veiled

underline *verb* 1 draw a line under 2 stress the importance of, emphasize

underling *noun* someone of lower rank

undermine *verb* do damage to, weaken gradually (health, authority *etc*)

▤ erode, wear away, weaken, sap, sabotage, subvert, vitiate, mar, impair

▨ strengthen, fortify

underneath *adj & prep* in a lower position (than), beneath: *look underneath the table/wearing a jacket underneath his coat*

undernourished *adj* not having enough nourishing food

underpants *noun plural* underwear covering the buttocks and upper legs

under par 1 not up to the usual level 2 unwell: *feeling under par*

underpass *noun* a road passing under another one

underpay *verb* pay too little

underpin *verb* support from beneath, prop up

underplay *verb* understate, play down

underprivileged *adj* not having normal living standards or rights

▤ disadvantaged, deprived, poor, needy, impoverished, destitute, oppressed

▨ privileged, fortunate, affluent

underrate *verb* think too little of, underestimate

▤ underestimate, undervalue, belittle, disparage, depreciate, dismiss

▨ overrate, exaggerate

underscore *verb* underline; emphasize

undersell *verb* 1 sell for less than the true value 2 sell for less than someone else

undersigned *noun*: the under-**signed** the people whose names are written at the end of a letter or statement

undersized *adj* below the usual or required size

▤ small, tiny, minute, miniature, dwarf, stunted, underdeveloped, underweight, puny

▨ oversized, big, overweight

underskirt *noun* a thin skirt worn under another skirt

understand *verb* (**understands, understanding, understood**) 1 see the meaning of 2 appreciate the reasons for, sympathize with: *I don't understand your behaviour* 3 have a thorough knowledge of: *do you understand economics?* 4 have the impression, take as true: *I understood that you weren't coming* ◇ **understandable** *adj*

▤ 1 grasp, comprehend, take in, follow, *informal* get, *informal* cotton on, fathom 2 make out, discern, perceive, see, realize, recognize, appreciate, accept 4 believe, think, know, hear, learn, gather, assume, presume, suppose, conclude

understanding *noun* 1 the ability to see the full meaning of something 2 someone's perception or understanding 3 an agreement or condition: *on the understanding that we both pay half* 4 appreciation of other people's feelings, difficulties *etc* ◇ *adj* able to understand other people's feelings, sympathetic

▤ *noun* 1 grasp, comprehension, knowledge, wisdom, intelligence, intellect, sense, judgement, discernment, insight, appreciation, awareness 2 impression, perception, belief, idea, notion, opinion, interpretation 3 agreement, arrangement, pact, accord 4 sympathy, empathy ◇ *adj* sympathetic, compassionate, kind, considerate, sensitive, tender, loving, patient, tolerant, forbearing, forgiving

▨ *adj* unsympathetic, insensitive, impatient, intolerant

understatement *noun* a statement which does not give the whole truth, making less of certain details than is actually the case ◊ **understate** *verb*

understudy *noun* (*plural* **understudies**) an actor who learns the part of another actor and is able to take their place if necessary

undertake *verb* (**undertakes, undertaking, undertook, undertaken**) **1** promise (to do something) **2** accept, take upon yourself (a task, duty *etc*): *I undertook responsibility for the food*

▣ **1** pledge, promise, guarantee, agree, contract, covenant **2** attempt, endeavour, take on, accept, assume

undertaker *noun* someone whose job is to organize funerals

undertaking *noun* **1** something which is being attempted or done **2** a promise **3** the business of an undertaker

▣ **1** enterprise, venture, business, affair, task, project, operation, attempt, endeavour, effort **2** pledge, commitment, promise, vow, word, assurance

under-the-counter *adj* hidden from customers' sight; illegal

undertone *noun* **1** a soft voice **2** a partly hidden meaning, feeling *etc*: *an undertone of discontent* **3** a subdued sound or shade of colour

undertow *noun* a current below the surface of the water which moves in a direction opposite to the surface movement

undervalue *verb* value (something) below its real worth

▣ underrate, underestimate, misjudge, minimize, depreciate, disparage, dismiss

▣ overrate, exaggerate

underwater *adj* under the surface of the water

underwear *noun* underclothes

underweight *adj* under the usual or required weight

underwent *past form* of **undergo**

underworld *noun* **1** the criminal world or level of society **2** the place where spirits go after death

underwrite *verb* **1** accept for insurance **2** accept responsibility or liability

for ◊ **underwriter** *noun* someone who insures ships

▣ **1, 2** endorse, authorize, sanction, approve, back, guarantee, insure, sponsor, fund, finance, subsidize, subscribe, sign, initial, countersign

undesirable *adj* not wanted

▣ unwanted, unwelcome, unacceptable, unsuitable, unpleasant, disagreeable, distasteful, offensive, objectionable

▣ desirable, pleasant

undies *noun plural, informal* underwear

undivided *adj* not split, complete, total: *undivided attention*

▣ solid, unbroken, intact, whole, entire, full, complete, combined, united, unanimous, concentrated, exclusive, wholehearted

undo *verb* (**undoes, undoing, undone, undid**) **1** unfasten (a coat, parcel *etc*) **2** wipe out the effect of, reverse: *undoing all the good I did* **3** *old* ruin, dishonour (*esp* a reputation)

▣ **1** unfasten, untie, unbuckle, unbutton, unzip, unlock, unwrap, unwind, open, loose, loosen, separate **2** nullify, invalidate, cancel, reverse, overturn, upset, quash, defeat, undermine, spoil, ruin, wreck, shatter, destroy

▣ **1** fasten, do up

undoing *noun* ruin, downfall

▣ downfall, ruin, ruination, collapse, destruction, defeat, overthrow, reversal, weakness, shame, disgrace

undoubted *adj* beyond question ◊ **undoubtedly** *adv* without doubt, certainly

undreamt-of *adj* more *etc* than could have been imagined

undress *verb* take your clothes off

undue *adj* **1** unjustifiable: *undue criticism* **2** too much, more than is necessary: *undue expense* ◊ **unduly** *adv*

▣ **1, 2** unnecessary, needless, uncalled-for, unwarranted, undeserved, unreasonable, excessive, inordinate, extreme, extravagant, improper ◊ **unduly** too, over, excessively, immoderately, inordinately, unreasonably, unjustifiably, unnecessarily

1, **2** reasonable, moderate, proper ◇ **unduly** moderately, reasonably

undulate verb **1** move as waves do **2** have a rolling, wavelike appearance ◇ **undulating** adj ◇ **undulation** noun

undying adj unending, never fading: *undying love*

unearth verb bring or dig out from the earth, or from a place of hiding

■ dig up, exhume, disinter, excavate, uncover, expose, reveal, find, discover, detect

◪ bury

unearthly adj **1** strange, as if not of this world **2** *informal* absurd, *esp* absurdly early: *at this unearthly hour*

■ **1** supernatural, ghostly, eerie, uncanny, weird, strange, spine-chilling **2** unreasonable, outrageous, ungodly

◪ **2** reasonable

uneasy adj anxious, worried ◇ **uneasiness** noun

■ uncomfortable, anxious, worried, apprehensive, tense, strained, nervous, agitated, shaky, jittery, edgy, upset, troubled, disturbed, unsettled, restless, impatient, unsure, insecure

◪ calm, composed

unemployed adj **1** without a job **2** not in use ◇ **the unemployed** unemployed people as a group

unemployment noun **1** the state of being unemployed **2** the total number of unemployed people in a country

unenviable adj not arousing envy, unpleasant: *unenviable task*

■ undesirable, unpleasant, disagreeable, uncomfortable, thankless, difficult

◪ enviable, desirable

unequal adj **1** not equal; unfair: *unequal distribution* **2** lacking enough strength or skill: *unequal to the job* ◇ **unequalled** adj without an equal, unique

■ **1** different, varying, dissimilar, unlike, unmatched, uneven, unbalanced, disproportionate, asymmetrical, irregular, unfair, unjust, biased, discriminatory

unequivocal adj clear, not ambiguous: *unequivocal orders*

■ unambiguous, explicit, clear, plain, evident, distinct, unmistakable, express, direct, straight, definite, positive, categorical, absolute, unqualified

◪ ambiguous, vague, qualified

unerring adj always right, never making a mistake: *unerring judgement*

uneven adj **1** not smooth or level **2** not all of the same quality *etc*: *this work is very uneven* ◇ **unevenly** adv

■ **2** irregular, intermittent, spasmodic, fitful, jerky, unsteady, variable, changeable, fluctuating, erratic, inconsistent, patchy

unexceptionable adj not causing objections or criticism

❗ Do not confuse: **unexceptionable** and **unexceptional**

unexceptional adj not exceptional, ordinary ◇ **unexceptionally** adv

unexpected adj not expected, sudden ◇ **unexpectedly** adv

■ unforeseen, unanticipated, unpredictable, chance, accidental, fortuitous, sudden, abrupt, surprising, startling, amazing, astonishing, unusual

◪ expected, predictable

unexpurgated adj not censored

unfailing adj never failing, never likely to fail: *unfailing accuracy*

unfair adj not just ◇ **unfairly** adv ◇ **unfairness** noun

■ unjust, inequitable, biased, prejudiced, bigoted, discriminatory, unbalanced, one-sided, undeserved, unmerited, unwarranted, uncalled-for, unethical, unscrupulous, unprincipled, wrongful, dishonest

◪ fair, just, unbiased, deserved

unfaithful adj **1** not true to one's marriage vows **2** failing to keep promises ◇ **unfaithfulness** noun

■ **1** adulterous, two-timing **2** disloyal, treacherous, false, untrue, deceitful, dishonest, untrustworthy, unreliable, fickle, inconstant

◪ **1** faithful **2** loyal, reliable

unfasten verb loosen, undo (*eg* a buttoned coat)

unfathomable adj not understandable, not clear

unfeeling *adj* harsh, hard-hearted
- insensitive, cold, hard, stony, callous, heartless, hard-hearted, cruel, inhuman, pitiless, uncaring, unsympathetic, apathetic
- sensitive, sympathetic

unfettered *adj* not restrained

unfit *adj* 1 not good enough, or not in a suitable state (to, for): *unfit for drinking/unfit to travel* 2 not in good condition physically
- 1 unsuitable, inappropriate, unsuited, ill-equipped, unqualified, ineligible, untrained, unprepared, incapable, incompetent, inadequate, ineffective, useless 2 unhealthy, out of condition, flabby, feeble, decrepit
- 1 fit, suitable, competent 2 healthy

unflagging *adj* not tiring or losing strength

unflappable *adj* imperturbable, always calm

unflinching *adj* brave, not put off by pain, opposition *etc*

unfold *verb* 1 spread out 2 give details of (a story, plan) 3 of details of a plot *etc*: become known
- 1 open, spread, flatten, straighten, stretch out, undo, unfurl, unroll, uncoil, unwrap, uncover 2 reveal, disclose, show, present, describe, explain, clarify, elaborate 3 develop, evolve
- 1 fold, wrap 2 withhold, suppress

unforgettable *adj* unlikely to ever be forgotten; memorable
- memorable, momentous, historic, noteworthy, notable, impressive, remarkable, exceptional, extraordinary
- unmemorable, unexceptional

unfortunate *adj* 1 unlucky 2 regrettable: *unfortunate turn of phrase* ◇ **unfortunately** *adv* 1 unluckily 2 I'm sorry to say: *unfortunately I can't go*
- 1 unlucky, luckless, hapless, unsuccessful, poor, wretched, unhappy, doomed, ill-fated, hopeless, disastrous 2 regrettable, lamentable, deplorable, adverse, unfavourable, unsuitable, inappropriate, inopportune, untimely, ill-timed
- 1 fortunate, happy 2 favourable, appropriate

unfounded *adj* not based on fact; untrue
- baseless, groundless, unsupported, unsubstantiated, unproven, unjustified, idle, false, spurious, fabricated
- substantiated, justified

unfurl *verb* unfold (*eg* a flag)

ungainly *adj* clumsy, awkward
- clumsy, awkward, gauche, inelegant, gawky, unco-ordinated, lumbering, unwieldy
- graceful, elegant

ungracious *adj* rude, not polite

ungrateful *adj* not showing thanks for kindness
- unappreciative, ill-mannered, ungracious, selfish, heedless
- grateful, thankful

unguarded *adj* 1 without protection 2 thoughtless, careless: *unguarded remark*
- 1 undefended, unprotected, exposed, vulnerable, defenceless 2 unwary, careless, incautious, imprudent, indiscreet, thoughtless, unthinking, heedless, foolish, foolhardy, rash, ill-considered
- 1 defended, protected 2 guarded, cautious

unguent *noun* ointment

unhand *verb*, *old* let go, release

unhappy *adj* 1 miserable, sad 2 unfortunate ◇ **unhappily** *adv* ◇ **unhappiness** *noun*
- 1 sad, sorrowful, miserable, melancholy, depressed, dispirited, despondent, dejected, downcast, crestfallen, long-faced, gloomy 2 unfortunate, unlucky, ill-fated
- 1 happy 2 fortunate

unhealthy *adj* 1 not well, ill 2 harmful to health: *unhealthy climate* 3 showing signs of not being well: *unhealthy complexion* ◇ **unhealthily** *adv* ◇ **unhealthiness** *noun*
- 1 unwell, sick, ill, poorly, ailing, sickly, infirm, invalid, weak, feeble, frail, unsound 2 unwholesome, insanitary, unhygienic, harmful, detrimental
- 1 healthy, fit 2 wholesome, hygienic, natural

unheard-of adj very unusual, unprecedented

■ unknown, unfamiliar, new, unusual, obscure

unhinged adj mad, crazy

unholy adj 1 evil 2 outrageous

uni- prefix one, a single

UNICEF abbrev United Nations Children's Fund

unicorn noun a mythological animal like a horse, but with one straight horn on its forehead

uniform adj the same in all parts or times, never varying ◇ noun the form of clothes worn by people in the armed forces, children at a certain school etc ◇ **uniformity** noun sameness

■ adj same, identical, like, alike, similar, homogeneous, consistent, regular, equal, smooth, even, flat, monotonous, unvarying, unchanging, constant, unbroken ◇ noun outfit, costume, livery, insignia, regalia, robes, dress, suit

◆ adj different, varied, changing

unify verb (**unifies, unifying, unified**) combine into one ◇ **unification** noun

■ unite, join, bind, combine, integrate, merge, amalgamate, consolidate, coalesce, fuse, weld

◆ separate, divide, split

unilateral adj 1 one-sided 2 involving one person or group out of several ◇ **unilateralism** noun action by one group only, esp the abandoning of nuclear weapons by one country ◇ **unilateralist** noun & adj

uninhibited adj not inhibited, unrestrained

■ unconstrained, unreserved, unselfconscious, liberated, free, unrestricted, uncontrolled, unrestrained, abandoned, natural, spontaneous, frank, candid, open, relaxed, informal

◆ inhibited, repressed, constrained, restrained

uninitiated adj not knowing, ignorant

uninterested adj not interested

■ indifferent, unconcerned, uninvolved, bored, listless, apathetic, unenthusiastic, blasé, unresponsive

◆ interested, concerned, enthusiastic, responsive

❗ Do not confuse with: **disinterested**

uninterrupted adj 1 continuing without a break 2 of a view: not blocked by anything

union noun 1 the act of joining together 2 partnership; marriage 3 countries or states joined together 4 an association of people with similar concerns, esp a trade union ◇ **Union Jack** the flag of the United Kingdom

■ 3 alliance, coalition, league, association, federation, confederation, confederacy

unionist noun 1 a member of a trade union 2 someone who supports the union of the United Kingdom

unionize verb start or join a trade union

unique adj without a like or equal: a unique sense of timing ◇ **uniquely** adv ◇ **uniqueness** noun

■ single, one-off, sole, only, lone, solitary, unmatched, matchless, peerless, unequalled, unparalleled, unrivalled, incomparable, inimitable

◆ common

❗ Do not confuse with: **rare**

unisex adj of or in a style suitable for either men or women

unison noun 1 exact sameness of musical pitch 2 agreement, accord ◇ **in unison** all together

unit noun 1 a single thing, person or group, esp when considered as part of a larger whole: army unit/storage unit 2 a fixed amount or length used as a standard by which others are measured (eg metres, litres, centimetres etc) 3 a whole number less than 10

unitary adj 1 forming a unit, not divided 2 using or based on units

unite verb 1 join together; become one 2 act together ◇ **united** adj

■ **1** join, link, couple, marry, ally, co-operate, band, merge, blend, unify

☲ **1** separate, sever

unity *noun* **1** complete agreement **2** the state of being one or a whole **3** *maths* the number one

universal *adj* **1** relating to the universe **2** relating to, or coming from, all people: *universal criticism* ◇ **universally** *adv*

■ **2** worldwide, global, all-embracing, all-inclusive, general, common, across-the-board, total, whole, entire, all-round, unlimited

universe *noun* all known things, including the earth and planets

university *noun* (*plural* **universities**) a college which teaches a wide range of subjects to a high level, and which awards degrees to students who pass its examinations

UNIX *noun* a type of computer operating system designed to allow multiuser access

unkempt *adj* untidy

■ dishevelled, tousled, rumpled, uncombed, ungroomed, untidy, messy, scruffy, shabby, slovenly

☲ well-groomed, tidy

unkind *adj* not kind; harsh, cruel ◇ **unkindly** *adv* ◇ **unkindness** *noun*

■ cruel, inhuman, inhumane, callous, hard-hearted, unfeeling, insensitive, thoughtless, inconsiderate, uncharitable, nasty, malicious, spiteful, mean, malevolent, unfriendly, uncaring, unsympathetic

☲ kind, considerate

unleaded *adj* of petrol: not containing lead compounds

unleash *verb* **1** set free (a dog *etc*) **2** let loose (*eg* anger)

unleavened /ʌnˈlɛvənd/ *adj* of bread: not made to rise with yeast

unless *conj* if not; except if: *unless he's here soon, I'm going* (*ie* if he's not here soon)

unlike *adj* different, not similar ◇ *prep* **1** different from **2** not characteristic of: *it was unlike her not to phone*

unlikely *adj* **1** not probable: *it's unlikely that it will rain today* **2** probably not true: *an unlikely tale*

■ **2** improbable, implausible, far-fetched, unconvincing, unbelievable, incredible, unimaginable, doubtful, dubious, suspect, suspicious

unload *verb* **1** take the load from **2** remove the charge from a gun

unlooked-for *adj* not expected: *unlooked-for happiness*

unloose *verb* **1** set free **2** make loose

unlucky *adj* **1** not lucky or fortunate **2** unsuccessful ◇ **unluckily** *adv*

■ **1** unfortunate, luckless, unhappy, miserable, wretched, ill-fated, doomed, cursed, unfavourable, inauspicious, unsuccessful, disastrous

unmanly *adj* weak, cowardly

unmask *verb* **1** take a covering off **2** bring to light (a plot *etc*)

unmatched *adj* without an equal

unmentionable *adj* not fit to be spoken of, scandalous, indecent

■ unspeakable, unutterable, taboo, immodest, indecent, shocking, scandalous, shameful, disgraceful, abominable

unmistakable or **unmistakeable** *adj* very clear; impossible to confuse with any other: *unmistakable handwriting* ◇ **unmistakably** or **unmistakeably** *adv*

■ clear, plain, distinct, pronounced, obvious, evident, manifest, patent, glaring, explicit, unambiguous, unequivocal, positive, definite, sure, certain, unquestionable, indisputable, undeniable

☲ unclear, ambiguous

unmitigated *adj* complete, absolute: *unmitigated disaster*

unmoved *adj* not affected, unsympathetic: *unmoved by my pleas*

■ unaffected, untouched, unshaken, dry-eyed, unfeeling, cold, indifferent, impassive, unresponsive, unimpressed, firm, adamant, inflexible, unbending, undeviating, unwavering, steady, unchanged, resolute, resolved, determined

☲ moved, affected, shaken

unnatural *adj* not natural, perverted
- abnormal, anomalous, freakish, irregular, unusual, strange, odd, peculiar, queer, bizarre, extraordinary, uncanny, supernatural, inhuman, perverted

unnecessary *adj* not necessary; avoidable ◇ **unnecessarily** *adv*
- unneeded, needless, uncalled-for, unwanted, non-essential, dispensable, expendable, superfluous, redundant, tautological
- ✦ necessary, essential, indispensable

unnerve *verb* disconcert, perturb ◇ **unnerving** *adj*
- daunt, intimidate, frighten, scare, discourage, demoralize, dismay, disconcert, upset, worry, shake, *informal* rattle, confound, fluster
- ✦ nerve, brace, steel

unobtrusive *adj* not obvious or conspicuous; modest
- inconspicuous, unnoticeable, unassertive, humble, modest, unostentatious, unpretentious, restrained, low-key, subdued, quiet, retiring
- ✦ obtrusive, ostentatious

unofficial *adj* not officially authorized or confirmed

unpack *verb* open (a piece of luggage) and remove the contents

unpalatable *adj* 1 not pleasing to the taste 2 not pleasant to have to face up to: *unpalatable facts*
- 1 unappetizing, distasteful, insipid, bitter, uneatable, inedible 2 unpleasant, disagreeable, unattractive, offensive, repugnant
- ✦ 1 palatable 2 pleasant

unparalleled *adj* not having an equal, unprecedented: *unparalleled success*
- unequalled, unmatched, matchless, peerless, incomparable, unrivalled, unsurpassed, supreme, superlative, rare, exceptional, unprecedented

unpick *verb* take out sewing stitches

unpleasant *adj* not pleasant, nasty ◇ **unpleasantly** *adv* ◇ **unpleasantness** *noun*
- disagreeable, ill-natured, nasty, objectionable, offensive, distasteful, unpalatable, unattractive, repulsive, bad, troublesome
- ✦ pleasant, agreeable, nice

unprecedented *adj* never having happened before

unpremeditated *adj* done without having been planned: *unpremeditated murder*

unprepossessing *adj* not attractive

unpretentious *adj* modest, not showy or affected
- unaffected, natural, plain, simple, unobtrusive, honest, straightforward, humble, modest, unassuming, unostentatious

unprincipled *adj* without (moral) principles

unprintable *adj* not suitable to be printed; obscene

unquestionable *adj* undoubted, certain

unravel *verb* (**unravels**, **unravelling**, **unravelled**) 1 unwind, take the knots out of 2 solve (a problem or mystery)
- 1 unwind, undo, untangle, disentangle, free, extricate, separate 2 resolve, sort out, solve, work out, figure out, puzzle out, interpret, explain
- ✦ 1 tangle 2 complicate

unreal *adj* 1 not real, imaginary 2 *informal* amazing, incredible
- 1 false, artificial, synthetic, mock, fake, sham, imaginary, visionary, fanciful, make-believe, *informal* pretend, fictitious, made-up, legendary, mythical, fantastic

unremitting *adj* never stopping, unending: *unremitting rain*

unrequited *adj* of love: not given in return, one-sided

unrest *noun* a state of trouble or discontent, *esp* among a group of people

unrivalled *adj* without an equal
- unequalled, unparalleled, unmatched, matchless, peerless, incomparable, inimitable, unsurpassed, supreme, superlative

unruly *adj* 1 badly behaved 2 not obeying laws or rules ◇ **unruliness** *noun*

▣ **1** uncontrollable, unmanageable, ungovernable, intractable, disorderly, wild, rowdy, riotous, rebellious, disobedient **2** lawless, disobedient, wayward, wilful, headstrong, obstreperous

unsavoury *adj* very unpleasant, causing a feeling of disgust

unscathed *adj* not harmed
▣ unhurt, uninjured, unharmed, undamaged, untouched, whole, intact, safe, sound
Ⓕ hurt, injured

unscrupulous *adj* having no scruples or principles ◇ **unscrupulously** *adv*

unseasonable *adj* **1** of weather: not usual for the time of year **2** not well-timed

unseat *verb* **1** remove from a political seat **2** throw from the saddle (of a horse)

unseemly *adj* unsuitable, improper: *unseemly haste*
▣ improper, indelicate, unbecoming, undignified, unrefined, disreputable, disreditable, undue, inappropriate, unsuitable
Ⓕ seemly, decorous

unseen *adj* not seen ◇ **sight unseen** (bought *etc*) without having been seen, at the buyer's risk

unsettle *verb* disturb, upset
▣ disturb, upset, trouble, bother, discompose, ruffle, fluster, unbalance, shake, agitate, *informal* rattle, disconcert, confuse, throw

unsettled *adj* **1** disturbed **2** of weather: changeable **3** of a bill: unpaid
▣ **1** disturbed, upset, troubled, agitated, anxious, uneasy, tense, edgy, flustered, shaken, unnerved, disoriented, confused **2** changeable, variable, unpredictable, inconstant **3** unpaid, outstanding, owing, payable, overdue

unsightly *adj* ugly
▣ ugly, unattractive, unprepossessing, hideous, repulsive, repugnant, off-putting, unpleasant, disagreeable
Ⓕ attractive

unsociable *adj* not willing to mix with other people
▣ unfriendly, aloof, distant, stand-offish, withdrawn, introverted, reclusive, retiring, reserved, unforthcoming, uncommunicative, cold, chilly, uncongenial, unneighbourly, inhospitable, hostile
Ⓕ sociable, friendly

unsolicited *adj* not requested: *unsolicited advice*

unsophisticated *adj* **1** simple, uncomplicated **2** naive, inexperienced
▣ **1** plain, simple, straightforward, uncomplicated, uninvolved **2** guileless, innocent, ingenuous, naive, inexperienced, unworldly, childlike, natural, unaffected

unsound *adj* **1** incorrect, unfounded **2** not sane **3** not solid or firm

unspeakable *adj* too bad to describe in words: *unspeakable rudeness*
▣ unutterable, inexpressible, indescribable, awful, dreadful, frightful, terrible, horrible, shocking, appalling, monstrous, inconceivable, unbelievable

unstinting *adj* unrestrained, generous

unstudied *adj* natural, not forced: *unstudied charm*

unsung *adj* not celebrated, neglected: *an unsung Scots poet*
▣ unhonoured, unpraised, unacknowledged, unrecognized, overlooked, disregarded, neglected, forgotten, unknown, obscure
Ⓕ honoured, famous, renowned

unsuspecting *adj* not aware of deceit or coming danger

unswerving *adj* solid, unwavering

untenable *adj* unjustifiable: *the government's position is untenable*

unthinkable *adj* **1** very unlikely **2** too bad to be thought of
▣ **1** inconceivable, unimaginable, unheard-of, unbelievable, incredible, impossible, improbable, unlikely **2** unreasonable, illogical, absurd, preposterous, outrageous, shocking

untie *verb* (**unties, untying, untied**) **1** release from bonds **2** loosen (a knot)

until *prep* up to the time of: *can you wait until Tuesday?* ◇*conj* **1** up to the time that: *keep walking until you come to the corner* **2** (with negatives) before: *not until I say so*

untimely *adj* **1** happening too soon: *untimely arrival* **2** not suitable to the time or occasion: *untimely remark*

■ **1** early, premature, unseasonable, ill-timed, inopportune, inconvenient **2** unsuitable, inappropriate, unfortunate, inauspicious

Fa **1** timely, opportune **2** suitable

unto *prep*, *old* to

untold *adj* **1** not yet told: *the untold story* **2** too great to be counted or measured: *untold riches*

■ **2** incalculable, innumerable, uncountable, countless, infinite, measureless, boundless, inexhaustible, undreamed-of, unimaginable

untouchable *adj* **1** not able to be handled or approached **2** not able to be equalled or surpassed **3** above the law

untoward *adj* **1** unlucky, unfortunate **2** inconvenient **3** improper

untrue *adj* **1** not true, false **2** unfaithful

■ **1** false, fallacious, deceptive, misleading, wrong, incorrect, inaccurate, mistaken **2** unfaithful, disloyal, untrustworthy, dishonest, deceitful, untruthful

Fa **1** true, correct **2** faithful, honest

untruth *noun* a lie ◇**untruthful** *adj*

unusual *adj* not usual, rare, remarkable ◇**unusually** *adv*

■ bizarre, unconventional, irregular, abnormal, uncommon, rare, unfamiliar, strange, odd, extraordinary, remarkable, exceptional, different, surprising, unexpected, left-field

Fa usual, normal, ordinary

unvarnished *adj* **1** not varnished **2** plain, straightforward: *the unvarnished truth*

unveil *verb* **1** remove a veil from **2** remove a cover from (a memorial *etc*) **3** bring to light, disclose ◇**unveiling** *noun*

unwaged *adj* **1** of work: unpaid **2** unemployed

unwarranted *adj* uncalled-for, unnecessary

■ unjustified, undeserved, unprovoked, uncalled-for, groundless, unreasonable, unjust, wrong

Fa warranted, justifiable, deserved

unwell *adj* not in good health

unwieldy *adj* not easily moved or handled ◇**unwieldiness** *noun*

unwind *verb* **1** wind off from a ball or reel **2** *informal* relax

■ **1** unroll, unreel, unwrap, undo, uncoil, untwist, unravel, disentangle **2** *informal* relax, wind down, calm down

Fa **1** wind, roll

unwise *adj* foolish

unwitting *adj* **1** unintended: *unwitting insult* **2** unaware ◇**unwittingly** *adv*

■ **1** inadvertent, unintentional, unintended, unplanned **2** unaware, unknowing, unsuspecting, unthinking, unconscious

Fa **1** deliberate **2** knowing, conscious

unwonted *adj* unaccustomed, not usual: *unwonted cheerfulness*

unworthy *adj* **1** of little merit **2** low, worthless, despicable **3** (with **of**) not deserving (*eg* of attention)

■ **2** shameful, disgraceful, dishonourable, discreditable, base, contemptible, despicable

unwritten *adj* **1** not written down **2** of a rule, law *etc*: generally accepted

up *adv* (**upper**, **upmost** or **uppermost**) **1** towards or in a higher or more northerly position: *walking up the hill/ they live up in the Highlands* **2** completely, so as to finish: *drink up your tea* **3** to a larger size: *blow up a balloon* **4** towards, as far as: *he came up to me and shook hands* **5** to or in a more erect position: *stand up* ◇*prep* **1** towards or in the higher part of: *climbed up the ladder* **2** further along: *walking up the road* ◇*adj* **1** ascending, going up: *the up escalator* **2** ahead in score or amount: *2 goals up* **3** better off, richer: *£50 up on the deal* **4** risen: *the sun is up* **5** of a given length of time: ended: *your time is up* **6** appearing in court ◇*verb* (**ups, upping, upped**) raise or increase: *up the price* ◇**up-and-coming** *adj* likely to succeed ◇**on the up and up** progressing steadily, getting better all the time ◇**up and about 1** awake **2** out of bed after an illness ◇**ups and downs** times of good and bad luck ◇**up to 1** until: *up to the present time* **2** capable of: *are you up to the job?* **3** dependent on, falling as a duty to: *it's up to you to decide* **4** doing: *up to his tricks again* ◇**up to date 1** modern, in touch with recent ideas, *etc* **2** belonging to the present time **3** containing all recent facts, *etc*: *an up-to-date account* ◇**up to scratch** of the required standard ◇**up to speed** fully competent at a new job *etc* ◇**what's up? 1** what's wrong? **2** what's happening?

■ **up to date 1** current, contemporary, modern, fashionable, *informal* trendy, latest, recent, new

🖪 **up to date 1** out of date, old-fashioned

upbeat *adj*, *informal* cheerful, optimistic

upbraid *verb* scold

upbringing *noun* the rearing of, or the training given to, a child

■ bringing-up, raising, rearing, breeding, parenting, care, nurture, cultivation, education, training, instruction, teaching

upcoming *adj* forthcoming

up-country *adv & adj* inland

update *verb* /ʌpˈdeɪt/ bring up to date ◇*noun* /ˈʌpdeɪt/ **1** the act of updating **2** new information: *an update on yesterday's report*

■ *verb* modernize, revise, amend, correct, renew, renovate, revamp

upend *verb* turn upside down

upfront or **up-front** *adj* **1** candid, frank **2** foremost ◇**up front 1** at the front **2** of money: paid in advance **3** candidly, openly

upgrade *verb* /ʌpˈɡreɪd/ **1** raise to a more important position **2** improve the quality of ◇*noun, comput* /ˈʌpɡreɪd/

a newer version of a software program

upheaval *noun* a violent disturbance or change

■ disruption, disturbance, upset, chaos, confusion, disorder, turmoil, *informal* shake-up, revolution, overthrow

upheld *past form* of **uphold**

uphill *adj* **1** going upwards **2** difficult: *uphill struggle* ◇*adv* upwards

■ *adj* **2** hard, difficult, arduous, tough, taxing, strenuous, laborious, tiring, wearisome, exhausting, gruelling, punishing

🖪 *adj* **2** easy

uphold *verb* (**upholds, upholding, upheld**) **1** defend, give support to **2** maintain, keep going (*eg* a tradition)

■ **1** support, stand by, defend, champion, back, endorse **2** maintain, promote, sustain

upholster *verb* fit (furniture) with springs, stuffing, covers *etc* ◇**upholsterer** *noun* someone who upholsters furniture ◇**upholstery** *noun* covers, cushions *etc*

upkeep *noun* **1** the act of keeping (*eg* a house or car) in a good state of repair **2** the cost of this

■ **1** maintenance, preservation, conservation, care, running, repair, support, sustenance, subsistence, keep

🖪 **1** neglect

upland *noun* **1** high ground **2** (**uplands**) a hilly or mountainous region

uplift *verb* raise the spirits of, cheer up ◇**uplifting** *adj*

up-market *adj* of high quality or price, luxury

upon *prep* **1** on the top of: *upon the table* **2** at or after the time of: *upon completion of the task*

upper *adj* higher, further up ◇*noun* **1** the part of a shoe *etc* above the sole **2** *slang* a stimulant drug ◇**upper hand** advantage; dominance, control

■ *adj* higher, loftier, superior, senior, top, topmost, uppermost, high, elevated, exalted, eminent, important

🖪 *adj* lower, inferior, junior

upper-case *adj* of a letter: capital, *eg*

A not *a* (*contrasted with*: **lower-case**)

upper-class *adj* belonging to the highest social class, aristocratic

uppercut *noun* a boxing punch which swings up from below

uppermost *adj* highest, furthest up
- highest, top, topmost, greatest, supreme, first, primary, foremost, leading, principal, main, chief, dominant, predominant, paramount, pre-eminent
- lowest

uppity *adj* putting on airs, haughty

upright *adj* **1** standing up, vertical **2** honest, moral ◇ *noun* an upright post, piano *etc* ◇ **uprightness** *noun*
- *adj* **1** vertical, perpendicular, erect, straight **2** righteous, good, virtuous, upstanding, noble, honourable, ethical, principled, incorruptible, honest, trustworthy
- *adj* **1** horizontal, flat **2** dishonest

uprising *noun* a revolt against a government *etc*

uproar *noun* a noisy disturbance ◇ **uproarious** *adj* very noisy
- noise, din, racket, hubbub, hullabaloo, pandemonium, tumult, turmoil, turbulence, commotion, confusion, disorder, clamour, outcry, furore, riot, rumpus

uproot *verb* **1** tear up by the roots **2** move (a person or people) from their usual home **3** leave your home and go to live in another place

upset *verb* (**upsets, upsetting, upset**) **1** make unhappy, angry, worried *etc* **2** overturn **3** disturb, put out of order **4** ruin (plans *etc*) ◇ *adj* distressed, unhappy *etc*, ill ◇ *noun* **1** distress, unhappiness, worry *etc* **2** something that causes distress
- *verb* **1** distress, grieve, dismay, trouble, worry, agitate, disturb, bother, fluster, ruffle **2** tip, spill, overturn, capsize, topple, discompose, unsteady **3** discompose, disconcert, confuse, disorganize ◇ *adj* distressed, grieved, hurt, annoyed, dismayed, troubled, worried, agitated, disturbed, bothered, shaken, disconcerted, confused ◇ *noun* **1** trouble, worry, agitation, disturbance, bother, disruption, upheaval, *informal* shake-up,

surprise, shock, *informal* whammy

upshot *noun* a result or end of a matter: *what was the upshot of all this?*
- result, consequence, outcome, issue, end, conclusion, finish, culmination

upside-down *adj* & *adv* **1** with the top part underneath **2** *informal* in confusion

upstage *adv* away from the footlights on a theatre stage ◇ *adj*, *informal* haughty, proud ◇ *verb* divert attention from (someone) to yourself

upstairs *adv* in or to the upper storey of a house *etc* ◇ *noun* the upper storey or storeys of a house ◇ *adj* in the upper storey or storeys: *upstairs bedroom*

upstanding *adj* **1** honest, respectable **2** strong and healthy **3** standing up

upstart *noun*, *derog* someone who has risen quickly from a low to a high position in society, work *etc*

upstream *adv* higher up a river or stream, towards the source

upsurge *noun* a rising, a swelling up

upswing *noun* an upward or positive swing, a recovery

uptake *noun*: **quick on the uptake** quick to understand

uptight *adj* nervous, tense

upturn *noun* a positive change, an improvement

upward *adj* moving up, ascending ◇ **upward** or **upwards** *adv* from lower to higher, up ◇ **upwardly** *adv* ◇ **upwardly-mobile** *adj* moving to a higher social status ◇ **upwards of** more than

uranium *noun* a radioactive metal

urban *adj* relating to a town or city (*contrasted with*: **rural**) ◇ **urbanization** *noun* ◇ **urbanize** *verb* make urban

urbane *adj* polite in a smooth way ◇ **urbanity** *noun* **1** smoothness of manner **2** (*plural* **urbanities**) urbane actions

urchin *noun* a dirty, ragged child

> Originally meaning 'hedgehog', the prickly sense of which survives in *sea urchin*

urge *verb* **1** drive (on) **2** try to persuade: *urging me to go home* **3** advise, recommend: *urge caution* ◇ *noun* a strong desire or impulse

■ *verb* **1** press, constrain, compel, force, push, drive, impel, hasten, induce, incite, instigate **2** encourage, implore, beg, beseech, entreat **3** advise, counsel, recommend, advocate ◇ *noun* desire, wish, inclination, fancy, longing, yearning, *informal* yen, itch, impulse, compulsion, impetus, drive, eagerness

Ea *verb* **1** deter, hinder **2** discourage, dissuade ◇ *noun* disinclination

urgent *adj* **1** requiring immediate attention **2** of a request *etc*: asking for immediate action ◇ **urgency** *noun* ◇ **urgently** *adv*

■ **1** immediate, instant, top-priority, important, critical, crucial, imperative, pressing, compelling **2** persuasive, earnest, eager, insistent, persistent

urine *noun* the waste liquid passed out of the body of animals and humans from the bladder ◇ **urinary** *adj* ◇ **urinate** *verb* pass urine from the bladder

URL *abbrev, comput* Uniform Resource Locator

urn *noun* **1** a vase for the ashes of the dead **2** a metal drum with a tap, used for making and pouring tea or coffee

US or **USA** *abbrev* United States of America

us *pronoun* used by a speaker or writer in referring to themselves together with other people (as the object in a sentence): *when would you like us to come?*

usage *noun* **1** the act or manner of using **2** the established way of using a word *etc* **3** custom, habit

■ **1** treatment, handling, management **3** tradition, custom, practice, habit, convention, etiquette, rule, regulation, form, routine, procedure, method

use *verb* **1** put to some purpose: *use a knife to open it* **2** (often with **up**) spend, exhaust (*eg* patience, energy) **3** treat (someone) in a way that benefits oneself: *he used his wife cruelly* ◇ *noun* **1** the act of using **2** value or suitability for a purpose: *no use to anybody* **3** the fact of

being used: *it's in use at the moment* **4** custom ◇ **usable** or **useable** *adj* ◇ **use up** use completely ◇ **no use** useless ◇ **used to 1** accustomed to **2** was or were in the habit of (doing something): *we used to go there every year*

■ *verb* **1** utilize, employ, exercise, practise **2** consume, exhaust, expend, spend, finish, exhaust, drain **3** treat, manipulate, exploit ◇ *noun* **2** usefulness, value, worth, profit, advantage, benefit, good **3** service, employment, operation, exercise

used *adj* **1** employed, put to a purpose **2** not new: *used cars*

■ **2** second-hand, pre-owned, cast-off, hand-me-down, nearly new, worn, dog-eared, soiled

Ea **2** unused, new, fresh

useful *adj* serving a purpose; helpful ◇ **usefully** *adv* ◇ **usefulness** *noun*

■ handy, convenient, practical, effective, productive, fruitful, profitable, valuable, worthwhile, advantageous, beneficial, helpful

Ea useless, ineffective, worthless

useless *adj* having no use or effect ◇ **uselessness** *noun*

■ futile, fruitless, unproductive, vain, idle, hopeless, pointless, worthless, unusable, broken-down, *slang* clapped-out, unworkable, impractical, ineffective, inefficient, incompetent, weak

Ea useful, helpful, effective

user *noun* someone who uses anything (*esp* a computer) ◇ **user-friendly** *adj* easily understood, easy to use ◇ **user name** a sequence of characters identifying a user to a computer system

usher, usherette *noun* someone who shows people to their seats in a theatre *etc* ◇ **usher** *verb* lead, convey

USSR *abbrev, hist* Union of Soviet Socialist Republics

usual *adj* **1** done or happening most often: *usual method* **2** customary: *with his usual cheerfulness* **3** ordinary ◇ *noun* a customary event, order *etc*

■ *adj* **1** normal, standard, regular, accepted **2** normal, typical, regular, routine, habitual, customary **3** common, everyday, general, ordinary, unexceptional, expected, predictable

Ea *adj* **1**, **2** unusual, strange **3** rare

usually *adv* on most occasions

■ normally, generally, as a rule, ordinarily, typically, traditionally, regularly, commonly, by and large, on the whole, mainly, chiefly, mostly

Ea exceptionally

usurer *noun* a moneylender who demands an excessively high rate of interest

usurp *verb* take possession of (*eg* a throne) by force ◇ **usurper** *noun*

usury *noun* the lending of money with an excessively high rate of interest

utensil *noun* an instrument or container used in the home (*eg* a ladle, knife, pan)

uterus *noun* (*plural* **uteri**) the womb

utilitarian *adj* concerned with usefulness, rather than beauty, pleasure *etc*

utility *noun* (*plural* **utilities**) **1** usefulness **2** a public service supplying water, gas *etc*

■ **1** usefulness, use, value, profit, advantage, benefit, avail **2** service, convenience

utilize *verb* make use of ◇ **utilization** *noun*

utmost *adj* **1** the greatest possible: *utmost care* **2** furthest ◇ **do your utmost** make the greatest possible effort

■ **1** extreme, maximum, greatest, highest, supreme, paramount **2** farthest, furthermost, remotest, outermost, ultimate, final, last

utopia *noun* a perfect place, a paradise ◇ **utopian** *adj*

> Literally 'no place', coined by Thomas More for his fictional book *Utopia* (1516)

utter[1] *verb* produce with the voice (words, a scream *etc*) ◇ **utterance** *noun* something said

■ speak, say, voice, vocalize, verbalize, express, articulate, sound, pronounce, deliver, state, declare, announce, proclaim, tell ◇ **utterance** statement, remark, comment, expression, articulation, delivery, speech, declaration, announcement, proclamation, pronouncement

utter[2] *adj* complete, total: *utter darkness* ◇ **utterly** *adv* ◇ **uttermost** *adj* most complete, utmost

■ absolute, complete, total, entire, out-and-out, downright, sheer, stark, arrant, unmitigated, unqualified, perfect ◇ **utterly** absolutely, completely, totally, fully, entirely, wholly, thoroughly, downright, perfectly

U-turn *noun* a complete change in direction, policy *etc*

UVA *abbrev* ultraviolet radiation

uvula /ˈjuːvjʊlə/ *noun* (*plural* **uvulas** or **uvulae**) the small piece of flesh hanging from the palate at the back of the mouth

uxorious *adj* of a man: extremely fond of his wife

Uzi *noun* a type of submachine-gun

v *abbrev* **1** against (from Latin *versus*) **2** see (from Latin *vide*) **3** verb **4** very **5** volume

vacancy *noun* (*plural* **vacancies**) **1** a job that has not been filled **2** a room not already booked in a hotel *etc*

▪ **1** opportunity, opening, position, post, job **2** place, room, situation

vacant *adj* **1** empty, not occupied **2** of an expression: showing no interest or intelligence ◇ **vacantly** *adv*

▪ **1** empty, unoccupied, unfilled, free, available, void, not in use, unused, uninhabited **2** blank, expressionless, vacuous, inane, inattentive, absent, absentminded, unthinking, dreamy

▪ **1** occupied, engaged

vacate *verb* leave empty, cease to occupy ◇ **vacation** *noun* **1** the act of vacating **2** a holiday

▪ leave, depart, evacuate, abandon, withdraw, quit

vaccinate *verb* give a vaccine to, *eg* by injection into the skin ◇ **vaccination** *noun*

vaccine *noun* a substance made from the germs that cause a disease, given to people and animals to try to prevent them catching that disease

vacillate *verb* move from one opinion to another; waver ◇ **vacillation** *noun*

vacuous *adj* **1** empty **2** emptyheaded, stupid ◇ **vacuously** *adv* ◇ **vacuousness** *noun*

vacuum *noun* a space from which all, or almost all, the air has been removed ◇ **vacuum cleaner** a machine which cleans carpets *etc* by sucking up dust ◇ **vacuum flask** a container with double walls enclosing a vacuum, for keeping liquids hot or cold ◇ **vacuumpacked** *adj* of food: sealed in a container from which air has been removed

vagabond *noun* **1** someone with no permanent home; a wanderer **2** a ras-

cal, a rogue ◇ *adj* wandering

vagaries *noun plural* strange, unexpected behaviour: *vagaries of human nature*

vagina *noun* the passage connecting a woman's genitals to her womb ◇ **vaginal** *adj* of the vagina

vagrant *adj* unsettled, wandering ◇ *noun* a wanderer or tramp, with no settled home ◇ **vagrancy** *noun* the state of being a tramp

vague *adj* **1** not clear; not definite: *vague idea/vague shape* **2** not practical or efficient; forgetful ◇ **vaguely** *adv*

▪ **1** ill-defined, blurred, indistinct, hazy, dim, shadowy, misty, fuzzy, nebulous, obscure, indefinite, imprecise, unclear, uncertain, undefined, undetermined, unspecific, generalized, inexact, ambiguous, evasive, loose, woolly

▪ **1** clear, definite

vain *adj* **1** conceited, self-important **2** useless: *vain attempt* **3** empty, meaningless: *vain promises* ◇ **vainly** *adv* ◇ **in vain** without success

▪ **1** conceited, proud, self-satisfied, arrogant, self-important, egotistical, *informal* bigheaded, *informal* swollenheaded, *informal* stuck-up, affected, pretentious, ostentatious, swaggering **2** useless, worthless, futile, abortive, fruitless, pointless, unproductive, unprofitable **3** hollow, groundless, empty

▪ **1** modest, self-effacing **2** fruitful, successful

vainglorious *adj* boastful ◇ **vaingloriously** *adv*

valance *noun* a decorative frill round the edge of a bed

vale *noun*, *formal* a valley

valediction /valɪˈdɪkʃən/ *noun* a farewell ◇ **valedictory** *adj* saying farewell: *valedictory speech*

valency *noun* (*plural* **valencies**) *chem-*

istry the combining power of an atom or group with hydrogen (*eg* in water, H_2O, oxygen shows valency two)

valentine *noun* **1** a greetings card sent on St Valentine's Day, 14 February **2** a sweetheart, a lover

valet /'valeɪ/ or /'valɪt/ *noun* a manservant

valetudinarian *noun* someone who is over-anxious about their health

valiant *adj* brave ◇ **valiantly** *adv*
- ■ brave, courageous, gallant, fearless, intrepid, bold, dauntless, heroic, plucky, indomitable, staunch
- ☒ cowardly, fearful

valid *adj* **1** sound, acceptable: *valid reason for not going* **2** legally in force: *valid passport* ◇ **validate** *verb* make valid ◇ **validity** *noun*
- ■ **1** logical, well-founded, well-grounded, sound, good, cogent, convincing, telling, conclusive, reliable, substantial, weighty, powerful, just **2** official, legal, lawful, legitimate, authentic, bona fide, genuine, binding, proper
- ☒ **1** false, weak **2** unofficial, invalid

Valium *noun, trademark* a brand name for diazepam, a tranquillizing drug

valley *noun* (*plural* **valleys**) low land between hills, often with a river flowing through it

valorous *adj* brave, courageous

valour *noun* courage, bravery

valuable *adj* of great value ◇ **valuables** *noun plural* articles of worth
- ■ precious, prized, valued, costly, expensive, dear, high-priced, treasured, cherished, estimable, helpful, worthwhile, useful, beneficial, invaluable, fruitful, profitable, important, worthy, handy
- ☒ worthless, useless

valuation *noun* **1** the act of valuing **2** an estimated price or value

value *noun* **1** worth; price **2** purchasing power (of a coin *etc*) **3** the quality of being a fair exchange: *good value for money* **4** usefulness or importance **5** *algebra* a number or quantity put as equal to an expression: *the value of x is 8* ◇ *verb* **1** put a price on **2** think highly of ◇ **value-added tax** a government tax raised on the selling-price of an article, or charged on certain services
- ▤ *noun* **1** cost, price, rate, worth **4** importance, desirability, benefit, advantage, significance, good, profit, worth, use, usefulness, utility, merit ◇ *verb* **1** evaluate, assess, estimate, price, appraise, survey, rate **2** prize, appreciate, treasure, esteem, hold dear, respect, cherish
- ☒ *verb* **2** disregard, neglect

valueless *adj* worthless

valuer or **valuator** *noun* someone trained to estimate the value of property

valve *noun* **1** a device allowing air, steam or liquid to flow in one direction only **2** a small flap of tissue controlling the flow of blood in the body

vamp ¹ *noun* the upper part of a boot or shoe ◇ *verb* **1** patch **2** play improvised music ◇ **vamp up** refurbish (something)

vamp ² *noun* a woman who sets out to attract men

vampire *noun* a dead person supposed to rise at night and suck the blood of sleeping people ◇ **vampire bat** a S American bat that sucks blood

van ¹ *noun* a covered or closed-in vehicle or wagon for carrying goods by road or rail

van ² *noun short for* **vanguard**

vandal *noun* someone who pointlessly destroys or damages public buildings *etc*

vandalism *noun* the activity of a vandal

vandalize *verb* damage by vandalism

vane *noun* **1** a weathercock **2** the blade of a windmill, propeller *etc*

vanguard *noun* **1** the leading group in a movement *etc* **2** the part of an army going in front of the main body **3** a leading position: *the vanguard of discovery*

vanilla *noun* a sweet-scented flavouring obtained from the pods of a type of orchid

vanish *verb* **1** go out of sight **2** fade away to nothing

▣ **2** disappear, fade, dissolve, evaporate, disperse, melt, die out, depart, exit, fizzle out, peter out

▣ **2** appear, materialize

vanity noun (plural **vanities**) **1** conceit **2** worthlessness **3** something vain and worthless

▣ **1** conceit, conceitedness, pride, arrogance, self-conceit, self-love, self-satisfaction, narcissism, egotism, pretension, ostentation, affectation, airs, informal bigheadedness **2** worthlessness, uselessness, emptiness, futility, pointlessness, unreality, hollowness, fruitlessness, triviality

▣ **1** modesty **2** worth

vanquish verb defeat

vantage point a position giving an advantage or a clear view

vapid /ˈvapɪd/ adj dull, uninteresting

vaporize verb change into vapour

vaporizer noun a device which sprays liquid very finely

vapour noun the air-like or gas-like state of a substance that is usually liquid or solid: water vapour

variable adj changeable; that may be varied ◇ noun something that varies eg in value

▣ adj changeable, inconstant, varying, shifting, unpredictable, fluctuating, fitful, unstable, unsteady, wavering, vacillating, temperamental, fickle, flexible

▣ adj fixed, invariable, stable

variance noun a state of differing or disagreement ◇ **at variance** in disagreement

▣ variation, difference, discrepancy, divergence, inconsistency, disagreement, disagreement, disharmony, conflict, discord, division, dissent, dissension, quarrelling, strife

▣ agreement, harmony

variant noun a different form or version ◇ adj in a different form

variation noun **1** a varying, a change **2** the extent of a difference or change: variations in temperature **3** music a repetition, in a slightly different form, of a main theme

▣ **1** change, difference, modification, novelty, innovation **2** diversity, variety, deviation, discrepancy

varicose vein a swollen or enlarged vein, usually on the leg

variegated adj marked with different colours; multicoloured

variety noun (plural **varieties**) **1** the quality of being of many kinds, or of being different **2** a mixed collection: a variety of books **3** a sort, a type: a variety of potato **4** mixed theatrical entertainment including songs, comedy, etc

▣ **1** difference, diversity, dissimilarity, discrepancy, variation, multiplicity **2** assortment, miscellany, mixture, collection, medley, pot-pourri, range **3** sort, kind, class, category, species, type, breed, brand, make, strain

▣ **1** uniformity, similitude

varifocals noun plural glasses allowing the user to focus on a range of distances

various adj **1** of different kinds: various shades of green **2** several different: various attempts ◇ **variously** adv

▣ **1** different, differing, diverse, varied, varying, assorted, miscellaneous, formal heterogeneous, distinct, diversified, mixed **2** many, several

varlet noun, old a rascal

varnish noun a sticky liquid which gives a glossy surface to paper, wood etc ◇ verb **1** cover with varnish **2** cover up (faults)

vary verb (**varies**, **varying**, **varied**) **1** make, be, or become different **2** make changes in (a routine etc) **3** differ, disagree ◇ **varying** adj

▣ **1** change, alter, modify, modulate, diversify, reorder, transform, alternate, inflect, permutate **3** diverge, differ, disagree, depart

vase /vɑːz/ or US /veɪz/ noun a jar of pottery, glass etc used as an ornament or for holding cut flowers

vasectomy noun (plural **vasectomies**) sterilization of a man by cutting, and removing part of, the sperm-carrying tubes

Vaseline *noun, trademark* a type of ointment made from petroleum

vassal *noun, hist* a tenant who held land from an overlord in return for certain services

vast *adj* of very great size or amount ◇ **vastly** *adv* ◇ **vastness** *noun*

■ huge, immense, massive, gigantic, enormous, great, colossal, extensive, tremendous, *informal* seismic, sweeping, unlimited, immeasurable, never-ending, monumental, monstrous

VAT or **vat** *abbrev* value-added tax

vat *noun* a large tub or tank, used *eg* for fermenting liquors and dyeing

vaudeville *noun* theatrical entertainment of dances and songs, usually comic

vault¹ *noun* **1** an arched roof **2** an underground room, a cellar

■ **2** cellar, crypt, strongroom, repository, cavern, depository, wine-cellar, tomb, mausoleum

vault² *verb* leap, supporting your weight on your hands, or on a pole

■ leap, spring, bound, clear, jump, hurdle, leap-frog

vaunt *verb* boast

VC *abbrev* Victoria Cross

VCR *abbrev* video cassette recorder

VD *abbrev* venereal disease

VDU *abbrev* visual display unit

veal *noun* the flesh of a calf, used as food

veg¹ /vɛdʒ/ *noun, informal* vegetables

veg² /vɛdʒ/ *verb, informal* (often with **out**) laze about

veer *verb* **1** change direction or course **2** change mood, opinions, *etc*

■ **1** swerve, swing, change, shift, diverge, deviate, wheel, turn, sheer, tack **2** swing, change, shift

vegan /viːgən/ *noun* a vegetarian who uses no animal products ◇ **veganism** *noun*

vegetable *noun* a plant, *esp* one grown for food ◇ *adj* **1** of plants **2** made from or consisting of plants: *vegetable dye/vegetable oil*

> *Vegetables include:*
> asparagus, artichoke, aubergine, baby corn, bean, broad bean, bok choy, broccoli, Brussels sprout, butter bean, cabbage, calabrese, capsicum, carrot, cassava (or manioc), cauliflower, celeriac, celery, chicory, courgette, cress, cucumber, daikon, *US* eggplant, endive, fennel, French bean, garlic, kale, kohlrabi, leek, lentil, lettuce, mange tout, marrow, mushroom, okra, onion, parsnip, pea, pepper, petit pois, potato, *informal* spud, pumpkin, radish, runner bean, shallot, soya bean, spinach, spring onion, squash, swede, sweetcorn, sweet potato, turnip, watercress, water chestnut, yam, *US* zucchini

vegetarian *noun* someone who eats no meat or fish ◇ *adj* consisting of, or eating, only vegetable or dairy foods ◇ **vegetarianism** *noun*

vegetate *verb* **1** grow as a plant does **2** lead a dull, aimless life: *sitting at home vegetating*

vegetation *noun* **1** plants in general **2** the plants growing in a particular area

veggie *adj, informal* vegetarian

vehement *adj* emphatic and forceful in expressing opinions *etc* ◇ **vehemence** *noun* ◇ **vehemently** *adv*

■ impassioned, passionate, ardent, fervent, intense, forceful, emphatic, heated, strong, powerful, urgent, enthusiastic, animated, eager, earnest, forcible, fierce, violent, zealous

▦ apathetic, indifferent

vehicle *noun* **1** a means of transport used on land, *esp* one with wheels: *motor vehicle* **2** a means of conveying information, *eg* television or newspapers ◇ **vehicular** *adj*

> *Vehicles include:*
> plane, boat, ship, car, taxi, cab, hackney-carriage, bicycle, *informal* bike, cycle, tandem, tricycle, *informal* boneshaker, penny-farthing, motorcycle, motorbike,

scooter, bus, omnibus, minibus, *informal* double-decker, coach, charabanc, caravan, caravanette, camper, recreational vehicle (or RV), *US* winnebago, train, Pullman, sleeper, wagon-lit, tube, tram, monorail, maglev, trolleybus, van, Transit®, lorry, truck, juggernaut, pantechnicon, trailer, tractor, fork-lift truck, steam-roller, tank, wagon, bobsleigh, sled, sledge, sleigh, toboggan, troika; barouche, brougham, dog-cart, dray, four-in-hand, gig, hansom, landau, phaeton, post-chaise, stagecoach, sulky, surrey, trap; rickshaw, sedan-chair, litter

veil *noun* **1** a piece of cloth or netting worn to shade or hide the face **2** something that hides or covers up ◇ *verb* **1** cover with a veil **2** hide ◇ **veiled** *adj* ◇ **take the veil** become a nun

▤ *noun* **2** cover, cloak, curtain, mask, screen, disguise, blind, shade ◇ *verb* **2** screen, cloak, cover, mask, shadow, shield, obscure, conceal, hide, disguise, shade

▧ *verb* **2** expose, uncover

vein *noun* **1** one of the tubes which carry the blood back to the heart **2** a small rib of a leaf **3** a thin layer of mineral in a rock **4** a streak of different colour in cheese *etc* **5** a mood or personal characteristic: *a vein of cheerfulness* ◇ **veined** *adj* marked with veins

▤ **5** mood, tendency, bent, strain, temper, tenor, tone, frame of mind, mode, style

Velcro *noun, trademark* a type of fastener made of two strips of specially treated fabric which interlock

veld or **veldt** /fɛlt/ or /vɛlt/ *noun* open grass-country with few or no trees, *esp* in South Africa

vellum *noun* **1** a fine parchment used for bookbinding, made from the skins of calves, kids or lambs **2** paper made in imitation of this

velocity *noun* (*plural* **velocities**) rate or speed of movement

velour /vəˈlʊə(r)/ *noun* a fabric with a soft, velvet-like surface

velvet *noun* a fabric made from silk *etc*, with a thick, soft surface ◇ *adj* **1** made of velvet **2** soft or smooth as velvet; silky ◇ **velvety** *adj* soft, like velvet

velveteen *noun* a cotton fabric with a velvet-like pile

venal *adj* **1** willing to be bribed **2** dishonest; unworthy

⚠ Do not confuse with: **venial**

vend *verb* sell ◇ **vending machine** a machine with sweets *etc* for sale, operated by putting coins in a slot ◇ **vendor** *noun* someone who sells

vendetta *noun* a bitter, long-lasting quarrel or feud

▤ feud, blood-feud, enmity, rivalry, quarrel, bad blood, bitterness

veneer *noun* **1** a thin surface layer of fine wood **2** a false outward show hiding some bad quality: *a veneer of good manners*

▤ **1** front, façade, appearance, coating, surface **2** show, mask, pretence, guise, finish

venerable *adj* worthy of respect because of age or wisdom

▤ respected, revered, esteemed, honoured, venerated, dignified, grave, wise, august, aged, worshipped

venerate *verb* respect or honour greatly ◇ **veneration** *noun* **1** the act of venerating **2** great respect

▤ revere, respect, honour, esteem, worship, *formal* hallow, adore

▧ despise, anathematize

venereal disease a disease contracted through sexual intercourse

Venetian blind a window blind formed of thin movable strips of metal or plastic hung on tapes

vengeance *noun* punishment given, harm done in return for wrong or injury, revenge ◇ **with a vengeance** with unexpected force or enthusiasm

▤ retribution, revenge, retaliation, reprisal, tit for tat

▧ forgiveness

vengeful adj seeking revenge
◇ **vengefully** adv

venial adj of a sin: not very bad, pardonable (*compare with*: **cardinal**)

> ❗ Do not confuse with: **venal**

venison noun the flesh of a deer, used as food

venom noun 1 poison 2 hatred, spite
◇ **venomous** adj 1 poisonous 2 spiteful
◇ **venomously** adv
▣ ◇ **venomous 1** poisonous, toxic, virulent, harmful, noxious 2 malicious, spiteful, vicious, vindictive, baleful, hostile, malignant, rancorous, baneful
▣ ◇ **venomous 1** harmless

vent noun 1 an opening to allow air or smoke *etc* to pass through 2 an outlet 3 a slit at the bottom of the back of a coat *etc* ◇ verb express (strong emotion) in some way ◇ **give vent to** express, let out
▣ noun 1 opening, hole, aperture, outlet, passage, orifice, duct ◇ verb air, express, voice, utter, release, discharge, emit

ventilate verb 1 allow fresh air to pass through (a room *etc*) 2 talk about, discuss ◇ **ventilation** noun ◇ **ventilator** noun a grating or other device for allowing in fresh air

ventricle noun a small cavity in the brain or heart

ventriloquist noun someone who can speak without appearing to move their lips and can project their voice onto a puppet *etc* ◇ **ventriloquism** noun

> Literally 'stomach speaker' and originally meaning someone possessed by a talking evil spirit

venture noun an undertaking which involves some risk: *business venture* ◇ verb 1 risk, dare 2 do or say something at the risk of causing annoyance: *may I venture to suggest* ◇ **venturesome** adj ◇ **venturous** adj
▣ noun risk, chance, hazard, speculation, gamble, undertaking, project, adventure, endeavour, enterprise, operation,

fling ◇ verb 1 risk, hazard 2 dare, advance, make bold, put forward, presume, suggest, volunteer

venue noun the scene of an event, *eg* a sports contest or conference

veracious adj truthful ◇ **veracity** noun truthfulness

> ❗ Do not confuse with: **voracious**

veranda or **verandah** noun a kind of terrace with a roof supported by pillars, extending along the side of a house

verb noun the word that tells what someone or something does in a sentence, *eg* 'I *sing*' / 'he *had* no idea'

verbal adj 1 of words 2 spoken, not written: *verbal agreement* 3 of verbs

verbatim adj in the exact words, word for word: *a verbatim account*

verbose adj using more words than necessary ◇ **verbosity** noun

verdant adj green with grass or leaves

verdict noun 1 the judge's decision at the end of a trial 2 someone's personal opinion on a matter
▣ 1 decision, judgement, finding, sentence 2 judgement, conclusion, adjudication, assessment, opinion

verdigris noun the greenish rust of copper, brass or bronze

verdure noun green vegetation

verge noun 1 the grassy border along the edge of a road *etc* 2 edge, brink: *on the verge of a mental breakdown* ◇ **verge on** be close to: *verging on the absurd*
▣ 1 border, edge, margin 2 limit, rim, brim, brink, boundary, threshold
◇ **verge on** approach, border on, come close to, near

verger noun a church caretaker, or church official

verify verb (**verifies, verifying, verified**) prove, show to be true, confirm
◇ **verifiable** adj able to be verified
◇ **verification** noun
▣ confirm, corroborate, substantiate, authenticate, bear out, prove, support, validate, testify, attest
▣ invalidate, discredit

verily *adv, old* truly, really

verisimilitude *noun* realism, closeness to real life

veritable *adj* 1 true 2 real, genuine

verity *noun* truth

vermicelli /vɜːmɪˈtʃɛlɪ/ *noun* a type of food like spaghetti but in much thinner pieces

vermilion *noun* a bright red colour

vermin *noun plural* animals or insects that are considered pests, *eg* rats, mice, fleas *etc* ◇ **verminous** *adj* full of vermin

vermouth /ˈvɜːməθ/ *noun* a kind of drink containing white wine flavoured with wormwood

vernacular *noun* the ordinary spoken language of a country or district ◇ *adj* in the vernacular
■ *noun* language, speech, tongue, parlance, dialect, idiom, jargon ◇ *adj* indigenous, local, native, popular, vulgar, informal, colloquial, common

vernal *adj* of the season of spring

verruca *noun* (*plural* **verrucas** or **verrucae**) a wart, especially on the foot

versatile *adj* 1 able to turn easily from one subject or task to another 2 useful in many different ways ◇ **versatility** *noun*
■ 1 adaptable, flexible 2 adaptable, multipurpose, multifaceted, adjustable, many-sided, general-purpose, functional, resourceful, handy, variable
Ea 1, 2 inflexible

verse *noun* 1 a number of lines of poetry forming a planned unit 2 poetry as opposed to prose 3 a short division of a chapter of the Bible ◇ **versed in** skilled or experienced in

version *noun* 1 an account from one point of view 2 a form: *another version of the same tune* 3 a translation
■ 1 rendering, interpretation, account 2 type, kind, variant, form, model, style, design 3 reading, translation, paraphrase, adaptation, portrayal

verso *noun* the left-hand page of an open book (*compare with:* **recto**)

versus *prep* against (*short form:* **v**)

vertebra *noun* (*plural* **vertebrae**) one of the bones of the spine

vertebrate *noun* an animal with a backbone ◇ *adj* having a backbone

vertex *noun* (*plural* **vertexes** or **vertices**) the top or summit; the point of a cone, pyramid or angle

vertical *adj* 1 standing upright 2 straight up and down ◇ *noun* a vertical line or direction ◇ **vertically** *adv*

vertigo *noun* giddiness, dizziness

verve *noun* lively spirit, enthusiasm
■ vitality, vivacity, animation, energy, dash, liveliness, sparkle, vigour, enthusiasm, gusto, life, relish, spirit, force
Ea apathy, lethargy

very *adv* 1 to a great extent or degree: *seem very happy/walk very quietly* 2 used for emphasis: absolutely: *the very same one* ◇ *adj* 1 used for emphasis: absolute: *the very top* 2 ideal, most suitable: *the very man for the job* 3 actual: *in the very act of stealing* 4 mere: *the very thought of blood*
■ *adv* 1 extremely, greatly, highly, deeply, truly, *informal* terribly, remarkably, excessively, exceeding(ly), acutely, particularly, really, absolutely, noticeably, unusually ◇ *adj* 2 exact, appropriate 3 actual, real 4 plain, mere, bare
Ea *adv* 1 slightly, scarcely

vespers *noun plural* a church service in the evening

vessel *noun* 1 a ship 2 a container for liquid 3 a tube conducting fluids in the body: *blood vessels*

vest *noun* 1 an undergarment for the top half of the body 2 *US* a waistcoat

vested *adj, law* belonging to a person ◇ **vested interest** interest in a system, company *etc* because one may benefit (*esp* financially) from it

vestibule *noun* an entrance hall; a lobby

vestige *noun* a trace, an indication of something's existence ◇ **vestigial** *adj* surviving only as a trace of former existence: *vestigial wings*
■ trace, suspicion, indication, sign, hint, evidence, inkling, glimmer, token, scrap, remains, remainder, remnant, residue

vestment *noun* a ceremonial garment, worn *eg* by a religious officer during a service

vestry *noun* (*plural* **vestries**) a room in a church in which vestments are kept

vet¹ *noun, informal* a veterinary surgeon

vet² *verb* (**vets, vetting, vetted**) examine, check

■ investigate, examine, check, scrutinize, scan, inspect, survey, review, appraise, audit

vet³ *noun, US informal* a veteran of the armed forces

vetch *noun* a plant of the pea family

veteran *adj* old, experienced ◇ *noun* **1** someone who has given long service **2** an old soldier **3** *US* anyone who has served in the armed forces

■ *adj* experienced, practised, seasoned, long-serving, expert, adept, proficient, old

■ *adj* inexperienced

veterinarian *noun, US* a veterinary surgeon

veterinary *adj* relating to the treatment of animal diseases ◇ **veterinary surgeon** a doctor who treats animals

veto /viːtəʊ/ *noun* (*plural* **vetoes**) **1** the power to forbid or block (a proposal) **2** an act of forbidding or blocking ◇ *verb* (**vetos, vetoing, vetoed**) forbid, block

■ *noun* **2** rejection, ban, embargo, prohibition, *informal* thumbs down ◇ *verb* reject, turn down, forbid, disallow, ban, prohibit, rule out, block, *informal* knock back

■ *noun* **2** approval, assent ◇ *verb* approve, sanction

Latin for 'I forbid', a phrase originally used by people's tribunes in the Roman Senate when objecting to proposals

vex *verb* annoy; cause trouble to ◇ **vexation** *noun* **1** the state of being vexed **2** something that vexes ◇ **vexatious** *adj* causing trouble or annoyance

■ irritate, annoy, provoke, pester, trouble, upset, worry, bother, *informal* put out, harass, *informal* hassle, *informal* aggravate, *informal* needle, disturb, distress, agitate, exasperate, torment, fret

■ calm, soothe

VHF *abbrev* very high frequency

via *prep* by way of: *travelling to Paris via London*

viable *adj* **1** able to be managed, practicable: *viable proposition* **2** of a baby or foetus: able to survive outside the womb

■ feasible, practicable, possible, workable, usable, operable, achievable, sustainable

■ impossible, unworkable

viaduct *noun* a long bridge taking a railway or road over a river *etc*

viands *noun plural, old* food

vibrant *adj* full of energy; lively, sparkling ◇ **vibrancy** *noun*

■ animated, vivacious, vivid, bright, brilliant, colourful, lively, responsive, sparkling, spirited

vibrate *verb* **1** shake, tremble **2** of sound: resound, ring ◇ **vibratory** *adj* of vibration

■ **1** quiver, pulsate, shudder, shiver, resonate, reverberate, throb, oscillate, tremble, undulate, shake

vibration *noun* **1** the act of vibrating **2** a rapid to-and-fro movement

vicar *noun* an Anglican cleric in charge of a parish ◇ **vicarage** *noun* the house of a vicar

vicarious *adj* **1** in place or on behalf of another person **2** not experienced personally but imagined through the experience of others: *vicarious thrill* ◇ **vicariously** *adv*

vice¹ *noun* **1** a bad habit, a serious fault **2** wickedness, immorality

vice² *noun* a tool with two jaws for gripping objects firmly

vice- *prefix* second in rank to: *vice-chancellor/vice-president*

viceroy *noun* a governor acting on royal authority

vice versa *adv* the other way round: *I*

needed his help and vice versa (ie he needed mine)

vicinity *noun* **1** nearness **2** neighbourhood

vicious *adj* **1** ferocious **2** wicked; spiteful ◊ **viciously** *adv* ◊ **viciousness** *noun* ◊ **vicious circle** a bad situation whose results cause it to get worse
☐ **2** wicked, bad, wrong, immoral, depraved, unprincipled, diabolical, corrupt, debased, perverted, *formal* profligate, vile, heinous, malicious, spiteful, vindictive, virulent, cruel, mean, nasty, slanderous, venomous, defamatory
☒ virtuous, kind

vicissitude *noun* **1** change from one state to another **2** (**vicissitudes**) changes of luck, ups and downs

victim *noun* **1** someone who is killed or harmed, intentionally or by accident: *victim of a brutal attack/victim of the financial situation* **2** an animal or person for sacrifice

victimize *verb* treat unjustly; make a victim of
☐ oppress, discriminate against, persecute, pick on, prey on, bully, exploit

victor *noun* a winner of a contest *etc*

victorious *adj* successful in a battle or other contest
☐ conquering, champion, triumphant, winning, unbeaten, successful, prizewinning, top, first
☒ defeated, unsuccessful

victory *noun* (*plural* **victories**) success in any battle, struggle or contest
☐ conquest, win, triumph, success, superiority, mastery, subjugation, overcoming
☒ defeat, loss

victuals /'vɪtəlz/ *noun plural* food

video *adj* **1** relating to the recording and broadcasting of TV pictures and sound **2** relating to recording by video ◊ *noun* (*plural* **videos**) **1** a videocassette recorder **2** a recording on videotape **3** *US* television ◊ *verb* (**videos, videoing, videoed**) make a recording by video ◊ **video game** an electronically-operated game played using a vi-

sual display unit ◊ **video recorder** a videocassette recorder

videocassette *noun* a cassette containing videotape ◊ **videocassette recorder** a tape recorder using videocassettes for recording and playing backTV programmes

videotape *noun* magnetic tape for carrying pictures and sound

vie *verb* (**vies, vying, vied**): **vie with** compete with, try to outdo
☐ strive, compete, contend, struggle, contest, fight, rival

view *noun* **1** a range or field of sight: *a good view* **2** a scene **3** an opinion or way of looking at something ◊ *verb* **1** look at **2** watch (television) **3** consider ◊ **in view 1** in sight **2** in your mind as an aim ◊ **in view of** taking into consideration ◊ **on view** on show; ready for inspecting ◊ **with a view to** with the purpose or intention of
☐ *noun* **1** sight, scene, vision, vista, outlook, prospect, perspective, panorama, landscape **3** opinion, attitude, belief, judgement, estimation, feeling, sentiment, impression, notion ◊ *verb* **1** examine, inspect, look at, scan, survey, witness **3** consider, regard, contemplate, judge, think about

viewpoint *noun* **1** a place from which a scene is viewed **2** a personal opinion (also **point of view**)
☐ **2** attitude, position, perspective, slant, standpoint, stance, opinion, angle, feeling

vigil *noun* **1** a time of watching or of keeping awake at night, often to watch over something, or before a religious festival **2** a peaceful, stationary demonstration for a cause

vigilance *noun* watchfulness, alertness ◊ **vigilant** *adj*
☐ **vigilant** watchful, alert, attentive, observant, on one's guard, on the lookout, cautious, wide-awake, sleepless, unsleeping
☒ **vigilant** careless

vigilante /vɪdʒɪ'lantɪ/ *noun* a private citizen who assumes the task of keeping order in a community

vignette /viːnˈjet/ *noun* **1** a small design or portrait **2** a short description, a sketch

vigorous *adj* strong, healthy; forceful: *vigorous defence* ◇ **vigorously** *adv*

■ energetic, active, lively, healthy, strong, strenuous, robust, sound, vital, brisk, dynamic, forceful, forcible, powerful, spirited, full-blooded, effective, efficient, flourishing, intense

☒ weak, feeble

vigour *noun* strength of body or mind; energy

Viking *noun, hist* a Norse invader of Western Europe

vile *adj* **1** very bad or wicked **2** disgusting, revolting ◇ **vilely** *adv* ◇ **vileness** *noun*

■ **1** base, contemptible, debased, depraved, degenerate, bad, wicked, worthless, sinful, mean, evil, impure, corrupt, despicable, disgraceful, degrading, vicious, appalling **2** disgusting, foul, nauseating, sickening, repulsive, repugnant, revolting, noxious, offensive, nasty, loathsome, horrid

☒ **1** pure, worthy **2** pleasant, lovely

vilify *verb* (**vilifies**, **vilifying**, **vilified**) say bad things about ◇ **vilification** *noun*

villa *noun* a house in the country *etc* used for holidays

village *noun* a collection of houses, not big enough to be called a town ◇ **villager** *noun* someone who lives in a village

villain *noun* a scoundrel, a rascal ◇ **villainy** *noun* (*plural* **villainies**) wickedness

villainous *adj* wicked

■ wicked, bad, criminal, evil, sinful, vicious, notorious, cruel, inhuman, vile, depraved, disgraceful, terrible

☒ good

vindicate *verb* **1** clear from blame **2** justify

■ **1** clear, acquit, excuse, exonerate, absolve **2** justify, uphold, support, maintain, defend, advocate, verify

vindictive *adj* revengeful; spiteful

■ spiteful, unforgiving, implacable, vengeful, relentless, unrelenting, revengeful, resentful, punitive, venomous, malevolent, malicious

☒ forgiving

vine *noun* **1** a climbing plant that produces grapes (also **grapevine**) **2** any climbing or trailing plant

vinegar *noun* a sour-tasting liquid made from wine, beer *etc*, used for seasoning or pickling ◇ **vinegary** *adj*

vineyard /ˈvɪnjəd/ *noun* an area planted with grapevines

vintage *noun* **1** the gathering of ripe grapes **2** the grapes gathered **3** wine of a particular year, *esp* when of very high quality **4** time of origin or manufacture ◇ *adj* **1** of a vintage **2** of wine: of a particular year **3** very characteristic of an author, style *etc*: *vintage Monty Python* ◇ **vintage car** one of a very early type, still able to run

vintner *noun* a wine-seller

vinyl /ˈvaɪnɪl/ *noun* **1** a tough plastic **2** a floorcovering made of this **3** plastic records as opposed to cassettes *etc*

viola¹ *noun* a stringed instrument like a large violin

viola² *noun* a member of the family of plants which include violets and pansies

violate *verb* **1** break (a law, a treaty *etc*) **2** harm sexually, *esp* rape **3** treat with disrespect **4** disturb, interrupt ◇ **violation** *noun* ◇ **violator** *noun*

■ **1** contravene, disobey, disregard, transgress, break **2** debauch, defile, rape, ravish, dishonour **3** debauch, defile, dishonour, desecrate, profane

violence *noun* **1** great roughness and force **2** violent behaviour

violent *adj* **1** forceful and intense: *violent storm* **2** caused or marked by violence: *violent death* **3** uncontrollable and aggressive: *violent temper* ◇ **violently** *adv*

■ **1** intense, strong, severe, sharp, acute, extreme, harmful, destructive, devastating, injurious, powerful, tumultuous, turbulent **2** painful, agonizing, forceful, forcible, harsh, ruinous, rough **3** cruel, brutal, aggressive, bloodthirsty, impetuous, hot-headed, headstrong, murderous, savage, wild, vicious, unrestrained, uncontrollable, ungovernable, passionate, furious, intemperate, maddened, outrageous, riotous, fiery

🖃 **1** calm, moderate **3** peaceful, gentle

violet *noun* a kind of small bluish-purple flower

violin *noun* a musical instrument with four strings, held under the chin and played with a bow ◇ **violinist** *noun* someone who plays the violin

violoncello *see* **cello**

VIP *abbrev* very important person

viper *noun* an adder

virago *noun* (*plural* **viragos**) a noisy, bad-tempered woman

viral *adj* of a virus

virgin *noun* someone who has had no sexual intercourse ◇ **virginal** *adj* of or like a virgin; chaste ◇ **the Virgin Mary** the mother of Christ

virile *adj* manly; strong, vigorous ◇ **virility** *noun* manhood; manliness; strength, vigour

virtual *adj* in effect, though not in strict fact: *virtual war* ◇ **virtually** *adv* ◇ **virtual reality** a computer simulation of a real or imaginary environment

🖿 effective, essential, practical, implied, implicit, potential ◇ **virtually** practically, in effect, almost, nearly, as good as, in essence

virtue *noun* **1** goodness of character and behaviour **2** a good quality, *eg* honesty, generosity *etc* **3** a good point: *one virtue of plastic crockery is that it doesn't break* ◇ **by virtue of** because of

🖿 **1** goodness, morality, rectitude, uprightness, worthiness, righteousness, integrity, honour, incorruptibility **3** quality, worth, merit, advantage, asset, credit, strength

virtuoso *noun* (*plural* **virtuosos**) a highly skilled artist, *esp* a musician ◇ **virtuosity** *noun*

virtuous *adj* good, just, honest

◇ **virtuously** *adv*

🖿 good, moral, righteous, upright, worthy, honourable, irreproachable, incorruptible, exemplary, blameless, clean-living, excellent, innocent

🖾 immoral, vicious

virulent *adj* **1** full of poison **2** bitter, spiteful **3** of a disease: extremely infectious or dangerous ◇ **virulence** *noun*

virus *noun* (*plural* **viruses**) a germ that is smaller than any bacteria, and causes diseases such as mumps, chickenpox *etc*

visa *noun* a permit given by the authorities of a country to allow someone to stay for a time in that country

visage /vɪzɪdʒ/ *noun* the face

vis-à-vis /viːzɑːˈviː/ *prep* in relation to, compared with

viscera /ˈvɪsərə/ *noun plural* the inner parts of the body ◇ **visceral** *adj* **1** of the viscera **2** gory, bloody

viscid /ˈvɪsɪd/ *adj* viscous

viscount /ˈvaɪkaʊnt/ *noun* a title of nobility next below an earl

viscountess *noun* a title of nobility next below a countess

viscous /ˈvɪskəs/ *adj* of a liquid: sticky, not flowing easily ◇ **viscosity** *noun*

visibility *noun* **1** the clearness with which objects may be seen or perceived **2** the extent or range of vision as affected by fog, rain *etc*

visible *adj* able to be seen or perceived ◇ **visibly** *adv*

🖿 perceptible, discernible, detectable, apparent, noticeable, observable, distinguishable, evident, unconcealed, undisguised, unmistakable, conspicuous, clear, obvious, manifest, open, plain, patent

🖾 invisible, indiscernible, hidden

vision *noun* **1** the act or power of seeing **2** something seen in the imagination **3** a strange, supernatural sight **4** the ability to foresee likely future events

🖿 **1** sight, seeing, eyesight **2** idea, ideal, conception, insight, view, picture, image, fantasy, dream, daydream **3** apparition, hallucination, illusion, delusion, mirage, phantom, ghost, chimera, spectre **4** far-sightedness, foresight

visionary *adj* seen in imagination only, not real ◇ *noun* (*plural* **visionaries**) someone who dreams up imaginative plans

▣ *adj* idealistic, romantic, dreamy, unrealistic, unreal, fanciful, prophetic, speculative, illusory, imaginary ◇ *noun* idealist, romantic, dreamer, daydreamer, prophet, mystic, seer, utopian, rainbow-chaser, theorist

▨ *noun* pragmatist

visit *verb* **1** go to see; call on **2** stay with as a guest ◇ *noun* **1** a call at a person's house or at a place of interest *etc* **2** a short stay

▣ *verb* **1** call on, call in on, *informal* drop in on, *informal* stop by, look in, look up, *informal* pop in, see **2** stay with

visitation *noun* **1** a visit of an important official **2** a great misfortune, seen as a punishment from God

visitor *noun* someone who makes a visit

visor or **vizor** /'vaɪzə(r)/ *noun* **1** a part of a helmet covering the face **2** a movable shade on a car's windscreen **3** a peak on a cap for shading the eyes

vista *noun* a view, *esp* one seen through a long, narrow opening

visual *adj* **1** relating to, or received through, sight: *visual image* **2** creating vivid mental images: *visual poetry* ◇ **visual display unit** a device like a television set, on which data from a computer's memory can be displayed

visualize *verb* form a clear picture of in the mind ◇ **visualization** *noun*

vital *adj* **1** of the greatest importance: *vital information* **2** necessary to life: *vital organs* **3** of life **4** vigorous, energetic: *a vital personality* ◇ **vitally** *adv*

▣ **1** critical, crucial, important, imperative, key, significant, basic, fundamental, essential, necessary, requisite, indispensable, urgent, life-or-death **4** alive, lively, spirited, vivacious, vibrant, vigorous, dynamic, animated, energetic

vitality *noun* life; liveliness, strength; ability to go on living

▣ life, liveliness, animation, vigour, energy, vivacity, spirit, sparkle, exuberance, *informal* go, strength, stamina

vitalize *verb* give life or vigour to

vitamin *noun* one of a group of substances necessary for health, occurring in different natural foods

---

Vitamins include:
aneurin (thiamine), ascorbic acid, bioflavonoid/citrin, biotin, calciferol, cholecalciferol, cyanocobalamin, ergocalciferol, folic acid, linoleic acid, linolenic acid, menadione, nicotinic acid (niacin), pantothenic acid, phylloquinone, pteroic acid, pyridoxine (adermin), retinol, riboflavin, tocopherol

---

vitiate /'vɪʃɪeɪt/ *verb* spoil, damage

vitreous *adj* of or like glass

vitrify *verb* (**vitrifies**, **vitrifying**, **vitrified**) make or become like glass

vitriol *noun* **1** sulphuric acid **2** bitter speech or criticism

vitriolic *adj* biting, scathing

vitro *see* **in vitro**

vituperate *verb* be rude to, abuse ◇ **vituperation** *noun* ◇ **vituperative** *adj* abusive, very rude

viva /'vaɪvə/ *noun* an oral examination ◇ *verb* examine orally

vivacious *adj* lively, sprightly ◇ **vivaciously** *adv* ◇ **vivacity** *noun* liveliness, spark

▣ lively, animated, spirited, high-spirited, ebullient, cheerful, sparkling, bubbly

vivarium *noun* a tank or other enclosure for keeping living creatures

vivid *adj* **1** creating striking, clear mental pictures: *a vivid account* **2** of a colour: bright and strong ◇ **vividly** *adv*

▣ **1** vigorous, expressive, dramatic, flamboyant **2** bright, colourful, intense, strong, rich, vibrant, brilliant, glowing, dazzling

vivisection *noun* the carrying out of experiments on living animals

vixen *noun* **1** a female fox **2** an ill-tempered woman

viz *adv* namely

vocabulary *noun* (*plural* **vocabularies**) **1** the range of words used by an individual or group **2** the words of a particular language **3** a list of words in alphabetical order, with their meanings

vocal *adj* **1** of the voice, spoken **2** expressing your opinions loudly and fully ◊ **vocalist** *noun* a singer ◊ **vocally** *adv* ◊ **vocal cords** two folds of tissue in the throat that vibrate to produce sound

☰ **1** spoken, said, oral, uttered, voiced **2** articulate, eloquent, expressive, noisy, clamorous, shrill, strident, outspoken, frank, forthright, plain-spoken

Ea **1** unspoken **2** inarticulate

vocation *noun* **1** an occupation or profession to which someone wants to dedicate themselves **2** a strong inclination to follow a particular course of action or work ◊ **vocational** *adj*

vociferous *adj* loud and forceful in speech, noisy ◊ **vociferously** *adv*

☰ noisy, vocal, clamorous, loud, obstreperous, strident, vehement, thundering, shouting

Ea quiet

vodka *noun* an alcoholic spirit made from grain or potatoes

vogue *noun* the fashion of the moment; popularity ◊ **in vogue** in fashion

voice *noun* **1** the sound produced from the mouth in speech or song **2** ability to speak **3** ability to sing **4** a way of speaking or singing **5** expression or a means of expressing: *gave voice to their feelings* ◊ *verb* express (an opinion)

☰ *noun* **1** speech, utterance, articulation, language, words, sound **4** tone, intonation, inflection, expression **5** say, vote, opinion, view, decision, will ◊ *verb* express, say, utter, air, articulate, speak of, verbalize, assert, convey, disclose, divulge, declare, enunciate

void *adj* **1** empty, vacant **2** not valid ◊ *noun* an empty space ◊ **void of** lacking completely

☰ *adj* **1** empty, emptied, free, unfilled, unoccupied, vacant, clear, bare, blank **2** annulled, inoperative, invalid, cancelled, ineffective ◊ *noun* emptiness, vacuum,

chasm, blank, blankness, space, cavity, gap, hollow, opening

Ea *adj* **1** full **2** valid

vol *abbrev* volume

volatile *adj* **1** of a liquid: quickly turning into vapour **2** of a person: changeable in mood or behaviour, fickle **3** of a situation: liable to change quickly

☰ **2** changeable, inconstant, unstable, variable, erratic, temperamental, unsteady, unsettled, fickle, unpredictable, capricious, restless, giddy, flighty, *informal* up and down, lively

Ea **2** constant, steady

volcano *noun* (*plural* **volcanoes**) a mountain with an opening through which molten rock, ashes *etc* are periodically thrown up from inside the earth ◊ **volcanic** *adj* **1** relating to volcanoes **2** caused or produced by heat within the earth

Named after *Vulcan*, the Roman god of fire

vole *noun* any of a group of small rodents, including the water rat

volition *noun* an act of will or choice: *he did it of his own volition*

volley *noun* (*plural* **volleys**) **1** a number of shots fired or missiles thrown at the same time **2** an outburst of abuse or criticism **3** *sport* a striking of a ball before it reaches the ground ◊ *verb* **1** shoot or throw in a volley **2** strike (a ball) before it reaches the ground

☰ *noun* **1** barrage, bombardment, hail, shower, burst, blast, discharge, explosion

volt *noun* the unit used in measuring the force of electricity

voltage *noun* electrical force measured in volts

voluble *adj* speaking with a great flow of words ◊ **volubility** *noun*

☰ fluent, glib, articulate, *formal* loquacious, talkative, forthcoming, garrulous

volume *noun* **1** the amount of space taken up by anything **2** amount: *volume of trade* **3** loudness or fullness of sound **4** a book, often one of a series

voluminous *adj* bulky, of great volume

■ roomy, capacious, ample, spacious, billowing, vast, bulky, huge, large

voluntary *adj* **1** done or acting by choice, not under compulsion **2** working without payment ◇ *noun* (*plural* **voluntaries**) a piece of organ music of the organist's choice played at a church service

■ *adj* **1** conscious, deliberate, purposeful, intended, intentional, wilful **2** free, gratuitous, optional, unforced, unpaid, honorary

volunteer *noun* someone who offers to do something of their own accord, often for no payment ◇ *verb* **1** offer help or services freely **2** give (information, an opinion *etc*) unasked

voluptuous *adj* **1** full of or fond of the pleasures of life **2** of a woman: attractively full-figured

vomit *verb* throw up the contents of the stomach through the mouth ◇ *noun* the matter thrown up by vomiting

voodoo *noun* a type of witchcraft

voracious *adj* very greedy, difficult to satisfy: *voracious appetite/voracious reader* ◇ **voracity** *noun*

⚠ Do not confuse with: **veracious**

vortex *noun* (*plural* **vortexes** or **vortices**) **1** a whirlpool **2** a whirlwind

votary *noun* (*plural* **votaries**) **1** someone who has made a vow **2** a devoted worshipper or admirer

vote *verb* **1** give your support to a particular candidate, a proposal *etc* in a ballot or show of hands **2** choose by voting ◇ *noun* **1** an expression of opinion or support by voting **2** the right to vote ◇ **voter** *noun* someone who votes

■ *verb* **1** ballot **2** elect, choose, opt, plump for, declare, return

vouch *verb* (with **for**) say that you are sure of or can guarantee: *I can vouch for his courage*

■ guarantee, support, back, endorse, confirm, certify, affirm, assert, attest to, speak for, swear to, uphold

voucher *noun* a paper which can be exchanged for money or goods

vouchsafe *verb* give or grant (a reply, privilege *etc*)

vow *noun* a solemn promise or declaration, *esp* one made to God ◇ *verb* make a vow

■ *noun* promise, oath, pledge ◇ *verb* promise, pledge, swear

vowel *noun* **1** a sound made by the voice that does not require the use of the tongue, teeth or lips **2** the letters *a*, *e*, *i*, *o*, *u* (or various combinations of them), and sometimes *y*, which represent those sounds

vox pop public or popular opinion (from Latin *vox populi*, voice of the people)

voyage *noun* a journey, usually by sea ◇ *verb* make a journey ◇ **voyager** *noun*

voyeur *noun* someone who gets sexual pleasure from watching other people secretly ◇ **voyeuristic** *adj*

VSO *abbrev* Voluntary Service Overseas

vulgar *adj* **1** coarse, ill-mannered **2** indecent **3** of the common people ◇ **vulgarian** *noun* a vulgar person ◇ **vulgarity** *noun* ◇ **vulgarly** *adv* ◇ **vulgar fraction** a fraction not written as a decimal, *eg* $\frac{1}{3}, \frac{1}{5}$

■ **1** unrefined, uncouth, coarse, common, crude, ill-bred, impolite, indecorous **2** indecent, suggestive, risqué, rude, indelicate **3** ordinary, general, popular, vernacular

vulnerable *adj* **1** exposed to, or in danger of, attack **2** liable to be hurt physically or emotionally ◇ **vulnerability** *noun* ◇ **vulnerably** *adv*

■ **1** unprotected, exposed, defenceless, wide open **2** susceptible, weak, sensitive

◙ **1** protected **2** strong

vulture *noun* a large bird that feeds mainly on the flesh of dead animals

Ww

W *abbrev* west, western

wad *noun* **1** a lump of loose material (*eg* wool, cloth, paper) pressed together **2** a bunch of banknotes
■ **1** chunk, plug, roll, ball, *informal* wodge, lump, hunk, mass, block

wadding *noun* soft material (*eg* cotton wool) used for packing or padding

waddle /'wɒdəl/ *verb* walk with short, unsteady steps, moving from side to side as a duck does ◇ *noun* such a walk
■ *verb* toddle, totter, wobble, sway, rock, shuffle

wade *verb* **1** walk through deep water or mud **2** get through with difficulty: *still wading through this book*

wader *noun* **1** a long-legged bird that wades in search of food **2** (**waders**) high waterproof boots worn by anglers for wading

wadi *noun* a rocky river-bed in North Africa, dry except in the rainy season

wafer *noun* **1** a very thin, light type of biscuit, as that eaten with ice-cream **2** a very thin slice of anything

waffle *noun* **1** a light, crisp cake made from batter, cooked in a **waffle-iron 2** pointless, long-drawn-out talk ◇ *verb* talk long and meaninglessly
■ *noun* **2** blather, prattle, wordiness, padding, nonsense, *informal* gobbledygook, *informal* hot air ◇ *verb* jabber, prattle, blather, *informal* rabbit on, *informal* witter on

waft *verb* carry or drift lightly through the air or over water

wag *verb* (**wags, wagging, wagged**) move from side to side or up and down ◇ *noun* **1** an act of wagging **2** someone who is always joking ◇ **waggish** *adj* always joking
■ *verb* shake, waggle, wave, sway, swing, bob, nod, wiggle, oscillate, flutter, vibrate, quiver, rock

wage *verb* carry on (a war *etc*) ◇ *noun* (often **wages**) payment for work
■ *verb* carry on, conduct, engage in, undertake, practise, pursue ◇ *noun* pay, fee, earnings, salary, wage-packet, payment, stipend, remuneration, *formal* emolument, allowance, reward, hire, compensation, recompense

wager *noun* a bet ◇ *verb* bet

waggle *verb* move from side to side in an unsteady manner ◇ *noun* an unsteady movement from side to side

wagon or **waggon** *noun* **1** a four-wheeled vehicle for carrying loads **2** an open railway carriage for goods

wagtail *noun* a small black and white bird with a long tail which it wags up and down

waif *noun* an uncared-for or homeless child or animal ◇ **waifs and strays** homeless children or animals

wail *verb* cry or moan in sorrow ◇ *noun* a sorrowful cry
■ *verb* moan, cry, howl, lament, weep, complain, *informal* yowl ◇ *noun* moan, cry, howl, lament, complaint, weeping

wain *noun*, *old* a wagon

wainscot *noun* a skirting-board ◇ **wainscoting** or **wainscotting** *noun*

waist *noun* the narrow part of the body, between ribs and hips

waistcoat *noun* a short, sleeveless jacket, often worn under an outer jacket

wait *verb* **1** (with **for**) remain in expectation or readiness for: *waiting for the bus to come* **2** put off or delay action **3** be employed as a waiter or waitress ◇ *noun* a delay ◇ **waiting list** a list of people waiting for something in order of priority ◇ **waiting room** a room in which to wait at a railway station, clinic *etc* ◇ **wait on 1** serve (someone) at table **2** act as a servant to

■ *verb* **1** await **2** delay, linger, hold back, hesitate, pause ◇ *noun* hold-up, hesitation, delay, interval, pause, halt

waiter, waitress *noun* someone whose job it is to serve people at table in a restaurant

waive *verb* give up (a claim or right) ◇ **waiver** *noun* **1** the act of waiving **2** a document indicating this

> ❗Do not confuse with: **wave** and **waver**

wake¹ *verb* (**wakes, waking, woken, woke** or **waked**) (often with **up**) (cause to) stop sleeping ◇ *noun* a night of watching beside a dead body ◇ **wakeful** *adj* not sleeping, unable to sleep

■ *verb* rise, get up, arise, rouse, came to, bring round, stimulate, stir, activate, arouse

wake² *noun* a streak of foamy water left in the track of a ship ◇ **in the wake of** immediately behind or after

waken *verb* wake, arouse or be aroused

walk *verb* **1** move along on foot **2** travel along (streets *etc*) on foot **3** lead or accompany in a walk ◇ *noun* **1** an act of walking **2** a manner of walking **3** a distance to be walked over: *a short walk from here* **4** a place for walking: *a covered walk* ◇ **walker** *noun* ◇ **walking stick** a stick used for support when walking ◇ **walk of life** someone's rank or occupation ◇ **walk the plank** *hist* be put to death by pirates by being made to walk off the end of a plank over a ship's side ◇ **walk out 1** of workers *etc*: leave the workplace in a body **2** depart abruptly in protest **3** (with **on**) abandon (someone)

■ *verb* **1** step, stride, pace, proceed, advance, march, plod, tramp, traipse, trek, trudge, saunter, amble, stroll, tread, hike ◇ *noun* **1** stroll, amble, ramble, saunter, march, hike, tramp, trek, traipse, trudge, trail **2** carriage, gait **4** footpath, path, walkway, avenue, pathway, promenade, alley, lane, pavement ◇ **walk of life** field, area, sphere, line,

activity, arena, course, pursuit, calling, métier, career, vocation, profession, trade

walkabout *noun* **1** a stroll by a celebrity through a crowd **2** a period of wandering

walkie-talkie *noun* a portable radio set for sending and receiving messages

Walkman *noun, trademark* a personal stereo

walkover *noun* an easy victory

■ *informal* pushover, *informal* doddle, child's play, *informal* piece of cake, *informal* cinch

wall *noun* **1** a structure built of stone, brick *etc* used to separate or enclose **2** the side of a building **3** an outer covering, *eg* of a cell ◇ *verb* (with **in, off** *etc*) enclose or separate with a wall ◇ **off the wall** unusual, eccentric ◇ **up the wall** *informal* angry; crazy

wallaby *noun* (*plural* **wallabies**) a small kind of kangaroo

wallet *noun* a small folding case for holding banknotes, credit cards *etc*

wallflower *noun* **1** a sweet-smelling spring flower **2** someone who is continually without a partner at a dance *etc*

wallop *verb, informal* beat, hit ◇ *noun* a hit

wallow *verb* **1** (often with **in**) roll about with enjoyment in water, mud *etc* **2** (often with **in**) to revel or indulge (in admiration, self-pity *etc*)

■ **1** loll, lie, roll, wade, welter, lurch, flounder, splash

wallpaper *noun* **1** paper used in house decorating for covering walls **2** a background pattern on a computer screen ◇ *verb* cover with wallpaper

wally /'wɒlɪ/ *noun* (*plural* **wallies**) *slang* a stupid or inept person

walnut *noun* **1** a tree whose wood is used for making furniture **2** the nut it produces

walrus *noun* (*plural* **walruses** or **walrus**) a large sea animal, like a seal, with two long tusks

waltz *noun* (*plural* **waltzes**) **1** a ballroom dance for couples with a circling movement **2** music for this dance, with three beats to each bar ◇ *verb* dance a waltz

WAN *abbrev, comput* wide area network

wan /wɒn/ *adj* pale and sickly looking ◇ **wanly** *adv*

wand *noun* a long slender rod used by a conjuror, magician *etc*

wander *verb* **1** roam about with no definite purpose; roam **2** go astray or digress **3** of thoughts *etc*: flit randomly ◇ **wanderer** *noun*

■ **1** roam, rove, ramble, meander, saunter, stroll, prowl, drift, range, stray, straggle **2** depart, go astray, swerve, veer, err, digress, diverge, deviate ◇ **wanderer** itinerant, traveller, drifter, rover, rambler, stroller, nomad, gypsy, vagrant, vagabond

wanderlust *noun* a keen desire for travel

wane *verb* **1** become smaller (*contrasted with*: **wax**) **2** lose power, importance *etc* ◇ **waning** *adj* ◇ **on the wane** becoming less

wangle *verb* get or achieve through craftiness, skilful planning *etc*

■ manipulate, arrange, contrive, engineer, fix, scheme, manoeuvre, work, pull off, manage, *informal* fiddle

wannabe /ˈwɒnəbiː/ *noun, informal* someone who desperately wants to be a particular thing: *filmstar wannabes*

want *verb* **1** wish for, desire **2** need: *the bin wants emptying* **3** (often with **for**) lack: *the child wants for nothing* ◇ *noun* **1** a desire **2** poverty **3** scarcity, lack

■ *verb* **1** desire, wish, crave, covet, fancy, long for, pine for, yearn for, hunger for, thirst for **2** need, require, demand **3** lack, miss, call for ◇ *noun* **1** desire, demand, longing, requirement, wish, need, appetite **2** poverty, privation, destitution **3** lack, insufficiency, deficiency, shortage, inadequacy

wanted *adj* **1** needed or desired **2** sought, *esp* by the police

wanting *adj* **1** absent, missing; without **2** not good enough

■ **1** absent, missing **2** inadequate, imperfect, faulty, defective, substandard, poor, deficient, unsatisfactory

🔁 **1** sufficient **2** adequate

wanton *adj* **1** thoughtless, pointless, without motive: *wanton cruelty* **2** immoral or lewd

■ **1** malicious, arbitrary, unprovoked, unjustifiable, unrestrained, rash, reckless, wild **2** licentious, immoral, shameless

WAP *abbrev* Wireless Application Protocol ◇ **WAP phone** a mobile phone using WAP and *usu* allowing Internet access

war *noun* an armed struggle, *esp* between nations ◇ *verb* (**wars**, **warring**, **warred**) (with **against**) fight in a war, make war against ◇ **on the warpath** in a fighting or angry mood

warble *verb* sing like a bird, trill ◇ **warbler** *noun* a type of songbird

war-cry *noun* words shouted aloud in battle, for encouragement

ward *verb* (with **off**) keep off, defend yourself against (a blow, illness *etc*) ◇ *noun* **1** a hospital room containing a number of beds **2** one of the parts into which a town is divided for voting **3** someone who is in the care of a guardian

■ *verb* avert, fend off, deflect, parry, repel, stave off, thwart, beat off, forestall, evade, turn away, block, avoid ◇ *noun* **2** division, area, district **3** charge, dependant, protégé(e), minor

warden *noun* **1** someone who guards a game reserve **2** someone in charge of a hostel or college

warder, wardress *noun* a prison guard

wardrobe *noun* **1** a cupboard for clothes **2** someone's personal supply of clothes

-ware *suffix* manufactured material: *earthenware/glassware*

warehouse *noun* a building where goods are stored

wares *noun plural* goods for sale

■ goods, merchandise, commodities, stock, products, produce, stuff

warfare *noun* the carrying on of war

■ war, fighting, hostilities, battle, arms, combat, strife, struggle, contest, conflict, contention, discord, blows

☲ peace

warhead *noun* the part of a missile containing the explosive

warlike *adj* **1** fond of war **2** threatening war

warm *adj* **1** fairly hot **2** of clothes: keeping the wearer warm **3** of a person: friendly, loving ◊ *verb* make or become warm ◊ **warmth** *noun* ◊ **warm-up** *noun* gentle exercising in preparation for vigorous exercise

■ *adj* **1** heated, tepid, lukewarm **3** friendly, amiable, cordial, affable, kindly, genial, hearty, hospitable, sympathetic, affectionate, tender ◊ *verb* heat (up), reheat, melt, thaw

☲ *adj* **1** cool **3** unfriendly

warm-blooded *adj* having a blood temperature higher than that of the surrounding atmosphere

warm-hearted *adj* kind, generous

warn *verb* **1** tell (someone) beforehand about possible danger, misfortune *etc*: *I warned him about the icy roads* **2** give cautionary advice to: *I warned him not to be late* **3** rebuke with the threat of future punishment

■ **1** caution, alert, admonish, advise, notify, counsel, put on one's guard, inform, *informal* tip off

warning *noun* a remark, notice *etc* that warns ◊ *adj* serving as a warning

■ caution, alert, admonition, advice, notification, notice, advance notice, counsel, hint, lesson, alarm, threat, *informal* tip-off

warp *verb* **1** become twisted out of shape **2** distort, make unsound: *his previous experiences had warped his judgement* ◊ *noun* **1** an unevenness or twist **2** a shift in a dimension, *esp* time **3** the threads stretched lengthwise on a loom, which are crossed by the weft

■ *verb* **1** twist, bend, contort, deform **2** distort, misshape, pervert, corrupt, deviate

warpath *noun*: **on the warpath** in angry pursuit

warrant *noun* a certificate granting someone a right or authority: *search warrant* ◊ *verb* justify, be a good enough reason for: *the crime does not warrant such punishment* ◊ **warranted** *adj* guaranteed ◊ **warranty** *noun* (*plural* **warranties**) an assurance of the quality of sold goods, and acceptance of responsibility for any repairs ◊ **I warrant you** or **I'll warrant** you may be sure, I assure you

warren *noun* **1** a collection of rabbit burrows **2** a building with many rooms and passages; a maze

warrior *noun* a great fighter

warship *noun* a ship armed with guns *etc*

wart *noun* a small hard growth on the skin

warthog *noun* a wild African pig

wary *adj* **1** cautious, on guard **2** (often with **of**) suspicious (of someone) ◊ **warily** *adv* ◊ **wariness** *noun*

■ **1** cautious, guarded, careful, on one's guard, on the lookout, prudent, heedful, attentive, alert, watchful, vigilant, wide-awake **2** distrustful, suspicious, unsure

☲ unwary, careless, heedless

was *past form of* **be**

wash *verb* **1** clean with water, soap *etc* **2** clean yourself with water *etc* **3** (with **off** or **out**) remove (a stain) by washing **4** of water: flow over or against **5** *informal* bear investigation: *that excuse won't wash* ◊ *noun* (*plural* **washes**) **1** a washing **2** a quantity of clothes *etc* for washing **3** the breaking of waves **4** a streak of foamy water left behind by a moving boat **5** a liquid with which anything is washed **6** a thin coat of paint *etc* ◊ **washbasin** or **washhand basin** a bathroom sink in which to wash your hands and face ◊ **wash your hands of** have nothing further to do with ◊ **wash down 1** wash (something) from top to bottom **2** ease (a pill) down one's throat, or accompany (food) with a drink ◊ **wash up** wash the dishes

■ *verb* **1** clean, cleanse, shampoo, launder, scrub, swab down, rinse, swill **2** bathe, bath, shower ◇ *noun* **1** cleaning, cleansing, bath, bathe, laundry, laundering, scrub, shower, shampoo, washing, rinse

washer *noun* **1** someone or something that washes **2** a flat ring of metal, rubber *etc* for keeping joints tight

washing *noun* **1** the act of cleaning by water **2** clothes to be or that have just been washed ◇ **washing machine** an electric machine for washing clothes

washing-up *noun* dishes to be washed

washout *noun* **1** an event stopped by rain **2** a failure

wasp *noun* a stinging, winged insect, with a slender, yellow and black striped body

wassail *verb, old* **1** have a festive drinking session **2** go from house to house singing carols

wastage *noun* **1** an amount wasted **2** loss through decay or squandering

waste *adj* **1** thrown away, rejected as useless: *waste paper* **2** of land: uncultivated, barren and desolate ◇ *verb* **1** spend (money, time, energy) extravagantly, without result or profit **2** fail to use (an opportunity *etc*) **3** throw away (*eg* uneaten food) **4** decay or wear away gradually ◇ *noun* **1** extravagant use, squandering **2** rubbish, waste material **3** uncultivated or devastated land
■ *adj* **1** useless, worthless, unwanted, unused, left-over, superfluous, extra **2** barren, desolate, empty, uninhabited, bare, devastated, uncultivated, unprofitable, wild, dismal, dreary ◇ *verb* **1** squander, misspend, misuse, fritter away, dissipate, lavish, spend, throw away, *informal* blow **4** consume, erode, exhaust, drain, destroy, spoil ◇ *noun* **1** squandering, dissipation, wastefulness, extravagance, loss **2** rubbish, refuse, trash, garbage, leftovers, debris, dregs, litter, scrap, slops, dross
🔁 *verb* **1** economize **2** preserve

wasteful *adj* causing waste, extravagant ◇ **wastefully** *adv*
■ extravagant, spendthrift, prodigal, profligate, uneconomical, thriftless, un-

thrifty, ruinous, lavish, improvident
🔁 economical, thrifty

waster or **wastrel** *noun* an idle, good-for-nothing person

watch *verb* **1** look at, observe closely **2** (often with **over**) look after, mind ◇ *noun* (*plural* **watches**) **1** the act of keeping guard **2** a sailor's period of duty on deck **3** a small clock worn on the wrist or kept in a pocket
■ *verb* **1** observe, see, look at, regard, note, notice, mark, stare at, peer at, gaze at, view **2** guard, look after, keep an eye on, mind, protect, superintend, take care of, keep ◇ *noun* **1** vigilance, watchfulness, vigil, observation, surveillance, notice, lookout, attention, heed, alertness, inspection, supervision

watchdog *noun* **1** a dog which guards a building **2** an organization which monitors business practices *etc*

watchful *adj* alert, cautious ◇ **watchfully** *adv* ◇ **watchfulness** *noun*
■ vigilant, attentive, heedful, observant, alert, guarded, on one's guard, wide awake, suspicious, wary, chary, cautious
🔁 unobservant, inattentive

watchman *noun* a man who guards a building *etc* at night

watchword *noun* a motto, a slogan

water *noun* **1** a clear, tasteless liquid which falls as rain **2** a collection of this liquid in a lake, river *etc* **3** a fluid secreted by the body, *esp* urine ◇ *verb* **1** supply with water **2** dilute or mix with water **3** of the mouth: fill with saliva **4** of the eyes: fill with tears ◇ **water biscuit** a crisp biscuit, a cracker ◇ **water polo** a ball-game played in a pool between teams of swimmers ◇ **water rat** a kind of vole ◇ **water down 1** dilute (something) with water **2** reduce the impact of (something)
■ *verb* **1** wet, moisten, dampen, soak, spray, sprinkle, irrigate, drench, flood, hose
🔁 *verb* **1** dry out, parch

water-closet *noun* a toilet, a lavatory (*short form*: **WC**)

watercolour *noun* **1** a paint which is mixed with water, not oil **2** a painting done with this paint

watercress *noun* a plant which grows beside streams, with hot-tasting leaves which are eaten in salads

waterfall *noun* a place where a river falls from a height, often over a ledge of rock

waterlily *noun* a plant which grows in ponds *etc*, with flat floating leaves and large flowers

waterlogged *adj* **1** filled with water **2** soaked with water

watermain *noun* a large underground pipe carrying a public water supply

watermark *noun* a faint design on writing paper showing the maker's name, crest *etc*

watermelon *noun* a large melon with red juicy flesh and a thick, green rind

watermill *noun* a mill driven by water

waterproof *adj* not allowing water to pass through ◇ *noun* an overcoat made of waterproof material

watershed *noun* **1** a ridge separating the valleys of two rivers **2** a crucial point after which events change

water-skiing *noun* the sport of gliding over water on skis, towed by a powered boat ◇ **water-skier** *noun*

watertight *adj* so closely fitted that water cannot leak through

waterway *noun* a channel along which ships can sail

waterwheel *noun* a wheel moved by water

waterworks *noun plural* **1** a place which purifies and stores a town's water supply **2** *euphem* the urinary system **3** *informal* tears

watery *adj* **1** full of water **2** too liquid, textureless
■ **1** liquid, fluid, moist, wet, damp **2** weak, watered-down, diluted, insipid, tasteless, thin, runny, soggy, flavourless, *informal* wishy-washy

watt *noun* a unit of electric power
◇ **wattage** *noun* electric power measured in watts

wattle *noun* **1** interwoven twigs and branches used for fences *etc* **2** an Australian acacia tree **3** a fleshy part hanging from the neck of a turkey

wave *noun* **1** a moving ridge on the surface of water **2** a ridge or curve of hair **3** a vibration travelling through the air carrying light, sound *etc* **4** a hand gesture for attracting attention, or saying hello or goodbye **5** a rush of an emotion (*eg* despair, enthusiasm *etc*) ◇ *verb* **1** make a wave with the hand **2** move to and fro, flutter: *flags waving in the wind* **3** curl, curve ◇ **wavy** *adj* having waves
■ *noun* **1** breaker, roller, billow, ripple, tidal wave, wavelet, undulation, *informal* white horse **5** surge, sweep, upsurge, rush, stream, flood ◇ *verb* **1** beckon, gesture, gesticulate, indicate, sign, signal, direct ◇ **wavy** undulating, rippled, curly, curvy, ridged, sinuous, winding

🚫 Do not confuse with: **waive**

wavelength *noun* the distance from one point on a wave or vibration to the next similar point

waver *verb* **1** be unsteady, wobble **2** be uncertain or undecided
■ **1** oscillate, shake, sway, wobble, tremble, totter, rock **2** vacillate, falter, hesitate, dither, fluctuate, vary
🔁 **2** decide

wax[1] *noun* **1** the sticky, fatty substance of which bees make their cells **2** a fatty substance in the ear **3** a quickly hardening substance used for sealing letters *etc* ◇ *adj* made of wax ◇ *verb* rub with wax ◇ **waxy** *adj* of, or like, wax

wax[2] *verb* grow, increase (*contrasted with*: **wane**)

waxen *adj* **1** of or like wax **2** pale

waxworks *noun plural* a museum displaying wax models of famous people

way *noun* **1** an opening, a passage: *the way out* **2** road, path **3** room to go forward or pass: *block the way* **4** direction:

he went that way **5** route: *do you know the way?* **6** distance: *a long way* **7** condition: *in a bad way* **8** means, method: *there must be a way to do this* **9** manner: *in a clumsy way* **10** someone's own wishes or choice: *he always gets his own way* ◇ **by the way** incidentally, in passing ◇ **by way of 1** travelling through **2** as if, with the purpose of: *by way of a favour* ◇ **give way 1** collapse **2** yield to pressure ◇ **in the way** blocking progress ◇ **make your way** go ◇ **no way** *slang* absolutely not ◇ **out of the way 1** remote **2** placed so as not to obstruct ◇ **under way** in motion; progressing

▤ **1** access, passage **2** path, road, channel, avenue, track **4** direction, course **5** route, course **8** method, approach, technique, procedure, means, mode, system ◇ **by the way** incidentally, in passing

wayfarer *noun, old* a traveller on foot

waylay *verb* (**waylays, waylaying, waylaid**) wait for and stop (someone)

-ways *suffix* in the direction of: *lengthways/sideways*

wayside *noun* the edge of a road or path ◇ *adj* located by the side of a road

wayward *adj* wilful, following your own way ◇ **waywardness** *noun*

▤ wilful, capricious, changeable, fickle, unpredictable, stubborn, unmanageable, headstrong, obstinate, disobedient, rebellious, insubordinate, intractable, unruly, incorrigible

▤ tractable, good-natured

WC *abbrev* water-closet

we *pronoun* used by a speaker or writer in mentioning themselves together with other people (as the subject of a verb): *we are having a party this weekend*

weak *adj* **1** not strong, feeble **2** lacking determination, easily persuaded **3** easily overcome: *weak opposition* **4** diluted: *weak tea* ◇ **weakly** *adv*

▤ **1** feeble, frail, infirm, unhealthy, sickly, delicate, debilitated, exhausted, fragile, flimsy **2** spineless, cowardly **3** powerless, impotent, ineffectual, poor, lacking, lame, inadequate, defective,

deficient, unconvincing, untenable **4** insipid, tasteless, watery, thin, diluted, runny

weaken *verb* make or become weak

▤ exhaust, debilitate, undermine, dilute, diminish, lower, lessen, reduce, moderate, mitigate, temper, soften (up), thin, water down, tire, flag, fail, give way, droop, fade, abate, ease up, dwindle

weak-kneed *adj* lacking determination

weakling *noun* someone or an animal lacking strength

weakness *noun* **1** lack of strength **2** a fault **3** a special fondness (for): *a weakness for chocolate*

▤ **1** feebleness, debility, infirmity, impotence, frailty, powerlessness, vulnerability **2** fault, failing, flaw, shortcoming, blemish, defect, deficiency **3** fondness, partiality, *informal* soft spot, penchant, appetite, liking

weal *noun* a raised mark on the skin caused by a blow from a whip

wealth *noun* **1** riches or possession of them **2** a large quantity: *wealth of information*

wealthy *adj* rich

▤ rich, prosperous, affluent, well-off, moneyed, opulent, comfortable, well-heeled, well-to-do, *informal* flush, *slang* loaded, *informal* rolling in it

▤ poor, impoverished

wean [1] *verb* **1** make (a child or young animal) used to food other than the mother's milk **2** (with **from** or **off**) make (someone) gradually give up (a bad habit *etc*)

wean [2] /wen/ *noun, Scot* a child

weapon *noun* **1** an instrument used for fighting, *eg* a sword, gun *etc* **2** any means of gaining advantage: *patience is our best weapon*

Weapons include:
gun, airgun, pistol, revolver,
automatic, Colt®, Luger®,
magnum, Mauser, six-gun, six-
shooter, rifle, air rifle, Winchester®
rifle, carbine, shotgun, blunderbuss,
musket, elephant gun, machine-

gun, kalashnikov, submachine-gun, Uzi, tommy-gun, sten gun, Bren gun, cannon, field gun, Gatling gun, howitzer, mortar, turret gun; knife, bowie knife, flick-knife, stiletto, dagger, dirk, poniard, sword, épée, foil, rapier, sabre, scimitar, bayonet, broadsword, claymore, lance, spear, pike, machete; bomb, atom bomb, H-bomb, cluster-bomb, daisy cutter, depth-charge, incendiary bomb, Mills bomb, mine, landmine, napalm bomb, thermobaric bomb, time-bomb; bow and arrow, longbow, crossbow, blowpipe, catapult, boomerang, sling, harpoon, bolas, rocket, bazooka, ballistic missile, Cruise missile, Exocet®, *informal* Scud, torpedo, hand grenade, flame-thrower; battleaxe, pole-axe, halberd, tomahawk, cosh, cudgel, knuckleduster, shillelagh, truncheon; gas, CS gas, mustard gas, nerve gas, tear-gas

wear *verb* (**wears**, **wearing**, **wore**, **worn**) **1** be dressed in, have on the body **2** arrange in a particular way: *she wears her hair long* **3** have (*eg* a beard, an expression) on the face **4** damage or weaken by use, rubbing *etc* **5** be damaged in this way **6** last: *wear well* ◇ *noun* **1** use by wearing: *for my own wear* **2** clothes *etc*: *school wear* **3** damage by use **4** the amount or type of use something gets: *heavy wear* ◇ **wearer** *noun* ◇ **wear and tear** damage by ordinary use ◇ **wear down 1** reduce by rubbing *etc* **2** tire or overcome (someone) through constant pressure ◇ **wear off** pass away gradually ◇ **wear on** become later: *the afternoon wore on* ◇ **wear out 1** make or become unfit for further use **2** exhaust
■ *verb* **1** dress in, have on **4** erode, corrode, consume, fray, rub, abrade, waste, grind ◇ *noun* **2** clothes, clothing, dress, garments, outfit, costume, attire **3** deterioration, erosion, corrosion, wear and tear, friction, abrasion ◇ **wear off** decrease, abate, dwindle, diminish, subside, wane, weaken, fade,

lessen, ebb, peter out, disappear ◇ **wear out 1** deteriorate, wear through, erode, impair, consume, fray **2** exhaust, fatigue, tire (out)

wearable *adj* fit to be worn

wearing *adj* tiring, exhausting
■ exhausting, fatiguing, tiresome, tiring, wearisome, trying, taxing, oppressive, irksome, exasperating
☒ refreshing

wearisome *adj* causing tiredness, boredom or impatience

weary *adj* **1** tired, having used up your strength or patience **2** tiring, boring ◇ *verb* (**wearies**, **wearying**, **wearied**) make or become tired, bored or impatient ◇ **wearily** *adv* ◇ **weariness** *noun* ◇ **weary of** tired of, bored with
■ *adj* **1** tired, exhausted, fatigued, sleepy, worn out, drained, drowsy, jaded, *informal* all in, *informal* done in, *informal* fagged out, *informal* knackered, *informal* dead beat, *informal* dog-tired, *informal* whacked
☒ *adj* **1** refreshed

weasel *noun* a small wild animal with a long and slender body, that lives on mice, birds *etc*

weather *noun* the state of the atmosphere, *eg* heat, coldness, cloudiness *etc* ◇ *verb* **1** dry or wear away through exposure to the air **2** come safely through (a storm, difficulty *etc*) ◇ **under the weather** *informal* unwell
■ *verb* **2** endure, survive, live through, come through, ride out, rise above, stick out, withstand, surmount, stand, brave, overcome, resist, pull through, suffer
☒ *verb* **2** succumb

weatherbeaten *adj* showing signs of having been out in all weathers

weathercock or **weathervane** *noun* a flat piece of metal that swings in the wind to show its direction

weave¹ *verb* (**weaves**, **weaving**, **wove**, **woven**) **1** pass threads over and under each other on a loom *etc* to form cloth **2** plait cane *etc* for basket-making **3** put together (a story, plan *etc*) ◇ **weaver** *noun* someone who weaves

▣ **3** create, compose, construct, contrive, put together, fabricate

weave² *verb* (**weaves**, **weaving**, **weaved**) move in and out between objects, or move from side to side: *weaving through the traffic*

Web *abbrev* the World Wide Web ◇ **web page** one of the linked pages of a website

web *noun* **1** the net made by a spider, a cobweb **2** the skin between the toes of ducks, swans, frogs *etc* **3** something woven

webbed *adj* of feet: having the toes joined by a web

webbing *noun* a type of strong, woven tape used for belts *etc*

webcam *noun* a camera for filming live broadcasts on the Internet

webcast *noun* a broadcast on the Internet

web-footed or **web-toed** *adj* having webbed feet or toes

website *noun* the location on the World Wide Web of information relating to a person or organization

wed *verb* (**weds**, **wedding**, **wedded**) marry

we'd *short for* **1** we would; we should **2** we had

wedding *noun* **1** marriage **2** a marriage ceremony

wedge *noun* **1** a piece of wood, metal *etc* thick at one end with a thin edge at the other, used in splitting wood, forcing two surfaces apart *etc* **2** anything shaped like a wedge ◇ *verb* **1** fix or become fixed with a wedge **2** push or squeeze (in): *wedged in amongst the crowd*

▣ *noun* **2** lump, block, chunk, wodge, chock ◇ *verb* **2** jam, cram, pack, ram, squeeze, stuff, push, lodge, block, thrust, force

wedlock *noun* the state of being married

Wednesday *noun* the fourth day of the week

wee *adj*, *Scot* small, tiny

weed *noun* **1** a useless, troublesome plant **2** a weak, worthless person ◇ *verb* clear (a garden *etc*) of weeds ◇ **weeding** *noun* clearance of weeds

weedy *adj* **1** full of weeds **2** like a weed **3** thin and puny, unmanly

▣ **3** thin, skinny, puny, scrawny, undersized, weak, feeble, frail, weak-kneed, insipid, *informal* wet, *informal* wimpish

▣ᴈ **3** strong

week *noun* **1** the sequence of seven days from Sunday to Saturday **2** any period of seven days **3** the traditional working days of the week, not Saturday and Sunday ◇ *adv* by a period of seven days before or after: *we leave Tuesday week*

weekday *noun* any day except Saturday and Sunday

weekend *noun* the time from Saturday to Monday

weekly *adj* happening, or done, once a week ◇ *adv* once a week ◇ *noun* (*plural* **weeklies**) a newspaper, magazine *etc* coming out once a week

weep *verb* **1** shed tears **2** ooze, drip: *weeping wound* ◇ *noun* a bout of weeping ◇ **weeping willow** a willow tree with drooping branches

▣ **1** cry, sob, moan, lament, wail, mourn, grieve, bawl, blubber, snivel, whimper, *informal* blub

▣ᴈ **1** rejoice

weevil *noun* a small beetle that destroys grain, flour *etc*

weft *noun* the threads on a loom which cross the warp

weigh *verb* **1** find out how heavy (something) is by putting it on a scale *etc* **2** have a certain heaviness: *weighing 10 kilogrammes* **3** raise (a ship's anchor) **4** of burdens *etc*: press down, be heavy or troublesome ◇ **weigh in** test your weight before a boxing match ◇ **weigh out** measure out a quantity by weighing it on a scale ◇ **weigh up** consider (a matter, point) carefully

▣ ◇ **weigh up** consider, contemplate, evaluate, meditate on, mull over, ponder, think over, examine, reflect on, deliberate

weighbridge *noun* a large scale for weighing vehicles

weight *noun* 1 the amount that anything weighs 2 gravitational force 3 a piece of metal weighing a certain amount: *a 100 gram weight* 4 a load, a burden 5 importance ◇ *verb* 1 make heavy by adding or attaching a weight 2 organize (something) so it has a bias ◇ **weightless** *adj* ◇ **weightlessness** *noun* absence of the pull of gravity

■ *noun* 1 heaviness, mass 2 gravity, pressure 4 burden, load, encumbrance 5 importance, significance, substance, consequence, impact, moment, influence, value, authority, *informal* clout, power, consideration ◇ *verb* 1 load, weigh down, oppress

weighty *adj* 1 heavy 2 important

■ 1 heavy, burdensome, substantial, bulky 2 important, significant, consequential, crucial, critical, momentous, serious, grave, solemn

☒ 1 light 2 unimportant

weir *noun* a dam across a stream

weird *adj* 1 mysterious, supernatural 2 odd, strange ◇ **weirdness** *noun* ◇ **weirdo** *noun*, *informal* someone who behaves oddly

■ 1 uncanny, eerie, creepy, supernatural, unnatural, ghostly, freakish, *informal* spooky 2 strange, mysterious, bizarre, *informal* far-out, *informal* way-out

☒ 1, 2 normal, usual

welcome *verb* 1 receive with warmth or pleasure 2 accept gladly: *I welcome the challenge* ◇ *noun* a welcoming, a reception ◇ *adj* received with pleasure ◇ **welcome to** permitted to do or take ◇ **you're welcome** used in reply to an expression of thanks

■ *verb* 1 greet, hail, receive, salute, meet 2 accept, approve of, embrace ◇ *noun* reception, greeting, *informal* salutation, acceptance, hospitality, *informal* red carpet ◇ *adj* acceptable, desirable, pleasing, pleasant, agreeable, gratifying, appreciated, delightful, refreshing

☒ *adj* unwelcome

weld *verb* 1 join (pieces of metal) by pressure, with or without heating 2 join closely ◇ *noun* a joint made by welding ◇ **welder** *noun*

welfare *noun* 1 comfort, good health 2 financial support to those in need ◇ **welfare state** a country with a health service, insurance against unemployment, pensions for those who cannot work *etc*

■ well-being, health, prosperity, happiness, benefit, good, advantage, interest, profit, success

well[1] *adj* (**better**, **best**) in good health ◇ *adv* 1 in a good and correct manner: *write well* 2 thoroughly: *well beaten* 3 successfully: *do well* 4 conveniently: *it fits in well with my plans* ◇ *exclam* expressing surprise, or used in explaining, narrating *etc* ◇ **as well as** in addition to ◇ **it is as well** or **it is just as well** it is a good thing, it is lucky

■ *adj* healthy, in good health, fit, able-bodied, sound, robust, strong, thriving, flourishing ◇ *adv* 1 rightly, correctly, skilfully, ably, expertly, adequately 2 thoroughly, greatly, fully, completely

well[2] *noun* 1 a spring of water 2 a shaft in the earth to extract water, oil *etc* ◇ *verb* (often with **up**) rise up and gush: *tears welled up in her eyes*

■ *noun* 1 spring, well-spring, fountain, fount, source, reservoir, well-head, waterhole ◇ *verb* flow, spring, surge, gush, stream, brim over, pour, flood, ooze, run, trickle, rise, seep

we'll *short for* we will; we shall

well-advised *adj* wise

wellbeing *noun* welfare; contentment

well-disposed *adj* (with **to**) inclined to favour

well-informed *adj* having or showing knowledge

wellingtons *noun plural* high rubber boots covering the lower part of the legs

well-known *adj* 1 familiar 2 celebrated, famous

■ 2 famous, renowned, celebrated, famed, eminent, notable, noted, illustrious

well-mannered *adj* having good manners

▤ polite, well-brought-up, mannerly, courteous, civil, refined, cultivated, cultured, genteel

▣ ill-bred

well-meaning *adj* having good intentions

well-meant *adj* rightly, kindly intended

well-off *adj* rich

▤ rich, wealthy, affluent, prosperous, well-to-do, thriving, successful, comfortable, fortunate

▣ poor, badly-off

well-read *adj* having read many good books

well-rounded *adj* 1 plump 2 having had a balanced upbringing and education

well-spoken *adj* having a refined way of speaking

well-to-do *adj* rich

well-wisher *noun* someone who wishes someone success

welsh rarebit a dish made of cheese melted on toast

welt *noun* 1 a firm edging or band, *eg* on the wrist or waist of a garment 2 a weal

welter *verb* roll about, wallow ◇ *noun* 1 great disorder or confusion 2 a muddled mass, a jumble: *a welter of information*

wench *noun* (*plural* **wenches**) *old* a young woman, a girl

wend *verb*: **wend your way** make your way slowly

went *past form of* **go**

wept *past form of* **weep**

were *past form of* **be**

we're *short for* we are

werewolf *noun* (*plural* **werewolves**) a mythical creature which changes periodically from a human into a wolf

west *noun* one of the four chief directions, that in which the sun sets ◇ *adj* in the west ◇ *adv* to or towards the west ◇ **the Wild West** *hist* the western United States in the early days of its settlement

westerly *adj* 1 lying or moving towards the west 2 of wind: from the west

western *adj* relating to, or in, the west ◇ *noun* a film or story about life among the early settlers in the western United States ◇ **westerner** *noun* someone from a western region or country

westward or **westwards** *adj & adv* towards the west

wet *adj* 1 soaked or covered with water or other liquid 2 rainy: *a wet day* 3 of paint *etc*: not yet dry 4 *slang* of a person: weak, ineffectual ◇ *noun* 1 moisture 2 rain 3 *slang* a weak, ineffectual person ◇ *verb* (**wets**, **wetting**, **wetted**) make wet ◇ **wetly** *adv* ◇ **wetness** *noun* ◇ **wet blanket** a dreary, negative person ◇ **wet suit** a suit that allows water to pass through but retains body heat

▤ *adj* 1 damp, moist, soaked, soaking, sodden, saturated, soggy, sopping, watery, waterlogged, drenched, dripping, spongy, dank, clammy 2 raining, rainy, showery, pouring, drizzling, humid ◇ *verb* moisten, damp, dampen, soak, saturate, drench, steep, water, irrigate, spray, splash, dip

whack *noun* a loud, violent slap or blow ◇ *verb* slap or hit violently

▤ *noun* smack, slap, blow, hit, rap, stroke, thump, cuff, box, bang, *informal* clout, *informal* bash, *informal* wallop ◇ *verb* hit, strike, smack, thrash, slap, beat, *informal* bash, bang, cuff, thump, box, buffet, rap, *informal* wallop, *informal* belt, *informal* clobber, *informal* clout, *informal* sock

whale *noun* a very large mammal living in the sea ◇ *verb* catch whales ◇ **whale oil** oil obtained from the blubber of a whale

whalebone *noun* a light bendable substance obtained from the upper jaw of certain whales

whaler *noun* a person or ship engaged in catching whales

whammy *noun*, *informal* a blow or upset

wharf noun (plural **wharfs** or **wharves**) a landing stage for loading and unloading ships

what adj & pronoun **1** used in questions and statements identifying a thing or person: *what day is this?* /*what are you doing?* **2** used for emphasis in exclamations: *what ties he wears!*/*what rubbish!* **3** that which, whatever: *that is what I thought* **4** anything that: *I'll take what you can give me* **5** used to ask for repetition: *what? I didn't catch that* ◇ adv used in questions or statements questioning extent: *what does that matter?* ◇ **what about?** used in asking whether the listener would like something: *what about a glass of milk?* ◇ **what if?** what will or would happen if : *what if he comes back?* ◇ **what with** because of: *what with having no exercise and being overweight, he had a heart attack* ◇ **so what?** why is that important?

whatever adj & pronoun **1** an emphatic form of **what**: *whatever shall I do?* **2** anything (that): *show me whatever you have* **3** no matter what: *whatever happens* **4** at all: *nothing whatever to do with you* **5** informal some or other: *it has disappeared, for whatever reason* **6** used to express uncertainty: *a didgeridoo, whatever that is*

whatsoever adj at all: *nothing whatsoever to do with me*

wheat noun a grain from which the flour used for making bread *etc* is made ◇ **wheaten** adj **1** made of wheat **2** wholemeal

wheatgerm noun the vitamin-rich embryo of wheat

wheatmeal noun meal made of wheat, *esp* wholemeal

wheedle verb beg or coax, often by flattery

▪ cajole, coax, persuade, inveigle, charm, flatter, entice, court, draw

▪ force

wheel noun **1** a circular frame or disc turning on an axle, used for moving things **2** an object similar to or functioning like a wheel ◇ verb **1** move or push on wheels **2** turn like a wheel or

in a wide curve **3** turn round suddenly: *wheeled round in surprise*

▪ verb **2** turn, rotate, circle, gyrate, orbit, spin, revolve, swivel **3** turn, whirl, twirl, whirl, swing

wheelbarrow noun a handcart with one wheel in front, two handles and legs behind

wheelchair noun a chair on wheels for an invalid

wheelie bin a large dustbin on wheels

wheeze verb breathe with difficulty, making a whistling or croaking sound ◇ noun **1** the sound of difficult breathing **2** informal a joke

▪ verb pant, gasp, cough, hiss, rasp, whistle

whelk noun a type of small shellfish, used as food

whelp noun **1** a young lion **2** a puppy ◇ verb of a lion, dog *etc*: give birth to young

when adv at what time: *when did you arrive?* ◇ conj **1** the time at which: *I know when you left*/*I fell when I was coming in* ◇ relative pronoun at which: *at the time when I saw him* **2** seeing that, since: *why walk when you have a car?*

whence adv & conj, old **1** from what place: *whence did you come?* **2** to the place from which: *he's gone back whence he came*

whenever conj **1** at any given time: *come whenever you're ready* **2** if ever; no matter when: *I go whenever I get the chance* ◇ adv **1** an emphatic form of **when**: *whenever did I say that?* **2** used to express uncertainty: *Pentecost, whenever that is*

where adv & conj **1** to or in what place: *where are you going?*/*I wonder where we are* **2** in which respect: *where did I go wrong?*/*that's where you went wrong* ◇ relative pronoun the place in which: *it's still where it was*

whereabouts adv & conj near or in what place: *whereabouts is it?*/*I don't know whereabouts it is* ◇ noun the place where someone or something is: *I don't* *know her whereabouts*

■ *noun* location, position, place, situation, site

whereas *conj* **1** when in fact: *they thought I was lying, whereas I was telling the truth* **2** but, on the other hand: *he's tall, whereas I'm short*

whereby *pronoun* by means of which

whereupon *adv & conj* at or after which time, event *etc*

wherever *adv* **1** an emphatic form of **where**: *wherever did you go?* **2** used to express uncertainty: *the Town Hall, wherever that is* ◊*conj & adv* to any place: *wherever you may go/take it wherever you want*

wherewithal *noun* the means of doing something, *esp* money

whet *verb* (**whets, whetting, whetted**) **1** sharpen (a knife *etc*) by rubbing **2** make (desire, appetite *etc*) keener

■ **1** sharpen, hone, file, grind **2** stimulate, stir, rouse, arouse, provoke, kindle, quicken, incite, awaken, increase

◨ **1** blunt **2** dampen

whether *conj* **1** used in indirect questions: *he asked whether it was raining* **2** if: *I don't know whether it's possible*

whetstone *noun* a stone on which to sharpen blades

whey *noun* the liquid part of curdled milk, as opposed to the **curd**

which *adj & pronoun* **1** used in questions or statements identifying a particular person or thing from a group: *which colour do you like best?/which is better?* **2** the one(s) that: *show me which dress you would like/animals which hibernate* ◊*pronoun* referring to the person or thing just named: *the chair which you are sitting on* ◊**which is which** which is one and which is the other: *they are twins and I can't tell which is which*

whichever *adj & pronoun* **1** any (one) that, no matter which: *I'll take whichever you don't want/I saw trees whichever way I turned* **2** used to express uncertainty: *the biscuit tin, whichever that is*

whiff *noun* a sudden puff or scent: *whiff of perfume*

■ breath, puff, hint, trace, blast, draught, odour, smell, aroma, sniff, scent, reek, stink

while or **whilst** *conj* **1** at the same time as: *she held the bowl while I stirred* **2** for as long as: *guards us while we sleep* **3** during the time that: *while I'm at the office* **4** although, whereas: *while I sympathize, I can't really help* ◊**while** *noun* a space of time ◊*verb* (with **away**) to pass (time) without boredom: *he whiled away the time by reading*

whim *noun* a sudden thought or desire

■ fancy, caprice, notion, quirk, freak, humour, conceit, fad, urge

whimper *verb* cry with a low, whining voice ◊*noun* a low, whining cry

■ *verb* cry, sob, weep, snivel, whine, grizzle, mewl, moan, *informal* whinge ◊*noun* sob, snivel, whine, moan

whimsical *adj* **1** full of whims, fanciful **2** humorous

■ **1** fanciful, capricious, playful, impulsive, eccentric

whimsy *noun* (*plural* **whimsies**) **1** fanciful or quaint humour **2** a whim

whin *noun* gorse

whine *verb* **1** make a high-pitched, complaining cry **2** complain unnecessarily ◊*noun* an unnecessary complaint

■ *verb* **1** cry, sob, whimper, grizzle, moan, wail **2** complain, carp, grumble, *informal* whinge, *informal* gripe, *informal* grouch, *US slang* kvetch ◊*noun* complaint, grumble, grouse, *informal* gripe, *informal* grouch

whinge *verb* (**whinges, whingeing, whinged**) whine, complain peevishly ◊*noun* a peevish complaint ◊**whingeing** *adj* ◊**whinger** *noun*

whinny *verb* (**whinnies, whinnying, whinnied**) of a horse: neigh ◊*noun* (*plural* **whinnies**) a neighing sound

whip *noun* **1** a lash with a handle, for punishing, urging on animals *etc* **2** a member of parliament who sees that the members of their own party attend to give their vote when needed **3** a notice sent by a parliamentary whip ◇ *verb* (**whips**, **whipping**, **whipped**) **1** hit or drive with a whip, with the force of a whip: *wind whipped our faces* **3** beat (eggs, cream *etc*) into a froth **4** snatch (away, off, out, up *etc*): *whipped out a revolver* **5** move fast, like a whip ◇ **whip up 1** arouse (a feeling) in (a crowd *etc*) **2** prepare (a meal *etc*) at short notice

◼ *noun* **1** lash, scourge, switch, birch, cane, horsewhip, riding-crop, cat-o'-nine-tails ◇ *verb* **1** beat, flog, lash, flagellate, scourge, birch, cane, strap, thrash, punish, chastise, discipline, *formal* castigate **4** pull, jerk, snatch, whisk **5** dash, dart, rush, tear, flit, flash, fly

whip-hand *noun* the advantage in a fight, argument *etc*

whiplash *noun* **1** the lash of a whip **2** an injury caused by sudden jerking of the head and neck

whippersnapper *noun* a small, unimportant, impertinent person

whippet *noun* a breed of racing dog, like a small greyhound

whipping *noun* a beating with a whip

whirl *verb* **1** turn round quickly **2** carry (off, away *etc*) quickly ◇ *noun* **1** a fast circling movement **2** great excitement, confusion: *in a whirl over the wedding arrangements*

◼ *verb* **1** swirl, spin, turn, twist, twirl, pivot, pirouette, swivel, wheel, rotate, revolve, reel, roll, gyrate, circle ◇ *noun* **1** spin, twirl, twist, gyration, revolution, pirouette, swirl, turn, wheel, rotation, circle, reel, roll **2** confusion, daze, flurry, commotion, agitation, bustle, hubbub, hurly-burly, tumult, uproar

whirlpool *noun* a place in a river or sea where the current moves in a circle

whirlwind *noun* a violent current of wind with a whirling motion

whirr or **whir** *noun* a sound of fast, continuous whirling ◇ *verb* (**whirrs**, **whirring**, **whirred**) move or whirl with a buzzing noise

whisk *verb* **1** move quickly and lightly,

sweep: *their car whisked past* **2** beat or whip (a mixture) ◇ *noun* **1** a quick sweeping movement **2** a kitchen utensil for beating eggs or mixtures

◼ *verb* **1** dart, dash, rush, hurry, speed, hasten, race **2** whip, beat

whisker *noun* **1** a long bristle on the upper lip of a cat *etc* **2** (**whiskers**) hair on the sides of a man's face, sideburns ◇ **whiskered** *adj*

whisky or *Irish* & *US* **whiskey** *noun* (*plural* **whiskies** or **whiskeys**) an alcoholic spirit made from grain

Based on Scottish Gaelic *uisge beatha*, meaning 'water of life'

whisper *verb* **1** speak very softly, using the breath only, not the voice **2** make a soft, rustling sound ◇ *noun* a soft sound made with the breath

◼ *verb* **1** breathe **2** hiss, rustle, sigh ◇ *noun* sigh, hiss

whist *noun* a type of card game for four players

whistle *verb* **1** make a high-pitched sound by forcing breath through the lips or teeth **2** make such a sound with an instrument **3** make any similar shrill sound ◇ *noun* **1** the sound made by whistling **2** any instrument for whistling

whit *noun* a tiny bit: *not a whit better*

white *adj* **1** of the colour of pure snow **2** pale or light-coloured: *white wine* **3** of a pale-coloured complexion **4** of coffee or tea: with milk or cream added ◇ *noun* **1** something white **2** someone with a pale-coloured complexion **3** the part of an egg surrounding the yolk ◇ **whiteness** *noun* ◇ **white elephant** something useless and costly or troublesome to maintain ◇ **white goods** large kitchen appliances, *eg* cookers ◇ **white knight** a company which comes to the aid of another facing an unwelcome takeover bid ◇ **white paper** a statement (printed on white paper) issued by the government for the information of parliament ◇ **white spirit** a clear liquid made from petroleum, used as a paint solvent

whitebait *noun* the young of herring or sprats

white-collar *adj* of workers engaged in *eg* clerical work rather than manual labour

white-hot *adj* having reached a degree of heat at which metals glow with a white light (hotter than **red-hot**)

white-knuckle *adj* causing alarm, frightening

whiten *verb* make or become white or whiter

▣ bleach, blanch, whitewash, pale, fade

▣ blacken, darken

whitewash *noun* a mixture of ground chalk and water, or lime and water, for whitening walls *etc* ◊ *verb* **1** put whitewash on **2** cover up the faults of, give a good appearance to

whither *adv* & *conj*, *old* to what place?

whiting *noun* a small type of fish related to the cod

whitlow *noun* an infected swelling beside the finger or toenail

Whitsun *noun* the week beginning with the seventh Sunday after Easter

whittle *verb* **1** pare or cut (wood *etc*) with a knife **2** (with **away** or **down**) make gradually less: *whittled away his savings*

▣ **1** carve, cut, scrape, shave, trim, pare, hew, shape **2** erode, eat away, wear away, diminish, consume, reduce, undermine

whizz or **whiz** *verb* (**whizzes, whizzing, whizzed**) **1** move with a hissing sound, like an arrow **2** move very fast ◊ **whizz kid** someone who achieves rapid success while relatively young

WHO *abbrev* World Health Organization

who *pronoun* **1** used in questions and statements identifying someone or some people (only as the subject of a verb): *who is that woman in the green hat? /the person who did this* **2** *informal* used as the object in a sentence (instead of **whom**): *who did you choose?* **3** referring to the person or people just

named: *do you know who those people are?*

whoever *pronoun* **1** no matter who; any person or people **2** an emphatic form of **who**: *whoever told you that?* **3** used to express uncertainty: *ask Eric, whoever he is*

whole *adj* **1** complete; all, with nothing or no one missing **2** in good health ◊ *noun* the entire thing ◊ **wholeness** *noun* ◊ **on the whole** when everything is taken into account

▣ *adj* **1** complete, entire, integral, full, total, unabridged, uncut, undivided, unedited, intact, unharmed, undamaged, unbroken, inviolate, perfect, in one piece, mint, unhurt **2** well, healthy, fit, sound, strong ◊ *noun* total, aggregate, sum total, entirety, all, fullness, totality, ensemble, entity, unit, lot, piece, everything ◊ **on the whole** generally, mostly, in general, generally speaking, as a rule, for the most part, all in all, all things considered, by and large

wholefood *noun* unprocessed food produced without the aid of artificial fertilizers

wholehearted *adj* enthusiastic, generous

▣ unreserved, unstinting, unqualified, passionate, enthusiastic, earnest, committed, dedicated, devoted, heartfelt, emphatic, warm, sincere, unfeigned, genuine, complete, true, real, zealous

▣ half-hearted

wholemeal *noun* flour made from the entire wheat grain

wholesale *noun* the sale of goods in large quantities to a shop from which they can be bought in small quantities by ordinary buyers (*compare with:* **retail**) ◊ *adj* **1** buying or selling through wholesale **2** on a large scale: *wholesale killing* ◊ **wholesaler** *noun*

wholesome *adj* giving health, healthy

▣ healthy, hygienic, salubrious, sanitary, nutritious, nourishing, beneficial, salutary, invigorating, bracing

▣ unhealthy

who'll *short for* who will; who shall

wholly *adv* entirely, altogether

☰ completely, entirely, fully, purely, absolutely, totally, utterly, comprehensively, altogether, perfectly, thoroughly, all, exclusively, only

🔁 partly

whom *pronoun* **1** used in questions and statements identifying someone or some people (only as the object of a sentence): *whom did you see?/to whom am I speaking?* **2** referring to the person or people just named: *the person whom I liked best*

whoop *noun* a loud cry, rising in pitch ◇ *verb* give a whoop

whooping-cough *noun* an infectious disease in which violent bouts of coughing are followed by a whoop as the breath is drawn in

whore *noun, offensive* **1** a female prostitute **2** a promiscuous woman

whose *adj & pronoun* **1** belonging to whom?: *whose handwriting is this?* **2** of whom or which: *the man whose wife I know*

why *adv & pronoun* for which reason?: *why did you not stay?* ◇ *conj* for, which: *no reason why I should get involved* ◇ *exclam* expressing surprise, impatience, etc: *why, you little monster!* ◇ **the whys and wherefores** all the reasons, details

wick *noun* the twisted threads in a candle or lamp which draw up the oil or grease to the flame

wicked *adj* **1** evil, sinful **2** mischievous, spiteful **3** *slang* excellent ◇ **wickedly** *adv* ◇ **wickedness** *noun*

☰ **1** evil, sinful, immoral, depraved, corrupt, vicious, unprincipled, iniquitous, heinous, debased, abominable, ungodly, unrighteous, shameful **2** naughty, mischievous, roguish

wicker *adj* of a chair *etc*: made of woven willow twigs ◇ **wickerwork** *noun* articles made from wicker

wicket *noun* **1** *cricket* the set of three stumps, or one of these, at which the ball is bowled **2** the ground between the bowler and the batsman

wide *adj* **1** broad, not narrow **2** stretching far, extensive: *wide support* **3** measuring a certain amount from side to side: *5 centimetres wide* ◇ *adv* **1** off the target: *the shots went wide* **2** to the fullest extent: *hold your arms wide apart* ◇ **wideness** *noun* ◇ **wide of the mark** off the target, inaccurate

☰ *adj* **1** broad, roomy, spacious, vast, immense **2** extensive, wide-ranging, comprehensive, far-reaching, general ◇ *adv* **1** astray, off course, off target, off the mark

wide-awake *adj* fully awake; alert

wide-boy *noun, slang* an astute or wily person

wide-eyed *adj* with eyes wide open in surprise *etc*

widely *adv* **1** over a wide area; among many: *widely believed* **2** far apart

widen *verb* make or become wide

☰ distend, dilate, expand, extend, spread, stretch, enlarge, broaden

🔁 narrow

widespread *adj* spread over a large area or among many people: *a widespread belief*

☰ extensive, prevalent, rife, general, sweeping, universal, wholesale, far-reaching, unlimited, broad, common, pervasive, far-flung

🔁 limited

widow *noun* a woman whose husband is dead ◇ **widower** *noun* a man whose wife is dead

width *noun* measurement across, from side to side

wield *verb* **1** swing or handle (a sword *etc*) **2** use (power, authority *etc*)

☰ **1** brandish, flourish, swing, wave, handle, manage, manipulate **2** have, hold, possess, employ, exert, exercise, use, utilize, maintain, command

wife *noun* (*plural* **wives**) **1** a married woman **2** the woman to whom a man is married

wig *noun* an artificial covering of hair for the head

wiggle *verb* move from side to side with jerky or twisting movements

◇ *noun* a jerky movement from side to side ◇ **wiggly** *adj*

wigwam *noun*, *hist* a conical tent of skins made by some Native Americans

wild *adj* **1** of an animal: not tamed **2** of a plant: not cultivated in a garden **3** of country: desolate or rugged **4** uncivilized **5** unruly, uncontrolled **6** of weather: stormy **7** frantic, mad: *wild with anxiety* **8** of a guess *etc*: rash, inaccurate ◇ *noun* (usually **wilds**) an uncultivated or uncivilized region ◇ **wild boar** a wild type of pig

◼ *adj* **1** untamed, undomesticated, savage, barbarous, primitive **3** uncultivated, desolate, waste, uninhabited **4** uncivilized, natural, ferocious, fierce **5** unrestrained, unruly, unmanageable, violent, turbulent, rowdy, lawless, disorderly, riotous, boisterous **6** stormy, tempestuous, rough, blustery, choppy **7** mad, *informal* crazy, frenzied, distraught, demented **8** reckless, rash, imprudent, foolish

◼ *adj* **1** civilized, tame **2** cultivated **4** restrained **7** cautious, considered

wildcard *noun* **1** someone allowed to compete in a sports event without qualifying **2** *comput* a symbol (*) representing any character or group of characters

wildcat *noun* an undomesticated type of cat ◇ *adj* **1** of a business scheme: risky **2** of a strike: not supported or permitted by trade union officials

wilderness *noun* a wild, uncultivated or desolate region

wildfire *noun* lightning without thunder ◇ **like wildfire** very quickly

wildfowl *noun* wild birds, *esp* those shot as game

wild-goose chase a troublesome and useless errand

wildlife *noun* wild animals, birds *etc* in their natural habitats

wile *noun* **1** a crafty trick **2** (**wiles**) charming ways

wilful *adj* **1** fond of having one's own way **2** intentional: *wilful damage*

◼ **1** self-willed, obstinate, stubborn, pigheaded, intransigent, inflexible, wayward, contrary **2** deliberate, conscious, intentional, voluntary, premeditated

◼ **1** flexible, good-natured **2** unintentional, accidental

will¹ *verb* **1** (*past form* **would**) also used to form future tenses of other verbs when the subject is **he**, **she**, **it**, **you** or **they**: *you will see me there* **2** *informal* often used for the same purpose when the subject is **I** or **we**: *I will tell you later* **3** used for emphasis, or to express a promise, when the subject is **I** or **we**: *I will do it if possible* (*see also* **shall**, **would**)

will² *noun* **1** the power to choose or decide **2** desire: *against my will* **3** determination: *the will to win* **4** a written statement about what is to be done with your property after your death ◇ *verb* (**wills**, **willing**, **willed**) **1** influence someone by exercising your will: *he willed her to win* **2** hand down (property *etc*) by will ◇ **at will** as or when you choose ◇ **with a will** eagerly

◼ *noun* **1** volition, choice, option, preference, decision, discretion **2** wish, desire, inclination, feeling, fancy, disposition, mind **3** purpose, resolve, resolution, determination, willpower, aim, intention ◇ *verb* **1** compel, wish **2** bequeath, leave, hand down, pass on, transfer, confer, dispose of

willing *adj* ready to do what is asked; eager ◇ **willingly** *adv* ◇ **willingness** *noun*

◼ disposed, inclined, agreeable, compliant, ready, prepared, consenting, content, amenable, biddable, pleased, well-disposed, favourable, happy, eager, enthusiastic

◼ unwilling, disinclined, reluctant

will-o'-the-wisp *noun* a pale light sometimes seen by night over marshy places

willow *noun* **1** a tree with long slender branches **2** its wood, used in cricket bats ◇ **willowy** *adj* slender, graceful

willpower *noun* the determination and self-discipline to achieve something

willy *noun, slang* a penis

willynilly *adv* whether you wish or not

> From the phrase *will I, nill I*, meaning 'whether I want or don't want'

wilt *verb* 1 of a flower or plant: droop 2 lose strength

■ 1 droop, sag, wither, shrivel 2 sag, flop, flag, dwindle, weaken, diminish, fail, fade, languish, ebb, sink, wane

wily *adj* cunning; devious

■ shrewd, cunning, scheming, artful, crafty, foxy, intriguing, tricky, underhand, shifty, deceitful, deceptive, astute, sly, guileful, designing, crooked

Ea guileless

wimp *noun, informal* an ineffectual person, feeble ◇ **wimpish** or **wimpy** *adj*

win *verb* (**wins**, **winning**, **won**) 1 gain by luck or in a contest 2 gain (something) by effort 3 come first in a contest 4 overcome a rival in (a war, election *etc*) 5 (often with **over**) gain the support or friendship of ◇ *noun* an act of winning; a victory ◇ **winner** *noun*

■ *verb* 1, 2 gain, acquire, achieve, attain, accomplish, receive, procure, secure, obtain, get, earn, catch, net 3 be victorious, triumph, succeed, prevail, overcome, conquer, come first, carry off, finish first ◇ *noun* victory, triumph, conquest, success, mastery

Ea *verb* 3 fail, lose

wince *verb* shrink or start back in pain *etc*, flinch: *her singing made me wince*

winch *noun* (*plural* **winches**) 1 a handle or crank for turning a wheel 2 a machine for lifting things, worked by winding a rope round a revolving cylinder ◇ *verb* lift up with a winch

wind[1] /wɪnd/ *noun* 1 a current of air 2 an influence pervading events: *a wind of change* 3 air or gas in the stomach 4 breath ◇ *verb* 1 put out of breath 2 make (a baby) burp ◇ **wind instrument** a musical instrument sounded by the breath ◇ **get the wind up** *informal* become afraid ◇ **get wind of** *informal*

hear about in an indirect way

■ *noun* 1 air, breeze, draught, gust, puff, blast, current, bluster, gale, hurricane, tornado, cyclone

wind[2] /waɪnd/ *verb* (**winds**, **winding**, **wound**) 1 turn, twist or coil 2 (sometimes with **up**) screw up the spring of (a watch, clockwork toy *etc*) 3 wrap closely ◇ **wind down** 1 slow down and stop working 2 begin to relax ◇ **wind up** 1 bring or come to an end: *wind up a meeting* 2 *informal* annoy, tease ◇ **wind your way** make your way circuitously ◇ **wound up** tense, agitated

■ 1 coil, twist, turn, curl, curve, bend, loop, spiral, zigzag, twine, encircle ◇ **wind up** 1 close (down), end, conclude, terminate, finalize, finish 2 annoy, irritate, disconcert, fool, trick, *informal* kid

windfall *noun* 1 a fruit blown from a tree 2 an unexpected gain, *eg* a sum of money

winding *adj* curving, twisting

windjammer *noun* a type of sailing ship

windlass *noun* a machine for lifting up or hauling a winch

windmill *noun* a mill driven by sails which are moved by the wind, used for pumping water, grinding grain *etc*

window *noun* 1 an opening in a wall, protected by glass, which lets in light and air 2 a gap in a schedule 3 *comput* a rectangular area displayed on a screen, which can be used as a separate screen

windpipe *noun* the tube leading from the mouth to the lungs

windscreen or *US* **windshield** *noun* a pane of glass in front of the driver of a motor-car *etc*

windsurf *verb* sail on a sailboard ◇ **windsurfer** *noun* ◇ **windsurfing** *noun*

windswept *adj* exposed to strong winds and showing the effects of it: *windswept hair*

windward *adj & adv* in the direction

from which the wind blows

windy _adj_ **1** of weather: with a strong wind blowing **2** of a place: exposed to strong winds

▤ **1** breezy, blowy, blustery, squally, wind-swept, stormy, tempestuous, gusty

▣ **1** calm

wine _noun_ **1** an alcoholic drink made from the fermented juice of grapes or other fruit **2** a rich dark red colour ◇ **wine gum** a fruit-flavoured jelly sweet

winepress _noun_ a machine which squeezes the juice out of grapes

wing _noun_ **1** one of the arm-like limbs of a bird, bat or insect by means of which it flies **2** one of the two projections on the sides of an aeroplane **3** a part of a house built out to the side **4** the side of a stage, where actors wait to enter **5** _football etc_ (a player positioned at) the edge of the field **6** a section of _eg_ a political party: _the left wing_ ◇ _verb_ **1** wound (a bird) in the wing **2** soar ◇ **winged** _adj_ **1** having wings **2** swift ◇ **wing commander** a high-ranking officer in the air force ◇ **on the wing** flying, in motion ◇ **under someone's wing** under the protection or care of someone

wink _verb_ **1** open and close an eye quickly **2** give a hint by winking **3** of lights _etc_: flicker, twinkle ◇ _noun_ **1** an act of winking **2** a hint given by winking **3** a flicker of light ◇ **forty winks** a short sleep

▤ _verb_ **1** blink, flutter **3** glimmer, glint, twinkle, gleam, sparkle, flicker, flash ◇ _noun_ **3** blink, flutter

winkle _noun_ a small edible shellfish (_also called:_ **periwinkle**) ◇ **winkle out** force out gradually

winning _adj_ **1** victorious, successful **2** charming, attractive: _winning smile_

▤ **1** conquering, triumphant, unbeaten, undefeated, victorious, successful **2** winsome, charming, attractive, captivating, engaging, fetching, enchanting, endearing, delightful, amiable, alluring, lovely, pleasing, sweet.

▣ **1** losing **2** unappealing

winnings _noun plural_ money _etc_ that has been won

winnow _verb_ separate the chaff from the grain by wind

winsome _adj_ charming

winter _noun_ the coldest season of the year ◇ _adj_ of or suitable for winter ◇ _verb_ pass the winter ◇ **winter sports** sports on snow or ice, _eg_ skiing, tobogganing _etc_

wintry _adj_ **1** cold, frosty **2** cheerless, unfriendly: _a wintry look_

▤ **1** cold, chilly, bleak, cheerless, desolate, dismal, harsh, snowy, frosty, freezing, frozen, icy

wipe _verb_ **1** clean or dry by rubbing **2** (with **away**, **out**, **off** or **up**) clear away **3** erase (a memory, data _etc_) ◇ _noun_ **1** the act of cleaning by rubbing **2** a piece of treated tissue used for cleaning _etc_ ◇ **wipe out 1** destroy or obliterate (something) **2** kill (someone)

▤ _verb_ **1** rub, clean, dry, dust, brush, mop, swab, sponge, clear **2**, **3** remove, erase, take away, take off, eradicate, obliterate, destroy, erase

wiper _noun_ one of a pair of moving parts which wipe the windscreen of a car

wire _noun_ **1** a thread-like length of metal **2** the metal thread used in communication by telephone _etc_ **3** _old_ a telegram ◇ _adj_ made of wire ◇ _verb_ **1** bind or fasten with wire **2** supply (a building _etc_) with wires for carrying an electric current **3** send a telegram

wireless _adj_ of communication: by radio waves ◇ _noun_, _old_ a radio set

wiry _adj_ **1** like wire **2** of a person: thin but strong

wisdom _noun_ **1** the quality of being wise **2** knowledge ◇ **wisdom teeth** four large back teeth which appear after childhood

▤ **1** discernment, penetration, reason, sense, astuteness, comprehension, enlightenment, judgement, judiciousness, understanding, intelligence, foresight, prudence **2** knowledge, learning, erudition

▣ **1** folly, stupidity

wise *adj* **1** very knowledgeable **2** judging rightly; sensible

- **1** discerning, sagacious, perceptive, rational, informed, well-informed, understanding, erudite, enlightened, knowing, intelligent, clever, aware, experienced **2** well-advised, judicious, prudent, reasonable, sensible, sound, long-sighted, shrewd
- **1** ignorant **2** foolish, ill-advised

-wise *suffix* **1** in the manner or way of: *crabwise* **2** with reference or regard to: *careerwise*

wish *verb* **1** feel or express a desire: *I wish he'd leave* **2** (often with **for**) long for, desire: *she wished for peace and quiet* **3** hope for on behalf of (someone): *wish someone luck* ◇ *noun* (*plural* **wishes**) **1** desire, longing **2** a thing desired or wanted: *her great wish was to live abroad* **3** an expression of a desire: *make a wish* **4** (**wishes**) expression of hope for another's happiness, good fortune *etc*: *good wishes* ◇ **wish someone well** feel goodwill towards them

- *verb* **2** desire, want, yearn, long, hanker, covet, crave, aspire, hope, hunger, thirst, prefer, need ◇ *noun* **1** desire, want, aspiration, inclination, hunger, thirst, liking, preference, yearning, urge

wishbone *noun* a forked bone in the breast of fowls

wishful *adj* wishing, eager ◇ **wishful thinking** basing your belief on (false) hopes rather than known facts

wishywashy *adj* **1** of liquid: thin and weak **2** feeble, not energetic or lively **3** lacking colour

wisp *noun* a small tuft or strand: *a wisp of hair* ◇ **wispy** *adj*

- **wispy** thin, straggly, frail, fine, attenuated, insubstantial, light, flimsy, fragile, delicate, ethereal, gossamer, faint
- **wispy** substantial

wistful *adj* thoughtful and rather sad: *a wistful glance* ◇ **wistfully** *adv*

- thoughtful, pensive, musing, reflective, wishful, contemplative, dreamy, dreaming, meditative, melancholy, sad, forlorn, disconsolate, longing, mournful

wit *noun* **1** the ability to express ideas neatly and humorously **2** someone who can do this **3** (often **wits**) intelligence, common sense ◇ **at your wits' end** unable to solve your difficulties, desperate ◇ **keep your wits about you** keep alert ◇ **to wit** namely, that is to say

- **1** humour, repartee, drollery, banter, jocularity, levity **2** humorist, comedian, comic, satirist, joker, wag **3** intelligence, cleverness, brains, sense, reason, common sense, wisdom, understanding, judgement, insight, intellect
- **3** stupidity

witch *noun* (*plural* **witches**) **1** a woman with magic power obtained through evil spirits **2** an ugly old woman ◇ **witch doctor** someone believed to have magical powers to cure illnesses *etc*

witchcraft *noun* magic performed by a witch

- sorcery, magic, wizardry, wicca, occultism, the occult, black magic, enchantment, necromancy, voodoo, spell, incantation, divination

witch-hazel *noun* **1** a N American shrub **2** a healing lotion made from its bark and leaves

with *prep* **1** in the company of: *I was walking with my father* **2** by means of: *cut it with a knife* **3** in the same direction as: *drifting with the current* **4** against: *fighting with his brother* **5** on the same side as **6** having: *a man with a limp* **7** in the keeping of: *leave the keys with me*

withdraw *verb* (**withdraws, withdrawing, withdrew, withdrawn**) **1** go somewhere more private **2** go back or away **3** take away, remove: *withdraw cash from your account/withdraw troops from the front line* **4** take back (an insult *etc*)

- **2** recoil, shrink back, draw back, pull back, depart, go (away), absent oneself, retire, remove, leave, back out, fall back, drop out, retreat **3** draw out, extract, pull out **4** recant, disclaim, take back, revoke, rescind, retract, cancel, abjure, recall, take away

withdrawal *noun* **1** an act of withdrawing **2** a removal of funds from a bank account **3** breaking of an addiction to drugs *etc*

■ **1** repudiation, recantation, disclaimer, disavowal, revocation, recall, departure, exit, exodus, retirement, retreat **2** extraction, removal

withdrawn *adj* of a person: unwilling to communicate with others, unsociable

■ reserved, unsociable, shy, introvert, quiet, retiring, aloof, detached, shrinking, uncommunicative, unforthcoming, taciturn, silent

▣ extrovert, outgoing

wither *verb* **1** fade, dry up or decay **2** make to feel very unimportant or embarrassed: *she withered him with a look*

■ **1** shrink, shrivel, dry, wilt, droop, decay, disintegrate, wane, perish, fade, languish, decline, waste

▣ **1** flourish, thrive

withering *adj* **1** drying up, dying **2** of a remark *etc*: scornful, sarcastic

■ **2** scornful, contemptuous, scathing, snubbing, humiliating, mortifying, wounding

▣ **2** encouraging, supportive

withers *noun plural* the ridge between the shoulder bones of a horse

withhold *verb* (**withholds**, **withholding**, **withheld**) keep back, refuse to give

■ keep back, retain, hold back, suppress, restrain, repress, control, check, reserve, deduct, refuse, hide, conceal

▣ give, accord

within *prep* inside the limits of: *keep within the law* ◇ *adv* on the inside

without *prep* **1** in the absence of: *we went without you* **2** not having: *without a penny* **3** not (showing or acting in a particular way): *answered without smiling* ◇ *adv, old* the outside

withstand *verb* oppose or resist successfully

■ resist, oppose, stand fast, stand one's ground, stand, stand up to, confront, brave, face, cope with, take on, thwart, defy, hold one's ground, hold out, last out, hold off, endure, bear, tolerate,

put up with, survive, weather

▣ give in, yield

witness *noun* (*plural* **witnesses**) **1** someone who sees or has direct knowledge of a thing **2** someone who gives evidence in a law court **3** proof, evidence ◇ *verb* **1** see, be present at **2** sign your name to confirm the authenticity of (someone else's signature) **3** give or be evidence ◇ **witness box** the stand from which a witness in a law court gives evidence ◇ **bear witness** give or be evidence of: *bear witness to his character*

■ *noun* **1** onlooker, eye-witness, looker-on, observer, spectator, viewer, watcher, bystander ◇ *verb* **1** see, observe, notice, note, view, watch, look on, mark, perceive **2** endorse, sign, countersign **3** testify, attest, bear witness, *formal* depose, confirm, bear out, corroborate

witticism *noun* a witty remark

wittingly *adv* knowingly

witty *adj* clever and amusing ◇ **wittily** *adv*

■ humorous, amusing, comic, sharp-witted, droll, whimsical, original, brilliant, clever, ingenious, lively, sparkling, funny, facetious, fanciful, jocular

▣ dull, unamusing

wizard *noun* a man believed to have the power of magic ◇ **wizardry** *noun* magic

wizened *adj* dried up, shrivelled: *a wizened old man*

woad *noun* **1** a blue dye **2** the plant from which it is obtained

wobble *verb* **1** rock unsteadily from side to side **2** of the voice: be unsteady ◇ *noun* an unsteady rocking

■ *verb* **1** shake, oscillate, tremble, quake, sway, teeter, totter, rock, seesaw, vibrate, waver, fluctuate

wobbly *adj* unsteady, rocking

■ unstable, shaky, rickety, unsteady, *informal* wonky, teetering, tottering, doddering, doddery, uneven, unbalanced, unsafe

▣ stable, steady

woe *noun* **1** grief, misery **2** a cause of sorrow, a trouble

woebegone *adj* dismal, sad-looking

woeful *adj* sorrowful; pitiful ◇ **woe-fully** *adv*

wolf *noun* (*plural* **wolves**) a wild animal like a dog that hunts in packs ◇ *verb* eat greedily: *wolfing down his food* ◇ **wolfish** *adj* like a wolf ◇ **cry wolf** give a false alarm ◇ **keep the wolf from the door** keep away hunger or want

wolfhound *noun* a large breed of dog

wolverine *noun* a wild animal of the weasel family

woman *noun* (*plural* **women**) **1** an adult human female **2** human females in general

womanhood *noun* the state of being a woman

womanish *adj* of a man: effeminate, not manly

womankind or **womenkind** *noun* women generally

womanly *adj* like, or suitable for, a woman ◇ **womanliness** *noun*

womb *noun* the part of a female mammal's body in which the young develop and stay till birth

wombat *noun* a small, beaver-like Australian animal, with a pouch

women *plural* of **woman**

won *past form* of **win**

wonder *noun* **1** the feeling produced by something unexpected or extraordinary; surprise, awe **2** something strange, amazing or miraculous ◇ *verb* **1** be curious or in doubt: *I wonder what will happen/I wonder whether to go or not* **2** feel surprise or amazement (at, that) **3** used to introduce requests: *I wonder if you can help me?* ◇ **no wonder** it is hardly surprising

■ *noun* **1** awe, amazement, astonishment, admiration, wonderment, fascination, surprise, bewilderment **2** marvel, phenomenon, miracle, prodigy, sensation, sight, spectacle, rarity, curiosity ◇ *verb* **1** meditate, speculate, ponder, ask oneself, question, conjecture, puzzle, enquire, query **2** marvel, gape, be amazed, be surprised

wonderful *adj* **1** arousing wonder; strange, marvellous **2** excellent

■ **1** amazing, astonishing, astounding, startling, surprising, extraordinary, incredible, remarkable, staggering, strange **2** marvellous, magnificent, oustanding, excellent, superb, admirable, delightful, phenomenal, sensational, stupendous, tremendous, *informal* super, *informal* terrific, *informal* brilliant, *informal* great, *informal* fabulous, *informal* fantastic

🖪 **1** ordinary **2** appalling, dreadful

wonderland *noun* a land of wonder, a fairy-like place

wonderment *noun*, *old* amazement

wondrous *adj*, *old* wonderful

wonky *adj*, *informal* not working properly, unsound

wont *adj*, *old* accustomed (to do something) ◇ *noun* habit: *as is his wont*

won't *short for* will not

won ton a spicy Chinese dumpling, often served in soup

woo *verb* (**woos**, **wooing**, **wooed**) **1** try to win the love of (someone) **2** try to win the support of (*eg* voters) ◇ **wooer** *noun*

■ **1** court, chase, pursue **2** encourage, cultivate, attract, look for, seek

wood *noun* **1** the hard part of a tree, *esp* when cut for use **2** a group of growing trees

woodbine *noun* the honeysuckle

woodchuck *same as* **marmot**

woodcock *noun* a game bird related to the snipe

woodcut *noun* **1** a picture engraved on wood **2** a print made from this engraving

woodcutter *noun* someone who fells trees, cuts up wood *etc*

wooded *adj* covered with trees

wooden *adj* **1** made of wood **2** dull, stiff, not lively: *a wooden speech* ◇ **woodenly** *adv*

■ **1** timber, woody **2** emotionless, expressionless, awkward, clumsy, stilted, lifeless, spiritless, unemotional, stiff, rigid, leaden, deadpan, blank, empty, slow

▣ 2 lively

Types of wood include:
timber, *US* lumber, hardwood, softwood, heartwood, sapwood, seasoned wood, green wood, bitterwood, brushwood, cordwood, firewood, kindling, matchwood, plywood, pulpwood, whitewood, chipboard, hardboard; afrormosia, ash, balsa, beech, cedar, cherry, chestnut, cottonwood, deal, ebony, elm, iroko, mahogany, African mahogany, maple, oak, pine, redwood, rosewood, rubberwood, sandalwood, sapele, satinwood, sheesham, teak, walnut, willow

---

woodland *noun* land covered with trees

woodlouse *noun* (*plural* **woodlice**) an insect with a jointed shell, found under stones *etc*

woodpecker *noun* a bird that pecks holes in the bark of trees with its beak, in search of insects

woodwind *noun* wind instruments, made of wood or metal, *eg* the flute or clarinet

woodwork *noun* **1** the making of wooden articles **2** the wooden parts of a house, room *etc*

woodworm *noun* the larva of a beetle that bores holes in wood and destroys it

woody *adj* **1** like wood **2** covered with trees

woof *noun* the sound of a dog's bark ◇ *verb, informal* bark

wool *noun* **1** the soft hair of sheep and other animals **2** yarn or cloth made of wool

woolgathering *noun & adj* daydreaming

woollen *adj* made of wool ◇ *noun* a knitted garment made of wool

woolly *adj* **1** made of, or like, wool **2** vague, hazy: *a woolly argument* ◇ *noun*

(*plural* **woollies**) a knitted woollen garment ◇ **woolliness** *noun*

▣ *adj* **1** woollen, fleecy, woolly-haired, downy, shaggy, fuzzy **2** unclear, ill-defined, hazy, blurred, confused, muddled, vague, indefinite ◇ *noun* jumper, sweater, jersey, pullover, cardigan

▣ *adj* **2** clear, distinct

word *noun* **1** a written or spoken sign representing a thing or an idea **2** (**words**) talk, remarks: *kind words* **3** news: *word of his death* **4** a promise: *break your word* ◇ *verb* choose words for: *he worded his refusal carefully* ◇ **word processor** an electronic machine, or computer program, which can store, edit and print out text ◇ **have words** *informal* quarrel ◇ **in a word** in short, to sum up ◇ **take someone at their word** treat what they say as true ◇ **take someone's word for something** trust that what they say is true ◇ **word for word** in the exact words ◇ **word of mouth** spoken word or conversation

▣ *noun* **1** name, term, expression, designation **3** information, news, report, communication, notice, message **4** promise, pledge, oath, assurance, vow, guarantee ◇ *verb* phrase, express, couch, put, say, explain, write

wording *noun* choice or arrangement of words

wordy *adj* using too many words

▣ verbose, long-winded, *formal* loquacious, garrulous, prolix, rambling, diffuse, discursive

▣ concise

wore *past form* of **wear**

work *noun* **1** a physical or mental effort to achieve or make something **2** a job, employment: *out of work* **3** a task: *I've got work to do* **4** anything made or done **5** something produced by art, *eg* a book, musical composition, painting *etc* **6** manner of working, workmanship: *poor work* **7** (**works**) a factory **8** (**works**) deeds: *good works* ◇ *verb* **1** be engaged in physical or mental work **2** be employed **3** run or operate smoothly and efficiently **4** of a plan *etc*: be successful **5** get into a position slowly and gradually: *the screw worked loose* ◇ **working class** the social class including manual workers ◇ **working-class** *adj* ◇ **working day** or **working hours** a day or the hours that someone spends at work, on duty *etc* ◇ **working party** a group of people appointed to investigate a particular matter ◇ **work on 1** use your powers of persuasion on **2** try to improve (something) **3** use (an idea *etc*) as the basis for decisions: *working on that assumption* ◇ **work out 1** solve **2** discover as a result of deep thought **3** of a situation: turn out all right in the end **4** perform energetic physical exercises ◇ **work up** arouse, excite: *working himself up into a fury*

■ *noun* **1** toil, labour, drudgery, effort, exertion, industry, *informal* slog, *informal* graft, *informal* elbow grease **2** occupation, job, employment, profession, trade, business, career, calling, vocation, line, livelihood, craft, skill **3** task, assignment, undertaking, job, chore, responsibility, duty **5** creation, production, achievement, composition, opus **7** factory, plant, workshop, mill, foundry, shop **8** actions, acts, doings ◇ *verb* **1** labour, toil, drudge, slave **2** be employed, have a job, earn one's living **3** function, go, operate, perform, run ◇ **work out 1** solve, resolve **2** calculate, figure out, puzzle out, sort out, understand, clear up ◇ **work up** incite, stir up, rouse, arouse, animate, excite, move, stimulate, inflame, spur, instigate, agitate, generate

workable *adj* able to be done, practical

workaday *adj* ordinary, unexciting

workaholic *noun, informal* someone addicted to work

worker *noun* someone who works at a job

workforce *noun* **1** the number of workers in an industry *etc* **2** the workers potentially available

workman *noun* someone who works with their hands

workmanlike *adj* done with skill

workmanship *noun* **1** skill shown in making something **2** manner of making or refining something

■ **1** skill, craft, craftsmanship, expertise, art, handiwork **2** technique, execution, manufacture, work, finish

workshop *noun* **1** a room or building where manufacturing, craftwork *etc* is done **2** a course of study or work on a particular project: *a theatre workshop*

workstation *noun* an area in an office where a person works, *usu* with a computer terminal

world *noun* **1** the earth and all things on it **2** the people of the world **3** any planet or star **4** the universe **5** a state of existence: *the next world* **6** a particular area of life or activity: *the insect world/the world of fashion* **7** *informal* a great deal: *a world of good* ◇ **on top of the world** *informal* supremely happy ◇ **out of this world** *informal* marvellous

■ **1** earth, globe, planet, nature **2** everybody, everyone, people, human race, humankind, humanity **4** universe, cosmos, creation **6** sphere, realm, field, area, domain, system, society, province

worldly *adj* concerned with material things such as money, possessions *etc*, not the soul or spirit

■ materialistic, selfish, ambitious, grasping, greedy, covetous, avaricious

worldwide *adj* extending throughout the world ◇ *adv* throughout the world ◇ **World Wide Web** a network of linked files accessed through the Internet

worm *noun* **1** a small creeping animal without a backbone, often living in soil **2** *informal* a low, contemptible person **3** something spiral-shaped, *eg* the thread of a screw **4** (**worms**) the condition of having threadworms *etc* in the intestines **5** *comput* a kind of virus ◇ *verb* **1** move gradually and stealthily (in or into) **2** (with **out**) draw out (information) bit by bit

wormwood *noun* a plant with a bitter taste

worn *adj* **1** damaged by use **2** tired, worn-out

■ **1** shabby, threadbare, worn-out, tatty, tattered, frayed, ragged **2** exhausted, tired, weary, spent, fatigued, careworn, drawn, haggard, jaded

☒ **1** new, unused **2** fresh

worn-out *adj* **1** damaged by use **2** tired, exhausted

worry *verb* (**worries, worrying, worried**) **1** annoy **2** make troubled and anxious **3** be troubled and anxious **4** of a dog: chase and bite (sheep *etc*) ◇ *noun* (*plural* **worries**) **1** uneasiness, anxiety **2** a cause of unease or anxiety ◇ **worrier** *noun*

■ *verb* **1** irritate, plague, pester, torment, upset, unsettle, annoy, bother, disturb, vex, tease, nag, harass, harry, perturb, *informal* hassle **3** be anxious, be troubled, be distressed, agonize, fret ◇ *noun* **1** anxiety, apprehension, unease, misgiving, fear, disturbance, agitation, torment, misery, perplexity **2** problem, trouble, responsibility, burden, concern, care, trial, annoyance, irritation, vexation

☒ *verb* **1** comfort **3** be unconcerned ◇ *noun* **1** comfort, reassurance

worse *adj* **1** bad or evil to a greater degree **2** more ill ◇ *adv* badly to a greater degree, more severely: *it's snowing worse than ever* ◇ **worse off** in a worse position, less wealthy *etc*

worsen *verb* make or become worse

■ exacerbate, aggravate, intensify, heighten, get worse, weaken, deteriorate, degenerate, decline, sink, *informal* go downhill

☒ improve

worship *verb* (**worships, worshipping, worshipped**) **1** pay honour to (a god) **2** adore or admire deeply ◇ *noun* **1** a religious ceremony or service **2** deep reverence, adoration ◇ **worshipful** *adj* **1** full of reverence **2** worthy of honour

worst *adj* bad or evil to the greatest degree ◇ *adv* badly to the greatest degree ◇ *verb* (**worsts, worsting, worsted**) beat, defeat ◇ **at worst** under the least favourable circumstances ◇ **if the worst comes to the worst** if the worst possible circumstances occur

worsted *noun* **1** a type of fine woollen yarn **2** a strong cloth made of this

worth *noun* **1** cost; price **2** importance **3** value or usefulness ◇ *adj* **1** equal in value to **2** deserving of: *worth considering* ◇ **worth your while** worth the trouble spent

■ *noun* **1** value, cost, rate, price **2** importance, significance **3** worthiness, merit, value, benefit, advantage

worthless *adj* of no merit or value ◇ **worthlessness** *noun*

■ valueless, useless, pointless, meaningless, futile, unavailing, unimportant, insignificant, trivial, unusable, cheap, poor, rubbishy, trashy, paltry

☒ valuable

worthwhile *adj* deserving time and effort

■ profitable, useful, valuable, worthy, good, helpful, beneficial, constructive, gainful, justifiable, productive

☒ worthless

worthy *adj* **1** (often with **of**) deserving, suitable **2** of good character ◇ *noun* (*plural* **worthies**) a highly respected person: *local worthy* ◇ **worthiness** *noun*

■ *adj* **1** worthwhile, fit, deserving **2** respectable, reputable, good, honest, honourable, excellent, decent, upright, righteous

would *verb* **1** the form of the verb **will**: *she said she would leave at 10* **2** used to express willingness or ability: *he would go if he could* **3** indicating habitual action: *would always phone at 6*

would-be *adj* trying to be or pretending to be: *would-be actor/would-be socialist*

wound /wuːnd/ *noun* **1** a cut or injury caused by a weapon, in an accident *etc* **2** a hurt to someone's feelings ◇ *verb* **1** make a wound in **2** hurt the feelings of ◇ **wounded** *adj* having a wound, injured, hurt ◇ **wounding** *noun, adj*

■ *noun* **1** injury, trauma, hurt, cut, gash, lesion, laceration, scar **2** hurt, distress, trauma, torment, heartbreak, harm, damage, anguish, grief, shock ◇ *verb* **1** damage, arm, hurt, injure, hit, cut, gash, lacerate, slash, pierce **2** distress, offend, insult, pain, mortify, upset, slight

WPC *abbrev* Woman Police Constable

wrack *noun* seaweed thrown onto the shore

wraith *noun* an apparition, a ghost

wrangle *verb* quarrel noisily ◇ *noun* a noisy quarrel

▣ *verb* argue, quarrel, disagree, dispute, bicker, altercate, contend, *informal* fall out, *informal* row, squabble, scrap, fight, spar ◇ *noun* argument, quarrel, dispute, controversy, squabble, tiff, *informal* row, bickering, disagreement, clash, altercation, contest, *informal* slanging match, *informal* set-to

wrap *verb* (**wraps**, **wrapping**, **wrapped**) **1** fold or roll round: *wrap it in tissue paper* **2** (with **up**) cover by folding or winding something round ◇ *noun* **1** a cloak or shawl **2** a tortilla wrapped around a filling of meat, vegetables *etc*

▣ *verb* **1** envelop, fold, enclose, cover, pack, wind, package, muffle, cocoon, cloak, roll up, bind, bundle up **2** wrap, pack up, package, parcel

wrapper *noun* a loose paper cover, *eg* round a book or sweet

wrath /rɒθ/ *noun* violent anger ◇ **wrathful** *adj* very angry

wreak *verb* **1** carry out: *wreak vengeance* **2** cause: *wreak havoc*

wreath *noun* **1** a ring of flowers or leaves **2** a curling wisp of smoke, mist *etc*

wreathe *verb* encircle

wreck *noun* **1** destruction, *esp* of a ship by the sea **2** the remains of anything destroyed *esp* a ship **3** *informal* someone whose health or nerves are in bad condition ◇ *verb* destroy ◇ **wrecker** *noun*

▣ *noun* **1** ruin, destruction, devastation, demolition, ruination **2** mess, write-off, disaster ◇ *verb* destroy, ruin, demolish, devastate, shatter, smash, break, spoil, play havoc with, ravage, write off

▣ *verb* conserve, repair

wreckage *noun* the remains of something wrecked

wren *noun* a very small type of bird

wrench *verb* **1** pull with a violent, often twisting, motion **2** sprain (your ankle *etc*) ◇ *noun* (*plural* **wrenches**) **1** a violent twist **2** a tool for gripping and turning nuts, bolts *etc* **3** sadness caused by parting from someone or something

▣ *verb* **1** yank, wrest, jerk, pull, tug, force **2** sprain, strain, rick, tear, twist

wrest *verb*, *formal* twist or take by force

wrestle *verb* **1** fight with someone, trying to bring them to the ground **2** (with **with**) apply yourself keenly to (a problem *etc*) ◇ **wrestler** *noun* someone who wrestles as a sport ◇ **wrestling** *noun* the sport in which two people fight to throw each other to the ground

wretch *noun* (*plural* **wretches**) **1** a miserable, pitiable person: *a poor wretch* **2** a worthless or contemptible person

▣ **2** scoundrel, rogue, villain, good-for-nothing, ruffian, rascal, vagabond, miscreant, outcast

wretched /ˈretʃɪd/ *adj* **1** very miserable **2** worthless, very bad ◇ **wretchedly** *adv* ◇ **wretchedness** *noun*

▣ **1** unhappy, sad, miserable, melancholy, depressed, dejected, disconsolate, downcast, forlorn, gloomy, doleful, distressed, broken-hearted, crestfallen **2** contemptible, despicable, vile, worthless, shameful, inferior, low, mean, paltry

▣ **1** happy **2** worthy

wriggle *verb* **1** twist to and fro **2** move by doing this, as a worm does **3** escape (out of a difficulty *etc*)

-wright *suffix* a maker: *shipwright/playwright*

wring *verb* (**wrings**, **wringing**, **wrung**) **1** twist or squeeze (*esp* water out of wet clothes) **2** clasp and unclasp (your hands) in grief, anxiety *etc* **3** cause pain to: *the story wrung every-*

body's heart **4** force (*eg* information) from someone ◇ **wringer** *noun* a machine for forcing water from wet clothes

■ **1** squeeze, twist, wrench, wrest, extract, mangle, screw **3** distress, pain, hurt, rack, rend, pierce, torture, wound, stab, tear **4** exact, extort, coerce, force

wrinkle *noun* a small crease or fold on the skin or other surface ◇ *verb* make or become wrinkled ◇ **wrinkly** *adj*

wrist *noun* the joint by which the hand is joined to the arm

writ *noun* a formal document giving an order (*esp* to appear in a law court)

write *verb* (**writes, writing, written, wrote**) **1** form letters, words *etc* with a pen, pencil *etc* **2** put into writing: *write your name* **3** compose (a letter, a book *etc*) **4** send a letter (to) **5** *comput* copy (a data file) ◇ **write-off** *noun* a car *etc* that has been damaged beyond repair ◇ **write down** record in writing ◇ **write off 1** write and send a letter of request **2** damage beyond repair **3** cancel (a debt) **4** discontinue or dismiss ◇ **write up 1** write in final form **2** bring (a diary *etc*) up to date **3** write about or review (something)

■ **1** pen, inscribe **2** jot down, set down, transcribe, scribble, scrawl **3** draft, draw up, copy, compose, create **4** correspond, communicate

writer *noun* someone who writes, an author

■ author, scribe, wordsmith, novelist, dramatist, essayist, playwright, columnist, diarist, journalist, hack, penpusher, scribbler, secretary, copyist, clerk

Writers include:
annalist, author, autobiographer, bard, biographer, calligraphist, chronicler, clerk, columnist, composer, contributor, copyist, copywriter, correspondent, court reporter, diarist, dramatist, editor, essayist, fabler, fiction writer, ghost writer, hack, historian, journalist,

leader writer, lexicographer, librettist, lyricist, novelist, penfriend, penman, pen-pal, *informal* penpusher, penwoman, playwright, poet, poet laureate, reporter, rhymer, satirist, scribe, scriptwriter, short-story writer, sonneteer, stenographer, *informal* storyteller, technical writer, web author

writhe /raɪð/ *verb* twist or roll about, *eg* in pain

writing *noun* **1** handwriting or script **2** a written text or texts

■ **1** handwriting, calligraphy, script, penmanship, scrawl, scribble, hand, print **2** document, letter, book, composition, letters, literature, work, publication

wrong *adj* **1** not correct **2** mistaken: *you are wrong if you think that* **3** unsuitable: *the wrong weather for camping* **4** not right or just **5** evil ◇ *adv* **1** incorrectly **2** badly ◇ *noun* **1** whatever is not right or just **2** an injury done to another ◇ *verb* do wrong to, harm ◇ **wrongly** *adv* ◇ **go wrong 1** fail to work properly **2** make a mistake or mistakes ◇ **in the wrong** guilty of injustice or error

■ *adj* **1** inaccurate, incorrect, mistaken, false, in error, imprecise **3** inappropriate, unsuitable, unseemly, improper, indecorous, unconventional, unfitting, incongruous, inapt **4** unjust, unethical, unfair, unlawful, immoral, illegal, illicit, dishonest, criminal, *informal* crooked, reprehensible, guilty **5** bad, wicked, sinful, iniquitous, evil ◇ *verb* abuse, ill-treat, mistreat, maltreat, injure, ill-use, hurt, harm, discredit, dishonour, misrepresent, malign, oppress, cheat

🔁 *adj* **1** correct, right **3** suitable, right **4** good, moral

wrongdoer *noun* someone who does wrong ◇ **wrongdoing** *noun*

wrongful *adj* not lawful or just ◇ **wrongfully** *adv*

■ immoral, improper, unfair, unethical, unjust, unlawful, illegal, illegitimate, illicit, dishonest, criminal, blameworthy, dishonourable, wrong, reprehensible

🔁 rightful

wrote *past form* of **write**

wrought /rɔːt/ *adj* of metal: hammered, rather than cast, into shape ◇ **wrought iron** a form of iron that can be shaped

wrung *past form* of **wring**

wry *adj* **1** slightly mocking or bitter: *wry remark* **2** of a facial expression: twisted ◇ **wryly** *adv*
▣ **1** ironic, sardonic, dry, sarcastic, mordant, mocking, droll **2** twisted, distorted, deformed, contorted, warped, uneven, crooked
▣ **2** straight

wuss /wʊs/ *noun*, *slang* a timid, weak person

WWW or **www** *abbrev* World Wide Web

WYSIWYG *abbrev*, *comput* what you see (on the screen) *is* *w*hat you *g*et (in the printout)

XL *abbrev* extra large

xenophobia *noun* hatred of foreigners or strangers ◇ **xenophobe** *noun* someone who hates foreigners ◇ **xenophobic** *adj*

Xerox *noun, trademark* **1** a photographic process used for copying documents **2** a copy made in this way ◇ *verb* copy by Xerox

Xmas *noun, informal* Christmas

X-ray *noun* **1** a ray that can pass through material impenetrable by light, and produce a photographic image of the object through which it has passed **2** a shadow picture produced by X-rays ◇ *verb* take a photographic image of with X-rays

xylophone /ˈzaɪloʊfoʊn/ *noun* a musical instrument consisting of a series of graded wooden plates which are struck with hammers

Yy

yacht /jɒt/ *noun* a sailing or motor-driven boat for racing, cruising *etc*
◊ **yachtsman, yachtswoman** *noun*

yak *noun* a Tibetan long-haired ox

yam *noun* a tropical root vegetable, similar to a potato

Yank or **Yankee** *noun, Brit informal* a person from the USA

> Originally a nickname for Dutch settlers in New England in the 18th century, possibly because of the Dutch forename *Jan*

yank *verb, informal* tug or pull with a violent jerk ◊ *noun* a violent tug
■ *verb & noun* jerk, tug, pull, wrench, snatch, haul, heave

yap *verb* (**yaps, yapping, yapped**) bark sharply

yard[1] *noun* **1** a measure of length (0.9144 of a metre, or 3 feet) **2** a long beam on a mast for spreading sails

yard[2] *noun* **1** an enclosed space used for a particular purpose: *railway yard/shipbuilding yard* **2** *US* a garden

yardstick *noun* **1** a standard for measurement **2** a yard-long measuring stick
■ **1** measure, gauge, criterion, standard, benchmark, touchstone, comparison

yarn *noun* **1** wool, cotton *etc* spun into thread **2** a long, often improbable, story
■ **1** thread, fibre, strand **2** story, tale, anecdote, fable, fabrication, tall story, *informal* cock-and-bull story

yarrow *noun* a strong-smelling plant with flat clusters of white flowers

yashmak *noun* a veil covering the lower half of the face, worn by Muslim women

yawl *noun* a small rowing boat or fishing boat

yawn *verb* **1** take a deep breath unintentionally with an open mouth, because of boredom or sleepiness **2** of a hole: be wide open, gape ◊ *noun* an open-mouthed deep breath

yd *abbrev* yard(s)

ye *pronoun, old* you

yea /jeɪ/ *exclam, old* yes

year *noun* **1** the time taken by the earth to go once round the sun, about 365 days **2** the period 1 January to 31 December **3** a period of twelve months starting at any point **4** (**years**) age: *wise for her years*

yearling *noun* a year-old animal

yearly *adj* happening every year, or once a year
■ annual, per year, per annum, perennial

yearn *verb* **1** long (for, to do something *etc*) **2** feel pity or tenderness (for)
■ **1** long for, pine for, desire, want, wish for, crave, covet, hunger for, hanker for, ache for, languish for, itch for

yearning *noun* an eager longing

yeast *noun* a substance which causes fermentation, used to make bread dough rise and in brewing

yell *verb* give a loud, shrill cry; scream
◊ *noun* a loud, shrill cry
■ *verb* shout, scream, bellow, roar, bawl, shriek, squeal, howl, *informal* holler, screech, squall, yelp, yowl, whoop ◊ *noun* shout, scream, cry, roar, bellow, shriek, howl, screech, squall, whoop
◄ *verb* whisper

yellow *noun* the colour of gold, egg-yolks *etc* ◊ *adj* **1** of this colour **2** *informal* cowardly ◊ *verb* become yellow, due to ageing

yellowhammer *noun* a finch with yellow plumage

yelp *verb* give a sharp bark or cry
◊ *noun* a sharp bark or cry
■ *verb* yap, bark, squeal, cry, yell, yowl, bay

yen[1] *noun* the standard unit of Japanese currency

yen[2] *noun, informal* a strong desire, longing: *a yen to return to Scotland*

yeoman /ˈjoʊmən/ *noun, hist* a farmer with his own land ◇ **yeomanry** *noun, hist* **1** farmers **2** a troop of cavalrymen serving voluntarily in the British army ◇ **Yeomen of the Guard** the company acting as ceremonial bodyguard to the British sovereign

yes *exclam* expressing agreement or consent ◇ *noun* **1** an expression of agreement or consent **2** a vote in favour

yesterday *noun* **1** the day before today **2** the past ◇ *adv* on the day before today

yet *adv* **1** by now, by this time: *have you seen that film yet?* **2** still, before the matter is finished: *we may win yet* **3** used for emphasis: *yet another mistake* ◇ *conj* but, nevertheless: *I am defeated, yet I shall not surrender*

Yeti *noun, another name* for the **Abominable Snowman**

yew *noun* **1** a tree with dark green leaves and red berries **2** its wood

YHA *abbrev* Youth Hostels Association

yield *verb* **1** give in, surrender **2** give way to pressure or persuasion **3** produce (a crop, results *etc*) ◇ *noun* an amount produced; a crop ◇ **yielding** *adj* giving way easily

◼ *verb* **1** surrender, renounce, abandon, abdicate, cede, part with, relinquish **2** give way, capitulate, concede, submit, succumb, give (in), admit defeat, bow, cave in, resign oneself, go along with, permit, allow, accede, agree, comply, consent **3** produce, bear, supply, provide, generate, bring in, bring forth, furnish, return, earn, pay ◇ *noun* return, product, earnings, harvest, crop, produce, output, profit, revenue, takings, proceeds, income

◼ *verb* **1** hold **2** resist, withstand

ylang-ylang /ˈiːlaŋˈiːlaŋ/ *noun* a SE Asian tree from whose flowers a fragrant oil is distilled

YMCA *abbrev* Young Men's Christian Association

yob or **yobbo** *noun* (*plural* **yobboes** or **yobbos**) a lout, a hooligan

yodel *verb* (**yodels, yodelling, yodelled**) sing in a style involving frequent changes between an ordinary and a very high-pitched voice

yoga *noun* **1** a Hindu system of philosophy and meditation **2** a system of mental and physical discipline involving special exercises

yoghurt or **yogurt** *noun* a semiliquid food product made from fermented milk

yoke *noun* **1** a wooden frame joining oxen when pulling a plough or cart **2** a pair of oxen or horses **3** a frame placed across the shoulders for carrying pails *etc* **4** a burden; something oppressive **5** something that joins together **6** a part of a garment fitting over the neck and shoulders ◇ *verb* **1** put a yoke on **2** join together

◼ *noun* **4** burden, bondage, enslavement, slavery, oppression, subjugation, servility ◇ *verb* **2** couple, link, join, tie, harness, hitch, bracket, connect, unite

yokel *noun, derog* an unsophisticated country person; a rustic

yolk *noun* the yellow part of an egg

Yom Kippur the Day of Atonement, a Jewish fast day

yonder *adv, old* in that place (at a distance but within sight) ◇ *adj* that (object) over there: *by yonder tree*

yonks *noun plural, informal* ages; a long time

yore *noun*: **of yore** *old* formerly, in times past

you *pronoun* **1** the person(s) spoken or written to, used as the *sing* or *plural* subject or object of a verb: *what did you say?/are you both free tomorrow?* **2** any or every person: *you don't often see that now*

you'd *short for* **1** you would; you should **2** you had

you'll *short for* you will; you shall

young *adj* **1** in early life **2** in the early part of growth ◇ *noun* **1** the offspring of animals **2** (**the young**) young people

◼ *adj* **1** youthful, juvenile, baby, infant, junior, adolescent **2** immature, early, new, recent, green, growing, fledgling, unfledged, inexperienced ◇ *noun* **1** offspring, babies, issue, litter, progeny, brood, children, family

▣ *adj* **1** adult, old **2** mature, old

youngster *noun* a young person

▣ child, boy, girl, toddler, youth, teenager, *informal* kid

your *adj* belonging to you: *it's your life*

you're *short for* you are

yours *pronoun* belonging to you: *is this pen yours?* ◇**Yours**, **Yours faithfully**, **Yours sincerely** or **Yours truly** expressions used before a signature at the end of a letter

yourself *pronoun* (*plural* **yourselves**) **1** used reflexively: *don't trouble yourself* **2** used for emphasis: *you yourself can't go* **3** your normal self: *you don't look yourself today* ◇**by yourself** on your own; without help

youth *noun* **1** the state of being young **2** the early part of life **3** a young person **4** young people in general ◇**youth hostel** a hostel where hikers *etc* may spend the night

▣ **2** adolescence, childhood, immaturity, boyhood, girlhood **3** adolescent,

youngster, juvenile, teenager, *informal* kid, boy, girl, young man, young woman **4** young people, the young, younger generation

youthful *adj* **1** young **2** fresh and vigorous, like a young person ◇**youthfully** *adv* ◇**youthfulness** *noun*

▣ **1** young, boyish, girlish, childish, immature, juvenile, inexperienced **2** fresh, active, lively, well-preserved

you've *short for* you have

yo-yo *noun*, *trademark* a toy consisting of a reel which spins up and down on a string ◇*verb* fluctuate wildly

yr *abbrev* year

yuan *noun* the main currency unit of The People's Republic of China

yucca *noun* a desert plant with thick spiky leaves

yuck *exclam*, *informal* expressing distaste ◇**yucky** *adj*

Yule *noun*, *old* Christmas ◇**Yuletide** Christmas time

yuppie or **yuppy** *noun*, *informal* (*plural* **yuppies**) a young well-paid urban professional

YWCA *abbrev* Young Women's Christian Association

Zz

zabaglione *noun* a custard made with egg yolks, sugar and sweet wine

zany *adj, informal* crazy, madcap ◇ **zanily** *adv* ◇ **zaniness** *noun*

■ comical, funny, amusing, eccentric, droll, *informal* crazy, clownish, *informal* loony, *informal* wacky

☢ serious

> After the name of a clownish character in the Italian *commedia dell'arte*

zap *verb* (**zaps, zapping, zapped**) **1** strike, shoot *etc* suddenly **2** move rapidly; zip

zeal *noun* enthusiasm; keenness, determination

■ ardour, fervour, passion, warmth, fire, enthusiasm, devotion, spirit, keenness, zest, eagerness, earnestness, dedication, fanaticism, gusto, verve

☢ apathy, indifference

zealot /'zɛlət/ *noun* a fanatical enthusiast

zealous *adj* enthusiastic; keen ◇ **zealously** *adv*

■ ardent, fervent, impassioned, passionate, devoted, burning, enthusiastic, intense, fanatical, militant, keen, eager, earnest, spirited

☢ apathetic, indifferent

zebra *noun* a striped African animal of the horse family ◇ **zebra crossing** a pedestrian street crossing, painted in black and white stripes

zeitgeist /'zaɪtgaɪst/ *noun* the present cultural climate

zenith *noun* **1** the point of the heavens exactly overhead **2** the highest point, the peak

■ **2** summit, peak, height, pinnacle, apex, high point, top, optimum, climax, culmination

zephyr *noun, formal* a soft, gentle breeze

zero *noun* **1** nothing or the sign for it (0) **2** the point (marked 0) from which a scale (*eg* on a thermometer) begins ◇ **zero hour** the exact time fixed for some action ◇ **zero option** a proposal to limit or abandon the deployment of nuclear missiles if the opposing side does likewise ◇ **zero in on 1** aim for **2** focus attention on

■ **1** nothing, nought, nil, bottom, cipher, *informal* zilch

zero-rated *adj* of goods: having no value-added tax

zest *noun* **1** relish, keen enjoyment **2** orange or lemon peel **3** sharp flavour ◇ **zestful** *adj* ◇ **zestfully** *adv*

■ **1** gusto, appetite, enthusiasm, enjoyment, keenness, zeal, exuberance, interest

☢ **1** apathy

zigzag *adj* having sharp bends or angles ◇ *verb* (**zigzags, zigzagging, zigzagged**) move in a zigzag direction

■ *adj* meandering, crooked, serpentine, sinuous, twisting, winding ◇ *verb* meander, snake, wind, twist, curve

☢ *adj* straight

zilch *noun, slang* nothing

zimmer *noun, trademark* a hand-held metal frame used to give support in walking

zinc *noun* a bluish-white metal

zingy *adj, informal* zestful, lively

zinnia *noun* a tropical American plant of the thistle family

zip *noun* **1** a fastening device for clothes, bags *etc*, consisting of two rows of metal or nylon teeth which interlock when a sliding tab is pulled between them **2** a whizzing sound, *eg* made by a fast-flying object **3** *informal* energy, vigour ◇ *verb* (**zips, zipping, zipped**) **1** fasten with a zip **2** whizz, fly past at speed **3** *comput* convert (a file *etc*) into a compressed form

zipper *noun*, *US* a zip fastener

zither *noun* a flat, stringed musical instrument, played with the fingers

zodiac *noun* an imaginary strip in space, divided into twelve equal parts ◇ **signs of the zodiac** the divisions of the zodiac used in astrology, each named after a group of stars within it

> *The signs of the zodiac (with their symbols) are*:
> Aries (Ram), Taurus (Bull), Gemini (Twins), Cancer (Crab), Leo (Lion), Virgo (Virgin), Libra (Balance), Scorpio (Scorpion), Sagittarius (Archer), Capricorn (Goat), Aquarius (Water-bearer), Pisces (Fishes)

zombie *noun* **1** a corpse reanimated by witchcraft **2** a very slow or overtired person

> After the name of a voodoo snake god

zone *noun* **1** any of the five main bands into which the earth's surface is divided according to temperature: *temperate zone* **2** a section of a country, town *etc* marked off for a particular purpose: *no-parking zone/smokeless zone* ◇ *verb* divide into zones

▤ *noun* **2** region, area, district, territory, section, sector

zonked *adj*, *slang* **1** exhausted **2** drunk; under the influence of drugs

zoo *noun* a place where wild animals are kept and shown to the public

zoological *adj* relating to animals ◇ **zoological gardens** *formal* a zoo

zoology *noun* the science of animal life ◇ **zoologist** *noun* someone who studies animal life

zoom *verb* **1** move swiftly, *esp* with a loud, low buzzing noise **2** of prices: increase sharply **3** use a zoom lens on a camera ◇ **zoom in** or **out** to close up (on something) or open out a shot again ◇ **zoom lens** *photog* a lens which makes a distant object appear gradually nearer without the camera being moved

▤ *verb* **1** race, rush, tear, dash, speed, fly, hurtle, streak, flash

zucchini /zʊˈkinɪ/ *noun* (*plural* **zucchini** or **zucchinis**) *US* a courgette